Jackson, Jamuel Macauley

The new Schaff-Herzog encyclopedia of religious knowledge

Vol. 7

Jackson, Jamuel Macauley

The new Schaff-Herzog encyclopedia of religious knowledge

Vol. 7

Inktank publishing, 2018

www.inktank-publishing.com

ISBN/EAN: 9783747768365

THE NEW

SCHAFF-HERZOG ENCYCLOPEDIA

OF

RELIGIOUS KNOWLEDGE

EDITED BY

SAMUEL MACAULEY JACKSON, D.D., LL.D.

(Editor-in-Chief)

WITH THE SOLE ASSISTANCE, AFTER VOLUME VI., OF

GEORGE WILLIAM GILMORE, M.A.

(Associate Editor)

AND THE FOLLOWING DEPARTMENT EDITORS

CLARENCE AUGUSTINE BECKWITH, D.D.
(Department of Systematic Theology)

HENRY KING CARROLL, LL.D.
(Department of Minor Denominations)

JAMES FRANCIS DRISCOLL, D.D.
(Department of Liturgics and Religious Orders)

JAMES FREDERIC McCURDY, PH.D., LL.D.
(Department of the Old Testament)

HENRY SYLVESTER NASH, D.D.
(Department of the New Testament)

ALBERT HENRY NEWMAN, D.D., LL.D.
(Department of Church History)

FRANK HORACE VIZETELLY, F.S.A.
(Department of Pronunciation and Typography)

VOLUME VII

LIUTPRAND — MORALITIES

FUNK AND WAGNALLS COMPANY

NEW YORK AND LONDON

EDITORS

SAMUEL MACAULEY JACKSON, D.D., LL.D.

(EDITOR-IN-CHIEF.)

Professor of Church History, New York University.

GEORGE WILLIAM GILMORE, M.A.

(ASSOCIATE EDITOR.)

New York,
Formerly Professor of Biblical History and Lecturer on Comparative Religion, Bangor Theological Seminary.

DEPARTMENT EDITORS, VOLUME VII

CLARENCE AUGUSTINE BECKWITH, D.D.,

(*Department of Systematic Theology.*)
Professor of Systematic Theology, Chicago Theological Seminary.

HENRY KING CARROLL, LL.D.,

(*Department of Minor Denominations.*)
Secretary of Executive Committee of the Western Section for the Fourth Ecumenical Methodist Conference.

JAMES FRANCIS DRISCOLL, D.D.,

(*Department of Liturgics and Religious Orders.*)
Rector of St. Gabriel's, New Rochelle, N. Y.

JAMES FREDERICK McCURDY, Ph.D., LL.D.,

(*Department of the Old Testament.*)
Professor of Oriental Languages, University College, Toronto.

HENRY SYLVESTER NASH, D.D.,

(*Department of the New Testament.*)
Professor of the Literature and Interpretation of the New Testament, Episcopal Theological School, Cambridge, Mass.

ALBERT HENRY NEWMAN, D.D., LL.D.,

(*Department of Church History.*)
Professor of Church History, Southwestern Baptist Theological Seminary, Fort Worth, Tex.

FRANK HORACE VIZETELLY, F.S.A.,

(*Department of Pronunciation and Typography.*)
Managing Editor of the STANDARD DICTIONARY, etc., New York City.

CONTRIBUTORS AND COLLABORATORS, VOLUME VII

HANS ACHELIS, Ph.D., Th.D.,
Professor of Theology, University of Halle.

JEAN GÉRARD RICHARD ACQUOY (†), D.D.,
Late Professor of Church History and the History of Dogma, University of Leyden.

OTTO WILHELM FERDINAND ALBRECHT, Th.Lic.,
Pastor at Naumburg-on-the-Saale.

JOHN ALEXANDER BAIN, M.A.,
Pastor of the Westport and Newport Presbyterian Churches, County Mayo, Ireland.

EDOUARD BARDE (†), D.D.,
Late Professor of New Testament Exegesis, School of Theology, Geneva.

CLARENCE AUGUSTINE BECKWITH, D.D.,
Professor of Systematic Theology, Chicago Theological Seminary.

HEINRICH BEHM, Ph.D.,
Superintendent in Doberan, Mecklenburg.

KARL BENRATH, Ph.D., Th.D.,
Professor of Church History, University of Königsberg.

IMMANUEL GUSTAV ADOLF BENZINGER, Ph.D., Th.Lic.,
German Orientalist and Vice-Consul for Holland in Jerusalem.

CARL ALBRECHT BERNOULLI, Th.Lic.,
Author at Arlesheim, near Basel.

CARL BERTHEAU, Th.D.,
Pastor of St. Michael's, Hamburg.

BERNHARD BESS, Th.Lic.,
Librarian, University of Halle.

WILLIAM LLOYD BEVAN, Ph.D.,
Assistant Editor of *The Churchman*, New York City.

EDWIN MUNSELL BLISS, D.D.,
Author of Books on Missions, Washington, D. C.

THEODORA CROSBY BLISS,
Writer on Missions.

HEINRICH BOEHMER, Ph.D., Th.Lic.,
Professor of Church History, University of Bonn.

HERMANN BOENIG,
Gymnasial Professor in Königsberg.

AMY GASTON CHARLES AUGUSTE BONET-MAURY, D.D., LL.D.,
Professor of Church History, Independent School of Divinity, Paris.

GOTTLIEB NATHANAEL BONWETSCH, Th.D.,
Professor of Church History, University of Göttingen.

FRIEDRICH HEINRICH BRANDES, Th.D.,
Reformed Minister and Chaplain at Bückeburg, Schaumburg-Lippe.

CHARLES AUGUSTUS BRIGGS, D.D., Litt.D.,
Professor of Theological Encyclopedia and Symbolics, Union Theological Seminary, New York.

JAMES MONROE BUCKLEY, D.D., LL.D.,
Editor of *The Christian Advocate*, New York City.

OSKAR GOTTLIEB RUDOLF BUDDENSIEG (†), Ph.D.,
Late Director of the Teacher's Seminary in Dresden.

FRANTS PEDER WILLIAM BUHL, Ph.D., Th.D.,
Professor of Oriental Languages, University of Copenhagen.

KARL BURGER (†), Th.D.,
Late Supreme Consistorial Councilor, Munich.

JACQUES EUGÈNE CHOISY, Th.D.,
Pastor in Geneva.

JOSEPH BOURNE CLARK, D.D.,
Editorial Secretary of the Congregational Home Missionary Society, New York.

FERDINAND COHRS, Th.Lic.,
Consistorial Councilor, Ilfeld, Germany.

HENRY COWAN, D.D.,
Professor of Church History, University of Aberdeen, Scotland.

AUGUST HERMANN CREMER (†), Th.D.,
Late Professor of Systematic Theology, University of Greifswald.

GUSTAV HERMAN DALMAN, Ph.D., Th.D.,
Professor of Old Testament Exegesis, University of Leipsic, and President of the German Evangelical Archeological Institute, Jerusalem.

SAMUEL MARTIN DEUTSCH (†), Th.D.,
Late Professor of Church History, University of Berlin.

HENRY MARTYN DEXTER (†), D.D.,
Late Editor of *The Congregationalist*, Boston.

MORTON DEXTER, M.A.,
Congregational Clergyman and Author, Boston.

WILHELM DILTHEY, Ph.D.,
Professor of Philosophy, University of Berlin.

PAUL GOTTFRIED DREWS, Th.D.,
Professor of Practical Theology, University of Halle.

JAMES FRANCIS DRISCOLL, D.D.,
Pastor of St. Ambrose's Church, New York City.

DUCHEMIN,
Pastor in Neuilly-sur-Seine, France.

FRIEDRICH HERMAN CHRISTIAN DUESTERDIECK (†), Ph.D., Th.D.,
Late General Superintendent, Osnabrück, Germany.

EMIL EGLI (†), Th.D.,
Late Professor of Church History, University of Zurich

RUDOLF EIBACH, Th.D.,
Consistorial Councilor, Dotzheim, near Wiesbaden, Germany.

HUBERT EVANS, Ph.D.,
Member of the Editorial Staff of the Encyclopædia Britannica Company, New York.

JOHN OLUF EVJEN, Ph.D.,
Professor of Theology in Augsburg Seminary, Minneapolis, Minn.

HERMANN AUGUST PAUL EWALD, Ph.D., Th.D.,
Professor of Dogmatics and New Testament Exegesis, University of Erlangen.

CHRISTIAN THEODOR FICKER, Ph.D.,
Emeritus Pastor at Eythra, near Leipsic.

DAVID HAY FLEMING, LL.D.,
Honorary Secretary of the Scottish Historical Society, Edinburgh.

FRITZ FLIEDNER (†), M.D.,
Late German Evangelist in Spain.

GUSTAV WILHELM FRANK (†), Th.D.,
Late Professor of Dogmatics, Symbolics, and Christian Ethics, University of Vienna.

GEORG FROBOESS,
Director for the Evangelical Lutheran Church in Prussia.

EMANUEL VOGEL GERHART (†), D.D.
Late Professor of Systematic Theology at Lancaster, Pa.

GEORGE WILLIAM GILMORE, M.A.,
Formerly Lecturer on Comparative Religion, Bangor Theological Seminary, Associate Editor of The New Schaff-Herzog Encyclopedia.

FRANZ GOERRES, Ph.D.,
Assistant Librarian, University of Bonn.

WILHELM GOETZ, Ph.D.,
Honorary Professor of Geography, Technical High School and Professor, Military Academy, Munich.

JOHANNES FRIEDRICH GOTTSCHICK (†), Th.D.,
Late Professor of New Testament Exegesis, Ethics, and Practical Theology, Evangelical Theological Faculty, University of Tübingen.

CASPAR RENÉ GREGORY, Ph.D., Th.D., D.D., LL.D., Dr.Jur.,
Professor of New Testament Exegesis, University of Leipsic.

PAUL GRUENBERG, Th.D.,
Pastor in Strasburg.

GEORG GRUETZMACHER, Ph.D., Th.Lic.
Extraordinary Professor of Church History, University of Heidelberg.

PETER REINHOLD GRUNDEMANN, Ph.D., Th.D.,
Pastor in Mörz, near Belzig, Prussia.

EDUARD GUEDER (†), Th.D.,
Late Preacher in Biglen, Canton of Bern, Switzerland.

HERMANN GUTHE, Th.D.,
Professor of Old Testament Exegesis, University of Leipsic

HEINRICH HAHN, Ph.D.,
Formerly Professor of History and German in the Luisenstadt Realgymnasium, Berlin.

ADOLF HARNACK, Ph.D., Th.D., Dr.Jur., M.D.,
General Director of the Royal Library, Berlin.

ALBERT HAUCK, Ph.D., Th.D., Dr.Jur.,
Professor of Church History, University of Leipsic, Editor in-Chief of the Hauck-Herzog *Realencyklopädie.*

HERMAN HAUPT, Ph.D.,
Professor, and Director of the University Library, Giessen.

JOHANNES HAUSSLEITER, Ph.D., Th.D.,
Consistorial Councilor, Professor of New Testament Theology and Exegesis, University of Greifswald.

MAX HEINZE (†), Ph.D., Th.D.,
Late Professor of Philosophy, University of Leipsic.

ERNST HENKE (†), Ph.D., Th.D.,
Late Professor of Theology, University of Marburg.

WILHELM HEYD (†), Ph.D.,
Late Oberstudienrat, Stuttgart.

KARL HOLL, Ph.D., Th.D.,
Professor of Church History, University of Berlin.

LOUISE SEYMOUR HOUGHTON,
Author and Translator.

JOHANN FRIEDRICH IKEN (†),
Late Pastor in Bremen.

HEINRICH FRANZ JACOBSON (†), Ph.D.,
Late Professor of Law, University of Königsberg.

ALFRED JEREMIAS, Ph.D., Th.Lic.
Privat-docent for Old Testament Exegesis, Leipsic.

GUSTAV ADOLF JUELICHER, Ph.D., Th.D.,
Professor of Church History and New Testament Exegesis, University of Marburg.

ADOLF HERMANN HEINRICH KAMPHAUSEN (†), Th.D.,
Late Professor of Old Testament Exegesis, University of Bonn.

FERDINAND FRIEDRICH WILHELM KATTENBUSCH, Ph.D., Th.D.,
Professor of Dogmatics, University of Halle.

PETER GUSTAV KAWERAU, Th.D.,
Consistorial Councilor, Professor of Practical Theology, and University Preacher, University of Breslau.

KONRAD KESSLER (†), Ph.D.,
Late Professor of Semitic Languages, University of Greifswald.

OTTO KIRN, Ph.D., Th.D.,
Professor of Dogmatics, University of Leipsic.

RUDOLF KITTEL, Ph.D., Th.D.,
Professor of Old Testament Exegesis, University of Leipsic.

FRIEDRICH EDUARD KOENIG, Ph.D., Th.D.,
Professor of Old Testament Exegesis, University of Bonn.

HEINRICH ADOLF KOESTLIN (†), Ph.D., Th.D.,
Late Privy Councilor in Cannstadt, formerly Professor of Theology, University of Giessen.

JULIUS KOESTLIN (†), Ph.D., Th.D., Dr.Jur.,
Late Professor of Theology, University of Halle.

THEODOR FRIEDRICH HERMANN KOLDE, Ph.D., Th.D.,
Professor of Church History, University of Erlangen.

RICHARD KRAETZSCHMAR (†), Th.D.,
Late Professor of Old Testament Exegesis, University of Marburg.

HERMANN GUSTAV EDUARD KRUEGER, Ph.D., Th.D.,
Professor of Church History, University of Giessen.

JOHANNES WILHELM KUNZE, Ph.D., Th.D.,
Professor of Systematic and Practical Theology, University of Greifswald.

GEORG RITTER VON LAUBMANN (†), Ph.D.,
Late Director of the Royal State Library in Munich.

WILLIAM LEE (†), D.D.,
Late Professor of Church History, University of Glasgow.

FRIEDRICH LEZIUS, Ph.D., Th.D.,
Professor of Church History, University of Königsberg.

RUDOLF LIECHTENHAN, Th.Lic.,
Pastor in Buch, Canton of Zurich, Switzerland.

FRIEDRICH LIST (†), Ph.D.,
Late Studiendirektor, Munich.

FRIEDRICH ARMIN LOOFS, Ph.D., Th.D.,
Professor of Church History, University of Halle.

JOHANN LOSERTH, Ph.D.,
Professor of History, University of Graz.

JAMES FREDERICK McCURDY, Ph.D., LL.D.,
Professor of Oriental Languages, University College, Toronto.

PEDER MADSEN, Th.D.,
Professor of Theology, University of Copenhagen.

WILHELM JULIUS MANGOLD (†), Th.D.,
Late Professor of Theology, University of Bonn.

THEODOR MEINHOLD,
Superintendent in Barth, Prussia.

JOHANNES MERZ, Ph.D.,
Consistorial Councilor, Stuttgart.

PHILIPP MEYER, Th.D.,
Supreme Consistorial Councilor, Hanover.

GEROLD MEYER VON KNONAU, Ph.D., Th.D.,
Professor of History, University of Zurich.

CARL THEODOR MIRBT, Th.D.,
Professor of Church History, University of Marburg.

WILHELM ERNST MOELLER (†), Th.D.,
Late Professor of Theology in Kiel.

RICHARD CARY MORSE, M.A.,
General Secretary of the International Committee of Young Men's Christian Associations.

GEORG MUELLER, Ph.D., Th.D.,
Inspector of Schools, Leipsic.

CHRISTOF EBERHARD NESTLE, Ph.D., Th.D.,
Professor in the Theological Seminary, Maulbronn, Württemberg.

ALBERT HENRY NEWMAN, D.D., LL.D.,
Professor of Church History, Southwestern Baptist Theological Seminary, Waco, Texas.

CONRAD VON ORELLI, Ph.D., Th.D.,
Professor of Old Testament Exegesis and History of Religion, University of Basel.

MARGARET BLOODGOOD PEEKE (†),
Late Inspectress-General of the Martinist Order for America.

CARL PFENDER,
Pastor of St. Paul's Evangelical Lutheran Church, Paris.

ERWIN PREUSCHEN, Ph.D., Th.D.,
Pastor at Hirschhorn-on-the-Neckar, Germany.

GOTTHILF PAUL EMIL LEOPOLD FRIEDRICH RANKE, Th.D.,
Head Pastor and Senior at Lübeck.

GEORG CHRISTIAN RIETSCHEL, Th.D.,
University Preacher and Professor of Practical Theology, University of Leipsic.

ROBERT WILLIAM ROGERS, M.A., Ph.D., LL.D.,
Professor of Hebrew and Old Testament Exegesis, Drew Theological Seminary, Madison, New Jersey.

FERDINAND SANDER,
Councilor for Schools in Bremen, Germany.

DAVID SCHLEY SCHAFF, D.D.,
Professor of Church History, Western Theological Seminary, Pittsburg, Pennsylvania.

PHILIP SCHAFF (†), D.D., LL.D.,
Late Professor of Church History, Union Theological Seminary, New York, and Editor of the Original Schaff-Herzog Encyclopædia.

REINHOLD SCHMID, Th.Lic.,
Pastor in Oberholzheim, Württemberg.

CARL WILHELM SCHOELL (†), Ph.D., D.D.,
Late Pastor of the Savoy Church, London.

THEODOR FRIEDRICH SCHOTT (†), Ph.D., Th.D.,
Late Librarian and Professor of Theology, University of Stuttgart.

JOHANN FRIEDRICH RITTER VON SCHULTE, Dr.Jur.,
Professor of Law, University of Bonn.

LUDWIG THEODOR SCHULZE, Ph.D., Th.D.,
Professor of Systematic Theology, University of Rostock.

REINHOLD SEEBERG, Th.D.,
Professor of Systematic Theology, University of Berlin.

EMIL SEHLING, Dr.Jur.,
Professor of Ecclesiastical and Commercial Law, University of Erlangen.

EDUARD SIMONS, Th.D.,
Extraordinary Professor of Practical Theology, University of Berlin.

PHILIPP FRIEDRICH ADOLPH THEODOR SPAETH, D.D., LL.D.,
Professor in the Lutheran Theological Seminary, Mt. Airy, Philadelphia.

GEORG EDUARD STEITZ (†), Th.D.,
Late Pastor in Frankfort-on-the-Main.

HERMANN LEBERECHT STRACK, Ph.D., Th.D.,
Extraordinary Professor of Old Testament Exegesis and Semitic Languages, University of Berlin.

ERNST PETER WILHELM TROELTSCH, Ph.D., Th.D.,
Professor of Systematic Theology, University of Heidelberg.

JOHANN GERHARD WILHELM UHLHORN (†), Th.D.,
Late Abbot of Lokkum, Germany.

SIETSE DOUWES VAN VEEN, Th.D.,
Professor of Church History and Christian Archeology, University of Utrecht.

JOHN VIÉNOT, Th.D.,
Professor of Church History, Independent School of Divinity, Paris.

JOHN VINSON,
Founder of the Church of the Living God.

WILHELM VOLCK (†), Ph.D., Th.D.,
Late Professor of Old Testament Exegesis, University of Rostock.

GUSTAV WARNECK, Ph.D., Th.D.,
Formerly Honorary Professor of the Science of Missions, Halle.

JOHANNES WEISS, Th.D.,
Professor of New Testament Exegesis, University of Heidelberg.

EDWARD ELIHU WHITFIELD, M.A.,
Retired Public Schoolmaster, London.

ALBERT EDMUND WILLIAMSON,
Pastor in Brooklyn, N. Y.

OTTO ZOECKLER (†), Ph.D., Th.D.,
Late Professor of Church History and Apologetics, University of Greifswald.

SAMUEL MARINUS ZWEMER,
Formerly Missionary in Arabia.

BIBLIOGRAPHICAL APPENDIX—VOLS. I—VII

The following list of books is supplementary to the bibliographies given at the end of the articles contained in vols. I.-VII., and brings the literature down to March, 1910. In this list each title entry is printed in capital letters. It is to be noted that, throughout the work, in the articles as a rule only first editions are given. In the bibliographies the aim is to give either the best or the latest edition, and in case the book is published both in America and in some other country, the American place of issue is usually given the preference.

ABRAHAM A SANCTA CLARA: *Werke in Auslese*, ed. H. Strigl, 6 vols., Vienna, 1904-07.

ADAM OF BREMEN: P. W. Kohlmann, *Adam von Bremen*, Leipsic, 1909.

ADENEY, W. F.: See below, GOD.

AFRICA: S. A. Donaldson, *Church Life and Thought in North Africa, A.D. 200*, London, 1909.
J. C. Lambert, *Missionary Heroes in Africa*, Philadelphia, 1909.

AGRICULTURE, HEBREW: F. Lundgreen, *Die Benutzung der Pflanzenwelt in der alttestamentlichen Religion*, Giessen, 1908.

AINGER, A.: E. Sichel, *The Life and Letters of Alfred Ainger*, London, 1910.

ALEANDRO, G.: J. Paquier, *Lettres familières de Jérome Aléandro (1510-40)*, Paris, 1909.

AMORITES: A. T. Clay, *Amurru, the Home of the Northern Semites; a Study showing that the Religion and Culture of Israel are not of Babylonian Origin*, Philadelphia, 1910.

ANDERSON, G.: *Hitherto Untold*, New York, 1910.

ANDREWES, L.: An edition of his *Manual for the Sick* is published, New York, 1909.

ANGELS: T. Laval, *Le Monde invisible, ou traité dogmatique et ascetique des anges*, Paris, 1909.

ANGELUS: *The Angelus and the Regina Coeli; with a few short Notes, explanatory and historical*, New York, 1910.

APOCRYPHA: H. M. Hughes, *The Ethics of Jewish Apocryphal Literature*, London, 1909.

APOLOGETICS: E. Boutraux, *Science and Religion in Contemporary Philosophy*, London, 1909.
H. C. King, *Letters on the Greatness and Simplicity of the Christian Faith*, Boston, 1909.
A. S. Peake, *Christianity: its Nature and its Truth*, New York, 1909.
W. S. Turton, *The Truth of Christianity. Being an Examination of the more Important Arguments for and against Believing in Christianity*, New York, 1909.
C. D. Williams, *A Valid Christianity for To-day*, ib. 1909.

ARABIA: O. Weber, *Eduard Glaser's Forschungsreisen in Südarabien*, Leipsic, 1909.

ARIANISM: D. H. von Schubert, *Das älteste germanische Christentum, oder der sogenannten "Arianismus" der Germanen*, Tübingen, 1909.

ARISTOTLE: The *Works* of Aristotle are to be translated into English under the editorship of J. A. Smith and W D. Ross; of this series there have appeared the *Parva naturalia*, *De lineus insecobilibus*, *Metaphysica*.
I. Bywater: *Aristotle on the Art of Poetry* (Text, Introduction, Transl.), London, 1908-1909.

ARNOLD, T.: H. M. Butler, *Ten Great and Good Men*, New York, 1909.

ART AND CHURCH: L. von Sybel, *Christliche Antike. Einführung in die altchristliche Kunst*, vol. ii., *Plastik, Architektur, und Malerei*, Marburg, 1909.

ASBURY, F.: G. P. Mains, *Francis Asbury*, London, 1910.

ATHANASIAN CREED: W. Hay, *The Athanasian Creed*, London, 1909.

ATONEMENT: E. DeW. Burto, and J. M. P and G. B. Smith, *Biblical Ideas of Atonement*, Chicago, 1909.

AUGUSTINE: *Scripta contra Donatistas*, pars iii., ed. M. Petschenig, Vienna, 1910.

BAALBEK: K. Maurer, *Baalbek*, Darmstadt, 1909.

BACON, B. W.: See below, JOHN THE APOSTLE.

BACON, R.: *Liber primus Communium naturalium; Partes prima et secunda* ed. R. Steele, New York, 1909, also *Metaphysica, de viciis contractis in studio*, ib., 1909.

BANKS, L. A.: *The Problems of Youth; A Series of Discourses for Young People on Themes of the Book of Proverbs*, New York, 1909.

BARNABAS: J. M. Heer, *Die versio Latina des Barnabasbriefes und ihr Verhältnis zur altlateinischen Bibel*, Freiburg, 1908.

BELLARMINE: J. de la Servière, *La Théologie de Bellarmine*, Paris, 1909.

BIBLE TEXT: *Der Codex Boernerianus der Briefe des Apostels Paulus in Lichtdruck nachgebildet*, Leipsic, 1909.

BIBLE VERSIONS: H. von Soden, *Das lateinische Neue Testament in Afrika zur Zeit Cyprians*, in *TU*, xxxiii., Leipsic, 1909.
Die aramäischen Bibel-Versionen (Targumim); Targum Jonatan ben Uzziel und Targum Jerusalem, Text, Umschrift, und Uebersetzung . . von M. Altschüler, vol. i., *Genesis*, Vienna, 1909.

The Octateuch in Ethiopic, According to the Text of the Paris Codex, With the Variants of Five Other MSS., ed. J. O. Boyd, part i., *Genesis*, in *Bibliotheca Abessinica*, ed. E. Littmann, Leyden, 1909.

S. Feist, *Etymologisches Wörterbuch der gotischen Sprache, mit Einschluss der sogenannten Krimgotischen*, part ii., Halle, 1909.

BIBLICAL CRITICISM: P. Fiebig, *Aufgaben der neutestamentlichen Forschung in der Gegenwart*, Leipsic, 1909.

BIBLICAL THEOLOGY: A. Schlatter, *Die Theologie des Neuen Testaments*, vol. i., *Das Wort Jesu*, Stuttgart, 1908.

S. E. Keeble, *The Social Teaching of the Bible*, New York, 1909.

F. S. Schenck, *The Sociology of the Bible*, ib., 1909.

M. Dibelius, *Die Geisterwelt im Glauben des Paulus*, Göttingen, 1909.

J. Adams, *Israel's Ideal; or Studies in O. T Theology*, Edinburgh, 1910.

BOTTOME, MARGARET: *Heart to Heart Letters; being Extracts from the Letters of Margaret Bottome to a Son*, New York, 1910.

BOURIGNON DE LA PORTE, A.: A. R. Macewen, *Antoinette Bourignon, Quietist*, London, 1909.

BUDDHISM: H. Hackmann, *Buddhism as a Religion; its Historical Development and present Conditions*, London, 1909.

BURIAL: S. Klein, *Tod und Begräbnis in Palästina zur Zeit der Tannaiter*, Berlin, 1909.

BUTLER, H. M.: *Ten Great and Good Men.* Lectures, New York, 1909.

CABALA: *Sepher ha-Zohar. Le Livre de la splendeur. Doctrine ésotérique des Israélites*, Paris, 1909.

CALVIN, J.: A. Rüegg, *Die Beziehungen Calvins zu Heinrich Bullinger und der von ihm geleiteten zürcherischen Kirche*, Zurich, 1909.

CAMPBELL, A.: J. Egbert, *Alexander Campbell and Christian Liberty*, St. Louis, 1909.

CAMPION, E.: *Works*, ed. P. Vivian, Oxford, 1909.

CEMETERIES: J. Wilpert, *Die Papstgräber und die Cäciliengruft in der Katakombe des heiligen Kallistus*, Freiburg, 1909.

CHASE, F. H.: *Confirmation in the Apostolic Age*, London, 1909.

CHINA: See below, KOREA.

S. P. Conger, *Letters from China*, London, 1909.

J. J. M. Degroot, *The Religion of the Chinese*, New York, 1910.

Feng-Shen-Yen-I. Die Metamorphosen der Götter. Aus dem Chinesischen by W Grube, vol. i., Leyden, 1909.

CHRISTMAS: R. Beck, *Das heilige Weihnachtsfest*, Regensburg, 1909.

CHRISTOLOGY: J. C. Granbery, *Outline of N. T Christology*, Chicago, 1909.

CHURCH: A. M. Fairbairn, *Studies in Religion and Theology; The Church in Idea and in History*, London and New York, 1910.

CHURCH HISTORY: S. A. Donaldson. See above, AFRICA.

K. Heussi, *Kompendium der Kirchengeschichte*, 2d half, 2d division, *Aufklärung. Neueste Zeit*, Tübingen, 1909.

A. C. Flick, *The Rise of the Mediæval Church*, London, 1909.

CLEMENT, VII.: C. F. Young, *The Medici*, i. 436–493, London, 1909.

CLEMENT OF ROME: H. Hemmer, *Clément de Rome, epitre aux Corinthiens. Homélie du ii. siècle*, Paris, 1909.

COLENSO, J. W.: A. T. Wirgman, *Life of James Green*, London, 1909. (Dr. James Green was the archopponent of Colenso, and this book in dealing with Green throws much light on Colenso.)

COMPARATIVE RELIGION: W S. Lilly, *Many Mansions; being Studies in Ancient Religions and Modern Thought*, London, 1907.

F. B. Jevons, *An Introduction to the Study of Comparative Religion*, New York, 1908.

W O. E. Oesterly, *The Evolution of the Messianic Idea. A Study in Comparative Religion*, London, 1908.

G. Galloway, *The Principles of Religious Development*, ib. 1909.

R. R. Marett, *The Threshold of Religion*, ib. 1909.

E. Mogk, *Die Menschenopfer bei den Germanen*, in the *Abhandlungen* of the Royal Saxon Academy, Philological-historical class, vol. xxvii., no. 17, 1909.

F. Cumont, *Les Religions orientales dans le paganisme romain*, 2d ed., Paris, 1909.

W. St. C. Tisdall, *Comparative Religion*, London, 1909.

CONDER, C. R.: *The City of Jerusalem*, London, 1909.

CONFIRMATION. See above, CHASE.

CONFUCIUS: L. H. Schütz, *Die hohe Lehre des Confucius*, Frankfort, 1909.

CONSCIENCE: G. Hughes, *Conscience and Criticism*, London, 1909.

CONSTANTINOPLE: E. M. Antoniadi, *Beschreibung der Hagia Sophia in Konstantinopel*, vol. i., Paris, 1909.

CONWELL, R. H.: *He Goeth before you*, Cleveland, 1910.

COSMAS INDICOPLEUSTES: *The Christian Topography of Cosmas . . , ed. with Geographical Notes* by E. O. Winstedt, Cambridge, 1910.

COUNCILS: C. J. Hefele, New French transl. of the *Conciliengeschichte*, *Histoire des conciles*, augmented with notes, vols. i. iii. 1, Paris, 1907–09.

CREATION: W. F. Warren, *The Earliest Cosmologies*, New York, 1909.

CREIGHTON, M.: *Lessons from the Cross*, London, 1910.

DANTE: W. H. V. Reade, *The Moral System of Dante's Inferno*, New York, 1909.

P Toynbee, *Dante in English Literature from Chaucer to Cary*, 2 vols., ib. 1909.

Quæstio de aqua et terra, ed. and transl. C. L. Shadwell, ib. 1910.

DEACONESS: W. M. Tippy, *The Socialized Church*, New York, 1909.

DIVORCE: J. P. Lichtenberger, *Divorce; a Study in Social Causation*, New York, 1909.

DOBSCHÜTZ, E. VON: *The Apostolic Age*, London, 1909.

DOCTRINE, HISTORY OF: O. Pfleiderer, *The Development of Theology in Germany since Kant*, New York, 1909.

DODS, M.: *Christ and Man*, ed H. R. Mackintosh, London, 1909.

DRIVER, S. R.: *Modern Research as Illustrating the Bible*, London, 1909; *Introduction to the O. T.*, 10th ed., 1909.

EDDY, M. B. G.: G. Milmine, *The Life of Mary Baker G. Eddy and the History of Christian Science*, New York, 1909.

EGLI, E.: *Schweizerische Kirchengeschichte*, vol. i., *1519–25*, Zurich, 1909.

EGYPT: J. O. Bevan, *Egypt and the Egyptians. Their History, Antiquities, Language, etc.*, London, 1910.
 E. Naville, *The Old Egyptian Faith*, ib. 1909.
 E. A. W Budge, new ed. of his transl. of the *Book of the Dead*, ib. 1909.

EGYPT EXPLORATION FUND: E. Naville, *The Temple of Deir el Bahari*, London, 1909. *The Monkey Tomb and the Gold Tomb*, by T. M. Davis. *King Siphtah and Queen Tansorit*, by G. Maspero. *The Excavations of 1905–07*, by E. Ayrton, ib. 1909.

ENGLAND, CHURCH OF: C. S. Carter, *The English Church in the Seventeenth Century*, New York, 1909.
 Church Congress held at Swansea Oct. 4–8, 1909, Official Report, London, 1909.

EPISTOLÆ OBSCURORUM VIRORUM: *The Latin Text, with an English Rendering, Notes, and an Historical Introduction* by Francis Green Stokes, London, 1909.

ERSKINE, T.: H. M. Butler, *Ten Great and Good Men*, New York, 1909.

EUSEBIUS OF CÆSAREA: *Kirchengeschichte. Die lateinische Uebersetzung des Rufinus bearbeitet . . . von T. Mommsen*, part 3, *Einleitungen, Uebersichten und Register*, Leipsic, 1909.

EXORCISM: F. J. Dolger, *Der Exorcismus im altchristlichen Taufritual*, Paderborn, 1909.

EZRA AND NEHEMIAH: G. Jahn, *Die Bücher Ezra (A und B) und Nehemja . . . , mit Erklärungen der einschlägigen Prophetenstellen und einem Anhang über hebräische Eigennamen*, Leyden, 1909.

FAIRBAIRN, A. M.: See above, CHURCH.

FAITH: R. J. Drummond, *Faith's Certainties*, London, 1909.
 G. Hoffmann, *Die Lehre von der Fides implicita*, Leipsic, 1909.

FÉNÉLON, F.: M. Cagnac, *Fénélon. Études critiques*, Paris, 1909.

FICKER, P. J.: *Anfänge reformatorischer Bibelauslegung*, i., parts 1–2, *Luther's Vorlesung über den Römerbrief 1575–1576*, Leipsic, 1908.

FOX, W. J.: R. Garnett, *The Life of W J Fox, Public Teacher and Social Reformer, 1786–1864*, New York, 1910.

FRANCIS, SAINT, OF SALES: M. Hamon, *Vie de S. Francis de Sales*, 2 vols., Paris, 1909.

FRIENDS, SOCIETY OF: Elizabeth B. Emmott, *The Story of Quakerism*, London, 1908.
 Amelia B. Gummere, *The Quaker in the Forum*, Philadelphia, 1910.

FUTURE PUNISHMENT: W. R. Savage, *The Resurrection of Judgment (St. John v. 29 R. V.); or, Eternal not Endless Punishment the Doctrine of Holy Writ*, London, 1909.

GARVIE, A. E.: *Life and Teaching of Paul*, Edinburgh, 1910.

GELZER, H., 1: Add to the works by him *Sextus Julius Africanus*, 2 parts, Leipsic, 1880–98; *Ausgewählte kleine Schriften*, 1907; *Byzantinische Kulturgeschichte*, 1909, the last two ed. his son Heinrich.

GENEVA: C. Borgeaud, *Histoire de l'Université de Genève*, Geneva, 1909.

GOD: W F. Adeney, *The Christian Conception of God*, London, 1909.
 L. Hill, *The Two Great Questions; The Existence of God and the Immortality of the Soul*, Chicago, 1909.

GOLTZ, E. FREIHERR VON DER: Add to the works by him *Ignatius von Antioch*, in *TU.* xiii. 3 (1895); *Nachrichten aus dem evangelischen Predigerseminar*, Wittenberg, 1909.

GOLTZ, H. FREIHERR VON DER: *Kirche und Staat*, and *Grundlagen der christlichen Sozial-Ethik*, both ed. his son, Berlin, 1907–08.

GORE, C.: *Orders and Unity*, London and New York, 1910.

GOSPELS AND GOSPELS: C. G. Montefiore, *The Synoptic Gospels . . . with Introduction and Commentary, additional Notes* by I. Abrahams, vols. i.–ii., London, 1909.
 W Fairweather, *The Background of the Gospels; or Judaism in the Period between the Old and New Testaments*, New York, 1909.
 J. C. Hawkins, *Horæ synopticæ. Contributions to the Study of the Synoptic Problems*, 2d ed., New York, 1910.

GOTTHEIL, R. J. H.: *Semitic Study Series*, ed. R. J. H. Gottheil and M. Jastrow Jr., Leyden, 1909.

GRAFTON, C. C.: *A Journey Godward of Doulos Iesou Christou (a Servant of Jesus Christ)*, Milwaukee, 1910 (autobiography).

HADES: M. Landau, *Hölle und Fegfeuer in Volksglaube, Dichtung und Kirchenlehre*, Heidelberg, 1909.

HALL, T. C.: *Social Solutions in the Light of Christian Ethics*, New York, 1910.

HAMBURG, ARCHBISHOPRIC OF: F. Curschmann, *Die älteren Papsturkunden des Erzbistums Hamburg*, Hamburg, 1909.

HAMMURABI: A. Ungnad, *Keilschrifttexte der Gesetze Hammurapis. Autographie der Stele sowie der altbabylonischen, assyrischen und neubabylonischen Fragmenta*, Leipsic, 1909.
 J. Kohler and A. Ungnad, *Hammurabis Gesetz*, vol. iii., ib. 1909.

HARMONY OF THE GOSPELS: H. M. Loudon, *The Life of Our Lord in the Words of the Evangelists*, London, 1909.

HARTMANN, K. R. E. VON: O. Braun, *Eduard von Hartmann*, Stuttgart, 1909.

HAWAIIAN ISLANDS: N. B. Emerson, *Unwritten Literature of Hawaii; The Sacred Songs of the Hula, collected and transl. with Notes and an Account of the Hula*, Washington, 1909.

HEINRICI, K. F G.: *Beiträge zur Geschichte und Erklärung des N. T.*, vol. v., *Des Petrus von Laodicea Erklärung des Matthäusevangeliums*, Leipsic, 1908.

HEXATEUCH: F. A. Jones, *The Dates of Genesis*, London, 1909.
 W. Engelkemper, *Heiligtum und Opferstätten in den Gesetzen des Pentateuch*, Paderborn, 1909.
 W. A. Van Es, *De Eigendom in den Pentateuch*, Kempen, 1909.

H. M. Wiener, *Essays in Pentateuchal Criticism*, Oberlin, 1910 (restates the conservative position).

HIBBERT LECTURES: 1909, W James, *Pluralistic Universe*, London and New York, 1909.

HINDUISM: R. B. L. B. Nath, *The Bhagwad Gita in Modern Life*, Calcutta, 1909.

HOBBES, T.: In *Cambridge Modern History*, vi. 785 sqq., New York, 1909.

HOLLAND: G. W Edwards, *Holland of To-day*, New York, 1909.
Jaarboek der Vereeniging voor nederlandsch-luthersche Kerkgeschiedenis, ed., J. W Pont, Amsterdam, 1909.

HOLY SPIRIT: A. C. Dawner, *The Mission and Ministration of the Holy Spirit*, London, 1909.

HOMILETICS: A. S. Hoyt, *The Preacher; his Person, Method, and Message*, New York, 1909.

HORSLEY, S.: H. H. Jebb, *A Great Bishop of One Hundred Years Ago. A Sketch of the Life of Samuel Horsley*, London, 1909.

HORT, F. J. A.: *The Epistle of St. James; Greek Text, Introduction, and Commentary as far as iv. 7*, London, 1909, New York, 1910.

HULSEAN LECTURES: 1909 10, W E. Chadwick, *Social Relationship in the Light of Christianity*, London, 1910.

HUME, D.: In *Cambridge Modern History*, vi. 819 sqq., New York, 1909.

IDEALISM : C. Werner, *Aristote et l'idéalism platonicien*, Paris, 1909.
R. C. Eucken, *Christianity and the New Idealism*, New York, 1909.

IGNATIUS OF LOYOLA: See below, JESUITS.
J. Thompson, *St. Ignatius of Loyola*, ed. J. H. Pollen, London, 1909, New York, 1910.

IMMORTALITY: See above, GOD.

INCENSE: E. G. C. F. Atchley, *A History of the Use of Incense in Divine Worship*, London, 1909.

INDIA: S. von Ketkar, *The History of Caste in India; Evidence of the Laws of Manu on the Social Conditions in India during the third Century A.D.*, vol. i., New York, 1909.
A. Lillie, *India in Primitive Christianity*, London, 1909.

INFALLIBILITY OF THE POPE: W J. S. Simpson, *Roman Catholic Opposition to Papal Infallibility*, London, 1909.

INGE, W. R.: *Faith and its Psychology*, London, 1909, New York, 1910.

ISAAC OF NINEVEH: *De perfectione religiosa*, ed. P Bedjan, Leipsic, 1910.

ISRAEL, HISTORY OF: E. E. Jessel, *The Unknown History of the Jews. Discovered from the ancient Records and Monuments of Egypt and Babylon*, London, 1909.
J. H. Kann, *Geschichte der jüdischen Literatur*, 2 vols., 2d ed., Hamburg, 1909.
N. Slouschz, *The Renaissance of Hebrew Literature (1743–1885)*, Philadelphia. 1909.
H. Brody and K. Albrecht, *The New Hebrew School of Poets of the Spanish Arabian Epoch*, London, 1909.
O. A. Tofteen, *The Historic Exodus*, Chicago, 1909.
B. H. Alford, *Old Testament History and Literature*, London, 1910.
D. W. Amram, *The Makers of Hebrew Books in Italy; being Chapters in the History of the Hebrew Printing Press*, Philadelphia, 1910.
A. T. Clay, *Amurru, the Home of the Northern Semites; a Study showing that the Religion and Culture of Israel are not of Babylonian Origin*, ib. 1910.
N. D. Davis, *Notes on the History of the Jews in Barbados*, ib. 1910.

JAINISM: U. D. Barodia, *History and Literature of Jainism*, London, 1909.

JAMES: See above, HORT.

JAPAN: See below, KOREA.
H. B. Montgomery, *The Empire of the East. A simple Account of Japan as it was, is and will be*, Chicago, 1909.

JEFFERSON, C. E.: *Talks on High Themes for Young Christians*, Boston, 1909.

JESUITS: In *Cambridge Modern History*, vi., 386 sqq., 591 sqq., New York, 1909.
A. Astrian, *Historia de la Compañia de Jesus en la Asistencia de España*, vol. iii., Madrid, 1909.
P. von Hoensbroech, *14 Jahre Jesuit. Persönliches und grundsätzliches*, Leipsic, 1909.
T. Hughes, *The History of the Society of Jesus in North America Colonial and Federal*, London, 1909.
Attention should be called to the important sources available in the *Monumenta historica societatis Jesu* in course of publication in several series at Freiburg since 1894, of which over thirty volumes have already been published, including J. A. de Polanco's *Vita Ignatii Loiolæ et rerum societatis Jesu historia*, 6 vols., 1894–98, and several series of *Epistolæ*.

JESUS CHRIST: W Bauer, *Das Leben Jesu im Zeitalter der neutestamentlichen Apokryphen*, Tübingen, 1909.
C. Mommert, *Zur Chronologie des Lebens Jesu*, Leipsic, 1909.

JESUS CHRIST, PICTURES OF: J. Burns, *The Christ Face in Art*, London, 1909.

JOHN THE APOSTLE: B. W. Bacon, *The Fourth Gospel in Research and Debate*, New York, 1910.

JOHN OF SALISBURY: C. I. Webb, *John of Salisbury*, 2 vols., Oxford, 1909.

KEMPIS, THOMAS A: J. Williams, *Thomas of Kempen*, London, 1909.

KING, H. C.: *The Ethics of Jesus*, New York, 1910; see also above, APOLOGETICS.

KLIEFOTH, T. F. D.: E. Haack, *Dr. Theodor Kliefoth*, 1910.

KNOX, G. W.: *The Gospel of Jesus the Son of God; an Interpretation for the Modern Man*, Boston, 1909.

KOREA: H. G. Underwood, *The Religions of Eastern Asia*, New York, 1910.
Miss A. L. A. Baird, *Daybreak in Korea*, New York, 1909.

LADD, G. T.: *Knowledge, Life, and Reality; an Essay in Systematic Philosophy*, New York, 1910.

LAMAISM: J. Sheepshanks, *My Life in Mongolia*, London, 1903.
H. Leder, *Das geheimnisvolle Tibet. Reisefrüchte aus dem geistlichen Reiche des Dalai-Lama*, Leipsic, 1909.
S. Hedin, *Transhimalaya*, New York, 1909.

LIST OF ABBREVIATIONS

Abbreviations in common use or self-evident are not included here. For additional information concerning the works listed, see vol. i., pp. viii.–xx., and the appropriate articles in the body of the work.

ADB . . . . . *Allgemeine deutsche Biographie*, Leipsic, 1875 sqq., vol. 53, 1907
Adv . . . . . *adversus*, "against"
AJP . . . . . *American Journal of Philology*, Baltimore, 1880 sqq.
AJT . . . . . *American Journal of Theology*, Chicago, 1897 sqq.
AKR . . . . . *Archiv für katholisches Kirchenrecht*, Innsbruck, 1857–61, Mainz, 1872 sqq.
ALKG . . . . . *Archiv für Litteratur- und Kirchengeschichte des Mittelalters*, Freiburg, 1885 sqq.
Am . . . . . American
AMA . . . . . *Abhandlungen der Münchener Akademie*, Munich, 1763 sqq.
ANF . . . . . *Ante-Nicene Fathers*, American edition by A. Cleveland Coxe, 8 vols. and index, Buffalo, 1887; vol. ix., ed. Allan Menzies, New York, 1897
Apoc . . . . . Apocrypha, apocryphal
Apol . . . . . *Apologia, Apology*
Arab . . . . . Arabic
Aram . . . . . Aramaic
art . . . . . article
Art. Schmal . . . . . Schmalkald Articles
ASB . . . . . *Acta sanctorum*, ed. J. Bolland and others, Antwerp, 1643 sqq.
ASM . . . . . *Acta sanctorum ordinis S. Benedicti*, ed. J. Mabillon, 9 vols., Paris, 1668–1701
Assyr . . . . . Assyrian
A. T. . . . . . *Altes Testament*, "Old Testament"
Augs. Con . . . . . Augsburg Confession
A. V . . . . . Authorized Version (of the English Bible)
AZ . . . . . *Allgemeine Zeitung*, Augsburg, Tübingen, Stuttgart, and Tübingen, 1798 sqq.
Baldwin, *Dictionary* . . . . . J. M. Baldwin, *Dictionary of Philosophy and Psychology*, 3 vols. in 4, New York, 1901–05
Bayle, *Dictionary* . . . . . *The Dictionary Historical and Critical of Mr. Peter Bayle*, 2d ed., 5 vols., London, 1734–38.
Benzinger, *Archäologie* . . . . . I. Benzinger, *Hebräische Archäologie*, 2d ed., Freiburg, 1907
BFBS . . . . . British and Foreign Bible Society
Bingham, *Origines* . . . . . J. Bingham, *Origines ecclesiasticæ*, 10 vols., London, 1708–22; new ed., Oxford, 1855
Bouquet, *Recueil* . . . . . M. Bouquet, *Recueil des historiens des Gaules et de la France*, continued by various hands, 23 vols., Paris, 1738–76
Bower, *Popes* . . . . . Archibald Bower, *History of the Popes . . . to 1758, continued by S. H. Cox*, 3 vols., Philadelphia, 1845–47
BQR . . . . . *Baptist Quarterly Review*, Philadelphia, 1867 sqq.
BRG . . . . . See Jaffé
Cant . . . . . Canticles, Song of Solomon
cap . . . . . *caput*, "chapter"
Ceillier, *Auteurs sacrés* . . . . . R. Ceillier, *Histoire des auteurs sacrés et ecclésiastiques*, 16 vols. in 17, Paris, 1858–69
Chron . . . . . *Chronicon*, "Chronicle"
I Chron . . . . . I Chronicles
II Chron . . . . . II Chronicles
CIG . . . . . *Corpus inscriptionum Græcarum*, Berlin, 1825 sqq.
CIL . . . . . *Corpus inscriptionum Latinarum*, Berlin, 1863 sqq.
CIS . . . . . *Corpus inscriptionum Semiticarum*, Paris, 1881 sqq.
cod . . . . . codex
cod. D . . . . . *codex Bezæ*
cod. Theod . . . . . *codex Theodosianus*
Col . . . . . Epistle to the Colossians
col., cols . . . . . column, columns
Conf . . . . . *Confessiones*, "Confessions"
I Cor . . . . . First Epistle to the Corinthians
II Cor . . . . . Second Epistle to the Corinthians
COT . . . . . See Schrader
CQR . . . . . *The Church Quarterly Review*, London, 1875 sqq.
CR . . . . . *Corpus reformatorum*, begun at Halle, 1834, vol. lxxxix., Berlin and Leipsic, 1905 sqq.
Creighton, *Papacy* . . . . . M. Creighton, *A History of the Papacy from the Great Schism to the Sack of Rome*, new ed., 6 vols., New York and London, 1897
CSCO . . . . . *Corpus scriptorum Christianorum orientalium*, ed. J. B. Chabot, I. Guidi, and others, Paris and Leipsic, 1903 sqq.
CSEL . . . . . *Corpus scriptorum ecclesiasticorum Latinorum*, Vienna, 1867 sqq.
CSHB . . . . . *Corpus scriptorum historiæ Byzantinæ*, 49 vols., Bonn, 1828–78
Currier, *Religious Orders* . . . . . C. W. Currier, *History of Religious Orders*, New York, 1896
D . . . . . Deuteronomist
DACL . . . . . F. Cabrol, *Dictionnaire d'archéologie chrétienne et de liturgie*, Paris, 1903 sqq.
Dan . . . . . Daniel
DB . . . . . J. Hastings, *Dictionary of the Bible*, 4 vols. and extra vol., Edinburgh and New York, 1898–1904
DCA . . . . . W. Smith and S. Cheetham, *Dictionary of Christian Antiquities*, 2 vols., London, 1875–80
DCB . . . . . W. Smith and H. Wace, *Dictionary of Christian Biography*, 4 vols., Boston, 1877–87
DCG . . . . . J. Hastings, J. A. Selbie, and J. C. Lambert, *A Dictionary of Christ and the Gospels*, 2 vols., Edinburgh and New York, 1906–1908.
Deut . . . . . Deuteronomy
De vir. ill . . . . . *De viris illustribus*
DGQ . . . . . See Wattenbach
DNB . . . . . L. Stephen and S. Lee, *Dictionary of National Biography*, 63 vols. and supplement 3 vols., London, 1885–1901
Driver, *Introduction* . . . . . S. R. Driver, *Introduction to the Literature of the Old Testament*, 5th ed., New York, 1894
E . . . . . Elohist
EB . . . . . T. K. Cheyne and J. S. Black, *Encyclopædia Biblica*, 4 vols., London and New York, 1899–1903
Eccl . . . . . *Ecclesia*, "Church"; *ecclesiasticus*, "ecclesiastical"
Eccles . . . . . Ecclesiastes
Ecclus . . . . . Ecclesiasticus
ed . . . . . edition; *edidit*, "edited by"
Eph . . . . . Epistle to the Ephesians
Epist . . . . . *Epistola, Epistolæ*, "Epistle," "Epistles"
Ersch and Gruber, *Encyklopädie* . . . . . J. S. Ersch and J. G. Gruber, *Allgemeine Encyklopädie der Wissenschaften und Künste*, Leipsic, 1818 sqq.
E. V . . . . . English versions (of the Bible)
Ex . . . . . Exodus
Ezek . . . . . Ezekiel
fasc . . . . . *fasciculus*
Fr . . . . . French
Friedrich, *KD* . . . . . J. Friedrich, *Kirchengeschichte Deutschlands*, 2 vols., Bamberg, 1867–69
Gal . . . . . Epistle to the Galatians
Gams, *Series episcoporum* . . . . . P. B. Gams, *Series episcoporum ecclesiæ Catholicæ*, Regensburg, 1873, and supplement, 1886
Gee and Hardy, *Documents* . . . . . H. Gee and W. J. Hardy, *Documents Illustrative of English Church History*, London, 1896
Gen . . . . . Genesis
Germ . . . . . German
GGA . . . . . *Göttingische Gelehrte Anzeigen*, Göttingen, 1824 sqq.
Gibbon, *Decline and Fall* . . . . . E. Gibbon, *History of the Decline and Fall of the Roman Empire*, ed. J. B. Bury, 7 vols., London, 1896–1900
Gk . . . . . Greek
Gross, *Sources* . . . . . C. Gross, *The Sources and Literature of English History to 1485*, London, 1900
Hab . . . . . Habakkuk

Haddan and Stubbs, *Councils*	A. W. Haddan and W. Stubbs, *Councils and Ecclesiastical Documents Relating to Great Britain and Ireland*, 3 vols., Oxford, 1869–78
Hær	Refers to patristic works on heresies or heretics, Tertullian's *De præscriptione*, the *Pros haireseis* of Irenæus, the *Panarion* of Epiphanius, etc.
Hag	Haggai
Harduin, *Concilia*	J. Harduin, *Conciliorum collectio regia maxima*, 12 vols., Paris, 1715
Harnack, *Dogma*	A. Harnack, *History of Dogma . . . from the 3d German edition*, 7 vols., Boston, 1895–1900
Harnack, *Litteratur*	A. Harnack, *Geschichte der altchristlichen Litteratur bis Eusebius*, 2 vols. in 3, Leipsic, 1893–1904
Hauck, *KD*	A. Hauck, *Kirchengeschichte Deutschlands*, vol. i., Leipsic, 1904; vol. ii., 1900; vol. iii., 1906; vol. iv., 1903
Hauck-Herzog, *RE*	*Realencyklopädie für protestantische Theologie und Kirche*, founded by J. J. Herzog, 3d ed. by A. Hauck, Leipsic, 1896–1909
Heb	Epistle to the Hebrews
Hebr	Hebrew
Hefele, *Conciliengeschichte*	C. J. von Hefele, *Conciliengeschichte*, continued by J. Hergenröther, vols. i.–vi., viii.–ix., Freiburg, 1883–93
Heimbucher, *Orden und Kongregationen*	M. Heimbucher, *Die Orden und Kongregationen der katholischen Kirche*, 2d ed. 3 vols., Paderborn, 1907
Helyot, *Ordres monastiques*	P. Helyot, *Histoire des ordres monastiques, religieux et militaires*, 8 vols., Paris, 1714–19; new ed., 1839–42
Henderson, *Documents*	E. F. Henderson, *Select Historical Documents of the Middle Ages*, London, 1892
Hist	History, *histoire, historia*
Hist. eccl.	*Historia ecclesiastica, ecclesiæ*, "Church History"
Hom.	*Homilia, homiliai*, "homily, homilies"
Hos	Hosea
Isa	Isaiah
Ital	Italian
J	Jahvist (Yahwist)
JA	*Journal Asiatique*, Paris, 1822 sqq.
Jacobus, *Dictionary*	*A Standard Bible Dictionary*, ed. M. W. Jacobus, . . . E. E. Nourse, . . . and A. C. Zenos, New York and London, 1909.
Jaffé, *BRG*	P. Jaffé, *Bibliotheca rerum Germanicarum*, 6 vols., Berlin, 1864–73
Jaffé, *Regesta*	P. Jaffé, *Regesta pontificum Romanorum . . . ad annum 1198*, Berlin, 1851; 2d ed., Leipsic, 1881–88
JAOS	*Journal of the American Oriental Society*, New Haven, 1849 sqq.
JBL	*Journal of Biblical Literature and Exegesis*, first appeared as *Journal of the Society of Biblical Literature and Exegesis*, Middletown, 1882–88, then Boston, 1890 sqq.
JE	*The Jewish Encyclopedia*, 12 vols., New York, 1901–06
JE	The combined narrative of the Jahvist (Yahwist) and Elohist
Jer	Jeremiah
Josephus, *Ant*	Flavius Josephus, "Antiquities of the Jews"
Josephus, *Apion*	Flavius Josephus, "Against Apion"
Josephus, *Life*	Life of Flavius Josephus
Josephus, *War*	Flavius Josephus, "The Jewish War"
Josh	Joshua
JPT	*Jahrbücher für protestantische Theologie*, Leipsic, 1875 sqq.
JQR	*The Jewish Quarterly Review*, London, 1888 sqq.
JRAS	*Journal of the Royal Asiatic Society*, London, 1834 sqq.
JTS	*Journal of Theological Studies*, London, 1899 sqq.
Julian, *Hymnology*	J. Julian, *A Dictionary of Hymnology*, revised edition, London, 1907
JWT	*Jaarboeken voor Wetenschappelijke Theologie*, Utrecht, 1845 sqq.
KAT	See Schrader
KB	See Schrader
KD	See Friedrich, Hauck, Rettberg
KL	*Wetzer und Welte's Kirchenlexikon*, 2d ed., by J. Hergenröther and F. Kaulen, 12 vols., Freiburg, 1882–1903
Krüger, *History*	G. Krüger, *History of Early Christian Literature in the First Three Centuries*, New York, 1897
Krumbacher, *Geschichte*	K. Krumbacher, *Geschichte der byzantinischen Litteratur*, 2d ed., Munich, 1897
Labbe, *Concilia*	P. Labbe, *Sacrorum conciliorum nova et amplissima collectio*, 31 vols., Florence and Venice, 1759–98
Lam	Lamentations
Lanigan, *Eccl. Hist*	J. Lanigan, *Ecclesiastical History of Ireland to the 13th Century*, 4 vols., Dublin, 1829
Lat	Latin, Latinized
Leg	*Leges, Legum*
Lev	Leviticus
Lichtenberger, *ESR*	F. Lichtenberger, *Encyclopédie des sciences religieuses*, 13 vols., Paris, 1877–1882
Lorenz, *DGQ*	O. Lorenz, *Deutschlands Geschichtsquellen im Mittelalter*, 3d ed., Berlin, 188
LXX	The Septuagint
I Macc	I Maccabees
II Macc	II Maccabees
Mai, *Nova collectio*	A. Mai, *Scriptorum veterum nova collectio*, 10 vols., Rome, 1825–38
Mal	Malachi
Mann, *Popes*	R. C. Mann, *Lives of the Popes in the Early Middle Ages*, London, 1902 sqq.
Mansi, *Concilia*	G. D. Mansi, *Sanctorum conciliorum collectio nova*, 31 vols., Florence and Venice, 1728
Matt	Matthew
MGH	*Monumenta Germaniæ historica*, ed. G. H. Pertz and others, Hanover and Berlin, 1826 sqq. The following abbreviations are used for the sections and subsections of this work: *Ant.*, *Antiquitates*, "Antiquities"; *Auct. ant.*, *Auctores antiquissimi*, "Oldest Writers"; *Chron. min.*, *Chronica minora*, "Lesser Chronicles"; *Dip.*, *Diplomata*, "Diplomas, Documents"; *Epist.*, *Epistolæ*, "Letters"; *Gest. pont. Rom.*, *Gesta pontificum Romanorum*, "Deeds of the Popes of Rome"; *Leg.*, *Leges*, "Laws"; *Lib. de lite*, *Libelli de lite inter regnum et sacerdotium sæculorum xi. et xii. conscripti*, "Books concerning the Strife between the Civil and Ecclesiastical Authorities in the Eleventh and Twelfth Centuries"; *Nec.*, *Necrologia Germaniæ*, "Necrology of Germany"; *Poet. Lat. ævi Car.*, *Poetæ Latini ævi Carolini*, "Latin Poets of the Caroline Time"; *Poet. Lat. med. ævi*, *Poetæ Latini medii ævi*, "Latin Poets of the Middle Ages"; *Script.*, *Scriptores*, "Writers"; *Script. rer. Germ.*, *Scriptores rerum Germanicarum*, "Writers on German Subjects"; *Script. rer. Langob.*, *Scriptores rerum Langobardicarum et Italicarum*, "Writers on Lombard and Italian Subjects"; *Script. rer. Merov.*, *Scriptores rerum Merovingicarum*, "Writers on Merovingian Subjects"
Mic	Micah
Milman, *Latin Christianity*	H. H. Milman, *History of Latin Christianity, Including that of the Popes to . . . Nicholas V.*, 8 vols., London, 1860–61
Mirbt, *Quellen*	C. Mirbt, *Quellen zur Geschichte des Papsttums und des römischen Katholicismus*, Tübingen, 1901
MPG	J. P. Migne, *Patrologiæ cursus completus, series Græca*, 162 vols., Paris, 1857–66
MPL	J. P. Migne, *Patrologiæ cursus completus, series Latina*, 221 vols., Paris, 1844–64
MS., MSS.	Manuscript, Manuscripts
Muratori, *Scriptores*	L. A. Muratori, *Rerum Italicarum scriptores*, 28 vols., 1723–51
NA	*Neues Archiv der Gesellschaft für ältere deutsche Geschichtskunde*, Hanover, 1876 sqq.
Nah	Nahum
n.d.	no date of publication
Neander, *Christian Church*	A. Neander, *General History of the Christian Religion and Church*, 6 vols., and index, Boston, 1872–81
Neh	Nehemiah
Niceron, *Mémoires*	R. P. Niceron, *Mémoires pour servir à l'histoire des hommes illustrés . . .*, 43 vols., Paris, 1729–45
NKZ	*Neue kirchliche Zeitschrift*, Leipsic, 1890 sqq.
Nowack, *Archäologie*	W. Nowack, *Lehrbuch der hebräischen Archäologie*, 2 vols., Freiburg, 1894
n.p.	no place of publication
NPNF	*The Nicene and Post-Nicene Fathers*, 1st series, 14 vols., New York, 1887–92; 2d series, 14 vols., New York, 1890–1900
N. T.	New Testament, *Novum Testamentum, Nouveau Testament, Neues Testament*
Num	Numbers
Ob	Obadiah

O. S. B.	*Ordo sancti Benedicti*, "Order of St. Benedict"
O. T.	Old Testament
OTJC	See Smith
P	Priestly document
Pastor, *Popes*	L. Pastor, *The History of the Popes from the Close of the Middle Ages*, 8 vols., London, 1891–1908
PEA	*Patres ecclesiæ Anglicanæ*, ed. J. A. Giles, 34 vols., London, 1838–46
PEF	Palestine Exploration Fund
I Pet	First Epistle of Peter
II Pet	Second Epistle of Peter
Platina, *Popes*	B. Platina, *Lives of the Popes from Gregory VII. to Paul II.*, 2 vols., London, n.d.
Pliny, *Hist. nat.*	Pliny, *Historia naturalis*
Potthast, *Wegweiser*	A. Potthast, *Bibliotheca historica medii ævi. Wegweiser durch die Geschichtswerke*, Berlin, 1896
Prov	Proverbs
Ps	Psalms
PSBA	*Proceedings of the Society of Biblical Archeology*, London, 1880 sqq.
q.v., qq.v	*quod (quæ) vide*, "which see"
R	Redactor
Ranke, *Popes*	L. von Ranke, *History of the Popes*, 3 vols., London, 1906
RDM	*Revue des deux mondes*, Paris, 1831 sqq.
RE	See Hauck-Herzog
Reich, *Documents*	E. Reich, *Select Documents Illustrating Mediæval and Modern History*, London, 1905
REJ	*Revue des études juives*, Paris, 1880 sqq.
Rettberg, *KD*	F. W. Rettberg, *Kirchengeschichte Deutschlands*, 2 vols., Göttingen, 1846–48
Rev	Book of Revelation
RHR	*Revue de l'histoire des religions*, Paris, 1880 sqq.
Richardson, *Encyclopaedia*	E. C. Richardson, *Alphabetical Subject Index and Index Encyclopaedia to Periodical Articles on Religion, 1890–99*, New York, 1907.
Richter, *Kirchenrecht*	A. L. Richter, *Lehrbuch des katholischen und evangelischen Kirchenrechts*, 8th ed. by W. Kahl, Leipsic, 1886
Robinson, *Researches*, and *Later Researches*	E. Robinson, *Biblical Researches in Palestine*, Boston, 1841, and *Later Biblical Researches in Palestine*, 3d ed. of the whole, 3 vols., 1867
Robinson, *European History*	J. H. Robinson, *Readings in European History*, 2 vols., Boston, 1904–06
Robinson and Beard, *Modern Europe*	J. H. Robinson, and C. A. Beard, *Development of Modern Europe*, 2 vols., Boston, 1907
Rom	Epistle to the Romans
RSE	*Revue des sciences ecclésiastiques*, Arras, 1860–74, Amiens, 1875 sqq.
RTP	*Revue de théologie et de philosophie*, Lausanne, 1873
R. V.	Revised Version (of the English Bible)
sæc	*sæculum*, "century"
I Sam	I Samuel
II Sam	II Samuel
SBA	*Sitzungsberichte der Berliner Akademie*, Berlin, 1882 sqq.
SBE	F. Max Müller and others, *The Sacred Books of the East*, Oxford, 1879 sqq., vol. xlviii., 1904
SBOT	*Sacred Books of the Old Testament* ("Rainbow Bible"), Leipsic, London, and Baltimore, 1894 sqq.
Schaff, *Christian Church*	P. Schaff, *History of the Christian Church*, vols. i.–iv., vi., vii., New York, 1882–92, vol. v., part 1, by D. S. Schaff, 1907
Schaff, *Creeds*	P. Schaff, *The Creeds of Christendom*, 3 vols., New York, 1877–84
Schrader, *COT*	E. Schrader, *Cuneiform Inscriptions and the Old Testament*, 2 vols., London, 1885–88
Schrader, *KAT*	E. Schrader, *Die Keilinschriften und das Alte Testament*, 2 vols., Berlin, 1902–03
Schrader, *KB*	E. Schrader, *Keilinschriftliche Bibliothek*, 6 vols., Berlin, 1889–1901
Schürer, *Geschichte*	E. Schürer, *Geschichte des jüdischen Volkes im Zeitalter Jesu Christi*, 4th ed., 3 vols., Leipsic, 1902 sqq.; Eng. transl., 5 vols., New York, 1891
Script	*Scriptores*, "writers"
Scrivener, *Introduction*	F. H. A. Scrivener, *Introduction to New Testament Criticism*, 4th ed., London, 1894
Sent	*Sententiæ*, "Sentences"
S. J.	*Societas Jesu*, "Society of Jesus"
SMA	*Sitzungsberichte der Münchener Akademie*, Munich, 1860 sqq.
Smith, *Kinship*	W. R. Smith, *Kinship and Marriage in Early Arabia*, London, 1903
Smith, *OTJC*	W. R. Smith, *The Old Testament in the Jewish Church*, London, 1892
Smith, *Prophets*	W. R. Smith, *Prophets of Israel . . to the Eighth Century*, London, 1895
Smith, *Rel. of Sem.*	W. R. Smith, *Religion of the Semites*, London, 1894
S. P. C. K.	Society for the Promotion of Christian Knowledge
S. P. G.	Society for the Propagation of the Gospel in Foreign Parts
sq., sqq	and following
Strom	*Stromata*, "Miscellanies"
s.v.	sub voce, or sub verbo
Swete, *Introduction*	H. B. Swete, *Introduction to the Old Testament in Greek*, London, 1900
Syr	Syriac
TBS	Trinitarian Bible Society
Thatcher and McNeal, *Source Book*	O. J. Thatcher and E. H. McNeal, *A Source Book for Mediæval History*, New York, 1905
I Thess	First Epistle to the Thessalonians
II Thess	Second Epistle to the Thessalonians
ThT	*Theologische Tijdschrift*, Amsterdam and Leyden, 1867 sqq.
Tillemont, *Mémoires*	L. S. le Nain de Tillemont, *Mémoires . . ecclésiastiques des six premiers siècles*, 16 vols., Paris, 1693–1712
I Tim	First Epistle to Timothy
II Tim	Second Epistle to Timothy
TJB	*Theologischer Jahresbericht*, Leipsic, 1882–1887, Freiburg, 1888, Brunswick, 1889–1897, Berlin, 1898 sqq.
TLB	*Theologisches Litteraturblatt*, Bonn, 1866 sqq.
TLZ	*Theologische Litteraturzeitung*, Leipsic, 1876 sqq.
Tob	Tobit
TQ	*Theologische Quartalschrift*, Tübingen, 1819 sqq.
TS	J. A. Robinson, *Texts and Studies*, Cambridge, 1891 sqq.
TSBA	*Transactions of the Society of Biblical Archæology*, London, 1872 sqq.
TSK	*Theologische Studien und Kritiken*, Hamburg, 1826 sqq.
TU	*Texte und Untersuchungen zur Geschichte der altchristlichen Litteratur*, ed. O. von Gebhardt and A. Harnack, Leipsic, 1882 sqq.
TZT	*Tübinger Zeitschrift für Theologie*, Tübingen, 1838–40
Ugolini, *Thesaurus*	B. Ugolinus, *Thesaurus antiquitatum sacrarum*, 34 vols., Venice, 1744–69
V. T.	*Vetus Testamentum, Vieux Testament*, "Old Testament"
Wattenbach, *DGQ*	W. Wattenbach, *Deutschlands Geschichtsquellen*, 5th ed., 2 vols., Berlin, 1885; 6th ed., 1893–94
Wellhausen, *Heidentum*	J. Wellhausen, *Reste arabischen Heidentums*, Berlin, 1887
Wellhausen, *Prolegomena*	J. Wellhausen, *Prolegomena zur Geschichte Israels*, 6th ed., Berlin, 1905, Eng. transl., Edinburgh, 1885
ZA	*Zeitschrift für Assyriologie*, Leipsic, 1886–88, Berlin, 1889 sqq.
Zahn, *Einleitung*	T. Zahn, *Einleitung in das Neue Testament*, 3d ed., Leipsic, 1907
Zahn, *Kanon*	T. Zahn, *Geschichte des neutestamentlichen Kanons*, 2 vols., Leipsic, 1888–92
ZATW	*Zeitschrift für die alttestamentliche Wissenschaft*, Giessen, 1881 sqq.
ZDAL	*Zeitschrift für deutsches Alterthum und deutsche Literatur*, Berlin, 1876 sqq.
ZDMG	*Zeitschrift der deutschen morgenländischen Gesellschaft*, Leipsic, 1847 sqq.
ZDP	*Zeitschrift für deutsche Philologie*, Halle, 1869 sqq.
ZDPV	*Zeitschrift des deutschen Palästina-Vereins*, Leipsic, 1878 sqq.
Zech	Zechariah
Zeph	Zephaniah
ZHT	*Zeitschrift für die historische Theologie*, published successively at Leipsic, Hamburg, and Gotha, 1832–75
ZKG	*Zeitschrift für Kirchengeschichte*, Gotha, 1876 sqq.
ZKR	*Zeitschrift für Kirchenrecht*, Berlin, Tübingen, Freiburg, 1861 sqq.
ZKT	*Zeitschrift für katholische Theologie*, Innsbruck, 1877 sqq.
ZKW	*Zeitschrift für kirchliche Wissenschaft und kirchliches Leben*, Leipsic, 1880–89
ZNTW	*Zeitschrift für die neutestamentliche Wissenschaft*, Giessen, 1900 sqq.
ZPK	*Zeitschrift für Protestantismus und Kirche*, Erlangen, 1838–76
ZWT	*Zeitschrift für wissenschaftliche Theologie*, Jena, 1858–60, Halle, 1861–67, Leipsic, 1868 sqq.

SYSTEM OF TRANSLITERATION

The following system of transliteration has been used for Hebrew:

א = ʼ or omitted at the beginning of a word.	ז = z	ע = ʻ
בּ = b	ח = ḥ	פּ = p
ב = bh or b	ט = ṭ	פ = ph or p
גּ = g	י = y	צ = ẓ
ג = gh or g	כּ = k	ק = ḳ
דּ = d	כ = kh or k	ר = r
ד = dh or d	ל = l	שׂ = s
ה = h	מ = m	שׁ = sh
ו = w	נ = n	תּ = t
	ס = s	ת = th or t

The vowels are transcribed by a, e, i, o, u, without attempt to indicate quantity or quality. Arabic and other Semitic languages are transliterated according to the same system as Hebrew. Greek is written with Roman characters, the common equivalents being used.

KEY TO PRONUNCIATION

When the pronunciation is self-evident the titles are not respelled; when by mere division and accentuation it can be shown sufficiently clearly the titles have been divided into syllables, and the accented syllables indicated.

ɑ as in *sofa*	e as in *not*	iu as in *duration*
ā " " *arm*	ō " " *nor*	c = k " " *cat*
a " " *at*	u " " *full*[2]	ch " " *church*
â " " *fare*	ū " " *rule*	cw = qu as in *queen*
e " " *pen*[1]	ʋ " " *but*	dh (*th*) " " *the*
ê " " *fate*	ū " " *burn*	f " " *fancy*
i " " *tin*	ai " " *pine*	g (hard) " " *go*
î " " *machine*	au " " *out*	H " " *loch* (Scotch)
o " " *obey*	ei " " *oil*	hw (*wh*) " " *why*
ō " " *no*	iū " " *few*	j " " *jaw*

[1] In accented syllables only; in unaccented syllables it approximates the sound of e in *over*. The letter ṇ, with a dot beneath it, indicates the sound of n as in ink. Nasal n (as in French words) is rendered n.
[2] In German and French names ü approximates the sound of u in dune.

THE NEW SCHAFF-HERZOG

ENCYCLOPEDIA OF RELIGIOUS KNOWLEDGE

LIUTPRAND, lūt′prand: Medieval Italian historian; d. about 970. He was of Lombard descent and was educated at the court of Pavia, where he attracted the attention of King Hugo, and later became the chancellor of King Berengar. In 949 he went to Constantinople on a mission for the king, but afterward became opposed to Berengar and went to the court of Otto I., who made him bishop of Cremona in 962. Six years later he made a second journey to Constantinople to gain the hand of a Greek princess for Otto II. His three works, none of which are complete, are as follows: *Antapodosis*, a history from 887 to 949, designed to requite the good and evil which he had experienced and directed especially against Berengar and Willa; *Liber de rebus gestis Ottonis magni imperatoris*, a history from 960 to 964; and *Relatio de legatione Constantinopolitana*, describing his second visit to the city. His style is attractive, but the subjectivity and unreliability of his writings render their historical value only secondary. (A. Hauck.)

Bibliography: His works are collected in *MGH*, *Script.*, iii (1839), 264 363, and in *MPL*, cxxxvi. 787 938. Consult: R. A. Köpke, *De vita et scriptis Liudprandi*, Berlin, 1842; C. Dändliker and J. J. Müller, *Luidprand von Cremona und seine Quellen*, Leipsic, 1871; F. Köhler, *Beiträge zur Textkritik Liudprands von Cremona*, in *NA*, viii (1883), 49-89; A. Zanelli, *Una legasione a Costantinopoli nel secolo x.*, Brescia, 1883; Wattenbach, *DGQ*, i (1885), 347, 391–396, i (1893), 372, 423–428; L. von Ranke, *Weltgeschichte*, viii. 634–655, Leipsic, 1887; Potthast, *Wegweiser*, 742–744 (for further literature).

LIVERMORE, ABIEL ABBOT: American Unitarian; b. at Wilton, N. H., Oct. 30, 1811; d. there Nov. 28, 1892. He was graduated at Harvard College (1833) and at the Harvard Divinity School (1836). He was pastor at Keene, N. H. (1836–50), Cincinnati, O. (1850–56), and at Yonkers, N. Y. (1857–63), editing while he was in Yonkers *The Christian Inquirer*. He was president of the Meadville, Penn., Theological School (1863–89). He wrote: Commentaries on the Gospels (2 vols., Boston and New York, 1850), Acts (1844), and Romans (1854); *Lectures to Young Men* (Keene, 1846); and the *Marriage Offering* (Boston, 1848).

LIVING GOD, CHURCH OF THE: An organization founded in 1894 in Indianapolis, Ind., by John Vinson (q.v.) and his mother, Mary Jane Vinson, and by others in other places. It is Congregational in polity; has as officers elders and deacons, serving the local churches; and believes in annual associations of all local churches by delegates. It lays stress upon the fact that its ministry is composed of men and women called by the Holy Spirit; makes the Bible its creed and book of discipline; and its ordinances are baptism of converted believers by immersion, the Lord's Supper, washing of feet, and the kiss of salutation, and it regards as of special importance the visitation of the sick and needy. The church also deems of special importance the doctrine of sanctification. It holds that Adam and Eve were created holy in soul, spirit, and body, and were possessed of free will; that both were allured by Satan and being led by him they disobeyed God's command, after which Satan in spirit entered into, and depraved them wholly. The depravity to which they were thus subjected affected by heredity only the bodies of their descendants, but soul and spirit of all infants, being the creation and gift of God at conception (Eccl. xii. 7; Zech. xii. 1; Heb. xii. 9), are pure until by voluntary yielding to Satan's temptations they become defiled by their own first act of sin, after the fashion of Adam and Eve. To meet this doctrine of sin and depravity they regard the true doctrine of sanctification to be the following. The act itself is a " setting apart," a " separation," in which there are six steps: (1) Universal Salvation through the blood of Jesus Christ of all infants from conception until the time when they voluntarily sin (Rom. v. 18; Matt. xix. 14). (2) Regeneration—conversion, by faith and repentance through the blood of Jesus, whereby the indwelling Satan, installed by the commission of the first act of sin, is turned out, when Jesus Christ, the Holy Spirit and love enter the believer by faith in the risen Lord (Luke xi. 24–26; Eph. ii. 2, iv. 22–23; Col. iii. 9–10; John i. 13; Rom. v. 5). (3) Instantaneous cleansing of soul, spirit and body, of all depravity, thus resulting in perfect holiness (II Cor. vii. 1; Heb. vi. 1), by the blood of Jesus Christ and the believer's faith and consecration (Rom. xii. 1; Heb. xii. 14, etc.). (4) Baptism by the Holy Spirit resulting in the full manifestation of the fulness of the Holy Spirit and of the fire of love (Matt. iii. 11; Acts i. 5, 8, ii. 1–21). (5) Resurrection, affecting the body on the final judgment day, the body being changed, cleansed from its vileness into the likeness of Christ's glorious body (Dan. xii. 2; Rom. viii. 23; I Cor. xv. 52–55; Phil. iii. 21). (6) The healing of the physical body from all diseases by and through the blood of Jesus and by the prayer of faith, diseases being caused directly or indirectly by Satan and his demons (Isa. liii. 4–5, R. V. margin; Matt. viii. 17; James v. 14–15; Mark ix. 21–29; Luke xiii. 11–17).

Statistics are not at hand, but the church reports two congregations in Indianapolis, Ind., and many scattered adherents elsewhere. JOHN VINSON.

LIVINGSTON, JOHN HENRY: The "father of the Reformed Dutch Church in America"; b. at Poughkeepsie, N. Y., May 30, 1746; d. in New Brunswick, N. J., Jan. 20, 1825. He attended Yale College (M.A., 1762) and began the study of law, but went to Holland in 1766 to study theology at the University of Utrecht (D.D., 1770). He was licensed by the Classis of Amsterdam in 1769, and in 1770 he became second English preacher in the Reformed Dutch Church in New York. Driven from the city by the Revolution, he preached at Kingston 1776, at Albany 1776–79, at Livingstone Manor 1779–81, and at Poughkeepsie 1781–83. In 1784 he was appointed by the general synod professor of didactic and polemic theology; and in 1810 the synod called him to New Brunswick to open a theological seminary there, and at the same time he was elected president of Queen's (now Rutger's) College. These two offices he held until his death. By his learning, piety, and dignity, he won the respect of both parties then existing in the church; and under his skilful management "the Conferentie" and "the Coetus" were united (1771). Thus the credit of forming the independent organization of the Reformed (Dutch) Church in America (q.v.) must be given to him. It was he, also, who principally shaped the constitution of this church, and prepared its first psalm- and hymn-book (1787). As a preacher he was much admired. His theological lectures are preserved in manuscript in the Sage Library, New Brunswick, but an abstract of them was published by the Rev. Alva Neal, New York, 1831, 2d ed. 1832. His publications include several sermons, also *Funeral Service, or Meditations adapted to Funeral Addresses* (New York, 1812); and *A Dissertation on the Marriage of a Man with his Sister-in-Law* (strongly condemning it as unlawful; New Brunswick, 1816).

BIBLIOGRAPHY: A. Gunn, *Memoirs of John Henry Livingston*, New York, 1829, condensed by T. W. Chambers, 1856.

LIVINGSTONE, DAVID: Explorer and missionary in Africa, was born at Blantyre (8 m. s.e. of Glasgow) Mar. 19, 1813, and died in Ilala, Central Africa, May 1, 1873. He grew up amid the austere Scotch piety of his home, with very limited schooling. At ten he went to work in a cotton factory, and formed the habit of putting most of his earnings into the acquisition of books (a Latin grammar, works on natural science, etc.), which he studied far into the night. His studies were so successful that in 1830 he was able to enter the University of Glasgow, with the object of studying medicine, supporting himself by factory work in the summer months. To this period belongs his awakening to personal Christianity. He describes his inner transformation as being similar to the curing of color-blindness. His desire to serve the kingdom of God was directed by an appeal of Gützlaff's toward the mission in China. He began to study theology with the design of going to China as an independent missionary. Some friends, however, induced him to join an organized mission. In 1838 he entered the service of the London Missionary Society, at whose expense he continued his studies. When these were completed, his proposed expedition to China was prevented by the outbreak of the Opium War. Through the influence of Robert Moffat, then in England, his thoughts were turned to South Africa, for which he was duly commissioned on Dec. 8, 1840.

Early Life and Education.

Early Missionary Labors.

At Moffat's station, Kuruman, Livingstone was to learn the language of the Bechuana people. While astonished at the results already achieved there, he was obliged to modify his earlier conceptions. In many particulars he was not in harmony with the existing methods. Before long his characteristic impulse to go further manifested itself. A few months after his arrival he made a journey of over 700 miles, winning the confidence of the natives wherever he went by his medical activity. Upon Moffat's return with the young missionary Edwards, Livingstone migrated with the latter to the Ba-katla tribe. Here, with great practical efficiency, he organized the Mabotsa station, to which in 1843 he brought Moffat's daughter as his wife. On account of difficulties arising apparently out of the wounded vanity of his colleague, who even brought charges against him before the missionary board of directors, Livingstone proceeded in 1846 to the country of the Bakwena, deserting the house and plantations at Mabotsa. He now founded a station on the river Kolobeñ to which Setshele, the chieftain, transferred his capital. This chief, who had known Livingstone since his first journey, was deeply impressed by his teaching, and when he made up his mind to abandon polygamy he was baptized. Unfortunately, but few of his subjects followed him. Concerning Livingstone's personal missionary labors at this period little is known, as his diaries have been lost. Since he refused to take in any but true believers, the congregation remained very small. He himself seems to have been far from satisfied with his labors here, which would never have made him famous.

His great nature impelled him onward. There was no rest for him at Kolobeñ. At the cost of laborious journeys, he was continually seeking new tribes. The immediate occasion was furnished by the destruction of his station by the Boers, who, having retreated before the English power into the interior, kept a sharp watch to prevent the natives from obtaining firearms, while Livingstone, a thorough free-trader, paid no attention to their wishes. So when Setshele failed to comply with the demand of the Boers that he should suppress this traffic in his tribe, a retaliatory expedition was undertaken against his capital, in which the mission station was destroyed. At the time Livingstone with his wife and child was on the journey in course of which he discovered Lake Ngami, and was paving the way by his acquaintance with Sebituane, chief of the Makololo, toward wider enterprises.

After escorting his family to Cape Town, he returned, and in 1853 began some preliminary missionary labor with the tribe at Linyanti on the River Tshobe, which was in time to spread abroad to the Barotse race, then subject to the Makololo, in the luxuriantly fertile Zambesi plain. A mission of this kind, however, required a direct and easy way of communication with home. In order to seek such a way, Livingstone, supplied by Sekeletu (son and successor of Sebituane) with a great company of bearers, undertook the journey to Loanda, where he arrived May 31, 1854. After a short rest he returned to the Makololo, whose capital, by his advice, was transferred to the north bank of the Zambesi. Next he proceeded down stream to the east, discovered Victoria Falls, and in the spring of 1856 reached the Portuguese colony of Tete, where he left his Makololo companions and returned by way of Kilimane to England.

Livingstone the missionary had become a world-renowned explorer. While writing the accounts of his travels, and in the midst of diverting influences, very extensive new plans took shape in his mind. A mission on vast lines, combined with colonization and trade, was contemplated. He severed his connection with the London Missionary Society, after it had sanctioned the founding of a Makololo mission, which he promised to support. He personally assumed the leadership of an expedition to the Zambesi with government support, in the capacity of British consul. With this was combined an enterprise of the Universities Mission looking toward the establishment of a "colonizing mission" in the Zambesi district. This second period of Livingstone's activity in Africa (1858–64) was full of difficulties, disappointments, and failures. In the ascent of the Zambesi, the expedition found little support among the Portuguese. What proved the most serious obstacle to Livingstone's plans was their toleration of the slave-trade. Meanwhile he explored the Shire, a left-bank tributary of the Zambesi; discovered Lake Shirwa and reached, by way of the south, Lake Nyasa, which had been recently discovered along its eastern shore by the German explorer Roscher. He then journeyed overland to the Makololo, among whom in the mean time a mission had been founded by the London Society amid the greatest difficulties, but fever had carried off its entire staff. Shortly afterward, in an uprising of the subject tribes, the Makololo were exterminated. Their tribal lands were assigned to the Barotse, among whom eventually the Paris mission assumed the labor toward which Livingstone had aspired in connection with that region. Bishop MacKenzie meanwhile had arrived with missionaries and colonists. The first station of the colonizing mission was founded near Lake Shirwa. But while Livingstone was occupied with the farther exploration of Lake Nyasa (1862), the new establishment once again succumbed to the ravages of fever, drought, famine, and the assaults of the savage slave-hunter Ajawa. After the bishop's death, the few remaining members removed the colony to the Shire. They succeeded no better here in effecting a permanent settlement; and thus the realization of Livingstone's favorite plan was frustrated. Besides all this, he had been troubled by dissensions among the officers of the expedition. A fresh reinforcement arrived, including Mrs. Livingstone, who desired to share her husband's journeys. A few weeks later, he had to commit his wife to the grave (1862). From the depth of mourning he roused himself to new labor. He sought to discover a better approach to Lake Nyasa and the interior by way of the Rovuma. Here again many difficulties and disappointments were encountered. It grew plainer and plainer that the objects of the expedition were not yet to be realized, and in 1864 it was recalled by the Government.

Explorations 1858–64.

Livingstone remained only a year in England. With the vigorous cooperation of persons of influence, he formed new plans, which no longer had to do with definite missionary labors, but contemplated the solution of that great problem of civilization, the opening up of central Africa, especial stress being laid on the suppression of the slave-trade. Directly after completing his second book, *The Zambesi and its Tributaries* (London, 1864), he sailed for Bombay with the idea of organizing a new expedition from that base. He recruited soldiers in India; and two native Africans, Chuma and Susi, trained in an Indian mission school, became his faithful servants. The bearers were recruited on Johanna Island. Provision was made for beasts of burden, including camels, buffaloes, mules, and asses. This imposing expedition was led by Livingstone, the sole European member of it, by way of Zanzibar to the mouth of the Rovuma. His plan was to pass around the Portuguese colony and open a route for legitimate trade communication and Christian influences all the way to the interior of the continent. As the expedition proceeded geographical exploration became more and more prominent in its work. Again, and very soon, unexpected difficulties occurred. In course of a few months the Indian soldiers had to be sent back as totally unserviceable. Livingstone understood the Africans very well, but not the Indians. The animals perished down to the last one. Lake Nyasa was reached with great efforts. Attacked by the savage Mafitu, the carriers from Johanna fled back to their home, and spread the report that Livingstone had been murdered, but he and the remnants of the caravan eluded the pursuers. While all Europe was mourning over his death, he still pushed on amid the greatest obstacles, sick, without medicine or proper food; and, falling in with an Arab caravan, arrived at Kasembe, thence discovering Lake Moero, and reaching Ujiji on Lake Tanganyika. Provisions were to await him here, but the Arab agent, weary of the delay, squandered them and embezzled the money. Despite all this, Livingstone so promptly recovered his strength in the wholesome air that he soon (1869), with his few attendants, undertook a new expedition westward through the district of the cannibal Manyema. At Nyangwe he reached the Lualaba, and supposed he had discovered the upper reaches of the Nile. He

Final Period of African Work, 1865–73.

sought vainly to obtain a boat of some kind, fell sick again, and wearily dragged himself, with three attendants, back to Ujiji. Here he was met by the intrepid explorer, Henry M. Stanley, who had been sent out in search of him. Under his fostering care Livingstone recovered, and they both undertook a journey of exploration to the north end of Tanganyika, ascertaining that this lake was not connected with the Nile. The search for the source of the Nile had come to be more and more Livingstone's preoccupation, and with this in view he withstood Stanley's entreaties to return with him to Europe. They parted with regret in Mar., 1872, and Livingstone turned to the exploration of the sources of the Lualaba. He discovered Lake Bangweolo, by a journey which took him largely through swampy and flooded country. His servants carried their sick master day after day, many a time through long reaches of water. At Tshitambo's village in Ilala they built him a hut and nursed him faithfully, until one morning they found his dead body in a kneeling posture by his couch. They embalmed his corpse, packed it in a bale of merchandise, and carried it in a wonderful funeral procession, amid many perils, to the coast. On Apr. 18, 1874, it was deposited in Westminster Abbey.

Livingstone the missionary developed into the pioneer of civilization, and ultimately into the geographical explorer. But he never lost sight of the fact that only the Gospel could bring true succor to the peoples of Africa. During his very last journey, he still observed regular devotions with his attendants, and, as long as his strength lasted, divine worship on Sunday. The latest entries in his diary evince unswerving profound piety. His discoveries were carried further with much success by Stanley, and the African continent was opened to European civilization and to the colonial enterprises of ambitious nations. Although this is unhappily not always directed by a Christian spirit, yet missionary work also has received a great impetus and achieved successful results in the spirit of the great pioneer, whose name can never be forgotten by the peoples of Africa. R. GRUNDEMANN.

BIBLIOGRAPHY: The works of Livingstone consist of his *Missionary Travels and Researches in South Africa*, London, 1857; *Narrative of an Expedition to the Zambesi and its Tributaries*, ib. 1865; and *Last Journals*, ed. H. Waller, 2 vols., ib. 1874. Besides the standard biography by W. G. Blaikie, London, 1888 and often, other lives have been written by: J. S. Roberts, ib. 1874; S. Mossman, in *Heroes of Discovery*, Edinburgh, 1877; idem, *Livingstone, the Missionary Traveller*, London, 1882; J. Marratt, ib. 1877; A. Gavard and A. Perier, Paris, 1878; T. Hughes, London, 1891 and often; H. H. Johnston, ib. 1891; T. B. Maclachlan, Edinburgh, 1901; B. K. Gregory, London, 1906; and in *DNB*, xxxiii. 384-396. Further material is found in: H. M. Stanley, *How I Found Livingstone*, London, 1872; W. D. Cooley, *Dr. Livingstone and the Royal Geographical Society*, London, 1874; C. F. Loriot, *David Livingstone et sa mission sociale*, Paris, 1881; R. Noel, *Livingstone in Africa*, London, 1895; and Sir Bartle Frere, in *Proceedings of the Royal Geographical Society*, vol. xviii., 1874.

LIVONIANS, CONVERSION OF THE. See ALBERT OF RIGA; and BERTHOLD OF LIVONIA.

LLORENTE, lyo-ren'tê, **JUAN ANTONIO:** Historian of the Spanish Inquisition; b. at Rincon de Soto (90 m. n.w. of Saragossa) Mar. 30, 1765; d. in Madrid Feb. 5, 1823. He studied at Saragossa and became both doctor and priest before he had reached the canonical age. He was appointed a commissioner in 1785, and secretary general of the Inquisition in 1789. The opportunity that was thus presented for becoming acquainted with the functions and the archives of those in authority was well utilized by Llorente. His endeavor to make the procedure public throughout was frustrated on the fall of his like-minded patrons, the Grand Inquisitor Manuel Abad y la Sierra, and the Minister Jovellanos. Llorente became so far involved in the latter's fall that he, too, was subjected to prosecution, which resulted, however, in his acquittal. Upon the downfall of the Bourbon Government in 1808, Llorente took the side of the followers of King Joseph. As member from 1808 of the Council of State, Llorente assumed the supervision of the abrogation of the cloisters, at which time he began to write the history of the Spanish Inquisition. This highly important work was first published in French, *Histoire critique de l'Inquisition d'Espagne* (4 vols., Paris, 1817–18); then in Spanish (10 vols., Madrid, 1822); then in German, English (London, 1826), Dutch, and Italian. The reactionary Government succeeded in punishing the author, for his ecclesiastical functions were annulled, and at the university there was even issued an order forbidding him to give instruction in his mother tongue, and when the *Portrait politique des Papes* (2 vols., Paris, 1822) appeared, he was banished. But being included under the universal political amnesty of 1820, he returned to Spain; he had scarcely reached Madrid, however, when his death occurred. The value of his principal work lies in the fact that it supplies extracts from documents no longer accessible. K. BENRATH.

BIBLIOGRAPHY: Sources for a biography are his own statements in the *Notice biographique*, Paris, 1818, and the life by his friend Mahul in *Revue encyclopédique*, xviii (1823). Consult further: C. J. von Hefele, *Der Cardinal Ximenes*, Tübingen, 1851, Eng. transl., London, 1860; P. Gams, *Zur Geschichte der spanischen Inquisition*, Regensburg, 1878; idem, *Die Kirchengeschichte von Spanien*, iii., part 2, ib. 1879; *KL*, viii. 56–59. The German transl. of Llorente's history of the inquisition appeared in 4 vols., Gmünd, 1810, and after the 3d ed. of the original, Stuttgart, 1824. The 2d ed. of the Italian transl. appeared, 6 vols., Milan, 1854.

LLOYD, WILLIAM: Bishop of Worcester; b. at Tilehurst (18 m. w. of Windsor), Berkshire, Aug. 18, 1627; d. at Hartleburg Castle (4 m. s. of Kidderminster), Worcester, Aug. 30, 1717. He studied at Oriel and at Jesus College, Oxford (B.A., 1642; M.A., 1646; B.D. and D.D., 1667), becoming a fellow of the latter college. He became a royal chaplain (1666), prebendary of Salisbury Cathedral (1667), vicar of St. Mary's, Reading, and archdeacon of Merioneth (1668), dean of Bangor and prebendary of St. Paul's (1672), vicar of St. Martin's-in-the-Fields (1677) and bishop of St. Asaph (1680). He was translated to the see of Lichfield and Coventry in 1692, and to the see of Worcester in 1700. He was one of the most indefatigable opponents of Romanism under James II., and was one of the seven bishops who were imprisoned in the Tower June 8–15, 1688, for protesting against the Second Declaration of Indulgence. With the other bishops he was tried and acquitted June 29. He assisted at the crowning of William and Mary and shortly afterward became lord high almoner. He furnished material for Burnet's *History of the Reformation of the Church of England* (3 parts, London, 1679-1715), wrote many tracts, and also one valuable work, *An Historical Account of Church Government as it was in Great Britain and Ireland when they first Received the Christian Religion* (London, 1684; reprinted in T. P. Pantin's edition of Stillingfleet's *Origines Britannicæ*, vol. ii., Oxford, 1842).

Bibliography: A valuable list of sources is appended to the article in *DNB*, xxxiii. 436-439. Consult: N. Salmon, *Lives of the English Bishops*, pp. 147-156, London, 1733; F. B. Howell, *Complete Collection of State Trials*, xii. 183-254, xiv. 545-560, ib. 1812; E. H. Plumptre, *Life of Bishop Ken*, i. 66, 140, 145, 293-316, ii. 1 10, 302, London, 1888; J. H. Overton, *The Church in England*, ii. 161 sqq., ib. 1897; W. H. Hutton, *The English Church (1625-1714)*, pp. 227 sqq., ib. 1903.

LOBO, lō'bō, **JERONIMO**: Portuguese Jesuit missionary; b. in Lisbon 1593; d. there Jan. 29, 1678. After teaching for a time in the Jesuit college at Coimbra he went as a missionary to India in 1621, arriving at Goa in 1622. In 1625 he settled in Abyssinia as superintendent of missions in the kingdom of Tigré, but some years later he was driven from the country, along with the patriarch and other Jesuit missionaries (see Abyssinia and the Abyssinian Church, § 8). After trying in vain to enlist the pope and the Spanish and Portuguese governments in a scheme to reclaim Abyssinia to the Romish Church by force of arms, he returned to India in 1640 and became provincial of the Jesuits at Goa. In 1656 he returned to Lisbon, where he spent the rest of his life. He wrote in Portuguese an account of his travels, which, it seems, has never been published. The manuscript is preserved in the monastery of St. Roque, Lisbon. Balthazar Tellez drew largely upon Lobo's work for his *Historia general de Ethiopia a Alta* (Coimbra, 1660), which has often been attributed to Lobo. Abbé Legrand translated Lobo's work into French under the title *Voyage historique de Abissinie* (Paris, 1728), which was translated by Dr. Johnson as *A Voyage to Abyssinia* (London, 1735; new ed., 1887).

LOBSTEIN, lob'stain, **PAUL**: German Protestant; b. at Epinal (264 m. e.s.e. of Paris), Department of the Vosges, France, July 28, 1850. He was educated at the universities of Strasburg, Tübingen, and Göttingen, and in 1876 became privat-docent at the first-named institution. In the following year he was appointed associate professor of theology at the same university, where he has been full professor since 1884. In theology he is a disciple of Reuss, A. Sabatier, and Ritschl. He has been associate editor of the works of Calvin in the *Corpus Reformatorum*, xxiii.-xxxii., xlv., and has written *Die Ethik Calvin's in ihren Grundzügen entworfen* (Strasburg, 1877); *Petrus Ramus als Theolog* (1878); *La Notion de la préexistence du Fils de Dieu* (Paris, 1883); *Études christologiques* (5 parts, 1885-94; the second part, *La Doctrine de la naissance miraculeuse du Christ*, 1890, was translated into English by V. Leuliette under the title *The Virgin Birth of Christ*, London, 1903); *La Doctrine de la Sainte-Cène* (Lausanne, 1889); *Réflexions sur le baptême des enfants* (Paris, 1892); *Essai d'une introduction à la dogmatique protestante* (Paris, 1896; Eng. transl. *Introduction to Protestant Dogmatics*, Chicago, 1902); *Études sur la doctrine chrétienne de Dieu* (Lausanne, 1906).

LOBWASSER, lōb-väs'ser, **AMBROSIUS**: Author of the well-known "Lobwasser Psalter"; b. at Schneeberg (20 m. s.s.w. of Chemnitz) Apr. 4, 1515; d. at Königsberg Nov. 27, 1585. He was educated at Leipsic, especially in jurisprudence (under his elder brother Paul, then professor of that subject); took his master's degree at twenty, and worked as a lecturer till 1550. During the next seven years he traveled as tutor to some young men of rank, and in 1557 became court councilor and chancellor at Meissen. At Bologna, in 1562, he attained the degree of doctor of laws. From 1563 to 1580, when he retired from active life, he was assessor and professor of law at Königsberg. He was a thorough and versatile scholar, and more than once filled the office of rector of the university. Although a Lutheran by conviction, he was viewed askance by his coreligionists for the reason that he based his translation of the Psalter of Beza and Marot not on the original text, but on the Reformed French Psalter. His object was to popularize in Germany the melodies of the French Psalter, of the beauty of which he had received a deep impression during a long sojourn in Berry; and thus he adhered to the texts which served as channels for these melodies, in order that the meter and versification might accord with the French model. His work was primarily designed for private edification. Accidental circumstances, above all a pestilential epidemic, afforded him the requisite leisure for the undertaking; a "noble Frenchman," Gaurier, gave him encouragement, and thus the Psalter was completely rendered into German by 1562. Duke Albert of Prussia, on whose patronage Lobwasser had doubtless reckoned, died in 1568, and the publication was deferred till 1573. The title reads: *Der Psalter des königlichen Propheten Davids, In deutsche reyme verstendiglich und deutlich gebracht, mit vorgehender anzeigung der reymen weise, auch eines jeden Psalmes inhalt: Durch den ehrvesten Hochgelarten Herrn Ambrosium Lobwasser, der Rechten Doctorn und Fürstlicher Durchlauchtigkeit in Preussen Rathe. Und hierüber bey einem jeden Psalmen seine zegehörige vier stimmen: Vnd laut der Psalmen andechtige schöne Gebet* (Leipsic, 1573).

The prayers appended to every psalm are translations of the *Oraisons* of Augustin Marlorat, preacher at Rouen. The summary preceding each psalm and the appended prayer stamp the work as a manual of edification. Although but a mediocre performance in point of language and practical objectiveness, the Psalter enjoyed a success not much inferior to that of the Huguenot Psalter itself. For nearly two hundred years, Lobwasser had almost unlimited sway in the German Reformed Church; and to this day, he is not quite out of date. He owed this success distinctly to the verbally exact adaptation of his version to the French melodies.

These melodies formed the common musical language of the Reformed of all tongues.

The work was recast musically in 1607 by Landgrave Maurice of Hesse, who sought to bring it into harmony with the declamatory style of singing at that time coming into fashion, and again by Samuel Marschall (Basel, 1606); by Crüger (Berlin, 1656); by Sultzberger (Bern, 1675) and others. The text was also rendered into other languages: Latin, by Andreas Spetke, 1596; Danish, 1662; Italian, by Planta, 1740, as well as earlier; by the daughter of Landgrave Maurice of Hesse, 1608; by Casimir, 1753; Nicolai, 1762, etc. The attempts of eighteenth-century taste to improve and expand the Lobwasser Psalter led gradually to its disuse. The appendix, which had at first comprised only the Decalogue Hymn ("Erheb' dein Herz, thu' auf dein Ohren") and the Song of Simeon, and had then been enlarged by the addition of German hymns, many of them Lutheran, grew continually stouter and heavier, till at last the "appendix" swallowed up the Psalter, and new hymnals arose in which only selected psalms were retained.

As the melodies lost their distinctive rhythm, their charm likewise vanished which the Lobwasser text, notwithstanding its stiff and far from poetic language, had possessed. The German hymns which had flourished, indeed, in the sixteenth century, although through the importance attached to Scriptural language and the charm of the French psalm melodies it had yielded to the latter, now gained the supremacy.

Besides his Psalter, Lobwasser also published a collection of *Hymni patrum und anderer gottseliger Männer, welche durchs ganze Jahr in den Kirchen gesungen werden, aus dem Latein ins Deutsch mit gleichen Reimen gebracht* (Leipsic, 1578–79). Some of these translations found acceptance in the Lutheran Church. H. A. Köstlin †.

Bibliography: Sources are: J. C. Wetzel, *Hymnopoegraphia*, ii. 79 sqq., Herrnstadt, 1721; M. Adam, *Vitæ Germanicorum jureconsultorum*, pp. 267 sqq., Heidelberg, 1620; C. Hartknoch, *Preussische Kirchenhistorie*, pp. 498 sqq., Frankfort, 1866. Consult: P. Wackernagel, *Das deutsche Kirchenlied*, i. 509 sqq., iv. 844 sqq., Leipsic, 1863–76; G. Döring, *Choralkunde*, pp. 52–57, 234, Danzig, 1865; E. Hopfner, *Reformbestrebungen auf dem Gebiet der deutschen Dichtung*, Berlin, 1866; E. Koch, *Geschichte des Kirchenliedes*, ii. 594–597, Stuttgart, 1867; F. Bovet, *Hist. du psautier des églises réformées*, Paris, 1872; O. Douen, *Clément Marot et le psautier huguenot*, ib. 1872; P. Wolfrum, *Die Entstehung und erste Entwickelung des deutschen evangelischen Kirchenliedes*, pp. 134 sqq., Leipsic, 1890; J. Zahn, *Die Melodien der deutschen Kirchenlieder*, vi. 56 sqq., Gütersloh, 1893; *ADB*, xix. 56–58; Julian, *Hymnology*, pp. 683–684.

LOCI THEOLOGICI: A term applied by Melanchthon to Evangelical systems of dogmatics and retained by many as late as the seventeenth century. The word was borrowed, as he himself says, from the usage of the classic rhetoricians, in whose works *topoi* or *loci* denote the places or sources from which proofs are deduced. Various systematized indexes of these *loci* were made from the days of Aristotle, and mere formal categories, such as "person," "nature," or "fortune," were also reckoned under this head. It was the particular task of the rhetorician, however, to trace the concrete case, or "hypothesis," to the general, or "thesis." Thus were evolved *loci communes*, or arguments which could be applied to many specific cases. The humanistic rhetoricians frequently confused *loci communes* with simple *loci*, or general basal concepts. This was especially true of Melanchthon, as is clear from his *De rhetorica libri tres* (Cologne, 1519), in which he sought to train students for disputation. He accordingly advised them to prepare lists of all possible *loci communes*, and to enter under the proper rubrics (*capita*) any examples gathered in the course of their reading. Among theological *loci communes* he lists "faith," "destruction of the body," "Church," "word of God," "patience," "sin," "law," "grace," "love," and "ceremony." Elsewhere he defines *loci communes* as "certain general rules of living, of which men are persuaded by nature, and which I might not unjustly call the laws of nature." These two definitions, however, are not clearly distinguished and the discussion of the *loci communes* is consequently somewhat vague. This criticism applies also to the *loci theologici* of his famous *Loci communes rerum theologicarum* (1521), which are primarily basal concepts appearing in the science of theology, to which all in it must be referred. He accordingly begins with his favorite list "God," "one," "triple," and "creation," and closes with "condemnation" and "beatitude." Although this list was derived from Peter Lombard, Melanchthon's treatment is not only more clear than that of his predecessor, but he draws his examples from the Bible instead of from the Church Fathers, and under Pauline influence deduces, in addition to *loci communes*, certain *loci communissimi*, such as "sin," "grace," and "law." In view of the long and powerful influence of this book, the result of his failure to give a methodical proof of his series of *loci* was that Lutheran dogmatics was slow in reaching inherent unity. The term *loci theologici* gradually came to denote the content, and thus the chief passages of the Bible as included in the individual *loci*, although this meaning was forced into the background when Melanchthon laid more stress on the development of doctrine.

For Lutheran theology Melanchthon's book had the same importance which the work of Peter Lombard possessed for scholasticism. His *loci* were the subject of commentary as late as Leonhard Hutter, and the term *loci communes* came to connote any work dealing with the sum of Christian doctrine. Among the Reformed the phrase *loci communes* was accepted by Wolfgang Musculus (Basel, 1560), Peter Martyr (London, 1576), Johannes Maccovius (Franeker, 1639), and Daniel Chamier (Geneva, 1653). After the middle of the seventeenth century, however, with the rise of a more systematic treatment of dogmatics the term fell into disuse. (Johannes Kunze.)

LOCK, WALTER: Church of England; b. at Dorchester (8 m. n. of Weymouth), Dorsetshire, July 14, 1846. He was educated at Marlborough College and Corpus Christi, Oxford (B.A. 1869), and was fellow of Magdalen College, Oxford, in 1869–72, where he has been honorary fellow since 1897 He was assistant to the professor of humanity at St. Andrews in 1869–70, and from the latter year to 1897 was tutor of Keble College, Oxford, as well as subwarden in 1880–97 and warden since 1897. Since 1895 he has been Dean Ireland's professor of the exegesis of Holy Scripture in the University of Oxford, and was also examining chaplain to the bishop of Lichfield in 1881–91 and to the archbishop of York since 1891, examiner in the Honour School of Theology in 1885–87, and select preacher to the university in 1889–90. He has edited Keble's *Christian Year* (London, 1895) and *Lyra Innocentium* (1899), and has written the essay on *The Church* in *Lux Mundi* (London, 1890); and on *The Bible* and *The Old Testament* in *Oxford House Papers* (1886–97); *John Keble, a Biography* (1892); *St. Paul, the Master Builder* (1899); and *The Bible and Christian Life* (1905).

LOCKE, JOHN: English philosopher; b. at Wrington (10 m. s.w. of Bristol) Aug. 29, 1632; d. at Oates, Essex, Oct. 28, 1704. He studied at the College of Westminster (1646–52), and at Christ Church, Oxford (B.A., 1655–56; M.A., 1658), there making the acquaintance of a circle of eminent men which included Edward Pococke and Robert Boyle (qq.v.), and continuing his residence there for some years. The Aristotelian-scholastic philosophy then dominant at Oxford left him unsatisfied; meanwhile, he was teaching privately, became Greek lecturer in 1660, lecturer on rhetoric in 1662, and censor in moral philosophy in 1663. He had also pursued the study of medicine, and had become interested in physical science. In 1665 Locke went as secretary of the English mission to the elector of Brandenburg, but the next year settled as a physician at Oxford, through his profession becoming a friend of the first earl of Shaftesbury, to whom he was in large part indebted for political preferments which continued to come to him through life. Thus, in 1672 Locke was appointed to a secretaryship which was, for the times, moderately well compensated. His health was not good, however, and he resided in France 1675–79, not in idleness, however, but making investigations along scientific, political, and social lines. After that he was in England until 1684, principally at Oxford, and then he went to Holland, remaining abroad till 1688–89, when he returned and became commissioner of appeals, an office which he retained till death.

The most important event in his life was the publication of the work which brought him lasting fame as a philosopher, his *Essay concerning Human Understanding* (London, 1690; five editions by 1706). The purpose was to investigate the origin, certainty, and extent of human knowledge. In this work Locke sought to prove that innate ideas do not exist, and that all knowledge comes through experience by sensation and reflection. He was thus the originator of the empirical philosophy of the eighteenth century which spread over England, France, and Germany and greatly influenced both the political and social theories of his times. His letters on *Toleration* (1689–90), *Two Treatises of Government* (1690), a work on the national currency (1692), and *Some Thoughts concerning Education* (1693) are further weighty productions of this period. Locke was a member of the council of trade (1696–1700), but because of failing health was obliged to decline other preferments.

Locke's influence continued dominant until the spread of Kantian ideas, and he is called "the founder of the analytic philosophy of mind" (J. S. Mill, *Logic*, book I., chap. vi.). His principles were either so carried out or so misapplied in theology that he became the object of sharp attack, to which he as sharply replied. This was especially the case with Bishop Edward Stillingfleet (q.v.), whose *Discourse in Vindication of the Doctrine of the Trinity* (London, 1696) brought on a controversy with Locke which continued till 1699. Locke has sometimes been regarded as the father of late English skepticism (see DEISM, §§ 4–5; ENLIGHTENMENT, THE, § 7). While in early life he had deliberately turned away from theology as a vocation, his interest never died out, and this came to its fruitage in his *Reasonableness of Christianity* (1695), and in his *Paraphrase* of the epistles to the Galatians, I and II Corinthians, Romans, and Ephesians (posthumous, 1705–07). Of his *Works* many editions have appeared (3 vols., London, 1714; best ed. by E. Law, 4 vols., ib. 1777); and his *Posthumous Works* (ib. 1706).

BIBLIOGRAPHY: Sources of knowledge are: *Some Familiar Letters between Mr. Locke and Several of his Friends*, London, 3d ed., 1737; *Original Letters of Locke, Algernon Sidney and Anthony Lord Shaftesbury*, ib. 2d ed., 1847; *Shaftesbury. Life, Unpublished Letters, and Philosophical Regimen*, ed. E. Rand, ib. 1900; J. Le Clerc's *Éloge historique de feu Mr. Locke*, Amsterdam, 1705; and the life prefixed to Law's ed. of the *Works*, ut sup. Consult further: G. W. von Leibnitz, *Nouveaux essais sur l'entendement*, Amsterdam, 1765, Eng. transl., *New Essays concerning Human Understanding*, London, 1896; J. G. Buhle, *Geschichte der neuern Philosophie*, iv. 238–438, Göttingen, 1803; F. Bowen, *Critical Essays*, pp. 1–32, Boston, 1842; A. H. Everett, *Critical and Miscellaneous Essays*, pp. 381–451, Boston, 1846; J. D. Morell, *Historical and Critical Review of the Speculative Philosophy of Europe in the 19th Century*, i. 91–147, London, 1846; R. Vaughan, *Essays in History, Philosophy, and Theology*, ii. 59–120, ib. 1849; E. Tagart, *Locke's Writings and Philosophy historically Considered*, ib. 1855; T. E. Webb, *The Intellectualism of Locke*, Dublin, 1857; V. Cousin, *La Philosophie de Locke*, Paris, 1863; J. Tulloch, *Rational Theology and Christian Philosophy in England in the 17th Century*, 2 vols., London, 1872; T. H. Green, *A Treatise on Human Nature by David Hume* (Introduction), ib. 1878; H. Marion, *J. Locke, sa vie et son œuvre*, Paris, 1879; J. Brown, *Horæ subsecivæ, Locke and Sydenham*, Edinburgh, 1882; P. King, *Life and Letters of John Locke; with Extracts from his Commonplace Books*, new ed., New York, 1884; H. Winter, *Darlegung und Kritik der lockeschen Lehre vom empirischen Ursprung der sittlichen Grundsätze*, Bonn, 1884; R. Falckenberg, *Geschichte der neuren Philosophie*, pp. 111–133, Leipsic, 1886; J. Fowler, *Locke*, London, 1887; M. M. Curtis, *An Outline of Locke's Ethical Theory*, Leipsic, 1890; W. L. Courtney, *Studies at Leisure*, London, 1892; G. F. von Hertling, *John Locke und die Schule von Cambridge*, Freiburg, 1892; P. Fischer, *Die Religionsphilosophie des John Locke*, Erlangen, 1893; J. McCosh, *Locke's "Theory of Knowledge," with a Notice of Berkeley*, New York, 1894; E. Fechtner, *John Locke*, Stuttgart, 1898; W. Graham, *English Political Philosophy*, London, 1899; E. E. Worcester, *The Religious Opinions of John Locke*, Geneva, N. Y., 1890; A. C. Fraser, *Locke*, Edinburgh, 1901; idem, *J. Locke as a Factor in Modern Thought*, London, 1905; J. Rickaby, *Free Will and Four English Philosophers*, London, 1906. Of importance, also, are the works on the history of philosophy, particularly those of J. E. Erdmann, Eng. transl., London, 1893; W. Windelband, Eng. transl., ib. 1893; A. Weber, Eng. transl., ib. 1896; and F. Ueberweg, Eng. transl., New York, 1874.

LOCUST: A common and familiar insect of the East. Locusts are counted among the small winged animals which "go upon all four" and were all regarded as unclean, with the exception of those which had two hind legs projecting above their feet "to leap withal upon the earth" (Lev. xi. 21-22). These legs for leaping are a characteristic of the locust, while other marks are a head set at right angles with the body, armed with strong mandibles and having two antennæ, large eyes, and a body formed of nine annulets. The four wings are of nearly equal length, but the rear ones are considerably broader than those in front. The female with her ovipositor thrusts the eggs, after they are fertilized, into the loose earth. In the spring, when the sun warms the ground, the larvæ creep out, greenish white or black, small as flies, in shape like the full-grown locusts, only without external sexual organs. They cast their skin four times; after the third casting the sexual parts appear and after the fourth the insects are able to fly. In Syria locusts begin to breed by the middle of April.

The two species which are most common in Syria (*Acridium peregrinum* and *Œdipoda migratoria*) are particularly dreaded on account of their voracity and their great numbers. When the desert winds drive the immense swarms through the air (Ex. x. 13; Prov. xxx. 27) they darken the sun like heavy clouds and the rattling of their wings sounds like the noise of chariots (Joel ii. 2, 5; Rev. ix. 9). Wherever they settle down, the verdure immediately disappears, even the Garden of Eden becomes a desert (Joel ii. 3). Those which are not yet winged crawl on the ground and no obstacle can stop them or divert them from the path they have chosen (Ex. x. 6; Joel ii. 7, 9). Broad ditches and large fires avail little to destroy the swarms, and even the red-hawk and the rosy grackle (*turdus roseus*), which fly along with them and devour many, scarcely lessen the swarms. Rain is their most dangerous enemy, as it destroys their eggs, and a severe storm does away with them altogether by sweeping them into the sea (Ex. x. 19; Joel ii. 20).

Locusts were looked upon as clean according to Lev. xi. 22, and they were eaten by the poor as they are to-day by the Bedouins (cf. Matt. iii. 4; Mark i. 5). By the Assyrians they were regarded as a delicacy. They are often mentioned in the Old Testament as a type of an enormous multitude (Judges vi. 5; Jer. xlvi. 23; Nah. iii. 15; Eccles. xliii. 17); of littleness, unimportance, and transitoriness (Num. xiii. 33; Ps. cix. 23; Isa. xl. 22; Nah. iii. 17); of greed (Deut. xxviii. 38; Isa. xxxiii. 4), and of destruction (Amos vii. 1). Their advancing in bands is described in Prov. xxx. 27; in their leaping and in their appearance they are compared to horses (Joel ii. 4; Rev. ix. 7). A plague of grasshoppers was one of the most dreadful judgments of God (Deut. xxviii. 38; I Kings viii. 37; Amos iv. 9). A highly poetical description of a swarm of locusts and the destruction and waste they left behind them is given by Joel (chaps. i.–ii).

The Old Testament has many names to designate locusts. The one most generally used, *'arbeh*, is a generic name (cf. Ex. x. 4 sqq.) as well as the name of a particular species, probably the flying, migratory locust (*gryllus migratorius*), which is said to bear this name in Bagdad at the present day. In Lev. xi. 22, *sal'am*, *ḥargal*, and *ḥaghabh* are named as different species; *ḥaghabh*, however, seems to be also a common designation. The names in Joel (i. 4, ii. 25) are popular expressions (cf. *ḥasil*, "the devourer," Deut. xxviii. 38; Ps. lxxviii. 46) which serve everywhere as general designations (Jer. li. 27; Amos iv. 9; Nah. iii. 16). To these may be added *gebh* and *gobh* (Isa. xxxiii. 4; Amos vii. 1; Nah. iii. 17)—an exceptional wealth of synonyms easily understood from the great part the locust played everywhere in the land. Some of these synonyms may have had their origin in the various dialects of the country. I. BENZINGER.

BIBLIOGRAPHY: S. Bochart, *Hierozoicon*, II., iv. 1, 3 vols., Leipsic, 1793–96; J. L. Burckhardt, *Notes on the Bedouins and Wahabis*, London, 1830; H. B. Tristram, *Natural Hist. of the Bible*, pp. 306 sqq., ib. 1880; A. Munro, *The Locust Plague and its Suppression*, ib. 1900; *DB*, iii. 130-131; *EB*, iii. 2807–10; *JE*, viii. 147; and the commentaries on Leviticus at xi. 22, and on Joel, particularly that by Driver, in the *Cambridge Bible*, containing an excursus on locusts and giving the literature.

LODENSTEIN, lō'den-stain, **JODOCUS VAN:** Reformed preacher and ascetic; b. at Delft Feb. 6, 1620; d. at Utrecht Aug. 6, 1677. He studied theology at Utrecht under Voetius, Schotanus and De Maets, and in 1642 went to Franeker in order to devote himself to the study of Oriental languages under the direction of Coccejus. In 1644 he became preacher at Zoetermeer near Delft, in 1650 at Sluis in Flanders, and in 1653 at Utrecht, where he labored until his death. He was the originator of a reformation of life and morals in the Netherlands, and was thus for the Dutch and German Reformed Church what Spener soon after became in the German Evangelical-Lutheran Church, and by the same analogy he was followed by a party of "Lodensteinians," who kept aloof from the external life of the Church without formally separating themselves, unlike the adherents of Labadie, who were outspoken dissenters. He was a reformer of practical life, not of doctrine. The Netherlands were at that time exceedingly prosperous, and the popular mind seemed to be entirely absorbed by secular pursuits. Lodenstein, however, made a wide-spread impression by his preaching, by his writings, and by his spiritual songs. Of his sermons many were published and often reprinted in various collections, such as *Geestelyke Opwekker* (Amsterdam, 1701); *Verralle Christendom* (Utrecht, 1711); *Heerlijkheid van een waar Christelijk leven* (Amsterdam, 1711); *Boetpredikatien over Jerem. xlv* (Utrecht, 1779). Of his important ascetic works must be mentioned especially *Weegschale der onvolmaacktheden* (Utrecht, 1664) and *Beschouwinge van Zion* (ib. 1674–76). A collection of his spiritual songs is in *Uytspanningen en andere Gedigten* (ib. 1676). (S. D. VAN VEEN.)

BIBLIOGRAPHY: P. I. Proost, *Jodocus van Lodenstein*, Amsterdam, 1880; M. Goebel, *Geschichte des christlichen Lebens in der rheinisch-westfalischen evangelischen Kirche*, ii. 160–180, Coblentz, 1852; H. L. J. Heppe, *Geschichte des Pietismus und der Mystik in der reformirten Kirche*, Leyden, 1879; A. Ritschl, *Geschichte des Pietismus*, i. 152 sqq., Bonn, 1880.

LOEBE, lōb'e, **AUGUST JULIUS:** German Lutheran; b. at Altenburg (24 m. s. of Leipsic) Jan. 8, 1805; d. at Rasephas (a suburb of Altenburg) Mar. 27, 1900. He was educated at the gymnasium of his native city and at the universities of Jena (1825–27; Ph.D., 1831) and Leipsic (1827–1828), after which he conducted a private school in Altenburg until 1839. Becoming deeply interested in Gothic, he determined on the first critical edition of the translation of Ulfilas (q.v.) in collaboration with Hans Conon von der Gabelentz; and for this purpose he visited Upsala in 1834 to inspect the famous Codex Argenteus, and in the following year went to Wolfenbüttel with Von der Gabelentz to study the Codex Carolinus of Ulfilas. The edition, which appeared under the title *Ulfilas: Veteris et Novi Testamenti versionis Gothicæ fragmenta quæ supersunt* (3 vols., Leipsic and Altenburg, 1836–46), was accompanied by Löbe's *Beiträge zur Textberichtigung und Erklärung des Skeireins* (Altenburg, 1839) and supplemented by the collaborators' *Nachschrift zu der Ausgabe des Ulfilas* (Leipsic, 1860).

In 1839 Löbe became pastor at Rasephas, where the remainder of his life was to be spent. Here he contributed largely to Pierer's *Universal-Lexikon*, and practically edited the fourth and fifth editions of the work (1857–64; 1867–72), as well as the three additional year-books incorporated in the same encyclopedia (1865–73). He also did most of the work on the edition planned by Preuss of the *Loci theologici* of Johann Gerhard (9 vols., Berlin and Leipsic, 1863–85). His third field of activity was the local and ecclesiastical history of Altenburg, represented by his *Geschichtliche Beschreibung der Residenzstadt Altenburg und ihrer Umgebung* (Altenburg, 1841), and the completion, in collaboration with his eldest son, Ernst Conon Löbe, of Sachse's *Altenburger Kirchengallerie* (3 vols., ib. 1886–91).

LOEHE, lō'e, **JOHANN KONRAD WILHELM:** Lutheran theologian and philanthropist; b. in Fürth (5 m. n.w. of Nuremberg) Feb. 21, 1808; d. at Neuendettelsau (12 m. s. of Nuremberg) Jan. 2, 1872. Descended from a pious middle-class family, he went from the gymnasium of Nuremberg to the University of Erlangen in 1826 to study theology. First the Reformed, then powerfully and inflexibly the Lutheran, view influenced him. In 1828 he spent a term at the University of Berlin, attracted not so much by the lectures of the professors as by the sermons of the famous preachers. In 1831 he became vicar at Kirchenlamitz where he drew large congregations by his original and fervent preaching. But the civil and ecclesiastical authorities on the charge of mysticism removed him after two years and he became assistant pastor of St. Giles in Nuremberg. Here his gift of preaching was fully developed. Like a prophet of old, Löhe denounced sin without fear, and thus set the magistracy of the city against him. He had, however, the support of the Church authorities. In 1837 he finally settled as preacher at Neuendettelsau, an inconsiderable and unattractive place, which after many a struggle he transformed into a busy Christian colony. From 1848 to 1852 the idea of leaving the Bavarian State Church frequently took hold of him, and his relations with its authorities became very strained. The reason for his dissatisfaction did not lie so much in actual conditions, but in the fact that Löhe measured these conditions by his ideal standards. It was the conflict between the ideal and the real that agitated him; he tried to identify the communion of saints with its visible organism. He planned originally not a reformation, but an entirely new formation of the Church. He addressed a petition signed by 330 people to the General Synod in which he demanded the withdrawal of secular supremacy over the Protestant Church, complete purification of confession, and the strictest adherence to the symbols of the Church. Although the synod tried to meet his demands as far as possible, Löhe was not satisfied and was several times actually on the point of secession; but his historical feeling and love for the traditions of the Church deterred him from the execution of his plan. As a strictly orthodox Lutheran, he was chiefly offended by the free intercourse between the Lutherans and the Reformed, and especially by their common celebration of the Lord's Supper, which threatened to eliminate the differences in doctrine, although no actual union existed. A proposition was made to suspend Löhe, but many voted against this measure, which, on account of his numerous following, would have led to an actual split within the Church of Bavaria. But these disagreeable conditions were changed when in 1852 the leadership of the consistory was entrusted to Harless, whose attitude toward Löhe was less hostile, and who effected a definite but peaceable separation between the Lutherans and Reformed. In his great work on the Church (*Drei Bücher von der Kirche*, 1845) Löhe propounds the strictest Lutheran orthodoxy. Impurity of doctrine is for him as bad as immoral conduct, and Lutheran doctrines are complete and perfect, in no need of development. But his zeal for orthodoxy was at times so excessive that it brought him dangerously near to Roman Catholicism, as for instance in his doctrine of a visible Church and his ideas of church government, the efficacy of works, self-denial, and celibacy. But he was so firmly rooted in the doctrine of justification that it is impossible to speak of a conscious inclination toward the Roman Catholic Church.

The personality of Löhe must, however, be judged in its entirety. He was not only a man of pure, although sometimes one-sided, orthodoxy, but a creative power in the field of charitable work. From 1840 he was active in educating spiritual workers for the German emigrants to America. He founded the Missouri Synod in union with the emigrant Lutherans of Saxony, the Franconian colonies in Michigan, and at a later time the Iowa Synod. Neuendettelsau possesses two stately buildings devoted to the education of missionaries for North America and Australia. In 1849 Löhe founded the Lutheran Society of Home Missions, and in 1853 an institution of deaconesses which was dedicated in the following year, the eighteenth in order of foundation, but the third or fourth in numbers of all Germany. Around this center there grew up with wonderful rapidity a number of institutions, such as asylums for idiots, a Magdalen asylum, hospitals for men and women, a chapel, industrial schools. etc. In 1865 a branch of the institution of deaconesses was founded at Polsingen near Oettingen, consisting of a department for male idiots, a district hospital, a reformatory, and an asylum for infants.

The characteristic trait in Löhe's personality was a healthy combination of orthodoxy with originality of thinking. Sin and grace, justification and sanctification, were the central points of his theology. As a preacher, he was among the greatest of the century. Originality of conception, vivid imagination, and prophetic fervor, were his chief characteristics in the pulpit. Löhe also made a profound study of liturgies and laid down his views in *Agende für christliche Gemeinden* (1848). He awakened everywhere the sense for liturgical order. But he was perhaps even greater as a pastor than as a preacher. Löhe was a man of striking appearance. His head was large, his forehead high; his mouth made the impression of great decision of character; his voice was powerful, and his eye bright and searching. He wrote not less than sixty works growing out of the experiences of his spiritual office and serving practical purposes. His earlier writings originated from his opposition to the State Church, *Unsere kirchliche Lage* (Nördlingen, 1850); *Aphorismen über die neutestamentlichen Aemter und ihr Verhältniss zur Gemeinde* (Nuremberg, 1849); *Kirche und Amt, neue Aphorismen* (Erlangen, 1851); *Die bayerische Generalsynode vom Frühjahr 1849 und das lutherische Bekenntnis* (Nuremberg, 1849). Of a permanent value are *Drei Bücher von der Kirche* (Stuttgart, 1845); *Rosenmonate heiliger Frauen* (1860); *Der evangelische Geistliche* (2 vols., 1852–58); *Sieben Predigten* (Nuremberg, 1836); *Predigten über das Vaterunser* (1837); *Sieben Vorträge über die Worte am Kreuze* (Stuttgart, 1859); *Erinnerungen aus der Reformationsgeschichte von Franken* (Nuremberg, 1847); *Haus-, Schul- und Kirchenbuch für Christen lutherischen Bekenntnisses* (Stuttgart, 1845); *Samenkörner* (Nördlingen, 1844). (A. Hauck.)

Bibliography: J. Deinzer, *W. Löhes Leben*, 3 vols., 3d ed., Gütersloh, 1901; H. Beck, *Die innere Mission in Bayern*, pp. 18 sqq., Hamburg, 1880; K. Eichner, *Wilhelm Löhe, ein Lebensbild*, Nuremberg, 1907.

LOEHR, lōr, MAX: German Protestant; b. at Stettin Apr. 30, 1864. He was educated at the universities of Königsberg and Göttingen (Ph.D., 1889), was member of the royal Domstift at Berlin (1889–90), and then became privat-docent for Old-Testament exegesis at Königsberg, and in 1892 associate professor of the same subject at Breslau. Became professor of the Old Testament at Königsberg, 1909. He was engaged at the German Archeological Institute in Jerusalem in 1903–04, edited the Syriac annotations of Bar Hebræus on the Pauline epistles (Göttingen, 1889) and wrote *Die Klagelieder des Jeremias erklärt* (for W. Nowack's *Handkommentar zum Alten Testament;* 1894); *Der Missionsgedanke im Alten Testamente* (Freiburg, 1896); *Geschichte des Volkes Israel* (Strasburg, 1900); *Untersuchungen zum Buche Amos* (Giessen, 1901); *Babel und die biblische Urgeschichte* (Breslau, 1902); *Seelenkämpfe und Glaubensnöte vor zwei Tausend Jahren* (Halle, 1904); *Der vulgärarabische Dialekt von Jerusalem* (Giessen, 1905); *Alttestamentliche Religionsgeschichte* (Leipsic, 1906); and *Die Stellung des Weibes zu Jahwe-Religion und -Kult* (1908). He likewise prepared the third edition of O. Thenius' *Kommentar zu den Büchern Samuelis* (Leipsic, 1898).

LOEN, lōn, JOHANN MICHAEL VON: German statesman and author; b. at Frankfort-on-the-Main Dec. 21, 1694; d. at Lingen (36 m. w.n.w. of Osnabrück), Hanover, July 26, 1776. He began the study of law at Marburg in 1711, but removed to Halle in 1712, and finally settled at Frankfort in 1723. As a prolific, open-minded writer, he attracted considerable attention in the literary world, and gained the notice of Frederick the Great, who, in 1753, conferred on him the offices of Prussian privy councilor and administrative president of the County of Lingen and Tecklenburg, which he held until his death.

His copious writings, of historical, esthetic, literary, political, ethical, and religious range, were published under the title *Gesammelte kleine Schriften* (ed. J. E. Schneider, 4 vols., Frankfort, 1749–1752). His standpoint is essentially that of the Enlightenment (q.v.), except that with him confessional indifferentism is still associated with a warm and genuine ethical religious interest. His aim of working in the cause of church union and a comprehensive type of Christianity expressed itself in his first work, the pseudonymous *Evangelischer Friedenstampel, nach Art der ersten Kirche entworfen* (Frankfurt, 1724). He made a German translation of Fénelon's spiritual writings; while his personal association with Zinzendorf resulted in *Der vernünftige Gottesdienst nach der leichten Lehrart des Heilandes* (Frankfurt, 1738 and often). The work which made Loen's name best known, yet brought upon him the most numerous and vehement attacks, was *Die einzige wahre Religion* (Frankfort, 1750). In the first half he shows this to consist solely in faith in God through Christ, and in a correspondingly devout and virtuous life according to the eternal law of love. The second part treats of the ideal union in the outward details of Christian life. This remarkable book combines liberalizing thoughts with the principles of the Roman Catholic hierarchy, and blends rationalistic and pietistic ideas in to its dream of one universal Christian Church. Carl Mirbt.

Bibliography: J. C. Strodtmann, *Das neue gelehrte Europa*, ii. 520–570, x. 426–439, Wolfenbüttel, 1753–56; J. A. Trinius, *Freydenker Lexikon*, pp. 545–575; F. G. Meusel, *Lexikon der . . . 1750–1800 verstorbenen teutschen Schriftsteller*, viii. 324–329, Leipsic, 1808; E. Heyden, in *Archiv für Frankfurts Geschichte und Kunst*, iii (1865), 534–562.

LOENER, lōn'er, KASPAR: German reformer and poet; b. at Markt Erlbach, near Baireuth, 1493; d. at Nördlingen (39 m. n.w. of Augsburg) Jan. 6, 1546. He received his early education in the monastery of Heilsbronn, and in 1508 entered the University of Erfurt; while in 1520 he was assistant priest at Nesselbach, combining this office with pastoral functions at the Cistercian monastery of Birkenfeld (near Neustadt-on-the-Aisch). There is reason to believe that he was already cautiously active in the cause of the Reformation, and the two conservative imitations of Luther's baptismal ordinal—*Ordnung der Tauff nach wirtzburgischer Rubricken von wort zu wort verteutscht* and *Ordnung der Tauff nach bambergischer Rubricken von wort zu wort verteutscht* (both subsequent to 1523)—are very plausibly ascribed to him. In 1524 the Margrave Frederick of Brandenburg transferred him to Hof, as his representative in the incumbency of St. Michael's. His Evangelical attitude, however, caused his speedy removal, and after preaching for a short time in the Franciscan church, he was obliged to leave Brandenburg and went to Wittenberg, where he matriculated at the university in 1526. After a brief visit to Markt Erlbach in Jan., 1527, and a short incumbency in Oelsnitz, the accession of Margrave George permitted him to return to Hof late in 1527 or early in 1528. Here he introduced Evangelical worship and also prepared an agenda, a hymnal, and a catechism for his congregation, the first-named forming the basis of the Naumburg agenda of Nikolaus Medler (1537–38) and Widmann's agenda of 1592.

Löner was equally independent as a hymnologist, and in 1527 twenty-six of his compositions were printed anonymously under the title *Gantz newe geystliche teütsche Hymnus vnd gesang;* while as late as 1561 hymns written by him, but hitherto unpublished, were still printed, so that their entire number amounts to something more than thirty-seven. In like manner his *Vnterricht des glaubens oder Christlicher kinderzucht jn LXXII. Fragen vnd Antwortt verfast* (Nuremberg, 1529) is an independent work, despite its indebtedness to Althamer's catechism and the earlier catechetical writings of Luther.

Löner took an active part in the preparation of the Brandenburg-Nuremberg agenda, but in May, 1531, his position became intolerable through the opposition which he had aroused, intensified by his attacks on the papacy, and in July he was expelled from Hof and retired to Oelsnitz. There, after a brief period of poverty with his wife and children, he resumed his pastorate through Melanchthon's influence, and there he published, under the title *Geistliche gesang, aus heiliger Schrift mit vleis zu samen gebracht, Vnd auffs new zu gericht* (Wittenberg, 1538), a collection of twenty of his hymns, three of them new. In 1539 he preached in Leipsic, but failed to secure the call he desired and contemplated retiring from pastoral work, declining a call to Oschatz. In 1542, however, he became preacher at the Naumburg cathedral, although the opposition of the canons gave him little scope for activity. In Jan., 1544, he became pastor of St. George's, Nördlingen, where he remained until his death, and where, as first superintendent, he organized ecclesiastical affairs as he would, sometimes with an excess of zeal, and prepared a new agenda, catechism, and hymnal. The agenda is essentially the same as the one he had prepared for Hof, while the catechism, despite its dependence on Luther's *Enchiridion*, is noteworthy for its division into six conversations with 128 questions and answers, its abundant meditations, and its seven original catechismal hymns. The hymnal, moreover, is of liturgical interest in its distribution of the hymns according to individual services and the seasons of the Christian year.

Bibliography: His *Briefbuch* is in *Beiträge zur bayerischen Kirchengeschichte*, ed. T. Kolde, vols. i.–iii., Erlangen, 1895–97. Other sources are the letters of Melanchthon in *CR*, v.–vi. passim, and of Luther in De Wette's ed. of Luther's letters, vols. iv.–v.; V. L. von Seckendorf, *Commentarius criticus . . de Lutheranismo*, i. 241, iii. 186, 219, 221, Leipsic, 1692. Modern treatment of the subject will be found in G. W. A. Fikenscher, *Gelehrtes Fürstentum Baireut*, v. 305–316, Nuremberg, 1803; P. Wackernagel, *Das deutsche Kirchenlied*, i. 386 sqq., 392, 408–409, 421–422, iii. 618–643, Leipsic, 1862 sqq.; G. Kawerau, in *ZKW*, x (1889), 467 sqq., 519–525; F. Cohrs, in *Monumenta Germaniæ pædagogica*, xxii. 463–480, Berlin, 1901; C. Geyer, *Aus der Reformationsgeschichte Nördlingens*, pp. 18–23, Nördlingen, 1901; *ADB*, xix. 152 sqq.

LOESCHE, lūsh'e, **GEORG KARL DAVID:** Austrian Lutheran; b. at Berlin Aug. 22, 1855. He was educated at the universities of Berlin, Bonn, and Tübingen (Ph.D., Jena, 1880; lic. theol., Berlin, 1883), was preacher to the German church in Florence, Italy (1880–85), and privat-docent for church history at the University of Berlin in 1885–1887. In 1887 he accepted a call to the Evangelical Protestant faculty at Vienna as associate professor of the same subject, and in 1889 became full professor. He is a privy councilor, president of the examining board for Evangelical theological candidates in Austria, and vice-president of the Austrian branch of the Gustav-Adolf-Verein and of the Gesellschaft für die Geschichte des Protestantismus in Oesterreich. In theology he is an adherent of the "modern" school. In addition to his work as editor of the *Jahrbuch der Gesellschaft für die Geschichte des Protestantismus in Oesterreich*, he has edited Johann Mathesius' *Ausgewählte Werke* (4 vols., Prague, 1896–1904) and Gustav Frank's *Die Theologie des neunzehnten Jahrhunderts* (Leipsic, 1905), and has written *Florenzer Predigten* (Halle, 1884); *Ernst Moritz Arndt, der deutsche Reichsherold* (Gotha, 1884); *Bellarmins Lehre vom Papst und deren actuelle Bedeutung* (Halle, 1885); *Analecta Lutherana et Melanchthoniana* (Gotha, 1892); *Johann Mathesius, ein Lebens- und Sittenbild aus der Reformationszeit* (2 vols., 1895); and *Geschichte des Protestantismus in Oesterreich* (Leipsic, 1902).

LOESCHER, lūsh'er, **VALENTIN ERNST:** German Lutheran; b. at Sondershausen Dec. 29, 1673; d. at Dresden Dec. 12, 1749. At the University of Wittenberg, where his father was professor of theology, he gave his attention mainly to philology and history, but out of respect to his father's wish he selected a theological subject for his master's dissertation, in which he opposed the Pietistic position. Subsequent study at Jena aroused his interest in church history. During travels undertaken at this time he formed the acquaintance of a number of influential anti-Pietistic theologians. In 1696 he began to lecture at Wittenberg on the origin of Deism and Pietism. After serving as superintendent at Jüterbog (1698–1701) and Delitzsch (1701–07) and professor of theology at Wittenberg (1707–09), he became pastor of the Kreuzkirche and superintendent in Dresden. Here he remained the rest of his life. His practical duties here turned his attention more particularly to the needs of the Church. His orthodoxy did not prevent him from admitting the truth of the claims of the Pietists concerning the prevailing perfunctoriness of religious life, which he ascribed to the negligence of orthodox pastors. He at once took earnest measures to encourage a deeper spiritual life in the Church. He had already begun the publication of his *Unschuldige Nachrichten von alten und neuen theologischen Sachen* (Wittenberg and Leipsic, 1701 sqq.), the first theological periodical. The comprehensive scope and able management of the magazine gave it great importance. Through it Löscher became the leader of the orthodox party, as opposed to the Pietistic and naturalistic factions in the Lutheran Church, and the representative of scientific Lutheran theology.

In opposition to the proposal that Pietism should be considered the best means of promoting the union of the Lutheran and the Reformed Churches (advocated at the time by the Prussian Government), Löscher published several works, including *Ausführliche Historia motuum zwischen den Evangelisch-Lutherischen und Reformierten* (3 parts, Frankfort, 1707–08). In the course of a controversy with the Pietist Joachim Lange, Löscher defended orthodoxy in his *Prænotiones et notiones theologicæ* (Wittenberg, 1708). However, his most comprehensive criticism of Pietism appeared in his magazine under the title *Timotheus Verinus*, in which work he held that the Pietists had a false conception of the relation between piety and religion and that their zeal for piety placed them in opposition to the doctrine of justification by faith. The work inspired a bitter reply from his Pietistic opponents, which called forth from Löscher his greatest work, *Vollständiger Timotheus Verinus* (2 parts, Wittenberg, 1718–22). In this he discusses the origin and rapid development of Pietism and elaborates upon its evils. Nevertheless he was unable to check the advance of Pietism or even to pass a true judgment upon the real significance of the movement. The importance of Löscher's part in the Pietistic controversy was not fully recognized until the return to Evangelical doctrine in the nineteenth century.

Löscher took an active part also in the controversy which at that time was being waged against the Roman Catholic Church in Dresden and contributed a number of studies to that cause, notably his *Vollständige Reformations-Akta und Documenta* (3 vols., Leipsic, 1720–29). He also opposed Wolff's system of philosophy, claiming that "philosophical indifferentism" portended a revolution in Christianity. (GEORG MÜLLER.)

BIBLIOGRAPHY: M. von Engelhardt, *V. E. Löscher nach seinem Leben und Wirken*, Stuttgart, 1856; G. W. Götte, *Das jetzt lebende gelehrte Europa*, ii. 169–233, Brunswick, 1736; J. J. Moser, *Beitrag zu einem Lexicon lutherischer und reformierter Theologen*, pp. 415–439, Züllichau, 1740; T. Crüger, *Leben Löscher's*, Dresden, 1751; G. Kramer, *August Herrmann Francke*, ii. 72–84, 272–319, 343, Halle, 1882; F. Blanckmeister, in *Beiträge zur sächsischen Kirchengeschichte*, viii. 330–344, Leipsic, 1893; idem, *Sächsische Kirchengeschichte*, pp. 224–254, 282–285, 304–331, Dresden, 1899; *ADB*, xix. 109–213.

LOGIA JESU. See AGRAPHA.

LOGOS.

On the influence which the doctrine of the Logos exerted on the general Christological development of the early Church see CHRISTOLOGY; and cf. TRINITY. This article will deal with the origin and signification of the term in Biblical literature, especially in the writings of John.

I. Content of the Term: The prologue of the Fourth Gospel sets forth the nature and work of Jesus primarily from the standpoint of the apparition of the Logos. The evangelist lays down first the essential nature of the Logos in relation to God, the world, and humanity, characterized by primeval existence before all worlds—an existence "with God" in the manner of personal relation (*pros ton theon*, cf. Matt. xiii. 56; II Cor. v. 8) and participation in the divine nature. All creation is by him; without him is no life or light of truth and salvation. Next comes his relation to the Baptist, who was born in time, a human prophetic messenger with the mission to bear witness to the Light, while the Logos is the mediator of a marvelous new life to all who receive him. Then comes the statement that the Word became flesh, revealing the glory of an only-begotten Son, full of grace and truth. This revelation can be made only by the Son, who has dwelt from all eternity in the bosom of the Father. After this the prologue returns to its starting-point, emphasizing the personal intercourse with God face to face as the incomparable privilege of the Logos conferred upon Jesus Christ, the only-begotten Son. Thus the conception originally laid down has gained in clearness not only by the exact definition of attributes, but by the identification of the person to whom the function of the Logos, the making known of God, is assigned.

The term Logos, then, denotes neither here nor anywhere else in the writings of John the "reason," but always the "Word," who is with God and comes into the world with the function of making known the thoughts and purposes of God. The Word is not an abstract revelation made to the world, but something greater, transcending the earthly sphere and belonging to that of the divine life. More exactly, the Word is a person communicating with God as with one of the same nature, then assuming a fleshly form and proclaiming, without loss of his supernatural being or unequaled closeness to God, that which he has seen of the Father and the Father's counsels. The personal nature of the Logos would not of itself follow from the identification with Jesus Christ, which might mean simply the assumption of a personality and a universal function, but it follows inevitably from verses 1 and 3 and the use made of the thought in verse 18. This is confirmed by other Johannine passages: in I John i. 1, the "Word of life," like the "life" which is afterward taken as equivalent, is the personal bearer of this life, first in the supernatural and then in the natural sphere; and still more obviously in Rev. xix. 13 the rider on the white horse, the triumphant executor of the divine judgments, is conceived as a person. It is safe, then, to say that in all the Johannine writings the Logos is conceived as a personal revelation of God for salvation or for judgment, a person who has an existence of his own with the Father before and after the duration of this world, as well as an existence here in time and in the flesh. Between the eternal and the temporal being of the Logos it is clear from the whole trend of the prologue that the difference is only one of manner and not of essence.

II. Source of the Term: To the question whence the author derived the term several different answers have been given: (1) It is simple enough to Hofmann, who asserts that the primitive Christian community designated as "the word of God" the Evangelical message. The author of the Fourth Gospel would thus associate himself only so far with this conception as to allow him to emphasize the personal content of the message. But more than one phrase in the prologue quite obviously precludes the acceptance of this view. (2) Others, especially Weiss, find the source of the term in the Old-Testament expressions concerning the Word of God. There is this much in favor of such a view, that the prologue plainly refers to the account of creation in Genesis, and that in the Psalms and prophets a poetical personification of the word of God as a creative and saving power sent forth into the world occurs not infrequently; but in these cases the spirituality and omnipotence of God are the fundamental thoughts, and the proclamation of his unconditioned unity leaves no place for a personal principle besides himself as the mediator of his activity in the world. Moreover, wherever on purely Hebraic soil in later times the idea of a creative intermediate cause appears, it is connected with the name not of the Word but of Wisdom (Prov. viii. 22–31; Ecclus. xxiv.), just as where the Word occurs (as in Wisdom ix. 1, xvi. 12, xviii. 15) the influence of Greek, especially Stoic, thought is discernible. The Johannine doctrine of the Logos may have taken up the Old-Testament notion of the word of God as operative in the world, but this can not be its sole source. (3) Still less can it be shown to have come from the use made of "Word of Yahweh" (*dibra dayay, meymra dayay*) in Palestinian theology. The *meymra* is used as an abstract term to conceal the name and spiritualize the idea of God; it is thus employed instead of "God" where his operation in history is spoken of or where the context contains anthropomorphic expressions. There is no hint of a concrete hypostasis of the Godhead or of a being mediate between him and the world. (4) The derivation of the Johannine doctrine from the Alexandrian religious philosophy, and especially from Philo, was taken up in the eighteenth century and accepted in the nineteenth by Lücke, De Wette, and the school of F. C. Baur. Philo, interested alike in the tradition of his people and the contemporary pagan culture, found in the Logos a means of reconciling the transcendence of the Jewish conception of God with the immanence taught in the philosophy of his day. A pupil of Heraclitus, familiar with the Platonic doctrine of ideas, and still more strongly influenced by the Stoic doctrine of the Logos as the active, rational, teleological principle which forms the passive matter, he attempts to connect these really pantheistic views with the Jewish conception of God, and thus gives the Logos an intermediate place between God and the world; his Logos is at once the world immanent in the divine thought and God operative in the world, a *mesitēs* in every sense—cosmological, moral, and religious. Stoic elements are most prominent in his idea, but there is room also for the Mosaic creative word and the later Jewish developments which add religious weight to the purely cosmological idea. But the religious motives and convictions in the two writers are, as might be shown by a detailed examination, too radically distinct to justify the theory of a definite borrowing from one by the other—though this only proves that the term Logos receives in the Gospel an entirely new direction when the historic redeeming work of Christ becomes its essential content, and not that there is not a considerable range over which the two are in harmony. If to these points are added a number of others throughout the Fourth Gospel which go to show that the author was well acquainted with Hellenic Judaism, either in the Philonic or some other popular form, the derivation to some extent of the Logos-idea from that source acquires a considerable degree of probability. But this by no means justifies an attempt to deduce the portrait of Christ in the Evangelical story from philosophic speculation, nor to confine the influence of the Logos-idea to the prologue, as Harnack has sought to do. The truth of the Johannine combination of an abstract idea with history is shown by the manner in which the eternal, inexhaustible personality of Christ not only permits but actually requires it.

III. Significance of the Term: In determining this it is necessary to read into it nothing from Philo or from the later church doctrine, but to confine oneself strictly to the account given by the evangelist. Its significance for him lies altogether in the religious department, giving him the answer to the questions "Who is God? How may I come to him and to participation in his life and light?" The cosmological interest is for him wholly subordinate; his use of the term serves only to place the whole human race on an equality with the favored people of Israel. The Logos, by whom the world was made, was made flesh for the world; but the mission which he is to perform in this universal field is the soteriological one of revealing God and thereby bringing grace and truth. When John identifies the person of Jesus Christ with the Logos, his purpose is to express in a universal way, comprehensible without as well as within the limits of Israel, that Jesus is set over the world, in union with God as the eternal mediator of his creative and redeeming will, and that therefore he is in his historical appearance the absolute and universal self-revelation of the Godhead, the exclusive conveyer of salvation. He does not so much as touch the metaphysical problems which from Justin onward make the Logos-idea a fertile source of questionings. Of the later theology on the subject it has been truly said that it subordinates the moral interpretation of the plan of salvation to the logical, and that it leads either to deistic or to pantheistic consequences, according as separation or union is principally emphasized in the conception of a *mesitēs* between God and the world. The Logos-idea as found in the Johannine writings is well adapted to guard against the Christology which sees in Jesus merely a prophet or a genius; it requires the recognition of his identity of being with God, without which the absoluteness of his historic mission can not be conceived. But it does not go into the metaphysical profundities from which it might be hoped to gain an insight into the inner recesses of the divine nature. It lights up history with the light of eternity; but it can show us eternity only in the light of history, not in its own supernatural radiance. (O. Kirn.)

Bibliography: On Jewish and ethnic doctrines of the Logos consult: A. Aall, *Der Logos; Geschichte seiner Entwickelung*, 2 vols., Leipsic, 1896–99; J. M. Heinze, *Die Lehre vom Logos in der griechischen Philosophie*, Oldenburg, 1872; Schürer, *Geschichte*, iii. 555–557, Eng. transl., II., iii. 374–376; works on O. T. theology, especially that of Schultz; and the literature under Philo.

On the Johannine doctrine: H. H. Wendt, *Das Johannesevangelium*, Gottingen, 1900; M. Stuart, in *Bibliotheca Sacra*, 1850, pp. 281–327; W. Emlicht, *Theophania; or, Scriptural View of the Manifestation of the Logos or pre-existent Messiah*, London, 1857; Röhricht, in *TSK*, 1868, pp. 299–315; J. Réville, *La Doctrine du Logos dans le quatrième évangile et dans les œuvres de Philon*, Paris, 1881; H. P. Liddon, *Divinity of our Lord and Savior Jesus Christ*, lecture v., London, 1885; H. W. Watkins, *Modern Criticism Considered in its Relations to the Fourth Gospel*, lecture viii., ib. 1890; A. Harnack, in *ZKT*, ii (1892), 189–231; idem, *Dogma*, vols. i.–iv (contains also the later development); G. B. Stevens, *Johannine Theology*, chap. iv., New York, 1894; W. Baldensperger, *Der Prolog des 4. Evangeliums*, Freiburg, 1898; Jannaris, in *ZNTW*, Feb., 1901, pp. 13 sqq.; W. R. Inge, *Personal Idealism and Mysticism*, lectures ii.–iii., New York, 1907; Lichtenberger, *ESR*, viii. 334–339; *DB*, iii. 132–136; *EB*, iii. 2811–2812; the commentaries on the Fourth Gospel, especially that of H. J. Holtzmann, Tübingen, 1893; the works on N. T. theology, particularly that of Beyschlag; and the works on the history of doctrine. The last-named class of works is also to be consulted for the later development of the doctrine, and further works of value are: L. Atzberger, *Die Logoslehre des heiligen Athanasius*, Munich, 1880; C. Bigg, *Christian Platonists of Alexandria*, London, 1886.

LOÏSTS, lō'ists: A pantheistic sect of the sixteenth century. The first mention of the sect of the Loïsts occurs in a letter of Luther's dated Mar. 27, 1525, in which he writes that some "new prophets" from Antwerp had appeared in Wittenberg, and that they put the mind and reason of man on terms of equality with the Holy Ghost. A disputation took place, in Luther's presence, between Melanchthon and the leader of this sect, a slater named Eligius (Loy) Pruystinck; and shortly afterward Luther directed a warning to his own adherents at Antwerp against dangerous "blustering and noisy spirits." Pruystinck was subjected to an examination by the Inquisition at Antwerp (Jan., 1526); he recanted, and was cleared with the sentence of public ecclesiastical penance. Nevertheless his doctrines in the following decades spread not only in Antwerp but also in the district about Cologne, in Brabant, and in Flanders. But an additional investigation ensued in the summer of 1544, ending in the execution of Pruystinck and of six of his followers, and completely disbanding their sect. The Loïsts' religious attitude may be defined as a corollary of practical pantheism. Man's intellectual nature is a spiritual substance; in other words, every one possesses the Holy Ghost. Since man's flesh and spirit are thoroughly independent, and with no influence upon each other, the spirit of man incurs no responsibility for the weakness of the flesh; hence the spirit, as such, is sinless. The final goal of man is to vanish into the divine being. The Loïsts based their doctrines upon forced exegesis of the Bible. There appears to have been no relation between the Loïsts and any sects antedating the Reformation, and they seem to have been wholly independent of the Baptists. [They certainly had much in common with the Beghards (q.v.) and the Brethren of the Free Spirit (see Free Spirit, Brethren of the). A. H. N.] It is fair to suppose that the pantheistic doctrines of the "Libertines," which from 1545 onward were combated notably by Calvin, in the Romance countries took their point of departure from the sect of the Loïsts disbanded at that very time. [David Joris was probably a disciple of Pruystinck, and the latter may have influenced Henry Nicolas, founder of the Family of Love (see Familists; and Antinomians), and through him several of the more recent varieties of Antinomians. A. H. N.] Herman Haupt.

Bibliography: A valuable collection of sources and history of the sect is given in J. Frederichs, *De secte der Loïsten of Antwerpsche libertijnen (1525–45)*, Ghent, 1891; idem, *Un luthérien français devenu libertin spirituel*, in *Bulletin historique et littéraire de la société de l'histoire du protestantisme français*, xli (1892), 250–269; idem, *La Moralité des libertins spirituels*, ib., pp. 502–504; A. Jundt, *Hist. du panthéisme populaire au moyen âge*, pp. 122 sqq., Paris, 1875.

LOISY, lwä''zī', **ALFRED FIRMAN:** French Roman Catholic; b. at Ambrières (6 m. n. of Mayenne) Feb. 28, 1857. He was educated at the Seminary of Châlons and was ordained to the priesthood in 1879, after which he was parish priest of Broussy-le-Grand and Landricourt (1879–81); became lecturer in Hebrew at the Institut Catholique, Paris, in 1881; was appointed associate professor in 1882 and titular professor of Holy Scripture in 1889. The freedom of his views, however, caused such distrust of his orthodoxy that in 1893 he was removed and appointed chaplain of the Dominican nuns at Neuilly-sur-Seine. In 1899 he retired to Bellevue, and in 1900–04 lectured at the Sorbonne on Assyriology, but in the latter year was again obliged by his superiors to cease lecturing. He then lived in retirement at Garnay, department of Eure-et-Loire. Became professor of the history of religions, College of France, Paris, 1909. His works attracted considerable attention, and five were placed, in 1903, on the Index, although Loisy claims to seek to refute the radicalism of A. Harnack (q.v.) and to defend the orthodox faith of the Church. He has written: *Histoire du canon de l'Ancien Testament* (Paris, 1890); *Histoire du canon du Nouveau Testament* (1891); *Le Livre de Job, traduit de l'hébreu* (1892); *Histoire critique du texte et des versions de la Bible* (2 vols., Amiens, 1892–93); *Les Mythes babyloniens et les premiers chapitres de la Genèse* (Paris, 1901); *Études bibliques* (1901); *La Religion d'Israel* (1901); *Études évangéliques* (1902); *L'Évangile et l'église* (1902; Eng. transl. by C Home, *The Gospel and the Church*, London, 1903);

Le Quatrième évangile (1903); *Autour d'un petit livre* (1903); and *Les Évangiles synoptiques* (1908).

BIBLIOGRAPHY: W. J. Williams, *Newman, Pascal, Loisy, and the Catholic Church*, London, 1906; *Publisher's Weekly*, Feb. 22, 1908, p. 884; *Expository Times*, Aug. 1909, pp. 488–495; A. Détrez, *L'Abbé Loisy*, Paris, 1909.

LOLLARDS.

1. Origin of the Lollards.

The name Lollards is applied both to a semi-monastic charitable society originating in Brabant in the fourteenth century and to the English followers of John Wyclif. The Brabantine Lollards are mentioned by J. Hocsem, a canon of Liége c. 1350, in a notice of the year 1309, and from his account it is obvious that they received their name from the Middle Dutch *loellen* ("to sing softly, hum"). They first appeared prominently on the outbreak of the plague in Antwerp c. 1350, devoting themselves to the care of the sick and the burial of the dead, and received the name Alexians (q.v.) from their patron saint. Suspected of heresy from the very start, they were tolerated conditionally after 1347, and their dubious reputation transferred their name to the adherents of Wyclif when he began in 1380 to assail the accepted teachings of the Church in regard to the Eucharist. The term was so used for the first time by Thomas Walden and the Cistercian Crompe in 1382, who applied it to Wyclif's friends Hereford and Repington. Five years later five itinerant preachers are described as Lollards, and the name henceforth appears frequently in English documents, finally losing all trace of its Dutch origin and becoming the national term of derision for Wyclif's followers from the fourteenth to the sixteenth century.

2. Wyclif and the Early English Lollards.

The middle of the fourteenth century was a period of religious transition for the English people, and the calm but intense conviction that the evils of the time must be overcome and that religious and social life must be reformed found expression in John Wyclif (q.v.). In 1378 he denied the teachings of the Roman Catholic Church, receiving the support of his university, the court, the nobles, and the knights. Finding his model in the mendicant monks, he sent his closest friends, including Hereford, Aston, Bedeman (all members of the University of Oxford), Purvey (his vicar at Lutterworth), Thorpe, Parker, and Swinderby, to preach among the farmers and the artizans. For the first time in English history an appeal was made to the people rather than to the scholars, and dogma was superseded by the Bible, which was made the sole source of faith and practise. Yet, though the stereotyped sermons of the mendicant orders were replaced by a new note of religious conviction, Wyclif had no ground of opposition to the ideals of St. Francis and St. Dominic, as is amply proven by his *Short Rule of Life* with its close affinities to the aims of St. Francis. Their followers, on the other hand, he bitterly assailed, not only for their teachings about the Eucharist, but also for their adherence to the two antipopes of the Great Schism (see SCHISM) after 1378, for their opposition to free preaching, and for their hostility to the Bible in the vernacular. Wyclif accordingly sent out his "Poor Priests" to invade the territory of the mendicant orders. Bound by no vows and no formal consecration, poor, and yet not mendicant, they wandered from village to village, barefoot, with a long staff in token of their pastoral vocation and coarse habits of reddish brown to symbolize poverty and toil. Prelates, priests, and abbots scorned and hated them, but the people loved them and flocked around them.

This was the beginning of the Lollard movement, which stirred England to its depths for nearly a century and a half and formed the essential basis of the Reformation. [It seems probable that Wyclif and his "Poor Priests" did not originate the type of Evangelical life and thought known as Lollardism. They rather evoked and made aggressive older forms of Evangelical life which survived the Roman Catholic conquest and may have been influenced by continental Evangelicals like the Waldenses, with whom they had much in common. The movement seems too extensive to be ascribed solely to the preaching of Wyclif's evangelists. A. H. N.] The ranks of the "Poor Priests" were soon increased by many of the laity, who boldly opposed the authority of the Church, while some of the nobility who did not fear the wrath of the powerful John of Gaunt, such as the count of Salisbury, likewise joined them. Among the common

3. Spread of Lollardism in England.

people their success was enormous, until their adherents were believed to number at least half the population. [This estimate is too high. It is not likely that one in ten was a Lollard. A. H. N.] Their weapon was the Bible in the vernacular, and true to their doctrine that each priest had the same power to bind and loose as pope or bishop, they ordained others to extend their work. By the middle of the fourteenth century the Lollards were at their zenith, at least numerically, but even during Wyclif's lifetime they met a rude shock when in 1382 Courtenay, archbishop of Canterbury, urged Parliament to take measures against the "Poor Priests," whom he accused of disobedience to their ecclesiastical superiors, stirring up class hostility, and propagating heresy. This was averted by Richard II., but on the insistence of the primate he placed the matter under the jurisdiction of the ordinaries, which were to proceed against the Lollards through their own episcopal officials. The result was the excommunication of Aston and the suspension of Hereford, Repington, and Bedeman from university privileges. On Dec. 31, 1384, Wyclif died, but the movement which he had inaugurated lived and grew.

A few years later Lollards were numerous in London, Lincoln, Salisbury, and Worcester, and their tenets, no longer restricted to religion, extended to economic and political life. In 1395, doubtless emboldened by the blunt refusal of Parliament to pass the archbishop's bill for the destruction of all Wyclif's translations of the Bible, the Lollards felt themselves sufficiently strong to present a memorial to Parliament and to demand the cooperation of that body in carrying out their reform. The twelve clauses of this memorial were as follows: Faith, love, and hope had vanished from the English daughter-church since she had been lost in worldly wealth through her association with her great stepmother of Rome; the Roman Catholic priesthood was not that of Christ; the priestly law of celibacy resulted in unnatural vice; transubstantiation was a feigned miracle and conduced to idolatry; prayers over bread, salt, wine, water, oil, wax, and the like were unlawful magic rites; it was contrary to the word of Christ (Matt. vi. 24) to have king and bishop or prelate and judge in one person; prayers for the dead were ineffectual, pilgrimages and the invocation of images were nearly idolatrous; auricular confession was not essential to salvation, but was a source of priestly arrogance and permission to sin; war was contrary to the New Testament, and death and pillage to the poor; the vows of nuns led to infanticide and unnatural impurity; and art was unnecessary and conducive to luxury and extravagance. [Cf. the text in *Fasciculi Zizaniorum*, ed. W. W. Shirley in *Rolls Series*, pp. 360–369, London, 1858; Wilkins, *Concilia*, III., p. 221; condensed transl. in Lechler's *John Wyclif*, ed. P. Lorimer, pp. 447–448.] In this memorial, however, the Lollards had overestimated their strength, and the king, who had taken no part hitherto in the episcopal proceedings against them, now admonished them sternly.

4. Lollard Memorial of 1395.

The decline of Lollardism now began. In 1396 Thomas Arundel, a bitter opponent of the movement, succeeded Courtenay as archbishop of Canterbury, and three years later Richard II. was murdered. The throne was then occupied by the Lancastrian Henry IV., who found it to his interests to follow the lead of the hierarchic and aristocratic faction which had given him the crown. In Jan., 1400, the bishops declared that they were unable to make headway against the heretics, and the statute *De comburendo hæretico* was accordingly passed. The first to be executed under its provisions was W. Sawtrey (Chartris), who died at the stake in the following month. The act was enforced with special severity in the counties of southern and middle England, while those who were not burned to death were either tortured into recantation or ended their lives in prison. Undismayed by these measures, the Lollards sought support in their struggle for religious and political freedom in the hatred of the oppressed peasantry for the priests who lived in luxury. Both the secular and the regular clergy, and especially the friars, were regarded as having long since deserted the principles of their founders and as having persecuted their own brethren, the Fraticelli, the Beghards, and the Lollards, for remaining faithful to the teaching of their fathers. In *Piers The Plowman's Creed* (c. 1394) a man in search of the true doctrines of Christ is represented as inquiring of the four mendicant orders in succession, only to meet the scornful reply that the words of Jesus are no longer remembered, and not until he finds the "Poor Priests" does he obtain what he desires. Popular approbation of the Lollards, however, could avail little against the power of the archbishop, who in 1408 extorted from the convocation of Oxford, then the center of the movement, the *Constitutiones Thomæ Arundel*, which were designed to crush the tenets of Wyclif. Among other prohibitions, these regulations forbade preaching without the permission of the bishop, as well as the punishment of the sins of the clergy by the laity, and required that the writings of Wyclif and the Lollards be destroyed. They likewise enacted periodical inspection of the residences of Oxford students, and all suspected of Lollardism were ruthlessly expelled. The success of the measure was complete, and within a few years the university was one of the foremost defenders of Roman Catholic orthodoxy.

5. Ecclesiastical Opposition to Lollardism.

6. The Constitutions of Arundel.

The movement of repression was now extended, and commoners in city and country alike were in peril of gallows, ax, and stake. On the other hand, many of the nobility remained true to their principles. Prominent among the latter was Sir John Oldcastle, Lord Cobham (see OLDCASTLE, SIR JOHN), who gave free scope to the Lollards on his Kentish estates, especially as he was protected against Arundel by his friendship with Henry IV. and the Prince of Wales, afterward Henry V. The date of his conversion to Lollardism is unknown, but was before 1410, when he was in high favor with the prince, whom he even sought to win over to his sect. During the reign of Henry IV. he had no need to fear the hostility of the bishops, who hated him for his denial of transubstantiation and his opposition to auricular confession, pilgrimages, and the adoration of images, as well as for the wealth which he expended on the preparation and maintenance of itinerant preachers. Henry V., however, lent a ready ear to the complaints of the archbishop and the convocation. Oldcastle refused to be convinced of his errors by the king, and left the court without permission, retiring to his castle of Cowley in Kent. Ignoring Arundel's citations, he was placed under the ban for contumacy and arrested by a royal warrant. He now formulated a reply to a committee consisting of Arundel and the bishops of Winchester and London, but his answers concerning transubstantiation and confession were unsatisfactory. After much urging, he finally declared himself ready to accept the teachings of the Church, but denied that the pope, the cardinals, or the prelates had the right to define these matters. He was accordingly brought before another episcopal court on Sept. 25. He refused to retract his opinions and sharply rebuked the pope and the clergy, where-

7. Sir John Oldcastle.

upon the archbishop delivered him over as a heretic to the secular arm. Henry vainly endeavored to induce him to recant, but he steadfastly refused and was imprisoned for weeks in the Tower. On Oct. 10, however, he escaped, and wild rumors spread through the country that the Lollards had resolved to kill the king and his brothers, as well as the archbishop and the clergy, to destroy all ecclesiastical edifices, and to make Oldcastle regent. There is no evidence that such a plot was actually formed, but on Jan. 11, 1414, about a hundred friends of Oldcastle, ignorant of his escape, gathered under the leadership of Sir Roger Acton in St. Giles to effect his liberation. They were dispersed without bloodshed, but some of the leaders were captured and executed, while two edicts were issued, one forbidding the reading of the Bible under penalty of death and the other declaring all Lollards heretics. Guarded by his friends, Oldcastle eluded capture for four years before he was taken in Wales by Lords Jeuan ab Gruffydd and Gruffydd Vychan of Garth. He was carried back to London and lodged in the Tower, where he was condemned to death Dec. 14, 1417, on the charges of high treason and heresy, his execution taking place on the same day.

With Oldcastle's death the hopes of Lollardism vanished. Minor recalcitrants were forced to choose between recantation and execution, and all political and social aspiration, if they had ever existed, disappeared. The Council of Constance (1414–18), moreover, had put an end to the Great Schism, and the Church, again able to devote its reunited energies to the suppression of heresy, forced the Lollards to seek refuge in secrecy and obscure hiding-places. Driven from the fields and the streets, they concealed themselves in hovels and barns, sand-pits and caves, while conventicles in the houses replaced preaching in the streets. Their numbers at first remained undiminished, and in some parishes the Lollards formed so large a proportion that pilgrimages and processions, as well as the observance of saints' days, were neglected. Some of the clergy were found among them, but after the execution of Oldcastle the leader was gone, although the Lollard hatred of the Church was occasionally manifested by rabid outbursts on the part of individuals. Executions for Lollardism continued long after the middle of the fifteenth century, and in 1476 the University of Oxford again had to proceed against some of its members for Wyclifite heresy. In 1485 and 1494 bishops preached in Coventry and Kyle against the "Bible Men," and in the first decade of the following century, before the thoughts of Luther had crossed the Channel, increasing numbers were condemned and burned for possessing Wyclif's writings, reading the Bible in the vernacular, and rejecting transubstantiation, auricular confession, the invocation of saints, and pilgrimages, the very things which had formed the point at issue in 1395. At Amersham, a Lollard center, thirty men were executed in 1506, and eleven years later sectaries called "Brethren in Christ" or "Known Men" (the latter name derived from a mistranslation of I Cor. xiv. 38) were cited before the courts.

8. Suppression and Decline of Lollardism.

In a certain sense, therefore, Lollardism, inherited for generations, was a real, though secret, precursor of the Reformation in England. With no Huss or Luther to lead them, they achieved what no other religious movement of the Middle Ages was able to do, when they succeeded in awakening and maintaining a longing for the Bible in the vernacular. The repeated efforts to secure an English Bible which were made by Tyndale, Coverdale, Taverner, Cranmer, the Geneva fugitives, and Parker were inspired primarily by the Lollard "Bible Men." From England Lollardism spread to Scotland. Oxford infected St. Andrews, and the teachers there were repeatedly accused of adhering to the doctrines of Wyclif's followers, while Knox expressly termed the Lollards of Kyle, Ayrshire, the forerunners of the Reformation and the descendants of the Lollards of the fifteenth century.

The tenets of the Lollards must be gleaned from the legal proceedings against them, contemporary accounts, the memorial of 1395, *Piers Plowman's Creed, Piers Plowman's Complaint, The Lanthorn of Light, The Plowman's Prayer*, and the *Repressor* of R. Pecock, but these documents must be used with caution. The scanty literature of the Lollards themselves, on the other hand, shows no trace of system. It is obvious from these sources, of which the most important is the *Repressor*, that Lollardism was based on the teachings of Wyclif and centered about the Bible, whence were derived all Lollard arguments and postulates. According to the Franciscan W Woodford, their chief dogma was that only what the pope and the cardinals could deduce from the Bible was true, all else being false, while if they could be convinced of the erroneous nature of this tenet, they would readily return to the Roman Catholic Church. *The Plowman's Prayer* makes true religion consist in love, fear, and trust in God above all things, and also declares that the soul of man, rather than an earthly temple, is the dwelling-place of the Lord. Pecock, in like manner, describes their faith as based on three postulates: Only what can be found in the Bible (especially in the New Testament) may be regarded as the command of God; each Christian man or woman of humble soul, and desirous to know the Scriptures, may comprehend their true meaning; whosoever has grasped the meaning of the Bible must refuse to accept any opposing arguments, whether derived from the Bible or reason. He also adds that the Lollards were called "Bible Men" because they memorized the New Testament in their mother tongue and found the reading of the Bible so profitable that they preferred it to instruction by scholars or priests. On the basis of these views, the Lollards protested against a series of ecclesiastical requirements which find no authority in the Bible. They rejected the use of images in the churches, pilgrimages to holy places, the right of the clergy to possess land, the orders of the hierarchy, the legislative power of the pope and bishops above the Bible, the institution of spiritual orders and the priestly mediation, the invocation of

9. Tenets of Lollardism.

10. Lollard Opposition to Roman Catholic Doctrines.

saints, the extravagant decoration of churches, mass and the sacraments, the obligation to take oaths, and the justification of war and the penalty of death. These eleven theses are all derived primarily from Wyclif, and are permeated with the principle, common both to Wyclif and to Luther, that the Bible is the sole source of religious truth. The Old Testament, however, was far inferior, in their opinion, to the New, so that everything outside the New Testament was regarded as erroneous and harmful. Herein the Lollards departed from the conservative attitude of Wyclif and Luther with regard to the Old Testament [and were at one with early continental Evangelicals such as the Waldenses, and with the Anabaptists of the sixteenth century. A. H. N.]. This principle explains the negations already noted. The doctrines of God and man, as well as of the person and office of Christ, are lost in the intensity of their opposition to the Roman Catholic teachings concerning the means of grace and the sacerdotal function, although this frequently led to a spirituality which was diametrically opposed to their Biblical objectivity, since it expected all from the spirit though it destroyed the means of intercommunication.

II. Lollard View of the Eucharist.

The faulty presentation in the scanty literature of the Lollards renders it difficult to tell whether they possessed a sharply defined system as opposed to the Roman Catholic teachings. Even their doctrine of the Eucharist nowhere receives a thorough proof, except that Oldcastle held that in the form of bread and wine the body and blood of Christ is present in the Eucharist after the consecration, although the elements still exist. This view accordingly represents the doctrine of the Real Presence as often taught by the Anglican Church, and approximates the position of Luther rather than that of Calvin. On the other hand, Walter Brute, of whom little is known, held that the presence of the body of Christ in the Eucharist is sacramental (i.e., symbolical), and not sacrificial, thus attacking the Roman Catholic doctrine of the mass. This is not found in the works of Wyclif. The view is also found that Christ has written his law in the hearts of believers, and fulfils through grace what the law can not fulfil through righteousness, so that the believer is justified by faith and not by works, a tenet almost identical with that of Luther. (RUDOLF BUDDENSIEG†.)

BIBLIOGRAPHY: The literature under WYCLIF, JOHN is of first importance, especially Lechler's work. For sources consult: Thomas Netter of Walden (?), *Fasciculi zizaniorum Johannis Wyclif cum tritico*, ed. W. W. Shirley, in *Rolls Series*, no. 5, London, 1858 (the only contemporary account of the rise of the Lollards, fitted by the editor with a masterly discussion of Wyclif and his times); R. Pecock, *The Repressor of Overmuch Blaming of the Clergy*, ed. C. Babington, in *Rolls Series*, no. 19, ib. 1860 (valuable as preserving arguments used by the Lollards against existing practises); Thomas Walsingham, *Historia Anglicana (1272–1422)*, ed. H. T. Riley, in *Rolls Series*, no. 28, I., 2 vols., ib. 1863–64; *Chronicon Angliæ, 1328–88*, ed. E. M. Thompson, in *Rolls Series*, no. 64, ib. 1874 (adverse to Lollards); Henry Knighton, *Chronicon*, ed. J. R. Lumby, in *Rolls Series*, 2 vols., London, 1889–95; *Apology for Lollard Doctrine, Attributed to Wicliffe*, ed. J. H. Todd for Camden Society, ib. 1842; *The Peasants' Rising and the Lollards, a Collection of Unpublished Documents*, ed. E. Powell and G. M. Trevelyan, ib. 1899. Documents relating to ecclesiastical action against the Lollards are in D. Wilkins, *Concilia Magnæ Britanniæ et Hiberniæ*, vol. iii., ib. 1737; parliamentary proceedings are given in *Rotuli parliamentorum*, vols. iii. iv., ib. 1808–34. Selections from T. Gascoigne's *Liber veritatum* were published as *Loci e libro veritatum*, Oxford, 1881, and contain much of value.

Of more modern works, aside from Lechler (ut sup.), consult: *The Lollards, some Account of the Witnesses for the Truth in Great Britain, 1400–1546*, London, 1843; S. R. Maitland, *Essays*, pp. 203–230, ib. 1852; A. Jundt, *Les Precurseurs de Jean Huss au 14. siècle*, Montauban, 1877; J. Gairdner and J. Spedding, *Studies in Eng. Hist.*, pp. 1–54, Edinburgh, 1881; W. Marshall, *Wycliffe and the Lollards*, ib. 1884; J. F. Latimer, in *Presbyterian Quarterly*, April, 1888; R. L. Poole, *Wycliffe and the Movement for Reform*, London, 1889; A. Snow, in *Dublin Review*, cxviii (1896), 40–62 (Roman Catholic); H. L. Cannon, *Poor Priests: a Study in the Rise of English Lollardry*, in American Historical Association's *Annual Report*, i (1899), Washington, 1900; G. M. Trevelyan, *England in the Time of Wycliffe*, London, 1904; W. H. Summers, *Our Lollard Ancestors*, ib. 1904; idem, *Lollards of the Chiltern Hills*, ib. 1906; Creighton, *Papacy*, i. 348 sqq.; J. Gairdner, *Lollardy and the Reformation in England*, 2 vols., London, 1908; and the literature on the church history of the period.

LOMAN, ABRAHAM DIRK: Dutch Protestant; b. at The Hague Sept. 16, 1823; d. at Amsterdam Apr. 17, 1897. After completing his studies at the Lutheran and Mennonite seminaries at Amsterdam, he traveled through Germany and Switzerland. Returning to Holland in 1846 he became assistant pastor of the Lutheran Church at Maastricht, where he was pastor for a year (1848–1849), after which he occupied a similar position at Deventer for seven years (1849–56). In 1856 he was appointed professor in the Lutheran seminary at Amsterdam, and in 1877, while still retaining his chair in the seminary, he became professor in the university of the same city, despite the fact that he had been totally blind since 1874. In 1803 he retired from active life.

As a theologian Loman belonged from the first to the so-called "modern school"; as early as 1861 he had advanced the view in *De Gids* that the Gospel account of the Resurrection was due to visions of the faithful. His main field was the New Testament, although his only book was his *Bijdragen ter inleiding op de Johanneische schriften des Nieuwen Testaments* (Amsterdam, 1865), of which the first part alone, on the testimony of the Muratorian Canon to the Fourth Gospel, was actually published. Later he devoted himself to the synoptic Gospels in his *Bijdragen tot de critiek der synoptische evangelien* (*ThT*, 1869–79). Here is manifest the beginning of the symbolic interpretation of the Gospels which he later developed. His view found its expression in his address on *Het oudste Christendom* before the "Free Congregation" at Amsterdam in Dec., 1881 (reprinted in *Stemmen uit de Vrije Gemeente*, Amsterdam, 1882), in which he declared that Christ was not a historic personality, but the incorporation of a series of concepts and the symbolization and personification of thoughts and principles which were first fully developed in the Christianity of the second century, the passion and resurrection being nothing more than the abasement and death of Israel and its revival as Christianity. The storm of opposition which this hypothesis aroused forced Loman to reconsider his attitude, and he granted, in 1882, the historicity of Christ, but denied that he had founded Christianity. He made still further retractations in his *De oorsprong van het geloof aan Jezus opstanding* in *De Gids*, 1888, in which all trace of novelty disappears from his theory, since he grants the historic personality of Christ and the fact that he actually founded Christianity, although still maintaining that the resurrection represents merely the metamorphosis of the Jewish Messianic community into the world-wide Christian Church.

Loman's symbolic theory of the Gospels now forced him to deny the authenticity of the Pauline epistles, for if they were actually written by Paul in the Apostolic Age, his Christological hypothesis would become untenable. In his *Quæstiones Paulinæ* (*ThT*, 1882-86), therefore, he distinguished between a "historic Paul" and a "canonical Paul," the former making a propaganda for the Jewish Messianic ideal outside Palestine, and the latter being merely a legendary figure.

Loman was not only a theologian, but also a musician, and composed a number of chorales and choruses, besides writing the libretto of an oratorio in four acts on the Song of Solomon.

Bibliography: H. U. Meyboom has contributed articles on Loman's life to *De Gids*, 1898, ii. 80-117, and to *Levensberichten der afgestorven medeleden van de Maatschappij der Nederlandsche Letterkunde*, 1898, 26-28, 69-72, and D. E. J. Völter has written in *Jaarboek van de koninklijke Akademie van Wetenschappen*, 1899, pp. 3-36.

LOMBARDS: A warlike Teutonic tribe of the period of migrations. They are first mentioned by Strabo. Their oldest abode on the Elbe is recalled by such names as Bardowik and Bardengau. While settled here they were defeated by the Romans in the year 5 A.D. A few centuries later, driven doubtless by hunger, they wandered southeastward into the Danube region. Under the heroic Alboin they destroyed the Gepidæ, and in 568 entered Italy. In the course of the next few years they conquered northern and central Italy, and erected Pavia (Ticinum) into a royal residence. They failed to acquire Venice and Naples and the Grecian coast strips, as also Rome and Ravenna.

The people they conquered became, for the most part, half free (*aldiones*). The few free men were excluded from public offices and army service, and all stood subject to Lombard law, and were obliged to make over to their district lords a portion of the fruits of the soil. The several divisions of the people, classed as nobles, freemen, half-free, and serfs, were governed by kings of noble descent, endowed with conquered or confiscated estates, and qualified as army leaders, judges, lawgivers, and administrators. The leaders of army divisions were at first dukes during only a life term, but afterward they became hereditary princes with almost royal power, not a few of them, such as the dukes of Spoleto and Benevento, being nearly independent. Unfortunately for the Lombards, King Alboin was murdered by his consort in 572, and in 574 his successor was murdered. Then followed, under thirty-five dukes, a decade of turmoil, until an invasion of the Franks led to the election of the powerful Autharis. He overcame the rebellious, concluded peace with the Franks, acquired the valley of the Po, and married the Catholic Bavarian Princess Theodelinda.

Under Theodelinda and her second consort, Agilulf, the Arian Lombards turned gradually to the Catholic faith. The royal pair founded and endowed churches and cloisters, as at Monza and Bobbio, installed Catholic bishops, and had their son baptized and brought up in the new faith. It was mainly Gregory the Great who contributed to this tranformation. Notwithstanding some relapses into Arianism, the orthodox faith continued to spread; and in towns where there were a Catholic and an Arian bishop the former took precedence over the latter. However, in relation to the pope, the bishop preserved an attitude of independence. After 653 all the rulers and all the bishops were of the orthodox faith, and Milan was the ecclesiastical center of the realm.

The reign of Rotharis (615), enlarger of the kingdom and subduer of formidable dukes, is distinguished by the promulgation of the *Edict of Rotharis* (643), comprehending penal and private law, and for the first time affording written law. Though barbaric in form it is humane in substance, and insures protection to the poor. Still more humane and equitable were the laws of Luitprand (712-744), under whom the kingdom achieved its greatest prosperity. He mitigated slavery and combated abuses, such as premature abjuration of cloister vows and duels. His piety manifested itself in the building of many churches, and in reverence of the popes, although the latter resisted his efforts toward the unity of Italy, which the fusion of Romans and Lombards, already initiated, was to consummate. After reiterated threats from Rome (under Gregory II. and III.), Pope Zacharias obtained peace from him (743), and the partial restoration of Lombard conquests; likewise, from his successor Ratchis (744-749), who was friendly to the Romans, the relinquishment of the siege of Perugia. Ratchis was succeeded by his warlike brother Astolphus, whose resumption of menacing projects of unity drove Pope Stephen II. to an alliance with the Frankish King Pepin. In the course of two campaigns (754 and 756) Pepin won the capital, forced Astolphus to pay tribute, swear fealty, and surrender the exarchate of Ravenna, Emilia and Pentapolis, and places not as yet ceded, thus furnishing the nucleus for the temporal dominion of the popes (see Papal States). Astolphus' successor, Desiderius (756-774), was at first accommodating to the pope and the Frankish rulers; but after his power was well secured, he fell out with both Adrian I. and Charlemagne. In 774 Charlemagne conquered Desiderius, sent him to a cloister, confiscated the kingdom, and called himself king of the Franks and Lombards. Thus the unity of major Italy and the sovereignty over Rome was consummated by a Frankish, instead of by a Lombard king. However, the conqueror, as well as his son Pepin, the governor and king of the Lombards, still had to fight several momentous conflicts with the kinsmen of Desiderius, the dukes of Friuli and Benevento.

The former obtained recognition of his Lombard possessions by way of Byzantium. H. HAHN.

BIBLIOGRAPHY: The sources are in the reports of such Greek and Roman writers as Strabo and Tacitus, in Byzantine writers such as Procopius (in *CSHB*, vols. i.-iii.), Theophylact (in Labbe's *Corpus Historiæ Byzantinæ*, Paris, 1648) and Theophanes (ed. C. de Boor, 2 vols., Leipsic, 1885-87); also in *MGH*, *Script. rer. Langob.*, ed. Waitz, 1878; *MGH*, *Leg.*, iv. 1868; C. Troya, *Codice diplomatico longobardo*, 6 vols., Naples, 1852–55; Dahlmann and Waitz, *Quellenkunde der deutschen Geschichte*, Leipsic, 1905. The *Historia Langobardarum* of Paulus Diaconus is translated by W. D. Foulke, New York, 1907. Consult: P. Balan, *Romani e Langobardi*, Modena, 1867; F. Dahn, *Langobardische Studien*, vol. i., Leipsic, 1876; idem, *Urgeschichte der germanischen und römischen Völker*, vol. iv., chap. 7, Berlin, 1889; F. Bertolini, *I Barbari. Storia delle dominazioni barbarische, 395–1024*, Milan, 1876; J. Weise, *Italien und die Langobardenherrscher*, Halle, 1887; J. Hodgkin, *Italy and her Invaders*, vols. v.–viii., Oxford, 1895–99; L. M. Hartmann, *Geschichte Italiens im Mittelalter*, vols. i.-iii., Gotha, 1900–08; P Villari, *The Barbarian Invasions of Italy*, 2 vols., London, 1902 (2d ed. of the Italian, Milan, 1905); L. Gauthier, *Les Lombards dans les Deux-Bourgognes*, Paris, 1907; Gibbon, *Decline and Fall*, chap. xlv. and vol. v. 517–518; Neander, *Christian Church*, vol. iii. passim.

LONDON POLYGLOT. See BIBLES, POLYGLOT, IV.; and WALTON, BRIAN.

LONG, ALBERT LIMERICK: American Methodist Episcopal missionary; b. at Washington, Pa., Dec. 4, 1832; d. in Liverpool, England, July 28, 1901. He was educated at the Western University of Pennsylvania, Pittsburg, and at Alleghany College, Meadville, Pa., graduating from the latter in 1852. He then studied theology in the Concord Biblical Institute (now Boston University), and entered the Methodist Episcopal ministry in 1857. In 1857 he was sent to Bulgaria as missionary of the Methodist Episcopal Church, where he labored until 1863, when he went to Constantinople to assist E. Riggs in revising the translation of the Bible into Bulgarian. From 1872 till his death he was a professor in Robert College, Constantinople. Besides the translation of the Bible, he wrote several hymns in the Bulgarian language, and also edited a Bulgarian periodical.

LONG BROTHERS. See MONASTICISM; and ORIGENISTIC CONTROVERSIES.

LONGLEY, CHARLES THOMAS: Archbishop of Canterbury; b. at Boley Hill, near Rochester (27 m. s.e. of London), July 28, 1794; d. at Addington Park, near Croydon (10 m. s.w. of Cambridge), Oct. 27, 1868. He received his preliminary education at Cheam, Surrey, and at Westminster; in 1812 entered Christ Church College, Oxford (B.A., 1815; M.A., 1818; B.D. and D.D., 1829); was reader in Greek in his college, 1822, tutor and censor, 1825–28, and proctor, 1827; meanwhile he took orders in 1818 and became curate at Cowley, then incumbent, 1823; was made rector of West Tytherley, Hampshire, 1827; was elected head master of Harrow, 1829, a post which did not serve to bring out his best qualities, since the discipline grew lax; became first bishop of the new see of Ripon, 1836, in this position gaining success in his opposition to Roman Catholic teaching, though at first he received much blame which changed to praise after several ministers became Roman Catholics; he was translated to the see of Durham, 1856; became archbishop of York, 1860, and a privy councilor the same year; was promoted archbishop of Canterbury, 1864. Two events of importance marked his primacy. The first was the deposition of Bishop John William Colenso (q.v.), in which Longley declared his belief in the unsoundness of Colenso's position respecting the documents of the Hexateuch and in the legality of his deposition. The second was the first meeting in 1867 of the Lambeth Conference (q.v.). His principal publications were charges and sermons.

BIBLIOGRAPHY: F. Arnold, *Our Bishops and Deans*, i. 161-168, London, 1875; A. R. Ashwell and R. G. Wilberforce, *Life of . S. Wilberforce*, passim, London, 1880–82; *DNB*, xxxiv. 121–122.

LONGBOARDS. See LOMBARDS.

LOOFS, lōfs, **FRIEDRICH ARMIN:** German Lutheran; b. at Hildesheim (21 m. s.s.e. of Hanover) June 19, 1858. He was educated at the universities of Tübingen, Göttingen, and Leipsic (Ph.D., 1881), and from 1882 to 1886 was privatdocent for church history at the latter university, becoming associate professor in 1886. In 1887 he went in the same capacity to Halle, where he has been full professor of church history since 1888. He is a corresponding member of the Berlin Academy of Sciences, and in theology belongs to the school of Ritschl. He has written *Zur Chronologie der auf die fränkischen Synoden des heiligen Bonifatius bezüglichen Briefe der bonifazischen Briefsammlung* (Leipsic, 1881); *De antiqua Britonum et Scotorum ecclesia* (1882); *Leontius von Byzanz und die gleichnamigen Schriftsteller der griechischen Kirche, i* (1887); *Die Handschriften der lateinischen Uebersetzung des Irenäus und ihre Kapiteltheilung* (1888); *Leitfaden zum Studium der Dogmengeschichte* (Halle, 1889; rev. and enl. ed., 1906); *Predigten* (2 vols., 1892–01); *Studien über die dem Johannes von Damaskus zugeschriebenen Parallelen* (1892); *Die Auferstehungsgeschichte und ihr Wert* (Tübingen, 1898); *Eustathius von Sebaste und die Chronologie der Basiliusbriefe* (Halle, 1898); *Schöpfungsgeschichte, Sündenfall und Thurmbau zu Babel* (Tübingen, 1899); *Anti-Haeckel, eine Replik nebst Beilagen* (Halle, 1900; Eng. transl., London, 1903); *Grundlinien der Kirchengeschichte in der Form von Dispositionen* (Halle, 1901); *Symbolik oder christliche Konfessionskunde, i* (Tübingen, 1902); and *Nestoriana, die Fragmente des Nestorius gesammelt, untersucht und herausgegeben* (Halle, 1905).

LOOMIS, lū'mis, **AUGUSTUS WARD:** American Presbyterian missionary; b. at Andover, Conn., Sept. 4, 1816; d. at San Mateo, Cal., July 26, 1891. He was graduated at Hamilton College (1841) and at Princeton Theological Seminary (1844). He was missionary in China, at Macao, Chusan, and Ningpo (1844–50); among the Creek Indians at Kowetah (1852–53); and among the Chinese in San Francisco (1859–91). He was stated supply at St. Charles, Mo. (1853–54), and at Lower Rock Island, Edwards, and Millersburg, Ill. (1854–59). He wrote: *Confucius and the Chinese Classics* (San Francisco, 1867), and *English and Chinese Lessons* (New York, 1872).

LORD: A term of address occurring in both the Old and the New Testament. In both A. V. and R. V. it occurs in three forms: "LORD," "Lord," and "lord," and represents both different words and different usages of the same word. (1) In the Old Testament "LORD" represents the divine name *Yahweh* or *Yah* (cf. I Kings viii. 39), translated in the Septuagint by *kurios*. It should be noted that in Gen. xv. 2, 8; Isa. xxv. 8, and other passages the collocation *'Adonai Yahweh* occurs in the Hebrew, and in Ex. xxiii. 17, xxxiv. 23, *'Adon Yahweh*, and in these cases *Yahweh* is rendered "God" to avoid the collocation "Lord LORD." (2) In the Old Testament "Lord" is employed to render *'Adonay* (a plural of excellence) when referring to deity, especially in theophanies (cf. Gen. xviii. 3, xx. 4); also to render *'Adon* in such passages as Ex. xxiii. 17 (Hebr. *'Adon Yahweh*), and the Aramaic *Mare*, Dan. ii. 47, v. 23. In the New Testament the A. V. usually renders *kurios* by "Lord" when referring to God or Christ; also *despotēs* in Luke ii. 29; Acts iv. 24; II Pet. ii. 1; Rev. vi. 10 (the R. V renders "Master" in the last two cases and in Jude 4 and puts the same word in the margin in the first two cases; in Jude 4 the A. V. translates "Lord God"). (3) In the Old Testament "lord" translates ten words which express various kinds of superiority of station or authority, including even the theophanic angel of Josh. v. 14. In the New Testament it translates *kurios*, *megistan*, and *rabboni*. Also see JEHOVAH; and YAHWEH.

LORD OF HOSTS. See SABAOTH.

LORD'S DAY: A designation of the first day of the week first found in Rev. i. 10, *te kuriakē hēmera*, Lat. *Dominica dies*. In the Didache, xiv. 1, *kuriakē* first appears as a noun with this meaning.

LORD'S PRAYER.

I. The Time and Place of Institution.	4. The Fourth Petition.
II. The Contents.	5. The Fifth Petition.
1. The Invocation.	6. The Sixth Petition.
2. The First Petition.	7. The Seventh Petition.
3. The Second and Third Petitions.	8. The Doxology.

I. The Time and Place of Institution: The text of the prayer is found in Matt. vi. 9-13 and in somewhat different form in Luke xi. 2-4. In Mark xi. 25 there is a reminiscence of Matt. vi. 9, 14, and 15. Compare these passages with Christ's teaching to the woman of Samaria; God is the Father and must be worshiped in spirit and in truth (John iv. 21). Matthew introduces the Lord's Prayer as supplementary to the Sermon on the Mount; Luke under altogether different circumstances, although he leaves time and place unspecified. It is immediately after the visit to Martha and Mary at Bethany (Luke x. 38-42) that the institution of the prayer is related and the Mount of Olives is traditionally pointed out as the place where this incident took place, although there is nothing in the text to warrant this idea. It was, however, the sight of Jesus himself in prayer that suggested to his disciples the request they made, "Lord, teach us to pray." His power and willingness to do this seemed all the more probable because his forerunner the Baptist had taught his disciples how to pray. In a Syrian fragment in the Bodleian Library an early fabrication of the Baptist's prayer is still extant and runs, "God make us worthy of thy kingdom and the joy that is therein, and show us the baptism of thy Son." On comparing Matthew's account with that of Luke the impression is produced that the prayer was on some occasion given not only to the personal companions of Christ but to the general multitude, after the delivery of the Sermon on the Mount and the calling of the twelve apostles (Luke vi. 20-49), and that the institution took place on two separate occasions. But a closer examination warrants the belief that there is no real connection as far as time and place are concerned between the giving of the prayer and the delivery of the Sermon on the Mount. Closely related with the text of the Lord's Prayer in Matthew is the prayer found in the Didache (viii. 2), "Do not pray as the hypocrites do, but as the Lord commanded in his Gospel, so pray ye," and then follows St. Matthew's version, with the variant "for thine is the power and the glory for ever."

II. The Contents: Examination of this prayer leads to the conclusion that it is not a new prayer in the sense that it introduces anything out of harmony with the historic traditions of Jewish piety and devotion. Thus the Kaddish or Synagogue liturgy begins with the words, "Glorified and hallowed be his great name in the world which he has created, according to his will, and may his kingdom prevail, and his redemption spring up, and may he send his Messiah and redeem his people." In the same tenor runs the great Jewish prayer, the Shemoneh 'Esreh, or prayer of eighteen petitions, which the Jews offered thrice every day. Yet from the sense in which Christ's words in the Lord's Prayer must be interpreted this composition may be fairly looked upon as a new prayer. It illustrates in the fullest degree the meaning of the proverb "if two say the same thing it is not the same," for while the Lord's Prayer can be used to-day by every Jew who may know nothing and wish to know nothing of Christ, yet it can only be properly offered by those who pray in the name of Jesus, and who know what is meant by praying in the name of the Crucified.

1. The Invocation: In the words, "Our Father which art in heaven," is summarized the whole Gospel, although in certain senses they might be used by Jews or heathen. In the Homeric poems the Greek prayed to Father Zeus, father of men and gods, and the Jews, although with much profounder consciousness of religion, called upon Yahweh, acknowledged him as their father and claimed the relationship of children (Deut. xxxii. 6; Isa. lxiii. 16, lxiv. 8). Yet the word "our" was not meant to include the disciples in the same relation of sonship as that in which Jesus stood to the Father. Jesus made a distinction to this effect when he said "my father" and "your father" (Matt. vii. 21; cf. v. 16, vi. 8). Nevertheless their belief in their master as a God-sent Messiah, as the bringer of redemption and reconciliation with God, placed them in a position toward God as their Father which rendered it neither impossible nor improper to join Jesus in his invocation of God as "our Father." That this prayer is not intended as an utterance of an individual but of believing disciples as a body appears in Luke's version from the fourth petition, and from Matthew's in the addition to the invocation "Our Father," etc. As the synagogue prayer was evidently congregational, so Jesus gave a prayer which was common and not individual. God is also addressed as Father in heaven (Matt. v. 48, vi. 14, 26, 32, xv. 13, xviii. 35, xxiii. 9) to indicate the distinction between him and a merely earthly father. With this may be compared the old Hebrew usage (Isa. xxxviii. 5), and in the Kaddish is read: "Let all Israel pray, and flee to the Heavenly Father." The Heavenly Father is the God unlimited by earthly bounds, who knows all, sees all, is the omnipotent. He is the Father who "seeth in secret" and hears the secret prayer (Matt. vi. 4, 6, 18). In other words he is the God who is spirit and life (John iv. 24, v. 26). In the earliest years of Jewish Christianity, for the use of which the first Gospel was written, the prayer was not considered a cast-iron form, but as the gift of Jesus which might be altered and expounded at will in the words which Jesus himself employed.

2. The First Petition: "Hallowed be thy name." The Greek translation of the original Aramaic uses throughout the aorist imperative, except in the fourth petition of Luke's version, *didou*. The aorist is employed to express an act at once completed (cf. I Pet. i. 13, where *teleiōs elpisate* expresses a hope continuing to the end). The petition is not expressed in the active voice, "Hallow thou thy name," but "let thy name be hallowed by men, especially by thy disciples." As Bengel says: "God is holy, that is God is God, he is therefore hallowed when he is acknowledged, worshiped and proclaimed to be what he is" (*Gnomon*, on Matt. vi. 9).

3. The Second and Third Petitions: "Thy will be done on earth as it is in heaven." Although it might be said that the full object of the prayer is attained when God's name is hallowed, yet this can actually never be realized until heaven and earth become one. God is manifested in his children, and his children walk as under his eye. Therefore Jesus directs the gaze of his disciples toward the future union of the heavenly and the earthly world. These two petitions must therefore be taken in an eschatological sense. "The kingdom of God, which we pray may arrive, tends unto the consummation of the age" (Tertullian, *De oratione*, v.; *ANF*, iii. 683). Then shall the world be changed from a state of sin and death into a land of peace and life and the perfect congregation of the saints shall praise their king whose will it is their delight to fulfil.

The next four petitions deal with the earthly interval which must elapse before the consummation of all things and the actual kingdom of God arrive. The disciples of Jesus are taught to pray that they may have strength to live in faith and love as children of God and thus hallow the name of the Father, who is asked to supply their material and spiritual needs.

4. The Fourth Petition: "Give us this day our daily bread" (Matthew), "Give us, day by day, our daily bread" (Luke). Bread is the staff of life, "all that pertains to the support and necessities of life" as Luther says. The followers of Jesus may well expect to receive daily the bread they need, as on the night of his passion Jesus asked his disciples: When I sent you without purse and scrip and shoes, lacked ye anything? (Luke xxii. 35). The anxiety of the Gentiles or pagans about food and clothing is put forth by Jesus as a warning in Matt. vi. 25–34. Although Cyprian ("On the Lord's Prayer," viii.; *ANF*, v. 452) and Tertullian (*De oratione*, vi.; *ANF*, iii. 683) emphasize the spiritual meaning of the word "bread," yet they admit that it is used here also in a material sense. Jerome in translating *epiousion* by *supersubstantialis* also attributes to it a spiritual meaning; still not only is this a false translation but it gives a false meaning to the words of Christ. Hugo Grotius is perhaps nearer the true interpretation when he says (*Critici sacri*, vol. vi.): "*Epiousia* is all that period of life which we have yet to live; unknown to us, known to God; *epiousion* what is sufficient for that period." In the same way Bengel interprets the word (*Gnomon*, on Matt. vi. 11), "Bread, as a single gift, is to be supplied to us for our whole life, but the giving of it is portioned off day by day."

5. The Fifth Petition: "And forgive us our debts, as we forgive our debtors" (Matthew), "And forgive us our sins; for we also forgive every one that is indebted to us" (Luke). The interval which the disciples of Jesus must spend before the coming of his glorious kingdom brings them not only in need of bodily nourishment but of permanent peace in the soul also. Man lives not by bread alone (Matt. iv. 4), especially sinful man. This is the connection of the fifth with the fourth petition. The forgiveness of sins prayed for refers to a daily forgiveness. The words imply that in comparison with God the suppliant is not good but evil (Matt. vii. 11); the spirit being willing but the flesh weak (Matt. xxvi. 41). It would be a sign of self-deceit against which Jesus gives express warning (Matt. vii.) for a man to consider himself sinless (John i. 8). The disciples of Jesus are to take an attitude exactly opposite to that indicated in the proud prayer of Apollonius of Tyana, "O ye gods pay the debts ye owe to me" (*Vita Apollonii*, II., i. 11, ed. Kayser, p. 10). The term debt, *opheilē*, *opheilēma*, is primarily used of money owed but not paid (Matt. xviii. 32); hence in a spiritual sense it becomes equivalent to *paraptōmata* "transgressions" (Matt. vi. 15), or *hamartiæ*, "sins" (Luke xi. 4; cf. Luke xiii. 4 and 2). But this prayer that God would remit our debts to him is not so much the appeal of slaves to a master (Luke xvii. 10) as of children to a father (Matt. xxi. 28–31), and the less the disciples of Jesus boast of their own perfection and the more conscious they are of their debts to God, so much the more when they utter this prayer will they have the consciousness of God's forgiveness and feel moved to forgive their brethren, even to the end (Matt xviii. 22; Luke xvii. 4). For when the disciple of Jesus forgives his neighbor it is by no means in the sense in which God forgives him. A man's "debtor" in a spiritual sense is not a debtor to him as he himself is a debtor to God. As Jesus bids the man who brings a gift to the altar while at variance with his brother first to be reconciled to his brother before he dare to offer it (Matt. v. 23, 24), so he enjoins his disciples to "lift up holy hands, without wrath and disputing" (I Tim. ii. 8), and to dismiss rancor and hatred from their hearts before they come with a prayer to their father (cf. Matt. vi. 14, 15). This is illustrated in the parable of the unmerciful servant (Matt. xviii. 23–35). A spirit of unmercifulness shuts the door of the father's mercy. This petition is even more pointed and earnest than parallel clauses in the Shemoneh 'Esreh: "Forgive us, our Father, for we have sinned; pardon us, our King, for we have transgressed." Polycarp recalls the intense devotion of this petition in the words: "If then we entreat the Lord to forgive us, we ought also ourselves to forgive; for we are before the eyes of the Lord" (Philippians, vi.; *ANF*, i. 34). Luther in his "Greater Catechism" (iii. 64) alludes to the spirit of the petition and says: "If you do not forgive, remember that God does not forgive you; but if you forgive others, you may have the certainty and consolation of knowing that you are forgiven in heaven."

6. The Sixth Petition: "And lead us not into temptation." The connection of the sixth with the fifth petition is evident. As the disciples of Jesus, during the time which elapses before the setting up of his kingdom in glory, utter the fifth petition with the consciousness of their sins, so they utter the sixth petition with the consciousness of their own weakness and of the ever-present danger of their sinning. In this connection may be recalled the words of Jesus to his disciples in Gethsemane: "Watch and pray, that ye enter not into temptation; the spirit indeed is willing, but the flesh is weak" (Matt. xxvi. 41). This temptation is especially imminent when men go out into the world, where pleasure or the force of evil influence surrounds them, or the power of the spiritual world and of the enemy of mankind seek an opportunity of sifting the disciples like wheat (Luke xxii. 31). This temptation is very different from the trial by which the faith of the disciples is actually strengthened (James i. 2). Watchfulness which avoids light-mindedness, overweening confidence, or cowardice, and sees all the dangers as they really are, prevents the falling into temptation, and the prayer against it insures at least that when temptation comes it may merely result in a sort of judgment in which only the unworthy fall (I Pet. iv. 17; cf. Rev. iii. 10; II Pet. ii. 9). When the spirit of the forgiving father produces in the disciples a strong disposition toward reconciliation with others, the deliverance from temptation asked of the father appears in their flight from sin, so that they do not seek out opportunities for sinning but avoid them. In strict accordance with the meaning of this sixth petition are such exhortations as those of St. Paul to the Corinthians (I Cor. vi. 18, x. 14). To be led into temptation is, however, sometimes a punishment from God, and Origen ("On Prayer," xxix. 16) observes: "Let us do nothing which shall cause us by the just judgment of God to be led into temptation."

7. The Seventh Petition: "But deliver us from evil" (not found in Luke). This petition merely puts in positive form the substance of the negative sixth petition. The Church Fathers have been divided as to the meaning of "the evil"—whether it means the Evil One (Satan), as Tertullian and the Greek fathers after Origin think, or the evil thing, sin, as Cyprian and the Latin fathers interpret it. The point seems to be decided by II Tim. iv. 18, where the exact words of the Evangelist are employed: "The Lord shall deliver me from every evil work."

8. The Doxology: "For thine is the kingdom and the power and the glory for ever and ever. Amen." The oldest form of the doxology, as would appear from the Didache, omits "the kingdom" and "Amen." The Amen probably did not appear in the original text of Matthew and Luke. At an early period, however, it was imported into the Christian liturgy from the synagogue prayers. In the Didache the Lord's Prayer was ordered to be repeated thrice a day, an order in which may be seen the influence of the Jewish custom, which was to recite the Shemoneh 'Esreh thrice a day. The variations in the versions of Matthew and Luke seem to intimate that the congregation of the disciples of Jesus when assembled in prayer were not bound in slavish bondage to the letter, but were united in the freedom and power of the spirit. (J. Haussleiter.)

Bibliography: The commentaries on Matthew and Luke are, of course, to be taken into account; many of them give considerable on the history of the exegesis of the Lord's Prayer. Patristic comment of note, other than that mentioned in the text, is by Cyprian, *De dominica oratione;* Augustine, *De sermone Domini in monte*, in *MPL*, xxxiv. 1229–1308; Origen, *Peri euchês;* Gregory of Nyssa, in *MPG*, xliv. 1120–1193. A collection of patristic comment is by G. Tillman, *Das Gebet, nach der Lehre der Heiligen dargestellt*, 2 vols., Freiburg, 1876. From the historical and critical side may be named: A. H. H. Kamphausen, *Das Gebet des Herrn*, Elberfeld, 1866; A. Tholuck, *Die Bergrede Christi*, Gotha, 1872; E. Achelis, *Die Bergpredigt nach Matthäus und Lukas*, Bielefeld, 1875; F. H. Chase, *The Lord's Prayer in the Early Church*, in *TS*, i., no. 3, Cambridge, 1891; G. Dalman, *Die Worte Jesu*, vol. i., Leipsic, 1898, Eng. transl., Edinburgh, 1902; O. Dibelius, *Das Vaterunser, Umrisse zu einer Geschichte des Gebets*, Giessen, 1903; E. Bischoff, *Jesus und die Rabbinen*, Berlin, 1905; G. Hönnicke, in *NKZ*, xvii (1906), 57–67, 106–120, 169–180; *DB*, iii. 141–144; *EB*, iii. 2816–23; *DCG*, ii. 57–63.

More of the homiletical is found in: N. Hall, *The Lord's Prayer; a practical Meditation*, Edinburgh, 1889; G. Karney, *Pater Noster; Studies on the Lord's Prayer*, London, 1889; H. J. Van Dyke, *The Lord's Prayer*, New York, 1891; J. Ruskin, *Letters to the Clergy on the Lord's Prayer and the Church*, late ed., New York, 1896; E. Wordsworth, *Thoughts on the Lord's Prayer*, ib. 1898; C. W. Stubbs, *Social Teaching of the Lord's Prayer*, London, 1900: L. T. Chamberlain, *The True Doctrine of Prayer*, New York, 1906; F. M. Williams, *Spiritual Instructions on the Lord's Prayer*, New York, 1907. Sermonic treatment is given by: H. Hutton, London, 1863; W. Gladden, Boston, 1881; H. W. Foote, ib. 1891; R. Eyton, ib. 1892; M. Dods, Cincinnati, 1893; F. W. Farrar, London and New York, 1893; W. J. S. Simpson, London, 1893; W. R. Richards, Philadelphia, 1910.

Important or interesting are: A. S. Cook, *Study of the Lord's Prayer in English*, in *American Journal of Philology*, xii. 59–66; idem, in *Biblical Quotations of Old English Prose Writers*, pp. 147 sqq., New York, 1898; *The Lord's Prayer in 500 Languages*, ed. R. Rost, London, 1905.

LORD'S SUPPER.

The Lord's Supper is one of the two sacraments generally recognized in the Christian Church, consisting in the blessing or consecration of bread and wine, the repetition of the words of institution (Matt. xxvi. 26–29; Mark xiv. 22–25; Luke xxii. 17–20; I Cor. xi. 23–26), and the eating and drinking of the consecrated elements. In connection with the treatment here given certain other articles should be consulted for the liturgy of the early Church and the method of celebration, the article EUCHARIST; for doctrine and liturgy of the Roman Church, MASS and TRANSUBSTANTIATION; for the Greek Church, EASTERN CHURCH, III., 5; and the special articles like EPIKLESIS; KISS OF PEACE; MYSTAGOGICAL THEOLOGY; SYMBOLISM, etc.

I. The New-Testament Doctrine: As to its origin, no one ever questioned that the Lord's Supper was instituted by the Lord himself for his Church before H. E. G. Paulus (*Commentar über das Neue Testament*, 4 vols., Lübeck, 1800–04; *Leben Jesu*, 2 vols., Heidelberg, 1828), followed by Kaiser in his *Biblische Theologie* (2 vols., Erlangen, 1813–1821). David Strauss apparently denied it in the first edition of his *Leben Jesu* (1835) but admitted its possibility in the later popular form of this work

1. Question of Christic Origin.

(1864), only questioning how far the details, as given by the Evangelists, are to be accepted. According to him, Paul gave the tradition as he found it on his entrance into the Church, but how much of this is the original fact and how much comes from subsequent Christian practise is difficult to determine. Rückert is inclined to believe that Jesus said nothing of a repetition of the observance, but that it was daily repeated from the beginning in the belief that this would be at least acceptable to him, and that thus the idea of an express command grew up. According to Weiss, the apostles had no express command either for this repetition or for the performance of the baptismal rite, but carried out what they understood to be the Master's intention, finding in both a bond of union for the disciples. Weizsäcker asserts positively that the sacrament rests on a distinct command; and Beyschlag calls the institution the most certain of all the facts recorded of Jesus. Recently Jülicher and Spitta have vigorously denied it, while Harnack accepts it, though giving the rite another meaning than that expressed in the New-Testament accounts.

The denial of the institutional character of Christ's action is based on the variation of the accounts—the words "This do in remembrance of me" being found only in two places (Luke xxii. 19 and I Cor. xi. 25). This variation is the more remarkable because in Codex D the text of the former passage omits altogether "which is given for you; this do in remembrance of me." The researches of Blass in the Acts render it very doubtful whether the text of Codex D can

2. Textual Basis for Denials.

be accepted absolutely, and appear to indicate that what seems a reminiscence of Paul may be a correction accepted by Luke himself rather than a later accretion. The relation of Luke to Paul, and the value of the latter's testimony to the view of the institution taken by apostolic Christianity, makes it improbable that a tradition existed which did not contain a trace of the intention of Christ to have it repeated. There is no analogy for the account of Luke as found in D, and the text of D may perhaps best be regarded as defective, if it is not rather an ancient corruption. Nor can the point be pressed that Matthew and Mark fail to mention the injunction of repetition. In both of them (Matt. xxvi. 28; Mark xiv. 24) the contents of the cup are designated "my blood of the covenant"; and Christ could scarcely have given his "blood of the covenant" in such a way as to offer it alone to the disciples there present, to say nothing of the reinforcement of this thought by the "many" following. Thus the accounts would have to be deprived of the presumably original form of Christ's words in order to sustain the hypothesis of an intention which did not include repetition. To this Paul's account would offer a further obstacle. When he says (I Cor. xi. 23) "for I received of the Lord that which also I delivered unto you," he uses *apo* instead of *para* to express the idea that he has received this from the Church as from the Lord himself. The analogy of Acts ii. 42, 46 shows that this must have been at the time of his baptism, and the basis of his account is thus put twenty years further back than the date of I Corinthians, into the very earliest days of Christianity; it becomes an evidence that the Christian Church never had any thought but that the institution was meant for repetition. The only real difficulty may be found in the fact that the Gospel of John is entirely silent as to the institution. The hiatus which has been looked for in this Gospel, in order to find a place where this originally might have been, is discovered by Spitta just before chap. xv. Here he thinks the account once was, vi. 51–59 having been afterward put in by another hand to supply its place when it had dropped out. But there is no need for this ingenious hypothesis. It is indubitable that when this Gospel was written the Lord's Supper was everywhere celebrated in the Church. The purpose of the Gospel presupposes an acquaintance with the whole story (cf. chap. vi.).

The real ground for the denial of the institution as an ordinance for the Church lies elsewhere than in the discrepancy of the accounts. Rückert finds it in the danger of externalism inevitably accompanying a formal rite. Spitta declares impossible the relation of the Supper to the death of Christ, since such a relation could be understood only in connection with the general New-Testament view of the person and office of Christ, which he and others decisively reject. Harnack's position on the question shows that it is not absolutely necessary on this account to deny Christ's intention to institute a permanent observance. In any case, the institution would lose its real abiding value if the view of it contained in all the sources were not recognized. What this view is must next be considered.

For the understanding of the purpose and meaning of the institution, consideration is limited to four accounts, the scantiness of which is in inverse ratio to the importance which the sacrament held from the beginning in the Christian assemblies, but is, on the other hand, a proof that the primitive community was untroubled by doubts as to what the Lord had left behind him. No part of the New Testament offers an exposition of the meaning of the Lord's Supper. What Paul gives in I Cor. x. 14–22, xi. 23 sqq., is not an exposition, but a reminder of what was self-evident to the Church, though perhaps in other places than Corinth (as is so often the case with self-evident truths) it was not sufficiently borne in mind. According to all the sources, the institution stands in immediate actual, not merely chronological, relation to the death of Christ. He gathers his disciples about him for the last time to celebrate the Passover. He stands face to face with death, which he has all along foreseen as in a special sense the purpose of his mission. He has repeatedly told his disciples, not only that they must not on that account lose faith in his Messiahship, but that they should have begun to understand something of the counsels of God (Matt. xvi. 23). They have not, however, understood. The hour of the Passover has come; of that sacred feast which pointed not only backward to the deliverance from Egypt, but also forward (as Ps. cxvi.–cxviii., sung at the feast, show) to the fulfilment of prophecy in the final redemption. What is to become of their hopes if Jesus dies? Where is the promised "new covenant" (Jer. xxxi. 31)? This is the last Passover of the old; one day he will celebrate it with them in a new manner in his kingdom (Luke xxii. 16–18, 29, 30). But they do not understand what lies between—his death; they do not believe it possible, as their strife for precedence shows. They are simply straining their eyes for the dawn of the new covenant. Jesus avails himself of a symbol. He takes the bread used in the paschal supper, gives it to them, and speaks words which lend it a new meaning. At the end of the supper, before the singing of the *Hallel*, he takes in like manner the cup of wine, which was passed from hand to hand four times during the paschal meal, and gives it to them with similarly significant words. Amid the variants, what were the *ipsissima verba* of Christ can not be determined; the only question is whether the more extended forms correspond to his thought, or whether they add something to it or depart from it. This question may be answered by considering the undoubted connection of the two distributions. If they are taken together, the mention of a covenant which is common to all the accounts in connection with the giving of the cup supplies a key. This term connects the institution with the Passover, which is closely connected with the old covenant, as this with the new. The giving of the body will thus have the same relation to the foundation of the new covenant as that of the blood, and both together will have reference to the sacrificial death (see Heb. x. 10) of Christ. The foundation of the new covenant is indicated by the shedding of the blood for many, for the remission of sins. In it the expression "my body given for you" finds its completion. No different thought is expressed in I Cor. x. 17 (taken in connection with xii. 27), where the words "for we being many are one bread, and one body" rest on the participation in the one bread; and this bread is (verse 16) "the communion of the body of Christ," as the cup is "the communion of the blood of Christ"—a community with the body and blood of Christ answering to that which those who ate of the sacrifices of the old law had with the altar, and that which those who took part in heathen sacrifices had with demons. The sacrificial conception dominates the whole Pauline doctrine on the subject, and contains the same interpretation of "my body given for you" which is to be taken from the connection of the bread and the cup and their relation to the "covenant." Thus what Jesus wished to symbolize for his disciples—and not to symbolize alone—was his coming death; but that death is not, as they suppose, a misfortune; it is to serve the purpose of the "covenant," to be a sacrifice. Promises and hopes have not come to naught; as the old covenant comes to an end, the new (Jer. xxxi. 31) is instituted.

3. The Basal Accounts.

But this is not all. The purpose of Christ is not merely to give his disciples the right point of view for the understanding of his death. It is to give them himself, in order that they may overcome the temptation to doubt into which the mere thought of his death has thrown them. What he now does stands on an entirely different footing from his discourse at Capernaum (John vi.). There he spoke, indeed, of the eating and drinking of his flesh and blood; but he spoke symbolically, with reference to the paradox of his

4. Christ's Purpose in the Institution.

lowly appearance, under which men must find the bread of heaven and of life. The image of eating and drinking represents the faith which lives by the humility of Jesus. Even verses 51 sqq. go no further than this, but declare that his humiliation must terminate in his death, and that men must accept him as he is, in flesh and blood, in order to live by him. The thought of a sacrifice does not appear. All this is merely symbolic. The institution of the Lord's Supper is entirely different. Here he acts, not merely talks. To be sure, both speech and action are primarily symbolical, but what he symbolizes is the sacrifice then approaching completion, and the appropriation by man of the benefits of that sacrifice. The symbol is but the means by which he gives them what he means to give them. He, who is about to offer himself in sacrifice, gives himself not only for but to his disciples for their own, in a way in which he has never before given himself to them. The last barrier which has separated them is removed. He has reached his goal; the old is past. He is, not only is about to be, the sacrifice; the few hours that intervene before the crucifixion do not count. The sacrifice is prepared—such a sacrifice as has never before been offered, and one in which they are to take part as none have ever taken part in any previous sacrifice. As their act of eating and drinking is both the symbol and the putting into operation of the faith by which they accept him, so his gifts are both the symbol and the realization of his utter self-devotion for them and to them. The distinction between these two latter aspects is that between the provision of salvation and its appropriation; and the appropriation takes place now. When they see the sacrifice offered, they can now say to themselves that it is theirs, that they have part in it. Thus the institution of the Lord's Supper is the extension of the line which passes through the language of John vi. about the eating and drinking of his flesh and blood. The gift of himself, as a sacrifice, for us and to us is the completion of his appearance in flesh and blood. The eating and drinking of his gifts in the Supper is the highest point of the eating and drinking mentioned in John vi.; and this may account for the fact that John's Gospel does not describe the institution. On this fact, then, that Jesus (as the new covenant requires) does not merely symbolize but gives what he symbolizes, rests the understanding of the words which he used, and the conception of the sacrament as an institution destined for all who accept the new covenant. Accordingly, wherever the Lord's Supper is celebrated after his institution, he gives himself in the manner in which he symbolizes his gift; symbol and reality are joined; he is present exactly as he said, as he symbolized, and as he accomplished—no otherwise and no less. There can be no question of the imparting of higher powers of life, as they are found in him, nor of nourishment for the resurrection body; but there is the sacrifice for the remission of sins, which he is for us, and which is ours.

The question remains how to understand the communion with Christ effected by the Lord's Supper, in what way the sacramental union with him takes place in it. Of course, if Christ is no more than any other man, distinguished from the rest of humanity only by his mission and his work, there can be no question of a partaking of his body and blood, and the conception of the thing which appears in all the accounts falls to the ground. The occurrences of that night must have been different, must mean something different, from what these accounts imply. The New-Testament view of the institution is indissolubly bound up with the New-Testament conception of the person of Christ expressed in the New Testament, proclaimed by the apostles, and received by the primitive Church. By entering human life and the human mode of existence, he has so completely incorporated himself with man that he is what he is to man through his human nature. As through and in this nature, in inseparable union with mankind, he became a sacrifice for us, so he continues to make us partakers of him under this same aspect of sacrifice. This is the meaning of his bodily presence in the Lord's Supper. In this gift of himself is concentrated all that he is and forever means to be to mankind in perpetual union. We can have him, we are meant to have him, for our own, as we can have no one else. It is no new relation into which he enters. That which he is for man, and (by virtue of his community of blood) with man, finds in this sacrament its highest expression, as the reception of the sacrament is the highest expression of the faith by which we accept him. And so the Lord's Supper, although, or rather because, it is the memorial of his death, is no *mysterium tremendum*, but something to be received, as the first Christians received it (Acts ii. 46), "in gladness." (H. Cremer†.)

5. Significance for Humanity.

II. The Church Doctrine (the teaching of the Fathers and the Early Church, the Greek Church, the Roman Catholic Church, and the Churches of the Reformation. See also the articles Mass and Transubstantiation).

1. In the East: Precisely because the New-Testament exegesis of the past did not succeed in giving a decisive answer to the questions which have made the love-feast of the primitive Church a battle-ground for contending creeds, a constant appeal to history has entered into the controversy. Early in the discussions of the sixteenth century, Œcolampadius appealed to the *vetustissimi auctores*, and in 1527 Luther found himself involved in a learned discussion with him on passages in Augustine, Tertullian, Irenæus, Hilary, and Cyprian. And so, in more recent times, the various beliefs of the opposing religious bodies have been found by their adherents mirrored in the history of eucharistic doctrine. Ponderous treatises have been written to prove that the Roman Catholic, or the Lutheran, or the Zwinglian view is that of antiquity; but they have not been fruitful in conversions. This lack of result is scarcely surprising, for little is really to be learned of the sense of the original institution from the history of the doctrine. The student finds too soon misconceptions and perversions, which are the result of non-Chris-

1. Difficulties of the Problem.

tian influences and superstitions within the Church. But the study of the question will be wholly unfruitful if it is pursued from the standpoint of sixteenth-century controversies. The oldest non-Scriptural sources give too little material, and as soon as more abundant testimony becomes available, it is in a world the civilization, education, and habits of thought of which are so totally different from those of the Reformation period as to give no premises for deducing the answer to the questions which agitated that period.

There were, prior to Irenæus and Tertullian, only three non-Scriptural authors who can be brought into the discussion: the author of the Didache, Ignatius of Antioch, and Justin Martyr. The indications of the first-named are particularly interesting. Here the Lord's Supper is still a family feast of the believers, taking its religious character from the thanksgiving (Gk., *eucharistia*) which precedes and follows the eating and drinking; the prayers, obviously received by the author from tradition, are of venerable antiquity and great beauty. But the treatise does not show in what manner the eucharistic food was regarded, except that it was considered as spiritual nourishment unto everlasting life. Nothing is said of the body and blood of Christ; and the total omission of any reference to his institution or to his death is so singular that the theory of these prayers forming the close of the Agape (q.v.), and thus having no reference to the sacramental feast which followed it, is worthy of consideration. Ignatius has, besides other brief allusions, two passages of especial importance, in which some have found a distinct affirmation of the real presence of the glorified body of Christ (*Ad Eph.* xx.; *Ad Smyrn.* vii. 1; *ANF*, i. 57–58, 89). But it is possible to lay too much stress on them. According to Ignatius, two special blessings—eternal life and mystical union with God—are received by means of Christ's incarnation and triumph over death. These latter Ignatius is forced to emphasize by his opposition to the Docetics; the flesh and blood of Christ are to him the tangible security for the life-giving union with God. Thus, just as he calls the Gospel, the proclamation of this tangible security, the "flesh of Jesus" (*Ad Phil.* v. 1; *ANF*, i. 82), so bread and wine, the tangible symbols of this blessing in the Eucharist, might equally well be called the body and blood of Christ. Ignatius preaches so strongly the "bodily and spiritual unity," connects the spiritual blessing so closely with its outward representation, that the denial of the outward would endanger for him the reality of the inward; yet that does not mean that he confuses the two, or considers the material elements as such to bring with them the divine. His view of the Lord's Supper, then, is certainly not purely symbolic; but it would be rash to conclude from this that he accepted the real presence of the glorified body of Christ.

2. The Didache and Ignatius.

It is just as difficult to draw precise conclusions from the words of Justin. Only one passage in his writings needs special consideration for our purpose—the long-debated *I Apol.* lxvi., which is worth quoting in full: "For not as common bread and common drink do we receive these; but in like manner as Jesus Christ our Savior, having been made flesh by the word of God, had both flesh and blood for our salvation, so likewise have we been taught that the food which is blessed by the prayer of his word, and from which our blood and flesh by transmutation are nourished, is the flesh and blood of that Jesus who was made flesh" (*ANF*, i. 185 [where the remark is made in a foot-note that "this passage is claimed alike by Calvinists, Lutherans, and Romanists; and, indeed, the language is so inexact, that each party may plausibly maintain that their own opinion is advocated by it."]) It is perfectly clear that Justin recognized the designation of the eucharistic food as the body and blood of Christ for a universal Christian usage. It may also be admitted that the clause "from which," etc., stands in inseparable relation to the "food which is blessed"; in other words, that by the Eucharist our flesh and blood is nourished "by transmutation" (*kata metabolēn*). The most probable explanation of this is that through the Eucharist our bodies are so nourished that they experience a change, namely, "so as to be incorruptible." The "drug of immortality" of Ignatius (*Eph.* xx. 2) is more than a parallel; the dependence of Justin upon the prevalent teaching of Asia Minor, as met in Ignatius, may be shown from other passages. Justin, like Ignatius, sees in some manner the body and blood of Christ in the Eucharist; and, following John vi., while he says nothing of remission of sins as a benefit conferred by it, he regards it as the food of immortality. There is no question of a change of the elements either in the Roman Catholic or the later Greek sense; nor is the body and blood of Christ so really present that they pass into the partaker "by transmutation," or are carnally eaten and drunk. The probable sense of the whole passage is this: as Jesus became man by the power of the Logos, so also the bread which is hallowed by the words of blessing derived from him becomes his flesh and blood; the Logos joins himself to the bread, as in the Incarnation he assumed flesh and blood. This theory, involving a real dynamic change of the elements, has been often repeated in later times; but it fails to tell anything of the fundamental meaning of the "this is" of the words of institution, and it is entirely foreign to the theories of the sixteenth century. So long as even the fuller expressions of later but still ancient times are studied in the light of that modern period, they can never be properly understood.

3. Justin Martyr.

It will not do, then, to impale the Fathers upon the horns of a modern dilemma. But it must equally be admitted that the primitive Church spoke of the eucharistic elements as the body and blood of Christ. Of course the teaching of the Church in the period about 150 did not bear the aspect of the later formal conciliar utterances; but Justin's word "we have been taught" shows that then (as thirty years later in Irenæus, V., ii. 2, and in the Apostolic Constitutions, viii. 12) the Church reiterated what the Gos-

4. Early Designations of the Elements.

pels gave it—" this is the body of Christ "—without troubling itself to reason at length on the meaning of the words. This view appears so self-evident in the above-cited passage of Ignatius (*Smyrn.* vii. 1) that he says the heretics abstained from the communion because they did not believe " the eucharist to be the flesh of our Savior, Jesus Christ." And even the Gnostic heretics, who (in spite of what Ignatius says) had some sort of a Eucharist of their own, apparently all retained the designation of the elements as the body and blood of Christ, in spite of their docetism and spiritualism; Irenæus argues against them (IV., xviii. 4) as if this designation were common ground. The practise of the Church bears out the same contention. Tertullian (*De corona*, iii.) and Origen (on Exod. xiii. 3) both speak, as of an old-established tradition, of the great care taken that no crumb or drop of the elements should fall to the ground. The oldest formula of administration known, going back certainly to the third century, is simply " the body of Christ, the blood of Christ, the cup of life." The same conception is evidenced by the reports of " Thyestean banquets " attributed by the heathen to the Christians in the second decade of the second century, in Asia (Pliny's letter to Trajan) and in Rome (Tacitus, *Annales*, xv. 44). In a word, following the "this is " of the Gospels, in the methods of speech used by the Church, catechetical as well as liturgical, in the popular belief, and in the practise based on that belief, the Eucharist was the body and blood of Christ.

5. Oriental Influences upon the Conception.

The very circumstance, however, that this same fact is met alike among Gnostics and their opponents, in the writings of an Origen and of a Tertullian, should warn against concluding from it the prevalence of a realistic conception (whether of a Roman Catholic or a Lutheran kind) in the early Church. The same thing may be inferred from the fact that no early apologist thinks it necessary to defend this designation of the elements as the body and blood of Christ against pagan opponents as anything irrational. Justin shows no consciousness that this must seem a stranger doctrine to the heathen than the incarnation or the resurrection; similar language is as much a matter of course to Origen writing against Celsus. But it would be equally unjustifiable to conclude that the language of the early Church may be understood in a Zwinglian or Calvinistic sense. The Fathers, whether Eastern or Western, must be interpreted by the presuppositions of their own times. Strauss draws a distinction (*Leben Jesu*, ii. 437, 1st ed.) between the Oriental mind, which thinks in images, and the more abstract Western habit of thought. Yet it must be remembere' that under the Empire the religious life of the West was permeated by Oriental influences. " Mysteries " were a natural concomitant of religion; and the idea that in a mystery earthly elements could " become " divine by the working of some invisible power without any change of their substance, was not unknown to the pagan philosophy of the West. It is now generally recognized that the Gnosticism of the second and third centuries understood or shaped Christian traditions according to the idea of mysteries; and, while it is not so universally admitted, it may safely be said that the same influence of pagan religious tradition which led in Gnosticism to " an acute Hellenizing of Christianity " (Harnack) began, about the same time, though more slowly and gradually, to have an effect on the Church which condemned Gnosticism. This is most clearly seen in the history of baptism and the Lord's Supper. The very name *sacramenta* is a token of this. Tertullian is the first author who can be shown to have spoken of *sacramentum baptismatis et eucharistiæ;* but the idea is found in Clement of Alexandria, and is not far off in Justin. The developed *Arcani Disciplina* (q.v.) of the fourth and following centuries must have been a consequence of this tendency, and thus later than the tendency itself. So, since the beginnings of the *disciplina* are found in Tertullian, the beginnings of the development which led to the Hellenizing of Christian worship must go back to the first half of the second century. The atmosphere of mystery thus inherited from the ancient world favored the leaving of the questions about which after ages contended without a definite and precise answer. A " symbolic " conception of the sacramental gift by no means excluded one which might be called " realistic." Harnack points out that whereas by " symbol " now is understood a thing which is not what it signifies, then it meant (for many people, at least) a thing which was, in some sense, what it signified. That the bread and wine were, in some sense, the body and blood of Christ was accepted in the second century, as has been seen. But this affirmation lay within the sphere of mystery, meaning different things to different persons according to the extent of their spiritual attainment; it was in no sense a defined dogma. This explains the fact that the doctrine of the Eucharist shows a much less regular development than the dogmas of the early Church, such as that of the Trinity or of the person of Christ.

6. Entrance of Sacrificial Conception.

The first important step in such development as there was is connected with the application of the idea of sacrifice to the Lord's Supper. The fact has often been overlooked that this application is unscriptural. It made its first appearance, to be sure, under the aspect of New-Testament thoughts. Prayer was spoken of as the sacrifice of the lips (Heb. xiii. 15; cf. Rev. v. 8, viii. 3; Hos. xiv. 2); to do good and to communicate was to offer a sacrifice with which God was well pleased (Heb. xiii. 16). So it was not far to considering in the same light the offerings of love which served for the Eucharist, and, so far as they were not needed for that, for the necessities of the poor (Polycarp, *Ad Phil.* iv. 2). But the thing soon went further than this; even the Didache (xiv. 3) regards the Lord's Supper, in the words of the famous prophecy of Malachi (i. 11), as the " pure offering " of the new covenant. This might have been of little consequence if the Eucharist had remained, as it appears in Ignatius and in the Didache, a real meal, or connected with one, and if the " giving thanks " had remained an act of the community, or of members specially adapted to it or visiting prophets (Didache, x. 7). To realize the significance of the change from this to the speaking of the eucharistic words as a specialized function of the officials, it is necessary only to remember how utterly distinct from what was called worship in heathen tradition, from all sacerdotal and theurgic action, were the earliest Christian assemblies—the gatherings "to edifying" of I Cor. xiv. 23, 26 and the agapæ of I Cor. xi 20. The distinction, then, grew less when the administration of the Eucharist became the function of appointed officials (cf. Ignat., *Ad Smyrn.* viii. 2; *ANF*, i. 89, "Let that be deemed a proper eucharist which is [administered] either by the bishop, or by one to whom he has entrusted it"). It grew still less when the Agape (q.v.) was gradually separated from the Lord's Supper. Alms and oblations, at first connected closely, began to be separated, the latter term designating the eucharistic elements, which alone received the mystical blessing of the bishop (Justin's "chief," Gk. *proestōs*); and it was an easy step to finding the sacrificial act in this blessing, instead of in the free-will offering by the members. But, however this development is traced, the terms used by Justin are certainly noteworthy. If it was the *proestōs* who "made the bread of the Eucharist a memorial of the suffering of Christ," it can hardly be denied that the distance is but short from this to the words of Cyprian: "the priest imitates that which Christ did and offers a true and complete sacrifice in the Church to God the Father" (*Epist.* lxiii.). Remembering that many of the ancient mysteries had their dramatic representations of sacred cult-legends, that the conception of the unbloody renewal of the sacrifice of Christ continued to shade off from a symbolic-imitative commemoration feast until after the time of Gregory the Great, and that the Greek Church in the final development of its mass approaches closely to a dramatic representation of the Passion, it will seem not too much to say that the above-quoted formula of Justin is in the direct line of development that leads to the Roman mass. The really important thing is that in the interval between Justin and Cyprian, the "sacrifice of praise" had become a priestly "sacrifice of propitiation." Immense as the change seems when judged by the New-Testament standard, it will not surprise any one acquainted with the Greco-Roman world of that period; the conception of sacrifice, once admitted, brought with it all its natural concomitants. Nor were connecting links wanting. Prayer was made for those who brought the oblations; to emphasize the communion with the departed, oblations were made for them too; and the "offerings for the dead" which Tertullian knows as a custom already ancient (*De corona*, iii.) show a more propitiatory character than those for the living. Tertullian still considered the giver of the oblations as the one who offered the sacrifice; commending his dead to God "through the priest" (*De exhortatione castitatis*, xi.). But even here a priestly mediation is assumed, and it is but a short step to the priestly sacrifice as the Church of the latter half of the third century knew it.

It has been necessary to discuss this development of the sacrificial conception of the Eucharist because it was the deciding factor in the final shape assumed by the conceptions of the early Church as to the sacramental gift. In attempting to discover what this latter was, it is expedient to discuss separately the development in the East and the West, though the examination will not be detailed. All that may be expected is a gradual assimilation of various views, without deliberate discussion, but under the influence of liturgical forms and popular conceptions; it is necessary here only to take up such views as offer a notion of one or other of the fundamental conceptions that were to be assimilated. Irenæus gives the first of these. He was appealed to in the *Formula Concordiæ* of Wittenberg (1536), as he had already been by Luther in 1527, to support the Lutheran view; and it was not difficult for those who then read his words in the light of their own beliefs to find such support. His words, however, must be considered in their simple objective meaning, apart from modern ideas. Irenæus' words are (*Hær.* IV., xviii. 5): "Then, again, how can they say that the flesh, which is nourished with the body of the Lord and with his blood, goes to corruption, and does not partake of life? For, as the bread, which is produced from the earth, when it receives the invocation of God, is no longer common bread, but the Eucharist, consisting of two realities, earthly and heavenly; so also our bodies, when they receive the Eucharist, are no longer corruptible, having the hope of the resurrection to eternity" (*ANF*, i. 486). And again (*Hær.* V., ii. 3), of the bread and wine, that, "having received the Word of God, they become the Eucharist, which is the body and blood of Christ" (*ANF*, i. 528). The interpretation of the first quotation hinges on the meaning given to the "heavenly reality," which has been variously explained by those who have forgotten the caution just given. If one must define precisely the "heavenly reality," it will appear, from the parallel between the "becoming the Eucharist" of the elements and the "becoming incorruptible" of the body, as well as from *Hær.* V., ix. 3, to be the Spirit of God, who is invoked upon the elements. But so precise a definition is not really needed. It is sufficient to observe that by the *ekklesis* or *epiklesis* (*Hær.* IV., xviii. 5) something heavenly is added to the elements, by which they become what they were not before—a food that guarantees the partaking of eternal life to the receiver. If this were the whole of Irenæus' conception, it would not be difficult to find in it a Greek view of the eucharistic mystery modified by the primitive thoughts about the resurrection of the flesh. But it is not the whole. Other passages, such as *Hær.* V., ii. 2, must be taken into account in the attempt to determine the teaching of Irenæus. As a theologian familiar with the Greek culture of his time, he took the view which he found in common Christian tradition (specifically that of the school of John and of Asia Minor)—that the Eucharist is in some sense the body and blood of Christ, intended as a food unto eternal

7. Doctrine of Irenæus.

life—and made it fit his own mental processes by a theory of the "consecration" of the elements, somewhat as Justin had done before him. He does not lessen the significance of the traditional belief by his theory, but enforces it by words which have a very material sound ("nourished with the body of the Lord and with his blood") without observing that his unsatisfying explanation of the received designation of the elements does not really fuse the two thoughts combined by him.

This peculiarity of Irenæus' view will appear more clearly when it is compared with that of the Alexandrian school. Clement need not here be considered; his view is practically the same as that found in a more developed form in his pupil Origen. The latter reproduces the same traditional belief discovered in Irenæus (*In Num. hom.* xvi. 9; *In Matt. ser.* lxxxvi.; *In Exod. hom.* xiii. 3; *In Ps. xxxvii. hom.* ii. 6). And here also, more intelligibly than in Irenæus, this traditional belief is put in the light of a mysterious consecration (*In Exod. hom.* xvi. 9; *Contra Celsum*, viii. 33; *In Lev. hom.* xiii. 5, 6). The difference is that in Origen scarcely anything but the mere words of tradition remain.

8. The Origenistic Doctrine.

The spiritualism of Origen was unable to conceive the notion of either the "body and blood" of the ascended Lord, or of eating unto life everlasting, or, in fact, of the resurrection of the flesh. Thus he says: "even if [Christ] was a man, at any rate he is no longer man" (*In Jer.* xv. 6); "he has ceased to be man" (*In Luc. hom.* xxix.): the material belongs only to this transitory world, and perishes with it; eating and drinking have nothing to do with the spiritual life; in the resurrection, the material will disappear more and more from us, until in us too the word is fulfilled, "he who shall have followed Christ will be no longer man" (*In Luc. hom.* ix. 11). Origen does not attempt to conceal the divergence of his view from the commonly received one; and he states with sufficient clearness what the eating of the body of Christ and similar liturgical expressions mean to him—the "body" in the Eucharist is a "typical and symbolic body," only pointing to the "true food," the Logos, the living Bread. We drink his blood "when we receive his words, in which is life," just as, when we read the words of his apostles, who also shed their blood "and attain unto life from them, we drink the blood of their wounds" (*In Num. hom.* xvi. 6). Accordingly, the eating and drinking of the body and blood of Christ are not confined to the Eucharist; the only preeminence which it has over other hearing of the word of God is in the fact that here the symbol is added to the word. In this spiritualism it is not alone the traditional Christian conception that disappears; there is really nothing left of the thought—more Greek than Christian—that the elements acquire a "helping power" (*In John,* xxxii. 16) by consecration.

These, then, are the two views of the Lord's Supper which have the greatest importance in the history of eucharistic doctrine—the spiritualism of Origen, and the realism of Irenæus. The most radical difference between them is that to the spiritualist everything is spiritual, and the Eucharist a food for the soul only; while Irenæus, though not excluding the spiritual effect, yet lays his emphasis on the imparting of immortality to the "body, made fit for the Spirit" by means of the Lord's Supper. But neither was realistic in the Roman Catholic or Lutheran sense. The realistic view of Irenæus was only realistic-dynamic.

9. The Symbolic-Sacrificial View.

The spiritual-dynamic view became the prevailing one with the theologians of that period. None of the great Fathers who followed Origen was, it is true, as extreme a spiritualist as he; none of them allowed the divergence of the spiritualist view and the received designation of the elements to appear as freely as he did; and even the most decided spiritualists among them, since they accepted the resurrection of the flesh, attributed to the faithful reception (following John vi. 54) a secondary significance also for the body. But Eusebius of Cæsarea, Basil the Great, Gregory Nazianzen, and Macarius the Elder must, in their treatment of this subject, be classed as Origenists. Athanasius, whom Steitz places wholly with them, was, it is true, strongly influenced in his eucharistic views by Origenistic conceptions, but Irenæus had a still greater influence on him. One term is of importance in the study of the Eastern doctrine because its meaning does not seem to fall under either of the two divisions adopted above, but rather points to a third view which was not without its effect on the later development. This is the expression employed by Gregory Nazianzen for the consecrated elements, "antitypes of the body and blood of Christ." Eusebius (*Demonstratio evangelica*, i. 10) uses the equivalent term "symbols" only in relation to the idea of sacrifice; and in Gregory too a reference to the sacrifice may lurk in the background. As objects of the "bloodless and reasonable sacrifice" (Eusebius, *Demonstratio evangelica*, ut sup.) or the "sacrifice without blood" (Gregory Nazianzen, *Oratio* iv. 52), the elements are symbols or antitypes of the real, historic body of Christ; as objects of reception, neither Eusebius nor Gregory could have called them by this name, since, in their view, the actual body and blood of Christ have nothing to do with the reception. Eustathius of Antioch, on the other hand, sees in Prov. ix. 5 a reference to the "antitype to the members of Christ's body," and thus must have found the elements as objects of reception antitypes of the actual body of Christ. In this use of the term Steitz and Harnack have seen a transference of the sacrificial idea to the sacramental. In connection with the latter, as soon as the thought of "offering the memorial of the great sacrifice" had taken the shape of "offering the body," a reference to the actual body of Christ was inevitable even for the Origenists. Thus the designation of the elements as "antitypes of the body and blood of Christ" might be taken as a spiritualistic reservation; and so it might well have been originally Alexandrian. But it is scarcely probable that Eustathius, who was a vigorous opponent of both Origen and Eusebius, would have taken up and developed an Alexandrian term; and there is no evidence of its use on definitely Alexandrian ground until later than his time. It is rather an independent tradition which meets us in Eustathius—the same that becomes evident concerning the Lord's Supper in a single passage in Theodore of Mopsuestia (on I Cor. xi. 34; *MPG*, lxvi. 889). Its essence consists in the subordination of the sacramental side to the sacrificial; as symbols of the body and blood of Christ, offered in sacrifice, the elements received communicate what was gained by the sacrifice of Christ, remission of sins and eternal life. Since Eustathius is in more than one aspect a precursor, if not a member of the school of Antioch, his words may be taken as a proof that he already entertained this Antiochian conception of the Lord's Supper. The record of the fragments of Irenæus edited by C. M. Pfaff (*Irenæi fragmenta*, The Hague, 1715), which seem to show a similar view, must be left out of the question as these fragments have by Harnack (*TU*, xx. 3, pp. 1–69, 1900) been shown to be falsifications. Not the second Pfaff fragment, but the passage cited from Eustathius, is the oldest Oriental testimony for this view of the Lord's Supper, influential also in the West. It may be called the "symbolic-sacrificial" view. The peaceful assimilation of the three conceptions described above resulted in the later eucharistic doctrine; and the one last set forth was distinctly influential. It had this advantage over the other two—that it brought the Lord's Supper into a clear relation to the real body and blood of Christ, while the Origenists only made use of the Logos in him, Irenæus only of the incorruptibility of his body. The acceptance of the term "symbols" or "antitypes" in a sacrificial context by Eusebius, Gregory Nazianzen, and Macarius is an instance of the influence exerted by the Antiochian eucharistic doctrine in the fourth and early part of the fifth century.

10. Cyril.

The Christological conflicts of the fifth century mark an epoch in the further development. Up to this point the views of the Fathers show a mixture, in varying proportions, of the three conceptions just analyzed. Since the idea has been widely prevalent that three of the Fathers of this period—Cyril of Jerusalem, Gregory of Nyssa, and Chrysostom—went beyond all three theories (which agree in the impossibility of conceiving a real presence of the actual body and blood of Christ), some reference must be made to the language used by them. One must begin by remembering that the liturgical tradition, becoming fixed and written by the fourth century, had still adhered closely, for all its increasing variety of expression, to the universal form of language in the Church. By its retention of the common designation of the elements, it could not fail to repress the spiritualism of theologians; and by its development of a "memorial of the great sacrifice," its emphasis on the "offering of the body of Christ," it brought the Eucharist into increasingly close connection with the real body and blood of Christ. The first of these three authors, Cyril, was teaching his newly baptized hearers about the Lord's Supper with especial reference to the words and usages of liturgical tradition. Bearing this in mind, and remembering how closely church teaching in Justin's time held to the "this is," it is not surprising to find the catechist coming down to the level of the *simplices*. As the object of the "holy and most awful sacrifice" ("Catechetical Lectures," v [xxiii.], 9) the "bloodless service" (ib. v [xxiii.], 8), he sets forth the "slain Christ" himself: "We offer up Christ sacrificed for our sins" (ib. v [xxiii.], 10); and the question as to the meaning of the eucharistic gifts is settled for him by the words of the Savior: "Since then he himself declared and said of the bread, 'this is my body,' who shall dare to doubt any longer? And since he has himself affirmed and said 'this is my blood,' who shall ever hesitate, saying that it is not his blood? He once in Cana of Galilee turned the water into wine, akin to blood, and is it incredible that he should have turned wine into blood?" (ib. iv [xxii.], 1–2; *NPNF*, 2 ser., vii. 151). As the cause of this "change" appears the invocation of the Holy Spirit; we pray God, he says "to send forth his Holy Spirit upon the gifts lying before him; that he may make the bread the body of Christ, and the wine the blood of Christ; for whatsoever the Holy Ghost has touched is surely sanctified and changed" ("Catechetical Lectures," v [xxiii.], 7; *NPNF*, 2 ser., vii. 154). The neophyte is to believe firmly that "the seeming bread is not bread, though sensible to taste, but the body of Christ; and that the seeming wine is not wine, though the taste will have it so, but the blood of Christ" ("Catechetical Lectures," iv [xxii.], 9; *NPNF*, 2 ser., vii. 152). Stronger or more positive language could scarcely be found; if his words were taken literally, they would necessitate the acceptance of a transubstantiation. But Cyril is speaking as a catechist. Even to him, as a matter of fact, the bread and wine are only so far transubstantiated as they are made more than common bread and wine; for him, too, the real sense of the eating and drinking the body and blood of Christ is the nourishment of the soul by the incarnate Word. What Cyril does show is how the transubstantiation theory grew up, by a sort of fusion of the realistic-dynamic and the symbolic-sacrificial views. But before it could proceed in a definite form from this fusion, it was necessary for the idea of a change to be carried further than the mere "sanctification," and for the symbolic part of the symbolic-sacrificial to be discredited. The latter result followed on the defeat of the Antiochian theology in the fifth century; the fulfilment of the former condition is usually attributed to Gregory of Nyssa.

11. Gregory of Nyssa and Chrysostom.

In his large catechetical work (chap. xxxvii.; *NPNF*, 2 ser., pp. 504–506) Gregory undertakes to show how the body, not only the soul, of the believer can attain "participation and mingling" with Christ. But a close study of his whole treatment shows that while Gregory has been often called the originator of the theory of transformation (rather than transubstantiation), he himself knew nothing of it, and carried the meaning of the Greek *metapoieisthai*, "to transform," no further than what was already understood by *hagiazesthai*, "to sanctify." His theory is the assumption-theory of Justin, which Alexandrians had spiritualized, and which now allied itself in a realistic form with that of Irenæus. In this shape it appears in Cyril of Alexandria. It is more difficult in regard to Chrysostom to sustain the assertion that the development had still gone no further than the sum of the three views described above. He speaks of the presence of Christ in terms which sound so material that the universal agreement to attribute to him a belief in a real reception of the actual body and blood is not surprising. But several things must be remembered. He belongs thoroughly to the school of Antioch, but unites its traditions with the realistic-dynamic theory in a form which spiritualism does not succeed in refining away; he brings out these really irreconcilable thoughts colored by all the rhetorical artifice of his style as a preacher, accustomed to the wording of liturgical tradition; and he pushes the Lord's Supper back, as no one before him except the older Alexandrians Clement and Origen had done, into the awe-inspiring obscurity that hangs around the mysteries. It will not do to attempt to find dogmatic formulas in the exuberance of his gorgeous rhetoric. In a word, then, the conception of a change of substance is to be dated neither from Cyril of Jerusalem, nor from Gregory of Nyssa, nor from Chrysostom. Realistic expressions which may seem to involve it are not rare in the fourth and fifth centuries; but they are usually brief unformulated protests against the acceptance of a purely symbolic presence of Christ. The definite theological theory leading up to transubstantiation is of later origin.

12. Doctrine in Fifth and Sixth Centuries.

The opposing views held in the fifth and sixth centuries as to the incarnation were reflected in very varied conceptions of the Eucharist. Theodore of Mopsuestia and Nestorius still represent the symbolic-sacrificial view of the school of Antioch, while Cyril of Alexandria and the Monophysites favored the view which corresponded to their general Christology, the realistic-dynamic in the form which it had assumed with Gregory of Nyssa. How far the former was discredited by the general overthrow of the school of Antioch may be seen in Theodoret. The Antiochian traditions, which he combines with other views into such a curious mixture, did not wholly die out; but the definitive victory of Cyril's Christology in the reign of Justinian stamped the corresponding eucharistic doctrine, the realistic-dynamic, as the accepted one. The fact pointed out under Irenæus (ut sup., § 6) that the older theologians attempted to combine two distinct meanings of the term "body of Christ" without success became less obvious when, in the iconoclastic controversy, popular devotion made the "dim religious light" of the mysteries still more dim. Even the iconoclastic council of 754 developed the view accepted as orthodox in Justinian's time: the bread and wine are only the images (types) of the humanity of Christ; this image of the body of Christ is made divine (a "divine body") through the "inspiration" (Gk. *epiphoitēsis*) of the Spirit. But even before the date of this synod, John of Damascus, the leading upholder of the images, had opposed the view expressed by it: "the bread and the wine are not types of the body and blood of Christ; let it not be thought; but it is the visible body of the Lord" (*De fide orthodoxa*, iv. 13). If, he goes on, certain of the holy fathers called the bread and wine "antitypes of the body and blood of the Lord," they referred not to the consecrated but to the unconsecrated elements. These explanations of John were repeated by the second council of Nicæa (787). Since that time the Greek Church has had a eucharistic dogma; it teaches the real presence of the body and blood of Christ after consecration. And from the same date it has a theory of the change, for John of Damascus, who developed it, has remained the standard theologian of the East. According to him, the Logos assumes the body constituted out of bread and wine in the same hypostatic manner as he assumed the body born of the Virgin; but as there is only one hypostasis of the incarnate Logos, the eucharistic body on earth and the glorified body in heaven are one body, by virtue of the one hypostasis to which they belong. This solution satisfied the theological needs of the age, and remained an axiom for those that followed, in the West as in the East. The Greek Church went no further for centuries; then, in the place of the theory of transformation (Gk. *metapoiēsis*), that of transubstantiation (Gk., *metousiōsis*) came in, probably as a result of the negotiations with the Western Church for reunion. The Greeks agreed to the term *metousiōsis* in 1274 and 1277, in a confession of faith proposed by Rome; but it did not come into use among them until the fifteenth century, after the Union of Florence, and it was not until the contests raised by Cyril Lucar (q.v.) in the seventeenth that it gained a complete triumph, with all its accompanying details.

2. Development in the West: The West was slower than the East to formulate a dogma on the point, not only because of the breach in continuity of intellectual development caused by the downfall of the empire, but because a different line was followed in the West. The result of the process is different, to begin with, and there is no parallel in the East for the preponderating influence exercised by Augustine in the West.

1. Tertullian and Cyprian.

The views of Tertullian and Cyprian must be first considered. The most essential point in regard to the latter is that he subordinates the sacramental aspect to the sacrificial: the Eucharist is "the sacrament of the Lord's passion and of our redemption." His thoughts being thus occupied with the crucifixion of the body and the shedding of the blood, it is not surprising that he does not think of them as really present. The sacrament is a symbolic commemoration of the Passion; its reception conveys, not nourishment to eternal life or anything of that sort, but the benefit of Christ's redeeming work, in which every one has a share who enters into union with him. Cyprian's whole view is clearly and simply the symbolic-sacrificial. The fact that an almost magical operation is attributed to the sacred symbol (as in *De lapsis*, xxv., xxvi.) is no proof to the contrary; the idea of some dynamic change in the elements was (unless spiritualized away) always connected in those days with that of consecration, and we practically never find a purely symbolic view in the modern sense. It will not, perhaps, do to say as positively that Tertullian held the same view, in a less developed form and occasionally combined with other thoughts; but there is much to show that this was the case. Bread and wine are, for him as for Cyprian, symbolic forms under which the body and blood of Christ are represented. The commentators have, however, usually forgotten to ask whether these symbols were primarily intended to be offered or to be received. That, as with Cyprian, the answer is the former, one may conclude from the facts that with Tertullian, too, the body is the crucified body and the blood that which was shed, and that to him the Eucharist is the Passover of the new covenant, as well as from certain passages the discussion of which would occupy too much space.

These symbolic-sacrificial ideas, which are inseparably connected with the actual body and blood of Christ, form the point of departure for the further development of Western doctrine. Thus

2. Transition to Transubstantiation.

they determine Ambrosiaster's conception of the sacrament: "It [the Eucharist] is a memorial of our redemption, that, mindful of the redeemer, we may be worthy to attain greater things by him the testament is made in blood, because blood is a testimony of the divine beneficence." Thus Ambrose says on John vi. 56: "You hear 'flesh,' and you hear 'blood,' and you recognize the sacred pledges of the Lord's death." (*De fide*, iv. 10). Thus for Augustine the Eucharist is the "memorial sacrament" by which since the ascension the real sacrifice of Christ is commemorated. When, accordingly, from the fourth century, Greek ideas had a stronger influence in the West than before, these symbolic-sacrificial conceptions prevented the dissociation of the real and the sacramental body which was often noticeable in the East; and the ideas of the realistic-dynamic type took on, under their influence, an appearance more "realistic" in the modern sense. This is most clearly the case with Ambrose, though no passage in his authentic works shows him a believer in the real presence of the actual body and blood. When, however, he says (*De fide*, iv. 10) "As often as we receive the sacramental elements, which by the mysterious efficacy of holy prayer are transformed (*transfigurantur*) into the Flesh and the Blood we do show the Lord's death," he comes close to connecting with the symbolic offering a change of the elements into the body and blood of Christ. It would thus not be inconceivable that Ambrose should have addressed his catechumens in the language found in the treatises *De mysteriis* and *De sacramentis* which pass under his name. Cyril of Jerusalem speaks strongly in the same way under the same circumstances (ut sup., § 9); and the writers of these two works do not accept the real presence. These treatises are of no small importance in the history of this question, even if they are not Ambrose's, since long before the ninth century they were thought to be his, and to the men of the Middle Ages it was "Ambrose" who led the way to the doctrine of transubstantiation. In fact, they are really more interesting if not his. If they had been, they must have been interpreted by his other expressions; but as products of a later period, they show that (just as in the East with Cyril of Jerusalem and Chrysostom) the realistic-dynamic conception, when it came under the influence of sacrificial ideas, approached ever nearer to the doctrine of a positive change—nearer than was the case with Ambrose himself.

The Western development would probably have reached the same conclusion as the Eastern at an even earlier period, if it had not been for Augustine.

3. Augustine's Check upon Development.

His position on the subject is the same as his general attitude in regard to the sacraments (see SACRAMENT): "the sacrament is one thing, the virtue of the sacrament, another"; ("On John's Gospel" xxvi. 11); "grace is the virtue of the sacrament" (*Enarratio in Psalmos*, lxxvii. 2). The *res sacramenti*, the benefit to which the *signum* points, is here also the "sanctification of invisible grace" (*Quæstiones in Heptateuchum*, iii. 84), with all that this includes. The sanctification by invisible grace is defined by him in three ways: either he thinks, in accordance with the traditional symbolic-sacrificial view, of the appropriation by faith of the redeeming work of Christ (*De doctrina Christiana*, iii. 16. 24); or, turning in a spiritualist direction, he considers the mystical union with Christ given with the sanctification (*De civitate Dei*, xxi. 25, 4); or, with a reference to I Cor. x. 17, he deals with the thought that grace incorporates us into the Church—the body of Christ ("On John's Gospel," xxvi. 15; *Sermo*, cclxxii.). Of an actual presence of the body and blood there is no mention; Christ is, indeed, "everywhere entirely present like God," but "in some place in heaven after the manner of a real body" (*Epist.*, clxxxvii. 13, 41). The fact that he uses expressions which sound "realistic" must not mislead in the light of his own explanation (*Epist.*, xcviii. 9): "For if sacraments had not some points of real resemblance to the things of which they are the sacraments, they would not be sacraments at all. In most cases, moreover, they do in virtue of this likeness bear the names of the realities which they resemble. As, therefore, in a certain manner the sacrament of Christ's body is Christ's body," etc. (*NPNF*, 1 ser., i. 410). There is scarcely a passage in the early literature so illuminating for our purpose—unless it be *De catechizandis rudibus*, xxvi. 50, where he warns the catechumen "that, if he hears anything even in the Scriptures which may carry a carnal sound, he should, even although he fails to understand it, nevertheless believe that something spiritual is signified thereby, which bears upon holiness of character and the future life" (*NPNF*, 1 ser., iii. 312). Here the "something spiritual" throws a light on the "heavenly reality" already discussed. But although Augustine's "realistic" expressions have no significance as regards his own position, they have much for the later history. He provided the later Roman Catholic development, which departed from his own symbolic-spiritualistic view, with a quantity of formulas, and made it possible for people to close their eyes to the fact that the most important teacher of the early Western Church held a doctrine of the Lord's Supper scarcely distinguishable from that of the "heretics" Berengar, Wyclif, Calvin, and their followers. But the result of his actual teaching was also an important one. He checked the development toward transubstantiation in the West.

Among the theologians of the last period of the early Church, Fulgentius of Ruspe, Facundus of Hermiane, and Isidore of Seville represent a more or less genuine Augustinian view, while besides the pseudo-Ambrose Cæsarius of Arles and Gregory the Great belong to the realistic-dynamic school in which the dynamic was growing less and less as the realistic assumed prominence. Both traditions came down side by side to the Carolingian age. The renaissance of Augustinianism which characterizes that period brought the symbolic view to the front among theologians, though not, of course, in the popular mind, and though the theologians admitted a real dynamic change in the elements and asserted as freely as Augustine that the bread "receiving the benediction becomes the body of Christ." The stage which had been reached may be seen in the controversy between Paschasius Radbertus and Ratramnus (qq.v.). There is little difference between their formulas; but Ratramnus showed a survival of the spiritualistic attitude, which was ended only in the conflict with Berengar (q.v., see also LANFRANC; TRANSUBSTANTIATION). Lanfranc went beyond Paschasius Radbertus only by the single important step of asserting the real presence for the unworthy as well as for the worthy; but other opponents of Berengar went further. Guitmund of Aversa was the first of the Western upholders of this change to assert clearly the *totus in toto et totus in qualibet parte*, "the whole in the whole and the whole in any particular"; he also used the terms *substance* and *accidents* in their later sense—asserting that the substance was changed, while the "accidents of the former essence" remained. This completed the doctrine of transubstantiation, though the word first became a dogmatic expression in the first half of the twelfth century (1215), and by its use in the confession of the fourth Lateran Council. The subtle minds of the schoolmen found much occupation in further refinements upon it, to which, however, little attention was paid in the final settlement of the Roman Catholic doctrine at the Council of Trent (see below, IV.). The *Catechismus Romanus*, indeed (II., iv. 42), borrows from Thomas Aquinas the distinction that Christ is present not "by way of quantity" but "by way of substance"; and the doctrine of concomitance, first brought up by Anselm, proved serviceable in defending the practise of the laity in communing only in one kind.

4. Transubstantiation.

Considering the infinity of varying views which the first fifteen centuries produced, we shall not be surprised to find that the Reformation period was able to evolve but few new ones. Many abuses which had grown up around the sacrament were swept away, many ideas which distorted and dishonored it were denied; the sacrifice of the mass, as a propitiatory offering, was no more; the adoration of the *sanctissimum*, exposition, the festival of Corpus Christi, were abolished, and communion in both kinds restored. But the positive ideas of the Reformation, even Luther's own, are scarcely any of them new. If Luther, after 1520, replaced transubstantiation by the presence of the body and blood of Christ in the untransformed elements, he was only following out a possibility already indicated by Nominalist schoolmen; he appeals to Pierre d'Ailly when he first brings forward this idea (*De captivitate Babylonica*, in *Werke*, vi. 508). He placed the benefit of the sacrament almost exclusively in the remission of sins, as the upholders of the symbolic-sacrificial view had done before him; and when he twice connected the immortality of the body with reception, he was adopting the Greek realistic-dynamic view which he knew from Irenæus. The doctrine of ubiquity on which he based his conception of the real presence (see UBIQUITY) was taken from the Nominalists, though carried further than scholasticism had carried it. [It seems probable that Luther's doctrine of ubiquity was closely connected with his doctrine of the Communicatio Idiomatum (q.v.), which latter came to him through mysticism from the Neo-Platonic Christian thought. If so, it had its root in realism rather than in nominalism and was essentially Eutychian. Luther's mind was not sufficiently philosophical to grasp the points at issue between realism and nominalism, to which fact were due in part his inconsistencies.—A. H. N.] The really new thing with Luther is the explanation of the "this is" by the grammatical figure of synecdoche, by which "one names a whole and means only a part," as when "a mother points to the swaddling-clothes in which her child is wrapped, saying, 'This is my child.'" Zwingli and Calvin followed Augustinian paths. The former accepted only the symbolic-sacrificial idea, separated, of course, from any thought of a sacrifice in the Eucharist; Calvin has also the notion of the "spiritual eating of the body and blood of Christ" in a form modified by realistic-dynamic ideas. That both of them found the symbolic part of the "this is my body" in "is" (= *significat*) has, it is true, no exact parallel in ancient days. But the point where they placed the symbol is comparatively unimportant—this "tropical" explanation was not new, and the gloss of Œcolampadius—"this is a figure of my body"—combines Augustine's sense with words of Tertullian.

5. Teaching of the Reformers.

In order to understand the sequence of events among the Lutherans, three things must be borne in mind: the extremely conservative character of Luther's original teaching and practise in this matter, Melanchthon's gradual departure from it, and the lateness of the real effect of Luther's teaching on ubiquity. The popular mind paid little heed to fine distinctions, and saw no great difference between transubstantiation and consubstantiation. Luther's catechisms, which soon became, if informally, the standard of teaching, asserted that "under" (or "in and under") "the bread and wine the true body and the true blood of our Lord Jesus Christ is imparted [to all receivers] as a certain pledge and sign of the benefit

6. Doctrine in the Lutheran Church.

of the sacrament (to the faithful only), the remission of sins." The manner in which the form of public worship was but slightly changed from the pre-Reformation mass produced a similar impression on the ordinary mind. The fact, then, was all the more notable that from 1531 Melanchthon drew away more and more from this position. As early as that date he dropped the doctrine of ubiquity, and somewhat later the "in the bread"; by 1535 he was sympathizing with the "tropical" meaning given to the words of institution, and then, though obscurely, abandoning the reception by the wicked; while toward the end of his life he agreed in all essentials with Calvin. About 1555 the doctrine of ubiquity began to have its effect. The Philippists (q.v.) were then directly attacked, after Melanchthon's death, as "crypto-Calvinists," and theological discussion turned with considerable heat to the question of the Lord's Supper, and to the doctrine of the Incarnation which the teaching on ubiquity connected closely with it. After the downfall of the Philippists in Saxony, it was possible to formulate definitely the anti-Philippist, anti-Calvinist teaching in article VII. of the *Formula Concordiæ* (see section IV and the article, FORMULA OF CONCORD).

Among the "Reformed" Churches—those which were neither Lutheran nor Anabaptist—there was a general agreement from Zwingli's time that "the body and blood of Christ" were not, as with Luther and the Roman Catholics, the "sign of the sacrament" but the benefit which only the faithful, "spiritually eating," received; that accordingly the "this is" must be taken in a figurative sense; that Christ, exalted "bodily" to the right hand of God, is present not "bodily" but according to his divinity and "efficacy." There were, however, differences on some points. In Zwingli's mind the rite was one which rather imposed obligations on the recipient than conferred benefits; "spiritual eating" was for him equivalent to the faith in the sacrifice of Christ which was professed by the congregation. It is true that he said more than once that the sacrament was a pledge and assurance of faith; but Bullinger emphasized much more strongly the side which gives, as in the general conception of a sacrament, so especially in the communion. Calvin, whose view may more easily be understood, and probably with more correctness, as a modification of Luther's, not of Zwingli's, insisted strongly on the "giving" character of the sacrament in opposition to what he thought the "profane" conception of Zwingli, and gave a much fuller meaning to the "spiritual eating." His views have ultimately been adopted by the great majority of the strictly "Reformed" bodies; but to take a wide general view of the infinite gradations between the strict Calvinistic belief and the rationalizing of the Zwinglian view into a mere observance in commemoration of Christ would require far too much space. (F. LOOFS.)

7. The Reformed Doctrine.

The position taken on the subject by the great Church of England divines represents a *via media* between the opposing views already cited, and differs essentially from that of any other reformed church. It is true that, with the extraordinary latitude allowed in that church to the teaching of the clergy, all possible views from absolute transubstantiation to flat Zwinglianism may be found at the present day; but none the less there is a traditional attitude which may be designated as characteristically Anglican. Its exponents call it simply the doctrine of the real presence, and lay distinguishing emphasis on the fact that "our doctrine leaves this subject in the sacred mystery with which God has enveloped it" (William Palmer, *Treatise on the Church of Christ*, London, 1838). The same idea is expressed at greater length by Bishop Andrewes (1555–1626) in his answer to Bellarmine: "The Cardinal is not unless 'willingly, ignorant' that Christ hath said 'This is my body,' not 'This is not my Body in this mode.' Now about the object we are both agreed; all the controversy is about the mode. The 'This is' we firmly believe; that 'it is in this mode' (the Bread, namely, being transubstantiated into the Body), or of the mode whereby it is wrought that 'it is,' whether in, or with, or under, or transubstantiated, there is not a word in the Gospel." In another place he quotes with approval, as does also Jeremy Taylor, a saying attributed to Durandus, "We hear the word, feel the effect, know not the manner, believe the Presence." Archbishop Laud (1573–1645) asserted in his conference with Fisher, "As for the Church of England, nothing is more plain than that it believes and teaches the true and real Presence of Christ in the Eucharist." The denial, in the so-called "Black Rubric" appended to the communion service, of the "*corporal* presence of Christ's *natural* Flesh and Blood" is intended, not to deny the real presence, but to strike at certain gross material views current among insufficiently educated people in the period just before the Reformation.

8. The Anglican Doctrine.

III. Confessional Statements:* The Roman Catholic doctrine is officially given in the *Canons and Decrees of the Council of Trent*, Sess. XIII., Oct. 11, 1551 (ii. 126–139). The principal points are:

"In the Eucharist are contained truly, really, and substantially, the body and blood, together with the soul and divinity of our Lord Jesus Christ, and consequently the whole Christ."—*Can.* 1.

"The whole substance of the bread is [converted] into the body," and "the whole substance of the wine into the blood."—*Can.* 2.

"The whole Christ is contained under each species, and under every part of each species, when separated."—*Can.* 3.

"The principal fruit of the most holy Eucharist is the remission of sins."—*Can.* 5.

"In the Eucharist, Christ is to be adored."—*Can.* 6.

"All and each of Christ's faithful are bound to communicate every year."—*Can.* 9.

"Sacramental confession is to be made beforehand, by those whose conscience is burdened with mortal sin."—*Can.* 11.

The same view is taught, though less distinctly, in the Greek Church in the *Orthodox Confession of the Eastern Church*, Ques. CVI., CVII. (ii. 380–385); in the *Confession of Dositheus* (ii. 427–432); in the *Longer Catechism of the Eastern Church*, Ques. 315:

"What is the *Communion?* A sacrament, in which the believer, under the forms of bread and wine, partakes of the very Body and Blood of Christ to everlasting life" (ii. 495).

* The references are to Philip Schaff, *The Creeds of Christendom*, 3 vols., New York, 1877.

"The true body and blood of Christ are truly present under the form of bread and wine, and are there communicated to and received by those that eat in the Lord's Supper" (iii. 13).

Afterward Melanchthon changed this article in the edition of 1540, substituting for *distribuantur* ("communicated") *exhibeantur* ("shown"). This departure occasioned much controversy. The Lutheran doctrine is thus given in the *Formula of Concord* (1576), Art. VII., *Affirmative:*

"We believe, teach, and confess that in the Lord's Supper the body and blood of Christ are truly and substantially present, and that they are truly distributed and taken together with the bread and wine" (iii. 137).

The authoritative teaching of the Reformed Churches is thus given: *First Helvetic Confession* (1536), XXIII.:

"The bread and wine [of the Supper] are holy, true symbols, through which the Lord offers and presents the true communion of the body and blood of Christ for the feeding and nourishing of the spiritual and eternal life" (iii. 225).

So also in the *Second Helvetic Confession*, Cap. XXI. (iii. 291–295).

The *French Confession of Faith* (1559), XXXVI., XXXVIII.:

"The Lord's Supper is a witness of the union which we have with Christ, inasmuch as he not only died and rose again for us once, but also feeds and nourishes us truly with his flesh and blood, so that we may be one in him, and that our life may be in common."

"The bread and wine in the sacrament serve to our spiritual nourishment, inasmuch as they show, as to our sight, that the body of Christ is our meat, and his blood our drink" (iii. 380, 381).

The *Scotch Confession of Faith* (1560), Art. XXI.:

"The faithful in the richt use of the Lord's Table do so eat the bodie and drinke the blude of the Lord *Jesus* that he remains in them and they in him" (iii. 467–474).

The *Belgic Confession* (1561), Art. XXXV.:

"Christ that he might represent unto us this spiritual and heavenly bread hath instituted an earthly and visible bread as a Sacrament of his body, and wine as a Sacrament of his blood, to testify by them unto us, that, as certainly as we receive and hold this Sacrament in our hands, and eat and drink the same with our mouths, by which our life is afterward nourished, we also do as certainly receive by faith (which is the hand and mouth of our soul) the true body and blood of Christ our only Savior in our souls, for the support of our spiritual life" (iii. 428–431).

The *Heidelberg Catechism* (1563), Ques. 76:

"What is it to eat of the crucified body and drink the shed blood of Christ? It is not only to embrace with a believing heart all the sufferings and death of Christ, and thereby to obtain the forgiveness of sins and life eternal, but moreover, also, to be so united more and more to his sacred body by the Holy Ghost, who dwells both in Christ and in us, that although he is in heaven, and we are upon the earth, we are nevertheless flesh of his flesh, and bone of his bones, and live and are governed forever by one Spirit, as members of the same body are by the one soul" (iii. 332, 333).

The *Thirty-Nine Articles of the Church of England* (1562), Art. XXVIII.:

"The Supper of the Lord is not only a sign of the love that Christians ought to have among themselves one to another; but rather it is a Sacrament of our Redemption by Christ's death: insomuch that to such as rightly, worthily, and with faith, receive the same, the Bread which we break is a [heavenly and spiritual] partaking of the Body of Christ; and likewise the Cup of Blessing is a partaking of the Blood of Christ" (iii. 505).

So the *Irish Articles of Religion* (1615; iii. 542, 543).

The *Westminster Confession of Faith* (1647), chap. XXIX.:

"The Lord's Supper [is] to be observed for the perpetual remembrance of the sacrifice of himself in his death, the sealing of all benefits thereof with true believers, their spiritual nourishment and growth in him, their further engagement in and to all duties which they owe unto him; and to be a bond and pledge of their communion with him, and with each other, as members of his mystical body."

"Worthy believers do inwardly by faith, really and indeed, yet not carnally and corporally, but spiritually receive and feed upon Christ crucified, and all the benefits of his death" (iii. 663–667).

The *Westminster Shorter Catechism* (1647), Ques. 96:

"What is the Lord's Supper? A sacrament wherein by the giving and receiving bread and wine, according to Christ's appointment, his death is showed forth, and the worthy receivers are, not after a corporal and carnal manner, but by faith, made partakers of his body and blood, with all its benefits, to their spiritual nourishment and growth in grace" (iii. 697).

The *Confession of the Society of Friends* (1675), Thirteenth Proposition:

"The communion of the body and blood of Christ is inward and spiritual, which is the participation of his flesh and blood, by which the inward man is daily nourished in the hearts of those in whom Christ dwells; of which things the breaking of bread by Christ with his disciples was a figure, which they even used in the Church for a time, who had received the substance, for the cause of the weak; even as 'abstaining from things strangled, and from blood'; the washing one another's feet, and the anointing of the sick with oil; all which are commanded with no less authority and solemnity than the former; yet seeing they are but the shadow of better things, they cease in such as have obtained the substance" (iii. 797).

Reformed Episcopal Articles of Religion (1875), Art. XXVII.:

"The Supper of the Lord is a memorial of our Redemption by Christ's death, for thereby we do show forth the Lord's death till he come. It is also a symbol of the soul's feeding upon Christ. And it is a sign of the communion that we should have with one another" (iii. 823).

IV. The Liturgy in the Churches of the Reformation.—1. Luther and the Lutheran Church: Although Luther hoped for a complete renewal of the whole life of the people by the preaching of a pure gospel, he did not try to attain this end by making his own external arrangement of the ordinances of public worship. Looking upon himself as a member of the one Church, and bearing in mind how the people were accustomed to liturgical forms, he concluded to retain as much of the Roman mass as did not conflict with the word of God. His order for the celebration of the Lord's Supper is, therefore, only to be fully understood by a comparison with the Roman Mass (q.v.). He kept the first part of it almost unchanged as far as the creed; but the introduction of a sermon at this point made a sharp division between the *missa catechumenorum* and the offertory and canon which followed. In regard to the offertory of the mass, Luther declares in his *Formula missæ* (1523) that from that point nearly everything savors of a sacrifice, and that accordingly, repudiating all that has this meaning, he has retained what is pure and holy. On this basis, he struck out the offertory and the five following prayers, and went on, after the creed and sermon, to (a) the preface of the Roman mass, somewhat abridged, and then immediately to (b) the words of institution in Latin, beginning, as in the mass, "*Qui pridie quam pateretur,*" but leaving out all

1. Luther's First Form.

the additions not found in the Scriptural text and adding the Scriptural words "*quod pro vobis datur*" after "*hoc est corpus meum*"; (c) the *Sanctus* and *Hosanna*, during the singing of which (d) the elevation was to take place. Then followed (e) the Lord's Prayer, (f) the *Pax Domini*, (g) the Communion, during which the choir was to sing (h) the *Agnus Dei*. He left optional a prayer from the mass, and the old formula of administration "*Corpus (Sanguis) Domini nostri Jesu Christi custodiat animam tuam.*" The service closed with (i) two post-communion prayers from the mass, (j) the *Benedicamus Domino*, to be sung invariably with the addition of Alleluia; (k) the blessing of Aaron (Num. vi. 24–27), which had never been used except in the Spanish liturgy.

2. Luther's Revised Form.

Three years passed between the publication of Luther's *Formula missæ* and his *Deutsche Messe und Ordnung des Gottesdienstes*. During this time a number of other services came into use. The earliest German mass known is that composed in 1524 by Kantz, a preacher of Nördlingen. There is a Latin one of 1524 at Nuremberg, which in the following year began to be used in German with a few changes; this is characterized by the introduction of a German exhortation to the communicants immediately before the *Pax*. The same feature is found in a Prussian vernacular service of 1525, but is lacking in the Strasburg order of the same year. Luther's new service of 1526 retained his earlier Latin form for week-days, but introduced the German form for Sundays. In the latter the preface was replaced by a paraphrase of the Lord's Prayer and an exhortation supposed to be written beforehand, of which Luther gives an example not intended to be binding; this was no innovation, but a medieval custom, which seems to have arisen in South Germany. During the communion of the people, either a German paraphrase of the *Sanctus*, or another German hymn, or the *Agnus Dei* was to be sung, followed by a new German prayer.

3. Variant Lutheran Forms.

Although Luther did not regard the form drawn up by him as in any way generally obligatory, the types appearing in these two services became models for the Lutheran liturgies of the sixteenth century. These *Kirchenordnungen* may be generally described as follows: At the beginning of the celebration, as prescribed by Luther, the communicants were to take their places in the choir, the men on the south and the women on the north. The preface was either retained as in Luther's two forms, or replaced for ordinary Sundays by an exhortation, or both preface and exhortation were used. In Southern Germany a general confession and absolution followed. The same variety appears in regard to the retention of the *Sanctus* and *Hosanna*, which were still sung in Latin in North Germany, elsewhere in either Latin or German. During the *Sanctus*, some liturgies prescribed three German prayers to be said by the celebrant; one for secular rulers, one for the ministers of the word, and one for Christian unity. Other new prayers were added in different places before the consecration. As the most important and indispensable part of the liturgy, all retained the words of institution, through which the real consecration of the elements for their sacred purpose was supposed to take place. Luther omitted the sign of the cross made over the elements, and no sixteenth-century service has it, while the Hanover form of 1536 directly forbids it. It is first mentioned in the Lutheran Church by Johann Gerhard in the begining of the seventeenth century as "an indifferent ceremony," possessing "no spiritual force"; and afterward it occurs not infrequently. The breaking of the bread and the placing of a fragment of it in the chalice were dropped because the former was connected with the Roman Catholic theory of sacrifice, and the latter with the denial of the cup to the laity. Unleavened bread was still generally used, but the mixture of wine and water was discontinued; the recitation of the words of institution was ordered to be in a loud voice, contrary to the Roman usage. The elevation of the elements after consecration was retained by Luther expressly for the sake of weak brethren who might be offended by too many striking changes in the service; and it was retained also in a number of sixteenth-century forms. The place of the Lord's Prayer, generally sung in German, varied. Though Luther had omitted the *Pax Domini* in his German mass, it was frequently retained in the light of a formula of absolution. The usual manner of distribution was for the minister to communicate first himself and then the people, placing the bread directly in their mouths. First the men and then the women were to approach; occasionally the young were to come before the old. Stress was frequently laid on provision that none of the consecrated elements should remain or be thrown away at the conclusion of the service. Luther first retained the Roman formula of administration as permissible, but gave no formula in his German mass. The other services show a great variety in this regard; but ultimately the struggle against Crypto-Calvinism (see PHILIPPISTS) brought about an agreement to adhere either to something like the Latin formula, or to the other one which had been frequently used, "Take and eat; this is the body of Jesus Christ, which is given for you." The later Lutheran formula came into use first in 1647 at Lübeck, where through Bugenhagen's influence no formula had previously been used. The blessing of Aaron generally concluded the service after Luther's example. The old liturgies tended more and more to fall into disuse, under the influence of Pietism, with its depreciation of liturgical forms, and still more under that of rationalism. The preface was almost universally omitted and replaced by exhortations in the spirit of the time. The words of institution, however, and the Lord's Prayer (the latter frequently in a weak paraphrase), were still considered essential.

2. Zwingli: Zwingli at first (1523), in relation to the order of divine service, adhered to the canon of the mass; but in his treatise *De canone missæ epichiresis* he expressed himself with much severity about this part of the mass. In place of the offertory he inserted a general prayer. Then he went on much like Luther: preface, *Sanctus*, prayer for a blessing on the reception, leading up to the words of institution, distribution, thanksgiving, the *Nunc dimittis* or Song of Simeon, and the blessing. In 1525 he worked out an independent form of service, which was to be said, not sung. The communicants being assembled in the choir, the minister first prayed, turning toward them, that they might be well prepared. Then followed the reading of I Cor. xi. 20–29; the *Gloria in excelsis*, recited alternately in German by the men and women; the salutation and response "The Lord be with you," "And with thy spirit"; the reading of John vi. 47–63; the Apostles' Creed, also recited alternately; a short exhortation on the comfort and the solemnity of the feast; the Lord's Prayer, and another prayer for worthy reception; and the words of institution. For the communion, unleavened bread on wooden plates and wine in wooden cups was given to the communicants, seated, by appointed assistants; each broke off a morsel of the bread for himself and took the chalice in his hands. Then, after the recitation of Psalm cxiii. and a short thanksgiving, the minister dismissed the congregation with "Go in peace." This form, which expresses the Zwinglian conception of the Lord's Supper as a profession of faith and devotion on the part of the congregation, was retained with slight variations in the later Zürich liturgies until 1675. According to the form of Œcolampadius, there was a preparation consisting of confession and absolution, psalm-singing, a general prayer, and reading of the Gospel account of the Passion, after which a simple form of celebration followed, consisting of exhortation, the Lord's Prayer, words of institution, communion, thanksgiving, and blessing.

3. The Reformed Services: After Farel had abolished the Roman mass in Geneva, Calvin instituted an independent liturgy in his *La manière de celebrer la cène.* The Lord's Supper was to be celebrated once a year, after a sermon on its significance and a prayer for worthy reception. The service then continued with the reading of I Cor. xi. 25–29 and an exhortation, which contained a solemn excommunication of grievous sinners and enemies of church unity, urged all to examine their consciences carefully, and gave comfort to those who were weak in the faith or tempted to despair. In the conclusion of this, the ancient *Sursum corda* was paraphrased according to Calvin's dogmatic conceptions: "Let us lift up our hearts and minds thither where Jesus Christ is in the glory of his Father . . for our souls will be well disposed to be nourished and vivified by his substance, when they are thus raised above all things earthly, to reach heaven itself and enter into the kingdom of God, where he dwells." Then followed the communion, with the provision that the minister himself should first receive it, then give it to the deacon and then to the whole congregation, who were to approach the holy table. The formula of administration was the following (in French): "Take and eat the body of Jesus, which was delivered up to death for you. This is the cup of the New Testament in the blood of Jesus, which was shed for you." During the communion Psalm cxxxviii. was sung, followed by a prayer of thanksgiving, the Song of Simeon, and the blessing. Calvin's type of service was followed by the scattered Reformed communities in Westphalia and on the Rhine. In Switzerland the Calvinistic and Zwinglian forms were combined and modified in such various ways that at least six different forms exist to-day. The order of service drawn up in 1550 by Johannes a Lasco (q.v.) for the Dutch refugees in England, the first complete order for the Calvinistic Reformed body, prescribes that on the day preceding the administration of the Lord's Supper, a sermon is to be delivered. At the time of the celebration, four cups and three pewter plates are to be set out on a table covered with a linen cloth. Another sermon is delivered, ending with an exhortation forbidding the approach of those who have not yet made their profession of faith and put themselves under Christian discipline or who have not given notice of their intention to receive. Then follow a prayer, the words of institution, and an exhortation to self-examination, after which the minister reads I Cor. v. 7, 8. The communion has the character of a family meal. The minister, elders, and members of the congregation sit around the table, as far as there is room. The minister takes a piece of the bread which is in the larger plate and, with the words, "The bread which we break is the communion of the body of Christ," divides it into small pieces on the other two plates, then handing it to those who sit near him with the words, "Take, eat, remember and believe that the body of our Lord Jesus Christ was given up to death upon the wood of the cross for the forgiveness of all our sins." The plates are then passed to those who sit further off and the same proceeding is observed in the administration of the cup, with corresponding words. First the men and then the women take their places around the table in turn, while John vi. and xiii.-xv. are read from the chancel. After the communion, the service closes with a word from the minister, thanksgiving, a psalm, and the blessing. The Dutch Reformed Church still maintains this order, in which is obvious the attempt to assimilate the celebration as much as possible to the brotherly fellowship at the table of the original institution. The Scotch Church also derives its form from the order of Johannes a Lasco, and, like the Reformed Church of France, gives a similar complexion to the celebration.

4. The Anglican Communion: In accordance with the general tendency of the English Reformation, a very large part of the Reformed service is taken more or less directly from the older liturgies, and even some parts which do not occur in the Roman mass have ancient precedent. Thus the prayer for the Church militant occupies the same position as the great intercession in the Gallican rite, and the recitation of the Ten Commandments, while probably due to the ethical tendency of the age, has been explained by some liturgical scholars as answering to the prophecy, or reading from the Old Testament, which in some other ancient liturgies preceded the epistle and Gospel. Several portions newly added were intended to emphasize the aspect of the service as a communion; thus the prayer of Humble Access, the Comfortable Words, and the position and wording of the confession and absolution presuppose the reception of the communion by the bulk of the congregation. The canon is much shortened, following the Roman closely in the essential part, and the Lord's Prayer, as scarcely ever elsewhere, follows the communion. The *Gloria in excelsis* retained its ancient position in the first Prayer-book of Edward VI., but was afterward moved to the end of the service, as an act of thanksgiving. See also COMMON PRAYER, BOOK OF.

V. Certain Points of Interest not Already Treated: In the primitive Church, the newly baptized were immediately admitted to communion; and with the growing frequency of infant baptism the same custom was still maintained. Cyprian (*De lapsis*, ix.) speaks of children who at the outset of their lives have received "the meat and drink of the Lord," and similar evidence may be collected from the Apostolic Constitutions, Dionysius the Areopagite, Paulinus of Nola (d. 431), and Gennadius of Marseilles (c. 492). The necessity of communion to salvation being taught on the basis of John vi. 53, this argument is applied to the communion of infants by Augustine and by Innocent I. But evidences of the practise are not confined to the first six centuries, as some have contended; on the contrary, they come down as late as the twelfth, in which Paschal II. (1118) prescribes that the two elements are to be separately administered "except to infants and those who are so weak that they can not swallow the bread," and Robertus Paululus speaks of the custom as extant, although beginning to disappear. A synodal ordinance of Odo, bishop of Paris, in 1175, and a canon of the Synod of Bordeaux in 1255 attest its cessation in France, the latter prescribing the administration of blessed bread (see EULOGIA) instead of the Host. It is a question whether the existence of the custom can be shown in Germany later than the twelfth century. The Council of Trent ruled finally (*Sessio* XXI. chap. 4) that children below the age of reason were bound by no necessity to sacramental communion of the Eucharist, "although antiquity is not to be condemned for observing this custom in certain places and times." The Greek Church has retained the practise to the present day. The Evangelical churches, making admission to communion dependent on spiritual maturity as evidenced by a special examination, have naturally not retained it. (GEORG RIETSCHEL.)

1. Infant Communion.

In the early Church it was customary to carry the consecrated elements immediately after service to the sick and to prisoners; and two passages in Tertullian (*Ad uxorem*, II., v.; *De oratione*, xix.) seem to imply the custom of communicating at home under the species of bread even apart from illness. Later we find the consecrated bread carried on journeys and used as an amulet, a practise against which more than one council legislated. With the introduction of communion in one kind, it became usual to carry the consecrated bread to the sick immediately after mass or from the tabernacle in which it was reserved; and the strict enforcement of the rule of fasting communion made it desirable as obviating the necessity of the priest's having to celebrate in the afternoon or evening for a person in sudden danger of death. In the Church of England a special service is provided for the celebration of the communion in the sick-room, somewhat shorter than the usual form; but in recent years, with the growth of the practise of reservation, the elements are not infrequently carried from the church and administered with a brief form of prayer. The Lutheran Church freely allows private communion, while the Reformed discourages it.

2. Communion of the Sick.

In the pre-Reformation Church the principal requirements for a worthy reception of the sacrament were freedom from sin and fasting from the previous midnight. Both of these are strictly required in the Roman Catholic Church at the present day. The former is imposed as a matter of absolute necessity in the case of mortal sin, when confession must invariably precede communion; in practise confession is usually recommended to infrequent communicants, even though they may not be conscious of having committed a mortal sin since their last communion. The question of the frequency of communion is one which has been much discussed at different times. It is generally admitted that in the Apostolic Age it was received, if not daily, at least on Sunday, Wednesday, and Friday. As the zeal of the days of persecution diminished, it became less frequent, and Chrysostom had to rebuke those who communicated only once a year. In Africa as late as Augustine's day once a week was the usual minimum. The second Synod of Tours (850) required at least three times a year; but by the Lateran Council of 1215 the Church had come to limit the actual requirement to once a year, at Easter. In the sixteenth century the frequency once more increased, under the influence of Ignatius and Philip Neri, and was spoken of as highly desirable by the Council of Trent. The Jansenist and Quietist movements in France (especially through Arnauld's treatise *De la fréquente communion*) tended to diminish it once more, and the laxity of modern times makes it usual for even fairly devout people to communicate at most once a month. In the Anglican communion, after the Reformation, the frequency of administration fell in most places to four times a year, or at most once a month, until the High-church revival of the nineteenth century restored it to normally once a week and in many places daily, with a consequent increase in the frequency of communion. In the other Protestant churches the quarterly administration is the most usual. The requirement of fasting, for which there is early evidence, was prescribed as a matter of reverence. In modern Roman Catholic practise the exceptions which excuse from it are serious illness and the necessity of protecting the sacred species from profanation or of completing the mass in the case of a sudden indisposition of the celebrant. This rule also is increasingly emphasized in the Anglican Communion under present conditions, but does not occur in the other Reformation churches, which content themselves with requiring

3. Requirements for Communicants.

a general condition of faith and repentance. As to the first admission to communion, they usually require a formal ceremony of recognition of membership or the like; according to the rubric of the Anglican Prayer-book "none shall be admitted to the Holy Communion except he be confirmed, or be ready and desirous to be confirmed."

The original Lutheran and Calvinist types of administration have been noted above. The mode of administration in non-Episcopal churches in America and England is almost uniform.

4. Practises Connected with Administration.

The elements are consecrated by prayer by the minister, who breaks as much bread and pours out as much wine as he deems sufficient. He repeats the words of institution; he then hands the elements for distribution to the elders or deacons, who serve him first and then pass to the other communicants sitting in their pews. In the Anglican Communion and also in many Lutheran churches the communicants kneel at the chancel rail. In the German Reformed Church they stand. On modern sanitary principles an agitation has recently been made in America for the introduction of individual communion cups, and the movement has slowly spread very widely. For communion in both kinds see MASS, II., 5.

BIBLIOGRAPHY: On the general subject the works cited under EUCHARIST should be consulted, as also those under TRANSUBSTANTIATION. On I. consult: The works cited in Biblical Introduction, II., especially those of Weiss and Beyschlag; J. G. Scheibel, *Das Abendmahl des Herrn*, Breslau, 1823; D. Schulz, *Die christliche Lehre vom Abendmahl nach dem Grundtext des N. T.*, ib. 1824; J. J. I. von Döllinger, *Die Lehre von der Eucharistie in den drei ersten Jahrhunderten*, Mainz, 1825; F. W. Lindner, *Die Lehre vom Abendmahl nach der Schrift*, Hamburg, 1831; K. F. A. Kahnis, *Die Lehre vom Abendmahl*, Leipsic, 1851; L. J. Rückert, *Das Abendmahl, sein Wesen und seine Geschichte in der alten Kirche*, ib. 1856; C. T. Keim, *Geschichte Jesu von Nazara*, iii. 266, Zurich, 1872, Eng. transl., 6 vols., London, 1875–82; H. Schultz, in *TSK*, 1886; P. Lobstein, *La Doctrine de la sainte cène*, Lausanne, 1889; Harnack, in *TU*, vii. 2, 1891; T. Zahn, *Brot und Wein im Abendmahl der alten Kirche*, Leipsic, 1892, cf. Harnack in *TLZ*, no. 15, 1892; A. Jülicher, in *Theologische Abhandlungen . . . K. von Weizsäcker gewidmet*, Freiburg, 1882; C. Weizsäcker, *Das apostolische Zeitalter*, pp. 574 sqq., Freiburg, 1892, Eng. transl., *The Apostolic Age*, 2 vols., London, 1894–95; F. Spitta, *Zur Geschichte und Literatur des Urchristentums*, vol. i., Göttingen, 1893; E. Grafe, in *Zeitschrift für Theologie und Kirche*, 1895, part 2, pp. 101–138; F. Schulten, *Das Abendmahl im N. T.*, Göttingen, 1895; A. C. McGiffert, *Hist. of Christianity in the Apostolic Age*, pp. 68 sqq. et passim, New York, 1897; A. Eichhorn, *Das Abendmahl im N. T.*, Leipsic, 1898; Schaff, *Christian Church*, i. 471–474; and the commentaries on the basal passages.

On II (history of the doctrine in the Church) consult: Harnack, *Dogma*, vols. i., ii., iv., v., vii. and, in general, the treatises on the history of doctrine; the works of Döllinger, Kahnis and Rückert, ut sup.; F. C. Baur, in *Tübinger Zeitschrift für Theologie*, 1839, pp. 56–144; J. H. A. Ebrard, *Das Dogma vom heiligen Abendmahl und seine Geschichte*, 2 vols., Frankfort, 1845–46; J. W. Nevin, *The Mystical Presence; Vindication of the Reformed or Calvinistic Doctrine of the Holy Eucharist*, Philadelphia, 1846; W. J. E. Bennett, *The Eucharist; its Hist., Doctrine, and Practice*, London, 1851; J. W. F. Höfling, *Die Lehre der ältesten Kirche vom Opfer*, Erlangen, 1851; R. Wilberforce, *The Doctrine of the Holy Eucharist*, London, 1853 (Anglican tractarian); A. W. Dieckhoff, *Die evangelische Lehre im Reformationszeitalter*, Gottingen, 1854; R. Halley, *The Sacraments*, part II., *The Lord's Supper*, London, 1855; P. Freeman, *The Principles of Divine Service*, 2 parts, London, 1855–62; E. Bickersteth, *A Treatise on the Lord's Supper*, ed. L. W. P. Balch, New York, 1857; E. B. Pusey, *The Real Presence of the Body and Blood of our Lord in the Holy Eucharist*, Oxford, 1857; G. F. Maclear, *The Witness of the Eucharist*, London, 1864; G. E. Steitz, in *Jahrbücher für deutsche Theologie*, ix (1864), 409–481, x (1865), 64–152, 399–463, xi (1865), 193–253, xii (1866), 211–286, xiii (1868), 3–66, 649–700; J. B. Dalgavins, *The Holy Communion, its Philosophy, Theology and Practice*, New York, 1868 (Roman Catholic); H. Schmid, *Der Kampf der lutherischen Kirche um Luthers Lehre vom Abendmahl im Reformationszeitalter*, Leipsic, 1868; J. Harrison, *Answer to Dr. Pusey's Challenge respecting the Doctrine of the Real Presence*, 2 vols., London, 1871 (Anglican Low-church); J. Macknaught, *Cœna Domini*, ib. 1878 (on the doctrine of the Anglican Church); H. Schultz, *Zur Lehre vom heiligen Abendmahl*, Gotha, 1886; L. Lanzoni, *The Names of the Eucharist*, Dublin, 1887; J. P. Lilley, *The Lord's Supper, . . . its Origin, Nature and Use*, Edinburgh, 1891; F. L. Renz, *Opfercharakter der Eucharistie nach der Lehre der Väter der drei ersten Jahrhunderte*, Paderborn, 1892; J. R. Milne, *Doctrine and Practice of the Eucharist*, London, 1895; J. Wilpert, *Fractio panis. Die älteste Darstellung des eucharistischen Opfers in der "Capella Græca,"* Freiburg, 1895; J. Smend, *Die evangelischen deutschen Messen bis zu Luthers Deutscher Messe*, Göttingen, 1896; J. Behringer, *Die heilige Kommunion in ihren Wirkungen*, Regensburg, 1898; A. Naegle, *Die Eucharistielehre des . . . J. Chrysostomus*, Freiburg, 1900; V. Schmitt, *Die Verheissung der Eucharistie bei den Vätern*, Würzburg, 1900; C. Gore, *The Body of Christ; an Inquiry into the Institution and Doctrine of Holy Communion*, London, 1901; W. Götzmann, *Das eucharistische Opfer nach der Lehre der ältern Scholastik*, Freiburg, 1901; A. G. Mortimer, *Eucharistic Sacrifice; historical and theological Investigation of the sacrificial Conception . . . in the Catholic Church*, London, 1901; R. M. Adamson, *Christian Doctrine of the Lord's Supper*, Edinburgh, 1905; J. C. Hedley, *The Holy Eucharist*, London, 1907.

On IV. consult: *Sammlung liturgischer Formulare der evangelisch-lutherischen Kirche*, part 3, Nördlingen, 1842; A. L. Richter, *Die evangelischen Kirchenordnungen des 16. Jahrhunderts*, Weimar, 1846; H. A. Daniel, *Codex liturgicus*, vols., ii.–iii., Leipsic, 1847–53; J. W. F. Höfling, *Liturgisches Urkundenbuch*, viii. 75 sqq., Schwerin, 1861; L. Schöberlein, *Schatz des liturgischen Chor- und Gemeindegesangs*, vol. i., Göttingen, 1865.

On V. consult: W. Vaux, *The Benefits Attached to Participation in . . . the Lord's Supper*, Oxford, 1826; A. N. Arnold, *Prerequisites to Communion*, Boston, 1860; T. W. Perry, *Historical Considerations Relating to the Declaration on Kneeling in . . . the . . . Book of Common Prayer*, London, 1863; F. Hall, *Fasting Reception of the Blessed Sacrament*, ib. 1882; J. W. Kempe, *Reservation of the Blessed Sacrament*, ib. 1887; R. Shiells, *The Story of the Token as Belonging to . . . the Lord's Supper*, New York, 1892; J. Hughes-Games, *Evening Communion*, London, 1894; R. V. Bury, *Vinum sacramenti; critical Examination of the Nature of the Wine of the Holy Communion*, Dublin, 1904; C. R. Davey Biggs, *The Lord's Supper; Text of the (Anglican) Service Explained*, Oxford, 1905; S. Phillips, *The Communion of the Sick*, London, 1905.

LORD'S TABLE. See ALTAR, III., 2, § 2.

LORETO, lo-rê'to: The most famous place of pilgrimage in Italy, and the principal seat for that country of the devotion to the Virgin Mary. It is situated 14 m. s.e. of Ancona on the road to Fermo, and is celebrated for its possession of what is alleged to be the house of the Virgin, transported thither from Nazareth by angels. The legend, although its first mention in literature is found in Flavius Blondus about the middle of the fifteenth century, seems to have grown up at the end of the crusading period. In its developed form, as found in Baptista Mantuanus (1576) and on a tablet on the wall of the church cited by Matthias Bernegger in 1619, it asserts that this is the actual portion of the dwelling of Mary at Nazareth in which she was born and brought up and received the angelic message, in which she lived after the ascension of her Son. The apostles, then, the legend goes on, made a church of it; St. Luke decorated it with a wooden figure of the Virgin holding the Child in her arms; and it was continuously used for worship until the fall of the kingdom of Jerusalem. Then, to save it from destruction by the unbelievers, angels appeared, caught it up into the air, and deposited it first at Raunitza in northern Dalmatia, between Fiume and Tersato (1291). Its genuineness was accredited by the healing of some sick people who prayed within it and by an apparition of the Virgin to Bishop Alexander of Tersato, who was himself miraculously healed of a long illness. Three years later the angels again picked it up and carried it to the opposite coast of Italy (Dec. 10, 1294) setting it down in a wood belonging to a pious woman named Laureta, from whom the shrine took its name. It was once more removed a mile nearer to Recanati, and reached its final resting-place Sept. 7, 1295. The second half of the fifteenth century saw a marked increase in devotion to the shrine. The earliest papal sanction of the devotion dates from Sixtus IV. (1471), who, as well as Julius II. (1507), uses the expression "as it is piously believed and the report is" in reference to the translation of the house. Sixtus V. (1587) founded a knightly order (Ordo et religio equitum Lauretanorum pontificiorum) for the protection of pilgrims, which as late as the eighteenth century had between two and three hundred members. Innocent XII. (d. 1700) sanctioned a special mass and office in honor of Our Lady of Loreto; and other popes granted special privileges, which, together with the munificent gifts of many Roman Catholic sovereigns, contributed to the spread of the devotion. At the beginning of the seventeenth century, not less than 200,000 pilgrims are said to have come to Loreto each year; but by the end of the eighteenth this number had much diminished, and in 1797 the French troops carried off nearly the whole of the enormous treasures of the shrine. Napoleon, however, made restitution of a part of them in 1800; and since the Roman Catholic revival of the nineteenth century the annual number of pilgrims has again exceeded 100,000. The artistic decoration of the shrine was carried on with great richness under Julius II., Leo. X., Clement VII., and Sixtus V. Numerous other shrines intended as reproductions of this have grown up in different parts of the world and attract many pilgrims. The Litany of Loreto, consisting of a long series of invocations of the Virgin under various titles, dates from the second half of the sixteenth century; the invocation *Auxilium Christianorum, ora pro nobis* was added in commemoration of the victory of Lepanto in 1571. The litany is now one of the most popular Roman Catholic devotions. (O. ZÖCKLER.)

BIBLIOGRAPHY: The account by Baptista Mantuanus is contained in his *Opera*, iv. 216 sqq., Antwerp, 1576. Consult further: B. Bartoli, *Le Glorie maestose del santuario di Loreto*, Macerata, 1712; Kirwan's *Romanism at Home*, pp. 99–107, New York, 1852; P. Arrighi, *Hist. de la demeure de la S. Vierge à Nazareth dans la basilique de Lorète*, Paris, 1889; W. Garratt, *Loreto, the New Nazareth*, London, 1890; *The Loretto Manual*, Dublin, 1891; W. F. H Garratt, *Loreto, the New Nazareth and its Jubilee*, London, 1895; Lichtenberger, *ESR*, viii. 371–372; *KL*, viii. 145–152. A long list of the polemical writings of Protestants and of the apologetics of Roman Catholics is given in Hauck-Herzog, *RE*, xi. 647.

LORETO SISTERS. See ENGLISH LADIES; and WOMEN, CONGREGATIONS OF.

LORIMER, GEORGE CLAUDE: American Baptist; b. in Edinburgh, Scotland, June 4, 1838; d. at Aix-les-Bains (40 m. s.s.w. of Geneva), France, Sept. 8, 1904. He came to the United States in 1856 and studied at Georgetown College, Ky. He was pastor at Harrodsburg, Ky. (1859); Paducah (1860–68); Albany, N. Y. (1868–70); Boston (1870–79); Chicago (1879–90); Boston (1891–1902); and New York (1902–04). He was the author of: *Under the Evergreens* (Boston, n. d.); *Great Conflict: Discourse concerning Baptists and Religious Belief* (1877); *Isms old and new* (Chicago, 1881); *Jesus, the World's Saviour* (1883); *Studies in Social Life* (1886); *Baptists in History* (Boston, 1893); *Argument for Christianity* (Philadelphia, 1894); *Messages of Today to the Men of Tomorrow* (1896); *Christianity and the Social State* (1898); *Christianity in the 19th Century* (1900); *Master of Millions* (New York, 1903); and *The Modern Crisis in Religion* (1904); and edited the *People's Bible History* (2 vols., Chicago, 1896).

LORIMER, PETER: English Presbyterian; b. in Edinburgh June 27, 1812; d. at Whitehaven (36 m. s.w. of Carlisle), Cumberland, July 29, 1879. He was the son of a master builder who occupied a good position in his native city. He received the elements of his education at George Heriot's Hospital, Edinburgh, and proceeded from the hospital to Edinburgh University. Here he passed through the classes of the arts curriculum with much credit, and also took his theological course, the professor of divinity at the time being Dr. Thomas Chalmers, to whom, as a teacher, Dr. Lorimer always acknowledged the highest obligations. In 1836 he was ordained as minister of the Presbyterian Church, River Terrace, London, connected with the Church of Scotland. In 1843, with his congregation, he cast in his lot with the Free Church. In 1845 he was appointed professor of Hebrew and Biblical criticism in the theological college of the English Presbyterian Church, then newly established in London, and in 1878 he was made principal. His most important writings are: a life of Patrick Hamilton (Edinburgh, 1857), the first of a projected series of works on the precursors of Knox; *The Scottish Reformation* (London, 1860); *John Knox and the Church of England* (1875), founded on the Knox papers preserved among the Morrice manuscripts; two lectures on *The Evidential Value of the Early Epistles of St. Paul* (1874); *The Evidence to Christianity Arising from its Adaptation to All the Deeper Wants of the Human Heart* (1875); and a translation with notes of vol. i (containing Wyclif's personal history) of G. V. Lechler's *Johann von Wiclif und die Vorgeschichte der Reformation* (*John Wiclif and his English Predecessors*, 2 vols., London, 1878; new eds. 1881, 1884).

W LEE†, revised by HENRY COWAN.

BIBLIOGRAPHY: *DNB*, xxxiv. 138.

LOS VON ROM.

Origin of Movement (§ 1).
Austria (§ 2).
Germany and France (§ 3).
Other Countries (§ 4).
Influence of "Modernism" (§ 5).

One of the most interesting features of recent religious life has been the growing movement away from Rome which has taken place during the past half century. In the beginning of the

1. Origin of Movement.

nineteenth century it seemed to be unquestioned that the bounds of Protestantism and Romanism were finally settled and that a new Reformation was not to be looked for. But the middle of the century saw a great intellectual, political, and religious awakening which was destined to have unexpected results in the ecclesiastical world. It became impossible to maintain the persecuting laws against Protestants which characterized all Roman Catholic countries, and these laws gradually disappeared or were mitigated, and mission work began. These missions have been carried on with varying success, partly by the small native Protestant Churches, partly by missionary societies in England, America, and Germany. But the movement away from Rome has not been due entirely or even mainly to these missionary efforts. It has been due to movements of various kinds inside the Church of Rome itself. The growth of political liberty made men dissatisfied with the despotism of the Vatican; and as the middle of the last century was characterized in the political sphere by a fierce struggle between absolutism and democracy, so in the ecclesiastical world there was a similar struggle between ultramontanism and the desire for greater freedom and elasticity of organization. In the political world democracy triumphed, but in the ecclesiastical ultramontanism won the day, and the result of its victory was the Vatican Council and the decree of papal infallibility (see VATICAN COUNCIL). Owing to the reluctance of Döllinger (q.v.) to create a schism and to the cowardice of some of the bishops who fought in the council against the decree, but accepted it when it had passed, the Old Catholic Church did not begin its career with numbers at all as large as were expected; but it has continued its course with a hopeful future in Holland, Germany, Switzerland, and Austria, and with a few followers in France, Italy, and Mexico. Its friendship for Protestantism has drawn it more and more away from the characteristic doctrines of Romanism, and in some places it serves as a temporary spiritual resting-place for those who are discontented with Rome, but not yet prepared for the decisive step of adopting a thoroughly Evangelical Protestantism. See OLD CATHOLICS.

A movement away from Rome which was at first very promising, but in the end proved more or less abortive, was that known as German Catholicism (q.v.). The remains of this move-

2. Austria.

ment are associated with the Union of Free Religious Congregations. This promising movement failed for want of a sufficiently vital religious and Evangelical element and from the excessive predominance of the political factor (see FREE CONGREGATIONS IN GERMANY). The German-speaking Roman Catholics, who furnished the greater part of these two movements, have recently given birth to a movement much more important than either of them, the "Los von Rom" movement in Austria. For a long time there has been a considerable alienation of both the German and Slav inhabitants of Austria from the Church of Rome and its services, but whether this would have led to a movement toward Protestantism and what form such a movement might have taken it is difficult to conjecture. The actual initiation of the movement toward Protestantism was due to a combination of racial and political influences which can only be referred to here. The war of 1866 with Prussia had transferred the leadership of the German states to that state, and eventually, after the defeat of France, had led to the formation of the German Empire, from which Austria was excluded. This loss of political position and power was keenly felt by the Austrian Germans, who saw themselves displaced by a new Protestant power from the position they had occupied for ages, and the explanation that forced itself on many minds was that Romanism had sapped the vigor of their race. Their resentment against Rome was intensified by the attitude Rome assumed in the racial struggles between Germans and Slavs. Having found France an ineffectual instrument for the promotion of its political aims, the Vatican began to throw its influence on the side of the Slavs against the Germans in order to build up a strong Slav Catholic power on which it could depend. Bitter anti-Roman political feeling was excited by this, and at length on Nov. 5, 1898, Schönerer, the leader of the German National Party, made an appeal for a secession from Rome, issuing the watchword by which it has been since known, "Los von Rom," i.e., Away from Rome, or Free from Rome. The movement has been pronounced purely a political maneuver, but this entirely misrepresents its character. The possibility of the political movement arose out of the religious dissatisfaction that existed, and many, even at the beginning, came out under the cover of the political passion of the moment, whose impelling motive was religious. The political element began rapidly to recede into the background, and after two or three years became entirely subordinate, till eventually it almost disappeared. In this transformation from the political to the religious a very deep influence has been exercised by the celebrated novelist Peter Rosegger, who has shown deep interest in the movement, though remaining nominally a Roman Catholic. The secessions have taken place almost entirely from the German-speaking portions of the population. Those who are most familiar with the Czech portions of Bohemia consider that the conditions exist for an important movement from Rome, but for the present the priests have succeeded in utilizing the strong racial hatred to prevent it by teaching their flocks that Protestantism is a German religion and to become Protestants is to be Germanized. The converts have joined one or other of the two Protestant confessions recognized by the government, the Augsburg or the

Helvetic, mainly the former, or the Old Catholic Church. Up to the end of 1908 over 51,000 had become Protestants and about 16,000 Old Catholics, besides a large number that worship in the Protestant churches who are prevented by fear of persecution from publicly enrolling themselves as Protestants. The conversions to Protestantism have during the past few years remained steadily about 4,500 annually, and the movement shows no sign of abating. See AUSTRIA.

3. Germany and France. In the German Empire (see GERMANY) there has been a growing movement away from Rome for many years while the conversions to Romanism have shown very slight increase. In the year 1890 3,105 Roman Catholics became Protestants, in 1895 3,895, in 1900 6,143, in 1905 9,339; while in the same years the conversions to Romanism were respectively 554, 588, 701, and 793. In the seventies the gains and losses of Protestantism were about equal. Mixed marriages, which at one time used in Germany and Austria to result almost invariably in gains to the Church of Rome, now generally mean gains to Protestantism. The losses in Germany from this cause alone for recent years have been estimated by a Roman Catholic authority as over 100,000, and the entire losses for the nineteenth century as at least a million. The revolt from Rome, though different in its nature, has been no less marked in France. It has there led to a considerable secession among the ranks of the priests. In 1895 André Bourrier, an able priest in the south of France, abandoned the Roman Church, and became two years later minister of the Protestant Church of Sèvres-Bellevue. He started a paper, *Le Chrétien Français*, which soon obtained a large circulation among the French priests, and through it he became the leader of an extensive revolt of the priests of France, which is one of the most remarkable of recent religious movements. His aim at first was the formation of a National Catholic Church, free from the tyranny and superstitions of Rome. The course of events has convinced him of the futility of hoping for a reformed Roman Catholic Church, and he is now working not for the organization of such a national Church, but for the conversion of Roman Catholics to Protestantism. His paper has at the same time changed its title to *Le Chrétien*. A somewhat similar work was carried on by another converted priest, Corneloup, in connection with his paper *Le Prêtre converti*. When the Separation Act was passed (1905) M. Meillon, Corneloup's successor, plunged into an agitation for the formation of "Associations cultuelles" by priests, and the consequent organization of an independent national Church, but the attempt failed. M. Meillon's work has been taken up with more success by M. Revoyre and his paper *Le Chrétien Libre*. There are no authentic statistics of the secessions from the priesthood, but those who are well informed believe that they amount to over a thousand, perhaps not far short of 1,500. A large proportion of these have become Protestants and some of them are working as pastors and Evangelists. Many have lapsed from Christian belief, but felt unable to continue preaching a creed they had ceased to hold, and have turned to civil life. The growth of Protestantism among the French people in numbers and influence has been considerable, but in the absence of religious statistics it can not be accurately estimated. Leading Roman Catholics are not blind to its reality, and have begun to speak in alarm of "the Protestant peril." This new movement from Rome, like that of the sixteenth century, has been closely associated with a fight with the monasteries. This struggle has reached a crisis first in France and has there issued in the dissolution of the greater number of them and the transfer of the education of the people to government schools. The attitude of the Church of Rome toward the monasteries and the schools convinced the leading French statesmen that it was necessary to disestablish that Church, and an act for that purpose was carried in 1905. It was thought that this act would lead to a secession of those priests and congregations who were restive under the spiritual tyranny of Rome, but the provision that the associations to which the Church property was transferred must be in connection with the general organization of the form of worship they propose to secure, prevented to a large extent the occurrence of a schism. The pope refused to allow the formation of the proposed associations for the management of the churches and other ecclesiastical property. Consequently the State seized the presbyteries, seminaries, and other buildings, and many of these have been put to secular uses. The Vatican apparently assumed that the government would also close the churches and thereby cause a reaction on the plea of religious persecution. But the government has not done so, and the priests have been allowed to continue their services, but the State endowments which were to have continued for four years have ceased on account of the refusal of the Church to accept the act. Some two or three hundred congregations have formed associations and have thereby set the papal decision at defiance. These may form the nucleus of a wider schism on those lines, but the outlook in that direction is not encouraging.

4. Other Countries. There is not space to follow the movement in detail through the different Roman Catholic countries. In Belgium there is a vigorous and growing mission church, almost exclusively composed of converts from Romanism and their children. In Italy the last half-century has seen a great revival of the Waldensian Church and the spreading of its organization and activities all over the peninsula, as well as the prosecution of mission work by different English and American churches. In Spain there was a promising revolt against the Church of Rome immediately after the granting of liberty of worship in 1868, but it was soon arrested and since then the work of Protestantism has been the slow and often discouraging gathering of units. But during the last few years there have been frequent manifestations of dissatisfaction with the papal domination, and a growing agitation against the power of the monasteries. Even Portugal has begun to move; greater liberty has been granted, and a recent decision of the supreme court has allowed the unreserved distribution of the Scriptures. The former colonies of Spain and Portugal have been moving more rapidly than their mother countries. Most encouraging mission work has been carried on in the Spanish republics of South and Central America, especially by the churches of the United States, and the power of Rome in those countries is rapidly decaying. In Brazil, for a long time one of the most hopeless fields, very remarkable progress is being made in recent years. In many respects the Philippines, since they came under the dominion of the United States, have presented the most remarkable revolt from Rome of modern times. Under the leadership of Aglipay an Independent National Philippine Church has been organized, which will probably grow into a vigorous Protestant communion. It claims at present to have the support of about half the population. In Canada and among the French Canadians in the United States the work inaugurated by Chiniquy has been most successful, and it is calculated that there are now over 30,000 French-Canadian Protestants in Canada and at least 40,000 in the United States. The exodus from the Church of Rome among the immigrants to the United States and their descendants has been very great, and Roman Catholic authorities estimate that they have lost in this way between twenty and thirty millions. It is known that in England Rome is losing by tens of thousands. The number of English Roman Catholics, when Irish and foreigners are excluded, is very small.

5. Influence of "Modernism."

But the hope of a revolt from Rome is probably derived by many more from the progress of Modernism (q.v.) inside that Church than from any other cause. This movement is wide-spread and varied in its character. It includes men like the late Professor Schell in Germany, Professors Ehrhardt and Wahrmund in Austria, Murri, Graf, Semeria, Minocchi, and Fogazzaro in Italy, Loisy and Houtin in France, Tyrrell in England, some of them men who recognize the impossibility of reconciling the scholasticism of Aquinas with the philosophical conceptions of the present day, men who desire to reconcile the Church with the democratic spirit of their time, men who desire to bring the Church into living contact with the great social movements of the present day and thereby infuse a Christian spirit into these movements, men who feel compelled to accept the results of modern criticism of the Bible and to hold these independently of the antiquated standpoint of the Vatican, and men who wish to see a more Christian and a less political spirit brought into all the activities of the Church. All such find themselves in irreconcilable conflict with the supreme authorities of their Church. Murri, Minocchi, and Loisy have been excommunicated by the Vatican, and Tyrrell died under the ban of the Church. The future alone can tell the issue of the conflict. It is difficult to see how they can permanently retain their position in a Church whose head is "infallible" and whose decisions are given promptly and unmistakably against them. Also see MODERNISM.

JOHN A. BAIN.

BIBLIOGRAPHY: Indispensable are the *Berichte über den Fortgang der Los von Rom Bewegung*, a series of publications edited by P. Bräunlich, Munich, 1899, still in progress, covering the different countries in which the movement exists. Consult also: J. A. Bain, *New Reformation, Recent Evangelical Movements in the Roman Catholic Church*, 2d ed., Edinburgh, 1909; A. Bourrier, *Ceux qui s'en vont*, Paris, 1905; H. Wegener, *Morgendämmerung in der Steiermark*, Mörs, 1904; A. Houtin, *La Crise du clergé*, Paris, 1907; A. Briand, *La Séparation des églises et de l'état*, ib. 1905; P. Rosegger, *Mein Himmelreich*, Leipsic, 1907; J. McCabe, *Decay of Church of Rome*, New York, 1909.

LOSERTH, lō′zārt, **JOHANN**: Austrian Protestant; b. at Fulneck (a village near Neutitschein, 26 m. e.n.e. of Prerau), Moravia, Sept. 1, 1846. He was educated at the University of Vienna (Ph.D., 1870), and after being a gymnasial professor in Vienna (1871–75) was professor of general history at the newly founded University of Czernowitz until 1893, when he was called to his present position of professor of history at Graz. He has devoted himself especially to the study of early Bohemian history, the Wyclif and Hussite movements, and the history of Anabaptism and the Counter-Reformation. Among his numerous publications, special mention may be made of the following: *Beiträge zur Geschichte der hussitischen Bewegung* (5 parts, Vienna, 1877–94); *Huss und Wiclif* (Prague, 1884; Eng. transl. by M. J. Evans, *Wyclif and Huss*, London, 1884); *Die Stadt Waldshut und die vorderösterreichische Regierung 1523–1526* (Vienna, 1891); *Der Anabaptismus in Tirol* (1893); *Balthasar Hubmaier und die Anfänge der Wiedertaufe in Mähren* (Brünn, 1893); *Studien zur englischen Kirchenpolitik im vierzehnten Jahrhundert* (2 parts, Vienna, 1894–1907); *Der Communismus der mährischen Wiedertäufer im sechzehnten Jahrhundert* (1895); *Die steirische Religionspazifikation* (Graz, 1896); *Der Sankt Pauler Formular, Briefe und Urkunden aus der Zeit König Wenzels II.*, (Prague, 1896); *Erzherzog Karl II. und die Frage der Errichtung eines Klosterrates für Innerösterreich* (Vienna, 1897); *Die Reformation und Gegenreformation in den innerösterreichischen Ländern im sechzehnten Jahrhundert* (Stuttgart, 1898); *Die Salzburger Provinzialsynode von 1549* (Vienna, 1898); and *Geschichte des späteren Mittelalters, 1197–1492* (Munich, 1903). He has likewise edited for the Wycliffe Society Wyclif's *De ecclesia* (London, 1886); *Sermones* (4 vols., 1887–90); *De eucharistia tractatus major* (1892); *Opus Evangelicum* (4 vols., 1895–96); *De civili dominio* (4 vols., 1900–04), *De potestate papæ* (1907); and *Das Archiv des Hauses Stubenberg* (Graz, 1908) as well as the collection of acts and correspondence for the history of the Counter-Reformation in Inner Austria under the Archdukes Karl II. and Ferdinand II. in the *Fontes rerum Austriacarum*, vols. l., lviii., lx. (Vienna, 1898–1907).

LOT: The son of Haran and nephew of Abram. According to the story in Genesis, in his migration from Haran to Canaan and Egypt, Abram was accompanied by Lot (Gen. xii. 4), but afterward Lot separated from Abram (xiii. 1 sqq.), and settled in the plain of Jordan at Sodom, where he was taken captive, but was liberated by Abram (xiv. 1 sqq.). He incurred still more danger in the catastrophe brought by God upon the vale of Siddim (xviii.-xix.). The angels, appointed to investigate the iniquity of the Sodomites, were hospitably received by Lot, who in order to fulfil the duties of hospitality was even ready to sacrifice his own family, while on the other hand the Sodomites, in their lust, trampled under foot the rights of the strangers. So the angels protected the family of the righteous Lot and rescued them from the judgment of Sodom. Lot's sons-in-law mocked at the warning and stayed in the city. Lot himself had to be torn away by force (xix. 16 sqq.). Lot was bidden not to look about him, neither to rest till he came to the mountains. But this was beyond his strength, so he begged leave to remain in Zoar, according to Gen. xiii. 10, the southernmost point of the vale of Siddim. Lot's wife could not refrain from looking back, and by thus transgressing that express prohibition she brought about her own punishment, for she was turned into a pillar of salt. (This detail is consistent with the nature of the Dead Sea, which is so saturated with salt that its vapor deposits a salty crust on surrounding objects.) Hence she stood conspicuous, a pillar of salt on the shore (Luke xvii. 32; cf. Wisdom, x. 7; Josephus, *Ant.*, I., xi. 4).

The judgment is described as a rain of fire and brimstone (cf. Ps. xi. 6; Ezek. xxxviii. 22), in consequence of which the whole region became desolate. That the latter was a historic event is undoubted. It profoundly impressed the surrounding peoples, and was borne in mind, especially in Israel, throughout all ages as a remarkable divine judgment (cf. Deut. xxix. 22; Amos iv. 11; Hos. xi. 8; Isa. i. 9, iii. 9; Jer. xx. 16, xxiii. 14; Zeph. ii. 9). The classic writers also speak of the catastrophe. Strabo, xvi. 2, knows of thirteen cities that were destroyed in that region; whereas he ascribes the origin of the sea to earthquakes, volcanic eruptions, and hot springs of both asphalt and brimstone. Tacitus, *Hist.* v. 7, tells of a monstrous fire that swept this district, kindled by lightning. Even the geographical nature of the Dead Sea might vouch for that violent eruption of destructive elements: at all events, to render it more easily conceivable. See PALESTINE. It is consistent with the Biblical narrative, according to which only the valley plain was stricken by the shower, that the surrounding mountain ranges exhibit no traces of volcanic disturbance. The Dead Sea, to be sure, did not owe its original existence to the catastrophe; it was then, however, that the southern tract of the sea subsided. Lot did not stay in Zoar, but went up into the mountains with his two daughters, and lived there in a cave. His daughters thinking they could obtain no husbands in that isolated situation, unlawfully contrived to get offspring of their father by stealth: a circumstance recalled by the Hebrews in the names Moab and Ammon (Gen. xix. 38). However, it might be noted that the story is possibly taken from the genealogical tradition of Moab and Ammon, since in the estimation of primitive antiquity, it was of so high importance for a woman to obtain posterity that in order to achieve this end she would not scruple even at incest, and that in fact people would regard such conduct of the tribal mothers even in a heroic light.

As touching the entire scope and content of the story of Lot, the same is no product of Jewish fancy, but rather arose from the tradition which was a common heritage of Abraham's people, and one very tenacious of local recollections. The whole tenor of the relation harmonizes with that patriarchal era when those simpler Semitic pastoral tribes contrasted to advantage, especially in matters of hospitality, with the inhabitants of the Canaanitic towns; and the most devout of them were supposed to enjoy more immediate conversation with the deity than was later the case with the people of God themselves. For description of the region see MOAB; PALESTINE. C. VON ORELLI.

BIBLIOGRAPHY: The commentaries on Genesis deal with the subject, as do some of the works on Old Testament theology. Consult: *DB*, iii. 150-152; *EB*, iii. 2824-25; *JE*, viii. 185-186. The Koran has many passages which embody traditions, partly of Talmudic origin, regarding Lot.

LOTS, HEBREW USE OF.

1. Urim and Thummim.

Apart from prophecy, the lot takes the first place in ancient Israel as a means of seeking counsel of the deity. In early times there existed various methods of casting lots, as by means of wooden staves or arrows (rhabdomancy, Hos. iv. 12; cf. Ezek. xxi. 21), employed also by Babylonians and by Arabs. But this and other methods of questioning the deity (necromancy, the conjuration of spirits, etc.) gradually fell into disrepute as heathenish magic, and the only legitimate form in the religion of Yahweh was that practised by the priest, the casting of lots by means of the Urim and Thummim (q.v.). The way in which these lots were handled shows that they stood in the closest connection with the priestly Ephod (q.v.). When therefore Saul or David wished to ask counsel of Yahweh through the casting of lots, they said to the priest: "Bring hither the ephod" (I Sam. xiv. 18, Septuagint; A. V. "Bring hither the ark of God"; cf. xxiii. 9, xxx. 7). From I Sam. xiv. 37 sqq., Septuagint, it appears that the two lots bore the names Urim and Thummim. Saul prays before questioning the oracle: "If the sin is upon me or upon Jonathan, let Urim appear: if it is upon the people, then let Thummim appear" (cf. S. R. Driver, *Hebrew Text of Samuel*, p. 89, Oxford, 1890). The proper explanation of the words Urim and Thummim is not certain: the most probable one is that the two lots symbolized the two divisions of the earth's rotation, light and darkness, life and death, yes or no. Urim is light or the full moon or the upper-world; Thummim (from a word meaning perfection) means sunset or under-world. Worn upon the breast, on the high priest's vestment, Urim and Thummim may be compared with the Babylonian tablets of fate which were given to Marduk, who wore them upon his breast.

Of what the lots consisted is nowhere stated. The principal facts concerning their use appear in several accounts in the Old Testament. The questions present a simple alternative which the lot is expected to decide. Sometimes they are simple questions to which Yahweh is expected to answer yes or no (cf. I Sam. xxiii. 9 sqq., xxx. 8; II Sam. ii. 1, v. 19; Judges xx. 23). At other times, the lot must decide between two possibilities; if, however, one possibility must be determined from among a number, by the exclusion of one possibility after another the number is reduced to two. An example of this is when Saul wishes to discover among the whole people the guilty one. Lots are first cast between the entire army on one side and Saul and Jonathan on the other (I Sam. xiv. 38 sqq.; similarly in I Sam. xx. 20 sqq.; Josh. vii. 16 sqq.). Hence the lots consisted of two objects of some sort (staves, stones, or similar objects), one of which signified yes and the other no. In special cases, however, any appropriate significance was attributed to one or the other. It may possibly be concluded from II Sam. xiv. 18 sqq. that Urim signified the affirmative, and Thummim the negative. Inquiry was made as to the sin of Saul and Jonathan; if Urim came out, the sin was proved, if Thummim came out, it signified a negative answer and therefore that the sin rested upon the army. From the prophetic books it has been conjectured that Urim and Thummim were two small idols, possibly teraphim, since teraphim are often mentioned in connection with the ephod (Hos. iii. 4; cf. Judges xvii. 5); they also appear alongside of spirits and ghosts as employed in the consultation of oracles (II Kings xxiii. 24). If Yahweh were angry, he did not reply; when, from certain happenings during the casting of the lots, the priest drew the conclusion that the divinity was not willing to answer, he ceased further questioning. By II Sam. v. 23–24 it is indicated that the priest, on his own initiative, added certain explanations which he perhaps deduced from some of the accompanying circumstances.

2. Methods of Employment.

It follows from the foregoing that the privilege of casting the lots belonged exclusively to the priest, whose characteristic duties were precisely the wearing of the ephod and the casting of the lots. In Deuteronomy the care of the Urim and Thummim is designated as an essential charge of the priest (Deut. xxxiii. 8). This possession may have contributed largely to make the priestly office hereditary, the knowledge and ability to handle the oracle being transmitted from father to son.

3. The Lot in Common Life.

In ancient times, the casting of lots played a prominent part in the life of the Israelites. It may be safely assumed that often the Israelites sought counsel of the deity in reference to possible eventualities just as they made use of the service of the seers (cf. I Sam. ix. 6 sqq.). According to the priestly writer, Joshua was directed to ask an answer from the lots by means of the priest (Num. xxvii. 21; cf. Josh. ix. 6 sqq.). In jurisprudence also the lots played a part; in intricate cases they were used to discover the guilty (Josh. vii. 16 sqq.; I Sam. xiv. 36 sqq.), and decisions in other cases were reached by their aid (Ezek. xxiv. 6; Prov. xviii. 18, xvi. 33; Matt. xxvii. 35). After the time of Solomon, the historical narratives cease to mention the lots of Urim and Thummim; internal evidence favors the assumption that they lost their importance. The prophets became more and more numerous, and it is to them that, for example, Ahaz turns with questions that David would have sought to solve by the sacred lots (I Kings xxii. 5). According to Jewish tradition, the Urim and Thummim no longer existed in the second temple. Alongside of the liturgical lots, secular lots (if this expression be permitted) were always in favor; booty taken in war was always divided by means of lots (Joel iii. 3; Nah. iii. 10; Ob. 11). In controversies regarding possession a decision was reached by casting lots (Prov. xviii. 18) and in similar ways (cf. also Zech. ii. 1). The lots, usually small stones, were shaken in the bosom, that is, in the fold of the dress in front, until one fell out (Prov. xvi. 33). At the time of the second temple, the casting of lots was still resorted to; for example, in the selection of the two goats on the Day of Atonement (Lev. xvi. 7–10), in the division of the days of office among the priests (Luke i. 9; cf. I Chron. xxiv. 5 sqq.), and in apportioning the contribution of wood for the altar (Neh. x. 34). I. BENZINGER.

BIBLIOGRAPHY: Consult the literature under DIVINATION; EPHOD; URIM AND THUMMIM; the articles under those words in the Bible Dictionaries; also the works mentioned under ARCHÆOLOGY, BIBLICAL, by Nowack and Benzinger, and others.

LOTZ, lots, **WILHELM PHILIPP FRIEDRICH FERDINAND:** German Lutheran; b. at Cassel Apr. 12, 1853. He was educated at the universities of Leipsic (Ph.D., 1879; lic. theol., 1883) and Göttingen, and in 1883 became privat-docent at the former institution. In the same year he went to Erlangen as privat-docent and tutor, but in 1884 accepted a call to Vienna as associate professor of Old-Testament exegesis in the Evangelical theological faculty. He was promoted to a full professorship there in 1884, a position which he held until 1897, when he was appointed to his present post of professor of Old-Testament exegesis at Erlangen. He has written: *Die Inschriften Tiglathpileser's I. in transscribiertem assyrischem Grundtext mit Uebersetzung und Kommentar* (Leipsic, 1880); *Quæstiones de historia sabbati* (1883); *Geschichte und Offenbarung im Alten Testament* (1891); *Die Bundeslade* (1901); *Das Alte Testament und die Wissenschaft* (1905); *Die biblische Urgeschichte in ihrem Verhältnis zu den Urzeitsagen anderer Völker, zu den israelitischen Volkserzählungen und zum Ganzen der Heiligen Schrift* (1907); and *Hebräische Sprachlehre* (1908).

LOTZE, lot'se, **RUDOLF HERMANN:** German philosopher; b. at Bautzen (31 m. e.n.e. of Dresden), Saxony, May 21, 1817; d. at Berlin July 1, 1881. He studied philosophy and medicine at the University of Leipsic, taking degrees in both subjects, and became extraordinary professor of philosophy there in 1842. He was called to Göttingen in 1844, and to Berlin in 1881, but here he was able to lecture only a part of one semester. Lotze was one of the most influential philosophers of the second half of the nineteenth century, and he has many followers, particularly among theologians. This is explained by the fact that in his speculation ethical and religious needs come into their full rights. His philosophy represents a reaction against the ideological pantheism of Hegel, which seemed to sacrifice all individuality and variety in existence to a formal and abstract scheme of development. Lotze characterized his philosophical standpoint as teleological idealism, and he regarded ethics as the starting-point of metaphysics. While enforcing the mechanical view of nature, he sought to show that mechanism, the relation of cause and effect, is incomprehensible, except as the realization of a world of moral ideas. Thus, each causal series becomes at the same time a teleological series. Lotze worked out this reconciliation of mechanism and teleology by combining with the monads of Leibnitz (q.v., § 2) the absolute substance of Spinoza (q.v.), in which individual things (monads) are grounded, and through whose all-inclusive unity interrelation is possible. Some of Lotze's more important works are: *Metaphysik* (Leipsic, 1841); *Logik* (1843); *Medizinische Psychologie oder Physiologie der Seele* (1852); *Mikrokosmus. Ideen zur Naturgeschichte und Geschichte der Menschheit* (3 vols., 1856–64; Eng. transl., 2 vols., Edinburgh, 1885), his principal work; *Geschichte der Aesthetik in Deutschland* (Munich, 1868); and the unfinished *System der Philosophie* (vol. i., *Logik*, Leipsic, 1874; vol. ii., *Metaphysik*, 1879; Eng. transl. of both, 2 parts, Oxford, 1884). After Lotze's death appeared *Diktate*, notes from his lectures on the various philosophical disciplines (8 parts, Leipsic, 1882–84; Eng. transl. by G. T. Ladd, *Outlines*, 6 vols., Boston, 1884–1887); also *Kleine Schriften* (3 vols., Leipsic, 1885–1894).

HUBERT EVANS.

BIBLIOGRAPHY: An excellent bibliography, including references to material which appeared in periodical literature, is in J. M. Baldwin, *Dictionary of Philosophy and Psychology*, III., i. 347–350. Consult: E. von Hartmann, *Lotze's Philosophie*, Leipsic, 1888; L. Stählin, *Kant, Lotze und Ritschl*, ib. 1888, Eng. transl., Edinburgh, 1889; G. Vorbrodt, *Principien der Ethik und der Religionsphilosophie Lotzes*, Dessau, 1891; H. Jones, *A Critical Account of the Philosophy of Lotze*, Glasgow, 1895; H. C. King, *An Outline of the Microcosmus of Hermann Lotze*, Oberlin, 1895; G. T. Ladd, *Lotze's Influence on Theology*, in *The New World*, iv (1895), 401–421; A. Tienes, *Lotze's Gedanken zu den Prinzipienfragen der Ethik*, Heidelberg, 1896; W. Wallace, *Lectures and Essays on Natural Theology and Ethics*, Oxford, 1898; G. Pape, *Lotze's religiöse Weltanschauung*, Erlangen, 1899; V. F. Moore, *Ethical Aspects of Lotze's Metaphysics*, New York, 1901.

LOUIS IX.: King of France and Roman Catholic saint; b. at Poissy (12 m. n.w. of Paris) Apr. 25, 1215; d. before Tunis Aug. 25, 1270. His father, Louis VIII., died when he was only eleven years old, and he ascended the throne under the regency of his mother, Blanche of Castile (Nov. 15, 1226). His mother, a pious and very capable woman, had him educated by brothers of the Franciscan and Dominican orders. During the first years of his reign his nobles and later the bishops of the realm gave him much trouble, but he at last restored order in his kingdom.

In fulfilment of a vow made on a bed of sickness he undertook a crusade (1248). In August he sailed for Cyprus, the rendezvous of the crusaders, with an army of 40,000. The next spring he set sail for Egypt, and landed at Damietta June 4, 1249. He took the town without a blow, then defeated a Mohammedan army and advanced up the Nile to Mansurah, whence he had to retreat, after fighting a battle with the Saracens. The king and his whole army were taken captive, but after tedious negotiations were set free for a large ransom. With the remnant of his army, scarcely 6,000 men, Louis sailed to Acre and stayed in the Holy Land four years, only returning to France when recalled by the death of his mother whom he had left as regent (Nov., 1252). He undertook a pilgrimage to Nazareth in thankfulness for his release from captivity. In 1270 he led another crusade to Tunis, landing in July at the site of Carthage, where a pestilence broke out in his army to which the king himself succumbed. His son Philip III. made peace with the emir and returned to France, carrying the ashes of his father.

Louis was canonized by Boniface VIII., Aug. 11, 1297; his day is Aug. 25. From his earliest childhood he was of a pious disposition and delighted in prayers and penances. Although naturally gentle, Louis was intolerant toward heretics and infidels, and was accustomed to say that the only way to deal with a Jew was to strike him with your sword. He was also superstitious; he brought back from the Holy Land the crown of thorns and a portion of the true cross, for which he built the Sainte-Chapelle in Paris. The authenticity of the famous Pragmatic Sanction of 1269 (q.v.) has been questioned. In this document he asserts the independence of the Gallican Church against the claims of the pope.

BIBLIOGRAPHY: The lives of Louis are very numerous; the most noted is by Le Nain de Tillemont, ed. J. de Gaulle, 6 vols., Paris, 1840–51. Others are by A. Mignon, ib. 1853; J. A. Faure, 2 vols., ib. 1865; F. P. G. Guizot, *Great Christians of France, St. Louis and Calvin*, London, 1869; Hermitte, ib. 1876; V. Verlaque, ib. 1885; C. V. Langlois, ib. 1886; H. Wallon, 2 vols., ib. 1887; M. Sepet, ib. 1898; M. H. F. Delaborde, ib. 1899. Consult further, P. Viollet, *Les Établissements de S. Louis*, 4 vols., ib. 1881–1886; J. Michelet, *Philippe-Auguste et S. Louis*, ib. n.d.; A. Lecoy de la Marche, *S. Louis, son gouvernement et sa politique*, ib. 1887; E. Berger, *S. Louis et Innocent IV.*, ib. 1893; S. de Froissart, *S. Louis et les croisades*, ib. 1898; M. Fromman, *Landgraf Ludwig III. der Fromme*, Jena, 1907; and the literature under CRUSADES.

LOURDES: A city of France in the department of the Hautes-Pyrénées, situated near the river Gave-du-Pau about 22 miles s.e. of Pau. Lourdes was a fortified town as far back as the time of the Cæsars and still possesses a château fort. The inhabitants number about 5,000. During the last half century Lourdes has become famous throughout the Roman Catholic world in consequence of the series of alleged apparitions of the Virgin Mary to Bernadette Soubirous, a child of the town, in 1858. The girl, who at that time was fourteen years of age, is described as being somewhat infirm in health, and inferior both in physical and mental development to the average child of her age. She belonged to a poor peasant family, and was simple and ignorant, knowing neither how to read nor write, and unable to speak French—her language being the patois of the locality. The story of the apparitions, which were seen only by Bernadette, is as follows: On Thursday, Feb. 11, 1858, in company with her sister Marie and Jeanne Abadie, a playmate of about the same age, she went to gather sticks for fire-wood along the banks of the Gave in the suburbs of the town. Arriving at a mill-race near a grotto in the mountain side, the two companions crossed over, and Bernadette, intending to do the same, remained behind a few minutes in order to remove her shoes and stockings. While thus occupied she was startled by a noise as of a great wind, though the atmosphere was at the time quite calm. In a moment her attention was drawn to a briar-bush growing beneath a kind of natural niche at the opening of the grotto. The bush seemed agitated; a "golden cloud" appeared above it, and above the cloud in front of the niche appeared the form of a woman. She was youthful and beautiful in appearance, robed in white with a blue sash around her waist. Her feet were bare but on each was a gold-colored rosette, and in her hands was a rosary of white beads strung on a golden chain. She smiled graciously and beckoned to Bernadette to approach. The latter obeyed and at the same time began instinctively to recite her beads. The lady then assumed an attitude of silent prayer, reciting, however, with Bernadette the *Gloria Patri* at the end of each decad. In the mean time the other two companions had returned. They were naturally surprised to find Bernadette on her knees praying in such a place, and seeing nothing themselves to account for her enraptured gaze, they laughed at her and brought her home. Here the experience was treated as an illusion and the girl was forbidden to return to the grotto. On the following Sunday, however (Feb. 14), she obtained permission to revisit the place in company with a few children of her own age. She again saw the same vision and soon went into an ecstasy from which she was aroused by a woman living near, who was attracted to the scene by the other girls who, though seeing nothing, were amazed and alarmed at the changed appearance of their companion. After this experience she was again restrained from going to the grotto, but a few ladies of the town moved by curiosity brought her back on Feb. 18. The mysterious lady appeared as before, and speaking to Bernadette asked her to return to the place daily for a fortnight. She promised to do so, and on the three following days (Friday, Saturday, and Sunday) the same experiences were enacted at the grotto in the presence of an ever-increasing crowd of spectators. Nothing was seen by any of them, but they were all deeply impressed by the ecstatic expression on the features of the little girl. Indeed, so great had become the crowd of onlookers that the civil authorities saw fit to interfere, and the day following a couple of policemen were detailed to accompany Bernadette to the grotto, but on this occasion nothing was seen. The next day, however, the vision again appeared and also on the following day (Feb. 24) on which occasion Bernadette received a command from the lady to dig a hole in the ground at the entrance of the grotto. This she did with her hands, and at once a stream of water appeared (the place had previously been perfectly dry) which gradually increased in volume until it became a settled perennial spring furnishing water in abundance for the piscinas and taps used by the pilgrims (about 33,000 gallons per day). The apparition was seen again on Feb. 26, and on the 27th, when Bernadette received the command to "go and tell the priests to build a chapel" at the spot. On Sunday, Feb. 28, the experience took place in the presence of more than 2,000 spectators. The phenomenon recurred on the two following days, but on Mar. 3 nothing was seen. Mar. 4 was the last of the fifteen days on which Bernadette had promised to visit the grotto. A multitude of 15,000 expectant persons crowded about the place; the vision came as usual, but nothing extraordinary occurred. Bernadette returned on the following days but nothing appeared until Mar. 25 (feast of the Annunciation), when in answer to Bernadette's request that the mysterious lady tell her name, she received the reply: "I am the Immaculate Conception." Twelve days passed without any further manifestation, but on Apr. 7 the vision was renewed, and still again three months later, July 16. This was the eighteenth and last apparition. From the outset the local ecclesiastical authorities held aloof and showed themselves scarcely less skeptical than the civil functionaries. Bernadette was put through long and trying interrogatory ordeals on the part of both, but she maintained her story even to its details without contradicting herself under severe cross-examination, and it remained the conviction of her examiners that she was truthful and sincere in relating her experiences. In this connection it is worth noting that she never sought notoriety or any pecuniary advantage as a result of the visions, and besides, it was freely admitted as inconceivable that one so young and so mentally deficient could concoct and successfully carry out a deceptive scheme of such magnitude. Shortly after the events above related she went to live with the Hospital Sisters established in the town, and it was only when she was eighteen years of age that she finished learning how to read and write. She later became a member of the order at the age of twenty-two and went to live in the convent of Nevers, where she died at the age of thirty-five. Apart from the apparitions at the grotto she never had any extraordinary psychic experience.

The great sensation produced by the apparitions, and the repeated assertion that miracles were being wrought at the grotto, made it necessary for the local church authorities to make an investigation, and an episcopal commission to that effect was appointed by Mgr. Laurence, bishop of Tarbes, in July, 1858. The inquiry referred not only to the apparitions, but also to the alleged miraculous occurrences, and the results were embodied in a report submitted to Mgr. Laurence four years later. It was favorable throughout to the miraculous and supernatural character of the episodes, and in Jan., 1862, the bishop issued a decision to the effect that: "these apparitions have all the characteristics of truth, and that the faithful are justified in believing them to be true. We humbly submit our decision to the judgment of the Sovereign Pontiff who governs the Universal Church." No official decision in the matter has been rendered by papal authority, but the three popes Pius IX., Leo XIII., and Pius X. are known to have expressed their personal belief in the reality of the apparitions and subsequent miracles. Official approbation has, however, been secured to the extent of allowing the liturgical office of Our Lady of Lourdes to be inserted in the breviary for certain localities, while churches bearing that name have been erected in many parts of the world. Lourdes soon became a rendezvous for pilgrims from all parts of the world, and in 1872 the national pilgrimages, viz., from the different provinces of France, were begun. These take place every year about Aug. 15, and on such occasions the town often receives at once as many as 60,000 pilgrims. The beautiful basilica which stands above the grotto was consecrated in 1876, and the Church of the Holy Rosary which stands on a lower level directly beneath the basilica was finished in 1901. [Before these churches is a park, the broad space in the middle of which is the scene of the procession of the Blessed Sacrament which takes place daily. The sick in all stages of disease are lined up on the edge of this space and so are passed by the consecrated Host and the attendant clergy and pilgrims, and then it is that miraculous cures are alleged to be performed.] JAMES F. DRISCOLL.

BIBLIOGRAPHY: For a description of Lourdes consult: G. Mares, *Lourdes et ses environs*, Bordeaux, 1894. For the phenomena from a sympathetic standpoint: G. Bertrin, *Histoire critique des événements de Lourdes. Apparitions et guérissons*, Lourdes, 1905, Eng. transl., *Lourdes; A Hist. of its Apparitions and Cures*, New York, 1908; H. Lasserre, *Les Episodes miraculeux de Lourdes*, Paris, 1886, Eng. transl., *Miraculous Episodes of Lourdes*, London, 1884; R. F. Clarke, *Lourdes, and its Miracles*, London, 1889. The critical or antagonistic point of view is set forth in E. E. C. A. Zola, *Lourdes*, Paris, 1884, Eng. transl., same title, London, 1894; Dozous, *La Grotte de Lourdes*, Paris, 1874; Justinus, *Lourdes in het licht der nieuwere wetenschap*, 's Hertogenbosch, 1895; J. B. Estrade, *Les Apparitions de Lourdes*, Lourdes, 1908.

LOVE: That disinterested and unselfish relation between persons, in which the personality of the one is lost in the other, in which each esteems the other better than himself (Phil. ii. 3). It is not only one of the most comprehensive of Biblical-Christian conceptions, having basal significance for dogmatics and ethics, but it also occupies a prominent place in the philosophy and literature of all peoples and times.

When John says, "God is love" (I John iv. 16), he does not mean to give a metaphysical definition of the essence of God, but to state God's feelings toward us. At the same time, the words open a profitable field of speculation in regard to the part love holds in the divine constitution. Augustine first, Richard of St. Victor next, and, after him, others, have endeavored to reconstruct the Trinity by the principle of love. Thus, the Father loves the Son, and the Son loves the Father (*redamando*); both loves are united in love for an object of common affection (*condilectio*), that is, in the Holy Spirit. But the attempt has been unsuccessful; for the Holy Spirit is a factor, not merely a product, of the divine love; and, besides, in the proposed scheme, the persons of the Godhead are not sufficiently distinguished. Yet it is undoubtedly true that love is a large element of the divine essence; and later theologians, as, for instance, Dorner, in discussing the problem of the Trinity, give it much space.

Love is a basal principle in creation, in redemption, and in Christian ethics. God created the world in order that he might have a field for the exercise of his love; not that the world was necessary in any way; but it delighted him to make the world and to fill it with creatures whom he could love; and God so loved the world that he sent his Son to die for it (John iii. 16). The Son, out of his free, divine love, laid down his life for our salvation (Matt. xx. 28). God was in Christ, reconciling the world unto himself (II Cor. v. 19); and this love of God in Christ is the only and exclusive ground of our salvation and of our sanctification (Acts iv. 12). Love is the source and center of the development of the new life in Christ. It is the chief of the Christian virtues. Our Lord set his approval upon the Mosaic summary of the law in the form of love to God and man (Matt. xxii. 37–40; cf. Deut. vi. 5; Lev. xix. 18), and gave his followers the "new commandment," that they should love one another (John xiii. 34). Paul calls love "the fulfilling of the law" (Rom. xiii. 10), and "the end of the commandment" (I Tim. i. 5); Peter exhorts to love as the fruit of holy living (I Pet. i. 22; II Pet. i. 7); John is particularly full upon love (I John ii. 5, iv. 7. 8), and James calls love of our neighbors "the royal law" (Jas. ii. 5, 8).

Love manifests itself in the two great directions, toward God and toward our neighbor, or in the contemplative and in the practical form; the former seen in Mary of Bethany, the latter in her sister Martha (Luke x. 38–42). Our Lord gave his preference to the former. It shows itself in prayer, meditation, worship, and in the communion. The practical form manifests itself in all works of benevolence and beneficence, far and near. It is incumbent upon the Christian to unite the two. The hardest burden our Lord lays upon his disciples is to love their enemies (Matt. v. 44). Among human relationships controlled by love, marriage occupies the first place (Eph. v. 22-33). It is noteworthy that the apostle who drew such a close parallel between conjugal love and the "great mystery" of Christ's love for the Church should treat married life so realistically (I Cor. vii.).

True love can exist only between rational beings. To speak of love for animals, or of love for a thing, is to use improper language. Self-love is also an inaccurate but indispensable term. What passes for love in literature and on the stage is too commonly mere sexual longing. Love for gold (I Tim. vi. 10) and love for the world (I John ii. 15) are perversions of love, to its destruction. KARL BURGER †.

LOVE, FAMILY OF. See FAMILISTS.

LOVE FEAST. See AGAPE.

LOVE, CHRISTOPHER: Presbyterian; b. at Cardiff, in Glamorganshire, 1618; educated at New Inn Hall, Oxford, 1635. After taking the master's degree he was obliged to leave Oxford for refusing to subscribe Archbishop Laud's canons. He went to London, and became domestic chaplain to the sheriff, and took a bold stand against the errors of the Book of Common Prayer and the religious tyranny of the times. He was cast into prison on account of an aggressive sermon at Newcastle, and in various ways persecuted in London. At the outbreak of the Civil War he was made preacher to the garrison of Windsor Castle, where he gave great offense to the prelatical party by his pointed utterances. He was one of the first to receive presbyterial ordination under the new organization in Jan. 23, 1644, at Aldermanbury, London; and became pastor of St. Laurence Jewry in London, where he was highly esteemed for the eloquence and vigor of his preaching. He was a strong Presbyterian, the leader of the younger men of that party. In this way he became involved in a treasonable correspondence with the Presbyterians of Scotland to restore Charles II.; and, with many others, was arrested May 7, 1651, and chosen to make an example of, to check the Presbyterian agitation against Cromwell and in favor of Charles II. He was condemned and beheaded on Tower Hill, Aug. 22, 1651. This excited the indignation and wrath of the entire Presbyterian party, which had petitioned, by ministerial bodies and parishes, in vain for his pardon. He went to his death as their hero and martyr. His funeral sermon was preached by Thomas Manton to an immense sympathizing audience. His sermons were published, after his death, under the auspices of the leading Presbyterians of London. The most important of his works are: *Grace, the Truth and Growth, and different Degrees thereof* (226 pp., London, 1652); *Heaven's Glory, Hell's Terror* (350 pp., 1653); *Combate between the Flesh and the Spirit* (292 pp., 1654); *Treatise of Effectual Calling* (218 pp., 1658); *The Natural Man's Case Stated* (8vo, 280 pp., 1658); *Select Works* (8vo, Glasgow, 1806–07, 2 vols.). C. A. Briggs.

Bibliography: D. Neal, *Hist. of the Puritans*, ed. J. Toulmin, 5 vols., Bath, 1793–97; W. Wilson, *Hist. and Antiquities of the Dissenting Churches in London*, i. 332, iii. 330, 4 vols., London, 1808–14; *Memoirs of the Life of Ambrose Barnes*, ed. W. H. D. Longstaffe for the Surtees Society, no. 50, Durham, 1867; W. A. Shaw, *Hist. of the English Church 1640–1660*, ii. 149, 321, 404, London, 1900; *DNB*, xxxiv. 155–157.

LOVE, WILLIAM DE LOSS: Congregationalist; b. at New Haven, Conn., Nov. 29, 1851. He was graduated from Hamilton College (A.B., 1873), and Andover Theological Seminary (1878); was instructor in mathematics and natural science in the Military Academy at Leicester, Mass., in 1873–1874, and principal of the Broadway Grammar School, Norwich, Conn., in 1874–75. After being pastor of the Evangelical Congregational Church, Lancaster, Mass., from 1878 to 1881, he traveled and engaged in commercial pursuits until 1885, besides acting as supply for the Second Congregational Church, Keene, N. H., for a year. Since 1885 he has been pastor of the Farmington Avenue Church, Hartford, Conn. He has written *The Fast and Thanksgiving Days of New England* (Boston, 1895) and *Samson Occom and the Christian Indians of New England* (1900).

LOW CHURCH. See England, Church of.

LOWDER, CHARLES FUGE: London mission preacher; b. at Bath June 22, 1820; d. at Zell-am-See (40 m. s.s.w. of Salzburg), Austria, Sept. 9, 1880. He studied at King's College School, London, and at Exeter College, Oxford (B.A., 1843; M.A., 1845), and took orders in 1843. He was curate at Walton, near Glastonbury, 1843–44, chaplain of the Axbridge workhouse 1844–45, curate of Tetbury, Gloucestershire, 1845–51, then curate at St. Barnabas' Church, Pimlico, 1851–56. In 1856 he entered upon his life-work as head of the mission at St. George's-in-the-East. The scene of his labors was in East London, among the lowest classes. Through his efforts was erected St. Peter's Church, London Docks, which was consecrated in 1866. Lowder became vicar of the new church and remained in this charge till his death. He held High-church views, was a strict ritualist, and resembled a Roman Catholic priest in his celibacy and his general mode of life. He published, besides some pamphlets, *Ten Years in St. George's Mission* (London, 1867); and *Twenty-one Years in St. George's Mission* (1877).

Bibliography: *Charles Lowder, a Biography*, London, 1882; *DNB*, xxxiv. 187.

LOWE, WILLIAM HENRY: Church of England; b. at Whaplode Drove (42 m. s.s.e. of Lincoln), Lincolnshire, Apr. 10, 1848. He was educated at Christ College, Cambridge (B.A., 1871; M.A., 1874). He was Hebrew lecturer in his college (1874–91), and chaplain there (1874–81). He was curate of Fen Ditton, Cambridgeshire (1873–75); Milton (1880–82); Willingham (1886–90); and vicar of Fen Drayton (1890–91); and since 1891 at Brisley, Norfolk. He has edited: *The Psalms, with Introductions and critical Notes* (in conjunction with A. C. Jennings; 2 vols., London, 1877); has written: *The Hebrew Student's Commentary on Zechariah* (1884); the commentaries on Zechariah and Malachi in Ellicott's *Bible for English Readers* (1884); and *A Hebrew Grammar* (1887); and translated: *Twelve Odes of Hafiz* (Cambridge, 1877); and *Muntakhab-i Tawarikh* (Calcutta, 1884).

LOWER SAXON CONFEDERATION: A federation of Reformed churches in Lower Saxony which has existed for more than two centuries. It is the one church body in Germany in which the Presbyterian system was fully carried out. In Electoral Hanover, especially in the cities of Celle, Lüneburg, Hameln, and Hanover, Huguenot fugitives had been received and had formed congregations, also in the neighboring territories of Schaumburg-Lippe and Brunswick. On Nov. 13, 1699, it was decided at Hanover to establish a closer union between these scattered members of the Reformed Church. German Reformed bodies in Hanover, Celle, and Bückeburg joined the confederation. The governments of Brunswick-Lüneburg and Schaumburg-Lippe gave permission for the establishment of the confederation, granting the union and its congregations self-government but reserving the so-called *jura circa sacra*. The first synod of the United Reformed churches in Lower Saxony was held in July, 1703, at Hameln. The government of Hanover expressly stipulated that the state commissary, who was to be present at every synod, have a seat, but not a vote. There were at first five French and three German congregations of the confederation. In 1708 a German-Dutch and a Huguenot congregation in Brunswick joined the confederation; in 1711 the German Reformed congregation of Münden (Hanover) was included, followed, in 1753, by the Reformed in Göttingen, and finally, in 1890, by the congregation of Altona. On account of the removal of Huguenots to the large cities, their congregations dwindled and were finally united with the local German congregations. The first to suffer this fate was the congregation at Bückeburg (1755), followed by those of Celle (1805), Brunswick (1811), and Hanover (1812), while the congregation of Hameln was dissolved altogether.

Since 1812 the confederation has consisted of the congregations of Brunswick, Bückeburg, Celle, Hanover, Göttingen, and Münden, with Altona since 1890. In 1824 the congregations of the kingdom of Hanover were recognized as possessing equal rights with the Lutheran churches, and as having the rank of state churches. In 1839 a new agenda for all congregations of the federation was adopted which guards the independence of the individual congregations but vests the ultimate authority in matters affecting church discipline and doctrine in a synod of the whole confederation. The State adheres to the right of its territorial power; and the resolutions of the synod must be confirmed by the State. The election of a minister formerly required the consent of the government, and the general state laws in Prussia still require that it be communicated to the provincial president, who may veto the election within thirty days. In sentences of synods in matters of discipline the right of an appeal *de abusu* to the government is recognized. The presbyteries and synods have remarkably advanced the life of the Church and of the educational institutions as well as the material resources of the communities. From the first the confederation provided for the surviving members of the families of their pastors, and at a later time also of their teachers. The widows' fund, founded in 1706, has a capital that would amount to 60,000 marks for each congregation. The confederation has sought to live in peace with its Lutheran neighbors. In the agenda of 1711 the synod adopted the resolution of the Conference of Charenton (1631), according to which Lutherans are permitted to take part in the worship of the Reformed Church without sacrificing their own confession. (F. H. Brandes.)

Bibliography: T. Hugues, *Die Konföderation der reformierten Kirchen in Niedersachsen*, Celle, 1873: the publications of the German Hugenotten-Verein, particularly the *Geschichtsblätter*, Magdeburg, 1891 sqq., in which the contributions of Drs. F. Albrecht, F. H. Brandes, H. Tollin and H. Villaret are especially pertinent.

LOWRIE, lau'ri, **SAMUEL THOMPSON:** Presbyterian; b. at Pittsburg, Pa., Feb. 8, 1835. He was graduated from Miami University (B.A., 1852) and Western Theological Seminary, Allegheny, Pa. (1855); remained for an additional year at Allegheny, after which he spent two semesters at the University of Heidelberg (1856–57). After being pastor of the Presbyterian church at Alexandria, Pa., from 1858 to 1863, he spent nine months at Berlin, and then held pastorates in his denomination at Bethany Church, Philadelphia (1865–69), and Abington, Pa. (1869–74). From 1874 to 1878 he was professor of New-Testament literature and exegesis in Western Theological Seminary, after which he returned to the ministry, being pastor of Ewing Church, near Trenton, N. J., in 1879–85 and chaplain of the Presbyterian Hospital in Philadelphia, as well as minister of a mission Sunday-school (now Emmanuel Presbyterian Church) in the same city, in 1886–89. From 1891 to 1896 he was co-pastor with T. W. J. Wylie, of the Wylie Memorial Church, Philadelphia. He was also corresponding secretary of the Presbyterian Historical Society from 1893 to 1906, when he retired from active life. In addition to assisting D. Moore in preparing the volume on Isaiah for the American Lange series (New York, 1878) and A. Gosman in preparing Numbers for the same series (1879), he has translated H. Cremer's *Ueber den Zustand nach dem Tode* (Gütersloh, 1883) under the title *Beyond the Grave* (New York, 1885), and written *Explanation of the Epistle to the Hebrews* (1884) and *The Lord's Supper* (1888).

LOWRIE, WALTER: Statesman and missionary secretary; b. near Edinburgh, Scotland, Dec. 10, 1784; d. in New York City Dec. 14, 1868. He was brought to America when eight years of age; studied for the ministry with marked zeal and swift progress, but, being prevented from finishing his studies, went into politics, and in 1811 was chosen to the senate of the State of Pennsylvania; after seven years' service there he was United States senator, Dec. 6, 1819–Mar. 3, 1825. At the expiration of his term he was made secretary of the senate of the United States, serving till 1836 when he became secretary of the missionary society of the synod of Pittsburg, which became, the year following, the Board of Foreign Missions of the Presbyterian Church. He was corresponding secretary of this organization until his retirement in 1868, shortly before his death, and to his faithful service much of the great success attained by the board must be attributed.

LOWRY, ROBERT: American Baptist; b. in Philadelphia Mar. 12, 1826; d. at Plainfield, N. J., Nov. 23, 1899. He was graduated at Lewisburg University (1854). He was pastor at West Chester, Penn. (1854–58); in New York (1858–61); in Brooklyn (1861–69); at Lewisburg, Penn. (1869–1875); and at Plainfield, N. J. (1876–85). He was professor of belles-lettres in Lewisburg University (1869–75). He was the editor of several popular hymnals, and also wrote a number of hymns, the best-known of which are "Shall we gather at the river," "One more day's work for Jesus," and "Where is my wandering boy to-night?"

Bibliography: S. W. Duffield, *English Hymns*, p. 479, New York, 1886; Julian, *Hymnology*, pp. 699–700.

LOWTH, lauth, **ROBERT:** Bishop of London; b. at Winchester Nov. 27, 1710; d. in London Nov. 3, 1787. He was a son of William Lowth (q.v.)

and studied at Winchester and at New College, Oxford (B.A., 1733; M.A., 1737; D.D., 1754). In 1735 he was instituted to the vicarage of Overton, Hampshire, and, in 1741, was appointed to the professorship of poetry at Oxford, which he held till 1750. He became archdeacon of Winchester in 1750, rector of Woodhay, Hampshire, in 1753, prebendary of Durham and rector of Sedgefield in 1755, and bishop of St. David's in 1766. He was translated to the see of Oxford the same year and to the see of London in 1777. In this position he remained till his death, having declined the primacy in 1783. Lowth achieved permanent fame by his lectures on Hebrew poetry, *De sacra poesi Hebrœorum prœlectiones academicœ Oxonii habitœ* (Oxford, 1753; 3d ed., 1775; ed. J. D. Michaelis, 2 parts, Göttingen, 1770; ed. E. F. C. Rosenmüller, Leipsic, 1815; reprinted, with notes by Rosenmüller, C. Weiss, K. F. Richter and others, Oxford, 1821; Eng. transl., 2 vols., London, 1787, and frequently); and by his *Isaiah, a New Translation, with Notes* (London, 1778; 13th ed., 1842; Germ. transl., 4 vols., Leipsic, 1779–81). Another important work by Lowth is his *Life of William of Wykeham* (London, 1758; 3d ed., Oxford, 1777). P. Hall collected and edited, with introductory memoir, his *Sermons and Other Remains* (London, 1834).

Bibliography: An anonymous *Memoirs of the Life and Writings of Bishop Lowth* appeared London, 1787; *DNB*, xxxiv. 214–216 gives a list of scattered references. Consult further: S. A. Allibone, *Critical Dictionary of English Literature*, i. 1140–1141, Philadelphia, 1891; C. A. Briggs, *Study of Holy Scripture*, pp. 226 sqq. et passim, New York, 1899; J. H. Overton and F. Relton, *The English Church (1714–1800)*, pp. 170–172 et passim, London, 1906.

LOWTH, WILLIAM: English theologian; b. at London Sept. 3, 1660; d. at Buriton (17 m. e.s.e. of Winchester), Hampshire, May 17, 1732. He was educated at the Merchant Taylors' School, London, and at St. John's College, Oxford (B.A. 1679; M.A., 1683; B.D. and D.D., 1688), where he became a fellow. With his *Vindication of the Divine Authority and Inspiration of the Old and New Testament* (London, 1692), an answer to Le Clerc, he attracted the attention of Peter Mew, bishop of Winchester, who made him his chaplain, gave him a prebend in Winchester Cathedral in 1696, and presented him to the living of Buriton and Petersfield, Hampshire, in 1699. While less eminent than his son, Robert Lowth, he was probably the profounder scholar of the two. Many scholars were indebted to him for valuable assistance. In addition to the work mentioned he published *Directions for the Profitable Reading of the Holy Scriptures* (London, 1708), a little work that has gone through many editions; and a now superseded commentary on the prophets (1714–25), which has been frequently reprinted as a continuation of Bishop Patrick's commentary.

Bibliography: S. A. Allibone, *Critical Dictionary of English Literature*, p. 1141, Philadelphia, 1891; *DNB*, xxxiv. 216–217.

LOYOLA. See Ignatius of Loyola.

LOYSON, lwä″son, **CHARLES JEAN MARIE AUGUSTIN HYACINTHE** (Father Hyacinthe): French Independent; b. at Orléans Mar. 10, 1827. He was educated privately and at the Seminary of St. Sulpice, Paris, where he studied from 1845 to 1849. He was ordained to the Roman Catholic priesthood in 1851, and was then professor of philosophy at the Seminary of Avignon in 1851–54, and of dogmatic theology at the Seminary of Nantes in 1854–56. Already a member of the Sulpician order, he was curate of St. Sulpice, Paris, in 1856–1857, but, determining to enter the monastic life, he made a six months' novitiate in the Dominican order in 1858. This not being sufficiently severe, he entered the order of Discalced Carmelites in 1862, and rapidly attained fame as a preacher. The freedom of his utterances, however, was such as to draw upon him the admonition of the general of his order, and in 1869 he was excommunicated. He then went to the United States, where he was greeted with fervor. By this time his break with the Church had become final, and in 1871 he attended the Old Catholic conference at Munich. In the following year Loyson went to Rome, where he established the *Esperance de Rome,* and in the same year still further manifested his antipathy for his former faith by marrying a widow who had long been working against certain distinctive doctrines of the Roman Catholic Church. From 1873 to 1874 he was an Old Catholic pastor at Geneva, but disapproving the rationalistic views of the Old Catholics, he again visited London, only to return before long to Paris, where he sought in vain to have his religious services authorized by the government. In 1877, however, he was permitted to hold private services, and speedily opened a "Catholic Gallican Church," which was legalized in 1883. Loyson remained at its head until 1884, since which year he has resided at Geneva, part of the time seeking to found a religious society in which Christians, Jews, and Mohammedans may all join in worship. Among his numerous writings, special mention may be made of the following: *La Famille* (Paris, 1867); *La Société civile dans ses rapports avec le christianisme* (1867); *De la réforme catholique* (1872; Eng. transl. by his wife, *Catholic Reform,* London, 1874); *Liturgie de l'église catholique de Genève a l'usage des fidèles* (Neuchâtel, 1873); *Catholicisme et protestantisme* (1873; Eng. transl., London, 1874); *Trois conférences au Cirque d'hiver* (Paris, 1877); *Les Principes de le réforme catholique* (1878; Eng. transl. by Lady Durand, London, 1879); *Liturgie de l'église catholique-gallicane* (1879); *La Réforme catholique et l'église anglicane* (1879; Eng. transl. by Lady Durand, London, 1879); *Ni cléricaux ni athées* (1890); *Mon testament* (1893; Eng. transl. by F. Ware, London, 1895); *Qui est le Christ? Pour les juifs, les chrétiens et les musulmans* (1900); and *L'Athéisme contemporaine* (1907).

Bibliography: Consult the Preface, by F. W. Farrar, to the Eng. transl. of *Mon testament*, ut sup.

LUARD, HENRY RICHARDS: Church of England; b. in London Aug. 17, 1825; d. at Cambridge May 1, 1891. He was educated at King's College, London, and at Trinity College, Cambridge (B.A., 1847; M.A., 1850; B.D., 1875; D.D., 1878). He became fellow of Trinity College (1849) and was assistant tutor in mathematics there (1855–

1865); junior bursar (1853-61); and registrary of the University of Cambridge (1862-91). He was ordained deacon and priest (1855) and was vicar of Great St. Mary's, Cambridge (1860-87). He wrote: *On the Relations between England and Rome during the Earlier Portion of the Reign of Henry III.* (Cambridge, 1877); and edited the *Diary of E. Rud* (1851); the *Correspondence of Richard Porson* (1851); *Lives of Edward the Confessor* (1858); *Bartholomæi de Cotton Historia Anglicana* (1859); *Roberti Grosseteste Epistolæ* (1861); *Annales monastici* (1864-69); *Matthæi Parisiensis Chronica majora* (1872); and *Flores historiarum* (1890); he also prepared a *Catalogue of the Manuscripts Preserved in the Library of the University of Cambridge* (1856); and *Graduati Cantabrigienses* (1884).

Bibliography: *DNB*, xxxiv. 225-226.

LUBBERTUS, SIBRANDUS: Dutch theologian; b. at Langwarden in East Friesland, 1556 or 1557; d. at Franeker (60 m. n.n.e. of Amsterdam) Jan. 11, 1625. He was educated in Bremen, afterward at Wittenberg, Marburg, and Geneva, where he became a follower of Beza. In 1577 he was at Basel, then removed to Neustadt, at that time the seat of the Evangelical theological faculty of Heidelberg. In 1583 he was active in visiting the poor in Emden, in 1584 went to Friesland as a preacher in order to advance there the cause of the Reformation. In 1585 he became professor at the University of Franeker, lecturing on dogmatics. He attracted many students, and as a preacher made a deep impression upon his hearers. He took an active part in the struggle with the Remonstrants, and combated Rome and Socinianism. From his innermost conviction he was a decided Calvinist, without sacrificing thereby his independence. He published: *De principiis Christianorum dogmatum libri septem* (Franeker, 1591-95); *De papa Romano libri decem, scholastice et theologice collati cum disputationibus R. Bellarmini* (1594); *De conciliis libri quinque* (Geneva, 1601); *De ecclesia libri sex* (Franeker, 1607); *Replicatio de principiis Christianorum dogmatum* (1608); *Replicatio de papa Romano* (1609); *De Jesu Christo Servatore libri quatuor contra Faustum Socinum* (1611); *Epistolica disceptatio de fide justificante, nostraque coram Deo justificatione* (Delft, 1612); *Declaratio responsionis D. Vorstii* (Franeker, 1611); *Commentarii ad nonaginta novem errores C Vorstii* (1613); *Responsio ad pietatem Hugonis Grotii* (1614); *Commentarius in Catechesin Palatino-Belgicam* (1618). S. D. van Veen.

Bibliography: E. L. Vriemoet, *Athenarum Frisicarum libri duo*, pp. 1-19, Leeuwarden, 1758; E. J. H. Tjaden, *Das gelehrte Ostfriesland*, i. 245-262, Aurich, 1785; C. Sepp, *Het godgeleerd onderwijs in Nederland*, i. 135-143, Leyden, 1873; W. B. S. Boeles, *Frieslands Hoogeschool en het Rijks Athenaeum te Franeker*, ii. 28-34, Leeuwarden, 1889.

LUCAS OF TUY (TUDENSIS): Spanish bishop; b. at Leon (112 m. n. of Salamanca) in the latter part of the twelfth century; d. at Tuy (60 m. n. of Oporto) 1250. After officiating as a canon in his native city, he went to Tuy as a deacon, and in 1227 made a pilgrimage to Palestine, visiting Gregory IX. and Elias of Cortona, the general of the Franciscans, in the course of his travels. In 1239 he was consecrated bishop of Tuy, where he spent the remainder of his life. Lucas was the compiler of an exhaustive chronicle of Spain, the first two books containing the history of Isidore with additions, and the last two that of Ildefonsus and Julian, together with a supplement of his own to 1236. He likewise wrote a refutation of the Albigenses and other heretics, consisting chiefly of excerpts from Gregory the Great and Isidore, but important for the history of sects in Spain and southern France. In this work he assailed those who denied the future life and he likewise rejected as heretical representations of God and the Trinity in human form, as well as crucifixes having both feet of Christ pierced with a single nail. It is uncertain whether the book on the miracles of St. Isidore which he mentions in the preface of his polemics is to be identified with the *Vita Isidori* edited by the Bollandists (*ASB*, Apr., i. 330). (R. Schmid.)

Bibliography: H. Florez, *España sagrada*, vol. xxii. 108 sqq., xxxv. 363-364, Madrid, 1754 sqq.; J. A. Fabricius, *Bibliotheca Latina mediæ et infimæ ætatis*, iii. 833, 6 vols., Hamburg, 1734-46; *KL*, viii. 192.

LUCIAN THE MARTYR: Presbyter of Antioch; b. probably at Samosata about the middle of the third century; d. at Nicomedia, Bithynia, 312. Of his life few details are known. He was educated at Edessa, and he may have studied at Cæsarea as well. He finally settled at Antioch, where he founded a school of exegesis. In the autumn of 311 Maximinus became sole emperor and immediately resumed his persecution of the Christians, although in the spring of the same year he had signed the edict of toleration promulgated by his colleague Galerius. Lucian, whose prominence rendered him especially odious to the emperor, was taken from Antioch to Nicomedia, where Maximinus himself was then residing. His profession of faith, though it made an impression on his hearers, was unavailing, and he suffered martyrdom early in the following year, the Church at Antioch celebrating the anniversary of his death on Jan. 7. His corpse was taken by the Christians to the city of Drepanum, which Constantine rebuilt in his honor, though he called it Helenopolis after his mother.

The scantiness of the data concerning Lucian receives at least a partial explanation from his doctrinal views. Alexander of Alexandria expressly states that Lucian accepted the teachings of Ebion, Artemas, and especially his fellow townsman Paul of Samosata, and consequently withdrew from the Church of Antioch during the bishoprics of Domnus, Timæus, and Cyrillus. It is probable that Lucian left the Church when Paul was deposed about 268, and the two were evidently in sympathy in their Christological views, so that, when Paul died, Lucian became the head of the nationalistic Syrian ecclesiastical party as opposed to the Greco-Roman faction. On the other hand, the agreement between these two teachers was neither complete nor lasting, and Lucian's doctrine of the antemundane creation of the Logos and its perfect incarnation in Jesus was a later development of his thought. His chief importance, however, lies in the fact that he was the real founder of Arianism, as was admitted by Arius himself, who was one of his numerous pupils, declared in a letter to Eusebius of Nicomedia, also a scholar of Lucian's school. Although it is clear from the statements of Alexander that Lucian returned to orthodoxy before he died, Epiphanius says that he was reckoned a martyr by the Arians, and Philostorgius, who praises him highly, declares that almost all the important Arian and semi-Arian theologians of the first half of the fourth century were pupils of Lucian. Nevertheless, his theological opponents were not altogether blind to his virtues. Eusebius, who mentions him but twice (*Hist. eccl.*, viii. 13, ix. 6), praises the purity of his life, his knowledge of the Scriptures, and his noble martyrdom; the pseudo-Athanasius terms him a great and holy ascetic and martyr; Chrysostom delivered a eulogy upon him; and the Church finally recognized the martyrdom of St. Lucian, especially as it was contained in the calendar of Nicomedia, the prototype of all Greek calendars.

Of the literary activity of Lucian scant remains survive. Jerome mentions his recension of the manuscripts of the Bible (his chief work), as do Suidas and Simeon Metaphrastes, and Jerome also alludes to his treatises on faith and his letters, to which must be added his defense preserved by Rufinus. A fragment of a letter is contained in the *Chronicon Paschale* (p. 277, ed. Ducange), describing the martyrdom of Bishop Anthimus, Paris, 1648 sqq. Lucian's apology (Rufinus, ed. Cacciari, i. 515) reveals the Christological standpoint of its author, postulating that "there is one God, revealed to us through Christ and inspired in our hearts by the Holy Spirit." The importance of Christ is restricted to his office as a teacher and lawgiver, who gave mankind an example of patience by his incarnation and death. Scarcely a trace of Lucian's writings on faith has survived, although they may form the basis of the statement of Epiphanius that Lucian and his followers affirmed that Christ had only a human body, but not a human soul, all human emotions being ascribed directly to the Logos, so that the Son was inferior to the Father, evidently a cardinal doctrine in his system. The creed adopted by the bishops assembled at Antioch in 341 is ascribed to Lucian by some writers of the early Church as well as by the semi-Arian Synods of Seleucia (359) and Caria (367), but this can at most mean little more than that part of his doctrines were accepted with many interpolations and additions. According to Jerome, Lucian's version of the Septuagint was received from Constantinople to Antioch, but varied widely from the current text. Of the recension of the New Testament Jerome speaks in terms of disapproval, and its use was forbidden by the *Decretum Gelasianum*. It was formerly supposed that in his New Testament Lucian adhered closely to the Peshitto, but it now seems inadvisable to attempt to trace any family of manuscripts to his work (see BIBLE VERSIONS, A, I., 1, § 5). Practically nothing is known concerning Lucian's exegetical treatises, although it is probable that he wrote on hermeneutics. (A. HARNACK.)

BIBLIOGRAPHY: *DCB*, iii. 748–749; *NPNF*, 2 ser., i. 360, col. i., note 4; Jerome, *De vir. ill.*, lxxvii.

LUCIAN OF SAMOSATA.

In the second half of the second century, with the single exception of Celsus, few of the cultivated classes of the Roman Empire paid more than a superficial attention to Christianity. Fronto, the friend of Marcus Aurelius, is said to have written against it, but nothing is certainly known of his book. Marcus Aurelius himself, Epictetus, Galen, and the orator Aristides mention the Christian religion only in passing. Nor did the great satirist Lucian think it necessary to take special notice of it. Only twice—cursorily in the *Alexander* and more at length in the *Peregrinus Proteus*—does he deal with the subject; but the interest of his account for modern times has led to frequent exaggeration of the interest which the topic had for him. His attitude toward Christianity has been represented in every possible light, from a fanatical hatred to a secret friendship. Still, Lucian's description of the Christians in the *Peregrinus* is actually one of the most interesting and instructive accounts of the early Christians which have been preserved from a pagan pen.

1. Lucian's Attitude toward Christianity.

The *Peregrinus* is a satire aimed at the Cynics, and more particularly, as Bernays has shown, at the contemporary Cynic philosopher Theagenes. This school, among whom a considerable proportion of unworthy elements existed, was antipathetic to Lucian. He was specially stirred up to this attack by the exaggerated admiration of Peregrinus expressed by the baser sort of Cynics, as well as by some of a higher class. Lucian had known the man personally; and when Theagenes, his closest associate, began to make a name for himself in Rome, the satirist felt that it was time to take the field. His work, addressed to the Platonist Cronius, gives an account of the life and death of Peregrinus, whom he calls, on grounds of personal knowledge, a common criminal. On reaching manhood, Peregrinus was, according to him, convicted of adultery and suitably punished in Armenia; then seduced a boy, and saved himself from the vengeance of the parents only by a money payment; and finally, in his birthplace, Parion on the Hellespont, murdered his father to get possession of his inheritance. Suspicion attaching to him, he was forced to flee, and after considerable wandering came to Palestine or possibly to Antioch. Here he became acquainted with the Christians, insinuated himself into their fellowship, and became a respected teacher. He was imprisoned as a Christian, but was released by the governor of Syria and returned to Parion, where he was able to meet the charge of parricide only by surrendering his portion of the inheritance, fifteen talents, to his fellow citizens. He had appeared there in the dress of a Cynic, but on his further journeys he was received and supported by the Christians as one of their own. Falling into discredit with them (Lucian thinks on account of eating forbidden meats), he

2. The *Peregrinus*.

resolved to simulate the life of a great ascetic, and after a training in Egypt went to Rome, where he attracted great attention by his cynical freedom of speech, especially by his unmeasured attacks upon the mild and just emperor. The prefect of the city banished him, which only increased his fame. He went to Greece, and continued his assaults on the social order, choosing the great Olympic gatherings for special manifestations. At the third which he attended, finding his reputation declining, he announced that he would burn himself alive at the next; and this Lucian says he actually did, claiming to have been an eye-witness of the occurrence as well as part author of the legends which were soon spread abroad in relation to the Cynic's death. He closes by relating some further instances of the baseness of Peregrinus, which he asserts that he witnessed on a voyage from Troas to Syria.

3. Historical Basis of the *Peregrinus*.

A brief investigation of the historical basis for this story is now in order. There is no reason to doubt the existence of a Cynic philosopher named Peregrinus Proteus. The oldest notice of him is possibly that of Aulus Gellius (xii. 11), who met him at Athens and speaks well of him. His remarkable suicide is mentioned by Athenagoras (" Apology," xxvi.; *ANF*, ii. 143), Tertullian (*Ad martyras*, iv.; *ANF*, iii. 695), and Eusebius (*Chron. ad ann. 2181; Marcus Aurelius*, v.), as well as by Philostratus (*Vitæ sophistarum*, II., i.) and Ammianus Marcellinus (XXIX., i. 39); there is no doubt that it caused a great sensation. A column was erected to him in his birthplace, and was supposed to be the seat of an oracle. Eusebius gives the date of his death as 165 A.D., and there is no reason to question this, or Lucian's statement that it was at the fourth Olympic meeting which he attended. The banishment from Rome would then fall at latest in 152–153; and the Christian episode between 140 and 150. That Tatian and the later apologists say nothing of his having been a Christian for a time is not surprising, even if they knew it. It is most unlikely that Lucian invented it; but it is, on the other hand, not probable that he got his details at first hand. Zahn's theory that he intended his account of the Cynic's death as a parody of Christian martyrdom will not hold. The whole point of the work, as directed against Cynicism, would be lost; and though Lucian knows that the Christians willingly give up their lives for their faith, so far from using this to explain the act of Peregrinus, he contrasts their sincere self-sacrifice with the mingled fear of death and mania for notoriety which he attributes to Peregrinus. Assuming the main facts—that Peregrinus was for a time a Christian, and as such was imprisoned, but afterward released, and that he later abandoned Christianity, it is worth while to see what Lucian knew of Christianity and what his judgment of it was, taking his sketch as a document belonging to about 170 and relating primarily to Syrian Christianity.

4. Lucian's Knowledge of Christianity.

The Christians are, then, a religious association in which a man crucified in Palestine is venerated. He has brought into life " new mysteries," and as the first lawgiver of the sect has convinced his followers that, when they have renounced the old gods and begun to worship him and live according to his laws, they are to consider themselves as brothers. They are persuaded that they are immortal, wherefore they despise death and meet it cheerfully and voluntarily. They consider all temporal goods as of small importance and hold them in common. They adhere closely to each other, and take incredible pains when any interest of the community is in question, considering it a general calamity when a brother is imprisoned. When Peregrinus was in prison, " very early in the morning aged widows and orphan children might be seen waiting near the place, and the leading men among them gained over the guards that they might pass the night with him. Many meals were sent in to him, their holy writings were read even from the cities of the province of Asia came certain who were sent by the Christians in the name of their communities, to aid, defend, or comfort him." Every detail in this account might be paralleled in Christian literature from the first epistle of Clement to Tertullian, *De jejunio*, and the detail of the envoys from the cities of Asia Minor is confirmed by the epistles of Ignatius—though there is not the slightest evidence of any direct employment by Lucian of Christian sources. The fact is simply that Lucian has named the essential characteristics of the Christian body as they presented themselves to a clear-sighted, disinterested observer, thus strengthening the evidence presented by Christian writers. So far from relying on Christian documents, Lucian does not seem to know the Christian writers of the second century; the prisoner in Syria has as little in common with Ignatius as the death of Peregrinus has with the martyrdom of Polycarp. While one can not assert positively that Lucian never read a line of a Christian author, the proof that he did is not forthcoming. For all this, his knowledge of Christianity is not so " vague and superficial " as Keim would have us believe. He brings none of the customary charges against the Christians, not even that of hostility to the empire. Christianity seems to be in his eyes a harmless movement. He considers it, indeed, without any token of sympathy; but he, the accomplished mocker, does not mock at the simplicity of the Christians which the impostor turns to his account. He finds it of course absurd that they should adore the crucified " sophist "; but their unshaken consciousness of brotherhood under all trials and their contempt for death are mentioned only as characteristic differentiæ. And it is these very Christians who, outside of the cultivated city-dwellers and the Epicureans, are the only people in the world to detect the hollowness of the pretentions of the false prophet Alexander of Abonoteichos; in fact, it is against them that the first denunciation of Alexander is uttered (*Alexander*, xxv., xxxviii.). In a word, in the *Peregrinus*, where he has poured out the fulness of his bitterest scorn upon the Cynics, he has contented himself with drawing an accurate picture of the Christians. It was not to be expected that he should set out to glorify them; what is remarkable is that he describes them not as deceivers, as criminals, or as revolutionaries, but merely as enthusiasts, credulous indeed, but capable of self-sacrifice and deep brotherly love. The single word "sophist" applied to Christ sufficed to stamp the great satirist as a blasphemer in the eyes of later generations, and cause them to neglect the historical value of the evidence which he supplies for the purity and uprightness of the Christian life and ideal as they were seen in his day. (A. Harnack.)

Bibliography: Perhaps the best edition of Lucian's works is by T. Hemsterhuis and J. F. Reitz, 3 vols., Amsterdam, 1743; a convenient one is by W. Dindorf, with Lat. transl., 3 vols., Paris, 1840; another is by F. Fritsche, 3 vols., Rostock, 1860–82; and still another is in the Tauchnitz series by C. H. Weise, 4 vols., Leipsic, 1867–77. There is an Eng. transl. by several hands, with life of Lucian by Dryden, 4 vols., London, 1711; one by T. Francklin, 4 vols., ib. 1781 (of great merit); and one by H. W. Fowler, 4 vols., ib. 1905. A Fr. transl. of the works is by L. Humbert, 2 vols., Paris, 1896, and an excellent Germ. transl. is by Wieland, 6 vols., Leipsic, 1788–89. Consult: J. Bernays, *Lucian und die Kyniker*, Berlin, 1879; C. T. Keim, *Celsus*, Zurich, 1862; J. M. Cotterill, *Peregrinus Proteus*, Edinburgh, 1879 (claims it is a forgery, perhaps by Henry Stephens the Reformation printer); M. Croiset, *Essai sur la vie et les œuvres de Lucien*, Paris, 1882; W. R. Smith, *Dictionary of Greek and Roman Biography*, ii. 812–822, London, 1890; *DCB*, iii. 744–748. The editions and translations have notes and introductions, and often a life of the author.

LUCIDUS, lū'sid-us: A Gallic priest of the second half of the fifth century. He held decided predestinarian views, going further even than Augustine and believing that at the fall man had utterly lost the freedom of his will, that God had determined beforehand that some were to be damned and others saved, and hence that Christ did not die for all but only for the elect, and finally that a "vessel unto dishonor" can never become a "vessel unto honor." A synod was summoned in 475 at Arles to condemn his views, and also one at Lyons in 476. Lucidus was compelled to recant chiefly through the influence of Faustus of Riez (q.v.), who, being a friend of Lucidus and also one of the most important members of the synod, had a lengthy correspondence with him on the subject. A letter to Lucidus by Faustus is in *MPL*, liii. 683.

LUCIFER (Hebr. *Helel*, "Shining one," R. V. "Day star"): A term applied by Isaiah to the king of Babylon (Isa. xiv. 12), and not occurring elsewhere in the Bible. By Tertullian, Jerome, and others the name was applied to Satan, and in the Middle Ages it became common in this sense. By Gunkel (*Schöpfung und Chaos*, pp. 132 sqq., Göttingen, 1895) the passage in Isaiah is regarded as embodying a reference to a nature myth.

LUCIFER OF CALARIS AND THE LUCIFERIANS: Bishop of Calaris (the modern Cagliari) in Sardinia, and his followers. The dates of Lucifer are uncertain; he died perhaps 371. He first appears in history as the envoy of Pope Liberius (q.v.) to the Emperor Constantius to urge the calling of a new synod. At the Synod of Milan, 355, he stood with the opposition, held firm with a few others, and, like these, was exiled. For a while he then lived at Germanicia in Commagene; next, at Eleutheropolis in Palestine, and afterward in the Thebaid. During his exile, he wrote some vehement polemics (ed. Hartel, in *CSEL*, vol. xiv., Vienna, 1886) against Emperor Constantius, as a patron of heretics and the enemy of the true faith. These writings may, with some degree of probability, be arranged in the following order: *De non conveniendo cum hæreticis, de regibus apostaticis, de Athanasio I* and *II.*, all prior to the autumn of 358; *De non parcendo in Deum delinquentibus*, after June, 359; *Moriendum esse pro Dei Filio*, 360 at the earliest, perhaps not until 361. Copious Biblical quotations give these documents no little value as bearing on the text of the Bible before Jerome and on the history of the canon. But, in other aspects, they are diffuse and repetitious, void of literary originality, and omit giving credit to authors from whom citations are made. Yet Lucifer's writings afford a vivid picture of the narrow yet honest zeal of a man loyal to his convictions.

The death of Constantius and the advent of Julian ended Lucifer's exile. In 362 he was at Antioch, trying unsuccessfully to settle the state of confusion there (see Meletius of Antioch). He combated with especial severity the lenient treatment of ecclesiastics who had become compromised by their defection from the right faith under Constantius, and insisted that they be stripped of their ecclesiastical offices. When at Naples, he refused church fellowship to Bishop Zosimus. He retired, eventually, and in sullen temper, to Calaris; where he lived revered, indeed, for his confessional constancy and his austere conversation, but in separation from a Church that he believed to be stained by indulgence of heretical doctrine. He was ever afterward the "Holy Sardinian"; and in 1623 his remains were deposited in the cathedral of Cagliari.

After his death Sardinia continued the center of the Luciferian coterie, a sect persistently entangling itself in the thought that the Church had become a harlot. The Luciferians were not confined to Sardinia, however. In Spain they reverenced Bishop Gregory of Elvira (q.v.); at Treves, their ideas were advocated by the Presbyter Bonosus; in Rome itself there was a Luciferian party (not to be confused with the followers of Ursinus, q.v.), against which Jerome wrote his *Altercatio Luciferiani et orthodoxi* (*MPL*, xxiii. 153–182); and Hilarius, the Roman deacon (q.v.), was a Luciferian. Ephesius, on a journey to the East (382 or 383), fell in with some Luciferians at Oxyrhynchos (Heptanomos, Egypt), who had for their bishop a monk Heraclidas, titular of Eleutheropolis (Palestine). And at Eleutheropolis were the two presbyters, Faustinus and Marcellinus, charged with holding assemblies for divine worship in the houses of their associates and opposed by the resident bishop. They complained against the bishop, and not in vain, to the Emperor Theodosius (see Faustinus), since a rescript of 384 forbade the persecution of those who stood in ecclesiastical fellowship with the Spaniard Gregory, and the oriental Heraclidas. By the irony of history, this imperial edict is the last intelligence concerning the Luciferians. G. Krüger.

Bibliography: The four most important treatments of the subject are: G. Krüger, *Lucifer, Bischof von Calaris, und das Schisma der Luciferianer*, Leipsic, 1886; W. von Hartel, in *Archiv für lateinische Lexikographie und Grammatik*, iii (1886), 1–58; L. Saltet, in *Bulletin de littérature ecclésiastique*, 1906, pp. 300–326 (claims for the Luciferians a great literary activity); and P. Lejay, *L'Héritage de Grégoire d'Elvire*, in *Revue Bénédictine*, xxv (1908), 435–457. Consult further: *DCB*, iii. 749–751; Ceillier, *Auteurs sacrés*, iv. 230–271; Harnack, *Dogma*, vols. iv.–v. passim; Neander, *Christian Church*, ii. 256–257, 441–442, 456–458, 559.

LUCIUS, lū'shĭŭs: The name of three popes.

Lucius I.: Pope 253–254. He was the successor of Cornelius, elected probably June 25, 253, and died Mar. 5 following. His election took place during the persecution which caused the banishment of Cornelius, and he also was banished soon after his consecration, but succeeded in gaining permission to return. From a letter of Cyprian's (lxviii. 5) it is evident that he took the same position as Cornelius in regard to the restoration of the lapsed after due penance. His tombstone is still extant in the cemetery of St. Calixtus. (N. BONWETSCH.)

BIBLIOGRAPHY: *Liber pontificalis*, ed. Mommsen, in *MGH*, *Gest. pont. Rom.* i (1898), 32; Jaffé, *Regesta*, i. 19–20; R. A. Lipsius, *Chronologie der römischen Bischöfe*, pp. 123 sqq., 207 sqq., Kiel, 1869; B. Platina, *Lives of the Popes*, i. 50–52, London, n. d.; Bower, *Popes*, i. 29.

Lucius II.: Pope 1144–1145. As Gerard, cardinal-priest of Santa Croce, he was active in the German controversies under Honorius II. and Innocent II. He became pope Mar. 12, 1144, and at first had a certain measure of success in suppressing the recalcitrant senate. But in the autumn his friendly relations with Roger of Sicily were disturbed; the Romans restored the senate, under the leadership of Giordano Pierleoni, who took the title of *patricius* and claimed all the regalian rights of the Roman Church. Lucius had recourse to arms against the citizens, and died Feb. 15, 1145. (A. HAUCK.)

BIBLIOGRAPHY: Jaffé, *Regesta*, ii. 7 sqq.; J. M. Watterich, *Pontificum Romanorum vitæ*, ii. 278 sqq., Leipsic, 1862; W. Giesebrecht, *Geschichte der deutschen Kaiserzeit*, iv. 222 sqq., Brunswick, 1877; F. Gregorovius, *Hist. of the City of Rome*, iv. 487–491, London, 1896; B. Platina, *Lives of the Popes*, ii. 43–44, ib. n.d.; Bower, *Popes*, ii. 476–477; Milman, *Latin Christianity*, iv. 242–243.

Lucius III.: Pope 1181–1185. As Hubald, bishop of Ostia, he was one of the most influential cardinals under Alexander III. He was elected pope Sept. 1, 1181, and consecrated on the following Sunday. His pontificate was an unsuccessful one. He was unable to control the Romans, and his residence in the city was limited to the period from the beginning of Nov., 1181, to the middle of Mar., 1182. The rest of the time he spent in various places, chiefly at Velletri and Anagni. The controversy over the succession to the inheritance of the Countess Matilda had been left unsettled by the peace of 1177, and the Emperor Frederick proposed in 1182 that the Curia should renounce its claim, receiving in exchange two-tenths of the imperial income from Italy, one-tenth for the pope and the other tenth for the cardinals. Lucius consented neither to this proposition nor to another compromise suggested by Frederick the next year; nor did a personal discussion between the two potentates at Verona in Oct., 1184, lead to any definite result. Meantime other causes of disagreement appeared, in the pope's refusal to comply with Frederick's wishes as to the regulation of German episcopal elections which had taken place during the schism, and especially as to the contested election to the see of Treves in 1183. In pursuance of his anti-imperial policy, he declined finally in 1185 to crown Henry VI. as Frederick's destined successor, and the breach between the empire and the Curia became wider on questions of Italian politics. Lucius died in Verona Oct. 25, 1185, having led up by his negative policy to the new contest between papacy and empire which soon broke out. (A. HAUCK.)

BIBLIOGRAPHY: Jaffé, *Regesta*, ii. 835 sqq.; J. M. Watterich, *Pontificum Romanorum vitæ*, ii. 650, Leipsic, 1862; P. Scheffer-Boichorst, *Friedrichs I. letzter Streit mit der Kurie*, pp. 20 sqq., Berlin, 1866; W. Giesebrecht, *Geschichte der deutschen Kaiserzeit*, vols. iv.–vi., Brunswick, 1888; J. Langen, *Geschichte der römischen Kirche*, iv. 557 sqq., Bonn, 1893; F. Gregorovius, *Hist. of the City of Rome*, iv. 609–612, London, 1896; B. Platina, *Lives of the Popes*, ii. 58–60, ib. n. d.; Bower, *Popes*, ii. 524–526; Milman, *Latin Christianity*, iv. 439–440.

LUCIUS, PAUL ERNST: German Protestant; b. at Ernolsheim (about 12 m. w. of Strasburg) Oct. 16, 1852; d. at Strasburg Nov. 27, 1902. He studied theology at Strasburg, Zurich, Paris, Jena, and Berlin. He was vicar at Sesenheim (1878–79); at Strasburg (1879–80); privat-docent there (1880–1883); professor extraordinary (1883–89); and professor (1889–1902). He wrote: *Die Therapeuten und ihre Stellung in der Geschichte der Askese* (Strasburg, 1879); *Der Essenismus in seinem Verhältnis zum Judenthum* (1881); *Die Kräftigung des Missionssinnes in der Gemeinde* (1885); *Zur äussern und innern Mission* (1903); and *Die Anfänge des Heiligenkults in der christlichen Kirche* (1904).

LUCKOCK, HERBERT MORTIMER: Church of England; b. at Great Barr (9 m. s.s.w. of Lichfield), Staffordshire, July 11, 1833; d. at Lichfield Mar. 24, 1909. He was educated at Jesus College, Cambridge (B.A., 1858; M.A., 1862), and was ordered deacon in 1860 and ordained priest in 1862. He was vicar of All Saints', Cambridge, in 1862–63 and 1865–75, rector of Gayhurst and Stoke-Goldington in 1863–65, and canon of Ely (of which he was honorary canon in 1874–75) in 1875–92, besides being principal of Ely Theological College in 1876–1887. From 1892 he was dean of Lichfield. He was also select preacher at Cambridge in 1865, 1874–75, 1883–84, 1892, and 1901, examining chaplain to the bishop of Ely in 1873–87, and proctor for the dean and chapter of Ely in 1892. Theologically he was an Anglo-Catholic, and wrote: *Tables of Stone* (sermons; London, 1867); *After Death, the State of the Faithful Dead and their Relationship to the Living* (1879); *Studies in the History of the Prayer Book* (1881); *An Appeal to the Church not to withdraw her Clergy from the Universities* (1882); *Footprints of the Son of Man as traced by St. Mark* (1884); *The Bishops in the Tower, a Record of Stirring Events affecting the Church and Nonconformists from the Reformation to the Revolution* (1886); *The Intermediate State between Death and Judgment* (1890); *The Divine Liturgy, being The Order for Holy Communion, historically, doctrinally, and devotionally set forth* (1889); *John Wesley's Churchmanship* (1891); *Who are Wesley's Heirs?* (1892); *History of the Church in Scotland* (1893); *History of Marriage, Jewish and Christian,* *with especial Reference to its Indissolubility and certain forbidden Degrees* (1894); *Footprints of the Apostles as traced by St. Luke in the Acts* (2 vols., 1897); *Four Qualifications for a Good Preacher* (1897); *The Characteristics of the Four Gospels* (1900); *Beautiful Life of an Ideal Priest; or, Reminiscences of Thomas Thelluson Carter* (1902); *Life and Works of Dr. Johnson* (1902); *Spiritual Difficulties in the Bible and Prayer Book: Helps to their Solution* (1905); and *Eucharistic Sacrifice and Intercession for the Departed* (1907). He also edited Bishop J. R. Woodford's *Great Commission: Twelve Addresses on the Ordinal* (London, 1886) and *Sermons* (2 vols., 1887).

LUD, LUDIM. See TABLE OF NATIONS.

LUDLOW, JAMES MEEKER: Presbyterian; b. at Elizabeth, N. J., Mar. 15, 1841. He was educated at Princeton (B.A., 1861), and Princeton Theological Seminary (1864). He was then pastor of the First Presbyterian Church, Albany, N. Y. (1864–68), Collegiate Reformed Dutch Church, New York City (1868–77), Westminster Presbyterian Church, Brooklyn, N. Y. (1877–85), and of Munn Avenue Presbyterian Church, East Orange, N. J. (1886–1909). He has written: *My Saint John* (New York, 1883); *Concentric Chart of History* (1885); *Captain of the Janizaries* (1886); *A King of Tyre* (1891); *That Angelic Woman* (1893); *History of the Crusades* (1896); *Baritone's Parish* (1897); *Deborah* (1901); *Incentives for Life* (1903); *Sir Raoul* (1905); *Jesse ben David* (1907); and *Judge West's Opinion, Reported by a Neighbor* (1908).

LUDOLF, lū'dolf, **HIOB:** German orientalist, founder of the study of the Ethiopic language and literature in Europe; b. at Erfurt June 15, 1624; d. at Frankfort-on-the-Main Apr. 8, 1704. He studied at Erfurt and Leyden, then traveled extensively. In Rome he learned Ethiopic from the Abyssinian Gregorius. He became tutor to the children of the duke of Saxe-Gotha in 1652, afterward aulic councilor, in 1675 chamberlain in Altenburg, and in 1691 president of the Collegium Imperiale Historicum in Frankfort, where he had settled in 1678. His principal works are: *Lexicon Æthiopico-Latinum* (3 parts, London, 1661; 2d ed., Frankfort, 1699); *Grammatica linguæ Æthiopicæ* (London, 1661; 2d ed., Frankfort, 1702); *Sciagraphia historiæ Æthiopicæ* (Jena, 1676); *Historia Æthiopica* (Frankfort, 1681; Eng. transl., London, 1684; French transl., Paris, 1684), to which he added a *Commentarius* (1691) and two appendices (1693–94); *Grammatica linguæ Amharicæ* (1698); and *Lexicon Amharico-Latinum* (1698). He also published the Ethiopic psalter, with Latin translation (1701).

BIBLIOGRAPHY: C. Junker, *De vita et scriptis Iobi Ludolphi*, Leipsic, 1710; J. Flemming, in *Beiträge zur Assyriologie*, vols. i.–ii., ib. 1890–91.

LUEBECK: One of the three city-states of the German Empire, comprising the inner city, with suburbs, and several enclaves in the surrounding country; area 115 square miles; population (1905) 108,857, of whom 101,724 were Evangelical Lutherans, 760 Reformed, 2,457 Roman Catholics, 638 Jews, and 231 sectarians (Baptists, Irvingites, Adventists, Mormons, etc.). The Reformation was established in Lübeck by Bugenhagen in 1531, and since that time the city has been Lutheran. Rigorous measures were taken against the Roman Catholics, and against adherents of the Reformed faith, though the former continued to hold religious services, and in 1693 the latter received permission to build a church and, under certain restrictions, hold their own service. Admission to the council was denied to all non-Lutherans till the beginning of the nineteenth century. The senate issued regulations for the Reformed parish in 1825, and for the Roman Catholics in 1841; and both denominations received full political and civil rights under the constitution of 1848 (revised 1851 and 1875). At present there are fourteen Lutheran parishes and fifteen churches. The present "Constitution of the Evangelical Lutheran Church in the State of Lübeck" went into effect in 1895. It vests the church government in the senate, which either exercises its authority directly through its Lutheran members, or delegates it to the ecclesiastical council, which is composed of two Lutheran senators, of whom one is chairman, the senior (chairman) of the clerical ministerium, and four other members, viz., a clergyman and three laymen, who are elected by the senate for a period of six years, the clergyman on the recommendation of the clerical ministerium, the laymen on the recommendation of the synod. In matters affecting ecclesiastical law, church taxes, the liturgy, and the boundaries of parishes, the acts of the ecclesiastical council have to be sanctioned by the synod and confirmed by the senate. The clerical ministerium includes all the clergy who have charges. This body has a word in all matters affecting the doctrine and formularies of the Church. Since 1902, in accordance with an agreement with the consistory of Schleswick-Holstein, candidates have been examined by the board of examiners in Kiel, those passing becoming eligible for appointment in Lübeck, as well as in Schleswick-Holstein. The synod consists of forty-seven members, of whom three are appointed by the ecclesiasical council, the remainder being members of the local parochial boards. Such a board is composed of the local clergy and a number of laymen, who are elected for six years. Each parish is divided into as many pastoral districts as it has clergy. The finances of the Church are regulated by a law of Jan. 18, 1895. The basis of the general church treasury is a fund of 150,000 marks formed by the surplus of the cloister of St. John, the Hospital of the Holy Ghost, and the Burg Cloister. The interest on this sum is supplemented by a yearly income of 16,000 marks from the cloister of St. John, and by a church tax. Church attendance on the part of adults is not good, and the number of communicants, which seems to be on the decrease, is less than sixteen per cent. of the population. Attendance by children is better. There are now services for children in every Lutheran parish of the city and suburbs. The oldest is that in the Church of St. James, which was established in 1875. The total attendance averages about 2,000. (L. F. RANKE.)

BIBLIOGRAPHY: *Lüb. Verordnungen und Bekanntmachungen*, ii. 291, iii. 25, 306; *Statist. Mittheilungen aus dem deutschen evangelischen Landeskirchen*, 1880; W. Deiss, *Geschichte der evangelisch-reformierten Gemeinde in Lübeck*, Lübeck, 1866; E. Illigens, *Geschichte der lübeckischen Kirche 1530–1896*, Paderborn, 1896; S. Carlebach, *Geschichte der Juden in Lübeck*, Lübeck, 1899.

LUEBECK, BISHOPRIC OF: An ancient episcopal see of northern Germany, established originally at Oldenburg by Otto I., probably in 968, and subject to the metropolitan jurisdiction of Hamburg. The first bishop, Egward, was consecrated by Archbishop Adaldag. His diocese included the whole of the Wendish territory, which was under Hamburg, or from the bay of Kiel southeast to near the southern boundary of the present Mecklenburg. The Wendish risings of 990 and 1018 destroyed the work here, and when it was revived by Archbishop Adalbert the diocese was restricted to eastern Holstein. It was not till the time of Vicelin (q.v.) that the work was established on a permanent basis, and in 1158 the see was transferred to Lübeck by his successor Gerold (1155–63). The bishopric never attained great importance, being overshadowed by the growing power of the city. (A. Hauck.)

The bishopric was made immediately subject to the empire under Conrad II. of Querfurt (1183–86). It had secular jurisdiction over a considerable territory; but the episcopal residence was usually at Eutin. The Reformation was first introduced under the influence of King Frederick I. of Denmark in 1524, and definitely established in 1530. It was not yet, however, possible to suppress or wholly to secularize the bishopric, so for a time bishops of Lutheran sympathies were elected. From 1586 the dignity was usually an appanage of the younger sons of the dukes of Holstein until 1706; and by the settlement of 1803 it was constituted a secular principality in favor of Peter Frederick William of Oldenburg and his heirs.

Bibliography: Sources are *Urkundenbuch des Bistums Lübeck*, ed. W. Leverkus, Oldenburg, 1856; Adam, *Gesta Hammenburgensis ecclesiæ*, ed. J. M. Lappenberg, in *MGH, Script.*, vi (1846), 267–389; Helmold, *Chronica Slavorum*, ed. idem, ib. xxi (1869), 1–99; Arnold, *Chronica Slavorum*, ed. idem, ib. pp. 100–250; *Annales Lubicenses*, ed. idem, ib. xvi (1859), 411–429; *Series episcoporum . . . Lubicensium*, ib. xiii (1881), 347. Consult: Hauck, *KD*, vols. iii.–iv.; E. A. T. Laspeyres, *Die Bekehrung Nord-Albingiens*, Halle, 1864; G. Dehio, *Geschichte des Erzbistums Hamburg-Bremen*, 2 vols., Berlin, 1876; C. Eubel, *Hierarchia catholica medii ævi*, 2 vols., Münster, 1898–1901.

LUECKE, lük'e, **GOTTFRIED CHRISTIAN FRIEDRICH:** German Lutheran theologian; b. at Egeln (16 m. s.w. of Magdeburg) Aug. 24, 1791; d. at Göttingen Feb. 14, 1855. He was educated at the cathedral school of Magdeburg and at the universities of Halle and Göttingen. In 1816 he went to Berlin, where the influence of Bunsen and Lachmann won him Schleiermacher's friendship and a position as licentiate and privat-docent in theology. He gladly took part in the "Evangelical union" which was sealed by the united communion service of Oct. 31, 1817. His publications in this period were *Grundriss der neutestamentlichen Hermeneutik und ihrer Geschichte* (Göttingen, 1816); *Ueber den neutestamentlichen Kanon des Eusebius* (Berlin, 1817); a new edition of Melanchthon's "Apology" (1818); and, in collaboration with De Wette, *Synopsis evangeliorum* (1818). In the autumn of 1818 he was called to the chair of theology in the new University of Bonn. Here for eight years he exercised a great and happy influence on the students, at the same time taking an active part in the reorganization of Evangelical church life in Rhenish Prussia. At Bonn he published his principal work, the *Kommentar über die Schriften des Evangelisten Johannes* (3 vols., 1820–25; Eng. transl. in part, Edinburgh, 1837). The first volume was hailed as a powerful support to positive theology, and was attacked with equal warmth by the rationalizing party under Paulus of Heidelberg. Toward the end of his stay at Bonn Lücke engaged in another controversy with Ferdinand Delbrück, who urged a return to the standards of the primitive *regula fidei* and the Apostles' Creed in place of the Scriptural basis of Protestant theology. With his colleagues Sack and Nitzsch, Lücke issued three open letters *Ueber das Ansehen der heiligen Schrift und ihr Verhältniss zur Glaubensregel in der protestantischen und in der alten Kirche* (Bonn, 1827), of which the third and longest was all his own. He was also associated with Schleiermacher and De Wette in publishing the *Theologische Zeitschrift* from 1819 to 1822, and with Gieseler in the short-lived *Zeitschrift für gebildete Christen der evangelischen Kirche* (1823); and in 1827, together with Nitzsch, Gieseler, Ullmann and Umbreit, he established the still flourishing *Theologische Studien und Kritiken* to represent, in a favorite phrase of his, "the alliance of the free scientific spirit with the power of the specifically Christian spirit."

Meantime, in the autumn of 1827, he had migrated to Göttingen to succeed Stäudlin, and there he spent the rest of his life, devoting himself rather to New-Testament exegesis and systematic theology instead of to church history which had been his special work at Bonn. In spite of the anxious days of the revolution of 1831 and the difficulties brought upon the university by the changes made in the constitution of Hanover in 1837 by King Ernest August, he declined calls to Kiel and Halle in 1838, to Jena in 1843, and to Leipsic in 1845. The government rewarded his constancy by the positions of councilor in the consistory at Hanover (1839) and of abbot of Bursfeld (1843). His later years were troubled by increasing theological isolation, as the younger men went off either to the radical camp of Baur and the Tübingen school, or to the strict Lutheran party of Harless, Kahnis, and Thomasius, with its center at Erlangen and Leipsic. Lücke and his friends attempted to hold a middle course between these two extremes, insisting in the spirit of Schleiermacher on the historical and permanent value of the Reformation confessions of faith, while avoiding any blind symbololatry and vindicating the clear and practical nature of theology.

Lücke's Göttingen period was also one of busy literary activity. He completed his earlier Johannine work by a *Versuch einer vollständigen Einleitung in die Offenbarung Johannis und die gesamte apokalyptische Litteratur* (Bonn, 1832), besides issuing two revised editions of the commentary itself (1833–36, 1840–56). He contributed a long series of important articles to periodicals and university publications, the most noteworthy of which was the treatise *Ueber das Alter und den Verfasser, die ursprüngliche Form und den wahren Sinn des kirchlichen Friedensspruches "In necessariis unitas, etc."* (Göttingen, 1850). Of practical importance, too, were four addresses delivered before the Göttinger Missionsverein between 1840 and 1842, which prepared the way for the founding of the "Seminar für innere Mission," the very name being taken from the last of them, though used not quite in his sense. (F. Sander.)

Bibliography: Lücke's biography was written by F. Sander, Hanover-Linden, 1891. There are notices by J. Müller in *ZKW*, 1855, nos. 16–17; by Redepenning in *Protestantische Kirchenzeitung*, 1855; and by Ehrenfeuchter, in *TSK*, 1855. Indications of further literature are given in Hauck-Herzog, *RE*, xi. 674.

LUEDEMANN, lü'de-män, **HERMANN KARL:** Swiss Protestant; b. at Kiel Sept. 15, 1842. He was educated at the universities of Kiel, Heidelberg, and Berlin from 1861 to 1867 (Ph.D., Kiel, 1870), and in 1872 became privat-docent at the university of his native city (where he also taught in a private school). In 1878 he was appointed associate professor of New-Testament exegesis at the same institution, and since 1884 has been connected with the University of Bern, where he has been professor successively of church history (1884–1891) and of systematic theology, dogmatics, and philosophy (since 1891). He is an adherent of the liberal school in theology, and has written: *Die Anthropologie des Apostel Paulus und ihre Stellung innerhalb seiner Heilslehre* (Kiel, 1872); *Die "Eidbrüchigkeit" unserer neukirchlichen (freisinnigen) Geistlichen* (1881); *Die neuere Entwicklung der protestantischen Theologie* (Bremen, 1884); *Reform und Täufertum in ihrem Verhältnis zum christlichen Prinzip* (Bern, 1896); *Individualität und Persönlichkeit* (1900); *Was heisst "biblisches Christentum"?* (1905) and *Religion und Leben* (1908).

LUETGERT, lüt'gärt, **WILHELM:** German Protestant; b. at Heiligengrabe (a village near Wittstock, 60 m. n.w. of Berlin), Brandenburg, Apr. 9, 1867. He was educated at the universities of Greifswald and Berlin from 1886 to 1889, and in 1892 became privat-docent for New-Testament exegesis and dogmatic theology at the former institution, where he was appointed associate professor of the same subjects in 1895. In 1901 he went in a similar capacity to Halle, where he was promoted to his present position of full professor in 1902. Besides assisting A. Schlatter since 1904 in editing the *Beiträge zur Förderung der christlichen Theologie*, he has written *Das Reich Gottes in den synoptischen Evangelien* (Gütersloh, 1895); *Die johanneische Christologie* (1899); *Die Liebe im Neuen Testament* (Leipsic, 1905); *Gottes Sohn und Gottes Geist, Vorträge zur Christologie und zur Lehre vom Geiste Gottes* (1905); *Im Dienste Gottes, Betrachtungen* (Berlin, 1907); *Jesus Christus für unsere Zeit* (Hamburg, 1907; in collaboration with several others); *Freiheitspredigt und Schwarmgeister in Korinth, Ein Beitrag zur Charakteristik der Christuspartei*, and *Die Irrlehrer der Pastoralbrife*, both in the *Beiträge*, ut sup. (1908–09).

LUETKEMANN, lüt'ke-män, **JOACHIM:** German Lutheran theologian; b. at Demmin (28 m. s. of Stralsund), Pomerania, Dec. 15, 1608; d. at Wolfenbüttel (8 m. s. of Brunswick) Oct. 18, 1655. Both his writings and his personality, which combined deep learning with the efficacious inner conviction of Pietism, had no slight influence in the same direction as those of Arndt and Johann Müller, while his controversy with the orthodox Lutherans as to the humanity of Christ in his death, though without abiding consequences, attracted much attention at the time. He was educated at the universities of Greifswald and Strasburg, afterward traveling through France and Italy and returning to Rostock to pursue his studies there. He became a lecturer in the philosophical faculty there in 1638, and five years later professor of metaphysics and physics. He had already become known as a preacher, and contributed much to the activity of religious life in Rostock. His work there was interrupted by a controversy in which he became engaged with the strict orthodox party in Mecklenburg, whom the duke favored. He put forth in what seemed to them a dangerous form a proposition already enunciated in the Middle Ages. To the concept of humanity, he said, there belongs besides the existence of soul and body the form of their joint existence, their unity; and with the dissolution of this unity in death the manhood of Christ was dissolved. The assertion of its permanence must take away something from the reality of the death of Christ, and thus from the reality of redemption. He attempted to save the belief in the divine-human character of Christ by the theory that the divinity was united not only with the soul but with the body; and when the soul left the body, the Godhead did not leave it, but the true, essential, eternal life still dwelt in the dead body. A vehement strife broke out over this apparent departure from the orthodox doctrine. Lütkemann defended himself in his *Dissertatio physico-theologica de vero homine*. The orthodox teaching seemed to imply that the body of Christ, as a necessary concomitant with the soul to the unity of human nature, was incorruptible. Two court preachers at Weimar, Coller and Bartholomäi, now expressed a doubt of this, and defended Lütkemann's view from this standpoint. The Rostock theologian Cothmann appeared as a violent opponent of Lütkemann, and used his influence with the duke to have him silenced both as a professor and as a preacher. In spite of the support of clergy and people, he was obliged to leave Rostock. Duke August of Brunswick, however, offered him the position of general superintendent and court preacher, and there he spent his remaining years, drawing up the excellent school ordinance of 1651 and the church order of 1657. He wrote a number of philosophical works, and one of the most popular books among the disciples of Arndt was his *Vorschmack der göttlichen Güte* (Wolfenbüttel, 1643). (W. Dilthey.)

Bibliography: A Life by Philipp Rethmeyer is prefixed to his *Vorschmack* in the later editions, e.g., Brunswick, 1740. Consult also: F. A. Tholuck, *Akademische Leben*, ii. 109, Hamburg, 1854.

LUKE.

I. **The Man:** The name appears three times in the New Testament as that of a man who belongs to the Pauline circle (Col. iv. 14; II Tim. iv. 11; Philemon 24), in the first case as that of "the beloved physician," in the last as a "fellow worker." Col. iv. 11 characterizes certain fellow workers as "of the circumcision" but does not include Luke among them, hence it may be concluded that Luke was not of Jewish blood and also not a Jewish proselyte. But it does not follow that he was personally known in Colosse, although known by reputation. It appears also that he was with Paul during the first imprisonment, helped him in his labors and perhaps as a physician was especially valuable in Paul's activity. So it appears from II Tim. that Luke was with the apostle in his second imprisonment as his only companion, and conjecture sees in this a reference to Luke's medical services, especially in view of the absence of Crescens, Tychicus, and Titus (II Tim. iv. 10). This exhausts all that the New Testament expressly says of Luke. The Lucius of Rom. xvi. 21 (a Jew) and of Acts xiii. 1 have nothing to do with the subject of this article. Formerly the "brother" of II Cor. viii. 18, or of 22, was identified with Luke, but this has not the foundation of tradition in its favor, only of traditional exegesis from before the time of Origen, and the identification is insecure. Testimony external to the New Testament derives Luke from Antioch (Eusebius, *Hist. eccl.*, III., iv. 7; A. Mai, *Patrum nova bibliotheca*, Rome, 1844–71, iv. 270; F. A. W. Spitta, *Brief des Julius Africanus*, Halle, 1877, pp. 69, 111). For this the singular reading of codex D in Acts xi. 28 (which describes the prophecy of Agabus as being delivered "while *we* were gathered together") can not be the basis, though the tradition may embody the facts. But many other traditions regarding the region of Luke's labors and the place of his literary activity have not in their favor the same degree of probability as inheres in that relating to the place of his nativity. Indeed, some of them palpably arise from misunderstanding of the New Testament, and others are purely conjectural and without solid foundation —e.g., that which connects Luke with the disciples at Emmaus, and that which makes of him an artist with the pencil as well as with the pen.

1. Early References to Him.

With the name of Luke three writings of the New Testament have been connected, the third Gospel, the Acts of the Apostles, and the Epistle to the Hebrews, though Luke's connection with the last is put forth as a mere hypothesis and requires no consideration. The tradition of his relation to the third Gospel goes back to a time earlier than Origen, and Paul's expression "my gospel" has been construed as a reference to that book. Irenæus, the Muratorian Canon, Clement of Alexandria, and Tertullian express what was evidently the opinion of their day, that Luke was the author of the third Gospel. And practically the same testimony assigns a Lucan origin to the Acts of the Apostles, while earlier hints to the same purport are discovered in the works of Marcion and Justin Martyr. It is now generally held that essentially the present Gospel of Luke lay before Marcion when the latter compiled his Gospel, while the reverse proposition, that Marcion's composition underlay Luke's, is universally given up. Until recent times there was no trace of a tradition adverse to Lucan authorship, while the title to the Gospel as given in the manuscripts testifies to the antiquity of the belief that Luke wrote this Gospel. Of course, modern criticism as well as Marcionitic rejected Lucan authorship, as did the encratitic Severians, the Ebionites, and the Manicheans, not on literary but on doctrinal grounds.

2. Traditions of His Authorship.

Acceptance of this tradition immediately results in a large increase of knowledge concerning the person and the fortunes of Luke. It must be recognized that he had more to do with the work of Paul than appears from the latter's epistles. Part of the narrative of the Acts of the Apostles is in the first person. If Luke is the author of the narrative of Paul's journeys in that book, the "we" passages testify that he was an eye-witness of the events, and this fits in well with the references in the epistles. And the occurrence of "we" in codex D of the clause noted above (§ 1) in a passage earlier than is found in the common text (Acts xi. 28) has caused Blass to suspect a double recension of the Acts by Luke's own hand. Neither Weiss' explanation (*TU*, xvii. 111, 1899) nor that of Ramsay (*St. Paul the Traveller*, New York, 1896, pp. 27, 210), which assume a correction of the original text arising in different ways, seems to have much probability in its favor. If Blass' supposition of a double text, both from the hand of Luke, be not accepted, the "we" must be original to the text. In that case the tradition of the Antiochian origin of Luke receives confirmation, and Luke must have been an associate of Paul in his early activities before either Timothy or Titus were connected with him. Moreover, Luke appears not only as a friend and close companion of Paul, as his personal medical attendant, but as a man well and broadly educated and with wide interests, possessing powers of keen observation and the ability to describe simply but vividly what he saw. If in spite of the modern adverse criticism tradition be accepted, Luke becomes a source of the first importance for the origins of Christianity and of the Christian Church.

3. Characteristics as a Historian.

II. **His Writings:** Doubts of Lucan authorship have been raised rather with regard to the Acts than the Gospel. In any case, the facts reported in the Gospel go farther back—the author does not claim to be an eye-witness or a sharer in the events.

1. Types of Modern Criticism. Still, suspicion regarding the Gospel inevitably followed that regarding the Acts. The hypothesis that the two books are from different authors is very seldom put forth and even then in a very guarded manner, while it is easily refuted by the many-sided similarities which are found in the books. Modern New-Testament criticism takes two principal directions in its discussion of the Lucan writings. In one case it asserts that they are "tendency writings," taking a part in the assumed burning contest between Paulinism and Judaism and endeavoring to furnish a middle ground upon which both could unite, blending the dogmatics, ethics, and practicality of Judaism with Pauline universalism. This makes the writings a peace proposal from a Pauline Christian. Of course, various forms of this hypothesis have been put forth. The other direction of modern criticism proceeds from a literary basis, and supposes that the books embody the editing of earlier sources, which expressed various tendencies and were of different origin and value, by a man who was not near enough to the facts to have complete mastery of them. Indeed, it is asserted that the interests of a later time than the authorship of Luke would admit appear in incidental details, that the report often shows that the time of Jesus and his apostles was already long past, while there is silence as to matters of importance which would not be expected from a man in the position of Luke. The question is, whether the objections are so grounded as to demand the rejection of a strong and consentient tradition, or whether, either by means of a more correct exposition or by a more exact appreciation of the intentions and situation of the traditional author, the possibility of the Lucan authorship may be more conclusively established. In order to gain securer results, an attempt must be made to delineate as a whole the historical and literary processes of apostolic times in order satisfactorily to examine the critical hypotheses with reference to their probability or possibility—an attempt which is excluded by the purposes of this article, which can give merely the indications.

The starting-point of any discussion is, of course, the Gospel, to which there is a preface. A prior question is whether this preface belongs only to the Gospel or also to the Acts. Although the question has been answered both ways, *prima facie* the preface belongs to the Gospel only.

2. The Preface to the Gospel. It indicates that the Gospel is written for a man of high position who has some certain knowledge of Christianity without necessarily being more than a catechumen, if even that. The Evangelist implies that Theophilus was not averse to such knowledge but was ready to receive further information. This knowledge was not to be of the dogmatic order, but rather historical and "accurate" (Luke i. 3), and by "accurate" was meant not simply "in chronological order" but rather the narration of events in their many-sided relationships. So far, there is nothing antagonistic to Lucan authorship. And no objection to such authorship is to be seen in the reference to previous writers of Gospel history in Luke i. 1, since enough material is known to justify the expression "many." The very growth of such a literature would emphasize for Luke its necessity not only for believing Christians to whom the oral impartation of the news was becoming increasingly rare, nor only for Jews and Jewish Christians to whom the Messianic consciousness of Jesus was of importance, but also for the heathen to whom Theophilus had belonged. It is continually becoming more completely established that the second Gospel, essentially in its present form, lay before the author of the third and was used by him. But comparison of the two Gospels shows marked differences in plan and conception. Thus Mark sets the story of Jesus in two great groups of events—Jesus' work in Galilee and the events between his departure from Galilee and Easter morning; Luke uses the same two groups but prefixes to the first the Gospel of the Infancy, inserts between them the account of the journey given in Luke ix. 51–xviii. 14, and adds to the second his account of the resurrection. Moreover, while Luke follows Mark in the main in the order of the events in the two groups, he effects transpositions and makes noteworthy omissions. Further, outside of the three great additions already indicated, the third Gospel makes single additions, such as the sermon on the mount, the story of Zaccheus, and very many others. All this indicates a special plan subordinated to a purpose different from that which the author of the second Gospel had before him and suited to a man whose antecedents were heathen, as were those of Theophilus.

But does this purpose, expressed in the preface, and its execution in the Gospel, agree with what is known of Luke? A difficulty raised here is that a man who stood as near to the events as did Luke,

3. The Character of the Gospel. and had such opportunities to meet eye-witnesses, in his departures from the narrative of Mark took so little the direction of the Fourth Gospel. This troubles little one who deals with the historicity of the Fourth Gospel, but the difficulty increases the more one deals with that historicity, and threatens to become fatal to the claim of Lucan authorship if, as many suppose, a long period of historical study (Luke i. 3) is involved. It may be conceded that the Lucan narrative contains parts tinged with Johannine coloring. But when the omission is noted of events given in the Fourth Gospel which are essential to the narrative of one who proposes to "trace the course of all things accurately from the first" (Luke i. 3), when it is remembered that the occurrences of John i.–iv., the visits to the feasts in Jerusalem of John v., vii., and x., and the Lazarus episode do not appear in the Lucan narrative, the authorship by the apostolic companion Luke seems impossible. For many of those events are not of a nature that permits their omission by one who proposes to give a résumé of the life of Jesus. Upon close observation the case seems otherwise. Luke did not know the Johannine material, but he considered that Mark really preserved the historical scheme in its principal outlines. His historical investigations therefore were limited in extent and need have lasted scarcely a year. Indeed, the *ensemble* of the Lucan Gospel is rather that of a narrative produced under the influence of the Marcan Gospel with the many additions, already noted, of events which seemed fully guaranteed, and which appeared, in accordance with the writer's scheme, to demand a place in the story. It presents also such omissions and transpositions as were necessary, in the plan conceived, to produce in new form a well-ordered history of the life of Jesus, such as would be adapted to the situation of the reader for whom it was ostensibly designed. So far as the preface is concerned, therefore, the Gospel might have proceeded from the pen of the historic Luke.

4. Bearing Upon Authorship.

Or does the pretended circumstance that the Gospel contains vague recollections or statements in conflict with certified fact compel one to suppose that the author or editor of sources lived at a later period? It may be admitted that in this or that one may think of legendary recasting or adornment. Such material many find in the Gospel of the Infancy and in other details. But these are practically paralleled in the Gospels of Mark and Matthew, which are rightly regarded as belonging to apostolic times, and failure has met the attempts to set the point at which these elements enter. So far as disagreement with other reports is concerned, it has first to be discovered which reports are correct, whether indeed reconciliation is not possible. Here is to be noted the relationship of Luke's history of the glorification of Jesus to I Cor. xv. 5 sqq., since the narrative of Luke has so little in common with the enumeration of Paul, though even here there are points which agree, and explanation of Lucan omissions is easy. On the whole, the Gospel would thus occupy an excellent position were it not that the Acts of the Apostles seems, under the methods of criticism, to draw it into the vortex of unreliability.

5. Character of the Acts of the Apostles.

The Acts of the Apostles appears as a continuation of the Gospel. The occasion calling it forth must have been something different from that which educed the Gospel, whether Theophilus had become a Christian or not. Christianity might have seemed to some an unjustified break with the past, an illy ordered revolutionary movement destined to fail. The Acts sets forth the development of the later from the primitive apostolic Christianity, its extension into the world of the heathen, especially by the instrumentality of Paul, whose figure is soon introduced into the picture. The purpose of the book seems to agree with that expressed in the preface to the Gospel. The old view that there is a paralleling of the fortunes of Peter and Paul, and the other exposition that the purposes of these two are harmonized, are no longer maintained. That Paul could in his epistles speak otherwise than he does in the speeches of the Acts goes without saying, whether the speeches reported in the Acts be actual reports or assumed addresses made up after the pattern of Greek historiography. There is no *a priori* reason why Peter should not early have found the way toward universalism, and it would be difficult to show that Paul could not have made use in the synagogues of the privileges of a born Jew (I Cor. ix. 19 sqq.).

6. Historical Difficulties of Acts xv.

The difficulty really lies where Luke has to do with Pauline accounts. The *locus classicus* is Acts xv. 1 sqq., compared with Gal. ii. 1 sqq. Earlier and later attempts to harmonize these passages upon the basis of another journey to Jerusalem must be rejected. The most frequent method of lightening the difficulty is to show that according to Luke's report the decree was applicable to the original community, that it was not an ordinance for converts from heathenism to which they were bound for the sake of salvation, that in general it involved nothing new so far as the general duty of Christians was concerned, and that therefore it was not necessary for Paul to mention it either to the Galatians or, indeed, later to make it a matter of injunction. This does not do away with the necessity for further attempts at enlightenment, and in view of the fact that the issuance of the decree can not be doubted while only the question of the occasion is in dispute, and further, since it is given by an author whose intention to be trustworthy appears from Luke i. 3, it is a duty not only of harmonistic interest but of historical exposition to attempt the solution of the problem. A beginning is to be made with a question of textual criticism. The οἷς οὐδὲ of Gal. ii. 5 has usually been regarded as relating the sentence to the circumcision of Titus. But in fact it may have been that this construction of the sentence influenced the introduction of those two words and that they are to be stricken out (so Ambrosiaster, Tertullian, Victorinus, Irenæus, Pelagius, and the codices D, d, and e). Verse 5 then may refer to the recognition on the part of Paul and Barnabas of the decree known to the Galatians. Paul is dealing with the calumnies uttered against him to the effect that he was a time-server (Gal. i. 10). He relates, therefore, the history of the events in his life which led up to the decree, states his independence as an apostle, tells of his exposition of his teaching before the authorities in Jerusalem, affirms that he had not yielded to the subjection of the "false brethren" (Gal. ii. 4) so far as Titus was concerned though he had yielded a point elsewhere; while so far as the meeting with Peter in Antioch was concerned, Peter had received the blame. When compared with Acts xv. this narrative seemed to be obscure, and relief was sought by the addition of the οἷς οὐδὲ in question in order to reconcile Paul and Luke. Paul was able to give adhesion to the decree so far as he did in permitting it to be sent to his congregations, indeed in personally imparting it to them (Acts xvi. 4), but he did not obligate himself to apply it to his mission field, though he was not personally opposed to it. While James could not disavow his own proposal (Acts xxi. 25), he could recognize that Paul was not bound to advance the matter and might have been ready to protect Paul in the latter's position. Finally Luke may have had an interest in informing Theophilus, who had perhaps already learned something of the affair, of the entire development.

If the course of this explanation should prove correct, it may be supposed that in other matters the author was well oriented, that in more or less weighty affairs his observation had been true and that his version is correct.

7. The Author's Methods. He handles the history rather in the way of adducing significant events than of a complete narration. With regard to the sections in which the first person is used, it is now seldom affirmed that they proceed from a man who falsely claims to have been present, and it is generally assumed that an eye-witness stands behind those sections. But it is sometimes held that the eye-witness is a different person from the author of the book, though against this is the lack of linguistic differences in the two portions of the text. Moreover, the time indications of the "we" sections agree well with those of the Pauline epistles concerning the companionship of Luke and Paul. If all the indications be taken together, the pronouncement of historians like Curtius and Ranke, of philologists like Blass and Vogel, and archeologists like Ramsay, as well as of a host of theologians, to the effect that the authorship by Luke of the Acts of the Apostles is best supported is not easily to be combated.

Some other questions remain for consideration. One is that of sources. A starting-point like that given for the Gospel in the parallel accounts is not furnished for Acts, and consequently no sure results are attained.

8. Remaining Problems. The relation of Acts to the Pauline epistles is also debated, one affirming the frequent use of them, another asserting that they were inaccessible to the author. It can not be definitely proved that literary dependence existed between the two sets of writings. A difficult question is that of the date, which can not be fixed at the conclusion of Paul's two years at Rome (Blass). The dependence of the Gospel upon Mark, which was not written before the death of Peter, gives the superior date. Krenkel in 1894 attempted to show literary dependence upon Josephus; in that case the earlier date would be 75–80 A.D. Tradition is silent as to the place of writing, though in Rome both writings were known at an early date. In the matter of the diffusion of these writings before the name of Luke was attached to them, the testimony of Clement of Rome (as implied by his citation of passages) is not easy to contest, and the same may be said of citations in Hermas, Barnabas, Ignatius, the Didache, Polycarp, and Papias. With respect to the text it may be said that in no other book of the New Testament is the text in so bad a condition as in Acts. It is due to Blass that a new stadium has been reached in its treatment. This scholar observes that in a number of manuscripts circulated in the East, of which D is the example among the uncials, one form of text is current which is no less original than that of the received text, and that of the two forms of text thus existent one is that of the original first draft while the other is the result of a revision by Luke's own hand. Blass in 1900 maintained that neither of these forms of the text is the original, but that both are the editions of a prior form (*TSK*, 1900, pp. 11, 19). That the hypothesis of the use of sources will be fully disproved in case of the establishment of this view is to be regarded as doubtful. (PAUL EWALD.)

BIBLIOGRAPHY: On the personality of Luke, consult the introductions prefixed to the commentaries and the pertinent sections in the works on Biblical introduction; also A. Harnack, *Lukas der Arzt*, Leipsic, 1906, Eng. transl., Edinburgh, 1907; W. M. Ramsay, *Luke the Physician and Other Studies*, New York, 1907; *DB*, iii. 161–162; *EB*, iii. 2830–33.

On matters of criticism consult the works cited under BIBLICAL INTRODUCTION II., particularly Zahn, and under PAUL. Special treatises on authorship, credibility, and the like are: H. H. Evans, *St. Paul the Author of the Third Gospel*, London, 1884–86; J. Friedrich, *Das Lukasevangelium und die Apostelgeschichte Werke desselben Verfassers*, Halle, 1890; A. C. Hervey, *Authenticity of Luke*, London, 1892; F. H. Chase, *Credibility of the Acts*, ib. 1901. On origins and sources consult: E. Zeller, *Die Apostelgeschichte nach ihrem Inhalt und . . Ursprung*, Stuttgart, 1854, Eng. transl., with Overbeck's Introduction to Acts, 2 vols., London, 1875; H. J. Litzinger, *Die Entstehung des Lukasevangeliums und der Apostelgeschichte*, Essen, 1883; F. Spitta, *Die Apostelgeschichte, ihre Quellen und deren geschichtlichen Wert*, Halle, 1891; J. Jüngst, *Die Quellen der Apostelgeschichte*, Gotha, 1895; B. Weiss, *Die Quellen des Lukasevangeliums*, Stuttgart, 1907; J. Horner, *Gospels of Matthew and Luke: a Vindication of their Agreement and Accuracy*, Pittsburg, 1908; A. Harnack, *Beiträge zur Einleitung in das N. T.*, III., *Die Apostelgeschichte*, Leipsic, 1908, Eng. transl., *New Testament Studies*, III., *The Acts*, London, 1908. Other problems are discussed in: F. Schleiermacher, *Ueber die Schriften des Lukas*, Berlin, 1817, Eng. transl., London, 1825; M. Schneckenburger, *Ueber den Zweck der Apostelgeschichte*, Bern, 1841; J. R. Oertel, *Paulus in der Apostelgeschichte*, Halle, 1868 (on the historicity); W. Stewart, *The Plan of Luke's Gospel*, Glasgow, 1873; W. M. Sanday, *The Gospels in the Second Century*, chap. viii., London, 1876; W. K. Hobart, *The Medical Language of Luke*, ib. 1882; A. Klostermann, *Probleme in Aposteltexte*, Gotha, 1883; P. Ewald, *Das Hauptproblem der Evangelienfrage*, Leipsic, 1890; J. M. Stifler, *Introduction to the Study of Acts*, New York, 1892; W. M. Ramsay, *The Church in the Roman Empire*, New York, 1893; idem, *St. Paul the Traveller*, ib. 1896; M. Krenkel, *Josephus und Lukas*, Leipsic, 1894; J. Weiss, *Ueber die Absicht und den literarischen Charakter der Apostelgeschichte*, Marburg, 1897 (makes Acts an apologetic work addressed to the heathen world); *DB*, i. 25–35, iii. 162–173; *EB*, i. 37–57, ii. 1761–1898.

For the Gospel the best commentary in English is A. Plummer, Edinburgh, 1897, which contains a good list of the earlier literature. Other commentaries are: C. W. Stein, Halle, 1830; J. Ford, London, 1851; J. H. Scholten, *Het paulinisch evangelie*, Leyden, 1870; M. Vernet, Paris, 1870; H. Cowles, New York, 1881; W. H. Van Doren, 2 vols., ib. 1881; P. Schanz, Tübingen, 1883; T. Lindsay, 2 vols., Edinburgh, 1887; F. Godet, 3 vols., Neuchâtel, 1875, Eng. transl. of earlier edition, Edinburgh, 1875; C. Robinson, New York, 1889; H. D. M. Spence, in *Pulpit Commentary*, London, 1889; H. Burton, ib. 1890; F. W. Farrar, in *Cambridge Bible*, Cambridge, 1890; A. Maclaren, New York, 1894; J. C. Ryle, 2 vols., London, 1896; P. Girodon, Paris, 1908; J. M. S. Baljon, Utrecht, 1908.

Commentaries on the Acts are: F. Blass, Göttingen, 1895, and an edition of the text, Leipsic, 1897; F. Rendall, London, 1897 (the two works just mentioned are the best); P. J. Gloag, 2 vols., Edinburgh, 1870 (ultra-conservative); J. S. Howson, *Companions of St. Paul*, London, 1871; J. R. Lumby, in *Cambridge Bible*, Cambridge, 1879; H. B. Hackett, Philadelphia, 1882 (long regarded as the best); C. F. Nösgen, Leipsic, 1882; A. C. Hervey, in *Pulpit Commentary*, 2 vols., London, 1884; T. M. Lindsay, Edinburgh, 1885 (very helpful); D. Thomas, London, 1889; W. Arnot, *The Church in the House*, New York, 1891; G. T. Stokes, in *Expositor's Bible*, 2 vols., London, 1891; J. M. Stifler, ib. 1894; B. B. Loomis, *Studies in the Acts*, New York, 1896; J. Belser,

Beiträge zur Erklärung der Apostelgeschichte, Freiburg, 1897 (takes especial note of codex D); J. Knabenbauer, Paris, 1899 (in Latin); R. B. Rackham, London, 1901; W. Robertson, *Studies in the Acts*, Edinburgh, 1901; A. Schlatter, Stuttgart, 1902.

LUKE OF PRAGUE: Bohemian bishop; b. probably at Prague about 1460; d. at Jungbunzlau (30 m. n.e. of Prague) Dec. 11, 1528. He studied at the University of Prague (B.A. about 1480). In 1480 he joined the Moravian Brethren (see BOHEMIAN BRETHREN, II.) and soon became one of their leaders. In 1491 the Brethren sent him to the East to discover if there were not some body of Christians there with whom the Brethren might make an alliance. In 1497 he was sent on a similar errand to the Waldensians and he also had dealings with Luther (q.v.), which, however, came to naught. In 1500 he was elected bishop of the Brethren. He was a voluminous writer in the departments of apologetics, hymnology, exegesis, and catechetics, more than eighty different works being ascribed to him.

BIBLIOGRAPHY: Consult the literature under BOHEMIAN BRETHREN.

LULLUS OF MAINZ: German ecclesiastic; b. in England about 705; d. at the monastery of Hersfeld (32 m. s.e. of Cassel) Oct. 16, 786. The son of well-to-do people in England, he was educated at the monastery of Malmesbury and subsequently at Nhutscelle [a monastery in Southamptonshire] while Boniface was teaching there. After a pilgrimage to Rome he followed Boniface to Germany, where he was consecrated deacon about 745. His relations with Boniface were very intimate, and the latter employed him repeatedly on important missions. In his old age Boniface made Lullus his associate and consecrated him bishop (752), to become at his death his successor at Mainz, although the dignity of archbishop was not conferred till later. Lullus was a stanch defender of the rights of the episcopate and endeavored to maintain episcopal supervision over monasteries and convents. In this way he became implicated in a controversy with Sturm, also a disciple of Boniface, abbot of Fulda, who maintained the independence of the monasteries. Thus the two great tendencies, the episcopal and the monastic, which were united in Boniface, were segregated in his disciples. Lullus assumed the control of the monastery of Fulda, and it was probably owing to his influence that Sturm was banished in 763 by King Pippin. Two years later Sturm was pardoned and in 767 assumed again the direction of the monastery. Thereupon Lullus founded in 768 or 769 his own monastery of Hersfeld which developed into a rival to Fulda. Sturm died in 779. Probably in the same year Lullus was made archbishop in connection with the renewal of the metropolitan constitution by Charlemagne. His influence as archbishop can not be compared with that of Boniface, and his relations with Charlemagne were not always peaceful. Under Lullus Cologne severed its relations with Mainz and developed its own archbishopric. He always maintained his connection with his native country, maintained strict canonical discipline and had the confidence of the higher clergy. It is not improbable that Lullus founded also the monastery of Bleidenstadt. (A. HAUCK.)

BIBLIOGRAPHY: The *Epistolæ* of Lullus, ed. E. Dümmler, are in *MGH*, *Epist.*, iii (1891), 207 sqq., and also in P. Jaffé, *BRG*, vol. iii. The *Vita* by Lambert of Hersfeld, ed. Holder-Egger with preface, is in *MGH*, *Script.*, xv. 1 (1887), 132–148 (contains only chaps. i.–xxii., the other five chapters are in the *Opera* of Lambert issued by the same editor, pp. 307–340, Hanover, 1894). Consult: *ASM*, iii. 2, pp. 392–401; C. Will, *Regesten zur Geschichte der Mainzer Erzbischöfe*, i., pp. xiv., xv., 34–45, Innsbruck, 1877; F. Falk, in *Der Katholik*, ii (1879), 662–667; A. Göpfert, *Lullus der Nachfolger des Bonifacius im Mainzer Erzbisthum*, Leipsic, 1881; H. Hahn, *Bonifaz und Lul*, ib. 1883; Holder-Egger, in *NA*, ix. 285–320, xix. 509; Hauck, *KD*, vols. i.–ii.; Rettberg, *KD*, i. 573 sqq.

LULLY, RAYMOND.

Raymond Lully (Ramón Lull, *Raymundus Lullus*) was born on Majorca (Balearic Islands) c. 1232; d. at sea near Cabrera, another of the Balearic Islands, June 30, 1315. As poet, philosopher, theologian, missionary, and martyr, he was one of the most remarkable personages of the Middle Ages for a combination of the most varied mental qualities, for adventurous and many-sided activity, and for the influence which he exercised not only on his own countrymen and contemporaries but on distant generations. His importance in the history of theology is due to the fact that, like his contemporary and fellow Franciscan Roger Bacon, he followed the path pointed out by St. Francis, that leading to the knowledge of God by study of the life of his creatures, in the direction of a scientifically organized natural theology; and also to the manner in which his fiery propagandist zeal anticipated the work done by his countryman Ignatius of Loyola 250 years later.

I. Life: Singularly little, however, is known with certainty about his life. Outside of the scanty biographical indications found in his works, the best source is the life by an anonymous disciple written in 1312. He came of a rich and noble family, and lived until he was thirty at the court of King James of Aragon, where he was grand seneschal. This period of his life was careless and worldly; he spent his time in the pursuit of pleasure and knightly exercises, including the practise of poetry in the manner of the courtly troubadours of the time. Suddenly convinced of the vanity of earthly pleasures, he turned to heavenly things and resolved to devote his life to the cause of Christ. He distributed most of his property among the poor, made pilgrimages to Compostela and other shrines, and returned to his native island with the intention of missionary labors among the mainly Mohammedan population of that and the neighboring lands. He learned Arabic from a Moorish slave, who made an attempt on his life. About the same time, certainly before 1275, he met the aged Dominican scholar Raymond of Pennaforte (q.v.), to whom he unfolded his plan of seeking knowledge at the University of Paris, but was dissuaded. He then withdrew to a hermitage he made for himself on his property in Majorca, broke off intercourse with his family, and gave himself up to meditation and study. He seems to have entered the third order of St. Francis; at least he brought thirteen young Franciscans as the first students to the college opened at Miramar in Majorca (Nov., 1276) for the study of the Arabic and Chaldean tongues, the direction of which he undertook with the sanction of Pope John XXI. He was also occupied at this time with the composition of his ambitious *Ars magna*. About 1285 he thought the time had come to carry out his extensive missionary plans, and went to Rome to obtain the sanction of Honorius IV. for his project of erecting missionary institutes in all countries of Christendom. But Honorius was dead when he reached Rome, and Nicholas IV. seemed little inclined to favor his views. He went to Paris, where he is said to have lectured on his philosophic method (1287–89), then to Montpellier, where he continued his lectures and studies. After about two years there and one at Genoa, he set sail from the latter port in the autumn of 1291 to attempt a missionary campaign in Africa, landed at Bugia in Tunis, preached against Islam, and challenged the fanatical Mohammedan scholars to a public disputation. His words made some impression, and the king, feeling that the Mohammedan supremacy was threatened, condemned him to death, which was commuted to banishment by the intercession of a learned man. He remained in concealment on a ship in the harbor for some time, seeking an opportunity to penetrate once more into the country, but finally lost hope and returned to Italy. He spent about a year (1292–93) in Naples, completing his *Tabula generalis* and writing his *Disputatio quinque sapientum*. His hopes revived with the election of Pope Celestine V., whose pontificate, however, was too short to accomplish anything, while his successor Boniface VIII. had other things to think about. After a sojourn of two years in Rome, during which he composed his poem *Desconort* and his treatise *Arbor scientiæ*, he went back to Genoa (1296), and then, after a short visit in Majorca, to Paris (1298-99). About 1300 01 is the most probable date for his visit to the Levant in pursuance of his plans for the conversion of the Mohammedans. The years 1302–05, full of literary activity, were spent between Genoa, Majorca, Montpellier, and Paris. In 1305 or 1306 he made a second attempt on North Africa, this time with the special design of opposing the Averroists. He ventured to appear once more in Bugia, passing through many perils and spending six months in rigorous captivity, only to be banished once more. On the return journey he was shipwrecked near Pisa and lost all his possessions, including his books. He now went to Avignon to see the new pope, Clement V., but again met with discouragement, and lectured once more in Paris (1309–11). In the latter year he appeared at the Synod of Vienne and addressed the assembled bishops several times, urging the condemnation of Averroism, the union of the spiritual orders of knighthood into one, the conquest of the Holy Land, and especially the erection of missionary colleges and chairs for instruction in the oriental languages. The last proposal was the only one adopted; professorships of oriental languages were created at Avignon, Paris, Bologna, Oxford, and Salamanca. From Vienne he seems to have gone first to Majorca, then to have been in Paris and Montpellier again, and to have sailed in the winter of 1314 from Messina for his last African missionary journey. After a short stay in Tunis, he returned to Bugia, where he lay concealed for a time with Christian merchants. Presently, however, he emerged into public notice with fresh fiery attacks on Islam. The Mohammedan population rose against him, drove him out of the city with sticks and stones, and left him half dead on the shore, where he was picked up by two Christian ship captains, but died the next day on the way to Majorca.

The dominant thought of all his later life and literary remains is the idea of Christian missionary enterprise, of which, in the modern sense, he may almost be called the pioneer. To proclaim in the very home of Islam, in the speech of the oriental peoples, the Gospel of Christ; to provide a new and simple scientific method, adapted to all subjects and capacities, for meeting both non-Christian and heretical opponents of the truth; to set before Christian people in the vernacular and in popular form the ideal of the Christian life, the fervor of mystical love of God, and finally to seal this testimony by the sacrifice of his life—such was the purpose and the achievement of nearly fifty years of his life.

II. Works: Of several hundred works left by him only a comparatively small part is printed; many manuscripts are extant in Spanish, French, and German libraries. It may be sufficient here, without going into the minute classification sometimes attempted, to give some account of the more important divisions of his work.

1. Poetical. Among his fellow countrymen he is still considered primarily as a poet. His *Obras rimadas* (ed. Rosello, Palma, 1859) count among the most valuable products of the medieval national literature of Spain, belonging to the Catalan-Provençal branch. The best known is *El Desconort*, composed of sixty-nine twelve-line stanzas in the form of a dialogue between the author and a pious hermit who tries to console him for the discouragement described above.

2. Methodical. Outside of Spain, he owes his fame principally to his scientific method (*Ars magna* or *generalis* or *universalis*), which has been as much overestimated by a distinct Lullist school as underestimated by others. Its essence consists in the arrangement of a number of partly formal, partly material concepts, which are designated by letters, in various circles or other mathematical figures, in such a way that by turning the circles or drawing connecting lines all possible combinations may readily be perceived. The concepts are not explained or made the basis of deductions, but are merely schematized. Mechanical as the whole process seems, it met a want of the age; and there were not only a number of enthusiastic Lullists in the thirteenth century who lauded him under the title of *Doctor illuminatus*, but later philosophers and theologians such as Agrippa of Nettesheim, Giordano Bruno, and Kircher were much interested in his system, which seemed to offer an easy road to the coordination of all sciences in one master science. However external and arbitrary the method may appear, it must not be forgotten that the whole scholastic method, built up on the traditional logic and metaphysic of Aristotle, was open to the same objection. Ritter points to the technical logical symbols attributed to Raymond's countryman Petrus Hispanus (d. 1297) as a possible model for the system; but it is more probable that he followed Jewish or Arabic predecessors; he himself uses *Kabbala* as an alternative title for his art, explaining it as "the reception of truth divinely revealed."

3. Scientific.

He attempted to employ this method for the solution of various problems in the individual sciences—not merely logic and metaphysic, grammar and rhetoric, but also geometry and arithmetic, physics and chemistry, anthropology, medicine and surgery, law, politics, and even military tactics. As with Roger Bacon, a remarkable tendency is apparent to the use of observation of nature and the attainment of real encyclopedic knowledge, in contrast with scholastic formalism.

4. Polemical.

His apologetic and polemical works are directed against two classes of adversaries, the "ignorant" who reject learning as dangerous to faith, and the "unbelieving" who reject the Christian doctrine as opposed to reason. He attacks specially the Averroistic view, then rather widely prevalent even in Christian circles, of the "double truth," according to which a man might believe as a catholic Christian what according to the laws of reason was impossible. A whole series of treatises is directed against Averroes. He considers faith and knowledge as inseparably connected, and the attempt to separate them as the greatest hindrance to the spread of Christianity, so dangerous to souls that he invokes the aid of the secular power against it. Some of the treatises against Mohammedanism are written in Arabic, such as the *Alchindi* and *Teliph* written at Miramar between 1275 and 1285. Lully is particularly fond of the dialogue form, which he uses with some skill. Noteworthy among the dialogues intended to serve his missionary aims is the *Liber de quinque sapientibus*, in which a Roman, a Greek, a Nestorian, and a Jacobite Christian dispute among themselves and with a Saracen, and a special attempt is made by the first-named (*Latinus*, i.e., Raymond himself) to instruct the Saracen in the errors of Islam. Another of somewhat similar form is the *Liber de gentili et tribus sapientibus*, in which the interlocutors are a pagan philosopher, a Jew, a Christian, and a Saracen. The *Disputatio Raymundi Christiani et Hamar Sarraceni* (1307) is an extended defense of the doctrines of the Trinity and the incarnation against the Mohammedan philosopher Hamar.

5. Dogmatic.

Under the head of specifically dogmatic writings the first place is taken by expositions of the existence and nature of God, especially of the Trinity. Others deal with the creation and fall of man and the doctrine of the atonement, which Raymond conceives, in a way reminding the reader of Anselm, as an infinite satisfaction offered by the God-Man for an infinite debt. In matters of ecclesiastical discipline he had a keen insight into the conditions of his time, and hit some of their most salient defects, as in his expressions on the value of pilgrimages and the excessive veneration of crosses and pictures, or in his portraiture of the various classes and orders in Christendom, their duties, virtues, and vices.

6. Ascetic.

Of special interest are the works written for practical edification, such as the *Liber mille proverbiorum ad communem vitam*, the *Liber de orationibus*, and the *Liber de contemplationibus in Deum;* several treatises on devotion to the Virgin; and a number still unprinted, such as *De centum signis Dei, De septem sacramentis*, and *De septem donis Spiritus Sancti*. A remarkable work is the religious romance *Blanquerna* (or *Bracherna*), written in glorification of Christianity and especially of monasticism; the hero is conducted through a great variety of situations, being successively a married man, a hermit, a monk, an abbot, a bishop, archbishop, cardinal, and pope, finally laying aside the tiara to end his days according to the ideal of Franciscan sanctity in mystical union with God and seraphic love.

III. Posthumous Fortunes: The Roman Catholic Church long wavered between honoring Raymond as a saint or condemning him as a heretic. The Dominican Nicolaus Eymericus, inquisitor of Aragon in the fourteenth century, brought charges against his works before Gregory XI., who forbade the reading of some of them, and subsequently (1376) condemned a hundred propositions extracted from them, apparently as leading to a rationalistic rebellion against church authority. The authenticity of this bull was early contested by the adherents of Raymond, while the Dominicans supported the attack on him. Paul IV. placed the writings condemned by Gregory XI. on the Index (1559), but they were removed in 1563 at the Council of Trent on petition of the Spanish bishops. The controversy still went on; some works by Raymond's disciples, especially pertaining to alchemy, were prohibited, and Benedict XIV expressly affirmed the authenticity of the bull of Gregory XI. though without renewing the condemnation—and Salzinger's edition of the works of the "Doctor illuminatus et martyr Raymundus Lullus" appeared without objection in his pontificate. Pius IX. authorized in 1847 an office of "the blessed Raymundus Lullus" for Majorca and conceded to the Franciscan order in 1857 the annual celebration of his feast-day on Nov. 27; but under the same pope in 1857 the officially authorized *Analecta juris pontificii* (II., 2480) upheld the authenticity of the bull of Gregory XI. (O. Zöckler†.)

Bibliography: The only edition of the works of Lully approaching completeness is that by I. Salzinger, 10 vols., Mainz, 1721–48, of which vols. vii.–viii. did not appear. The earliest life, by an unnamed contemporary, which, however, only came down to the year 1312, is in Latin transl. in *ASB*, June, v. 661–668, and in *Histoire littéraire de la France*, xxix., pp. 4–46, with further discussion, pp. 47–386; it is also to be found in Salzinger's edition of the works, ut sup., vol. i. Later accounts are: N. Antonio, *Bibliotheca Hispanica vetus*, ii. 122–123, Madrid, 1788; H. Löw, *De vita Raymundi Lulli*, Halle, 1830; Delecluze, in *Revue des deux mondes*, Nov. 15, 1840 (an excellent account of the life); A. Helfferich, *Raymund Lull und die Anfänge der catalonischen Litteratur*, Berlin, 1858; W. Brambach, *Des Raymund Lulls Leben und Werke*, Carlsruhe, 1893; M. Andre, *Le Bienheureux R. Lulle*, Paris, 1900; S. M. Zwemer, *Raymund Lull, First Missionary to the Moslems*, New York, 1902; W. T. A. Barber, *Raymond Lull, the Illuminated Doctor*, London, 1903; G. F. Maclear, *Apostles of Mediæval Europe*, pp. 269–288, ib., 1908; Neander, *Christian Church*, iv. 61–71 et passim; *KL*, x. 747–753; *Encyclopædia Britannica*, xv. 63–64.

For consideration of his works consult: A. R. Pasqual, *Vindiciæ Lullianæ*, 4 vols., Avignon, 1778; X. Rousselot, *Études sur la philosophie dans le moyen âge*, iii. 76–141, Paris, 1842; K. Prantl, *Geschichte der Logik*, iii. 145–177, Leipsic, 1867; J. R. de Luanco, *Ramon Lull considerad como alquimista*, Barcelona, 1870; F. de P. Canalejas, *Las Doctrinas del Ramon Lull*, Madrid, 1872; J. B. Haureau, *Histoire de la scolastique*, vol. ii., Paris, 1880; F. H. Reusch, *Der Index der verbotenen Bücher*, i. 26–33, Bonn, 1883; O. Keicher, *Raymundus Lullus und seine Stellung zur arabischen Philosophie*, Münster, 1909.

LUMBER RIVER MISSION. See MISCELLANEOUS RELIGIOUS BODIES, 14.

LUNA, PEDRO DE. See BENEDICT XIII.

LUND, ARCHBISHOPRIC OF: A former metropolitan see in Denmark (now in Sweden), founded about the middle of the eleventh century, and raised to metropolitan dignity probably in 1103–04, replacing the former jurisdiction of the archbishops of Hamburg-Bremen. This transfer was not recognized by Innocent II. and was long contested by the Germans; it was confirmed, however, by Adrian IV., with the addition of the title of primate of Denmark and Sweden. The last Roman Catholic archbishop was imprisoned in 1536, to be released only on condition of withdrawing his opposition to the change of religion, and in 1537 the first Lutheran bishop took possession of the see. In 1660 it was transferred to Copenhagen.

BIBLIOGRAPHY: The occupants of the see are named, with their terms of office, in Gams, *Series episcoporum*, p. 330. Consult further: *Acta pontificum Danica 1316–1536*, Copenhagen, 1904; *KL*, viii. 295–300.

LUPUS, lū'pus, SERVATUS: French Benedictine; b. probably in the archdiocese of Sens c. 814; d. at Ferrières (23 m. s.w. of Sens) 862. He was a scion of a distinguished family and received his education in the monastery of Ferrières from Abbot Aldric, later archbishop of Sens. Dissatisfied with instruction there, however, he went to Fulda and studied under Rabanus Maurus, remaining there from 830 to 836 and forming close friendships not only with his teacher but also with other German scholars, especially with the famous Einhard, the author of the biography of Charlemagne. He returned to Ferrières in 836, but in the following year accompanied his abbot, Odo, to Germany. His activity as a teacher at Ferrières, of which traces are still extant in his pupils' notes of his lectures, quickly made him famous, and in 838 he enjoyed the favor of the Emperor Louis the Pious and the Empress Judith. In the civil wars which followed the death of the emperor, Lupus took the side of Charles the Bald, who made him abbot of Ferrières (842) in place of Odo, the latter having been a partizan of Lothair, the rival of Charles. In the troublous times which followed his appointment he proved his fidelity to his king, whom he accompanied on his unlucky expedition against Aquitaine. He was taken prisoner in the defeat of the Franks on June 14, 844, but returned to his monastery on July 5. The wars had brought the cloister into dire poverty and in 846 he was obliged to beg for money. Ascribing the misfortunes of Ferrières to Charles' alienation of the cell of St. Judocus, which he had enfeoffed to a temporal dignitary, Lupus finally succeeded in regaining it in the latter part of 848. In the following year he was sent by Charles on a mission to Rome, where for the first time he came into direct contact with the controversy between Gottschalk and Hincmar. Lupus, as a firm adherent of Augustine, favored the former, and both orally and in his *De tribus quæstionibus* opposed the doctrine of the freedom of the will and defended the teaching of election, although he did not press it to the extent of predestination to condemnation. On the other hand, he carefully refrained from any personal appeal on behalf of the imprisoned Gottschalk and remained on friendly terms with Hincmar. After 850 his letters contain scarcely any allusions to the controversy. He was now busily employed in restoring his cloister and was steadily increasing in favor with the king. He remained at the court for months both as a diplomat and scholar and as a boon companion. His fidelity to his monarch was unshaken even after the disasters of 858, when Charles lost his throne to Louis the German and retired to Burgundy. There he was followed by Lupus and Hincmar, but the excitement and the privations shattered the abbot's health and brought on a fatal illness.

The writings of Lupus, in addition to the work already noted, which is one of the best theological contributions of the time, include the *Vita Wigberti* and the *Vita Maximini*. The theory that he was the author of the pseudo-Isidorian Decretals is unsupported by evidence. On the other hand, he edited the canons of the Synod of Verneuil (843), which were directed primarily against the misuse of ecclesiastical property by princes. His most important writings were his letters, which are characterized by personal charm and at the same time form valuable historical documents, especially as he corresponded with almost all the important men of the period, including kings, popes, and ecclesiastics. (R. SCHMID.)

BIBLIOGRAPHY: The *Opera* of Lupus, including his *Epistolæ*, ed. E. Baluze, appeared at Paris, 1664, Antwerp, 1710, and in *MPL*, cxix. A very excellent issue of his *Epistolæ*, ed. Desdevizes du Dezert, appeared Paris, 1888. Consult: F. Sprotte, *Biographie des Abtes Servatus Lupus von Ferrières*, Regensburg, 1880; *Histoire littéraire de la France*, v. 255 sqq.; G. Phillips, *Vermischte Schriften*, i. 196 sqq., Vienna, 1856; B. Nicolas, *Études sur les lettres de Servat-Loup*, Paris, 1862; E. Ebert, *Allgemeine Geschichte der Litteratur des Mittelalters*, ii. 203–209, Leipsic, 1880; Giry, in *Études d'histoire du moyen âge dédiées à G. Monod*, Paris, 1896; Hauck, *KD*, ii. 609 sqq. et passim; *KL*, viii. 300–304.

LUTHARDT, lūt'hārt, CHRISTOPH ERNST: German Lutheran theologian; b. at Maroldsweisach

(55 m. n.n.w. of Nuremberg) Mar. 22, 1823; d. at Leipsic Sept. 21, 1902. He studied theology at Erlangen and Berlin (1841–45) and was teacher in the Munich gymnasium (1847–51). He was privat-docent at Erlangen (1851–54), extraordinary professor at Marburg (1854–56), and ordinary professor of systematic theology and New-Testament exegesis at Leipsic (1856–1902). He became constitutorial councilor (1865) and privy ecclesiastical councilor (1887). Luthardt was a voluminous writer of the Erlangen school of theologians, one of the attractions of the University of Leipsic, an eloquent preacher, and an ecclesiastical statesman.

Among his works may be mentioned: *Das johanneische Evangelium nach seiner Eigenthümlichkeit geschildert und erklärt* (2 vols., Nuremberg, 1852–53, Eng. transl. by C. R. Gregory, 3 vols., Edinburgh, 1865–78); *Die Lehre von den letzten Dingen* (Leipsic, 1861); *Die Lehre vom freien Willen und sein Verhältniss zur Gnade* (1863); *Apologetische Vorträge über die Grundwahrheiten des Christenthums* (1865; Eng. transl., *Apologetic Lectures on the Fundamental Truths of Christianity*, Edinburgh, 1865); *Compendium der Dogmatik* (1865); *Die Ethik Luthers in ihren Grundzügen* (1867); *Apologetische Vorträge über die Heilswahrheiten des Christenthums* (1867; Eng. transl., *Apologetic Lectures on the Saving Truths of Christianity*, Edinburgh, 1868); *Die Ethik Aristoteles im Unterschied von der Moral des Christenthums* (1869); *Vorträge über die Moral des Christenthums* (1873; Eng. transl., *Apologetic Lectures on the Moral Truths of Christianity*, Edinburgh, 1873); *Der johanneische Ursprung des vierten Evangeliums* (1874; Eng. transl. by C. R. Gregory, *St. John the Author of the Fourth Gospel*, Edinburgh, 1875); *Die modernen Weltanschauungen und ihre praktischen Konsequenzen* (1880); *Licht und Leben* (1885); *Die antike Ethik in ihrer geschichtlichen Entwickelung als Einleitung in die Geschichte der christlichen Moral dargestellt* (1887); *Geschichte der christlichen Ethik* (1888–93; Eng. transl., *History of Christian Ethics*, Edinburgh, 1889); *Die vier Evangelien* (1899); *Die christliche Glaubenslehre* (1898); and *Kompendium der theologischen Ethik* (1898). He was editor of the *Allgemeine evangelische lutheranische Kirchenzeitung*.

BIBLIOGRAPHY: J. Kunze, *Christoph Ernst Luthardt*, Leipsic, 1903; F. J. Winter, *Die Theologie des D. Luthardt*, ib., 1883.

LUTHER, MARTIN.

Early Life and Religious Training (§ 1).
Initial Changes of View (§ 2).
The Doctrine of Grace (§ 3).
The Ninety-five Theses (§ 4).
Denial of the Power of the Pope (§ 5).
Development of Views on Eucharist, Priesthood, Church, and Works (§ 6).
Appeal to the Laity for Reform (§ 7).
Doctrine of the Sacraments (§ 8).
At the Diet of Worms (§ 9).
In Hiding at the Wartburg (§ 10).
Opposition to Extreme Radicalism (§ 11).
Correspondence with Other Sectaries and Break with Erasmus (§ 12).
Polemics Against Carlstadt and Münster (§ 13).
Transformations in Liturgy and Church Government (§ 14).
Eucharistic Views and Controversies (§ 15).
The Diet of Augsburg and the Question of Civil Resistance (§ 16).
The Authority of Church Councils Denied (§ 17).
Attacks on Zwingli, and Recognition of the Bohemian Brethren (§ 18).
Luther as a Preacher and Exegete (§ 19).
Theory of Confession and the Law (§ 20).
Establishment of Consistories and the Marriage of Philip of Hesse (§ 21).
Renewed Eucharistic Controversies (§ 22).
The Death of Luther (§ 23).
Summary of Luther's Doctrinal Development (§ 24).
Theory of the Church and the World (§ 25).
The Style of Luther (§ 26).
The Personal Life of Luther (§ 27).
His Hymns (§ 28).

Martin Luther, the German Reformer, was born at Eisleben (23 m. w. of Halle) Nov. 10, 1483, and died there Feb. 18, 1546. His father, Hans, was a miner, formerly living at Möhra, while his mother, Margarete (*née* Ziegler), came from a family of the middle class. At the age of six months, Luther was taken by his parents to Mansfeld, and was there brought up in an atmosphere of strictness and probity.

1. Early Life and Religious Training.

His father's financial condition gradually improving, Luther was sent to the Latin school, first at Mansfeld, then at Magdeburg (probably to an institution conducted by Brethren of the Common Life) in 1497, and finally, in 1498, at Eisenach, where his mother had relatives. There, with other poor students, he was obliged to sing in the streets begging for bread, and there he gained the sympathy of Ursula, the wife of Kunz Cotta. From Eisenach he went, in 1501, to the University of Erfurt, where his principal teachers were the nominalists Trutvetter and Arnoldi, and where he was a friend of at least some of the young humanistic "poet" circle. He received his bachelor's degree in 1502 and the master's degree three years later; and was destined by his relatives for a legal career.

Brought up in the strict religious atmosphere of the Roman Catholic Church, but without any knowledge of the Bible, Luther was terrified by thoughts of the wrath of God, intensified by the sudden death of a friend. He resolved to become a monk, and on July 17, 1505, entered the Augustinian monastery at Erfurt, to the grief of his father, and without a clear comprehension of his act. In 1507 he was ordained to the priesthood, but his theological studies brought him no inward peace, and he eagerly followed the advice of an old master of studies in the monastery, who urged him to center his hopes in the article of the forgiveness of sins. He was also aided by the instruction of Johann von Staupitz, the vicar of the order, but the decisive change was brought about by his study of the Scriptures. In 1508, at the suggestion of Johann von Staupitz, the Elector Frederick appointed Luther professor of philosophy at Wittenberg, where he received the degree of *baccalaureus ad biblia* in the following year. He was then recalled for some unknown reason to Erfurt, but in 1511 (or possibly in 1510) went to Rome in the interests of his order. Returning to Wittenberg, he received the doctorate of theology on Oct. 18, 1512, and three years later was appointed Augustinian vicar for Meissen and Thuringia, being also active as a preacher both in his own monastery and in Wittenberg.

Even at this time his radical change of views had become evident. Turning from philosophy, he sought the kernel of the trust of salvation in the Bible, especially in the Epistle to the Romans and in the Psalms, which he interpreted entirely from the New Testament.

2. Initial Changes of View.

He next lectured on Galatians, Hebrews, Titus, and Judges, his lectures being partly published and partly preserved in manuscript. Of the Fathers, Augustine had the profoundest influence on him, though he grasped more deeply than his teacher the meaning of the faith which is the direct road to the righteousness of God. Among medieval teachers he was most impressed by Bernard of Clairvaux, while in 1516 he came under the influence of the mysticism of Tauler.

Although still devoted to the Roman Catholic Church, Luther had now reached essentially the conclusions which were to lead him to combat her claims. Resting salvation entirely on the grace of God, he held that all the good works of the natural man are sin, and that divine grace comes solely through the eternal election and predestination of God. Luther also held with Paul that man is purified by faith inwrought by the divine spirit and word of grace, and that the spirit of God then works inward righteousness in them that believe. Nevertheless, those who are thus regenerate still sin constantly and are without honor or merit, persisting only through pardoning grace and through faith before God. Like the mystics, Luther's concept of the plan of salvation is based on the relation of the individual to God and Christ in faith. Faith is identical with entire devotion, renunciation of all self-righteousness, and surrender of all self-will. Both faith and hope are directed only to Christ, who alone fulfilled the law and bore our sins; while man is justified solely by the imputation of God. While inward righteousness is included in justification, it follows the forgiveness of sins which forms a part of faith. From faith Luther also derives love, and the strength, impulse, and delight to do good. Christ, who dwells in man through faith, himself does all and conquers all; but the deeds of the just are not for his own righteousness, but for the service of God and man. All this grace is bestowed by the Word, in which dwells Christ, the bread of life; and this bread of life is given outwardly in preaching and the Eucharist, and inwardly by "God's own teaching." That the current ecclesiastical views were opposed to those which formed the center of his belief and life was still unknown to Luther. In contradistinction to the prevailing custom, he held that the bishops should regard preaching as their prime duty, and that sermons should be free from false legends and the opinions of men, nor should the subjects longer be restricted to character and works, but should be devoted especially to faith and justice. Nevertheless, Luther entertained no doubt of the authority of the visible Church, and obedience to her was to him identical with obedience to Christ. The sources for his views at this period are his lectures on the Psalms, Latin sermons beginning with 1515, a preface to Tauler's *Deutsche Theologie* (1516), a German exegesis of the seven penitential Psalms, theses in Bernhardis of Feldkirchen and Günther's *Disputation* (1516–1517), sermons on the Decalogue (Latin ed., 1518), and a German exegesis of the Lord's Prayer (1517), besides the letters of these years.

3. The Doctrine of Grace.

The sale of indulgences by Johann Tetzel near Wittenberg incited Luther to a polemic attitude, yet not, in his opinion, against the Church, but for her honor. He began by assailing the misuse of indulgences, while his dogmatic views concerning them gradually developed out of the cardinal principles of his belief. On Oct. 31, 1517, he nailed his ninety-five theses on the castle church at Wittenberg, though he had no intention of making a decisive attack nor did he wish them to be generally circulated. The content of the theses was in accord with his sermons: penance was repentance, not priestly confession and satisfaction; mortification of the flesh, implying punishment until entrance into the kingdom of heaven, must coexist with inward repentance; this punishment only is remitted by papal indulgence, which can not remove the actual guilt of the smallest sin, being able to grant remission only in virtue of the proclamation and confirmation of divine pardon; the merit of Christ and the saints work grace to the inner and death to the outer man without the cooperation of the pope; the true "treasure of the Church" is the Gospel of the grace of God, though God subjects those whom he forgives to the priests as his representatives. Luther accordingly restricted indulgences to the penalties and works prescribed by the Church, and herein he purposed to express the true intention of the pope, who could scarcely know how they were misused.

4. The Ninety-five Theses.

Luther's theses spread throughout Germany in two weeks, gaining an unanticipated notoriety. He was egged on still further by his opponents, Tetzel, Silvester Prierias (the papal "master of the palace," q.v.), Johann Eck (prochancellor of Ingolstadt and his chief adversary; q.v.), and Hoogstraten, to all of whom he replied individually, though his most important work on the questions involved in the controversy was his *Resolutiones disputationum de indulgentiarum virtute* (1518). Meanwhile he took part in an Augustinian convention at Heidelberg, where he presented theses on the slavery of man to sin and on divine grace. In the course of the controversy on indulgences the question arose of the absolute power of the pope, since the doctrine of the "treasure of the Church" was based on a bull of Clement VI. Luther saw himself branded as a heretic, and the pope, who had determined to suppress his views, summoned him to Rome. Yielding, however, to the unwillingness of the Elector Frederick to part with his theologian, the pope did not press the matter, and the cardinal legate Cajetan was deputed to receive Luther's submission at Augsburg (Oct., 1518). The latter, while professing his implicit obedience to the Church, boldly denied the absolute power of the pope, and appealed first "from the pope not well informed to the pope who should be better informed" and then (Nov. 28) to a general council. Luther now declared that the papacy formed no part of the original and immutable essence of the Church, and he even began to think that Antichrist ruled the Curia. He had already asserted at least the potential fallibility of a council representing the Church, and, denying the church doctrine of excommunication, he was led by his con-

5. Denial of the Power of the Pope.

cept of the way of salvation to the new tenet that the Church is the congregation of the faithful. Still wishing to remain on friendly terms with the elector, the pope made a last effort to reach a peaceable conclusion with Luther. A conference with the papal chamberlain K. von Miltitz at Altenburg in Jan., 1519, led Luther to agree to remain silent so long as his opponents should, to write a humble letter to the pope, and to prepare a work to testify his honor of the Roman Church. The letter was written, but was not sent, since it contained no retraction; while in a German treatise later prepared, Luther, while recognizing purgatory, indulgences, and the invocation of the saints, denied all effect of indulgences on purgatory. When, moreover, Eck challenged Luther's colleague Carlstadt to a disputation at Leipsic, Luther joined in the debate (June 27–July 16, 1519), denying the divine right of the papacy, and holding that the "power of the keys" had been given to the Church (i.e., to the congregation of the faithful), affirming besides that belief in the preeminence of the Roman Church was not essential to salvation and maintaining the validity of the Greek Church.

6. Development of Views on Eucharist, Priesthood, Church, and Works.

There was no longer hope of peace. His writings were now circulated most widely, reaching France, England, and Italy as early as 1519, and students thronged to Wittenberg to hear Luther, who had been joined by Melanchthon in 1518, and who now published his shorter commentary on Galatians and his *Operationes in Psalmos*, while at the same time he received deputations from Italy and from the Utraquists of Bohemia. These controversies necessarily led Luther to develop his doctrines further, and in his *Sermon von dem hochwürdigen Sakrament des Leichnams Christi* (1519) he set forth the significance of the Eucharist (see LORD'S SUPPER, II., 2, § 5, IV., 1, §§ 1–2), interpreting the transubstantiation of the bread as the transformation of the faithful into the spiritual body of Christ, i.e., into fellowship with Christ and the saints. The basal concept of the Eucharist, moreover, according to him, is the forgiveness of sins; and his entire theory is closely connected with his mystic view of the all-embracing participation in salvation shared by the believer with Christ and his Church. At the same time, he advocated that a council be called to restore communion in both kinds, and denied the doctrine of seven sacraments (letter of Dec. 18, 1519). He likewise stripped the priesthood of all meaning other than the general priesthood taught in the Bible, and cast doubt on the entire doctrine of purgatory. The Lutheran concept of the Church (see CHURCH, THE CHRISTIAN, IV., § 2), wholly based on immediate relation to the Christ who gives himself in preaching and the sacraments, was already developed in his *Von dem Papsttum zu Rom*, a reply to the attack of the Franciscan Alveld at Leipsic (June, 1520); while in his *Sermon von guten Werken*, delivered in the spring of 1520, he controverted the Roman Catholic doctrine of good works and works of supererogation, holding that the works of the believer are truly good in any secular calling ordered of God.

7. Appeal to the Laity for Reform.

From the time of his disputation at Leipsic, Luther came into relations with the humanists, particularly with Melanchthon, Reuchlin, Erasmus, and Crotus. The last was intimately associated with Ulrich von Hutten (q.v.), who in his turn influenced Franz von Sickingen (q.v.), so that, when it became doubtful whether it would be safe for Luther to remain in Saxony if the ban which threatened should be pronounced against him, both Franz von Sickingen and Silvester of Schauenburg invited him to their fortresses and their protection. Under these circumstances, complicated by the crisis then confronting the German nobles, Luther issued his *An den christlichen Adel deutscher Nation* (Aug., 1520), committing to the laity, as spiritual priests, the reformation required by God but declined by the pope and the clergy. The subjects proposed for amelioration were not points of doctrine, but ecclesiastical abuses: diminution of the number of cardinals and the demands of the papal court; the abolition of annats (see TAXATION, ECCLESIASTICAL); recognition of secular government; renunciation of claims to temporal power on the part of the pope; abolition of the interdict, abuses connected with the ban, harmful pilgrimages, the misdemeanors of the mendicant orders, many holidays which led only to disorder; the suppression of nunneries, beggary, and luxury; the reform of the universities; abrogation of the celibacy of the clergy; and reunion with the Bohemians; besides demanding a general reform of public morality and denying transubstantiation in favor of the doctrine of the true presence of the natural body of Christ in the natural bread.

8. Doctrine of the Sacraments.

The climax of Luther's doctrinal polemics was reached in his *De captivitate Babyloniaca*, especially in regard to the sacraments. As concerned the Eucharist, he denied transubstantiation, the sacrificial character of the mass, and the withholding of the cup. In regard to baptism, he taught that it brought justification only when conjoined with belief, but that it contained the foundation of salvation even for those who might later fall. As for penance, its essence consists in the words of promise given to belief. Only these three can be regarded as sacraments, in virtue of the promises attached to them; and strictly speaking baptism and the Eucharist alone are sacraments, as being a "sign divinely instituted." The sacrament of unction was discarded by Luther with his doubts of the authenticity of the Epistle of James. In like manner, the acme of Luther's doctrine of salvation and the Christian life was attained in his *Von der Freiheit eines Christenmenschen*. Here he required complete union with Christ by means of the Word through faith, entire freedom of the Christian as a priest and king set above all outward things, and perfect love of one's neighbor. These three works may be considered the chief writings of Luther on the Reformation. [For their English translation by Buckheim and Wace see below.]

In Oct., 1520, at the instance of Miltitz, Luther sent his *De libertate Christiani* to the pope, adding the significant phrase: "I submit to no laws of interpreting the word of God." Meanwhile it had been rumored in August that Eck had arrived at Meissen with a papal ban, which was actually pronounced there on Sept. 21. This last effort of Luther's for peace was followed on Dec. 12 by his burning of the bull, which was to take effect on the expiration of 120 days, and the papal decretals at Wittenberg, a proceeding defended in his *Warum des Papstes und seiner Jünger Bücher verbrannt sind* and his *Assertio omnium articulorum.* The execution of the ban, however, was prevented by the pope's relations with the elector and by the new emperor, who, in view of the papal attitude toward him and the feeling of the Diet, found it inadvisable to lend his aid to measures against the Reformer.

9. At the Diet of Worms.

The final judgment of the Roman Catholic Church had been pronounced on Luther in the ban, but the papal legate, Aleander, was obliged to acquiesce in the desire of the Diet to summon Luther under a safe-conduct to Worms. Luther quietly awaited the result, occupied with polemics against Emser and the Dominican Ambrosius Catharinus, and with work on a postilla. Entering Worms on Apr. 16, he was brought before the Diet on the following day and asked simply whether he acknowledged his writings, which were laid before him and read by title, and whether he retracted their contents or persisted in them, all debate on the truth of their statements being excluded by the emperor's agreement with Aleander. Luther requested a day for consideration, and on the evening of Apr. 18 replied to the question of Johann von Eck, the official of the elector of Treves, who asked whether he defended all his writings or would retract some, by distinguishing three divisions of them: those on faith and life, recognized as harmless and even useful by his opponents; against papal institutions and claims injurious to body and soul, of which he would retract none; and polemics against protagonists of that falsehood and tyranny, where again he would make no retraction of matter. His demand that he be refuted by arguments from the Bible was met by referring him to the decisions of the Church, particularly at the Council of Constance, on similar heresies. The debate which followed resulted in a stormy adjournment, though not before Luther had declared: "Unless I shall be convinced by the testimonies of the Scriptures or by clear reason, I neither can nor will make any retraction, since it is neither safe nor honorable to act against conscience; God help me! Amen!" (other versions vary slightly, having, "I can naught else! Here I stand! God help me!"; "Here I stand! I can naught else! God help me!"; and "God come to my help! Amen! Here I am!"). The archbishop of Treves still sought to change Luther's views, but in vain, since he persisted in the tenet, condemned by the Council, that "the Church universal is the number of the elect." On May 25 he was declared an outlaw, and, leaving Worms on the following day, he was seized, with his own connivance, by the Elector Frederick and taken to the Wartburg, where he remained in hiding under the name of Junker Georg.

10. In Hiding at the Wartburg.

With Luther's residence in the Wartburg began the constructive period of his career as a reformer; while at the same time the struggle was inaugurated against those who, claiming to proceed from the same Evangelical basis, were deemed by him to swing to the opposite extreme and to hinder, if not prevent, all constructive measures. In his "desert" or "Patmos" (as he called it in his letters) of the Wartburg, moreover, he began his translation of the Bible, of which the New Testament was printed in Sept., 1522 (see BIBLE VERSIONS, B, VII., § 3). Here, too, besides other pamphlets, he prepared the first portion of his German postilla and his *Von der Beichte*, in which he denied compulsory confession, although he admitted the wholesomeness of voluntary private confessions. He also wrote a polemic against Archbishop Albrecht, which forced him to desist from reopening the sale of indulgences; while in his attack on Jacobus Latomus (q.v.) he set forth his views on the relation of grace and the law, as well as on the nature of the grace communicated by Christ. Here he distinguished the objective grace of God to the sinner, who, believing, is justified by God because of the justice of Christ, from the saving grace dwelling within sinful man; while at the same time he emphasized the insufficiency of this "beginning of justification," as well as the persistence of sin after baptism and the sin still inherent in every good work.

11. Opposition to Extreme Radicalism.

Meanwhile some of the Saxon clergy, notably Bernhardi of Feldkirchen, had renounced the vow of celibacy, while others, including Melanchthon, had assailed the validity of monastic vows. Luther in his *De votis monasticis*, though more cautious, concurred, on the ground that the vows were generally taken "with the intention of salvation or seeking justification." With the approval of Luther in his *De abroganda missa privata*, but against the firm opposition of the prior, the Wittenberg Augustinians began changes in worship and did away with the mass. Their violence and intolerance, however, were displeasing to Luther, and early in December he spent a few days among them. Returning to the Wartburg, he wrote his *Eine treue Vermahnung vor Aufruhr und Empörung;* but in Wittenberg Carlstadt and the ex-Augustinian Zwilling demanded the abolition of the private mass, communion in both kinds, the removal of pictures from churches, and the abrogation of the magistracy [i.e., the noninterference of the civil ruler in ecclesiastical matters.—A. H. N.]. About Christmas Anabaptists from Zwickau added to the anarchy. Thoroughly opposed to such radical views and fearful of their results, Luther entered Wittenberg Mar. 7, and the Zwickau prophets left the city. The canon of the mass, giving it its sacrificial character, was now omitted, but the cup was at first given only to those of the laity who desired it. Since confession had been abolished, communicants were now required to declare their intention, and to seek consolation, under acknowledgment of their faith and longing for grace, in Christian confession. This new form of service was set forth by Luther in his *Formula missæ et communionis* (1523), and in 1524 the first Wittenberg hymnal appeared with four of his own hymns. Since, however, his writings were forbidden by Duke George of Saxony, Luther declared, in his *Ueber die weltliche Gewalt, wie weit man ihr Gehorsam schuldig sei*, that the civil authority could enact no laws for the soul, herein denying to a Roman Catholic government what he permitted an Evangelical.

Luther watchfully followed the effect of his preaching, commending the town of Leisnig when it introduced a new agenda in 1523, honoring the memory of two martyrs in Brussels (1523) and of Henry of Zütphen (1524, see MOLLER), and counseling those of like views in Riga, Reval, Dorpat, and elsewhere. At this same period he entered into correspondence with the Bohemian Brethren, and in this connection he wrote the *Vom Anbeten des Sakraments* (1523), in which he maintained the natural presence and actual physical participation. In 1522 Luther wrote the Bohemian Estates to continue firm against the pope, and in the following year he sent, through the Bohemian Gallus Cahera, his *De instituendis ministris* to Prague, defending the right of a congregation to provide themselves with new ministers of the Word if their clergy withheld the Gospel from them, his argument being based upon the theory of the universal priesthood. Soon, however, the Bohemians, headed by Cahera himself, sought reconciliation with the pope, and Luther is not known to have had further dealings with them. At the same time he answered the criticisms of Henry VIII. of England on his *De captivitate Babylonica* in his *Contra Henricum regem*, a work of characteristic coarseness, for which he apologized in 1525 humbly, but in vain. The most important event in Luther's war with the Roman Catholic Church at this period was his break with Erasmus, who was followed by a large body of humanists in his return to the Church. Erasmus had long been offended by Luther's harshness and coarseness, while the latter charged his former friend with timidity and lack of recognition of the grace of God, which alone brought salvation. In 1524 Erasmus published his *De libero arbitrio*, to which Luther replied in 1525 with his *De servo arbitrio*. Here he identified foreknowledge and predestination, and distinguished between God as preached and God himself. Though the lost perish through the unconditioned will of God, this is right because God wills it, the reason, into which man may not inquire, being one of the mysteries of the divine majesty. Free will can, accordingly, be predicated only of God, never of man, whose duty it is simply to trust to the Word, accepting the inconceivable as such until the Son of Man shall reveal it.

12. Correspondence with Other Sectaries, and Break with Erasmus.

It now became Luther's task to war on the spirit of false freedom which had arisen within his own followers. Carlstadt denied the presence of the body of Christ in the Eucharist, while, on the basis of the Old Testament, he forbade pictures, but permitted polygamy. Others, likewise claiming the Old Testament as their support, sought to secure the restoration of the Mosaic year of jubilee; while Münster, the leader of the Zwickau fanatics, who had become pastor at Allstedt in 1523, plotted a revolution to establish a kingdom of his "saints." Luther attacked the entire tendency in his *Wider die himmlischen Propheten* (1525), in which he declared that the Mosaic law had been abrogated by Christ, who was the end of the law, the only law of the Christian being that written in the heart of every man. Nevertheless, the revolution, really caused by the political, economic, and social conditions of the peasants, was still threatening, especially as they hoped to find in the new religious movement a confirmation of the rights and freedom which they claimed. Luther therefore sought to show them that Christian freedom might coexist with earthly bondage, and that they must not attack their temporal superiors. On the other hand, he sharply criticized the princes and nobles; but when the Peasants' War actually broke out, he urged its merciless suppression, though he advocated clemency after the victory had been won (cf. his *Ermahnung zum Frieden; Wider die mörderischen Rotten; Sendbrief von dem harten Büchlein;* etc.). During this time of conflict, Luther, learning of attempts on his life and already feeling himself old and near death, married the ex-nun Katharina von Bora (q.v.) on June 13, 1525. His motive was not love, but defiance of his opponents, and at the same time to testify his esteem of the married state and to obey his father's desire for posterity.

13. Polemics against Carlstadt and Münster.

Luther marked a further step in his revision of the liturgy by his *Deutsche Messe* in 1526, making provision for week-day services and for catechetical instruction. He strongly objected, however, to making a new law of the forms, and urged the retention of other good liturgies. The gradual transformation of the administration of baptism was accomplished in the *Taufbüchlein* (1523, 1527); and in May, 1525, the first Evangelical ordination took place at Wittenberg. Luther had long since rejected the Roman Catholic sacrament of ordination, and had replaced it by a simple calling to the service of preaching and the administration of the sacraments. The laying-on of hands with prayer in a solemn congregational service was considered a fitting human rite. Conditions now seemed to Luther to require the introduction of a higher official authority. As early as 1525 he had complained of the state of affairs, and he held that the secular authorities should take part in the administration of the Church, as in making appointments to ecclesiastical office and in directing visitations. Nevertheless, the discharge of these functions did not appertain to the secular authorities as such, and Luther would gladly have vested them in an Evangelical episcopate, had he known of any persons

14. Transformations in Liturgy and Church Government.

suited for that office. He even declared in 1542 that the Evangelical princes themselves "must be necessity-bishops," and even went so far as to meditate (letter of Mar. 29, 1527) a "congregation of Christians" with full ecclesiastical powers, but determined to be guided by the course of events and to wait until parishes and schools were provided with the proper persons. Since, however, the result of the Saxon visitation gave no encouragement to this project, it was deemed far more important first to win non-Christians to the faith through the Gospel, preserving the external form of the Church as it was at the beginning of the Reformation. The visitation accordingly took place in 1527–29, Luther writing the preface to Melanchthon's *Unterricht der Visitatoren an die Pfarrherrn*, and himself acting as a visitor in one of the districts after Oct., 1528, while, as a result of his observations, he wrote both his catechisms in 1529. At the same time he took the keenest interest in education, conferring with Georg Spalatin (q.v.) in 1524 on plans for a school system, and declared that it was the duty of the civil authorities to provide schools and to see that parents sent their children to them. He also advocated the establishment of elementary schools for the instruction of girls.

15. Eucharistic Views and Controversies.

In the mean time the nature of the Eucharist had become a theme on which Luther found himself obliged to state his doctrines both fully and polemically. Rejecting transubstantiation, he nevertheless maintained the actual presence of the body of Christ, while Zwingli, Leo Jud, and Œcolampadius, on the other hand, rejected this doctrine, interpreting the "is" of the words of institution as "signifies." Luther was sorely disturbed by this doctrine, which he regarded as closely akin to the teachings of Carlstadt and the "fanatics" in general. In the controversy which ensued, Luther replied to Œcolampadius in the preface to the *Syngramma Suevicum*, and also set forth his views in his *Sermon von den Sakramenten Wider die Schwärmgeister* and *Dass diese Worte noch feststehen* (spring, 1527), while he sought to give a final and most thorough statement in his *Vom Abendmahl Christi Bekenntnis* (1528). In view of the perils to Protestantism in the measures of the Diet of Speyer (q.v.) in 1529 and the coalition of the emperor with France and the pope, the Landgrave Philip desired a union of all the adherents of the Reformation, but Luther declared himself opposed to any alliance which might aid heresy. He accepted, however, the landgrave's invitation to a conference at Marburg (Oct. 1–3, 1529; see MARBURG, CONFERENCE OF) to settle the matters in controversy, and there opposed Œcolampadius, while Melanchthon was the antagonist of Zwingli. Although he found an unexpected harmony in other respects, no agreement could be reached regarding the Eucharist; and he therefore refused to call them brethren, even while he wished them peace and love. [It was Luther's conviction that God had blinded Zwingli's eyes so that he could not see the true doctrine of the Lord's Supper. He denounced Zwingli and his followers at this time as "fanatics," "patricides," "matricides," "fratricides," "devils," "knaves," "heretics," "rioters," "hypocrites," and the like. A. H. N.] The princes themselves then made subscription to the Schwabach Articles, upheld by Luther, a condition of alliance with them. Luther's reason for his Eucharistic doctrine was not a mere literal interpretation of the words of institution, but rather thankfulness for such an individual sealing and giving of the forgiveness won by the death of this body in the administering of the very same body, doubts as to the possibility of such a presence being silenced by remembering the absolute unity of the divine with the human in Christ. While Christ's presence is "repletive" (filling all places at once), his omnipresence in the Eucharist is especially "definitive" (unbound by space). On the other hand, Luther taught with equal clearness that participation in itself is of no avail without faith. [He insisted that the impious and even beasts in partaking of the consecrated elements partake of the body and blood of Christ, but the unworthy partake unto damnation. A. H. N.] While, moreover, he combated the view that the Eucharist is a mere memorial, he fully recognized the commemorative element in it. As regards the effect of the Sacrament on the faithful, he laid special stress on the words "given for you," and hence on the atonement and forgiveness through the death of Christ.

16. The Diet of Augsburg and the Question of Civil Resistance.

Under the same perilous conditions which had made desirable an alliance of all adherents of the Reformation, the estates convened with the emperor at Augsburg in 1530, when the relation of the empire to Protestantism was definitely to be determined. Luther, despised by emperor and empire, remained at Coburg, but the confession there presented by Melanchthon was essentially based upon his labors. The latter, while refraining from an authoritative attitude, was little pleased by the smooth and cautious procedure of Melanchthon, and saw no chance of harmony of doctrine except in abolishment of the papacy, although he hoped for official toleration of both religions in the empire. While the recess of the diet gave the Protestants only a short time to make their submission, the emperor, urged on by threatened war with the Turks and by the Schmalkald League of the Protestant princes and cities, made further attempts to secure harmony, which led to the Religious Peace of Nuremberg in 1532 (q.v.), to last until a general council should be called to make a final decision. Since the Diet of Speyer (1529) the question had become vital whether, in case the emperor refused peace, the princes were justified in, or even bound to, armed resistance. Until now Luther had held that even wrongful acts of the emperor in no way released his subjects from obedience, and had been unfavorable to offensive and defensive alliances between Evangelical princes, preserving this attitude even in regard to the Schmalkald League. His position was somewhat modified, however, by the opinions of the jurists that in cases of public and notorious injustice the existing imperial laws ("the emperor himself in his laws") warranted such resistance. Accepting this, he nevertheless referred judgment on the present conditions to the jurists, and not to the theologians. In his *Warnung an die lieben Deutschen* (1531), nevertheless, he openly advocated resistance in a righteous cause, while in letters written in 1539 he went back still further to the general requirements of natural law.

The pope declaring himself ready to call a council, peaceable negotiations were renewed with the Roman Catholic Church, and in Nov., 1535, the papal nuncio Vergerius conferred with Luther in Wittenberg. While Luther had no faith in the pope's sincerity, he agreed to attend the council, wherever it might be held, although it was convened expressly for the extirpation of Lutheran heresy. At the instance of the elector, he prepared articles for the council in which he bitterly attacked Roman Catholic dogmas and the Roman Catholic Church, and termed the pope antichrist. The diet at Schmalkald (Feb., 1537) declined to take part in the council, and in 1539 Luther developed his views on councils in general in his *Von den Concilien und Kirchen*. Here he declared that not only could no reformation be hoped for from the pope and a papal council, but even the early councils and Fathers could not be regarded as the source for a reform. The entire system of Christian belief was to be derived, not from the Fathers and the councils, but from the Bible, the one task even of the four chief councils being simply and solely the defense of clear fundamental doctrines of the Scriptures. He therefore denied the right of any council which, he declared, should include laymen, to posit new articles of belief, to command new good works, or to require ceremonies; and he restricted their functions to juristic pronouncement of judgment according to the Bible in cases of peril to the faith. In this same treatise he reiterated his view that the Church consists solely of the congregation of the faithful, and is recognizable by the use of the means of grace and the power of the keys, as well as by prayer, the bearing of the cross, and uprightness of life, in that her members are sanctified by the Holy Spirit.

17. The Authority of Church Councils Denied.

In the mean time, efforts had been made to unite the Protestants upon the doctrine of the Eucharist, and Butzer (q.v.) had conferred with Luther on the matter at Coburg as early as 1530. Luther himself could yield nothing, for he could not see why, if his opponents really acknowledged the true presence of the body of Christ, they would not grant external participation in the case of the unworthy. He accordingly expressed the utmost disapproval of Zwingli and warned against any acceptance of his teaching. Since, however, he found the other Southern Germans unexpectedly yielding, he reached a formal agreement with them at Wittenberg in 1536, wherein they renounced Zwingli's teachings and recognized the true presence. On the other hand, since he did not, evidently through some uncertainty regarding the question, demand recognition of the reception of the elements by the actually "impious," he left a loophole for Butzer's opinion that only Christians who, even though unworthy, believed the words of institution, received, but not those who "mocked at all and believed naught." In 1537 he wrote a friendly letter to the burgomaster of Basel and to the Swiss cities, who could not, however, be won over, and in the following year he informed Bullinger that since the Marburg conference he had considered Zwingli personally an "excellent man." Luther's desire for all possible union with those of kindred views was shown still more clearly by his recognition of the Bohemian Brethren (q.v., II.). In 1533 and again five years later he had written the prefaces to the apology and confession which they had presented to the Margrave George of Brandenburg and King Ferdinand, even though in their new apology their theory of justification and of the Eucharist was not in agreement with his own.

18. Attacks on Zwingli, and Recognition of the Bohemian Brethren.

However much Luther took part in visitations and the like, his chief activity within his Church consisted not so much in external organization as in preaching, exegesis, spiritual counsel, and the preparation of treatises on the truths of salvation. As a preacher he now labored at the city church together with his friend Bugenhagen, and also visited the sick and performed other duties of private pastoral care. During the years following his return from the Wartburg, he delivered exegetical sermons on I and II Peter and Jude (1522–24), as well as on Genesis and Exodus (1523–27), besides preaching on the pericopes. In 1524–25 he had lectured on Deuteronomy, and in 1524–26 he delivered lectures on the minor prophets, Ecclesiastes, and Isaiah. In 1526 he published his exegeses of Jonah and Habakkuk, and that of Zechariah in the following year. Among his other lectures the most important were those on Galatians (1531–35; the chief presentation of his doctrine of salvation) and on Genesis (1536–45); of his sermons the most noteworthy, besides those on the pericopes, were delivered on Matthew and John. His postilla, the second half not edited by himself, was completed in 1527; while the sermons which Luther, prevented by ill health from delivering publicly, preached to his children and household in 1532 formed the basis of his *Hauspostille*. The translation of the Bible was completed in 1534, although he made emendations until 1545.

19. Luther as a Preacher and Exegete.

Within his own church questions repeatedly arose which led Luther to more explicit statements on weighty points of doctrine. While he had rejected Roman Catholic auricular confession, he laid great stress on Evangelical private confession, not because of any power of the confessor, but because of the words of promise with which forgiveness is declared, provided that the penitent is filled with faith. Although the words of forgiveness should be proclaimed in every sermon, he held private confession conducive to the ascertainment of the penitent's spiritual state; but declaration of forgiveness could be withheld only in case of manifest un-

20. Theory of Confession and the Law.

belief and impenitence. In 1533, and again in 1536, Luther approved the retention of public general absolution together with private confession at Nuremberg, and even drew up a formula for such absolution. Nevertheless, holding that absolution was not conditioned by priestly judgment (though it was an objective and effectual conferring of forgiveness), he later declared that it might be conferred by one layman on another in virtue of the "power of the keys." On the other hand, in 1538 he stated that those capable of instructing themselves need not make a formal confession before receiving the Eucharist. In 1537 a controversy broke out with Johann Agricola on the nature of the law (see AGRICOLA, JOHANN; and ANTINOMIANISM). Sharply opposed by Luther in theses of 1537-38 and the *Wider die Antinomer* (1539), Agricola held that the Mosaic law had been abrogated, and that repentance should be preached only on the basis of the Gospel (the word of grace in Christ), not because of the law. Luther, on the contrary, maintained that the word of salvation could not awaken faith in the sinful heart unless it had first been broken by the law and its resultant terrors of conscience. This is, indeed, not true repentance, but is a preparation for it; and stress was also laid by Luther on the fact that wherever in the New Testament sin, wrath, and judgment are revealed, the law, and not the Gospel, prevails.

21. Establishment of Consistories and the Marriage of Philip of Hesse.

The most important part in Church organization yet in store for Luther was the establishment of consistories. These were especially needed for the regulation of marriage. Luther, proceeding on his theory of the relation of the secular to the Mosaic law, and regarding marriage as a secular, though holy estate, relegated it to the State; and held that the clergy were concerned with it in so far as, from its very nature, it led to questions of conscience more than any other secular state (see MARRIAGE, I., § 6, II. 2, § 5). The first consistory was established at Wittenberg in 1539 with Luther's approval. The chief importance of the consistory for the organization and life of the Church, however, came from the fact that the duty entrusted to it was discipline. This, it was thought, would lead to the introduction of the public ban, with its civic consequences, but when opposition was raised in Wittenberg in 1539 on the matter, Luther set forth very clearly the ban he would be willing to establish—one based on Matt. xviii. 15 sqq. There is no record, however, that such a plan, so eminently in accord with the Evangelical concept of the Church, was anywhere carried out; nor had Luther himself much hope of the consistories' actual disciplinary powers. The end of Luther's life was now approaching, and he had already received warning in a sharp attack of calculus at Schmalkald in 1537. Beneath his external bravery, he felt himself aging, and while full of gratitude for the grace of the Gospel, he felt the world an alien to it in precept and practise, and looked forward to a time of distress and judgment for the Church. He was pained most of all by the attitude of the masses and of the nobility toward the Gospel, illustrated by the marital relations of Philip of Hesse. The latter, though married, was enamored of a girl of the nobility, and asserted that he was compelled by most urgent reasons of conscience to search for another wife. He conceived the idea of a double marriage, and as early as 1526 asked Luther's opinion on it, renewing his inquiries most urgently through Butzer after 1539. Though Luther held that monogamy was the original institution of God, he nevertheless granted the possibility of cases in which a dispensation was admissible, even among Christians, especially as such a double marriage was preferable to an illegal divorce. This dispensation, however, could be given only as confessional advice, and could not alter the law, which recognized only a single wife; and it must, therefore, remain absolutely secret to avoid scandal. While sharply admonishing Philip of his sins and his duty, Luther and Melanchthon granted that his was a case for a dispensation, and the wedding took place on Mar. 3, 1540. Luther insisted that the affair be kept secret, and that the new wife be represented to the emperor as a mistress, knowing that he could not justify his attitude to the world, though he thought he might to God.

22. Renewed Eucharistic Controversies.

The impossibility of peaceable relations with the Roman Catholic Church was felt still more keenly by Luther in these last years when new attempts at reconciliation were made. He was obliged to deliberate with his colleagues in Jan., 1540, with only the passing hope that the emperor might convene a national council, for there was no remedy unless doctrines contrary to Scripture should first be openly renounced. He accordingly felt little sympathy with the Regensburg Conference in 1541 (q.v.), headed by Melanchthon and Cruciger, condemning their attitude toward both the Eucharist and the doctrine of justification. When, however, the emperor sought to reopen negotiations in 1545, Luther subscribed to Melanchthon's proposal to reunite with the episcopate, but his diatribes against the Roman Catholic Church were even more bitter than ever, as is amply illustrated by his *Wider das Papsttum zu Rom*, which appeared in the year before his death. He gave a very real ground of offense, moreover, to his opponents, when in 1542, despite the protests of the chapter, he made Nikolaus von Amsdorf bishop of Nuremberg, an act which he defended in his *Exempel einen rechten christlichen Bischof zu weihen*, wherein he sought to establish from the Evangelical point of view the validity of the consecration which he had performed. With the growth of dissension between the two Saxon houses after 1542 came a break in the unity of the Evangelicals. Luther had never ceased warning against the doctrines of Zwingli, and he now found his suspicions increased by the fact that Zurich refused to give up these tenets. He formally renounced fellowship with the preachers of Zurich, but deemed that the heresy had entered Germany through the Cologne scheme of reformation drawn up by Butzer and Melanchthon, who made reception of the Eucharist simply a heavenly work and a matter of faith. Aroused to fresh elucidations, finally, by Schwenckfeld (q.v.), he published, toward the end of 1544, his *Kurze Bekenntnis des Sacraments*, containing no new doctrinal development, but savage criticisms of those who disagreed with him, renewed in the following year in his attacks on the theologians of Louvain, where he declared "the Zwinglians and all blasphemers of the Sacrament" to be heretics and cut off from the Christian Church. He had likewise protested against the Eucharistic doctrine of the Bohemian Brethren in 1541, being suspicious of their views, but in the following year he received Augusta in friendly fashion in Wittenberg and gave him the hand of fellowship for his coreligionists. A still more striking proof of his recognition of unity of spirit despite difference of opinion is seen in his attitude toward Melanchthon, against whose synergistic passages in the later editions of his *Loci* Luther could never be persuaded to polemize. As early as 1537 Melanchthon was charged with Zwinglian views on the Eucharist, but Luther, though finding much suspicious in his writings, nevertheless desired "to share his heart with him." He also gave high tribute to the *Loci* and the entire theological activity of his colleague in the preface to the first volume of his Latin works (1545); but Melanchthon is said to have foretold in his illness (1537) that after his death there would be no peace among the theologians associated with himself.

23. The Death of Luther.

More and more pronounced became Luther's conviction that bitter trials were to come on Germany, whether from the Turks or from internecine strife. While the whole world seemed to him to be in the state it had been in before the flood or the Babylonian exile or the destruction of Jerusalem, he was especially shocked by the immorality in Wittenberg, so that he threatened in 1545 that he would never revisit it. But he felt his death approaching. In 1544 he declined to prepare a church discipline on the plea of old age and exhaustion, and when, in 1545, he completed his lectures on Genesis, he expressed his longing to die. On Jan. 23, 1546, he went from Wittenberg to Eisleben to settle a mining dispute between the counts of Mansfeld, and was successful. But amid his preoccupations his health had been neglected; a fontanel which he had long had in his thigh had cicatrized; and he had caught a severe cold on his journey. On the evening of Feb. 17 he felt a heavy pressure on his chest, and on the following morning he died, still declaring his adherence to the faith he had preached. His corpse was solemnly buried in the castle church at Wittenberg, where it was rediscovered on the morning of Sunday, Feb. 14, 1892, by two men who had taken part in the restoration of the church ordered by William I., thus disposing of the story that during the Schmalkald War the corpse had been exhumed and buried in a neighboring field.

Surveying the entire course of Luther's life and activity, and especially the development of his theories and teachings, their important and positive content is seen clearly formulated when he entered upon his struggle in 1517; while their logical results, particularly as opposed to the Roman Catholic Church and the papal claims, were fully evolved at the time of his return from the Wartburg. The Peasants' War, often termed the great incentive to his subsequent career, was really important only as accentuating his boldness in the practical task of reformation. After that, modifications in his doctrine entered only in so far as he emphasized one or another factor, as circumstances required.

24. Summary of Luther's Doctrinal Development.

His basal principle was ever "justification by faith in Christ," as set forth especially by Paul and experienced by himself. Curious as it may seem, however, he never understood the Pauline doctrine of justification as a declaration or assumption of righteousness in man; but he took it rather as an inward process, in the believer, of becoming justified. The first step is the forgiveness of sins by grace alone, after which justification and the imputation of righteousness proceed from the Spirit which is given to those thus forgiven. It is clear, moreover, from his controversy with Agricola, that from the first Luther held that the rousing of conscience by the mandatory and punitive word of God was a necessary preliminary to belief. A further characteristic of his views on the divine influence on faith and the divine part in those who were justified through faith was the realism with which he asserted the actual and full presence of God in the Holy Ghost. In regard to God, he held that he could never be known from human speculation or from a merely natural revelation, but that man may rise to him from his perfect self-manifestation in Christ, even while refraining, in trusting faith, from penetrating into what is here concealed. In his concept of the historic Christ, it is noteworthy that he insisted on the most intimate identification of the divine and human, instead of contenting himself with a mere coexistence of the two natures.

25. Theory of the Church and the World.

Luther's doctrine of the Church, or congregation, of Christ and the means of grace conferred by it, was of the highest importance in his activity as a reformer. This was, in his opinion, the congregation of the faithful, who become sanctified by the means of grace and must exercise them continually in the name of God. As regards the moral status of the Christian in this world, proceeding from faith and the Holy Ghost, Luther held that he already shared in heavenly blessings and was exalted above the world, serving God and himself in the temporal ordinances and estates ordered of God, and partaking thankfully of the earthly blessings vouchsafed him. While he took a warm interest in the problems of secular, civil, and social life, he was a reformer here only in so far as he urged that they be considered according to the importance God had given them and with the proper attitude of mind. If, finally, the inquiry be made whence Luther gained the entire basis of his belief and doctrine, the answer must be that he ever defended the supreme authority of the Bible against the claims of the Roman Catholic Church. This faith is also based on the inner witness which the spirit of God bears to the believer in the right use of the

Scriptures, not merely as regards its authority, but also its content, so that he considered himself permitted to distinguish the higher character and value of individual books included in the Bible, and to make a further distinction between statements referring to divine revelation and those alluding to secular affairs.

26. The Style of Luther.

The style of Luther was naturally strong, simple, and clear; and, despite its depth and keenness, it was as free from excess of feeling of fantasy as from dialectic subtlety. But, as he himself said, he must always storm and fight. His basal concept of salvation ever occupied the foreground and center of his writings, even in the exegesis of texts where, strictly speaking, it scarcely applied. On the other hand, historical and linguistic accuracy were frequently imperfectly considered. The force of allegorical interpretation he denied, yet employed it as suggestive and enlightening. In his sermons, next to the requirement that Christ should be their theme, he sought intelligibility for the masses. They lack technical form, but combine exegesis and application, strictly following the thought and exhortation to be developed, though lacking an explicit theme.

27. The Personal Life of Luther.

In conformity with his recognition of the free activity of man in secular affairs, Luther possessed a lively interest in such matters. He highly valued all noble arts and sciences, and he had a keen appreciation of proverbs, fables, and the like. His married life was marked by nothing noteworthy, yet it was true, happy, and patient, as is clearly shown by his letters and table-talk. He was generous with his modest wealth, and among his friends his conversation was brisk and natural, though frequently far too coarse for a refined ear. In food he was extremely temperate, despite his corpulency, and he often fasted for several days in succession. His inner life was one of humble struggle, amid the strongest temptations (due, in great part, to the bodily infirmities from which he frequently suffered), for his own salvation, a phenomenon the more remarkable in view of his unswerving conviction of the truth of his belief and his resolute attitude in the face of external dangers. He never formed far-reaching plans for the future, feeling that speedy death awaited him. Throughout his life he seemed to feel the impulse of a higher power constraining him to toil and fight; and in his obedience to the call he knew neither fear nor anxiety, but calmly awaited the results from on high. (JULIUS KÖSTLIN †.)

28. His Hymns.

For his contributions to hymnody Martin Luther deserves and receives the thanks of the Christian world. His activity in this direction included not only the writing of hymns but the compilation of hymnals, of which nine are on record, issued between 1524 and 1545, five of these being revisions of his *Geistliche Lieder*. These hymnals always contained a large proportion of his own compositions; thus the *Etlich christlich Lider Lobgesang uñ Psalm* (Wittenberg, 1524) contained eight hymns of which four were his own, the *Geistliche Lieder* of Wittenberg, 1543, contained sixty-one hymns, of which he composed thirty-five. His own hymns were not all new, some of them being translations from the Latin, some revisions of pre-Reformation German hymns, while others were versions of Psalms or paraphrases of other portions of Scripture. In all Luther left thirty-eight hymns, the most celebrated of which is his "battle hymn," *Ein' feste Burg ist unser Gott*, known best to those who worship in English in the version of Rev. F. H. Hedge, "A mighty fortress is our God," though the translation by Thomas Carlyle, "A safe stronghold our God is still," is justly celebrated on account of its strength and fidelity to the original. Other hymns which have passed into common use in English are *Nun freut euch lieben Christengemein*, many times translated, but known best in the version of Mrs. Charles, "Dear Christian people, all rejoice"; and *Gelobet seist du Jesu Christ*, anonymously translated into "All praise to thee, eternal Lord." More than all other work of Luther, excepting only his translation of the Bible, his hymns have become the household possession of the German people, while his great battle hymn was sung by Gustavus Adolphus before the battles of Leipsic and Lützen, and by others in times almost as critical.

BIBLIOGRAPHY: The Works of Luther have appeared in seven major editions: (1) the Wittenberg edition, 19 vols., 1539–58; (2) the Jena edition, 13 vols., 1555–58, with two supplementary vols., Eisleben, 1564–65; (3) the Altenburg edition, 10 vols., 1661–64, with additional volume, Halle, 1702; (4) the Leipsic edition, 23 vols., 1729–40; (5) the Walch edition, 24 vols., Halle, 1740–1753; (6) the Erlangen-Frankfort edition, 103 vols., 1826–1898; and the Weimar edition, begun in 1883, of which 35 vols. are issued (1909). Notes upon these editions will be found in Hauck-Herzog, *RE*, xi. 720–721. A standard edition of the *Works* in English is in course of publication by the Lutherans in All Lands Co., Minneapolis, 1904 sqq. The principal collection of the "Letters" is still that of W. M. L. de Wette and J. K. Seidemann, 6 vols., Berlin, 1825–56, though other collections are by C. A. H. Burkhardt, Leipsic, 1866; and D. C. A. Hase, Leipsic, 1878 (cf. G. Veesenmeyer, *Litterargeschichte der Briefsammlungen . von Dr. Martin Luther*, Berlin, 1821). Note should be made also of *The Letters of Martin Luther. Selected and translated by Margaret A. Currie*, London and New York, 1908. The best edition of the *Tischreden*, "Table Talk," is by C. E. Förstemann and H. E. Bindseil, 4 vols., Berlin, 1844–48. Of the Table Talk there are many English translations, e.g., by Capt. Henrie Bell, London, 1652, republished, Lewes, 1818; by W. Hazlitt, London, 1846; and the Centenary edition, ib. 1883. The Latin form, *Colloquia*, ed. H. E. Bindseil, 3 vols., Detmar, 1863–66. Luther's *Dichtungen* were collected by K. Gödeke, Leipsic, 1883; and by G. Schleusner, Wittenberg, 1892. Among selections from his works mention may be made of E. Lessing's *Martin Luther als deutscher Klassiker*, Hamburg, 1908 (from Luther's poetical and popular prose writings); and R. Neubauer's *Martin Luther; eine Auswahl aus seinen Schriften in alter Schriftform*, Halle, 1908.

Lives written by contemporaries were: by Melanchthon, in his preface to vol. ii. of the Latin Works in the Wittenberg edition; by M. Ratzeberger, first published by C. G. Neudecker, Jena, 1850; and by J. Mathesius, ed. G. Lösche in the *Werke* of Mathesius, vol. iii., Prague, 1898. The best life, made from the sources, is J. Köstlin, *Martin Luther, sein Leben und seine Schriften*, 5th ed. by G. Kawerau, 2 vols., Berlin, 1903; and the most accessible for English readers is H. E. Jacobs, *Martin Luther, the Hero of the Reformation*, New York, 1898. Among the immense literature upon Luther the following lives may be mentioned: M. Michelet, 2 vols., Paris, 1835, Eng. transl., London, 1846; M. Meurer, 3 vols., Dresden, 1843–1846; K. Jürgens, 3 vols., Leipsic, 1846–47; H. Lang, Berlin, 1870; G. A. Hoff, Paris, 1873; K. J. Ledderhose,

Carlsruhe, 1883; W. Rein, Leipsic, 1883, Eng. transl., New York, 1883; G. G. Evers, 6 vols., Mainz, 1883–91; T. Kolde, Gotha, 1884–93; J. von Dorneth, 3 vols., Hanover, 1886–89; P. Bayne, 2 vols., London, 1887; C. Müller, Munich, 1892; G. Freitag, Leipsic, 1901; M. Rade, 3 vols., Tübingen, 1901; G. Buchwald, Leipsic, 1902; T. M. Lindsay, *Luther and the German Reformation*, New York, 1903; A. Hausrath, 2 vols., Berlin, 1905; J. Dose, Düsseldorf, 1906; J. L. Nuelsen, Cincinnati, 1906; and P. Bess, *Unsere religiösen Erzieher*, vol. ii., Leipsic, 1908.

On various phases of Luther's activity consult: W. Beste, *Dr. Martin Luthers Glaubenslehre*, Halle, 1845; E. Jonas, *Die Kanzelberedsamkeit Luthers*, Berlin, 1852; C. H. Weisse, *Die Christologie Luthers*, Leipsic, 1852; T. Harnack, *Luthers Theologie*, 2 vols., Erlangen, 1862–1886; C. E. Luthardt, *Die Ethik Luthers*, Leipsic, 1875; H. C. Mönckeberg, *Luthers Lehre von der Kirche*, Hamburg, 1876; H. Hering, *Die Mystik Luthers*, Leipsic, 1879; S. Lommatzsch, *Luthers Lehre*, Berlin, 1879; Danneil, *Luthers Geistliche Lieder*, Frankfort, 1883; F. W. F. Kattenbusch, *Luthers Stellung zu den ökumenischen Symbolen*, Giessen, 1883; T. Kolde, *Luther auf dem Reichstag zu Worms*, Halle, 1883; A. W. Dieckhoff, *Luthers Lehre in ihrer ersten Gestalt*, Rostock, 1887; G. Schleusner, *Luther als Dichter*, Wittenberg, 1892; E. Wagner, *Luther als Pädagog*, Langensalza, 1892; E. Schäfer, *Luther als Kirchenhistoriker*, Gütersloh, 1897; P. Frotscher, *Luther und die Bauern*, Leipsic, 1899; J. Köstlin, *Luthers Theologie*, 2 vols., Stuttgart, 1901. For his share in Philip of Hesse's bigamous marriage, see W. W. Rockwell, *Die Doppelehe des landgrafen Philipp von Hessen*, Marburg, 1903, and literature under PHILIP OF HESSE. In English the best book on Luther's hymns is *The Hymns of Martin Luther set to their Original Melodies, with an English Version*, ed. L. W. Bacon and N. H. Allen, New York, 1883 (contains Luther's four prefaces to his hymn-books and versions of all the hymns; cf. Julian, *Hymnology*, pp. 703–704 and references there to other pages where the hymns are annotated). On Luther as a translator of the Bible see BIBLE VERSIONS, B, VII., § 3. For further discussions consult the works on the church history of the period, especially Schaff, *Christian Church*, vol. vi (where a good list of sources is given), and, in general, the literature under REFORMATION. A valuable review of recent Luther-literature is in *Theologische Rundschau*, Oct. and Dec., 1906.

LUTHERANS.

I. State Churches in Europe: The Lutheran Church in Europe is the oldest and probably the largest of the Evangelical denominations which sprang from the Reformation of the sixteenth century. It was named after the great leader, first, in derision, by Roman Catholics, then by the followers of Luther, though he protested against a sectarian use of his name. Its usual title is "Evangelical Lutheran Church." In Prussia and other countries of Germany where the union between Lutherans and Reformed has been introduced (since 1817), the name "Lutheran" has been abandoned as a church title for "Evangelical" or "Evangelical United." This Church has its home in Germany, where it outnumbers all other Protestant denominations, and in Scandinavia (Denmark, Sweden, Norway), where it is the established or national Church. It extends to the Baltic provinces of Russia, and follows the German emigration and the German language to other countries, especially to the United States, where it is now one of the strongest denominations (see below, III.). The total membership, including all branches, is estimated at about sixty millions. Its history may be divided into five periods: (1) The pentecostal or formative period of the Reformation, from the promulgation of Luther's ninety-five theses in 1517 to the publication of the "Book of Concord" in 1580. (2) The period of polemical orthodoxy, in which the doctrinal system of the church was scholastically defined and analyzed in opposition to Romanism, Calvinism, and the milder and more liberal Melanchthonian type of Lutheranism (as represented by Calixtus), 1580–1689. (3) The period of Pietism (Spener, d. 1705; and Francke, d. 1727), or a revival of practical piety in conflict with dead orthodoxy, from 1689 (when Francke began his *Collegia philobiblica* in Halle) to the middle of the eighteenth century. The Pietistic movement is analogous to the Methodist revival in the Church of England, but kept within the limits of the Lutheran state churches and did not result in secession. (4) The period of rationalism, which gradually invaded the universities, pulpits, and highest judicatories, and effected a complete revolution in theology and church life to such an extent that the few Moravian communities were for some time almost the only places of refuge for genuine piety in Germany. (5) The period of revival of Evangelical theology and religion at the third centennial celebration of the Reformation, and the publication of Claus Harm's ninety-five theses against the rationalistic apostasy (1817). In the same year Prussia took the lead in the union movement which brought the Lutheran and Reformed confessions under one system of government, but called forth the "Old Lutheran" reaction and secession (see UNION, ECCLESIASTICAL). Since then there has been a constant conflict between Evangelical and rationalistic tendencies in the Lutheran and the United Evangelical Churches of Germany.

1. Name and History.

The Lutheran Church acknowledges the three ecumenical creeds (the Apostles', the Nicene, and the Athanasian), which it holds in common with other orthodox churches, and, besides, six specific confessions which separate it from other churches.

2. Creed and Theology. These are: (1) The Augsburg Confession (see AUGSBURG CONFESSION AND ITS APOLOGY), drawn up by Melanchthon and presented to the Augsburg Diet in 1530, afterward altered by the author in the tenth article, on the Lord's Supper, 1540. This is the fundamental and most widely accepted confession of this church; some branches accept no other as binding. (2) The Apology of the Augsburg Confession, also by Melanchthon (1530). (3) and (4) Two catechisms of Luther (1529), a Larger and a Smaller (see CATECHISMS; LUTHER'S TWO CATECHISMS); the latter, for children and catechumens, is, next to Luther's German Version of the Bible (see BIBLE VERSIONS, B, VII., § 3), his most useful and best-known work. (5) The Schmalkald Articles (q.v.) by Luther (1529; strongly antipapal). (6) The Formula of Concord (q.v.), prepared by six Lutheran divines for the settlement of the Melanchthonian or synergistic controversy (see SYNERGISM), the Crypto-Calvinistic controversy (see PHILIPPISTS), and other doctrinal disputes which agitated the Lutheran Church after the death of Luther and Melanchthon. These nine symbolical books, including the three ecumenical creeds, were officially published by order of Elector Augustus of Saxony, in Latin and German, under the title *Concordia* (Leipsic and Dresden, 1580; best editions, outside the *editio princeps*, by J. G. Walch, Jena, 1750, and J. F. Müller, 6th ed., 1886; best Eng. transl. by H. E. Jacobs, *The Book of Concord*, Philadelphia, 1893).

Two tendencies have always been in evidence in the Lutheran Church in its relation to the Reformed or Calvinistic Churches—one rigid and exclusive, which is represented by the Formula of Concord, the Lutheran scholastics of the seventeenth century, and the "New Lutheran" school

3. Relation to the Reformed Church. in Germany; the other moderate and conciliatory, represented by the altered Augsburg Confession of 1540, by Melanchthon in his later period after the death of Luther, Calixtus, John Arndt, Spener, Francke, Mosheim, the Swabian Lutherans, and those moderate Lutheran divines who sympathize with the Union and regard the differences between the two confessions as unessential and insufficient to justify separation and exclusion from communion at the Lord's table. The Lutheran Church is, next to the Church of England, the most conservative of the Protestant denominations, and retains many usages and ceremonies of the Middle Ages which the more radical zeal of Zwingli, Calvin, and Knox threw overboard as unscriptural corruptions. The strict Lutheran creed differs from the Reformed or Calvinistic in four points (as detailed in the semi-symbolical Saxon Visitation Articles of 1592), viz.: (1) Baptismal regeneration, and the ordinary necessity of baptism for salvation. (2) The real presence of Christ's body and blood "in, with, and under" the bread and wine during the sacramental fruition, usually called by English writers Consubstantiation (q.v.), in distinction from the Roman Catholic Transubstantiation (q.v.); but the term is not used in the Lutheran symbols and is rejected by the Lutheran divines, as well as the term "Impanation" (q.v.). Body and blood are not mixed with nor locally included in, but sacramentally and mysteriously united with, the elements. (3) The *Communicatio Idiomatum* (q.v.) in the doctrine of Christ's person, whereby the attributes of the divine nature are attributed to his human nature, so that Ubiquity (q.v.), or conditional omnipresence, is ascribed to the body of Christ, enabling it to be really and truly, though not locally and carnally, present wherever the communion is celebrated. (4) The universal vocation of all men to salvation, with the possibility of a total and final fall from grace; yet the Formula of Concord teaches at the same time (with Luther, *De servo arbitrio*) the total depravity and slavery of the human will, and an unconditional predestination of the elect to everlasting life. It is therefore a great mistake to identify the Lutheran system with the later Arminian theory. Melanchthon's synergism may be said to have anticipated Arminianism, but it was condemned by the Formula of Concord.

The foundation of the ritual of the Lutheran Church was laid in Luther's work *Von ordenung gottes dienst ynn der gemeyne* (Wittenberg, 1523), and his Latin and German missals (1523, 1526). It was his intention to retain all that was good in

4. Ritual and Worship. the service of the Roman Catholic Church, while discarding all unevangelical doctrines and practises. Thus, in his Latin and German litanies, which were in use in 1529 at Wittenberg, he made certain corrections and additions. The Lutheran Church uses a liturgy. The first complete form, or Agenda, was that of the Duchy of Prussia, 1525 (see AGENDA for a history of Lutheran liturgy). There is no authoritative form for the whole Church. A movement was set on foot in 1817 by Frederick William III. of Prussia to introduce a uniform Agenda, but it created intense excitement and caused the Old-Lutheran secession (see below, II.). The various states of Germany have their own forms, which differ, however, only in minor particulars. Luther introduced the use of the vernacular into the public services, restored preaching to its proper place, and insisted upon the participation of the congregation in the services, declaring "common prayer exceedingly useful and healthful." He rejected auricular confession as practised and required in the Roman Catholic Church, but advocated private and voluntary confession. This practise has been mostly given up. The rite of exorcism, which the Reformed Churches abandoned, was retained and recommended by Luther and Melanchthon. Hesshusius, in 1583, was the first to propose its omission, and it has since fallen into disuse in the Lutheran Church. The popular use of hymns was introduced by Luther, who was himself an enthusiastic singer, and by his own hymns became the father of German hymnody (see HYMNOLOGY, VI., § 1; LUTHER, § 28). Congregational singing continues to form one of the principal features in the public services. The great festivals of the Church, such as Christmas, Easter, Pentecost, the Days of the Twelve Apostles, are observed with religious services, and the Reformation is commemorated on Oct. 31. Pictures are admitted into the churches.

5. Government. The doctrinal development of the Lutheran Church was matured much earlier than its organization and polity. Luther was not an organizer. The necessity of organization, however, was deeply felt; and in 1529 a visitation of the churches of Saxony was prosecuted, and superintendents were appointed for the oversight of the congregations and schools. The Order of Discipline of the Church in Saxony became the model for other books of discipline. The priesthood of all believers is a fundamental doctrine, and the parity of the clergy is recognized. In Sweden, when the whole country passed over to the Lutheran communion, the Roman Catholic bishops and archbishops retained their titles. The validity of the Swedish orders, from the standpoint of the Church of England, is a matter of dispute. The Danish Church likewise retains the title "bishop," but no claim is made to apostolic succession. The first bishops under the new Danish régime were called superintendents (1536), and were consecrated by Bugenhagen. In Germany, church government is executed by consistories (composed of ministers and laymen) and superintendents. These officers are appointed by the government, examine candidates for the ministry, appoint and remove pastors, fix salaries, and perform other duties. In Germany, as in Denmark and Sweden, the Lutheran Church is under the governmental patronage of the various states; the support of the congregations and the construction of church edifices are provided for out of the national revenues. The supreme consistory of Prussia since 1852 has been composed in part of Lutheran and in part of Reformed members. PHILIP SCHAFF†.

[For further information regarding the Lutheran Church in Germany the reader is referred to the biographies of the German Reformers, to the articles on the separate states of the German Empire (Anhalt, Baden, Bavaria, Brunswick, Alsace-Lorraine, Hesse, Mecklenburg-Schwerin, Mecklenburg-Strelitz, Oldenburg, Prussia, Saxe-Altenburg, Saxe-Coburg-Gotha, Saxe-Meiningen, Saxe-Weimar-Eisenach, Saxony, and Württemberg); see also DENMARK; GERMANY; NORWAY; and SWEDEN. Such articles as AGENDA; AUGSBURG CONFESSION AND ITS APOLOGY; CHURCH GOVERNMENT; FORMULA OF CONCORD; PHILIPPISTS; PROTESTANTISM; and UNION, ECCLESIASTICAL will be found abounding in information in regard to origins, development, doctrine, polity, and the like.]

II. **Separate Lutherans.—1. In Prussia:** The Lutheran free churches in Germany do not recognize the position of the secular ruler as supreme head of the Church, and have organized independent congregations without the aid of the State. Originating primarily in hostility to the introduction of the Union (q.v.) between the Lutheran and Reformed Churches, they do not, however, reject the State Church altogether.

1. Scheibel at Breslau. The oldest and largest free church in Germany is the Evangelical Lutheran Church in Prussia, also known as Old Lutherans. It originated from the opposition to the Union, which was introduced into Prussia in 1817 and gradually carried through by 1830 (see I., § 1, above). Johann Gottfried Scheibel, assistant preacher at St. Elisabeth's in Breslau, was the leader of the opposition. He attacked the Union in his writings, from the pulpit, and at synods, and pleaded in vain to be permitted to explain to the king his scruples of conscience in a personal interview. Refusing to sign a statement of the Breslau clergy which recommended the amalgamation of the Lutherans and Reformed into one church, Scheibel was suspended from office for fourteen days. Several hundred members of Scheibel's congregation appeared before Scheibel, declaring that they would remain faithful to the Church of their fathers. The new congregation regarded itself as the continuation of the Lutheran Church hitherto legally acknowledged in Prussia, and asked the king to grant them a constitution. The authorities, however, saw in the new congregation only revolutionaries and dissenters, and their petitions long remained unanswered. Since Scheibel was strictly forbidden to officiate, the members of his congregation received the sacraments from Berger in Hermannsdorf, two miles from Breslau, who still used the old Lutheran agenda. When this too was forbidden, the heads of the families themselves baptized their children, and the Lord's Supper was distributed by lay elders, because of a total lack of Lutheran clergymen. In a ministerial order, dated June 13, 1831, Scheibel was required to use the new agenda, and the formation of a special Lutheran church was refused.

Meanwhile Baron von Kottwitz had pleaded for the Lutherans before the king in Berlin. The king tried to remove their scruples against the agenda by the concession of the Lutheran formula of distribution, but he refused the formation of a dissenting church on the ground that with it the purity of the Lutheran Church within the Union was openly denied. In 1832, after being deposed from his offices in the church and the university, Scheibel left Breslau and settled in Dresden that he might advance the cause of the Lutheran Church by writing, unhindered by Prussian censorship. The former members of his congregation held meetings conducted by laymen, or turned to the few pastors in Silesia who had not yet adopted the new agenda.

2. Movement Elsewhere before 1840. In the neighborhood of Züllichau, Juliusburg, and Strehlen the Separate Lutheran movement began, without special interference by the clergy, in lay circles holding services and prayer-meetings. On Apr. 4, 1834, three pastors, four theological candidates, and thirty-nine laymen united in a synod at Breslau and solemnly protested against the violation of the rights granted to the Lutheran Church in Prussia. A petition sent

VII.—6

by them to the authorities in Berlin was flatly refused, and the cabinet orders of Mar. 9 and 10, 1834, in which the State had prepared for the struggle, were now executed. The first was directed against "conventicles," and the second against the "unauthorized administration of spiritual official acts"; while the third referred to the obligation of all Evangelical parents to send their children to Evangelical schools. The church services of the Lutherans were suppressed, the official acts of their clergy were declared invalid, and no child was permitted to leave school before he had been confirmed by a clergyman of the Evangelical State Church. These and other oppressive measures only spread the movement. In 1835 another synod was formed at Breslau, but all clergymen participating in it were imprisoned. Some congregations even found themselves compelled to emigrate; a part of them went to Australia under the leadership of their pastors Kavel and Fritzsche and formed the nucleus of the Lutheran Church of Australia; others followed Grabau to North America where they entered the Buffalo Synod (see below, III., 5, § 2). The king was deeply grieved at the outcome of his measures, yet he could not make up his mind to annul them and grant the Lutheran congregations their right of existence.

It was only after Frederick William IV. had ascended the throne in 1840 that conditions became more favorable for the Old Lutherans. One of the new ruler's first measures was to release the imprisoned Lutheran ministers, and at the request of the government, after some preliminary negotiations, the Lutherans presented a memorial on the conditions under which the Evangelical Lutheran Church was to be acknowledged as legal by the Prussian State. Before an answer had arrived, however, the first public Old-Lutheran General Synod met on Sept. 15, 1841. It established a comprehensive church order which is still in force in all essentials. The government of all churches was entrusted to a board of clergy and laity. A General Synod, meeting every four years, was to form the supreme court of appeal, to which the ecclesiastical board was also responsible. In 1841 the first attempt was made at a synodical constitution of the Lutheran Church upon German soil, and this organization found a certain measure of recognition by the State in the so-called general concession of July 23, 1845. The dissenting congregations were freed from taxes payable to the State Church, and the official acts of their clergy were recognized by the State, but their places of worship were not recognized as churches. In a special concession of Aug. 7, 1847, the board in Breslau was also officially recognized, and twenty-one congregations in the provinces of Silesia, Brandenburg, Pomerania, Prussia, Posen, and Saxony were granted corporate rights. At the meeting of the General Synod in 1860 the total number of 18,644 members in 1845 had increased to 55,017 in sixty-two parochial districts, with sixty-three ministers, thirty-four Lutheran schools, and forty-four teachers.

3. Accession of Frederick William IV.

At the same synod a discord arose which shook the Lutheran Church in Prussia to its depths and led to a fatal schism, the question concerning the importance of church government. Several ministers were not willing to recognize church government as an organic part of the Church. The General Synod of 1860 did not fully decide the question, but referred it to a committee for further investigation. Diedrich, the schismatic Old-Lutheran pastor at Jabel, with his congregation soon renounced the supervision of the ecclesiastical board. A conference in Berlin in Oct., 1861, tried in vain to remove the difficulties in the doctrine of church government. A number of preachers sided with Diedrich and accused the ecclesiastical board of false doctrine. The rupture became irremediable when, on July 21, 1864, these preachers under the leadership of Diedrich organized a special body, the Immanuel Synod (see below). In a "Public declaration concerning the disputed doctrines of the Church, the church government and the church orders," issued in 1864, the ecclesiastical board stated that the external institutional side of the Church could not be separated from its essence and conception, although the church government with regard to its special formation is based upon human right. In recent times the Lutheran Church, subject to the ecclesiastical board in Breslau, has recovered from the shock of the schism caused by the separation of the Immanuel Synod. In 1883 there was established a theological seminary. The Church possesses also its own institution for deaconesses, a pension fund for old pastors, for the widows of pastors, and 140 churches. It numbers about 51,600 members in sixty-four parishes with seventy-five ministers. The Evangelical Lutheran Immanuel Synod was formed in 1864 at Magdeburg, by Ehlers, Diedrich, and other preachers in consequence of the disputes on church government that had arisen within the Evangelical Lutheran Church in Prussia. Its leading idea is that the pastors as the sole incumbents of the spiritual office are bound to care for the church orders, and that the laity can freely take part in synods, with no restriction in number; the synod has properly no power of discipline over the ministers. The general concession of the State did not apply to the congregations of the Immanuel Synod, because they no longer were under the board of dissenting Lutherans recognized by the special concession of 1847. Consequently they had no corporate rights, and the official acts of their pastors had no validity before the State, but the civil law of 1874 removed the latter disability. The synod numbers about 5,300 persons, with thirteen ministers.

4. Schism of 1860.

2. Elsewhere: The Independent Evangelical Lutheran Church in the Hessian lands originated in the opposition of the strictly Lutheran clergy to the new united church constitution introduced into the grand duchy of Hesse-Darmstadt Jan. 6, 1874. It is true, the Union had been practically introduced into several parts of the country since 1822, but the pastors of a stricter confessional tendency had united since 1851 for the defense of their old rights. A synodical constitution pub-

1. Churches in Hesse.

lished in 1870 tried to unite all congregations without regard to confession. Seven protesting Lutheran ministers were deposed from office (June 25, 1875). Consequently they separated from the State Church and formed five congregations. In 1877 they formed a synod. In 1878 their number was augmented by confederation with a part of the dissenters in Lower Hesse, the so-called "Homberg Konvent." In 1880 both church bodies united with the Lutheran Free Church in Hanover, and by a complete union of the congregations of Hesse-Darmstadt with those of the Homberg Konvent into one church body there came into being the Independent Evangelical Lutheran Church in the Hessian lands which comprises now about 1,800 members with ten parishes and ten ministers. An ordinance for the organization of a common consistory for the Lutheran, Reformed, and Union Churches in the district of Cassel on June 13, 1868, called forth the protest of many clergymen. When it was actually established in 1873, forty-two Reformed preachers of Lower Hesse under the leadership of Vilmar and Hoffmann as well as one Lutheran preacher in Upper Hesse refused to be subject to the new consistory, and adhered to the old Hessian church order. The consistory applied the severest measures, fines, suspension, and deposition, against the dissenting pastors. A few only being supported by their congregations, they were forced to emigrate. Those remaining in Hesse were forbidden to officiate until a decree of the higher tribunal in 1876 declared the deposed preachers laymen as regards the State, and thus protected their official acts against the decrees of punishment of the penal code. The Nonconformist Church of Lower Hesse comprises now about 2,400 members.

2. Churches in Hanover and Baden.

The Evangelical Lutheran Free Church in Hanover had its origin in the ecclesiastical struggles due to the annexation of the kingdom of Hanover and the danger of the Prussian Union. In spite of the promise of King William to maintain the existing order, the Union made great progress. Open hostilities broke out on the occasion of the change in the wording of the marriage contract in connection with the introduction of the civil status law in 1876. A number of clergymen under the leadership of Harms in Hermannsburg refused to use the new wording, seeing in it a denial of what he conceived to be the Christian nature of marriage. In 1878 they separated from the State Church and founded the Evangelical Lutheran Free Church in Hanover. It is governed on the basis of the Lüneburg church order by a board composed of clergy and laity. There are at present eight parishes with about 3,050 members and ten ministers. The Hermannsburg Free Church originated from a split in the Evangelical Lutheran Free Church in Hanover. It numbers about 2,800 members and two ministers. In the grand duchy of Baden the confessional union of the Lutheran and Reformed Churches was executed in 1821 without opposition. Only the awakening faith in Germany and the Lutheran movement instigated by Löhe in Bavaria created in Baden also a desire for a clear and unambiguous confession of the Lutheran Church. Karl Eichhorn, a preacher in Nussloch, started a Lutheran movement which led to the formation of small Lutheran congregations which soon petitioned for recognition, but were flatly refused. Eichhorn was repeatedly thrown into prison and finally banished into a remote place, but the Lutheran movement increased from year to year, and at last, in 1856, toleration was granted to its adherents. The congregations in Baden number about 1,330 members.

3. Churches in Saxony.

The Evangelical Lutheran Free Church in Saxony and other states has an entirely different character from that of the other Lutheran free churches in Germany. While the others were called forth more or less by the opposition against the Union, this Free Church was formed in the midst of Lutheran territories, partly even of such as had separated already from the State Church on account of the Union. It stands in connection with the Missouri Synod in America (see below, II., 5, § 1), and declares all other Lutheran state and free churches unfaithful to the confession. The occasion for the formation of the Free Church in Saxony was the change into a mere vow of the oath of religion binding upon Lutherans. Many protested against this change, seeing in it a concession to infidelity. On the recommendation of Walther, the leading spirit of the Missouri Synod, an association of strict Lutherans called Ruland from America to Saxony, who in the most violent manner criticized the defects of the Saxon State Church and made separation from it as well as from all other State Churches a duty of conscience. On Nov. 6, 1876, all dissenting congregations in Saxony united to form the Evangelical Lutheran Free Church in Saxony and other states. The addition "and other states" shows that this Free Church intends to gather around its banner the strict Lutherans from all Lutheran churches in Germany. At the end of 1901 it numbered about 2,230 members and seven pastors in Saxony, and 1,350 members with eight pastors outside of Saxony. Besides these free churches in Germany there are also congregations that arose frequently only from local conflicts with the State Church. The common aim of all free churches to found the church on Holy Scripture and the Lutheran confession alone can easily be justified; for this was the aim of the Reformation and is in harmony with the early Christian Church. The form of royal supremacy over the Protestant Church seems to be irreconcilable with the modern State, but it is also feared that the Lutheran Church, unless it were a State Church, might lose its hold upon the people, but the development of the Lutheran Church in North America shows that this is not necessarily the case. (G. Froböss.)

III. Lutherans in America:—1. Early Settlements; According to the testimony of the Jesuit Isaac Jogues in the year 1643 Lutherans were living in Manhattan (New Amsterdam—New York) along with Calvinists, Puritans and Anabaptists. The recognized religion of the colony of New Netherlands was the strict Calvinism of the Synod of Dort, and the Lutherans were treated harshly, especially by Peter Stuyvesant, the general director. Their children had to be brought to Calvinistic preachers for baptism, and they were forced to accept the doctrines of the Synod of Dort. The Lutherans were fined and imprisoned even for holding informal services for the reading of the Word of God. They applied to the directors of the Dutch West India Company in Holland for better treatment and to the Lutheran consistory in Amsterdam for a faithful Lutheran pastor. The Rev. John Ernest Goetwater arrived on June 6, 1657, in America, but through the influence of the Calvinistic preachers Megalopolensis and Drisius was forbidden to exercise his ministry and forced to return to Europe. When New Amsterdam was captured by the British in 1664 the Lutherans secured freedom in matters of worship and discipline. In the year 1669 Jacob Fabricius had been sent over from Holland, but his ministry in New York was a disappointment. He was succeeded by Bernhard Anton Arensius (1671–91) who also served the Lutherans at Albany. As no additional preachers could be obtained from Amsterdam, the New York Lutherans (1701) applied to the Lutheran Swedes on the Delaware, who sent Andreas Rudman (July, 1702). He recommended as his successor Justus Falckner (born 1672 in Saxony) who was ordained for the Lutheran ministry by Rudman, Bjoerk, and Sandel in the Swedish Church at Philadelphia in Nov., 1703—a German, ordained by Swedes to serve a Dutch congregation in America! His parish included the territory from New York to Albany on both sides of the Hudson and on Long Island. After his death, 1723, the Lutheran Consistory of Amsterdam at the request of the New York congregation sent as his successor in 1725 Wilhelm Christoph Berkenmeyer (born 1686 in Lüneburg, died 1751) a man of great energy and the strictest adherence to the Lutheran Confessions. Under his pastorate and that of his successor Michael Knoll the transition was made in the Lutheran congregations in New York from the Dutch to the German and English languages.

1. Dutch Lutherans.

Through William Usselinx of Antwerp the Swedish King Gustavus Adolphus had been sufficiently interested in the New World to grant a charter to the "South Company" in Stockholm (June 14, 1626) which, in addition to its work of colonization, was, from the very beginning, to undertake the propagation of the Gospel on this Western Continent. After the death of the king his great chancellor Oxenstierna continued to work for the realization of the plan. Peter Minuit, general director of New Netherlands, joined in the Swedish enterprise and sailed two Swedish vessels into the Delaware river (1638) where Fort Christina was built and an extensive territory was purchased from the Iroquois Indians. Reorus Torkillus was the first Lutheran pastor in New Sweden (died 1643). He was succeeded by John Campanius, who had arrived with Governor Johan Printz. He consecrated the first Lutheran church in the new world, on the island of Tinicum, near Philadelphia. He also translated Luther's Smaller Catechism into the language of the Indians. He returned to Sweden in May, 1648, where he died in 1683. When the Dutch took possession of New Sweden, the adherents of the Augsburg Confession obtained the guaranty of their religious liberties (1655). This was also secured to them when the British occupied New Sweden (1674). During the last quarter of the seventeenth century the Swedish Lutherans on the Delaware were much neglected, until King Charles IX. sent them such pastors as Rudman, Erik Bjoerk, and Jonas Auren. These were followed by other godly men, such as Karl Magnus Wrangel, whose name occurs again in the history of the German Lutherans, and Israel Acrelius, author of the *History of New Sweden* (English by Dr. W. M. Reynolds, Philadelphia, 1874). All these pastors sent over from Sweden were salaried by the king and, as a rule, returned to their native church after a few years of American service. The last among them, Nils Collin, arrived in America in 1771. Under him the union with the Swedish mother church was formally dissolved. He took Episcopal ministers for his assistants and thus opened the way for the use by these Swedish Lutheran Churches of the English language and their transition into the communion of the Protestant Episcopal Church. He died in 1831.

2. Swedish Lutherans.

William Penn had visited Germany in 1671 and 1677 with a view to obtaining settlers for his young American colony, Pennsylvania. It was not the interest of trade and commerce, as in the case of the Dutch, nor the colonial policy of far-seeing statesmen, as in the case of the Swedes, that brought the German immigration to America, but foremost the desire of unlimited freedom of worship, and the insecurity of life and property under the constant raids of their French neighbors from which particularly the Palatinate had to suffer. The first German colony, under the leadership of Frank Pastorius, arrived in 1683 and founded Germantown, now a part of Philadelphia. These first immigrants, however, consisted mostly of separatistic elements. There was one isolated German Lutheran congregation in New Hanover, some thirty-five miles from Philadelphia, whose origin can be traced as far back as 1703. With the beginning of the eighteenth century the German immigration assumed larger dimensions. Lutherans and Reformed crossed the ocean in considerable numbers, and there are now more regularity and vitality in the newly established Lutheran congregations. A number of Lutheran immigrants under Pastor Joshua Kocherthal (d. 1719) from Landau (Palatinate) arrived in 1709 in New York and settled on the Hudson above West Point. There they founded the town of Newburg, for which they had received a grant of 2,200 acres of land, 500 of which were to be devoted to church purposes. During the summer of 1709 Kocherthal returned to England to obtain additional favors and privileges for his colonists. Of the thousands of German emigrants from the Palatinate, Alsace, and Württemberg, that had been kept by the British government on "Black Heath," about 3,000 were brought to America in 1710, where they settled on both shores of the Hudson river at the

3. German Lutherans.

foot of the Catskill Mountains. In 1712 hundreds of them wandered northward to the Schoharie, where they were kindly received by the Indians. Eleven years afterward a considerable number of these colonists turned southward along the Susquehanna river to found new homes in Pennsylvania. Kocherthal's successors in the service of the German congregations in the State of New York were Justus Falckner, Wilhelm Christoph Berkenmeyer, and Michael Knoll, who at the same time ministered to the Dutch Lutherans. Isolated groups of German Lutherans with modest beginnings of congregational organization are found in the eighteenth century along the whole Atlantic coast as far as Georgia, in New Jersey, Virginia, North and South Carolina. Most prominent among them was the colony of Lutheran Salzburgers in Georgia, near Savannah. A number of the Salzburg Lutherans who were expelled by Archbishop Firmian, in 1731, had been recommended to the English court and were offered most favorable terms by the British government. They embarked at Rotterdam in the fall of 1733, with two pastors, John Martin Boltzius and Israel Christian Gronau. Governor Oglethorpe gave them a hearty welcome and they established the colony of Ebenezer, about twenty-five miles inland from Savannah. Wesley and Whitefield took a kindly interest in those immigrants and gave them material support. In eastern Pennsylvania up to the middle of the eighteenth century some 30,000 German Lutherans had settled, for whose spiritual wants there was, at first, no adequate provision. Much disorder and offense was caused by unworthy subjects who assumed the office of the ministry without proper call and qualification. In order to secure faithful ministers three congregations, New Hanover, New Providence (Trappe), and Philadelphia united in an application to Friedrich Michael Ziegenhagen, court preacher at St. James' Chapel, London, and Gotthilf August Francke in Halle. Negotiations were carried on in an extended correspondence, from 1734 to 1739. In the year 1741 Count Ludwig Zinzendorf arrived and, under the name of Herr von Thuernstein, offered his services to the Lutherans in Pennsylvania as "Evangelical-Lutheran inspector and pastor." He secured a call from a number of German Lutherans in Philadelphia, to whom he preached his famous "Pennsylvania discourses." John Christopher Pyrlaeus, whom he had appointed as a substitute in his place, was violently expelled by the Lutherans in 1742. In the fall of the same year there appeared Valentin Kraft, formerly pastor in Zweibruecken, Palatinate, a man of questionable character, whose activity among the German Lutherans helped to increase the general confusion.

2. Organization under Mühlenberg: Henry Melchior Mühlenberg (q.v.) was encouraged by Dr. Francke in Halle to accept the call to Pennsylvania, Sept. 6, 1741. In April, 1742, he arrived in London where the formal vocation from the three Pennsylvania congregations was handed to him by Frederick Michael Ziegenhagen. Leaving London on June 11 he arrived in Charleston, S. C., Sept. 23, 1742, as he had been commissioned to visit the Salzburg colonies in Georgia. He reached Philadelphia Nov. 25, and at once proceeded to New Hanover and New Providence. In Philadelphia he preached his first sermon Dec. 5, and three weeks afterward was formally recognized as the rightful pastor of the Lutheran congregation. He at once curbed the pretensions of Valentin Kraft and also succeeded in maintaining in a dignified manner his position against Count Zinzendorf, who attempted to call him to account in the presence of the officers of the Lutheran Church of Philadelphia. The magistrate of the city ordered Zinzendorf to give up the records and communion vessels of the Lutherans, and the count left the city and the country Jan. 1, 1743. Now Mühlenberg's work of church-organization began under many difficulties. The three congregations from whom he had a direct call were thirty-five miles apart, and to serve them regularly with the means of grace involved many hardships and dangers. As soon as the influence of his work of organization became known, his services in removing difficulties and restoring order were asked by other congregations, such as Tulpehocken, Germantown, Lancaster, and York. In the spring of 1743 the cornerstone of St. Michael's Church in Philadelphia, and that of the Augustus Church (Trappe) were laid. The latter church is still standing and close to its walls Mühlenberg is buried. Until the time of the revolutionary war the directors of the Francke institutions at Halle, together with Dr. Ziegenhagen in London, had full control of the congregations organized by Mühlenberg and his colaborers who were sent after him from Halle. Regular reports were sent over to Halle and were published under the title "Halle Reports of the United German Evangelical Lutheran Congregations in North America, particularly Pennsylvania" (1744–87, new ed., with valuable historical annotations and additions, ed. Drs. W J. Mann, B. M. Schmucker, and W Germann, Allentown, Pa., 1886). The most important step taken by Mühlenberg for the permanent organization of the Lutheran Church on this continent was the founding of the Synod of Pennsylvania, Aug. 26, 1748. There were present on this occasion the Swedish Provost Sandin and Pastors Hartwig of New York, Mühlenberg, Brunnholtz, Handschuh, and Kurz, who was ordained at this first meeting.

1. Preliminary Labors.

The character of this first synodical organization was, however, in the beginning rather loose and informal. No regular constitution was adopted, not even a formal election of a presiding officer. As a matter of course the position of leadership was accorded to Mühlenberg. The Collegium pastorum received the reports and requests of the lay delegates and acted on them. The latter had no vote, which was accorded to them only in the year 1792. The relation between the ministers and the lay element was one of patriarchal or apostolic simplicity. The unselfish devotion and faithfulness, the pastoral wisdom and experience of the leading men, above all, of Mühlenberg himself, secured the full confidence of the congregations, without any fear of hierarchical presumptions or aggressions on the part of the ministers. The

2. Character of the Organization.

doctrinal and confessional position of those fathers was unequivocally that of the historical standards of the Lutheran Church. The liturgy adopted at the first meeting of the synod, which was made obligatory for all pastors and congregations, was based on the Saxon and North German orders with which Mühlenberg had been familiar in Germany, such as those of Lüneburg 1564, Calenberg 1569, Saxony 1712, and Brandenburg-Magdeburg 1739. From 1748 to 1786 this first Pennsylvania agenda existed only in manuscript form. From 1754 to 1760 no regular meetings were held and the young synod seemed to be threatened with extinction. But in 1760, particularly through the influence of the Swedish Provost Karl Magnus Wrangel, the intimate friend of Mühlenberg, the body was revived and from that time on there is no break in its regular meetings. The constitution of the Evangelical Lutheran Ministerium of North America gradually took shape and was entered in the minute book in the year 1781. In those years Mühlenberg also prepared the first constitution for the mother congregation in Philadelphia (St. Michael's) which was formally adopted in 1762 and became the model for most of the Lutheran congregations in the East, giving the administration of congregational affairs into the hands of the church council, consisting of pastors, elders, and deacons. In 1766 Mühlenberg encouraged the Philadelphia congregation to undertake the erection of a new church, Zion's, which was completed in 1769, and, with its 2,500 sittings, was considered the largest and most beautiful sanctuary in North America. In this building Congress held its memorial service for George Washington. Before the death of Mühlenberg the second Lutheran Synod in America, the Ministerium of New York, was founded by his son, Frederick August Conrad Mühlenberg, pastor of the German Lutheran Christ Church in New York City (1773). Mühlenberg's son-in-law, the scholarly John Christopher Kunze (q.v.), took a leading position in this body, over which he presided from 1785 till his death in 1807.

3. Period of Deterioration, 1787–1820: The prevailing rationalism of the close of the eighteenth and the beginning of the nineteenth century did not affect the Lutheran Church of North America quite as strongly as it did the churches of England and Germany. With few exceptions the Lutheran pastors in America adhered to the confession of Christ, the Son of God, and the Word of the Cross.

1. Effects of Rationalism.

The traveling preachers of the mother synod did active missionary work in the West and Southwest, organizing congregations and conferences which formed the nucleus for new synods in Virginia, Ohio, Tennessee, North Carolina, Maryland, and western Pennsylvania. Among the tracts and religious literature which they distributed the Augsburg Confession had a prominent place. The parish schools were numerous and in flourishing condition. In the year 1820 not less than 206 parochial schools are reported by eighty-four congregations of the Pennsylvania Ministerium. Nevertheless, there were unmistakable signs that the strict confessionalism of the early Lutherans was beginning to weaken and to yield to indifferentism and subjectivism. The altered constitution of the Pennsylvania Ministerium of 1792 made no reference to the confessional standards, though the pastors continued to pledge their adherence to the symbolical books at their ordination. After Kunze's death Frederick Henry Quitmann became the leader of the New York Ministerium. He was a pupil of Semler, a decided adherent of the common rationalism, and it was through his influence that the old Lutheran Catechisms, Hymn-books, and Agenda gave way to modern publications, which were to have "due regard to the needs of the rising generation." The same tendency manifested itself in Pennsylvania, where the Hymn-book of 1817 (*Das Gemeinschaftliche Gesangbuch*) for the use of Lutheran and Reformed Churches, and the Agenda of 1818 represented a complete falling away not only from the historical, conservative order of service, but also from positive Lutheran doctrine, in the orders for baptism, communion, and ordination. In 1797 the New York Ministerium resolved that, on account of the close relation between the Lutheran and Protestant Episcopal Church and their similarity of doctrine, it would never recognize an English Lutheran church in a locality where the services of the Episcopal church could be attended by the Lutherans. This resolution, which was, however, cancelled after seven years, revealed the strong antagonism of the Germans to the English language.

The conflicts arising in this period through the transition from the use of German to that of English greatly retarded the progress and healthy development of the Lutheran Church. In New York the English became the official language of the ministerium in the year 1807 and held that position until 1866, when at the formation of the General Council, the English element seceded and the German took the lead. In Philadelphia the language controversy led to a split in the mother congregation. The English element, under the leadership of Peter Mühlenberg, had demanded the appointment of a third pastor who should officiate in the English language. This request being refused, St. John's Church was organized in 1806 as the first English Lutheran congregation. The Ministerium of Pennsylvania, the decision of which had been asked in the language controversy, resolved in 1805 forever to remain a German-speaking body. But it recommended the formation of English congregations and provided for their admission into the synod on condition that they accept its constitution. In other towns of Pennsylvania the language difficulty adjusted itself in a more peaceful manner. The German congregations first became German-English, with two pastors for the two languages. Gradually the English gained the ascendency and dismissed the German element with sufficient financial assistance, so that new German churches could be built. By this peaceable process of transition the descendants of the old Lutheran families were retained in the church of their fathers, in the English language, while in Philadelphia multitudes were lost to the

2. Change in Language.

English denominations of another faith. The national and linguistic feeling was stronger with the Germans than their ecclesiastical and Lutheran consciousness. They felt themselves nearer to the Reformed Germans than to the English-speaking Lutherans, and the venerable Charles Frederick Schaeffer (q.v.) of New York voiced the general sentiment when he said, in a letter addressed to the Pennsylvania Synod in 1819, that "as the Lutherans and Reformed in Germany had been brought together in one united church, so the true Germans in America should, in this respect, follow the example of the Germans in Germany."

4. The General Synod: At this critical period in the history of the Lutheran Church in America the first steps were taken toward the formation of a Lutheran General Synod, in order to stop the threatening disintegration, to unite more firmly the scattered members of the Lutheran Church on this continent, and to secure for her a recognized position. The mother synod of Pennsylvania took the initiative at its convention in Harrisburg, 1818. An organization was effected in Hagerstown, Pa., in 1820, and in the following year the first regular convention was held in Frederick, Md., the Synods of Pennsylvania, North Carolina, and Maryland-Virginia being represented. New York sent no delegates until 1837. Ohio and Tennessee stood aloof. Pennsylvania withdrew again in 1823, yielding to the unreasonable anxiety of some of its country congregations who feared the danger of hierarchical oppression on the part of the general body. Thus, for eight years the General Synod consisted of the small synods of North Carolina, Maryland-Virginia, and West Pennsylvania. The Hartwick Synod, in the State of New York, entered in 1831, the synod of South Carolina in 1835; New York in 1837 At all times the General Synod represented only a minority of Lutherans in America. For a considerable period the mother synod of Pennsylvania alone outnumbered the general body. The General Synod undoubtedly was a courageous and determined attempt to perpetuate the Lutheran Church and to give her a standing and recognition in America, such as she had not enjoyed before. It succeeded in organizing the educational and missionary work of the church. The establishment of the theological seminary in Gettysburg, the sending of a delegation to Germany to rouse the sympathies of the fatherland and to collect contributions for the Lutheran Church in America, the formation of the Parental Educational Society, the Central Missionary Society, and the Foreign Missionary Society were measures of the highest importance, looking to the vital interests of the Lutheran Church in her new western home. There was, from the beginning, an element that sought to remain in contact with the faith of the fathers and the historical Lutheran Church and manifested a certain consciousness and appreciation of the peculiar gifts and responsibilities of the Lutheran Church and an endeavor to assert and preserve her individual character. But then there was, on the other side, a broad and powerful current of unionism and indifferentism which declared, in an official communication to the Evangelical Church in Germany (1845): "In most of our church principles we stand on common ground with the Union Church of Germany. The distinctive doctrines which separate the Lutheran and the Reformed Churches we do not consider essential. The tendency of the so-called old Lutheran party seems to us to be behind the time. Luther's peculiar views concerning the presence of the Lord's body in the communion have long been abandoned by the majority of our ministers." While in the Pennsylvania Synod, during the thirty years of its separation from the General Synod, a more conservative and churchly spirit had gradually gained the ascendency, it nevertheless maintained friendly relations with the General Synod. On several occasions approaches were made by prominent men of the General Synod toward the restoration of the union. The Pennsylvania Liturgy and Hymn-Book were adopted by the General Synod. And the Pennsylvania Synod endowed a professorship in Pennsylvania College, Gettysburg, belonging to the General Synod. Thus the way was prepared for the formal return of the mother synod to the General Synod, which took place in 1853. The step was taken in the hope of strengthening the conservative element in the General Synod and with the reservation, that "should at any time the General Synod violate its constitution and require of our synod, or of any synod, as a condition of admission to or continuation of membership, assent to anything conflicting with the old and long-established faith of the Evangelical Lutheran Church, then our delegates are hereby required to protest against such action, to withdraw from its sessions, and to report to this body."

1. Organization and Purpose.

In order to define more clearly the position of American Lutheranism, which was claimed to be the position of the General Synod in its majority, Samuel Simon Schmucker published in 1855 the *Lutheran Manual*, an American recension of the Augsburg Confession, the "Definite Platform," in which the seven articles on abuses are entirely omitted, and of the twenty-one doctrinal articles twelve are more or less altered, particularly those treating of the sacraments. The effect of this publication was a disappointment to the author and his party. It opened the eyes even of the indifferent and undecided ones and caused them to reflect. On all sides strong protests arose against this attack on the venerable Augustana. Only a few Western synods adopted the "Definite Platform." While, even then, an open rupture was for the time avoided, the "Definite Platform" certainly hastened the crisis in the General Synod. During the Civil War the Southern churches had withdrawn and established the General Synod of the Evangelical Lutheran Church in the Confederate States of America (1863). The second, far more important rupture dates from the convention of the General Synod in York, Pa., 1864. The Franckean Synod, New York State, applied for admission into the General Synod. It had never formally adopted the Augsburg Confession, and had been declared Sabellian and Pelagian by the

2. Dissentient Movements.

civil courts. It was received into the General Synod by a vote of ninety-seven to forty. The Pennsylvania delegation protested and withdrew. A number of delegates from other synods joined in the protest of the Pennsylvanians. To avoid the threatening rupture the doctrinal basis of the General Synod was amended so as to recognize the Augsburg Confession as a correct exhibition of the fundamental doctrines of the divine Word, and of the faith of the Church founded upon that Word. But the important question, which doctrines were to be considered as fundamental, remained open, most of the American Lutherans considering the distinctive doctrines that separated Lutherans and Reformed as non-fundamental. The action at York was answered by the Pennsylvania Ministerium in the establishment of her own theological seminary at Philadelphia, in July, 1864 (first faculty: Drs. C. F. Schaeffer, W. J. Mann, C. P. Krauth, C. W. Schaeffer, G. F. Krotel; present faculty: A. Spaeth, H. E. Jacobs, J. Fry, G. F. Spieker). The Pennsylvania Ministerium, still considering itself a member of the General Synod, appointed delegates to represent it at the next convention of the General Synod in Fort Wayne, 1886. Here the final crisis occurred through the action of the presiding officer, S. S. Sprecher, who refused to accept the credentials of the Pennsylvania delegates when the roll of the synods was called, declaring that synod to be "out of practical union with the General Synod." Nothing was left to the delegation but to withdraw again and to report to their ministerium, which now formally severed its connection with the General Synod and issued a fraternal letter, inviting all Evangelical Lutheran Synods in the United States and Canada to unite in the formation of a new general body, "first and supremely for the maintenance of unity in the true faith of the Gospel, and in the uncorrupted Sacraments, as the Word of God teaches and our Church confesses them; and furthermore for the preservation of her genuine spirit and worship, and for the development of her practical life in all its forms." In response to this fraternal address the "Reading Convention" was held, in Dec., 1866, at which Pennsylvania, New York, Ohio, Pittsburg, Wisconsin, Michigan, Minnesota, Iowa, Missouri, Canada, the Norwegian Synod, and the Swedes were represented. The "Fundamental Articles of Faith and Church Polity," drawn up by Charles Porterfield Krauth, were discussed and unanimously adopted. The organization of "The General Council of the Evangelical Lutheran Church in North America" was resolved.

At present the following synods belong to the General Synod: Maryland, West Pennsylvania, Hartwick, East Ohio, Franckean (N. Y.), Allegheny (Pa.), East Pennsylvania, Miami (Ohio), Wittenberg (Ohio), Olive Branch (Ind., Ky., Tenn.), Northern Illinois, Central Pennsylvania, Iowa, Northern Indiana, Pittsburg (W. Pa.), Susquehanna (N. E. Pa.), Kansas, Nebraska, New York and New Jersey, Wartburg (German, West and South), California, Rocky Mountains (Colorado, New Mexico, Wyoming), Nebraska (German), Central Illinois, Southern Illinois, numbering a total of 1,322 ministers, 1,734 congregations, 265,459 communicants. The General Synod has 5 theological seminaries with 22 professors and 103 students. It has foreign mission stations in the Telugu land, East India, and in Liberia, East Africa, with 30 missionaries, 550 native helpers, 34,053 native Christians, 10,500 pupils in mission schools, and 3,900 candidates for baptism.

5. Confessional Lutherans in the West: About a quarter of a century before the revival of confessional Lutheranism in the General Synod led to disruption and to the organization of the General Council, Lutheran immigrants from Saxony, Prussia, and Bavaria, who had left the fatherland on account of their faith, undertook the foundation of strictly Lutheran bodies, which, though frequently engaged in sharp controversies, were remarkably successful in gathering the large Lutheran population of the West into strong ecclesiastical organizations.

1. The Synod of Missouri.

In the month of Nov., 1838, hundreds of earnest Lutherans, under the leadership of Martin Stephan, pastor of the Bohemian Church at Dresden, resolved to emigrate to America. The hopeless condition of their home church, the opposition to the Lutheran confession, and the prevalence of rationalism, drove those people out of their native land where they despaired of seeing their ideal of the Church realized. Stephan was distinguished by his remarkable eloquence in the pulpit, his knowledge of men, and his pastoral ability in dealing with souls in a state of despondency under severe spiritual trials. Though he had had difficulties with the ecclesiastical authorities in Saxony, no charges had affected his character. His adherents had absolute confidence in him and trusted him not only with their spiritual guidance but even with the administration of their worldly possessions. They numbered altogether about 700 persons, among them several faithful pastors of the Lutheran Church in Saxony, like O. H. Walther, C. F. W. Walther, E. G. W. Keyl, and G. H. Loeber. One of the vessels on which the immigrants embarked was lost at sea with all on board. The others landed in Jan., 1839, at New Orleans and settled in St. Louis and in Perry Co., Mo. Soon after their arrival Stephan was found to be unworthy, guilty of defalcation and gross immorality. They cast him off, and Carl Ferdinand Wilhelm Walther (q.v.) became their principal leader. When the catastrophe of Stephan's exposure overwhelmed the Saxon immigrants, and they themselves were in doubt, whether they still were a Christian Church and their pastors real officers of the church by divine right, it was Walther who brought light and encouragement to the downcast little band. He founded the semimonthly *Der Lutheraner* and later on the theological monthly *Lehre und Wehre*. By means of these publications he gathered a number of like-minded men, and prepared the way for the organization of the synod of Missouri, which met for the first time in Chicago, Ill., Apr. 26, 1847. In the same year the educational institution founded by W. Loehe in Fort Wayne, Ind., was transferred to the synod of Missouri, and the theological seminary of the Saxon immigrants in Perry Co. was moved to St. Louis, where Walther became the head of the faculty. From the very beginning the synod of Missouri placed itself on the foundation of the Lutheran confessions as contained in the Book of Concord of 1580, rejecting all kinds of unionism and syncretism with those of another faith. Continued doctrinal discussions at synods, conferences, and congregational meetings, regular visitations of the churches, and the faithful training of the children in their parochial schools were the means of not only holding the synod itself firmly together in one spirit, but also of enlarging it rapidly in every direction. Special emphasis was laid on the rights of the congregation, and all "High-church" ideas concerning the ministry were repudiated. The authority of the synod in its relation to the congregations is advisory in character. The right of vote at synodical meetings is confined to the delegates of congregations and to those pastors who actually serve congregations in full connection with the synod. All other pastors, teachers, and professors are only advisory members. The wisdom and consistency of Walther's management proved a powerful attraction, which succeeded in overcoming and assimilating even antagonistic elements. At its second convention the synod numbered fifty-five ministers, among them many who had enjoyed a thorough theological training at German universities, who knew how to adapt themselves admirably to their new American environments, and who worked together with the greatest personal devotion and self-denial. In 1909 the synod of Missouri extended from the Atlantic to the Pacific, and from Canada to the Gulf of Mexico and Brazil. Including the English Synod (1888) and the Slovak Synod (1902) it numbered 2,086 ministers, 2,584 congregations, 498,409 communicants. It had two theological seminaries with 12 professors and 396 students.

The Missouri Synod in Brazil.—In the year 1899 Pastor Brutschin of Rio Grande do Sul, Brazil, applied to the synod of Missouri with the request that pastors be sent to that territory. The General Committee for Home Missions of the Missouri Synod sent C. J. Broders to examine the field in 1900. He was followed by other pastors in 1901 who took up the work in the interest of the Missouri Synod in the district of San Lorenzo. In the year 1902 W Mahler, henceforth the leader of the Missouri pastors in Brazil, established himself in Porto Allegre. In 1903 the publication of a periodical in the interest of the Missouri Synod was undertaken and an institution founded for the training of pastors and teachers, which, after a temporary interruption, was reopened at Porto Allegre in 1907. In 1904 the synod of Brazil was organized as a separate district of the Missouri Synod. It numbers at present 20 pastors, ministering to 8,251 souls, including 3,943 communicants, and 1,234 voting members. In Europe (Germany and Denmark) the Missouri Synod numbers 29 pastors, in Australia, in two districts, 36 pastors, in New Zealand 3 pastors.

2. The Buffalo Synod.

Following the Saxon emigrants, in 1839 another band of German Lutherans left their home on account of their faith and started for America. Their leader was Johann Andreas August Grabau, born 1804 near Magdeburg, pastor of St. Andrew's Church at Erfurt. He had been repeatedly imprisoned on account of his opposition to the Prussian Union and to the introduction of the king's Agenda. About 1,000 adherents followed him, the most of them from Erfurt, Magdeburg, and the surrounding country. The greater number settled in Buffalo, N. Y., but some went as far west as Wisconsin. In the year 1845 Grabau with his friends, P. v. Rohr, L. Krause, and Kindermann, founded the "Synod of Lutherans immigrated from Prussia," afterward called the Buffalo Synod. Its theological seminary was connected with the Martin-Luther-Collegium in Buffalo. In distinction from the Saxon Lutherans Grabau entertained high-churchly ideals of the office of the ministry and ordination, making the reality and efficacy of the means of grace dependent on the office, and depriving the congregation of its right to discipline and excommunicate its members. Even in the management of the temporal affairs of the congregation the members were bound to strict obedience toward their pastors. Walther and his friends were convinced that in these views the hierarchical tendencies of Stephan were revived, from whose bondage they had just escaped. A violent controversy ensued between the "Prussians" and the "Saxons." After a colloquy held in 1866 eleven pastors of the Buffalo Synod joined the Missouri Synod. The small remnant again broke into two sections, one of which ceased to exist in 1877. At the present time the Buffalo Synod numbers 30 pastors, 41 congregations, and 5,556 communicants. It has a theological seminary in Buffalo with five teachers and eleven students. In recent times there has been brought about an amicable understanding between the Buffalo Synod and the Ministerium of New York. Several conferences have been held with satisfactory results, both synods recognizing each other and admitting their members to pulpit and altar fellowship.

3. The Iowa Synod.

In the year 1841 the Rev. Frederik Wyneken, pastor of the Lutheran congregations in and near Fort Wayne, Ind., sent forth a touching appeal to the mother church in Germany, appealing in behalf of the Lutherans in the western States of North America for help in supplying them with the means of grace. The venerable W. Loehe, pastor in Neuendettelsau, Bavaria, and founder of the deaconess institution in that village, was deeply moved with sympathy for his brethren in the faith in America. He established a missionary institute and began the publication of a paper (*Kirchliche Mitteilungen aus und über Nord Amerika*) through which he awakened and nourished an active interest in the condition of the Lutherans in America. The first two missionaries sent by him attached themselves to the synod of Ohio and to the Michigan Synod. But in 1845 they and their sympathizers left the synod of Ohio and established the theological seminary at Fort Wayne under the presidency of Wilhelm Sihler. This step was taken because they were not satisfied with the confessional position of their synod in respect to the unionistic tendencies of the time. The institution at Fort Wayne was opened in 1846 with sixteen pupils, most of whom had received their preparatory training at Neuendettelsau. The ground and the buildings were acquired chiefly through contributions coming from Loehe and his friends.

Loehe himself advised his friends to associate themselves with the Saxon Lutherans. Several conferences were held at St. Louis and Fort Wayne, and the parties united in the formation of the synod of Missouri in which the emissaries of Loehe outnumbered the "Saxons." Soon, however, serious differences arose between Loehe and the leaders of the Missouri Synod, particularly on the doctrines concerning the Church and the ministry. To avoid a threatening rupture Wyneken and Walther were sent to Germany to confer personally with Loehe, but no agreement was reached. Consequently the adherents of Loehe, G. M. Grossmann and J. Deindoerfer, to avoid friction with the Missouri Synod, went further west, to carry on the American Mission work of Loehe beyond the Mississippi. Together with S. Fritschel and M. Schueller they founded the synod of Iowa at Dubuque, Ia., Aug. 24. 1854. This synod means to represent a strictly confessional yet ecumenical Lutheranism. Accepting the symbolical books without reservation it distinguishes between what is confessed in the symbols as a direct doctrine of faith, and what those standards contain in their exegetical, historical, and explanatory material. From the very beginning there was a conflict between the synods of Missouri and Iowa. No agreement was reached in the conference at Milwaukee, 1867. The points of difference are essentially the following: (1) Concerning the office of the ministry, Missouri holds that the spiritual priesthood of believers involves the ministry of the Word, while the congregation, possessing the priesthood and all ecclesiastical authority, transfers to the individual the authority of exercising the rights of the spiritual priesthood publicly, in behalf of the congregation. Iowa draws the distinction between the spiritual priesthood and the office of the Word as a special vocation, and holds that the Missouri doctrine on this particular point was not fixed in the confessions of the Church, and therefore, even if correct, should not divide the Church. (2) Concerning the authority of the confessions both agree that all doctrines of faith in the confessions are binding. But Iowa limits those doctrines to such articles as are taught *ex professo*, without accepting their theological exposition as binding in every case. (3) Concerning "open questions" Iowa teaches that there are points on which different opinions may be held without disturbing church fellowship, such as the doctrines concerning Antichrist and the conversion of Israel. Missouri at first maintained that nothing that was taught in the Scriptures could be considered an open question in this sense. But later on, when difficulties arose in the Missouri Synod itself concerning the subject of usury, it was publicly declared that there was, indeed, a difference between articles of faith and other Scripture doctrines which must not necessarily be considered as such. (4) Concerning Antichrist and all eschatological doctrines Missouri insists that all prophecies of things preceding the last day are actually fulfilled, including the prophecy concerning Antichrist, whose fulfilment is found in the pope. Iowa, while admitting the antichristian character of popery, holds that it should not be condemned as unlutheran to expect some future culmination of the prophecy concerning Antichrist in a person that is yet to appear. (5) Concerning chiliasm (see MILLENNIUM, MILLENARIANISM) both agree to accept the seventeenth article of the Augsburg Confession and reject any doctrine of the millennium which would rob the spiritual kingdom of Christ of its character as a kingdom of grace and of the cross. But the doctrine of a first resurrection, though not taught by the Iowa Synod as such, is not considered a fundamental error, as Missouri considers it. From the beginning there have been pleasant and kindly relations between the Iowa Synod and the General Council, though the former never entered into organic connection with the latter. At most of the conventions of the General Council the Iowa Synod was represented by delegates. It took an active part in the preparation of the General Council's church-book and uses it in all its congregations. The Iowa Synod numbers 487 ministers, 927 congregations, 99,895 communicants, scattered over nineteen States and British Columbia. It has a theological seminary in Dubuque, Ia., with 4 teachers and 45 students.

4. The Joint Synod of Ohio.

In the year 1805 for the first time traveling preachers of the Pennsylvania Ministerium reached the State of Ohio, where they founded a conference in connection with the mother synod. The organization of the synod dates from the year 1818 and its present name, Joint Synod of Ohio, from the year 1833. Though a number of ministers, like Dr. Sihler and the missionaries sent by Loehe, had left the synod because they were not satisfied with its confessional position, the synod developed more and more in a decidedly Lutheran direction and in 1847 adopted all the symbolical books as the basis of its confession. Conferences held between Missouri and Ohio led to a gradual approach between the two bodies, and in the year 1872 the Joint Synod of Ohio united with the Missouri Synod and other western bodies in the formation of the synodical conference. But the controversy on predestination led to the withdrawal of the synod of Ohio in 1881. There followed an approach between Ohio and Iowa which culminated in a mutual recognition. The synod at present numbers 556 ministers, 733 congregations, 110,-877 communicants. There are two theological seminaries, in Columbus and St. Paul, with 9 teachers and 101 students.

5. The Synodical Conference.

The Synodical Conference, at present the strongest in the Lutheran Church in America, was founded in the year 1872 on the basis of the Concordia of 1580. It embraced the following synods: Missouri, Ohio, Wisconsin, Minnesota, Illinois, Michigan, and the Norwegian Synod, and numbers at present 2,444 ministers, 3,101 congregations, and 643,599 communicants. The synod of Wisconsin was founded by Rev. J. Mühlhäuser, formerly in Rochester, N. Y., and afterward in Milwaukee (1848–68). This synod at first belonged to the General Council, but left it in 1872 to join the synodical conference. It numbers 242 pastors, 350 congregations, 100,000 communicants, with a theological seminary at Wauwatosa, near Milwaukee (3 professors, 32 students). The synod of Minnesota was the fruit of the missionary labors of Father C. F Heyer (1793–1873), born at Helmstädt, Germany, for many years an active missionary among the Telugus in India, died as chaplain of the theological seminary in Philadelphia. The synod was founded in 1860 at West St. Paul. It numbers 86 pastors, 123 congregations, 35,685 communicants. In 1867 it joined the General Council but left it in 1871 and afterward connected itself with the synodical conference. The synod of Michigan was the outcome of the missionary labors of the Rev. F. Schmid, Ann Arbor, Mich. It was founded in 1860, joined the General Council in 1867, and afterward went over to the synodical conference, in which it is now represented by 14 pastors, 22 congregations, 4,225 communicants. These three synods, of Wisconsin, Minnesota, and Michigan, united in the synod of the Northwest, in 1892, with their common seminary in Milwaukee. But the original Michigan Synod, dissatisfied with this step, left the synodical conference in 1896, and is, since that time, without connection with a general body. It numbers 37 pastors, 54 congregations, 7,933 communicants. Another, more serious rupture took place in the synodical conference in consequence of the predestinarian controversy. Since 1868 there has appeared a tendency of the Missouri leaders to condemn as Pelagian and synergistic the so-called *Intuitu fidei* doctrine of the old Lutheran dogmaticians, and to teach an absolute, unconditional, particular decree of God, by which a certain limited number of men were elected to salvation. Professor Asperheim, in the seminary of the Norwegian Synod, raised a voice of warning and was forced to resign his professorship and to leave his synod. Professor F. A. Schmidt, formerly one of the champions of Missouri, protested against the teaching of Walther, the great leader of the Missouri Synod. The professors of the Ohio Synod sided with him. A colloquy, lasting five days, held in Milwaukee, had no favorable result, and in 1881 the Ohio Synod left the synodical conference. The Norwegian Synod to which Dr. F. A. Schmidt belonged was divided into two parties, and, in order to avoid a rupture in its own midst in 1884, it also left the synodical conference.

6. The Scandinavian Lutherans: About the middle of the nineteenth century a new tide of Swedish immigration set in. Rev. Lars P Esbjoern organized the first Lutheran congregations at Andover, Galesburg, Moline (Ill.), and New Sweden (Iowa). In 1851 he joined the synod of northern Illinois, belonging to the General Synod. Faithful pastors were called over from the mother country, like T. N. Hasselquist (afterward professor of the theological seminary of the Augustana Synod), Erla Carlson, Jonas Swensson, and young men like E. Norelius were ordained for the ministry. In 1860 the Scandinavians withdrew from the General Synod and organized the "Scandinavian Evangelical Lutheran Augustana Synod of North America." In 1870 the Swedes and Norwegians separated peacefully. The Swedish Augustana Synod joined the General Council at the time of its organization and has ever since formed one of the most prominent bodies in this connection. In the seventies the Augustana Synod had to contend against the influence of the "Mission Friends" (Waldenstroemians). Their college and seminary were moved to Rock Island. Other preparatory institutions are the Gustavus Adolphus College at St. Peters, Minn., Bethany College at Lindsborg, Kansas, and the Lutheran Academy at Wahoo, Neb. The Augustana Synod is in reality the Swedish General Synod of North America, extending over the whole Union from the Atlantic to the Pacific. It numbers 574 pastors, 1,052 congregations, 154,390 communicants, and has seven orphans' homes, two deaconess homes, three hospitals, and several immigrant and seamen's missions.

1. Swedes. Augustana Synod.

A small colony of Norwegian immigrants settled at Rochester, N. Y., in 1825 and nine years afterward moved to Illinois. The first step toward a church organization was the founding of (1) the Evangelical Lutheran Church of North America, Hauge Synod, through the influence of Elling Eielsen (1804–83), originally a lay preacher and adherent of Hauge, of Pietistic tendency. Several secessions took place and in 1876 there was a reorganization under the name: "The Norwegian Evangelical Lutheran Hauge Synod," with 122 pastors, 290 congregations, 21,181 communicants. Eielsen with a few adherents kept aloof, and there is at the present time still a separate Eielsen Synod with 6 pastors, 26 congregations, 1,200 communicants. (2) The Norwegian Evangelical Lutheran Synod of North America was founded in 1853 by the more conservative elements, under the leadership of C. L. Claussen, A. C. Preus, H. A. Preus, U. V. Koren, J. A. Ottesen, and P. L. Larsen, in sympathy with the Missouri Synod, in whose theological seminary at St. Louis they were represented by professors of their own (Larsen, Preus, F. A. Schmidt). Afterward the synod established its own seminary in Madison, Wis. The predestinarian controversy, as above stated, led to the withdrawal of this Norwegian Synod from the synodical conference, and finally to a separation in the synod itself (1887). It numbers at present 350 pastors, 1,050 congregations, 87,000 communicants with a theological seminary at St. Paul, Minn., and a college at Decorah, Ia. (3) The initiative toward the founding of the United Norwegian Lutheran Church in North America was taken by the anti-Missourian party in the Norwegian Synod, who sought to unite the Hauge Synod, the Norwegian Augustana Synod, and the Norwegian-Danish Conference. The Hauge Synod did not join in this movement, but the others united in 1890 at Minneapolis. The united synod numbers 480 pastors, 1,335 congregations, 154,055 communicants, with a theological seminary at St. Paul, Minn., and colleges at Canton, S. D., Moorhead, Minn., and Northfield, Minn., and two orphans' homes, two deaconess motherhouses, and seven hospitals. (4) The Norwegian Lutheran Free Church was founded in 1893 by G. Sverdrup and Sven Oftedahl, formerly members of the Norwegian-Danish Conference, and reports 148 pas-

2. The Norwegians.

tors, 340 congregations, 42,738 communicants, with a theological seminary at Minneapolis, Minn., and a college, an orphans' home, and a deaconess mother-house.

(1) The Danish Evangelical Lutheran Church in North America, formerly the Church Mission Society, was founded in 1872, and numbers 61 pastors, 117 congregations, 11,737 communicants, with a theological seminary at Des Moines, Ia. (2) The United Danish Evangelical Lutheran Church in America was founded in 1896 in Minneapolis, and has 106 pastors, 202 congregations, 9,261 communicants, a college and theological seminary at Blair, Neb., and another college at Hutchison, Minn. The Icelandic immigration in North America dates from the year 1870. The first congregation was organized by Rev. Paul Thorlacksohn in 1875. The synod of Icelanders was founded in 1885 under the presidency of Rev. Bjernason in Winnipeg. Delegates from that body were in attendance at the convention of the General Council in Chicago, 1899. The synod numbers 9 pastors, 43 congregations, 4,451 communicants. The Finnish immigration is of quite recent date. The Suomi Synod was organized in 1889 and numbers 24 pastors, 110 congregations, 13,201 communicants, with a theological seminary in Hancock, Mich.

6. Other Scandinavians.

7. Lutherans in the South: Lutheran congregations were first organized in the South at Woodstock, Winchester, and New Market, Va., Salisbury and Concord, N. C., Orangeburg, Lexington, Newberry, and Charleston, S. C., and in the Salzburg colonies of Georgia. At the time of the Civil War the Southern General Synod seceded from the General Synod, consisting of the synods of Virginia, Southwestern Virginia, North Carolina, South Carolina, and Georgia. The Apostolic and Nicene Creeds, together with the Augsburg Confession, as setting forth the fundamental doctrines of the Word of God, constituted the confessional basis, with the distinct understanding that there should be liberty of private judgment with reference to some articles of the Augustana. With the gradual development of a stricter confessional position this reservation disappeared. In 1886 a new general body was formed, called The United Synod in the South, accepting essentially the same doctrinal and confessional position as the General Council. It includes the following synods: North Carolina (organized 1803), Tennessee (1820), South Carolina (1824), Virginia (1829), Southwest Virginia (1842), Mississippi (1855), Georgia (1860), and the Holston Synod in Tennessee (1861). The United Synod numbers 235 pastors, 458 congregations, 47,514 communicants. It has a theological seminary at Mount Pleasant, Charleston, S. C., and colleges at Hickory, N. C., and Newberry, S. C.

8. The General Council: The history of the origin of this body has been told in 4 above. Its first convention was held in Fort Wayne, Ind., Nov., 1867. Its doctrinal basis is stated in the fundamental articles of faith and Church polity as follows: "We accept and acknowledge the doctrines of the unaltered Augsburg Confession in its original sense as throughout in conformity with the pure truth of which God's Word is the only rule. The other Confessions of the Evangelical Lutheran Church, inasmuch as they set forth none other than its system of doctrine and articles of faith, are of necessity pure and Scriptural and are, with the unaltered Augsburg Confession, in the perfect harmony of one and the same Scriptural faith." At the first convention of the General Council the Joint Synod of Ohio, which had not adopted the constitution and was not ready to enter into organic union with the General Council, laid before that body four questions on its relation to chiliasm, altar and pulpit fellowship, and secret societies. Similar questions, except that on chiliasm, were also presented by the Iowa Synod. The discussion of these four points and the successive declarations on the same, at Pittsburg (1868), Lancaster, O. (1870), Akron, O. (1871), and Galesburg (1875), showed a steady growth in the fuller appreciation of the confessional principle underlying those points and a determination to carry the principle into practical execution. This position has been reached in spite of the hasty withdrawal of the very synods which from the beginning appeared as the champions of the confessional principle, viz., Wisconsin, Minnesota, Illinois, and Michigan. Much care was bestowed by the General Council on the production of sound books of worship for the use of its members in the family, the school, and the church. In this field it has been most successful. The German and English official literature published by authority of the General Council may justly be called a model of its kind. It is based upon the most careful and comprehensive studies in liturgics and hymnology, and in its preparation the best and most reliable sources have been used. It is pure in doctrine and complete in the material which it contains. More than any other Lutheran general body of this country the General Council represents the peculiar mixture, in the American Lutheran Church, of German, Scandinavian, and English-speaking elements, and that critical period of transition from the church of the immigrant to that of the native English-speaking American population. Its great task is to transfer into the sphere of the English tongue a genuine Lutheranism, sound in doctrine, government, and form of worship.

The Lutherans in the South initiated the important movement toward the Common Service for all English-speaking Lutherans in the United States. The General Council, in 1879, declared itself ready to cooperate in this matter on condition that the pure Lutheran Agenda of the sixteenth century should be recognized as the norm and standard for this work. This rule having been adopted by the United Synod of the South and the General Synod, the work on the Common Service was actually begun in 1884 and the orders for the main service, matins, and vespers were finished in 1888 and adopted by the three general bodies and the English Synod of Missouri. The English version of the Augsburg Confession was revised on the basis of Taverner's translation of 1536, and a new translation of Luther's Small Catechism was prepared for all English-speaking Lutherans.

The General Council, according to the latest statistics, embraces the following synods: The Ministerium of Pennsylvania (organized 1748), with 388 ministers, 554 congregations, 145,215 communicants; the Ministerium of New York (1773), 150 ministers, 149 congregations, 65,000 communicants; Pittsburg Synod (1845), 138 ministers, 190 congregations, 31,392 communicants; English District, Synod of Ohio (1857), 49 ministers, 82 congregations, 14,245 communicants; Augustana Synod, Swedish (1860), 574 ministers, 1,052 congregations, 154,390 communicants; Canada Synod (1861), 38 ministers, 76 congregations, 12,096 communicants; Chicago Synod (1871), 40 ministers, 58 congregations, 5,981 communicants; English Synod of the North West (1891), 29 ministers, 34 congregations, 5,060 communicants; Manitoba Synod (1897), 18 ministers, 51 congregations, 4,000 communicants; Pacific Synod (1901), 13 ministers, 20 congregations, 1,313 communicants; New York and New England Synod (1902), 52 ministers, 56 congregations, 15,192 communicants; Nova Scotia Synod (1903), 8 ministers, 25 congregations, 2,545 communicants. Total: 1,497 ministers, 2,347 congregations, 456,429 communicants, with three theological seminaries, at Philadelphia, Rock Island, and Chicago, numbering 15 professors and 163 students; 7 colleges with 127 teachers and 2,107 students; 6 academies with 49 teachers and 902 students; 3 deaconess institutions, 12 orphans' homes, 8 asylums for the aged and infirm, 5 seamen's missions.

In addition to the synods that have thus far been treated, the following independent synods are to be mentioned: The Texas Synod, consisting of those members of the original Texas Synod who refused to unite with the Iowa Synod in 1895, numbering 15 ministers, 23 congregations, 2,200 communicants. Immanuel Synod, German, organized 1886, numbering 17 pastors, 11 congregations, 3,250 communicants.

The grand total of the Lutheran Church in North America shows: 8,052 ministers, 13,142 congregations, 2,012,536 communicants, with 24 theological seminaries, 96 professors, and 1,137 students; 39 colleges with 433 teachers and 7,535 students, 49 orphans' homes, 24 homes and asylums for the aged, 28 hospitals, 9 deaconess motherhouses. Of these there are in Canada 92,550 Lutherans (in Ontario 48,100, in Manitoba 16,550, in the Northwest Territories 12,100), where since 1891 they have increased 44.5 per cent.

The number of Lutherans in Central and South America is estimated at about half a million, in the Danish West Indies they are in connection with the State Church of Denmark, in South America they are partly supported by the Lutherische Gotteskasten in Germany, and partly under the supervision of the Prussian State Church and assisted by it. ADOLPH SPAETH.

The Lutheran Church, while largely augmenting its strength for many years by immigration, has not been indifferent to the demands of missionary effort in the United States. As usual, this effort began in sporadic forms. As early as 1836 Rev. Ezra Keller, sent out by the Ministerium of Pennsylvania, had explored the territory now comprised in West Virginia, Ohio, Kentucky, Indiana, and Illinois, laying foundations for the present churches of that region. In 1837, Rev. Carl Friedrich Heyer reported to the General Synod that he had explored the entire Mississippi Valley and found places for, at least, fifty missionary pastors. But it was not until 1845 that the Home Missionary Society of the General Synod was organized. In the early fifties missionary aid was given to the Indians in Michigan, and to a number of missionary points in Wisconsin and Canada. The New York Ministerium sent strong help to the establishment of the Mother Churches in Buffalo, Rochester, Utica, Syracuse, Lyons, and others in that State. The Ohio Synod was all missionary territory, and twenty pastors in this synod ministered to not less than 195 congregations. Between 1857 and 1859 the General Synod was supporting sixty-seven missionaries, while the district synods of New York and Allegheny had their independent work, rivaling that of the general body. Progress in Minnesota, under the aged Father Heyer, was particularly encouraging. In recent years the Pennsylvania and New York Synods have cooperated in the support of an immigrant mission at the port of New York and in the founding of an Emigrant House for the care of incoming Germans. The Lutheran Church at the present time is receiving and expending for home missions from three-quarters of a million to a million dollars a year. J. B. CLARK.

BIBLIOGRAPHY: Some of the principal literature is named in the text; that cited under the articles in this work to which cross-reference is made in the text is, much of it, pertinent, e.g., under AGENDA; AUGSBURG CONFESSION AND ITS APOLOGY; FORMULA OF CONCORD; LUTHER; MELANCHTHON; and PHILIPPISTS; for bibliographies cf. J. G. Morris, *Bibliotheca Lutherana*, Philadelphia, 1876; H. E. Jacobs, in *American Church History Series*, iv. pp. ix.–xvi., New York, 1893. For statistics cf: *Kirchliches Jahrbuch* (published at Gütersloh), the *Lutheran Church Annual*, and *Lutheran Year Book* (annual). On the doctrines, besides the work of Jacobs on the Book of Concord, cf.: Schaff, *Creeds*, i. 220–253, ii. 1–189; C. P. Krauth, *The Conservative Reformation and its Theology*, Philadelphia, 1871; A. L. Richter, *Die evangelischen Kirchenordnungen des 16. Jahrhunderts*, Leipsic, 1871; idem, *Lehrbuch des Kirchenrechts*, ib. 1874; S. A. Holman (ed.), *Lectures on the Augsburg Confession*, Philadelphia, 1888; H. Schmid, *The Doctrinal Theology of the Evangelical Lutheran Church*, Philadelphia, 1889; *The Distinctive Doctrines and Usages of the General Bodies of the Evangelical Lutheran Church in the United States*, Philadelphia, 1893; S. Fritschel, *Die Unterscheidungslehren der Synoden von Iowa und Missouri*, Waverly, 1893; *The Lutheran Church, her Communion and her Service*, Philadelphia, 1906 (two sermons given as authoritative expositions of the doctrinal standpoint); L. Cristiani, *Luther et le lutheranisme*, Paris, 1908.

For the history of Lutherans consult: *Nachrichten von den vereinigten deutschen ev.-lutherischen Gemeinden in Nord Amerika, absonderlich in Pennsylvanien. Mit einer Vorrede von D. Johann Ludewig Schulze*, 2 vols., Halle, 1750-1787, republication with notes begun by W. J. Mann, B. M. Schmucker, and W. Germann, Allentown, Pa., 1886, Eng. transl. begun by C. W. Schaeffer, Part I., Reading, Pa., 1882 (left incomplete); E. L. Hazelius, *History of the American Lutheran Church, 1685–1842*, Zanesville, Ohio, 1846; P. A. Stroebel, *History of the Salzburgers*, Baltimore, 1885; Clay, *Annals of the Swedes on the Delaware*, Philadelphia, 1858; D. H. Focht, *The Churches Between the Mountains*, Baltimore, 1862; C. W. Schaeffer, *Early History of the Lutheran Church in America*, Philadelphia, 1868; W. B. Sprague, *Annals of the American Pulpit*, vol. ix., New York, 1869; G. D. Bernheim, *History of the German Settlements and of the Lutheran Church in North and South Carolina*, Philadelphia, 1872; Schirmer, *Historical Sketches of the Evangelical Lutheran Synod of South Carolina*, Charleston, 1875; J. G. Morris, *Fifty Years in the Lutheran Ministry*, Baltimore, 1878; W. Sihler, *Lebenslauf*, St. Louis, 1880 (autobiography); W. J. Mann, *Life and Times of Henry Melchior Mühlenberg*, Philadelphia, 1881; Schierenbeck, *Lebensbeschreibungen von lutherischen Predigern in Amerika*, Selinsgrove, Pa., 1881–83; *Amerikanische Beleuchtung*, Philadelphia, 1882; C. Hochstetter, *Geschichte der Missouri Synode*, Dresden, 1885; A. Spaeth, *The General Council*, Philadelphia, 1885; idem, *Chas. Porterfield Krauth, Memoir*, vol. i., New York,

1898; idem, *Dr. W J. Mann. Ein deutsch-amerikanischer Theologe*, Reading, 1903; B. M. Schmucker, *The Organization of the Congregation in the Early Lutheran Churches in America*, Philadelphia, 1887; Andersen, *Den evang. lutherske Kirke's Historie*, New York, 1888; J. Nicum, *Geschichte des Ministeriums von New York*, Reading, 1888; F. C. Guenther, *F. W Walther, Lebensbild*, St. Louis, 1890; S. Henkel, *Hist. of the Evangelical Lutheran Tennessee Synod*, New Market, 1890; D. L. Roth, *Acadie and the Acadians*, Philadelphia, 1890; H. E. Jacobs, *The Lutheran Movement in England and its Literary Monuments*, Philadelphia, 1890; idem, in *American Church History Series*, vol. iv., New York, 1893, Germ. transl. with important additions by G. Fritschel, Gütersloh, 1896; E. J. Wolf, *The Lutherans in America*, New York, 1889, the same in German with important additions by J. Nicum, New York, 1891; A. L. Graebner, *Geschichte der lutherischen Kirche in America*, St. Louis, 1892 (reaching to the year 1820); J. Nicum, in *Proceedings of American Society of Church History*, New York, 1892; J. N. Lenker, *Lutherans in All Lands*, Milwaukee, 1894; J. F. Sachse, *The German Pietists of Provincial Pennsylvania, 1694 1708*, Philadelphia, 1895; A. Spaeth, H. E. Jacobs, and G. F. Spieker, *Documentary History of the Ministerium of Pennsylvania, Containing the Proceedings of the Convention 1748 1821*, New York, 1895–1899; J. Deindorfer, *Geschichte der evangelisch-lutherischen Synode Iowa*, Chicago, 1897; H. E. Jacobs and J. A. W. Haas, *The Lutheran Cyclopedia*, New York, 1899; *Proceedings of the First Free Lutheran Diet, 1878, Proceedings of the Second Free Lutheran Diet, 1879, General Conference of Lutherans*, ed. H. E. Jacobs, Philadelphia, 1899; F. Nippold, *Handbuch der neuesten Kirchengeschichte*, 5 vols., Berlin, 1901; G. H. Gerberding, *The Lutheran Pastor*, Chicago, 1903; T. Schmauk, *A History of the Lutheran Church in Pennsylvania, 1638–1820*, vol. i., Philadelphia, 1903.

LUTHER'S TWO CATECHISMS: Even while a Roman Catholic priest, Luther had repeatedly treated in his sermons the main divisions of the catechism. Some of the sermons which he preached on the Commandments and the Lord's Prayer in 1516 and 1517 have been preserved. More important, however, as a preparation was his work in the confessional, where he learned to know the detrimental influence of the formal lists of sins which were considered useful, and to appreciate in contrast the unparalleled excellence of the ten commandments, of which, as well as of the Apostles' Creed and the Lord's Prayer, he early began to write short expositions: in 1518 *Kurze Auslegung der zehn Gebote Gottes, ihrer Erfüllung und Uebertretung*, in 1519 *Kurze Unterweisung wie man beichten soll*, and in the same year several expositions of the Lord's Prayer and one on the Apostles' Creed; then in 1520 he combined these treatises under the title *Kurze Form der zehn Gebote, des Glaubens, des Vaterunsers*. Here is found the first combined treatment of these three articles, and therefore the most important work of preparation for the catechisms. In 1522 Luther edited the *Betbüchlein*. All these writings were intended primarily to be used in preparation for confession, but he had the instruction of youth also in his mind.

When, after Luther's return from the Wartburg, Evangelical principles were introduced at Wittenberg, especial attention was paid to the religious instruction of children. In the spring of 1521 Johann Agricola was appointed catechist at the principal church, and gave regular instruction in religion to the children. The custom of preaching regular sermons on the catechism began about this time. After the abolition of compulsory confession Luther announced in 1523 that every person intending to partake of the Lord's Supper should give notice to the pastor and submit to an examination. To facilitate the preparation for such an examination, he arranged short questions on the Lord's Supper; but soon he conceived the idea of writing a small book that should serve for the instruction of youth, form the basis for sermons on the catechism, and make possible a more comprehensive preparation for the Lord's Supper. The *Kinderfragen* of the Bohemian Brethren, with which Luther became acquainted at least as early as 1523, may have suggested the idea of such a manual. Nicolaus Hausmann, preacher at Zwickau, to whom Luther announced his intention, confirmed him in it. In a letter to Hausmann (1525) Luther states that Jonas and Agricola had been commissioned to prepare a catechism; but their work does not seem to have progressed rapidly, and when Agricola removed to Eisleben, Luther himself took charge of the matter. Before it was finished, there appeared in 1525 a book in Low German entitled *Eyn Bökeschen vor de leyen vnde kinder*, which in the same year was translated into High German. It is not known to what extent Luther was concerned in the publication of this book, but there is no doubt that it originated under his influence, since it appeared at a time when he had already conceived the idea of adding the two sacraments to the original three articles discussed in his *Kurze Form* of 1520. In 1526 Luther seems to have already sanctioned its official use in the Church. As the *Büchlein für Laien* forms the basis for the text of the catechisms, so do Luther's catechetical sermons of 1528 for their interpretation in his more comprehensive work, called the larger catechism; for the larger catechism is nothing but an interpretation of the smaller ones on the basis of sermons which he preached in 1528 at Brunswick in the absence of Bugenhagen, and was necessitated chiefly by the ignorance of preachers revealed to him at the visitations of 1528 and 1529.

While Luther was working in 1529 on his larger catechism, the idea of issuing a smaller catechism, as an epitome of the larger, occurred to him, and he published it before the latter in two series in the form of tables, according to a wide-spread custom of the time. The *tabulæ* have not been preserved, but their contents are pretty well known. The first table was in circulation as early as Jan. 20, 1529, and was a real children's catechism, including the Ten Commandments, the Creed, the Lord's Prayer, and some other prayers. The second table, which appeared in the middle of March, treated of the sacraments of baptism and of the Lord's Supper, and was intended chiefly for adults. This distinction between the catechism proper and the doctrine of the sacraments was clearly expressed by Luther in his catechetical sermons of 1528, then in the larger catechism, and again in 1530. Only by degrees did it disappear and the sacraments come to be considered an inseparable part of the catechism. The *tabulæ* were first put into book form in a Low German translation (Hamburg, 1529). The larger catechism appeared in the same month of Apr., 1529, and retained in the main its original form in the numerous later editions, of which a second followed in the same year and a third in 1530. Like the *tabulæ*, the larger catechism was translated into Low German (1529) and in the same year twice into Latin. By May 16, 1529, Luther's own smaller catechism was published in book form, and soon went into a second edition. No copies of the original Wittenberg printings of either edition are extant, but there are three reprints, evidently independent, two made at Erfurt and one at Marburg. According to these the title of the first editions in book form was *Der kleine Catechismus für die gemeine Pfarherr und Prediger. Mart. Luther.* Besides the material of the *tabulæ* they contained a preface, morning and evening prayers, and devotional exercises for the family, and a marriage service. The third edition was out by June 13, 1529, under the title *Enchiridion. Der kleine Catechismus für die gemeine Pfarherr und Prediger, gemehret und gebessert.* Of the editions which appeared prior to Luther's death, those of 1531, 1535, 1536, 1537, 1539, and 1542 are known. Two Latin translations (with some alterations) appeared in 1529, both at Wittenberg. One of these, *Simplicissima et brevissima catechismi expositio*, appeared as an appendix to the *Enchiridion piarum precationum*, the Latin translation of the *Betbüchlein*. Its author is not known. The other translation, *Parvus Catechismus pro pueris in schola*, was made by J. Sauermann and was incorporated into the "Book of Concord." A third Latin translation originated with Justus Jonas and is contained in his Latin translation of the Nuremberg *Kinderpredigten* of 1539. A Greek translation by Johann Mylius was printed at Basel in 1558 at the instigation of Michael Neander, who republished it in 1564 together with Sauermann's translation. In 1572 J. Clajus composed his German-Latin-Greek-Hebrew polyglot. For the translations into modern languages and the position of Luther's smaller catechism in the history of catechisms, see CATECHISMS.

The excellent points of the smaller catechism have been stated as follows: (1) The smaller catechism does not attempt to give a complete system of doctrine—it is not a manual of dogmatics for children; (2) it avoids carefully the scholastic language of the theologians; (3) it avoids all polemics; (4) it does away with the traditional division of the Apostles' Creed into twelve articles, and makes it an exposition of the God of revelation as showing himself in his works and blessing the Christian life. It was soon forgotten that the larger catechism was the authoritative exposition of the smaller. In 1750 Johann Georg Walch pointed out in the introduction to his edition of the symbolical books that the catechism must be explained by Luther himself. This principle has been observed in the modern works of A. Nebe, *Der kleine Katechismus ausgelegt aus Luthers Werken* (Stuttgart, 1891); Th. Hardeland, *Der kleine Katechismus nach Luthers Schriften ausgelegt* (Göttingen, 1889); idem., *Die katechetische Behandlung des kleinen Katechismus Luthers in Unterredungen* (Berlin, 1899). (FERDINAND COHRS.)

BIBLIOGRAPHY: Besides the lives of Luther by Köstlin, Kolde, and others, consult: J. C. W. Augusti, *Versuch einer historisch-kritischen Einleitung in die beyden Haupt-Katechismen der evangelischen Kirche*, Elberfeld, 1824; G. Veesenmeyer, *Nachrichten von einigen evangelischen catechetischen Schriften*, Ulm, 1830; K. F. T. Schneider, *D. Martin Luthers kleiner Katechismus*, Berlin, 1853; T. Harnack, *Der kleine Katechismus Luthers in seiner Urgestalt*, Stuttgart, 1856; C. Mönckeberg, *Die erste Ausgabe von Luthers kleinem Katechismus*, Hamburg, 1868; E. Göpfert, *Wörterbuch zum kleinen Katechismus Luthers*, Leipsic, 1889; A. Ebeling, *Luthers kleiner Katechismus*, Hanover, 1890; F. Fricke, *Luthers kleiner Katechismus in seiner Einwirkung auf die katechetische Litteratur des Reformationsjahrhunderts*, Göttingen, 1898; F. Cohrs, *Die evangelischen Katechismus-Versuche vor Luthers Enchiridion*, Berlin, 1900; H. E. Jacobs, *Martin Luther*, pp. 274 sqq., New York, 1898; *Luther's Small Catechism Developed and Explained, Published by the General Synod*, Philadelphia (current).

LUTZ, luts, **JOHANN LUDWIG SAMUEL:** Swiss theologian; b. at Bern Oct. 2, 1785; d. there Sept. 21, 1844. He was educated at Bern, Tübingen, and Göttingen, and in 1812 was appointed professor at the gymnasium and rector of the Litterarschule of his native city. The lack of harmony between his views and those of the citizens of Bern, as well as his share in certain movements for social and political reform which rendered the municipal authorities suspicious of him, led him to leave the school for the pulpit in 1824. He served as pastor first in Wynau and later in Bern, where in 1833 he was appointed professor of Old- and New-Testament exegesis. In addition to his academic duties, he was for many years a member of the department of education and of the Evangelical Church committee, and also dean of the theological faculty and the chapter of Bern, and president of the synod and of the Protestant charitable association. In his lifetime he published little except a few occasional and academic addresses, but after his death his pupil, R. Rüetschi, edited a volume of his lectures under the title *Biblische Dogmatik* (Pforzheim, 1847) and A. Lutz published a second entitled *Biblische Hermeneutik* (1849). (E. GÜDER†.)

BIBLIOGRAPHY: F. Lutz, *Der Gottesgelehrte J. L. S. Lutz*, Bern, 1863 (by his son); the *Gedächtnisrede* was by Baggesen, ib. 1844; C. B. Hundeshagen, . . *Professor Lutz in Bern; ein theologisches Charakterbild*, ib. 1844; *Berner Taschenbuch*, 1855, pp. 229–240; E. Müller, *Die Hochschule Bern 1834–84*, ib. 1884.

LUTZ (LUCIUS), SAMUEL: Swiss Pietist; b. at Bern Aug. 10, 1674; d. at Diessbach (near Thun, 16 m. s.s.e. of Bern) May 28, 1750. He received a thorough classical training from his father, who was pastor at Biglen, but a strong tendency toward mysticism developed early in his life and led him to abandon his original studies. He studied at the University of Bern, where he came under the influence of the strongly orthodox Rudolf Rudolf, although his personal religious trend was little in accord with the scholastic theology of his time. Scarcely had the Swiss theologians attempted to reaffirm the orthodoxy of Dort as contrasted with its modifications by the Saumur school, before a system of Pietism closely allied with that of Germany, though marked by Anabaptist and other separatistic tendencies, began to develop in Switzerland, especially in Bern. After a brief hesitation the government of Bern, which was not inclined to toleration, assumed a position of extreme hostility toward the movement, and brought legal penalties to bear upon the Pietists. Among the adherents of Pietism Lutz was especially mentioned. He was a close friend of Samuel König, who had been banished for his views four years previously, and it was but natural that he should be placed under surveillance and receive his ordination comparatively late. It was not until 1703 that he was appointed to the obscure pastorate of Yverdun, where he labored twenty-three years, winning the affection and esteem of both the French and German inhabitants of the place. His Pietism nullified the official call to Köthen, Pfalz-Zweibrücken, Büdingen, and Zerbst, and he likewise declined a professorship at Lausanne. In 1726, however, he accepted a call to the pastorate of Amsoldingen and twelve years later went in a similar capacity to Diessbach, where he spent the remainder of his life.

Although not altogether free from a certain self-complacency, Lutz strove with patience, energy, and skill against the formalism prevailing in theological and religious life. His attitude at Yverdun at first excited considerable opposition in the canton of Vaud, especially on account of his admonitions to repentance and conversion, but the government paid scant attention to the complaints lodged against him and even tacitly ignored his reluctance to take the oath rigidly exacted from other pastors. On the other hand, Lutz himself grew more moderate in course of time, nor was he a reformer of the visible Church, being devoted only to the spiritualities of the kingdom of God. In his desire to proclaim his doctrines as widely as possible, he preached in no less than 108 pulpits both in Switzerland and abroad, until it became necessary to direct him to restrict his activity to his own congregation. He attributed special importance to catechetical instruction, and had a daily hour for prayer in his church. He was likewise closely associated with circles of like sympathies in Zurich, Basel, Schaffhausen, St. Gall, and Grisons, in addition to conducting a correspondence with such men as Zinzendorf, Denhöfen, and Heinrich Ernst of Stollberg-Wernigerode, who brought him into contact with Christian VI.

Lutz also exercised a powerful influence by his writings, which began to appear in quick succession after 1721. Of these thirty-six are enumerated without exhausting the list. The most important were republished in two collections, *Wohlriechender Strauss von schönen und gesunden Himmelsblumen* (2 vols., Basel, 1736–37) and *Ein neuer Strauss* (1756). All his works are ascetic in tendency, partly treatises on the spiritual life, partly detailed considerations of individual truths, and partly sermons of almost interminable length. His basal postulate was that each visible object bears the stamp of a heavenly and spiritual essence, so that all things earthly must be interpreted by the celestial. According to a credible tradition, the Lutheranizing and mildly antinomistic sect of Heimberg Brethren, who are now centered around Saanen and Adelboden, were first inspired by the teachings of Lutz. (E. GÜDER†.)

BIBLIOGRAPHY: K. R. Hagenbach, *History of the Church in the 18th and 19th Centuries*, Lecture 9, 2 vols., New York, 1869; E. Bloesch, *Geschichte der schweizisch-reformierten Kirchen*, ii. 47 sqq., Bern, 1899; W. Hadorn, *Geschichte des Pietismus in den schweizisch-reformierten Kirchen*, pp. 262 sqq., Constance, 1901.

LUXEMBURG: A grand duchy of Europe with a capital of the same name, bounded by the Rhine province of Prussia on the northeast and east, Lorraine on the south, France on the southwest, and Belgium on the west; its area is 998 square miles, and its population (1900) 236,543, of whom 29,549 are foreigners. Of the entire population 233,073 are Roman Catholics, 2,269 Protestants, and 1,201 Jews. The country was an apostolic vicariate 1840–70, and in 1870 was raised to a bishopric by Pius IX., though the vicar had been since 1863 bishop in partibus infidelium. In 1873 the episcopal office was duly ratified by legislative act and an episcopal living was established, controlling 13 deaneries, 255 parishes, 83 chaplaincies, and 82 vicarages. In 1845 a seminary for priests was established. The Protestant population of the capital is due chiefly to the fact that Prussian troops were garrisoned there 1815–66, some of whom remained there after the duchy became independent. Not until the former grand duke (d. 1908) came to the throne (1890) did the Protestant Church receive either recognition or support from the state. It was then furnished with a consistory, the control of affairs pertaining to administration and government being vested in six members of consistory, whose head is the pastor. Vacancies are filled by cooptation. W. GÖTZ.

BIBLIOGRAPHY: N. von Werveke, *Beiträge zur Geschichte des Luxemburger Landes*, 3 parts, Luxemburg, 1886–87; F. Bonnardot, *Les Archives de l'état de Luxemburg*, ib. 1890; T. H. Passmore, *In Further Ardenne*, London, 1905.

LUZ: The name of two cities. (1) The early Canaanitic name for Bethel (Gen. xxviii. 19, xxxv. 6; Josh. xviii. 13; but cf. Josh. xvi. 2). (2) A city founded, according to Judges i. 26, in "the land of the Hittites" by the survivors of the ancient city when it was taken by the Hebrews. The location is unknown.

LYCAONIA, lic"a-ō'ni-a: A region of Asia Minor mentioned in the Bible only in Acts xiv. in connection with the journeys of Paul. Normally bounded north by Galatia, east by Cappadocia, south by Cilicia, and west by Phrygia, its boundaries fluctuated greatly during the Roman period, its territories being in part included within those of the neighboring provinces. See ASIA MINOR IN THE APOSTOLIC TIME, VII.

BIBLIOGRAPHY: W. M. Ramsay, *Historical Geography of Asia Minor*, passim, London, 1890; idem, *The Church in the Roman Empire*, pp. 48 sqq. et passim, New York, 1893; idem, *St. Paul the Traveller and the Roman Citizen*, pp. 110–111, ib. 1896.

LYCIA. See ASIA MINOR, VIII.

LYDDA, LOD: A city of Ephraim, situated in the plain of Sharon, 10 m. s.e. of Joppa on the road to Jerusalem, identified with the Arab village of Ludd. It is mentioned in the Old Testament as Lod in I Chron. viii. 12; Ezra ii. 33; Neh. vii. 37, xi. 35, and as Lydda in I Macc. xi. 34. In the New Testament it appears only Acts ix. 32–38 as visited by Peter, who healed there the paralytic Eneas. After the fall of Jerusalem it was famous as a seat of rabbinic learning, Rabbi Eliezer and Rabbi Akiba being reckoned among its scholars. In the second century its name was changed to Diospolis, though the older name persisted. In the third century it became the seat of a bishop, but the bishopric seems to have lapsed in the sixth century. Legend makes it the birthplace of St. George, whose head is said to have been buried there, and a church, built on the spot, was destroyed by the Mohammedans, rebuilt by the Crusaders, and again destroyed by Saladin in 1191.

BIBLIOGRAPHY: G. A. Smith, *Historical Geography of the Holy Land*, pp. 160 sqq., London, 1897; Robinson, *Researches*, ii. 244–248; Schürer, *Geschichte*, i. 184–185, ii. 181–186 et passim, Eng. transl., I., i. 190, 191, 245–246, II., i. 157–159 et passim.

LYDIUS, lid'i-us: The name of a Dutch family which produced several Reformed theologians in the sixteenth and seventeenth centuries.

1. Martin Lydius: Professor of theology at Franeker; b. at Lübeck (to which his parents had fled from Deventer, seeking refuge from the Spaniards) in 1539 or 1540; d. at Franeker June 27, 1601. About 1560 he entered the University of Tübingen, but in 1565 migrated to Heidelberg, where he became a teacher in the Collegium Sapientiæ in 1566 or 1567. On the death of the Elector Frederick III. (1576), Lydius, after a brief residence in Frankfort, became a pastor in Antwerp, whence he was called in 1579 to Amsterdam. In 1585 he accepted a call to the newly founded University of Franeker and became its first rector in 1586. He sought to avoid religious controversy, yet his part in the struggle between the infralapsarians and the supralapsarians led him to contribute toward the rise of Arminianism, for when, in 1589, an infralapsarian treatise was submitted to him for his opinion, he referred it to the young Amsterdam preacher Jacobus Arminius (q.v.). The result for Arminius was a complete reversal of his views on predestination. When, however, Arminius was accused of Pelagianism in 1592, Lydius sought to mediate in the controversy. Besides letters to Beza, Ursinus, Arminius, Lipsius, Joseph Scaliger, J. G. Vossius, and others, also several orations and poems, he wrote *Apologia pro Erasmo* (edited by his son and included in the Leyden edition of Erasmus, x. 1759-80), but no theological works.

2. Balthasar Lydius: Elder son of Martin Lydius; b. at Umstadt (a suburb of Darmstadt) in 1576 or 1577; d. at Dort Jan. 20, 1629. Educated at Leyden, he was chosen assistant pastor at Dort in 1602, and became full pastor in 1604, retaining this position until his death. Though irenic in temperament like his father, he became a bitter opponent of the Remonstrants, especially at the Synod of Dort, which he both opened (Nov. 13, 1618) and closed (May 29, 1619), and of whose protocol he was one of the editors. He made a reputation by his *Waldensia, id est conservatio veræ ecclesiæ* (2 vols., Rotterdam and Dort, 1616–17), which, however, though still of value, is both incomplete and incorrect, and is little more than a collection of documents on the Taborites and Bohemian Brethren. He also wrote, among other works, *Dry historische Tractaetgens* (Amsterdam, 1610), on the Church from the apostles to the Reformation, on the various names of the Waldenses, and on the faith of the Waldenses. As an archeologist he wrote *Super loco Mosis de cruentato sponsarum linteo et aliis virginitatis signis* and *De Lyncuro lapide* (nos. 5 and 16 of J. Beverwyck's *Epistolicæ quæstiones cum doctorum responsis*, Rotterdam, 1644), and assisted in the preparation of Mellinus' *Groot-Martelaarsboek* (Dort, 1619).

3. Johannes Lydius: Younger son of Martin Lydius; b. at Frankfort in 1577; d. at Oudewater (12 m. s.w. of Utrecht) in 1643, where he had been pastor since 1602, after a year's pastorate at Aarlanderveen. Like his brother, he was an opponent of Arminianism, but his literary activity was restricted to editing G. du Préau's *Narratio conciliorum omnium ecclesiæ Christianæ* (Leyden, 1610); R. Barnes' and J. Bales' *Vitæ Pontificum* (1610); and the works of Nicholas de Clémanges (2 vols., 1613) and J. Wessel (1617).

4. Jacob Lydius: Third son of Balthasar Lydius; b. at Dort about 1610; d. there in 1679. Educated at Leyden, he was pastor at Bleskensgraaf from 1633 to 1637, after which he was pastor at Dort until his death, except in 1643–45, when he was chaplain of the English embassy of the States General. This period resulted in his *Historie der beroerten van Engelandt, aangaende de veelderley secten, die aldaer in de Kercke Jesu Christi zijn ontstaen* (Dort, 1647). His exegetical learning was evinced by his *Florum sparsio ad historiam passionis Jesu Christi* (Dort, 1672), and his patristic studies by his *Agonistica sacra, sive syntagma vocum et phrasium agonisticarum quæ in sancta Scriptura, imprimis vero in epistolis sancti Pauli apostoli, occurrunt* (Rotterdam, 1657). High praise was given his *Cœna dominica litteratorum* (Dort, 1669). S. van Til edited his posthumous *Syntagma sacrum de re militari, nec non de iureiurando* (1698). As a poet he wrote *Vrolicke uren des doodts ofte der wijsen vermaek* (Dort, 1640), while his *Belgicum gloriosum* (1668; Dutch transl. by himself, 1668) was an ostensible ground for the declaration of war against Holland by Charles II. in 1672. His greatest fame, however, was gained by his anonymous *Den Roomschen Uylen-spiegel* (Amsterdam, 1671), a savage but witty satire on the Roman Catholic Church. In the ensuing controversy between him and the Jesuit Cornelis Hazart of Antwerp, he wrote, besides other polemics, *Antwerpschen uyl in doodsnood* (1671); *Het overlijden van den Antwerpschen uyl* (1671); *Laetst olyssel van den Antwerpschen uyl in doodtsnoot;* and the posthumous *Laetsten duyvelsdreck, ofte ongehoorde grouwelen van paepsche leeraers onser eeuwe* (Dort, 1687), all works of importance for a knowledge of the relations between the Reformed and the Roman Catholics in Holland in the seventeenth century. (S. D. VAN VEEN.)

BIBLIOGRAPHY: E. L. Vriemoet, *Athenarum Frisiacarum libri*, pp. 20–28, Leeuwarden, 1758; G. D. J. Schotel, *Kerkelijk Dordrecht*, i. 257–284, 391–423, Utrecht, 1841; B. Glasius, *Godgeleerd Nederland*, ii. 414–421, 3 vols., 's Hertogenbosch, 1851–56; H. C. Rogge, in *Kalender voor de Protestanten in Nederland*, 1857, pp. 228 sqq.; C. Sepp, *Het Godgeleerd onderwijs in Nederland*, i. 125–135, Leyden, 1873.

LYNCH, THOMAS TOKE: English Independent; b. at Dunmow (32 m. n.e. of London), Essex, July 5, 1818; d. in London May 9, 1871. He was educated at Islington, London, and attended Highbury College for a short time. He was pastor of the Independent Church at Highgate (1847–49); of a church in Mortimer Street, which afterward moved to Grafton Street (1849–52); and of one in Gower Street, afterward Mornington Church (1860–1871). Lynch had little success as a preacher, but as a hymn-writer he obtained great celebrity. His hymns, however, have been considered to betray too ardent a love of nature to be entirely suited to use in Christian worship. The best-known is "Gracious Spirit, dwell with me." He first came into prominence through the publication of *The Rivulet: a Contribution to Sacred Song* (London, 1855), which gave rise at the time to a fierce controversy because of the charge that it was pantheistic in tone. His chief opponents were James Grant and Dr. John Campbell; his chief supporters, Newman Hall and Thomas Binney. Lynch was his own best defender, writing under the *nom de plume* of "Silent Long." Among his other writings are *Memorials of Theophilus Trinal* (largely autobiographical, 1850); *Essays on some of the Forms of Literature* (1853); *Lectures in Aid of Self-Improvement* (1854); *The Mornington Lecture* (1870); and *Sermons for my Curates* (1871).

BIBLIOGRAPHY: His *Memoirs*, ed. W. White, appeared London, 1874, and a small *Critical and Descriptive Notice of T. T. Lynch* was published London, 1874. Consult: S. W. Duffield, *English Hymns*, p. 191, New York, 1886; Julian, *Hymnology*, pp. 705–706; *DNB*, xxxiv. 338–339.

LYNE, JOSEPH LEYCESTER (called Father Ignatius): Anglican monk: b. in London Nov. 23, 1837; d. at Camberley (31 m. s.w. of London) Oct. 16, 1908. He was educated at Trinity College, Glenalmond, and was ordered deacon in 1860. He was then curate of St. Peter's, Plymouth, in 1860–62, and in 1862–63 was St. George's missioner under Father Lowder. In 1863 he entered upon the monastic life, and resided successively in the monasteries at Claydon (Suffolk), Norwich, and Laleham (Chertsey), for seven years. In 1870 he purchased an estate near Abergavenny, Monmouthshire, where he established Llanthony Abbey, of which he was chosen superior. In this abbey he introduced the Benedictine rule and the Sarum Missal. Refusing to leave off the monastic habit even while being ordained to the priesthood, he remained a deacon until 1898, when he accepted advancement from the schismatic Bishop Villatte. Later recognizing the error of his action, which was commonly considered a desertion of Anglican orders, he did not attempt to exercise the priestly office, but remained in simple lay communion with the Church of England. He was particularly successful as a missioner, and in 1890–91 visited the United States and Canada in this capacity. In later years, however, he declined to preach in churches on account of his firm opposition to rationalism and higher criticism, he himself being a vigorous champion of orthodoxy. In addition to many sermons and pamphlets in defense of his position, in which he was frequently assailed, he wrote *All for Jesus* (London, 1867); *The Holy Isle: a Legend of Bardsey Abbey* (1870); *Leonard Morris, or, The Benedictine Novice* (1870); *Brother Placidus, and why he became a Monk: A Tale for the young Men of the Times* (Brighton, 1870); *Our Glorious Reformation* (London, 1884); and *Mission Sermons and Orations* (1887).

BIBLIOGRAPHY: Father Michael, O. S. B., *Father Ignatius in America*, London, 1893; Baroness de Bertouch, *Life of Father Ignatius, O. S. B., Monk of Llanthony*, ib. 1904.

LYON, DAVID GORDON: Baptist; b. at Benton, Ala., May 24, 1852. He was educated at Howard College, Marion, Ala. (A.B., 1875), Southern Baptist Theological Seminary, Louisville, Ky. (1876–79), and the University of Leipsic (Ph.D., 1882). Since 1882 he has been Hollis professor of divinity in Harvard University, and has also been curator of the Harvard Semitic Museum since its foundation in 1890. In 1906–07 he was director of the American School for Oriental Study and Research in Palestine. In theology he is a progressive conservative. Besides a number of briefer contributions, he has written *Die Keilschrifttexte Sargon's, Königs von Assyrien (722–705 v. Chr.), nach den Originalen neu herausgegeben, übersetzt und erklärt* (Leipsic, 1883) and *An Assyrian Manual for the Use of Beginners in the Study of the Assyrian Language* (Chicago, 1886).

LYON, MARY: American educator; b. at Buckland, Mass., Feb. 28, 1797; d. at South Hadley, Mass., Mar. 5, 1849. She was educated at several academies, notably at Ashfield and Byfield, and later at Amherst College. She taught at the Adams Female Seminary at Londonderry, N. H. (1824–28), and at Miss Grant's school in Ipswich (1828–34). In 1834 she left teaching to raise funds for building a female academy, which was finally opened at South Hadley on Nov. 8, 1837. Of this school, called the Mount Holyoke Seminary (now College), she was principal until her death. Under her care the school was, as it still is, a nursery of missionaries and it still keeps its reputation for piety and efficiency.

BIBLIOGRAPHY: E. Hitchcock, *Power of Christian Benevolence Illustrated in the Life and Labors of Mary Lyon*, Northampton, 1851, new ed., New York, 1858; F. Fiske, *Recollections of Mary Lyon*, Boston, 1866; *Mary Lyon*, in *Old South Leaflets*, no. 145, ib. 1904.

LYONS, ARCHBISHOPRIC OF: An ancient metropolitan see in France. The town, which became a Roman colony in 43 B.C., acquired considerable importance under the Empire; in it Augustus spent three years; here Claudius was born; and when the town was rebuilt after a conflagration, Nero gave it precedence over all the other Roman towns of Gaul. Christianity was probably introduced within the first century. As at Marseilles, the earliest Christians were of Greek origin. The first bishop is supposed to have been Pothinus or Photinus, sent by Polycarp from Smyrna between 140 and 150. With many of his flock, he suffered martyrdom in 177, and was succeeded by Irenaeus (q.v.). A long line of devoted bishops followed. Lupus (d. c. 542) is usually reckoned as the first archbishop, with four suffragan sees, Autun, Langres, Macon, and Châlons—to which in the middle of the eighteenth century were added the newly founded sees of Dijon and Saint-Claude. After the Revolution Châlons and Macon were suppressed, and Grenoble was taken from the province of Vienne, which metropolitan see was then united with Lyons. After the surrounding territory became part of the Frankish kingdom in 532, the temporal sovereignty of Lyons was exercised by the archbishops, and this continued practically the case while it was nominally a part of the Empire, from 1032 to 1312. Philip the Fair erected a county of Lyons, but left it attached to the archiepiscopal see; the secular jurisdiction was not assumed by the king until 1563.

Bibliography: The occupants of the see are given in order in Gams, *Series episcoporum*, pp. 569–572, supplement, p. 38. Consult: J. Perrier, *Hist. des archevêques de Lyon*, Lons-le-Saunier, 1887; *Cartulaire des fiefs de l'église de Lyon, 1173–1521*, Lyons, 1893; J. B. Martin, *Obituaire de l'église primatiale de Lyon*, ib. 1902; idem, *Conciles et bullaire du diocèse de Lyon, des origines à , 1312*, ib. 1905; *Martyrologe de la sainte église de Lyon*, Paris, 1902.

LYONS, COUNCILS OF. For the council of 1245, see Innocent IV.; for that of 1274, see Gregory X.

LYRA, li′rā′, NICOLAUS DE (NICOLAUS LYRAMUS): French exegete; b. at Lyre (a small village in the diocese of Evreux) c. 1270; d. at Paris Oct. 23, 1340. In 1292 he entered the Franciscan order at Verneuil, and later went to Paris, where he spent the remainder of his life as a teacher at the Sorbonne. These are the only certain details of his life, and are given on his epitaph in the Minorite monastery at Paris. Other sources, however, add that in 1325 he was appointed provincial of his order for Burgundy according to the provisions of the will of Jeanne, queen of Philip the Tall. The statement that he taught in Oxford is baseless, as is the tradition that he was of Jewish descent. He doubtless acquired his knowledge of Hebrew in Paris, where oriental studies in the interest of polemics against Judaism and Mohammedanism were not unknown. Immediately after entering the monastery he began his commentary on the Bible; in 1322 he was working on Genesis, and in 1326 on Isaiah. The work reached a temporary conclusion in 1330, but was not published until after his death, when it received additions from other hands, particularly the prefaces to the individual books and the general introduction *De libris canonicis et non canonicis.* His *Postillæ* include fifty books of running commentary on the entire Bible, including the Apocrypha, which, however, are treated as non-canonical. Then follow thirty-five books of *moralia*, and the whole is preceded by three prologues. The first of these is a conventional eulogy of the Scriptures and a recommendation of their study. The second is devoted to method and is based on the theory of the double meaning of the text, one literal and the other mystical. The third prologue develops the mystical meaning in three categories, and the whole is summed up in the passage:

"The fact dwells in literal meaning, allegorical is thy belief;
The moral defineth thine actions, thine end anagoge doth tell."

The characteristic feature of Nicolaus is his sobriety as an exegete and his ability to restrict himself to the literal sense of the Bible, avoiding the peril of allegorical interpretation as well as mystic and dogmatic excursus. It is noteworthy in this connection that the Jewish exegete whom he almost transcribed was Rashi, who had introduced an anti-allegorizing epoch into Jewish hermeneutics. Of Greek Nicolaus shows little knowledge, but he had a source for Aramaic and Arabic in the *Pugio fidei* of Raymond Martin. In addition to the Church Fathers, he made much use of Thomas Aquinas. His *Postillæ* enjoyed extraordinary popularity in the Middle Ages, and were repeatedly edited, generally with the adverse criticisms of Paul of Burgos and the rejoinders of Matthæus Döring, a German Minorite. Luther in his interpretation of Genesis consulted Nicolaus in almost every sentence and owed to him his rabbinical knowledge, while Melanchthon, Urbanus Rhegius, and other Reformers were also acquainted with his work. From this fact originated the well-known doggerel of Peter of Pflug, *Si Lyra non lyrasset, Lutherus non saltasset*, or, according to another version, *Si Lyra non lyrasset, nemo doctorum in Bibliam saltasset,* "If Lyra had not played the lyre, Luther (or, those learned in the Bible) would not have danced." The remaining works of Lyra are of little interest. He proved his right to be considered a scholastic by his commentaries on Peter Lombard and the *Quodlibeta*, and wrote three books against the Jews. His alleged authorship of the treatises *De idoneo ministrante* and *Contemplatio de vita et gestis sancti Francisci* is doubtful. (R. Schmid.)

Bibliography: For a bibliography of the early editions consult J. Le Long, *Bibliotheca sacra*, ed. A. G. Masch, II., iii. 359 sqq., and cf. J. F. T. Graesse, *Trésors des livres rares et précieux*, 6 vols., Dresden, 1859–69. Consult: S. Davidson, *Sacred Hermeneutics*, Edinburgh, 1843; Siegfried, in *Archiv für Erforschung des A. T.*, vol. i., 1867; idem in *ZWT*, 1894; L. Diestel, *Geschichte des A. T. in der christlichen Kirche*, pp. 195 sqq., Jena, 1868; F. W Farrar, *Hist. of Interpretation*, pp. 274–278, New York, 1886; Maschkowski, in *ZATW*, 1891.

LYSANIAS. See Abilene.

LYTE, HENRY FRANCIS: British hymn-writer; b. at Ednam (3 m. n.n.e. of Kelso), Roxburghshire, Scotland, June 1, 1793; d. at Nice, France, Nov. 20, 1847. He was educated in Ireland, first at the royal school of Enniskillen, then at Trinity College, Dublin, where he was graduated in 1814. He took orders in 1815, and, after holding curacies at Taghmon (near Wexford), Marzion (Cornwall), and Lymington (Hampshire), entered upon the perpetual curacy of Lower Brixham, Devonshire, in 1823. This appointment he held till his death. Lyte's hymns were published partly in *Poems, chiefly Religious* (London, 1833), and partly in *The Spirit of the Psalms* (1834). Many of them are in common use. His "Abide with me, fast falls the eventide" is generally regarded as one of the few fine hymns in the language. Other well-known hymns by Lyte are, "Pleasant are Thy courts above," "Far from my heavenly home," "God of mercy, God of grace," "Praise, my soul, the King of heaven," and "Jesus,

I my cross have taken." Lyte also published *Tales in Verse* (London, 1826), and an appreciative *Memoir* of Henry Vaughan, prefixed to Vaughan's *Sacred Poems* (London, 1847). His daughter edited his *Remains* (1850), which consists of poems, sermons, and letters. The poems in this volume were reprinted in Lyte's *Miscellaneous Poems* (1868).

BIBLIOGRAPHY: Besides the *Memoir* in the *Remains*, consult: J. Miller, *Singers and Songs of the Church*, pp. 431–433, London, 1869; Julian, *Hymnology*, pp. 706–707.

LYTTELTON, GEORGE, first **BARON LYTTELTON:** English author and statesman; b. at Hagley (6 m. n.e. of Kidderminster), Worcestershire, Jan. 17, 1709; d. there Aug. 22, 1773. He studied at Eton and Christ Church, Oxford, but took no degree. He entered parliament in 1735 as member for Okehampton, Devonshire, and continued to represent this borough till 1756, when he was elevated to the peerage. He was lord commissioner of the treasury 1744–54, and chancellor of the exchequer 1755–56. Though he was a good debater, he became prominent in parliament chiefly because of his influential political connection. With Lord Cobham, his uncle, William Pitt, a relation by affinity, and the Grenvilles, his first cousins, Lyttelton formed the powerful political clique known at first as the "Cobhamites," then, after Lord Cobham's death, as the "Grenville Cousins." He was a liberal patron of literature and enjoyed the friendship of Pope, Thomson, Shenstone, Fielding, and others. His principal works are, *Observations on the Conversion and Apostleship of St. Paul* (London, 1747; new ed., 1879), which Dr. Johnson characterized as "a treatise to which infidelity has never been able to fabricate a special answer"; *Dialogues of the Dead* (1760; 4th ed., enlarged, 1765; new ed., 1889); and *The History of the Life of Henry II.* (4 vols., 1767; 3d ed., 6 vols., 1769–73), a work of much careful research, which has, however, been superseded. His verse, which is inferior to his prose, was chiefly included in *Poems* (Glasgow, 1773), and in his *Poetical Works* (London, 1785). His nephew, C. E. Ayscough, collected his *Works* (London, 1774; 3d. ed., 3 vols., 1776), including both verse and prose. Sir Robert Phillimore edited his *Memoirs and Correspondence* (2 vols., 1845).

BIBLIOGRAPHY: An excellent list of authorities is given at the end of the sketch in *DNB*, xxxiv. 369–374, and a *Life* is found in A. Chalmers, *Works of the English Poets*, vol. xiv., London, 1810. Consult also: E. S. Creasy, *Memoirs of Celebrated Etonians*, ib. 1876; and the works on the history of the times.

M

MAAS, mās, **ANTHONY JOHN:** American Jesuit; b. at Bainkhausen, a village of Westphalia, Germany, Aug. 23, 1858. He was educated at the gymnasium of Arnsberg from 1874 to 1877, when he entered the Society of Jesus. He then left Germany for the United States, and after studying at Manresa, N. Y., from 1877 to 1880, studied philosophy at Woodstock College, Woodstock, Md., until 1883. He was then professor of classics at Frederick, Md., for a year, after which he returned to Woodstock and studied theology until 1888. Except for the year 1893–94, spent in Manresa, Spain, he has been connected with Woodstock College since 1885, where he has been professor of Hebrew since 1885, librarian since 1888, professor of Scripture since 1891, prefect of studies since 1897 and president since 1907. In addition to numerous minor contributions, he has written: *Life of Jesus Christ according to the Gospel History* (St. Louis, 1891); *Day in the Temple* (ib., 1892); *Christ in Type and Prophecy* (2 vols., New York, 1893–96); and *Commentary on the Gospel of St. Matthew* (Boston, 1898), and has prepared the fourth edition of Z. Zitelli Natali's *Enchiridion ad sacrarum disciplinarum cultores accomodatum* (Baltimore, 1892).

MABILLON, mā"bī"lyēn, **JEAN:** French Roman Catholic; b. at St. Pierremont in Champagne Nov. 23, 1632; d. in Paris Dec. 27, 1707. He entered the Congregation of St. Maur in 1653, and was professed in the following year. After some years spent in different houses of the order, he was at Saint-Denis in 1663, and the next year at the abbey of Saint-Germain-des-Prés in Paris, the literary headquarters of the congregation, where he assisted D'Achery (see ACHERY, JEAN LUC D') in the compilation of the last six volumes of the *Spicilegium*. In 1667 appeared two folio volumes of the works of St. Bernard, edited from the oldest and best manuscripts, the beginning and the model of the editions of the Fathers which the congregation was to issue thenceforth in rapid succession. Mabillon's most important life-work, however, was the history of the Benedictine order, for which D'Achery had collected a mass of materials. In 1668 appeared the first volume of the *Acta sanctorum ordinis sancti Benedicti*, relating to the sixth century. After thirty-four years of work, nine folio volumes had appeared, bringing the work down to 1100, and the material for a tenth was in shape. On this foundation Mabillon began to work at his most mature production, the *Annales ordinis sancti Benedicti* (6 vols., Paris, 1703–39), of which four volumes had been published before his death; the fifth was published by R. Massuet (1713), and the sixth, to the year 1137, by E. Martène (1739). He won perhaps even greater fame in another department of scholarship, owing to a controversy with the Jesuits, brought on by a dissertation of the Bollandist Papebroch in the second volume of the *Acta sanctorum* for April (1675). Papebroch set down most of the early documents conveying monastic privileges, and especially the Merovingian archives of Saint-Denis, as forgeries. The Benedictines, in whose possession most of these were, regarded this as an attack on themselves, and Mabillon answered it in his *De re diplomatica* (1681), which is still a classic in this department, and as to Merovingian paleography has never been surpassed. In 1682 Colbert, to whom it was dedicated, sent Mabillon to Burgundy to make a study of the archives there which concerned the royal house; and he made further journeys of the sort, to Germany in 1683, to Italy in 1685–86, publishing some of his results in the *Vetera analecta* (4 vols., 1675–85) and in *Musæum Italicum* (2 vols., Paris, 1687–89). He took part in the controversy as to the authorship of the *Imitatio Christi* between the Benedictines and the Augustinians (see KEMPIS, THOMAS À, III.), in his *Animadversiones in vindicias Kempenses* (an answer to a book published by the Augustinian Testelette) deciding for the mythical Italian Benedictine abbot John Gersen. Against the Trappist De Rancé (see TRAPPISTS), who had declared that scholarship was a hindrance to monastic perfection, Mabillon maintained, in his *Traité des études monastiques* (1691) that learning was necessary to monastic clergy and no violation of the rule of St. Benedict. Other important works of his are the *De liturgia Gallicana* (1685); the edifying little book *La Mort chrétienne* (1702), and the *Dissertatio de pane eucharistico, azymo et fermentato* (1674), the last of which is printed with other smaller treatises and a number of letters in the *Ouvrages posthumes de Mabillon et de Ruinart* (3 vols., Paris, 1724). Another portion of his extensive correspondence is contained in Valery's *Correspondance inédite de Mabillon et de Montfaucon avec l'Italie* (3 vols., Paris, 1846); and a complete edition of his letters is in preparation. (G. LAUBMANN†.)

BIBLIOGRAPHY: T. Ruinart, *Abrégé de la vie de . . J. Mabillon*, Paris, 1709; C. de Malan, *Hist. de Mabillon et de la congrégation de St.-Maur*, ib. 1843; H. Jadart, *Dom Jean Mabillon*, Reims, 1879; E. de Broglie, *Mabillon et la société de l'abbaye de St.-Germain-des-Prés*, 2 vols., ib. 1888; S. Bäumer, *J. Mabillon*, Augsburg, 1892; Lichtenberger, *ESR*, viii. 520–521.

McALL MISSION (Mission populaire évangelique): A French undenominational, evangelistic mission founded in Paris in 1872 by Robert Whitaker McAll (q.v.). The immediate impulse to this act was the remark of a French working man that the French common people, though opposed to an imposed religion of forms and ceremonies, were ready to hear, if some one would teach them a religion of freedom and earnestness. The mission is addressed, not to Roman Catholics, but to free-thinkers, whether atheists or well disposed to religion, but it is conscientiously opposed to the Church of Rome. Some converts from Roman Catholicism have been made, but the majority of the converts are from the ever-increasing class in France which has broken with all religion.

The opening, Jan. 17, 1872, of a small shop as an evangelistic hall in Belleville, the communistic quarter of Paris, was the pioneer act of modern city missions in any country. French Protestant pastors and church officers welcomed it and freely lent their aid; the government, still guarding itself sedulously against the dangers inherent in meetings of working men, was quick to perceive that the *Mission aux ouvriers*, as it was at first called, tended to order; and authorized McAll to open as many halls as he would. In 1888 the work attained its largest number of halls, 130; forty-two being in Paris and its environs, and the others in thirty-three departments, Algeria, Tunis, and Corsica. In 1906 there were but fifty-eight halls, a number of those formerly worked by the mission having been taken over by Protestant churches, and others closed in the interest of better methods. The work is thus far more extensive than in the days of more mission halls, in part owing to boat work and itineracy, in part to larger and more varied use of the halls.

Sunday-schools were introduced into the mission in Jan., 1873, and immediately afterward McAll took advantage of the Thursday half-holiday to open supplementary schools for religious instruction, an example followed by the Roman Catholic and Protestant churches. The first adult Bible class in France was established in a McAll hall. The Christian Endeavor movement was introduced into France by C. E. Greig, then in charge of work among the young in the mission halls, and, after McAll's retirement, the director of the mission. The Christian Endeavor Society is of inestimable value in regions where there are no Protestant churches with which the converts may unite.

Although the one purpose of the mission is evangelization, many agencies contribute to this end. The halls are centers of temperance and dispensary work, mothers' meetings, fraternal societies, lending libraries, Bible and tract distribution, and an extensive domestic visitation. The first industrial school in France was established in a McAll hall in 1874. The first social settlement in France was founded in 1899 in connection with the work of the mission in Roubaix, and several others have since been opened elsewhere.

In 1878, 1889, and 1900 the McAll Mission, in cooperation with the British and Foreign Bible Society, and the French and the London Tract Societies, carried on evangelistic work in connection with the expositions of these years, with continuous religious meetings and an extensive sale and distribution of religious literature.

In 1882, desiring to put the work upon a permanent basis, McAll formed a Board (*Comité de direction*) of French, English, and American residents of Paris. At that time the name of the work was changed from *Mission aux ouvriers de Paris*, which it had hitherto borne, to its present name, *Mission populaire évangélique de France*. The board, however, wishing to associate the founder's name with the work, voted to add the sub-title "The McAll Mission." The president of the board was a prominent business man of Paris, Louis Saalter.

In 1885–88, the London Seaman's Mission loaned one of its boats to McAll for work in the coast cities, several permanent stations being the outcome. One of these boats, going up the Seine to Paris, aroused an immense interest there. Subsequently two chapel boats, *Le Bon Messager* and *La Bonne Nouvelle*, were built for service in the inland waterways of France, and have carried the gospel to many sequestered villages, in some of which permanent work has been established. In numerous cases they have been the means of recalling to their ancestral faith the scattered descendants of Huguenots, for generations destitute of religious privileges.

The McAll Mission neither invests money in buildings nor founds churches. Its halls are hired shops, its converts are sent to join the nearest church, in many cases forming the major part of the new accessions. Certain of the converts, mainly Roman Catholics of advanced age, prefer to remain in their own communion, though regularly attending the mission meetings. Exceptions to the rule not to establish churches have been found necessary in Corsica, and in certain parts of France where no Protestant church existed; but in these cases the converts themselves have supplied the funds for building.

The mission is supported by voluntary contributions from Great Britain, America, Protestant Europe, the descendants of Huguenots in South Africa, and an ever-increasing amount from the Protestants of France. In 1883 the American McAll Association, numbering in 1906 sixty-one auxiliaries, was formed to collect funds for the mission, and similar associations have since been formed in England, Scotland, Ireland, and Canada.

The economy with which this mission is worked is without precedent, due in part to the large proportion of unsalaried workers, and in part to the marvelous genius of its founder for organization. At no time has the average expenses of the halls exceeded a thousand dollars a year, including rent, salaries, running expenses, the due proportion of administrative expenses, and of the extensive itinerating and boat work.

Not being an effort to convert Roman Catholics, and polemics being rigidly excluded from the halls, the mission has been wonderfully exempt from opposition. Through all the evidences of animosity to religion manifested in the French Parliament in recent years no opposition to the mission has found expression. In the early days some atheists of the Belleville quarter made an attack upon it. They were frankly answered and became stanch supporters of the work. In 1898-99, during the virulent anti-Protestant campaign, the mission received some small share of abuse, but it was so strongly entrenched in public confidence that the attack fell powerless.

On Jan. 17, 1892, the twentieth anniversary of the mission was celebrated with signal evidences of the gratitude of the community and the appreciation of the State. Shortly after, McAll resigned the direction of the mission into the hands of his colleague, C. E. Greig, and removed to England. So well had he established the mission that its success has continued to increase and its importance to be recognized. In 1905 the Board of Direction gave to Greig a colleague, S. de Grenier Latour, a young man of noble Huguenot extraction, and created the office of Foreign Corresponding Secretary for America, to which they called Henri Merle d'Aubigné, son of the historian of the Reformation, and for years a worker in the mission. LOUISE SEYMOUR HOUGHTON.

BIBLIOGRAPHY: H. Bonar, *The White Fields of France; or the Story of Mr. M'All's Mission*, New York, 1879; idem, *Life and Work of Rev. G. Theophilus Dodds . . . in Connection with the McAll Mission*, ib. 1884; *Cry from the Land of Calvin and Voltaire; Records of the McAll Mission*, ib. 1887; Mrs. L. S. Houghton, *Cruise of the "Mystery" in McAll Mission Work*, ib. 1891.

McALL, ROBERT WHITAKER: English Congregationalist, and the founder of the McAll Mission (q.v.); b. at Macclesfield (17 m. s. of Manchester), Cheshire, Dec. 17, 1821; d. in Paris May 11, 1893. He was the son of a Congregational minister, but at first proposed to take up the profession of architecture. Almost at the outset of a promising career, however, he felt himself drawn to the ministry, as his father had wished; and after completing his studies at the Free College of Theology at Whalley Range, near Manchester (1844-48), he was called to the pastorate of the Congregational church at Sunderland. Subsequently he held charges at Leicester, Birmingham, Manchester, and Hadleigh, his sermons everywhere being marked by their simplicity, force, and elegance. While at Leicester, he became distinguished as a street preacher, and in all his pastorates he did extensive work in the villages, where he was eminently successful in enlisting the services of young men. In Aug., 1871, while on a ten days' visit to France with his wife, he heard, at Paris, the words of a working man which determined his future career. Convinced that there was an opportunity for evangelistic work in France among those who had abandoned religious faith, McAll, having consulted prominent French Protestant pastors, and having secured the consent and cooperation of his church at Hadleigh, returned to Paris, where, with the permission of the Government, he began evangelistic work in the communistic quarter of Belleville (Jan. 17, 1872). The work was at first carried on by the private means of McAll and his wife; but within a year interest was aroused in the undertaking, and contributions came in generously. In 1882, wishing to put the mission on a permanent foundation, McAll formed a board of directors, who in turn made him honorary director for life. This office he resigned in 1892 and returned to England to raise the funds which were urgently needed to carry on the work. Early in the following spring, becoming seriously ill, he went once more to Paris, where he died, and was buried with military honors. His wife, who died at Paris May 6, 1906, gave her last years to the mission with a devotion equal to that of her husband. McAll was the author of ninety-seven published works, chiefly tracts, many of which were written in French; and he also wrote or translated fifty hymns for the *Cantiques populaires*, the hymnal used in the McAll missions and by many other French Protestants. LOUISE SEYMOUR HOUGHTON.

BIBLIOGRAPHY: *R. W. McAll, Founder of the McAll Mission, Paris: a Fragment by himself, a Souvenir by his Wife*, London, 1896; and literature under MCALL MISSION.

MACARIUS, ma-cā'ri-us: A name of frequent occurrence in the history of the early Church (cf. the *DCB*, s.v., and Stadler and Heim, *Heiligenlexicon*, iv. 2-10, where more than forty of the name are mentioned). The most noteworthy are:

1. Macarius The Egyptian, called also **The Elder** or **The Great:** Head of the monks of the Scetic desert; b. in Upper Egypt about 300; d. in the Scetic desert, 391. He was won to the religious life at an early age by St. Anthony and when thirty years old became a monk. Ten years later he was ordained priest, and for the remainder of his life presided over the monastic community in the Scetic desert, except for a brief period during which he was banished, with other adherents of the Nicene Creed, to an island in the Nile by the Emperor Valens. The day appointed for his feast in the Eastern Church is Jan. 19, while the Western Church celebrates it four days earlier. Certain monasteries of the Libyan desert still bear the name of Macarius, and the neighborhood is called the Desert of Macarius and seems to be identical with the ancient Scetic district. The ruins of numerous monasteries in this region almost confirm the local tradition that the cloisters of Macarius were equal in number to the days of the year. Although Gennadius recognizes as the only work of Macarius a letter addressed to the younger monks, there seems to be no reason to deny the genuineness of the fifty homilies ascribed to him. The *Apophthegmata* edited with the homilies may also be genuine, but the seven so-called *Opuscula ascetica* edited under his name by P. Possinus (Paris, 1683) are merely later compilations from the homilies, made by Simeon the Logothete, who is probably identical with Simeon Metaphrastes (d. 950). Macarius likewise seems to have been the author of several minor writings, including an *Epistola ad filios Dei*, and a number of other letters and prayers. The teachings of Macarius are characterized by a mystical and spiritual mode of thought which has endeared him to Christian mystics of all ages, although, on the other hand, in his anthropology and soteriology he frequently approximates the standpoint of St. Augustine. Certain passages of his homilies assert the entire depravity of man, while others postulate free will, even after the fall of Adam, and presuppose a tendency toward virtue, or, in semi-Pelagian fashion, ascribe to man the power to attain a degree of readiness to receive salvation.

2. Macarius The Younger, or Macarius of Alexandria: A somewhat younger contemporary of the preceding, was a monk in the Nitric desert, where he died c. 406. He was an extreme ascetic, and numerous miracles were ascribed to him. He presided over the 5,000 Nitric monks with the same success as had the elder Macarius in the Scetic desert. According to oriental tradition, he died on Jan. 2, but he is also commemorated on the same days as Macarius the Egyptian, with whom he is often confused. In addition to a monastic rule and three brief apothegms, a homily "On the End of the Souls of the Righteous and of Sinners" is ascribed to him, although excellent Vienna manuscripts assign the latter to a monk named Alexander. Palladius and Sozomen also mention a Macarius the Younger of Lower Egypt, who lived in a cell for more than twenty-three years to atone for a murder which he had committed.

3. Macarius Magnes: Probably to be identified with the bishop of Magnesia who, at the Synod of the Oak in 403, brought charges against Heraclides, bishop of Ephesus, the friend of Chrysostom (see CHRYSOSTOM, § 4). He seems to have been the author of an apology against a Neo-Platonic philosopher of the early part of the fourth century, contained in a manuscript of the fifteenth century discovered at Athens in 1867 and edited by C. Blondel (Paris, 1876). This work agrees in its dogmatics with Gregory of Nyssa, and is valuable on account of the numerous excerpts from the writings of the opponent of Macarius. These fragments are apparently drawn from the lost "Words against the Christians" of Porphyry or from the "Truth-Loving Words" of Hierocles. Like Macarius the Younger, this Macarius is frequently confused with Macarius the Egyptian.

4. Macarius of Jerusalem: A bishop who took part in the Council of Nicæa and also received a long letter from Constantine the Great with reference to the building of the Church of the Redeemer at Jerusalem. Of his life no details are known. (O. ZÖCKLER†.)

BIBLIOGRAPHY: 1. The *Opera* are in *MPL*, xxxiv. 409–822; a Germ. transl. in 2 vols. appeared at Sulzbach, 1839; fifty *Homiliæ* were edited by J. G. Pritius, Leipsic, 1598; and H. J. Floss issued *Epistolæ, homiliarum loci, preces*, Cologne, 1850, and *Zwei Fragmente des heiligen Makarius*, Bonn, 1866. Consult: J. Stoffels, *Die mystische Theologie Makarius des Aegypters und die ältesten Ansätze christlicher Mystik*, Bonn, 1908; B. Lindner, *Symbolæ historiæ theologicæ mysticæ: de Macario*, Leipsic, 1846; T. Förster, in *Jahrbücher für deutsche Theologie*, 1873, pp. 439–501; R. Löbe, in *Kirchliches Jahrbuch für Sachs.-Altenburg*, 1900, pp. 37–38.

2. The *Regula monastica* ascribed to Macarius, a homily, and three apothegms are in A. Gallandi, *Bibliotheca veterum patrum*, vol. vii., 14 vols., Venice, 1765–81. Consult: Floss, ut sup.; O. Zöckler, *Askese und Mönchtum*, pp. 226–227, 247, 335, 375, Frankfort, 1897; O. Bardenhewer, *Patrologie*, pp. 232–233, Freiburg, 1901.

3. C. Blondel, *Macarii Magnetis quæ supersunt*, Paris, 1876; L. Schalkhausser, *Zu den Schriften des Macarius von Magnesia*, in *TU*, 1907; L. Duchesne, *De Macario Magnete*, Paris, 1877; W. Möller, in *TLZ*, 1877, no. 19; T. Zahn, in *ZKG*, iii. 450–459; C. J. Naumann, *Scriptorum Græcorum . quæ supersunt*, fasc. iii., Leipsic, 1880; O. Bardenhewer, ut sup., pp. 331–332.

MACARTHUR, JAMES: Church of England, bishop of Southampton; b. at Dawsholme, Dumbartonshire, June 6, 1848. He was educated at the University of Glasgow (M.A., 1868), and after being called to the Scottish Bar in 1871 and to the Inner Temple in 1874, entered Cuddesdon Theological College, where he studied in 1877–78, being ordered deacon in 1878 and ordained priest in the following year. He was successively curate of St. Mary's, Redcliff, Bristol, in 1878–80, rector of Lamplugh, Cumberland, in 1880–87, and vicar of St. Mary's, Tothill Fields, Westminster, in 1887–92 and of All Saints', South Acton, Middlesex, in 1892–1893. He was also rural dean of Ealing in 1894–1898, and in the latter year was consecrated bishop of Bombay, a diocese which he retained until 1903. He was acting metropolitan of India in 1902, and in the following year was translated to his present see of Southampton (suffragan to the bishop of Winchester). In addition to charges, addresses, and sermons, he has written *Christianity and Indian Nationality* (London, 1903).

MACARTHUR, ROBERT STUART: Baptist; b. at Dalesville, P. Q., July 31, 1841. He was educated at the University of Rochester (A.B., 1867) and Rochester Theological Seminary, from which he was graduated in 1870. Since the latter year he has been pastor of Calvary Baptist Church, New York City. He was for many years a correspondent of *The Chicago Standard*, and was long connected editorially with *The Christian Inquirer* and *The Baptist Quarterly Review*. In addition to compiling a number of hymnals, of which the most important is the *Calvary Selection of Hymns and Spiritual Songs* (in collaboration with C. S. Robinson; New York, 1879) and *Laudes Domini* (in collaboration with C. S. Robinson; 1889), he has written *Calvary Pulpit* (New York, 1890); *Divine Balustrades* (Chicago, 1892); *Quick Truths in Quaint Texts* (2 series, 1895–1907); *The Attractive Christ, and other Sermons* (Philadelphia, 1898); *Current Questions for Thinking Men* (1898); *Bible Difficulties and their Alternative Interpretations* (New York, 1899); *Celestial Lamp* (Philadelphia, 1899); *Old Book and Old Faith* (New York, 1899); *Round the World* (Philadelphia, 1899); *The Land and the Book* (1900); *The Questions of the Centuries* (Cleveland, 1905); *Advent, Christmas, New Year, Easter, and Other Sermons* (1908); and *The Christian Reign, and Other Sermons* (1909).

McAULEY, CATHARINE ELIZABETH: Founder of the Sisters of Mercy; b. at Gormanstown House, near Dublin, Ireland, Sept. 29, 1787; d. at Dublin Nov. 11, 1841. She was born in the Roman Catholic faith, but, having been left an orphan, was brought up in a Protestant family. At the age of eighteen she was adopted by Mr. and Mrs. Callahan of Coolock House (north of Dublin), whom she converted to Roman Catholicism, and on the death of Mr. Callahan in 1822 she inherited his fortune. She now erected in Lower Baggot Street, Dublin, the House of our Blessed Lady of Mercy, which was completed in 1827. She and two companions then underwent the novitiate in the Presentation convent of George's Hill, Dublin. They returned to Baggot Street in Dec., 1830, and in Jan., 1831, gave the religious dress to six sisters who had been in charge during their absence. Thus was founded the order of Sisters of Mercy (see MERCY, SISTERS OF).

BIBLIOGRAPHY: *Life of Catharine McAuley*, New York, 1866; *Dublin Review*, March, 1847, pp. 1–25; *DNB*, xxxiv. 420–421.

McAULEY, JEREMIAH: Methodist missionary; b. in Kerry, Ireland, about 1839; d. in New York Sept. 18, 1884. He had no schooling and when he was thirteen years old emigrated to America. There he assisted his sister's husband in his business in New York, but soon, falling in with evil companions, he left his home and became a river thief. When only nineteen years old he was arrested for highway robbery and although innocent of the charge was convicted and sentenced to fifteen years' imprisonment at Sing Sing (Jan., 1857). While in prison he was converted, largely through the medium of Orville Gardner, a fellow convict, and he himself converted many others in the prison. Governor Dix, after proof was laid before him of McAuley's innocence of the charge against him, pardoned him (Mar. 8, 1864). On leaving prison he had no friends to help him lead an honest life, and relapsed into his old ways. In 1872 he found Christian friends who assisted him, and in October of that year he opened at 316 Water Street a "Helping Hand for Men," where he did a great amount of good and saved many a man from evil courses. In 1876 the old building was replaced by a better one, and the mission was incorporated as the McAuley Water Street Mission. In 1882 he began another mission on Thirty-second Street, near Sixth Avenue, where he labored until his death. Himself an ex-convict, he knew the hardships and temptations of such men and therefore could aid and save them far better than many a man who had not had his experience.

BIBLIOGRAPHY: R. M. Offord, *Jerry McAuley; his Life and Work*, New York, 1885; H. Campbell, *The Problem of the Poor; Record of quiet Work in unquiet Places*, ib. 1882; *Jerry McAuley, an Apostle to the Lost*, 5th ed., ib., 1908 (by a number of writers).

McBEE, SILAS: Protestant Episcopal layman; b. at Lincolnton, N. C., Nov. 14, 1853. He was educated at the University of the South, Sewanee, Tenn., from which he was graduated in 1876. Since 1896 he has been editor of *The Churchman* (New York). He is a member of the board of managers of the Prayer Book Society in America, and in theology describes himself as "a Catholic (in its real and not sectarian sense) Churchman."

MACBRIDE, JOHN DAVID: English orientalist; b. at Plympton (5 m. n.n.e. of Plymouth), Devonshire, June 28, 1778; d. at Oxford Jan. 24, 1868. He studied at Exeter College, Oxford (B.A., 1799; M.A., 1802), where he received a fellowship in 1800. In 1813 he was appointed principal of Magdalen Hall and lord almoner's reader in Arabic. These positions he held till his death. Though he was a layman, he frequently lectured on theology. His principal work was *The Mohammedan Religion Explained* (London, 1857). He also published *Lectures Explanatory of the Diatessaron* (2 vols., Oxford, 1835); *Diatessaron, or the History of our Lord Jesus Christ compiled from the Four Gospels* (1837); *Lectures on the Articles of the United Church of England and Ireland* (1853); *The Syrian Church in India* (1856); and *Lectures on the Acts of the Apostles and on the Epistles* (1858).

BIBLIOGRAPHY: *DNB*, xxxiv. 429–430.

McBURNEY, ROBERT ROSS: General secretary of the New York City Young Men's Christian Association; b. at Castleblayney (12 m. s.e. of Monaghan), County Monaghan, Ireland, Mar. 31, 1837; d. at Clifton Springs, N. Y., Dec. 27, 1898. He was the son of a physician of repute. When seventeen he came to New York, where he learned the hatter's trade. Eight years later he became "librarian" of the New York Y. M. C. A., then occupying rooms on the second floor at 659 Broadway. Here he was associated with a group of young men who later became leading business men in the city, and together they were instrumental in building up the organization till in Dec., 1869, its first building, at Twenty-third Street and Fourth Avenue, costing with site $487,000, was completed and occupied. The following figures briefly contrast the work at the time he took charge of it and near the end of his secretaryship: In 1862: 150 members, two small rented rooms, and an annual expenditure of $1,700; in 1897: 7,309 membership, work conducted at fifteen points, nine buildings valued at $2,000,000, annual budget $175,000.

McBurney was for thirty years a member of the Y. M. C. A. International Committee; and as its corresponding member he in 1866 called the first New York State convention which he for three years served as president. He was seven times a delegate to the triennial World's Conference, held in Europe; in 1871 he was one of the founders and till his death was a leader of the Association of General Secretaries of North America. He was active outside of the association; he was a lifelong member and for many years an official of St. Paul's Methodist Episcopal Church; from 1867 an active member of the executive committee of the Evangelical Alliance. Besides these activities, he was an active participant and director in many enterprises and institutions directed to philanthropic and religious ends. He was not a college graduate, but he read widely and carefully. He was a close student of the Bible and a successful teacher. He traveled extensively in America, visited Europe many times, and made a tour of Egypt and the Holy Land. He was distinguished for his sturdy Scotch character, strong common sense, energy, tact, and executive ability, with an integrity and conscientiousness that were never questioned. He was above all a lover of young men and his large-hearted and practical sympathy never failed. Perhaps no other man in his generation touched and helped so many young men. RICHARD C. MORSE.

BIBLIOGRAPHY: L. L. Doggett, *Life of Robert R. McBurney*, Cleveland, O., 1902.

McCABE, CHARLES CARDWELL: Methodist Episcopal bishop, better known as Chaplain McCabe; b. at Athens, O., Oct. 11, 1836; d. in New York City Dec. 19, 1906. He entered Ohio Wesleyan University, Delaware, O., in 1854, but did not complete the course, which he frequently interrupted to do evangelistic work. His health gave way and on his recovery he taught the high school at Ironton, O., 1858–60. He joined the Ohio conference and was ordained deacon Sept. 23, 1860, and appointed to Putnam, since incorporated into the city of Zanesville, O. He pleaded the Union cause so vigorously and successfully that it was largely owing to him that the 122d regiment of Ohio Volunteers was raised. He was ordained elder at Zanesville Sept. 7, 1862, and appointed chaplain of the regiment on Oct. 8, 1862. He proved himself efficient; indeed has been styled "the most popular and distinguished chaplain" in the volunteer army. He was during the rest of his life called "chaplain," whatever other designation his office entitled him to. On June 16, 1863, he was captured on the field of battle at Gettysburg, Pa., and sent by Major General J. A. Early to Libby Prison, Richmond. He did much to relieve the tedium of confinement, showed himself indefatigable in getting up entertainments, a son of consolation to the downcast, and ardent in impressing religious truth upon his associates. But on Sept. 25 he came down with typhoid fever and was very ill. In October he was exchanged and allowed to leave the prison. He resigned his chaplaincy, Jan. 8, 1864, received his commission as a delegate of the United States Christian Commission (Mar. 29, 1864) and was one of its most active members. "Whether pleading for money throughout the North or singing (he had a remarkable gift of song) and preaching to the soldiers in Southern camps, he was equally happy and successful." At the close of the war he was appointed (Sept., 1865) to Spencer Chapel in Portsmouth, O., and had a series of revivals until he left it to be centenary agent of Ohio Wesleyan University in 1866. He exhibited great ability as a money-raiser and was continuously employed by his denomination for this purpose. In 1868 he was elected financial agent of the Church Extension Society, in 1872 the title was dropped and he was elected assistant corresponding secretary. In 1884 he was elected secretary of the missionary society of his church. He stirred great enthusiasm by proposing that the society should raise a million dollars for missions, foreign and domestic, in 1885. Unsuccessful in the first effort, although nearly $96,000 advance had been made, he renewed the effort and reached his point in 1887 In 1896 he was elected a bishop. To this office he brought his great popularity and tireless energy, his spiritual enthusiasm and Evangelical fervor. He did noteworthy service in Mexico and South America in 1899–1902. In Dec., 1902, he was elected chancellor of the American University. But under this accumulation of duties and under the strain of trying to finance his gigantic schemes he sank and died of apoplexy. He was able to raise large sums by his lecture, frequently repeated and yet never wholly repeated, "The Bright Side of Life in Libby Prison."

BIBLIOGRAPHY: F. M. Bristol, *The Life of Chaplain McCabe*, New York, 1908 (it contains a summary of the famous lecture).

M'CABE, JOSEPH: English ex-Franciscan; b. at Macclesfield (15 m. s.e. of Manchester), Cheshire, Nov. 11, 1867. He was educated at St. Francis' College, Manchester (1883–84), Holy Trinity, Killarney (1884–85), St. Anthony's, London (1885–91), and the University of Louvain (1893–94). In 1891 he was ordained to the Roman Catholic priesthood and appointed professor of scholastic philosophy at St. Anthony's College, London, where he taught in 1891–93 and 1894–95. In 1895–96 he was rector of St. Bernardine's College, Buckingham, but in the latter year abandoned the Church on account of his adoption of agnostic views, and since that time has been a private secretary, lecturer, journalist, and author. Besides translating E. Haeckel's *Riddle of the Universe* (London, 1900); *Wonders of Life* (1904); *Evolution of Man* (1905); and *Last Words on Evolution* (1906); F. K. C. Büchner's *Last Words on Materialism* (1901); and W. Bölsche's *Haeckel* (1906), he has written *From Rome to Rationalism* (London, 1896); *Modern Rationalism* (1897); *Twelve Years in a Monastery* (1897); *Life in a modern Monastery* (1898); *Can we Disarm?* (1899); *The Religion of the Twentieth Century* (1899); *Peter Abé-*

lard (1901); *Saint Augustine and his Age* (1902); *Haeckel's Critics answered* (1905); *Religion of Woman* (1905); *The Origin of Life* (1906); *Secular Education* (1906); *Talleyrand* (1906); *The Bible in Europe; an Inquiry into the Contribution of the Christian Religion to Civilisation* (1907); *Life and Letters of George Jacob Holyoake* (2 vols., 1908); and *The Decay of the Church of Rome* (1909).

MACCABEES. See HASMONEANS.

MACCABEES, BOOKS OF: See APOCRYPHA, A, IV., 9–11.

MACCABEES, FESTIVAL OF THE: The celebration on Aug. 1 of the martyrdom of the seven brothers and of their mother under Antiochus Epiphanes (cf. II Macc. vii.). The festival dates from the fourteenth century.

BIBLIOGRAPHY: H. Wace, *The Apocrypha*, ii. 589 sqq., in "Speakers Commentary," London, 1888.

MacCARTHY, WELBORE: Church of England, bishop of Grantham; b. at Cork, Ireland, Apr. 11, 1840. He was educated at Trinity College, Dublin, and St. Aidan's Theological College, Birkenhead, and was ordered deacon in 1867 and ordained priest in the following year. He was successively curate of Preston-Patrick, Westmoreland (1867–68), Ulverston (1868–71), Christ Church, Battersea (1871–72), and Balham, Surrey (1872–73). He then went to India, where he was chaplain at Jhansi, Northwestern Provinces (1874–75), Rangoon, Burma (1875–1877), St. Paul's Cathedral, Calcutta (1877–82 and 1889–98), Mussooree (1882–84), Meerut (1884–85), Shahjahanpur (1885–87; all three in the Northwestern Provinces), and Lucknow (1888–89). He was likewise commissary to the bishop of Calcutta in 1879–82 and 1891–98, as well as acting archdeacon of Calcutta in 1891–92 and archdeacon in 1892–98. Returning to England in 1898, he was rector of Ashwell in 1898–1901 and vicar of Gainsborough in 1901–05, besides being assistant chaplain of St. George's, Cannes, France, in 1900–05, and rural dean of Corringham and prebendary of Lincoln in 1901–1905. In 1905 he became vicar of Grantham, and in the same year was consecrated bishop of Grantham (suffragan to the bishop of Lincoln).

McCAUL, ALEXANDER: Church of England; b. at Dublin, Ireland, May 16, 1799; d. at London Nov. 13, 1863. He studied at Trinity College, Dublin (B.A., 1819), and in 1821 went to Warsaw, Poland, as a missionary of the London Society for Promoting Christianity among the Jews. At the close of 1822 he returned to England, took orders and became curate of Huntley, near Gloucester, but on his marriage in 1823 he returned to Warsaw, where he lived as head of the Jewish mission and English chaplain till 1830. Settling in London he continued to cooperate with the London Society, which in 1840 made him principal of the Hebrew college in London. In 1841 he was given the professorship of Hebrew and rabbinical literature in King's College, London, to which the chair of divinity was added in 1846. He became rector of St. James's in 1843, prebendary of St. Paul's in 1845, and rector of the parish of St. Magnus, St. Margaret, and St. Michael on Fish Street Hill, in 1850. On the revival of Convocation in 1852 he was elected proctor for the London clergy, whom he represented till his death. He published a large number of single sermons and pamphlets, but his principal works are two series of Warburtonian lectures: *Lectures on the Prophecies* (London, 1846) and *The Messiahship of Jesus* (1852). He wrote also *Rationalism and the Divine Interpretation of Scripture* (1850); *Notes on the First Chapter of Genesis* (1861); *Testimonies to the Divine Authority of the Holy Scriptures* (1862), and *An Examination of Bishop Colenso's Difficulties with Regard to the Pentateuch* (2 parts, 1863–64).

BIBLIOGRAPHY: J. B. McCaul, *A Memorial Sketch of Alexander McCaul*, Oxford, 1863; *DNB*, xxxv. 1–2.

McCHEYNE, mak-shên, ROBERT MURRAY: Church of Scotland; b. at Edinburgh May 21, 1813; d. at Dundee Mar. 25, 1843. He studied at the University of Edinburgh, where he distinguished himself by his poetical talent, being awarded a prize by Professor John Wilson ("Christopher North") for a poem on *The Covenanters*. In 1831 he took up the study of theology at the Divinity Hall of the university under Thomas Chalmers and David Welsh, and on Nov. 7, 1835, he began his ministerial labors at Larbert, near Falkirk, as assistant to John Bonar. On Nov. 24, 1836, he was ordained to the pastorate of St. Peter's Church, Dundee, which he held till his death. In 1839 he was a member of the committee sent to Palestine by the General Assembly of the Church of Scotland to collect information respecting the Jews. On his return he entered upon a successful evangelistic campaign, first at Dundee, then at other places in Scotland and northern England. In the controversy that finally led to the disruption of the Scottish Church he took very decided ground on the non-intrusion side. McCheyne was a fine example of the true Gospel preacher. Long after his death he was constantly referred to as "the saintly McCheyne." His principal works are, *Narrative of a Mission of Inquiry to the Jews in 1839* (in collaboration with A. A. Bonar; Edinburgh, 1842); *Expositions of the Epistles to the Seven Churches of Asia* (Dundee, 1843); *The Eternal Inheritance two Discourses* (1843); *Memoirs and Remains* (ed. A. A. Bonar, Edinburgh, 1843, and often; new ed., 1897); and *Additional Remains, Sermons, and Lectures* (1844). The *Remains*, which have done much to perpetuate McCheyne's memory, consist of sermons, fugitive pieces, and hymns, including the popular "When this passing world is done."

BIBLIOGRAPHY: The principal work is the *Memoir and Remains* by A. A. Bonar, ut sup., abridged ed., Edinburgh, 1865. Consult further the short *Life* by J. L. Watson, London, 1881; *DNB*, xxxv. 3.

MACCHI, mä″chî, LUIGI: Cardinal; b. at Viterbo (42 m. n.n.w. of Rome), Italy, Mar. 3, 1832; d. at Rome Mar. 29, 1907. He was ordained to the priesthood in 1859, and was soon appointed privy chamberlain by Pius IX. After being made domestic prelate, vice-president of the hospice for the poor in the Baths of Diocletian, and an incumbent of other offices, he was appointed, in 1875, *mæstro di camera*, an office in which he was confirmed by Leo XIII. In 1886 he became major domo and prefect of the apostolic palaces, and in the former capacity successfully carried out the jubilee of the Pope's ordination to the priesthood. In 1889 he was created cardinal-deacon of Santa Maria in Aquiro, and after 1896 was cardinal-deacon of Santa Maria in Via Lata. Although not a bishop, the cardinal was made abbot *in commendam* of San Benedetto di Subiaco in 1890, and was secretary of the Congregation of Briefs and great chancellor of all papal orders of knights, as well as a member of the congregations of the Council, Rites, Ceremonies, and Indulgences.

McCLELLAN, JOHN BROWN: Church of England; b. in Glasgow, Scotland, Mar. 7, 1836. He was educated at Trinity College, Cambridge (B.A., 1858; M.A., 1861). He was fellow of his college (1859–61). Ordained deacon in 1860, and priest in 1861, he was vicar of Bottisham, Cambridgeshire (1861–80); and rural dean of first division of Camp's deanery (1871–77). In 1880 he was appointed principal of the Royal Agricultural College at Cirencester, Gloucestershire. He is the author of: *Fourth Nicene Canon and the Election and Consecration of Bishops* (London, 1870); and *The New Testament: A New Translation* (only one vol. published; 1875).

McCLINTOCK, JOHN: Methodist Episcopalian; b. in Philadelphia Oct. 27, 1814; d. at Madison, N. J., Mar. 4, 1870. He was graduated from the University of Pennsylvania in 1835 and was received as a traveling preacher in the New Jersey Annual Conference the same year. From 1836 to 1848 he taught in Dickinson College, Carlisle, Penn., holding the chair of mathematics 1836–40, and that of Greek and Latin 1840–48. He was then editor of *The Methodist Quarterly Review* 1848–56. In 1857 he went to England as a delegate to the Wesleyan Methodist Conference. He was pastor of St. Paul's Methodist Church, New York, 1857–60, and pastor of the American Chapel, Paris, 1860–64. During the Civil War in America his pen was constantly active in the interest of the Union cause. In 1864 he was recalled to St. Paul's, but ill health forced him to resign a year later. From 1867 till his death he was president of the newly established Drew Theological Seminary, Madison, N. J. He was an eloquent and impressive preacher and one of the best scholars that his denomination has produced. In addition to a popular series of Greek and Latin text-books and numerous articles in periodicals, he published *Analysis of Watson's Theological Institutes* (New York, 1842; a translation of Neander's *Life of Christ* (1847); *Sketches of Eminent Methodist Ministers* (1852); *The Temporal Power of the Pope* (1853); and a translation of Bungener's *History of the Council of Trent* (1855). His most important work, however, was the *Cyclopædia of Biblical, Theological, and Ecclesiastical Literature* (10 vols. and Supplement 2 vols., New York, 1867–87). In collaboration with James Strong he began to collect materials for this work as early as 1853, but lived to see only three volumes through the press. After his death there appeared *Living Words* (1870), a volume of sermons; and *Lectures on Theological Encyclopædia and Methodology* (1873).

BIBLIOGRAPHY: G. R. Crooks, *Life and Letters of Rev. John McClintock*, New York, 1876.

McCLOSKEY, JOHN: American cardinal; b. in Brooklyn Mar. 20, 1810; d. in New York Oct. 10, 1885. He studied at Mount St. Mary's College, Emmitsburg, Md., was ordained priest in 1834, and then pursued postgraduate studies in theology at the Roman College. Returning to America in 1837 he was assigned for parish duty to St. Joseph's Church, New York City. When St. John's College, Fordham, was opened in 1841 he was appointed its first president, but the year following he returned to his parish work at St. Joseph's. In 1844 he was appointed coadjutor to Bishop Hughes of the diocese of New York, being made titular bishop of Axiere, *in partibus infidelium*. He was consecrated Mar. 10, and though assisting the bishop in his episcopal functions, he retained his position as pastor of St. Joseph's parish. In 1847 he was transferred from New York to become the first bishop of the newly erected diocese of Albany, and this post he filled during the ensuing seventeen years. The new diocese included nearly all of the northern and eastern portions of the state of New York, and throughout this vast territory Roman Catholics were relatively few and without resources; there were in all only about forty churches and many of these were without priests. During his administration conditions were greatly improved and much was done by way of organization and development. Thus in Albany he built the fine cathedral of the Immaculate Conception, which was dedicated in 1852; new parishes were established in great numbers throughout the diocese; many schools and homes were erected, and in 1864 St. Joseph's Provincial Seminary for the training of ecclesiastical students was opened in Troy. In May of the same year he was appointed to succeed Archbishop Hughes in the metropolitan see of New York. In this capacity he attended the Vatican Council in 1870, and was a member of the committee on ecclesiastical discipline. In 1875 he was made cardinal by Pius IX. with the title of *Sancta Maria supra Minervam*. On the death of Pius IX. in 1878 he left for Rome in order to attend the conclave in which Leo XIII. was elected, but arrived too late to take part in the proceedings. He had a distinguished career as a churchman, having taken an important part in the remarkable development of the Roman Catholic Church in New York during that period. He was a prelate of more than ordinary scholarship, and though mild and gentle in character, he possessed the firmness necessary to the leader, together with great executive ability JAMES F. DRISCOLL.

BIBLIOGRAPHY: J. G. Shea, *Hist. of the Catholic Church within the Limits of the United States*, vol. iv., passim, New York, 1892; *Lives of the Clergy of New York and Brooklyn*, ib. 1874.

McCLURE, JAMES GORE KING: Presbyterian; b. at Albany, N. Y., Nov. 24, 1848. He was educated at Yale (A.B., 1870) and Princeton Theological Seminary, from which he was graduated in 1873. He was ordained to the Presbyterian ministry in 1874, and from that year until 1879 was pastor at New Scotland, N. Y., after which he traveled in Europe for two years. He was then pastor at Lake Forest, Ill., until 1905, and also president of Lake Forest University from 1897 until his resignation in 1901. Since 1905 he has been president of McCormick Theological Seminary. He was also president of the College Board of the Presbyterian Church in the United States of America in 1903-04. He has written: *Possibilities* (Chicago, 1896); *The Man who Wanted to Help* (1897); *The Great Appeal* (1898); *Environment* (1899); *For Hearts that Hope* (1900); *A mighty Means of Usefulness* (1901); *Living for the Best* (1903); *The Growing Pastor* (1904); *Loyalty the Soul of Religion* (1905); and *Supreme Things* (sermons; 1908).

McCLYMONT, JAMES ALEXANDER: Church of Scotland; b. at Girvan (17 m. s.w. of Ayr), Ayrshire, May 26, 1848. He was educated at the universities of Edinburgh (M.A., 1867; B.D., 1870) and Tübingen, and was assistant in Dundee Parish Church from 1871 to 1874. Since the latter year he has been minister of Holburn Parish, Aberdeen, as well as chaplain to the Gordon Highlanders. He was examiner in Hebrew in Aberdeen University in 1894 and in Hebrew and Biblical criticism in 1906–08, and is also convener of the Business Committee of the Aberdeen Synod and a member of the General Committee of the Church of Scotland. In theology he describes himself as an "Evangelical Broad Churchman." Besides his work as joint editor (with A. H. Charteris) of the *Guild Text-Books* (Edinburgh, 1890 sqq.) and the *Guild Library* (London, 1895 sqq.), he has translated J. T. Beck's *Pastorallehren des Neuen Testamentes* (Gütersloh, 1880) under the title *Pastoral Theology of the New Testament* (in collaboration with T. Nicol; Edinburgh, 1885); and has written *The New Testament and its Writers* (1892); *St. John's Gospel* in *The Century Bible* (1901); and *Greece* (London, 1906).

McCOOK, HENRY CHRISTOPHER: Presbyterian; b. at New Lisbon, O., July 3, 1837. He was educated at Jefferson College (B.A., 1859) and at the Western Theological Seminary, Allegheny, Pa. (1859–61). He was first lieutenant, and afterward chaplain, in the Forty-first Regiment Illinois Volunteers. He has held pastorates at Clinton, Ill. (1861–63); St. Louis, Mo. (1863–69); and at Philadelphia, Pa. (1869-1902; since 1903, pastor emeritus). He has written: *Object and Outline Teaching: Guide Book for Sunday School Workers* (St. Louis, 1871); *Teacher's Commentary on Gospel Narrative of Last Year of our Lord's Ministry* (Philadelphia, 1871); was a contributor to the *Tercentenary Book* (of the Heidelberg Catechism; 1863); *Natural History of the Agricultural Ant of Texas* (1879); *Honey Ants of the Garden of the Gods and the Occident Ants of the American Plains* (1881); *Tenants of an Old Farm: Leaves from the Note-Book of a Naturalist* (New York, 1885 [1884]); *Women Friends of Jesus* (1886 [1885]); *Gospel in Nature* (Philadelphia, 1886); *American Spiders, and their Spinning Work* (3 vols., 1890–93); *Old Farm Fairies* (1895); *The Latimers: Tale of the Western Insurrection of 1794* (1898 [1897]); *Martial Graves of our Fallen Heroes in Santiago de Cuba* (1899); *The Senator: a Threnody* (1905); *Nature's Craftsmen: Popular Studies of Ants and other Insects* (New York, 1907); and *Ant Communities* (1909).

McCORMICK, JOHN NEWTON: Protestant Episcopal bishop coadjutor of western Michigan; b. at Richmond, Va., Feb. 1, 1863. He was educated at Randolph-Macon College, Va. (A.B., 1883) and Johns Hopkins University (1886–88). From 1883 to 1893 he was a Methodist Episcopal minister, but entering the Protestant Episcopal Church he was rector successively of St. Paul's, Suffolk, Va., 1893 to 1895, of St. Luke's, Atlanta, Ga., 1895, and of St. Mark's, Grand Rapids, Mich., 1898. In 1906 he was consecrated bishop coadjutor of western Michigan. He has written: *Distinctive Marks of the Episcopal Church* (Milwaukee, 1902); *The Litany and the Life* (1904); and *Pain and Sympathy* (1907).

McCOSH, JAMES: Presbyterian divine and educator; b. at Carskeoch (36 m. s.s.w. of Glasgow), a farm in the parish of Straiton, Ayrshire, Scotland, Apr. 1, 1811; d. at Princeton, N. J., Nov. 16, 1894. He was destined at an early age for the ministry by his father, who put him under the tuition of a pious man, one Quentin Smith. In 1824 he entered the University of Glasgow, and in 1829 he removed to the University of Edinburgh (M.A., 1834), where he studied divinity under Chalmers. He was licensed by the presbytery of Ayr in 1834 and was settled first in Arbroath, a parish of sailors and artizans, but in 1838 he was appointed pastor at Brechin, Forfarshire. At the disruption of 1843 he entered the Free Church and became superintendent of a mountainous district in Forfarshire. In 1850 he was called to Queen's College, Belfast, as professor of logic and metaphysics. There he not only devoted himself to the duties of his chair, but also interested himself in Evangelical work in Smithfield, establishing a church and founding schools. He took great interest in Irish affairs and was a firm advocate of the national system of schools. He desired the abolition of the *Regium Donum*, yet he suggested a sustentation fund, as he had done before in Scotland. In the summer of 1858 he traveled in Germany; and in 1866 he made a journey to the United States, investigating chiefly the system of education in use here. In May, 1868, he was elected president of the College of New Jersey, Princeton, which position he retained until his resignation in 1888. McCosh was one of Princeton's most influential presidents; he introduced, but with more restrictions than at Harvard and at Yale, the elective system. He was a firm, although kind, disciplinarian. After his resignation he still showed interest in the college, continuing his lectures there on philosophy for two years. As a philosopher McCosh takes a high rank; he was a firm believer in realism and strongly opposed both to idealism and to materialism. He always strove to keep abreast of the times, from the start giving his assent to the doctrine of evolution and showing how it could be reconciled with the Gospel teachings, in which he was always a firm believer. Of his voluminous works the more important are: *The Method of Divine Government, Physical and Moral* (Edinburgh, 1850); *Typical Forms and Special Ends in Creation* (1855), in collaboration with G. Dickie; *The Intuitions of the Mind, Inductively Investigated* (London, 1860); *The Supernatural in Relation to the Natural* (Cambridge, 1862); *A Defense of Fundamental Truth; being an Examination of Mr. J. S. Mill's Philosophy* (London, 1866); *The Laws of Discursive Thought* (1870); *Christianity and Positivism* (New York, 1871); *The Scottish Philosophy, Biographical, Expository, Critical* (London, 1874); *The Emotions* (1880); *Psychology: the Cognitive Powers* (1886); *Psychology: the Motive Powers, Emotions, Conscience, Will* (1887); *The Realistic Philosophy Defended* (1887); *The Religious Aspect of Evolution* (1888); *Gospel Sermons* (1888); *The First and Fundamental Truths* (1889); and *Our Moral Nature* (1892).

Bibliography: *Life of James McCosh, a Record chiefly Autobiographical*, ed. W. M. Sloane, New York, 1896 (contains a list, by J. H. Dulles, of the published writings of Dr. McCosh).

MACCOVIUS, mā-cō'vī-ʊs, JOHANNES (Jan Makowsky): Polish Reformed theologian; b. at Lobzenic, Poland, 1588; d. at Franeker, Holland, June 24, 1644. After visiting various universities as the tutor of young Polish nobles, and holding disputations with Jesuits and Socinians, he entered the University of Franeker in 1613. There he became privat-docent in 1614 and professor of theology in 1615 Theologically he was a rigid Calvinist of the extreme supralapsarian school, and theses of a corresponding character, defended in 1616 by one of his pupils, involved him in a controversy with his colleague Sibrandus Lubbertus (q.v.) which was settled only by the Synod of Dort in 1619. The synod, while neither approving nor condemning his supralapsarianism, acquitted Maccovius of the charges of heresy brought against him, but advised him to be more cautious and peaceable. Nevertheless, he became involved in another controversy at Dort with his subsequent colleague William Ames (q.v.) by asserting that all things that must be believed are not necessarily true, that no impulse toward regeneration and effecting it exists in the unregenerate, and that Christ is the object of faith because of whom, but not in whom, man must believe. Maccovius' theory of Scripture was very free, and he distinguished sharply between scholarship and beliefs essential to salvation. His fame attracted many students to Franeker. His chief works are: *Collegia theologica* (Amsterdam, 1623); and the posthumous *Maccovius redivivus sive manuscripta eius typis exscripta* (Franeker, 1647) and *Loci communes* (1650). (S. D. van Veen.)

Bibliography: A. Kuyper, Jr., *Johannes Maccovius*, Leyden, 1899; E. L. Briemoet, *Athenarum Frisiacarum libri*, pp. 151-160, Leeuwarden, 1758; J. Heringa Ez, in *Archief voor Kerkelijke Geschiedenis*, 1831, iii. 503-564; W. B. S. Boeles, *Frieslands Hoogeschool en het Rijks Athenaeum te Franeker*, ii. 90-94, Leeuwarden, 1889.

MacCRACKEN, HENRY MITCHELL: Presbyterian; b. at Oxford, O., Sept. 28, 1840. He was educated at Miami University, Oxford, O. (A.B., 1857), United Presbyterian Theological Seminary, Xenia, O. (1860-62), Princeton Theological Seminary (from which he was graduated in 1863), and the universities of Tübingen and Berlin (1867-68). In 1857-58 he was a teacher of classics in Grove Academy, Cedarville, O., and in 1858-60 was superintendent of the Union Schools of South Charleston, O., after which he was pastor of the Westminster Presbyterian Church, Columbus, O. (1863-67), and the First Presbyterian Church, Toledo, O. (1868-81). He was then chancellor of Western University, Pittsburg, Pa., for three years (1881-1884), and from 1884 to 1891 was professor of philosophy and vice-chancellor of New York University, and from 1891 to 1910 chancellor of the same institution. He was a deputy to the General Assembly of the Free Church of Scotland in 1867 and to the General Assembly of the Irish Presbyterian Church in the same year and in 1884. He has edited, translated, and enlarged F. Piper's *Evangelischer Calender* (Berlin, 1875) under the title *Lives of the Leaders of our Church Universal* (Philadelphia, 1880).

McCRIE, THOMAS: The name of two prominent Scotch Presbyterians.

1. The biographer of John Knox; b. at Dun (36 m. e.s.e. of Edinburgh), Berwickshire, Nov., 1772; d. at Edinburgh Aug. 5, 1835. After teaching for a time in the neighboring elementary schools he studied at the University of Edinburgh (1788-1791), but did not graduate. In 1791 he opened an "anti-burgher" school at Brechin, where he resided for three years, except during the few weeks which were annually required for attendance at the theological seminary of the General Associate Synod (anti-burgher) at Whitburn. He was licensed in 1795 by the associate presbytery of Kelso, and in 1796 he was ordained pastor of the Potterrow Church, Edinburgh. In 1806, owing to differences about the province of civil magistrates in religious affairs, a schism occurred in the anti-burgher denomination, and McCrie and three other ministers withdrew from the General Associate Synod and on Aug. 28, 1806, organized the Constitutional Associate Presbytery, which in 1827 was merged in the Synod of Original Seceders. At the end of a lawsuit McCrie was ejected from the Potterrow Church in 1809. His congregation then built him the West Richmond Street Church, where he continued his ministrations till his death. During the years 1816-18 he filled the chair of divinity in the theological seminary of his denomination. McCrie's works grew chiefly out of investigations which the controversies of the time led him to make into the early history of the Church of Scotland. His most important work is his *Life of John Knox* (2 vols., Edinburgh, 1812; 2d ed., enlarged, 1813), which not only placed McCrie in the front rank of the authors of his day, but also produced a great change of popular sentiment in regard to Knox. It was distinguished by original, painstaking research, independence of judgment, judicial fairness of mind, and singular clearness of style; and its effect on the general estimate of Knox among men was not unlike that produced, in the succeeding generation, in reference to Cromwell, by the publication of Carlyle's monograph. There is reason to

believe that the impulse given by it to the study of the history of the Scottish Reformation, and the principles involved in the subsequent conflicts of the Scottish Church, did much to bring about that movement which resulted in the disruption of 1843. Other works are, *The Life of Andrew Melville* (2 vols., 1819); *History of the Progress and Suppression of the Reformation in Italy* (1827); and *History of the Progress and Suppression of the Reformation in Spain* (1829). Posthumous were, *Sermons* (1836) and *Miscellaneous Writings, Chiefly Historical* (1841). His son, Thomas McCrie, edited his *Works* (4 vols., 1855-57).

BIBLIOGRAPHY: A *Memoir*, by his son, was prefixed to the *Works*, ut sup., and a *Life of Thomas McCrie, D.D.*, by the same, appeared Edinburgh, 1840; *DNB*, xxxv. 13-14. There is also a *Memoir* of Dr. McCrie by A. Crichton in the latter's ed. of McCrie's *Life of John Knox*, Edinburgh, 1840.

2. Son and biographer of the preceding; b. at Edinburgh Nov. 7, 1797; d. there May 9, 1875. He studied at the University of Edinburgh, entered the ministry of the Original Secession Church in 1820, and, after holding pastorates at Crieff and Clola, succeeded his father in 1836 as minister of the West Richmond Street Church, Edinburgh. The same year he was given the chair of divinity at the Original Secession Hall. In 1852 he joined the Free Church of Scotland, at the union with it of the larger part of the Original Secession Church. He took a prominent part in the deliberations necessary for effecting this union and in 1856 was moderator of the Free Church assembly. In 1866 he became professor of church history and systematic theology in the Presbyterian College, London. His principal works are, *Life of Thomas McCrie* (Edinburgh, 1840); *Sketches of Scottish Church History* (1841); *Lectures on Christian Baptism* (1850); *Memoirs of Sir Andrew Agnew* (1850); and *Annals of English Presbytery, from the Earliest Period to the Present Time* (London, 1872).

BIBLIOGRAPHY: *DNB*, xxxv. 14.

M'CURDY, JAMES FREDERICK: Presbyterian; b. at Chatham, New Brunswick, Feb. 18, 1847. He was educated at the University of New Brunswick (A.B., 1866), and after being principal of Restigouche County Grammar School, Dalhousie, New Brunswick, in 1867-68, entered Princeton Theological Seminary, from which he was graduated in 1871 and where he studied two additional years (1871-72). He was then assistant professor of Oriental languages in the same institution from 1873 to 1882, after which he studied at the universities of Gottingen and Leipsic until 1884. He was lecturer at Princeton Theological Seminary on the Stone foundation in 1885-86, and in the latter year was appointed lecturer on Oriental literature in University College, Toronto, where he was promoted to his present position of professor of the same subject in 1888. In addition to numerous contributions to *The Jewish Encyclopedia*, Hasting's *Dictionary of the Bible*, and the *Standard Bible Dictionary*, to theological periodicals, and besides preparing the sections on the Psalms, Hosea, and Haggai for the American edition of J. P. Lange's commentary on the Bible (New York, 1872-76) he has written: *Aryo-Semitic Speech: A Study in Linguistic Archæology* (Andover, 1881); *History, Prophecy, and the Monuments* (3 vols., London, 1894-1901); and *Life of D. J. Macdonnell* (Toronto, 1897).

MACDONALD, DUNCAN BLACK: Presbyterian; b. at Glasgow, Scotland, Apr. 9, 1863. He was educated at the university of his native city (M.A., 1885; B.D., 1888), where he was later scholar and fellow, and then studied Semitics at the University of Berlin (1890-91, 1893). Since 1892 he has been professor of Semitic languages in Hartford Theological Seminary. He was Haskell lecturer in comparative religion in the University of Chicago in 1905-06. He is editor of the Mohammedan section of J. Hastings' *Encyclopædia of Religion and Ethics*, and is editor of the concordance of the Peshitta being prepared under the auspices of Hartford Theological Seminary. He has written: *Development of Muslim Theology, Jurisprudence, and Constitutional Theory* (New York, 1903); and *Religious Attitude and Life in Islam* (Chicago, 1909; Haskell lectures).

MACDONALD, FREDERIC WILLIAM: English Methodist; b. at Leeds Feb. 25, 1842. He was educated at Owens College, Manchester (B.A., 1862), and after being a Wesleyan minister from 1862 to 1881, was professor of systematic theology in Handsworth College, Birmingham, from 1881 to 1891. From the latter year until 1905 he was secretary of the Wesleyan Missionary Society, of which he has since been honorary secretary, and in 1899-1900 was likewise president of the Wesleyan Methodist Conference. He was also joint editor of the *London Quarterly Review* from 1871 to 1875, and in 1880 represented the British Methodist Conference at the General Conference of the Methodist Episcopal Church of America. He has written: *Life of Fletcher of Madeley* (London, 1885); *Life of William Morley Punshon* (1887); *Latin Hymns in the Wesleyan Hymn-Book* (1900); and *In a Nook with a Book* (1907).

McDOWELL, WILLIAM FRASER: Methodist Episcopal bishop; b. at Millersburg, O., Feb. 4, 1858. He was educated at Ohio Wesleyan University (A.B., 1879) and Boston University (S.T.B., 1882), and from 1882 to 1890 held successive pastorates at Lodi, O. (1882-83), Oberlin, O. (1883-1885), and Tiffin, O. (1885-90), after which he was chancellor of the University of Denver for nine years (1890-99). From 1899 to 1904 he was corresponding secretary of the Board of Education of the Methodist Episcopal Church, and in 1904 was elected bishop of his denomination. He was a member of the Colorado State Board of Charities and Corrections in 1894-99 and president of the Religious Education Society in 1905-06, while since 1899 he has been a member of the International Committee of the Young Men's Christian Association.

MACDUFF, JOHN ROSS: Church of Scotland; b. at Bonhard in the parish of Scone, Perthshire, May 23, 1818; d. at Chislehurst (10 m. s.e. of London), Kent, England, Apr. 30, 1895. He was educated at the University of Edinburgh, and was pastor successively of Kettins, Forfarshire (1843–1849), of St. Madoes, Perthshire (1849–55), and of Sandyford parish, Glasgow (1855–70). In 1870 he retired to Chislehurst and devoted himself to the composition of religious literature. His publications were very numerous. They are mostly small devotional manuals, characterized by a devout and practical imagination, and have been read by thousands in his own country and in America. Possibly of these the two most famous volumes are *The Morning and Night Watches* (in one vol., London, 323d thousand in 1904); and *The Mind and Words of Jesus* (in one vol., 341st thousand). He wrote also verse, of which he issued a collected edition, *Matin and Vesper Bells* (2 vols., 1898). Two of his hymns have found their way into hymn-books, "Christ is coming," and "Everlasting Arms of love." His autobiography, *Reminiscences of a Long Life, by the Author of Morning and Night Watches*, appeared 1896.

Bibliography: Consult, besides the *Reminiscenses*, ut. sup. edited by his daughter, S. W. Duffield, *English Hymns*, pp. 86–87, New York, 1886; Julian, *Hymnology*, p. 708.

MACEDONIA IN THE APOSTOLIC AGE: After the battle of Pydna (168 B.C.) Macedonia passed under Roman dominion and was divided into four districts. In 146 B.C. it became a province, and under Augustus it passed to the senate; under Tiberius and Claudius it was an imperial charge and was united with Achaia; but after 44 B.C. it belonged again to the Senate. In the third and fourth centuries it was again divided into four provinces. Ptolemæus (iii. 13) thus describes its extent: "On the east the river Nestus formed the boundary toward Thracia, so that Philippi politically belonged to Macedonia. [This agrees with Acts xvi. 9, where the 'man of Macedonia' appeared to Paul asking him to come over into Macedonia, who went by way of Samothrace directly to Neapolis-Philippi, passing around Thrace.] On the north, Macedonia bordered on Dalmatia-Illyricum; in the west, on the Adriatic Sea. The southern boundary is uncertain." As in other provinces, there was also a provincial council for Macedonia which probably met in Thessalonica, which was called the "first [city] of Macedonia." The principal cities were connected by the *Via Egnatia*, a fine military road, which Paul used from Neapolis to Thessalonica. From Neapolis, opposite to the island of Thasos, the road led to Philippi, a city founded by Philip of Macedonia. Octavianus planted a Roman colony there (cf. Acts xvi. 12) which was considerably enlarged after the battle at Actium. The population was almost entirely Roman, as the many Latin inscriptions prove. The masters of the prophesying slaves (Acts xvi. 16–21) were Romans. The officers also were Romans (prætors, not politarchs). The number of Jews in Philippi seems to have been not very large, for Paul intended to stay there only a few days, and a congregation seems not to have existed at all. Acts xvi. 13 says nothing of a synagogue (as in xvii. 1), it mentions only a praying-place for women outside of the gate by the river. The next two stations on the *Via Egnatia*, at which Paul only touched, were Amphipolis and Apollonia. Then comes Thessalonica, formerly called Thermæ. According to Philip it was a free city, the capital of the province. In the time of Strabo it was very populous. It had its politarchs (Acts xvii. 6), though their number is uncertain, also a council (*demos*, Acts xvii. 5). The politarchs had police jurisdiction and were responsible to the provincial authorities for order and quiet in the city (xvii. 6 sqq). That Paul selected this important commercial city as a missionary field is in accord with his custom; in the Acts a further motive was the fact that a synagogue of the Jews was there. This "would mean that the Jews of the entire district, including those of Amphipolis and Apollonia, centered their worship at Thessalonica" (Zahn). Thus is explained also why the apostle passed by Amphipolis and Apollonia. The influence of the Jews in Thessalonica must have been very great; it was felt even at Berea, the first city to go over to the Romans after the battle of Pydna. This last was one of the most populous cities of Macedonia. (J. Weiss.)

Bibliography: J. Marquardt, *Römische Staatsverwaltung*, i. 316–321, Leipsic, 1881; W. M. Leake, *Travels in Northern Greece*, vol. iii., London, 1835; T. A. Desdevizes-du-Dezert, *Géographie ancienne de la Macédoine*, Paris, 1863; L. Heuzey, *Mission archéologique de Macédoine*, Paris, 1876; B. Niese, *Geschichte der griechischen und makedonischen Staaten seit der Schlacht bei Chaeronea*, 3 parts, Gotha, 1893–1903; W. M. Ramsay, *Church in the Roman Empire*, pp. 149, 151, 156, 158, 160, London, 1893; idem, *St. Paul the Traveller and Roman Citizen*, chaps. ix.–x., ib. 1897.

MACEDONIUS, mas″e-dō′ni-us, AND THE MACEDONIAN SECT.

Toward the end of the fourth century the name of Macedonius, bishop of Constantinople, became accepted as that of a heresiarch. Jerome, writing in that city about 380, mentions him as intruded into the see by the Arian party, and says that the Macedonian heresy takes its name from him. About the same time Damasus, in his twenty-four anathemas against various heresies, pronounced one against "the Macedonians, who, coming out of the Arian stock, changed their name but not their perfidy"; and in 383 and 384 Theodosius enforced repressive measures not only against Eunomians and Arians but also against Macedonians. From this time his name was known in the West as that of a heresiarch. Rufinus relates (c. 402) that the Arians split about 361 into three groups, Arians proper, Eunomians, and Macedonians, and Augustine about the same time enumerates the eastern heretics similarly, and afterward (428) places the Macedonians, "whom the Greeks call also Pneumatomachi," in his list of heretics. The term Macedonians must have been common in Constantinople about 380–384; but it is not met in the older eastern literature—neither in Athanasius, nor in Basil, nor in the list of heretics given by Epiphanius; nor is it used by the council of 381 in the canon (i.) which condemns the "Semi-Arians or Pneumatomachi." Canon vii., which deals with the reception into the Church of "Mace-

1. Early Accounts.

donians," is some eighty years later than the council. Theodoret mentions briefly that after his deposition Macedonius became "the leader of a heresy of his own"; but otherwise he names him only in quoting the anathemas of Damasus. The historians Socrates and Sozomen, writing in Constantinople, are the first to make frequent mention of him and his party, and it is through them that the Macedonians became a well-known group of heretics in the East. The definite name of Macedonians can not be shown to have been used in the East before 380.

These and other similar facts can be explained only by saying that Macedonius had an importance rather for Constantinopolitan than for general church history. The circumstances of his life are not easy to trace accurately; but a glance at the indications given will be useful. According to Socrates and Sozomen, on the death of Alexander of Constantinople (c. 340), Macedonius was put up by the Arian party as their candidate in opposition to the properly elected and orthodox Paul, whom the Emperor Constantius set aside through a synod and replaced by Eusebius of Nicomedia. After Eusebius' death there was another contest between the same two candidates. Once more Constantius, at the cost of much popular disorder, expelled Paul, and tacitly allowed Macedonius to take possession of the see. Paul went to Rome and Julius awarded him his see, which he claimed in person, while the Arians, gathered at Antioch, protested against the interference of Julius in eastern matters. Constantius had Paul seized and banished to Thessalonica, and Macedonius was forcibly installed, after a riot in which many lives were lost. Constans took up the cause of Paul, but without success until, after the Council of Sardica (347) had declared in favor of Paul, Athanasius, and Marcellus, he induced his brother by actual threats of war to restore them. When, however, Constans died in 350, Constantius reversed his action, and Paul was banished to Cucusus and strangled there. Macedonius, now in undisturbed possession, persecuted the orthodox party, but ultimately fell into disgrace with Constantius and was deposed at a synod in Constantinople (360), after which he broke away from the Acacians and founded a sect of his own.

2. Apparent Facts in Life of Macedonius.

A thorough examination, however, of these statements shows that they are not reliable in several particulars; and a more trustworthy account may be made up from the acts of the Council of Sardica and the statements of Athanasius (*Historia Arianorum*, vii., and *Apologia de fuga*, iii.), and of Jerome. From these sources it appears that Paul had been banished to Pontus by Constantine, and that he had already been bishop of Constantinople for some time before Eusebius was set up (at latest in 338), and that Macedonius, who had once accused him in the presence of Athanasius, was then his presbyter. When Eusebius set his mind on winning the bishopric, the old charges were revived; Constantius banished him in chains to Singara in Mesopotamia, then to Emesa, and finally to Cucusus, where his persecutors put him to death with the help of the Prefect Philippus. The letter of the Council of Sardica does not mention him naming only Athanasius, Marcellus, and Asclepas. The eastern bishops there asserted that he had assented to the condemnation of Athanasius; that he was himself condemned long before 342; that in 342 he went into exile; and that it was Maximin of Treves who entered into communion with him and effected his restoration. Paul was, according to all the indications here given, not at Sardica, nor at the time bishop of Constantinople, but apparently in exile. The most probable conclusion from the whole difficult matter is that Paul died at the earliest in 351. In any case Macedonius was in sole possession of the see of Constantinople from 342 or 343. It is impossible to decide how much truth there is in the accounts by Socrates and Sozomen of his fierce persecution of the orthodox, though it is credible that he filled as many sees as he could reach with his partizans. The statement of Socrates and Sozomen that he adhered to the Acacian or court party until 360 is certainly wrong; Philostorgius relates that Basil of Ancyra won him to his side, Sabinus of Heraclea reckons him among the Homoiousians, Epiphanius calls him a partizan of Basil, and the letter addressed to him in 358 by George of Laodicea proves that he was all along on the Homoiousian side. With this party he supported Basil in Seleucia against the Acacians, and as a member of it he was deposed at the synod of 360. That his death followed soon afterward is a natural inference from the fact that he is not mentioned in connection with the actions of his party after 364. Thus he would scarcely have had time to found a separate sect after his deposition; and his views on the doctrine of the Holy Spirit were not peculiar to him, but were shared by all the Homoiousians. Nor was this question much debated in Constantinople and Asia Minor before 367.

3. Critical Account of His Life.

The development of the "Macedonian" sect, held to be heretical on this point, began in Alexandria. During his third exile (356–362) Athanasius heard of people who regarded the Holy Ghost as a creature, and in four letters to Bishop Serapion of Thmuis defended the *homoousia* of the Spirit as the only true doctrine. To him, after his long residence in the West (where since Tertullian this doctrine had been firmly established) it could present no difficulties, and fell in easily with his general doctrine of the Trinity. But the case was different with the Homoiousians and with the so-called "young Nicene" party, brought up in Origenistic traditions. Hence it was possible for Gregory Nazianzen to say about 381: "Of the wise amongst us, some hold the Holy Spirit to be a power (*energeia*), others a creature, others for God, and still others are unwilling to decide, out of reverence (as they say) for the Scriptures, which do not speak plainly on the matter." The question how it came to an open breach between the supporters of the various views is impossible to answer with certainty; the decisive elements were probably the authority of Athanasius, the requirement of the Synod of Alexandria that the *homoousia* of the Holy Spirit should be acknowl-

4. The Sect.

edged, and the prompt response of Meletius of Antioch. The breach between Basil of Cæsarea and Eustathius in 373 seems to have marked a turning-point in the controversy. The Pneumatomachi were regarded as semi-Arians, and condemned as such in 381, although it is doubtful whether any of them were heterodox in their Christology. Gregory Nazianzen, preaching in Constantinople on the Pentecost of that year, speaks of them as "sound in regard to the Son," and efforts were made to win them in a brotherly spirit by reminding them of their acceptance of the Nicene Creed—which, it must be remembered, did not attempt to define the doctrine of the Holy Spirit. Refusing to treat and leaving the council to the number of thirty-six, they were condemned as heretics, and, after fruitless negotiations in 383, became subject to the edicts of Theodosius. But Macedonius had nothing to do with the development after 360. That the Pneumatomachi in Constantinople were named after him about 380–387 was due to the fact that his disciples there, holding aloof from the dominant Homoians, were not strong enough after his death to set up a bishop of their own, and were thus still called after the man whose deposition had inaugurated their separation from the Homoians. In a word, it has seldom been the ill fortune of a man to win the name of a heresiarch on such slight grounds as have sufficed in the case of Macedonius. According to Socrates, none of the separatist groups were persecuted or disturbed in their worship except the Eunomians, and Nestorius was the first, at Constantinople and Cyzicus, to take away the churches of the "Macedonians" and thus force some of them back into the orthodox fold. The rest probably died out by degrees. See ARIANISM. (F. LOOFS.)

BIBLIOGRAPHY: The sources are indicated in the text. Consult further: the *Opera* of Damasus in *MPL*, xiii. 109–442; J. Vogt, *Bibliotheca historicæ hæresiologicæ*, i. 1, pp. 165–199, Hamburg, 1723; F. Loofs, *Eustathius von Sebaste*, Halle, 1898; J. Gummerus, *Die homöusianische Partei bis zum Tode des Konstantius*, Leipsic, 1900; Neander, *Christian Church*, v. 186: Moeller, *Christian Church*, i. 392–393; Schaff, *Christian Church*, iii. 639–640, 664.

MacEWEN, ALEXANDER ROBERTSON: United Free Church of Scotland; b. at Edinburgh May 14, 1851. He studied at Glasgow (1866–70), Balliol College, Oxford (B.A., 1874), Göttingen, and the United Presbyterian Hall, Glasgow (1877–80). In 1874–75 he was deputy professor of Greek, and from 1875 to 1877 assistant professor of Latin in the University of Glasgow, where he was also classical examiner for degrees in 1881–84. He was pastor of the United Presbyterian Church at Moffat (1880–1886), of Anderston Church, Glasgow (1886–89), and of Claremont Church, in the same city (1889–1901). Since 1901 he has been professor of church history in New College, Edinburgh. He is secretary of the Christian Unity Society for Scotland. In theology he describes himself as liberal and Evangelical, and as belonging to the historical school, as well as a "resolute advocate of central and unifying beliefs," although non-controversial and declining to be ranked with any party. He has edited John Ker's *Lectures on Preaching* (London, 1886), and has written: *Life of Alexander MacEwen, D.D.*, his father (Glasgow, 1875); *Origin of Roman Satiric Poetry* (Oxford, 1876); *St. Jerome* (London, 1878); *The Eastern Church in Greece* (1890); *Life and Letters of Principal Cairns* (1894); and *The Erskines, Ebenezer and Ralph* (Edinburgh, 1900).

McFADYEN, JOHN EDGAR: Presbyterian; b. at Glasgow, Scotland, July 17, 1870. He was educated at the universities of Glasgow (M.A., 1890), Oxford (B.A., 1895), and Marburg, and at the Free Church College, Glasgow, and was successively Snell exhibitioner, Oxford (1890–93) and George A. Clark fellow, Glasgow (1893–97). Since 1898 he has been professor of Old-Testament literature and exegesis at Knox College, Toronto. In theology he is "a believer in reverent but fearless investigation." He has written: *The Messages of the Prophetic and Priestly Historians* (New York, 1900); *The Divine Pursuit* (Chicago, 1900); *In the Hour of Silence* (1902); *Old Testament Criticism and the Christian Church* (New York, 1903); *The Messages of the Psalmists* (1904); *Introduction to the Old Testament* (1905); *The Prayers of the Bible* (1906); *Ten Studies in the Psalms* (1907); and *The City with Foundations* (1909).

McFARLAND, JOHN THOMAS: Methodist Episcopalian; b. at Mt. Vernon, Ind., Jan. 2, 1851. He was educated at Iowa Wesleyan University, Simpson College, Indianola, Ia. (A.B., 1873), and the School of Theology, Boston University (B.D., 1878). His principal pastorates, since he entered the ministry in 1873, have been at the First Methodist Episcopal Church, Peoria, Ill. (1880–82), Grace Methodist Episcopal Church, Jacksonville, Ill. (1891–96), New York Avenue Methodist Episcopal Church, Brooklyn, N. Y. (1897–99), and First Methodist Episcopal Church, Topeka, Kan. (1899–1905). He was vice-president of Iowa Wesleyan University from 1882 to 1884, and president from 1884 to 1891, and since 1894 has been secretary of the Sunday-school Union and editor of the Sunday-school literature for his denomination.

McGARVEY, JOHN WILLIAM: Disciple; b. at Hopkinsville, Ky., Mar. 1, 1829. He was educated at Bethany College, Bethany, W. Va. (A.B., 1850), and after conducting a private school for boys from 1850 to 1852 and being the head of a boarding-school from 1856 to 1858, besides holding pastorates at Fayette, Mo., Dover, Mo., and Lexington, Ky., was appointed professor of sacred history at the College of the Bible, Lexington, in 1865, a position which he still retains. Since 1895 he has also been president of the same institution. He was president of the Kentucky Christian Missionary Society for nearly forty years and of the Christian Education Society for over thirty, and has been editor of the department of Biblical criticism in *The Christian Standard* (Cincinnati) since 1893. In theology he is strongly conservative on questions connected with Biblical criticism. He has written: *Commentary on the Acts of the Apostles* (Cincinnati, O., 1863); *Commentary on Matthew and Mark* (1867); *Lands of the Bible* (1881); *Text and Canon of the New Testament* (1886); *Credibility and Inspiration of the New Testament* (1891); *McGarvey's*

Sermons (1894); *Jesus and Jonah* (1897); and *The Authorship of Deuteronomy* (1902).

McGARVEY, WILLIAM: Roman Catholic; b. at Philadelphia Aug. 14, 1861. He was educated by private tutors and at the General Theological Seminary, from which he was graduated in 1886. He was ordained to the priesthood of the Protestant Episcopal Church (1886); was curate of the Church of the Evangelists, Philadelphia (1886–96); rector of St. Elizabeth's, Philadelphia (1896–1908); but in 1908, together with his assistant clergy, embraced Roman Catholicism, the immediate cause of his conversion being his fear that a so-called "open pulpit" would be permitted in the Episcopal Church. While in his former communion he was superior of the Congregation of the Companions of the Saviour and chaplain general of the Sisters of Saint Mary in the United States. He has written: *The Ceremonies of a Low Celebration* (Milwaukee, 1891); *Liturgiæ Americanæ* (Philadelphia, 1895); *The Doctrine of the Church of England on the Real Presence* (Milwaukee, 1900); and *Ceremonies of the Mass* (in collaboration with C. P. A. Burnett; New York, 1905).

McGIFFERT, ARTHUR CUSHMAN: Congregationalist; b. at Sauquoit, N. Y., Mar. 4, 1861. He was educated at Western Reserve College (A.B., 1882), Union Theological Seminary (from which he was graduated in 1885), and France, Italy, and Germany (Ph.D., Marburg, 1888). Returning to the United States in 1888, he was appointed instructor in church history in Lane Theological Seminary, a position which he held until 1890, when he was promoted to a full professorship of the same subject. Three years later (1893), he was appointed to his present position of professor of church history in Union Theological Seminary, New York. In theology he belongs to the critical school, and has written, in addition to translating the "Ecclesiastical History" of Eusebius (New York, 1890), *Dialogue between a Christian and a Jew entitled ἀντιβολὴ Πανίσκου καὶ Φίλωνος Ἰουδαίου πρὸς μόναχόν τινα* (New York, 1888); *A History of Christianity in the Apostolic Age* (1897); *The Apostles' Creed* (1902); and *The Christian Point of View* (in collaboration with F. Brown and G. W. Knox; 1902).

McGREADY, JAMES: Presbyterian; b. in western Pennsylvania about 1758 or 1760; d. at Henderson, Ky., Feb., 1817. He was educated for the ministry at a school in Cannonsburg, Pa., and was licensed to preach on Aug. 13, 1788. His first parish was in Orange County, N. C., but in 1796 he moved to Logan County, Ky., where, beginning in 1797, he took a prominent part in the great revival, holding the first camp-meetings there in July, 1800. It was partly due to his influence in ordaining young men who were without a classical education that the Cumberland Presbyterian Church seceded from the main body (see PRESBYTERIANS). McGready, who had really never seceded, was speedily reconciled to his church, having been prohibited from preaching for only a year or two, and was sent in 1811 as a missionary to found churches in southern Indiana. His sermons were edited by J. Smith (vol. i., Louisville, 1831; vol. ii., Nashville, 1833). See REVIVALS OF RELIGION, III., 2, § 2.

BIBLIOGRAPHY: E. H. Gillett, *Hist. of the Presbyterian Church, U. S. A.*, passim, Philadelphia, 1864; R. V. Foster, in *American Church History Series*, xi. 260, 261, 268, 272, New York, 1894.

MACHÆRUS: A fortress in Peræa, nine miles east of the northern end of the Dead Sea, identified with the modern Mkawr. It was built by Alexander Jannæus, destroyed by Gabinius, rebuilt by Herod the Great. Josephus points it out as the place in which the beheading of John the Baptist took place.

BIBLIOGRAPHY: Sources are: Josephus, *War*, I., v. 8, II., xviii. 6, VII., vi. 1–2, 4; *Ant.*, XIV., v. 4, XVIII., v. 1–2; Pliny, *Hist. nat.*, v. 16, 72. Consult: G. A. Smith, *Historical Geography of the Holy Land*, pp. 569–570, London, 1897; Schürer, *Geschichte*, i. 438–441 et passim, Eng. transl., I., ii. 250–251 et passim.

MACHPELAH: The name of the cave, or of the place near Hebron where the cave was situated, which Abraham bought of Ephron the Hittite for a family sepulcher. The name occurs only Gen. xxiii. 9, 17, 19, xxv. 9, xlix. 30, l. 13; and according to these passages and their context Abraham and Sarah, Isaac and Rebekah, Jacob and Leah were buried there. The place which holds what is traditionally regarded as the cave is surrounded by a wall 194 feet long and fifty-eight feet high, constructed of huge stones, and reminding one, both in design and workmanship, of the foundation of the temple in Jerusalem. Within this enclosure is a Mohammedan mosque; and strangers, that is, non-Mohammedans, are rigidly excluded from the building. In 1862 the Prince of Wales, accompanied by Dean Stanley, visited Hebron; and, on special orders from Constantinople, the mosque was opened to them. In 1882 the same courtesy was extended during a visit paid by Princes Albert Victor and George of Wales, accompanied by Canon Dalton, Sir Charles Wilson, and Capt. Conder.

BIBLIOGRAPHY: An indispensable account, historical in method and summarizing the accounts of travelers from the fourth century on, as well as giving exact references to collections and sources, is found in *DB*, iii. 197–202. Consult further: W. M. Thomson, *The Land and the Book*, ii. 381–388, 586, New York, 1859; A. P. Stanley, *Lectures on the History of the Jewish Church*, i. 535 sqq., ib. 1863; J. Fergusson, *Holy Sepulchre and the Temple*, London, 1865; C. Ritter, *Comparative Geography of Palestine*, iii. 305–323, Edinburgh, 1866; P. Schaff, *Through Bible Lands*, pp. 212 sqq., New York, 1878; PEF, *Memoirs, Survey of Western Palestine*, iii. 305, London, 1883.

McILVAINE, CHARLES PETTIT: Protestant Episcopalian; b. at Burlington, N. J., June 18, 1799; d. at Florence, Italy, Mar. 14, 1873. He graduated at Princeton in 1816, then spent two years in the Princeton Theological Seminary. He was minister of Christ Church, Georgetown, D.C., 1820–25, chaplain to the United States senate 1822 and 1824, professor of ethics and chaplain in the United States Military Academy, West Point, 1825–1827, pastor of St. Ann's Church, Brooklyn, 1827–1832, professor of the evidences of revealed religion and sacred antiquities in New York University 1831–32, and bishop of the diocese of Ohio 1832–1873. He was also president of Kenyon College,

Gambier, O., 1832–40, and the head of the theological seminary of his diocese. During the Civil War he was a member of the sanitary commission, and in 1861, in company with Archbishop Hughes and Thurlow Weed, he went to England on a semi-official mission in connection with the Trent affair. He was a pronounced "Evangelical," and for years he was regarded as the leader of the Low-church party in the Protestant Episcopal Church. His principal works are, *The Evidences of Christianity* (New York, 1832), lectures delivered at New York University; *Oxford Divinity compared with that of the Romish and Anglican Churches* (Philadelphia, 1841), which was regarded as a good refutation of the Oxford school; *The Holy Catholic Church* (1844); and *The Truth and the Life* (New York, 1855), twenty-two sermons.

BIBLIOGRAPHY: W. Carus, *Memorials of Rev. C. P. McIlvaine*, New York, 1881; W. S. Perry, *The Episcopate in America*, p. 65, ib. 1895.

MACK, ALEXANDER. See DUNKERS, I., §§ 1–2.

MACKAY, ALEXANDER MURDOCH: Missionary to Uganda; b. at Rhynie (31 m. n.w. of Aberdeen) Oct. 13, 1849; d. at Uganda Feb. 4, 1890. He studied at the Free Church Training School for Teachers at Edinburgh, at Edinburgh University, and in Berlin. He displayed a great aptitude for mechanics, and spent several years as a draftsman in Germany. In 1875 he offered his services as a missionary to the Church Missionary Society, was accepted, reached Zanzibar on his way to his field May 30, 1876, and Uganda in Nov., 1878. There, largely through his knowledge of practical mechanics, he enjoyed the protection of Mutesa; but when Mwanga came to the throne in 1884, Mackay's position became difficult because of the king's opposition, and there was little change when Kiwewa succeeded to the throne in 1888. Mackay still held on, however, and it is largely due to his courage, energy, and devotion that the mission in Uganda is in its present flourishing condition (see AFRICA, II., Uganda). He fell a victim to malarial fever, and succumbed after four days of illness, having spent fourteen years in Africa without once having visited his native country.

BIBLIOGRAPHY: *Alexander M. Mackay, Pioneer Missionary of the Church Missionary Society in Uganda; by his Sister*, new ed., London, 1899; *Alexander Mackay, Missionary Hero of Uganda*, ib. 1893.

MACKAY-SMITH, ALEXANDER: Protestant Episcopal bishop-coadjutor of Pennsylvania; b. at New Haven, Conn., June 2, 1850. He was educated at Trinity College, Hartford, Conn. (A.B., 1872), and received his theological training partly in the General Theological Seminary and partly in England and Germany. He was ordered deacon in 1876 and advanced to the priesthood in the following year. After being successively curate of Grace Church, Boston (1877–80), and St. Thomas's, New York City (1880–86), he was first archdeacon of New York from 1887 to 1893, and from the latter year to 1902 was rector of St. John's, Washington, D. C. In 1902 he was consecrated bishop-coadjutor of Pennsylvania, after having declined the coadjutor-bishopric of Kansas.

McKENZIE, ALEXANDER: Congregationalist; b. at New Bedford, Mass., Dec. 14, 1830. He was educated at Phillips Academy, Andover, Harvard College (A.B., 1859), and Andover Theological Seminary, graduating in 1861. Ordained in 1861, he became pastor of the South Church in Augusta, Me., in 1861, and of the First Church in Cambridge, Mass., in 1867. In 1882 he acted as lecturer on theology of the New Testament in Andover Theological Seminary and in Harvard Divinity School. He wrote: *Two Boys* (Boston, 1870); *History of First Church in Cambridge* (1873); *Cambridge Sermons* (1883); *Some Things Abroad* (1887); *Christ Himself* (1891); *A Door Opened* (1898); *Divine Force in Life of the World* (1899); and *Getting One's Bearing* (New York, 1903).

MACKENZIE, CHARLES FREDERICK: Bishop of Central Africa; b. at Portmore (5 m. n. of Peebles), Peeblesshire, Scotland, Apr. 10, 1825; d. on the island of Malo (at the confluence of the Shire and Ruo rivers; 415 m. w.s.w. of Mozambique), British Central Africa, Jan. 31, 1862. He was educated at Cambridge (B.A., 1848; M.A., 1851), and became fellow of Caius College and curate of Haslingfield, Cambridgeshire, in 1851. In 1855 he accompanied J. W. Colenso, bishop of Natal, to Africa. He officiated as priest among the English settlers, first at Durban, and afterward at a post on the Umhlali river. In 1859 he returned to England, but in 1860 he sailed for Cape Town as head of the Universities' Mission to Central Africa. There he was consecrated bishop of Central Africa Jan. 1, 1861. He settled at Magomero, in the Manganja territory, and labored there for almost a year. While hurrying to meet Livingstone he fell ill of a fever and died.

BIBLIOGRAPHY: H. Goodwin, *Memoir of Bishop Mackenzie*, London, 1865; Francis Awdry, *An Elder Sister: a short Sketch of Annie Mackenzie and her Brother, the Missionary Bishop*, London, 1878; *DNB*, xxxv. 136–138.

MACKENZIE, JOHN KENNETH: Medical missionary; b. at Yarmouth, Eng., Aug. 25, 1850; d. at Tien-tsin, China, Apr. 1, 1888. His education was in a Bristol private school, his conversion took place in one of the Moody and Sankey meetings held in Bristol in 1867, where he had held a clerkship for a couple of years. He then joined the Presbyterian Church. Determining to become a medical missionary he studied at Bristol and London from 1870 to 1874 and went to China under appointment of the London Missionary Society. He opened the medical station at Hankow in 1875 and stayed there till 1879, when from motives of health he moved to Tien-tsin where he conducted the hospital till his death. He was a man of unusual gifts and by his professional skill, his ability to win the confidence of the Chinese, and his devoted life ranks with the best of the missionaries, although his career was so short.

BIBLIOGRAPHY: Mrs. Mary Isabella Bryson, *John Kenneth Mackenzie, Medical Missionary in China*, London, 1891.

MACKENZIE, WILLIAM DOUGLAS: Congregationalist; b. at Fauresmith (80 m. s.e. of Kimberley), Orange Free Colony, South Africa, July 16, 1859. He was educated at the University of Edinburgh (M.A., 1881), the Congregational Theological Hall, Edinburgh, and the universities of Göttingen and Marburg (1881–82). He then entered the ministry of his denomination, and held successive pastorates at Montrose, Kincardineshire (1882–1889), and Morningside, Edinburgh (1889–95). From 1895 to 1903 he was professor of systematic theology in Chicago Theological Seminary, and since 1904 has been professor of the same subject and president of Hartford Theological Seminary. He has written: *The Ethics of Gambling* (London, 1893); *The Revelation of the Christ* (1893); *Christianity and the Progress of Man* (Chicago, 1897); *South Africa: Its History, Heroes, and Wars* (1900); and *John Mackenzie, South African Missionary and Statesman* (biography of his father; New York, 1902).

McKIBBIN, WILLIAM: Presbyterian; b. at Pittsburg, Pa., May 24, 1850. He was educated at Princeton College (A.B., 1869), and after studying law at Philadelphia, entered Western Theological Seminary, Allegheny, Pa., from which he was graduated in 1873. He then held successive pastorates at the Seventh Presbyterian Church, Pittsburg (1873–74), Central Presbyterian Church, St. Paul, Minn. (1874–79), Second Presbyterian Church, Pittsburg (1880–88), and First Presbyterian Church, Walnut Hills, Cincinnati, O. (1888–1904). Since 1904 he has been president and professor of systematic theology in Lane Theological Seminary, Cincinnati.

MACKIE, GEORGE MONRO: Scotch Presbyterian; b. at Banchory (15 m. s.w. of Aberdeen), Kincardineshire, Oct. 27, 1853. He was educated at the University of Aberdeen and the Divinity Hall of Edinburgh University, and since 1880 has been minister of the Anglo-American congregation and missionary of the Church of Scotland Jewish Mission at Beirut, Syria. In addition to his missionary and pastoral work, he has devoted himself to the study of oriental life as illustrative of the Bible, and in theology holds " that a man becomes a Christian by giving himself to Christ as a dwelling-place for His Spirit; that this indwelling will show itself in likeness to Christ personally, and socially in kindness to all in whom the same Spirit is already dwelling or desiring to dwell; and that in the statesmanship of the Gospel, while all past and present forms of church membership and government have rendered in their day most important service, they are quite unable to produce that conception of a great citizenship that is necessary for a kingdom that is destined to conquer the world for Christ." He has written *Bible Manners and Customs* (Edinburgh, 1898).

McKIM, JOHN: Protestant Episcopal bishop of Tokyo, Japan; b. at Pittsfield, Mass., July 17, 1852. He was educated at Griswold College, Davenport, Ia. (A.B., 1876), and Nashotah House, Nashotah, Wis., from which he was graduated in 1879. He was ordered deacon in 1878 and advanced to the priesthood in the following year. After working for a brief time in the diocese of Chicago, he went to Japan as a missionary (1880), where in thirteen years he was able to report seventeen stations and substations, with headquarters at Osaka. In 1893 he was consecrated missionary bishop of Tokyo.

McKIM, RANDOLPH HARRISON: Protestant Episcopalian; b. at Baltimore, Md., Apr. 15, 1842. He was educated at the University of Virginia (A.B., 1861), and served in the Confederate Army throughout the Civil War. He was ordered deacon in 1864 and ordained priest in 1866, after having been curate of Emanuel Church, Baltimore, in 1865–66. He then held successive rectorates at St. John's, Portsmouth, Va. (1866–67), Christ Church, Alexandria, Va. (1867–75), Holy Trinity, New York City (1875–86), and Trinity, New Orleans, La. (1886–88). Since 1889 he has been rector of the Church of the Epiphany, Washington, D. C. He was likewise president of the House of Clerical and Lay Deputies from 1904 to 1907, and has written: *A Vindication of Protestant Principles* (New York, 1879); *The Nature of the Christian Ministry* (1880); *Future Punishment* (1883); *Bread in the Desert, and other Sermons* (1887); *Christ and Modern History* (1893); *Leo XIII. at the Bar of History* (Washington, D. C., 1897); *Present Day Problems of Christian Thought* (New York, 1900); *The Gospel in the Christian Year* (1902); *The Confederate Soldier, his Motives and Aims* (Washington, 1904); and *The Problem of the Pentateuch* (New York, 1906).

McKINNEY, ALEXANDER HARRIS: Presbyterian; b. in New York City July 28, 1858. He was educated at the College of the City of New York (A.B., 1881), Union Theological Seminary (from which he was graduated in 1886), and New York University (Ph.D., 1891). He taught school in 1881–83, and has held successive pastorates at Romeyn Chapel, New York City (1886), and Olivet Memorial Church in the same city (1887–99). From 1899 to 1903 he was superintendent of Interdenominational Sunday-school Work in New York State, and in 1904 was associate editor of the *Westminster Lesson Helps*, while since 1905 he has been assistant pastor of the First Presbyterian Church, Newark, N. J. In theology he describes his position as that of one " always working toward the best." He has written: *The Bible School Manual* (New York, 1898); *Bible School Pedagogy* (1900); *The Child for Christ* (Chicago, 1902); *After the Primary, What?* (1904); and *The Pastor and Teacher Training* (Nashville, 1905).

MACKINTOSH, CHARLES HENRY: Plymouth Brother; b. in County Wicklow, Ireland, in 1820: d. at Cheltenham (7 m. n.e. of Gloucester) Nov. 2, 1896. He was schoolmaster at Westport, County Mayo, Ireland, for a few years. But for the greater part of his life he devoted himself to evangelism and pastoral ministry as well as to religious journalism, as editor of the monthly periodical *Things New and Old;* and to religious literature. He was the author of the *Notes* by C. H. M. on all the books of the Pentateuch, which enjoyed great popularity, being sold in enormous quantity, especially in the United States; so that the initials "C. H. M." under which they were issued were very familiar while probably the name they stood for was not. Mr. Gladstone commended his English style; Spurgeon, while dissenting from their "Darbyism," commended the *Notes*, especially the volume on Exodus. EDWARD E. WHITFIELD.

MACKNIGHT, JAMES: Scotch divine and Biblical scholar; b. at Irvine (10 m. n. of Ayr), Ayrshire, Sept. 17, 1721; d. at Edinburgh Jan. 13, 1800. He was educated at the universities of Glasgow and Leyden; preached for a short time at Gorbals, Renfrewshire; was then assistant minister at Kilwinning, Ayrshire; pastor at Maybole, 1753–69; at Jedburgh, 1769–72; and of Lady Yester's Church, Edinburgh, from 1772 till his death. His fame rests chiefly upon his *Harmony of the Gospels, in which the Natural Order of each is Preserved, with a Paraphrase and Notes* (2 vols., London, 1756; 7th ed., 1822; Latin transl., 3 vols., Bremen, 1772–79), a work which for over half a century remained the standard. The notes are very copious and make of the work practically a complete life of Christ so far as the knowledge of the period permitted. He also wrote: *The Truth of Gospel History* (1763; on the evidences for the Gospels); and *A New Literal Translation from the Original Greek of all the Apostolical Epistles, with a Commentary and Notes* (4 vols., 1795; subsequent editions varying in the number of volumes, those subsequent to 1806 prefaced by a *Life* by his son; 7th ed., 1843). The last-named work was printed both with and without the Greek text.

BIBLIOGRAPHY: Besides the *Life* by his son, ut sup., consult: S. A. Allibone, *Critical Dictionary of English Literature*, ii. 1188–89, Philadelphia, 1891 (cites several varying opinions of Macknight's work); *DNB*, xxxv. 184–185.

MACLAGAN, WILLIAM DALRYMPLE: Church of England, former archbishop of York, primate of England, and metropolitan; b. at Edinburgh June 18, 1826; d. at London Sept. 19, 1910. He received his early education in Edinburgh, and 1847–52 served in the Indian army, retiring with the rank of lieutenant. He then entered Peterhouse, Cambridge, (B.A., 1856), and was ordered deacon in 1856 and ordained priest in the following year. He was curate of St. Saviour, Paddington, London (1856–58), and St. Stephan's, Marylebone, London (1858–60), after which he was secretary of the London Diocesan Church Building Society for five years (1860–1865). He was curate in charge of Enfield (1865–1869), rector of Newington (1869–75), and vicar of Kensington (1875–78), as well as honorary chaplain in ordinary to the queen (1877–78) and prebendary of Reculverland in St. Paul's Cathedral (1878). In 1878 he was consecrated bishop of Lichfield, and was translated in 1891 to the archdiocese of York, from which post he resigned in 1908. He edited, in collaboration with A. Weir, *The Church and the Age, Essays on the Principles and Present Position of the Anglican Church* (London, 1870), and wrote *Pastoral Letters and Synodal Charges* (1892).

McLAREN, ALEXANDER: English Baptist; b. in Glasgow Feb. 11, 1826; d. at Edinburgh May 5, 1910. He was educated at Stepney (Regent's Park) College, London, and was minister of Portland Chapel, Southampton, 1846–58. He was then pastor, later pastor emeritus, of Union Chapel, Manchester, and in 1909 retired and moved to Scotland. He wrote: *Sermons Preached in Manchester* (3 series; London, 1864–73); *Week-Day Evening Addresses* (1877); *The Life of David as Reflected in his Psalms* (1880); *The Secret of Power, and other Sermons* (1882); *A Year's Ministry* (1884); *Epistles of St. Paul to the Colossians and Philemon* (1887); *Modern Miracles: Manifestation of God's Love and Power* (1888); *The Unchanging Christ, and other Sermons* (1889); *Holy of Holies* (sermons on the Gospel of John; 1890); *God of the Amen, and other Sermons* (1891); *Gospel of St. Luke* (1892); *Gospel of Matthew* (2 vols., 1892); *Gospel of John* (1893; in 3 vols., 1907); *Gospel of Mark* (1893); *The Wearied Christ, and other Sermons* (1893); *Acts of the Apostles* (1894; in 2 vols., 1907); *Christ's Musts, and other Sermons* (1894); *The Beatitudes, and other Sermons* (1896); *Triumphant Certainties and other Sermons* (1896); *The Victor's Crown* (sermons; 1897); *Leaves from the Tree of Life* (1899); *A Rosary of Christian Graces* (1899); *After the Resurrection* (1902); *Last Sheaves* (sermons; 1903); *The Book of Genesis* (1904); *Books of Isaiah and Jeremiah* (2 vols., 1905–06); *The Books of Deuteronomy, Joshua, Judges, Ruth and I Samuel* (1906); *The Books of Exodus, Leviticus, and Numbers* (1906); *The Second Book of Samuel and the Books of Kings to II Kings vii.* (1907); *Pulpit Prayers* (1907); and *Expositions of Holy Scripture* (6 vols., 1908); and other volumes, including Psalms in *The Expositor's Bible* (3 vols., London, 1893–94) and *Pulpit Prayers* (1909).

MACLAY, ROBERT SAMUEL: Methodist Episcopalian; b. at Concord, Pa., Feb. 7, 1824. He was educated at Dickinson College, Carlisle, Pa. (A.B., 1845). In 1847 he went to China as a missionary, and was stationed first at Foochow, whence he was transferred to Japan in 1872. In both these countries he took an active part in translating the New Testament, besides being secretary and treasurer in both missions. He was one of the founders of the Anglo-Chinese College at Foochow in 1881 and of the Anglo-Japanese College at Tokyo in 1883, and also established the Philander Smith Biblical Institute in the latter city in 1882. In 1884 he began mission work in Korea by permission of the king. He was likewise president of the Anglo-Japanese College from 1883 to 1887 and dean of the Philander Smith Biblical Institute from 1884 to 1887, as well as delegate from Japan to both the Ecumenical Methodist Conference at London in 1881 and the General Conference of the Methodist Episcopal Church at New York in 1888. From 1888 to his retirement from active life in 1893 he was dean of the Maclay College of Theology, San Fernando, Cal. Besides contributing the sections on the Japanese mission of his denomination to J. M. Reid's *Missions and Missionary Societies of the Methodist Episcopal Church* (2 vols., New York, 1879) and on Shintoism to the same theologian's *Doomed Religions* (1882), he has written: *Life among the Chinese* (New York, 1861) and *Dictionary of the Chinese Language in the Dialect of Foochow* (in collaboration with C. C. Baldwin; Foochow, 1871).

MACLEAN, ARTHUR JOHN: Church of England; bishop of Moray, Ross, and Caithness; b. at Bath, England, July 6, 1858. He was educated at King's College, Cambridge (B.A., 1880; M.A., 1883), and was ordered deacon in 1882 and ordained priest in the following year. After being missionary chaplain of Cumbræ Cathedral in 1882–1883, he was priest in charge of St. Columba, Portree, with Stornoway and Caroy, in 1882–86. He then went to the Orient as head of the archbishop's Assyrian (East Syrian) mission, where he remained until 1891, being at the same time honorary canon of Cumbræ from 1883 to 1892. Returning to England, he was successively rector of Portree from 1891 to 1897, and of St. John the Evangelist, Selkirk, from 1897 to 1903, and Pantonian professor and principal of the Theological College of the Episcopal Church in Scotland from 1903 to 1905. He was likewise dean of Argyll and the Isles in 1892–1897 and canon of Cumbræ during the same period, besides being canon of St. Mary's Cathedral, Edinburgh, in 1903–05, being honorary canon of the same cathedral since the latter year. In 1904 he was consecrated bishop of Moray, Ross, and Caithness. Besides editing *East Syrian Lectionary* (London, 1889); *Old and New Syriac Grammars* (in vernacular Syriac; 1890); *East Syrian Liturgies* (2 parts, 1890–92); and *Modern Syriac and English Verb Vocabulary* (1891), and in addition to translating *East Syrian Daily Offices* (London, 1894); *The Testament of Our Lord* (in collaboration with J. Cooper; 1902); and *East Syrian Epiphany Rites* (in F. C. Conybeare's *Rituale Armenorum*, 1905), he has written: *The Catholicos of the East and his People* (in collaboration with W. H. Browne; London, 1892); *Grammar of the Dialects of Vernacular Syriac as spoken by the Eastern Syrians of Kurdistan, North-West Persia, and the Plain of Mosul* (Cambridge, 1895); *Dictionary of the Dialects of Vernacular Syriac as spoken by the Eastern Syrians of Kurdistan, North-West Persia, and the Plain of Mosul* (Oxford, 1901); and *Recent Discoveries illustrating Early Christian Life and Worship* (London, 1904).

MACLEAR, GEORGE FREDERICK: Church of England; b. at Bedford Feb. 3, 1833; d. at Canterbury Oct. 19, 1902. He was educated at Trinity College, Cambridge (B.A., 1855; M.A., 1860; B.D., 1867; D.D., 1872). He was ordained deacon in 1856 and priest in 1857. He was assistant minister of Curzon Chapel, Mayfair, and of St. Mark, Notting Hill; and from 1865 to 1870 assistant preacher at the Temple Church (all three churches in London). He was head master of King's College School from 1866 to 1880; and Boyle lecturer in 1879–80. In 1880 he became warden of St. Augustine's College, Canterbury, and in 1885 honorary canon of Canterbury cathedral. His works include: *A Class-Book of Old Testament History* (Cambridge, 1862); *A Class-Book of New Testament History* (1862); *A Class-Book of the Catechism of the Church of England* (1868); *Apostles of Mediæval Europe* (London, 1868); *Conversion of the Celts, of the English, of the Northmen* (London, 1878) *and of the Slavs* (1879); *Evidential Value of the Holy Eucharist* (1883); *An Introduction to the Creeds* (1889); *The Village Church and what it Teaches* (1893); and (together with W. W. Williams) *An Introduction to the Articles of the Church of England* (1895). He also edited in the *Cambridge Bible for Schools*, Joshua (1880) and Mark (1879); and in the *Cambridge Greek Testament for Schools*, Mark (1883).

MACLEOD, DONALD: Church of Scotland; b. at Campsie (15 m. s.w. of Stirling), Stirlingshire, Mar. 18, 1831. He was educated at the University of Glasgow (B.A., 1850), after which he spent two years in travel. In 1858 he was ordained minister of Lauder, and four years later was called to the parish of Linlithgow. Since 1869 he has been minister of Park Parish, Glasgow. He was appointed one of the chaplains in ordinary to the queen in 1872 and to the king in 1901; and was convener of the Home Mission Committee of the Church of Scotland from 1888 to 1900 and moderator of the Church of Scotland in 1895–96. In theology he terms himself a "conservative Broad churchman." Besides his activity as editor of *Good Words* from 1872 to 1905, he has written *Memoir of Norman Macleod* (London, 1874); *The Reformation, 1559 to 1572 A.D.* (1881); *Sunday Home Service* (1885); *The Parochial System* (1886); *Christ and Society* (1892); and *The Doctrine and Validity of the Ministry and Sacraments of the National Church of Scotland* (Baird lecture; Edinburgh, 1903).

MACLEOD, NORMAN: Church of Scotland; b. at Campbeltown (38 m. w. by s. of Ayr), Argyllshire, June 3, 1812; d. in Glasgow June 16, 1872. In his *Reminiscences of a Highland Parish* (London, 1867) will be found an animated account of the old Highland family—especially as represented by his grandfather, the patriarchal minister of Morven—from which he was proud to be descended, as well as graphic descriptions of the wild scenery, and free, out-of-door life, in the midst of which some of the happiest days of a happy boyhood were spent. It was, however, chiefly with the town of Campbeltown and its seafaring associations that the boy was familiar. On his impressible and sympathetic nature all the circumstances of those early years appear to have exercised a lasting influence. He entered the University of Glasgow, after an irregular classical training, in 1827, where he shone more in the students' social and political meetings than in the classrooms. Of general literature, however, he appears to have read much in those days, his favorite author in poetry being Wordsworth. In 1831 he removed to the University of Edinburgh, that he might take his theological course under Dr. Thomas Chalmers, then professor of divinity in that university. Before receiving license in 1837, he spent three years in the family of a Yorkshire gentleman, Mr. Preston of Moreby, as tutor to his son, during most of the time residing at Weimar, or elsewhere on the continent of Europe. This first of many visits abroad had an important influence on the development of the young man's character. "His views were widened, his opinions matured, his human sympathies vastly enriched; and, while

Early Life.

all that was of the essence of his early faith had become doubly precious, he had gained increased catholicity of sentiment, along with knowledge of the world" (*Memoir*, vol. i., p. 49).

Macleod's first charge, to which he was ordained in 1838, was Loudoun, in Ayrshire, a parish partly agricultural, but with a considerable weaving population. There he gave himself with all the ardor of his nature and the enthusiasm of youth to his parochial duties, especially among the working classes. His *Cracks about the Kirk for Kintra Folk*, published in 1843 shortly before the disruption, had a large circulation and exerted considerable influence. In Dec., 1843, he was translated to Dalkeith. During his ministry there he became one of the founders of the Evangelical Alliance in 1847, and also editor of the Edinburgh *Christian Magazine*. In 1851 he was appointed to the large and important parish of the Barony, Glasgow, embracing at that time 87,000 souls, and here he showed preeminently his gifts as a parish minister, above all his powers of organization, his large-hearted sympathy with all classes of his parishioners, and his eloquence as a preacher. One of his special aims in the Barony was to reclaim the non-churchgoing population; for which purpose, among other schemes, he introduced with success Sunday services open exclusively to working people in their working clothes. He also founded the first congregational penny savings-bank in Glasgow, and established places of resort for working men, to counteract the temptations of the public-house. In 1857 he was appointed one of her majesty's chaplains, and he enjoyed in an eminent degree the royal favor and confidence (cf. *Journal of our Life in the Highlands* by Queen Victoria, London, 1868, pp. 147, sqq.).

Ministry.

Dr. Macleod took an active part in the general work of the Church. In 1845 he was one of a deputation to visit the Scottish churches in Canada. In 1864 he became chairman of the Foreign Mission Committee of his church, and in this capacity paid a visit to India as a deputy from the church in 1867. His last great public effort was a memorable speech in the General Assembly of 1872, when he resigned this position. In 1865 he became involved in a controversy regarding the Sabbath; while strenuously upholding the religious observance of the Lord's day, he refused to base that observance on the perpetual obligation of the Fourth Commandment. In 1869 he was elected moderator of the General Assembly. Two memorial windows were placed by Queen Victoria in Crathie Church, Aberdeenshire, where he had often conducted service; in one of these he is described as "a man eminent in the Church, honored in the State, and in many lands greatly beloved." He married Catherine Ann Mackintosh Aug. 11, 1851.

In 1860 Dr. Macleod undertook the editorship of *Good Words*, one of the ablest and most successful of the religious magazines of the day. Some of the more popular of his contributions to general literature were written about the same time, many of them originally appearing in *Good Words*. They include: *The Earnest Student* (Edinburgh, 1854), a memoir of his wife's brother, John Mackintosh of Geddes; *The Gold Thread* (1861); *The Old Lieutenant and his Son* (1862); *Wee Davie* (London, 1864); *Eastward* (London, 1866); *Simple Truth Spoken to Working People* (1867); *The Starling* (2 vols., 1867); *Peeps at the Far East* (1871); *Character Sketches* (1872); *The Temptation of our Lord* (1873).

Writings.

W. Lee†, revised by Henry Cowan.

Bibliography: Donald Macleod (his brother), *Memoir of Norman Macleod*, London, 1876; A. Strahan, *Norman Macleod*, ib. 1872; Stanley, in *Good Words*, 1872; Jean L. Watson, *Life of Norman Macleod*, ib. 1881; R. Flint, in *Scottish Divines* (St. Giles Lectures), London, 1883; A. H. Japp, *Good Men and True*, ib. 1890; J. Wellwood, *Norman Macleod*, Edinburgh, 1897; John N. Macleod, *Memorials of Rev. Norman Macleod*, ib. 1898; *DNB*, xxxv. 217-218.

MACMILLAN, HUGH: United Free Church of Scotland; b. at Aberfeldy (22 m. n.w. of Perth) Sept. 17, 1833; d. in Edinburgh May 24, 1903. He was educated at the University of Edinburgh and was minister at Kirkmichael (1859-64), Glasgow (1864-78), and Greenock (1878-98). He made his reputation by his first two books, *Footnotes from the Page of Nature, or First Forms of Vegetation* (Cambridge, 1861), and *Bible Teachings in Nature* (London, 1866), of which 30,000 copies had been sold in Great Britain up to 1907, and which had been translated into French, German, Italian, Danish, and Norwegian, and reprinted and widely sold in America. In these two books he first revealed his ability to interest persons in his favorite theme, the intimate relations between the natural and the spiritual. This was the theme of many subsequent volumes, some of which were travels and many of which were collections of sermons and essays. Of these may be mentioned: *Holidays in High Lands, or Rambles and Incidents in Search of Alpine Plants* (1869); *The Sabbath of the Fields* (1876); *Two Worlds are Ours* (1880); *Roman Mosaics* (1888); *Gleanings in Holy Fields* (1899); his book of verse, *The Christmas Rose* (1901); his two volumes of collected addresses to children, *The Gate Beautiful* (1891), and *The Corn of Heaven* (1901); posthumous were *Rothiemurchus* (1907), and *The Isles and the Gospel* (1907, with a prefatory memoir by George A. Macmillan).

M'NEILL, JOHN: Mission Preacher; b. at Houston (11 m. w. of Glasgow), Renfrewshire, July 7, 1854. He received his early education in the Free Church schools at Houston and Inverkip, after which he was in the railway service from 1869 to 1877. In the latter year he resolved to prepare for the ministry, and studied successively at Edinburgh University (1877-80), Glasgow University (1880-81), and Free Church Divinity Hall, Glasgow (1881-85). In 1886 he was ordained to the ministry and became pastor of M'Crie-Roxburgh Free Church, Edinburgh, where he remained until 1889, when he went to London as minister of Regent Square Presbyterian Church. In 1892 he left the regular ministry to become a mission preacher, and in this capacity traveled throughout Great Britain, in addition to visiting India, South Africa, Australia, Tasmania, New Zealand, the United States, and Canada. In 1908 he became pastor of Christ Church (Congregational), London. He has written: *Sermons* (3 vols., London, 1890–91); *The Brazen Serpent, and other Addresses* (1893); and *The Lord our Shepherd, and other Addresses* (1898).

MÂCON (MATISCO): A city of Burgundy, in which three synods were held. One, in 581, at which twenty-one bishops were present, issued nineteen canons, of which the seventh threatens with excommunication any civil judge who dares to proceed against a clerk, except in criminal cases, while canons 13–16 are aimed at the Jews. Another, in 585, at which forty-three bishops were present in person, and twenty were represented by deputies, issued twenty canons, of which the eighth forbade any one who had sought refuge in the sanctuary to be touched without the consent of the priest; while the ninth and tenth forbade the civil power to proceed against a bishop, except through his metropolitan, or against a priest or deacon, except through his bishop. The third was held between 617 and 627, and decided against an attempt to do away with the rule of St. Columban. The acts and canons are not extant.

BIBLIOGRAPHY: Hefele, *Conciliengeschichte*, iii. 36–41, 74, Eng. transl., iv. 402–409, 444.

MACRINA, ma-cri'na: The name of two female saints of the early Church.

1. Macrina the Elder: Grandmother of Basil the Great and Gregory of Nyssa; d. at Neocæsarea c. 340. Of her life little is known. She seems to have married into a rich and distinguished family of Pontus, and Basil assumes (*Epist.* cciv.) that she was remembered in Neocæsarea for more than a generation after her death. He says that she told him stories of Gregory Thaumaturgus, and influenced his life by her teaching in his childhood. Gregory mentions (*Vita Macrinæ junioris, MPG*, xlvi. 961–980) that she suffered persecution, together with her husband, for her faith; and Gregory Nazianzen in his panegyric on Basil (*Oratio* xliii.; *MPG*, xxxvi. 501) states that they took refuge in the forest of Pontus and remained there considerable time. Neither the date nor the duration of this voluntary exile is certain, since the statements of Gregory Nazianzen that it lasted seven years and took place during the reign of Maximinus (who ruled only from 311 to 313) do not agree with each other. Her day is Jan. 14.

2. Macrina the Younger: Granddaughter of the preceding and the sister of Basil the Great and Gregory of Nyssa; b. in Pontus c. 329; d. at a family estate on the Iris in the same province in the latter part of 379. She was the oldest of ten children and was betrothed at the age of twelve to a young jurist of distinguished family. He died, however, before the marriage, and Macrina seems to have seized this pretext to adopt a life of celibacy and asceticism. After the death of her father, Basilius, she remained with her mother Emmelia until Basil returned from his studies about 358, when she, together with her mother and her servants and slaves (now ranked as her sisters), retired to the banks of the Iris to lead the life of a nun. To her brothers, particularly the youngest, Peter, who afterward became bishop of Sebaste, this place was a school of earnest Christianity, and it was also visited by Gregory Nazianzen and Eustathius of Sebaste. When Emmelia died shortly before 370, Macrina became the head of the community. Her brother Gregory was present at her death and has preserved the memories of the scene both in his *Vita Macrinæ* and in his treatise *On the Soul and the Resurrection*. Her day is July 19. (F. LOOFS.)

BIBLIOGRAPHY: 1. The sources are indicated in the text. Consult: *ASB*, Jan., i. 952–3; *DCB*, iii. 779; and the literature under BASIL, SAINT; and GREGORY OF NYSSA. 2. The life is most accessible in *ASB*, July, iv. 589–604; *DCB*, iii., 779–781; and ut sup. under 1.

McTYEIRE, HOLLAND NIMMONS: American Methodist Episcopal (South) bishop; b. in Barnwell Co., S. C., July 28, 1824; d. at Nashville, Tenn., Feb. 15, 1889. He was educated at Randolph-Macon College, Va. (A.B., 1844) and entered the Methodist ministry in 1845. He was pastor at Williamsburg, Va., Mobile and Demopolis, Ala., Columbus, Miss., New Orleans, La., and Montgomery, Ala. (at the last-named place during the Civil War). He was elected bishop in 1866, and made president of Vanderbilt University in 1873. He became editor of the *Christian Advocate* (New Orleans) in 1851, and of the *Christian Advocate* (Nashville) in 1858. He wrote: *A Catechism on Church Government* (Nashville, 1869); *A Catechism on Bible History* (1869); *Manual of the Discipline* (1870); *History of Methodism* (1884); and *Passing through the Gates* (1889).

BIBLIOGRAPHY: O. P. Fitzgerald, *Holland N. McTyeire*, Nashville, 1896.

McVICKAR, WILLIAM NEILSON: Protestant Episcopal bishop of Rhode Island; b. in New York City Oct. 19, 1843. He was educated at Columbia College (A.B., 1865), the Philadelphia Divinity School (1865–66), and the General Theological Seminary, from which he was graduated in 1868. He was ordered deacon in 1867, and, after being curate of St. George's, New York City, for a year, was advanced to the priesthood in 1868. From the latter year until 1875 he was rector of Holy Trinity, New York City, after which he was rector of Holy Trinity, Philadelphia, until 1897, declining both the rectorship of St. Paul's, Boston, and a tutorship in Columbia. In 1898 he was consecrated bishop coadjutor of Rhode Island, and in 1903, on the death of Bishop Thomas M. Clark, became bishop of the same diocese. He was a deputy to the General Convention from 1883 to 1895, and was also president of the Southwest Convocation, a manager of the General Missionary Society, and a member of the Diocesan Board of Missions and of other diocesan bodies.

MADAGASCAR, MISSIONS IN: While having all the evil traits of a heathen people, including infanticide, polygamy, and the slave-trade, the Malagasy believed in a supreme being called Zangahara, whom they greatly feared and reverenced. At death, good men go to be happy forever with Zangahara, while bad men go to be tormented by the evil lord, Anggatyr. From 1540 to 1640 numerous colonies were founded by the Dutch and English as well as by the Portuguese, all accompanied by

Prior to 1818.

slavery, all preaching Christianity, and all resulting in failure and repeated massacres in retaliation for ill-treatment. From 1642 to 1686 several French companies also made efforts to colonize the island, enslave and Christianize the Malagasy, but these also failed, and for a time the island was left to become a rendezvous for pirates and buccaneers. In 1754 a further attempt at colonization was made by France, which was broken up by a general massacre. During the next half century occasional French trading-posts were established, which met with little success. The Malagasy were not attracted by the rapacity, licentiousness, and cruelty of the exponents of the new religion, and during 160 years but one convert is mentioned. Not until the accession of Radama I. in 1808 were there any successful relations with the outside world. In 1818 Radama entered into a treaty with England, in which, for certain considerations, he agreed to abolish the slave-trade, while England was to reduce the Malagasy language to writing, and establish schools. This treaty was ratified in 1820, and Madagascar was open for Christian effort.

With the ratification of the treaty assured, in 1818 the London Missionary Society sent the Rev. **1818 to 1835.** Thomas Bevan and David Jones with their families as their first missionaries in Madagascar. They opened a station at Andovoranto, on the east coast; but within two months all of them, except Mr. Jones, died of the fever, and he was obliged to flee for his life. Returning in 1820 with Mr. Hastie, the government agent, with the consent of King Radama, he located in Antananarivo, the capital, where the first school was opened in Dec., 1820. A large force of missionaries was sent out, the Malagasy language was reduced to writing, and the beginnings of a literature were made; more schools were opened, and the work was developed and made rapid progress along educational, industrial, and evangelistic lines. Before 1828 more than one hundred schools had been established, and nearly 5,000 pupils had received the rudiments of education. Preaching services were held regularly in the capital and the surrounding villages, and a beginning was made in the Vonizongo district, a day's journey westward. In Jan., 1828, the Gospel of Luke was printed in the Malagasy language, and other Scriptures were being translated as rapidly as possible. The outlook was most promising, when in July of this year Radama died, and was succeeded by one of his twelve wives, Ranavalona I., an utter heathen and of a turbulent disposition. A reign of terror ensued. The British resident was ordered to leave the country, and for several years a desultory warfare was maintained with the French. Expecting opposition, the missionaries worked at high pressure; in 1831 the first native churches were formed, and within a few months there were nearly 2,000 members; by 1833 the translation and printing of the New Testament was completed, and that of the Old Testament was pushed as rapidly as possible. But a crisis was approaching. In 1834 the queen forbade any but the government employees to learn to read or write. In Jan., 1835, formal accusations were made against all Christians, and the following month the missionaries were notified that Christian worship and teaching were banned. All natives were commanded to renounce Christianity, and the missionaries were ordered to leave the island.

In spite of this edict, David Johns and Edward Baker succeeded in remaining till 1836, finishing the translating and printing of the entire **From 1835 to 1883.** Bible and also of the Pilgrim's Progress. This year over a thousand people were massacred. The persecution continued till 1842; there was then a lull till 1849, when it broke out afresh and over 2,000 were tortured or slain outright. This continued with a short intermission in 1852, till the welcome death of the bloody queen in 1861. She was succeeded by her son Rakoto as Radama II. His first official act was to proclaim freedom of worship to all; Christians in captivity were released, the banished recalled, and the missionaries invited to return and continue their work. By 1862 three clergymen, a physician, a teacher, and a printer were busily gathering up the lines laid down in 1836; at this time there were some twenty-five congregations with about 900 communicants and 7,000 adherents. Religious freedom continued during his short rule and that of his successor, Queen Rosaherina; and with the accession and conversion of Queen Ranavalona II. in 1868, there was a great revival especially in the central province of Imerina, from which it spread southward to the province of Betsileo. In 1869 the idols were publicly burned, and steps were taken toward building up a Christian civilization. Up to this time the London Missionary Society had been alone in Madagascar, but during the next decade several other organizations entered the field, the first being the Society for the Propagation of the Gospel in 1864, followed by the Norwegian Mission Society of Norway (Det Norske Missions Selskab) in 1866, the Friends of England and America in 1867, the Church Missionary Society in 1868, and a number of Roman Catholic priests from France. The work developed rapidly. Memorial churches were erected on the four sites where many martyrs fell, schools were multiplied. By 1870 there were 250,000 converts and at least 1,500,000 people desiring Christian instruction. Missionaries and teachers were sent by the queen to the still heathen tribes. Then followed a period of harvesting as well as seed-sowing.

In 1883 France demanded a protectorate over northwestern Madagascar. On being refused war was declared, which resulted in a French protectorate for the entire island, with an **Since 1883.** influx of Roman Catholic priests who at once began an active propaganda against the Protestants. In 1892 the Norwegian Lutheran Church of America established a mission, followed three years later by the Lutheran Free Church. New openings came among the Sakalavas and several smaller tribes, while there were extended revivals in the principal towns of Imerina and Betsileo, and Madagascar was making progress toward a Christian civilization when in 1895 France annexed the island, and two years later the queen was deposed. At this time there was a total of 75 Protestant missionaries representing 7 societies, over 1,000 native pastors, 97,800 communicants, 393,099 adherents, and 126,000 pupils in the schools. There were 7 hospitals and 10 dispensaries. The number of Roman Catholic Malagasy was estimated at 60,500. Bitter opposition to the English Protestant missions followed. Church buildings were confiscated, and ruin threatened their schools through the enforced use of the French language. At this crisis, the Evangelical Society of Paris took over some 1,200 schools and 62,000 pupils, and much of the work of the London Missionary Society in the two provinces of Imerina and Betsileo, and finally succeeded in obtaining for the non-French Evangelical societies a reasonable amount of religious liberty. The work of the Friends suffered but little from French control, and that of the Norwegians hardly at all. For several years there was friction through the Jesuits trying to gain possession of the Protestant mission properties, but this was stopped by the government. In 1905 and again in 1907 new laws were enacted aiming at the absolute suppression of mission schools, and ordering that no private school be located in buildings used for religious purposes, thus closing 270 of the 300 educational institutions of the Paris Society, and affecting the other missions in like degree. Later the Y. M. C. A. was closed; family prayers were prohibited if any but members of the immediate family were present; an address could not be made or a prayer offered at a public funeral; Evangelists were forbidden to continue their work; and many of the churches were closed. The Paris Society, representing all the Protestant bodies in Madagascar, entered a formal complaint with the secretary of the French colonies, and the governor-general was called to France to explain his actions, but the situation in 1908 was rapidly becoming worse.

There were, in 1907, 51 Roman Catholic missionaries with 348 stations and outstations, and 79,000 communicants and adherents. Five Protestant societies had 227 missionaries and 5,816 native helpers, 1,852 stations and outstations, 355,717 adherents, 1,951 schools and colleges with 92,126 pupils, 9 hospitals and dispensaries, 7 orphanages and 4 leper settlements. Many schools have been closed since these statistics were obtained. THEODORA CROSBY BLISS.

BIBLIOGRAPHY: W. Ellis, *Hist. of Madagascar, . . Progress of the Christian Mission*, 2 vols., London, 1838; idem, *Three Visits to Madagascar*, ib. 1860; idem, *Madagascar Revisited*, ib. 1867; idem, *The Martyr Church*, ib. 1870; J. Sibree, *Madagascar and its People*, ib. 1870; idem, *The Great African Island*, ib. 1879; idem, *Madagascar before the Conquest*, ib. 1896; idem, *Madagascar Mission*, ib., 1907; De la Vaissière, *Hist. de Madagascar, ses habitants et ses missionnaires*, Paris, 1884; G. Shaw, *Madagascar of To-day*, London, 1886; W. E. Cousins, *Madagascar of To-day*, ib. 1895; J. J. K. Fletcher, *Sign of the Cross in Madagascar*, ib. 1901; C. Keller, *Madagascar, Mauritius and Other African Islands*, ib. 1901; H. Froidevaux, *Les Lazaristes à Madagascar au 17. siècle*, Paris, 1902; A. van Gennep, *Tabou et Totémisme à Madagascar*, Paris, 1904; T. T. Matthews, *Thirty Years in Madagascar*, London, 1904; H. O. Dwight, *Blue Book of Missions for 1907*, pp. 23–24, New York, 1907.

MADHAVACHARYA: Hindu Philosopher. See INDIA, I., 2, § 2.

MADRIGAL. See MUSIC, SACRED, II, 2, § 3.

MADSEN, PEDER: Danish theologian; b. in Vinding parish near Holstebro (160 m. n.w. of Copenhagen), Denmark, Aug. 28, 1843. He studied at Viborg and was graduated from the University of Copenhagen, 1868; taught in private schools, 1868–72; spent two years in travel and study; was called to teach dogmatics and exegesis at the University of Copenhagen, 1874; was appointed professor of theology, 1875; was rector 1889–90 and 1903–04; and became bishop of Zealand 1909. He cooperated in working out a new series of Pericopes (q.v.), 1879–81, and assisted in reconstructing the liturgical parts of the church hymnal; represented the theological faculty on the church council, 1884–1886; is on the committee directing Danish missions in America, assists in directing home missions, and is active in Sunday-school work. He has also been for many years president of the Bethesda conventions which are doing for Denmark what the Eisenach Conference (q.v.) does for Germany. He is a member of the body which is considering new lines of polity for the Church in Denmark. Elected bishop of Zealand, 1909.

He gained his doctorate with the thesis *De kristnes aandelige Præstedömme* (1879). Other works are his university programs: *Det kirkelige Embede* (1890); *Embedet og Menighedens Samvirken i det kirkelige Arbejde* (1894); and *Ordinationens Betydning indenfor den luth. Kirkeafdeling* (1904), supporting the Lutheran traditional view of ministry and congregation. He had defended the same view in *Bornholmerne eller den saakaldte lutherske Missionsforening* (1886). JOHN O. EVJEN.

MAGARITA, MAGARITES: A name given by some writers of the Middle Ages to apostates from the Christian religion, particularly those who went over to Mohammedanism. The derivation of the term is unknown. Cf. Du Cange, s.v.

MAGDALENE, ORDERS OF ST. MARY: Several orders established at various times and in different places for the reformation of fallen women. The oldest community of penitents under the patronage of St. Mary Magdalene was probably that established at Metz, which traces its history, doubtless with some exaggeration, back to 1005, while a similar institution is said to have been founded at Treves about 1148. In the early part of the thirteenth century several convents of magdalens were established, influenced in great part by the revival inaugurated by St. Francis, the most noteworthy being those at Goslar about 1215, and at Worms and Strasburg between 1220 and 1230. Bulls confirming the privileges of such orders were issued by Gregory IX. and Innocent IV. between 1227 and 1251. The inmates followed the Augustinian rule and were supervised by provosts appointed by the general provost of the entire order. About the middle of the thirteenth century, convents of magdalens existed at Erfurt, Prenzlau, Malchow, Vienna, Regensburg, and elsewhere, attaching themselves now to one of the great orders and again to another. Refuges for fallen women were established at Marseilles in 1272, at Naples in 1324, and at Prague about 1372. One was founded at Paris in 1492, at Rome by Leo X. in 1520, at Seville in 1550, and at Rouen and Bordeaux in 1618.

At first the discipline in the convents for magdalens was extremely severe, but gradually it grew lax, especially through the admission of those for whom the order was not originally intended, until in 1637–40 a reformation was enforced at Paris, Marseilles, Bordeaux, Rouen, and elsewhere by St. Vincent de Paul. According to the new rule, which was officially approved in 1640, the order was to be divided into three grades. The first of these was the Congregation of St. Mary Magdalene with strict vows, which were assumed after a novitiate of two years, and required fasting throughout Advent, and on all Fridays, as well as frequent retreats, and other acts of penance. The second grade of the order was the Congregation of St. Martha, which required no vows and permitted those who were truly penitent and reformed to reenter the world and marry. The third grade was the Congregation of St. Lazarus, which forcibly detained those who were entrusted to its care for reformation.

Numerous other Roman Catholic orders of more recent times have devoted themselves to the rescue of fallen women, noteworthy among them being the Order of Our Lady of Refuge, founded at Nancy by Elisabeth de la Croix (d. 1649), the Sisters of St. Joseph, established in 1821, and the Order of the Good Shepherd, founded at Angers in 1828. The first impulse toward similar work in Evangelical circles was given by the work of Theodor Fliedner (q.v.; see also DEACONESS, III., 2, a, § 2) at Kaiserswerth beginning with 1833, and his example has since found numerous followers. (O. ZÖCKLER†.)

MAGDEBURG, ARCHBISHOPRIC OF: A former archbishopric, named from an ancient city of Germany, situated on the Elbe, 88 m. w.s.w. of Berlin. The town was an important commercial center as early as the reign of Charlemagne, and its oldest church is supposed to date from this period. In the tenth century, when the city belonged to the diocese of Halberstadt, it contained a parish church, and on Sept. 21, 937, Otho I. founded there a Benedictine monastery, which he endowed richly. Later he conceived the plan of transferring the episcopal palace from Halberstadt to Magdeburg, incorporating the monastery with it, and transforming the bishopric into an archbishopric for the Wends. In 955 he assured himself of the papal sanction through Abbot Hadamar of Fulda, but his plans failed on account of the opposition of Archbishop William of Mainz, who refused to relinquish Halberstadt and proposed to separate Magdeburg from the diocese of Halberstadt and create of it a new bishopric among the Wends. This plan was carried out. In the Roman synod of Feb. 12, 962, Magdeburg was made an archbishopric with jurisdiction over all future Wendish dioceses, according to the emperor's wish. The final negotiations took place at Ravenna in Oct., 968, when Archbishop Hatto II., who had succeeded William seven months previously at Mainz, agreed to the creation of the new archbishopric. Otho appointed Adalbert, abbot of Weissenburg in Alsace, the first archbishop. The archdiocese of Magdeburg comprised the dioceses which already existed in Brandenburg and Havelberg, as well as the new bishoprics of Merseburg, Meissen, and Zeitz, thus stretching from the Saale and Elbe in the west to the Oder in the east. (A. HAUCK.)

BIBLIOGRAPHY: Sources are the *Gesta archiepiscoporum Magdeburgensium*, and the *Catalogi*, ed. W. Schum, in *MGH*, *Script*, xiv (1883), 361 sqq., 484–486; *Annales Magdeburgensis*, ed. G. H. Pertz, ib., xvi (1859), 105–196; G. A. von Mülverstedt, *Regesta archiepiscopatus Magdeburgensis*, 4 vols., Magdeburg, 1876–99; and *Die Magdeb. Schöppenchronik*, ed. W. Janicke, in *Chroniken der deutschen Städte*, vol. vii., Leipsic, 1869; Gams, *Series episcoporum*, p. 288. Consult: F. W. Hoffmann, *Geschichte der Stadt Magdeburg*, 2 vols., Magdeburg, 1885–86; W. Kawerau, *Aus Magdeburgs Vergangenheit*, Halle, 1886; K. Uhlirz, *Geschichte des Erzbistums Magdeburg*, Magdeburg, 1887; C. Eubel, *Hierarchia catholica medii ævii*, 2 vols., Münster, 1898–1901; Hauck, *KD*, vols. iii.–iv.

MAGDEBURG CENTURIES: The first attempt to write the history of the Church from the Evangelical point of view. The plan of this work was conceived by Matthias Flacius (q.v.). He projected a church history from the original sources showing that the Church of Christ since the time of the apostles had deviated from the right course, a documentary history of anti-Christianity in the church of Christ from its beginnings to its highest development up to the restoration of true religion in its purity by Luther. From 1553 Flacius gave his efforts to the securing of patrons to aid the work financially, whom he found among German noblemen and wealthy citizens, in Augsburg, Nüremberg, and elsewhere, and in obtaining collaborators. The active interest and assistance manifested by the Imperial Councilor Niedbruck, curator of the Royal Library in Vienna, proved especially valuable. Libraries had to be searched for sources and documents; for this purpose Flacius himself undertook journeys in Germany, and his assistant Marcus Wagner of Friemar near Gotha with great success traveled through Denmark, Scotland, Austria, Bavaria, and other territories, while many manuscripts and books were purchased or donated by patrons. In Magdeburg Flacius, Johann Wigand, and Matthäus Judex stood at the head of the project and worked out the details of the plan. The Councilor Ebeling Alemann, and the physician, Martin Copus, were treasurers; assistants were trained in furnishing the necessary excerpts, which two learned masters put into shape. From Jena Flacius directed the entire work. Thus there appeared in Basel, 1559–74, the *Ecclesiastica historia secundum singulas centurias per aliquot studiosos et pios viros in urbe Magdeburgica*, hence called the Magdeburg Centuries. Centuries seven to thirteen were elaborated especially by Wigand in Wismar. Wigand and subsequently Stangewald afterward worked on the three following centuries without completing them (the sixteenth century, compiled by Wigand, is in Wolfenbüttel in manuscript form); attempts made by several persons in the eighteenth century to bring the work down to date were also without result. The "Centuries" mark immense progress in ecclesiastical historiography, not only by the tracing of the sources and the completeness with which the material was collected, but also because there is applied in them the pragmatic method of historical development. The anti-Roman interest sharpened the vision and helped the authors of the work to critical achievements that marked a new epoch. While the division into centuries was an obstacle to a good grouping of the material, and the one-sided polemical anti-Roman interest formed a barrier to an unprejudiced appreciation of the development of church history; nevertheless, there was achieved the utmost that was possible within the limits of the sharply defined dogmatic standpoint, and the work furnished the weapons which Protestantism needed in its struggle. The work, *pestilentissimum opus*, as it was called by the Roman opponents, made a very strong impression upon the Roman Church. Canisius urged the most learned theologians to attack it, and many pens were set in motion until in Cæsar Baronius (q.v.) there was found an able opponent who drew his material from the Roman sources themselves. (G. Kawerau.)

Bibliography: F. C. Baur, *Die Epochen der kirchlichen Geschichtsschreibung*, pp. 39 sqq., Tübingen, 1852; B. ter Haar, *De Historiographie der Kerkgeschiedenis*, pp. 121 sqq., Utrecht, 1870–73; A. Jundt, *Les Centuries de Magdebourg*, Paris, 1883; Schaumkell, *Beitrag zur Entstehungsgeschichte der Magd. Centurien*, Ludwigsburg, 1898; Schaff, *Christian Church*, i. 37–38.

MAGEE, WILLIAM; Archbishop of Dublin; b. at Enniskillen (70 m. s.w. of Belfast), County Fermanagh, Mar. 18, 1766; d. at Stillorgan (5 m. s.e. of Dublin) Aug. 18, 1831. He was educated at Trinity College, Dublin (B.A., 1785), and became fellow in 1788, and senior fellow and professor of mathematics in 1800. Ordained deacon in 1790, he became dean of Cork in 1813, bishop of Raphoe in 1819, and archbishop of Dublin in 1822. He was a determined opponent of the Roman Catholics but still more of the Unitarians, against whom he wrote several pamphlets. He wrote among other works: *Discourses on the Scriptural Doctrines of Atonement and Sacrifice* (London, 1801). His works were collected in two volumes (London, 1842).

Bibliography: Consult, besides the Memoir by A. H. Kenney, prefixed to his collected *Works*, ut sup., *DNB*, xxxv. 313–315, where further literature is given.

MAGEE, WILLIAM CONNOR: Archbishop of York; b. at Cork Dec. 17, 1821; d. in London May 5, 1891. He was a grandson of William Magee (q.v.). He was educated at Trinity College, Dublin (B.A., 1842; M.A. and B.D., 1854; D.D., 1860). He became curate of St. Thomas', Dublin, in 1844; of St. Saviour's, Bath, in 1848; minister of the Octagon Chapel, Bath, in 1850; perpetual curate of Quebec Chapel in 1859; rector of Enniskillen in 1860; dean of Cork in 1864; dean of the Chapel Royal, Dublin, in 1866; bishop of Peterborough in 1868; and archbishop of York in 1891. He was Donellan lecturer at Dublin in 1865–66. He was the author of: *Sermons Delivered at St. Saviour's Church, Bath* (Bath, 1852); *Sermons at the Octagon Chapel, Bath* (Bath, 1854); *The Gospel and the Age* (London, 1884); *The Atonement* (1887); *Growth in Grace* (1891); *Christ the Light of all Scripture* (1892); and *Speeches and Addresses* (1892).

Bibliography: J. C. MacDonnell, *The Life and Correspondence of William Connor Magee*, 2 vols., London, 1896; idem, in *DNB*, xxxv. 313–315.

MAGIC.

Magic is the alleged art of producing supernatural results by means of occult agencies, although in the widest sense of the term it includes Divination (q.v.), and thus coincides with occultism. In the present article, however, the discussion of magic is restricted to the causation of supernatural phenomena by mystic conjurations or incantations which may be either benevolent or malevolent. In this form magic coincides in great part with Witchcraft (q.v.), although it is distinguished, on the one hand, by a more scientific method, and, on the other, by a social trend which aims at a unification of magic operations by occult traditions. Magic is divided, according to the means employed, into demonistic (operating with the aid of spirits), religious (regulated by the priesthood and the cult), and natural (working simply through hidden powers of nature), while with regard to its beneficent or maleficent intent it is termed "white" and "black" magic respectively.

1. Definition and Scope.

Magic is an element of the empirical religion of all times and peoples, and belongs, like asceticism, sacrifice, and purification, to the constantly recurring and ineradicable factors of the social life of mankind (see Comparative Religion, VI., 1, a, § 5). Among many wild tribes religion seems to consist almost entirely of magic, although the theory that all religion is a development of witchcraft and magic is open to grave objections. The question may even be raised whether magic is not a phase of religious degeneration rather than evolution. The view prevailing in many circles that the religious conditions of modern savages constitutes the norm for reconstructing the religion of primitive man fails to recognize that the evidence in the life of ancient and of modern peoples shows a slow process of religious decay. It must be noted, furthermore, that savages are not found to advance from fetishism or animism (see Comparative Religion) to a higher stage of religious life, nor are magic and witchcraft (q.v.) the most primitive forms of the religion of the civilized nations of antiquity. Neither in Egypt nor in Babylonia does religious development reveal polydemonistic magic as the source of their mythology and their cult, however early magic rites and formulas were used among both nations. Magic is, then, essentially a symptom of religious decay and belongs to the latest period of religious evolution. In cases where it appears at a relatively early stage in a given people, it is seldom developed by the people in question, but is usually of foreign origin, being imported from degenerate neighboring tribes.*

2. Place in Religion.

* For the presentation of another view of ethnic magic, see Comparative Religion, VI., 1, a, § 5.

The Babylonians are usually regarded as the nation among whom magic, in the strict sense of the term, first appeared, although it must be borne in mind that Babylonian here connotes Sumerian, and that the Babylonian Semites first became acquainted with magic through their Sumerian neighbors. The Medes and Persians were strongly opposed to magic and sturdily resisted the priests of magic coming from Babylonia, India, and Egypt.

3. In Babylonia. Neither the Medes nor the Persians can be regarded as the authors of the magic art which later spread from the Orient to Greece and Rome, but the real source of magic was the proto-Babylonian priesthood of the region of the lower Euphrates, whose incantations, written in Sumerian, are doubtless the oldest documents of their class. The Sumerians seem to have been a "Turanian" people who left their original home in Central Asia and became fused with the Aryan stock south of the Caspian, especially with the Medes, and also with the Semites of the Euphrates valley (see BABYLONIA, V., §§ 1–2). This worship of the elements and their spirits to which the peoples of central and northern Asia were devoted thus penetrated into the southwestern part of the continent. In the older magic texts, preserved in numerous clay tablets in the library of Asshurbanipal (see ASSYRIA, VI., 3, § 14), witchcraft is essentially a system of incantation to avert the power of evil demons, while various gods, especially Ea, Marduk, Gibil-Nusku, and Sin, are invoked as protectors. The entire object was the averting of physical ills and the exorcism of disease-demons, thus presenting numerous parallels with the arts of shamanistic medicine men. It was only this older Babylonian magic, which was still influenced by Sumerian traditions, that was medical, for after the consolidation of the Babylonian kingdom in the second millennium B.C., divination superseded all other forms of magic in Babylonia while astrology spread from Chaldea throughout the west and made the terms Chaldean and astrologer almost synonymous.

4. In Egypt. In Egypt, which, like Babylonia, was one of the earliest homes of Oriental magic, witchcraft never became overlaid with divination, but always remained essentially a system of medical exorcism, practised by priestly medical magicians, and based on sympathetic cures, the conjuration of hostile powers of nature, and the banishment of sickness by amulets and the like. The magic papyri of the New Kingdom contain incantations against crocodiles and other noxious creatures, especially serpents, as well as against all sorts of demons, against the evil eye, and against sickness of every kind, and many of their mystic words of power are Assyro-Babylonian in origin.

5. Among the Hebrews. The ancient Hebrews, surrounded and influenced by two neighboring peoples which were adepts in magic art, also showed a strong tendency to witchcraft, as is clear from the rigid but ineffectual prohibitions in the legal code (Ex. xxii. 18; Deut. xviii. 10–11; comp. II Kings xxi. 6; Isa. viii. 19, 20, lvii. 3; Micah v. 11). Both the divination of the Babylonians and the medical exorcisms of the Egyptians seem to have exercised a strong influence on Israel, and the later development of pre-Christian Judaism favored an increased devotion to these forbidden arts. This is shown by many of the Apocrypha and Pseudepigrapha of the Old Testament, especially Tobit iii., vi.; Enoch lxix., the Testaments of the Twelve Patriarchs, the late Jewish Testament of Solomon and various other Solomonic legends and incantations connected with the tradition of the queen of Sheba based on I Kings x. 1–10.

6. In India. Throughout the Aryan and non-Aryan peoples which surrounded the Semites of southwestern Asia magic is seen to appear at a relatively early period, although it did not exist in the very beginning. Nor did it disappear with development of civilization and learning, but, on the contrary, increased in extent and refinement. So it was among the Hindus (see BRAHMANISM), whose earliest phase of religion, as represented in the Rig Veda, was a simple nature worship free from magic accretion, while the rise of the Brahmanic priesthood produced an extreme formalism with a tendency to exercise power over the gods by means of a correct performance of the prescribed offerings, prayers, and invocations. The Atharva Veda contains a vast number of examples of formulas to be employed in such acts of magic, and the Sutras, or compendiums of ritual for the Brahmanic sacrifice, mark a still further advance in religious formalism. Even the Buddhistic reform was unable to suppress the witchcraft underlying Hinduism, and it was in Buddhism that the popular belief in a cult of magic appropriate to the spirits of earth, trees, mountains, fields, and houses found its most luxuriant development. If this be true of Hindu Buddhism it is still more characteristic of the Mongolian and Tatar neighbors of India, especially the Chinese and the shamanistic tribes of central and northern Asia. In modern China (q.v.) Buddhist bonzes vie with Taoist priests in the practise of magic and divination.

7. In Persia. In Persia (see ZOROASTER, ZOROASTRIANISM), in like manner, magic forced itself upon a Mazdaism which was originally free from witchcraft. The Avesta bitterly opposed the magic arts of the "wizards" who derived their skill either from "Turan" or from Babylon, but toward the end of the Achæmenian period, as well as under the Arsacids, magic began to play so prominent a part in the popular religion of the Persians that the name Magian became a designation for the priesthood of Persia. Even the efforts of the Sassanians to restore the ancient pre-Magian faith had only temporary success. As far as this later Persian or Parthian magianism was predominantly astrological or mantic in character, it must be regarded as borrowed from Babylonia, but its magic elements in the narrower sense of the term, such as conjuration and amulets, doubtless came from the "Turanian" or Scythian peoples in the north.

Among the ancient Teutons a cult of the divinity of the fields and forests connected with the practise of magic was an important feature of religion at a very early period, although it reached its zenith only to be crushed by Christianity. Among the Celts, in like manner, religion was strongly infused with magic elements which had reached a degree of refinement and complexity unknown to the popular Teutonic witchcraft. This was due in great part to the organized priesthood of the Druids (q.v.), who were especially skilled in medical magic.

8. Among Teutons and Celts.

In Greece magic was an important religious factor even in the Homeric and early post-Homeric periods, as is clear from the story of Media in Argonautic legend, Circe in the Odyssey, the magic goddess Hecate, Hermes the protecting herald of the gods and giver of dreams, and all other patron deities. That these ancient Hellenic traditions of magic were native in origin and not borrowed from the East is shown by abundant evidence, especially that which alludes either to Thrace or Thessaly as the early home of witchcraft. Yet at an early time foreign magic found its way into Greece both from Egypt and Babylonia or Persia. Nor did the refinement of Greek civilization prevent the warmest welcome and the most varied imitations of the magic arts of oriental "barbarians." The medical magic of Egypt found no bar to its entrance, and neither the rationalism of the followers of Hippocrates nor the mockeries of Lucian could shake the pseudo-philosophy of the wizards of the Nile who flocked to Greece in increasing numbers. Equally successful was the divination of Persia and Babylon. All forms of prophecy, by astrology, the raising of the dead, psychomancy, invocation of the gods, clidomancy, hydromancy, lecanomancy, and anthropomancy, were in constant use; while the defense of "Persian" magicians as priestly sages by Aristotle, Dio Chrysostom, Apuleius, and Celsus shows the esteem and influence enjoyed by these adepts of eastern occult art among the Greeks during the dynasty of the Diadochi and the Roman period.

9. In Greece.

Rome also possessed its magic and divination, which in their beginnings reached back to the regal epoch and were domiciled among the tribes living on the banks of the Tiber. The Etruscans introduced the cult of the *Dii Averrunci* and all forms of auguries into Rome, although other neighboring peoples, such as the Marsi, likewise contributed their quota. The introduction of eastern magic was bitterly opposed by legislation as early as the reigns of Augustus, Tiberius, and Claudius, while Caracalla condemned magicians to be burned alive or thrown to the beasts. Nevertheless the occult wisdom of the East was irresistible, and the diatribes of Pliny and Tacitus proved unavailing. Even the emperors favored magic; Nero accepted invitations to magic feasts, and Otho was a pronounced patron of magic, while Vespasian, Hadrian, and Marcus Aurelius were at least tolerant toward it and Alexander Severus gave it official subvention. In the reign of the latter and his immediate predecessors magic reached its climax in Rome, and not till the triumph of Christianity was it checked, and even then not extirpated.

10. In Rome.

The early Church was at times not unfavorable to magic. Thus Origen, in his commentary on Genesis (cited in Eusebius, *Præparatio Evangelica*, book VI., chap. xi., Eng. transl., i. 280 sqq., Oxford, 1903), drew a distinction between divine and demonic astrology, and in his polemic against Celsus ascribed a certain reality and justification to the power of those who healed through magic. It was especially the Christian Alexandrians who expressed such views, following, on the one hand, such Hellenistic predecessors as Philo, and, on the other, such neo-Platonic philosophers as Iamblichus and Synesius, one of the earliest sources of this nature being the philastrological dialogue known as *Hermippus* (*Anonymi Christiani Hermippus de astrologia dialogus*, ed. W. Kroll and P. Viereck, Leipsic, 1895), which probably dates from the fifth or sixth century. The New Testament, however, except for the reference to the "wise men from the East," which was regarded as the fulfilment of Messianic prophecy (Ps. lxxii. 10, 15; Isa. lx. 1 sqq.), was unfavorable to magic. Thus the Samaritan Simon is characterized as a false prophet, as is the Jew Bar-Jesus, who is termed a "child of the devil" (Acts viii. 9–11, xiii. 6–11). The tractate of "The Two Ways" at the beginning of the Didache (q.v.) and at the close of the epistle of Barnabas contains an explicit warning against magic, which is ranked with witchcraft, idolatry, drunkenness, impurity, and infanticide. After the middle of the second century the Gnostics were condemned by the Church Fathers as the representatives of accursed magic arts, and Irenæus traced all heretical Gnosticism back to Simon Magus. The same charge of magic was made against Menander, the Carpocratians, the Marcosians, the Elkesaites, the Ophites, and heretics of every description. Side by side with this gnostic magic ran the ancient pagan belief in the power of witchcraft. After the beginning of the fourth century influential heads of the neo-Platonic school sought to extend both theurgic and mantic magic, and the opposing measures of such Christian emperors as Constantine, Valentinian I., Valens, and Theodosius I. had but temporary efficacy. Even during the centuries of the barbarian wars the aid of Tuscan magicians was repeatedly sought, despite the fulminations of Church Fathers like Ephraem Syrus, Isaac of Antioch, Chrysostom, Augustine, Gregory the Great, and Isidore of Seville.

11. Magic and the Early Church.

Throughout the Middle Ages the conflict continued. In the East collections of oracles and Apocrypha ascribed to Zoroaster, Daniel, Methodius, Leo the Wise, and other famous names were multiplied and formed the basis of commentaries of Psellus the Younger, Roger Bacon, and Albertus Magnus, and also of such protagonists of the Renaissance as Pletho and Ficinus. The Cabala added its quota to occultism, furnishing the magic pentagram, the *Shem ha-Mephorash*, and the *Agla*. Innumerable ecclesiastical prohibitions failed to crush magic, though the early disapproval of witchcraft as a foolish superstition gradually developed, after the period of the crusades, into attacks upon a

12. Mediæval Magic.

crass belief in witches and the devil. With his adoption of the later view Thomas Aquinas prepared the way for the bull issued against witches by Innocent VIII. in 1484 and for the *Omnipotentis* of Gregory XV. in 1623, which condemned magic resulting in death to punishment by the secular arm and requited minor magic injuries with imprisonment for life. The freedom of thought and doctrine prevailing from the time of the Reformation gradually destroyed belief in devils and demons, while it developed medicine and surgery from the magic art of healing and the doctrines of Paracelsus, and evolved astronomy from astrology, and chemistry and physics from alchemy and the hermetic art.

13. Black Magic.

The term "black magic" has been applied, especially by the humanists and during the period of the Reformation, to the practise of those occult sciences which profess to invoke the aid of evil spirits or to make a compact with the devil. The Reformers, Luther, Melanchthon, Camerarius, and Bullinger, all expressed their belief in the black art, while at the same period many asserted that they had formed compacts with the devil and had thus acquired supernatural power. With the decay of the belief in witches after the eighteenth century, however, the idea that superhuman power might thus be gained gradually disappeared, although certain Roman Catholic theologians, such as Oswald and Heinrich, still adhere to the older view.

14. White Magic.

The name "white magic," on the other hand, was given to the occult arts practised, especially in the sixteenth century, by various scholars, by which they professed to produce supernatural results either by the aid of good spirits or by peculiar gifts and powers of the human soul. The acme of this form of magic was reached by the *De occulta philosophia* of Agrippa von Nettesheim (Cologne, 1510), which distinguished between "natural magic," "celestial magic" (astrology and the casting of nativities), and "religious magic" (meditation and purification of the heart). Through "natural magic," which is based on a knowledge of the "quintessence," or all-pervading cosmic spirit, the human soul may gain the "hidden powers" by which it can often control nature, and rule the souls of the departed. Proceeding from the same theory of the "quintessence" or "macrocosm," Paracelsus made the concept of the mystic sympathy of all things the basis of his art of healing. Increasing rationalism and the advance of science, however, has caused the meaning of the term "white magic" to degenerate until it now connotes little more than legerdemain.

The adherents of modern occultism protest strongly against the interpretation of all phenomena of magic by rationalism, although they do not wish to be considered representatives of common superstition, since they regard the secret doctrines which they profess and practise as equal in dignity to other sciences of the present day. In their judgment a large residue of mysterious facts and phenomena do not fall within the scope of ordinary investigations of nature, but are to be reserved for the future science of the spirit. The endeavor to realize such a higher magic or occultism must be admitted to be legitimate,

15. Magic and Modern Occultism.

but as yet there is no uniformity regarding principles or method, and even the name is not decided. Two tendencies may be distinguished, one extending into the obscure realm of the future life and the world of spirits (see PSYCHICAL RESEARCH AND IMMORTALITY), and the other restricted to the sphere of the human soul. Leaving out of consideration the former class, there remains a long list of names and methods for the purely anthropological system of occultism, which has variously been termed "animal magnetism," "mesmerism," "electrobiology," "somnambulism," "psychic power," "psychism," "transcendental physics," "practical magic," "occultism," "cryptic science," "frontier science," and even "cryptology," "acrology," "adelology," and "horology." Among the various subdivisions of natural magic mention may also be made of hypnotism and mind-reading. (O. ZÖCKLER†.)

BIBLIOGRAPHY: For primitive magic special attention is called to the literature given under COMPARATIVE RELIGION, particularly to the works of Chantepie de la Saussaye, Tylor, Brinton, Frazer, Jevons, Mannhardt, Borchart, Haddon, Lenormant, King, Davies, Budge, Skeat, and Lang, which together comprise a literature on the subject. Most of the works on the religions of Assyria, Babylonia and Egypt (see bibliographies under those articles), and India (see bibliography under BRAHMANISM; HINDUISM) deal adequately with magic in those countries. Note also the works named under ZOROASTER, ZOROASTRIANISM. Much material will also be found in the Hibbert Lectures (q.v.), and especially in the *Annual Reports of the American Bureau of Ethnology*. Consult further: P. Scholz, *Die Götzendienst und Zauberwesen bei den alten Hebräern und deren Nachbarvölkern*, Regensburg, 1877; J. Lippert, *Die Religionen der europäischen Kulturvölker in ihrem geschichtlichen Ursprung*, Berlin, 1881; J. Réville, *Die Religion in Rom unter den Severern*, Leipsic, 1888; V. von Strauss, *Der altägyptische Götterglaube*, 2 vols., Heidelberg, 1889; K. du Prel, *Studien über Geheimwissenschaften*, 2 vols., Leipsic, 1890; idem, *Die Magie als Naturwissenschaft*, Jena, 1899; J. Sepp, *Die Religion der alten Deutschen und ihr Fortbestand bis zur Gegenwart*, Munich, 1890; R. Smend, *Alttestamentliche Religionsgeschichte*, Freiburg, 1893; F. T. Elworthy, *The Evil Eye, an Account of this Ancient and Widespread Superstition*, London, 1895; É. Reclus, *Le Magisme*, Paris, 1895; H. Zimmern, *Beiträge zur Kenntnis der babylonisch-assyrischen Religion*, Leipsic, 1896–1901; W. Kroll, *Antiker Aberglaube*, Hamburg, 1897; Uriarte, *Die Magie des 19. Jahrhunderts*, Berlin, 1897; W. J. Flagg, *Yoga; or Transformation: comparative Statement of the various religious Dogmas concerning the Soul . . . and of Magic*, New York, 1898; W. Caland, *Altindisches Zauberritual*, Amsterdam, 1900; C. Grüneisen, *Der Ahnenkult und die Urreligion Israels*, Halle, 1900; R. C. Thompson, *Reports of the Magicians and Astrologers of Nineveh and Babylon*, 2 vols., London, 1900; idem, *The Devils and Evil Spirits of Babylonia*, London, 1903; idem, *Semitic Magic, its Origin and Development*, London, 1908; A. J. Evans, *The Mycenean Tree and Pillar Cult*, London, 1901; J. Oppert, *Sechshundert drei und fünfzig. Eine babylonische magische Quadrattafel*, Strasburg, 1902; J. Hunger, *Becherwahrsagung bei den Babyloniern nach zwei Keilschriften aus der Hammurabi-Zeit*, Leipsic, 1903; F. L. Griffith and H. Thompson, *The Demotic Magical Papyrus of London and Leiden*, 2 vols., London, 1904–05; V. Henry, *La Magie dans l'Inde antique*, Paris, 1904; A. Boissier, *Choix de textes relatifs à la divination assyro-babylonienne*, Geneva, 1905; W. L. Hare, *Babylonian Religion, Chaldean magic*, London, 1905; K. L. Parker, *The Euahlayi Tribe*, London, 1905; A. Wiedemann, *Magie und Zauberei im alten Aegypten*, Leipsic, 1905; A. C. Haddon, *Magic and Fetishism*, London, 1906; Mary Hamilton, *Incubation*, London, 1906; W. Bousset, *What is Religion*, pp. 45–47, New York, 1907; A. Bros, *La Religion des peuples non civilisés*, chap. iii., Paris, 1907; E. Doutté, *Magie et religion dans l'Afrique du Nord*, Paris, 1908; T. Scherman, *Griechische Zauberpapyri*, Leipsic, 1909. For later and modern magic consult: J. Braid, *Magic, Witchcraft, Animal Magnetism, Hypnotism and Electrobiology*, London, 1852; J. Burckhardt, *Die Kultur der Renaissance in Italien*, vol. ii., Basel, 1860, Eng. transl., *Civilization of the Renaissance in Italy*, 2 vols., London, 1878; C. Pazig, *Treatyse of Magic Incantations*, Edinburgh, 1886; A. Dieterich, *Abraxas; Studien zur Religionsgeschichte des späteren Altertums*, Leipsic, 1891; C. Kiesewetter, *Geschichte des neuren Occultismus*, 2 vols., Leipsic, 1891–94; F. Hartmann, *Magic, White and Black*, London, 1893; A. Thompson, *Magic and Mystery*, London, 1894; S. L. M. Mathers, *The Book of the Sacred Magic of Abra-Melin the Mage*, London, 1898; A. E. Waite, *The Book of Black Magic and of Pacts*, Edinburgh, 1898; H. Weinel, *Die Wirkungen des Geistes und der Geister im nachapostolischen Zeitalter bis auf Irenæus*, Freiburg, 1899; F. L. Gardner, *Catalogue raisonné of Works on the Occult Sciences*, London, 1903; F. Hartmann, *Die weisse und schwarze Magie oder das Gesetz des Geistes in der Natur*, Leipsic, 1903; J. Körmann-Alzech, *Schwarze und weisse Magie. Aegyptische Mysterien, Hexenwesen, Faust's Höllenfahrt, Höllenzwang. Indische Wunder. Die Fakire*, Leipsic, 1904; F. Unger, *Die schwarze Magie, ihre Meister und ihre Opfer*, Cothen, 1904; L. Thorndike, *Place of Magic in the Intellectual History of Europe*, New York, 1905; H. R. Evans, *The Old and New Magic*, Introduction by P. Carus, Chicago, 1906; F. C. Conybeare, *Myth, Magic, and Morals*, London, 1909. A copious magazine literature on magic is indicated in Richardson, *Encyclopædia*, p. 660. See also FETISHISM; SUPERSTITION. The reader will find the best materials for original study in books of travel among primitive peoples.

MAGISTER SACRI PALATII ("Master of the Sacred Palace"): An official of the papal court, who unites the functions of chief chaplain and theological adviser of the pope. The first incumbent of this office is said to have been St. Dominic, and it is still filled invariably by a Dominican. Perceiving that the retainers of the cardinals and other dignitaries used to while away their time in idle amusements during the attendance of their masters on the pope, St. Dominic is said to have urged the pope to appoint some one to instruct them during these intervals in the Bible and in Christian doctrine. The saint himself was commissioned to do this, and met with such success that about 1218 Honorius III., according to tradition, established the office of Master of the Sacred Palace. The legendary character of this tradition, however, is evident from the fact that the first incumbent whose existence can be indubitably established was Bartholomæus de Brigantiis, who filled the office about 1236 under Gregory IX. Gradually other duties were added to homiletic instruction, and, in collaboration with the cardinal-vicar, the Master of the Sacred Palace exercised a censorship over all books, while he also controlled the import and export, as well as the purchase and sale, of books in Rome, besides attending the sessions of the Congregation of the Index. These multifarious duties rendered the office of Master of the Sacred Palace very important. Its incumbent was a member both of the Holy Office and of the Congregation of Rites. In the course of time many of the duties and privileges of this official of the Sacred Palace became obsolete. The office has been filled by many Dominicans of distinction, such as Albertus Magnus (supposed to have held this position in 1255–56) and Thomas Aquinas (1262–68). (O. ZÖCKLER†.)

BIBLIOGRAPHY: Fontana, *Syllabus magistrorum sacri palatii apostolici*, Rome, 1663; J. Quétif and J. Échard, *Scriptores ordinis prædicatorum*, vol. ii., p. xxi., Paris, 1721; J. Catalani, *De magistro sacri palatii apostolici*, Rome, 1751; F. A. Zaccaria, *La Corte di Roma*, vol. ii., ib. 1774; G. Phillips, *Kirchenrecht*, vi. 545, Regensburg, 1857; F. H. Reusch, *Der Index der verbotenen Bücher*, passim, Bonn, 1883; H. Denifle, in *ALKG*, ii (1886), 167–248; *KL*, viii. 163–165.

MAGNIFICAT: The common liturgical designation of the hymn of praise in Luke i. 46–55; so called from its initial word in the Latin. It is more formally called the Canticle of the Blessed Virgin, in accordance with the tradition which refers it to the lips of the Lord's mother, in verse 46. This tradition is based on all the Greek and the majority of the Latin manuscripts, and on countless ancient witnesses: notably Irenæus (*Hær.* III., x. 2) and Tertullian (*De anima*, xxvi.), who confirm the traditional reading of verse 46. The authority for this designation has been recently questioned by G. Morin in his edition of the treatise *De psalmodiæ bono*, ascribed to Nicetas, bishop of Remesiana in Dacia, about the close of the fourth century, which in two passages assumes Elisabeth to be the singer (for critical discussion see *Revue Bénédictine*, xiv [1897], 385–397). Both on this ground and on the ground of the other evidences for the reading "Elisabeth" in verse 46, as well as on internal evidence, Fr. Jacobé challenges the received interpretation; while, independently of Morin and Jacobé, it has been decisively contested by A. Harnack. On the other hand, the traditional view is supported by A. Durand, against Jacobé and by O. Bardenhewer against Harnack. The controversy can not be here discussed in detail.

The use of the *Magnificat* in public worship dates back to the early Christian centuries. In the Eastern Church, it constitutes an element of the morning prayers. Between each verse is a response addressed to the Virgin. While it is being sung the deacon incenses the altar.

In the Western Church, the *Magnificat* certainly appears before 600, in the second Gallican liturgy, while Bingham (*Origines*, XV., ii. § 7) refers its introduction to Cæsarius of Arles (d. in 542). Since the time of Gregory the Great or St. Benedict it has been assigned to the vesper service, which, as an "evening sacrifice of praise and thanksgiving," culminates in the *Magnificat*, corresponding to the *Benedictus* at lauds. While the Song of Zacharias proclaims the coming redemption, the *Magnificat*, at evening, celebrates the fulfilment of the promise. The *Gloria patri*, subjoined to the hymn, generalizes Mary's thanksgiving into the Church's. At the same time it receives a coloring appropriate to the special manifestation of salvation commemorated by the particular day or season, through the antiphon, which is sung entire both before and after it on all but the lowest class of festivals (see ANTIPHON).

With the vesper service the Evangelical Church also retained the *Magnificat*, "forasmuch as it is an excellent hymn of praise" (*Kirchenordnung* of Brunswick-Lüneburg, 1544). Along with the Latin version of the *Magnificat*, assigned to the choir, or instead of it, the German version was early used, in accordance with the Evangelical principle of having the congregation take part in divine worship. For instance, the Wittenberg Order of 1533 prescribes that "before a particular feast, and after the (afternoon) sermon, they shall sing the German *Magnificat*, as usual, with a German versicle, in the midst of the Church, with the people." In short, their first practise was to sing the plain German version, adhering exactly to the Latin melody; afterward, the metrical *Magnificat*, paraphrased into the form of a German hymn: or both together, sometimes in the guise that each verse of the Latin, or German and Latin, *Magnificat* would serve as "text," to be followed by a German hymn strophe by way of "elucidation."

As concerning the liturgically musical presentation of the *Magnificat*, the Roman Catholic custom is to sing it, whatever the psalm tone employed, somewhat higher and slower, in its quality of a New-Testament canticle, with a festival intonation for each verse. The Evangelical Church in Germany adheres to this custom as regards the Latin *Magnificat;* whereas, for the German version, it is usual to select the ninth psalm tone (*tonus peregrinus*). The *Magnificat* was made a favorite theme for artistic elaboration, and masters in every style of church music have applied their skill to it. In the Evangelical Church, also, the *Magnificat* is an attractive focus for the development and expansion of musical art. Out of the practise of playing organ interludes between the verses, there grew up a special department of organ literature (see ORGAN). The structure of the text itself becomes an important factor in the development of Evangelical church music, and exhibits all forms and styles of the same, from the closed choral motet (as with Dietrich, Hassler, Vulpius, Frank, Crüger, etc.); or, in case of the metrical *Magnificat*, from the polyphonic choral hymn, down to the highly elaborate cantata, comprising all modes of church music in one complicated artistic creation, such as Johann Sebastian Bach's quintet *Magnificat*. See CHURCH MUSIC. (H. A. KÖSTLIN†.)

BIBLIOGRAPHY: F. Jacobé, in *Revue d'histoire et de littérature religieuse*, ii (1897), 424–432; A. Durand, in *Revue biblique*, vii (1898), 74–77; A. Harnack, in *SBA*, xxvi (1900), 538–556; O. Bardenhewer, *Biblische Studien*, vi (1901), parts 1–2; H. A. Köstlin, in *Zeitschrift für die Neutestamentliche Wissenschaft*, 1902, pp. 139 sqq.; Julian, *Hymnology*, p. 711. Consult also: B. Thalhofer, *Handbuch der katholischen Liturgik*, ii. 478, Freiburg, 1883–90; S. Kümmerle, *Encyklopädie der evangelischen Kirchenmusik*, ii. 124–127, 180–186, Gütersloh, 1890; G. Rietschel, *Lehrbuch der Liturgik*, pp. 345, 443, Berlin, 1899.

MAGNUS: The name applied to a saint remarkable for his early missionary labors among the Swabians. The narrative of his life, however, by a process of incorporation not uncommon in medieval literature of the kind, is made up by the fusion of incidents belonging to two distinct persons, one in the seventh and the other in the eighth century —the former connected with St. Gall, the latter with the monastery of Füssen on the Lech, although he also probably came originally from St. Gall. Maginold and Theodo accompanied the Irish monk to the wilderness on the Steinach in 613; after his death they remained there, and Maginold is said to have lived until about the middle of the seventh century. The Füssen legend speaks of a monk Magnus, from his name presumably of Romaic origin, not Teutonic, like Maginold, as a contemporary of Wichbert, the first demonstrable bishop of Augsburg, toward the middle of the eighth century. Wishing to convert a last pagan corner of his diocese, he sent to St. Gall for monks; and Magnus, with Theodo or Dieto (an analogy with the older legend), went forth to help him, the former working in the valley of the Lech and founding the monastery of Füssen, where he died about the middle of the eighth century. When about 851 Bishop Lanto of Augsburg translated his relics, a life was made up, based on tradition, but tradition a century old, and attributed to the contemporary Dieto, here called Theodore. In the last decade of the ninth century the abbot-bishop Solomon III. erected the church St. Magnus at St. Gall, and obtained relics of the patron from Füssen, together with the life, which then at St. Gall was fused with the story of the local Maginold. (G. MEYER VON KNONAU.)

BIBLIOGRAPHY: The literature is indicated in Potthast, *Wegweiser*, p. 1444. The Vita mentioned in the text is with other material in *ASB*, Sept., ii. 700–781, cf. *ASM*, ii., pp. 505–510. Consult: Rettberg, *KD*, ii. 146–151; Friedrich, *KD*, ii. 654–656.

MAGOG. See GOG AND MAGOG; and TABLE OF THE NATIONS.

MAGUIRE, JOHN ALOYSIUS: Roman Catholic archbishop of Glasgow; b. at Glasgow Sept. 8, 1851. He was educated at St. Aloysius' College, Glasgow, Stonyhurst College, the University of Glasgow, and the College of the Propaganda, Rome, until 1875, and after being an assistant at the St. Andrew's Cathedral at Glasgow, from 1875 to 1879, was appointed secretary of the diocese, a position which he held four years. He was incumbent of Partick in 1883, but in the following year became canon of the cathedral of Glasgow, vicar-general in 1885, and provost of the chapter in 1893. In 1894 he was consecrated titular bishop of Trocmadæ and appointed to assist the archbishop of Glasgow, whom he succeeded in the archiepiscopal office in 1902.

MAHAFFY, JOHN PENTLAND: Church of Ireland; b. near Vevey (11 m. e.s.e. of Lausanne), Switzerland, Feb. 26, 1839. He was educated at Trinity College, Dublin (B.A., 1859; M.A., 1863), and was ordered deacon in 1864 and ordained priest two years later. He was elected fellow of his college in 1864, where he has been senior fellow and registrar since 1899, as well as a member of the University Council since 1892. He was also precentor of Trinity College in 1867 and chaplain to the Lord Lieutenant of Ireland in 1880. He was assistant regius professor of Greek at Trinity College in 1864–65, 1867–68, 1870–74, 1877, and 1896, assistant in Archbishop King's divinity lectures in 1870–79, junior dean in 1869, junior proctor in 1871, Donellan lecturer in 1876, and examiner repeatedly in various subjects, besides being evening preacher in 1865–67 and university preacher in

1868-70. From 1869 to 1900 he was professor of ancient history at Trinity College, and was also High Sheriff of County Monaghan in 1901 and a commissioner for intermediate education. In theology he is a Broad Churchman. Among his numerous publications, chiefly on classical subjects, special mention may be made of the following: *Twelve Lectures on Primitive Civilization* (London, 1869); *Prolegomena to Ancient History* (1871); *Greek Social Life from Homer to Menander* (1874); *Greek Antiquities* (1876); *A History of Classical Greek Literature* (1880); *The Decay of Modern Preaching* (1882); *The Story of Alexander's Empire* (in collaboration with A. Gilman; 1887); *Greek Life and Thought from Alexander to the Roman Conquest* (1887); *Greek Pictures drawn with Pen and Pencil* (1890); *The Greek World under Roman Sway* (1890); *The Empire of the Ptolemies* (1895); *The Silver Age of the Greek World;* and *What have the Greeks Done* (1909); and contributed vol. iv. to Petrie's *History of Egypt;* in addition to numerous editions of classical, historical, and philosophical works and *The Petrie Papyri Deciphered and Explained* (3 vols., Dublin, 1892–1905).

MAHAN, ASA: American Congregationalist educator; b. at Vernon, N. Y., Nov. 9, 1800; d. at Eastbourne (65 m. s. of London), England, Apr. 4, 1889. He was graduated at Hamilton College, Clinton, N. Y., in 1824, and at Andover Theological Seminary in 1827 He was pastor at Pittsford, N. Y. (1829–31); Cincinnati, O. (1831–35); Jackson, Mich. (1855–57); and Adrian, Mich. (1857–60). He was president of Oberlin College (1835–50), Cleveland University (1850–54), and Adrian College, Mich. (1860–71). In 1871 he retired to Eastbourne, England, to devote himself to literary work. His works include: *Scripture Doctrine of Christian Perfection* (Boston, 1839); *System of Intellectual Philosophy* (New York, 1845); *Doctrine of the Will* (Oberlin, 1846); *The True Believer* (New York, 1847); *System of Moral Philosophy* (Oberlin, 1848); *Election, and the Influence of the Holy Spirit* (London, 1850); *Modern Mysteries Explained and Exposed* (Boston, 1855); *The Science of Logic* (New York, 1856); *Science of Natural Theology* (Boston, 1867); *Theism and Antitheism* (Cleveland, 1872); *Phenomena of Spiritualism Scientifically Explained and Exposed* (1875); *Misunderstood Texts of Scripture Explained and Elucidated* (1876); *Critical History of the Late American War* (1877); *System of Mental Philosophy* (Chicago, 1882); *Autobiography; Intellectual, Moral, and Spiritual* (London, 1882); and *Critical History of Philosophy* (2 vols., New York, 1883).

MAHDI, mā'dī: The title given by Mohammedans to the person who according to their expectation is to exercise functions not unlike those attributed to the Jewish Messiah. He is to complete the work of Mohammed, convert or destroy the infidels, inaugurate the reign of justice and truth upon earth, and lead the faithful to Paradise. The word means "directed," hence, "one fit to guide others." The Mohammedan world is divided between those who believe that Mahdi has already come but is concealed until the time of his final manifestation (Shiahs; see MOHAMMED, MOHAMMEDANISM), and those who still await his appearance (Sunnis). As in the case of the cognate Jewish belief, from which in part it sprang, the possession of the idea has led to many attempts to realize it. These attempts have been made both by impostors and by those who were self-deluded. One of these was the famous veiled prophet al-Mokanna, Hakim ibn Allah, who conducted a revolt against Mohammed ben Mansur (c. 780 A.D.), while this Mohammed himself assumed the title of Mahdi; another was Ubayd Allah al-Mahdi in North Africa, 909–934, founder of the Fatimid dynasty; almost as celebrated was Ibn Tumart, the founder of the Muwahhid Berber dynasty, also in North Africa. A recent example is Mohammed Ahmed (1843–85), "the mad mullah," whose revolt in the region south of Egypt caused so great fear of a holy war, and to whose capture of Khartum the death of General Gordon was due. The head of the brotherhood of al-Sanusi also claims to be the Mahdi. GEO. W. GILMORE.

BIBLIOGRAPHY: E. Müller, *Beiträge zur Mahdilehre des Islams*, Heidelberg, 1901; J. Darmesteter, *The Mahdi, Past and Present*, New York, 1885; D. B. Macdonald, *Development of Muslim Theology, Jurisprudence, and Constitutional Theory*, pp. 244–249 et passim, New York, 1903.

MAI, mā'ī or mai, **ANGELO:** Roman Catholic scholar; b. near Bergamo, Italy, Mar. 7, 1782; d. near Albano Sept. 9, 1854. He entered the Jesuit order in 1799, and taught in their college at Naples from 1804. At Orvieto, in the intervals of priestly duties, he applied himself to paleography, and especially to the deciphering of palimpsests. His activity as an editor of ancient works dates from 1813, when he went to Milan as keeper of the Ambrosian Library; his field comprised both classical and ecclesiastical authors. In 1819 Pius VII. appointed him prefect of the Vatican library; and he was made a cardinal in 1838. The writings he edited are mainly embraced in four general collections: *Veterum scriptorum nova collectio* (10 vols., Rome, 1825–38); *Classici auctores* (10 vols., 1828–1838); *Spicilegium Romanum* (10 vols., 1839–44); *Sanctorum patrum nova bibliotheca* (6 vols., 1844–1871); and the posthumous *Appendix ad opera edita ab Angelo Mai* (1879).

BIBLIOGRAPHY: *KL*, viii. 483–486 (appreciative).

MAIMBOURG, man"būr', **LOUIS:** French Jesuit and ecclesiastical historian; b. at Nancy in 1610; d. in Paris Aug. 13, 1686. In his sixteenth year he entered the Society of Jesus, and after completing his theological studies in Rome was made professor at the Jesuit college in Rouen. Although he had no high oratorical gifts, he acquired considerable renown as a preacher; but it is as a historian that his name survives. Here again his equipment was quite ordinary; his works, tedious by their length, full of inaccuracies, and totally lacking in impartiality, served him as weapons to strike at those from whom he differed or as means to win favor for himself. His most valuable service to posterity consists in his having, by his *Histoire du Luthéranisme* (Paris, 1680), called forth the remarkable work of Seckendorf. In his *Histoire de l'Arianisme* (1682) he indirectly attacks and calumniates the Jansenists of Port Royal; in the *Histoire de l'hérésie des Iconoclastes* (1674) he seeks to win the favor of Louis XIV. by upholding his rights against the Roman see, and then attempts to soothe Innocent XII. by his *Histoire du schisme des Grecs* (2 vols., 1680); but soon after he took such a strong stand in favor of Louis XIV. against the pope that he was obliged to leave the order. The king named him historiographer, and used his practised pen against the Huguenots in the *Histoire du Calvinisme* (1682). His collected historical writings (14 vols., 1686–87) include histories of the League (Eng. transl. by Dryden, *History of the League*, London, 1684), the Crusades (Eng. transl., 1686), the Wycliffites, Gregory the Great, and Leo the Great. (C. PFENDER.)

BIBLIOGRAPHY: L. Ellies Dupin, *Bibliothèque des auteurs ecclésiastiques*, Paris, 1689–1711; P. Bayle, *Dictionary Historical and Critical*, iv. 63–66, London, 1737; idem, *Critique générale de l'histoire du calvinisme de M. Maimbourg*, 2 vols., Amsterdam, 1714; F. H. Reusch, *Index der verbotenen Bücher*, pp. 583–882, Bonn, 1885; Lichtenberger, *ESR*, viii. 554–556.

MAIMONIDES, mai-mon'i-dêz or -diz, **MOSES** (Grecized from Maimuni), also called **Rambam** (formed acrostically from Rabbi Moses ben Maimun), and by the Arabians **Abu Amran Musa Obeidallah alkortobi:** Jewish rabbi and philosopher; b. at Cordova Mar. 30, 1135; d. at Old Cairo, Egypt, Dec. 13, 1204. He received his early education in the house of his father, and was instructed in natural science and philosophy by Mohammedan teachers. When in 1148 the Almohade Abdelmuman took Cordova and interdicted Judaism, his father fled, and finally settled in 1159 at Fez with his family, where they lived as Mohammedans. The first work of young Maimuni was a justification of this position. In the *Iggereth hashemadh*, written in Arabic about 1162, he showed that Mohammedanism required neither idolatry, murder, nor unchastity, but simply acknowledgment of Mohammed as prophet, a mere formality, by which one may avoid martyrdom, though it is best to seek a country where one can live according to his religion. [Some good authorities doubt the genuineness of this work.] In April, 1165, Maimuni's family left Morocco and after a short residence in Palestine settled at Old Cairo. There Maimuni spent the remainder of his life. For a time he practised medicine, at the same time preparing his commentary on the Mishna which he completed in 1168. Two years later the government appointed him head of all Jewish congregations in Egypt, and ten years later, about 1180, he completed his legal code, the *Mishneh Torah*, which soon spread his fame abroad. In 1190 he published his religio-philosophical work, *Moreh Nebhukhim*, and soon afterward his treatise on the resurrection of the dead; both works were in Arabic. He was buried at Tiberias in Palestine. Maimuni's importance rests on his writings. The first important work was his "Commentary on the Mishna." Before him, aside from the two Talmuds, only glossatory expositions of the Mishna existed. He assumed the task of classifying and explaining the matter contained and implied in that work. In elaborate introductions he discoursed on the nature of prophecy, interjecting remarks on the natural sciences and philosophy. In the special introduction to the chapter called *Ḥelek* in the treatise Sanhedrin, he for the first time defined and formally laid down thirteen articles of the Jewish creed, which in an abbreviated form were received into the Jewish ritual. These articles state: (1) That there is one God, creator of all things; (2) that he is One in the sense that no other shares his divinity (a disavowal of the doctrine of the Trinity); (3) he is incorporeal and formless; (4) he is eternal; (5) he alone is to be worshiped and without any mediator (against Christianity); (6) he ordained prophecy; (7) Moses was the greatest prophet, to whom revelation was delivered in a most complete manner (against Islam); (8) law and tradition are the complete expression of the revelation of God; (9) neither can ever be changed (against Christianity and Islam); (10) God is omniscient; (11) he rewards and punishes the acts of men; (12) Messiah is still to be expected (against Christians and unbelieving Jews); (13) the dead shall rise again. A truly monumental work was his *Mishneh Torah*, i.e., "Deuteronomy," also called *Yadh ha-Ḥazakah*, i.e., "The Mighty Hand," or simply *Yadh*. It is a cyclopedia comprising every department of Biblical and Jewish literature. [Portions of this work have been translated into English by Bernard: *Main Principle of the Creed and Ethics of the Jews*, Cambridge, 1832.] As an appendix to the *Yadh* he published the "Book of Laws" on the [613] precepts. His third and most important work was the "Guide for the Perplexed," Arabic *Dalālat elhāīrīn* [translated into Hebrew under the title *Mōreh Nebūkim*], consisting of three parts. The first part is devoted to the explanation of all expressions which are employed in the Bible in connection with deity. The second part develops his theory of creation, and shows Gen. i.–iv. to be in accord with his cosmology; it deals also with prophecy. The third part deals with the first vision of the prophet Ezekiel, the relation of God to the world, treats of the opposition of good and evil in the world, of God's providence and omniscience, all with the purpose of encouraging the more intelligent to a thorough investigation of the Old Testament. This work contributed more than any other to the progress of rational reformatory efforts in Judaism. Being translated into Latin a short time after its composition, it influenced Christian scholasticism. But it must be stated in praise of the latter that it never explained away the contents of revelation in favor of "reason" to the same degree as did the Jewish scholasticism which preceded it, whose most prominent representative was Maimuni. The anathemas of French rabbis against the study of the "Guide" and its burning by the Inquisition on the basis of its condemnation in 1233 were indeed foolish and without effect, but not without occasion in the rationalizing notions of the author. (G. DALMAN.)

BIBLIOGRAPHY: The editions of the works of Maimonides are numerous, mostly published in parts which deal with sections of his productions. The *editio princeps* of the *Mishneh Torah* is without place and date; numerous editions followed, e.g., Soncino, 1490; Constantinople, 1590; 4 vols., Amsterdam, 1702; Hebrew and Eng., H. H. Bernard, Cambridge, 1832; Hebrew and German, Vienna, 1889; Eng. by J. W. Peppercorne, London, 1838, 1863. His "Guide for the Perplexed" appeared first without place or date (before 1480); then in Hebrew, Venice, 1551; Berlin, 1791; in Latin, Paris, 1520; Basil, 1629;

in Arabic and French, 3 vols., Paris, 1856-66; in German, Krotoschin, 1839; Italian, Livorno, 1879-81; English, 3 vols., London, 1885 and 1904. The Commentary on the Mishna was first published Naples, 1492, and is accessible in the Latin transl. of Surenhusius, in his *Mishna*, Amsterdam, 1698-1703. Great activity has been manifested in recent years in publishing the works of Maimonides. This activity can be traced and the places and dates of publication learned by combining Hauck-Herzog, *RE*, xii. 80, with the *Schlagwort-Katalog* (described in this work, vol. i., p. xiii.; the *Schlagwort-Katalog* was brought down to 1907 in 1909) under "Maimonides"; cf. also Baldwin, *Dictionary*, vol. iii., part i., p. 358. For the life and work of Maimonides consult: I. Grossman, *Maimonides*, Vienna, 1892; *Maimonides*, in *Jewish Worthies Series*, London, 1903; P. Beer, *Leben und Wirken des Rabbi Moses ben Maimon*, Prague, 1834; S. B. Scheyer, *Das psychologische System des Maimonides*, Frankfort, 1845; A. Benisch, *Two Writings on the Life and Writings of Maimonides*, London, 1847; A. Geiger, *Moses ben Maimon*, Rosenberg, 1850; M. Jöel, *Die Religionsphilosophie des Moses ben Maimonides*, Breslau, 1859; S. Rubin, *Spinoza and Maimonides*, Vienna, 1868; M. Eisler, *Vorlesungen über die jüdischen Philosophen des Mittelalters*, Vienna, 1870; D. Rosin, *Die Ethik des Maimonides*, Breslau, 1876; D. Kaufmann, *Geschichte der Attributenlehre*, pp. 363 sqq., Gotha, 1877; J. H. Weiss, *Rabbi Moses ben Maimon*, Vienna, 1881; W. Bacher, *Die Bibelexegese Moses Maimunis*, Strasburg, 1897; L. Dünner, *Die älteste astronomische Schrift des Maimonides*, Würzburg, 1902; J. Münz, *Rabbi Moses ben Maimon. Sein Leben und seine Werke*, part i., Mainz, 1902; and W. Bacher, M. Brann, D. Simonson, and J. Guttmann, *Moses ben Maimon. Sein Leben, seine Werke, und sein Einfluss. Zur Erinnerung an dem 700. Todestag*, Leipsic, 1908. An excellent article, with supplementary literature, is found in *JE*, ix. 73-86. A considerable amount of periodical literature, some of it important, is indicated in Richardson, *Encyclopaedia*, p. 670, 1907.

MAINS, GEORGE PRESTON: Methodist Episcopalian; b. at Newport, N. Y., Aug. 7, 1844. He was educated at Wesleyan University, Middletown, Conn. (A.B., 1870), after having served under Admiral Porter in the North Atlantic Squadron in 1864–65. He was admitted to the New York East Conference of his denomination in 1870, and his pastorates were as follows: Hamden Plains, Conn. (1869–71), Ansonia, Conn. (1871–73), Chapel Street Church, New Haven, Conn. (1873–76), First Church, New Britain, Conn. (1876–79), First Church, Bristol, Conn. (1879–80), Grace Church, Brooklyn, N. Y. (1880–83), First Church, Waterbury, Conn. (1883–84), New York Avenue Church, Brooklyn, N. Y. (1887–92), and First Church, Mt. Vernon, N. Y. (1896–97). He was likewise presiding elder of the New York District in 1884–87, as well as superintendent of Seney Hospital, Brooklyn, N. Y., in 1885–87 and of the Brooklyn Church Society in 1892–96. Since 1897 he has been publishing agent of the Methodist Book Concern, New York City.

MAINZ, maints: A city of Germany, 20 m. w.s.w. of Frankfort, formerly the seat of an archbishopric and once the most important ecclesiastical center of Germany. The beginning of the Christian Church there is involved in obscurity, although the statement of Irenæus (*Hær.* I., x. 2) that Christian communities existed in Germany in his time renders it probable that Christians then lived in Mainz. Old Christian inscriptions from the city are almost entirely lacking, but Ammianus Marcellinus (xxvii. 10) states that in 368 a large portion of the population was Christian. According to Jerome (*Epist.* cxxiii. 16), thousands were killed in the church when Mainz was taken by the Germans in the early part of the fifth century, yet the effects of this disaster were only transitory, and ancient churches were still standing about the middle of the century, the Christian community having become Teutonized in the mean time.

Although the bishopric of Mainz certainly existed as early as 550, Christianity scarcely flourished there, for the local church was involved in the decay of the Frankish Church in the closing years of the Merovingians. The revival first began when Boniface became bishop in 745 or 746, and it was then that the bishopric commenced to extend. Originally it seems to have embraced only the Frankish territories on the Rhine and Main, for bishoprics were erected in Buraburg and Erfurt in 741, although they seem to have lapsed after the death of their first bishops and then formed part of the bishopric of Mainz. The diocese thus became larger than any other in Germany, stretching from Donnersberg in the south to the Harz in the north, and from the upper portion of the Saale in the east beyond the Nahe in the west. Between 780 and 782 the successor of Boniface, Lullus (see LULLUS OF MAINZ), was raised to the rank of an archbishop and Mainz became the metropolitan city. The province later comprised the Frankish bishoprics of Würzburg, Eichstätt, Worms, and Speyer; the Swabian bishoprics of Augsburg, Constance, Strasburg, and Chur; the Saxon bishoprics of Paderborn, Hildesheim, Halberstadt, and Verden; and the bishoprics of Bamberg, Prague, and Olmütz. In 1047, however, Bamberg was detached from Mainz and made immediately subject to the holy see; and after the elevation of Prague into an archbishopric in 1343 the Czech sees were taken from Mainz. (A. HAUCK.)

From the episcopate of Christian I. (1165-83), who had been chancellor to Frederick Barbarossa before his consecration, this office became permanently connected with the see of Mainz; and when the electoral system had its first beginning in 1125, largely at the suggestion of Adalbert I. (1109-37), it was natural that he should be one of the electors. When the number was later fixed at seven, of whom three were ecclesiastics (the archbishops of Mainz, Cologne, and Treves), the archbishop of Mainz, who in any case took precedence over the other princes of the empire, ranked as the first. In the period of the Reformation, the fifty-sixth and fifty-seventh archbishops, Albert II. of Brandenburg (1514-45) and Sebastian von Heusenstamm (1545-1555) governed with wisdom and moderation, and checked the spread of Protestantism without recourse to violence. The see maintained its dignity down to the French Revolution, at which period the archbishop had an income of 1,400,000 gulden, and was both temporal and spiritual ruler of a population of 400,000. The territory of the see was incorporated with the dominions of the French Republic in 1797; and by the Peace of Luneville (1801) a settlement was made which, when the last archbishop, Frederick Charles Joseph, Baron von Erthal (1774-1802), died, allowed his coadjutor Dalberg to retain, with the title of arch-chancellor, the principalities of Aschaffenburg and Regensburg and the county of Wetzlar, the see being transferred to Regensburg. After the Concordat of 1801 had gone into effect, Napoleon arranged for the elevation of Mainz once more to the position of a bishopric, and the cathedral, which had been almost ruined in the wars, was finally restored. The territory of the ancient see was incorporated in 1814 with the grand duchy of Hesse-Darmstadt. The diocese was vacant from 1818 to 1830, when, on the creation of the ecclesiastical province of the Upper Rhine, it was placed under the metropolitan jurisdiction of the archbishop of Freiburg.

Bibliography: J. F. Böhmer, *Regesta archiepiscoporum Maguntinensium*, ed. C. Will, 2 vols., Innsbruck, 1877-86; G. C. Joannis, *Rerum Moguntiacarum libri*, 3 vols., Frankfort, 1722-27; V. F. de Gudenus, *Codex diplomaticus anecdotorum res Moguntinas illustrantium*, 5 vols., Göttingen, 1743-58; S. A. Würdtwein, *Dioecesis Moguntina in archidiaconatus divisa*, 4 vols., Mannheim, 1769; *Monumenta Moguntina*, ed. P. Jaffe, Berlin, 1866; C. G. Bockenheimer, *Die Mainzer Bischöfe des 19. Jahrhunderts*, Mainz, 1886; J. Jaeger, *Beiträge zur Geschichte des Erzstifts Mainz*, Osnabrück, 1894; J. Schmidt, *Die katholische Restauration in den Kurmainzer Herrschaften*, Erlangen, 1902; J. Simon, *Stand und Herkunft der Bischöfe der Mainzer Kirchenprovinz im Mittelalter*, Weimar, 1908; and literature under Boniface, Saint; Lullus of Mainz; Rabanus Maurus.

MAIR, mar, **WILLIAM:** Church of Scotland; b. at Savoch, Scotland, Apr. 1, 1830. He was educated at the University of Aberdeen (M.A., 1849), and was minister successively at Lochgelly (1861-64), and Ardoch (1864-69). From 1869 until his retirement from active life in 1903, he was minister of Earlston. Since the latter year he has resided in Edinburgh. He was likewise moderator of the Church of Scotland in 1897, and has written, in addition to numerous briefer contributions, *A Digest of Laws and Decisions, Ecclesiastical and Civil, relating to the Constitution, Practice, and Affairs of the Church of Scotland* (Edinburgh, 1887); *The Truth about the Church of Scotland* (1891); *Speaking* (1900); *Churches and the Law* (1904); and *The Scottish Churches* (1907).

MAISTRE, mêtr, **JOSEPH MARIE, COMTE DE:** French Roman Catholic diplomat; b. at Chambéry (55 m. e. of Lyons) Apr. 1, 1754; d. at Turin Feb. 26, 1821. He was educated by the Jesuits and afterward studied law in Turin. In 1788 he became a member of the Piedmontese senate, but when the French troops invaded the country in 1792 he took refuge in Lausanne, where he stayed until he was summoned to Turin by Charles Emmanuel II. In 1798, when the French took Turin, he had to retreat to Venice, but in 1799 the king called him to Sardinia as grand chancellor. From 1803 till 1817 he was ambassador of the king of Sardinia at St. Petersburg. He then returned to Turin and became regent of grand chancery and minister of state for Victor Emmanuel I. Maistre was the leader of the Ultramontanists and a steadfast opponent of Gallicanism. In his works, especially in his *Du pape*, he maintained the doctrines of the infallibility of the pope, and of his supreme temporal power, and that the Reformation was the cause of all the evils that had overtaken France. He was also a vigorous advocate of legitimacy. Among his numerous works may be named: *Considerations sur la France* (Paris, 1796); *Du pape* (2 vols., Lyons, 1819; new ed., Tours, 1891; Eng. transl., *The Pope*, London, 1850); *Les soirées de Saint-Pétersbourg, ou entretiens sur le gouvernement temporel de la Providence, suivies d'un traité sur les sacrifices* (2 vols., Paris, 1821; new ed., 1888); and *Examen de la philosophie de Bacon* (2 vols., Paris, 1836). His *Œuvres* (7 vols., Brussels, 1838) have appeared in a new edition, including posthumous works and inedited correspondence, with a biographical preface by R. de Maistre (14 vols., Lyons, 1884-87).

Bibliography: Accounts of the life have been written by: R. de Chantelause, Paris, 1859; J. C. Glaser, Berlin, 1865; L. I. Moreau, Paris, 1879; A. de Margerie, ib. 1882; F. Descostes, ib. 1893; and G. Cogordan, ib. 1894. Consult further: Mme. C. T. Woillez, *Le Génie de De Maistre*, Paris, 1861; R. de Sezeval, *Joseph de Maistre, ses détracteurs*, ib. 1865; M. F. A. de Lescure, *Le Comte Joseph de Maistre et sa famille*, ib. 1892; F. Paulhan, *Joseph de Maistre et sa philosophie*, ib. 1893; and works on the history of modern philosophy.

MAITLAND, SAMUEL ROFFEY: Church of England; b. in London Jan. 7, 1792; d. at Gloucester Jan. 19, 1866. He studied at St. John's and Trinity colleges, Cambridge, and was called to the bar in 1816, but was ordained deacon in 1821 and appointed curate of St. Edmund, Norwich. In May, 1823, he became perpetual curate of Christ Church, Gloucester, but resigned in 1827. In 1838 he was appointed librarian and keeper of the manuscripts at Lambeth Palace, which position he retained until 1848, when he retired to Gloucester. Among other works he wrote: *An Enquiry into the Grounds on which the Prophetic Period of Daniel and St. John has been Supposed to Consist of 1260 Years* (London, 1828); *Eruvin, or Miscellaneous Essays on Subjects Connected with the Nature, History, and Destiny of Man* (1831); *Facts and Documents Illustrative of the History, Doctrines, and Rites of the Ancient Albigenses and Waldenses* (1832); *The Dark Ages* (1844); *An Index of such English Books, Printed before the Year MDC, as are now in the Archiepiscopal Library at Lambeth* (1845); *Essays on Subjects Connected with the Reformation in England* (1849); and *Illustrations and Enquiries Relating to Mesmerism* (1849); and translated *The Holy War* of St. Bernard (Gloucester, 1827).

Bibliography: An appreciative Memoir is in *DNB*, xxxv. 371-373, where references to other literature is given.

MAJAL, MATHIEU: French pastor of "the Desert," known as Désubas from his birthplace, Désubas, near Vernoux (50 m. s. of Lyons), Department of Ardèche; b. 1720; executed at Montpellier Feb. 2, 1746. As pastor of Vivarais he sat in the "national synod" of French Protestants which met in Bas Languedoc Aug. 18, 1744, and which gave offense to the court at Versailles and led to rigorous measures. Majal was arrested Dec. 12, 1745, and taken to Vernoux, where his arrival occasioned a riot and several persons were killed (the "massacre of Vernoux"). On his trial at Montpellier he strenuously denied all treasonable acts or designs and convinced the court of his innocence, but was condemned by order of the king and shot. A ballad of the peasants of Vivarais relates the trial and death of the young pastor.

BIBLIOGRAPHY: D. Benoit, *Une victime de l'intolerance au XVIIIe siècle*, Toulouse, 1879; Charles Coquerel, *Histoire des églises du désert*, i. 287 sqq., 387 sqq., Paris, 1841.

MAJOR (MAIER), GEORG: Lutheran theologian; b. at Nuremberg Apr. 25, 1502; d. at Wittenberg Nov. 28, 1574. At the age of nine he was sent to Wittenberg, and in 1521 entered the university there. When Cruciger returned to Wittenberg in 1529, Major was appointed rector of the Johannisschule in Magdeburg, but in 1537 he became court preacher at Wittenberg and was ordained by Luther. In 1545 he was made professor in the theological faculty, in which his authority increased to such an extent that in the following year the elector sent him to the Conference of Regensburg (see REGENSBURG, CONFERENCE OF), where he was soon captivated by the personality of Butzer. Like Melanchthon, he fled before the disastrous close of the Schmalkald war, and found refuge in Magdeburg. In the summer of 1547 he returned to Wittenberg, and in the same year became cathedral superintendent at Merseburg, although he resumed his activity at the university in the following year. In the negotiations of the Interim he took the part of Melanchthon in first opposing it and then making concessions. This attitude incurred the enmity of the opponents of the Interim, especially after he cancelled a number of passages in the second edition of his *Psalterium* in which he had violently attacked the position of Prince Maurice of Saxony, whom he now requested to prohibit all polemical treatises proceeding from Magdeburg, while he condemned the preachers of Torgau who were imprisoned in Wittenberg on account of their opposition to the Interim. He was even accused of accepting bribes from Maurice. In 1552 Count Hans Georg, who favored the Interim, appointed him superintendent of Eisleben, on the recommendation of Melchior Kling. The orthodox clergy of Grafschaft Mansfeld, however, immediately suspected him of being an interimist and adiaphorist, and he tried to defend his position in public, but his apology resulted in the so-called Majoristic Controversy (q.v.). At Christmas, 1552, Count Albrecht expelled him without trial and he fled to Wittenberg, where he resumed his activity as professor and member of the consistory. Thenceforth he was an important and active member in the circle of the Wittenberg Philippists. From 1558 to 1574 he was dean of the theological faculty and repeatedly held the rectorate of the university. He lived long enough to experience the first overthrow of Crypto-Calvinism (see PHILIPPISTS) in electoral Saxony, and Paul Crell, his son-in-law, signed for him at Torgau in May, 1574, the articles which repudiated Calvinism and acknowledged the unity of Luther and Melanchthon. Among his writings, special mention may be made of the following: A text edition of *Justini ex Trogo Pompejo historia* (Hagenau, 1526); an edition of Luther's smaller catechism in Latin and Low German (Magdeburg, 1531); *Sententiæ veterum poetarum* (1534); *Quæstiones rhetoricæ* (1535); *Vitæ Patrum* (Wittenberg, 1544); *Psalterium Davidis juxta translationem veterem repurgatum* (1547); *De origine et auctoritate verbi Dei* (1550); *Commonefactio ad ecclesiam catholicam, orthodoxam, de fugiendis blasphemiis Samosatenicis* (1569); as well as commentaries on the Pauline epistles and homilies on the pericopes. (G. KAWERAU.)

BIBLIOGRAPHY: Major's *Opera* appeared in 3 vols., Wittenberg, 1569–70, though the edition is incomplete. Some letters of his are in *CR*, vols. ii., vi., vii., and x.; in J. Voigt, *Briefwechsel der berühmtesten Gelehrten der Reformation*, pp. 424 sqq., Königsberg, 1841; and in A. Schumacher, *Gelehrter Männer Briefe an die Könige in Dännemark, 1522–1663*, ii. 99–247, 3 vols., Leipsic, 1758–1759. A worthy biography is yet to be written. Consult bibliography under MAJORISTIC CONTROVERSY.

MAJOR, JOHN: Scotch Roman Catholic historian and scholastic divine; b. at Gleghornie (22 m. n.e. of Edinburgh) in 1469; d. at St. Andrews (32 m. n.n.e. of Edinburgh) 1550. He studied at the universities of Cambridge and Paris (M.A., of Paris, 1496; D.D., 1505), became a regent of the latter university in 1496, also a fellow and teacher in arts and philosophy; accepted the position of principal regent and professor of philosophy and divinity at the University of Glasgow, 1518; returned to the University of Paris, 1525; went to St. Andrews in 1531, and was made provost of St. Salvator's College in the university there, 1533, holding the position till his death. In theology Major was in essentials a stanch Roman Catholic, denouncing sternly the Hussite, Wyclifite, and Lutheran movements, but also opposing the luxurious living and tendency to expensive and grandiose architecture manifested by the monastic orders; intellectually he was a schoolman, opposed to the newer spirit then entering the universities. One of his titles to fame is the part he had in the education of John Knox (q.v.). The work by which he is now best known is *Historia Majoris Britanniæ, tam Angliæ quam Scotiæ* (Paris, 1521, republished, Edinburgh, 1740; Eng. transl. in the *Scottish History Society's Publications*, vol. x., Edinburgh, 1892, containing also a life of Major, an estimate of his character and writings, and a collection of his prefaces). Other works were a new edition of H. Pardo's *Medulla dyalectices* (Paris, 1505); a volume on logic (1508); commentaries on the "Sentences" of Lombard (1509–17; new ed., 3 parts, 1510–28); and a commentary on the Gospels (1529).

BIBLIOGRAPHY: Besides the life in the Eng. transl. of his "History," ut sup., consult: P. H. Brown, *George Buchanan*, Edinburgh, 1890; idem, *John Knox*, i. 13, 14, 20–28, 50–52, et passim, London, 1895; T. G. Law, in *Scottish Review*, July, 1892; *DNB*, xxxv. 386–388.

MAJORISTIC CONTROVERSY: A Lutheran controversy of the sixteenth century regarding the doctrine of justification by faith. The sixth article of the Augsburg Confession, like Melanchthon, maintained the necessity of good works as the necessary outcome of faith, not with the intention of attributing any merits to good works in themselves, but only to emphasize the necessary connection between faith and works. In his report on the Conference of Regensburg (see REGENSBURG, CONFERENCE OF), Major had unmistakably taught the doctrine of faith and grace and had sharply attacked the view which maintained that the justified fulfil the law through works. The Leipsic Interim, it is true, repudiated any merits of good works for justification, yet it advocated the necessity of works in virtue of the divine commandment, not for their intrinsic value, but for the sake of Christ's merit and promise. When Major was about to enter upon his activity at Eisleben, Amsdorf (q.v.) published his treatise *Dass Dr. Pommer und Dr. Major Aergernis und Verwirrung angerichtet* (1551), in which he accused the latter of teaching the necessity of good works for salvation, and Major replied with his pamphlet *Auf des ehrwürdigen Herrn N. von Amsdorf's Schrift Antwort* (Wittenberg, 1552), affirming his full belief in *sola fide*, although at the same time he defended the thesis that good works are necessary for salvation, for as none are saved by evil works, none are saved without good works. Thereupon Amsdorf, Flacius, and Gallus, each in a special treatise, roused the whole Lutheran Church. The clergy of Mansfeld, who had received Major with suspicion at Eisleben, requested him to give an account of his teachings; and after Count Albrecht had expelled him from the city without a trial, he published a sermon on Paul's conversion (Leipsic, 1553), in which he argued that faith can not exist without works, just as the sun can not exist without splendor. Works, according to him, are not required as meritorious, but as a token of obedience, and are not needed to gain salvation, but to retain it. Where they are not present, it is a sure sign that faith is dead. This explanation, however, failed to satisfy his opponents. Amsdorf still maintained that Major was a Roman Catholic, in that he taught the necessity of merit and the cooperation of faith and works in the attainment of righteousness and salvation, while Flacius pointed out that it would be impossible, according to Major's view, to convert the dying or save children. Gallus more pertinently attacked the sentence that salvation must be retained by good works, and showed how liable to misunderstanding these words were, although he did not acknowledge that the object of his critique was not a false doctrine, but only the awkward expression of a correct thought. The Mansfeld theologians, on the other hand, conceded in their *Bedenken* (Magdeburg, 1553) that there was nothing offensive in Major's doctrine, and contented themselves with the statement that, for various reasons, his phraseology should be avoided. In his further publications Major sought to guard his view against misinterpretations, but was unwilling to surrender the wording of his disputed sentence. The controversy still raged, however, and in 1562 he finally decided to sacrifice the misinterpreted passage, although he could not refrain from giving vent to his anger at Flacius and his adherents, and thus exposed himself to renewed attacks. The only theologian of reputation who defended Major was Justus Menius (q.v.), who was accused by Amsdorf, Schnepf, and Stolz of being an adherent of Major, while John Frederic forbade him to teach. He fled to Wittenberg, where he discussed the matter with Melanchthon, but soon returned to Gotha after the court had assured him of his safety. His treatise *Von der Bereitung zum seligen Sterben* (1556) offered, however, a new opportunity for attack, since he maintained that the beginning of the new life as wrought by the Holy Spirit in the faithful was "necessary for salvation," and that salvation could be lost by sin, unless preserved in a pious heart, a good conscience, and a true faith. Thereupon Flacius accused Menius of renewing the heresy of Major. Menius was suspended from office, summoned to Eisenach, and tried by Victorin Strigel, whereupon Amsdorf and his adherents drew up seven theses and insisted upon the signature of Menius. To their surprise he signed them without hesitation, declaring that his teachings had always conformed to them. The adherents of Flacius looked upon this act as a recantation, but they actually obtained nothing but a strict censorship which was soon to involve them in their turn, while the final decision was merely that Major and Menius had confused faith and works. Amsdorf, however, who had maintained as early as 1554 that good works are not necessary for salvation, now went so far as to declare that good works are injurious to salvation, but Menius escaped these unfortunate dissensions by resigning his offices in Thuringia.

Melanchthon had at first held aloof from these controversies, but after Major had been publicly accused by the theologians of Weimar in their fatal protest at Worms in 1557, he declared that Major's words had been evoked by the Antinomians, who considered justification by faith compatible with a sinful life; while he also believed that men like Amsdorf should be restrained by the thesis that new obedience is necessary according to the divine order and the sequence of cause and effect. The controversy of Major was revived in the March of Brandenburg from 1558 to 1563 between J. Agricola and A. Musculus as opposed to Provost Buchholzer in Berlin and Professor Abdias Prætorius in Frankfort-on-the-Oder. It ended with the defeat of the adherents of Melanchthon. The theses of both Major and Amsdorf are rejected in the fourth article of the Formula of Concord, which upholds the necessity of good works in so far as faith is never alone. Works belong to faith as heat and light to fire, and are, therefore, not injurious, but are proofs of eternal life in the faithful. (G. KAWERAU.)

BIBLIOGRAPHY: C. Schlüsselburg, *Catalogus hereticorum*, book vii., Frankfort, 1599; C. A. Salig, *Historie der augsburgischen Confession*, i. 637 sqq., iii. 38 sqq., Halle, 1730; G. J. Planck, *Geschichte der Entstehung . unsers protestantischen Lehrbegriffs*, iv. 469 sqq., Leipsic, 1796; W Preger, *M. Flacius*, i. 356 sqq., Erlangen, 1859; F. H. R. Frank, *Theologie der Concordienformel*, ii. 148 sqq., 4 vols., Erlangen, 1858–65; G. L. Schmidt, *Justus Menius*, ii. 184 sqq., Gotha, 1867; J. C. L. Gieseler, *Church History*, ed. H. B. Smith, iv. 438, New York, 1868; G. Wolf, *Zur Geschichte der deutschen Protestanten 1555–59*, Berlin, 1888; Kurtz, *Church History*, ii. 352, New York, 1894; F. Loofs, *Dogmengeschichte*, pp. 898 sqq., Halle, 1906; Moeller, *Christian Church*, vol. iii. passim.

MAKEMIE, mā'kê-mî, **FRANCIS:** American Presbyterian; b. at Rathmelton (32 m. n.e. of Donegal), Ireland, 1658; d. in Accomac Co., Va., in the summer of 1708. He was educated at Glasgow University and was ordained as a missionary to America by the presbytery of Laggan, Ireland, in 1682. He itinerated in Maryland, Virginia, and

Barbados, and is said to have founded the church at Snow Hill, Md. In 1704 he went to England to secure aid for the Presbyterian Church in America, and on his return in 1706 he helped to organize at Philadelphia the first presbytery in America. In 1707 he was arrested at Newtown, L. I., for preaching without a license and had to pay heavy costs besides being confined in jail for several weeks. He wrote a catechism which was attacked by G. Keith, when he wrote a spirited reply praised by I. Mather. He has been regarded as the founder of Presbyterianism in America, but there are records of at least two other ministers before him.

Bibliography: C. A. Briggs, *American Presbyterianism*, New York, 1885; W. B. Sprague, *Annals of the American Pulpit*, iii. 1-4, ib. 1858; G. P. Hays, *Presbyterians*, pp. 63, 74-76, ib. 1892; R. E. Thompson, *American Church History Series*, vol. vi., ib. 1895; J. H. Patton, *Popular Hist. of the Presbyterian Church, U. S. A.*, ib. 1900; C. L. Thompson, *The Presbyterians*, ib. 1903; *DNB*, xxxv. 390-391.

MALACHI, mal'a-cai, **BOOK OF:** The book which, in the English Version, closes the Old Testament. It is debated whether Malachi is a personal name, or merely official ("my messenger"), or used symbolically. Against the supposition that it is a personal name Hengstenberg uses the following arguments: (1) the superscription gives no information respecting his antecedents; (2) the oldest Jewish tradition appears to know nothing about him; (3) it is derived from iii. 1, and is impossible as a personal name since to a prophet it could not be given by men, but by God alone. Hengstenberg, therefore, considers the name as either ideal, or an official title. The first of these arguments was by Hengstenberg himself regarded as not cogent in view of the meager knowledge possessed concerning other prophets. The second can not be accepted, since the translators of the Septuagint rendered the word "my messenger" in iii. 1, but put *Malachias* (as a personal name) in the title. As to the third, the name may be abbreviated from a form *Malachiah*, "Messenger of Yahweh," which would satisfy the form in the Greek, and meet the objection of Hengstenberg.

The Title.

The date of the prophecy is disputed. Recently Stade, Cornill and Kautzsch have argued for a date prior to the time of Ezra, although the entire point of view of the book, resting upon the institution of the law, implies that Ezra had already come. Stade's argument, based upon the fact that Malachi makes no reference to Ezra's measures against mixed marriages, to a publication of the law, while it regards the priests as Levites, loses force inasmuch as the same features are found in Neh. xiii., which deals with events later than Ezra's measures. The book can belong neither before Ezra nor under his leadership, since in that case mention of it would have been made in the book of Ezra, as is seen by the reference to Haggai and Zechariah in Ezra v. 1, vi. 14; and the absence of mention in Nehemiah is against the activity of the prophet during Nehemiah's governorship. Nägelsbach, Köhler, Orelli, and Reuss rightly place the book in the period between the two visits of Nehemiah, the ground being the reference to the "governor" in Mal. i. 8, who, however, can not be Nehemiah (cf. Neh. v. 8, 10, 14-18) and suits best the governor of the time between Nehemiah's visits. The content of the book agrees with this period, since reference is made to three points, marriage with foreign women, observance of the Sabbath, and maintenance of the temple services through stated offerings (cf. Neh. x. 28 sqq.). Neh. xiii. has Neh. x. in view, and Malachi agrees in standpoint with Neh. xiii. At the coming of Ezra the temple service was a charge on the state treasury; later under Nehemiah the Jews undertook to support the temple by their own contributions as a fulfilment of the law (Neh. x. 33), but became lax in performance after Nehemiah's departure. Out of this arose the reproaches which appear both in Malachi and in the book of Nehemiah, which therefore fix the date.

The Date.

The prophet takes in at a glance past, present, and future. Starting with the past, he sets plainly before his hearers the love which led Yahweh to choose Jacob while he rejected Esau. In contrast to this love of long standing, the prophet sets the present conduct of the people. People and priest sin in that they bring diseased offerings, reduce the temple revenues, and disgrace the divine name by mixed marriages. For these things comes the judgment, which is to be ushered in by a great messenger, whom Yahweh calls emphatically "my messenger," but who, in turn, is only the forerunner of a still greater, the angel of the covenant, with whom Yahweh himself will appear, and this messenger, as the counterpart of Moses, will reveal the new law to God's people. The prophet determines yet more closely the time of the coming of the forerunner, when he says that he is the prophet Elijah, who will come to convert young and old. Then the Lord will return to his temple, and the great and terrible day of judgment will begin. But the judgment has two sides, the destruction of the ungodly, and the refining and purification of the righteous. While Malachi's minatory sermon seems to lay stress upon mere externals, upon the outward observance of the law, in reality he cites the cases of disobedience merely as examples in order to exhort the people to such conduct as befits those in the presence of the day of final reckoning. Israel's duty—this is his exhortation—is in general and in particular conscientiously to obey the law. Malachi has, upon the basis of passages like i. 11, iii. 3, been charged with laying undue emphasis upon sacrifice and thus with being in sharp contrast with the earlier prophets. But alongside of these passages should be placed i. 10, which (like Isa. i. 10 sqq.) shows that not sacrifice in itself but as an evidence of righteous intention is what the prophet has in mind. (W. Volck†.)

The Contents.

Bibliography: The earlier commentaries are obsolete. Modern commentaries are by G. A. Smith, *The Book of the Twelve*, London, 1898; L. Reinke, Giessen, 1856; A. Köhler, Erlangen, 1865; C. F. Keil, Eng. transl., Edinburgh, 1868; W. Drake, in *Bible Commentary*, London, 1876; T. T. Perowne, in *Cambridge Bible*, Cambridge, 1890; C. von Orelli, *Twelve Minor Prophets*, New York, 1893; W. Nowack, Göttingen, 1903; E. B. Pusey, *Minor Prophets*, latest ed., London, 1907; O. Isopescul, Czernowitz, 1908. Consult also: E. W. Hengstenberg, *Beiträge* zur *Einleitung in das Alte Testament*, 3 vols., Berlin, 1831–1839; W. Böhme, in *ZATW*. vii (1887), 210 sqq.; F. W. Farrar, *The Minor Prophets*, London, 1890; J. Wellhausen, *Kleine Propheten*, Berlin, 1898; C. C. Torrey, in *JBL*, xvii. 1, 1898 (important); works cited under Biblical Introduction; Messiah; also *DB*, iii. 218–222; *EB*, iii. 2907–2910; *JE*, viii. 275–276.

MALACHY, mal'u-ki, **O'MORGAIR, SAINT:** Archbishop of Armagh; b. at Armagh, Ireland, between 1093 and 1095; d. at Clairvaux (33 m. s.e. of Troyes), France, Nov. 2 or 3, 1148. He came of a noble family, and received the usual education at the hands of Irish monks and clergy, after which he attached himself to the recluse Iomhar, who lived in a cell adjoining the church of Armagh. Iomhar (d. in Rome, 1134) was a strong supporter of the Roman tendency, and won his disciple for the same cause. Malachy was ordained priest about 1119, to be chosen a bishop shortly afterward and assigned to the district of Armagh. Determined to introduce Roman customs as far as possible, he felt the need of knowing them more thoroughly and of forming closer relations with like-minded prelates in the south of Ireland, so he spent some time with Bishop Malchus at Lismore in Munster. In 1124 he was chosen bishop of Connor in Ulster; but the see was laid waste two years later by one of the northern chieftains, and he and his clergy were driven out. He found a refuge at Ibrach in Kerry, where he founded a monastery; but in 1129 he was recalled to Armagh by the choice of Bishop Celsus on his dying bed as his successor. This was an uncanonical *coup d'état* on the part of Celsus, who was an adherent of the Roman party, and the conservative party refused to recognize Malachy and set up a claimant of their own who gained possession of the see. In 1132 the papal legate Gilbert and Malchus of Lismore took a second revolutionary step by solemnly creating Malachy archbishop of Armagh, and urged him to go and assert his rights. The rival prelate, however, retained his footing in the city until his death in 1134. His successor was driven out by violence, and a compromise finally reached with him by a money payment. In 1136 Malachy appointed the monk Gelasius as his successor at Armagh and took himself the bishopric of Down in Ulster. He could now set to work at his plans for reorganizing the Irish Church, and in 1139 he went to Rome to ask that the pallium be given to two Irish archbishops, another to be named for Cashel in the south. Innocent II. made him papal legate for Ireland and sanctioned the erection of the archbishopric of Cashel, but refused to grant the pallia until they should be requested by the unanimous voice of a general Irish council. Malachy returned in 1140, passing by Clairvaux to consult with St. Bernard as to the introduction of Cistercian monks into Ireland, and renouncing only at the papal command his desire to take the cowl himself in the famous abbey. He busied himself in the duties of his station, and won universal reverence by his saintly humility and asceticism, earning also the reputation of a miracle worker. In 1148 he succeeded in inducing a council at Innispatrick to ask for the pallia again, and so to win formal papal sanction for the reorganization of the Irish Church. He started on this mission, but fell ill at Clairvaux, and died a fortnight later, St. Bernard preaching the sermon at his funeral in the abbey church.

Malachy's importance in Irish ecclesiastical history is analogous to that of Boniface in the German. The result of his work was indeed a loss of independence for his people, but it was more than compensated by the gain in order, discipline, and higher culture. His life was written before 1152 by his admiring friend Bernard, and is one of the most finished works of the greatest of medieval stylists. It doubtless contributed to his canonization, which was pronounced by Clement III. in 1190. The works attributed to him by later writers are almost certainly not his; some of them may belong to an Irish Franciscan of the same name who was at Oxford about 1390. The famous prophecy bearing his name, which consists of 141 mottos for all the popes from Celestine II. to the end of time, was first published by the Benedictine Wion in 1595, and is now thought to have been written by a partizan of Cardinal Simoncelli to support his candidacy in the conclave of 1590. (H. Böhmer.)

Bibliography: J. O'Hanlon, *Life of St. Malachy O'Morgair*, Dublin, 1859; A. Bellesheim, *Geschichte der katholischen Kirche in Irland*, vol. i., Mainz, 1890; *KL*, viii. 539–542. On the prophecy consult: C. F. Menestrier, *Refutation des propheties . . sur les elections des papes*, Paris, 1689; J. J. I. von Döllinger, *Fables Respecting the Popes*, New York, 1872; The Marquis of Bute, in *Dublin Review*, Oct., 1885.

MALALAS, JOHN: Greek chronographer; lived at Antioch in the first half of the sixth century. He is presumably identical with a Johannes Rhetor whose work Evagrius (q.v.) used as one of his sources; he was probably a Syrian of Greek training and by profession an advocate (*malal=rhetōr*). Under his name the Greek text of a general Chronicle (Chronographia) has been transmitted (ed. L. Dindorf in *CSHB*, Bonn, 1831; reprinted *MPG*, xcvii. 9–970) which reaches, in its present form, to 563, but was originally, perhaps, continued as far as 573. Whether the work, in its whole extent of eighteen books, is by but one author, is fairly open to question. Books i.–xvii. and the early portion of xviii. appear to have been written prior to 540; whereas the greater part of book xviii., wherein Constantinople, not Antioch, is the center of the situation, was not closed till after the death of Justinian, and was then consolidated with the other books. The dogmatic character is not uniform, the original Monophysite treatment bearing the appearance of having been revised by an orthodox editor. Book xviii. certainly emanates from an orthodox writer. The last four books, which narrate the events from Emperor Anastasius down, are important as a source for ecclesiastical history, in spite of the puerility of conception and the narrow horizon. Being in high favor as a book for the people, the Chronicle was repeatedly transcribed and copied, but ultimately it was superseded by later annalists (Theophanes, Georgius Monachus, Zonaras), and has thus been preserved in only one manuscript, while even this is an abridged revision (Codex Baroccianus of the twelfth century in the Bodleian library at Oxford; cf. J. B.

Burg in *Byzantinische Zeitschrift*, vi., 1897, pp. 219–230). G. Krüger.

Bibliography: Krumbacher, *Geschichte*, pp. 325–334 (contains a very full and adequate list of the earlier literature); E. Patzig, in *Byzantinische Zeitschrift*, vii (1898), 111–128; C. E. Gleye, in the same, viii (1899), 312–327; J. Haury, in the same, ix (1900), 337–356; *DCB*, iii. 787–788; *KL*, viii. 544–545.

MALAN, mɑ̈''lɑ̄n', CÉSAR HENRI ABRAHAM: Swiss Reformed preacher; b. at Geneva July 7, 1787; d. there May 18, 1864. He descended from a family which settled in the twelfth century at Mérindol in Dauphiné. Expelled from France by the annulment of the edict of Nantes, Peter Malan, grandfather of César, settled in 1722 at Geneva. At an early age César showed a strong inclination for study. The example of his parents fostered this, and he developed a strong feeling for art and a vivid sense of the beautiful in nature. At the age of seventeen he served a short time as apprentice in a business house and the following year returned to Geneva, where he began his theological studies. The theological instruction which he received there was not congenial, since the Bible was almost entirely neglected; however, he passed his examinations successfully. In 1809 he received a position as teacher in the fifth class of the Latin school in Geneva, where he soon proved himself to be an excellent pedagogue. In 1810 he was ordained, and in 1811 he married the daughter of a merchant who had settled in Geneva; his wife became an important aid in the development of his faith. Some genuinely Evangelical sermons which he heard, conversations with genuine believers and the influence of a society called "friends," modeled after the congregation of Brethren, were the means of leading him to the truth. His new faith assumed that decided character and determined form which never left him, by which his standpoint in theology became essentially dogmatic. While it is true that his inability to appreciate fully the ideas of others was in some respects an element of weakness, such a man was needed at a time when the fundamental principles of Christianity were controverted. The conversion of Malan may be dated from 1816. It was strengthened and confirmed in the following year by a visit of the Haldanes (see Haldane, Robert and James Alexander) in Geneva. The fearless promulgation of Christian truth on the part of Malan gave great offense to the clergy of Geneva. In 1817 he was forbidden to preach in town and country. An order had been issued by a union of clergymen in which the preaching of the following themes was prohibited: (1) Union of both natures in the person of Jesus Christ; (2) hereditary sin; (3) the manner in which grace works its effects; (4) predestination. Malan refused at first to submit, but at the close of the year, after some confused explanations and somewhat uncertain promises had been given him, he yielded and was allowed to preach. Malan, however, was not able to suppress his personal convictions and soon was definitely excluded from all pulpits of the canton. He still kept his position as teacher of the Latin school where his instruction was greatly appreciated. But after he tried to introduce here also his own Christian principles, he was threatened with removal unless he changed his method, and was finally deposed. As he was not willing to stop preaching, he began to hold meetings at his residence, and, as the number of his hearers increased, he built a chapel on his premises at his own expense. The building of the chapel was looked upon as an act of insubordination, and Malan was deprived of the right to exercise his ministerial functions. He wrote to the council of state that he intended to leave the Protestant church of the canton as she then existed, whereupon he was dismissed as preacher on the eighteenth of Sept., 1828. But these violent measures did not induce Malan to cause a split in the church. He ceased to administer the Lord's Supper in his own church and participated in the celebration in the national church, where he also had his children baptized. Similarly, he did not join the newly established Church *du Bourg de four* because he was averse to its principle of separation. Nevertheless, his spiritual activity increased from day to day. His chapel grew into a church. His doctrinal differences with the Church *du Bourg de four* became more pronounced in the course of time and led in 1830 to a rupture in consequence of which a third of the members of his congregation left him. But his activity was in no way restricted by this event. He became a missionary. Without leaving Geneva permanently, he frequently undertook extensive travels to different countries where numerous friends awaited him. His fame spread especially in England and Scotland, and he found there an enthusiastic reception in his six visits, 1826–43. He was endowed with peculiar gifts as an itinerant preacher and often preached daily for several weeks. He traveled also through France, Belgium, Holland, some parts of Switzerland and Germany, and through the valleys of the Waldenses in Piedmont, preaching everywhere. In his conversations, as well as in his sermons, he manifested the dogmatic character of his mind. In his method he conceded perhaps too prominent a place to reason; salvation was with him almost a logical conclusion. He clung to the harshest formulas of Calvinism, and yet loved souls so fervently that his benevolence often conquered the people who were at first repelled by his theology. He preached predestination without glossing even the most repulsive features, without shrinking from the consequences, but still with the simplicity of a child and the joy of a conqueror. His severance from the state church caused him great pain, and he was willing to reenter it whenever the free preaching of the Gospel should be permitted. Several attempts were made by him to be received again into fellowship, but without avail. He succeeded, however, in becoming a member of the Scottish Church. It is only just to ascribe to him since 1830 a beneficent and lasting influence upon the religious movement in the countries where French is used and even in Holland. It was chiefly through him that the religious awakening of that period was not lost in mere sentimentality. Of his works may be mentioned a polemical treatise, *Jesus Christus ist der ewige im Fleisch geoffenbarte Gott* (1831), Malan's reply to a treatise of Professor Chenevière, who had openly denied the divinity of Jesus Christ. Another polemical treatise, *Pourrai-je entrer jamais dans l'église romaine?* (Paris, 1837), was directed against Abbé Baudry. Other works of Malan are, *Quatre-vingt jours d'un missionaire* (Geneva, 1842); *Le véritable ami des enfants* (4th ed. in 4 vols., Geneva, 1844); *Êtes-vous heureux, mais pleinement heureux? Sincères aveux de quelques amis* (Geneva, 1851); *Vingt tableaux suisses, tous esquissés d'après nature* (Geneva, 1854). Malan wrote also a large number of religious tracts which had great popularity, a very considerable number of them being translated, as were many of his stories and sermons, into English. He composed more than a thousand hymns, some of which have become the common property of all Christian churches. (E. Bardet.)

Bibliography: C. Malan (his son), *La Vie et les travaux de César Malan*, Geneva, 1869, Eng. transl., *The Life, Labours, and Writings of Cæsar Malan*, London, 1869; *Histoire véritable des mômiers de Genève*, Paris, 1824; *The Late Rev. Dr. Cesar Malan of Geneva*, London, 1864.

MALAN, SOLOMON CÆSAR: Orientalist; b. at Geneva Apr. 22, 1812; d. at Bournemouth (24 m. w.s.w. of Southampton), England, Nov. 25, 1894. He was of an old Waldensian family, and the son of César Henri Abraham Malan (q.v.). He was educated at St. Edmund Hall, Oxford (B.A., 1837; M.A., 1843), and was ordered deacon in 1838 and ordained priest in 1843. From 1838 to 1840 he was classical lecturer at Bishop's College, Calcutta. He was then curate of Alverstoke, Hampshire (1843–44); Crowcombe, Somersetshire (1844–45); vicar of Broadwindsor, Dorsetshire (1845–85); rural dean (1846–53); and prebendary of Salisbury cathedral (1870–75). Malan was a good linguist, being acquainted with twenty-five to thirty languages. He made two or three journeys to the East after his return from India, one in particular to Nineveh, passing through the Caucasus and preaching in Georgian at Kutais. Among his numerous works may be mentioned: *Outline of Bishop's College and of its Missions* (London, 1843); *Plain Exposition of the Apostles' Creed* (1847); *Systematic Catalogue of the Eggs of British Birds* (1848); *Vindication of the Authorised Version of the English Bible* (1856); *Aphorisms on Drawing* (1856); *Magdala: a Day by the Sea of Galilee* (1857); *Bethany: a Pilgrimage* (1857); *Coasts of Tyre and Sidon* (1858); *Letters to a Young Missionary* (1858); *On Ritualism* (1867); *Outline of the English Jewish Church* (1867); *Holy Sacrament of the Lord's Supper, According to Scripture, Grammar, and the Faith* (1868); *Parables of Jesus Christ, Explained to Country Children* (2 vols., 1872); *Miracles of Our Lord, Explained to Country Children* (1881); and *Original Notes on the Book of Proverbs* (3 vols., 1889–93). He also translated many works, chiefly religious, from the Russian, Welsh, Armenian, Arabic, Syriac, Coptic, Ethiopic, Georgian, Chinese, Japanese, and other languages; among them: the *San Tsze King* (from the Chinese; 1856); the *Gospel according to St. John* (from the eleven oldest versions; 1862); *History of the Georgian Church* (from the Russian; 1866); *Life and Times of St. Gregory the Illuminator* (from the Armenian; 1868); *Conflicts of the Holy Apostles* (from the Armenian; 1871); *Misawo, the Japanese Girl* (from the Japanese; 1871); *History of the Copts, and of their Church* (from the Arabic; 1873); and *The Book of Adam and Eve* (from the Ethiopic; 1882).

Bibliography: A biography was written by his son, A. N. Malan, London, 1897, and a notice by Macdonnell appeared in the *Journal of the Royal Asiatic Society*, 1895; cf. *DNB*, Supplement, vol. iii. 133–134.

MALAY ARCHIPELAGO: A chain of four large and numerous small volcanic islands, lying to the southeast of Asia, extending from the Malay Peninsula to New Guinea, also known as the Dutch East Indies. They are divided into the Larger Sunda Islands—Sumatra, Java, Borneo, Celebes; the Lesser Sunda Islands—Bali, Lombok, Sumbawa, Flores, Sumba, Sawu, Timor, etc.; and the Moluccas—Buru, Ambon, Ceram, Almaheira, Ternate, the Sangi, and the Talaut Islands, etc.; area, 943,000 square miles; population (estimated), 32,435,000. The Philippine Islands (q.v.) are sometimes included in the group. An area of about 84,000 miles on North Borneo is under British control, while Portugal has 7,500 square miles of territory on East Timor; the rest of the archipelago is under Dutch control. The majority of the inhabitants are Malays, divided into the savage and semi-civilized tribes. There are over half a million Chinese, 60,000 Dutch, and about 3,000 Europeans and other foreigners.

A Hindu invasion antedating the Christian era was followed first by a Buddhist and later by a Brahmin wave, each leaving its impress on the natives. A Mohammedan invasion in the twelfth century resulted in a wide-spread Mohammedanism, and Arab influence was paramount till the coming of the Dutch in 1521. In 1602 the Dutch East India Company established itself in the archipelago and at once began the work of civilizing and Christianizing the people, which was demanded by its charter. The Malay language was reduced to writing, and numerous schools were established; by 1688 the New Testament was given to the people, and in 1733 the Old Testament was also completed. But the work of these missionaries of the company was largely perfunctory; any person so desiring was baptized and ranked thereafter as a Christian, though heathen in habit. The company dissolved in 1795, and no further Protestant mission work was attempted till 1812, when the Netherlands Society sent its first missionaries. They were followed by the English Baptists (1820), the American Board (1834), the Netherlands Mennonite Mission Union (1847), the Java Committee (1855), the Ermelo Missions Society (1856), the Netherlands Missions Union (1858), the Missions of the Reformed Churches in the Netherlands (1859), the Utrecht Missionary Society (1859), and the Netherlands Lutheran Church (1882). Other societies are the Rhenish Society (1835), the Society for the Propagation of the Gospel (1837), the Neukirchen Missions Institute (1882), and the Methodist Episcopal Society (1889).

However, the results of missionary work were meager, largely owing to the attitude of the government toward Mohammedanism, which flourished under Dutch rule, and to the fact that the missions were uniformly poorly manned, with the exception of those of the Rhenish Society. There was a lack of aggressive work, and heathen remained heathen or became Mohammedan. Even the Christian communities that resulted from the early missions were neglected. Dutch missionaries were scattered throughout the archipelago, their most successful work being in the Minahassa district of Celebes, which is practically Christianized. The Rhenish Society has worked among the Dyaks of Borneo, the Bataks of Sumatra, and on the smaller islands of Nias and Mentawei. The Society for the Propagation of the Gospel occupies British Borneo, with stations in North Borneo, Sarawak, and Labuan, and the Methodist Episcopal Society (U. S. A.) has a small work in Java, Sumatra, and Borneo. The English Baptists and the American Board both attempted to establish missions in Sumatra early in the nineteenth century, but the English missionaries abandoned the field, and the Americans were massacred by the natives. The most successful work of the Dutch societies in the Celebes, Moluccas, and adjacent isles was taken over by the Colonial State Church in 1865, but their " missions helpers " were restricted to work among the nominal Christians, and did nothing for the heathen multitudes. In 1888 the secretary of state for the Netherlands Colonies notified the Protestant Netherlands societies that " the government would value it highly if they would increase their staff of missionaries so as to counteract the growing influence of Islam." Nothing came of it, and the Dutch mission force still remained inadequate at the beginning of the present century, and the Dutch government continued to obstruct the work of Christians while giving free scope to the Mohammedans. At that time there were about 315,000 Protestant and 30,000 Roman Catholic Christians. Of late years the attitude of the government has been more friendly, the spread of Mohammedanism has had a decided check, and there has been progress all along the line. There are 11 Protestant societies, working in 521 stations and outstations; 269 missionaries and 592 native helpers; 492 schools, with 23,108 scholars; 3 hospitals and dispensaries; 148,708 professed Christians. The Roman Catholics have 38 stations and outstations, 50 priests, 29 schools and 6 orphanages; and 50,000 communicants and adherents. Their missionaries are under the apostolic vicar of Batavia, and come from the Foreign Missionary Society of Paris. They are working in both British Borneo and throughout the Dutch possessions, making special efforts in the islands where the Protestants are doing least. Their work is noteworthy for the large number of orphanages. The work throughout the archipelago is noted for the number of converts from the Mohammedans. The number of converts during the last twenty-five years is estimated at 20,000. THEODORA CROSBY BLISS.

BIBLIOGRAPHY: For description of the people consult: A. C. Haddon, *Headhunters, Black, White, and Brown*, London, 1901; W H. Furness, *Home-Life of Borneo Head-Hunters*, Philadelphia, 1902; H. Breitenstein, *21 Jahre in . Borneo, Java, Sumatra*, 2 vols., Leipsic, 1899–1900. For missions consult: H. Needham, *"God First"; or, Hester Needham's Work in Sumatra*, London, 1899; H. Dijkstra, *Het evangelie in onze Oost*, 2 vols., Leyden, 1900–01; S. Coolsma, *De Zendingseeuw voor Nederlandsch Oost-Indië*, Utrecht, 1901.

MALCOM, HOWARD: American Baptist; b. in Philadelphia Jan. 19, 1799; d. there Mar. 25, 1879. He was educated at Dickinson College, Pa., and Princeton Theological Seminary. Ordained in 1820, he was pastor at Hudson, N. Y. (1820–26), Boston (1827–35), and Philadelphia (1849–51). He was president of Georgetown (Ky.) College (1840–49), University of Lewisburg (1851–1857), and Hahnemann Medical College (1874–79). He was general secretary of the American Sunday School Union (1826–27); from 1835 to 1838, as deputy of the Baptist Missionary Society, he traveled in India, Burma, Siam, China, and Africa. He wrote: *A Bible Dictionary* (Boston, 1828); *Travels in Southeastern Asia* (2 vols., 1839); and *Index to Religious Literature* (Boston, 1868).

MALDONATUS, mal″do-nā′tus, **JOHANNES (JUAN MALDONADO):** Roman Catholic exegete; b. at Las Casas de la Reina (a village in the Spanish province of Estremadura) 1534; d. at Rome Jan. 5, 1583. He was educated at Salamanca, where he attained such distinction that on the completion of his studies in 1556 he was appointed professor, giving instruction for a short time in philosophy, and then accepting the chair of theology. He was preeminently successful, but his very fame alarmed him, lest he should thus be won from the life of renunciation of the world on which he had long since determined. In 1562 accordingly he resigned his professorship and went to Italy, where on Aug. 10 he was received into the order of Jesus as a novice, and at the expiration of a year was ordained priest and appointed to a chair in the Collegium Romanum. In 1563 he was sent by the general to Paris, where he was made professor in the College of Clermont, although the hostility manifested toward the Jesuits prevented him from beginning his lectures until the following year. He lectured at first on philosophy and attracted large audiences, but in Oct., 1565, he was appointed professor of theology, the Jesuits wishing to counteract the Gallicanism of the Sorbonne and disapproving of its too moderate opposition to Calvinism. Here again his popularity was phenomenal, but in 1570 his activity in Paris ceased for a time when he and nine companions were sent by the general of the order to Poitiers to establish a house for the instruction and conversion of young Calvinists. He met with little success, however, and on Oct. 10 resumed his lectures at Paris, interrupting his activity only by a missionary trip of a few weeks to Sedan and Lorraine. Until Aug., 1576, he taught with ever-increasing prestige, although he was confronted with the growing jealousy of the Sorbonne. He was accused of having influenced the dying Montbrun, president of St. André, to make a will in favor of the Jesuits, but was speedily acquitted, only to have a more serious charge brought against him on account of doubts concerning the Immaculate Conception. Herein he was in accord with the Council of Trent, but the Sorbonne, which had accepted the dogma in 1497 in harmony with a decree of the Council of Basel, was impatient of such deviation from its views, and accused him of heresy in 1574. The archbishop of Paris, Pierre de Gondy, acquitted Maldonatus of the charge, whereupon the Sorbonne again accused him of heresy for having expressed the opinion, in a lecture delivered six years before, that no soul would be required to remain in purgatory more than ten years in all, whereas the usual view postulated seven years of expiation for each sin unatoned for during life. Twisting this mere opinion into a categorical statement, the Sorbonne lodged charges against Maldonatus before parliament, and the debate dragged wearily on until Pope Gregory XIII., at the request of both parties, interfered and declared Maldonatus orthodox in his teachings. The latter accordingly resumed his lectures, which he had declined to deliver during the trial, on May 6, 1576, but his reluctance to remain longer in Paris, combined with the pope's desire to reconcile the Sorbonne and Clermont, resulted in his transfer to the College of Bourges, where he found a little leisure to devote to literary work. In the latter part of 1578 he was appointed visitor of his order in the province of France, and in this capacity devoted much energy to the development of the University of Pont-à-Mousson, which had been founded by Cardinal Guise in 1573 and placed under Jesuit control. Exhausted by his duties, he retired for a brief rest to Bourges, but on Aug. 1, 1580, Everard Mercurian, the fourth general of the order, died, and Maldonatus was sent to Rome as the deputy of the province of France to attend the election fixed for Apr., 1581. He accordingly hastened to Italy, was invited to preside at the election, and in this capacity proclaimed his compatriot, Aquaviva, the fifth general of the Jesuits. His new superior detained him in Rome at the Collegium Romanum to give him leisure and materials for the completion of his commentary on the Bible, and at the same time the pope appointed him a member of the committee for the revision of the Pentateuch, but he did not live to complete the latter task. The works of Maldonatus are as follows: *Commentarii in quattuor Evangelia* (2 vols., Pont-à-Mousson, 1596–97; new ed. by F. Sausen, 5 vols., Mainz, 1840, abridged by K. Martin in two vols., Mainz, 1850; Eng. transl. of the commentary on Matthew by G. J. Davie, 2 vols., London, 1888–89); *Commentarii in Prophetas quattuor Jeremiam, Baruch, Ezechielem et Danielem* (Tours, 1611); and *Tractatus de cærimoniis missæ* (best edited by P. Zaccaria, *Bibliotheca Ritualis*, iii., Rome, 1781). His *Opera varia theologica* were edited by two doctors of the Sorbonne, Dubois and Faure (3 vols., Paris, 1677). (W. J. Mangold†.)

Bibliography: J. M. Prat, *Maldonat et l'université de Paris au xvi. siècle*, Paris, 1856 (somewhat one-sided); R. Simon, *Histoire critique des principaux commentateurs du N. T.*, pp. 618–632, Rotterdam, 1693; L. E. Du Pin, *Nouvelle bibliothèque des auteurs ecclésiastiques*, xvi. 125 sqq., Amsterdam, 1710; P. Bayle, *Dictionary Historical and Critical*, iv. 76–82, London, 1737; Aberle, in *TQS*, 1855, pp. 121 sqq.; A. and A. de Backer, *Bibliothèque des écrivains de la Société de Jésus*, ed. C. Sommervogel, v. 403 sqq., Paris, 1891 sqq.; Lichtenberger, *ESR*, viii. 598–601; *KL*, viii. 547–551.

MALEBRANCHE, mal"brānsh', **NICOLAS:** French philosopher; b. in Paris Aug. 6, 1638; d. there Oct. 13, 1715. He studied theology at the Sorbonne, then at the age of twenty-two entered the Congregation of the Oratory, and spent the rest of his life in seclusion. The reading of Descartes' *Traité de l'homme* led him to devote himself exclusively to philosophy, in the history of which he appears as the most prominent disciple of Descartes, at some points developing and carrying farther the ideas of his master. He is the father of Occasionalism. This depends upon the Cartesian distinction between spirit and matter, soul and body. The relation between these two opposites, which Descartes left unexplained or only vaguely explained, Malebranche made the subject of his deepest meditation. Hence resulted his peculiar doctrine, that events taking place in the one sphere occasioned God to effect corresponding readjustments in the other, so that nothing could be truly understood unless "seen in God." The principal representation of his system is found in his first work, *De la recherche de la verité* (Paris, 1674; two Eng. translations appeared in the same year, each in two vols., Oxford and London, 1694); but further developments are found in his *Conversations chrétiennes* (1677), *De la nature et de la grâce* (1680; Eng. transl., 1695), *Méditations chrétiennes et métaphysiques* (1683), *Traité de morale* (2 vols., 1694; Eng. transl., London, 1699), and especially in his *Entretiens sur la métaphysique et sur la religion* (2 vols., 1688). His *De la nature et de la grâce* deprived him of the favor of Bossuet, and implicated him in a long and bitter controversy with Antoine Arnauld. His doctrines were often said to incline toward Spinozism, but on this point he found a warm defender in Leibnitz. While his metaphysics have now only very little interest, the noble piety of his works still impresses and the elegance of the representation exercises its charm. His works, first published in Paris, 1712, were again edited by Genoude and Lourdoueix (2 vols., Paris, 1837); also by J. Simon (1842, new ed., 1859; in 4 vols., 1871, incomplete).

Bibliography: H. Joly, *Traité de morale de Malebranche*, Paris, 1882; idem, *Malebranche*, ib. 1901; J. P. Damiron, *Essai sur l'hist. de la philosophie*, pp. 352–396, ib. 1846; E. A. Blampignon, *Étude sur Malebranche*, ib. 1862; F. Bowen, *Modern Philosophy*, pp. 73–86, New York, 1877; P. André, *De la vie de* . *Malebranche*, Paris, 1886; E. Farny, *Étude sur la morale de Malebranche*, Chaux de Fonds, 1886; E. Caird, *Essays on Literature and Philosophy*, 2 vols., New York, 1892; and, in general, works on the history of modern philosophy.

MALLET, FRIEDRICH LUDWIG: German pulpit-orator; b. at Braunfels (37 m. e.n.e. of Coblenz) Aug. 4, 1793; d. at Bremen May 5, 1865. He was educated in the universities of Herborn and Tübingen, and during his student days served in the Napoleonic wars of 1814–15. In Dec., 1815, he became assistant in St. Michael's Church, Bremen, and succeeded the aged pastor, Buch, two years later. In 1827 he was chosen third pastor at the large church of St. Stephen in Bremen, where he officiated for the remainder of his life, becoming first pastor after the deaths of his superiors, Müller and Pletzer.

Mallet was preeminently a preacher of simplicity and orthodoxy, as may be seen from the collection of his sermons and addresses edited by his son at Bremen in 1867. He was also active as an editor, and in 1832 founded at Bremen the *Bremer Kirchenbote*, which ran until 1847, when it was replaced by the *Bremer Schlüssel* (1848–50) and the *Bremer Post* (1856–60). He polemized against the Roman Catholics and against rationalism, to both of which he was bitterly opposed. In this spirit he wrote *Ueber den Heiligen- und Bilderdienst in der römischen Kirche* (Bremen, 1842), *Zeugnisse* (2 parts, 1845), *Geständniss* (1845), and *Memoiren eines Weltmannes* (1847). From 1848 to 1852 he was involved in a controversy with the pantheistic pastor, Rodolf Dulon, against whom he wrote several pamphlets and who was finally dismissed from his position. Mallet's activity in all movements for Christian union and missions was untiring. In 1819 he assisted in the establishment of the first Bremen missionary society, and in 1834 in the foundation of the first young men's association and a society for the dissemination of Christian tracts, while in 1844 he devoted much of his energy to the furtherance of the Gustav-Adolf-Verein. His principal writings, in addition to those already mentioned, are: *Die Weisen aus dem Morgenlande* (Bremen, 1852); *Passions- und Festpredigten* (Frankfort, 1859); *Altes und Neues* (Bremen, 1864); and the posthumous *Neues und Altes*, edited by his son (Bremen, 1868). (J. F. Iken†.)

Bibliography: C. A. Wilkens, *Friedrich Mallet, . . . eine Biographie*, Bremen, 1872 (a model biography); H. Hupfeld, *Friedrich Ludwig Mallet*, ib. 1865; W. H. Meurer, *Zur Erinnerung an Friedrich Ludwig Mallet*, ib. 1872.

MALMESBURY, WILLIAM OF. See William.

MALTA, KNIGHTS OF. See John, Saint, Knights of.

MALVENDA, TOMAS: Spanish Dominican; b. at Xativa (43 m. s.s.w. of Valencia) 1566; d. at Valencia May 7, 1628. He devoted his chief efforts to the text of the Bible, although he also wrote on dogmatics and church history. In 1600 he submitted to Cardinal Baronius a list of passages in the *Annales ecclesiastici* and the Roman Martyrology which he deemed incorrect, and the cardinal thereupon summoned him to Rome, where the general of his order entrusted him with the correction of the Dominican breviary, missal, and martyrology, his work appearing in 1603. At the direction of the Congregation of the Index, Malvenda revised the *Bibliotheca patrum* of Margarin de la Bigne (9 vols., Paris, 1575-76), and in 1607 published at Rome his critical notes on this work. About the same time he began his *Annales ordinis fratrum prædicatorum*, but carried it only through thirty years (ed. D. Gravina, 2 vols., Naples, 1627). In 1610 Malvenda was recalled to Spain and appointed by the grand inquisitor on a committee to prepare a Spanish *Index librorum prohibitorum*. His chief work, however, was his commentary on the Bible, together with a new translation from the Hebrew, as far as Ezek. xvi. (5 vols., Lyons, 1650). Among his numerous other writings special mention may be made of his *Libri novem de Antichristo* (Rome, 1604) and his *De paradiso voluptatis* (1605). (O. Zöckler†.)

Bibliography: J. Quétif and J. Échard, *Scriptores ordinis prædicatorum*, ii. 454-455, Paris, 1721; L. E. Du Pin, *Nouvelle bibliothèque des auteurs ecclésiastiques*, xvii. 86-93, 35 vols., Paris, 1698–1711; H. Hurter, *Nomenclator literarius theologiæ recentioris*, i. 312–314, Innsbruck, 1892; F. H. Reusch, *Der Index der verbotenen Bücher*, i. 554–555, Bonn, 1883; *KL*, viii. 582.

MAMACHI, mā-mā'chī, **TOMMASO MARIA:** Italian Roman Catholic; b. in the island of Chios Dec. 3, 1713; d. at Corneto, near Montefiascone (50 m. n.n.w. of Rome), June 7, 1792. He was taken to Italy by his parents at an early age and was educated in the cloister of St. Mark at Florence by the Dominicans, of whose order he afterward became a member. In 1736 he was ordained priest and was made by Benedict XIV. a doctor of divinity and a member of the Congregation of the Index. Under Pius VI. he became master of the holy palace and in 1779 secretary of the Index. Among his works may be named: *De ratione temporum Athanasianorum, deque aliquot synodis iv. seculo celebratis, epistolæ iv* (Rome, 1748), directed against G. D. Mansi; *Originum et antiquitatum Christianarum libri xx* (four books only were published; 6 vols., 1749–55; new ed., 6 vols., 1839–51); *De' costumi de' primitivi Cristiani libri tre* (3 vols., Venice, 1757; new ed., 2 vols., Florence, 1853; Germ. transl., 3 vols., Augsburg, 1796); *Del diritto libero della chiesa di acquistare e di possedere beni temporali* (3 vols., Rome, 1769–70); and *De ratione regendæ Christianæ reipublicæ, deque legitima Romani pontificis auctoritate* (3 vols., Rome, 1776–1778), directed against J. N. von Hontheim (q.v.).

Bibliography: H. Hurter, *Nomenclator literarius*, iii. 412-413, Innsbruck, 1886; *KL*, viii. 583–584; Lichtenberger, *ESR*, viii. 622-623.

MAMERTUS. See Claudianus Mamertus.

MAMMON: Aramaic for "wealth" or "gain." It is a word of uncertain etymology, and is found in the Aramaic ("what one has saved"), in Syriac, and in Carthaginian and Phenician (*lucrum*, "wealth"), possibly in the Arabic ("a deposit"). The Targum of Onkelos renders by it the Hebrew for "ransom" (Ex. xxi. 30; Num. xxxv. 31), also the word "gain" (Gen. xxxvii. 26; Ex. xviii. 21). Accordingly in Matt. vi. 24 and Luke xvi. 9, 11, 13, the word must mean "possession," "wealth," or "money." The meaning was not necessarily sinister; the accompanying adjectival expression gives it that sense in the Targum on I Sam. viii. 3; Isa. xxxiii. 15; Ezek. xxii. 27; Hos. v. 11; Prov. xv. 27; Hab. ii. 9; and Ezek. xxii. 13. In Luke xvi. 9 sqq. the meaning is not that money sinfully acquired is best spent in alms (Holtzmann), but that the earthly possessions of the children of the kingdom of God are called "unrighteous" because not properly held by them, since their rightful possession is the kingdom of God. The good which is foreign [to one's nature] he is to bestow in order to obtain that possession which is really his own. There is known no god or demon "mamon" as Weiss (on Luke xvi. 9) supposed. (G. Dalman.)

Bibliography: The commentaries on the passages cited, particularly that of Plummer on Luke xvi. 9-13 (New

York, 1896); the lexicons (Hebrew, Aramaic, and Greek) on the word; *DB*, iii. 224; *EB*, iii. 2912–15; *JE*, viii. 278 (elaborate).

MAMRE. See JUDEA, II., 1, § 5.

MAN.

I. Origin of Man.
II. Unity of the Human Race.
III. Antiquity of Man.

While in man the natural realm finds the culmination of its development, there develops in him at the same time a new realm, the kingdom of the spirit. The noblest philosophical thinkers, ancient and modern, as well as the Scripture, corroborate this view of the twofold nature of man. They place man in close connection with the preceding works of creation, and at the same time represent him as the product of a new creative thought and act (Gen. i. 26, ii. 7).

I. Origin of Man: Man was created in God's image. The *consensus gentium* bears testimony to the truth of this Biblical sentence. According to most pagan myths of creation, the human race was created by the gods or the deity. Some anthropologists like to base their theories upon legends in natural religions (India, Tibet, etc.), which trace the original man back to the ape; but other legends as numerous and as old as those (ancient Mexico, West Africa, South Arabia, Indo-China) consider apes as degenerated and fallen descendants of men. More important are the traditions of the civilized nations of antiquity, which almost unanimously agree that man is the creature of God. Of these may be mentioned the Chinese tradition about Fo-hi or Pao-hí, the Babylonian, with its many points of agreement with the Biblical account; the Egyptian Book of the Dead, with its praise of the "Divine Architect, who made the world to be the home of man, the image of the Creator"; Hesiod's and Ovid's poems.

It is only since the middle of the eighteenth century that the materialistic philosophy of men like Lamettrie, Holbach, Helvetius (qq.v.) degraded man to a mere animal, or even a machine. In recent times many anthropologists have adopted the same view. Carolus Linnæus (1707–1778) classified man with the ape as the highest representative of the vertebrates, but pronounced him to have been "created with an immortal soul, after the divine image," and called him "the only one among the creatures blessed with a rational soul for the praise of God" (*Systema Naturæ*, 6th ed., 1748). J. F. Blumenbach (1752–1840), the real founder of anthropology as a science, never doubted that man was distinguished from the whole animal world by his upright walk, perfectly developed hands, protruding chin, and articulate speech. Other investigators, basing their theories on the study of embryology, paleontology, and experiments in breeding animals and plants, have come to the conclusion that man is the result of a process of development, some primeval type of ape being his immediate ancestor (see EVOLUTION). This view has been advanced especially by Charles Darwin, Thomas H. Huxley, John Lubbock, E. B. Tylor, and in Germany by Ernst Haeckel, Oskar Schmidt, H. Schaaffhausen, O. Caspari, and others.

This theory, however, is only a hypothesis the scientific untenableness of which is evident from the following facts: (1) There are anatomical differences between man and even the most developed apes (gorilla, chimpanzee, etc.), so important that the assumption of their common origin is subject to the greatest difficulties. According to the investigations of Æby, Bischoff, R. Owen, and others, the capacity of the lowest human skull (the natives of New Holland) is seventy-five cubic inches; while the largest capacity of the gorilla is thirty-four cubic inches. The average weight of the brain of a European is fifty-seven ounces; that of the negro, from thirty-eight to fifty-one ounces; but that of the gorilla from seventeen to nineteen ounces. (2) No validity can be attached to the embryological proof, consisting in the supposed identity of the fetal phases of the development of man with those of the higher mammals, especially the apes. The exact repetition of lower animal forms of existence in the steps of the development of the embryo does not take place in reality, as Haeckel has asserted. His, Goette, Kölliker, and other authorities on the doctrine of evolution decidedly disagree with Haeckel in many details. (3) The proof from paleontology is also full of gaps and deficiencies. The assumed human apes (*pithecanthropi*) have so far been found neither in a living nor in a fossil condition. Neither the Neanderthal skull, nor the Engis skull, nor the Cro-Magnon skull, nor any other human remains excavated in a fossil condition show an essential approach to the type of the ape. (4) The doctrine of descent assumes for the sake of certain analogies genealogical relations of affinity and changes of organisms in great numbers, but not one case of a definite and permanent change of an organic species into another has been accurately observed. It assumes a process of natural selection such as a gardener or a breeder pursues; but as far as empirical knowledge goes, the character of the individual vegetable and animal species has never changed. In order to substantiate its view, its advocates postulate millions of years; but whether the epochs of geological formation really require such an immense amount of time as Darwin needed for his hypothesis is still doubted by geologists. Geology, too, shows that the specific groups of organic beings were distinct from the very beginning. The truth of the Biblical words that "God created everything after its kind," is confirmed as much by the natural life of the present world as by the facts of the former ages of geology. (5) The Darwinian hypothesis of descent does not give due consideration to the great difference between man and animal in a psychological respect. Man represents an entirely new phase of existence, being distinguished from the preceding organisms by his freedom, self-consciousness, and endowment of speech. Conservative investigators like Agassiz, Rudolf Wagner, Wigand, and Dubois-Reymond have always ridiculed the hypothesis that considers the higher nature of man the product of a purely natural development. In the same way, men like A. de Quatrefages and the French physiologists following him, E. Bouchut, Tandon, and others, and recent German critics of Darwin like Hans Driesch, Haacke, and Gustav Wolff acknowledge the radical distinction between man and animal; and Wallace, who with Darwin is the author of the theory of natural selection, holds that in the case of man, the natural selection was the work of God.

II. Unity of the Human Race: The fact that the human race descended from one pair (Gen. i. 27) is confirmed by numerous traditions of paganism. It is true, however, that there appeared also polygenism or autochthonism, the theory of eponymous ancestors (see EPONYM), which was represented especially by the Greeks and revived in the period of the Renaissance. Blumenbach opposed polygenism in his work, *De generis humani varietate nativa* (Göttingen, 1795); similarly Prichard, John Herschel, the two Humboldts, and others. Since the appearance of Darwin's doctrine of evolution the theory of monogenism has been adopted more generally. Several of the most important ethnologists, Oskar Peschel, T. Waitz, A. de Quatrefages, Keane, adhere to the theory of the unity of the human race, or at least to its origin from a common hearth, if not from one single pair. In favor of Biblical monogenism may be advanced: (1) The different races of men do not lose their power of procreation by intermarriage. Blumenbach, Buffon, Johann Müller, Waitz, Quatrefages, and others have emphasized this fact as decisive for the unity of the race. (2) Among all human races, the skeleton, the period of pregnancy, and the average duration of life are the same. (3) Apparent divergencies of the races in the formation of the skull, the quality of skin, hair, etc., may be explained by climatic conditions. (4) Linguistic objections against monogenism do not stand upon a solid basis, since in the course of hundreds and thousands of years languages are subject to considerable changes. (5) Archeology and the science of religions furnish important material for the proof of the original unity of the human race. The wide circulation of certain religious traditions in primitive history, especially of the legends of the flood, can hardly be explained otherwise than by the assumption of primitive relations of affinity. Moreover, the legends of the American people pointing to repeated immigrations of their ancestors from Eastern Asia contradict the assumptions of American autochthonism or nativism, as it was represented by George Squier, H. Bancroft, Lorenz Diefenbach, J. G. Müller, and others. (6) The different races of humanity reveal a thoroughgoing uniformity and spiritual relationship also in a psychological and ethical respect. Even the most barbarous tribes are capable of participating in the higher spiritual interests of humanity. The idea of the impotence of the Christian religion as a civilizing power over against the stupid resistance of lower races (cf. De Gobineau, *Essai sur l'inégalité des races humaines*, Paris, 1853) has been amply refuted by the activity of Christian missionaries among the savages of all parts of the world.

III. Antiquity of Man: The usual system of Biblical chronology makes the period from Adam to Christ cover 4,000 years (see TIME, BIBLICAL RECKONING OF). Such a short period seems to be inconsistent with the alleged unity of the race, but the effects of sin must not be left out of account in determining this question. There is much in the chronological tables of the Old Testament to make any calculation based upon them of questionable accuracy. There is at any rate some truth in the words of Chalmers, that "the sacred writings do not fix the antiquity of the globe," and those of Le Hir and De Sacy, "There is no Biblical chronology." It is quite possible that the lists of the patriarchs in Gen. v. and xi. are incomplete. The Bible, in fact, seems to allow for a longer duration of the human race by several thousands of years than the usually accepted chronology makes out. The records of Egyptian history seem to make an extension of the chronology necessary (see EGYPT). The primitive history of Babylonia may be traced back even further than that of Egypt. From recent discoveries in Babylonia (q.v., III., § 6), especially those of Hilprecht (since 1893) it seems to be sufficiently evident that South Babylonia possessed a royal dynasty already before Sargon, so that it may be safely assumed that the beginnings of Babylonian culture date back at least 5,000 years (see BABYLONIA, V., § 1, VI., 1–2). Of less value are the arguments based upon geological calculations according to which the age of man is measured by ten thousands of years. There is as yet no reliable geological chronometer, but it is proved by recent discoveries in caves that man must have lived at the close of the great ice period, that is, during the great geological deluge; but when this period began and when it ended, remains still a matter of uncertainty. Quatrefages justly criticizes the lavish extravagance with which many Darwinians calculate time. Even Lyell was obliged, in the later edition of his *Geological Evidences of the Antiquity of Man* (London, 1863), to modify his earlier statements. E. B. Tylor, it is true, in his *Anthropology* (London, 1881) holds that some dozens of centuries within the period of historical time are not sufficient to explain the gradual development of the distinctions of the human race, but, on the other hand, he declares the oldest human remains from the earliest stone period as "lying back out of the range of chronology."

From the very beginning the spirit of man has been the principal factor of his being. It is his true Ego. Judged according to its original conception and its higher divine destiny, humanity is a thoroughly good and noble principle; but by the invasion of sin into the development of the race its innate nobility has degenerated. Without redeeming help from above, without the intervention of the incarnate Son of God, a return to the normal and original condition would be impossible. While humanity is still far removed from the full realization of its ideal in an ethical and religious respect, faith in the final victory of the good in humanity over the evil must not be given up, as little as the striving after the highest development of culture must cease. The realm of Christ and the realm of true humanity form concentric circles; the ideal of humanity is very little distinguished from the Christian ideal of life. The true aim of humanity is rightly understood only by those of its apostles who see in the pioneers of foreign and home missions of Christianity their self-evident allies, and in the holy spirit of Christ the perfection toward which all spiritual life of humanity must tend. (O. Zöckler†.)

Bibliography: On the Biblical doctrine of man consult the works in and under the article Biblical Theology, especially the treatises by H. Schultz, and W. Beyschlag. For the treatment in systematic theology consult the section on Anthropology in the works cited under Dogma, Dogmatics. Further works in the same line are: M. Hopkins, *Outline Study of Man*, New York, 1876; idem, *Scriptural Idea of Man*, ib. 1883; J. Laidlaw, *Bible Doctrine of Man*, Edinburgh, 1879; and Bishop Butler's famous *Sermons*, new ed., Edinburgh, 1888.

From the scientific standpoint the reader is referred to the article Evolution and the literature under it, particularly the works of Darwin, Huxley, Fiske, Mivart, Wallace, Romanes, Le Conte, Weismann, Croll, McCosh, Dodson, Calderwood, Haeckel. Consult further: the Duke of Argyll, *Primeval Man*, London, 1869; L. Figuier, *Primitive Man*, ib. 1870; C. Lyell, *Antiquity of Man*, ib. 1873; H. Spencer, *Descriptive Sociology*, 8 vols., ib. 1873–1882; J. F. McLennan, *Studies in Ancient History*, ib. 1886; A. Quatrefages, *The Human Species*, ib. 1886; J. Lubbock, *The Origin of Civilization and Primitive Condition of Man*, ib. 1881; C. F. Keary, *The Dawn of History*, ib. 1888; H. Lotze, *Microcosmus*, books iv. sqq., Edinburgh, 1888; E. Clodd, *Childhood of the World*, London, 1889; G. F. Wright, *Ice-Age of America and its Bearings on the Antiquity of Man*, New York, 1889; O. Ziemssen, *Makrokosmus; Grundideen zur Schopfungsgeschichte und zu einer harmonischen Weltanschauung*, Gotha, 1893; A. H. Keane, *Ethnology*, Cambridge, 1896; B. Platz, *Der Mensch*, Leipsic, 1898; C. Gutberlet, *Der Mensch, Ursprung und Entwicklung*, Paderborn, 1903; E. B. Tylor, *Primitive Culture*, new ed., London, 1903; A. H. Wallace, *Man's Place in Nature*, New York, 1903; L. H. Morgan, *Ancient Society*, reprint, New York, 1907.

MANASSEH, ma-nas'e: Thirteenth king of Judah, son and successor of Hezekiah. His dates, according to the old chronology, are 696–641 B.C., according to Kamphausen, 685–641, according to R. Kittel (*Geschichte des Volkes Israel*, ii. 516 sqq., Gotha, 1909), 697 or 686–641. In order to understand the reign of Manasseh, it is necessary to bear in mind the events which took place toward the end of Hezekiah's reign—the inroad of Sennacherib into Judah and the rescue which followed, a result of which was a revival of faith in Yahweh. With the enthronement of Manasseh came a revulsion and a reversal of the religious tendencies, restoration of the sanctuaries closed by Hezekiah and of the heathenish or semi-heathenish rites formerly practised, particularly that of child-sacrifice. This was accompanied by a persecution of the religion of the prophets who had led in Hezekiah's reform. Manasseh was swayed more by the sentiments of the masses of the people than by the little circle of earnest followers of the Yahweh cult. Undoubtedly the chief occasion of this change was the political situation. Assyria had reached the height of its power, and the vigorous Esarhaddon sat on the throne and conducted victorious campaigns in the Syrian region and against the Phenicians, the Arabs, and the Egyptians. He was followed by his equally able son Asshurbanipal, who established the Assyrian power in those districts on a still firmer basis. Manasseh, therefore, abandoned the pro-Egyptian policy of his father and threw himself, politically and religiously, into the arms of Assyria, in spite of the predictions of the coming fall of that empire. The apparent success of the gods of Assyria influenced the religious situation, and the anti-Yahwistic acts of Manasseh were probably met by the resistance of the faithful, which resulted in the persecution of the latter. The Chronicler (II Chron. xxxiii. 1–20) reports that Manasseh was taken prisoner and carried bound to Babylon and afterward restored to his kingdom. This statement has been much questioned, since it did not seem probable that as an Assyrian prisoner Manasseh would be carried to Babylon [McCurdy, *History, Prophecy and the Monuments*, vol. ii., changes "Babylon" to "Nineveh"]; but this is answered by the fact that in his later years Asshurbanipal often dwelt at Babylon. The Chronicler also mentions that Manasseh added to the defenses of Jerusalem. (R. Kittel.)

Bibliography: The sources are II Kings xxi. 1–18 (of which verses 5 and 7–15 are by a later hand), and II Chron. xxxiii. 1–20. Consult the pertinent sections in the literature under Ahab; Israel, especially R. Kittel, ut sup.; and Kittel's commentary on Kings and Chronicles, Göttingen 1900; the articles in the Bible Dictionaries, and S. R. Driver, in D. G. Hogarth, *Authority and Archæology*, pp. 114–116, London, 1899.

MANASSEH BEN ISRAEL: Jewish theologian and patriot; b. at La Rochelle (78 m. s. of Nantes), France, in 1604; d. at Middelburg (47 m. s.w. of Rotterdam), Holland, Nov. 20, 1657. He received his education at Amsterdam, where he became a noted pulpit orator. He is best known for his service to his people by securing for them through personal intercession with Cromwell permission to settle under protection in England, erect a synagogue in London, and purchase ground there for a cemetery. His principal work was *El Conciliador* (part 1, Frankfort, 1632, parts 2–4, Amsterdam, 1641–51), an attempt to reconcile all passages in the Old Testament which seem to conflict.

Bibliography: *JE*, viii. 282–284; *DNB*, xxxvi. 13–14.

MANASSEH, PRAYER OF. See Apocrypha, A, IV., 4.

MANCHESTER, CHARLES: Church of God; b. at Burritt, Ill., Dec. 28, 1858. He was educated at Park College, Mo. (A.B., 1883), and Oberlin Theological Seminary (B.D., 1886). Having been ordained a minister in his denomination as early as 1879, he held pastorates at Mt. Carroll, Ill. (1886–1888), Decatur, Ill. (1888–89), and Milmine and Lodge, Ill. (1889–90), while from 1890 to 1896 he was preacher in a church at Barkleyville, Pa., and also principal of the academy in the same place. He was then connected with Findlay College, Findlay, O., from 1896 to 1904, being successively professor of Greek and philosophy (1896–1901), and professor of philosophy and theology (1901–04), in addition to being acting president of the same institution from 1896 to 1900, and president from that year to 1904. Since 1904 he has been pastor of a church of his denomination at Wooster, O. He was secretary of the Board of Missions of the General Eldership of the Church of God from 1893 to 1901, and was editor of the *Missionary Signal*, which he founded, from 1893 to 1896 and of the *Findlay College News* from 1897 to 1904.

MANDÆANS.

The many Gnostic sects against which the Church Fathers strove left little literature to survive till the present. The Mandæans, who still are found in scanty numbers in Persia and the region of southern Babylonia, are an exception; and their rich literature is very suggestive of the varied sources of Gnostic systems. This sect, belonging to ophitic Gnosticism, to form its system combined elements from Judaism, early Christianity, and Sassanian Parseeism with an original Babylonian and early Aramaic basis of religion. Connection is to be found also with the heretical sect of disciples of John the Baptist, and derivation is allowed by the Mandæans themselves from the Sabians of pre-Mohammedan Arabia (Koran, ii. 59, v. 73, xxii. 17). Indeed, "Sabian" is an Arabized word meaning "baptist." In their principal sacred work, the Ginza or the Sidra Rabba ("Great Book"), the Mandæans call themselves *Naṣorayya*, the "Nazarenes." In the same source the name *Mandayya* is also employed, from the word *madda'*, "knowledge," with which is combined *hayya*, "life," in the sense of *gnosis* or knowledge of life (see GNOSTICISM). Theodore bar Choni gives them other names, as *Mashkenayye*, from *Mashkena*, the Mandæan word for church; *Dosti*, from Persian *dost*, "friend"; and Adonæans, from their assumed founder, Ado, who was perhaps a reformer or leader of a party. Theodore makes Ado come from Adiabene to the district of Maishan (Mesene) on the lower Euphrates and Tigris, where he lived as a mendicant (perhaps like the Brahmanic *bhikshu* or fakir), surrounded by disciples. Ado is then said to have heard of a man named Papa on the upper course of the river Ulai (the modern Karun), of whom he sought shelter. There he settled by the wayside to beg from travelers. Theodore gives also the names of Ado's father, mother, and brothers, which names all have significance in the Mandæan religion. On account of the honor which they pay to John the Baptist, the Mandæans bear also the name Christians of St. John, though there is little in their life and nothing in their dogma which merits the name Christian, their doctrine of redemption going back to the god Marduk (see BABYLONIA, VII., 2, § 10).

1. Origin and Names.

The first knowledge of this sect in modern times was brought to Europe by the Carmelite missionary Ignatius a Jesu, who in the middle of the seventeenth century lived many years in Basra and converted some of the adherents to Christianity (see bibliography below for his book). He regarded them as descendants of disciples of John the Baptist, who had fled thither from persecution, being led to this view by the honors paid by them to the Baptist, their many legends of him, and their practise of baptizing only in rivers. He gave their number as from 20,000 to 25,000 families, scattered through Babylonia, Persia, Goa, Ceylon, and India, in the latter country reckoning to them the Thomas-Christians (Nestorians). Further information came through Abraham Ecchellensis (q.v.), the missionary Angelus a Sancto Josepho, Pietro della Valle, Jean Thévenot, Carsten Niebuhr, and others. The reports of these writers have considerable value, dealing as they do with a time when the sect was relatively large. The sources of first importance for knowledge of the Mandæans are their own writings, especially the Ginza, which are, however, only fragments of a once large religious literature. The older parts of the Ginza date back to the early Mohammedan period, 700–900 A.D. Besides the great collections of the sect, there are many tracts for priests and for laity, dealing with sickness and demoniacal possession, often employed as amulets and worn on the breast. The present Mandæan religion has, under Mohammedan influence, taken on a monotheistic form. But study of the Ginza shows that this is the result of development; the early form was polytheistic (cf. W. Brandt, *Die mandäische Religion*, Leipsic, 1889) and dealt with theogony and cosmogony; this was succeeded by a combination of Jewish-Christian sources under Indian influence. The next stage appears to have been under the ascendancy of Persian thought, especially in its eschatology, followed by a period of confusion, which in turn gave way to a monotheistic type of theology with a "Great King of Light" as the chief deity, from which the step to Allaha as God was easy.

2. Recent Reports. The System Outlined.

The earliest priestly form of the religion dealt, as did the systems of Phenicia and Babylonia, with the origins of gods and of the world. There stand out in this two forms, now distinct, now united, the "Great Fruit" (cf. Hebr. *periy*), Pira Rabba, and Mana Rabba, "Great Spirit."

Pira Rabba is the All, the comprehensive basis of things, bounded only by itself, from which all things came. It is the "golden egg" of the Brahmanic cosmogony which, at first a unit in which rests Brahma or Purusha, divides into heaven and earth. It is regarded as an independent and spontaneous deity and as creator. This is a conception not peculiar to India and the Mandæans. With Pira Rabba is closely connected Ayar Ziwa Rabba, "Great Lustrous Ether" (cf. Syr. *a'ar*, Gk. *aēr*), or Yora Rabba, "Great Brilliance," from which last sprang the "Great Jordan" or stream of heaven. In Pira Ayar appears as a personal spirit Mana Rabba de eḳara, "Great Spirit of Excellence," usually called in the system Mana Rabba (ut sup.). While the origin and meaning of this last term are not clear, derivations are given from the Indo-Persian *man*,

3. The Earliest Theogony and Cosmogony.

"thought," and Arabic *ma'na*, "mind," "meaning." It probably corresponds to the Indian *atman*, "principle of life or individuality." With it, as female potency, Demutha, "image," is joined, and a triad of Pira-Ayar, Mana Rabba, and Demutha is formed. Thus far no visible world or life existed, only the transcendental. Hence there appears Ḥayye Kadmaye, "First Life," formed from Mana Rabba; and in Mandæan prayers he is always the first invoked. From him proceeded the countless emanations of gods, eons, and angels, whose task it was to create the visible world. (This theogony is not the only one present in the system, since other parts speak of a Nitufta, "Material of Life," corresponding to Ḥayye Kadmaye; another name given is Nebat, "sprout," who creates 800 eons and other beings.) From Mana Rabba proceed in fantastic completeness other Manas, called also Piras, more commonly Uthriyye (Uthras), "dominions" or "powers." From "First Life" emanated Ḥayye Tinyaniyye, "Second Life," called also Yoshamin (cf. Hebr. *shamayim*, "heavens"), who evoked Uthras, erected dwellings, and called a "Jordan" into existence. Three of these Uthras desired to enter upon the work of creation, to which Second Life agreed, but First Life was averse and called into existence Kebar Rabba or Manda de ḥayye, "Spirit of Life," which personifies knowledge of life. This last creation becomes the center of Mandæan theology and its preexistent Christ, with which Hibil Ziwa, the power acting as redeemer in the world of fact, was identified. Yet this redemption and this "Christ" are not at all parallel to the conceptions carried by the same names in the Christian system. Manda de ḥayye is to be derived from Marduk, and his work may be equated with Marduk's in vanquishing the monster Tiamat. Many epithets applied to Marduk are applied also to Manda de ḥayye, such as "beloved son," "good shepherd," "word of life"; and, like Marduk, Manda de ḥayye became potent in creation, acting in opposition to the presumptuous Uthras and Second Life. Before this, however, he had to make a "descent into hell," during which he came into conflict with the powers of darkness, including one Ruḥa (Heb. *ruaḥ*, the "Spirit of God" of Gen. i. 2, converted by the Mandæans in their anti-Christian bias into a chief devil), conquered them and appointed as their punishment that their food should be fire and their drink foul water. He created Gabriel, who was to be the demiurge (known also as Petahil, who appears elsewhere as an emanation of "Second Life"). The seven planets and the twelve signs of the zodiac are created, land, water, and the firmament follow in order, then the first man, in whose creation Hibil, Sitil, and Anos (cf. the Biblical Abel, Seth, and Enos), "brothers" of Manda de ḥayye, cooperate, after which they marry Adam to Eve. The "seven" (planets) attempt to lead the pair into sin, but are prevented by the creators of man; vain attempts are also made to destroy man. Yet the evil spirits maintain their hold on the world, the "twelve" (zodiacal signs) divide the world-age among themselves, and the "seven" found false religions and call into existence beasts of prey and other evil beings.

4. Later Theogony and Cosmogony.

When the religion began to develop toward monotheism (ut sup., § 2, end), the divine figures took another form. Pira, Ayar, Yora, and Mana disappear, and instead of them the "great king of light" reigns alone. The portrayal of the world of light, in which this being sits enthroned, agrees with the Manichean picture of the "kings of the paradise of light." The address to him at the beginning of the Ginza is noteworthy: "Praised, blessed, glorified, celebrated and highly honored be thou, O god of truth, whose might is great, who hast no bounds, who art pure glory and sheer light which nothing dims; a gracious, approachable and spiritual existence [art thou], a kind deliverer of all who are faithful, supporting and upholding all good in strength and wisdom." The bridge to the creation of the visible world is found, according to this phase of Mandæan thought, in the unfolding of the light-god in his shining ether. From this early epitome of light go forth the numerous eons (*'Uthre*, "splendors"), Second Life, sometimes called Yoshamin ("Yahweh of the heavens"), then Manda de ḥayye, the life-spirit, mediator and savior of Mandæan theology, the first man. Second Life seeks to gain supremacy over First Life, fails, and is exiled from the world of pure ether into that of dimmer light. Then there issue a series of emanations, the first of whom are Hibil, Sitil and Anos (ut sup.). The last is John the Baptist. These appear both as brothers and as sons of Manda de ḥayye, and also in other relationships. Of these Hibel, or Hibil Ziwa, is the most celebrated. He receives the same titles as Manda, has the same activity, and indeed is merged as though he were the same being. From Second Life also emanate sons, the last one named variously Third Life and Abathur, the "Ancient One," also called Father of Uthra. He sits at the outermost bound of the world of light, where is the great gate which leads to the middle and lower regions; there he weighs the deeds of the departed who come to him, returning to the lower regions those spirits whose deeds prove too light, while to the others Abathur opens the way to the higher regions of light. In the beginning there was under Abathur an immense void, and at the bottom the troubled black water. As he looked into this and saw his image reflected, Petahil (the material nature of the deep of Chaos) came into existence as his son to become the demiurge of the Mandæans, equivalent to the Yaldabaoth ("Chaos-son") of the Ophites. He was commanded by his father to create the earth and man. Some passages make him do this alone, others assign to him demons as his helpers, especially the seven spirits of the planets. From this point confusion exists as to the sequence of events. Here begin "the entanglements of Mandæan theology" (A. J. H. W. Brandt, ut. sup., pp. 48–55). The course of action follows in part the usual Semitic cosmogony—Petahil erects the heaven, reduces the diffused, floating matter into form as the earth and fixes it in position, and creates the bodies of Adam and

Eve, but can not give them life, which was accomplished by Hibil, Sitil, and Anos, who obtained life from Mana Rabba. Petahil, because of his failure, was by his father Abathur excluded from the world of light until the judgment day, when he will be raised by Hibil, be baptized and made king of the Uthras, and receive worship.

The underworld, described in the Ginza, consists of four entrances and three hells. Each of the entrances is governed by a king and queen. The kingdom of darkness is divided into three stories, each ruled by an old king. These kings, named from above downward, are S'dum, the "Warrior," Giv, the "Great," and Krun or Karkum, the oldest and mightiest, most often called the "Great Mountain of Flesh." The entrances to hell contain filthy, slimy water; in hell there is no water, and in the lowest hell (Krun's) there are only ashes, dust, and vacancy. In these regions fire continually burns, but, though it consumes, it gives no light. From these kings Hibil Ziwa took away all power by descending, clothed with the might of the god of light, Mana Rabba, into the lowest hell and wresting from Krun the knowledge of the secret name of darkness (see NAME). Above the entrances to hell is the dwelling-place of Ruḥa, a mighty she-devil, mother of Kin, queen of the fourth entrance. She was brought out from the underworld by Hibil and prevented from returning thither. The conception of Ruḥa finely illustrates Mandæan hostility to Christianity, since she is the Syriac *ruha deḳudsha*, "the Holy Ghost" (cf. Gen. i. 2). She corresponds to the Manichean Ḥawwa (Eve). She is the mother of Ur, Fire, the most fearful of all devils, corresponding to the original devil of the Manicheans. Ur attempted to take by storm the world of light, but was by Hibil cast back into the "black waters," chained there, and surrounded by seven iron and seven golden walls. While Petahil was engaged in the work of creation, Ruḥa bore to her son Ur first seven sons, then twelve, and finally five more, all of whom Petahil set in the heavens, the seven as the planets, the twelve as the zodiacal signs, while what the five were is as yet undetermined. The planets are the sun, Venus, Mercury, the moon, Saturn, Jupiter, and Mars, and the names given to the last five are the old Babylonian names. These planets were set in the seven heavens; the sun is the ruler and is in the middle (fourth) heaven. They were intended by the creator to be helpers of man, but instead they sought to do him harm. They are the sources of evil. They have their stations to which they return after completing their heavenly journeys, and these stations are fixed on anvils which rest upon the belly of the conquered Ur. Heaven is by the Mandæans regarded as created out of the purest, clearest water, but so solidified that even the diamond will not cut it. On this water the planets and other stars sail; these are all, like evil demons, dark by nature, but are illuminated by radiant crosses carried by angels. The clearness of the firmament enables man to look through all seven heavens to the polar star, the central sun about which the other bodies revolve, and to which Mandæans turn their face at prayer. The earth they regard as a circle, inclining somewhat to the south, and surrounded on three sides by the sea. On the north is a great mountain of turquoise, the reflection of which causes the sky to appear blue. Behind this mountain is the world of the blessed, a kind of lower paradise, where the Egyptians reside who did not perish with Pharaoh in the Red Sea. They are regarded as the ancestors of the Mandæans, since Pharaoh had been high priest and king of the Mandæans. Both worlds are surrounded by the Yamma rabba d'suf, the outer sea.

5. Mandæan Cosmology.

The period of duration of the earth is fixed at 480,000 years, divided into seven epochs, each of which is governed by a planet. According to the Ginza, the human race has been three times destroyed by water, fire, sword, and pestilence, only one couple remaining alive after each time. At the time of Noah, the world was 466,000 years old. After him rose many false prophets. The first prophet was Abraham, who came 6,000 years after Noah, when the sun ruled the world. Then came Moses, in whose time the Egyptians had the true religion. After him came Solomon, to whom the demons yielded obedience. The third false prophet is Yishu Mesiḥa (i.e., Jesus the Messiah), the planet Mercury, a sorcerer. Forty-two years before him lived, under King Pontius Pilate, the only true prophet, Yahya, or Yuhana bar Zikaryâ (i.e., John, son of Zacharias; Luke i. 13), whose mother was Enishbai (Elizabeth); Yahya, being deceived by the Messiah, baptized him. He is an incarnation of Hibil, who had preached repentance in the time of Noah. As a contemporary of the Messiah and John the Baptist lived Anos Uthra, a younger brother of Hibil, who had descended from heaven, was baptized by John, wrought miracles, healed the sick, raised the dead, was the cause of the crucifixion of the false Messiah, proclaimed the true religion, and, before his return to the world of lights, sent 360 prophets into the world to proclaim his teaching. Jerusalem, which was once built at the command of Adunay̑ (Adonai), was destroyed by Anos, while the Jews were dispersed into all the world, having killed John the Baptist. Two hundred and forty years after the appearance of the Messiah, 60,000 Mandæans came out of the world of Pharaoh. Their high priest settled in Damascus, and their sacred writings are concealed there in the cupola of the mosque of the Omayyade. The last of the false prophets was Mohammed, called "the Perverter." After 4,000 or 5,000 years, mankind will again be destroyed by a terrific storm; but the earth will be again repeopled by a man and a woman from the upper world, whose descendants will dwell on earth for 50,000 years in piety and virtue. Then will Ur destroy the earth and the other middle worlds, after which, bursting asunder, he will fall into the abyss of darkness, to be annihilated there with all worlds and powers of darkness. Then the universe will become a realm of light, enduring forever.

6. Chronology and Eschatology.

The weekly holy day of the Mandæans is Sunday, which is celebrated by abstention from work and by divine service, with reading of the scriptures by the priest. Modern travelers record the use of Thursday also as holy and as sacred to Hibil Ziwa.

7. System of Ceremonial. The Ginza does not enjoin other sacred seasons, but it seems clear that certain festivals have been long in use. New Year's Day is mentioned in the Ginza as a time to abstain from ablutions in running water, probably on the ground that on that day the angel who protects the waters is engaged in celebrating a festival and consequently the evil powers find their opportunity for assailing men; Mandæans are therefore on that day not to leave the house and especially not to approach water. Yet scholars testify to the celebration of a New Year's festival, called Nauruz rabba, beginning on the first day of the first winter month and continuing six days, or seven, if with them be reckoned the last day of the old year. On the first day of the year the priests and scholars forecast the prospects of that year. From the eighteenth to the twenty-second of the fourth month is celebrated the feast of the ascension of Hibil Ziwa from the regions of darkness to his own realm of light. The five days intercalated between the eighth and ninth months of the year are a great festival of baptism during which all Mandæans must bathe three times daily, before meals, and dress wholly in white. The first day of the eleventh month is a feast in honor of the 360 Uthras. The first day of the fifth month is employed to commemorate the Egyptians who perished in the Red Sea. The last day of the old year is preparatory to the New Year's festival. The Mandæan year is solar, divided into twelve months of thirty days each, with five days intercalated between the eighth and ninth months. The year is further divided into seasons of three months each, beginning with winter. The week has seven days, named after the planets. In the matter of the time for prayer there is some contradiction; one passage seems to require it three times a day and twice in the night, another seems to forbid it during the darkness. Prohibition of fasting appears as a mark of opposition to Christianity, though a pretense of fasting is said now to be made because of fear of the Mohammedans. Yet spiritual fasts are enjoined in keeping the members and organs of the body from sinning; moreover, there are times when the priests abstain from flesh. Mandæans may not eat of the blood of animals, of anything that is pregnant, or of that which still has life or which a beast of prey has pulled down. What has been killed with iron, cleansed, and purified is edible, provided it has not been prepared by others than the faithful. There is no distinction made between what in the natural world is clean and unclean, since "all things which Petahil has made were made for Adam." Of Mandæan sacraments the chief is baptism, with which is bound up communion. Unbaptized children are not reckoned as belonging to the Mandæan community. Baptism must be performed in running water and not in pools or tanks, and is by complete and trine immersion. The baptism of adults is required in a great number of cases; when demanded by an act of consecration or of sin, on Sunday and festivals, on return from a foreign land, after contact with a corpse, after being bitten by a snake or a wild animal, or when a ceremony has been omitted. In the Eucharist are used two elements, corresponding to the Host and wine of Catholic ceremonial. Its purpose is to consecrate the participant by imparting special strength. Prerequisities are baptism, good repute, and adherence to the Mandæan faith. It is received at the festivals. The bread is prepared from fine white flour by priests, without salt or leaven, divided into small portions, and baked in a new oven. It is kept in the priest's house, and is received directly into the mouth from the priest's fingers. Another usage connected with baptism and with Sunday observance is the giving of the hand, called by the Mandæans *kusta* ("fidelity"), which may be understood from a corresponding Manichean custom to signify mutual support. As a provision against sudden death, unprovided with the common consecration, there is a sort of mass for the soul by the bishop, by which the beneficiary is obligated to an ascetic life. The church building proper of the Mandæans is for the priests and their helpers only; the laity remain at the entrance. It is small, holding only a very few persons, has only two windows, and the door is always at the south, so that the entrant may look at the North Star. It contains no altar and no ornament, but has a few shelves in the corners for vessels. It is always near running water. At the consecration of a church a dove is sacrificed—a trace of the old Ishtar worship. The injunction to marry and people the earth is stringent, and condemnation of Christian asceticism severe.

8. The Clergy. The Mandæan ministry has three grades. The first is that of *Shkanda*, deacon. The candidate must be without physical blemish, and is generally taken from the family of a priest or a bishop. He undergoes a preliminary training of twelve years under priests, accompanying them on their journeys, and at the age of nineteen is ordained and begins to assist the priest or bishop in the services. After a year in this grade, he is admitted to the second grade, that of *Tarmida*, priest or presbyter, being ordained by a bishop and two priests or by four priests empowered by the bishop, but only on condition that the candidate is approved by the community. The period of probation involves a trial lasting over at least sixty-two days, and may through inadvertence or accident in the conduct of the trial be prolonged for several months. A part of the ceremony is bathing three times daily in a river in full clothing, the wet robes being changed only after the candidate has completed a ritual of prayer. The ordination is terminated by baptism, in which the candidate's wife and mother participate, if they are still living, and a feast in which presents are given to the poor. The highest grade is *Ganzivra*, "treasurer," or bishop. The candidate, who is chosen from among the presbyters, must show his ability to explain difficult passages in the Mandæan scriptures. Still another grade is reported by Petermann, that of *Rish amma*, "head of the people," a rank corresponding to that of patriarch or pope. This grade, according to the Mandæans, has been filled only twice, once before

John the Baptist by Pharaoh, and once since, by a certain Adam abu al-farash, both of whom were not of this world but came from the upper world. Women are admitted to the clergy. They enter the diaconate as virgins and become presbyters only after marriage with one of the higher orders. The official dress of the clergy is white throughout, consisting of breeches, tunic, girdle, stole, and turban, and on the little finger of the right hand the priest wears a gilt and the bishop a golden ring, on which is inscribed *shum Yawar ziwar,* " name of Yawar Ziwa," i.e., of Hibil Ziwa. In exercising their ministerial functions the clergy go barefooted.

9. Last Rites; the Soul's Hap.

Man consists of three parts, the body, the animal soul, and the heavenly soul. On the approach of death a Mandæan is attended by a deacon and two or more nurses, is bathed with warm and then with cold water, and then clothed in the funeral robes consisting of seven pieces. The body is laid out with the head to the south so that the eyes are directed to the polar star, and the grave is dug so that the body maintains the same position, and prayers are offered at the interment. The soul of the dead passes out of the earth-region into the sphere of light, and according to some passages of the scriptures is accompanied by an Uthra, who comes for that purpose from the kingdom of light, finally passing a stream which constitutes the last hindrance to its approach to the " house of life." At the door of this house sits Abathur with his scales to weigh the deeds of the departed; after passing this ordeal, the soul is received and clothed in garments of light. Those whose deeds do not permit their reception are remitted to the lower regions, there to receive punishment of stripes without end. The end of the world is called " the day of the end " and " the second death," and is brought about by the serpent Leviathan which destroys all not belonging to the world of light and the earth itself. Mandæans are not willing to disclose their beliefs to strangers for fear of arousing the fanaticism of the Mohammedans. Part of the knowledge gained came through the son of a priest who became a convert to Roman Catholicism and communicated information to M. N. Siouffi, the French consul in Mosul 1874–75.

10. Present Conditions; the Language.

While in the seventeenth century the numbers of the Mandæans were given at about 20,000 families, at present there is only a small remnant of about 1,500 persons, living south of Bagdad along the Tigris and Euphrates and in Khuzistan, plying the trades of goldsmiths, blacksmiths, builders, and carpenters. They are not to be confused with the Mohammedan sect of Nosairiyah in Lebanon. Externally the Mandæans do not distinguish themselves from Mohammedans. Since the latter arrogate to themselves white clothing, which the Ginza regards as holy, Mandæans usually wear brown raiment or brown with white stripes. Mandæans speak Arabic or Persian, but the language of their scriptures is an Aramaic dialect of great value for the student of language and is related lexically and grammatically to that of the Babylonian Talmud and to the Nabatæan tongue. It was probably the native tongue of Mani, and the Ginza doubtless contains long passages from the Manichean writings (see MANI, MANICHEANS, § 13). Nevertheless, the pronunciation as at present employed by Mandæans has not been correctly transmitted. The vocabulary is Aramaic in groundwork, with loan words from Jewish, Syrian-Christian, and especially Persian sources, while the later writings are mixed with Arabic. The alphabet, which probably arose in Babylonia and combines the early Aramaic and Palmyrene elements, has twenty-two letters.

11. Sources of Mandæan Doctrines.

The origins of Mandæan doctrine, it must firmly be maintained, are to be sought in the religion of Babylonia; and Babylonia itself was the place where it arose. A Jewish or Christian source in Palestine is out of the question. Mandæans are not the descendants of the disciples of John the Baptist, although he and the Jordan are so frequently mentioned in their writings. The tradition of the people themselves that they arose in Galilee, were persecuted in Jerusalem and driven thence by the caliphs is historically worthless. They are to be compared with such sects as the Hemerobaptists of the Church Fathers (Eusebius, *Hist. eccl.*, IV., xxii. 6; *NPNF*, 2 ser., i. 199; Epiphanius, *Hær.* xvii.; " Clementine Recognitions," i. 54: " Some even of the disciples of John, who seem to be great ones, have separated themselves from the people and proclaimed their own master as the Christ "; *ANF*, viii. 92). The reputed founder and other Biblical characters and coloring have come into the religion through the syncretistic process. To connect them with these early sects is no more right than to associate them with the *Nazaraioi* of Epiphanius (*Hær.* xviii.). The mistake arose in the misapprehension of missionaries of the seventeenth century, who mistook them for a kind of Christians on account of their practise of baptism and related them with the Baptist and with Galilee. It is true that during the second and third centuries the religion passed through a period of sympathetic feeling for Christianity and was influenced by its ritual. Thus Biblical reminiscences and nomenclature, from Adam to John and Jesus, including even the terminology of parts of the Jewish ritual, went to the building of the Mandæan scriptures and teaching. But the antichristian bias appears in making Moses a false prophet, Jesus the evil planet Mercury, and the Holy Ghost the most devilish evil spirit, as well as in the polemics against Christian monasticism and other Christian institutions. Still more observable is the antijudaic bias, especially in the utter abhorrence of circumcision. While the constant use of the name " Jordan " might seem to imply derivation of the sect from people who once dwelt on that river, the usage is to be compared with that in Hippolytus (*Hær.* v. 2; *ANF*, v. 52), where the " great Jordan " is employed in the Naassene system to express the idea of the great sanctifying element of life in the world of light. Thus the name of the Biblical Jordan was employed in the earliest Gnostic systems, and notably in that of the Peratæ (who were in the Euphrates region), who also employed "Egyptians" and "Red Sea" in just such a metaphorical sense as did the Mandæans. Indeed, the question of the sources of Mandæism is just that of the sources of Ophitism and Gnosticism in general. These systems are not traceable to the teachings of the Persian Zarathustra, nor to Phenician heathenism, nor to the Greek mysteries, but simply to the Babylonian-Chaldean national religion, which was domiciled in the region where Ophites, Peratæ, and Mandæans lived, and where they were distinguished from Christians (cf. W. Anz, *Zur Frage nach der Ursprung des Gnostizismus*, pp. 59 sqq., Leipsic, 1897). While some fundamental conceptions are changed, as when the names of Babylonian deities become the names of the planets and are regarded as evil spirits, yet the derivation is so clear upon investigation that no doubt can be entertained upon this point.

12. Babylonian and Manichean Ideas Borrowed.

The Mandæan baptism can not be derived from the Jewish baptism of proselytes, nor is it Christian baptism taken over and exaggerated; the Mandæan practise is diametrically opposed to both. Christian baptism implies *metanoia*, ethical rebirth, and it marks the inauguration of an ethical renewing of the heart after the pattern of the Savior; the Mandæan rite, so frequently repeated, is a theurgic-magical operation and aims at an ever-increasing insight into the secrets of the kingdom of light through the mediation of water, the element of the king of light. The Mandæan light-god Mana Rabba is to be identified with the Babylonian Ea (see BABYLONIA, VII., 2, § 3), and his emanation Manda de ḥayye or his son Hibil Ziwa with Ea's son Marduk (see BABYLONIA, VII., 2, § 10). Ea, the god of profound knowledge, father of the mediator Marduk, enthroned in the world-sea, whose holy element is water, is the Ea of the brilliant ocean of heaven, as comes out in the Ayar-yora and the heavenly Jordan of the Mandæans. Similarly, as Marduk, the conqueror of Tiamat, appears in various incarnations like that of Gilgamesh, so do Hibil Ziwa and his successors. The parallels of Ishtar's descent into hell and that of Hibil Ziwa, the division of the planetary worlds into a system of seven, and the seat of Ea in the North with the Mandæan direction of worship to that quarter are sufficiently obvious. Similar relationship can be established with Manicheanism. Mani was in his youth an adherent of the Babylonian *Mu'tasilah* ("baptizers"), an early Babylonian sect. Palestinian Hemerobaptists, Elkesaites (q.v.), Nazarenes, and Ebionites (q.v.) were sects which propagated in the West under Jewish influence Babylonian ideas, especially those of a mediator and the closely connected rite of baptism; these sects took form in pre-Christian times and later were hostile to Christianity. John the Baptist gave to the rite of baptism, thus derived, a new ethical content by connecting with it the Old-Testament expectation of a Messiah. Similarly the second sacrament of the Mandæans, the Eucharist, must be explained upon usage grounded in nature-religions, in honor paid to the pure elements of nature and its gifts, and not as a perversion of the Christian mystery. The original teaching of Mani could not have been very different in this matter from the common Mandæan-Gnostic doctrine (see MANI, MANICHEANS). The conception of eons and of the *ruḥ al-ḥayat*, "spirit of life," are alike in the two systems (cf. the Valentinian *Zōē*). Similarly the work of the original man in combating the original devil is practically the same in Mandæism and Manicheanism, though the former has made the development more complex by introducing a stratum of Aramaic thought in the names of angels and devils. While, then, the religious system of the Mandæans has especial interest rather in connection with the universal history of religion than with the theology of Christianity, yet there is much in it which can shed light upon the history of doctrine. In particular, the form of the Mandæan sacraments affords ground for thought to the investigator of the history of the Christian sacrament of baptism. (K. KESSLER.)

BIBLIOGRAPHY: The *Ginza*, called also the *Sidra rabba*, is best consulted in the ed. of H. Petermann, *Thesaurus sive liber magnus, vulgo "Liber Adami,"* vol. i., Berlin, 1867, vol. ii., Leipsic, 1867 (based on a comparison of four MSS. of 16th and 17th centuries). A prior ed. was by M. Norberg, *Codex Nasaræus, liber Adami appellatus*, vols. i.–iv., Copenhagen, vol. v (onomasticon), Lund, 1817 (misleading, being a Syriac transcription, but has Latin transl.). A Germ. transl., with notes, has been issued by W. Brandt, Göttingen, 1893, and the same scholar gives the titles of the tracts or books of which the *Ginza* is composed in his very scholarly *Mandäische Religion*, pp. 207–209, Leipsic, 1889. Other Mandæan writings published are: *Qolasta*, by J. Euting, Stuttgart, 1867 (a liturgical work); parts of the *Sidra de Yahya* ("Book of John"), in Germ. transl. by G. W. Lorsbach, in *Beiträgen zur Philosophie und Geschichte*, v (1799), 1–44. Mandæan inscriptions have been published: H. Pognon, *Inscriptions mandaïtes des coupes de Khouabir*, 2 vols., Paris, 1898–99 (cf. the review by M. Lidzbarski in *TLZ*, 1899); idem, *Une incantation contre les genies malfaisants en Mandaïte*, Paris, 1892; M. Lidzbarski, in *Ephemeris für semitische Epigraphik*, i. 1 (1900), 89–106; cf. J. H. Mordtmann and D. H. Müller, *Sabäische Denkmäler*, Vienna, 1883.

For early reports concerning the Mandæans consult: F. Ignatius a Jesu, *Narratio originis, rituum et errorum Christianorum S. Joannis*, Rome, 1652; Abraham Ecchellensis, *Eutychius patriarcha Alexandrinus vindicatus*, pp. 310–336, Rome, 1660; Jean Thévenot, *Voyage au Levant*, Paris, 1664; J. Chardin. *Journal du voyage en Perse*, London, 1686; C. Niebuhr, *Reisebeschreibung nach Arabien und andern . Ländern*, 3 vols., Hamburg, 1774–1837, Eng. transl., 2 vols., Edinburgh, 1792. The two important modern works, besides that of W. Brandt, ut sup., are by H. J. Petermann, *Reisen im Orient*, 2 vols., Leipsic, 1861; and M. N. Siouffi, *Études sur la religion des Soubbas ou Sabéens, leurs dogmes, leurs mœurs*, Paris, 1880. Not to be overlooked is W. Brandt, in *JPT*, xviii (1892), 405–438, 575–603. Consult further: J. Matter, *Hist. du gnosticisme*, ii. 394–422, Paris, 1828; L. E. Burckhardt, *Les Nazoréens ou Mandai-Jahja* (*disciples de Jean*), Strasburg, 1840 (based on Norberg); D. Chwolsohn, *Die Ssabier*, i. 100–138, St. Petersburg, 1856; J. M. Chevalier Lycklama, *Voyages . dans la Mésopotamie*, vol. iii., book 3, chap. iv., Paris, 1868; Babelon, in *Annales de philosophie chrétienne*, 1881; E. Bischoff, *Im Reiche der Gnosis. Die mystischen Lehren des jüdischen und christlichen Gnosticismus, Mandäismus und Manichäismus und ihr babylonisch-astraler Ursprung*, Leipsic, 1906; an important body of magazine literature is indicated in Richardson, *Encyclopaedia*, pp. 674–675; *Encyclopædia Britannica*, xv. 407. For the language: T. Nöldeke, *Mandäische Grammatik*, Halle, 1875; idem, in *Abhandlungen der Göttinger Gesellschaft*, 1862; H. Pognon, *Inscriptions*, ut. sup., pp. 257–308.

MANDE, mān'de, **HENDRIK**: Dutch mystic of the Windesheim community; b. at Dort c. 1360; d. in the monastery of Sion, near Beverwijk, 1431.

Very little is known regarding his life. When his biographer, Jan Busch (q.v.), entered the monastery of Windesheim, Mande was already an old man. All known of his early life is that he was physically frail and weak and that his education enabled him to fill the position of court scribe with William VI., count of Holland, under difficult conditions. He was deeply impressed by Groote's sermons (see Groote, Geert), and, as a result of visions of the Crucified One with his stigmata, he resolved to enter a monastery and chose that of Windesheim at Deventer, taking the vows in 1395. On account of his health he never became *canonicus*, in spite of the great veneration inspired by his visions and his gracious personality. He cultivated intimate relations with the prominent members of the new devotion. In a little tractate he has given an account of his visions; this Busch translated into Latin and added some accounts of the author derived from his associates. In the monastery—which he rarely left, and only in its service—he occupied himself with copying manuscripts. His death occurred during a journey with Busch directed by the authorities at Windesheim.

Of Mande's writings in French and German, composed for the brethren, fourteen are mentioned by Busch. They did not become widely known in spite of their graceful diction and depth of meaning. Mande was strongly influenced by Ruysbroeck, but was simpler and more easily understood. He was indeed called the Ruysbroeck of northern Holland. Only in 1854 were his writings rediscovered. They are as follows: *Liber unus quomodo veterem hominem cum actibus suis eruere debemus et Christo nos unire.* The Dutch manucript was found by G. Visser and printed in his *H. Mande. Bijdrage töt de Kennis der Noord-Nederlandsche Mystiek*, The Hague, 1899. *Liber de intimis domini nostri J. Christi et septem viis quibus itur ad ea,* found by S. Becker and published by C. K. de Bazel, Leyden, 1886, new ed. in Visser, ut sup. Mande refers to Bonaventura's *Itinerarium mentis*, more especially to the section *de septem itineribus æternitatis. Liber de perfecta amoris altitudine et de viis ad eam perveniendi*, ed. Visser after a Brussels manuscript. *De sapida sapientia*, according to Visser; it exists in an Amsterdam manuscript and treats of the seven gifts, under the title: *Van der gave der smakender wijsheit. Speculum veritatis*, also in the Amsterdam manuscript, *Een spiegel der waerheit*, printed in Visser, ut sup., appendix V.; *De luce veritatis*, extant in the same manuscript; *De tribus statibus hominis conversi, in quibus consistit perfectio vitæ spiritualis.* This is Mande's most important and best known writing, based on Joel ii. 12, 13. In it Mande has explained his whole conception of the spiritual life. *Amorosa querela amantis animæ Deum suum pro liberatione tenebrarum defectuumque suorum*, extant in several manuscripts and printed by W. Moll in the *Kalender voor Protestanten in Nederland*, 1860, p. 113. *Allocutio brevis amantis animæ cum amato suo*, printed in W. Moll's *Joh. Brugmann*, i. 310, Amsterdam, 1854. *De preparatione internæ nostræ habitationis*, in Moll, *Brugmann*, i. 293. *Dialogus sive collocutio devotæ animæ cum Deo amato suo et responsio ejus ad animam devotam*, supposed by Visser to be in the third part of an Amsterdam manuscript (cf. Visser, ut sup.). *De raptibus et collocutionibus cum Deo et Dei secum decem* (cf. Visser, in the *Nederlandsche Archief van Kerkgeschiedenis*, 1901, p. 249. In the issue for 1902 the *dietsche text van H. M. apokalypsis* is printed).

Of the writings mentioned by Busch there are missing *De vita spirituali et devota* and *De vita contemplativa;* these are probably developments of parts of the *De tribus statibus.* The tractate *Van den gheesteliken opgave*, found by Borssum in Amsterdam and published in the *Archief* for 1896, has not yet been proved to be by Mande.

According to Busch, all the writings of Mande enumerated were written in his own hand but without the addition of his name. During the disorders succeeding the Reformation and the suppression of the monasteries the tradition of authorship was lost. Mande's mysticism as described by Visser is less grandiose than Ruysbroeck's. Mande is simpler, more sentimental, and more Biblical, and he may be looked upon as the precursor of Thomas à Kempis, who popularized him. L. Schulze.

Bibliography: The one source is the *Chronicon Windeshemense* of J. Busch, ed. K. Grube, Halle, 1887. Consult W. Moll, *J. Brugmann*, i. 260, Amsterdam, 1854; idem, *Kerkgeschiedenis van Nederland voor de Hervorming*, 2 vols., ib. 1864–71; J. G. R. Acquoy, *Het Klooster te Windesheim*, i. 260, Utrecht, 1875; *ADB*, xx. 165; above all, the monograph by G. Visser mentioned in the text.

MANDEVILLE, BERNARD. See Deism.

MANEGOLD OF LAUTENBACH: German Augustinian monk; b. about 1060; d. after 1103, probably on May 24. At an early age he entered the cloister of Gebweiler in Alsace, but when it was destroyed by partizans of Henry IV., he went, after a period of wandering, to Bavaria about 1086, and found refuge in the cloister of Raitenbach. After 1090 he lived in the cloister of Marbach, near Colmar in Alsace, ultimately becoming prior, and opposing Henry to the very last. The great importance attached to the pamphlet of the scholastic Wenrich of Treves (q.v.) moved Manegold to compose his *Liber ad Gebehardum* (*MGH*, *Lib. de lite*, i., 1890, 308–430), dedicated to Archbishop Gebhard of Salzburg, and written in the lifetime of Gregory VII., though not published until after his death. Manegold reveals himself as an enthusiastic partizan of the Gregorian party, and upholds the pope's views in all the disputes of the period, though from a radically democratic platform. Thus royalty, in his view, is not an ordinance of God, but an office bestowed by the people, and the relation between king and people is in the nature of a treaty, breach of which by the king enables the people to recede from the treaty and to dissolve the subject relation. In the light of these principles, Manegold vindicated the pope's right to release the Germans from their oath of allegiance to Henry IV., though without being clear concerning the relation of such an exercise of popular sovereignty to the papal act of nullifying the oath. In his *Opusculum contra Wolfelmum Coloniensem* (ed. A. Muratori, *Anecdota*, iv. 163–208, Padua, 1713; cf. *Lib. de lite*, i. 303–308), Manegold assails the assumption of a compatibility of the teachings of the ancient philosophers with Christian dogma.

Manegold of Lautenbach has often been confused with the philosopher Manegold (*Histoire littéraire de la France*, ix. 280–290, Paris, 1750), who probably likewise came from Alsace, and gained much renown as a teacher in France between 1070 and 1090. CARL MIRBT.

BIBLIOGRAPHY: W. von Giesebrecht, in *Sitzungsberichte der Münchener Akademie*, 1868, ii. 297–330; N. Paulus, in *Revue catholique d'Alsace*, 1886, pp. 209–221, 279–289, 337–345; W. Martens, *Gregor VII.*, Leipsic, 1894; C. Mirbt, *Die Publizistik im Zeitalter Gregors VII.*, passim, ib. 1894; G. Meyer von Knonau, *Jahrbücher des deutschen Reichs unter Heinrich IV und V.*, vol. iii., ib. 1900; J. A. Endres, in *Historisch-politische Blätter*, cxxvii (1901), 389–401, 486–495; G. Koch, *Manegold von Lautenbach*, Berlin, 1902; *KL*, viii. 597–598.

MANETHO: Egyptian historian. He was probably a native of Sebennytus, chief town of the nome of that name, flourished in the third century B.C., during the reign of Ptolemy Soter and possibly of Ptolemy Philadelphus, and was a priest of On (Heliopolis). He wrote in Greek for the temple archives an "Epitome of Things Physical," on Egyptian philosophy and theology, and what is cited by Josephus (*Ant.* I., iii. 9) as "Egyptian History." Only fragments of these works are extant, in citations. Of the "Epitome" the most extensive fragments are in Plutarch's *De Iside et Osiri* (chaps. viii., ix., xlix., lxii., lxxiii.). Of the "History" the most important fragment is a catalogue of the kings of Egypt of dynasties I.–XXX. (Menes–Nectanebo II.), preserved in part in Julius Africanus and Eusebius. The fragments have been collected in C. and T. Müller, *Fragmenta historicorum Græcorum*, vol. ii (Paris, 1848).

BIBLIOGRAPHY: F. J. Lauth, *Manetho und der Turiner Königspapyrus*, Munich, 1865; G. F. Unger, *Chronologie des Manetho*, Berlin, 1867; J. Krall, *Composition und Schicksale des manethonischen Geschichtswerkes*, Vienna, 1879.

MANGOLD, WILHELM JULIUS: German Lutheran; b. at Cassel Nov. 20, 1825; d. at Bonn Mar. 1, 1890. He entered the University of Halle in 1845; later he spent a year and a half at Marburg, and so distinguished himself here that in the autumn of 1848 he was urged by his examiners to embrace an academic career. Until Sept., 1849, he devoted himself at Göttingen to ecclesiastical history, and in the following year served with success as private tutor to two sons of the elector. On Thiersch's retirement Mangold chose the vacant department of New-Testament theology in place of ecclesiastical history. Having acquired a considerable reputation both as teacher and author, he received in 1863 a call to Vienna, from the Evangelical faculty of theology there, but at the same time, in spite of the intrigues of his adversaries, he was at last, by command of the elector, appointed regular professor of theology at Marburg. Here, besides his constant application to his specialty of Biblical instruction, and to his other university duties, including the rector's office, which he filled in 1869–1870, he took much interest in the Reformed congregation at Marburg and in the extraordinary Hessian Synod, in whose behalf he labored as a member of the Prussian House of Deputies. His call to Bonn in 1872 was due to the minister Falk. Here he labored indefatigably and successfully for over seventeen years, in the spirit of his chosen motto, "Speaking the truth in love." He was largely influenced by his teacher and veteran colleague, Ernst Henke, his memorial tribute to whom (Marburg, 1879) clearly reflects his own theological attitude. Although he fully understood honest orthodox zeal and was patient with ignorance, he had abundant occasion in Bonn for decided opposition to arbitrary traditionalism. However, he soon became one of the best loved teachers of the university, which in 1876–77 elected him rector.

Omitting his numerous minor works, of which a complete list is given in the *Protestantische Kirchenzeitung* for 1890, no. 17, it is necessary to mention here the following larger books: *Die Irrlehrer der Pastoralbriefe* (Marburg, 1856); *Der Römerbrief und die Anfänge der römischen Gemeinde* (1866); and an independent work, not merely a recasting of the last-named work, *Der Römerbrief und seine geschichtlichen Voraussetzungen* (1884). He was also widely known for his two greatly enlarged new editions of his predecessor Friedrich Bleek's *Einleitung in das Neue Testament* (Berlin, 1875; 1886). He left Bleek's text as it stood, but amplified it by excellent supplements, thereby prolonging the usefulness of Bleek's remarkable work by coordinating it with the progressive development of New-Testament scholarship. A. KAMPHAUSEN.

BIBLIOGRAPHY: *Protestantische Kirchenzeitung*, 1890, no. 17.

MANI, MANICHEANS.

When Christianity had won its fight and been declared in the fourth century the State religion, its doctrines had been in conflict with many opposing forms of belief. But its doughtiest opponent was not the decrepit faith in the gods of Greece and Rome. A more dangerous foe was found in ancient philosophy, especially in its latest form of Neoplatonism, which strove for spiritual control of the world and combined the theoretical with the practical. The one lack of Neoplatonism was a personal center around which to gather its forces, for want of which, as contrasted with Christianity, it failed to attain popularity. Even more dangerous than this was a religion which, rising in the Orient, united in itself the charms of the new with the allurements of the old as represented in the mysteries — which were so attractive to the peoples of that time. This was Mithraism, of which Renan once rightly remarked,

1. The Religion Characterized.

"If the world had not become Christian in the fourth century, it would have become Mithraic." See MITHRA, MITHRAISM. When this enemy had been conquered by the polemics of the Fathers, Babylonia, the cradle of Mithraism, sent a dreadworthy successor to the West, the religion of Mani, or Manicheism. Of Babylonian-Persian origin, the teaching of Mani found its way smoothed by its predecessor, Mithraism. Christianity fought its hardest battle with this new religion, which, though too far removed from Christianity to become a Christian sect, yet combined in itself all the elements which made Gnosticism, with its emphasis upon higher wisdom, so dangerous to Christianity. Manicheism had an existence of nearly a thousand years. It united to Ophitism, the oldest and purest form of Gnosticism, the best elements of the teachings of Marcion and Bardesanes, and so built up the most important of all Gnostic systems. Yet it had, at least as respects Christianity, all the advantages of independence; and it confidently claimed ability to supply a universal need. Its basis was pagan as contrasted with the Christian foundation of other forms of Gnosticism. Mani's object was to give to the Persians of Sassanian times a better religion than that of Zoroaster; he had not apostolic Christianity in view as an opponent. Hence he utilized the sources found in the metropolis of metropolises, Babylon, and built upon the foundations of religion laid there so many centuries earlier. That he later had regard to the Christianity of the West and to the Buddhism of the East is indeed not to be denied; but the influence of Christianity is small compared with the abounding paganism worked into his system. The elements, then, out of which Mani created the religion which he gave to his disciples to propagate, were the Babylonian-Aramaic beliefs of his time, with Parseeism controlling the theory, Buddhism influencing the ethics and life, Christianity furnishing holy names and external analogies, and Mandæism giving its "king of light." A great literature arose about this faith. Concerning the founder Christians and non-Christians wrote; Church Fathers and professional polemists as well as philosophers and historians who had no bias, litterateurs of the East and of the West were engaged in discussing it. Christian sources are in Greek, Latin, Syriac, Armenian, and a few in Arabic; the non-Christian mainly in Arabic or Persian, and the latter, as belonging to the soil on which the religion grew and because of the natural sympathy and habits of writing of the East, are the most valuable as giving the purest forms of tradition.

The native name of the founder is Mani (Gk. *Manes*, *Manichaios*, Lat. *Manes* or *Manichæus*), the etymology of which is doubtful. It is not of Persian but of Babylonian-Aramaic derivation, and is to be connected with the *Mana* so frequently occurring in Mandæan writings (see MANDÆANS).

2. Mani's Origin; Legendary Accretions.

The *Acta Archelai* gives the founder's original name as Curbicius, changed later into Curbicus and Urbicus. Mani's father's name is given as Fatak (Patak), and his family is said to have been of distinguished Persian origin, to have emigrated from Ecbatana in Bactria and settled near Ctesiphon. His mother is reputed to have belonged to the Arsacidæ. Mani is said to have been born in the city of Mardinu in 215-216; he was crucified at Gundev Shapur in 276. A cycle of legend surrounds the circumstances of his birth. According to reports, his father took the boy under his especial care, removed him from his mother, and, in consequence of a change in his religious convictions, joined a South Babylonian sect, the Mu'tasilah, "baptizers," and took up his residence in the district of Mesene on the lower Tigris, where he gave his son instruction until his twelfth year, at which time Mani reached independent conclusions on the matter of religion. Reports indicate that Fatak was essentially a religious leader who used his son to further the diffusion of his teachings. The *Acta Archelai* mentions two supposed forerunners of Mani, Scythianus and Terebinthus. The former is reported to have been a "Saracen" merchant of Arabia who went to Egypt and absorbed all the wisdom of that land during a residence there, and through his disciple Terebinthus wrote a number of books. He then went to Judea to propagate his doctrines but was worsted in a disputation and lost his life. Terebinthus fled to Babylonia with his master's books and treasures, there took the name of Buddas (or Baiddas), engaged in a disputation with Persian priests of Mithra, but was worsted, gaining as convert only an old widow who fell heir to his books and treasures, and bought as a slave Curbicius (see above), who in turn came into possession of the treasures of Scythianus. But this whole story arises in a misconception. "Terebinthus," though it might be used as a proper name, means "pupil," and embodies also a development of the term *rubbiya*, having the same general meaning. Mani is spoken of as the disciple of his father, is identified with Terebinthus, and his father with Scythianus, as coming from the country of the Scythians, while the term "Saracen" (see above) is explicable from Fatak's settlement in Mesene (Characene). This explanation fits well with the varied sources drawn upon in the construction of the system. Allegorical reconstruction then accounts for the story of Scythianus and Terebinthus given above.

Manichean tradition places the first independent development in the religious life of Mani in his twelfth year. The traveled youth received then a revelation from the king of light through the angel Elta'um ("El [God] is allied," cf. the name of the Talmudic angel Tumiy'el, in which the elements are the same, only reversed in order) directing him to withdraw from the Mu'tasilah and purify himself by ascetic practises.

3. Mani's Life.

The next twelve years were spent in preparation for his work, especially in the study of Babylonian religion; during this time he was in contact with the Christians of South Babylonia. Mani's first public appearance is set by a trustworthy Manichean source on the coronation day of Shapur I., Mar. 20, 242, and he is asserted to have begun his work as a religious teacher in his twenty-eighth year. While the occasion, the collection of a large concourse of people, was happily chosen, the disfavor of the king compelled

Mani to leave the kingdom, and he is said to have lived abroad forty years, extending his travels to Khorassan, Bokhara, China, and India. The statement that Mani had as disciples Thomas, Addas, and Hermas, two of whom he sent to Syria and Egypt, is unhistorical. Bar Hebræus asserts that Mani chose twelve disciples. The early Manichean tradition knows only of a personal propaganda of Mani to the north and east of the Persian realm, in which he declared himself to be the last of a series of divinely sent ambassadors of the true God who had commissioned Zoroaster, Buddha, and Jesus. This conception is the same as appears in the Clementine literature, the "great prophet" of Elkesaite thought. Still, how little Mani intended to accept Jesus as a forerunner appears in the later Persian report that Mani's system made Jesus a devil. After long wandering, in which possibly Manichean communities were established in Turkestan and India, Mani returned to Persia, where his followers had increased. He attempted to win over the brother of Shapur, though political circumstances must have predisposed the king to reject overtures on account of dangers to the dynasty from the Persian priesthood; the teacher, however, appears personally to have impressed Shapur favorably. Freedom to practise their religion is said to have been granted his followers, though it appears that this favor was subsequently withdrawn, since Mani had twice to flee the realm. Concerning the remainder of Mani's life little that is reliable has come down. His following increased at various points in the empire; and he is said to have enjoyed the favor of Hormisdas I., the successor of Shapur I., and to have received a city in Khuzistan as his residence. On the accession of Bahram I. he was crucified and flayed, and his skin was stuffed with straw and nailed to the gate which long bore his name. A severe persecution of his followers began immediately after the death of the master. Of Mani's personal characteristics little is known, but the *Fihrist* says that he had a physical defect, a malformed leg. He had fine philosophical and linguistic endowments, profound religious knowledge, and a decided aptitude for literary work. His moral precepts make his character worthy of all honor.

4. Manichean Cosmogony.

As the basis for the study of the system of Mani the *Acta Archelai* and the reports of Augustine are no more employed, but rather the *Kitab al-Fihrist* and the reports of Theodore bar Choni, which depend upon early Manichean writings. The fundamental part in this system is the theory of the origin of the world, which is rooted in Persian dualism. The world began in a mixing of two opposing elements, light and darkness, one essentially good, the other essentially evil. The original light was self-existent, and was called "the first (or original) excellence," i.e., the source of the derived "excellences" or eons, also "the king of the paradise of lights." This entirely spiritual existence consisted of five elements, eternal existences, which composed the body and soul of the divine being; the five corporeal elements were mildness, knowledge, understanding, secrecy, and discernment; the five spiritual elements were love, faith, fidelity, generosity, and wisdom. The kingdom of light, coeternal with the king, included an ether of light and an earth of light; the ether was composed of the same material elements as the body of the king of light, while the earth had as its elements breath, wind, light, water, and fire. This earth of light was under the government of a special light-deity, who was surrounded by twelve excellences of like nature. It was a transcendental correlative of the present earth. From above and at the sides this light world was unbounded, but beneath it met the realm of darkness, which was without limits from below and at the sides. This darkness was also a personal being, who filled his world in a manner like that of the light-god, though he is never called "god" by Mani. The representation of darkness resembles that of the early Babylonian Tiamat, the personified chaos. Darkness was also constituted of five elements, cloud, burning, burning wind, air, and darkness, and the regions were divided as were those of light, while the description follows in part the exposition of the Mandæan lower regions (see MANDÆANS, § 5). The first step toward the commingling of the two elements and the forming of earth came about through the formation of Satan in the realm of darkness, who came into being out of the eternal elements of darkness. He is pictured with the head of a lion, the body of a dragon, the wings of a bird, the tail of a fish, and with four feet. He moved about in the darkness and discovered a gleam of light which appeared to him of the nature of a challenge and he moved to attack it. The king of light put forward the "original man" (*primus homo*) to meet the assault. Different accounts follow of the way the combat proceeded and of the combatants actually engaged; but the fight ended in victory over man, who was bound and surrounded by the elements of darkness. The king of light entered the conflict with other deities of light, rescued the original man, and put to flight the powers of darkness. Among the helping eons were "the friend of lights," "the spirit of life," and "gladness." Victory seems to have been gained in part by the mystic power of knowledge of the secret name of darkness, though the accounts vary in different authorities.

5. Commingling of Light and Darkness.

Meanwhile the elements of the world of light combined, pair by pair, to produce the world of sense. To this commingling of elements diverse in nature is due the varying effects of matter upon substances and upon man, the elements of light producing effects corresponding to their character, beneficent and pleasant, the elements of darkness causing destructive and maleficent results. Thus, fire has a twofold agency, it preserves and warms or it consumes and destroys. In the progress of creation the spirit of life through his three sons slew the three powers taken prisoner by man, killed and flayed them, and from their skins was made the vault of heaven. The regions of the universe were divided off, angels were appointed to support the heavens, others the earths. According to one account, there were ten heavens and eight earths. The cosmology was worked out in definite detail, and the geography of each region laid down. The sun and moon were set in place; the former became the home of the "original man," of the "friend of lights," and of the "spirit of life"; in the moon resided the "mother of life" (Ishtar) and the "maiden of light." Both bodies were created out of the purest material of light possible after the commingling of elements—the sun of good fire, the moon of good water—and both sail on the ocean of heaven. The sun and moon exercise a cleansing efficiency, separating the elements of pure light from the elements of darkness until the smallest possible residuum of admixture is left. All the light remaining in the present universe mingled with darkness and awaiting deliverance is named collectively by the oriental Manicheans after a Christianized terminology "the suffering Jesus, suspended from every tree," and in pantheistic fashion African Manicheans saw in objects that show brilliancy or light or glowing color, particularly in the bloom and fruitage of the plant world, the suffering Jesus or "light-souls." They have brought into connection with this the suffering servant idea of the Deutero-Isaiah and the expectant creation of Rom. viii. 18 sqq. The princes of darkness, named archons, who were taken prisoners in the combat between the two sets of powers, were set by the spirit of life in the heavens as stars.

The power of the princes of darkness continued even after their conquest in the lower world. In order to retain power over the light which had been captured, the chief archon allied himself in marriage with five evil feminine powers and begot Adam, the first man. Adam combined in himself the natures of light and of darkness; his body belonged to the lower class of dark matter, while in his soul were the concentrated elements of light. As a consequence the two elements were at war in him. A second result from the marriage of the archon was the birth of Eve, in whom the evil part was by far preponderant, the reverse of Adam's case. Recognizing their evil condition, both begged for help from the higher eons, and Jesus was sent, who instructed Adam regarding the difference between the two kingdoms, about the commingling of the two elements, concerning the possibility of a release of the light still commingled with darkness, and warned him against connection with Eve, who as the servant of the demons would lead him farther into the material world. Still other accounts of the origin of Adam are given in the narrative of Theodore bar Choni, according to which Adam was the son of Ashkelon, the son of the king of darkness, while Jesus is made to come and wake Adam out of his death sleep. The *Fihrist* reports that the earth archon had by Eve the hateful red-haired Cain, to whom Eve bore Abel of fair complexion and also two daughters, "the worldly-wise" and the "daughter of greed"; the last Cain took as his wife, giving the other to Abel as his wife. Abel's wife, akin by nature to the light elements, became by an angel of light the mother of two daughters; Abel charged Cain with the paternity, and Cain in anger slew Abel and married the widow. To offset the loss of Abel, the archon taught Eve witchcraft in order to enable her to secure Adam as a husband. She bore Adam a son, Shatil or Seth, who was, however, so filled with the elements of light that the archon sought to kill him with the aid of Eve. But Adam took the child and fed it, called to his help the powers of light, and succeeded in foiling the designs of the archon and of Eve. Eve was enabled by the chief devil to recall Adam to live with her, but the reproaches of Seth brought about the separation of the pair, and Seth and Adam wandered to the East and after their death entered paradise, as did the daughters of Abel's wife, while Eve, Cain, and the "daughter of greed" wander in the hells.

6. Origin of Man.

7. The End of the World.

The purpose which underlies the process of world development, viz., the release of the imprisoned elements of light, is carried out through the followers of the teaching of Mani. During the moon's first half, the ship of the moon fills itself with the ascending particles of light, including the souls of the upright, in the last half these are transferred to the sun. When all the light is thus freed, the end of the world of sense comes, the signal being given by "the Third Ancient One," who is also the "friend of lights" (see above). The spirit of life, the original man, the gods of light, and the saints gather, the angels which sustain heaven and earth remove their support, all material things fall together and a universal fire enwraps them and burns for 1,468 years, the imprisoned light is set free and complete separation is made between light and darkness. The government of the kingdom of light is once more completely established, while the world souls return to their grave in the deep, where the darkness lies immovable.

8. Two Classes of Manicheans.

The Manichean community falls into two parts, adepts, and hearers. Entrance is conditioned upon the result of a trial of the candidate's ability to govern his sensual tendencies. Failing in this, he remains outside; but if he still would show his sympathy with the faithful, he may become a hearer. The true Manichean must first of all suppress lust of every kind. To him is forbidden the heaping up of riches, eating of flesh, drinking of wine, witchcraft, hypocrisy, and use of such handicrafts as exhibit the injurious effects of fire and water. All forbidden things were classed together in the conception of "the three seals." The seal of the mouth prohibited impure words and impure foods; that of the hands referred to all affairs which injured the world of light; that of the breast referred to the purification of thought and motive. To adepts marriage was forbidden, to hearers it was permitted conditionally as a matter of necessity. For the hearers Mani composed a decalogue. This class was to deal with the matters of this world as little as possible, to plant no tree, to build no house, though they might sustain the family relation, engage in commerce, and hold office. The honor in which the hearers held the adepts was noteworthy; the latter were regarded as immaterial existences of light and were supported by the hearers upon the best that was obtainable, the hearers kneeling as they offered their services. On account of these services to the adepts, the hearers were often called "protectors" and "warriors for religion," the latter expression having a connection with Mithraism, in which *miles*, "soldier," was a grade of the clergy. The number of the adepts could never have been great.

9. Fasts, Feasts, and Prayer.

Manicheism had, as a rule, seven fast-days in each month upon which monthly and yearly fasts were celebrated. Concerning the details the sources differ greatly. Augustine and Leo the Great report that the Manicheans of the West in the fifth century fasted, as a rule, on Sunday and Monday, the adepts on both days, the hearers only on Sunday, and with this the *Fihrist* agrees. These fasts were in honor of the sun and moon, or rather of the spirits whose seat was placed in those bodies. The two days after new moon constituted a monthly fast. Another fast was when the sun was in Sagittarius at the end of the third quarter of the year and the moon was full, approximately Nov. 22–23. A fast took place also on dates corresponding nearly to Dec. 21–22. A partial fast of a month, food being taken only after sunset, coincides with the Mohammedan Ramadan, and was possibly borrowed by Mohammed from the Manicheans. Doubtless Babylonian fasts lie at the basis of this whole series. The great special feast was that in memory of the execution of Mani, and was called *Bema* and celebrated in March, when a pulpit, elaborate in its adornment, with five steps, was set up, but was not occupied. Possibly this was instituted by the founder in imitation of Christ's institution of the Lord's Supper. In general, Manicheans observed the festivals of the country in which they lived, so as to obliterate as far as possible discernible differences between themselves and the rest of the population. Worship among the Manicheans knew no sacrifice, but prayer was held of supreme importance. Four seasons of prayer daily were prescribed, at midday, in the afternoon before sunset, in the evening after sunset, and at night three hours after sunset. For prayer the Manichean prepared himself by washing with flowing water, standing erect; he then turned to the sun, if it were day, to the moon if it were night and the moon were visible, otherwise to the north, prostrated himself, and so directed his petitions. It was not, however, to the sun and moon in themselves that the Manicheans addressed their prayers, but in these bodies they saw the chief visible representations of the world of light, while the north was the seat of the king of light. At each season of prayer twelve prostrations occurred and twelve prayers were uttered. The general tenor of these prayers was that of praise of the various powers or instruments of light which had a place in the hierarchy of the system. They bore a very close relation to the Mandæan formula, and to Babylonian hymns. The attributes ascribed to the beings worshiped were often derived, even borrowed, from those ascribed to Marduk, Shamash, and Sin in the Babylonian system.

10. The Church.

The confession of every member contained in brief four articles which each must know, though only the adepts appreciated their full significance. These were faith in God, in his light, in his might, and in his wisdom, which are named "the four excellences." These have a Christian sound, but in fact God is the king of the paradise of light, his light is the sun and the moon, his might is the five angels, and his wisdom is the religion, that is, the Manichean church. The five grades of the Manichean church are symbolized by the five steps of the Bema; the highest grade is composed of teachers, "sons of mildness"; the second of servers, "sons of knowledge"; the third of presbyters, "sons of understanding"; the fourth of the true (adepts), "sons of secrecy"; and the fifth of the adherents (hearers), "sons of discernment." Thus, the church visible consists of the last two classes; a select number of the adepts furnish the clergy, and the community is made up of the rest of the adepts and the hearers or adherents. Augustine gives practically the same arrangement, but applies to the grades the Christian terms master, bishop, presbyter, elect, and auditors or hearers. The epithets applied to these five grades (given above in quotation marks) all have significance in the terminology of the system. Thus the lowest class are called sons of discernment because they have discerned in Mani's teaching the most perfect religion. The three upper grades correspond closely to the three grades of the Mandæan clergy. Augustine's statement that there were twelve teachers and seventy-two bishops is a further indication of Mani's borrowing from the Christian system, for this arrangement is not to be derived from Babylonia. Both Augustine and the *Fihrist* mention a head of the church who corresponded to the *Rish amma* of the Mandæans or to the pope of the Roman Church. Holy offices, like the sacraments of the Christian Church, arose among the Manicheans, but were employed only among the adepts; to this is due the lack of information concerning them. The Church Fathers speak of a Manichean baptism and service of communion. In a time like the fourth century, when the sacraments of the Christian Church were part of a secret discipline, it is not strange that on the one side the Manicheans kept their rites secret, nor, on the other, that the foes of the Manicheans charged them with travesties of Christian rites. The baptism of the Manicheans should doubtless be brought into connection with the employment of water in nature-religions, and the Eucharist may also be so referred, as in the case of the Mandæans (q.v., § 7). In the Eleusinian mysteries, in Parseeism, and in Mithraism there was a kind of Eucharist. The Manicheans of the Middle Ages had instead of baptism a laying-on of hands by which hearers were advanced to the grade of adept. The churches were like those of the Mandæans, small and unadorned. Bloody sacrifice had no part in the system.

When one of the adepts dies and his soul leaves his body, the original man sends a light-god in the form of a wise guide, i.e., Jesus, and with him three other light-deities and a light-maiden, who carry five articles which symbolize relationship to the kingdom of light—a water vessel, a cloak, a headband, a crown, and a wreath of light. The number five corresponds to the five elements of the light-deity, and derivation from Babylonian-Aramaic sources is clear. Resemblances to Mandæan characteristics also are noticeable in some of these particulars. Outside of these sources, a close dependence upon Zoroastrianism is discoverable, as, for instance, in the light-maiden as compared with the fravashi of Zoroaster. At the death of the adept, however, the devil of greed and the devil of lust are alert to assail the soul, which cries to the light-deities for help; they approach and the devils retreat. The symbolic articles are received by the soul, which then ascends to the moon, thence to the sun, thence to "the mother of the living," and finally to the "highest light" in the paradise of light, where the soul attains to its original condition before the commingling of the two sets of elements. At the death of the hearer the same vain attempt is made by the devils as in the case of the adept, but the help of the divine is found. The soul wanders a long time, however, in a state like that of a man who has a bad dream, seeing horrible shapes and expecting to sink into slime and filth. Finally its constituents of light are liberated and it enters the company of the adepts. Over the souls of those who do not belong to this faith, the devils have full power to seize and torment, especially by the production of shapes of fearful form. Their cries to the light-deities are met only by reproaches and reminders of their evil deeds. Their torture continues till the end of this world, and then they are cast into the hells. The transmigration of souls does not appear to have been taught by Mani, though it may have been hinted.

11. The Future Life.

The character under which Mani promulgated his system appears in a formula of prayer and also in a citation from his "gospel": "Blessed be our leader, the paraclete, the ambassador of light." Indeed, his employment of New-Testament terminology in matters other than this naming of himself "the paraclete" comes out in a number of particulars. Chapters in his chief work, "The Book of Secrets," deal with "the son of the poor widow, whom the Jews crucified," with "Jesus' testimony to himself in his relations with the Jews," and with "the testimony of Adam concerning Jesus." Mani regarded Jesus as a devil, as did the Mandæans, though humanly speaking he was the "son of a poor widow"; contemporary with Jesus, however, was the real savior, but he was present in a body which had only the appearance of reality (the Docetic doctrine). This real savior came from the world of light to bring a larger knowledge of divine things, as he long before had come to Adam. To this real savior Mani, in spite of his rejection of the historical Christian savior, gave the name Jesus, and to discriminate between the two Mani usually spoke of the Christian savior as the Messiah, just as did the Mandæans. The real savior of Mani had no objective existence, his whole human course, including his sufferings, being only apparent. The Fathers of the Greek and Roman Churches refer to a redeeming Christ in the system of Mani whose seat is in the sun and the moon; this is the "original man," and he cooperates as savior with the heavenly Jesus. This doctrine of a double savior is one of the characteristic teachings of Manicheism, and the connection with Gnosticism comes out in the diffusion of knowledge as one of the functions of the redeemer. It follows from Mani's doctrine regarding the union of heavenly and infernal elements in the work of Christ that he made a sharp distinction between genuine and spurious writings in the Bible, particularly of the New Testament. The Gospels were not by the disciples of Christ, but were written, or at least interpolated, from the Jewish standpoint. Therefore Mani wrote a new "gospel" (the title of one of his books). The Acts of the Apostles is spurious and the Pauline epistles are not uninterpolated, though Paul was the most enlightened of the apostles. The teaching of Christ, originally in parables and obscure form, has been misunderstood and perverted; yet the light peeps out often even in the corrupt Gospels, as where Jesus deals with his descent from heaven and his superhuman might. The seeming crucifixion is itself a parable of the suffering of the light commingled with darkness in nature and in the human soul. The Old Testament is treated even more severely, since it originates with the Jews. The God of the Old Testament is the prince of darkness and the prophets were lying servants of the devil. Moses is expressly called an apostle of darkness, and his law proceeded from the Archon. Mani proclaimed himself the last of the prophets, his predecessors being Adam, Seth, Noah, Abraham, Buddha, Zoroaster, the messiah as "the word of God," and Paul.

12. Mani's Attitude toward the Bible.

Mani was the author of a series of greater writings, seven in number, and of many smaller tracts which dealt with individual points. His followers continued to imitate him in putting forth tracts (often as letters), and the *Fihrist* speaks of seventy-six titles of this character. Unfortunately Manichean literature has almost entirely perished, owing to the persecutions of the religion. Accounts of Mani's literary activity come from various sources, Syriac, Arabic, and Greco-Roman. Al-Nadim reports in the *Fihrist* that Mani wrote one book in Persian and six in "Syriac," i.e., Babylonian Aramaic. Mani seems to have used a sort of cipher, but the Sassanian-Persian became the customary script of Manichean writings. The books alleged to be written in Syriac are: (1) The "Book of Secrets," mentioned by Epiphanius and Titus of Bostra (q.v.) as *Mysteria*, and among Christians it was described as the book which seeks to destroy the law and the prophets. It probably contained Mani's dogmatics and polemics. The titles of the chapters as given in the accounts which have been transmitted appear mere riddles, though some of them probably relate to recognized fundamentals in the system. (2) The "Book of Giants" dealt with cosmogony and demonology, and Gen. vi. 1–4 probably exerted an influence upon this conception. The Babylonian myth of the contest

13. Manichean Literature.

between gods and demons was not without effect. (3) The "Book of Chapters" is concerned with directions for the "elect," a sort of catechism, and was probably the book with which Augustine dealt in his celebrated *Contra epistolam Manichæi quam vocant Fundamenti* (Eng. transl. in *NPNF*, 1 ser., iv. 129–150). The Manichean Felix asserted that it contained "the beginning, middle and end," i.e., the entire teaching concerning the history of the gods to the end of men. It was written in epistolary form in imitation of Paul's method, and was designed by the author to be the fundamental book of instruction. It began with a description of the original relations of light and darkness before the commingling, and proceeded with a fantastic development of the *pleroma* of light, etc. (4) The title of the fourth work was probably *Shapurakan* ("for Shapur"). According to Biruni, Mani wrote this book for Shapur I., son of Ardashir, in order to win him to the faith. The *Fihrist* sums it up in three chapters dealing with the death of the adherent, of the apostate, and of the sinner. This book was probably not known in the western world. (5) The "Book of Making Alive" was probably that known to Epiphanius, Photius, and Augustine as *Thesaurus*. It was of considerable size, since Augustine cites a seventh book. (6) The *Pragmateia* was possibly the original title of another work which is otherwise unknown. The seventh of Mani's main works, written in Persian, was his *Engeliun* (*Evangelion*, "Gospel"). Biruni says of it that it was of a character entirely different from the Christian Gospels, that the Manicheans regarded it as the only correct one and called it the "Gospel of the Seventy," and that it was arranged in the order of the twenty-two letters of the old Aramaic alphabet. It was written during the author's exile in Turkestan, and the initial capitals were, in Persian fashion, worked in ornamental designs, from which among the Persians Mani was known as "the painter," a characterization not known to the Arabs or in the West. Possibly the reference in this title has something to do with the pictorial character of Mani's representations of heaven and hell. Biruni ascribes to Mani also a "Book of Books." The first, third, fifth, and last of the works named above were ascribed to Scythianus (§ 2 above); part of Mani's work may have originated with his father and been enlarged by himself. Not to be overlooked in this survey is the *Canticum amatorium*, a liturgical hymn to the eternal father of light often mentioned by Augustine. Of the lesser Manichean writings those issued by Mani and those by later writers can not be distinguished. Some are directed to cities or regions; thus three are to India, six to Kashgar (Chitral), seven to Armenia, ten to Ctesiphon, etc. Others are directed to persons who are otherwise unknown. The subjects dealt with are very varied and range from the theories of the system to the conduct of life. Greco-Roman sources recognize a like number of lesser writings, but the titles given do not afford data for identification with those mentioned in the *Fihrist*. A collection of these minor documents was made later and was known as "the Book of Epistles." The *Acta Archelai* and Epiphanius have preserved genuine fragments of one writing, other fragments are collected in Fabricius-Harles, *Bibliotheca Græca*, vii. 311 sqq. In these fragments dependence can not be placed upon the forms of the names of the persons addressed.

In spite of the severe persecution which Bahram I. instituted against the Manicheans, the system spread rapidly in all directions. The Manicheans fled into Turkestan, and thence they were scattered in other directions under further persecutions. After reaching the West, they adopted many ideas from the Christians, as has been suggested in the preceding account. With growing numbers differences regarding special points arose, and so came sects. In accordance with the founder's direction, the entire church was under a chief called Imam, who was obligated to reside in Babylonia. The first successor of Mani was named Sis or Sisinius, to whom some of the lesser writings are attributed. One cause of division among Manicheans was a dispute respecting the residence of the Imam; a party known as the *Dinawarier*, "religious," split off and settled along the Oxus, but later became reconciled with those who remained in Babylonia. A later division, in the early part of the eighth century, produced the Miklasites, named from Miklas, successor of a Persian ascetic named Zadhurmuz, and their leading principle was laxity in observing the rules of separation from non-Manicheans. The number of Manicheans became very great in the northern part of the Persian highlands, the refuge of all sects. New persecutions arose in the eighth century under Shapur II. and Chosroes I. The religion had already spread eastward, and though probably the founder did not reach India, in the first persecution after his death his followers reached Malabar, which became a new center for the diffusion of the faith. By about 930 A.D. a strong Turkish tribe on the border of China had embraced the religion, inscriptional traces of which fact are known (Marquart, in *Wiener Zeitschrift für Kunde des Morgenlandes*, xii., 1898, 157–200). By about 980 the number of Manicheans in Bagdad was small, though in the villages they were more numerous. In spreading westward the religion first reached Syria and Palestine, where Titus of Bostra opposed it; then it spread into Egypt and through Roman North Africa, where its success was great. Proconsular Africa was one of the chief Manichean regions, and an edict of Diocletian is known directing the prosecution of the "sect derived from the hostile Persian kingdom." They were again assailed in edicts after the year 377, but in Augustine's time their church was in flourishing condition in North Africa, having a good organization, numerous communities, and zealous leaders. Indeed, this branch is of especial interest because of Augustine's nine years' connection with it as an adherent and his later polemics against it. On account of these facts, fuller information has come down than would otherwise have been the case, especially in regard to the teachers who then were prominent. Among these were Felix and Faustus of Mileve, who settled in

14. History of the Religion.

Carthage in 383. By Faustus' reputation Augustine was much attracted, but he was soon undeceived, since on close association he found Faustus shallow and uninspiring. Faustus wrote a polemic against the Catholic Church, which Augustine answered in his *Libri xxxiii. adversus Faustum* (Eng. transl. in *NPNF*, 2 ser., iv. 155–345). Felix was more intimately connected with Augustine, and a disputation between them in the church at Hippo lasted two days, the principal matter of which is reported in Augustine's *De actis cum Felice Manichæo*, while the result was the defeat of Felix and his renunciation of Manicheism. Under the Vandals the Manicheans of North Africa suffered severe persecution. In Italy, especially at Rome, the religion gained a firm foothold and large numbers of adherents; Leo the Great sought the assistance of the civil authorities against them, and governmental measures were taken to suppress them under Valentinian III. and Justinian. The religion spread as far as Spain, where it was connected with Priscillianism (see Priscillian, Priscillianists). The Manicheans of later times were the Cathari of South France in the eleventh and twelfth centuries (see New Manicheans, II.), while in the East their doctrines were continued in the teachings of the Paulicians (q.v.).

15. Component Sources of the System.

The great success of this system of belief is to be found in two particulars: first, its completeness of development as a Gnostic creation, using so fully, richly, and immediately the original sources of all Gnostic forms of faith, viz., the Assyrian-Babylonian religion with its wealth of mythical material; second, the genius of its founder, who systematized this material and developed it into a coherent and artistic unity. All the questions which were raised by the inquiring thought of his times, questions which concerned the being, destiny, and duties of God and man, questions which related to past, present, and future, were answered in a manner wholly self-consistent. Where earlier Gnostic systems were weak, Mani's was strong. The problem of necessity and free will he solved by the hypothesis of the original duality of being and the subsequent commingling of the two elements. While the founder was a philosopher, he clothed his ideas in full mythological dress. This dress, however, was not of his own creation, built out of his fancy, in this respect differing from earlier Gnostic doctrines. It was borrowed from the sources already sufficiently indicated, from the surroundings in which Mani's youth and manhood were passed. The "king of light" is clearly Ea (see Babylonia, VII., 2, § 3), originally the ocean of heaven, the deity of profoundest knowledge, enthroned in the deep of the world-sea. In the Manichean system water becomes light, while the Mandæans retained water as the sacred element. Marduk, son of Ea, reappears in Mani's teaching as the "original man," and his wanderings are the antetype of the adventures of the type as developed in Manichean-Elkesaite and Mandæan doctrines. The model for the "spirit of life" was Ramman (see Assyria, VII., § 4; Babylonia, VII., 2, § 6), with recollections of Shamash and Sin, while the original devil is the Babylonian Tiamat (see Creation, Babylonian Accounts). The mechanism of redemption follows the Babylonian pattern, and the *bema* recalls in form the ziggurat. These particulars do no more than suggest the wholesale appropriation of the material ready at hand in Babylonian religion. On the other hand, it is noticeable that Mani made the stars evil spirits and forbade the witchcraft and magic which had so large a part in the old faith. The period of transition from the older faith and the break from its control were under the influence of the Mu'tasilah, to which some of the practical details of the religion may be due. To Zoroastrianism something must be accredited, though far less than was formerly thought necessary. Both religions deal fundamentally with light, and many forms in the two systems are identical, while the influence of the Zoroastrian prayer and eschatology is easily discernible. The great chasm between the two faiths is found in the conception of darkness. In Zoroastrianism Ahriman is a creation of Ormazd become perverted; in Manicheism, darkness is as essentially eternal as the light and originally evil in nature. Similarly, the Parsee conception of man is that the body is a pure creation of Ormazd, who also gave the soul, while Mani makes it a structure of darkness and the prison of the soul. The view of Baur that Manichean morals were drawn from Buddhism can not be substantiated, the one close connection here being the similarity between the idea of the adept and the Buddhist striver after Nirvana. (K. Kessler†.)

Bibliography: Owing to the various persecutions of the Manicheans their writings as a whole are lost. Portions of them are almost certainly embodied in the *Ginza* of the Mandæans (q.v.). Other fragments are found in the Syriac of Theodore bar Choni, and in the Arabic in the *Fihrist* (see below). The source of first importance is the *Fihrist al-'ulum* (finished 988 A.D.) of Muhammad ibn Ishak, generally known as Al-Nadim, the part concerning Mani being edited with transl. and commentary by G. Flügel, Leipsic, 1882. Next to the *Fihrist* as a source is (Abu Fath Muhammad al-) Shahrastani (d. 1153), *Kitab almilal wannuhal*, ed. W. Cureton, i. 188–192, London, 1842, in Germ. transl. by T. Haarbrücker, 2 vols., Halle, 1850–51. Interesting details from Mani's writings, in Arabic transl., are furnished by (Muhammad ibn Ahmad al-) Biruni in his "Chronology of the Oriental Peoples," written about 1000 A.D., ed. E. Sachau, pp. 207–209, Leipsic, 1878, Eng. transl., London, 1879 (cf. K. Kessler, *Mani*, i. 304–323, Berlin, 1889), and in his "India," ed. E. Sachau, London, 1887, Eng. transl., ib. 1888. A discussion of Mani's life and teaching is contained in the Nestorian "Chronicle" of 'Amr ibn Matta, ed. H. Gismondi, Rome, 1896–97, though the basis is the *Acta Archelai* and Epiphanius. Further minor Arabic sources are indicated in Hauck-Herzog, *RE*, xii. 194. From the Syriac the matter derivable from Ephraem Syrus is collected in Kessler's *Mani*, ut sup., pp. 262–302. Items of information may be gathered from the Syriac martyrologies in the collections of Assemani, 2 vols., Rome, 1748, and Bedjan, Paris, 1890 sqq. Theodore bar Choni's *Eskolion* (in H. Pognon, *Inscriptions mandaïtes des coupes de Khouabir*, 2 vols., Paris, 1898–99) is of great value, since the author cites long passages from the Manichean originals. The Middle-Persian Pahlavi texts sometimes contain material. Such are: the *Shikand-gumanik Vigar*, in Eng. transl. in *SBE*, vol. xxiv., consult pp. 243–251; the *Dinkard*, ed. with Eng. transl. by Peshotun D. B. Sungana, 6 vols., Bombay. The New-Persian Firdausi has some material in the *Shahnameh*, for which cf. Kessler, ut sup., pp. 373–376. The report of the Armenian Esnigh is accessible in *ZHT*, ii (1840).

Of Western sources the first is the *Acta disputationis*

Archelai, most accessible in M. J. Routh, *Reliquiæ sacræ*, v. 1–206, Oxford, 1848, in Eng. transl. in *ANF*, vi. 179–235, cf. H. von Zittwitz, in *ZHT*, 1873, pp. 467–528. Next to this come the Anti-Manichean writings of Augustine, the most important of which are in vols. i., viii. of the Benedictine ed. of his works. Some of these are translated in *NPNF*, 2 ser., iv. 37–365, with *Introductory Essay on the Manichæan Heresy* by A. H. Newman, ib., pp. 3–29. Epiphanius dealt with Manicheism in *Hær.*, lxvi. Consult also *Alexandri Lycopolitani contra Manichæi opiniones disputatio*, published Leipsic, 1895, Eng. transl. in *ANF*, vi. 241–252. Other Greek sources are given in Hauck-Herzog, *RE*, xii. 196–197, as is the Western literature between 1700 and 1800.

Of later works on the subject the first place is due to Kessler's *Mani*, ut sup., of which only vol. i. is published, though vol. ii. is promised, and to his *Untersuchungen zur Genesis des manichäischen Religionssystems*, Berlin, 1876. Perhaps of next importance is G. Flügel, *Mani, seine Lehre und seine Schriften*, Leipsic, 1862. Consult further, A. von Wegnern, *Manichæorum indulgentiæ*, Leipsic, 1827; F. C. Baur, *Das manichäische Religionssystem*, Tübingen, 1831; F. C. Trechsel, *Ueber Kanon, Kritik und Exegese der Manichäer*, Bern, 1832; F. Spiegel, *Eranische Alterthumskunde*, ii. 185–232, Leipsic, 1873; A. Geyler, *Das System des Manichäismus und sein Verhältniss zum Buddhismus*, Jena, 1875; E. Rochat, *Essai sur Mani et sa doctrine*, Geneva, 1897; A. Dufourcq, *De Manichæismo*, Paris, 1900; A. Brückner, *Faustus von Mileve. Ein Beitrag zur Geschichte des abendländischen Manichäismus*, Basel, 1901; F. W. K. Müller, *Handschriften-Reste in Estrangelo-Schrift aus Turfan, Chinesisch-Turkestan*, Berlin, 1904; C. Salemann, *Ein Bruchstück manichäischen Schrifttums*, St. Petersburg, 1904; idem, *Manichäische Studien*, Leipsic, 1908; E. Bischoff, *Im Reiche der Gnosis*, ib., 1906; F. Cumont, *Recherches sur le Manichéisme. I. La Cosmogonie d'après Théodore bar Khôni*, Brussels, 1908; Harnack, *Dogma*, passim, consult Index; Neander, *Christian Church*, i. 479–506 et passim.

MANIPLE. See VESTMENTS AND INSIGNIA, ECCLESIASTICAL.

MANN, CAMERON: Protestant Episcopal missionary bishop of North Dakota; b. in New York City Apr. 3, 1851. He was educated at Hobart College (A.B., 1870) and the General Theological Seminary, from which he was graduated in 1873, and was ordered deacon in the latter year and advanced to the priesthood in 1876. After being a missionary at Branchport and Dresden, N. Y., in 1873–74 and curate of St. Peter's, Albany, N. Y., in 1875, he was rector successively of St. James', Watkins, N. Y., from 1876 to 1881 and of Grace, Kansas City, Mo., from 1881 to 1901. In 1902 he was consecrated missionary bishop of North Dakota. In theology he is a liberal High-churchman, and has written *Future Punishment* (New York, 1888) and *Comments at the Cross* (1893).

MANN, WILHELM JULIUS: Lutheran theologian; b. in Stuttgart, Germany, May 29, 1819; d. in Boston, Mass., June 20, 1892. He received his preparatory education in the Latin school at Blaubeuren and the excellent gymnasium of his native town. In his early school-days he became the intimate friend of Philip Schaff, "the presiding genius of international theology" as he afterward used to call his learned friend. In 1837 he took up the study of theology at the University of Tübingen, where Professor Christian Friedrich Schmidt exerted the greatest influence on him. In 1845 he came to America through the invitation of Philip Schaff. He first taught in Mercersburg, Pa., and for some time was assistant pastor of Salem's Reformed Church in Philadelphia. In 1848 he became coeditor, with Dr. Schaff, of *Der deutsche Kirchenfreund*, becoming editor-in-chief in 1854. In 1850 he accepted a call to the Evangelical-Lutheran Zion's congregation in Philadelphia, founded by Henry Melchior Muehlenberg (q.v.) and entered the Lutheran Ministerium of Pennsylvania, where he found his proper spiritual home and field for his pastoral and theological activity in this country. Twice he held the office of president of the Ministerium and wrote, in connection with his friend, Dr. G. F Krotel, an exposition of Luther's Catechism, which was published by the synod and is still in use. In the confessional controversy which agitated the Lutheran Church about the middle of the nineteenth century, he took strong ground against "American Lutheranism" and its champion, Dr. Samuel Simon Schmucker (q.v.). Against the latter's *Definite Platform* (1855) Dr. Mann wrote his *Plea for the Augsburg Confession* (Philadelphia, 1856) and in the following year his *Lutheranism in America: an Essay on the present Condition of the Lutheran Church in the United States.* When the Ministerium of Pennsylvania founded its own theological seminary in Philadelphia (1864) Dr. Mann was elected a member of the first faculty, together with Drs. Charles Porterfield Krauth and Charles William Schaeffer. For twenty-seven years he held his position as professor of Hebrew, New-Testament exegesis, German homiletics, symbolics, and ethics. He prepared a little text-book for his students in ethics: *General Principles of Christian Ethics: the first Part of the System of Christian Ethics by C. F. Schmidt* (1872). During the last part of his life his literary activity was chiefly confined to the sphere of American, particularly Pennsylvanian, church history. His principal works in this field are: *Life and Times of Henry Melchior Mühlenberg* (Philadelphia, 1887), written for the centennial of Mühlenberg's death; and the new edition of the Halle Reports prepared by Dr. Mann in connection with Drs. Beale Melanchthon Schmucker and W Germann, in Germany. Only the first volume of this important and valuable publication was completed by him. Another valuable book is his life of William Penn, in German (Reading, Pa., 1882). ADOLPH SPAETH.

BIBLIOGRAPHY: Emma T. Mann, *Memoir of the Life and Work of W. J. Mann*, Philadelphia, 1893 (by his daughter); A. Spaeth, in *Lutheran Church Review*, Jan., 1893, also published in pamphlet form, *Dr. W. J. Mann, ein deutsch-amerikanischer Theologe, Erinnerungsblaetter*, Reading, 1895; H. E. Jacobs, in *American Church History Series*, vol. iv., passim, New York, 1893.

MANNING, HENRY EDWARD: English cardinal; b. at Totteridge (12 m. s.w. of Hertford) July 15, 1807; d. in London Jan. 14, 1892. He received his preparatory education at Harrow, and went in 1827 to Balliol College, Oxford. His chief distinction in the university was as a debater, rather than as a scholar. At this period of his life his interests were primarily political, but the financial losses sustained by his father rendered a parliamentary career impossible for him, and after graduating with first-class honors in 1830 he obtained a subordinate position in the colonial office. Coming under Evangelical influence he resigned in 1832 and returned to Oxford. There he was

Early Life and Education.

elected a fellow of Merton College and was ordained priest on Dec. 23. He was soon appointed curate to John Sargent, the Evangelical rector of Lavington, Sussex, and in the following year he was instituted to the rectory as Sargent's successor. In this same year (1833) he married a daughter of his late rector, but his wife died four years later. This blow Manning felt keenly, and his sorrow, added to tendencies long at work within him, doubtless predisposed him still more to the principles of the Oxford Movement (see TRACTARIANISM). At the time of his ordination he believed in the doctrine of baptismal regeneration, and before long modified his view of the Eucharist and accepted the tenets of apostolic succession and the value of tradition. He was likewise active in the promotion of a system of education which should be under religious control, and aided in the establishment of diocesan boards in cooperation with the National Society for Promoting the Education of the Poor. In Dec., 1840, he was appointed archdeacon of Chichester, and two years later select preacher at Oxford. At this period of his life he published his *Unity of the Church* (London, 1842), in which he ably defended the doctrines of Anglo-Catholicism. In 1838 he had visited Rome and had seen Wiseman, but he was still totally out of sympathy with Roman Catholicism.

Activity in the Anglican Church.

The conversion of W. G. Ward and Newman to Roman Catholicism left Manning at the head of the High-church party in the Anglican Church. In 1847, however, he was compelled by illness to take a continental tour, which lasted until July, 1848, and took him through Belgium and Germany to Italy. Most of this time, however, was spent in Rome, and in April and May, 1848, he was received in audience by Pius IX. His doubts concerning the catholicity of the Anglican Church were meantime increasing, although there is no evidence that he seriously contemplated withdrawing from her communion. Events shortly after his return to England, however, turned the tide of his convictions. The consecration of the unorthodox Hampden to the see of Hereford and the decision in the famous Gorham case seemed to him evidence that the Church of England was not a part of the Church catholic, and though he presided at a meeting of the Chichester clergy to protest against the so-called "Papal Aggression" in the creation of Roman Catholic dioceses in England in 1850, he resigned his archdeaconry and went to London. There he placed himself under the instruction of the Jesuits, and on Passion Sunday, Apr. 6, 1851, was received into the Roman Catholic Church. On the following Sunday he received minor orders, and was ordained priest on June 14. In the following year Manning went to Rome, where he spent the next three years in study at the Accademia dei Nobili Ecclesiastici. Receiving his doctorate from the pope in 1854, he began regular work in England, and three years later was made provost of the chapter of Westminster and superior of the Congregation of the Oblates of St. Charles. For eight years he labored with unceasing activity, preaching, writing, and working among the poor. A strong ultramontanist, he was appointed by the pope in 1860 domestic prelate and pronotary apostolic with the title of Monsignor. He consistently objected, therefore, to the welcome accorded Garibaldi on his visit to England in 1864, even though his general ultramontane course aroused the suspicion of a large body of English Roman Catholics.

Steps Leading to his Conversion to Roman Catholicism.

In 1864 Cardinal Wiseman died, and the pope, ignoring the names submitted to him by the chapter, nominated Manning his successor as archbishop of Westminster, London. He was consecrated at the pro-cathedral of St. Mary's, Moorfields, June 8, received the pallium at Rome on Michaelmas Day, and was enthroned at St. Mary's Nov. 6. A rigid disciplinarian, he spared neither himself nor others, and worked consistently in an ultramontane spirit to advance Roman Catholicism in England. He accordingly opposed Newman's plan of founding a Roman Catholic hall at Oxford, and, believing that the Roman Catholic Church should provide education for its own members, he made an unsuccessful attempt to establish a Roman Catholic university at Kensington, which remained open only from 1874 to 1878. On the other hand, he was more than successful in the promotion of parochial schools, and was unswerving in his opposition to all that was at variance with the teaching of his Church. He gained additional prominence in 1870 by his advocacy of the doctrine of papal infallibility, and in 1875 replied to Gladstone in his *Vatican Decrees in their Bearing on Civil Allegiance*. On Mar. 15 of the same year he was created a cardinal, although he did not receive the hat until Dec. 31, 1877, when he was in Rome. After the death of Pius IX. (Feb. 7, 1878), Manning attended the conclave and, although some of the Italian cardinals were prepared to vote for him as pope, he cast his ballot for Cardinal Pecci (Leo XIII.). With the new pope, however, he was less in sympathy, and for the remainder of his life his chief interests were social questions, especially total abstinence, for the advancement of which he founded a "League of the Cross," which in 1874 numbered some 30,000 members in London alone. He was likewise extremely active in the cause of labor, and his urgent advocacy of the claims of the working classes drew upon him the charge of socialism, although he rightly denied the truth of the assertion. In 1889 he assisted in settling the strike of the longshoremen, while he was also active in movements for the suppression of the East African slave-trade and Hindu child-marriage, in addition to advocating the raising of the minimum age for child labor.

Labors for his New Faith.

Philanthropic Interests.

Cardinal Manning was a prolific writer, and his works betoken a man of sincere conviction, earnest faith, and noble character. He was preeminently an ecclesiastic and a diplomat, even though in matters of mere intellect he was inferior to certain others of his period. His chief works, written for the most part under the press of manifold ecclesiastical and public duties, are as follows: *The Unity of the Church* (London, 1842); *Sermons* (4 vols.,

1842-50); *Sermons Preached before the University of Oxford* (Oxford, 1844); *The Grounds of Faith* (London, 1852); *Sermons on Ecclesiastical Subjects* (3 vols., Dublin, 1863-73); *The Temporal Mission of the Holy Ghost* (London, 1865); *England and Christendom* (1867); *Petri privilegium* (1871); *National Education and Parental Rights* (1872); *The Internal Mission of the Holy Ghost* (1875); *The Vatican Decrees in their Bearing on Civil Allegiance* (1875); *The Infallible Church and the Holy Communion of Christ's Body and Blood* (1875); *The True Story of the Vatican Council* (1877); *Miscellanies* (3 vols., 1877-88); *National Education* (1889); and the posthumous *Pastimes* (1893).

Bibliography: Lives have been written by E. S. Purcell, 2 vols., London, 1895; A. Zimmermann, 1880; A. W. Hutton, London, 1892; J. R. Gasquet, ib. 1895; F. de Pressensé, Paris, 1896, Eng. transl., London, 1897 (reviewed by G. Grabinski, *Uno Studio sul Card. Manning*, Florence, 1897); H. M. Hemmer, Paris, 1898; and W. P. Ward, in *Ten Personal Studies*, New York, 1898. Consult further: J. Lemire, *Le Cardinal Manning et son action sociale*, Paris, 1893; *Cardinal Manning: a Character Sketch or Foreshadowings. Being Extracts from his earlier Sermons*, ed. H. E. H. King, London, 1895; S. Roamer, *Cardinal Manning as Presented in his own Letters and Notes*, London, 1896; J. A. Nicholson, *The Adoration of Christ. A Vindication of the Catholic Doctrine and Refutation of the Heresies taught by Card. Manning in the Devotion to the Sacred Heart*, ed. C. E. Roney-Dougal, London, 1897; *DNB*, xxxvi. 62-68 (the bibliography contains reference to much incidental matter). A noteworthy list of magazine literature is indicated in Richardson, *Encyclopaedia*, pp. 676-677.

MANNING, JAMES: Baptist preacher and educator; b. near Elizabethtown, N. J., Oct. 22, 1738; d. at Providence, R. I., July 29, 1791. He studied at Hopewell Academy in New Jersey, and at Princeton College (B.A., 1762). After about a year of evangelistic preaching in several colonies, he was urged by members of the Philadelphia Association to join them in an effort to establish a Baptist university. At about the same time the association voted its approval of an effort to enlist the entire Baptist body in an effort to found such an institution in Rhode Island. Manning was sent to Rhode Island in 1763 to confer with leading brethren and to promote the enterprise (see Baptists, II., 2, § 3). In 1764 the legislature granted a charter in accordance with which the president and a majority of the trustees must always be Baptists, but all the leading denominations of the colony shall have representation on the board and members of all Evangelical denominations shall be eligible for professorships, etc. Pending the raising of funds and the fixing of the location of the college, Manning accepted the pastorate of the church at Warren, R. I., and conducted there an academy which should prepare the way for the future college. The Calvinistic Baptists of New England had been so zealous for absolute independency that they had never united in associations. In 1767 Manning led in the formation of the Warren Association, which was to become a factor in the struggle for religious liberty and in the promotion of educational and missionary work. In 1770 he led in the negotiations for the permanent location of the college, which resulted in the choice of Providence. He accepted the pastorate of the Providence church, then in a weak and discouraged condition, and soon brought it to great prosperity. The raising of funds and the erection of college buildings, the duties of administration, heavy teaching duties, and denominational leadership, together with the pastorate, gave him abundant occupation. He sought and secured the help of English Baptists in the equipment and endowment of the college. His college duties were suspended during the war, Rhode Island having been early captured by the British who turned the college buildings into barracks. In 1782 the college was reopened. In 1786 he was chosen by the Rhode Island General Assembly to represent the State in the national convention for the framing of the federal constitution. He used his great influence in favor of the adoption of the constitution by Rhode Island and other New England States, where there was much opposition. He was an eloquent and impressive preacher, master of an elegant and forceful literary style, while his attainments gave him a commanding position among his contemporaries. His theological views were moderately Calvinistic. A. H. Newman.

Bibliography: R. A. Guild, *Life, Times and Correspondence of . James Manning, and the Early Hist. of Brown University*, Boston, 1864; W. B. Sprague, *Annals of the American Pulpit*, vi. 89-97, New York, 1860; F. Piper, *Lives of the Leaders of our Church Universal*, transl. and ed. H. M. MacCracken, pp. 608-614, Philadelphia, 1879; A. H. Newman, in *American Church History Series*, vol. ii., ib. 1894.

MANNIX, DANIEL: Irish Roman Catholic; b. at Charleville (33 m. n.n.w. of Cork), County Cork, Mar. 4, 1864. He was educated at the Christian Brothers' School, at St. Colman's College, Fermoy, and St. Patrick's College, Maynooth (1882-1890). Since 1891 he has been connected with the latter institution, where he has been professor of mental and moral philosophy (1891-94), professor of theology (1894-1903), and president (since 1903). In 1906 he was appointed domestic prelate to the pope, and in 1907 was made a senator of the Royal University of Ireland.

MANSEL, HENRY LONGUEVILLE: Church of England; b. at Cosgrove (33 m. s. of Northampton), Northamptonshire, Oct. 6, 1820; d. in London July 30, 1871. He was educated at the University of Oxford, where his course was exceptionally brilliant; was ordained deacon (1844) and priest (1845). After graduation he tutored privately, meanwhile prosecuting studies in ancient and modern languages and in ecclesiastical history. He was appointed reader in mental and modern philosophy in Magdalen College (1855); Bampton lecturer (1858); Waynflete professor of moral and mental philosophy (1859); "professor fellow" of St. John's (1864); professor of ecclesiastical history (1866); and dean of St. Paul's, London (1868).

Mansel was eminent both as an author and as a teacher in the department of logic, and a fruit of this side of his activities is his edition of H. Aldrich's *Artis logicæ rudimenta* (London, 1862). His favorite themes, however, were those of metaphysics, but he passed into this realm by the path of psychology, a result of which was his *Prolegomena logica, an Inquiry into the Psychological Character of Logical Processes* (1851, 2d ed., 1860). In spite of his preference for metaphysics, he commanded a lesser degree of attention there than he had in the logical field. His *Metaphysics; or the Philosophy of Consciousness Phenomenal and Real* (Edinburgh, 1860) is concerned with psychological problems, including causality and ethics; his *Philosophy of the Conditioned* (London, 1866) is a defense against Mill of the philosophy of Hamilton; but the best results of his work as a metaphysician are to be found in a prior work, the Bampton Lectures, *The Limits of Religious Thought Examined* (Oxford, 1858), in which he sought to apply Hamilton's philosophy of the conditioned to apologetic uses. Other works, showing the range of his activity, are: *Demons of the Wind and Other Poems* (London, 1838); *Letters, Lectures and Reviews* (posthumous; 1873); and *Gnostic Heresies of the First and Second Centuries*, ed. J. B. Lightfoot (1875). When he died, he was at work on a commentary on Matthew for the *Bible Commentary* which he left unfinished. He also edited, in collaboration with John Veitch, Hamilton's *Lectures on Metaphysics and Logic* (4 vols., Edinburgh, 1859–60), and published a volume of *Lenten Sermons* (1863), as well as individual sermons on occasional topics.

Bibliography: J. W. Burgon, *The Lives of Twelve Good Men*, ii. 149–237, London, 1889; *DNB*, xxxvi. 81–83.

MANSI, GIOVANNI DOMENICO: Italian prelate and scholar; b. at Lucca Feb. 16, 1692; d. there Sept. 27, 1769. In 1708 he joined the "Regular Clerks of the Mother of God," founded at Lucca in 1583 by Giovanni Leonardi, devoted himself to theological teaching and writing, and became archbishop of Lucca in 1765. His literary productions are partly original, partly new and revised editions of famous older works. He issued new editions of Baronius' *Annales* together with the continuation of Raynaldus and the criticisms of Pagi (38 vols., Lucca, 1738–56), of Natalis and Graveson's *Historia ecclesiastica*, of Reiffenstuel's and later of Laymann's *Theologia moralis*, of the *Vetus et nova ecclesiæ disciplina* of Thomassin, and a number of others. He began his original work with a treatise on reserved cases in 1724; and his *Epitome doctrinæ moralis et canonicæ* (Venice, 1770), taken from the works of Benedict XIV., has been often reprinted. But his most celebrated works were concerned with the councils of the Church. In 1746 he published a chronological investigation of the councils of Sirmium and Sardica, and not long afterward began his renowned *Sanctorum conciliorum et decretorum collectio nova* (6 vols., Lucca, 1748–52), intended as a supplement to the collection of Labbe, Cossart, and Coleti. It contains 320 papal briefs, the acts of 200 councils previously omitted, and notes on 380 councils whose acts are lost. At the request of the Venetian publisher Zatta, he undertook to reduce to unity and further supplement and annotate the labors of his predecessors; and the *Sacrorum conciliorum nova et amplissima collectio* was the result. He delivered the complete manuscript to the printer in 1765; thirty-one folio volumes appeared up to 1798, when its publication ceased with the Council of Florence (1439). Beginning in 1900, a facsimile of the earlier part has been coming out in Paris, which is intended to bring the work down to the end of the nineteenth century in forty-five volumes. (G. Laubmann†.)

Bibliography: The biography by his associate Franceschini is in vol. xix. of Mansi's collection of councils; that by Dominic Pacchi is in J. A. Fabricius, *Bibliotheca latina mediæ et infimæ ætatis*, i., pp. xi.–xix., Florence, 1858. Consult also: A. Zatta, *Commentarius de vita et scriptis J. D. Mansi*, Venice, 1772; Lichtenberger, *ESR*, viii. 634–635; *KL*, viii. 626–627.

MANT, RICHARD: Church of Ireland; b. at Southampton Feb. 12, 1776; d. at Ballymoney (12 m. n.n.w. of Belfast), Ireland, Nov. 2, 1848. He was educated at Winchester and at Trinity College, Oxford (B.A., 1797; M.A., 1801). Ordained deacon in 1802 and priest in 1803, he was curate of Buriton, Hampshire (1804–08); Crawley, Hampshire (1808–09); and Southampton (1809–10); vicar of Great Coggeshall, Essex (1810–13); and rector of St. Botolph, London (1815–20); and East Horsley, Surrey (1818–20). He was Bampton lecturer in 1811 and domestic chaplain to the archbishop of Canterbury from 1813 to 1815. In Apr., 1820, he was consecrated bishop of Killaloe and Kilfenora and in Mar., 1823, he was translated to Down and Connor, to which Dromore was added in 1842. Mant was a very voluminous writer, both in prose and verse; of his works the most important are: *Sermons for Parochial and Domestic Use* (3 vols., Oxford, 1813); his annotated Bible, in collaboration with George D'Oyly (3 vols., Oxford, 1814; see Bibles, Annotated, II., § 9); *Sermons Preached before the University of Oxford* (1816); *The Book of Psalms in a Metrical Version* (1824); *The Gospel Miracles, in a Series of Poetical Sketches* (London, 1832); *The British Months, a Poem* (1835); *Ancient Hymns from the Roman Breviary* (1837); and *History of the Church of Ireland, from the Reformation* (2 vols., 1840). Of Mant's numerous hymns may be mentioned: "For all thy saints, O God" and "Come, Holy Ghost, my soul inspire!"

Bibliography: Memoirs were written by W. B. Mant, the bishop's son, London, 1857, and by E. Berens, ib. 1849. Consult further: *DNB*, xxxvi. 90–95; S. W. Duffield, *English Hymns*, pp. 152, 153, 221, 342, 488, New York, 1886; Julian, *Hymnology*, pp. 713–714.

MANTELETTA. See Vestments and Insignia, Ecclesiastical.

MANTON, THOMAS: English nonconformist; baptized at Lydiard St. Lawrence (38 m. s.w. of Bristol), Somersetshire, Mar. 31, 1620; d. in London Oct. 18, 1677. He was graduated from the University of Oxford (B.A., 1639; B.D., 1654; D.D., 1660), and was ordained deacon in 1640. He settled at Stoke Newington, London, in 1644 or 1645, and became rector of St. Paul's, Covent Garden, in 1656. He was one of the three scribes to the Westminster Assembly, and during the commonwealth preached many times before parliament. Despite his close relations with the commonwealth, he favored the restoration and was made in 1660 one of the twelve chaplains to the king, though he never performed the duties or received the emoluments of the office. In the same year he was offered the deanery of Rochester, but declined to subscribe. In 1662 he left St. Paul's and held meetings at first in his own house, and, as the attendance increased, elsewhere; these meetings were ignored till 1670, when Manton was arrested and kept in prison for six months. In 1672 he became one of the first six preachers for the merchants and citizens of London in Pinners' Hall. Manton was exceedingly attractive in the pulpit, pacific in spirit, and a man without enemies. He wrote commentaries on James (London, 1651 and often; latest issue, 1844), on Jude (1658), and on the Lord's Prayer (1684); many of his sermons were printed separately, while collections, with memoirs, etc., were made by W. Bates (5 vols., 1678–1701) and by R. Baxter (1 vol., 1679; reprinted, Achill, 1842), and individual sermons figure in sermon anthologies.

Bibliography: W. Harris, *Some Memoirs of the Life and Character of T. Manton*, London, 1725; R. Baxter, *Christian Biography*, pp. 199–226, ib. 1768; Walter Wilson, *Hist. of Dissenting Churches*, iii. 545–566, ib. 1810; W. A. Shaw, *Hist. of the English Church . . . 1640–1660*, vol. ii. passim, ib. 1900; *DNB*, xxxvi. 101–104.

MANUEL, NIKLAUS: One of the notable personalities at the closing period of the Reformation; b. at Bern 1484; d. there Apr. 30, 1530. Until 1522 he devoted himself almost exclusively to art. At the same time he figured as a satirical poet and as such helped very successfully the cause of the Reformation, especially in Bern. In 1512 he was elected into the great council of Bern, and in 1523 was appointed prefect in Erlach. After the disputation of Baden in 1526 the Reformation in Bern made rapid progress. Haller abolished the mass and, after six gilds of the town had joined his cause, received Guillaume Farel and Franz Kolb (qq.v.) as assistant preachers. In 1528 at the Disputation of Bern (see Bern, Disputation of) Manuel took an active part. Shortly afterward he entered the small council of Bern. After that he was almost entirely alienated from art, and the poet gave way to the statesman. Manuel now became an enthusiastic itinerant. Between 1528 and 1530 he advocated in more than thirty assemblies and conferences the cause of the Reformation and of Bern, and gathered new friends for the new teaching. His considerateness and kindness made him appreciated everywhere. In May, 1528, he became member of the board which occupied itself with the organization of the new church, superintended the moral condition of the congregation, and settled matrimonial disputes. In the autumn of the same year Manuel advanced to the position of Venner of Gerbern, acting as judge and taking part in the government of the state. While he has a place in the history of German painting, popular poetry, drama and satire, and was influential in the political development of his native city of Bern, most significant was his attitude toward the religious change of his time. As among the powerful men in Germany Hutten was the most ingenuous ally of Luther, so Manuel was the most popular ally of Zwingli in German Switzerland. Fight against Rome was the watchword of the day, and Manuel served this fight by the satire of his brush, pen, and spoken word, and he became the spiritual father and champion of the Reformation in Bern. He acquired his greatest fame and exercised his chief influence as a poet in the service of the Reformation. Satire and polemics form the core and essence of his poetical productions. His two moralities—*Vom Papst und seiner Priesterherrschaft* and *Von Papsts und Christi Gegensatz*—performed at Bern in 1522, completely destroyed there the authority of the bishop of Lausanne and induced the council of Bern to allow the free preaching of the Gospel. Thus Berchthold Haller (q.v.) had free scope for the development of his reformatory work. No less effect had his satires—*Ablasskrämer* (1526) which belongs to the best satirical productions of the Reformation; *Ecks und Fabers Badenfahrt* (1527), a satire on the disputation of Baden and especially directed against Dr. Eck; *Krankheit* (1528); *Klagred der armen Götzen* (1528); *Elsli Tragdenknaben und Uly Rechenzan* (1530), a merry carnival play. (F. List†.)

Bibliography: Biographies are by S. Scheurer, in *Bernerischen Mausoleum*, 1742; K. von Grüneisen, Stuttgart, 1837 (against this Rettig wrote his *Ueber ein Wandgemälde von Niklaus Manuel*, Bern, 1862); J. Bächtold, Frauenfeld, 1878 (a masterpiece); B. Händcke, ib. 1889. Further literature of minor interest is given in Hauck-Herzog, *RE*, xii. 241.

MAON, MAONITES: A place and people mentioned in the Old Testament. The place-name occurs in Josh. xv. 55 (see Judea), and there is mention in Judges x. 12 of a people called Maonites. Modern critics, following the lead suggested by the best Septuagint readings, correct this to Midianites (cf. the commentaries on Judges of Moore, Budde and Nowack). Traces of a place or territory of the name "Maon" are found in the Meunim (Mehunim) of I Chron. iv. 41 (Hebr. and R. V.); II Chron. xx. 1 (R. V. margin), xxvi. 7. In these passages the Meunim appear in company with nomads, for the most part, and are located in mount Seir. The data used by the chronicler, therefore, implied the existence of a stock of Meunim who about 860–700 B.C. came from the south and assailed Judah. This agrees with the fact of a modern site named Ma'an, fifteen and a half miles southeast of Petra. In case this is correct, it might be that the Meunim of Ezra ii. 50 and Neh. vii. 52 were the descendants of some of these who had been made prisoners in the campaigns noted by the chronicler and had been assigned to service in the temple (cf. Ezek. xliv.7). The fact that the Meunim are represented as parties to an alliance with important peoples like the Moabites and Ammonites suggests that they are to be connected with the early Arabic stock of the Minæans, whose sway was overthrown by the Sabians (see Arabia). Winckler and Hommel connect the Minæans with the North Arabian Muẓri (see Assyria, VI., 2, § 1). (H. Guthe.)

Bibliography: E. Glaser, *Skizze der Geschichte und Geographie Arabiens*, ii. 14–15, 21 sqq., 450–451, Berlin, 1890, and cf. another view by Sprenger, in *ZDMG*, xliv. 505 sqq.; F. Hommel, *Ancient Hebrew Traditions as Illustrated by the Monuments*, pp. 251, 272, London, 1897; idem, *Aufsätze und Abhandlungen*, iii. 273 sqq., Munich, 1892; F. Buhl, *Geschichte der Edomiter*, pp. 40 sqq., Leipsic, 1893; Winckler, in Schrader, *KAT*, pp. 140 sqq.; *DB*, iii. 240; *EB*, iii. 2934–35.

MAORI. See New Zealand.

MAPPA: The linen cloth with which the communion-table, and afterward the altar, was covered. See ALTAR, III., 1, a, § 2.

MARAIS, JOHANNES ISAK: Dutch Reformed; b. at Capetown, South Africa, Aug. 23, 1848. He was educated at South African College, Capetown (B.A., Board of Examiners, Cape of Good Hope [now University of the Cape of Good Hope], 1867), the Dutch Reformed theological seminary, Stellenbosch (from which he was graduated in 1870), and the universities of Edinburgh and Utrecht (1871–1873). From 1873 to 1877 he was minister of the Dutch Reformed church at Hanover, Cape Colony, and since the latter year has been professor of apologetics and speculative philosophy in the theological seminary at Stellenbosch. He has likewise been president of the council of Victoria College, Stellenbosch, since 1883, and lecturer in Hebrew there since 1890, while since 1884 he has also been a member of the council of the University of the Cape of Good Hope.

MARAN, mā″rān′, **PRUDENT:** French Benedictine; b. at Sézanne (40 m. s.s.w. of Reims) Oct. 14, 1683; d. in Paris Apr. 2, 1762. In his twentieth year he became a member of the Congregation of St. Maur, and the rest of his life is mainly a record of scholarly activities. In 1734, on account of his agitation against the constitution *Unigenitus*, he was expelled from the abbey of Saint-Germain-des-Prés, but returned to Paris a few years later. Evidence of his profound knowledge of dogmatics and ecclesiastical history is found not only in his original works but also in his exhaustive introductions to critical editions of the Fathers. He completed three such editions after the death of their first projectors—Cyril of Jerusalem, begun by Touttée (Paris, 1720); Cyprian, begun by Baluze (1726), an edition which was the standard until the appearance of Hartel's text (Vienna, 1868–71); and Basil, begun by Garnier (1730). His most important work, however, was his edition of Justin, Tatian, Athenagoras, Theophilus, and Hermas (1742). His original works, anonymous like his editions, include a *Dissertation sur les sémiariens* (Paris, 1722), written in defense of Touttée's introduction to Cyril; *Divinitas Domini nostri Jesu Christi manifesta in scripturis et traditione* (1742); *La Divinité de Jésus-Christ prouvée contre les hérétiques et les déistes* (3 vols., 1751); *La Doctrine de l'écriture et des pères sur les guérisons miraculeuses* (1754); and *Les Grandeurs de Jésus-Christ avec la défense de sa divinité* (1756). (G. LAUBMANN†.)

BIBLIOGRAPHY: D. Tassin, *Hist. littéraire de la congrégation de Saint-Maur*, pp. 741–749, Brussels, 1770.

MARANOS: A name given the "New Christians" of Spain from the fact that they included Moors. See SPAIN.

MARBACH, mār′bāн, **JOHANN:** German Reformer; b. at Lindau, Bavaria, Apr. 14, 1521; d. at Strasburg Mar. 17, 1581. He began his studies at Strasburg in 1536, and three years later went to Wittenberg, where he lived in the same house with Luther and took his doctor's degree in 1543. After holding temporary positions at Jena and Isny, in 1545 he accepted a call to Strasburg, which was to be the field of his lifelong labor. Here, from 1545 to 1558, he was pastor of the Church of St. Nicholas; canon at St. Thomas' from 1546; professor from 1549, and from 1552 president of the Church Convocation. In 1551 he was an envoy from Strasburg to the Council of Trent. Until Butzer's departure for England (1549) Marbach was on the most cordial terms with the recognized head of the Strasburg Church, and remained a regular correspondent until Butzer's death (1551). By degrees, however, Marbach developed a tendency toward a more exclusive Lutheranism than that represented by the Strasburg Reformers. In the violent opposition to the Swiss, Calvinistic, and Unionistic elements in Strasburg, Marbach was leader. The result of this conflict was the "Lutheranizing" of Strasburg, as evidenced in the Strasburg *Kirchenordnung* of 1598, principally Marbach's work.

During his sojourn at Strasburg (1538–41), Calvin had founded and served a congregation of French refugees, which to the younger generation of Strasburg theologians appeared more and more like a foreign body in the local church. From 1553 complaints began to be urged against the pastor of the French congregation, Garnier, because he did not hold the doctrine of the Strasburg church on the Lord's Supper. He was obliged to leave Strasburg in 1555. In the same year, Peter Martyr, a teacher at the High School, betook himself to Zurich to escape making stricter declarations on the same subject. The last prominent advocate of a Unionistic-Calvinistic theology at Strasburg was Jerome Zanchi (1516–90), a teacher in the High School, and member of the French congregation. When in 1560 Marbach reprinted at Strasburg the treatise of the ardent Lutheran Tilemann Hesshusen, *De præsentia corporis Christi in cœna Domini* with the author's vehement preface against the Elector Palatine Frederick III. and the Palatine theologians in Strasburg, open strife broke out between Zanchi and Marbach. The main points of contention were the doctrines of the Eucharist, of Ubiquity (q.v.), just then coming into prominence, and of the perseverance of the elect and predestination. This controversy gave occasion for a thorough discussion of predestination between the Lutheran and the Reformed theologians. Marbach advocated his own standpoint in his three principal writings: *Christlicher und wahrhaftiger Unterricht von den Worten der Einsetzung des heiligen Abendmahls* (1565); *Christlicher Unterricht und wahrhaftige Erweisung, dass Jesus Christus durch die persönliche Vereinigung der göttlichen und menschlichen Naturen in alle göttliche Herrlichkeit erhaben und versetzt sei* (1567); *Antwort und gründliche Widerlegung der vermeinten Trostschrift Tossani, in der er den Zwinglischen Sakramentsschwarm aufs neue die Bahn bringt* (1579).

Amid all these conflicts Marbach's course was determined not by vainglory nor personal malevolence, but by a sincere love of purity in doctrine and of ecclesiastical discipline and order, as he conceived them. His standpoint in the question as to creed subscription was always that in accepting the "Wittenberg Concord" (1536) Strasburg acceded to the

Lutheran Confession; and he understood this confession just as the later Lutheran theologians generally understood it. The sole canon which he applied in theological controversies was pure Lutheranism. From this doctrinal position he combated not only the Calvinists but the Schwenkfeldians and Anabaptists, who were still active at Strasburg; while, on the same platform, he accomplished the introduction of the Lutheran catechism at Strasburg (1554), and strove for the use of uniform hymnbooks and a common liturgy, though not with immediate success. He instituted private confession in the Church of St. Nicholas, and kept up there the rite of confirmation when it began to fall into disuse in other Strasburg churches. In the interest of a "uniform doctrine and confession," Marbach also took an active part in bringing about the acceptance of the Formula of Concord (q.v.), as is shown by his correspondence from 1567 with Jacob Andreä and Martin Chemnitz. Moreover, he prevailed with the Strasburg theologians to sign the Zerbst Formula (1571), while the official acceptance of the Formula of Concord was opposed by the town council. In the Palatinate he assisted Elector Ludwig, in 1576, to restore Lutheranism after the death of Frederick III. He was likewise eminently active (1564–78) in Zweibrücken (see Wolfgang, Count Palatine). This lean, stirring, industrious little man was by no means lacking in sincere piety, which did not exclude personal irritability, petty intrigues, and doubtful methods in the heat of conflict. Against the Jesuits and the superstitions favored by them he published a vigorous treatise, *Von Mirakeln und Wunderzeichen* (1571). Paul Grünberg.

Bibliography: Sources are Marbach's own writings; *Die Strassburger Kirchenordnung* of 1598; the *Christliche Leichpredigt*, Strasburg, 1612; G. Obrecht, *Patriotische Gedenkrede*, ib. 1659; J. Fecht, *Hist. eccl. sæculi xvi., supplementum*, Durlach, 1683. Consult: W. T. Röhrich, *Geschichte der Reformation im Elsass*, vol. iii., Strasburg, 1832; various essays in W. Horning, *Beiträge zur Kirchengeschichte des Elsasses*, ib. 1881–93; W. Horning, *Dr. Johann Marbach, Beiträge zu dessen Lebensbild*, ib. 1887; idem, *Handbuch der Geschichte der evangelisch-lutherischen Kirche in Strassburg*, ib. 1903; F. Hubert, *Die Strassburger liturgischen Ordnungen im Zeitalter der Reformation*, Göttingen, 1900; J. M. Reu, *Quellen zur Geschichte des kirchlichen Unterrichts . . . 1530–1600*, i. 1, pp. 141–154, Gütersloh, 1904; T. Gerold, *Geschichte der Kirche St. Niklaus in Strassburg*, Strasburg, 1904.

MARBECK, PILGRAM: Anabaptist leader and author; b. at Rattenberg (23 m. e.n.e. of Innsbruck) about the end of the fifteenth century; d. in or near Augsburg c. 1547. He was brought up in the Roman Catholic communion, but left it in early manhood and about 1522–23 became a "promulgator of the Wittenberg Gospel." But he found that "where God's word was preached in the Lutheran way a fleshly freedom followed in its trail" and soon became dissatisfied with Lutheranism. About 1525–26 he "accepted baptism as a witness of the obedience of faith, having regard in this solely to God's word and command" (his own account in his disputation with Butzer). He became an expert engineer and in 1525 was appointed by the Austrian government to a responsible position in connection with the mines of that region. Early in 1528 he was in danger of being arrested and punished as an Anabaptist and made his way to Augsburg, where he hoped to find toleration and employment (J. Walch, *Decas fabularum humani generis*, Augsburg, 1606). But persecution had already begun in Augsburg and in October he went to Strasburg, where his engineering skill was called into use. At this time Strasburg contained a greater number and a greater variety of Anabaptist leaders than any other city. Marbeck's force of character, attractive personality, intellectual vigor, blameless Christian walk, literary skill, and generosity brought him marked consideration among his fellow believers and at first won the highest praise from the leading Evangelical pastors, Butzer, Capito, Zell, and Blaurer. He gained the friendship of Margaretha Blaurer (q.v.) to such an extent that she protected him as far as she was able from persecuting measures when Butzer turned against him and rebuked Butzer for his intolerance. Profoundly convinced of the evil of infant baptism, he was zealous in his efforts to win not only the masses but the preachers to antipedobaptist views. The publication of two books in support of his position led to his imprisonment (October, 1531); but because of his engineering skill he was liberated without promising to desist. On Dec. 9, at his own request, he engaged in a discussion with Butzer, the record of which has been preserved. In twenty-eight articles he defended the antipedobaptist position with a logical acumen rarely excelled. But the council decreed his banishment and after an earnest plea for the Anabaptists he departed for Ulm and soon settled again in Augsburg. Until his death he was the guiding spirit of the antipedobaptist congregations in the neighborhood of Ulm and Augsburg. In 1542 he published an exposition of his views on baptism, sin, hereditary sin, divine worship, magistracy, and the Lord's Supper (*Vermahnung auch ganz klarer grundlicher und unwidersprechlicher Bericht zu wahrer Christlicher ewig bestandiger Brüder-Vereinigung*). This brought him into controversy with Schwenckfeld and his followers. A. H. Newman.

Bibliography: J. Loserth, *Zwei biographische Skizzen aus der Wiedertäufer in Tirol*, Innsbruck, 1895; T. W. Röhrich, *ZHT*, 1860; C. A. Cornelius, *Geschichte des münsterischen Aufruhrs*, vol. ii., Leipsic, 1860; J. W. Baum, *Capito und Bucer*, Elberfeld, 1860; L. Keller, *Ein Apostel der Wiedertäufer*, Leipsic, 1882; C. Gerbert, *Geschichte der Strassburger Sectenbewegung zur Zeit der Reformation*, Strasburg, 1889; A. H. Newman, *Hist. of Anti-Pedobaptism*, pp. 249–253, Philadelphia, 1897. Sidelights are cast by the writings and letters of the contemporary religious leaders, Bucer, Capito, Luther, Zwingli, and others.

MARBURG BIBLE. See Bibles, Annotated, I., § 3.

MARBURG, CONFERENCE OF: A gathering of Protestant theologians at Marburg Oct. 2–4, 1529. The controversy on the Lord's Supper had already assumed considerable dimensions, when in the summer of 1526 the Diet of Speyer convened; therefore the Protestants took pains to come to an agreement in order to present a united front to their opponents. The efforts at harmony originated among the Strasburg theologians, but were frustrated by Luther's firm adherence to his convictions. An attempt of Butzer in the summer of 1526 to influence Luther through Justus

Preliminary Negotiations.

Jonas was also without result. Jonas first suggested that perhaps by a personal meeting of the leaders a remedy might be found; but it was Johann Haner, former preacher of the cathedral in Würzburg, who approached Landgrave Philip of Hesse with the proposal of a conference. Ulrich of Württemberg used his influence upon the young prince for the same purpose. From the beginning political machinations were a factor in the efforts at harmony. In Feb., 1528, Duke Ulrich invited Œcolampadius and Butzer to the court of the landgrave at Marburg, probably for the purpose of winning the support of Philip for the South Germans. Philip, however, was very anxious to bring together Luther and Œcolampadius, and the development of affairs at the Diet of Speyer about 1529 made it necessary to strive for agreement. The Strasburg theologians presented at Speyer a formula of the Lord's Supper which so skilfully concealed the opposition of the contending parties as to offer a basis for a temporary alliance between Saxony, Hesse, Nuremberg, Strasburg, and Ulm on Apr. 22, 1529. The leading authorities, however, saw that these preliminary negotiations would lead to a result only in case of a real agreement on the Lord's Supper. The landgrave therefore invited Zwingli on the same day to a religious conference, and Zwingli declared his willingness to attend. The theologians of Wittenberg took a different attitude. Melanchthon was evidently offended by the political nature of the proposed alliance, and Luther dissuaded the elector from giving his consent because "no improvement was to be hoped for among the principal opponents" (Zwingli), even if the members of the conference should come to an agreement. After June 10 the theologians of Wittenberg received a formal invitation from Philip to meet at Marburg. Under the influence of the elector, Luther and Melanchthon gave their final consent on July 8, but unwillingly and with no hope of good results. The landgrave, however, persevered, and Zwingli was full of zeal, both aiming at a great political alliance of all Evangelical states. Neither the Wittenberg theologians nor the elector knew of the political intentions of the landgrave.

On Sept. 27, 1529, Zwingli and Ulrich Funk from Zurich, Œcolampadius and Rudolph Frey from Basel, Butzer, Hedio, and Jacob Sturm from Strasburg arrived at Marburg. Even before the arrival of Luther, Zwingli had come to an understanding with the landgrave on political questions; but in order to make it effective, it was necessary to reconcile Luther. He arrived at Marburg on Sept. 30, with Melanchthon, Jonas, Cruciger, Veit Dietrich and Georg Rörer from Wittenberg, Myconius from Gotha, Menius and Eberhard von der Thann from Eisenach. Duke Ulrich of Württemberg arrived the same night. The colloquy began on Oct. 2, after the arrival of the South German Lutherans Osiander, Brenz, and Stephan Agricola. Although a great crowd had gathered at Marburg, only fifty to sixty persons were admitted. At the beginning it was agreed that the question of the Lord's Supper should be the primary point of discussion. Luther adhered to the plain and simple words of Christ, "This *is* my body," which he wrote with a piece of chalk on the table, rejecting any metaphorical interpretation. Œcolampadius, who replied first, started from John vi. and then pointed to the existence of numerous metaphors in Holy Scripture, which Luther, of course, did not deny. What he demanded, however, was justification for the assumption of a metaphor in the passage on the Lord's Supper where the text is clear without it. He also declared that he in no way rejected the spiritual eating, as mentioned in John vi. 53; he even regarded it as necessary, but from this, he said, it did not follow that the bodily eating instituted and commanded by Christ was of no use or unnecessary. This was the point on which the controversy hinged—whether beside spiritual eating which both parties equally emphasized, bodily eating was also necessary. A further point of debate was the question of the ubiquity of the body of Christ, which Zwingli rejected on the basis of Rom. viii. 3; Phil. ii. 7; Heb. ii. 7. The characteristic difference in the fundamental conceptions of Zwingli and Luther showed itself in their estimate of reason. Luther conceded to it no right of decision in questions of faith, while Zwingli replied that God would not propose to us for our belief anything inconceivable. At the end of the debate nothing had been accomplished. Then Butzer, as chief representative of the Strasburg theologians, stated their doctrine of the Trinity, original sin, baptism, etc., and asked Luther for a testimony of his orthodoxy, but Luther did not comply with his request. "Our spirit and your spirit do not agree," he said; for the same spirit could not, in his opinion, dwell in people who simply believed the word of Christ and those who vehemently combated it and gave it the lie. Therefore he wished to leave his opponents to the judgment of God; they might teach as they thought it justifiable before God.

The Conference.

Thus the official negotiations were ended, but still the landgrave hoped to succeed by personal influence in his efforts at union. Luther now declared himself willing to draw up a statement of the most important points of doctrine on which an agreement was possible. Thus originated on Oct. 4 the so-called "Articles of Marburg." Fourteen theses testified to agreement on the doctrine of the Trinity, the person of Christ, faith and justification, the Word of God, baptism, good works, confession, secular authority, tradition or human order, and infant baptism. The fifteenth article, on the sacrament of the body and blood of Christ, confesses as uniform doctrine the necessity of partaking of it in both kinds and rejection of the mass, and also that the spiritual eating of the body and blood is principally necessary for every Christian. As to the disputed point in the Lord's Supper, Christian charity should be shown toward each other. The document was signed in three copies by the ten official participants in the colloquy, Luther, Jonas, Melanchthon, Osiander, Agricola, Brenz, Œcolampadius, Butzer, Hedio, and Zwingli. By signing the articles, Zwingli had evidently gone to the extreme limit of concession in the interest of his great plans. Not entirely without reason, Melanchthon thought that the Swiss had "followed Luther's

Articles of Marburg.

opinion." As the Wittenberg circle had no idea of the political machinations which called forth Zwingli's love of peace, they naturally carried away an impression of the complete humiliation of their opponents. But Zwingli ascribed the victory not less to himself and explained the articles in his own sense. It soon became obvious that instead of bridging over the opposition, the conference of Marburg had brought it to fuller expression. (T. KOLDE.)

BIBLIOGRAPHY: The Articles were printed by H. Heppe, *Die 15 Marburger Artikel*, Cassel, 1854; by Bindseil, in *CR*, xxvi. 122–127; and by T. Kolde, in *Die Augsburgische Konfession*, pp. 119 sqq., Gotha, 1896. Sources for the history are the *Opera* of Zwingli, ed. Schuler and Schultheiss, vols. vii.–viii.; the *Briefe* of Luther, ed. De Wette, vols. iii.–iv., or Enders' *Luthers Briefwechsel*, vol. vii.; in T. Kolde, *Analecta Lutherana*, Gotha, 1893; the *Briefwechsel* of J. Jonas, ed. Kawerau, Halle, 1884 sqq.; the reports of contemporaries such as Melanchthon, in *CR*, i. 1099 sqq.; of Jonas, ib., p. 1095; of Butzer in his Commentary on the Gospels, Strasburg, 1530. Consult further: L. K. Schmidt, *Das Religionsgespräch zu Marburg, 1529*, Marburg, 1840; J. Kradolfer, *Das Marburger Religionsgespräch, 1529*, Berlin, 1871; Schirrmacher, *Briefe und Akten zur Geschichte des Religionsgesprächs zu Marburg, 1529*, Gotha, 1876; M. Lenz, *ZKG*, iii (1879), 28 sqq., 220 sqq., 429 sqq.; A. Erichson, *Das Marburger Religionsgespräch, 1529*, Strasburg, 1880; Egli, in *Theologischer Zeitschrift aus der Schweiz*, i (1884), 1 sqq.; F. H. Foster, in *Bibliotheca Sacra*, April, 1887, pp. 363–369; Schaff, *Christian Church*, vi. 629–653; T. M. Lindsay, *Hist. Ref.*, i. 352–359; the literature under JONAS, JUSTIN; LUTHER; MELANCHTHON; ZWINGLI; and also the principal works on the REFORMATION.

MARCA, mār"cā', PIERRE DE: French theologian and prelate; b. at the château of Gant, near Pau (56 m. e.s.e. of Bayonne), Jan. 24, 1594; d. in Paris June 29, 1662. He was educated first at Auch and then at the University of Toulouse, and took up the study of law, beginning his public life in 1615 at Pau, as a member of the Council of Béarn. When the country was annexed to France in 1620 he rendered important services to Henry IV., and was named president of the *parlement* which replaced the former independent council. He occupied this post till 1639, when he was summoned to Paris to join the council of state. He had already published some small treatises and a *Histoire de Béarn* (Paris, 1640; new ed., Pau, 1894), and now took part in the exciting discussion on the liberties of the Gallican Church at the request of Richelieu. His *De concordia sacerdotii et imperii seu de libertatibus ecclesiæ Gallicanæ* (vol. i., 1641) was put on the Index in 1642; but Richelieu rewarded him by the nomination to the bishopric of Conserans in 1643. He was not yet, however, in orders; and his book prevented him from obtaining papal confirmation until 1648, when, after he had published a submission to the censure of the Holy See (1646) and another book, *De singulari primatu Petri* (1647), in which he controverted the theory that the Church had originally had two heads, Peter and Paul, he was taken back into favor. He was ordained priest in 1648, but could not take possession of his bishopric until 1651. In the following year he was named archbishop of Toulouse, but again, owing to the suspicion of Jansenism, did not obtain the papal confirmation until 1654. In 1656, however, he supported the condemnation of Jansenism in the assembly of the French clergy. The king employed him in both political and ecclesiastical affairs, and after Mazarin's death in 1661 wished to have him near at hand. He was accordingly named for the archbishopric of Paris in Feb., 1662, and confirmed by the pope in June, but died three days after the news of his confirmation arrived. Baluze issued a new edition of his *De concordia*, which now appeared complete in print for the first time (1663). Although it was again condemned by the Congregation of the Index the next year, Baluze issued new editions in 1669 and 1704, and it has been several times reprinted since. Collections of smaller treatises were posthumously published by De Faget in 1669 and by Baluze in 1681. (J. F. VON SCHULTE.)

BIBLIOGRAPHY: Brief biographies appeared in the editions by Baluze and De Faget; P. Bayle, *Dictionary Historical and critical*, iv. 98–104, London, 1737 (quotes from sources which well illustrate the text).

MARCELLA: Roman Christian of the fourth and fifth centuries. She came of a wealthy family and married early, but when her husband died seven months after the marriage, she made a vow of perpetual celibacy and gave all her goods to her relatives and the poor. When Jerome came to Rome in 382 she became his friend and studied the Scriptures with him. When Rufinus translated Origen's work "On First Principles" she herself went to Pope Anastasius and showing him the heretical passages induced him to condemn the doctrines of Origen. At the sack of Rome in 410, she was tortured by the Goths, who sought to make her reveal her supposed wealth, and died shortly afterward.

BIBLIOGRAPHY: The chief source of information on her life and character is Jerome's letters, especially no. 127, Eng. transl. in *ANF*, vi. 253–258; cf. *DCB*, iii. 803.

MARCELLIANS: The followers of Marcellus of Ancyra (q.v.).

MARCELLINISTS: A heretical sect of the latter part of the second century, consisting of the adherents of Marcellina, a pupil of Carpocrates (q.v.), whose system of Gnosticism she taught with much success in Rome while Anicetus was bishop (cf. Irenaeus, *Haer.*, I., xxv. 6, *ANF*, i. 351).

MARCELLINUS, mār"cel-lī'nus: Pope June 30, 296, probably to Oct. 25, 304. He is mentioned by Jerome, Nicephorus, and the *Chronographon Syntomon;* other early sources omit his name on account of the apostasy ascribed to him. Eusebius says that Marcellinus succeeded Caius in the twelfth year of Diocletian (a statement confirmed by the *Catalogus Liberianus*), and adds (*Hist. eccl.*, VII., xxxii. 1) that "persecution overtook him." While this implies more than that the persecution merely occurred during his bishopric, it does not necessarily denote that Marcellinus was a martyr, despite the statement of Theodoret (*Hist. eccl.*, i. 2) that he distinguished himself during the persecution. The *Liber pontificalis*, on the authority of a lost *Passio Marcellini*, probably dating from the fifth century, expressly states that Marcellinus, a Roman by birth and the son of Projectus, became a *thurificus* in the persecution, but quickly repented of his apostasy and was beheaded. This is denied by Augustine, but the Donatists knew of the accusation and it is also mentioned in the acts of a Council of Sinuessa forged in 501. There seems to be no good reason to doubt that he actually lapsed for a time and later made atonement, but his martyrdom is improbable. The only detail known concerning his administration is that he enlarged the Roman catacombs. The Pseudo-Isidore contains two spurious decretals of this pope. (A. HARNACK.)

BIBLIOGRAPHY: The sources are indicated in the text. Consult *Liber pontificalis*, ed. Mommsen in *MGH, Gest. pont. Rom.* i (1898), 41–42; and the critical sketch in *DCB*, iii. 804–806, where the sources are adequately discussed.

MARCELLUS: The name of two popes.

Marcellus I.: Pope 308–309. According to the *Liber pontificalis* a Roman by birth, he succeeded Marcellinus after a vacancy of four years (not seven as the *Liber pontificalis* and the *Catalogus Liberianus* give) due to the persecution. He was banished by Maxentius, not, however, as a Christian, but on account of the fierce quarrels which then vexed the Roman church as to the treatment of the lapsed, and induced the emperor to seek peace by the banishment of the heads of both parties. He seems not to have died in exile, and was apparently buried in the cemetery of Priscilla. Little else is known of him with any certainty. The assertion that he delivered the sacred books to the heathen and offered incense rests on a confusion with his predecessor arising from the similarity of their names. (A. HARNACK.)

BIBLIOGRAPHY: *Liber pontificalis*, ed. Mommsen in *MGH, Gest. pont. Rom.*, i (1898), 43–44, ed. Duchesne, i. 165, Paris, 1886; B. Platina, *Lives of the Popes*, i. 64–65, London, n.d.; Bower, *Popes*, i. 40–41.

Marcellus II. (Marcello Cervini): Pope 1555; b. at Montefano, in the March of Ancona, May 6, 1501; d. at Rome May 1, 1555. He became a cardinal under Paul III. in 1539, and was papal legate during the opening period of the Council of Trent. He belonged to the party which strove for a reform of the Church on medieval principles. Great hopes were entertained of the results to follow from his pontificate, but it lasted only from Apr. 10 to May 1, and gave him no time to take any decisive steps. (A. HAUCK.)

BIBLIOGRAPHY: P. Polidoro, *De vita, gestis et moribus Marcelli II.*, Rome, 1744 (depends upon a MS. life by the brother of Marcellus); Ranke, *Popes*, i. 212, iii. 153–155; Bower, *Popes*, iii. 318.

MARCELLUS: The name of five Christian martyrs besides Marcellus I., bishop of Rome (q.v.).

1. A certain Marcellus is said to have been martyred by the Prefect Priscus at Chalon-sur-Saône during the reign of Antoninus Pius, probably in 140. His festival is appointed for Sept. 4, but some throw doubt on the historicity of the legend.

2. **Marcellus the Centurion,** beheaded at Tingis (Tangier) on the birthday of the Emperor Diocletian, probably in 298, for refusing to celebrate the occasion with sacrifices.

3. A third Marcellus, born at Rome, was martyred, according to tradition, at Argenton-sur-Creuse (165 m. s.w. of Paris) during the reign of Aurelian. Fleeing from the persecutions of this emperor to the city where he was fated to die, he attracted the attention of the Prefect Heraclius by his miracles and was scourged and roasted without being harmed. He was accordingly beheaded, while his friend Anastasius was scourged to death. Both these martyrs are commemorated on June 29.

4. **Marcellus, Bishop of Apamea** (the modern Kalaat al-Madik, 120 m. n.e. of Beirut) was burned to death during the reign of Theodosius the Great by a pagan mob roused by his destruction of their temples.

5. **Marcellus, Bishop of Die,** was born at Avignon, and died a prisoner of the Arians at Die (100 m. n. of Marseilles), early in the sixth century. He succeeded his brother as bishop and at his consecration a dove descended on his head. Refusing to accept Arian teachings, however, he was imprisoned until his death. His festival is appointed for Apr. 9. (G. UHLHORN†.)

MARCELLUS OF ANCYRA: Bishop of Ancyra (the modern Angora, 220 m. s.e. of Constantinople); b. probably in the latter part of the third century; d. about 374. He took part as bishop in the synod held at Ancyra apparently in 314, and eleven years later was a somewhat inconspicuous opponent of the Arians at Nicæa. In 335, however, he attracted attention by a book of which little is known, being extant only in fragments. His work was evoked primarily by a treatise of the Lucianistic Asterius, although it formed a general attack upon both the living and the dead leaders of the great Eusebian party. His polemic was aimed against the Eusebian and Arian doctrine of three divine hypostases, which had been received from the teachings of Origen. Perceiving the pagan basis of this doctrine, Marcellus opposed not only the doctrine of Christ's inferiority which it implied but also its polytheistic coloring. A rigid defender of monotheism, he acknowledged only one God, although he recognized a certain differentiation in him. Previous to the creation of the world God had been simply a "monad," but with the formation of the universe the first period of salvation was introduced by the "procession" of the Logos, which was eternal in God and has since remained the "operative activity" of God. In the incarnation of the Logos it became, in a somewhat stronger form, "divided from the Father by the weakness of the flesh," though it existed potentially in the Father not only throughout the period between the creation and the incarnation, but also afterwards, so that God and the Logos are not to be separated, and the eye of faith accordingly sees the Father in Christ (John xiv. 9). In like manner Marcellus regards the Spirit as contained within the Logos until Jesus breathed on his disciples and bade them receive the Holy Ghost (John xx. 22), after which it proceeded operatively from the Father and the Son. Up to the time of the outpouring of the Holy Spirit, therefore, Marcellus taught binitarianism, but after this event "the monad was extended into a triad." Nevertheless, this "extension" did not produce a disruption of the "monad," which is "potentially indivisible," so that the Father, the Logos, and the Spirit are one God. After the parusia, when

Early Life; Trinitarian Doctrine.

Doctrine of the Trinity.

Christ will appear in the flesh, both the Logos and the Spirit will be wholly reunited with God, and the "monad" will again exist as it existed before the creation of the world. The kingdom of the man Christ will then have an end (cf. I Cor. xv. 28), but the Logos, whose power has neither beginning nor interruption, will then, again existing in the Father, retain the divine omnipotence which he had never lost.

Marcellus of Ancyra accordingly taught trinitarian monotheism, which in its development from a "monad" to a "triad" formed part of the plan of salvation, and in this teaching his theological interests were centered. He emphasized the thought that the "non-incarnate Word" is called merely Logos and not Son in the Scriptures, and he accordingly referred the terms "Son of God," "image of the invisible God," and "first-born of every creature" (Col. i. 15), as well as all Biblical designations of Christ except the Logos-concept, to the incarnate Logos. He thus escaped the Eusebian assumption of a "creation" of the Logos, which destroyed the doctrine of its eternity, and at the same time found a confirmation of his theory that the historic Christ was "God appearing in human form" and at the same time "the perfect man."

The Eusebian Synod of Constantinople in 336 condemned the work of Marcellus as heretical, since it assumed that the Son began with his birth by Mary and also postulated an end of his kingdom.

Teachings Condemned; Later Life.

He was accordingly anathematized, the destruction of his book was ordered, his followers, who seem to have been numerous in Galatia, were bidden to return to orthodoxy, and Basil was apparently appointed to succeed him as bishop of Ancyra. Where Marcellus went after his deposition is unknown, but the death of Constantine in 337 permitted him to return to his see. That he was formally reinstated seems scarcely probable, but at all events his reappearance in Ancyra resulted in tumultuous scenes. He was again condemned at a second synod in Constantinople in the latter part of 338 or the early part of 339, and in the summer of the latter year went to Rome, where he was declared to be innocent. He then left Rome, and is next found at the Synod of Sardica in 343, where he was condemned for the third time by the Eastern Church, but was again acquitted by the Western. Of his subsequent fortunes little is known. According to Sozomen, he returned to Ancyra as bishop, only to be again expelled in 350, but the assertion is supported by scant evidence. He was repeatedly condemned both by the Homoiousians and the younger Nicene school, while in the West, on the other hand, his doctrines were not discussed at any synod between 343 and c. 380, although Basil complained that the Occident had no words of blame for the teachings of Marcellus. Where he passed the last thirty years of his long life is unknown, nor are the place and exact date of his death determined. He is said by Jerome to have written many works against the Arians, although none are now extant. At the time of his death he had many followers in Galatia, though it is uncertain how far they actually understood and accepted his teachings. A committee sent apparently in the early part of the eighth decade of the fourth century, from Ancyra to Athanasius, who was mistrustful of Marcellus, though he never polemized against him, presented a symbol which accepted the definition of the Son given in the Nicene Creed, but spoke of only one hypostasis of the Trinity, and also revealed other traces of the influence of Marcellus. He left no representative of his theology, however, and Marcellianism remained an impersonal heresy. It was condemned by Pope Damasus c. 380, and with the acceptance of the first canon of the synod held at Constantinople in 381, the name of Marcellus was placed on the list of heretics in the West after the middle of the fifth century.

While it is true that the Christology of Marcellus recalls the doctrine of Paul of Samosata (see MONARCHIANISM), if the historic Christ be regarded as the "new man" and the Logos or Spirit in him be considered undivided from God, on the other

Position in the History of Dogma.

hand, the historic Christ is, in his teaching, also "God manifest in the flesh." Both these views appear side by side in the system of Marcellus, as they do in almost all the Christology of the early Church before Apollinaris and the Nestorian controversy. Any estimate of the position of Marcellus in the history of dogma must proceed, therefore, from the twofold assumption that his general conception of Christianity was closely akin to that of Irenæus and that the creed of Sardica represented his economic trinitarian "monotheism." A remarkable similarity with the latter document is shown by the views of Phœbadius of Aginnum and the older writings of Hilary, while both Tertullian and Novatian are in harmony with Marcellus in their development of the "monad" into a "triad" in the course of the plan of salvation. These points of resemblance, as well as the agreement of Marcellus with Irenæus, find their explanation in the fact that he represents the tradition of the pre-apologetic age, as it is found in the "binitarianism" of Hermas, the Epistle of Barnabas, and the Second Epistle of Clement, as well as in many Gnostic systems; nor is it impossible that these traditions may have originated in Asia Minor, where both Marcellus and Irenæus lived, and where both modalistic Monarchianism and Montanism flourished. (F. LOOFS.)

BIBLIOGRAPHY: In *Marcelliana* (Göttingen, 1794) C. H. G. Rettberg carefully collected the fragments of Marcellus' writings, cf. *MPG*, xviii.; they are also in Klostermann's ed. of Eusebius' "Against Marcellus," Leipsic, 1906. Earlier discussions are antiquated by T. Zahn, *Marcellus von Ancyra*, Gotha, 1867. Consult further: Hefele, *Conciliengeschichte*, vol. i.; Harnack, *Dogma*, passim, consult Index; R. Seeberg, *Lehrbuch der Dogmengeschichte*, i. 175–176, Leipsic, 1895; F. Loofs, in *Sitzungsberichte der Berliner Akademie, philosophisch-historische Klasse*, 1902; idem, in *Abhandlungen der Berliner Akademie*, 1909, pp. 1 sqq.; *DCB*, iii. 808–813 (excellent).

MARCH, DANIEL: Congregationalist; b. at Millbury, Mass., July 21, 1816; d. at Woburn, Mass., Mar. 2, 1909. He was educated at Yale College (A.B., 1840) and Yale Divinity School, from which he was graduated in 1845, after having been principal of Chester Academy, Vt., and Fairfield Academy, Conn. He held successive pastorates at Cheshire, Conn.

(1845–48). First Congregational Church, Nashua, N. H. (1848–54), First Congregational Church, Woburn, Mass. (1855–61, 1870–93), and Clinton Street Presbyterian Church, Philadelphia (1861–76). After 1893 he was pastor emeritus of the First Congregational Church, Woburn. In theology he advocated "practical, common-sense interpretation of the Gospel of Christ." He wrote *Religion for Heart and Home* (Woburn, Mass., 1858); *Walks and Homes of Jesus* (Philadelphia, 1866); *Night Scenes in the Bible* (1868); *Our Father's House* (1869); *Home Life in the Bible* (1873); *From Dark to Dawn* (1878); *Days of the Son of Man* (1881); *The First Khedive: Lessons in the Life of Joseph* (Philadelphia, 1887); *Morning Light in Many Lands* (Boston, 1891). Several of his works were translated into Swedish and German.

MARCIANITES. See MESSALIANS.

MARCION, MARCIONITES.

1. Marcion's Life.

The facts of the early career of Marcion are difficult to establish, partly because of the tendency of ecclesiastical writers, from whom information of him is gained, to believe and report damaging stories concerning heretics. The principal sources for his life are the writings of Justin Martyr, Hippolytus, Irenæus, Epiphanius, and Tertullian, and these writers are not in entire accord. His birthplace is given as Sinope, in Paphlagonia, on the Euxine, and he is described as a shipmaster of Pontus. Tertullian tells of his coming from Pontus (c. 140) and joining the Christian community at Rome, in the first warmth of his faith making them a present of 200,000 sestertii (Tertullian, "Against Marcion," iv. 4; *Præscriptio*, xxx.; *ANF*, iii. 349, 257). He speaks of his differences with the Roman community, of his excommunication, of the return of his gift, and of his attaching himself afterward to the Gnostic teacher Cerdo (q.v.). According to the same authority the Marcionites dated the time of their master's separation from the Church 115 years and six months from the time of Christ ("Against Marcion," i. 19; *ANF*, iii. 285). This would be the autumn of 144. Justin in his first apology written about 150 (chaps. xxvi., lviii.) notices the great activity of Marcion. Irenæus (*Hær.* III., iv. 3) speaks of Marcion's flourishing under the episcopate of Anicetus (154–165) and tells how Polycarp met Marcion and addressed him as the first-born of Satan (*Hær* III., iii. 4, iv. 3). These give the few certain facts in regard to Marcion's life, his separation from the church in 144, his study of Gnosticism, and his foundation of a separate Christian community.

Of the genesis of Marcion's thought tradition gives only a slight insight. He was a disciple of Cerdo, and, according to Irenæus, Cerdo taught that the God announced in the law and the prophets could not be the father of Jesus Christ. The one was known and the other unknown; one was only just, the other good. On this basis Marcion erected and developed his idea of the complete and absolute distinction between Christianity and Judaism.

2. His System.

His comprehensive work bore the title "Antitheses," and was a semi-dogmatic treatise contrasting contradictory sentences from the law and the Gospel. Tertullian made industrious use of this work in his reply to Marcion. Origen knew of it, perhaps, and also Ephraem, but Epiphanius and Hippolytus did not use it. Antithetical sentences were used as the chief arguments, but they were fortified by examples taken from other passages. Marcion's teaching is especially remarkable for its lack of interest in metaphysical questions. It is certain, however, that he did not regard the Cosmos as the creation of the supreme God; it was the production of a demiurge. "Marcion has with the help of demons in all countries largely contributed to the expression of blasphemies and to the refusal to recognize as God the creator of our world. He acknowledges another God who because he is essentially greater has done greater deeds than the other" (Justin Martyr, I., xxvi; cf. *ANF*, i. 171). Marcion differs entirely from Valentinus in failing to discuss eons. Marcion's thought concerns itself entirely with the religious records of the Jews and the Christians. His demiurge is the creator and lord of all men, who has, however, a chosen people, and is the God of the Jews, the God of the Old Testament. Marcion's reading of the Old Testament convinced him that the principle of retributive justice found in the Old Testament could not be reconciled with that of love and goodness as represented by the God of the new covenant (Tertullian, "Against Marcion," I., vi.; *ANF*, iii. 275). The creating God is just according to the maxim, "an eye for an eye, a tooth for a tooth"; this maxim was expressly annulled by the good God (Matt. v. 38–39). The God of creation caused fire to come down from heaven, the good God in Christ forbade his disciples from doing this (II Kings i.; Luke ix. 54–55); stealing was encouraged by the God of creation of the Old Testament (Ex. xii. 35–36) and forbidden in the New; the creation God is neither omnipotent nor omniscient; he had to investigate what Adam was doing and find out what was going on in Sodom. The good God knows all things and is all-powerful. The Old Testament with its ceremonial law and its low standard of morality is quite fitted to the creation God, but neither he nor his book should have recognition among Christians. Marcion did not employ the allegorical method of interpretation, he accepted the letter of the Old Testament with its miracles and its prophecies. He acknowledged that the creation God was to send a Messiah to collect the chosen people in his kingdom to rule over the whole earth and to exercise judgment upon heathen and sinners. It is at this point that the good God is introduced; before this he was unknown in the world of the demiurge who did not even suspect his existence, but the plan of the demiurge the good God could not allow to be carried out. He wishes to be merciful to sinners and to free all from the bonds of the God of the Jews. He determined therefore to appear in the world in the person of Christ, but Marcion took no interest in the nature of the union between the two, though on this point he must be called a docetist (see DOCETISM; GNOSTICISM). In the Gospel of St. Luke Marcion made an arbitrary change in the text in order to provide for an immediate appearance of God in the world: "In the fifteenth year of the Emperor Tiberius God came down to Capernaum and taught on the sabbath days." In order to influence the Jews, Christ attempted to adapt himself to their conditions, calling himself the Messiah; but in all his activity he showed himself the opposite of the demiurge; while the demiurge only approved of just persons, Christ called to himself publicans and sinners and those who were weary and heavy laden. According to the law lepers were unclean; Christ touched them. Elisha healed one individual by water; Christ healed many through his word. The demiurge sent bears against the children in order to avenge their mockery of Elisha; Christ bade children to come unto him. The Messiah of the demiurge was sent to gather together the Jews of the dispersion, Christ is to free all men. Judaism is restricted to one people; all peoples furnish converts to Christianity. Jewish hopes are concerned with an earthly kingdom; Christ promises to his own a kingdom heavenly and eternal. Only as time went on did the demiurge understand the significance of Christ's career. When he saw his law being rejected he abandoned the Messiah to the believers in the demiurge who crucified him. Here again his victory over the good God was only apparent. The dead Christ he sent down to Hades; but Christ preached and found believers even there who rejected the God of the Jews. The veiling of the sun at the time of the crucifixion was the work of the demiurge. The Messiah of the demiurge has still to appear and will establish an earthly kingdom to last 1,000 years, a realm opposed to the heavenly kingdom of Christ where those who have risen from the dead live and reign, released from the impediment of matter after laying aside their earthly bodies. But the good God continues to be the God of love. Those who do not follow him but cling to fellowship with the demiurge he refuses to punish; he simply gives them over to the demiurge in whose fire they will burn. For believers in the heavenly father there is no judgment; they exist in God's love and nothing seems more inconceivable to Marcion than the notion of a Christ returning for judgment.

In all these speculations there is one great fundamental thought, viz., the idea of the absolute originality and independence of Christianity. This was brought out in Marcion's dispute with the Roman presbyters, in which he quoted from Luke v. 36–37, vi. 43. In applying this to Christianity Marcion indicated his conviction that its connection with Judaism should be entirely severed. For Marcion's New Testament see CANON OF SCRIPTURE, II., 3, § 1. His position was that the original Christian records as they were handed down in the Church had either been intentionally falsified or been written by men to whom the spirit of Christ was foreign. The first place in his class of false apostles was occupied by Peter, James, and John, and he was careful to support this position by citing the Epistle to the Galatians. For him Paul alone was the true apostle; yet he disregarded the Jewish elements in Paulinism. The favorite Pauline antitheses between the law and the Gospel, anger and grace, works and faith, flesh and spirit, sin and righteousness, death and life, were congenial to his thought and germane to his method. In Marcion's system the Gospel of the free grace of God in Jesus Christ is given so much weight that it caused him to view the Church conception of the Gospel as an unpermissible falsification.

3. Relation to Christianity and the New Testament.

As to whether Marcion was a Gnostic or not it must be said that in many different directions he was distinct from the Gnostics, whose orientalism was absent from his system. He was not interested in religious philosophy, and recognized no distinction between faith and gnosis. The Gnostic division of classes with different standards of conduct and different aims he did not accept, and the teaching concerning eons he entirely omitted. His work is chiefly important from the point of view of Christian ethics. All works of the creating God, he affirmed, were to be rejected. He preached the strictest asceticism, denied the lawfulness of marriage, and issued strict provisions in regard to fasting (Tertullian, "Against Marcion," I., xxix., IV., xvii., xxix., xxxiv., xxxviii., xliv., etc.). The type of his propaganda also differed from the Gnostics'. A purified church in which all were to have a place was his aim. He kept many of the church customs in their entirety, baptizing with water and with the trinitarian formula. He did not, however, distinguish between the baptized and catechumens (see CATECHUMENATE), but it was especially his strict asceticism which opposed an obstacle to the growth of his party. Marcion was highly reverenced in his communities, being called the most holy master. His antitheses were given a canonical position. His popularity and his wide influence over the masses made his work the gravest danger to the Church in the second century. He exerted a power never attained by the Valentinians and other Gnostic groups, and was especially dreaded by the orthodox. Possibly the baptismal creed of Rome was prepared to counteract his teaching.

4. His Affiliations and Significance.

Many of Marcion's followers did not adhere strictly to his teachings. Some of them agreed with their master in recognizing two principles, others insisted that there were three. Apelles, the Marcionite about whom most is known (Tertullian, *Præscriptio*, xxx.; *ANF*, iii. 257), seems to have engaged in magical practises and paid great attention to visions, to the utterances of oracles, and to the prophetical revelations of a woman named Philumene, his companion. He differed also from Marcion in his metaphysical interests. His rule of faith began with the words: "There is one good God and one beginning and one power unnamable" (Epiphanius, *Hær.*, xliv. 1–2). But he denied with the Marcionites that the

5. His School and Sect.

world was created by the good God. He taught a fully developed system of angelic mediation, in which there was a creative angel, a fire angel, an angel who spoke to Moses. The ancient authorities differed as to the number of these beings in his system. Apelles differed also from Marcion in his Christology. Christ did not merely seem to have appeared; in truth he took on flesh, he had real flesh and body. He really appeared in the world, and was truly crucified and truly buried and truly rose again. But Apelles did not accept the virgin birth of Christ, and according to him Christ had a sidereal body. He agreed with Marcion as to the origin of the Old Testament and its unsuitability for Christians, the whole volume being unworthy of credence. He wrote a book to show that whatever Moses had written about God was untrue. He called the story of the ark a fable on the ground that it could not have held more than four elephants. The orthodox party accused him of picking and choosing according to his inclinations, to which he replied by quoting Christ's well-known apochryphal saying "be ye skilful money-changers" (see AGRAPHA, 5). Altogether his teaching shows a return to Gnosticism. Three other Marcionites appear in early Christian literature, Lucian, Megethius, and Mark. Some of these recognized three principles, a good and evil principle in addition to the demiurge. The only complete account of any late Marcionite system is found in the Armenian writer Eznik. He speaks of three principles, of the creation being due to a just God, while the creation God succeeds in getting it into his power, and then forming an alliance with Adam. Matter by itself produces diabolical creation. This chaotic condition is cured by the supreme God sending his son from heaven. Those who believe on him as he is revealed through Paul are saved. Marcionite communities seem to have been found especially throughout the East, but also in the West. Their ardor in braving persecution was equal to that of the orthodox, and Marcionite martyrs are frequently mentioned in Eusebius. Near Damascus a description of a Marcionite church has been found proving that in the year 318 the Marcionites were allowed to worship freely (P. Le Bas and W. H. Waddington, *Inscriptions Grecques*, vol. iii. p. 582, no. 2558, Paris, 1870). But a few years later the sect was prohibited by Constantine (Eusebius, *Vita*, iii. 64). It disappeared earlier in the West than in the East, where it lasted still for a number of centuries. Theodoret, for example, claims to have converted 1,000 Marcionites in eight villages (*MPG*, lxxxv. 1316). They were also numerous in Armenia. Perhaps the Paulicians (q.v.) originated from the Marcionites. (G. KRÜGER.)

BIBLIOGRAPHY: The principal sources, though indicated in the text, may be stated again here for convenience: Tertullian's "Against Marcion" (the main source), "Prescription against Heretics," "On the Flesh of Christ," and "On the Resurrection of the Flesh," all in Eng. transl. in *ANF*, vol. iii.; Justin Martyr, I., xxvi., lviii.; Irenæus, *Hær.*, I., xxviii., IV., xxxiii. sqq.; Hippolytus, *Philosophumena*, VII., xxix.; Epiphanius, *Hær.*, xlii.; Philaster, *Hær.*, xlv.; and Esnik, Germ. transl. from the Armenian, by J. M. Schmid, Vienna, 1900, cf. C. F. Neumann, in *ZHT*, iv (1834).

The subject is treated in most of the works on GNOSTICISM—consult especially the books by Neander, Baur, Matter, Lipsius, Harnack, Mansel, and King—and in those mentioned in and under DOCTRINE, HISTORY OF (q.v.). A monograph is by H. U. Meyboom, *Marcion en de Marcioniten*, Leyden, 1888. Of the highest value is Harnack, *Geschichte*, i. 191–197, 839–840, ii. 1, pp. 297 sqq., 591, ii. 2, pp. 537 sqq. et passim, consult index under Marcionites; also his *Dogma*, i.–iii. passim, consult index; cf. *ZWT*, xix (1876), 80–120. Other references are A. Lipsius, *Quellen der ältesten Ketzergeschichte*, Leipsic, 1875; A. Hilgenfeld, *Die Ketzergeschichte des Urchristenthums*, 2 vols., ib. 1884–86; idem, *Cerdon und Marcion*, in *ZWT*, xxiv (1881), 1–37; F. Kattenbusch, *Das apostolische Symbol*, vol. ii. passim, Leipsic, 1900; R. Liechtenhan; *Die Offenbarung im Gnosticismus*, pp. 34–40, Göttingen, 1901; A. C. McGiffert, *The Apostles' Creed*, New York, 1902; Schaff, *Christian Church*, ii. 482 sqq.; Neander, *Christian Church*, i. 458–473 et passim; Krüger, *History*, pp. 77–82; *DCB*, iii. 816–824.

For Marcion's relation to the canon consult the works cited under CANON OF SCRIPTURE, especially that of Zahn. Other works pertinent are: A. Hahn, *Das Evangelium Marcions in seiner ursprünglichen Gestalt*, Königsberg, 1823; G. Volkmar, *Das Evangelium Marcions*, Leipsic, 1852; W. Sanday, *The Gospels in the Second Century*, London, 1876; [W. R. Cassels], *Supernatural Religion*, 3 vols., 1879. On Apelles consult A. Harnack, *De Apellis gnosi monarchica*, Leipsic, 1874; and *TU*, vi. 3 (1890), 109–120, xx. 3 (1900), 93–100.

MARCUS: Pope Jan. 18–Oct. 7, 336, successor of Sylvester. According to the *Liber pontificalis* he was a Roman by birth, the son of Priscus, and was buried in the cemetery of Balbina on the Via Ardeatina. He may have been archdeacon during the pontificate of Melchiades. The *Liber pontificalis* attributes to him the provision that the pope should be consecrated by the bishop of Ostia, and states that he held two ordinations in Rome in the month of December; but he did not live to see that month. He built two basilicas, and received large gifts from Constantine, of which a list is given in the *Liber pontificalis*. The Pseudo-Isidore attributes to him a reply to a letter from Athanasius. (A. HARNACK.)

BIBLIOGRAPHY: *Liber pontificalis*, ed. T. Mommsen, in *MGH*, *Gest. pont. Rom.*, i (1898), 73–74; B. Platina, *Lives of the Popes*, i. 75–77, London, n.d.; Bower, *Popes*, i. 54; *DCB*, iii. 825.

MARCUS AURELIUS ANTONINUS: Roman emperor Mar. 7, 161–Mar. 17, 180; b. at Rome Apr. 26, 121; d. probably at Sirmium (260 m. n. of Dyrrhachium, the modern Durazzo) Mar. 17, 180. He was the son of Annius Nerus, who died c. 130, and was adopted and educated by his grandfather, Marcus Annius Verus. As a child he enjoyed the favor of Hadrian, and became versed in philosophy at an early age. In 138 he was adopted by Antoninus Pius, whose daughter he married, apparently in 145, and the year after Antoninus ascended the throne, Marcus Aurelius became consul for the first time. In 146 he received the tribunician power and then became coregent though he did not bear the title *imperator*. Proposed as the successor of Antoninus, he was *autocrator* after Mar. 7, 161. He immediately made Lucius Verus coregent and placed him in charge of the Parthian war. He assumed the cognomens of *Armeniacus* shortly after 163 and *Parthicus Maximus* and *Medicus* in 166, the same year in which both emperors seem to have assumed the title *pater patriæ*. In this same year he triumphed over the Parthians, and after crushing the Marcomanni bore the cognomen *Germanicus* in 172, while three years later, after his expedition against the Iazygi, he termed himself *Sarmaticus*. In the latter year he made an expedition to Asia, returning by way of Smyrna and Athens, where he was initiated in the Eleusinian mysteries, and arrived in Rome in 176, when he celebrated a triumph over the Germans and Sarmatians. He then associated his son, Commodus, with him in the government, but in 177 both were called to Germany, and during this expedition Aurelius died, apparently of the plague.

Despite the fact that his reign was a period of almost unceasing war, Marcus Aurelius found time for literary activity. His philosophical standpoint was that of eclectic Stoicism, and the writings of Epictetus were his favorite reading; in religion he sought to avoid every form of folly, as he shunned all sophistry and pedantry in philosophy. His ideal of life and his efforts to attain it are given in his *Meditations*, but the extent of his knowledge of Christianity is uncertain. His view that the contempt of death manifested by the Christians was based on obstinacy was merely the general opinion of the philosophers of his period, and any apparent affinity between his *Meditations* and Christian thought is merely accidental and undesigned.

The position of the Church during his reign was practically what it had been under his predecessors, although local persecutions were more frequent and received encouragement in 176 by his stringent laws against superstitious and foreign religions. On the other hand he expressly confirmed Trajan's policy of pardon for all who should recant, and the tradition of his policy toward the Christians in the early Church was accordingly twofold. The older view, represented by Tertullian and Lactantius, ignores the sufferings of the Christians under the "good" emperor or refers them to the machinations of evil counselors, while the later tradition, as given by Sulpicius Severus, Chrysostom, and Orosius, brands his reign as the age of the fifth persecution. The most trustworthy records of the condition of the Church at this period are: the account of the martyrdom of Justin and his companions at Rome, written between 163 and 167; the *Peregrinus Proteus* of Lucian, composed shortly after 165; the letters of Dionysius of Corinth; the works of Melito of Sardis, especially his "Apology," written in the second half of the reign of Aurelius; the lost "Apologies" of Apollinaris and Miltiades, and the extant "Apology" of Athenagoras, composed in the closing years of the reign; the authentic account of the persecutions at Lyons and Vienne given by Eusebius, the most important and detailed source; the account of the martyrdom of Carpus, Papylus, and Agathonice; and scattered references to the Christians in the fragments of the older anti-Montanistic writers preserved by Eusebius, as well as in the works of Lucian, Aristides, Fronto, and Celsus. It is evident, from these sources, that the persecutions became more numerous in the latter part of the reign of Aurelius, and that the rule laid down by Trajan was not always followed, although the government sought to suppress the disorders and thus issued decrees which the Christians construed as acts of toleration. The letter of Marcus Aurelius (usually appended to Justin Martyr's first "Apology"; Eng. transl. in *ANF*, i. 187), dealing with the "thundering legion," is a forgery, though it may be based on a genuine letter. According to this the army under Marcus Aurelius was saved in the face of a vast army of Germans by answer to the prayer of the Christians in the shape of a refreshing rain which fell on the Romans but was a withering hail as it reached the Germans. The "thundering legion" long bore this title, but did not derive its name from this miracle. (A. Harnack.)

Bibliography: There is an excellent list of works in Baldwin, *Dictionary*, iii. 1, pp. 365-366. The *editio princeps* of the "Meditations" was by G. Xylander, Greek and Latin, Zurich, 1559; best ed., by T. Gataker, London, 1643, Cambridge, 1652, Eng. transl., by George Lang, London, 1880; late ed., by C. Cless, Berlin, 1900. Numerous transls. exist in English and continental languages. Among the sources are the *Vita* by Capitolinus; Dion Cassius, lxxi.; the letters of Marcus Cornelius Fronto (ed. A. Mai, Milan, 1815, Rome, 1823); and the Letter of the Churches of Vienne and Lyons, cf. Eusebius, *Hist. eccl.*, IV., xiv.-V., viii. The subject is treated in the works on the history of Rome; in those on the history of philosophy, e.g., by Ueberweg, Erdmann, and Windelband; in those on the persecutions of the Christians, in the works on the history of the early church; and in the classical dictionaries. Lives are by J. Capitolin, Paris, 1850; E. Renan, Paris, 1882, Eng. transl., London, n.d.; B. Gabba, Milan, 1884; P. B. Watson, London, 1884. Consult further: L. M. Ripault, *Histoire philosophique de Marcus Aurelius*, etc., 5 vols., Paris, 1830; M. E. de Suckau, *Étude sur Marc-Aurèle: sa vie et sa doctrine*, Paris, 1857; A. Noël des Vergers, *Essai sur Marc-Aurèle*, Paris, 1860; M. Königsbeck, *De stoicismo Marci Antonini*, Königsberg, 1861; E. Zeller, *Vorträge und Abhandlungen*, pp. 82-177, Leipsic, 1865; A. Bodek, *M. Aurelius Antonius als Freund und Zeitgenosse des Rabbi Jehuda ha-Nasi*, Leipsic, 1868; F. W. Farrar, *Seekers after God*, London, 1891; L. Alston, *Stoic and Christian in the 2nd Century. A Comparison of the ethical Teaching of Marcus Aurelius with that of contemporary and antecedent Christianity*, London, 1906; Schaff, *Church History*, ii. 326–330.

MARCUS EREMITA.

Marcus Eremita, ascetic and theologian, flourished apparently in the first half of the fifth century and died after 430. He first became known by a series of treatises described by Photius in his *Bibliotheca*, although no details of his life are given there. The nine tractates named and summarized by Photius, however, agree with those now extant, with the exception of the "Ascetic Chapters." Marcus was identified by Bellarmine with a monk of the same name, who about 900 prophesied ten additional years of life to the wounded Emperor Leo VI., and the same scholar also advanced the hypothesis that the writings ascribed to the Eremite had been fabricated or corrupted by the heretics of his time. Although this theory was later refuted, Marcus attracted little attention until his treatise against the Nestorians, previously unknown, was published by Papadopulos Kerameos (St. Petersburg, 1891), and since that time it has been shown that all the writings as-

1. Identification and Early Citations.

cribed to Marcus by Photius were actually written by him, or at least by a single author. The first certain mention of Marcus Eremita dates from the seventh century, when he was twice cited by Dorotheus, a Palestinian archimandrite. In the same century he was quoted by Isaac of Nineveh, Anastasius Sinaita, John of Damascus in the eighth century, and Theodore the Studite in the ninth. An important historical note concerning this author is given by Nicephorus Callistus, who states that the ascetics Euphymius, Simon the Stylite, Nilus, Isidore of Pelusium, and the "famous Marcus" were almost contemporary. The last three he designates as pupils of Chrysostom, a statement which is particularly important in the case of Marcus, since neither his writings nor any tradition connect him with this saint. A divergent tradition identifies Marcus Eremita with an ascetic of the same name living in the Egyptian monastic colony of Cellia. According to this identification, Marcus would have attained an extreme age in 395, even if he were not already dead.

2. Ascetic and Polemic Treatises. The first two works of Marcus are treatises "On the Spiritual Law and On Them that Think they are Justified by Works." They originally formed a single work entitled "On the Spiritual Law," and contained 412 mystic and ascetic aphorisms devoted to the interpretation of the law of the spirit (Rom. vii. 14). The underlying thought is monastic renunciation of the world, and the conception is characterized by a combination of a mystic concept of grace with ascetic zeal, the object of all human activity being the removal of obstacles through grace. The treatise of Marcus "On Repentance" is an exposition of penitence required by the commandment of God. Essentially a matter of the heart and the conscience, it need not be manifested openly since it consists in mortification of desires, continual prayer, and bearing of sorrow. It is requisite for all the descendants of Adam, though in itself it can not win the kingdom of heaven.

The treatise "On Baptism," devoted to the efficacy of baptism with respect to regeneration and the new moral life of the Christian, is the most valuable source for Marcus' doctrine of salvation. He holds that baptism is perfectly efficacious for the destruction of sin, but all good works are merely an outworking of the perfect gift of grace conferred through it, according to man's fulfilment of the commandments, so that God and not man is responsible for all good, while the individual and not Adam is to answer for all sin.

The "Salutary Admonitions to Nicholas" are addressed to a young monk who had asked for counsel in his struggle against anger and fleshly lusts, while the "Disputation with a Lawyer" is a dialogue of "an aged ascetic" (the author himself) with a lawyer concerning the two monastic requirements not to invoke the law and to refrain from works of the flesh. The "Colloquy of the Mind with the Soul" is an apostrophe in which the author's mind accuses itself and the soul of ascribing the responsibility of the sins which they themselves commit to Adam, Satan, or mankind in general. In the treatise "On Fasting," Marcus seeks the ethical mean for monastic fasts, so they may actually serve to correct the heart and not to make it proud. In contradistinction to these ascetic treatises, the tractate "On Melchizedek" is exegetic and dogmatic in character, and is a polemic against a heretical view prevailing in the author's time, despite episcopal anathemas. Those who maintained these false teachings, while orthodox in the main, even in their Christology, held that they might teach "deeper mysteries than the apostles" with reference to the account of Melchizedek in Heb. vii. They regarded him as essentially divine and as a true son of God in the sense that he was a theophany of the "non-incarnate Logos." To these treatises must be added the recently discovered polemic against the Nestorians, which is indubitably genuine. In a somewhat obscure fashion Marcus seeks to prove that the Scriptures regard the incarnate Logos invariably as a single Christ, the God-Man being neither mere God nor mere man, but both in virtue of "essential unity." Internal evidence dates this polemic in the beginning of 430 or 431.

3. Spurious Writings. Four treatises are incorrectly ascribed to Marcus Eremita. These are a *Parænesis*, which is identical with the fifth homily of Macarius (q.v., 1); "On Paradise and the Spiritual Law," closely similar to the thirty-seventh homily of Macarius, but with a long preface which is lacking in the edition of Macarius; a fragment of the so-called second letter of Marcus which corresponds to a passage in Macarius; and the incomplete "Ascetic Chapters," the greater part of which is contained in the ascetic *Centuries* of Maximus Confessor, while the remainder are repeated almost word for word in Macarius. The ascription of these writings of Macarius to Marcus is doubtless due in great measure to the similarity of the names. That these treatises were not composed by Marcus is shown both by the fact that Photius does not mention them and also by their partial or complete identity with the works of other authors, this correspondence being nowhere found in the eremite's genuine treatises. The "Ascetic Chapters" seem to be excerpts of some late author.

4. Details of his Life. The writings of Marcus Eremita render it evident that he was a monk of authority and that he composed all his ascetic tractates for monks or ascetics. It may be inferred, moreover, from his "Salutary Admonitions to Nicholas," that before he went to the desert Marcus had been the abbot of a monastery in Ancyra. The *Colloquy* implies that he became an anchorite late in life, although it is not known what desert he chose. Since, however, his writings were best preserved in the laura of Sabas, the region where his memory was retained the longest, and since he resided in Asia and his creed is Asiatic and non-Egyptian in character, there is good foundation for the supposition that he sought the Syrian rather than the Egyptian desert. Johannes Moschus, moreover, in his *Pratum spirituale* makes certain statements "about Father Marcus the Anchorite," who lived in the Syrian desert. The date of Marcus is approximately fixed by the monastic system which was at once developed yet free in form, the mention of the Council of Nicæa as an event of the past, the development of the doctrine of the three hypostases of the Godhead, his independence of tradition, and his creed in his polemic against the Nestorians, as well as by the omission of all mention of the Antiochian Creed of 433 or of the Chalcedonian Creed.

5. His Theology.

As a theologian Marcus was ethical rather than dogmatic, feeling that it was more important to keep the commandments of Christ than to speculate concerning the miracles of God. Convinced that the truth was contained in the apostolic tradition of the Church, and needed only to be guarded against innovations, he never dogmatized except when obliged to do so, and then based his arguments directly on the Bible so far as he could. He accordingly decided Christological controversies by referring the predicates both of exaltation and humility to Christ, guided by his belief in the uncombined yet essentially indivisible union of the Logos and the flesh, since the deeds of a mere man could not give salvation. The general theological position of Marcus closely approximates that of Chrysostom, Nilus, Isidore of Pelusium, and, in Biblical doctrine, of Theodore of Mopsuestia. His ethical attitude is in harmony with his theology. His asceticism is practical rather than mystical, and he attaches little value to mere formalism. In his teachings concerning sin and grace Marcus Eremita held that man was mortal since and because of the sin of Adam, inasmuch as he, being himself condemned to die, could beget none but mortal offspring. Though this death is termed sin and punishment, he denies original sin in so far as he restricts sin to voluntary acts. Death is defined as "estrangement from God," which must be obviated by the atonement of Christ, yet the view is nowhere expressed that death is the cause of sin, but the opinion is maintained that the prevalence of sin is the fault of the individual, though all are subject to a captivity and impurity which can be removed only by the grace of Christ. Grace accordingly consists, on the one hand, of the ransom from death by the death of Christ, and, on the other, in the mystic gift of the Holy Ghost through the baptism of the Catholic Church, which thus restores the perfect freedom of the will hindered by the dominion of sin. The power to fulfil the commandments of Christ is conferred by grace, though the human will is a necessary condition of the manifestation of grace according to Phil. ii. 13. Nevertheless, in all good works hidden grace alone is revealed, and all self-righteousness is thus excluded, while grace so completely annihilates the entire "fault of Adam" that the death of the baptized is traced to their own iniquities. On the other hand, death is necessary for the attainment of complete perfection, for while man remains in the flesh, his human nature renders it impossible for him to become unchanging. (JOHANNES KUNZE.)

BIBLIOGRAPHY: The works of Marcus are found most handily in *MPG*, lxv. 903–1140, with prefatorial matter, pp. 893 sqq. One of his hitherto unknown writings (§ 1 above) is printed by P. Kerameus in *Analekta Hierosolymitikês stachyologias*, i. 89–113, St. Petersburg, 1891. For Syriac translations cf. J. S. Assemani, *Bibliotheca orientalis*, iii. 1, pp. 96, 194, Rome, 1728; W. Wright, *Catalogue of Syriac MSS. in the British Museum*, London, 1871; E. Sachau, *Verzeichnis der syrischen Handschriften . zu Berlin*, Berlin, 1899. Consult: J. Kunze, *Marcus Eremita, ein neuer Zeuge für das altkirchliche Taufbekenntnis*, Leipsic, 1895; idem, in *TLB*, xix (1898), 393–398; C. Oudin, *Commentarius de scriptoribus ecclesiasticis*, i. 902–908, Leipsic, 1722; G. C. Hamburger, *Zuverlässige Nachrichten von den vornehmsten Schriftstellern*, iii. 1–3, Lemgo, 1760; Fabricius-Harles, *Bibliotheca Græca*, ix. 267–269, Hamburg, 1804; T. Ficker, in *ZHT*, xxxviii (1868), 402 sqq.; U. Chevalier, *Répertoire des sources historiques*, Paris, 1877–86; J. Fessler, *Institutiones patrologiæ*, ed. Jungmann, ii. 143–146, Innsbruck, 1892; Ceillier, *Auteurs sacrés*, xi. 634–643; H. G. Floss, *Macarii Ægyptii epistolæ*, in *MPG*, lxv. 877 sqq.; *DCB*, iii. 826–827; *KL*, viii. 684.

MARESIUS, SAMUEL. See DES MARETS, SAMUEL.

MARGARET OF NAVARRE: Daughter of Duke Charles of Orléans-Angoulême, duchess of Alençon, and later Queen of Navarre, patron of the Reformation in France; b. at Angoulême Apr. 11, 1492; d. at the château of Odos, near Tarbes, Dec. 21, 1549.

Social Position; Patronage of Letters.

After her father's death, she was sent by her mother, the witty and ambitious Louise of Savoy, to the court of Louis XII., her guardian, where she received an excellent education. Endowed with rare mental qualities, including eagerness for knowledge and a warm appreciation of everything beautiful, she studied philosophy and theology in addition to the living and dead languages. On Dec. 1, 1509, she married Charles, last Duke of Alençon, and on the accession of Francis I. in 1515, was introduced to the court. The king was very fond of his sister, for whose intellect he had a high esteem, and often asked her advice in difficult matters. Like him, she was the patron of many scholars and men of letters, who clustered about her at her court at Nérac. Among them were some of a serious turn of mind, who spoke to her of religion, such as Lefèvre d'Etaples (see FABER STAPULENSIS, JACOBUS) and his friend Gérard Roussel (q.v.), Michel d'Arande, Clement Marot (q.v.), and Guillaume Briçonnet, bishop of Meaux (q.v.), who with the help of D'Arande, of Evangelical tendencies, was trying to awaken in his diocese a religious life that would lead to a study of the Bible. Between 1521 and 1524 she kept up a correspondence with Briçonnet, through which she became acquainted with "the wisdom of learned ignorance," the art of contemplating God without intermediary (neglecting all scholastic deductions and even the use of the sacraments) and finding union with him only through an intense faith and increasing love.

Attitude Toward Reform.

These letters also discuss the need of reform in the Church. In his reforming zeal Briçonnet had chosen Lefèvre d'Etaples as his vicar-general, and sent Michel d'Arande to Margaret as her chaplain. The latter expounded the Scriptures in private to Margaret and her brother and mother, who, she says, often expressed the wish to reform the Church; and she mentions the spreading of the idea that "divine truth is not heresy." It was on suspicion of heresy, however, that the Franciscans arraigned Briçonnet before the Parlement of Paris in 1524. He was coerced into giving up his reforming projects; but Michel d'Arande, Lefèvre d'Etaples, and Gérard Roussel remained in the private circle of the princess. In 1525 her husband died, and she spent the first period of her widowhood at Lyons, where D'Arande preached before large audiences. During the captivity of Francis I. the persecution of the Huguenots began. When Louise of Savoy was regent, although she had seemed unfriendly to the monastic orders and favorable to reforming ideas, she allowed the introduction into France of the Inquisition. Lefèvre and Roussel, abandoned by Briçonnet, took refuge at Strasburg, whither Michel d'Arande soon followed them. On June 24, 1527, Francis gave his sister in marriage to Henri d'Albret, king of Navarre, eleven years her junior. In her new position Margaret remained faithful to her Evangelical convictions, which were shared by her husband. With his assent she tried to reform the Church in their little kingdom. Gérard Roussel was made abbot of Clairac and later bishop of Oloron. Through her influence with Francis I., Lefèvre was appointed librarian of the château of Blois, and when he was persecuted by the Sorbonne, she had him brought under her protection at Nérac. In Strasburg, where Lefévre and Roussel had praised her dispositions, great things were expected of her for the cause of reform in France. In 1527 Sigismund von Hohenlohe, dean of the cathedral there, imbued with Lutheran ideas, entered into communication with her, expressing the desire to come to France to help the cause. In May, 1528, Capito dedicated to her his commentaries on Hosea, saying "All eyes are turned toward you; you are the hope of all Reformers." As duchess of Alençon, she had done much in that neighborhood for the revival of letters and for reform in religion. In the duchy of Berry, which she had ruled since 1518, the university of Bourges flourished under her protection, and it was here that Calvin and Beza were inclined toward Protestantism under Wolmar's teaching. She intended to found a college in Béarn, to which Sturm and Latomus were to be called (1533); but her plan was not destined to be realized until her daughter Jeanne d'Albret founded the Academy of Orthez. Staying in Paris with her husband in 1533, she caused Gérard Roussel to preach the Evangelical doctrine in the chapel of the Louvre, and his boldness of speech raised a storm not only against him but against his patroness. The *Miroir de l'âme pécheresse* (see bibliography) was condemned and prohibited by the Sorbonne, because it made no mention of the saints or of purgatory. Francis, exasperated by the insults directed against his sister, banished several of the most prominent reactionary clergy. By the help of his confessor Guillaume Petit, bishop of Senlis, he opened a process before the University of Paris for the reversal of the condemnation of the *Miroir*, and the sentence of the Sorbonne was annulled. To allay the popular excitement, Francis ordered both Roussel and his antagonists to keep silence on controverted points. Margaret took a lively share in her brother's correspondence with Melanchthon and Butzer with the view of working out a plan which might promote the reunion of Christendom by mutual concessions. When, however, Francis definitely took the side of the persecutors, Margaret lost all her influence over him in religious matters, and retired in disgust to Navarre, where she and her husband devoted themselves to promoting the cause of reform.

Favoring of the Reformation in Navarre.

Searching the Scriptures, she became far more advanced, in all that concerned dogma, than her teachers D'Arande, Roussel, and even Lefèvre d'Etaples. This is manifest in her book *Les Marguerites de la Marguerite*, and in her last verses, *Dialogue de l'homme et de Dieu* and *Les Prisons*. She adopted Calvin's doctrines of salvation and the sacraments, and rejected confession, indulgences, and prayer to the saints. As to the external forms of religion, which appeared to her non-essential, she kept up at the same time most of the old rites, because, although opposed to clerical abuses, she had always hoped for a reform without a complete breach with Rome. But she did not wish to retain unity at the cost of renouncing the newly recovered truths or of employing compulsion. She ordered that justification by faith should alone be preached in the kingdom of Navarre. The service was held, and the psalms were sung, in the vernacular. Many monastic abuses were reformed, and only godly and Evangelical priests appointed to parishes. These improvements, established by Margaret in the churches of Béarn and later introduced by Roussel in his diocese of Oléron, paved the way for a more thoroughgoing reform which was made later by Jeanne d'Albret, and explains the latter's success. The little mountain kingdom became the refuge of persecuted Protestants, for all of whose needs Margaret provided. As long ago at Alençon she had sheltered Sainte-Marthe, who had escaped from the gallows at Grenoble, so now she begged mercy from Francis I. for persecuted heretics, such as Louis de Berquin, Etienne Dolet, and the Waldenses of Provence. She spent most of her time either at Nérac with her court around her, or in the convent of Tusson, whither she retired during her mourning after Francis I.'s death (1547), and set an example of Christian virtue. At all critical conjunctures she prayed without ceasing. From this period of her life date most of her religious poems, many of which were printed in the *Marguerites de la Marguerite des princesses*, while some remain in manuscript in the Bibliothèque Nationale.

Other Interests in Life.

But her whole time was not given up to religious pursuits. She was by nature a lover of mirth and gaiety. She had comedies performed at Nérac and at Mont de Marsan by Italian players, and wrote a series of lively tales entitled *Heptaméron des nouvelles*, in the style of Boccaccio's *Decameron*, in which she drew from the example of human frailty the moral lesson that one can not rely on one's own strength but should have recourse in all circumstances to God. During the last illness of Francis I. she went to him, and her presence seemed to revive him; but scarcely had she returned to Nérac when she heard of his death (Mar. 31, 1547). The income of 24,000 livres which he granted her was used largely for charity. In 1538 she established a foundling asylum under the name of "Hospice des enfants de Dieu le Père," commonly known from the costume of the inmates as "Les enfants rouges." On Oct. 20, 1548, she unwillingly gave her decidedly Protestant daughter, Jeanne d'Albret, in marriage to the vain and untrustworthy Antoine de Bourbon. Little more than a year later, after a long illness, she died, and was lamented and eulogized by native and foreign poets, as she well deserved to be. G. BONET-MAURY.

BIBLIOGRAPHY: Her works include: *Le Miroir de l'âme pécheresse, au quel elle recongnoist ses faultes et péchez, aussi les grâces et bénefices à elle faictz par Jésus Christ son espoux*, Alençon, 1531, and elsewhere often, e.g., Paris, 1533, Lyons, 1538, Eng. transl. by Princess Elizabeth, *A Godly Medytacion of the Christen Sowle*, London (?), 1548; *Poésies et dialogue entre Marguerite de France et . Charlotte de France*, Alençon, 1533; *Les Marguerites*, ut sup., 2 vols., Lyons, 1547; *L'Heptaméron*, Paris, 1559, and elsewhere in innumerable editions and translations. Her letters are scattered in *Lettere di xiii. Huomini illustri*, Venice, 1564; J. C. Wibel, *Lebensgeschichte des . Siegmung von Hohenlohe*, Nuremberg, 1748; Genin, *Lettres de Marguerite d'Angoulême*, Paris, 1841; A. Champollion, *Captivité de François I.*, ib. 1842, and in A. L. Herminjard, *Correspondance des reformateurs*, Paris, 1878-97.

The most authoritative biography is in F. Frank's ed. of *Les Marguerites de la Marguerite des princesses*, Introduction, 4 vols., Paris, 1873. Consult: P. de Bourdeilles, Seigneur de Brantôme, *Vie des dames illustres*, discours v., ib. 1665-66; V. Durand, *Marguerite de Navarre*, 2 vols., ib. 1849; Miss M. W. Freer, *Life of Marguerite, Queen of Navarre*, 2 vols., London, 1857; H. A. Blind, *Marguerite de Navarre dans ses rapports avec la réforme*, Strasburg, 1858; H. de la Ferrière Percy, *Marguerite d'Angoulême*, Paris, 1862; V. Lüro, *Marguerite d' Angoulême*, ib. 1866; P. Albert, *Littérature française au xvi. siècle*, ib. 1881; J. Bonnet, in *Bulletin de la société du protestantisme français*, xxxvii. 109-114; F. Lotheissen, *Königin Margareth von Navarra; ein Kulturbild aus der französischen Reformation*, Berlin, 1885; Mary Robinson, *Margaret of Angoulême*, London, 1886; A. Lefranc, *Les Idées religieuses de Marguerite de Navarre*, Paris, 1898; P. A. Becker, *Marguerite . . et G. Briçonnet*, ib. 1901; E. Sichel, *Women and Men of the French Renaissance, 1498-1547*, London, 1901; Lichtenberger, *ESR*, viii. 679 sqq.

MARGARET, SAINT: Queen of Scotland; b. in Hungary c. 1045; d. at Edinburgh Nov. 16, 1093. She was of the royal family of England, granddaughter of Edmund Ironside, the last English king before the Danish usurpation (d. 1016). Her father and his brother were sent out of the country by Canute, and, as tradition has it, ultimately came to Hungary and there Margaret was born. She probably accompanied her father to England in 1057. Her marriage with Malcolm III. of Scotland took place in 1067 according to some authorities, in 1069 or 1070 according to others. She applied to Lanfranc, archbishop of Canterbury, for instruction in the way of God's service, became distinguished for her austere and ascetic life, and did much to introduce Roman usages into the Scottish Church.

BIBLIOGRAPHY: A' *Vita*, by a contemporary, probably her confessor, Turgot, is in *ASB*, June, ii. 320-340, an Eng. transl. of which is edited by W. Forbes-Leith, 3d ed., Edinburgh, 1896. Consult: W. F. Skene, *Celtic Scotland*, ii. 344-354, Edinburgh, 1877; W. J. Rees, *Lives of the Cambro-British Saints*, pp. 219-231, 540-553; Llandovery, 1853; A. P. Forbes, *Kalendars of Scottish Saints*, pp. 387-391, Edinburgh, 1872.

MARGARET, SAINT: One of the Helpers in Need (q. v.).

MARGARITA: The term applied in the Greek Church to the vessel containing the consecrated host, while the portions of the host reserved for the sick by the priests in special receptacles are called *margaritai* ("pearls"). These *margaritai* are then placed in the consecrated wine, dipped from it with a spoon, and given to the sick.

MARGOLIOUTH, mār″go-lī′ūth, **MOSES:** Church of England; b. at Suwalki (150 m. n.e. of Warsaw), Poland, Dec. 3, 1820; d. in London Feb. 25, 1881. Of Jewish parentage he pursued rabbinical studies in Poland, but having been induced on a visit to England in 1837 to read the Hebrew New Testament he embraced Christianity and was baptized in Apr., 1838. He entered Trinity College, Dublin, in Jan., 1840, and was ordained curate of St. Augustine's, Liverpool, in 1844. He served in many places as curate and vicar and in 1877 became vicar of Little Linford, Buckinghamshire. He wrote many books, chiefly on Hebrew subjects. His chief works are: *Fundamental Principles of Modern Judaism* (London, 1843); *Pilgrimage to the Home of my Fathers* (2 vols., 1850); *History of the Jews in Great Britain* (3 vols., 1851); *Curates of Riversdale* (3 vols., 1860); *Vestiges of the Historic Anglo-Hebrews in East Anglia* (1870); and *Poetry of the Hebrew Pentateuch* (1871).

BIBLIOGRAPHY: Consult: Margoliouth's *Curates of Riversdale*, ut sup.; the autobiography prefixed to his *Fundamental Principles of Modern Judaism*, ut sup.; and *DNB*, xxxvi. 159.

MARGRETH, JOHANN JAKOB: German Roman Catholic; b. at Hamburg May 29, 1873. He was educated at the University of Münster (1892-94, 1900-01) and the Gregorian University, Rome (1894-1900), studying philosophy from 1892 to 1896 (Ph.D., Gregorian University, 1896) and theology from 1896 to 1900 (D.D., Gregorian University, 1900). After being a theological tutor in the dioceses of Osnabrück (1900-02) and Hildesheim (1902-03), he became privat-docent for apologetics at Münster in 1903. Three years later he was appointed to his present position of professor of moral theology at the Seminary of Mainz. He has written *Das Gebetsleben Jesu Christi des Sohnes Gottes* (Münster, 1902).

MARHEINEKE, mar-hai′nê-ke (until 1823 **MARHEINECKE), PHILIPP KONRAD:** German Protestant theologian; b. at Hildesheim (21 m. s.s.e. of Hanover) May 1, 1780; d. at Berlin May 31, 1846. After completing his theological education at Göttingen he became lecturer there, and in 1805 was appointed professor extraordinary and second university preacher at Erlangen. Two years later he was called as professor to Heidelberg, where he remained until he went to Berlin in 1811. His pretentiousness and bombastic style rendered him unpopular with his colleagues, nor were his sermons at the *Dreifaltigkeitskirche*, where he preached after 1820 as the colleague of Schleiermacher, well received. He began his literary career with his *Universalkirchenhistorie* (Erlangen, 1806) and with his *Allgemeine Darstellung des theologischen Geistes der kirchlichen Verfassung und kanonischen Rechtwissenschaft in Bezug auf die*

Moral des Christenthums und die ethische Denkart des Mittelalters (Nuremberg, 1807). To this same period belongs his *Christliche Predigten zur Belebung des Gefühls fürs Schöne und Heilige* (Erlangen, 1805). His general history of the church was overladen with philosophy, but a better reception was accorded to his *Geschichte der deutschen Reformation* (2 vols., Berlin, 1817). Marheineke was the first to make a scientific study of symbolics, his works on this subject being *Christliche Symbolik* (3 vols., Heidelberg, 1810–14), *Institutiones symbolicæ, doctrinarum Catholicorum, Protestantium, Socinianorum, Ecclesiæ Græcæ, minorumque societatum Christianorum summam et discrimina exhibentes* (Berlin, 1812) and his lectures on *Christliche Symbolik* (1848). His works are marked by an extravagant admiration of Protestantism and of Luther. In his *Grundlegung der Homiletik* (Hamburg, 1811) he deduced all homiletics from the eternal concept of sacrifice and advocated spiritual asceticism, while in briefer writings he made a revival of ecclesiastical life conditional upon the acceptance of a new creed, and pleaded for a more general emphasis on dogma.

The obscurity enveloping Marheineke's thought was dissipated by Hegelianism, and he became one of the leaders of the Hegelian school, writing in this spirit *Vorlesungen über die Bedeutung der hegelschen Philosophie in der christlichen Theologie* (Berlin, 1842). Long before, in his *Christliche Dogmatik* (1819) and his *Lehrbuch des christlichen Glaubens und Lebens* (1823), he had endeavored to develop the external form of religion to a speculative science, regarding the principle of dogmatics as the immediate consciousness of God or as the reason which solves all mysteries in virtue of its knowledge of God and its identity with the idea. The stages of the development of religion were three: the religion of fancy and opinion in paganism; the religion of reflection and recollection in Judaism; and the religion of revelation or the spirit in Christianity. The basal mystery of all religions and ages, even of nature herself, is the Trinity. The undifferentiated substance is the Father; the eternal outgoing of God from himself, the inward self-differentiation of substance and subject, is the Son; and the Holy Ghost reconciles the differentiations between the Father and the Son, thus restoring their unity. In his *System der theologischen Moral* (Berlin, 1847) Marheineke's dogmatics reached its fullest development. The cleavage of the Hegelian school was at first greeted by him as a proof of energy, but the *Leben Jesu* of Strauss was a bitter blow to him, the unceasing opponent of rationalism. In his *System der christlichen Dogmatik* (Berlin, 1847) he replied to Strauss, holding that Christ was the central figure in the history of the world and that Strauss, by his identification of the God-man with humanity, had confused the center with the circumference. Unfavorable in the extreme to the philosophy of Kant, Marheineke approved of the earlier teachings of Schelling, although for his later views he had only the antipathy which he expressed in his *Zur Kritik der schellingschen Offenbarungsphilosophie* (Berlin, 1843). Marheineke became in his closing years a representative of free-thinking piety, holding that the principle of the Evangelical church was that because a thing was true it was in the Bible, not that because a thing was in the Bible it was true.

Marheineke collaborated on the *Studien* edited by C. Daub and F. Creuzer (Frankfort, 1805–11) and on B. Bauer's *Zeitschrift für spekulative Theologie* (Berlin, 1836–38), edited Hegel's *Vorlesungen über die Philosophie der Religion* (Berlin, 1832) and, with T. W Dittenberger, C. Daub's *Philosophische und theologische Vorlesungen* (7 vols., 1838–1841). His own theological lectures were edited by S. Matthies and W. Vatke (4 vols., Berlin, 1847–1849). (G. Frank†.)

Bibliography: K. G. Bretschneider, *Theologische Systeme von Schleiermacher, Marheineke, Hase*, Leipsic, 1828; A. Weber, *Le Système dogmatique de Marheineke*, Strasburg, 1857; *ADB*, xx. 338.

MARIA DE AGREDA, mā-rī'ā dê ā-grē'dā (**Maria Coronel, Maria de Jesu**): A nun of the Franciscan order of the Poor Clares, mother superior of the convent of the Immaculate Conception at Agreda (135 m. n.e. of Madrid) in Old Castile; b. at Agreda Apr. 2, 1602; d. there May 24, 1635. She left a work, alleged to have been divinely inspired, *La mystica ciudad de Dios* (first published in Spanish, 3 vols., Madrid, 1670, afterward also in Latin and other languages)—a tendency writing in favor of the Scotist Franciscan doctrine of the immaculate conception of Mary. The supposed revelations to the author are the wildest flights of imagination. Mary, the immaculately conceived, is carried directly after her birth at divine command into the uppermost heaven, where she beholds the Trinity; 900 angels, under command of the Archangel Michael, are appointed to her service; she is praised as God's eternal wisdom (cf. Prov. viii. 22 sqq.), as ruler of the world, who was present at the transfiguration of Christ on Mount Tabor as well as at his Last Supper, who rose again after her death at Jerusalem, and ascended to heaven no less than twice, and the like. Pope Innocent XI. prohibited the book in 1681, chiefly on the ground of its one-sided espousal of an uncanonized dogma and the heretical teaching propounded therein, viz., that Mary's flesh and blood were present *propria specie* in the Eucharist. But Charles II. of Spain interfered in behalf of the work, which his subjects not only loved but almost idolized. He obtained from the pope a suspension of the decree, at least for Spain. An effort to induce Innocent's successor, Alexander VIII., to revoke the edict for all Christendom, was in vain; the new pope confirmed the suspension brief of his predecessor (1690). Alexander's successor, Innocent XII., to please the king, appointed a commission to examine the work, but never published its decision. This reservation of his opinion seemed the more necessary, as during Innocent's pontificate the Sorbonne of Paris condemned the work after the publication of a French edition (*La Mystique Cité de Dieu*, Marseilles, 1695). The controversy grew more complicated, as the authorship was repeatedly denied to Maria of Agreda and ascribed to the Franciscan Joseph Ximenes Sammaniejo. Pope Benedict XIV (in an edict of Jan. 1748) declared the authorship to be uncertain, and

Clement XIV. and Pius VI. were also compelled to take notice of the book. A German adaptation in two volumes was published at Regensburg as late as 1890 (2d ed., 1893). O. ZÖCKLER†.

BIBLIOGRAPHY: S. J. Baumgarten, *Nachrichten von merkwürdigen Büchern*, iv. 214 sqq., Halle, 1753; J. Görres, *Die christliche Mystik*, i. 482–495, Regensburg, 1836; A. M. da Vicenza, *Della mistica citta di Dio*, Bologna, 1873; Germ. transl. of a brief life from this book by B. M. Lierheimer, Regensburg, 1875; J. Hergenröther, *Kirchengeschichte*, iii. 526–528, Freiburg, 1886; F. H. Reusch, *Der Index der verbotenen Bücher*, ii. 253–257, Bonn, 1885.

MARIAMNE, mār″i-am′ne: The name of three women connected with the family of Herod. See HEROD AND HIS FAMILY, I., §§ 2–4, II., § 4.

MARIANA, JUAN DE: Spanish Jesuit; b. at Talavera de la Reina (68 m. s.w. of Madrid) 1536; d. at Toledo Feb. 17, 1624. He entered the order of Jesus in 1554, and seven years later was appointed professor at the Collegium Romanum, where his chief subject was exegesis, in which his ability was shown by his *Scholia in Vetus et Novum Testamentum* (Madrid, 1619). In 1565 he was transferred to Sicily, and from 1569 to 1574 taught in Paris, where he gained distinction by his lectures on Thomas Aquinas, until his health forced him to return to Spain. The last fifty years of his life were spent in Toledo, and in this period falls his literary activity. His *Historiæ de rebus Hispaniæ libri viginti-quinque* (Toledo, 1592; later extended to thirty books, Frankfort, 1603; Eng. transl., to the death of Ferdinand the Catholic, by J. Stephens, 2 vols., London, 1699) won him the title of "the Spanish Livy."

Mariana's fame is chiefly due to his *De rege et regis institutione libri tres* (Toledo, 1599), which, sanctioned by his ecclesiastical superiors, contains one of the boldest defenses ever written of the sovereignty of the people and their right of rebellion against tyranny. The attack made by Mariana in his *De monetæ mutatione* on the changes proposed in the coinage by Philip III. resulted in his imprisonment for a year in the Franciscan monastery at Madrid. This tractate, together with six others, some of which were subjected to censorship, was included in his *Tractatus septem tum theologici tum politici* (Cologne, 1609), which comprises *De adventu beati Jacobi Apostoli in Hispaniam; De editione vulgata sanctorum bibliorum; De spectaculis; De monetæ mutatione; De die et anno mortis Christi; De annis Arabum cum nostris annis comparatis;* and *De morte et immortalitate libri tres.* In the closing decade of the sixteenth century Mariana wrote his *De erroribus qui in forma gubernationis Societatis Jesu occurrunt.* This was first printed in French at Bordeaux in 1624 during the struggle of the Jesuits with the University of Paris, and later appeared in Latin and Italian, as well as in the original Spanish (Geneva, 1631), but was placed on the Index when the Italian version appeared in 1628. Mariana was also the author of a number of minor works, and edited the *Contra Albigensium errores* of Lucas Tudensis (Ingolstadt, 1612). O. ZÖCKLER†.

BIBLIOGRAPHY: F. Buchholz, *Juan de Mariana*, Berlin, 1804; P. Bayle, *Dictionary Historical and Critical*, iv. 124–133, London, 1837; L. Ranke, *Sämtliche Werke*, xxiv. 230–236, xxxiv. 60 sqq., Leipsic, 1872–73; F. H. Reusch, *Index der verbotenen Bücher*, ii. 281–282, 341–344, Bonn, 1883; idem, *Beiträge zur Geschichte des Jesuitenordens*, pp. 1–23, Munich, 1894; P. Krebs, *Die politische Publizistik der Jesuiten*, pp. 108–121, Halle, 1890; A. and A. de Backer, *Bibliothèque des écrivains de la société de Jésus*, ed. Sommervogel, v. 547–567, 7 vols., Liége, 1891 sqq.; H. Hurter, *Nomenclator literarius recentioris theologiæ catholicæ*, i. 310–312, Innsbruck, 1892; Ranke, *Papacy*, ii. 8, 86; *KL*, viii. 795–800.

MARIANISTS (Knights of the Glorious Virgin; *Fratres Gaudentes*): A Roman Catholic order established among the nobility of Bologna about 1233 by the Dominican Bartolomeo de Bragantiis. Its object was to promote public safety during the struggles of the Guelphs and Ghibellines, and to assist widows, orphans, and all in distress. The first Grand Master was Loderino Andalo of Bologna. The Marianists were divided into conventuals and married, the rule of the order permitting not only marriage but also the possession of property and secular life, thus giving rise to the epithet of "Joyous Brothers" as applied to the knights. The habit of the knights was white, with an ashen-gray mantle bearing a red cross, while the conventuals wore a white or gray habit. Commanderies were gradually established in Modena, Mantua, Treviso, and several other cities of northern Italy, but by the end of the sixteenth century the Marianists declined, and at the death of their last commendator, Camillo Volta, in 1589, Sixtus V. presented their estates to the college of Montalto.

The Teutonic Knights were occasionally termed "Marianists" or "Knights of St. Mary," and a community of regular clergy established in 1588 by Giovanni Adorno of Genoa and St. Francisco Caraccioli of Naples was at first termed "Regular Clerks of St. Mary," although, at the wish of Sixtus V., this name was soon exchanged for "Regular Minor Clerks." In 1816 two French missionary societies were founded bearing the name of the Virgin: the "Oblates of the Immaculate Virgin Mary," founded by the Provençal Bishop J. E. de Mazenod (d. 1861) and soon numbering seventy houses in five provinces (three European and two American); and the "Society of Mary," founded by the Abbé Colin, which was confirmed in 1836 and has since worked chiefly in Oceania. (O. ZÖCKLER†.)

MARINUS, ma-rai′nus *or* ma-rī′nus: The name of two popes.

Marinus I.: Pope 882–884. He was the son of a priest named Palumbus, of Gallese in Tuscany, was a subdeacon under Leo IV. (847–855), and became a deacon in 862 or soon after. In 866 he was sent as one of Nicholas I.'s envoys to the eastern emperor, but was stopped on the Greco-Bulgarian frontier and forced to return to Rome. He was in attendance upon the eighth ecumenical council as legate of Adrian II., Nov., 869–Feb., 870, and was recognized as the most capable Roman representative. He next became treasurer (*arcarius*) of the Roman see, archdeacon, and bishop of Cære in Etruria. He represented John VIII. in the negotiations of 879–880 with Charles the Fat, and went again to Constantinople in the latter year to persuade Photius into submission, but failed and was imprisoned. He was elected pope in Dec., 882, the first case of the breach of the ancient rule forbidding the translation of bishops from one see to another. He came to terms with Charles the Fat in June, 883, and succeeded in reconciling the adherents of Formosus, whom he recalled to Rome and to the occupancy of his see of Porto. He excommunicated Photius (q.v.), and maintained friendly relations with the English King Alfred, dying in the middle of May, 884. (H. Böhmer.)

Bibliography: *Liber pontificalis*, ed. Duchesne, ii., p. lxvii., 224, Paris, 1892; J. M. Watterich, *Pontificum Romanorum vitæ*, i. 29, Leipsic, 1862; J. Hergenröther, *Photius*, ii. 650–651, Regensburg, 1868; R. Baxmann, *Die Politik der Päpste*, vol. ii., Elberfeld, 1869; F. Gregorovius, *Hist. of the City of Rome*, iii. 205–206, London, 1895; Bower, *Popes*, ii. 292–293; Milman, *Latin Christianity*, iii. 101; Mann, *Popes*, iii. 353–361 et passim.

Marinus II.: Pope 942–946. He was chosen under the influence of Alberic, who retained entire control of his actions until his death.

It should be noticed that the two popes above named are in the later lists designated as Martin II. and III., so that the second Martin (1281–85) is counted as Martin IV. (H. Böhmer.)

Bibliography: *Liber pontificalis*, ed. Duchesne, ii., pp. lxix.–lxx., Paris, 1892; J. M. Watterich, *Pontificum Romanorum vitæ*, i. 40, Leipsic, 1862; R. Baxmann, *Politik der Päpste*, ii. 94 sqq., Elberfeld, 1869; F. Gregorovius, *Hist. of the City of Rome*, iii. 318–321, London, 1895.

MARISTS. See Society of Mary.

MARIUS: Bishop of Aventicum 574–94. In the process of Frankish conquest between 530 and 540, a considerable part of what is now Switzerland was incorporated, and with it the old Roman colony of Aventicum Helvetiorum. Toward the end of the sixth century it was made the seat of a bishopric, and Marius is the first well-attested bishop. He was born in the diocese of Autun in 530 or 531, probably of Gallic-Roman blood, and received an excellent education with a view to the priesthood. In 585 he took part as bishop of Aventicum in the Frankish Synod of Macon. He died in 594, on Dec. 31, according to a necrology of the church of Lausanne, where he was buried. The chronicle written by him, the manuscript of which is in the British Museum, is a continuation, without separate title, of that of Prosper, covering the years 455–581, and contains scanty but useful contributions to the history of Valais and Burgundy. The saintly life attributed to him by his epitaph is one of the bright spots in a dark period. (Emil Egli†.)

Bibliography: The *Chronicon*, ed. J. Rickly, is in *Mémoires et documents de la société de l'hist. de la Suisse Romande*, xiii. 19–56, Lausanne, 1853; *MPL*, lxxii. 793–802, and in W. Arndt, below. The chief source for a life is the *Cartularium Lausannense*, reproduced in full in *Mémoires et documents de la société de l'hist. de la Suisse Romande*, vol. vi., Lausanne, 1851; cf. *MGH, Script.*, xxiv (1880), 794 sqq., and *MGH, Auct. ant.*, xi (1893), 227 sqq. Consult: J. D(ey), in *Mémorial de Fribourg*, i (1854), 49–55; W. Arndt, *Bischof Marinus von Aventicum*, Leipsic, 1875; Holder-Egger, in *NA*, 1876, p. 254; *KL*, viii. 868 869. The very scattered references are well collected in Potthast, *Wegweiser*, p. 768.

MARIUS MERCATOR: Ecclesiastical writer of the fifth century; d. after 451. But little is known of his life. His cast of thought, dogmatic views, style, acquaintance with Augustine, and knowledge of African affairs, point to North Africa as his birthplace. He appears to have been a cultivated layman, with a lively interest in theology, well read in Scripture, and able in polemics. What is known of him rests wholly on his writings, on a mention of him by Possidius, in *Index librorum Augustini*, iv.; and on a letter to Marius from Augustine, who thanks him for two tracts against the Pelagians, which the "young" author in 418 (hence he was hardly born prior to 390) had sent over to him from Rome (*NPL*, xlviii. 193). It is possible that he then followed, at Rome, the vocation of a public teacher; at all events, Augustine styles him *doctor*. He must have removed to Constantinople before 429, where he took part in the last stage of the Pelagian agitations and in the Nestorian dispute. In these matters he so keenly advocated the interests of Rome that he gives the impression of having served the Roman see in some official capacity. He vigorously urged the condemnation of Julian of Eclanum and his companions, and to this end in 429 he addressed a memorial in Greek to the congregation in Constantinople, submitting a copy to the Emperor Theodosius II. and translating the same into Latin (*Commonitorium super nomine Cœlestii*). As a result the Pelagians were banished from the capital, and their ecclesiastical condemnation followed at the Council of Ephesus of 431. In the same year Marius issued a second and ampler tract against the Pelagians (*Commonitorium adversus hæresin Pelagii et Cœlestii vel etiam scripta Juliani;* also under the title *Subnotationes in dicta quædam Juliani ad Pientium presbyterum*, with extracts from Julian's writings). His remaining literary activity is confined to translation from Greek into Latin of documents bearing upon the Pelagian and Nestorian controversies. Of particular importance in this regard, especially in view of the meager transmission of the original texts, are his translations from writings of Nestorius (e.g., *Sermones V adversus Dei genetricem Mariam*).

Marius is not to be rated very highly as an author. As exhibited in his writings, he was a close adherent of orthodox doctrine and an ardent admirer of Augustine and Cyril. His polemics included not only Pelagianism and Nestorianism, but also the theology of the Antiochian school. His dogmatic position is that of a rather narrow orthodoxy; his judgment is borrowed, his polemics is impassioned; he is often unjust, at times coarse and vulgar. His style is harsh and frequently ignoble. Nevertheless, his writings and literal translations are of permanent value for the history of the Pelagian and Nestorian controversies, inasmuch as not a few of the weightiest of the original documents are preserved exclusively through him. G. Krüger.

Bibliography: The first collected edition of Marius' works was by J. Garnier, Paris, 1673; the best is by S. Baluze, ib. 1684, reproduced in Gallandi, *Bibliotheca veterum patrum*, viii. 613–768, Venice, 1772; *MPL*, xlvi. reproduces in the main the poorer text of Garnier. Consult: F. Loofs, *Nestoriana*, Halle, 1905; J. Fessler, *Institutiones patrologiæ*, ii. 2, pp. 151–165, Innsbruck, 1896; O. Bardenhewer, *Patrologie*, pp. 447–449, Freiburg, 1901; *DCB*, iii. 834–835; *KL*, viii. 869–871; W. Smith, *Dictionary of Greek and Roman Biography*, ii. 1045–46, London, 1890 (gives list of the writings); Ceillier, *Auteurs sacrés*, viii. 498–508.

MARK.

I. The Man: In Acts xii. 12, 25, a John Mark is named as one of the Christians of Jerusalem, at whose mother's house the meetings of the community were held, who was also a companion of Barnabas and Paul on their missionary journey to Antioch and Cyprus (Acts xiii. 5) but left them when they reached Asia Minor. Because of this defection, Paul refused to take him along on the second missionary journey, and this caused a separation between Barnabas and Paul, Barnabas and Mark going together and Paul and Silas becoming companions. A Mark is mentioned by Paul several times in his epistles (Col. iv. 10, "Mark, the cousin of Barnabas"; II Tim. iv. 11; Philemon 24), always in favorable terms. In I Pet. v. 13 is mentioned one of the name as "Mark my son." These notices do not suffice to prove the existence of two men of the name (Schleiermacher and Kielen in *TSK*, 1843), but the historicity of at least one Mark is apparent. He was a Jew (Col. iv. 11), and, like the Jesus Justus of that passage and other Jews of the period, took a Roman name in addition to his Jewish name. Acts xii. 12 suggests that his father was already dead in the early years of Christianity. Mark appears to have been younger than Paul and Peter, but still old enough to have been an adult at the time of the crucifixion. Tradition identifies him with the man described in Mark xiv. 13 as "bearing a pitcher of water" and with the young man of verses 51–52, and also makes him one of the seventy disciples; it does not follow from I Pet. v. 13 that he was converted and baptized by Peter. His missionary activity is abundantly recognized by Paul, and the last historical datum is that of his presence in Rome about 63 A.D. Legend makes him the founder of the Church in Egypt and bishop of Alexandria (Eusebius, *Hist. eccl.*, IV., xv.). The predicate "stump-fingered" applied to him in Hippolytus, *Hær.*, VII., xxx., is possibly a misunderstanding arising from the fact that the Gospel ascribed to him is without such introduction and conclusion as the other Gospels have.

II. The Gospel: Universal tradition ascribes to Mark the authorship of the shortest of the Gospels, and almost as unanimously regards Peter as the authority behind Mark (Tertullian, *Adv. Marcion*, IV., v.). Bound up with this is the legend that Mark was the convert of Peter.

1. External Testimony to Authorship. Irenæus (*Hær.*, III., i. 2) reports that Mark wrote the Gospel after Matthew was written and after the death of Peter, and Origen adds (Eusebius, *Hist. eccl.*, VI., xxv. 5) that it was written before the Gospels of Luke and John. Clement of Alexandria reports (Eusebius, *Hist. eccl.*, VI., xiv. 6–7) that the writing was undertaken at the request of the converts at Rome, and that Peter neither favored nor hindered the undertaking. These reports may well be based upon the words of Papias recorded in Eusebius (*Hist. eccl.*, III., xxxix. 15). This celebrated passage asserts that the Gospel was based not on Mark's own knowledge of Jesus, whom he had not heard, but on the preaching of Peter, and that this Mark faithfully recorded but did not observe chronological order. This is not to be pressed farther than is legitimate as the report of a well-informed man of the Church of Asia Minor in the immediate postapostolic period; it is evident both that the Gospel is not a full record and that the order of events is not that of history. Papias says nothing of the method or occasion of writing the Gospel, only it is clear that he thinks of it as composed in Greek, and he calls Mark "the interpreter of Peter." "Interpreter" has often been understood as a synonym of "author" of the written expression of Peter's teaching; but it is better to take the word in its nearer sense of "translator," since the fact that the Gospel contains reports of Jesus' words and the other fact that Mark is expressly said not to have heard Jesus seem to demand a documentary basis. There is no necessity, however, to doubt the Marcan origin of the second Gospel, especially in view of Justin Martyr (*Trypho*, cvi.) and of the fact that it is ascribed to a man of the second rank when tradition might have assigned the authorship to an apostle.

The Gospel contains no title which gives the author's name. Some scholars regard i. 1 as a title; but since verses 2–3 are not in the style of the citations usually employed in this Gospel, it is better to take verse 1 as the predicate after "John came," verse 4.

2. Internal Testimony. Then the report of "the beginning of the Gospel" reaches through i. 13, while verses 14–15 report Jesus' assumption of the work begun by John. The rest of chapter i. reports the initial success of Jesus; with ii. 1 is registered the beginning of conflict with scribes and Pharisees; iii. 6 notes the purpose of these opponents to destroy Jesus; in rapid succession follow the story of recognition of him as Son of God by the demons, his teaching of the disciples, his wonder-working, the sending of the twelve to preach and heal, his celebrity (reaching even to Herod's court), his Galilean activity and his journey through Peræa, his announcement of his coming death, his last conflicts with the ecclesiastical authorities, his final instructions to the disciples, his suffering and death and resurrection. Evidently the intent of the evangelist was to detail in chronological order the facts of Christ's life, and time notes (viii. 1, cf. vi. 34, ix. 2) show that this purpose was kept in mind, though sometimes the relation of cause and connection is preferred to that of time. Thus the impression the whole Gospel gives is that of a development which proceeds inevitably to the end. But the evangelist never asserts himself as an eye-witness of the events which he narrates; there is no more reason to connect him with the "certain young man" of xiv. 51 than with the "certain one" of verse 47. Of greater consequence is the matter of trustworthiness. To be noted are the lively freshness of tone, the loving lingering on little episodes, the definiteness of reference to details of place, time, and person, the result of which is to impress the reader with the fact that this book is a triumph of the writer's art and with the antiquity and originality of its account. Attempts to make out of the Gospel a "tendency writing" are failures; one view makes it the production of the mediating party, another sees in it a Pauline production, another would make it Petrine—all of which contain a portion of the truth. The author was certainly not a Judaizer, as certainly the Gospel was meant for the heathen; Pharisaism was condemned, while the Davidic origin of Jesus is asserted, not proved. The universalism of the author is Pauline in its emphasis upon faith and upon the effect of Christ's death. The fundamental interest of the Gospel in the Messiahship of Jesus and in him as the completion of salvation through suffering and death is of early Christian cast. The legendary elements make it difficult to assume Peter's responsibility for all the details, though a leading interest in that apostle may be granted. He is first mentioned (i. 16), and last (xvi. 7), and most frequently, while of certain episodes he is the center; yet some matters can hardly go back to him as the reporter (viii. 33, xiv. 54–72). If Peter was so important in the councils of the twelve as appears from the Pauline epistles, this alone might account for the frequency with which he figures in the Gospel. Without the report of Papias no one would with so great assurance have ascribed the virtual authorship to Peter. It can not be granted that the evangelist related without arrangement and with omissions what he gives, since a very definite plan fully carried out is evident in the book. That a man who had dwelt in Jerusalem and had in the first decade associated with all the apostles, Paul included, should set down in his Gospel merely what he received from Peter and what Peter used in his preaching seems not at all to fit with probabilities. John Mark, the friend and companion of a Peter and a Paul, whom tradition names as the author of this Gospel, presents the figure of the person whom, apart from tradition, the Gospel itself presupposes—a man born a Jew but acquainted with Greek, well but not rabbinically educated, wishing to further the speedy conquest of the world by the Gospel. He wrote not as a historian but as a propagator of religious ideas, and put forth his Gospel with the same independence as he showed in his first missionary journey, not to fit with a Pauline or a Petrine statement but to suit the needs of those whose requirement was salvation. If Mark is the author, the date is probably not later than 75 A.D. On the other hand, the development of the material given seems to require several decades. It is debated whether Jerusalem had fallen, since, e.g., chap. xiii. seems to contain reminiscences of the beginning of the Jewish War. The earliest tradition names Rome as the place of writing. Chrysostom's mention of Alexandria seems connected with an attempt to gain honor for that city by relating to it the Gospel of the traditional first bishop. Latinisms favor the Roman origin (xii. 42, xv. 15). The story, first appearing in Ephraem Syrus, that Mark wrote his Gospel in Latin needs no refutation, however; the book was evidently written for readers of Greek. Explanations of facts or expressions which for Jews would need no explanation appear with considerable frequency (iii. 17, v. 41, vii. 11, xii. 18, xiv. 12).

The hypothesis of Griesbach, accepted in substance by Strauss, Baur, Schwegler, and Keim, makes of Mark an abbreviated compilation from Matthew and Luke. It is based principally upon the fact that Mark has little peculiarly his own apart from single verses and the sections iv. 26–29, vii. 32 37, viii. 22–26. Such literal agreement between works can not be fortuitous, literary relationship alone explains. In that case the priority of Mark is most probable, and that is the conclusion strongly supported by scholarship.

3. Relation to the Other Synoptics.

The arguments in favor of Marcan priority are: (1) the arrangement of Mark prevails in Matthew and Luke; (2) this hypothesis best explains the omissions by the other Synoptics of details found in Mark; (3) in the verbal agreements of Matthew and Luke with Mark, the turns of phrasing and expression are Marcan; (4) the dissonance of Matthew and Luke in the history of the infancy and of the passion strongly confirms the hypothesis of their dependence on Mark where the matter is common to all three. On the other hand, the arguments of the opponents of the priority of Mark have some force, since there are Marcan passages which seem to be excerpts or to be in form of statement grounded upon misconception or references to an earlier text. Moreover, there are to be explained the agreements of Matthew and Luke in passages not found in Mark and not containing the words of Jesus. Accordingly there has been supposed an early Mark, and an early Matthew used by Mark, or at least one written source used in both, and indeed these hypotheses have been combined. While it is possible that the original text of Mark is to be distinguished from that which received official recognition, tradition gives no basis for this supposition such as would be afforded by dissonance in reports regarding the book. Fully as difficult to decide is the question whether there were written sources in Mark's possession, or at least prior works of which he knew. Unless the work of a century of investigation is worthless, the present Matthew can not be a source. On the other hand, a collection of the words of Jesus ("apostolic source," "Logia," "Ur-Matthew," "Urevangelium," see MATTHEW), alleged to have been compiled by Matthew, might have lain before Mark as early as 70 A.D.; but there is no proof that such was the case. While passages like Mark iv. 1-34 and chap. xiii. impress one as the result of a working over or editing, they do not necessarily presuppose a prior documentary basis. The impression which the book makes is that the author wrote not after books but from the heart and with all the joy that attends a new project. He doubtless knew of many words of Jesus which he did not record, not because they were dissonant from his purpose, but because his ideal was not that of completeness.

The Gospel has met some severe misfortune. Despite the sturdy attempt of Dean Burgon (see bibliography) to defend them as original, the verses Mark xvi. 9–20 appear as a compilation from Luke and John. The manuscripts B and ℵ close the

Gospel with xvi. 8, so also the Sinaitic Syriac and the best manuscripts of the time of Eusebius and Jerome. An alternative ending is known to exist in shorter form, and indeed appears in some manuscripts alongside the longer form of conclusion.

4. Mark xvi. 9–20.

This testifies to the need felt for a fitting ending, and shows also that whoever composed the shorter form did not know of the longer. The shorter ending can be traced to the fourth century, the longer perhaps into the second. The suspicion that Aristion wrote it (so Conybeare, Resch, Rohrbach, Harnack) has little support outside of a manuscript of the Armenian version. Yet Mark hardly closed his book with the words "for they feared." Equally unsatisfactory are the hypotheses that Mark died before he finished and gave it to his friends who published it and that the last leaf was lost from the original copy. It is most probable that the original close was in times before Papias stricken out by some ecclesiastical authority because its account of the resurrection conflicted with that of the other Gospels. In manuscripts where it still existed it was marked with the obelus, and like so many other obelized passages has perished. (G. A. JÜLICHER.)

BIBLIOGRAPHY: A large amount of pertinent matter is to be found in the literature cited under GOSPELS; LUKE; MATTHEW. The reader should consult also the pertinent sections of the works on N. T. introduction (see BIBLICAL INTRODUCTION), particularly those of Holtzmann, Weiss, Zahn, and Jülicher. Works on the apostolic age are also to be consulted, such as E. Renan, *Les Évangiles*, Paris, 1877; C. Weizsäcker, *Das apostolische Zeitalter*, Freiburg, 1892, Eng. transl., London, 1894–95; A. C. McGiffert, *Hist. of Christianity in the Apostolic Age*, New York, 1897.

On the man consult: R. A. Lipsius, *Die apokryphen Apostelgeschichten und Apostellegenden*, ii. 2, pp. 321–353, Brunswick, 1884; T. Zahn, *Einleitung in das N. T.*, ii. 199–220, Leipsic, 1899; *DB*, iii. 245–248; *EB*, iii. 2937–2941. H. B. Swete, in his commentary, London, 1902, has an illuminating chapter on "the personal history of St. Mark."

On questions of introduction, besides the general works already referred to, the following are suggested: F. Hitzig, *Ueber Johannes Marcus und seine Schriften*, Zurich, 1843; F. C. Baur, *Das Marcusevangelium nach seinem Ursprung und Charakter*, Tübingen, 1851; K. R. Köstlin, *Der Ursprung und die Komposition der synoptischen Evangelien*, Stuttgart, 1853; A. Klostermann, *Das Marcus-Evangelium*, Göttingen, 1867; J. H. Scholten, *Het oudste Evangelie*, Leyden, 1868; G. Volkmar, *Das Evangelium, oder Marcus und die Synopsis der . Evangelien*, Leipsic, 1869; W. Weiffenbach, *Die Papiasfragmente über Marcus*, Berlin, 1878; P. Corssen, in *TU*, xv. 1, 1896; A. Link, in *TSK*, 1896, pp. 405 sqq.; W. Hadorn, *Die Entstehung des Marcus-Evangeliums*, Gütersloh, 1898; T. Calmes, *Comme se sont formés les évangiles*, Paris, 1899; P. Wernle, *Die synoptische Frage*, Tübingen, 1899; E. A. Abbott, *Diatessarica*, part 2, *Corrections of Mark adopted by Matthew and Luke*, London, 1901; A. Menzies, *The Earliest Gospel; Historical Study of . Mark*, ib. 1901; A. Bolliger, *Marcus der Bearbeiter des Matthäus-Evangelium*, Basel, 1902; R. A. Hoffmann, *Das Marcusevangelium und seine Quellen. Ein Beitrag zur Lösung der Urmarcusfrage*, Königsberg, 1904; E. Wendling, *Ur-Marcus. Versuch einer Wiederherstellung der ältesten Mitteilungen über das Leben Jesu*, Tübingen, 1905; idem, *Die Entstehung des Marcus-Evangeliums*, ib., 1908; B. W. Bacon, in *JBL*, xxvi., part 1, 1907 (on the prologue); idem, *The Beginnings of Gospel History*, New Haven, 1909; Harnack, *Litteratur* (consult the indexes); *DB*, iii. 248–262; *EB*, ii. 1761–1898. On the last twelve verses: P. Rohrbach, *Der Schluss des Marcus Evangeliums*, Berlin, 1894; J. W. Burgon, *Last Twelve Verses of . . Mark*, Oxford, 1871; F. C. Conybeare, in *Expositor*, 1893, 241 sqq., cf. 1894, 219 sqq., 1895, 401 sqq.

Of the host of commentaries the following may be mentioned: J. Calvin, in Eng. transl., 3 vols., Edinburgh, 1845–46; C. F. A. Fritzsche, Leipsic, 1830; J. Ford, Oxford, 1862; A. Klostermann, Göttingen, 1867; B. Weiss, Berlin, 1872; idem, *Die vier Evangelien im berichtigten Text*, Leipsic, 1900; R. Wenger, Stuttgart, 1879; C. A. Keil, Leipsic, 1879; L. Bonnet, Lausanne, 1880; M. Riddle, New York, 1881; P. Schanz, Freiburg, 1881 (Roman Catholic, excellent); R. F. Weidner, Philadelphia, 1881; G. F. Maclear, in *Cambridge Bible*, London, 1883; E. H. Plumptre, New York, 1883; J. A. Alexander, ib. 1884; T. M. Lindsay, ib. 1884; G. A. Chadwick, London, 1887; E. Bickersteth, in *Pulpit Commentary*, 2 vols., ib. 1888; C. S. Robinson, *Studies in Mark's Gospel*, New York, 1888; H. S. Solly, London, 1893; J. Morison, London, 1894 (regarded as one of the best); E. Gould, in *International Critical Commentary*, New York, 1896; F. L. H. Millard, ib. 1901; J. Weiss, *Das älteste Evangelium*, Göttingen, 1903; J. Wellhausen, 2d ed., Berlin, 1909; A. Maclaren, 2 vols., London, 1906; W. H. Bennett, *The Life of Christ according to St. Mark*, ib. 1907.

MARKOS EUGENIKOS: Metropolitan of Ephesus; b. at Constantinople in the latter part of the fourteenth century; d. 1443 (according to others, 1447 or 1449). He was educated by the famous Joseph Bryennios, and at the age of twenty-five became a monk. About 1436, against his will, the emperor made him metropolitan of Ephesus, and both in this capacity and as the representative of the patriarch of Antioch he attended the Council of Ferrara and Florence. After his return he resided at first in Constantinople, but his ecclesiastical polity debarred him both from that city and from Ephesus. He sought refuge in Athos, but was imprisoned at least once. In learning, Markos was inferior to such scholars as Gennadius and Gemistos Plethon, despite his thorough training in the theology and philosophy of his countrymen. He was, however, a powerful though simple orator, and was characterized by unyielding firmness. His importance in the history of the Church is due to his opposition to union with Latin Christianity; both before and after the Council of Florence he refused to sign the decree of union unless the pope would permit the use of leavened bread in the sacrament, or at least strike out the *Filioque* from the creed. According to his panegyrist Syropulos, he defended himself before the emperor, the patriarch, and the pope; but this seems doubtful, especially as Hierotheus of Monembasia states that he fled to Constantinople instead. His unswerving opposition to the union was not improbably the cause of its failure. His polemic nature is shown by the majority of his writings (collected in *MPG*, clx.), in which he considers almost all the points of controversy with the Latins, such as the doctrine of the Trinity, the question of purgatory, the signification of the Epiklesis (q.v.) in the Eucharist, and the problem of the Tabor light (see HESYCHASTS). The respect in which he was held is clear from the fact that he was placed among the saints at an early date. An *Acoluthia* was composed in his honor in the fifteenth century, and a decree of the synod held by the Patriarch Seraphim in 1734 expressly termed him a saint. (PHILIPP MEYER.)

BIBLIOGRAPHY: A list of the pertinent literature, mainly in Greek, is given in Hauck-Herzog, *RE*, xii. 287. The early life by Manuel Peloponnesius, of the 15th or 16th century, was edited by Arsenij, Moscow, 1886. Consult Fabricius-Harles, *Bibliotheca Græca*, xi. 670–677, Hamburg,

1808; A. C. Dematracopulus, *Græcia orthodoxa*, pp. 98-105, Leipsic, 1872; Krumbacher, *Geschichte*, pp. 115-116; and the literature under FERRARA-FLORENCE, COUNCIL OF.

MARLORAT DU PASQUIER, mār"lā"rū' dü pās"kyē', **AUGUSTIN:** French Reformer; b. at Bar-le-Duc (158 m. e. of Paris) about 1506; executed at Rouen Oct. 31, 1562. At the age of eight he was placed in an Augustinian monastery, where he took the vows and was ordained priest in 1524. Nine years later he was abbot of a monastery at Bourges, but, becoming indoctrinated with the principles of Protestantism, he was forced to flee from France in 1535 and took refuge in Geneva, where he gained a precarious living as a proof-reader for Greek and Hebrew. At the recommendation of Viret he was appointed to a pastorate in Crissier near Lausanne, and there married. From Crissier he was called to Vevey, where he remained until 1559. The dismissal of Viret in the controversy on excommunication, however, led Marlorat, who approved the rigidly Calvinistic procedure, to resign, and after a brief sojourn in Geneva he was sent in July to Paris as pastor of the Evangelical congregation there. After a year he accepted a call to Rouen as first preacher. In that city, three years previously, the Protestants had formed a community of their own and were still struggling to secure the right to hold public services. On the accession of Charles IX. in Dec., 1560, they addressed a petition, written by Marlorat, to the parliament and the king, requesting permission to use a church. The petition was refused, but the 10,000 Protestants of Rouen felt themselves able to defy the edict of July 25, 1561, and hold their services in the halls of the ancient tower. Marlorat likewise addressed a printed petition to Catharine de' Medici, in which he asserted the loyalty of the Protestants, and in August of the same year he was summoned to Poissy to attend the religious disputation to be held there. In this conference Marlorat was an important figure, and in the debates with the doctors of the Sorbonne, in Jan., 1562, on images, baptism, and similar points of controversy, he was one of the three spokesmen of the Protestants.

Returning to Rouen, Marlorat presided over the provincial synod held on Jan. 25, 1562. After the massacre at Vassy on Mar. 1, 1562, the Protestants of Rouen resolved to seize their city. On the night of Apr. 15 they carried out their purpose, and Marlorat was appointed one of the three heads of the new government, which still professed to be loyal to the king. Rouen was speedily fortified, and on May 27 the city was invested by an army under the command of the Duc d'Aumale, who, however, was forced to retire on June 12. On Sept. 29 a second force led by Charles himself, Anthony of Navarre, and others appeared before the city. Rouen was gradually reduced, but Montgomery, who commanded the besieged, like Marlorat, would accept no terms which did not include free exercise of the Protestant religion, and on Oct. 26 the city was carried by storm. Marlorat and his family were captured and imprisoned. Three days later he was tried before the parliament on the charge of high treason, and on Oct. 30 was condemned to be executed before the church in which he had lately preached, the sentence being carried out on the following day.

The chief works of Marlorat were: *Novi Testamenti catholica expositio ecclesiastica* (Geneva, 1561); similar commentaries on Genesis (1561), the Psalms, and the Song of Solomon (1562); posthumous commentaries on Isaiah (1564) and Job (1585); and especially his concordance, *Thesaurus in locos communes rerum, dogmatum et phraseon . ordine alphabetico digestus* (ed. W. Fenguereius, London, 1574). English translations were made of his commentary on Mark and Luke by T. Timme (London, 1583), on John by the same (1575), on II and III John by N. Baxter (1578?), and on Revelation by A. Golding (1574). Marlorat likewise prepared the index to the *Institutio* of Calvin, which has since formed an integral portion of the work. (T. SCHOTT †.)

BIBLIOGRAPHY: T. Beza, *Hist. eccl.*, vol. i. passim, ii. 610 sqq., Antwerp, 1580; *CR*, vols. xvii.-xxi. passim. Sketches of the life have been written by C. D. Kromayer, Strasburg, 1851; in *Bulletin de la société de l'histoire du protestantisme français*, vi (1857), 109 sqq.; and by Osmont de Courtisigny, Caen, 1862. Consult also H. M. Baird, *Hist. of the Rise of the Huguenots*, i. 509, 539, ii. 80, London, 1880.

MARNIX, PHILIPS VAN.

Philips van Marnix, Baron Sainte-Aldegonde, renowned as a Dutch Protestant theologian and statesman, was born at Brussels in 1538 and died at Leyden Dec. 15, 1598. After receiving a thorough education, he resided for a time in Geneva, where he formed a friendship with Calvin and Beza. Returning to his native country between 1560 and 1562, he lived for a time in retirement, from which he was summoned to the struggle to free the Netherlands from Rome and Spain.

1. Early Career.

Here his first activity was the preparation of the "Compromise" by which the Dutch nobles pledged themselves to resist the introduction of the Inquisition, while the petition to the Regent Margaret of Parma (Apr. 5, 1566) on the same subject was also written by him. He defended the iconoclastic riots in Antwerp in Aug., 1566, in his *Van de beelden afgheworpen in de Nederlanden in Augusto 1566* and *Vraye narration et apologie des choses passées au Pays-Bas.* Before long he also took up arms in the cause of the Reformation, but, with his brother and Brederode, was repulsed at Austruweel (Mar. 13, 1567) in an attempt to raise the siege of Valenciennes, and fled successively to Breda and Germany. He was banished by the "Council of Blood," Aug. 17, 1568, and his estates were confiscated; but in this exile he became the life-long friend of William the Silent, in whose honor he wrote late in 1568 or early in 1569 the famous "William's Lay," a poem which is still a favorite folk-song in Holland. Meanwhile he had entered the service of the Reformed elector-palatine, Frederick III., and at Heidelberg he wrote on Christology and the Eucharist, besides composing his *De biënkorf der heilige roomsche kercke* (Emden, 1569) and attending the convention at Wesel (Nov., 1568) and the synod at Emden (Oct. 4–14, 1571).

Holland soon claimed the services of Marnix, whose principal political activity was exercised between 1572 and 1585. In the former year he was the plenipotentiary of William and secured the promise of the Estates to renew the war with Spain.

2. Diplomat and Soldier. On Nov. 4, 1573, however, he was himself captured by the Spaniards at Maaslandssluis. He was taken first to The Hague and then to Utrecht, where he was induced to make vain negotiations for peace. He was exchanged on Oct. 15, 1574, and from March to June of the following year he acted as William's deputy at the fruitless conferences at Breda. Holland and Zeeland declared themselves independent of Spain and offered the crown, under certain conditions, to Elizabeth of England, Marnix being the head of the embassy which remained in England from Christmas, 1575, to Apr., 1576, in a vain endeavor to persuade Elizabeth to become the sovereign of the Dutch. In the latter year, moreover, he was a leader in the "Pacification of Ghent." Don John of Austria, the Spanish viceroy, who carried through the "Eternal Treaty" (Feb. 17, 1577), recognizing in Marnix a dangerous enemy of Roman Catholicism, now unsuccessfully demanded his expulsion from Brussels. The Spanish attack on the citadel of Namur (July 24, 1577) roused the Dutch to a sense of their situation. Don John was retired from his office on Dec. 7, and three days later the second Brussels union was concluded for mutual protection and toleration. Marnix, as privy councilor after Dec. 29, 1577, first put down the revolts in Groningen and Artois, and, at the Diet of Worms (May 7, 1578), secured German neutrality in the Dutch struggle with Spain.

At this juncture, Marnix and William were attacked in an anonymous pamphlet, to which the former replied in his *Response apologétique* (see below, § 4) which is particularly interesting for its numerous details of his own life.

3. Decline of Power. After a fruitless visit to the Diet of Cologne in 1580, he entered upon the more hopeful endeavor to induce Duke Francis of Alençon-Anjou, the youngest son of Catharine de' Medici, to accept the throne of the revolted Dutch provinces. At the head of an embassy sent to France for this purpose, he reached Plessis (near Tours) on Sept. 9, 1580, and ten days later the treaty of Plessis-lez-Tours was signed, in which Marnix ably defended the civil and religious liberties of the Dutch. He remained in France until Mar. 8, 1581, and on July 22 of the same year Philip was declared deposed in favor of Francis, Marnix himself preparing the act (*Acte de deschéance de Philippe II. de sa seigneurie des Pays-Bas*). In November he went to England, where Francis was paying court to Elizabeth, and on Feb. 19, 1582, he returned with the new ruler. Francis, however, madly attempted (Jan. 15–17, 1583) to seize Antwerp and the most important cities by treason or a *coup d'état*. He was defeated and forced to leave the Netherlands, while Marnix and William, as his allies, were exposed to such suspicion that the former retired to his estates in West-Souburg, near Flushing. He was called from this seclusion to become first burgomaster in Antwerp, Nov. 30, 1584. A few days later the siege of the city by Alexander of Parma began, ending on Aug. 17, 1585, by its honorable surrender, though without recognition of Protestantism. A storm of indignation broke over Marnix, who defended his surrender of the city in his *Bref récit de l'éstat de la ville d'Anvers du temps de l'assiègement*. But his political activity was at an end, although he visited England in 1590, France in 1591, and Orange in 1597. He resided at West-Souburg until 1596, when he removed to Leyden.

4. Theological Position and Bible Translation. Theologically Marnix was an enthusiastic partizan of Calvin and Beza, and in this spirit he secured the rejection of the Wittenberg Concord at the Synod of Antwerp (Aug. 20, 1566). He was also instrumental in securing a Calvinistic Presbyterian organization, culminating in a general synod, for the exiled congregations of his coreligionists. Here, too, belong his polemics against the fanatics and Anabaptists, exemplified in his *Ondersoeckinge ende grondelijcke wederlegginge der geestdrijvische leere*, written in 1595. This was followed by a series of other polemics, the most important being the *Response apologétique à un libelle fameux* (Leyden, 1598), a reply to an anonymous attack by Emmery de Lyere. He was a stern opponent, moreover, of all revelation of God alleged to exist outside the Bible and creation, and was a genuine Calvinist in his assertion that the secular arm had authority to suppress religious error. He was active as a translator of the Bible and the Psalms. After ten or twelve years of labor, he issued a rimed version of the latter (Antwerp, 1580), but this, though the subject of many debates in the synods, never gained a place in the liturgy, despite its scholarly and literary merits. Like previous Dutch versions of the Psalms, the early Dutch translation of the Bible was essentially faulty, and in 1578 the Synod of Dort deputed Marnix and Dathen to seek suitable revisers. The commission was never executed, but Marnix had already begun to translate the Psalms and some of the Minor Prophets, when, in 1586, the Synod of The Hague made unsuccessful overtures to him for an entire new translation. It was not, however, until 1594, when he was formally requested by the States General to perform this task, that he consented, but he lived to complete only the Psalms and Genesis, though he left fragments of Exodus, Deuteronomy, Isaiah, Daniel, and other books (see Bible Versions, B, III.).

5. Other Works. His most important contribution to theology was the *Biënkorf* already mentioned. It is a biting satire on the Roman Catholic Church, written by a supposed adherent of that communion, and ridiculing all its arguments against Protestantism. The book, which is clearly modelled on the *Epistolæ obscurorum virorum* (q.v.), has won for Marnix a place among the great satirists of all time. The work ran through more than twenty editions (the last at Groningen, 1862) and was translated into most European languages (Eng. transl. by G. Gilpin, London, 1579). After his death appeared his *Traicté du sacrament de la saincte cene du Seigneur* (Leyden, 1599), an intensely Calvinistic attack on the doctrine of the Mass. He also carried on a controversial correspondence on the same subject with the Louvain professor Michael Bajus, which he published under the title *Opuscula quædam Domini Sanct Aldegondii* (Franeker, 1598); while in his *Trouwe vermaninge aen de christlike Gemeynten van Brabant, Vlanderen, enz.* (Leyden, 1589) he urged his coreligionists to be patient under their afflictions. There is no complete edition of the works of Marnix, but select works were edited by E. Quinet, *Œuvres de P. de Marnix de Sainte-Aldegonde* (9 vols., Brussels, 1857–60), while his theological writings were collected by J. J. van Toorenenbergen, *Philips van Marnix van St. Aldegonde godsdienstige en kerkelijke geschriften* (3 parts, The Hague, 1871–91). (S. D. van Veen.)

Bibliography: The life of Marnix has been written by: J. Prins, Leyden, 1782; W. Broes, 3 vols., Amsterdam, 1838–40; E. Quinet, Paris, 1854; T. Juste, The Hague, 1858; A. Lacroix and F. van Meenen, Brussels, 1858; J. van der Have, Haarlem, 1874; P. P. M. Alberdingk Thijm, Leuven, 1876; and G. Tjalma, Amsterdam, 1896. Consult also: P. Fredericq, *Marnix en zijne Nederlandsche geschriften*, Ghent, 1881; *Cambridge Modern History*, iii. 201 sqq., New York, 1905; A. Elkan, *Philipp Marnix von St. Aldegonde*, Part i., *Die Jugend Johanns und Philipps von Marnix*, Leipsic, 1909.

MARONITES.

1. Character and Claims. The Maronites are a Syrian people, forming within the Christian Church a peculiar half-independent community or sect. Its members live scattered all over Syria; congregations are gathered in Aleppo, Damascus, Nazareth, and the Island of Cyprus; but the proper home of the community is the Lebanon region, from Tripoli in the north, to Tyre and the Lake of Gennesaret in the south. The districts of Kesrawan, n.e. of Beirut, and Bsherre (26 m. s.e. of Tripoli) are inhabited exclusively by Maronites; while in other places Maronites, Greeks, Jacobites, Druses, and others live as neighbors. The total number of the Maronite inhabitants of Lebanon is somewhat over 200,000, according to the newest reports. They pursue agriculture and cattle-breeding, and succeed well in the cultivation of the silk-worm. Their native tongue has for centuries been the Arabic, but they are of Syrian descent. The liturgy employed in their divine service is in Syriac, though only a few understand that language; the readings from the Gospels, however, are in Arabic. They like to consider themselves a distinct nation; and they have, indeed, always succeeded in maintaining a certain measure of political independence. They are governed by sheiks, elected from among their own nobility; and to the Ottoman sultan, who appoints a Christian pasha over them, they pay a variable tribute. At the head of their church (the *Ecclesia Maronitarum*) stands a patriarch, who is elected by themselves and has the title of patriarch of Antioch and all the East. He is elected by a two-thirds' vote of the archbishops and bishops. He resides during summer in the monastery Kanobin, in the Lebanon, and during winter at Bkerki. He receives confirmation from the pope; for from the latter part of the twelfth century there has existed a relationship between the see of Rome and the Maronites. Although this relationship depends more upon an external basis and upon adjustments made from time to time, and though real unity in doctrine or worship has never existed, the claim of later Maronite authors is often to the effect that from apostolic times their church has maintained an undisturbed orthodoxy, essentially that of the Roman Catholic Church. Authors who have written in this strain are Abraham Ecchellensis (q.v.) and Faustus Nairon, in *Dissertatio de origine, nomine ac religione Maronitarum* (Rome, 1679). These writers follow somewhat closely a few Roman Catholic writers, though there have been manifest traces of monothelite tendencies.

On the Orontes, between Hamath and Emesa, lay an old monastery dedicated to St. Maron. In the sixth century it was repaired by Justinian, according to Procopius (*De ædificiis*, v., ix.), and was the most prominent among the Syrian monasteries.

2. Origin of the Name. Early Accounts. The Maron after whom the monastery was named is generally considered identical with the hermit whose life Theodoret has described (*Religiosa historia*, xvi.), the monk and presbyter of whom Chrysostom speaks so highly (*Epist.* xxxvi.), who probably lived about 400. But the great age and the celebrity of the monastery make it more probable that it took its name from some saint much older, perhaps from Mari, missionary to Babylon, who was buried in the monastery Deir Mar Mari, near Seleucia, on the Tigris; or from Mari the Persian, mentioned by Ibas of Edessa (W. Wright, *Hist. of Syriac Literature*, London, 1894, pp. 48–49, 59). However this may be, it is from the monastery that the Maronites themselves derive their name; some scholars, however, derive it from Maronea, a village thirty Roman miles east of Antioch; and others from Johannes Maron (see below). The name does not occur until the eighth century, when it is used by John of Damascus to designate a heretical sect. Exactly in the same manner it occurs later in the writings of Christian authors in Egypt (who wrote in Arabic), such as Eutychius (Ibn Batrik, beginning of the tenth century), Benassalus (Ibn el-Assāl, thirteenth century), and others (cf. E. Renaudot, *Hist. patriarcharum Alexandrinorum*, Paris, 1713, pp. 419 sqq.). Eutychius says: "At the time of the Emperor Mauricius there lived a monk Marun who taught that Christ had two natures, one will, and one activity (? operation). The most of his adherents, named Maronites after him, dwelt in Hamath, Ḳinnesrin and 'Awasim. After his death, the citizens of Hamath built the cloister Deir Marun and openly professed his teaching." Benassalus distinguishes Maronites from Melchites (orthodox Greeks) and from Franks (Latins), and reports that the Maronites went over to the religion of the Franks. William of Tyre (q.v.) states that a people dwelling in the neighborhood of Byblos, who for 500 years had followed the teaching of the heresiarch Maron, had in 1182 come into relations with the Patriarch Aimerich of Antioch, forsworn their heresy, accepted the orthodox faith, and received bishops of the Roman Catholic Church. These writers show a bias against the Maronites, and William of Tyre is in this matter dependent upon Eutychius, and, further, he does not seem to intend to imply that all Maronites went over to the Roman Catholic Church. Yet, that Maronites were not regarded as orthodox appears from efforts continuing into the eighteenth century to make their teaching conform to the Roman system. The Maronites, in asserting their early and continuous orthodoxy, appeal to the fact that in the acts of the sixth synod (680), which condemned the Monothelites, the Maronites are not mentioned. But other testimony which they adduce for their orthodoxy is taken from later writers whose productions are more or less suspicious both because of their late date and because of an admixture of legend in their accounts of Johannes Maron, which are derived from an Arabic source not earlier than the fourteenth or fifteenth century.

3. The First Patriarch, Johannes Maron.

The account given of Johannes Maron, whom the Maronites acknowledge as their first patriarch, is that he was born at Sirûm, near Antioch, was educated in Antioch and the monastery of St. Maron. Later he studied in Constantinople, became monk in St. Maron, was ordained priest, and wrote against the heretics. He was introduced to the papal legate in Antioch, and by him made bishop of Botrus in 676. He then converted all the Monophysites and Monothelites in the Lebanon region to the Roman faith, ordained priests and consecrated bishops, and gave the Maronites their political and military constitution. When Theophanes, patriarch of Antioch, died, in the second year of the reign of Justinian II., Johannes happened, it is said, to be present in the city, and was unanimously elected patriarch. It is also reported that he journeyed to Rome, and was consecrated by Pope Honorius; that he built a new monastery near Botrus after the Greeks destroyed the old one, and that he died there in 707. But this story contains anachronistic elements, since Honorius lived nearly a century before that time. As no one but the biographer of Maro knows about a patriarch of Antioch of that name, the story of his patriarchate seems to be a fabrication. Renaudot even goes so far as to deny the very existence of Maron; but there is no reason to doubt that he really was elected bishop of Lebanon, and exercised great influence there in steady opposition to the Greeks. The Maronites celebrate him on Mar. 2. A singular characteristic of this history of Johannes Maron is that it erroneously identifies the Mardaites and the Maronites and ascribes to the latter the doughty deeds narrated of the former—a matter which has given rise to variant explanations of no historic value.

4. Relation to Monothelitism and Monophysitism.

Early reports give no insight into religious and ecclesiastical conditions prior to the seventh century. If in that century Maronites were Monothelites, they may have received the Monophysite doctrine spread by Jacobus Baradæus (see JACOBITES) in Syria. And if, as is reported, the monks of the monastery of Maron were made martyrs because of their agreement with the deliverances of the Council of Chalcedon, they could not have been supported by their countrymen. The Maronites confess that heretical passages have gotten into their literature, but they assert that these were smuggled in by Monophysites and Monothelites. In their zeal for Rome they have burned many books of this character, and they boast of the correctness of their later literature, especially that printed in Rome! Their historians declare that at the beginning of the twelfth century a certain Thomas, archbishop of Kafar Tab, near Aleppo, preached among the Maronites the doctrine of the Monothelites and in consequence had a controversy with the Greek patriarch of Antioch. This may have been the schism referred to by William of Tyre, ended by the agreement of Maronites and the Roman Church in 1182, and may have furnished the pretext for preaching the doctrine to the Maronites who lived in Cyprus, where the heresy lingered till the time of Pope Eugenius IV

5. Relations with Rome.

The great conversion to Romanism in 1182 was not complete. An anti-Roman reaction set in and was punished by a papal interdict, from which the country was not absolved until 1215. Rome took great pains to maintain the union, as, for example, in 1445, in consequence of the Council of Florence. A national synod was held at the command of Clement VIII. in 1596, in the monastery of Kanobin, to which Girolamo Dandini, a Jesuit, went as papal legate, charged with the revision of all Maronite affairs. According to his report (*Missione apostolica al patriarca e Maroniti del Monte Libano*, Cesena, 1656; Fr. transl. by Richard Simon, *Voyage du Mont Liban*, Paris, 1685), the council resulted in submission to the Roman see, and an agreement with respect to doctrines. The differences, however, were neither few nor unimportant. The Maronites retained the celebration of the Lord's Supper under both kinds, the Syriac liturgy, the marriage of the priests, their own fast-days, and their own saints. A new council was held in 1736 in the monastery of Mary, at Luweiza, in the district of Kesrawan. The celebrated Maronite scholar J. S. Assemani was sent from Rome as papal legate; and the object was to secure among the Maronites acceptance of the canons of the Council of Trent. How incomplete the success of this mission was is shown by the remark of a Maronite monk: "(The Maronites) recognize the pope as head (of the Church); outside of that they have nothing essentially Catholic." The principal concessions by the Maronites were that they accepted the *filioque* and kneeling at the consecration, and acknowledged the councils of 787 (second Nicene), 869 (Constantinople), 1439 (Florence), and the Council of Trent; the Roman catechism (in Arabic) and the Gregorian calendar were introduced; the Tridentine exposition of the doctrine of transubstantiation was established; the marriage of the clergy was confined to the lower degrees; the name of the pope was introduced in the prayers and the mass. Other provisions dealt with the preparation of the host, its reception by the clergy in both kinds, but by the laity in the form of a sop; the orders of the clergy and their ordination, and the general constitution of the Church. While this synod settled the modern form of the Maronite organization, in many particulars there has been reversion to the earlier customs.

In 1581 Gregory XIII. founded the Collegium Maronitarum in Rome, and from that institution issued a number of celebrated scholars—Georgius Amira, Gabriel Sionita, Abraham Ecchellensis, the Assemanis, and others. An earlier Maronite scholar of note was Theophilus, court astrologer to the Caliph al-Mahdi, who compiled a "Chronicle" and translated Homer into Syriac. But before the agreement with Rome there was little literary activity among the Maronites. Even afterward, the people remained backward in culture, in spite of schools established among them, and retained many of their early customs.

6. Modern Conditions.

Two printing-presses were established at Mar Hanna in 1795, and at Kashia in 1802; but they awakened no interest in reading. For a long period the Maronites maintained a kind of supremacy over the Druses; but after 1840 their power became greatly weakened, feuds arose between them and the Druses, by which the country was often fearfully devastated. As a consequence the Maronite Church has greatly suffered. The priests are poor, being supported only by free-will offerings and fees for masses. The monasteries participate also in the general poverty, and many have been destroyed. The clergy includes, besides the patriarch, archbishops and bishops, presbyters, deacons, sub-deacons, readers and cantors. The temporal power is exercised by an emir, who is responsible to the pasha of Saida. (K. KESSLER†.)

7. In the United States.

The superior of the Syro-Maronite Church in the United States is the Rt. Rev. Joseph Yazbek, chorbishop, and rector of the Maronite church of Boston, which was dedicated in 1898. The ceremony of the preconization of the pastor of the church of Boston to the chor-bishopric took place there in 1900. The decree was conferred by the Maronite patriarch, and was approved by the Roman Catholic archbishop of Boston. The title of chorbishop, it should be added, is equivalent to the title of a vicar *in partibus*. It gives the right to use the miter.

The church of New York was organized in 1893. There are also churches in Philadelphia, St. Louis, Buffalo, Scranton, Pa., Youngstown, O., and Lawrence, Mass., about ten in all, with an equal number of priests. The sect claims a membership of about 35,000 in the United States.

The Maronite priests in the United States, although appointed by the Maronite patriarch, are under the immediate protection and at the call of the Roman Catholic bishops in whose dioceses their churches are located. A. A. STAMOULI.

BIBLIOGRAPHY: Sources for doctrine are their ecclesiastical books: *Missale chaldaicum juxta ritum . Maronitarum*, Rome, 1592–94, 2d ed., 1604; their service for the Eucharist was printed at Kozchaya in the Lebanon, 1816, 1855; *Liber ministri missæ juxta ritum . Maronitarum*, Rome, 1596; *Officia sanctorum*, 2 parts, Rome, 1656–66; *Officium feriale*, Beirut, 1876. Historical sources are John of Damascus, in *MPG*, xciv. 485, 1432; the presbyter Timotheus, in *MPG*, lxxxv. 165; J. S. Assemani, *Bibliotheca orientalis*, i. 496 sqq., iii. 2, pp. 22 sqq., Rome, 1719; Faustus Nairon, *Enoplia fidei catholicæ Romanæ historico-dogmatica*, ib. 1694; a collection of sources is in M. Le Quien, *Oriens Christianus*, iii. 1–100, Paris, 1740. An excellent religious orientation of Christian peoples in Syria is by H. H. Jessop, in *History . . . of the Sixth Session of the Evangelical Alliance*, ed. P. Schaff and S. I. Prime, pp. 634–642, New York, 1874. Consult further: Robinson, *Researches*, vol. iii.; G. Guy, *Séjour . . . à Beirout et dans le Liban*, 2 vols., Paris, 1847; H. Petermann, *Reisen im Orient*, vol. i., Leipsic, 1860; C. H. Churchill, *Mount Lebanon*, vol. iv., *Druzes and Maronites*, London, 1862; A. Pichler, *Geschichte der kirchlichen Trennung*, ii. 533–557, Munich, 1865; *KL*, viii. 891–902; A. de Piolant, *Au pays des Maronites*, Paris, 1882; F. J. Bliss, in PEF, *Quarterly Statements* for 1892 (valuable); J. Debs, *Perpétuelle Orthodoxie des Maronites*, Arras, 1896; F. Nau, *Opuscules Maronites. Œuvres inédites de J. Maron*, Paris, 1899; J. Parisot, *Rapport sur une mission scientifique en Turquie d'Asia*, ib. 1899; K. Beth, *Orientalische Christenheit*, Berlin, 1902; F. Tyan, *Sous les cèdres du Liban; la nationalité Maronite*, La Chapelle-Montligeon, 1905.

On the synod of 1736 consult: S. E. Assemani, *Bibliothecæ Medicæ*, pp. 118 sqq., Florence, 1742; *Nouveaux mémoires des missions de la compagnie de Jésus dans le Levant*, viii. 353 sqq., Paris, 1745; while a summary of the Acts was given by C. F. Schnurrer, in *De ecclesia Maronitica*, Tübingen, 1810–11, cf. *Archiv für Kirchengeschichte*, i (1814), 32–82. Consult also J. S. Assemani, *Synodus provincialis a patriarcha Antiocheno, archiepiscopis et episcopis, necnon clero Maronitarum*, Rome, 1820.

MAROT, mä″ro′, CLÉMENT: French poet and Protestant leader; b. at Cahors (60 m. n. of Toulouse) c. 1497; d. at Turin in Aug., 1544. In 1518 he entered the service of the Princess Margaret of Orléans-Angoulême, better known as Margaret of Navarre (q.v.), and thus came into contact with Protestant teachings. In 1525 he accompanied Francis I. to Italy, and was wounded and taken prisoner with him at Pavia. When he returned to France he began to attack the abuses of the Roman Catholic system, and was imprisoned. On his release in Nov., 1527, he openly declared his adhesion to Protestantism. In 1530 he published a collection of his early poems, some of which were by no means edifying, under the title *L'Adolescence clémentine*. Accused of heresy, he escaped by the protection of the king and his sister. Believing that Francis was inclined to favor the Evangelical doctrines, he wrote for him a poem on the fundamental principles of the New Testament (*Sermon du bon pasteur et du mauvais*). At this time he also began to translate the Psalms into verse. But in Oct., 1534, when the *affaire des placards* brought on a severe persecution of the Protestants, he fled to Ferrara, where he remained under the protection of Renée, daughter of Louis XII. of France (see RENÉE OF FRANCE). In 1536 he renounced Protestantism at Lyons, went back to the court, and worked at his poetical version of the Psalms from the Latin version of Vatable, thus rendering a valuable service to the French Protestant churches, which were in need of a hymn-book. The first Calvinistic hymn-book (Strasburg, 1539) contains eighteen psalms, twelve of which are Marot's. In 1542 he published thirty psalms with a dedication to the king; but the general adoption of them by the Protestants compelled him once more to seek safety in flight, reaching Geneva at the end of the year and remaining there a twelvemonth. Calvin induced him to translate twenty more psalms, which he published with the others in 1543, under the title *Cinquante pseaumes*. He was unable, however, to submit to the ecclesiastical discipline of Geneva, and went to Turin. His version of the Psalms is accurate and renders admirably the beauties of the Hebrew text. Its success was remarkable. In 1562 the French Protestant hymn-book was completed by the addition of 101 psalms translated by Beza to forty-nine of Marot's. Between 1562 and 1565 not less than sixty-two editions were printed; and it was ultimately translated into twenty-two languages. EUGÈNE CHOISY.

BIBLIOGRAPHY: The one edition of the *Œuvres* to be consulted is by G. Guiffrey, vols. ii.-iii., Paris, 1875-81. Consult: F. Bovet, *Hist. du psautier des églises réformées*, Paris, 1872; O. Douen, *Clément Marot et le psautier huguenot*, 2 vols., ib. 1878-79 (cf. T. Dufour, in *Revue critique*, Jan. 31 and Feb. 7, 1881); E. Doumergue, *Jean Calvin*, i. 233 sqq., 585 sqq., Lausanne, 1899. Consult also: Julian, *Hymnology*, p. 714; Lichtenberger, *ESR*, viii. 734-737.

MARPRELATE TRACTS: A series of seven publications which appeared in England under the pseudonym of "Martin Marprelate, Gentleman," between Nov. or Dec., 1588, and July, 1589. They were violent attacks upon the Church, episcopacy, and certain bishops in particular, impudent, personal, and scurrilous in passages, so that they were not approved even by the Puritans; but their keen and apt if somewhat broad and vulgar wit, their logical argument, and their evident sincerity made them effective for the ends for which they were intended. Their success occasioned numerous imitations and more numerous and ponderous replies, giving rise altogether to "the greatest religious controversy of Elizabeth's reign." The tracts were printed surreptitiously, at first at East Moulsey (opposite Hampton Court), Surrey, afterward at hiding-places in Northamptonshire and Warwickshire. Extraordinary but unsuccessful efforts were made by the authorities to discover the author. It was suspected at the time, and has been generally believed since, that they were written by the Welshman John Penry (q.v.). Dr. Dexter's argument for Henry Barrow is not conclusive. It was Penry beyond question who superintended the printing and distribution. He had more or less help and encouragement from John Udall (q.v.); Job Throckmorton, a country gentleman of Hasely, Warwickshire; Robert Waldegrave, a London printer; Sir Richard Knightly, a Puritan squire of Fawsley, Northamptonshire; John Hales, of Coventry; and Robert Wigston, of Wolston, Warwickshire.

The titles of the tracts are very long; abridged they are: (1) *An Epistle;* (2) *An Epitome;* (3) *Certain Mineral Conclusions;* (4) *Ha y' any Worke for Cooper?* (5) *The Protestation;* (6) *Theses Martinianæ* or *Martin Junior;* (7) *The Censure of Martin Junior.* Nos. 1, 2, and 4, with *An Admonition to the People of England* by Thomas Cooper, bishop of Winchester, prepared in reply to the *Epistle*, and two other anti-Martin publications, were reprinted with introductions and notes by John Petheram under the title of *Puritan Discipline Tracts* (London, 1843-47). Udall's *Diotrephes*, the *Epistle*, and Cooper's *Admonition* were reprinted with introductions by Edward Arber in the *English Scholar's Library* (London, 1879-82).

BIBLIOGRAPHY: W. Maskell, *A History of the Marprelate Controversy*, London, 1845; M. Dexter, *Congregationalism of the Last Three Hundred Years*, pp. 131-202, New York, 1880; E. Arber, *An Introductory Sketch to the Martin Marprelate Controversy*, *English Scholar's Library*, no. 8, London, 1879; W. Law, *Defence of Church Principles*, 2d ed., ib. 1894; idem, *Wholly for God the Christian Life, with Introduction*, ib. 1894; G. H. Curteis, *Dissent in its Relation to the Church of England*, p. 76, ib. 1897; J. H. Overton, *The Church in England*, i. 474-476, ib. 1897; W. H. Frere, *The English Church (1558-1625)*, pp. 249-254, ib. 1904; W. Pierce, *An Historical Introduction to the Marprelate Tracts; a Chapter in the Evolution of religious and civil Liberty in England*, New York, 1909.

MARQUARDT, JULIUS: German Roman Catholic; b. at Plässwich (37 m. s.w. of Königsberg), East Prussia, Mar. 24, 1849. He was educated at the Lyceum of Braunsberg and the universities of Münster (lic. theol., 1874), Würzburg, and Munich. In 1874 he became privat-docent at Braunsberg, where he was appointed associate professor of moral theology in 1878 and promoted to a full professorship of the same subject in 1882. He became a canon of Frauenburg in 1900 and since 1903 has been honorary professor of moral theology at Braunsberg. In addition to a number of briefer contributions, he has written *Cyrillus Hierosolymitanus baptismi, chrismatis, eucharistiæ mysteriorum interpres* (Leipsic, 1882).

MARQUETTE, JACQUES: Roman Catholic missionary and explorer and discoverer of the Mississippi; b. at Laon (87 m. n.e. of Paris), France, in 1637; d. in Michigan near the Marquette River May 18, 1675. He entered the Society of Jesus in 1654; became priest in 1666, and the same year went to Canada, taking up his residence among the Algonquin and Huron Indians and studying their languages; in 1668 he went to Lake Superior to Sault Sainte Marie, renewing there the abandoned mission first established in 1641, where he built a church and made many converts; later he moved to La Pointe du St. Esprit, and then in 1671 to Mackinaw, where he founded the mission of St. Ignatius; in 1673 he joined the expedition of Louis Joliet, keeping a diary which is of permanent interest (*Voyage et découverte de quelques pays et nations de l'Amérique Septemtrionale*, printed often, e.g., in M. Thevenot, *Recueil de voyages*, Paris, 1681; Eng. transl. in J. G. Shea, *Discovery and Exploration of the Mississippi*, New York, 1852); in 1674 he started to establish a mission, under orders, in Illinois, but was taken ill on the way, and did not reach Kaskaskia until the following spring, where he accomplished his object; the following year he set out for Mackinaw, being compelled by illness to leave Kaskaskia, and died on the way. His grave was discovered at Point St. Ignace, Mich., in 1877.

Bibliography: R. G. Thwaites, *Father Marquette*, New York, 1902; idem, in *Jesuit Relations and Allied Documents*, Cleveland, 1896 sqq.; J. Sparks, *Library of American Biography*, vol. x., Boston, 1838; H. H. Hurlbut, *Father Marquette at Mackinaw and Chicago*, Chicago, 1878; S. Hedges, *Father Marquette, Discoverer of the Mississippi*, New York, 1903.

MARQUIS, DAVID CALHOUN: Presbyterian; b. in Lawrence Co., Pa., Nov. 15, 1834. He was educated at Jefferson College, Cannonsburg, Pa. (A.B., 1857), and after teaching for three years (1857–60), studied at Western Theological Seminary, Allegheny, Pa. (1860–62), and the Theological Seminary of the Northwest (now McCormick Theological Seminary, Chicago), from which he was graduated in 1863. He then held successive pastorates in his denomination at Decatur, Ill. (1863–1866), North Church, Chicago (1866–70), Westminster Church, Baltimore, Md. (1870–78), and Lafayette Park Church, St. Louis, Mo. (1878–83), and since 1883 has been professor of New-Testament literature and exegesis at McCormick Theological Seminary. He was also moderator of the General Assembly of the Presbyterian Church at Minneapolis, Minn., in 1886.

MARRIAGE.

I. History of Marriage: In the general use of the term, marriage is a union between a man and a woman which is intended to be permanent and is recognized by society. The views concerning the number, rights, and duties of married persons and concerning the dissolubility of marriage have differed much and still differ in various places. The Christian view, based on Mark x. 6–8, is that the union of one man and one woman for life is the order intended by the creator; but Gen. ii. 18–24 has lost its authoritative force as a proof text since sociology shows that monogamy is a result late in its development.

1. Marriage in Primitive Society.

According to the researches of Bachofen, Morgan, McLennan and others concerning the matriarchate, an extensive community in women was the first stage; with the origin of the patriarchate and of private property woman took the position of a chattel, polygamy was originated, after which the rights of private property and of inheritance led to monogamy. It is true, the conclusions concerning the evolution of marriage on the basis of the researches of Bachofen concerning the matriarchate and of Morgan concerning the system of affinity of the Indians have been contested by Grosse, Westermarck, and others, on the ground that occasional underlying facts, which have been interpreted as remnants of older periods, admit and even demand another interpretation, since such conceptions presuppose paternal right and the view that the wife was the property of the husband. But in spite of these modifications, even the possibility that monogamy was the original form of marriage has not been shown. The conditions of monogamy, namely, a higher estimation of woman, the individualization of spiritual life, and consciousness of immorality of illegitimate intercourse, are the results of an extended historical development. Even in Israel the status in Gen. i. and ii. was preceded by a lower moral status such as is involved in polygamy, purchase of the bride, and the slavery of women. But Christian judgment is not refuted by the fact that its idea of marriage has only gradually unfolded under the cooperation of economic and other factors in the development of culture, since the same is true of the individual. Its basis, however, must be different; instead of using tradition, it must employ the idea of inner necessity. Since God has created nature for a moral purpose, the ethical gifts developed from the distinction of sex must be understood as the original purpose of God in creating man and woman just as they are independent of the economic conditions which cooperated in their origin. The same applies also to indissoluble monogamy if it be necessary for the conservation of those gifts. For Jewish conceptions and practise see Family and Marriage Relations, Hebrew.

Among the Greeks and Romans the dignity of marriage as an institution having divine sanction was based upon its importance for the family (which was a group of citizens with full civil and political rights, consisting of several generations and consolidated by its own cult) and for the State. Its purpose was the birth of legitimate sons to continue the family cult and to form a body of citizens.

Marriage was desired out of reverence for the family and the State, also because of the support during life and in old age thus secured and to provide for the payment of the last honors to the dead. Sons competent for these duties could proceed only from a woman who had been received into the family cult. The results were monogamy, and the elevation of the position of woman. It is true that family interests decided the husband's choice and that the wife stood under the legal guardianship of the husband; but in so far as she brought a dowry, administered the affairs of the household, and educated the children, she was relatively independent and highly esteemed. There may have been possible a comprehensive and intimate communion of husband and wife as an ethical gift resulting from marriage, especially in Rome, where woman enjoyed freedom of movement outside of the home and took an interest in the activity of man, while in Athens her seclusion in the house made this impossible for her; but such a communion was impeded by the dissipations of sexual intercourse which was still estimated in a naturalistic manner and might be indulged in by any man, so that Demosthenes says significantly: "We keep courtesans to be amused, concubines to be nursed, wives for the bringing forth of legitimate children and as faithful watchers of the house." Changes in the manner of economic production and in the relations of the family brought about unfavorable consequences. The principal duties of woman lost their significance when degeneration of the family cult and of economic production took place. As the power of the head of the family was restricted, woman became legally more independent. Thus matrimony became merely a civil contract with no higher purpose, and might be dissolved with the consent of both parties and was frequently so dissolved. The male's desire for legitimate sons vanished with decay of reverence for the family and of interest in the state. The sole incentive of marriage remaining, namely, hope of increase in influence and fortune, did not supply a permanent ethical bond. On the other hand, marriage was beneficially influenced by the birth of the philosophic idea of spiritual and ethical personality. Sexual intercourse, which for Neo-Pythagorean spiritualism was under any circumstance contamination of the spirit, was, in consequence of the Stoic idea of control of the sensual desires by rational purpose, declared admissible only in matrimony and for the purpose of producing children. It was regarded as incumbent on the husband to be faithful in marriage and the idea of a harmonious ethical life communion of husband and wife was developed, without accomplishing, however, any noteworthy change either in theory or in actual life.

2. Marriage Among Greeks and Romans.

Christianity first brought about such a change by applying stronger motives than philosophy furnished, namely, such religious sentiments as reverence for God's commandments and fear of his punishment, to which the power of higher morals and the penitential discipline of the congregation contributed. It is true, expectation of the imminent end of the world obstructed the development of a complete doctrinal system of marriage and hindered appreciation of the importance which it has in the evolution of history and in the universal mission of Christianity. Nevertheless, the contrast of the fundamental conceptions of Christianity with Jewish and pagan morals immediately brought about great progress. Christ condemned the laxity of the Jewish laws of divorce; he declared every separation as disobedience of God's commandment (the addition "saving for the cause of fornication," Matt. v. 32, is wanting in I Cor. vii. 10, 11, and disagrees with the uncompromising attitude of the Sermon on the Mount), because a relation of communion which, on account of its divinely created impulse, takes precedence even over the relationship to father and mother can not be dissolved by the arbitrary act of man. Paul emphasizes the unconditional objectionableness of fornication (which among the pagans, at least among the men, was not considered an offense) upon the basis of the idea of holiness, of the duty of the man who has been called to be a member of God's people and even elevated to be a temple of God and a member of Christ to devote even the physical life to the honor of God and to avoid self-pollution by indulging in the impulses of the flesh (I Cor. vi. 13, 20; I Thess. iv. 7, 8). It is owing to the emphasis upon this factor, which was derived from later Judaism and was intensified by the Hellenistic dualism of spirit and flesh, and also to eschatological expectation that for Paul virginity was the higher ideal and that matrimony was a means conceded for the prevention of a worse evil, fornication, though marriage was a state which, for persons not specially blessed with the grace of abstinence, was not only permissible, but preferable (I Cor. vii. 2, 36, 38). Furthermore, celibacy recommends itself to him as more convenient in view of the sufferings of the last days (ib. vii. 26 sqq.), also because zeal for the Lord might easily be encroached upon by worldly cares (32-34). The Pauline cast of thought reappears in Rev. xiv. 4; I Tim. iii. 2, 12, iv. 3–5. In view of the expectation of the end of the world, the moral purposes which had urged pagans and Jews to marry receded, and the idea that the bringing forth of children is a means of accomplishing the purposes of God had not yet arisen. This "low" view of matrimony, which nevertheless in connection with the prohibition of all fornication signifies progress, did not, however, hinder idealization of the mutual relations of husband and wife through the Christian view that husband and wife are of equal value in Christ (Gal. iii. 28); hence conjugal union represented itself as an ethical union between persons of equal position whose differences consisted only in the distinctions of nature, although the continuation of the legal and social subordination of the wife to the husband was demanded, not only out of regard to unbelievers, but as the order of God (Col. iii. 18; I Pet. iii. 1-6) and as proved from the history of man (I Cor. xi. 3–15; Eph. v. 22; I Tim. ii. 11–14). Man should use his superior position not for the purpose of asserting legal claims but to show due respect and love to woman (Eph. v. 25,

3. New-Testament View of Marriage.

33). The subordination of woman appears only as a special act of subordination under God and Christ and under the general duty of love (Col. iii. 18; Eph. v. 22–24).

The ancient church spread these views and customs into larger circles. Marriage received a greater sanctity in so far as it was transformed from a private and civil act into a religious and public ceremony. It took place under the sanction of the Church with the accompaniments of bestowal of eucharistic oblations, congregational intercession, and priestly blessing. After the time of Augustine it was regarded as a sacrament, i.e., a sign of invisible gifts, namely, union of Christ with the congregation, which furnishes a further reason for its indissolubility, even in cases of unfaithfulness and lack of children. The communion of faith, of religious exercises, of works of charity on a footing of equality—and the marriage tie was to be consummated only between Christians—brought about a closer union between husband and wife (Tertullian, *Ad uxorem*, ii. 9). Notwithstanding, a proper appreciation of the ethical significance of marriage for the Christian failed to develop. While the systematic condemnation of marriage by the Gnostics as contamination was refuted on the basis of faith in God as the creator, there reigned a sentiment that the communion of the sexes actually contaminated because it involved sensual appetite. Augustine saw in this appetite a consequence of sin. Thus abstinence appeared to take higher rank. Conjugal intercourse, according to him, was not sin if its purpose was the generation of children; it was deadly sin if its purpose was concupiscence. A second marriage was regarded as a sign of excess of sensuality. The reason for regarding matrimony as simply a protection against unchastity is to be found both in the ascetic ideal and in the fact that the expectation of the imminent end of the world hampered the appreciation of a positive ethical ideal. Tertullian considered it absurd for a Christian to desire children; for why should a man desire heirs or rejoice in possession of them if he must wish their speedy removal from this dangerous world? According to Augustine the truly pious desires only spiritual children. Whoever enters the state of matrimony must, of course, look for children who are to be born again (*generare regenerandos*) and upon educating them accordingly. With a general abstinence humanity would die out, but the coming of the kingdom of God would be only hastened. In the course of time such arguments became merely a dialectic means for the defense of the ascetic ideal which praised abstinence as the anticipation of angelic life, as the spiritual and therefore superior counterpart of marriage, and as communion in love of God and of Christ, explicit expression of which matrimony also tries to discover.

4. Marriage in the Primitive Church.

This conception, which is intelligible from the condition of primitive Christianity, persisted after the Church had learned to endure the prospect of a long future upon earth and of the task of educating other peoples in the Christian religion, but it was used by Christianity in order to gain among the representatives of a higher perfection fit instruments for the accomplishment of its world dominion.

5. Medieval Estimate of Marriage.

Thus the estimate of matrimony in comparison with the sanctity of the monastical and priestly states remained low. The unchastity of many monastics and celibates and a low valuation of marriage induced in the laity a moral degeneracy which was intensified toward the end of the Middle Ages by the coarseness which literature took on, by habitual slander of woman, and by the humanistic renascence of pagan lasciviousness and contempt of matrimony.

6. Luther's Conception.

In contrast with religious and secular contempt of marriage, Luther paid the institution due honor. He regards sexual appetite as a consequence of the fall of man which becomes defensible only through the order of God. Therefore for him also matrimony is an infirmary, and also a state necessary to all to whom has not been granted the rare gift of abstinence. From this point of view he praises the glory of matrimony. While the estimate of celibacy rests upon the illusion that God is pleased by self-chosen achievements, the state of matrimony is an institution of God. Consequently a wife is a gift of God. Thus a good conscience is secured for him who uses matrimony and becomes a protection against temptations to infidelity. The hardships which marriage entails become precious through the assurance that God is pleased with them. Finally matrimony fosters a chaster spirit than celibacy. By thus paying due regard to matrimony as a divine order of nature, Luther opposed arbitrary ecclesiastical restrictions of natural impulse. From such motives are to be explained the blunders which he committed to alleviate the distress of those to whom matrimony through the fault of either husband or wife offered no protection against temptation. But he conceded to nature only its right, not its dominion, in matrimony. He demanded moderation of the sexual instinct, and this he looked for from a deepening of physical fidelity to love and harmony, and not from casuistic guidance in the confessional. The real glory of matrimony Luther found in the ethical purpose for which God created man and woman, and upon the ethical gifts the development of which is their "nature." Children are not only to be born but are to be brought up in the fear of God and for his service. Upon this fact Luther based his judgment that no state is better before God than that of matrimony, and it especially takes precedence of virginity. His reasoning proceeded from the belief that nothing pleases God more than the saving of souls, particularly as it is done by parents, who are the apostles and bishops of children. "Particularly in the state of matrimony children are educated in the fear of God and in honor and virtue; for the natural love of parents makes the task of education a pleasure, and in parental love, which is similar to the love of God, children find an image of the divine heart." Here finally dawned that knowledge which Christianity should have acquired previously along with the conception of its task in universal history—the knowledge that the natural purpose of marriage, the birth and education of children, is a valuable ethical task, especially for Christians. God still has for humanity a plan and needs for its fulfilment faithful servants in Church and State and in all conditions of life; he is, therefore, interested not only in the conversion of men who are now living, but also in the birth of ever new generations. Furthermore, the divine sanction of the marriage state rests for Luther upon the fact that it is a school of faith and love inasmuch as it calls for the constant exercise of sympathy, sacrifice, and patience. It is indeed this state which offers the best opportunity to obtain in faith and love what the contemplative life strives after, a life above the world. This estimate of marriage expresses the spirit of Christianity inasmuch as it unites the conviction that man has to live for the eternal purpose of the kingdom of God with the faith that God as creator has ordained nature to be a means of achieving his eternal ethical purpose.

In his valuation of marriage Luther had in mind the average state of matrimony which has its motives in sexual desire as well as in interests of economy and of the family. The ideal of matrimony was heightened and the ethicality of prohibition of fornication and divorce was enforced when the independent ideas of ethical personality and individuality were applied in the general sphere of Protestantism. Kant and Fichte, starting from this notion of ethical personality and having in view the satisfaction of sexual appetite, reach the conclusion that the immoral degradation of woman is absent only when husband and wife yield up each to the other the entire personality, as in monogamous lifelong matrimony. Such a union, according to Fichte, removes from sexual communion its animal taint, gives it a character worthy of a rational being, and is a school of ethical ennoblement for which there is no substitute. To these ideas Schleiermacher gave clear and full expression. He thus formulated the ideal of chastity as applied to all sensual enjoyments. Sensual pleasure need not be lacking, but it must not be the impulsive force and must be under control of the spirit. This conception is as far removed from the Neo-Pythagorean-Augustinian view of lust as from the assertion of the right of esthetically sublimated sensuality which appeared in the Renaissance and developed into a cult of the flesh. It lies within the sphere of Christian judgment which not only does not deny the gifts of nature, but rather appreciates them in so far as they may be subordinated to the ethical spirit. A second idea is that of individuality. The individual must not only place himself under the general moral code, but must also develop his own personal gifts under the guidance of the universal norm of ethics so as to represent humanity within himself in a peculiar manner. This thought fits in well with the Christian judgment of the relation of nature to the moral spirit and with the Reformed estimate of man's worth. In accordance with this idea Schleiermacher opposed merely prudential matches. His notion of matrimony involved that two individualities should mutually supplement each other and by virtue of this fact be mutually attracted, the result being that they foster each other's moral growth and by perfect communion of life become one will and even one being. In accordance with the individualistic character of the time he at first transferred the purpose of marriage entirely into the mutual ethical relation of husband and wife, abstracting its natural purpose of serving for the propagation of humanity, and he was in danger of applying his idea so absolutely that for the sake of realizing his ideal he would dissolve a marriage which did not correspond to that ideal. After the time of Friedrich Schlegel, this last idea became so dominant that not only was the annulment of marriages which did not fill these conditions declared moral, but the cooperation of society in promoting matrimony as the result of a feeling which is not under control was declared immoral. Divested of its esthetic nimbus, the illusion of the claim made by the individual's changing passion as against the objective order of society first appears with Bebel. During the turbulent times of war, Schleiermacher's eyes were opened to the moral importance of the community, so that he was led to correct himself, whereupon his ethical individualism lost its one-sidedness. Accordingly, he regards the duties involved by marriage and the resulting domestic education as specific means for the cultivation of the heart. He rejects polygamy and the right of divorce because there would then be lacking the fundamental conditions of education, viz., the permanent spiritual communion of the parents. The significance of marriage under Christianity results for him from the knowledge that the moral growth of the individual is conditioned by society. The Christian family is the most efficacious means for the expansion of Christianity.

7. Kant, Fichte, and Schleiermacher.

Thus from the principle of distinction in sex there have developed in history two ethical possessions that can be realized only in monogamous and lifelong marriage, viz., family life as a pedagogic in morals and the mutual ethical advancement of two individualities which supplement each other. Both are independent of changes in economic, social, and political conditions. The socialistic prediction of the disappearance of family life as a consequence of the abolition of the household and the incorporation of private property into the State can not be fulfilled so long as there remains a call for the individualization of the material conditions of life, for bodily and spiritual recreation and for family life, and while the superiority of parental instruction over all public education is so decided. Moreover, love itself, in its inception and its disappearance, is not altogether independent of will and may by the use of the opportunities offered in marriage and family be elevated to the rank of an ethical intercourse, of perpetual sympathy. Thus the two ethical possessions of matrimony form the purpose of creation of male and female, and monogamous, lifelong marriage is the order of God's creation. Matrimony with its two possessions is a means for the coming of the kingdom of Christ on earth. The superior purpose is the social; for the ethical purpose of matrimony

8. Ethical Basis of Marriage.

must be analogous to its natural purpose, and mutual ethical supplementing of two individualities can be realized only if both are perpetually united by their special ethical purposes. But owing to the different vocations of husband and wife such a union takes place as a rule only when the education of the children gives them a common purpose.

From the purpose of matrimony follow its basal principles. The individual purpose demands not only free choice but also a reverence for the families of husband and wife. The conditions for the realization of the ideal marriage are mutual inclination, relative equality of education and rank, and possession of the highest aims in life. An ideal marriage between Christians and non-Christians is therefore impossible, as also between Protestants and non-Protestants. Since marriage has to depend upon public recognition and in its effects touches public life, it is a duty to submit to public regulations regarding it, while the Christian should also seek the sanction of the Church. In theory, marriage should be indissoluble, but owing to the guilt of sin this ideal can not always be realized. The Christian must always feel that separation from a living husband or wife contradicts duty. Where divergencies of temperament or moral defects in either party hamper the realization of the ideal, one must, according to Matt. v. 29–30, save his soul, even if in that way the individual life is shortened. In case of unfaithfulness, Christian love must strive to condone even such guilt. The statement that adultery is *de facto* annulment of marriage, rests upon a one-sided emphasis upon the physical phase of marriage. Adultery may be committed also without the sin of the flesh (I Cor. vii. 2–15). But it may be right or even a duty for the married to discontinue living together if the moral power is not sufficient to bear the burden thus imposed by guilt or if pardoning love sees no prospect of change in the guilty party; and, in case of second marriage on the part of the guilty person, one's own moral danger may justify a new marriage. These ideal ethical norms can not immediately be transformed into legal norms for State and Church, for both must take into consideration the weakness of their members and must adjust their legal measures to the greatest possible ethical effects. When the death of husband or wife has intervened, a second marriage should not be contested, since it does not involve unfaithfulness to the deceased. The abiding relationship is by death transferred to the spiritual world. (J. Gottschick †.)

9. Practical Considerations.

The development of class distinctions in Germany up to the sixteenth century shows, in addition to the serfs, the three sharply differentiated classes of nobles, knights (the lower nobility), and freemen. By the principle of equality of birth, marriages between members of these classes were considered misalliances, and the wife of lower birth was not raised to her husband's rank, while the children belonged to their mother's class. This condition of affairs was partly obviated by the introduction of the Roman law, except for the nobility, which, in virtue of its autonomy, was able by family laws and agreements to prevent the principles of Roman jurisprudence from interfering with their family rights, and thus to conserve the traditional theories of Teutonic law. In the ancient German kingdom, as to-day, the nobility were able to restrict the concept of the misalliance, so that the marriage of members of noble families with those not belonging to the high nobility was to be considered in conformity with class requirements. The so-called morganatic, Salic, or left-hand, marriage (*matrimonium ad morganaticam, ad legem Salicam*) is normally a marriage between persons of unequal rank, but differs from the misalliance in the strict sense of the term in that its effects are based on a special contract instead of on law and custom. The term "morganatic" is apparently derived from the morning-gift (Germ. *Morgengabe*) which was usually given at such marriages. The expression *matrimonium ad legem Salicam*, which is yet employed, is unexplained. The phrase "morganatic marriage" is now the one in common use, and such marriages still take place only in ruling families and those of the high nobility. (E. Sehling.)

10. Misalliance and Morganatic Marriage.

Under the head of wedding customs may be conveniently treated several details relating to betrothal or marriage. The preliminary examination is for the purpose of finding out whether any civil or ecclesiastical impediment to the marriage exists, and whether the parties understand the duties of the married state; the Roman ritual instructs the pastor to see whether they know the rudiments of the faith, so that they may teach them to their children. Such an examination is prescribed in some Evangelical churches. The modern usage of having groomsmen and bridesmaids is a relic of ancient usage (cf. John iii. 29; Matt. xxv. 1–13). The custom of having a *paranymphus* for the bridegroom and a *paranympha* for the bride remained usual in the East; they were compared to the sponsors in baptism. In the West the custom is referred to as regular by the Fourth Synod of Carthage (398). It fell in with the old Teutonic law, which required the bride to be handed over to her husband by her former guardian.

11. Wedding Customs.

The wedding-ring is a symbol of great antiquity. Rings were used in Roman law for symbols of other mutual contracts, but especially of marriage (Pliny, *Hist. naturalis*, xxxiii. 1). The Christian Church early adopted the use, which is mentioned by Tertullian (*Apol.*, vi.). That as late as the seventh or even the ninth century the ring was given at the first betrothal is attested by Isidore of Seville and by Pope Nicholas I. Later it was given at the wedding, and frequently two rings were exchanged. The ceremony of giving the ring varies in different places. According to the Roman ritual, it is blessed by the priest and placed by the bridegroom upon the bride's third finger. The reason for the selection of this finger is the ancient belief that a large vein led from it directly to the heart. The use of wreaths as part of the bridal attire was avoided by the early Christians in order to differ from the pagans and Jews (Justin, *I Apol.* ix.; Tertullian, *De corona*, v. 13). Later it not only came in but acquired a special significance. In the Greek Church it became customary for the priest to place wreaths or "crowns" upon the heads of both bride and groom, though the strict rule forbade this except where the bride was a virgin. In the West the custom never attained so much importance, because the veil was early preferred, as is shown by Ambrose, Isidore, and Nicholas I. In Germany, however, wreaths long remained very common, and the restriction of their use to virgins was in many places definitely laid down by both civil and ecclesiastical law. At the present day such matters depend upon local custom. (H. F. JACOBSON†.)

II. Marriage Law.—1. History of Marriage Law: From the Christian doctrine of marriage, even in its ecclesiastical development, no new marriage law could be deduced because the relation of marriage is not a part of the plan of redemption. Nevertheless, it became necessary that, under its influence, both usage and marriage law itself should experience a partial renewal in Christendom. It became incumbent upon the Church to lay down principles; and gradually, together with the development of the dogma that marriage among Christians is a sacrament, the concept developed in the Western Church that the Church has the exclusive right of making marriage laws for Christians. The Council of Trent confirmed this dogma with great firmness and precision (Sess. xxiv., Can. 1: "Whoever shall affirm that matrimony is not truly and properly one of the seven sacraments of the Evangelical law, instituted by Christ Our Lord, but that it is a human invention introduced into the Church, and does not confer grace, let him be anathema"; and also, as the inference [Canon 12]: "Whoever shall affirm that matrimonial causes do not belong to the ecclesiastical judges, let him be anathema"). Jurisdiction in matrimonial affairs is here expressly asserted by the Church, which also indirectly claims control of the laws, since, according to the Roman system, it is a matter of course that ecclesiastical judges can decide only according to ecclesiastical laws and not after secular legal norms, unless the latter are acknowledged by the Church. Long before the Reformation a complete ecclesiastical marriage law had developed and become a part of the canon law in the West, and had obtained exclusive authority, especially in Germany.

1. Development of Ecclesiastical Jurisdiction over Marriage.

Luther controverted the sacramental character of matrimony and declared it to be a purely secular relation, subject to the laws of the civil authority ("Apology," xiii.). That marriage is commanded of God and has divine promises was decidedly asserted, as well as that Christian authorities are bound to be guided in making and executing marriage laws by the utterances of divine revelation. The supplement to the Schmalkald Articles, §§ 80-81, declares the establishment of special courts for marriage affairs to be an ecclesiastical necessity. In accordance with these ideas in German Evangelical countries, Scriptural corrections of the canonical marriage laws were introduced into the church disciplines promulgated by the rulers in accordance with the advice of theologians, and the consistories were charged with matrimonial jurisdiction. Marriage legislation and its execution were based entirely upon the harmonious cooperation of Church and State. Toward the middle of the eighteenth century, following the example of Prussia, a complete transformation of these relations was gradually brought about. In Prussia, by an edict dated May 10, 1749, the jurisdiction of the consistories in general, especially in marriage affairs, was abolished and transferred to the regular secular courts; while the laws were soon modified in such a way that marriage was contracted exclusively from a secular point of view without the aid of the Church. Nevertheless, though the religious significance of marriage was entirely disregarded, the religious ceremony of marriage was inadvertently retained.

2. Marriage Secularized by Protestantism.

The fundamental idea of this legislation, foreign to the Reformers and to the Evangelical Church, according to which civil legislation pays no regard to the religious meaning of marriage, but leaves it entirely to the Church to assert these relations of marriage by influencing the conscience, had its origin in the Roman Catholic Church of France, where the debate arose concerning what in Christian marriage constitutes the *materia sacramenti* and what the agent or *minister sacramenti*. A distinction should be made, according to the opinion which prevailed in France, between the *contractus naturalis* and *sacramentalis*. The contract made by the parties received its sacramental character from the priest (as the *minister sacramenti*) through his benediction (*materia*). The State must fix the conditions under which the civil marriage contract could be made and annulled. The priest could only bless the marriage (which was valid as a civil marriage contract), and this he need not do in case of ecclesiastical impediments; but his withholding the blessing must not prejudice the validity of the marriage, provided it was contracted in a form recognized by the law of the State (cf. E. Friedberg, *Recht der Eheschliessung*, Leipsic, 1865, pp. 546 sqq.). The popes always rejected this doctrine without plainly deciding what was to be regarded as *materia* and who as *minister sacramenti* in the marriage, though both by their rejection and by the enactments of the Council of Trent (see below) the Roman Catholic Church indirectly taught that the *materia sacramenti* was the intended union of man and wife in accordance with ecclesiastical law, and that the parties to the marriage were the *ministri sacramenti*. The French theory here set forth has been made the basis of civil legislation by the Roman Catholic states of Germany, with the addition of an obligatory civil marriage form, following the example of the French law of 1792.

3. Minister and Materia Sacramenti in Marriage.

Upon the theory that the Church has authority to make a partial marriage law is based the distinction between *ratum* and *legitimum matrimonium*, i.e., between a marriage answering to the ecclesiastical demands and one meeting the requirements of secular legal provisions (cf. *Corpus juris canonici*, causa xxviii., quæstio 1, dictum of Gratian). According to canon law, a *matrimonium ratum non legiti-*

mum is conceivable among Christians, but not a *matrimonium legitimum non ratum;* for a marriage answering only to secular and not to ecclesiastical law can not, by canon law, be considered a marriage among believers, whereas to contract marriage in disregard of secular law does not diminish the sacramental character of matrimony, even when secular law does not recognize such a union as marriage. Only by the French theory can a *matrimonium legitimum non ratum* exist among believers. In the ecclesiastical Protestant concept, this distinction is impossible, since it does not regard the Church as having authority to pass laws on marriage. A civilly valid marriage, therefore, can no more be ecclesiastically invalid than a civilly invalid marriage can be ecclesiastically valid, provided that the enactments of the civil law are not absolutely inconsistent with the divine Word. From a Protestant point of view the question of a *matrimonium legitimum non ratum* could exist only in the figurative sense of a marriage not approved by the Church and hence not blessed.

4. Ratum and Legitimum Matrimonium.

2. Theory and Contracting of Marriage: Roman law distinguished between betrothal and marriage, defining the latter as "the union of a man and a woman," which might also be contracted by a simple informal agreement to enter at once upon the wedded state; and considering betrothal as "a declaration and counter-promise of future marriage." The Church recognized the validity of the Roman law on marriage, but never held that a divine command defined the form of contracting marriage, though it always regarded it as a necessary expression of Christian piety not to marry without ecclesiastical approval and without "thanksgiving and sanctification through the word of God and prayer." On the other hand, it never made the legal status of marriage dependent on the fulfilment of these demands of Christian piety. Like the Roman law, the Church regarded the consent of the parties as the sole necessary condition for marriage. Though the Roman practise was essentially adopted, the distinction between betrothal and marriage was drawn less sharply, even while betrothals were blessed, and while marriage after betrothal was regarded as stronger than had been the case among the Romans. Moreover, the Bible terms the marriage of Mary and Joseph a betrothal, and for these reasons the Fathers distinguished betrothal and marriage less clearly. Necessity, however, demanded a distinction. Betrothal was soluble, whereas marriage was regarded by the Church as indissoluble; betrothal was no sacrament but marriage was, though the precise reason was doubtful, since the existence of non-sacramental marriages was also acknowledged. The questions whether marriage is a sacrament, and whether or for what reasons marriage is indissoluble, were much disputed, and formed the basis of profound differences of opinion.

1. Influence of Roman Law.

To substantiate their views, the schoolmen and canonists found themselves obliged to adduce citations, especially those passages of the Bible in which Joseph and Mary are called *sponsus* and *sponsa.* The difficulties of the interpretation were overcome by distinctions. Gratian distinguished between the *desponsatione* (i.e., *consensu*) *initiatum* and the *copula perfectum coniugium* (only the latter being sacramental and indissoluble); while the schoolmen, beginning with Hugo of St. Victor, distinguished two kinds of espousals, one having the effect of the Roman betrothal, and the other that of the Roman marriage, *sponsalia de futuro* and *sponsalia de præsenti* (the latter being sacramental and indissoluble even without a *copula*). In Germany the Church likewise found a national law of marriage, and retained it like the Roman in the Roman Empire. Teutonic law did not everywhere answer to the general development of the Teutonic state and law, and it is a vain effort to deduce a uniform picture from the many tribal laws. Nevertheless, certain general characteristics can be fixed. According to these, the marriage contract diminished from an actual purchase of the wife to a purchase of *mund*, or power (*mundium*), over the wife from him who had it. Thus the marriage normally followed in consequence of the surrender of the *mund* and the payment of the purchase money. The contract, or betrothal, preceding the marriage, as to the future surrender of the bride and the amount of the purchase money, indeed had its effect, which was greater than in the case of the Roman betrothal, so that the betrothal could not be dissolved without monetary damages, although it was not considered a real marriage. Whereas the marriage originally took place by the acquisition of the *mund* (normally by its transfer from its owner to the groom), while the will of the bride was a matter of no concern, her wishes became more and more important, until they, and not the acquisition of the *mund*, were the decisive factor. Thus the actual purchase became fictitious. The Teutonic development accordingly came to coincide with the Roman principle that the consent of the parties brings about the marriage.

2. Teutonic Elements.

Canon law seriously interfered with this evolution, for, although it had hitherto acknowledged, and had been obliged to acknowledge, the validity of the laws of individual peoples, since the secular courts alone determined the validity of marriage, a change took place in the time of Alexander III. The Church now acquired jurisdiction over marriage, and with it the power of carrying out her principles. As concerned the contracting of marriage, the Church took her stand on the simple maxim of Roman law, *consensus facit nuptias*, and expressed this maxim in the scholastic form of both espousals. The consent with reference to the future (*accipiam te*) produced a betrothal in the Roman sense (*sponsalia de futuro*); the consent with reference to the present (e.g., *accipio te in uxorem* [or *in maritum*]) produced marriage (*sponsalia de præsenti*). If the *copula carnis* was conjoined with the *sponsalia de futuro*, it was considered a *præsumptio iuris et de iure* for the conjugal consent, and required marriage. Nevertheless, all this was merely a new terminology for the simple principles of Roman law.

3. Relation of Canon to Roman and Teutonic Law.

In the original Teutonic marriage law there was no place for the cooperation of a priest, but this now became possible. The German people adhered to the ancient formality of giving away; but since in reality nothing more was to be given away, a third person chosen by the parties, hence the priest, could perform the formality. As a matter of fact, it was the will of the parties which made the marriage. This church marriage, however, did not become general in Germany, nor indeed did the Church regard its cooperation as necessary to validity, since mere consent, however expressed, was sufficient. Herein lay the peril to ecclesiastical marriage law, nor was it until the Council of Trent that it was enacted that in future the declaration of consent to wed must be made before the proper priest in the presence of two or three witnesses if the marriage was to be valid.

4. Decline of the Importance of the Betrothal.

In the Protestant Church the decided rejection of the validity of secret marriages by no means made their validity dependent on their solemnization by the Church, but resulted at first merely in the non-recognition of clandestine betrothals looking toward immediate marriage, and later in the compulsory completion of public betrothals, whether unconditional or followed by cohabitation, by church marriages. It soon became a general custom, however, to celebrate the marriage by a church wedding; while the decline of the custom of regarding an unconditional public betrothal as a marriage facilitated the prescriptive law which had become firmly established in Switzerland and Germany by the beginning of the eighteenth century, and which fixed the religious ceremony as the proper and necessary form. The movement inaugurated in Evangelical circles by Just Jenning Böhmer against the theory of betrothal in canon law naturally conditioned the importance of the marriage ceremony, which it considered the real marriage act. In England this was first established by the Hardwicke Act in 1753. In Scotland the pre-Tridentine canonical marriage law is still in force, thus explaining the famous marriages in Gretna Green, which, following that law, take place by a mere *sponsalia de præsenti* without a formal marriage.

5. Theory of Marriage in Early Lutheran Rituals.

For the cooperation of the Church in contracting marriage Protestantism retained essentially unchanged the church banns and marriage by the Church. Luther's marriage ritual makes the ceremony take place before the church, only the Scripture lesson and the prayer of benediction being given at the altar. In Luther's book and in most Protestant rituals the marriage form reads: "I pronounce you joined in wedlock in the name of the Father, Son, and Holy Ghost." The Nördlingen agenda of 1676 has the fuller form: "I pronounce and give you joined in wedlock in like manner as God joined our first parents in Paradise, and this in the name," etc. Some rituals, especially in South Germany, read like the Brandenburg-Nuremberg agenda: "The marriage vows which ye have pledged one to the other in the presence of God and his holy congregation, I here confirm at the command of the Christian congregation in the name," etc. In other rituals both forms are combined, as in the Eisleben manual of 1563: "This marriage, ordered and ordained by God Almighty between you, I confirm as a minister of the Church in his stead, and in the presence of this congregation I here pronounce you publicly joined in wedlock in the name," etc. From this it follows that the real and essential meaning of the "joining together" in the name of the Trinity represents the divine joining together in wedlock, but that it does not imply that the marriage is performed by the act of the minister. Marriage was originally held to be contracted by the engagement preceding the ceremony and the banns. In the introduction to the marriage ritual it is sometimes said (as in the Lower Saxon agenda of 1585): "The persons here present have, in the customary manner, with the knowledge of their parents on both sides, etc., entered into the holy estate of matrimony." The wedded life already begun was merely completed by the church ceremony. When, at a later time, the distinction between *inchoatum* and *consummatum matrimonium* was disregarded, and a sharp line was again drawn between betrothal and wedded life (marriage being deemed necessary for the latter), the "pronouncing together" in the name of God came to denote the declaration of marriage, which could be celebrated only by such a declaration. Nevertheless, this new development did not supersede the original and main significance of the "pronouncing together," for as a religious act it never lost this meaning, its declarative aspect arising from the legal character which it had now assumed in addition to its religious functions. The actual validity of the marriage contract was always held to reside in the mutual agreement of the parties concerned, as expressed in their assent to the questions in the marriage ceremony. They themselves thus contracted with each other the marriage which the minister merely confirmed solemnly by his declaration, although the latter ceremony was necessary for the validity of the marriage. Herein Protestant canon law finally differed from Tridentine Roman Catholic, the latter holding that a formal wedding was not necessary to the validity of marriage, if a declaration of mutual consent had previously been made.

6. Development of Civil Marriage.

Various grave difficulties arising from the requirement of a religious ceremony for the legal validity of marriage led to the development of a civil marriage service, which then became either sufficient for or necessary to its civil validity. This civil ceremony, as found in the sixteenth century in Holland, and in France in 1787, had for its object the protection of the liberty of conscience of sectaries or members of Protestant communities which were merely tolerated; since by observing a prescribed civil form of marriage they were enabled to obtain the same public recognition for it as could properly be obtained only by the cooperation of the State Church. A French law of 1792 made the civil ceremony obligatory upon all citizens, on the principle that "the citizen belongs to the State, irrespective of religion," the legal basis being the distinction between *contractus sacramentalis* and *naturalis* (see above). The obligatory civil ceremony thus introduced was adopted in the civil *Code Napoléon*, and remained authoritative in those parts of Germany where it had become naturalized under French rule. The same theory forms the basis of the obligatory civil ceremony in Holland, Italy, Chile, Mexico, Rumania, Hungary, and Japan [and in some parts of the United States]. In England, Scotland, and Ireland the civil ceremony was introduced in 1653 to free the Church from secular affairs. Abolished at the Restoration (1660), civil marriage was again introduced as optional into England for practical reasons in 1836. In Germany the obligatory civil ceremony, first introduced by the law of Feb. 6, 1875, was based on the principle of the separation of Church and State according to the Belgian precedent. In case the State permits a marriage when a religious ceremony is impossible, the civil ceremony is employed in Austria, Denmark, Sweden, Norway, Spain, Portugal, and Russia. In North America, where the principle prevails that *consensus facit nuptias*, both ministers of the different denominations and judicial officers have the right to perform marriages.

According to the law of the Roman Catholic Church, a marriage performed by a civil magistrate may become *ratum* and *legitimum matrimonium* only where the Tridentine Decree has not been promulgated; where it has been promulgated, or is practised without being promulgated, the civil ceremony becomes a *ratum matrimonium* only by a subsequent religious marriage according to the form prescribed by the Decree. The Protestant Church, on the contrary, must consider marriage as binding the conscience from the instant the civil ceremony is performed, and can not, therefore, regard a subsequent religious ceremony as a marriage.

The validity of marriage in the Roman Catholic Church underwent a very important development under Pius X. by the constitution "*Provide*" of 1906 (see below) and by the decree "*Ne temere*" of Aug. 2, 1907 By the decree "*Ne temere*" there was introduced a special form for betrothal (a written contract to be signed by the parties, the priest, or ordinary, or by at least two witnesses); the validity of the Tridentine form of consummating marriage (which, of course, is acknowledged everywhere) is made actual by the presentation of the decree "*Ne temere*" to the diocesan bishop and extends to all people baptized in the Roman Catholic Church and to those that have returned to her from heresy or schism. The declaration in contracting a marriage must take place before the priest whose presence has been requested, who officiates of his own will (these are innovations), and before two witnesses. The priest must be chosen from the proper diocese; but if that is not the case, marriage is not declared void as formerly, provided the priest officiates within his own official district.

3. Impediments to Marriage: Impediments to marriage, or those circumstances which impede the proper or legal state of marriage, fall into certain general categories: (*a*) Public and private impediments (*impedimenta publica* and *privata*), according as the impediment has the character of the marriage itself, or exists merely in the rights of individuals, so that the impediment concerns either the community or only individuals. Thus, a public impediment is too close consanguinity; a private impediment is coercion. (*b*) Diriment and obstructing impediments (*impedimenta dirimentia* and *tantum impedientia*), according as the impediment either renders void the legal status of the marriage, or, while it exists, merely delays the proper conditions of its contraction. In case of the latter, the marriage is simply to be postponed till they are removed; but if this is not done, the marriage does not therefore become invalid, but is at most punishable. In case of diriment impediments, on the other hand, the marriage may be annulled if the causes are private, and must be annulled if the causes are public; but such annulment must not be construed as divorce, being merely a declaration of the invalidity or nonexistence of the marriage. Diriment impediments are, e.g., a previous marriage still existent, and the impotence or sterility of one of the parties, the former being a public, and the latter a private, diriment impediment. Obstructing impediments are betrothal (*sponsalia de futuro*) and the times when matrimony is forbidden. (*c*) Absolute or relative impediments, according as the cause impedes the legality of the marriage in general or only between certain persons. Thus, an absolute impediment is impuberty, and a relative one is difference in religion.

1. Classification of Impediments.

The various canonical impediments are as follows: (*a*) Impuberty, i.e., when the male is not yet fourteen years of age, and the female not yet twelve years old. The law both of the Roman Catholic and the Protestant Church considers this a public diriment impediment; but in canon law this holds only when the marriage has not been consummated because of the previous development of puberty. The civil law has everywhere raised the age of marriage. (*b*) A previous and still existing marriage of one of the contracting parties (*impedimentum ligaminis*) is a public diriment impediment, since by its very nature marriage can exist only between one man and one woman. Ignorance of the continuance of a former marriage precludes only the crime of bigamy, but not the necessary severance of the second marriage, the latter being a sham marriage which can not be legalized even by the consent of the injured party or by a dispensation, since the impediment must be considered as based upon divine law. (*c*) The impediment which exists in consequence of a still existing marriage is found by canon law in the reception of a higher consecration and in the solemn vow of chastity taken when entering a religious order approved by the Holy See. (*d*) On account of consanguinity the Mosaic law (Lev. xviii. 7 sqq., xx. 17 sqq.; Deut. xxvii. 20 sqq.) forbids a man to marry his mother, sister (whether uterine or not), granddaughter, and paternal or maternal aunt. In Roman law marriages between relatives in the ascending and descending lines are unrestricted, but wedlock is forbidden between brothers and sisters (whether uterine or not) and between all collat-

2. Canonical Impediments.

eral relatives who "stand to each other in the stead of parents and children," the one party being born of the common stock. According to earlier law, marriage among cousins was also prohibited, and this prohibition was temporarily renewed by Christian emperors under the influence of the Church, which rejected such marriages, so that it does not exist in the Justinian code. In both Mosaic and Roman law it was immaterial whether the relationship was legitimate or illegitimate. According to the Decretals, which in this respect are still authoritative in the Roman Catholic Church, marriages among collateral relations to the fourth degree inclusive are prohibited, whereas formerly the prohibition was extended to the seventh degree. These relationships were computed by the Teutonic theory, which assumed as many degrees of relationship as acts of procreation were required to bring about the relations of the one relative to the other, the more distant line being taken in case of an inequality of the collateral relatives. The Reformers rejected the canon law and went back to the Mosaic and Roman law, adopting from the latter the impediment of "regard to kinship." Although by no means uniform, the extension of the impediment was generally made to the third degree of canonical computation. With the theory prevailing in the eighteenth century that the Mosaic law was not to be considered divine in this regard, the sovereign's right of dispensation gained wide scope; but even after the State had greatly limited the impediment of relationship, the Evangelical Church maintained a portion of the former law in the form of an impediment to religious marriage.

3. Consanguinity.

The relation of one of a married pair to the kin of the other constitutes affinity. For this reason the Mosaic law expressly prohibits marriage with a stepmother, the wife of a paternal uncle, a daughter-in-law, the wife of a brother, a stepdaughter, and a step-granddaughter. Marriage with the wife's sister was forbidden only during the lifetime of the wife, polygamy in itself still being permissible. Marriage with the widow of a childless brother, the levirate marriage, was required (Deut. xxv. 5). According to Roman law, affinity was an absolute impediment. Marriage with brothers and sisters of a deceased husband or wife was first prohibited by the laws of Christian emperors. Even in the older laws an impediment to marriage, based on a feeling of honor, was felt to exist in the quasi-affinity between one betrothed and the kin of the party of the other part in a direct line, as well as between stepchildren and step-parents, or between a man and his divorced wife's daughter by a second marriage. According to Roman law, legal marriage alone established real affinity, whether the marriage was consummated or not; and when marriage ceased, affinity ceased, although it continued to be an impediment to marriage. Unlawful sexual intercourse generally formed no impediment for the marriage of the one party with the relatives of the other, only concubinage and marriage with slaves effecting an impedimental affinity similar to that of lawful marriage.

4. Affinity.

Canon law derived the impediment of affinity less from marriage than from the "union of flesh" effected by sexual intercourse, so that it made the impediment of affinity coincide with that of kinship, extending it even to marriages between the kin of the husband and children by the second wife. Even an *affinitas secundi generis*, between one of the married pair and the *affines* (*primi generis*) of the other, and, in certain cases, an *affinitas tertii generis* (the relation to the *affines secundi generis* of the other party to the marriage) were considered an impediment. Through non-matrimonial intercourse an affinity also originated, whence arose an impediment between the one guilty party and the kin of the other (*affinitas illegitima*). The opinion likewise prevailed that marriages should be annulled for an *affinitas superveniens*, arising from adultery on the part of one of the married pair with one of the kin of the other. By the law of 1215 Innocent III. entirely abolished the prohibitions of marriages in *secundo et tertio genere affinitas*, and also permitted marriage between kindred of the husband and children by his wife's second marriage, besides limiting the prohibition of *affinitas primi generis* to the fourth degree. He likewise decided that the *affinitas illegitima superveniens* should entitle the injured party only to refuse marital rights. The Council of Trent limited the impediment of the *affinitas illegitima* (*antecedens*) to the second degree; while the Roman quasi-affinity through betrothal was made coterminous, under the name *impedimentum quasi affinitatis*, with real affinity. The Council of Trent limited the impediment to the first degree, but without abolishing the extension of the impediment of affinity *ex matrimonio rato non consummato* to the fourth degree, although, as in the former case, it was only an *impedimentum publicæ honestatis*. Early Protestant church legislation, doctrine, and practise appropriated the canonical concept of the impediment of affinity, and in general likewise accepted the resultant deductions of canon law, so that legitimate and illegitimate affinity acted as impediments to marriage within the same degrees as consanguinity. At the same time, the prohibitions of Roman law on account of quasi-affinity were retained, and even sometimes extended, despite their abolition by Innocent III. by the entire abrogation of the impediment of the *affinitas secundi generis*. After the regulation of the impediment by civil law (see below), the Evangelical Church went beyond it in establishing impediments to religious marriage.

5. Affinity in Canon Law and Early Protestantism.

Imitative or artificial relationship is connoted by *legalis* and *spiritualis cognatio*. The former was recognized as a public diriment impediment by canon law, which, however, laid down no new regulations defining its extent; and the canon law regarding this impediment has been retained by the Protestant Church. The marriage impediment of the spiritual relationship has its basis in the code of Justinian (XXVI., v. 4), which prohibits marriage between a sponsor and the person to be baptized. In medieval

6. Spiritual Relationship and Difference of Religion.

canon law it was greatly extended. According to the decrees of the Council of Trent (sess. xxiv., can. 2), spiritual kinship is an impediment only to marriage between the one who baptizes or confirms and the sponsors on the one hand, and the person baptized or confirmed and his parents on the other hand. Evangelical agenda have sometimes prohibited marriages between sponsor and godchild; but in later Protestant Church law a spiritual relationship is no longer a marriage impediment. Difference of religion (*cultus disparitas*) did not become a public diriment impediment through a church law, but through a general ecclesiastical right prescriptive, and as such was acknowledged in the Protestant Church, although Luther repeatedly disapproved of it, in part overlooking the difference between contracting and continuing a marriage between Christians and non-Christians, and in part one-sidedly emphasizing the secularity of marriage. While the law of the State nowhere recognizes difference of religion as a marriage impediment, it is always to be considered an impediment to a religious wedding. The Church can not bless and consecrate a marriage in which one of her members regards it as quite immaterial for the closest union of life whether the other professes Christ or not. The mere difference of Christian confession, on the other hand, is considered even by the Roman Catholic Church merely as an obstructing impediment (see below on mixed marriages).

Physical incapacity to consummate the marriage by sexual union (*impotentia cœundi*) is a diriment private impediment according to canon law since, in case it exists and is incurable at the beginning of the marriage (or can be cured only by an operation which would imperil life), it entitles the other party to have the marriage annulled. Sixtus V. (1587) prescribed a public impediment only for eunuchs. In the Roman Catholic Church the prevailing opinion, at present at least, is that the effect of this impediment is the same whether it was known to the other party at contracting the marriage, or not. Protestant doctrine and practise, on the other hand, have always held that annulment of marriage on the ground of impotence (or sterility) can be demanded by the healthy party only on condition that he (or she) contracted the marriage without knowing of the defect of the other party. Adultery (*impedimentum criminis*) is, according to the latest canon law, a public diriment impediment as regards marriage with the person accessory to adultery, in case either that the adulterers have promised to marry one another, or have actually contracted a marriage, or that one of the adulterers has successfully attempted the life of the injured party. In case one of a married pair is killed by the other with the assistance of a third person to render possible the marriage of the latter two, such an act, as a matter of course, is an impediment to marriage, even though only one party intended to make it possible when perpetrating the deed. The latest canon law on this point became the law of the Protestant Church, although Luther had objected: " Vice and sin are to be punished by other punishments than by prohibiting marriage."

7. Impotence and Adultery.

The impediment of error is recognized by canon law only as regards the person of the other part, but not as regards quality or condition (with the single exception of freedom). Here error as regards the person arises especially when the party believed to be the party of the second part is known to the party of the first part, who here makes the error, only by virtue of quality or condition, provided this is distinctly characteristic of the party of the second part (*error qualitatis in personam redundans*). Some Evangelical agenda of the sixteenth century consider the absence of virginity, the actual pregnancy of the bride by a third person (with reference to the Mosaic law), and incurable contagious diseases as conditions justifying a claim for an annulment of marriage on the plea of error. Later Protestant doctrine and practise are inclined to attribute that effect to every physical or moral defect which in a similar degree affects the nature of the marital relation. So far as the fact of error is considered impedimental, it makes no difference whether it was caused or used through fraud or not. The canon law does not recognize fraud as an absolute impediment. In the Evangelical Church the opposite opinion has never become the general consensus, though it has often been stated with very different bases and limitations, and has occasionally been enforced and made the subject of special legislation.

8. Error.

Canon law allows marriage to be contracted under postponing conditions. The contracting parties are lawfully, but not conjugally, united. As soon as the conditions are complied with, the marriage takes place. The deficient condition forms an *impedimentum deficientis conditionis appositæ*. Impossible or immoral conditions are not considered binding, but a secondary stipulation nullifying one of the *tria bona matrimonii* (*fides, proles, sacramentum*) makes the marriage illegal. The permission of the bishop and notice to the officiating priest are necessary. Lack of parental consent is considered an *impedimentum impediens* in canon law, since the conjugal sacrament is brought about by the contracting parties themselves, and since a third party should not be allowed to decide on the validity of the sacrament. Protestant law, however, referring to the Fifth Commandment, and civil law differ here from canon law, although both provide temporary limitations and afford protection against arbitrariness on the part of the parents. A simple obstructing impediment is raised by the *tempus clausum*, or the seasons of Advent and Lent, in which, according to ancient ecclesiastical custom, marriages were considered inadmissible, though the Council of Trent (sess. xxiv., canon x.) restricted this prohibition to marriage festivals. The custom was retained among Protestants, but with modifications in detail. An obstructing impediment is given by the *vetitum* or *interdictum ecclesiæ*, by which the provisional prohibition of marriage issued by ecclesiastical authority because of the suspected presence of a diriment impediment or objection does not militate against the validity of a marriage legal in itself, yet contracted in spite of the prohibition; although, until this prohibition is

9. Obstructing Impediments.

removed, it naturally makes the marriage in question unpermitted and subject to the punishment of the Church. The effect of an obstructing impediment is also possessed by betrothal in the narrower sense, and, in Roman Catholic canon law, by the simple vow of chastity. [In some countries the *annus luctus*, "year of mourning," is a period during which a widow may not contract marriage, unless she has born a child after the death of her husband. The object of this provision is to prevent ambiguity in the matter of paternity.]

The removal of impediments takes place of itself where they are based on transient reasons, although this does not validate a marriage contracted under conditions invalidated because of impediments.

10. The Removal of Impediments. Private impediments arising from lack of consent or faulty consent can be removed only by later full consent of the parties concerned. If, however, the marriage is to become valid, Roman Catholic practise requires a *renovatio consensus* in the Tridentine form, where this has been introduced, unless the impediment has been kept secret. Public impediments which can not be removed of themselves can be removed only by dispensations; but this course is possible only in cases which are not considered to be based on divine law. Roman Catholic practise, therefore, absolutely denies the possibility of dispensation in the case of an impediment of an existing marriage, or of relationship in the direct line and the first like degree of the collateral line. On the other hand, the impediments of difference in religion of affinity proper in the direct line, and of *crimen ex occisione coniugis cum adulterio* later becoming publicly known are held to be only generally incapable of dispensation. By the third canon of the twenty-fourth session of the Council of Trent it was expressly declared that the Church can grant dispensations in certain degrees of consanguinity and affinity mentioned in Leviticus. In the Evangelical Church all Mosaic prohibitions of affinity and relationship, usually with generalizing extensions, were formerly considered as incapable of dispensation, with the exception of marriage with a brother's widow, from which the law itself granted a certain degree of dispensation in the levirate marriage. In more recent times it has become the prevalent opinion in the Evangelical Church that only the impediments of relationship and affinity in the direct line and of consanguinity in the first degree of the collateral line are absolutely debarred from dispensation. In the Roman Catholic Church the pope has the exclusive right of granting dispensations from all diriment impediments, as well as from the obstructing impediments of *mixta religio* and of the simple vows of perpetual chastity or of entrance into a religious order. All other dispensations are granted by the bishops, each in his own diocese, although the pope delegates to the bishops the exercise of varying portions of the power of dispensation reserved for him.

4. Dissolution of Marriage: Dissolution of marriage, according to canon law, which is followed by all modern civil legislations, takes place *ipso jure* only through death; during the lifetime of both parties a marriage, even though existing simply *de facto*, can be dissolved only by legal decision or by dispensation, except in the case of the annulment

1. Classes of Dissolution of Marriage. of an unconsummated marriage by a vow, possible according to the laws of the Roman Catholic Church. In general a distinction must be drawn between a dissolution of the nuptial tie (*a vinculo matrimonii*), thus permitting remarriage, and mere separation from bed and board (*separatio a toro et mensa*), which, according to the law of the Roman Catholic Church, can be only for life (*perpetua*), but according to Protestantism may be merely temporary (*temporaria*). In the dissolution of marriage distinction must be made between dissolution on account of a marriage impediment (annulment) and dissolution of legal matrimony (divorce, q.v.). The bull *Dei miseratione* of Benedict XIV. (Nov. 3, 1741) contains strict rules for the proceeding of the ecclesiastical courts with reference to the annulment of marriage; and among these regulations is the very pertinent principle, retained in later civil law, that in all procedure for annulment of marriage there must be an official "Defender of the marriage tie" (q.v.) to protect the interests of the religious or civil community in maintaining the marriage. It is characteristic of Roman Catholic Church law that the entrance of one of the parties into a monastery or a papal dispensation can annul a marriage not yet consummated, and hence not yet sacramental.

Real divorce, as an arbitrary deed of one party, legally permitted under certain conditions by Mosaic and Roman law, is referred to in the well-known sayings of Christ, and is opposed by his

2. In the Early Church. words: "What God hath joined together, let not man put asunder." The Church, therefore, has always regarded, and must ever regard, divorce as incompatible with true Christian sentiment. From this the Roman Catholic Church has drawn the inference that the law must treat a consummated (and thus sacramentalized) marriage as so absolutely indissoluble that all divorce, even for adultery, is precluded, even though it may be granted by the courts. Augustine (*De fide et operibus*, iv. 19) considered it at least doubtful whether in that case sanction might be given to a simple separation of the innocent party, who was not, however, to be permitted to marry again until the death of the guilty party. An African synod of 407 expressly recognized the right of the Church to prevent the remarriage of the guilty party, though only by means of church discipline; since to secure the legal impossibility of such remarriage, the Church could only request the passage of an imperial law. Among the Germanic nations even the Roman Catholic Church allowed real divorces, at least by way of "dissimulation," as late as the ninth century.

As soon as the Western Church obtained entire jurisdiction and legislation concerning marriage, however, every indulgence ceased; although it was clearly recognized that while real divorce was no longer possible, it was imperatively necessary that a separation should be allowed which should maintain the marriage and yet abrogate cohabitation, permanently in case of adultery. The consequences of such a separation were the same as those of a real divorce so far as property-rights were concerned; and the separation, like the divorce, presupposed legal procedure and decree. If the words of Christ with regard to divorce were taken as a legal prohibition of it, the phrase "saving for the cause of fornication" (Matt. v. 32; cf. xix. 9) must necessarily be interpreted as a legal permission of at least *perpetua separatio* in such a case. The law of the Roman Catholic Church is, accordingly, that upon motion a separation for a definite or indefinite time (*temporaria separatio a toro et mensa*) is to be granted in case of greater or lesser impairment of conjugal life, in case of temptation to immoral acts or crimes, in case of endangered safety, and the like. Perpetual separation (*perpetua separatio*), however, can be granted only for adultery or unnatural crimes, although in such cases the motion may be opposed by the plea of compensation (adultery practised by the plaintiff), pandering or connivance, and condonation.

3. In the Roman Catholic Church.

Protestant divorce law had its beginning in the proposition laid down in the appendix to the Schmalkald Articles: "Unjust also is the tradition which forbids an innocent person to marry after divorce" (cf. H. E. Jacobs, *Book of Concord*, i. 351, Philadelphia, 1893). The positive rules which the magistrates were to lay down with the advice of the Church concerning divorce in the strict sense of the term (though the Church itself could make no independent legislation on the subject) were to be based on the relevant passages of the Bible submitted to a conscientious exegesis unhampered by ecclesiastical tradition. The result was to substantiate the words of Luther, in his exegesis of the Sermon on the Mount (Erlangen ed., xliii. 117): "Christ (and, of course, Paul as well) here makes no ruling or enactment like a jurist or regent in things external, but simply as a preacher who instructs the conscience so that the law of divorce may be rightly used." The question is, then, not one of "Scriptural grounds for divorce," as if the Bible assigned certain grounds which granted one married party a legal right to separate from the other and the liberty of marrying again; for even in this sense the adultery of the other party is not a Scriptural ground for divorce. The sole problem, on the contrary, is what forms of actual separation or guilt of the one party, in harmony with the Scripture, should be true grounds for the civil authorities to come to the aid of the innocent party by granting a dissolution of the legal bond of marriage. If, from this point of view, the grounds for divorce be considered those for which a petition for judicial separation would be entertained by the civil authorities for the protection of the sanctity of marriage and the defense of the innocent against the guilty, then the most undoubted Scriptural grounds for divorce are adultery and wilful desertion. These were generally expressly and exclusively recognized as such by the Evangelical agenda of the period of the Reformation. On the other hand, it can not be termed contrary to Scripture that the most recent Protestant law of divorce, developed with ecclesiastical sanction, permits judicial separation for other reasons, which, like adultery and wilful desertion, imply *dolosa fidei coniugalis violatio* on the part of one of the married pair.

4. Divorce in the Protestant Church.

The remarriage of divorced persons can no longer be impeded by the refusal of the Church to perform the wedding ceremony, though she must disapprove such unions from the point of view of Christian ethics. Still less can she be prevented by the State from wishing to guard her conscience and to lend active emphasis to her Scriptural teachings on divorce. She must be the more earnest in this respect, since she no longer helps to contract the marriage by the wedding ceremony, the latter being [on the continent of Europe] simply a solemn recognition and declaration that the marriage in question is a union in conformity to the divine will, not so much in virtue of the motives with which it is contracted as with regard to objective requirements. This must be the basis of judgment whether the ceremony is to be granted or refused to the divorced; and for this very reason general principles can and must be established, their applicability to individual cases in which differences arise between the officiating clergyman and those who desire the ceremony being determined by the ruling of the Church.

5. Remarriage of the Divorced.

5. Mixed Marriages: Mixed marriages are those contracted between persons of different Christian confessions, especially between Protestants and Roman Catholics. Since they render impossible that perfect harmony between husband and wife which is demanded by the ethical and religious concept of marriage, inasmuch as the family thus founded necessarily comes under the influence of two antagonistic churches, while almost insuperable difficulties arise regarding the religious training of the children, each Church must disapprove of them and dissuade its members from such marriages.

While this should be especially the case with the Roman Catholic Church, it has never regarded mixed marriages as illegal or as lacking sacramental character. Nevertheless, it fully applied the prohibitions of the early Church regarding marriages between Catholic Christians and heretics to marriages between Roman Catholics and Protestants, despite the fact that the latter were recognized by the State as members of churches on a par with the Roman Catholic Church, and without regard to the circumstance that these Protestant churches were essentially different from the sects to which the prohibitions in question referred. The Roman Curia accordingly maintained that an obstructing impediment based on general Church laws existed for mixed marriages between Roman Catholics and Protestants. A dispensation for such a marriage could be granted by the pope alone; and by him, generally speaking, only on condition that Protestantism was abjured by the Protestant party to the marriage, with the promise that all children born of the union should be educated in the Roman Catholic faith. Moreover, the full applicability of Roman Catholic canon law to such marriages was asserted on the ground that Protestants belong by baptism to the Roman Catholic Church and are

1. The Roman Catholic Position.

lawfully subject to its statutes. Under certain circumstances a temporary exception was made from the strict execution of these principles by express papal favor or "dissimulation." The abjuration of Protestantism was the point least insisted upon, but special stress was laid on the assurance that the children should be educated in the Roman Catholic faith. On principle the Roman Catholic Church always endeavors to prevent mixed marriages altogether, and then at least to render them difficult; but in any case where it assists in their contraction, it expresses its disapproval of the desecration of the sacrament of marriage which it sees in every mixed union. Absolute prevention, however, even from the point of view of its own law, is possible only where the Tridentine Decree on the contraction of marriage has either been promulgated or is practised without formal promulgation. On the other hand, where the pre-Tridentine canon law is authoritative in this respect, a *ratum matrimonium* may also be brought about by informal consent, even though the Church should refuse to cooperate. Difficulties may always be raised by the special conditions made in case a dispensation, either compulsory or voluntary, is asked. Disapproval may be expressed by refusing the banns and by withdrawing active assistance in declaring the consent of the parties to the marriage, the cooperation of the Church thus being restricted to the so-called passive assistance outside the Church and without priestly vestments, or at least by refusal to celebrate the nuptial mass with its benediction, or by omitting the simple benediction connected with the marriage ceremony. Where more or less sweeping exceptions to these principles are made, they are due to a desire to avoid greater evils to the Church. Toward the end of the eighteenth century mixed marriages were very mildly treated by the Roman Catholic Church; but in the nineteenth century she revived the full severity of her strict principles, the modifications conceded by Pius VIII. for the archdiocese of Cologne (1830) and for Bavaria (1832), or by Gregory XVI. for Austria (1841) being merely temporary.

2. Present Roman Catholic Usage.

According to the present legal status, the pope, or the bishop as his delegate, removes the *impedimentum mixtæ religionis*. The Roman Catholic ceremony is required, except in countries to which the declaration of Benedict XIV. (Nov. 4, 1741) for Holland and Belgium has been extended. The priest gives merely *assistentia passiva*. The grant of dispensation presupposes the fulfilment of certain conditions. The Roman Catholic party promises to attempt the conversion of the Protestant, while the latter is pledged to make no such effort; both are bound to bring up all their children in the Roman Catholic faith and are required to waive an Evangelical marriage ceremony. By a decree of the Inquisition (June 17, 1864), the Roman Catholic ceremony in addition to the Protestant is inadmissible. If the Roman Catholic ceremony is desired after the Protestant, the priest is to perform it, but must impose some penance on the Roman Catholic party. Should the priest hear that the parties intend also to have the Evangelical ceremony, he is to dissuade them, although emphasis is not to be laid so much on this point as upon the other conditions, especially the one referring to the education of the children. In the constitution "*Provide*" of January 18, 1906, Pope Pius X. decreed for Germany that mixed marriages of Catholics with non-Catholics not consummated according to the Tridentine Decree are subject to penalty, but valid, also that marriages of non-Catholics among each other in Germany are not subject to the Tridentine Decree for their validity. The State has repeatedly objected to the Roman Catholic regulation of mixed marriages; but through the introduction of the obligatory civil marriage the question has lost its acute character so far as the State is concerned, and has become primarily a controversy of the different confessions. The contraction of a mixed marriage after the divorce of the Protestant party would necessarily be considered absolutely unlawful by the Roman Catholic Church, even did she not consider Protestants bound by her laws, since according to her dogma the marriage union existing between two who have been baptized can not be dissolved by a judicial separation. Even did she concede the legal right of divorced Protestants to contract a new marriage, she could never allow her members to contract a marriage with those who, according to Roman Catholic belief, are still bound together by a former marriage. Only in case the divorce is found by a Roman Catholic ecclesiastical court to have affected a marriage which was null and void, can the Roman Catholic Church allow such a mixed marriage.

3. Lutheran Usage.

In the Protestant Church mere difference of religious Christian confession, at least in Germany, has never been regarded as an actual impediment to marriage requiring a formal dispensation, although in Saxony, as late as the seventeenth and the early eighteenth centuries, a marriage between Lutherans and Roman Catholics needed a special license of the higher consistory, which was granted only on certain conditions, especially that of bringing up all the children in the Lutheran faith. For many years, however, the church ceremony has been generally allowed for mixed marriages, except where the Protestant party has agreed to bring up all the children in the Roman Catholic faith.

Legal statutes limiting the liberty of parents to decide as to the religious education of children born of a mixed marriage can be enacted only by the State, since those made by ecclesiastical authority can be binding only on the party to the marriage subject to such authority. E. SEHLING.

BIBLIOGRAPHY: On primitive marriage consult: E. Westermarck, *Hist. of Human Marriage*, new ed., London, 1901, Fr. transl., *Origine du mariage dans l'espèce humaine*, Paris, 1895; L. Dargum, *Mutterrecht und Raubehe und ihre Reste*, Breslau, 1883; A. Girard-Teulon, *Les Origines du mariage*, Geneva, 1884; J. F. McClellan, *Studies in Ancient Hist.*, 2 series, London, 1886–96; idem, *The Origin of Exogamy*, in *English Historical Review*, Jan., 1888 (both the last are of high importance); C. Letourneau, *The Evolution of Marriage and the Family*, New York, 1891; L. Tillier, *Le Mariage, sa genèse, son évolution*, Paris, 1898; E. Crawley, *The Mystic Rose; a Study of primitive Marriage*, London, 1901; Smith, *Kinship*; L. H. Morgan, *Ancient Society*, reissue, New York, 1907; N. W Thomas, *Kinship Organizations and Group Marriage in Australia*,

New York, 1908; and the literature on totemism under COMPARATIVE RELIGION.

On the history of Christian marriage consult: Bingham, *Origines*, passim (using the index); *DCA*, ii. 1092–1115; G. E. Howard, *A History of Matrimonial Institutions, chiefly in England and the United States*, 3 vols., Chicago, 1904; E. Saalfeld, *Luthers Lehre von der Ehe*, Leipsic, 1882; W. Kawerau, *Die Reformation und die Ehe*, Halle, 1892; J. F. Bingham, *Christian Marriage; the Ceremony, History and Significance*, New York, 1900.

On the theory of marriage consult: W. Glock, *Christliche Ehe und ihre modernen Gegner*, Carlsruhe, 1881; C. Thönes, *Die christliche Anschauung der Ehe*, Leyden, 1881; W. Humphrey, *Christian Marriage*, London, 1886 (Roman Catholic); A. H. Huth, *Marriage of Near Kin*, ib. 1887; A. Richard, *Marriage and Divorce*, ib. 1888 (religious, practical and political); H. A. Smith, in *Is Marriage a Failure?* ib. 1888 (a popular handbook); O. D. Watkins, *Holy Matrimony*, ib. 1895; A. M. Caird, *The Morality of Marriage*, ib. 1897; D. F. Wilcox, *Ethical Marriage*, Ann Arbor, 1900; M. W. Allen, *Marriage, its Duties and Privileges*, Chicago, 1901; P. A. Morrow, *Social Diseases and Marriage*, Philadelphia, 1904; L. F. Post, *Ethical Principles of Marriage and Divorce*, Chicago, 1906; H. H. Henson, *Christian Marriage*, London, 1907.

On the law of marriage and its history consult: J. P. Bishop, *Commentaries on the Law of Marriage and Divorce*, 2 vols., Boston, 1881; G. Mansella, *De impedimentis matrimonii dirimentibus*, Rome, 1891; P. Brillaud, *Traité des empêchements de mariage*, Paris, 1884; J. Freisen, *Geschichte des canonischen Eherechts*, Tübingen, 1888; A. Esmein, *Le Mariage en droit canonique*, 2 vols., Paris, 1891; F. Heiner, *Grundriss des katholischen Eherechts*, Münster, 1892; F. H. Geffcken, *Zur Geschichte der Ehescheidung vor Gratian*, Leipsic, 1894; G. Revesz, *Das Trauerjahr der Witwe*, Stuttgart, 1902; L. Gaugusch, *Das Ehehindernis der höheren Weihe*, Vienna, 1902; M. Leitner, *Lehrbuch des katholischen Eherechts*, Paderborn, 1902.

For marriage law and the general status in different countries, consult for France: E. Kelly, *The French Law of Marriage*, London, 1885; G. Baidry-Lacantinerie, *Du contrat de mariage*, 3 vols., Paris, 1901. For Germany: C. Barazetti, *Das Eherecht*, Hanover, 1895; C. Sartorius, *Kommentar zum Personenstandgesetz in der vom Jan. 1, 1900, an geltenden Fassung*, Munich, 1902. For England: W. Ernst, *Treatise on Marriage and Divorce*, London, 1879; J. T. Hammick, *The Marriage Law of England*, ib. 1887; D. M. Ford, *Matrimonial Law*, ib. 1888, C. Crawley, *The Law of Husband and Wife*, ib. 1892. For the United States: J. Fulton, *The Laws of Marriage*, New York, 1883; W. L. Snyder, *The Geography of Marriage*, New York, 1889 (on the complexities of marriage law in the U. S.); C. D. Wright, *Report on Marriage and Divorce in the U. S.*, Washington, 1889; L. J. Robinson, *Law of Husband and Wife*, Boston, 1890; J. P. Bishop, *Commentaries on Marriage, Divorce and Separation*, 2 vols., Chicago, 1891; F. Keezer, *Law of Marriage and Divorce*, Boston, 1906; J. M. Donovan, *Law of Marriage, Annulment, Domicile, Divorce*, Sioux Falls, 1908.

MARROW CONTROVERSY, THE: A Scotch ecclesiastical dispute occasioned by the republication in 1718 by James Hog of Carnock of *The Marrow of Modern Divinity, . by E. F.* (2 parts, London, 1645-49), possibly wrongly ascribed to Edward Fisher, an English Calvinist of the seventeenth century noted for spirituality and learning (cf. *DNB*, xix. 55–56). The work consists of religious dialogues of an original and sprightly kind, discusses the doctrine of the atonement, and aims to guide the reader safely between Antinomianism (q.v.) and Neonomianism. A copy of it was brought into Scotland by an English Puritan soldier, and years afterward found by Thomas Boston (q.v.), who was much pleased with it, and spoke of it to several; and so it was republished with a commendatory preface by James Hog. The book displeased the Neonomians, and they were the leading men in the Church of Scotland. One of their number, Principal Haddow of St. Andrews, assailed it in his opening sermon at the Synod of Fife, Apr., 1719; and a " committee for preserving the purity of doctrine " was chosen at the Assembly that year, the business of which was to discredit the book. This was attempted by garbled extracts. In their report in 1720 the committee condemned the book as Antinomian, and the Assembly approved. Then the friends of the book rallied to its defense. Twelve men, who were called " the Representers," formally called the attention of the Assembly to the anomaly that it had condemned, because taught in the book, propositions which were couched in Scripture language, and others which were expressly taught in their symbolical books. The Neonomians, however, gained a moderate victory, and in the Assembly of 1722 the twelve Representers were solemnly rebuked; subsequently every effort was made by the Neonomians to prevent the settlement of ministers holding the *Marrow* doctrines. No action was taken against the Representers, and the controversy in the church courts ended. But the irritation lasted, and ultimately led to the formation of the Secession Church (see PRESBYTERIANS).

BIBLIOGRAPHY: W. M. Hetherington, *Hist. of the Church of Scotland*, chap. ix., pp. 342, 344–347, New York, 1881; C. A. Briggs, *American Presbyterianism*, pp. 254 sqq., ib. 1885.

MARSAY, mär"sê', CHARLES HECTOR DE ST. GEORGE, MARQUIS DE: Quietist and mystic; b. at Paris 1688; d. at Ambleden (an estate near Wolfenbüttel), Brunswick, Feb. 3, 1753. He was a descendant of a noble family of Reformed faith, which had emigrated from France to Germany and Switzerland, and from childhood he was acquainted with such books of devotion as those of Thomas à Kempis and Jurieu. He served as an ensign in an Anglo-Hanoverian regiment in Belgium during the Spanish War of Succession. During a severe illness he was urged by two friends to resign his commission and withdraw entirely from the world. The three retired in 1711 to Schwarzenau, in the county of Wittgenstein, where they lived as hermits, practising self-castigation, observing silence so far as possible, and toiling diligently. Not receiving from this mode of life the edification which he sought, De Marsay withdrew from his companions and in 1712 entered into a marriage of absolute continence with Clara Elisabeth von Callenberg. The pair lived in a small house near Gersdorf, suffering the extremes of poverty and distressed by fears concerning their spiritual welfare. After 1713 De Marsay and his wife made repeated visits to his kinsmen in Geneva in the hope of reconciling his mother, who was displeased with her son's course of life. In Switzerland they came in frequent contact with the " awakened," and De Marsay learned of the writings of Madame Guyon, which were henceforth to control him. Gradually withdrawing from ascetic extremes, De Marsay and his wife devoted themselves more to practical work, became partially reconciled with his family, and accepted a pension from his father's estate. Now all his former struggles seemed to him self-righteousness, and he regarded himself as a child with neither light nor certainty. Then began, according to his conviction, the renewal of the "center," or the foundation of his soul, through the spirit of God, although for many years his spiritual life knew neither rest nor constancy.

Meantime serious controversies resulted from his association with Pietists of like tendencies. In 1726 he conceived the plan of emigrating to Pennsylvania, and in 1730 Zinzendorf sought to interest him in forming the separatists in Schwarzenau and Berleburg into a Moravian community, and also wished to send him to France to win the scattered and oppressed Reformed for his cause. For a time De Marsay and his wife were favorably impressed, but both later rejected the proposal. He now withdrew from mystic meetings and resumed a hermit's life in Schwarzenau and Berleburg. After 1732 he resided for some years at the castle of Hayn near Berleburg as the spiritual adviser of the Von Fleischbein family. In this period fall a number of his works. All these writings, of which the most important are his *Freimütige und christliche Diskurse* (3 parts, 1735–39; Eng. transl., *Discourses on Subjects Relating to the Spiritual Life*, Edinburgh, 1749), *Zeugnis eines Kindes von der Richtigkeit der Wege des Geistes* (8 parts, 1736–41), and *Christliche Gedanken über verschiedener Materien der Gottseligkeit* (1750), show the influence both of French mysticism and of the theosophy of Jakob Böhme and Gottfried Arnold (qq. v.). After the death of his wife in 1742, De Marsay lived for three years in Schwarzenau, and then resided in various places. Coming into contact with pietistic Evangelical pastors, through their influence he abandoned separatism, took part in public worship and the communion, and accepted the Evangelical doctrine of justification by faith. His importance is due to the fact that he introduced the quietistic mysticism of French Roman Catholicism into Germany, although he was one of the last representatives of his school. (K. Holl.)

Bibliography: The main source for a life is the autobiography, existing in MS. in the provincial ecclesiastical archives at Coblenz, reproduced substantially in De Valenti, *System der höheren Heilkunde*, ii. 153 sqq., Elberfeld, 1827. Consult further: H. Corrodi, *Kritische Geschichte des Chiliasmus*, iii. 456 sqq., Zurich, 1783; *ZHT*, 1855, pp. 349 sqq.; M. Göbel, *Geschichte des christlichen Lebens in der rheinisch-westphälischen evangelischen Kirche*, iii. 193 sqq., Coblenz, 1860; G. Heppe, *Geschichte der quietistischen Mystik in der katholischen Kirche*, pp. 506 sqq., Berlin, 1875; A. Ritschl, *Geschichte des Pietismus*, i. 425, ii. 379 sqq., Bonn, 1880–84; R. A. Vaughan, *Hours with the Mystics*, ii. 291–295, 8th ed., London, n.d.

MARSDEN, SAMUEL: Church of England; b. at Horsforth (5 m. n.w. of Leeds) July 28, 1764; d. at Windsor (30 m. n.w. of Sydney), New South Wales, May 12, 1838. He was educated at the grammar-school in Hull, and then assisted his father in his shop in Leeds. He was converted and joined at first the Methodist Church, but afterward united himself to the Church of England, and entered St. John's College, Cambridge. He was ordained in 1793, and in 1794 sailed to Australia as chaplain to the penal colony at Paramatta, near Sydney. He established a farm there which eventually became one of the finest in Australia, and endeavored to train the convicts to habits of industry. In 1807 he returned to England to make a report on the condition of the colony, and tried to interest the Church Missionary Society in the Maoris of New Zealand, but in vain. He succeeded, however, in inducing W. Hall and J. King, two laymen, to return to Australia with him, and in 1814, after he had fitted out a small vessel at his own expense, he and his two assistants sailed to New Zealand. The natives welcomed him gladly and he labored among them at intervals until his death, making in all seven visits to the islands, the last in 1837. He believed that civilization should precede the Gospel, and therefore his chief efforts were in that direction. In New South Wales also he was very influential in the cause of civilization, establishing schools and a seminary.

Bibliography: J. B. Marsden, *Memoirs of the Life and Labours of . Samuel Marsden*, London, 1858; J. L. Nicholas, *Narrative of a Voyage to New Zealand . . in 1814-15, . with Rev. S. Marsden*, ib. 1817; *DNB*, xxxvi. 205–206.

MARSEILLES, BISHOPRIC OF: An ancient episcopal see in the south of France, said by tradition to have been founded by the Lazarus who was raised from the dead. He is supposed to have come hither with his sisters Mary and Martha in the year 63, to have been bishop here fifty years, and to have met a martyr's death. The first bishop known to authentic history is Oresius, who signed the decrees of the Synod of Arles in 314. Proculus (381–428) attempted to claim metropolitan rights, which were conceded to him personally but not to his successors by the Synod of Turin in 401. During his episcopate Semipelagianism made such progress in southern Gaul that its adherents were sometimes known as Massilians. The see continued to be of considerable importance. During a part of the episcopate of Paul de Sade (1404–34), the antipope, Peter de Luna (Benedict XIII.), resided here. The bishopric, which had remained a suffragan see of Arles, was suppressed in 1801, and restored in 1821, but is now under the metropolitan jurisdiction of Aix.

Bibliography: Gams, *Series episcoporum*, pp. 573–574, supplement, pp. 38, 42 (for list of bishops); *Gallia Christiana*, i. 631–704, appendix, pp. 106–118, Paris, 1715; F. X. de Belzance de Castelmoron, *L'Antiquité de l'église de Marseille et la succession de ses évêques*, 3 vols., Marseilles, 1747–51; A. Ricard, *Les Évêques de Marseille*, Paris, 1872.

MARSH, HERBERT: Bishop of Peterborough; b. at Faversham (44 m. e.s.e. of London), Kent, Dec. 10, 1757; d. at Peterborough May 1, 1839. He was educated at the King's School, Canterbury, and St. John's College, Cambridge (B.A., 1779; M.A., 1782; B.D., 1792; D.D., 1808). In 1779 he became a fellow of his college. In 1785 he traveled on the continent and studied at Leipsic for some years with interruptions. In 1807 he was appointed Lady Margaret professor of divinity at Cambridge, where he instituted an innovation by delivering his lectures in English instead of Latin. In Aug., 1816, he was made bishop of Llandaff, and in 1819 he was transferred to Peterborough. As bishop he introduced many reforms in the administration of his dioceses. Marsh was a zealous opponent both of Calvinism and of Roman Catholicism and wrote many controversial pamphlets. Some of his more important works are: *The History of the Politicks of Great Britain and France* (2 vols., London, 1800);

A Course of Lectures, containing a Description of Divinity (6 parts, 1809–22); *A Comparative View of the Churches of England and Rome* (Cambridge, 1814); *Horæ Pelasgicæ* (only part 1 published, 1815); *Lectures on the Criticism and Interpretation of the Bible* (1828); and *Lectures on the Authenticity and Credibility of the New Testament, and on the Authority of the Old Testament* (London, 1840). He also translated the *Introduction to the New Testament* of J. D. Michaelis (4 vols., Cambridge, 1793–1801).

Bibliography: T. Baker, *Hist. of the College of St. John, Cambridge*, ed. J. E. B. Mayor, ii. 735–898, Cambridge, 1869; I. Milner, *Strictures on Some of the Publications of Rev. H. Marsh*, London, 1813; *DNB*, xxxvi. 211–215.

MARSHALL, JOHN TURNER: English Baptist; b. at Farsley (5 m. w. of Leeds), Yorkshire, May 13, 1850. He was educated at Rawdon College and Owens and Baptist Colleges, Manchester (B.A., London University, 1870). From 1877 to 1898 he was classical tutor in Manchester Baptist College, and since the latter year has been president of the same institution, while since 1904 he has also been lecturer on the history of Christian doctrine in Manchester University. He was president of the Baptist Union, 1909–10. He is an able Aramaic scholar, and is applying this knowledge to the criticism of the Greek text of the Gospels in an interesting and instructive manner. In theology he is "Evangelical, with a frank outlook on all that is well grounded in Biblical criticism." He has written commentaries on Job and Ecclesiastes (Philadelphia, 1903) and *Job and his Comforters* (London, 1905).

MARSHALL, STEPHEN: Westminster divine; b. at Godmanchester in Huntingdonshire, England, at an unknown date; educated at Emmanuel College, Cambridge; became minister at Wethersfield, and then at Finchingfield in Essex, where he was silenced for non-conformity. In 1640 he was made lecturer at St. Margaret's, Westminster. He was one of the chiefs in the Smectymnuan controversy (see Calamy, Edmund) with Bishop Hall in 1641; was made member of the Westminster Assembly of Divines in 1643. He was the greatest preacher of his times and the most popular speaker. He was an active man, and a judicious adviser in all ecclesiastical affairs. He preached before Parliament, the Lord Mayor, and the Assembly, more frequently than many others combined. He was the most influential member of the Westminster Assembly in ecclesiastical affairs. He represented the English Parliament in Scotland in 1643; attended the commissioners sent to the king at Newcastle for the accommodation of peace in 1646; attended the commissioners at the treaty of the Isle of Wight in 1647. He was a moderate and judicious Presbyterian under Cromwell's administration, and as an acknowledged chief was appointed one of the committee to draw up a catalogue of fundamentals as a basis of toleration, to be presented to the House of Commons in 1654, and became one of the Tryers. He died in November, 1655; and his remains were interred in Westminster Abbey, but were shamefully dug up at the Restoration.

Large numbers of his sermons on special occasions were published. These, notwithstanding the faults in method and style characteristic of the times, are models of eloquence and fervor. Among these may be mentioned: *A Peace-Offering to God*, Sept. 7, 1641; *Reformation and Desolation*, Dec. 22, 1641; *Meroz cursed*, Feb. 23, 1641 (2); *Song of Moses the Servant of God, and the Song of the Lamb*, June 15, 1643; *Sacred Panegyricks*, 1644; *Sermon of the Baptizing of Infants*, 1644; *Right Understanding of the Times*, Dec. 30, 1646; *Unity of the Saints with Christ the Head*, April, 1652. The only systematic work he published was *A Defence of Infant Baptism* against John Tombes, London, 1646, 4to, pp. 256. C. A. Briggs.

MARSHMAN, JOSHUA: English Baptist missionary; b. at Westbury Leigh (21 m. n.w. of Salisbury), Wiltshire, Apr. 20, 1768; d. at Serampur (12 m. n. of Calcutta), India, Dec. 5, 1837. He had almost no schooling as a boy, but was a weaver like his father till he was twenty-six years old. By diligent and persistent private study he fitted himself to take in 1794 the position of master of a school in Bristol, while he studied Latin, Greek, Hebrew, and Syriac at the Bristol Academy. He was led by reading about the labors of W. Carey in India to offer himself for that work, and in May, 1799, he sailed for India together with W. Ward, arriving at Serampur Oct. 13, 1799, and was soon afterward joined there by Carey. He was not allowed to enter British territory, so he and his companions remained in Serampur, which at that time was under Danish rule, and established their mission there. Marshman and his wife opened two boarding-schools for European children, which met with great success and with the income derived from them he maintained his mission. His relations with the Baptist Missionary Society in England soon became much strained and in 1826 he returned to England to settle matters, but not succeeding in his purpose in 1827 the Serampur mission was separated from the others. In 1823 Ward died, and in 1834 when Carey died Marshman was left alone. In 1818 he started a newspaper in Bengali, the *Sumachar-Durpun* or "Mirror of News." Marshman was learned not only in Bengali and other Indian tongues, but had also made a deep study of Chinese. He not only translated parts of the Bible into several languages, including Bengali, Telinga, and Chinese, but also wrote much original matter. Among his chief works may be mentioned: *A Dissertation on the Characters and Sounds of the Chinese Language* (Serampur, 1809); and *Clavis Sinica* (1814). He also translated the works of Confucius (1809) and in connection with Carey the *Ramayana* (1806).

Bibliography: J. C. Marshman, *Life and Times of Carey, Marshman, and Ward, Embracing the History of the Serampore Mission*, 2 vols., London, 1859, abridged ed., 1864, New York, 1870; *DNB*, xxvi. 255–256.

MARSILIUS, mar-sil'i-us, **OF PADUA:** With William of Occam, the most important of the learned publicists who supported Louis the Bavarian in his struggle with Rome. He was born at Padua soon after 1270; d. between Oct. 28, 1336, and Apr. 10, 1343. His family name was either De Raimundinis, as his friend Albertus Mussatus calls him, or De Mainardinis, as official church documents and other contemporary sources have. In choice of a vocation he hesitated between law and medicine, apparently served the houses of della Scala in Verona and Visconti in Milan for a while, and by 1312 was in Paris with a master's degree and priest's orders. Here he fell in with William of Occam and John of Jandun, and all three took an active share in the controversy which raged so fiercely under John XXII., especially after 1322, in the Franciscan order with reference to the poverty of Christ and the apostles, taking the side of the strict Observantists against the pope. Though Marsilius escaped the imprisonment that befell Occam and others, he was undoubtedly in some danger, and looked to the emperor, Louis IV. the Bavarian, for protection. Louis was at that time in conflict with the pope, and welcomed Marsilius and John of Jandun to his side. They were soon busy with the preparation of the great work which was to make the name of Marsilius remembered, the *Defensor pacis*, and in two months had it ready to take to Germany to the emperor. This was between 1324 and 1326, so that the date of a Vienna manuscript (June 24, 1324) may be the exact one. Louis took them into his suite, declaring later that he had welcomed them simply as accomplished scholars who might be useful to him, without committing himself to their theological subtleties. The influence of Marsilius was probably important in determining Louis to march toward Rome and to set up the Franciscan Peter of Corbara as antipope under the title of Nicholas V. Marsilius himself was named papal vicar of Rome, and is reported also to have been appointed archbishop of Milan. The failure of the imperial expedition ended the preponderant influence of Marsilius. Louis humbled himself to ask for a reconciliation with the pope whom he had deposed, and promised that Marsilius also should submit or forfeit the imperial protection. Fortunately for Marsilius, neither John nor his successors, Benedict XII. and Clement VI., accepted Louis' offer.

In his oration of Apr. 10, 1343, the pope declared that he had never read a more shockingly heretical book than the *Defensor pacis*, while Flacius, on the other hand, in his *Catalogus testium*, says that among the older (i.e., pre-Reformation) works there is no more sound, scholarly, bold and pious book against the papal power. The work as a whole may be divided into two parts, the first book developing, on an Aristotelian basis, the political theory, and the second dealing with the constitution of the Church, the relations of which to the State are finally discussed. For his age, Marsilius is strikingly bold and sharp-sighted, far surpassing his forerunners Dante, Johannes Parisius, etc. In abstract politics he lays down the aphorism that the sovereignty of the people, or a majority of them, is the source of all power. In spiritual things he affirms the validity of the New Testament as law, but says that it is to be enforced only by internal means, not by temporal punishment. Speaking of dignities in the Church, he deduces from the New Testament and Jerome the assertion that bishops and presbyters were originally the same, and derives the later episcopal power from human convention, denying also that one bishop surpasses another by any divine right. He vehemently combats the claim of the hierarchy to withdraw all its property and its followers from secular jurisdiction, and asserts the right of the "human legislator" to use wholly or in part such temporal possessions as are over what the Church needs for divine worship, the support of the clergy, and the necessities of the poor. He looks for reformation of the ills of the time from councils and synods consisting of bishops, priests, and faithful laymen, and called by the secular authority. These remarkable conclusions, though proceeding rather from Aristotelian reasoning than, as in Luther's case, from pious instinct, are important features of the preparation for the Reformation. (F. SANDER.)

BIBLIOGRAPHY: Apparently the editio princeps of the *Defensor* was Basel, 1522. Subsequent editions were Frankfort, 1592, 1692; Heidelberg, 1599, 1612; and also in M. Goldast, *Monarchia*, ii. 154–312, Frankfort, 1614. An Eng. transl. is by Wyllyam Marshall, London, 1553. Consult: P. E. Meyer, *Étude sur Marsile de Padoue*, Paris, 1870; G. Lechler, *Johann von Wiclif und die Vorgeschichte der Reformation*, Leipsic, 1873; S. Riezler, *Die litterarischen Widersacher der Päpste*, ib. 1874; C. Müller, *Der Kampf Ludwigs des Baiern mit der römischen Kurie*, 2 vols., Tübingen, 1879–1880; B. Labanca, *Marsilio da Padova*, Padua, 1882; *Vatikanische Akten zur deutschen Geschichte in der Zeit Kaiser Ludwig des Bayern*, Innsbruck, 1891; Pastor, *Popes*, i. 76–81, 86, 159, 178; Neander, *Christian Church*, v. 25–35, 38, 93, 147, consult index for other references; *KL*, viii. 908–911.

MARTÈNE, mār"tên', EDMOND: French Benedictine scholar; b. at Saint Jean de Lône (17 m. s.e. of Dijon) Dec. 22, 1654; d. in Paris June 20, 1739. He entered the Benedictine order Sept. 8, 1672, and was influenced by the work of Johannes Trithemius on the Benedictine rule to write on the subject himself. The superiors of his abbey, St. Remi at Reims, sent him to Saint Germain des Prés at Paris, the headquarters of the literary activity of the congregation of Saint-Maur, to assist in editing the Fathers. There he studied under D'Achery and Mabillon, and published his first book, a commentary on the rule of St. Benedict (1690). Almost simultaneously appeared his *De antiquis monachorum ritibus* (2 vols., Lyons, 1690), a mine of information on monastic antiquities. Next he spent some time in the monastery of Marmoutier, where he was influenced in an ascetic direction by Claude Martin, whose life he wrote (Paris, 1697). Not long after he was sent to the house of Saint-Ouen at Rouen to help Dom de Sainte-Marthe in his edition of Gregory the Great. He now published his *De antiquis ecclesiæ ritibus* (3 vols., Rouen, 1700–02), an expansion of his earlier work; the cognate *Tractatus de antiqua ecclesiæ disciplina in celebrandis officiis* (Lyons, 1706); and a completion of D'Achery's *Spicilegium* (Rouen, 1700). In 1708 he was chosen as a collaborator on the *Gallia christiana*, and spent six years in documentary research throughout France. The result of his investigations appeared in the *Thesaurus novus anecdotorum* (5 vols., Paris, 1717), as well as in the celebrated *Voyage littéraire de deux religieux bénédictins* (ib. 1717). A further achievement of Martène and his fellow-worker Durand was the *Veterum scriptorum et monumentorum amplissima collectio* (9 vols., Paris, 1724–33). His last published work was the sixth volume of his *Annales* in 1739; his *Histoire de la congrégation de Saint-Maur* remained in manuscript until 1747. By his death the order lost one of its most learned members and at the same time a saintly, humble, and amiable man. (FRANZ GÖRRES.)

BIBLIOGRAPHY: D. Tassin, *Hist. littéraire de la congrégation de S. Maur*, pp. 542–571, Brussels, 1770; C. G. Jöcher, *Gelehrtenlexikon*, iii. 218–219, Leipsic, 1751, iv. 810–814, Bremen, 1813; C. de Lama, *Bibliothèque des écrivains de . . S. Maur*, pp. 145–147, Paris, 1882; K. Schorn, *Eiflia sacra*, ii. 80–82, 148 sqq., 340, Bonn, 1888; *KL*, viii. 911–913; Lichtenberger, *ESR*, viii. 742–743.

MARTENSEN, HANS LASSEN.

Life (§ 1).
Theological Development (§ 2).
Character of His Theology (§ 3).
Mystic and Theosophic Elements (§ 4).
Polemic and Other Activities (§ 5).

Hans Lassen Martensen, a Danish bishop and theologian, was born at Flensburg (41 m. n.w. of Kiel, Germany) Aug. 19, 1808; d. at Copenhagen Feb. 3, 1884. He was educated in Copenhagen, both in school and at the university, from which he took his degree in theology in 1832. From 1834 to 1836 he made further studies in Germany and Paris. Returning to Copenhagen, he became a licentiate and privat-docent in theology in 1837, and was appointed reader in 1838 and professor of systematic theology in 1840, and in 1845 became also court preacher. On the death of the bishop of Zealand, J. P. Mynster (q.v.), in 1854, Martensen was chosen by the government as his successor, and in this, the highest ecclesiastical office of the country, he displayed great zeal both for the performance of the duties of his office and for the defense of the faith by his pen. In the last year of his life, conscious of failing strength, he resigned, and died a few days afterwards.

1. Life.

As a theologian, he adhered without wavering to the philosophy which sees the spiritual explanation of all things in the light of the Christian revelation, and finds the person of Christ the centerpoint of the universe and of all its thoughts. Under the influence of Sibbern's teaching at Copenhagen, he early came to the conclusion that Christianity was to be accepted because its truth appeals to the reason as the one source of a comprehensive philosophy of life. He sought the unity of faith and knowledge, and could not be content with any scheme which did not offer this. But he was even more strongly influenced by the philosophy of Schleiermacher and Hegel. Schleiermacher he met personally in 1833, and was an enthusiastic admirer of his mystical depth and the structural completeness of his dogmatics; but he could not hold with his subjective attitude, in contradistinction from which he found himself powerfully attracted by the objective, all-embracing system of Hegel. Here, on the other hand, he felt the lack of system and of the recognition of religion as a higher sphere than mere philosophy. These deficiencies he found supplied in the teaching of Franz Baader (q.v.) at Munich, who strongly emphasized the principle that philosophy must be religious, and that only one who has a personal sense of religion can philosophize about it.

2. Theological Development.

His dissertation of 1837, *De autonomia conscientiæ sui humanæ, in theologiam dogmaticam nostri temporis introducta*, lays down a definite series of propositions, to which he always adhered. Philosophy is not outside of or above his religion, but speculation needs religion (revelation) as its principle; in matters of conscience (the kernel of religion) man is conscious of himself not primarily as one who knows God but as one who is known of God. Human knowledge must remain in this dependence established by the conscience, and recognize that human powers will not avail to find the truth. Man can not place himself in the theocentric standpoint, for that would involve the denial of his qualities of a creature and a sinner. Regeneration and faith in revelation are prerequisites for a right insight into things both divine and human; faith is the condition of the entrance of the divine idea into the soul. Thus he rejected the autonomous standpoint of Kant and Schleiermacher on one side and of Hegel on the other. His system is more fully developed in his *Christelige Dogmatik* (Copenhagen, 1849), which Landerer calls "unquestionably the best reconstruction of ecclesiastical dogmatics from the standpoint of nineteenth-century knowledge." The peculiarity of his speculative position lies in his determined adherence to the teaching of Scripture and the Church. Scripture is to him at once the critical and the organic norm. His aim was not to discover or establish new doctrines, but to put new life into the old.

3. Character of His Theology.

To the speculative element which is the most characteristic of his theology the mystic and theosophic were added in increasing measure as time went on. In his youth he had been a diligent student of Eckart, on whom he wrote in 1840; but his studies along these lines bore their ripest and best fruit in his *Christelige Ethik* (3 vols., 1871–78), throughout which he assumes an intimate acquaintance with mystical experiences in relations with God. The theosophic element appears later and more gradually. It is found in his *Dogmatik*, not so much in the discussion of the being of God as in the passages which deal with the participation of nature and the universe in the renovation and perfecting of the Spirit. Jesus Christ is the second Adam, whose coming has not only a spiritual and a moral significance, but also a deep cosmological one; miracles are an inchoate, if not a continuing transfiguration of nature; the sacraments are mysteries of nature, especially the Lord's Supper considered as nourishment for the future spiritual body. A still closer approximation to theosophical views is seen in the controversial treatise *Vom Glauben und Wissen* (1867), partly no doubt owing to Schelling's later philosophy which had in the mean time been published. His conception of the Deity reached its greatest fulness in his work on Jakob Böhme (1881). This work closes his strictly theological production, which forms an unusually harmonious whole, allowing his genius full development on all its sides. His works

4. Mystical and Theosophic Elements.

found wide-spread approval wherever Protestant theology was studied, and even beyond those limits.

Outside of this connected theological production, he took part in the discussion of many questions of his day. Thus he opposed the Baptists in *Den christelige Daab* (1843), where he laid down the principles more fully developed later in his *Dogmatik*. His conception of the relation between faith and knowledge was strongly opposed by S. A. Kierkegaard (q.v.), who between 1843 and 1851 published a long series of writings, tending to show that Christianity and speculation were things of different orders, and to reduce Christianity to the absurd and paradoxical which must be believed in spite of reason. With the appearance of Martensen's *Dogmatik*, some of Kierkegaard's followers opened a campaign against his views, under the leadership of R. Nielsen; but to these attacks, lasting for a generation, Martensen seldom replied. When a young candidate for ordination set forth the view that the operation of the sacraments depended on the faith of the minister, and Grundtvig defended him, he published two small works (1856, 1857) against this position, and in 1863 subjected the peculiarities of this view to a thorough criticism in his *Til Forsvar mod den saakaldte Grundtvigianisme* (1863). He broke a lance with the Roman Catholics in *Katholicisme og Protestantisme* (1874), and published two treatises on constitutional questions affecting the Danish national church. In his episcopal duties he devoted himself principally to preaching and visitation. Of his sermons eight volumes were published, besides three more of ordination addresses, and a number of occasional discourses. As bishop of Zealand he was the principal adviser of the government in ecclesiastical affairs. In 1849 the king divided his power in these matters with the national assembly, and a minister of public worship was charged with its administration, although he might be a man of no churchly affiliations. In the discussions which followed, Martensen decidedly opposed the abstract individualism which would leave every man free to follow his own conscience, but was not prepared to support altogether the proposal for a synodal form of government, preferring rather to follow traditional Lutheran lines of consistorial organization, which in Denmark amounted to placing the power in the hands of bishops. At first his ideas met with little success; but just before his death a step in that direction was taken by the organization of an episcopal council, which was to be later expanded into a synod — although this was abolished in 1901, and has not yet been replaced by any other system. (P. MADSEN.)

5. Polemic and Other Activities.

BIBLIOGRAPHY: Martensen's works were widely circulated through translations in German, English and other languages. In English appeared his *Christian Dogmatics*, Edinburgh, 1865; *Christian Ethics*, 3 vols., ib. 1873-82; *Jacob Böhme*, London, 1885. On his life the principal authorities are his autobiography, Copenhagen, 1882-83, Germ. transl., 3 parts, Carlsruhe, 1883-84, and *Briefwechsel zwischen H. L. Martensen und I. A. Dorner*, 2 vols., Berlin, 1888. Consult further: V. Nannestad, *H. L. Martensen*, Copenhagen, 1897; *London Quarterly Review*, lxii (1883), 74 sqq.; *Athenæum*, 1884, i. 214 sqq.; *British and Foreign Evangelical Review*, xxxv (1886), 272 sqq.; *Methodist Quarterly*, xlvi (1886), 701 sqq.

MARTI, KARL: Swiss Reformed; b. at Bubendorf (10 m. s.e. of Basel) Apr. 25, 1855. He was educated at the universities of Basel, Göttingen, and Leipsic from 1873 to 1878, after which he held Reformed pastorates successively at Buus (1878-85) and Muttenz (1885-95), both in Baselland. From 1881 to 1894 he was also privat-docent for theology at the University of Basel, where he was appointed associate professor in the latter year. In 1895 he left the ministry and accepted his present position of full professor of theology at the University of Bern, where he has also been professor of Semitic philology since 1901. He has written: *Der Prophet Jeremia von Anatot* (Basel, 1889); *Der Prophet Sacharja, der Zeitgenosse Serubbabels* (Freiburg, 1892); *Der Einfluss der Ergebnisse der neueren alttestamentlichen Forschungen auf Religionsgeschichte und Glaubenslehre* (Brunswick, 1894); *Kurzgefasste Grammatik der biblisch-aramäischen Sprache* (Berlin, 1896); and *Die Religion des Alten Testaments unter den Religionen des vorderen Orients* (Tübingen, 1906; Eng. transl., *The Religion of the Old Testament*, London, 1907). He likewise edited the second edition of August Kayser's *Theologie des Alten Testaments* (Strasburg, 1894; the third, fourth, and fifth editions, 1897-1907, bearing the title *Geschichte der israelitischen Religion*), and *Kurzer Hand-Commentar zum Alten Testament*, in collaboration with I. Benziger, A. Bertholet, K. Budde, B. Duhm, H. Holzinger, and G. Wildeboer (20 vols., Tübingen, 1897-1904), to which Marti himself contributed the volumes on Isaiah (1900), Daniel (1901), and the Minor Prophets (1904). He is also the editor of *Zeitschrift für die alttestamentliche Wissenschaft*.

MARTIANAY, mār"tī"ā"nê', **JEAN:** French Benedictine of St. Maur; b. at St. Sever-Cap (75 m. s. of Bordeaux) Dec. 30, 1647; d. in Paris June 16, 1717. He entered the Benedictine order in 1668 and devoted himself to the study of Greek and Hebrew. In opposition to Paul Pezron, he defended the traditional Biblical chronology in his *Défense du texte hébreu et de la chronologie de la vulgate* (Paris, 1689; supplement, 1693); while in his *Divi Hieronymi prodromus* (Paris, 1690) he roused hopes of a new edition of Jerome which were not fulfilled in the edition itself (5 vols., 1693-1706; the first volume in collaboration with A. Pouget). His work was sharply criticized by R. Simon in his *Lettres critiques* (Basel, 1699) and by J. Clericus in his *Quæstiones Hieronymianæ* (Amsterdam, 1700), as well as by D. Vallarsi in his edition of Jerome (Verona, 1734-42). Martianay also wrote a *Vie de St. Jérôme* (Paris, 1706), which, unfortunately, abounds in chronological errors. He likewise wrote on the Itala, not only in the preface to his edition of Jerome, but also in the introduction to his *Vulgata antiqua latina et itala versio evangelii secundum Matthæum* (Paris, 1695) and in his *Remarques sur la version italique de l'évangile de St. Matthieu* (1695). His hermeneutic principles, based on Augustine and Jerome, are developed in his *Traité méthodique ou manière d'expliquer l'écriture par le secours de trois syntaxes, la propre, la figurée et l'harmonique* (Paris, 1704), in which he subordinated the metaphorical interpretation to the literal, and urged a rigid observance both of context and of syntax. (G. LAUBMANN.)

BIBLIOGRAPHY: D. Tassin, *Hist. littéraire de la congrégation de Saint-Maur*, pp. 382–397, Brussels, 1770; J. B. Vanel, *Les Bénédictins de Saint-Maur 1630–1792*, pp. 112–115, Paris, 1896; Lichtenberger, *ESR*, viii. 743–744; *KL*, viii. 914–916.

MARTIGNY, mār″ti″nyī′, JOSEPH ALEXANDRE: French Roman Catholic; b. at Sauverny (8 m. n. of Geneva) Apr. 22, 1808; d. at Bâgé-le-Châtel (60 m. w. of Geneva) Aug. 18, 1880. Ordained priest in 1832, he served at a village near Belley, and was then archpriest of Bâgé-le-Châtel from 1849 to 1880, also titular canon of the cathedral of Belley. He was noted for his archeological researches, the results of which he embodied in his greatest work, the *Dictionnaire des antiquities chrétiennes* (Paris, 1865; 2d ed., 1877), now undergoing reconstruction as *Dictionnaire d'archéologie chrétienne et liturgie* (ed. F. Cabrol, 1903 sqq.).

MARTIN: The name of five popes.

Martin I.: Pope 649–653. He came originally from Tubertinum (Todi) in Umbria. Before ascending the papal throne as successor to Theodore I., in July, 649, he was apocrisiary, or papal envoy, in Constantinople. His ordination was solemnized without the approval of Emperor Constans II. Further, in Oct., 649, at the Lateran Synod, Martin condemned the Monothelite doctrine, together with the imperial edict (*Typos*) forbidding further controversy on the subject (see MONOTHELITES). The emperor now ordered Olympius, exarch of Ravenna, to proceed to Rome and seize the pope; but for some reason or other Olympius failed to execute this commission. Probably he hoped for support from the pope in connection with his treasonable designs of founding an Italian kingdom independent of Byzantium. On the death of Olympius, the Exarch Kalliopa proceeded with greater energy. In the night of June 17–18, 653, he caused the pope to be seized in the Church of the Lateran, and carried captive to Constantinople. According to the usual acceptation, he was first detained a year or so on the island of Naxos, and reached Constantinople not before Sept. 17, 654. But possibly (cf. E. Michael in *ZKT*, xvi. 1892, pp. 375–380) he reached there in the autumn of 653. In the face of a brutal arraignment Martin exhibited an extraordinary firmness of character. It appears that he escaped the penalty of quartering, with which he was threatened, through the intercession of Patriarch Paul of Constantinople. On Mar. 26, 655 (or 654), Martin was conveyed to Cherson in the Crimea, where he died on Sept. 16 of the same year. The Greek Church venerates him as confessor on Apr. 11, the Church of Rome as martyr on Nov. 12. G. KRÜGER.

BIBLIOGRAPHY: The letters are collected in Mansi, *Concilia*, x. 785–853, 1170–88, and in *MPL*, lxxxvii. 119–204, cf. Jaffé, *Regesta*, i. 230–234. The *Commemoratio eorum quæ . . . acta sunt . . . in . . . Martinum papam*, is also in Mansi, x. 853–864. Consult: *Liber pontificalis*, ed. L. Duchesne, i. 336–340, Paris, 1886, ed. T. Mommsen, in *MGH, Gest. pont. Rom.*, i (1898), 181–184; J. Langen, *Geschichte der römischen Kirche*, vol. i., Bonn, 1885; F. Gregorovius, *Hist. of the City of Rome*, ii. 144–149, London, 1894; Mann, *Popes*, i. 385–405; Hefele, *Conciliengeschichte*, iii. 212–239, Eng. transl., v. 97 sqq.; Bower, *Popes*, i. 446–450; Milman, *Latin Christianity*, ii. 276–280; Platina, *Popes*, i. 153–155; *DCB*, iii. 848–857.

Martin II. See MARINUS I.

Martin III. See MARINUS II.

Martin IV.: Pope 1281–1285. Simon de Brion, of a family in Touraine, had already held ecclesiastical positions at Rouen, later at Tours, when he was appointed chancellor of France by Louis IX. in 1260 and created a cardinal by Urban IV. in 1261. As papal legate in France he conducted the negotiations with Charles of Anjou concerning the assumption of the Sicilian crown; and it was due to the influence of Charles that the conclave at Viterbo, after the death of Nicholas III., unanimously elected Cardinal Simon pope on Feb. 22, 1281. In honor of Saint Martin of Tours, Simon adopted the name of Martin. His pontificate was entirely subservient to the policy of France. After his coronation at Orvieto Mar. 22, 1281 (for the Romans would not receive him within their walls), Martin bestowed on Charles of Anjou the office of a Roman senator, and sought at the same time, with the Sicilian king's assistance, to take possession of the Romagna. The complete dependence of Martin IV. on Charles of Anjou became evident when the pope, in deference to the king's desires and aims toward the sovereignty of Greece, fulminated excommunication against Emperor Michael Palæologus. In the strife that broke out between the Greek emperor and the king of Sicily, the pope supported the latter to the extent of a six years' loan of the Church tithes accruing from Sardinia. But scarcely had he taken this step when Charles of Anjou's dominion over Sicily was terminated by the Sicilian vespers, Mar. 31, 1282. The consequent insurrection in Rome led to the deposition of Charles of Anjou as senator, and to the election of a tribune of the republic; and Martin, who sojourned at Orvieto, was obliged to make prompt acknowledgment of these decisions. Martin died Mar. 28, 1285. CARL MIRBT.

BIBLIOGRAPHY: Sources are: *Les Registres de Martin IV.*, in *Bibliothèque des écoles françaises d'Athènes et de Rome*, 2 ser., vol. xvi., Paris, 1901 sqq.; F. F. Böhmer, *Regesta imperii*, vi. 1, ed. O. Redlich, Innsbruck, 1898; A. Potthast, *Regesta pontificum Romanorum*, pp. 1756–95, Berlin, 1874; *Mitteilungen aus dem vatikanischen Archive*, vol. i., ed. F. Kaltenbrunner, vol. ii., ed. O. Redlich, Vienna, 1889–94; *Martini Oppaviensis chronicon pontificum et imperatorum, continuatio* , ed. L. Weiland in *MGH, Script.*, xx (1868), 477 sqq.; and the early life to be found in L. A. Muratori, *Rerum Italicarum scriptores*, iii. 1, pp. 608–610, 25 vols., Milan, 1723–51. Consult: F. Gregorovius, *Hist. of the City of Rome*, v. 492–501, London, 1897; H. C. Lea, *Hist. of the Inquisition*, i. 89, 525, ii. 121, 248, iii. 190, 196, New York, 1906; Hefele, *Conciliengeschichte*, vi. 209 sqq.; Bower, *Popes*, iii. 29–34; Milman, *Latin Christianity*, vi. 143–171; Platina, *Popes*, ii. 111–114. A full list of scattered references is given in Hauck-Herzog, *RE*, xii. 381.

Martin V.: Pope 1417–31. Oddo Colonna was born probably at Genazzano (26 m. e. of Rome) in 1368. He was educated at the University of Perugia and became prothonotary under Urban VI. In 1405 Innocent VII. made him cardinal deacon of St. George in Velabro. Under Gregory XII. he left his Roman obedience, took part in the Council of Pisa and became an adherent of John XXIII. On Nov. 11, 1417, at the Council of Constance (q.v.), he was unanimously elected pope, after the deposition of John XXIII., Gregory XII. and Benedict XIII. Thus the unity of the Church was restored after the forty years' schism (see SCHISM). Martin was filled with the idea of a papal autocracy, a regeneration of ancient Roman imperialism consistently applied to the papacy. There was no means of harmonizing that autocratic ideal with the ideas of the reformers of the council; but Martin had the prudence to avoid an open conflict. He never confessed his adherence to the decrees of the council, and thwarted the plan of a uniform reform of the Church by the innovation of national concordats. He left Constance May 16, 1418, but was not able to enter Rome till Sept. 28, 1420. He found the States of the Church in the most desolate condition, but owing to his energy and tenacity they were soon restored in their former extent. In conformity with a decree of the Council of Constance that a new council be called within five years, he called a council at Pavia in 1423, which was immediately transposed to Siena. Here, as at Constance, antipapal tendency began to spread, and Martin found it advisable to dissolve the assembly, using the small attendance and the dissension of the powers as a pretext. He intended to satisfy the reformers by a bull issued on May 16, 1425, but the demand for a general council became more urgent. The future council was to be held at Basel; but Martin showed no indulgence, being a decided opponent of conciliarism. He died suddenly at Rome Feb. 20, 1431. (B. BESS.)

BIBLIOGRAPHY: The early sources for a life are collected in L. A. Muratori, *Rerum Italicarum scriptores*, iii. 2, pp. 857-868, 1121-22, 25 vols., Milan, 1723-51. Martin's bulls are in Mansi, *Concilia*, vol. xxviii. Consult A. von Reumont, *Geschichte der Stadt Rom*, ii. 1162 sqq., iii. 56 sqq., Berlin, 1868-70; B. Jungmann, *Dissertationes selectæ*, vol. vi., Regensburg, 1886; Funk, in *TQ*, lxx (1888), 451-465; F. Bernet, in *Revue des questions historiques*, li (1892), 373-423; H. C. Lea, *Hist. of the Inquisition of the Middle Ages*, passim, vols. i.-iii., New York, 1906; Pastor, *Popes*, i. 208-282; Creighton, *Papacy*, ii. 100-163; Bower, *Popes*, iii. 201-218; Milman, *Latin Christianity*, vii. 513-535; Platina, *Popes*, ii. 200-213; and much of the literature under CONSTANCE, COUNCIL OF. A list of scattered notices may be consulted in Hauck-Herzog, *RE*, xii. 382-383.

MARTIN OF BRAGA: Spanish bishop of the sixth century; b. in Pannonia about 510; d. about 580. Knowledge of his life is based on a few scattered notices in his own works and in those of his contemporaries Gregory of Tours and Venantius Fortunatus, with a little help from Isidore of Seville. He became a monk, acquired, for his time, great learning, especially in Greek, and visited the East, including the Holy Land. Falling in with some Spanish pilgrims, he was determined by them to go to Galicia and devote himself to the conversion of the partly Arian, partly half-pagan population. He arrived in Spain about 550 and was soon made a bishop, according to Gregory, although he may have spent some time in founding monasteries, especially that of Dumio, over which he presided as abbot and later as bishop. In the latter capacity he was present at the Synod of Braga in May, 561. Later he became archbishop of Braga or Bracara, and presided as such over the second (incorrectly called third) synod there in 572. As a missionary, an ecclesiastical organizer, and an intermediary of Christian culture between East and West, he was one of the most remarkable and influential men of the latter half of the sixth century. The position which he held is evidenced not only by the work done by him in the two synods of Bracara, but by the frequent requests of King Miro for his counsel and by the visits of Spanish and foreign bishops for the same end.

Martin's most important work is his *Collectio orientalium canonum sive Capitula Martini* (Mansi, *Concilia*, ix. 845 sqq.), a systematic arrangement of Eastern (and a few Western) canons, with a view to giving a more correct and intelligible version of the Greek canons, as a guide to the legislation of his own day and country. The *Epistola ad Bonifatium de trina mersione* (*Collectio maxima conciliorum Hispaniæ*, ii. 506, Rome, 1693) answers the question of a Spanish bishop whether baptism was administered in his province with not only a threefold immersion but a threefold repetition of the formula, which would seem to carry a suspicion of Arianism, by saying that the formula was used only once, but asserting the orthodoxy of the threefold immersion. The small treatise *De pascha* (Gallandi, *Bibliotheca veterum patrum*, xii. 287 sqq., 14 vols., Venice, 1765-81) defends the practise of making Easter a movable feast, and mentions it as an old custom of the Gallican Church to celebrate it on Mar. 25, the traditional date of the actual resurrection. Ethical treatises extant include *Formula vitæ honestæ*, *De differentiis quatuor virtutum* and *De ira* (all in Gallandi, xii. ut sup.), of which the first two enter the province of philosophic morality, with Seneca for their model; in fact, they have been more than once printed as works of Seneca. The *Formula* gives a picture of the Christian life, adapted especially for the laity, on the moderate lines of the four cardinal virtues. His ascetic works include a collection of *Sententiæ patrum Ægyptiorum* (*MPL*, lxxiv. 381 sqq.), translated by Martin from the Greek, and a similar compilation from the old monastic traditions of the Egyptian desert, *Verba seniorum* (*MPL*, lxxiii. 1025 sqq.). Mention must also be made of a sermon, *De correctione rusticorum* (*MPL*, lxxii. 21-52; first complete ed. by Caspari, ut inf.), which has considerable historical interest. It was written to correct the tendency of the rural population to pagan superstitions. The gods of the heathen, he says, are but demons, of whom there are a number in rivers, and fountains, and forests, venerated by ignorant rustics, who also employ superstitious practises like augury and magic. God sent his Son "to lead them back from the error of the devil to the worship of the true God; and after he had taught, he was pleased to die for the human race." The Christian is to win the kingdom of God by good works; otherwise he will fall into damnation by evil works. In baptism he has renounced the devil and promised faith in God. Superstition is the abandonment of this faith and the breach of this compact. No sign is permitted to the Christian except the sign of the cross, no incantation except the creed and the Lord's Prayer. No one should doubt the mercy of God, but do penance; and true penance is "that a man shall do no more the evils that he has done, but seek remission of his past sins." There are also interesting remarks on baptism and its ceremonies, and on the observance of Sunday. Gregory mentions verses written by this Martin on his namesake of Tours, which are extant in the three short poetical inscriptions published by Sirmond, Migne, and others. (R. SEEBERG).

BIBLIOGRAPHY: C. P. Caspari, *Martin von Bracaras Schrift De correctione rusticorum*, Christiania, 1883; *ASB*, March, iii. 86–90; P. B. Gams, *Kirchengeschichte von Spanien*, ii. 471 sqq., Regensburg, 1874; O. Bardenhewer, *Patrologie*, pp. 579 sqq., Freiburg, 1901; Ceillier, *Auteurs sacrés*, xi. 350–352, 406, 885–886, 891–892; *DCB*, iii. 845–848.

MARTIN OF TOURS, SAINT: Bishop of Tours; b. at Sabaria (perhaps the modern Sárvár in Hungary, 80 m. s. of Vienna) in 316 or 317; d. at Candes in Gaul Nov. 11 of one of the years 397–401. He came of a Roman family of pagan faith, and was educated at Pavia; he early came under the influence of Christianity, was a catechumen at ten years of age, and was baptized at eighteen. From his fifteenth to his twentieth year he served as a soldier in Gaul. Within a few years after leaving military service, Martin went to Hilary of Poitiers and was made an exorcist. Soon after, on returning home, he suffered scourging at the hands of the Arians on account of his orthodoxy and thus gained the title of confessor. His orthodoxy resulted later (356) in his expulsion from Milan. After living as a hermit for a time, he returned to Hilary in Gaul, and about 370 gathered a company of monks near Poitiers, probably the first monastic establishment of the West. In 371 or 372, he was elected bishop of Tours, and established a second convent at what is now Marmoutier, where he built a church and gathered eighty monks around him. Martin acquired renown as a miracle-worker, and his zealous Evangelical activity met great success in spreading the Christian faith into the surrounding country.

On the occasion of an interview about 384 with the Emperor Maximus, Martin interceded unsuccessfully in behalf of the followers of Priscillian (q.v.), not out of sympathy with them but because of his strong sense of justice. Martin was professedly a man of practical life and held a simple faith resting upon trinitarian symbolism, the worship of relics and the revelations of good and evil spirits. While his predilections for monastic asceticism blinded him to the requirements of the commonly accepted rules of life, he at the same time advocated a gospel of service, in sharp contrast with the quiet life of contemplation followed by the Oriental hermits. As the molder of the popular faith of the Frankish people, Martin has become their patron saint and has made Tours a popular goal of pilgrimage. To his name was given a prominent place in the saint worship of the Middle Ages and it entered largely into the epic and legendary lore of both the French and the German language. [The most famous story concerning him is that while yet a catechumen and a young soldier he was stationed at Amiens, and there on an uncommonly severe day of midwinter encountered a poor man without clothes. Martin himself had on only his single military cloak and his arms. He cut his cloak in two with his sword and gave half to the beggar. In recognition of this deed Christ appeared to him the next night clad in the half cloak he had given, and he heard Christ say to the attendant angels, "Martin gave me this cloak!"] (C. A. BERNOULLI.)

BIBLIOGRAPHY: The early life by Sulpicius Severus, ed. Halm, is in *CSEL*, vol. i.; a later account, dating from about 475 A.D., is vol. xvi. of *CSEL*, and is also in *MGH, Auct. ant.*, iv. 1 (1881), 293–370; the working over of these by Gregory of Tours, ed. B. Krusch, is in *MGH., Script. rer. Merov.*, i (1885), 584–662. A large list of literature is given in Potthast, *Wegweiser*, pp. 1459–61. Among the more recent accounts may be named: A. Dupuy, *Histoire de S. Martin . de Tours*, Schaffhausen, 1855; J. H. Reinkens, *Martin von Tours*, Breslau, 1866; F. Chamard, *Saint Martin et son monastère de Ligugé*, Poitiers, 1873; J. Rabory, *Vie de S. Martin, apôtre des Gaules*, Abbeville, 1894; the lives by A. Lecoy de la Marche, Paris, 1895, and H. Bus, ib., 1897; *DCB*, iii. 838–845. To these are to be added the notices in J. H. Newman, *Historical Sketches*, vol. iii., "Martin and Maximus," 185–210, London, 1873; A. Marignan, *Études sur la civilisation française*, vol. i., Paris, 1899; and C. A. Bernoulli, *Die Heiligen der Merovinger*, Tübingen, 1900; also J. G. Bulliot and F. Thiollier, *La Mission et le culte de S. Martin d'après les légendes populaires*, Paris, 1892.

MARTIN, ALEXANDER: Free Church of Scotland; b. at Panbride (11 m. n.e. of Dundee), Forfarshire, Nov. 25, 1857. He was educated at Watson's College, Edinburgh, Edinburgh University (M.A., 1880), and New College (the theological hall of the same institution), from which he was graduated in 1883. He was assistant to the professor of moral philosophy at Edinburgh University from 1880 to 1883 and examiner in mental philosophy at the same university from 1886 to 1888, while from 1884 to 1897 he was minister of Morningside Free Church, Edinburgh. Since 1897 he has been professor of apologetics and practical theology in New College. In theology he belongs to the modern Evangelical school. He has written *Winning the Soul* (Edinburgh, 1897) and *The Present Position of Apologetics* (1897).

MARTIN, CHALMERS: Presbyterian; b. at Ashland, Ky., Sept. 7, 1850. He was educated at Princeton College (A.B., 1879) and Princeton Theological Seminary, from which he was graduated in 1882, and where he was fellow in Hebrew in 1882–1883. He was a missionary in Laos, northern Siam, in 1883–86, after which he held successive pastorates at Moorestown, N. J. (1888–91) and Port Henry, N. Y. (1891–92). He was then Eliott F. Shepard instructor in Old Testament in Princeton Theological Seminary and instructor in Hebrew in Princeton University from 1892 to 1900, and president of Pennsylvania College for Women, Pittsburg, Pa., from 1900 to 1903. Since 1903 he has been professor of Old-Testament history and literature in the University of Wooster, Wooster, O., and was also students' lecturer on missions in Princeton Theological Seminary in 1895 and 1901. He has been a member of the General Assembly's Permanent Committee on Systematic Beneficence since 1903, and in the same year became a member of the Religious Education Society. In theology he is a Calvinist of the conservative type, and a firm believer in the traditional view of Biblical criticism. Besides a number of briefer contributions, he has written *Apostolic and Modern Missions* (New York, 1898).

MARTIN, mār″tan′, **DAVID:** French Protestant; b. at Revel (167 m. w. of Marseilles) Sept. 7, 1639; d. at Utrecht Sept. 9, 1721. He was educated at Montauban and Nîmes, and at the Protestant academy at Puy-Laurens. Ordained in 1663, he was a pastor at Espérausses and Lacaune, but on the revocation of the Edict of Nantes he fled to Utrecht, where he spent the remainder of his life, declining many honorable calls to other charges. Martin wrote a *Traité de la religion naturelle* (Amsterdam, 1713; Eng. transl., 1720), but his chief reputation was won by his Biblical studies, which comprised *Le Nouveau Testament expliqué par des notes courtes et claires* (Utrecht, 1696); *Histoire du Vieux et du Nouveau Testament* (2 vols., Amsterdam, 1700); and especially by his revision of the Geneva translation under the title *La Sainte Bible expliquée* (2 vols., 1707), the latter serving as the standard French version until recent years (see Bible Versions, B, VI., § 3). (John Viénot.)

Bibliography: E. Petavel, *La Bible en France*, Paris, 1864; O. Douen, *Hist. de la société biblique protestante de Paris*, ib. 1868; idem, in Lichtenberger, *ESR*, viii. 750–751.

MARTIN, mār′tin, **GEORGE CURRIE:** English Congregationalist; b. at Portobello (3 m. e. of Edinburgh), Scotland, July 9, 1865. He was educated at the University of Edinburgh (M.A., 1888), New College, London, and the University of Marburg. He held successive Congregational pastorates at Nairn, Scotland (1890–95), and Reigate, Surrey (1895–1903), and since 1903 has been professor of New-Testament exegesis and patristics in the United College, Bradford, Yorkshire, and the Lancashire Independent College, Manchester. He was examiner in Old-Testament and New-Testament languages and literature in the Congregational Theological Hall, Edinburgh, in 1894–95 and has held similar positions in other institutions. He was an honorary organizer of the Young People's Union of the Congregational Union of England and Wales in 1901–03 and president in 1904, as well as honorary secretary of the Congregational Historical Society in 1900–03. In theology he holds that "the fullest revelation of God comes to us in the person of Jesus. God, however, reveals himself in many ways, and therefore the judgments of pure reason are in no way to be rejected, and the universe can be rationally interpreted. In dealing with the Old and New Testaments the greatest liberty of criticism must be permitted, since neither they nor the Church are the final seats of authority, but only the word of Jesus Christ through his Spirit." He has written *Catechism on the Teaching of Jesus* (London, 1897); *Great Mottoes with Great Lessons* (1901); and *Foreign Missions* (1905); besides editing *Ephesians, Colossians, Philemon, Philippians,* and *Proverbs* in *The Century Bible* (1902 sqq.).

MARTIN, WILLIAM ALEXANDER PARSONS: Presbyterian; b. at Livonia, Ind., Apr. 10, 1827. He was educated at Indiana State University (B.A., 1846) and the Theological Seminary at New Albany, Ind., from which he was graduated in 1849. In 1850 he went to China, where he was a missionary at Ning-po (1850–59) and Peking (1863–67). He was captured by Chinese pirates in 1855. In 1858 he acted as interpreter to the United States minister, William B. Reed, in negotiating the treaty of Tientsin, and in the following year accompanied John E. Ward, United States minister, to Peking and Yeddo, Japan. In 1866 he also visited the colony of Chinese Jews at Ho-nan. From 1867 to 1894 he was president and professor of international law in Tung Wen College, Peking, and during this period was adviser in international law to the Chinese government in several disputes, notably in the conflict with France in 1884–85. He was president of the Imperial University of China from 1897 to 1902 and was in Peking during the siege of the city by the foreign allies (1900). From 1902 to 1905 he was president of the University of Wu-chang, and since 1905 has been engaged in literary work. Theologically he is progressively orthodox. In addition to numerous independent works in Chinese and Chinese translations of standard works on international law, his standard work on Christian apologetics, in Chinese, and besides his activity as editor of the Chinese "Peking Scientific Magazine" (1875–78) and "Science Monthly" (1897–98), he has written: *The Chinese: Their Education, Philosophy, and Letters* (London, 1881); *Essays on the History, Philosophy, and Religion of the Chinese* (Shanghai, 1894); *Chinese Legends and other Poems* (1894); *A Cycle of Cathay; or, China South and North, with personal Reminiscences* (Chicago, 1896); *The Lore of Cathay; or, Intellect of China* (1901); *The Analytical Reader: A short Method for Learning to Read and Write Chinese* (Shanghai, 1897); *The Siege in Peking* (Chicago, 1900); and *Awakening of China* (New York, 1907). He has likewise contributed extensively on Chinese subjects to various learned and literary periodicals.

MARTINEAU, mār″ti-nō′, **JAMES:** English Unitarian philosopher and educator; b. at Norwich Apr. 21, 1805; d. in London Jan. 11, 1900. He was educated at the Norwich grammar-school, at Dr. Lant Carpenter's private school at Bristol, and at Manchester College, then at York (1827). He taught for a year in the school at Bristol; became in 1828 junior minister in the Eustace Street "Presbyterian" Church in Dublin; at the death of his colleague, in 1831, Martineau would have succeeded to the sole pastorate had he not entertained conscientious scruples concerning the *regium donum* (a bounty originating in a gift of Charles II. amounting to £100 a year) on account of which he resigned; he was immediately called as co-pastor to the Paradise Street Chapel, Liverpool, and was sole pastor 1835–57, with an interval of study in Germany (1848–49); and was minister of Little Portland Street Chapel, London, 1859–72. Meanwhile he had become professor of mental and moral philosophy in Manchester New College in 1840, and principal in 1869, resigning both posts in 1885, though during 1886–87 he was again principal. During all this time his literary activity had been great, a remarkable series of essays, criticisms and reviews

His Life.

from his pen appearing in several of the periodicals devoted to literary and philosophical themes.

His Philosophy and Theology.

Martineau's intellectual and spiritual development began in his contact at school with the stimulating Lant Carpenter (q.v.). His youth was spent in close connection with Unitarian institutions and amid the contest for full civil and religious rights waged by dissenters in England during the first third of the nineteenth century, to the settlement of which he contributed. He went to his first pastorate an ardent disciple of Joseph Priestley (q.v.), holding the normal doctrines of Unitarianism, believing in Christ as the mediator between God and man who had opened by his life and death a new and living way of salvation. The doctrines of the Trinity and the Atonement were not rejected merely as contrary to reason but as unscriptural. Revelation was a communication of faith certified by miracles. At this time Martineau's view of the universe was necessarian and his test of character utilitarian. From this position, normal to the Unitarian, Martineau first dissented in his *Rationale of Religious Enquiry* (London, 1836), in which he insisted on the supremacy of reason in judging any statement: "No seeming inspiration can establish anything contrary to reason, against whose judgments Scripture can not have any authority." In 1839, in lectures delivered at Liverpool, he placed the Fourth Gospel above the Synoptics in historic worth; in other lectures delivered in 1845 he gave up the apostolic authorship of this Gospel, holding it to be later in composition than the time of Justin Martyr. By 1840, he had placed the power of Christ as a revealer of the divine character not in his precepts but in his person. His matured philosophy is expressed in: *A Study of Spinoza* (1882); *Types of Ethical Theory* (2 vols., Oxford, 1885); *Study of Religion* (2 vols., 1888); *Seat of Authority in Religion* (London, 1890); and *Essays, Reviews and Addresses* (4 vols., London, 1890–91). In these works he made large contributions to epistemology, exposed the weak points of sensational idealism, laid a firm basis for a philosophical theism, offered a thoroughgoing criticism of agnosticism and materialism as represented by Herbert Spencer and Professor Tyndall, and assailed with equal force irrational dogmatism in theology and antitheistic assumptions in science. His theism was built upon the idea that God is most intimately revealed in man's rational, moral, and spiritual nature, emphasis being laid upon the ethical. God is the eternal will on whom the natural world depends for its existence, and the sole causes in the universe are God and rational beings—unconscious second causes are excluded. In his opposition to pantheism (*Study of Spinoza*) Martineau admits the immanence of God, but insists strongly that the divine Being transcends his manifestation in the universe. His philosophy involved an adequate spiritual cause for the cosmos and the ethical experience of a superhuman presence and authority in the conscience. Thus he wrought out the statement of the harmony between the religion of nature and the religion of conscience—both are expressions of an activity directed to conscious purpose. In the practical affairs of life, he said, morality is not always choice of a moral good over a natural good or between an absolute good and an absolute bad; it is often between better and not so good. The absolute depravity of man and his moral helplessness were held by him to be dogmas absolutely incompatible with man's intuitional nature.

General Activities.

The intense literary activity which he displayed, carried into his ninth decade, tells but a part of his life story. He was intensely interested in the development of knowledge on the scientific as well as the philosophic side. His interest in total abstinence was vital and active, and he worked ardently in the early campaigns for international peace. He is a fine example of a man forced against his inclination into the leadership of thought by the virility of his mental processes; of a faithful pastor, giving to his congregation ungrudgingly his best efforts; of an inspiring teacher, kindly in his methods; withal so humble and sincere as to be surprised beyond measure yet sweetly proud when on his eighty-third birthday the leaders in the literary, academic, and even political circles of England, Europe, and America united in paying tribute to the services which he had rendered to religion and to the spirit of fellowship with all Christians exemplified in his personal life. Not the least memorable of his accomplishments are his contributions to hymnody in the two choice hymns "Thy way is in the deep, O Lord!" and "A voice upon the midnight air." Besides the works named above, he published three hymnals, one for his Dublin church (1831), *Hymns for the Christian Church and Home* (1840), and *Hymns of Praise and Prayer* (1874). In addition he wrote the larger part of *Unitarianism Defended* (Liverpool, 1839), a controversial work in reply to attacks on Unitarianism by clergymen of the Church of England; *Endeavours after the Christian Life* (2 vols., London, 1843–47), sermons; *Miscellanies* (ed. T. S. King, Boston, 1852); *Essays, Philosophical and Theological* (1866); and *Hours of Thought on Sacred Themes* (2 vols., 1876–80).

GEO. W. GILMORE.

BIBLIOGRAPHY: J. Drummond, *Life and Letters of James Martineau. Survey of his Philosophical Work by C. B. Upton*, 2 vols., New York, 1902; A. W. Jackson, *Dr. James Martineau, a Biography and a Study*, London, 1900; A. H. Craufurd, *Recollections of James Martineau, with an Essay on his Religion*, Edinburgh, 1903; C. B. Upton, *Dr. James Martineau's Philosophy, a Survey*, London, 1905; J. E. Carpenter, *James Martineau, Theologian and Teacher*, ib. 1905; A. Hall, *James Martineau*, ib. 1906.

MARTINELLI, SEBASTIANO: Cardinal; b. at Lucca Aug. 20, 1848. He was educated at Genazzano and Rome, and was ordained to the priesthood in 1871, after having entered the Augustinian order while in Genazzano. In 1889 he was elected general of the order, and in 1896 was consecrated titular archbishop of Ephesus and sent as apostolic delegate to Washington, D. C. There he remained five years, until, in 1901, he was created cardinal-priest of San Agostino, Rome.

MARTINIST ORDER, THE: "A spiritualized freemasonry." The order was founded by Martinez de Pasqualis, a Portuguese emigrant to France at the end of the eighteenth century, who selected individuals, some of them of prominent position, who seemed to him adapted to the purpose and taught them by a severe, systematic, and persistent discipline to develop their inner and hidden powers. To his initiates Pasqualis applied the name "elect priests." As he left the system it had seven degrees. After his death two of his pupils, Jean Baptiste Willermoz and Louis Claude de Saint-Martin (q.v.), assumed direction of the order and reduced the degrees to three. Willermoz devoted his energies to founding lodges; Saint-Martin applied himself to personal development, and gave to the ritual the name of the rectified rite of St. Martin. There are two parts in the order: the inner or spiritual, open to those who become adepts; and the exterior or practical and scientific, open to "men of desire." The government is in five degrees: the supreme council (located at Paris, France; president, Dr. Geront Encausse); inspectors, appointed by the supreme council; delegates, appointed by the inspectors; lodges, and groups. It differs from freemasonry in that it admits men and women on equal footing; does not require fees for initiations, dues, or instruction; aims to bring man into pristine relations with God; and it receives orders from the unknown philosopher and thus depends from the invisible world. It was introduced into America in the year 1894, the government there being by an inspector- (inspectress-) general.

Margaret B. Peeke†.

MARTINIUS (MARTINI), MATTHIAS: German Reformed theologian and philologist; b. at Freienhagen (a village in Waldeck) 1572; d. at Kirchtimke, near Bremen, June 21, 1630. He was educated at Herborn, and at the age of twenty-two was chaplain to the court of Nassau-Dillenburg, going in the following year to Herborn as professor and pastor. In 1607 he went to Embden as pastor, but after three years accepted a call to Bremen as professor of theology and rector of the Gymnasium Illustre. There he officiated for the remainder of his life, attracting pupils not only from the Reformed portions of Germany but also from Switzerland, Hungary, Denmark, Norway, Scotland, France, Spain, and especially from the nobility of Bohemia and Moravia. As a mild predestinarian he took part in the Synod of Dort in 1618–19, and it was largely through his influence that infralapsarianism gained the victory over supralapsarianism. After his return he resumed his professorial activities, and continued them until his sudden death from apoplexy. Martinius was a prolific writer in philology and theology, the latter category including dogmatics, exegesis, and polemics against the Lutherans, although he esteemed Luther highly. His chief works were his *Christianæ doctrinæ summa capita* (1603), and his *Lexicon philologico-etymologicum* (Bremen, 1623, Utrecht, 1697–98). (J. F. Iken†.)

Bibliography: A *Vita* was printed in the Utrecht ed. of the *Lexicon;* cf. J. F. Iken, in *Bremisches Jarhbuch*, xii. 11 sqq. Earlier literature is indicated in Hauck-Herzog, *RE*, xii. 391.

MARTINMAS: A festival celebrated on Nov. 11, in honor of St. Martin of Tours. In Germany the festival is called Martinalia. In England and Scotland in olden days a cow or ox fattened to be killed about Martinmas was called a "mart."

MARTYN, HENRY: English missionary; b. at Truro (10 m. n.e. of Falmouth), Cornwall, Feb. 18, 1781; d. at Tokat (58 m. n.w. of Sivas), Asia Minor, Oct. 16, 1812. His father, who had been a miner, rose to a place of comparative ease as chief clerk in a store, and was able to send his son to the grammar-school, which he attended from 1788 till 1797, when he entered St. John's College, Cambridge (B.A., 1801; M.A., 1804; B.D., 1805), and became senior wrangler in 1801. In 1802 he was chosen fellow of St. John's College, taking the first prize in Latin prose composition. His college subsequently elected him twice public examiner. In 1802 Martyn formed the resolution of devoting his life to missionary labors. To this state of mind he had been brought, in part, by the perusal of the biography and diary of David Brainerd. He offered himself to the Society for Missions to Africa and the East; but, suffering from pecuniary losses which gave him some anxiety about the support of a sister, he ultimately went to India as a chaplain of the East India Company. He had served from 1803 as the curate of Charles Simeon at Cambridge; and July 17, 1805, he sailed for his new home.

He arrived at Calcutta in April, 1806. The impression made upon his mind by idolatry was most painful. He wrote of seeing natives bow before a hideous image: "I shivered as if standing, as it were, in the neighborhood of hell." He did not go to his station, Dinapur, till October, remaining in the mean time at Calcutta. His tolerant Christian spirit was displayed in the cordial friendship which sprang up between himself and the Serampore missionaries. In 1806 Carey wrote, "A young clergyman, Mr. Martyn, is lately arrived, who is possessed of a truly missionary spirit. We take sweet counsel together, and go to the house of God as friends" (Marshman's *Life of Carey*, i. p. 246). In Apr., 1809, Martyn was transferred to Cawnpur. In addition to his labors among the soldiers and English residents, he preached to the natives, and prepared translations in the vernacular. Endowed with rare linguistic talents, he speedily became fluent in the Hindustani; and his preaching was so attractive that, at the time failing health obliged him to quit Cawnpur, he had as many as eight hundred in his audiences.

Martyn's most permanent influence was exerted through his translations. He had by Feb. 24, 1807, completed a translation of a part of the Book of Common Prayer into the vernacular (Calcutta, 1814), and in March, 1808, he completed a Hindustani version of the New Testament (Serampore, 1814). At the urgency of his friends, he also undertook the supervision of a Persian version of the New Testament. In this task he was less successful, and his version was referred back to him for revision. Never strong, his health gave way in 1810; so that he determined to take a trip to England in the hope of restoring it, when the rejection of his Persian version induced him to take a journey to Persia, for recreation and the revision of the version. Starting in Jan., 1811, Martyn reached Shiraz, where he not only finished the Persian New Testament (St. Petersburg, 1815; revision, Calcutta, 1816), but made a Persian version of the Psalms (London, 1824). His learning and skill in disputing with the Mohammedans awakened a sensation in the city and aroused the professor of Mohammedan law to engage in a public dispute with him. The professor followed the discussion up with a tract in defense of Mohammedanism, to which Martyn replied in defense of Christianity. Anxious to present a copy of the New Testament to the Shah of Persia, Martyn directed his steps to Tabriz to secure a letter of introduction from the British minister, Sir Gore Ouseley. On this journey his body was racked with fever and chills, and he barely escaped with his life. In Tabriz he likewise engaged in animated discussion with the Mohammedans, risking his life by the fearless confession of Christ as the Son of God. He failed to put his Testament into the hands of the Persian monarch, but left it with Sir Gore, who did it for him, and afterward saw it through the press. Martyn then turned his horse's head toward Constantinople, fifteen hundred miles away. Fever and ague were racking his system, but with unflagging patience the sufferer pushed on. He got no further than Tokat. His body rests in the Armenian cemetery there. In addition to the translations mentioned above there have appeared: *Sermons of Henry Martyn* (Calcutta, 1822); *Controversial Tracts on Mohammedanism and Christianity* (Cambridge, 1824); and his *Journals and Letters* (ed. S. Wilberforce, 2 vols., London, 1837). D. S. SCHAFF.

BIBLIOGRAPHY: Lives have been written by J. Sargent (*Life and Letters*), London, 1819, new ed., 1885; Mary Seeley (in *Later Evangelical Fathers*), ib. 1879; C. D. Bell, ib. 1880; J. Page, New York, 1890; G. Smith, London, 1892.

MARTYN, WILLIAM CARLOS: Presbyterian; b. in New York City Dec. 15, 1841. He was educated at Union Theological Seminary, from which he was graduated in 1869. He was ordained to the ministry of his denomination in the same year, and held successive pastorates at the Pilgrim Church, St. Louis, Mo. (1869–71), Portsmouth, N. H. (1871–1876), Thirty-fourth Street Reformed Dutch Church, New York City (1876–83); Bloomingdale Reformed Dutch Church, New York City (1883–90); First Reformed Dutch Church, Newark, N. J. (1890–92); and Sixth Presbyterian Church, Chicago, Ill. (1892–1894). Since 1894 he has been engaged in literature and lecturing, and from 1897 to 1903 was director of the Abbey Press, New York City. In addition to editing *The American Reformers Series* (New York, 1890–96), he has written *John Milton* (New York, 1866); *Life of Martin Luther* (1866); *History of the English Puritans* (1867); *History of the Huguenots* (1868); *The Dutch Reformation* (1869); *The Pilgrim Fathers of New England* (1870); *Wendell Phillips* (1890); *William E. Dodge* (1891); *John B. Gough, the Apostle of Cold Water* (1893); *Christian Citizenship* (1897); and *Sour Saints and Sweet Sinners* (1898).

MARTYRARIUS: The cleric who had charge of a *martyrium*, that is a church containing the grave of a martyr. Deacons, presbyters, and even abbots have been *martyrarii*. During the Middle Ages there were such clerics in various countries; at Rome they were called *custodes martyrum;* the name *martyrarius* occurs, as far as is known, only in France. (H. ACHELIS.)

MARTYRIANS. See MESSALIANS.

MARTYRS AND CONFESSORS: Names applied in the early Church to those who gave up their lives for their Christian faith, or underwent great sufferings short of death for the same cause. The name "martyr" (Gk. *martyr*, "witness") is applied in the New Testament both to those who were eye-witnesses of the life and resurrection of Jesus and to those who sealed their testimony with their blood (Acts xxii. 20; Rev. ii. 13, xvii. 6, cf. vi. 9, xx. 4). Such witnesses under persecution were never lacking from the time of the stoning of Stephen and the slaying of James; and down to the middle of the third century there was not a decade, scarcely a year, without its martyrs. Throughout the early literature runs the scarlet thread; numerous passages might be cited to show how joyfully the disciples met their death, although it was expressly forbidden to seek it. The full account of the martyrs of Lyons given in Eusebius (*Hist. eccl.*, V., i.–iii.) shows the attitude of the Church. God gives the martyrs strength, suffers in them, and by them overcomes the adversary; in them, the athletes of Christ and of his beauteous bride, is a sweet savor as of ointment. As a proof of their humility it is mentioned that they did not claim the name of martyrs, but called themselves only confessors, still needing the grace of perfection. The right of intercession for sinners is thus early recognized, here and elsewhere (cf. Eusebius, *Hist. eccl.*, V., xviii. 7; Tertullian, *Ad martyres*, i.). Tertullian speaks of it as their prerogative to attain glorification immediately after death. The number of the martyrs has been disputed; Dodwell was the first to work out a smaller total than that previously deduced from the legends and the early acts (see ACTA MARTYRUM). By degrees the treatment of those who had fallen away under the fear of torture became an urgent question (see LAPSED), with which was connected that of the intercessory privilege of the confessors; Cyprian's letters (*Epist.*, xv. 22, ii. 23, 27) show how strongly this claim was urged, and he was obliged to oppose the extension of the practise. The origin of the Donatist schism was the uncompromising procedure of Cæcilian against the party which exaggerated the duty of suffering martyrdom and the honor paid to the Carthaginian martyrs. Evidences begin to appear of superstitious veneration paid to the martyrs (Optatus, i. 16; Eusebius, *Hist eccl.*, VIII., vi.); the possession of their relics was a cause of eager rivalry, and these assumed the position almost of tutelary deities in the eyes even of such men as Basil and Gregory Nazianzen. Martyrdom was from the beginning designated as a "baptism of blood," supplying the place of that by water, and even, according to Cyprian (*Ad Fortunatum*, iv.), "greater in grace, more exalted in power, more precious in honor." On the anniversaries of the martyrs' deaths, considered as their birthdays into a higher life, special oblations were brought as early as Tertullian's day (*De corona*, iii.), and Cyprian prescribes the special observances to be practised (*Epist.*, xii. 2, xxxix. 3).

When, with the proclamation of Christianity as the State religion, martyrdom became a thing of the past, and at the same time the influence of pagan superstition was felt in the Church, the honor paid to the martyrs increased greatly. Prudentius and Fortunatus celebrated their deeds in verse; altars were erected over their places of sepulture, and great confidence was placed in their intercession with God—though even now a Jovinian was found to protest against exaggerated devotion to them and a Vigilantius to oppose the veneration of their relics (Jerome, *Adversus Jovinianum*, II., xx.; *Adversus Vigilantium*, i.).

Martyrs were not lacking, however, in the later ages of the Church. In Persia, Armenia, Arabia, and elsewhere the Christians were the objects of pagan persecution shortly after Constantine's conversion, and later in other parts of the world they suffered at the hands of the Arian Germans and of the followers of Mohammed, while the dominant Church learned to apply the same treatment to heretics. The Donatists had already used this as a proof that the Catholic was not the true Church. The persecuting spirit pervades the Middle Ages and marks with blood the story of the Waldenses, the strict Franciscans, the Apostolic Brethren, the Lollards, and the disciples of the martyred Huss. After the Reformation Luther soon had occasion to write hymns in celebration of its martyrs, and the Anabaptists have left us a number of theirs to attest the joy with which they endured persecution. The Reformed Church of France was a martyr-church. In the mission fields, especially in Japan and China, many Christians of the Roman obedience sealed their testimony with their blood; and on the Evangelical side the blood of the martyrs has proved, in Tertullian's phrase, "the seed of the Church" in Madagascar and more recently in Uganda, China, and elsewhere. The Evangelical church canonizes no martyrs, and believes it to be as great a thing to live for Christ as to die for him; but it, too, cherishes the examples of those who have been, in the literal sense, "faithful unto death." (N. Bonwetsch.)

Bibliography: Quite adequate literature is given under Acta Martyrum, Acta Sanctorum; Saints, and the Veneration of Saints. The customs and early literature are well indicated in Bingham, *Origines*, XIII., iii. 2–3, ix. 5, XIV., iii. 14, XVI., iii. 4, XVIII., iv. 10, XX., vii. Consult further: *Analecta Bollandiana*, Paris, Brussels, and Geneva, 1882 sqq.; Gass, in *ZHT*, 1859; H. Delehaye, *L'Amphithéâtre Flavien et ses environs dans les textes hagiographiques*, Brussels, 1897; E. Amélineau, *Les Actes des martyres de l'église copte*, Paris, 1900; H. Achelis, in *Abhandlungen der Göttinger Gesellschaft*, 1900; F. Kattenbusch, in *ZNTW*, iv (1903), 111 sqq.; F. Augar, in *TU*, xxviii (1905); A. Linsenmayer, *Die Bekämpfung des Christentums durch den römischen Staat*, Munich, 1905.

MARTYRS, THE FORTY: Forty soldiers who suffered martyrdom at Sebaste (the modern Sivas, 165 m. s.w. of Trebizond) in the beginning of the Licinian persecution, probably in 320. Remaining true to their faith, as is stated by Basil the Great, Ephraem, Gregory of Nyssa, and Gaudentius of Brescia, they were exposed naked on the ice throughout a night in the coldest winter. All froze to death except one who recanted, and he died from a warm bath given him to counteract the effects of his exposure. When the pagan guard learned of this, he became a convert to Christianity, and suffered martyrdom by freezing, thus completing the number forty. The corpses were burned and the ashes thrown into the water. The later *Acta* (*ASB.*, Mar., ii. 19–21) records the names of the forty martyrs and gives the details of their sufferings with many embellishments, but the essential portion of the account, including the names, is undoubtedly historically true. Their day is appointed for Mar. 9 or 10. (O. Zöckler†.)

MARUTHAS, ma-rū'thas: The name of two bishops. **1.** Bishop of Maipherkat; d. about 420. Maruthas was sent twice by the Emperor Theodosius II. as ambassador to Jezdegerd I. Ebedjesu mentions among his works a book on martyrdoms, church poetry, and a translation of the canons of Nicæa (on which cf. *Synodicon Orientale*, ed. J. B. Chabot, Paris, 1903, p. 259) and has his name among the members of that synod. The "Martyrs' Anthem" has been translated by Maclean (*East Syrian Daily Offices*, London, 1894, pp. 12–23). His most important work, if it be his, is the "History of the Persian Martyrs" under Sapor II., Jezdegerd I., and perhaps Behnam V., 341–379 A.D. (ed. S. E. Assemani, *Acta Sanctorum Martyrum*, Rome, 1748; and by P. Bedjan, *Acta Martyrum et Sanctorum*, ii., Paris, 1891, 57–396, Germ. transl. P. P. Zingerle, *Monumenta Syriaca*, vol. i., Innsbruck, 1836). Kmosko doubts whether the work is his; he ascribes to him only the Greek translation, which was used already by Sozomen (*Hist. eccl.*, II., ix.–xiii.; Eng. transl., *NPNF*, 2 ser., ii. 264–267) for the lives of Simeon bar Sabaë, Pusai (Pusices), Tarbula and Akebsima (Acepsimas). There are also ascribed to him the "Acts of the Council of Seleucia" of the year 410 (ed. J. Lamy, Louvain, 1868). His commemoration is on the sixth Friday of Moses. His brother Julian is said to have surrounded with a wall the cloister of Mar Babai on Mount Izla, which contained one thousand monks. E. Nestle.

Bibliography: Sources are Socrates, *Hist. eccl.*, vi. 15, vii. 8, Eng. transl., *NPNF*, 2 ser., ii. 148–149, 156–157; Sozomen, *Hist. eccl.*, viii. 16, Eng. transl., *NPNF*, 2 ser., ii. 409; Bar Hebræus, *Chronicon*, ii. 45. Consult: J. S. Assemani, *Bibliotheca orientalis*, ii. 45, 3 vols., Rome, 1719–1728; W. Wright, *Short Hist. of Syriac Literature*, p. 44, London, 1894; R. Duval, *La Littérature syriaque*, Paris, 1899, 2d ed., pp. 132–133, 428; A. Harnack, in *TU*, xix., part 2, 1899.

2. Bishop of Takrit; d. 649. He is not to be confounded with Maruthas of Maipherkat (ut sup.). He was born in the diocese of Beth Nuhadre, Persia, studied for some time at Edessa, became bishop of Takrit and the first maphrian, or primate, of the Jacobites (see Jacobites). His life has been written by his successor Dencha. He composed a liturgy (in the *Missale* of the Maronites, Rome, 1594, p. 172; E. Renaudot, *Liturgiarum Orientalium collectio*, ii., Paris, 1716, 261); a commentary on the Gospels (two extracts in G. Mösinger, *Monumenta Syriaca*, ii., Innsbruck, 1878, 32), homilies and hymns. E. Nestle.

Bibliography: Consult the literature under 1, noting in Wright, p. 137, and in Duval, p. 374.

MARY, MOTHER OF JESUS CHRIST.

I. Mary in the New Testament: The question which naturally arises first in regard to the history of Mary is that concerning her ancestry, which has been much discussed and cannot yet be decisively settled. Both of the genealogies of

1. Family Relations.

Jesus at the opening of the Gospels, those of Matthew and Luke, demonstrate the descent of Joseph, not Mary, from David; but the very incompleteness of the lists lends support to the theory that Mary's descent from David was presupposed as an accepted fact by the evangelists. Her descent from the priestly tribe of Levi may be supported by the fact that Elisabeth, wife of the priest Zacharias, is called her cousin in Luke i. 36, though this need not refer to any closer connection than one arising from a marriage between a priestly ancestor of Elisabeth's with a descendant of David. Thus a double genealogy of Jesus, from David through Joseph, and from the sacerdotal family through his mother, might be shown. The question of her maternal relationship to Jesus on the one hand and to the "brethren of the Lord" on the other is a less difficult one. The designation of Jesus as her "first-born son" (Luke ii. 7) and the statement as to her relations with Joseph (Matt. i. 25, cf. i. 13) seem to point to the conclusion that the persons called in the Gospels and in Acts i. 14 the brethren of the Lord were the younger sons of Joseph and Mary. For various reasons the theory of Jerome that they were cousins, and that of Epiphanius that they were children of Joseph by a former marriage, are untenable. The unprejudiced reader of the New Testament can not avoid the view represented in antiquity by Helvidius and stamped as heresy after Jerome and Ambrose, that they were the children of Joseph and Mary, while Jesus was the son of Mary in a miraculous manner, by the Holy Ghost. The latter assertion rests upon distinct passages of Scripture (Matt. i. 18–25; Luke i. 26–38, ii. 7–14), whereas the rationalist and Ebionite view that he also was the son of Joseph and Mary finds no support either in the Gospels or elsewhere in the New Testament. The fundamental fact of a supernatural birth was evidently unquestioned by Paul. This is plain from passages like I Cor. xv. 47; II Cor. viii. 9; Phil. ii. 9, 10, and especially Gal. iv. 4, where the mention of Christ's birth simply "of a woman" is explained by the fact that Paul had no thought of an earthly father.

But while the witness of the New Testament is clear in favor of a supernatural birth, it is equally free from the decorative traits with which later legend loved to adorn the story of the birth and childhood of Jesus and the history of his mother. The Gospels neither tell anything of the birth and childhood of Mary, nor place her noticeably in the foreground in his earthly ministry. She is depicted as a pure maiden, full of childlike innocence and humble piety. It is noteworthy that she understands as little as Joseph her son's profound saying at the age of twelve. At the marriage of Cana she presses him in loving impa-

2. Her Character.

tience for the anticipation of the time to reveal his power, and has to be rebuked by him. She is apparently, at least, passive when his brethren show their unbelief in him, and is included in his reproof of them (Matt. xii. 46–50). Her bearing at the cross is human and motherly, and Jesus commends her to John as an evidence of his filial love and reverence for her (John xix. 25–27). After the ascension she appears in the circle of the apostles (Acts i. 14), but without any specially prominent position. Thus the New Testament affords no ground for the undue exaltation of Mary which was later so common; in fact, Jesus utters a warning (Luke xi. 27, 28) against it which ought to be sufficient.

II. Early Growth of Devotion to Her: The first tendency toward this exaggeration of her importance was the outgrowth of the Christological development. The more the awe and reverence of the early Church for the God-Man attempted to find adequate expression, the more

1. Causes of Increased Veneration.

natural it was that a portion of it should be transferred to his mother, the vehicle of his redeeming incarnation. As early as the middle of the second century, she appears as the antitype of Eve, bringing life into the world as Eve brought death (Justin, *Dialogue*, c.; Irenæus, III., xxii. 4, V., xix. 1; Tertullian, *De carne Christi*, vii.); and later the Western Church applied Gen. iii. 15 to her (in the Vulgate version with the feminine pronoun, *ipsa conteret caput tuum*). A further impulse was given to the devotion to Mary by the exaggerated reverence for the ascetic life and for celibacy, as spread by monasticism from the fourth century. She became the type and ideal of virginity. Tertullian had admitted her marriage (*De monogamia*, viii.), and Basil had recognized (*Homilia in Christi generationem*, v.) that the natural sense of Matt. i. 25 favored this view. But Epiphanius (*Hær.*, lxxviii.) controverted as heretics (under the name of Antidicomarianites, q.v.) those who said that she had married Joseph and had children by him. From this time on the title of "Virgin" became an inseparable predicate of hers. Pope Siricius (c. 392) confirmed the sentence of the Illyrian bishops against Bonosus on the charge of sharing the heresy of Helvidius. The theory of a merely nominal marriage was generally accepted; Origen accounts for it by the necessity of concealing the mystery of the virgin birth from the princes of this world (*Homilia in Lucam*, vi.).

These developing views took shape as legends in

a long series of Apocryphal narratives. The most important of these is the *Protevangelium Jacobi*, some features of which were known to Justin and Tertullian. According to it, Joachim and Anna, long childless, prayed fervently for offspring, and vowed their child, if they should have one, to the service of the Lord. Mary was born and solemnly dedicated. When she was twelve, all the widowers were assembled and their staves blessed in the temple. Out of that of Joseph emerged a dove which settled on his head, designating him as the destined guardian of the maiden. Miraculous signs accompanied the birth of her child; the visit of the Magi and the massacre of the Innocents came in their proper places, but instead of the flight into Egypt the concealment of the child in a corner of the inn, followed by the miraculous rescue of Elisabeth and John the Baptist and the murder of Zacharias by command of Herod. Although the Apocryphal literature was officially repudiated, not a few features of it crept into the tradition of the Church, such as the names of Mary's parents, her education in the Temple, and the nominal marriage with Joseph, already an aged man. A further series of legends deal with the life of Mary after the Ascension, especially in the Apocryphal narrative *De transitu Mariæ*, dating from the middle of the fourth century. In the differing versions the duration of her life after the Ascension is variously given as from two to twenty-four years. A tradition assigning her later life (under the care of the apostle John) and death to Ephesus was known to Epiphanius (*Hær.*, lxxviii. 11); other ancient traditions give Jerusalem for both (for the legend of her assumption see below, III.). Yet in spite of all this development of glorifying tradition, there was no tendency before the end of the fourth century to promote a regular cultus of the Virgin, or even to address prayers to her. The change which took place about that time may have been partly due to the great influx of pagans into the Church. Their old religions, largely growing out of nature-worship, and emphasizing the opposition of the sexes, passed by an easy transition to the Gnostic *syzygiai*, and thus to the idea of the cooperation of a created principle in the work of redemption. This principle was naturally found in Mary, the second Eve. Epiphanius (*Hær.*, lxxix.) condemns the Collyridians (q.v.), a sect of fanatical women calling themselves priestesses of Mary, who on festival days solemnly offered cakes to her and then feasted upon them, as in the pagan Thesmophoria and in Jer. vii. 18, xliv. 59.

2. Apocryphal Legends.

The Nestorian controversy (see NESTORIUS) marked the most important turning-point in the development of devotion to Mary. Although in essence Christological, it centered around the question debated between the Alexandrian and Antiochian schools, on the basis of their differing views as to the relations of the two natures in Christ and the communicability of the divine attributes to humanity, as to whether Mary was to be called the mother of God (*Theotokos*) or merely the mother of Christ. The former was officially adopted at the council of Ephesus in 431, and the devotion became increasingly fervent throughout the whole Church with each succeeding century. The veneration of the martyrs had already spread to such an extent that it was a simple completion to place Mary at their head as queen of the heavenly hosts. Prayer to her became a universal custom. Churches and altars were erected in her honor, and her picture was exposed for veneration. When, in spite of the dogma of Chalcedon, the humanity of Christ had been, in the popular mind, swallowed up in the divinity, the need was felt of further human mediation through which the divine Majesty might be approached and the severity of the awful Judge mitigated. From the lowly recipient of grace, she became a source and giver of grace. The Iconoclastic controversy served still further to enhance the veneration of her (see IMAGES AND IMAGE-WORSHIP, II.). The second Council of Nicæa (787) declared that veneration paid to her image passed on to her, and that he who adored (*ho proskunōn*) the image adored the original. A regular tradition grew up as to her appearance: the most celebrated picture of her was that attributed to St. Luke, which existed in numerous copies, each with its own tradition; others in Italy and Spain were believed to have been painted by angels.

3. Theotokos and Iconoclastic Controversies.

The reverence for woman mentioned as early as Tacitus among the traits of the Germanic peoples developed into the romantic service of medieval chivalry, and Mary was still further exalted as the crowning glory of womanhood, enthroned even above the angels. Among ecclesiastical writers, Ildephonsus (q.v.; d. 667) demonstrated her perpetual virginity once more against the long-departed Jovinian and Helvidius and against the Jews in his book *De illibata beatæ virginis virginitate*. Ratramnus wrote c. 845 against those who asserted that Jesus was born in some miraculous manner different from the ordinary; but this view was supported by Paschasius Radbert. A still higher level of Marian devotion was reached in the eleventh century. Peter Damiani sings the praises of Mary as the perfect creature, asserts that nothing is impossible to her, and says that she restores hope to the despairing. Bernard of Clairvaux (*Sermo in nativitatem*, iv.) asks: "Dost thou fear the divine Majesty in the Son? Wilt thou find an advocate before him? Flee to Mary; in her humanity is pure. The Son will listen to the mother, and the Father to the Son." Many more equally strong expressions might be collected from medieval theologians; and liturgical formulas kept pace with theological teaching. Scholasticism attempted to satisfy scrupulous consciences by making a distinction between *latria*, the worship due to God alone, and *dulia*, the veneration which might be lawfully paid to saints and sacred objects; the highest form of the latter, or *hyperdulia*, was assigned to Mary. From the eleventh century a special office of the Blessed Virgin was recited in the monasteries, which the Synod of Clermont (1095) extended to the clergy in general. Nothing, however, contributed so largely to the spread of daily

4. The Middle Ages.

devotion to her as the introduction of the *Ave Maria* or angelic salutation as a normal supplement to the Lord's Prayer in popular devotions. After the middle of the twelfth century it spread from France, where St. Bernard aided its diffusion, to Germany, England, Spain, and other countries, and by the end of the thirteenth was practically universal in western Christendom. The introduction of the recitation of the Angelus (q.v.) three times a day and of the Rosary (q.v.), with its ten Aves for one Pater noster, tended to increase the influence of this short and easily remembered form of prayer. Devotion to Mary was promoted zealously by the religious orders. The Teutonic Knights chose her for their patroness; the Dominicans aided with the rosary from 1270; the Franciscans were ardent advocates of the doctrine of the Immaculate Conception; the Carmelites boasted of her special favor, asserting that their sixth general, St. Simon Stock, had seen a vision (1246) in which she gave him a scapular with the promise that he who died wearing it should be delivered from the eternal fire.

III. Feasts of Mary: The development of the cultus of the Virgin is marked all along its course by the multiplication of festivals in her honor. The feast of the **Annunciation,** the annual commemoration of the Incarnation, was probably observed as early as the fourth century (see ANNUNCIATION, FEAST OF THE). The feast of the **Purification** of the Virgin Mary, or of the Presentation of Christ in the Temple (known in old English usage as Candlemas), based on Luke ii. 22 sqq., and thus reckoned also among the feasts of Christ, occurs forty days after Christmas (Feb. 2), according to Lev. xii. 2–7. It is said by Georgius Hamartolus and Cedrenus to have been instituted under Justin I. (c. 526), by Nicephorus under Justinian in 541. Western writers (Ildephonsus, and later Durand) connect it with the ancient Roman lustrations which Numa is said to have instituted in February in honor of Februus, the purifying god, and to take the place of which the Christian festival was established. In the West, its celebration was specially referred to the Virgin. In Bede's time it was usual to go in procession through the towns with burning candles. The feast of the **Nativity** was unknown in the time of Augustine. Early evidences for its existence are Andrew of Crete (c. 650), for Rome the *Calendarium Frontonis*, for Spain Ildephonsus, for France Paschasius Radbert. The reason for its assignment to Sept. 8 is unknown. The feast of the **Assumption** commemorates the assumption or corporal translation of Mary into heaven after her death. The festival in its later signification is based on Apocryphal sources, dating from about 400. The legend contained in these writings (whose ecclesiastical use was forbidden by Gelasius I.) was accepted as true by the pseudo-Dionysius and by Gregory of Tours, the latter of whom gives it in the following form. All the apostles were assembled in the house of Mary to watch by her death-bed, when Jesus appeared with his angels, received her soul, and gave it over to the archangel Michael. When on the following day they were about to carry her body to the grave he appeared again and took it up in a cloud to paradise, there to be reunited with the soul. The legend appears in a more extended form in John of Damascus; not only the angels but the patriarchs stand around the death-bed with the apostles, and even Adam and Eve are there, calling their descendant blessed for removing the curse which through them came into the world (see ASSUMPTION, FEAST OF THE). The feast of the **Presentation,** attested in the ninth century by the homilies of George of Nicomedia, was ordained in the twelfth for the whole Eastern Empire by Manuel Comnenus. In 1372, at the request of King Charles IV., it was sanctioned by Gregory XI. for France, and fixed on Nov. 21. It commemorates, following the Apocryphal gospels, the presentation of Mary in the Temple at the age of three, in pursuance of a vow of her parents. The **Visitation,** found only in the Western Church, commemorates the visit of Mary to Elisabeth, and is first found in the list of festivals drawn up by the Synod of Mans in 1247. After the Franciscans had adopted it as a feast of the order in the general chapter at Pisa in 1263, Urban VI. extended it to the whole of Christendom in 1389. The feast of the **Espousal** of Mary with Joseph has apparently been celebrated on Feb. 23 since the fourteenth century. It was extended to the whole of Christendom by Benedict XIII. in 1725. The **Seven Dolors** are celebrated on the Friday before Palm Sunday. These are variously enumerated as beginning either with the prophecy of Simeon and the flight into Egypt, or with the parting between Jesus and his mother at the commencement of the Passion, ending in both cases with the crucifixion and burial. Among the numerous hymns written for this festival from the thirteenth century, in which it seems to have originated in the Servite order, the most famous is the *Stabat Mater* of the Franciscan Jacopone da Todi (q.v.). The feast of the **Joys of Mary** (Sept. 24) is a parallel commemoration suggested by the "joyful mysteries" of the rosary. The festival of **St. Mary of the Snows** is a local Roman feast celebrated on Aug. 5 in memory of the foundation of the church of Santa Maria Maggiore. The legend relates that the patrician John and his wife were directed by a vision to build the church in a certain spot on the Esquiline, designated by a miraculous fall of snow in mid-summer. Other festivals, such as the **Expectation of Mary** (Dec. 18), the **Holy Name of Mary** (Sunday after her Nativity), **Our Lady of Mt. Carmel or of the Scapular** (July 16), **Our Lady of Ransom** (Sept. 24), the **Patronage of Our Lady** (third Sunday in November), are of minor importance. The feast of the **Immaculate Conception,** which has assumed great importance since the Reformation, is purely western (see IMMACULATE CONCEPTION).

IV. Devotion to Mary since the Reformation: The Reformation churches returned in this regard to the standpoint of primitive Christianity. While Luther in 1516 was still so much under the influence of the Scotist tradition as to call Mary (with a play on one interpretation of her name) "the only pure drop in the ocean of human perdition," in 1521, in his exposition of the *Magnificat*, he dwelt on the humility of this handmaiden of God, "who is no helping goddess, who gives us nothing,

1. In Protestant Churches.

in whom rather God as the only giver of all things is to be praised." The fact that he held to the traditional belief in the perpetual virginity of Mary did not lessen his decided opposition to the practise of asking for her intercession. The same position was taken by the other principal leaders of the German Reformation.

2. Growth of Roman Catholic Devotion. In the Roman Catholic countries, however, devotion to Mary received scarcely even a temporary check. The Jesuit order put a new enthusiasm into this as into all other medieval institutions; and the same tendency was furthered by the foundation of a number of female religious orders bearing her name or specially devoted to her during the sixteenth and seventeenth centuries. A certain reaction against this attitude was the result of the freer spirit of Jansenism and similar movements, and of literary undertakings after the middle of the seventeenth century, such as those of Théophile Raynaud (*Diptycha Mariana*, Grenoble, 1643), J. de Launoy (1676), and A. Baillet (1693). This opposition was carried still further by the reform movement of the Emperor Joseph. By his orders in 1784, the gold and silver hearts, hands and feet, and other votive offerings were removed from the shrines of Mary and from the churches, and the further distribution of scapulars, medals, and amulets forbidden. After the Congress of Ems (q.v.) and the Synod of Pistoja in 1786, however, Pius VI. defeated the anti-ultramontane opposition, and brought to nothing the hopes of those who had looked for thorough and permanent expulsion of the Jesuit spirit from the Church. Especially in Southern Italy, a more exaggerated devotion than ever surpassed the most extreme assertions of medieval theologians. In the *Glorie di Maria* of Liguori (q.v.), which found a wide circulation outside of Italy, Mary's mediatorial power was celebrated as even greater than that of her Son. All this prepared the way for the complete triumph of the upholders of the Immaculate Conception theory in the decree of Pius IX. in 1854 (see IMMACULATE CONCEPTION). The increasing enthusiasm of the Roman Catholics in devotion to Mary was not, however, so strongly promoted by this decision on a technical point as by other factors, especially the institution of the **Feast of the Rosary,** on the first Sunday in October (a Dominican institution, extended to the whole Church by Gregory XIII. in 1583), and the introduction by the Jesuits of the **May Devotions,** by which the entire month of May acquired the character of a season consecrated to the special honor of the Virgin. These latter arose at the end of the eighteenth century in Italy as an ecclesiastical antithesis to the irreligious spring festivals introduced by the French Revolution, and gradually spread to France, Belgium, Austria and Germany. Pius VII. commended the custom by a brief of Mar. 21, 1815, and attached numerous indulgences to it. A further help to the promotion of Marian devotion has been found in the sodalities or congregations of the blessed Virgin, originating in the sixteenth century but flourishing especially in the later epoch of Jesuit influence (see CONFRATERNITIES, RELIGIOUS).

3. Pilgrimage-Places. It is impossible to enumerate the pilgrimage-places which serve as local centers of the cult, on account of miraculous pictures or relics. Every century since the beginning of the Middle Ages has seen new places of this sort arise; and the nineteenth has not been behind the others. France has had La Salette (1846) and Lourdes (1851), Italy New Pompeii (1880), and Germany Marpingen near Treves (1876) and Dietrichswalde in Eastern Prussia (1877). As long ago as 1672, Gumppenberg's *Atlas Marianus* could describe more than twelve hundred miraculous pictures or images, of which about half were in Germany. Many of these, of course, have long since fallen into decay; but others, especially the newer ones, retain their attraction in spite of all criticism. The miraculous picture of the *Madonna di Pompeji*, originally bought from an antiquary for four francs, now reposes on a throne valued at one hundred and fifty thousand francs; the image was solemnly crowned by Cardinal Valletta in 1887 before a throng of devotees numbering many thousands. In Russian Poland the miraculous Madonna of Czenstochau is venerated as "Queen of Poland" and protectress of the Polish race. In France the famous miraculous spring at Lourdes (q.v.), designated to the fourteen-year-old Bernadette Soubirous by a vision on Feb. 11, 1858, attracts thousands of pilgrims every year, and the cures wrought there have been so remarkable as to engage the serious attention of men of science. Among the more ancient which have preserved their fame undiminished through centuries, mention should be made of those of Assisi (the Portiuncula) and Loreto (q.v.) in central Italy, of Maria Einsiedeln and Maria Stein in Switzerland, of Monserrat del Pilar and Guadalupe in Spain, of Hall in Belgium, and in Germany of Kevelaer, with its miraculous picture much visited since 1642, and Aachen, where for nearly a thousand years the alleged garment of the Virgin and swaddling-clothes of the infant Jesus have been preserved and occasionally exhibited.

V. The Glorification of Mary in Art: The date of the earliest artistic representations of the Virgin has been a subject of controversy between Roman Catholic and Protestant writers. The latter usually ascribe to the period of the Theotokos controversy, the fifth century, those which may properly be called Madonna-pictures, while the former date them earlier than the Nestorian heresy, some even tracing their origin to the sub-apostolic age. The true solution of this difference of opinion is probably found in the view that the pre-Nestorian period produced a number of pictures in which Mary appeared as part of a group, but that the origin of separate pictures of her intended to be used as objects of religious veneration can not be placed so early.

1. Early Stages. In the oldest Christian works of art, Mary appears invariably as a member of the composition—connected, that is, with scenes from the life of Jesus, especially the Annunciation, the Adoration of the Magi, or the Presentation in the Temple. The oldest representations of the Annunciation, including the famous one from the catacomb of Priscilla (certainly before the time of Constantine), keep close to scriptural lines; and the same is true of the numerous representations of the Adoration of the Magi, such as those in the catacomb of Domitilla and in SS. Pietro e Marcellino. Not even where Mary appears simply with her Child or in the Holy Family are there any traces in these early days of her elevation to a supernatural dignity; and the influence of Apocryphal legends enters comparatively late into art. The commemoration of Mary by architectural monuments dedicated to her can not be clearly shown before the fifth century, especially the time of the triumph of the Theotokos-doctrine at Ephesus in 431. The church in which the council met received at that time its dedication to "the Holy Mother of God." The first church with this dedication at Rome, Santa Maria Maggiore, was built soon after 432 by Sixtus III. on the site of a basilica erected a century earlier by Liberius and dedicated for the first time to the Virgin by Sixtus. It is at least half a century earlier than Santa Maria in Trastevere, of which the first written record dates from 499. Not till the eighth or ninth century does the legend of the Assumption begin to influence the imagination of artists. About the same time were made some extant representations of the figure of Mary enthroned in heaven holding her Child, such as the mosaics put up about 816 by Paschal I. in the churches of St. Cecilia and Santa Maria della Navicella. But the attribution of actually regal attributes to her does not yet occur in this period of transition to the Middle Ages.

2. Development of Types in Painting.

After the iconoclastic controversy there is a marked separation between Eastern and Western artistic traditions on this subject. The Byzantine type of the Madonna shows no further development after the termination of this controversy in the middle of the ninth century. In the Western Church, however, there was a constant progression following the lines of ecclesiastical architecture, as they passed through the various periods of Byzantine, Romanesque, Gothic, and Renaissance. In painted representations of the Madonna it is possible to trace quite distinctly the same four periods as named above—only that the duration of the first or partially Byzantine type extends somewhat later into the Middle Ages than is the case with architecture, occurring as late as the end of the crusades. The second, with its tendency to humanize the ideal Madonna, coincides closely with the fourteenth century; the third, whose principal characteristic is the emphasis laid on the spotless virginity of the Queen of Heaven, is contemporary with the late Gothic, practically covering the fifteenth century; while the fourth, distinguished by an almost wholly naturalist type of Madonna, corresponds both in conception and in date to the period of the Renaissance. For the first period scarcely any names of artists have been preserved. In the second, the leading names are those of Giotto and the two Sienese painters Guido and Simone Martini. Fra Angelico shows a transition to the next period, marked by the names of Masaccio, Mantegna, Perugino, Pinturicchio, and Filippi Lippi in Italy, Master Stephen, the unknown painter of the great picture in Cologne cathedral, and Hans Memling in Germany. With all the varieties of artistic invention in the sixteenth and seventeenth centuries, there is a constant tendency to subordinate the religious factor to the realistic. Raphael, Correggio, and Titian endow their Italian beauties with the fulness of human charm, and in the two latter at least religious devotion is almost lacking. In the Madonnas of Dürer and Holbein the fervor of devotion is less prominent than the chaste and pious feeling of their German ideals of family life. Murillo, in ardent subjection to the Franciscan and Jesuit type of devotion, succeeds in transfiguring the delicate features of his Spanish beauties so far as to approach, with the use of apocalyptic symbols, the realization of the mystery of the Immaculate Conception. It is impossible to estimate the effect upon modern Protestant feeling of the splendors which art has consecrated to this subject; but, while the Evangelical Christian may perfectly well admire these as works of art, it does not follow that he must approve the insidious attempts made by some of recent years to bring back something scarcely to be distinguished from the doctrinal basis which inspired such painting in bygone years. (O. ZÖCKLER†.)

BIBLIOGRAPHY: The Biblical side of the subject is treated with more or less completeness in the works on the life of Christ. An extensive bibliography, particularly of the earlier works on the entire subject, appears in Hauck-Herzog, *RE*, xii. 309, 314, 323-324. Among the sources should be included the Apocryphal gospels which deal with the life of Mary, especially those which are translated in *ANF*, viii. 361-415. For Mary in the Bible, in early patristics and in the Apocrypha of the N. T., consult: F. W. Genthe, *Die Jungfrau Maria, ihre Evangelien und ihre Wunder*, Halle, 1852; K. Benrath, in *TSK*, lix (1886), 1-28 (cf. the reply to Benrath by F. Linsenmann, in *TQ*, 1888, pp. 265-299); F. A. von Lehner, *Die Marienverehrung in den ersten Jahrhunderten*, Stuttgart, 1886 (Roman Catholic); J. B. Lightfoot, in his commentary on Galatians, London, 1890; T. Livius, *Mary in the Epistles*, ib. 1891; idem, *The Blessed Virgin in the Fathers of the First Century*, ib. 1893 (also Roman Catholic); O. Bardenhewer, *Der Name Maria*, in *Biblische Studien*, i., part 1, Freiburg, 1895; J. Nirschl, *Das Grab der heiligen Jungfrau Maria*, Mainz, 1896; A. Schäfer, *Die Gottesmutter in den heiligen Schrift*, Münster, 1900; J. Richard, *La Maternité de Marie chez les pères du 2. siècle*, Lyons, 1901; *DB*, iii. 286-293; *EB*, iii. 2952-69; *DCG*, ii. 140-142.

On the history of various phases of development of the cult consult: J. C. W. Augusti, *Handbuch der christlichen Archäologie*, i. 559-565, Leipsic, 1836; *Review of Mariolatry, Liturgical, Devotional, Doctrinal*, London, 1869; K. Benrath, in *TSK*, lix (1886), 197-267 (on the Middle Ages); F. G. Holweck, *Fasti Mariani*, Freiburg, 1892; J. C. L. Dubosc de Pesquidoux, *L'Immaculée Conception, Hist. d'un Dogme*, 2 vols., Tours, 1898; B. Saint John, *The Blessed Virgin in the 19th Century*, London, 1903; E. Bishop, *Origins of the Feast of the Conception of the Virgin Mary*, ib. 1904; J. Lemann, *La Vierge Marie dans l'hist. de l'orient chrétien*, Paris, 1904; S. Beissel, *Geschichte der Verehrung Marias in Deutschland während des Mittelalters*, Freiburg, 1909; Schaff, *Christian Church*, ii. 281-284, iii. 409 sqq., 425 sqq., 716 sqq., 807, v. 1, pp. 831 sqq.; idem, *Creeds*, i. 108-128; Neander, *Christian Church*, vols. ii.-v. passim; Harnack, *Dogma*, vols. ii. vii. passim; *KL*, viii. 711-727, 802-826, 831-859.

Controversial or dogmatic presentations are: J. E. Tyler, *Worship of the Blessed Virgin Mary . . . Contrary to Holy Scripture*, London, 1847; E. B. Pusey, *Eirenicon*, pp. 101-190, Oxford, 1865 (cf. J. H. Newman, *Letter to Pusey on his Eirenicon*, pp. 28-159, London, 1866); F. Preuss, *The Romish Doctrine of the Immaculate Conception Traced from its Source*, Edinburgh, 1867; A. Kurz, *Mariologie oder Lehre der katholischen Kirche über die*

Jungfrau Maria, Regensburg, 1881; H. Lasserre, *Our Lady of Lourdes*, Leamington, 1886; idem, *Miraculous Episodes of Lourdes*, ib. 1884; R. Montague, *The Sower and the Virgin*, ib. 1887 (against the Immaculate Conception); J. B. Terrien, *La Mere de Dieu*, 2 vols., Paris, 1900 (Roman Catholic); J. J. I. von Döllinger, *Das Papstthum*, pp. 282 sqq., 533–534, Munich, 1892; J. Wilhelm and T. B. Scannell, *Manual of Catholic Theology*, ii. 122–126, 208–224, London, 1898; J. S. Mulholland, *The World's Madonna; a Hist. of the Blessed Virgin Mary*, ib. 1909.

On Mary in literature and art consult: W. B. Marriott, *The Catacombs*, pp. 1–63, London, 1870; J. S. Northcote and W. S. Brownlow, *Roma Sotteranea*, ii. 133 sqq., ib. 1879; V. Schultze, *Archäologische Studien über altchristliche Monumente*, Vienna, 1880; idem, *Die Katakomben*, pp. 150 sqq., Leipsic, 1882; B. Eckl, *Die Madonna als Gegenstand christlicher Kunstmalerei*, Brixen, 1883; J. Liell, *Darstellungen der . Jungfrau auf den Kunstdenkmälern der Katakomben*, Freiburg, 1887; A. Mussafia, in *Sitzungsberichte der Wiener Akademie*, vols. cxiii., cxv., cxix., 1887–89 (on medieval legends); H. A. Guerber, *Legends of the Virgin with Special Reference to Art*, London, 1896; E. M. Hurll, *The Madonna in Art*, ib. 1898; A. Venturi, *The Madonna. A pictorial Representation of the Mother of Christ*, London, 1902; E. L. Taunton, *The Little Office of our Lady*, ib. 1903; Mrs. A. B. Jameson, *Legends of the Madonna*, ib. 1904; A. Bartle, *The Madonna of the Poets*, ib. 1906; M. Siebert, *Die Madonnendarstellung in der altniederländischen Kunst von Jan van Eyck bis zu den Manieristen*, Strasburg, 1906.

MARY MAGDALENE (Mary of Magdala): The most devoted of the female followers of Jesus. She has been confused with two other persons mentioned in the New Testament; with the "woman which was a sinner" of Luke vii. 36 sqq., by reason of which she has been supposed to have been of profligate character, and with Mary of Bethany. The first of these identifications is probably due to the mention of Mary in Luke viii. 2, but is made unlikely by the statement in Luke viii. 1, while it appears from verse 2 and Mark xvi. 1, that Mary Magdalene had been healed by Jesus of a mental disease. The second identification is shown unlikely by the total difference appearing in the accounts of the two. Mary of Bethany belonged to a highly respected family living near Jerusalem, and remained in the immediate circle of her family, while, according to her name, Mary of Magdala belonged to a place in Galilee (Matt. xv. 39), and devoted herself wholly to the service of the Master. She was the first visitor to the grave on Easter morning and was the first to see Jesus after his resurrection (John xx.). She has a considerable part in the legend and art of the Church. One legend takes her to France and makes her an ascetic there. The eastern story carries her to Ephesus and makes her a companion of John. The paintings which depict her as a penitent are many and well known. The mystery plays of the Middle Ages also portrayed her as in league with Lucifer until Jesus appeared and effected her conversion. It is time that her name be dissevered from the associations with which it has so long been connected and that she be given her due as a devoted disciple of Jesus. (KARL BURGER†.)

BIBLIOGRAPHY: *DB*, iii. 214–216; *EB*, iii. 2970–71; *KL*, viii. 735–739 (identifies Mary of Magdala, Mary of Bethany, and the sinner of Luke vii.). On Mary in art: J. E. Wessely, *Iconographie Gottes und der heiligen*, pp. 288 sqq., Leipsic, 1874; Mrs. Jameson, *Sacred and Legendary Art*, i. 363–404, Boston, 1893. On the mystery plays, H. Kurz, *Geschichte der deutschen Literatur*, i. 722 sqq., Leipsic, 1853.

MASON, FRANCIS: Baptist missionary; b. at York, England, Apr. 2, 1799; d. at Rangoon, Burma, Mar. 3, 1874. He was educated at home by a retired naval officer and in 1818 came to the United States, where he worked at the shoemaker's trade until 1824. In 1827 he entered the Newton Theological Seminary and in 1830 was sent to Burma by the Baptist Missionary Union. There he became the successor of G. D. Boardman in his work among the Karens. He learned not only the Karen language in all its dialects, but also many other Eastern tongues. He translated the Bible into two of the Karen dialects, the New Testament into a third, also several religious works, and edited the *Morning Star*, a Karen monthly. He wrote: *The Karens or Memoir of Ko Thah-Byu* (Tavoy, 1842); *Synopsis of the Grammar of the Karen Language* (1846); *Natural Productions of Burmah* (Maulmain, 1850); *Flora Burmanica* (Tavoy, 1851); *Tenasserim, or the Fauna, Flora, Minerals, and Nations of British Burmah and Pegu* (1852; 2d edition, enlarged, Rangoon, 1860); *Pali Grammar* (Toungoo, 1868); and *Story of a Working Man's Life* (an autobiography; New York, 1870); he also translated Kachchayano's *Pali Grammar* (Calcutta, 1848).

MASON, JOHN MITCHELL: Associate Reformed divine and educator; b. in New York Mar. 19, 1770; d. there Dec. 26, 1829. He was graduated from Columbia College in 1789; studied theology with his father for two years, then went to Edinburgh for further study in 1791; was pastor of the Cedar St. Church, New York (his father's), 1793–1810; founded a new church, subsequently located in Murray St., New York, 1810; was provost of Columbia College, 1811–16; president of Dickinson College, Carlisle, Pa., 1821–24. In 1822 he transferred his ecclesiastical relations to the Presbyterian Church. He became eminent in his denomination through his services to the cause of education of the ministry and by his advocacy of a more frequent communion service. In the latter connection his pamphlet *Letters on Frequent Communion* (New York, 1798) was noteworthy; in the former his services in calling the attention of his coworkers to the necessity of providing a supply of ministers educated in America for the American churches led to his being appointed in 1802 on a commission to draft a plan for a theological seminary, and finally to his appointment as first professor of the institution in 1804. It was opened, apparently in his home in New York city, November 1, 1805. The course of study lasted five years. He established *The Christian's Magazine* in 1807 and himself wrote most of what appeared in its pages, the substance being a friendly controversy with Bishop Hobart on episcopacy. He was also one of the founders of the American Bible Society. Dr. Mason was eminent as a preacher, speaking without notes and with great eloquence; and he was often called upon as orator on national and patriotic occasions. His writings were collected by his son Ebenezer (4 vols., New York, 1832, new ed. enlarged, 1849).

BIBLIOGRAPHY: J. Van Vechten, *Memoirs of John Mitchell Mason*, 2 vols., New York, 1856; W. B. Sprague, *Annals of the American Pulpit*, iv. 1–26, ib. 1858.

MASON, LOWELL: Musical composer and educator; b. in Medfield, Mass., Jan. 8, 1792; d. in Orange, N. J., Aug. 11, 1872. He early developed a remarkable talent in musical matters, and in 1812 began to give public instruction in that branch in Savannah, Ga.; in 1827 he removed to Boston, Mass., whence his activities spread through all New England, exciting popular interest and educating taste for music. By his instrumentality the Boston Academy of Music was established, and an enormous impetus given to musical education. In 1837 he visited Europe for purposes of study. He was especially devoted to the bettering of the musical services of the churches, and to that end paid attention to the training of church choirs. He was indefatigable also in the preparation of handbooks and manuals for use in churches, Sunday-schools and singing-classes. His collections, from his first (*Boston Handel and Haydn Society's Collection of Church Music*, Boston, 1821) to his last (*The Song Garden*, 1866), number more than forty. He also composed many hymn tunes which are still in use. In 1855 the University of the City of New York made him a "doctor in music," the first degree of the kind given in the United States.

Bibliography: *American Annual Encyclopædia*, xii. 495-500, New York, 1873 (contains a very full list of Mason's works); G. Grove, *Dictionary of Music and Musicians*, ii. 225, London, 1880; J. D. Champlin and W. F. Apthorp, *Cyclopedia of Music and Musicians*, ii. 532-533, New York, 1893.

MASORAH, mās'o-rā: The Jewish tradition regarding the textual readings of the Pentateuch in particular and of the Old Testament in general, meaning by this the consonantal text.

Content of the Masorah. After the return from the Exile the Law of Moses was the central point of the common life of the people, and an absorbing care for the textual basis was the natural consequence. Instruction in the Law began in early youth, and in the synagogues passages were read from this part of Scripture, to which there came to be added also selections from the prophets. Very early there were formulated exact directions regarding the copying of the Scriptures, especially for the making of synagogue rolls. Soon there were devised also checks in order to control in the matter of accuracy. The verses, words, and letters of the entire Old Testament and also of parts of it were counted, and note was taken of the number of times single words occurred in the whole or in parts of the volume. Thus the tradition that there are in the Old Testament 23,203 verses is as old as the persecution under Hadrian. Moreover, peculiarities were noted and arranged in groups, as in cases where marginal readings were preferred (see Keri and Kethibh). In cases where these singularities were supposed to have particular significance, note was made of them so that omission or change became difficult or impossible, and sometimes an explanation of the phenomenon was given. Examples of these are the suspended "nun" in the name "Manasseh," Judges xviii. 30, and the two methods (*scriptio plena* and *defectiva*) of spelling the proper name Ephron in Gen. xxiii. 16, of which fanciful explanations were given.

There is no indication in the Talmuds or in the older Midrashim that materials of this sort were committed to writing, but it is presumed that they were transmitted orally, at least until the seventh century. The division of the Law into paragraphs (in Palestine so as to be read through in three years, in Babylonia in one year) and into

Oral Transmission; Textual Variations. verses was known at this early date, indicated by the 290 open and 379 closed sections. It appears that after the pronunciation handed down by tradition was indicated in the manuscripts, the notes of peculiarities and the results of the examination of the text began to be written on the margin of the manuscripts or at the end of the volume or of the individual books, sometimes, however, on separate manuscripts. The different development which Judaism underwent at home and abroad (in Palestine and Babylonia) produced variations and diversities in the texts, and thus a diversity of "authority" has been produced. Concerning these the Masorah is not wholly consistent, and the older manuscripts show great varieties of reading. The general agreement among most codices of the Old Testament is due to a leveling process under the influence of the Masoretes. The origin of the three systems of punctuation known to exist has not with certainty been discovered.

Masoretic studies were long prosecuted in Tiberias, a fact that is registered in marginal references on the codices to the "men of Tiberias," where in particular the family of Aaron ben Moses ben Asher was active from the end of the eighth century; and the Masoretic punctuation must have taken shape there, at least in its essentials. Many names of noted Masoretes are known,

Eminent Masoretes and Texts. among them the contemporary of Aaron ben Moses ben Asher, Moses ben David ben Naphthali, and something more than the name of Moses Moḥeh and Rabbi Pinḥas. A manuscript of singular notoriety is also known by name—the Maḥazora rabba, cited as early as Ben Naphthali; and of other codices citations are extant which are still of value. The points in which Ben Naphthali differed from Ben Asher are preserved in lists and in numerous marginal notes. But the most celebrated of all the Masoretes is Aaron ben Moses ben Asher (flourished at Tiberias early in the tenth century), who is quoted as the highest authority upon the text; and it has been claimed that a codex from his hand, supplied with punctuation and Masorah, is extant at Aleppo. Modern textual criticism seeks particularly to employ the means left by Aaron ben Asher. After him come the so-called Nakdanim or punctuators, eminent among whom are Moses, Samson (both called Nakdan), and Jekuthiel ben Judah ha-Kohen. Later copyists and grammarians cite them and their model codices with frequency. Of the Masoretic handbooks named and cited since the middle of the twelfth century the most important is that called *Oklah weoklah* (*Ochlah weochlah*), though an older work is the tract *Sopherim*. Mention should also be made of the codices from Yemen which combine grammar with Masorah.

Jacob ben Ḥayyim ibn Adonijah undertook to

collect and arrange all the material accessible to him in manuscripts, the complexity of which task only the most expert can appreciate.

Masorah Parva, Magna, and Marginalis.

The results are employed in the second of Daniel Bomberg's Bibles (4 vols., Venice, 1524–25), and the text of the Masorah given there, practically reproduced as it is in the later rabbinic Bibles, must in spite of its incompleteness and gaps be considered the *textus receptus* of the Masorah. The Masorah is distinguished into *Masorah parva* and *magna* (together called *Masorah marginalis*). In rabbinic Bibles text and Targum are printed in parallel columns, between which stands the Masorah parva, which concerns the Keri and gives the number of occurrences of a form. Above and below the text stands the Masorah magna, which contains references to the parva and general matters such as concordances of words which have certain peculiarities. At the end of the fourth volume is the Masorah finalis, a kind of lexicon in alphabetical order containing also references to the Masorah marginalis and statements of differences between Ben Asher and Ben Naphthali and between Oriental and Occidental readings. This is practically the arrangement of the manuscripts, though there are differences both of content and of order. That the eastern or Babylonian Jews differed in their text from the western or Palestinian Jews was known in early times only through Jacob ben Ḥayyim's list of 216 variants. It is now known that variations exist in the Pentateuch and concern vowels and accents, that they show differences from the Masoretic tradition, and that the Orientals were not in entire agreement with each other. See Bible Text, I., 1–2. (H. L. Strack.)

Bibliography: References to the earlier literature are given in Hauck-Herzog, *RE*, xii. 393 sqq. On the introduction to the Masorah the best single work is C. D. Ginsburg, *Introduction to the Massoretico-Critical Edition of the Hebrew Bible*, pp. 1–468, London, 1897. Helpful studies are: A. Geiger, in *Jüdische Zeitschrift für Wissenschaft und Leben*, iii (1864–65), 78–118; E. le Savoureux, *Études historiques et exégétiques sur l'A. T.*, pp. 191–224, Paris, 1887; I. Harris, in *JQR*, i (1889), 128–142, 223–257; W. Bacher, in Winter and Wünsche, *Die jüdische Litteratur*, ii. 121–132, Treves, 1894; idem, in *JQR*, iii (1891), 785–790. Elias Levita's work, *Sepher massoreth ha-massoreth* was published, Venice, 1536, Basel, 1539, cf. C. D. Ginsburg, *The Massoreth ha-massoreth of Elias Levita, . . in Hebrew with Eng. transl. and . Notes*, London, 1867; idem, *The Massorah Compiled from MSS. alphabetically and lexically Arranged*, vols. i.–iii., London, 1880–85. On the Syrian punctuation consult: J. P. Martin, *Histoire de la ponctuation ou de la Massore chez les Syriens*, Paris, 1875; A. Merx, *Hist. artis grammaticæ apud Syros*, Leipsic, 1882; G. Diettrich, *Die Massorah der östlichen und westlichen Syrer*, London, 1899. On punctuation in general consult M. Schwab, *Des points-voyelles dans les langues sémitiques*, Paris, 1879. On the supralinear system consult: F. Prætorius, in *ZDMG*, liii (1899), 181–196; G. Margoliouth, in *PSBA*, 1893, pp. 164–205. On a third system read: C. Levias, in *American Journal for Semitic Language and Literature*, xv (1898–99), 157–164; and P. Kahle, in *ZATW*, 1901, pp. 273–317. On the accents: A. Büchler, *Untersuchung zur Entstehung und Entwickelung der hebräischen Accente*, Vienna, 1891; W. Wickes, *Treatise on the Accentuation of the . Poetical Books of the O. T., . . and of the . . . Prose Books*, 2 vols., Oxford, 1881–87; F. Prætorius, *Ueber die Herkunft der hebräischen Accente*, Berlin, 1901; P. Kahle, in *ZDMG*, 1901, pp. 167–194.

For discussion of points touched on in the text consult: Zunz, *Zur Geschichte und Litteratur*, pp. 105–122, Berlin, 1845 (on the punctuators); S. Pinsker, *Einleitung in das babylonisch-hebräische Punktationssystem*, Vienna, 1863, and H. L. Strack, in G. A. Kohut, *Semitic Studies*, pp. 560–572, Berlin, 1897 (on the eastern Masorah); S. Frensdorff, *Das Buch Ochlah W'ochlah*, Hanover; C. D. Ginsburg, *Jacob ben Chajim ibn Adonijah's Introduction to the Rabbinic Bible, Hebrew and English, with Explanatory Notes*, London, 1867; L. Löw, *Graphische Requisiten und Erzeugnisse bei den Juden*, p. 71, Leipsic, 1870 (on the care exercised on the text); the tract Sopherim was edited by Joel Müller, Leipsic, 1878; H. T. de Graaf, *De Joodsche weigeleerden in Tiberias 70–400 A.D.*, Groningen, 1902 (on Jewish learning in Tiberias); P. Kahle, *Der masoretische Text des A. T.'s nach der Ueberlieferung der babylonischen Juden*, Leipsic, 1902.

MASORETIC TEXT. See Bible Text, I.

MASS.

I. The Doctrine.—1. The Name "Mass": The subject of consideration is the history of the idea of sacrifice as an element of Christian worship—an idea connected specially with the name "mass," given to the ceremony which the Roman Church in other connection calls "communion" and the Greek Church calls *leitourgia* (earlier *koinōnia* and *synaxis*). The Greek Church also imports the idea of sacrifice, but less absolutely than the Roman. Neither Church has forgotten the name "Eucharist," but it serves more as a dogmatic than as the cultic designation of the mystery. Roman Catholic theology distinguishes between the "Eucharist as sacrament" and the "Eucharist as sacrifice." The following discussion of the doctrine of the mass should be compared with the articles Lord's Supper and Transubstantiation; special articles like Epiklesis, Kiss of Peace, etc., may also be consulted.

The English "mass" comes from the Latin *missa*. How early the latter was used to designate the eucharistic sacrifice is uncertain. The first to remark on the expression is Isidore of Seville (d. 636), who says that "*missa* is the time of sacrifice, when the catechumens are dismissed and for this reason is it called *missa*, because those who are not yet regenerated can not be present at the sacrifice of the altar" (*Etymologiæ* vi. 19).

1. Etymology and Meaning.

He clearly understands *missa* as equivalent to *missio* with the meaning "dismissal," and he is right in so far as he conceives of *missa* as a noun. Explanations which make it a participle, connecting it with the formula of dismissal (*Ite, missa est*) and completing the latter by supplying *oratio* or *hostia* ("the prayer or the sacrifice has been sent [to God, by an angel]") or *concio* ("the assembly is dismissed") are to be rejected. Isidore's interpretation, however, may be called in question. Probably *missa* as a by-form of *missio* has two meanings, one in which it signifies the rite of dismissal and another in which it serves as translation of the Greek *leitourgia*, and only in the latter sense is *missa* the mass. It is used from the fourth century and probably earlier for all sorts of divine service, especially for ritual ceremonies in the church, therein corresponding exactly to *leitourgia*, which meant first a public service at Athens performed by the richer citizens for the community, then any public service or work and specially the public service of the gods, whence it was transferred in Christian usage to the service or ministry of priests (Septuagint) and public worship generally, more particularly to the Eucharist. It thus approximates to the English "mission," which is the duty or service on which one is sent. Against the interpretation "dismissal" and the connection with *Ite, missa est* is the following consideration. The Greek Church had its *apolysis*, corresponding to the *Ite, missa est*, but it did not transfer the name to the entire service, as would be expected if the Latin Church did so, since the liturgical terminology of the two Churches is essentially parallel. If the Latin *missa* is not the translation of the Greek *leitourgia*, the Latin Church has no parallel expression for *leitourgia*. Silvia of Aquitaine (later fourth century) repeatedly uses *missa* for the dismissal (=*apolysis*), but also in connections where it clearly means the entire service (=*leitourgia;* cf. *Peregrinatio Silviæ*, ed. G. F Gamurrini, pp. 82, 87, 99, 101, Rome, 1888). Proof of a like use of the word after 400 is given by Rottmanner. The distinction between the *missa catechumenorum* and *missa fidelium* in the sense of a twofold "mass" was first made probably in the twelfth century (Ivo of Chartres); *missa* in these phrases, at any rate in the passages thus far cited, means simply "dismissal."

2. New Testament and Early Catholic Ideas: The Lord, when he founded the Supper, neither performed nor instituted a sacrificial act. All that he did with the bread and the wine was directed to the disciples; in the later terminology it indicated a sacrament, not a sacrifice. But it had reference to his death as a sacrifice, and was intended to impress upon the disciples that he in his death was the sacrifice of the new covenant, wherein the new covenant was made perfect. It was in connection with

1. The New Testament.

the cup that the thought of sacrifice first entered, this act having a somewhat different significance from that with the bread (cf. C. von Weizsäcker, *Apostolisches Zeitalter*, pp. 576–577, Freiburg, 1890). Paul, the oldest witness (cf. Luke xxii. 19–20; Matt. xxvi. 26, sqq. and Mark xiv. 22 sqq., represent a later tradition), applies the bread or the "body" to the congregation, the church, the members of which represent their communion (*koinōnia*) with one another and with their Head when they break it together, and prove themselves the "body of Christ" (cf. the course of thought in I Cor. xi. 20 sqq.; also xii. 13, 27; Col. i. 18, ii. 19; Eph. i. 23). The thought of Jesus may have been that even in the future, when his followers broke the bread in his memory, he would be with them, would himself "nourish" them as if he were present "in the body." His own have his "body," that is, himself, always with them like bread for their nourishment. His act corresponded in ritual form to the promise of Matt. xviii. 20. The counterpart to the "body" in the second transaction is not the "blood," but the "new covenant." The Lord did not offer his "flesh," but his "body"—it was a change of far-reaching consequences when the Church began to talk of the "flesh" instead of the "body"—and he did not offer his "blood" but the "new covenant." Paul speaks nowhere of drinking the "blood," but always of the "cup." So far as he sets the acts with the bread and the cup parallel, he seems to bring the latter into relation with the "one spirit" of the congregation (I Cor. xii. 13, which really proves only that Paul did not have a "dogma" about the Supper). If the thought of Jesus were as just stated, this in connection with the "cup of the covenant," which was made by the "blood," by a sacrifice, could lead to the notion that the Supper of the Lord had some, though a limited, resemblance to a sacrificial meal. Paul drew a parallel between the "table of the Lord" and the sacrificial meals of both Jews and Gentiles (I Cor. x. 18 sqq.); but this must not be pressed. Paul has in mind here only the close relationship of the participants to one another in case of the Jews, the relationship with their gods in case of the heathen. In the Epistle to the Hebrews (xiii. 10 sqq.) the combination between the celebration of the Supper and the sacrificial meal is developed further. The conception that "we [the Christians] have an altar," from which others may not eat, is not expressed by Paul, though he may have suggested it. Just how far the idea of the writer went is not made plain. His thought may have been that the congregation of Jesus "ate" directly from the cross as its altar, that it continually renewed a "sacrificial meal" in addition to the "offering once for all." But he may have meant that in the Lord's Supper the congregation renewed the "sacrifice" in cultic-commemorative manner, that the eucharistic ceremony was a repetition of what had taken place on Calvary. In any case the Epistle to the Hebrews shows how easily the conception of the Lord's Supper passed over into that of a sacrificial meal, even of a sacrificial act. That it eventually became only a sort of dramatic memorial of the sacrificial death of Jesus is easily comprehended.

In the Didache the ceremony in all its relations is called uniformly *hē thusia* (xiv. 1, 2)—a real "offering," but it is not made plain whether anything more than prayers and alms is meant, unless, possibly, xiv. 3 gives a hint by citing Mal. i. 11. Justin applies this passage to the bread and the cup (*Trypho*, xxviii.–xxix., xli., cxvi.–cxvii.). If the Didache is by one writer, it must belong to the time when the agape and the Lord's Supper had been separated (see AGAPE). How early and where this first happened is not certain. The Epistle to the Hebrews may presuppose the separation. Justin attests it for Rome (*I Apol.* lxv.). It can hardly have been due to purely practical considerations; a tendency to idealization must have given the first impulse. Most probably, in course of time, perhaps under Paul's influence in the first instance, the ceremony in reference to the "body of Christ" and the "new covenant in his blood" took on such a character that "one bread" (I Cor. x. 17) and "one cup" were set apart and came to be regarded as so superior to all other bread and wine, which served merely to satisfy natural needs, that it was found necessary to separate the agape and the Supper. When the tendency to such a separation had once developed, a new conception of the "this do" (*touto poieite*) was made easy. Neither Jesus nor Paul thought of the words as a command to "offer" anything. But as early as the second century the *poieite* was interpreted as "offer." Of course "to do something" can acquire the meaning "to offer" only from the connection (as when the thought is to "do something to God," expressed or implied; cf. Ex. xii. 47 sqq., Septuagint, where *poiein* is used to render the Hebrew *'asah*), and the use of "eat" before and after the "this do" may have suggested the idea of sacrifice. But the most effective impulse came from the effort to accommodate early Christian concepts to Greco-Roman thought. The "new covenant" was wholly unfamiliar to non-Jews. The Latins translated it *novum testamentum*, not *novum fœdus*, and the Greeks too, for the most part, understood the *diathēkē* as a last will and testament prescribing doctrines and ordinances, of which the chief was the Eucharist. The contents of the cup now come to the foreground. Neither Jesus nor Paul had spoken of the wine, and there is nothing to indicate that the former thought of the wine as representing his blood. But the notion of sacrifice called up the thought of his blood, and it was an intelligible idea that he sealed the covenant by a holy drink. The blood thus came to take the place of the new covenant in the second part of the Supper. The notion of the "wine-blood" brought with it that of the "bread-flesh." To be sure, people still said "body" (*sōma*), but they thought "flesh." The twofold conception of Jesus that his followers would always have, and commemorate both his living presence among them and the new covenant with God, became transformed into the thought that the Lord was present in twofold manner, viz., that one saw his flesh in the bread and his blood in the cup. It was then almost inevitable that the ancient mind should conceive of the Lord's Supper as a mysterious sacrificial institution. It is possible that even in the second century the development had not gone beyond the conception of a sacrificial meal. But the association of ideas must soon have led farther. That in the second century and perhaps from the beginning the Eucharist had in a certain sense the character of a sacrificial act is not contested. It was called "Eucharist" because of the prayers of thanksgiving, and early Christianity designated prayer as "offering." Also the agape was held with gifts of the rich, which were brought as "offerings" (*prosphorai*) before God and consecrated to God. For a long time after the "Lord's Supper" was separated from the "common meal" (the agape), the "elements" were furnished by the congregation in such profusion that a considerable surplus remained for the poor and the clergy. Such gifts of the congregation were consecrated by prayer and passed as "offerings." Höfling and others maintain that "offering" in connection with the Supper means no more than prayers and alms till the third century. But once the ideas of the "body and covenant" were displaced by the "flesh and blood," the thoughts that the Eucharist was a representation of the sacrifice on Calvary and was essentially a sacrifice must have entered. A time when sacrifice was everywhere a living institution of the cult, while it noted the symbolism and spirituality of all Christian worship in the eucharistic service, could not fail to discern also in it the thought of an offering of Christ beside the offerings of prayer and alms.

2. Further Development.

The important sources after the Didache are Justin, Ignatius, Irenæus, Clement of Alexandria, and Tertullian. For Justin, taking all in all, the Eucharist was a "sacrifice" (*Trypho*, xxviii.–xxix., xli., cxvi.–cxvii.; *I Apol.*, lxv.–lxvi.). Ignatius speaks of the Eucharist and prayer (*eucharistia* and *proseuchē*) as two things ("Smyrnæans," vii. 1), and the former "is the flesh which suffered [*sarx pathousa*] of our Savior Jesus Christ." He does not directly call the Eucharist a sacrifice. But he knows an altar of the congregation ("Philadelphians," iv.; "Trallians," vii. 2), the congregation itself is the temple and altar of God, and the true priest in it is Jesus ("Magnesians," vii. 2; "Philadelphians," ix. 1). His thought is that Jesus, in that he is present at the Eucharist as the "flesh which suffered," presents himself here in the name of the congregation, living, as a sacrifice to God. Irenæus in the passage which needs chiefly to be considered (*Hær.*, iv. 29–32) is writing from the apologetic side and makes no attempt to set forth the real character of the Eucharist. But he applies the prophecy of Mal. i. 10–11 to the Lord's Supper and calls the "body" and "blood of Christ" the "offering of the New Testament" and, later, the "pure sacrifice." Clement of Alexandria and Tertullian had little occasion to speak of the Lord's Supper except as a meal; in so far as they refer to it as sacrifice at all, they set forth no theory. Clement often speaks of the "offerings" of Christians, meaning prayer and alms. But he calls the Eucharist the "offering" (*prosphora*; *Strom.*, i. 19), meaning the entire ceremony collectively. Tertullian, when he speaks of the "sacrifices" or "offerings" of the Christians, generally means prayers. But there are passages where he applies to the Supper as a whole the expressions "sacrifice," "offering," or "to offer" (*De cultu feminarum*, ii. 11; *Ad uxorem*, ii. 8; and elsewhere). Only *De oratione*, xix., however, can be adduced as direct proof that he does not restrict "offering" to prayers, alms, and the like. This passage assumes that the ceremony of the Eucharist is a unit, and that it necessarily closes with the "reception" of the body of the Lord. Its significance lies in a distinction between the "prayers of the sacrifices" (plural) and "participation in the sacrifice" (singular). To be sure it proves in itself no more than that Tertullian knew of the view of the Supper as a sacrificial meal. But taking it with the expressions of earlier writers, it is

3. The Sources.

probable that he had also in mind a sacrificial offering of the body of the Lord. Tertullian is the first to speak of "offerings" or "sacrifices" for the dead (*De corona*, iii.; *De monogamia*, x.; *De exhortatione castitatis*, xi.). It is uncertain just how they were carried out; but the thought here can not be merely that of giving thanks.

3. Patristic Teachings: By the time of Cyprian (d. 258) and Origen (d. 251) the apostolic congregation had been organized into a single Church, and the elaboration of "dogmas" was soon making rapid strides. Not many new ideas were propounded, however; the chief characteristic was a fixing and systematizing process exercised upon concepts already at hand. It should be remembered that the history of the doctrine of the Lord's Supper is nowhere a logical progress of thought, but was conditioned by fixed rites and absolutely binding words, with which a multitude of individual opinions was interwoven. The ceremony early became a mystery. From about 200 also the notion of a privileged priesthood stood in the background. Furthermore, it must not be overlooked that till the end of the fourth century sacrifice was everywhere a vital institution of public life. Everybody knew what a "sacrifice" was. But when the "Christian sacrifice" was the only one remaining, there arose need of explanations and "doctrines." At this very time, however, other dogmatic problems claimed attention. Thus different factors worked together to the detriment of the doctrine of the Lord's Supper.

It has been usual to date an epoch in the development of the doctrine of the sacrificial character of the Eucharist from Cyprian—probably because he has left a much fuller exposition of his views on the subject than earlier writers. The occasion was furnished by the spread of the custom of celebrating the Supper with water instead of wine,

1. Cyprian and Origen.

which Cyprian treats at great length in his sixty-third letter (*Ad Cæcilium*). He sets forth here a theory of the Supper as sacrifice, with certain limitations, which was probably widely held. In the most varied terms he designates the transaction with the cup and the entire ceremony as a "sacrifice" and an "offering." When Jesus poured the wine into the cup he fulfilled a whole cycle of prophecies which all looked forward to his suffering and redemption through his blood (chaps. iii. sqq.). Jesus offered the Supper as "sacrifice" to God (chap. xiv.). The wine "expresses the blood of Christ" (chap. xi.), and the Supper is the "offering of the blood of Christ" (chaps. ix., xv.). The mixing of wine and water in the cup is interpreted mystically, the water representing the congregation (chaps. xii., xiii.). Cyprian is still able to define the import of the sacrifice as "thanks," but the thought prevails with him that the petition is promoted by the "memorial of the passion of Christ" (i. e., the Supper), although he nowhere speaks directly of a "propitiatory" effect of the eucharistic offering. Nor does he express the thought that the "offering of the body and blood of Christ" is a "sacrifice" in an independent sense; it is such only in relation to the "representative sacrifice" in the Lord's Supper. Origen was less of a hierarch than Cyprian. The latter apparently thought a "priest" necessary. Origen does not deny the importance of the priest, but he bases it on the need of "order" and the priest's personal gifts. He believes that "everyone" can sacrifice. He has gone a step beyond any extant expression of Cyprian's in that he attributes "atoning" efficacy to the Lord's Supper. As theologian he was dominated by the idea of a "higher" sense, the allegorical interpretation, which he sought in the Eucharist and sacrifice as everywhere else. All sacrifice has the aim of cleansing from sin (*Hom. in Num.*, x. 2; *Hom.* xxiv. 1). What the Old-Testament sacrifices merely prefigured became truth in Christ's death. But Origen regarded Christ's sacrifice and high-priesthood, not as a thing of the past, but as continuing. Christ continually sacrifices and intercedes for the faithful in heaven, at the altar of heaven; and Origen inferred from the Old-Testament type that Christ sacrifices in heaven with the coals from our altar and with the incense from our hands (cf. *Hom. in Lev.*, ix. 8). It is hardly credible that Origen did not have in mind here the "body and blood of Christ" in the Eucharist. Elsewhere (*Contra Celsum*, viii. 33) he says that the bread of the Eucharist is not mere bread, but also a "body , a holy thing which sanctifies those who use it with right intention." It is true that Origen nowhere actually sets forth a theory of the Lord's Supper as an offering of the body of Christ; but he shows clearly enough that it had such significance for him (cf. *Hom. in Lev.*, xiii. 3). He sometimes alludes to an offering of the blood of Christ in the Eucharist. According to his whole mode of thinking, Origen could have conceived only of a symbolic "offering" of Christ in the Eucharist. But there was nothing to hinder his seeing in it a "commemorative" renewal of the atoning work of Christ.

Ambrose and Augustine brought together two ideas which before them had been current separately; that is, they connected the thought of the "body of Christ," which is sacrificed, with Christians themselves individually and collectively,

2. Ambrose and Augustine.

Augustine directly combining the former with the conception of the Church as the "body of Christ." Thereby the sense of the duty of Christians to present themselves, their thoughts and works, and their whole life to God as the weightiest sacrifice, came into close connection with the idea of the Lord's Supper as sacrifice. What Origen was able to connect with the Supper only by the medium of allegory, these two Western Fathers regarded as the content and import of the sacred act. Thus they gave the church ceremony a practical significance which tended to counteract the superstitious notions of mere sacramental magic. Of course the thought of the "blood of Christ" received their attention. Ambrose says that the "flesh of the Savior" has its significance "for the welfare of the body," his blood was poured out "for our soul." Augustine interprets the pouring of the wine into the mouth of the communicant as a figure of the "shedding" of the blood. But the most important thing with each is that he brings closely together the two acts, of priest and of congregation, since this lessened the danger that the Supper as a sacrifice should be set apart and become a purely hierurgic transaction. For Ambrose it will suffice to cite merely the *Enarratio in Psalm xxxviii.*, nos. 25, 26. He says that the "priests" offer the "body of Christ," i. e., the elements with their true content perceived by faith, viz., "Christ himself." But the truth of the matter is for Ambrose this, that Christ continually offers to God in heaven the "perfect man," i. e., the Christian who has actually received Christ at the hands of the priest. Ambrose regards the eucharistic bread and wine as "medicine"; the conception of a "sacrificial meal" has quite disappeared. With Augustine (*De civitate Dei*, x. 4 sqq.) a sacrifice is something which is addressed to God that we may have close connection with God. Every "visible sacrifice" is only a "sacrament of an invisible sacrifice." The sacrifice of the death of Christ makes it possible that "the congregation of saints be presented a general sacrifice to God by the great high priest, who also in his passion sacrificed himself for us that we might be the body of so great a head." The thought that the "body of Christ" in the Lord's Supper is the Church—"in a sacrament"—and the question, whether merely bread and wine or a wonder in reference to the real body of Christ constituted the sacrament, are discussed further in Sermon cclxxii. In *Contra Faustum Manichæum*, xx. 15 sqq., all of Augustine's thoughts on the Christian sacrifices are summed up. The influence of both Ambrose and Augustine on the interpretation of the eucharistic sacrifice has always been great. And the rich subjective passion-mysticism which Roman Catholicism connects with the sacrifice of the mass is derived chiefly from the Ambrosian-Augustinian tradition.

3. Gregory the Great. Passing over the theologians of the next two centuries, at the boundary between the patristic and the medieval time stands Gregory the Great, theologically without originality, yet by his position one of the greatest of teachers, and even more so because of the popular, pastoral manner in which, with citation of many examples preferably from his own knowledge and experience, he expounded what seemed to him of most practical importance. The official dogmas are not prominent in his works. But questions of the cult and of the spiritual discipline interested him both as preacher and writer. He considers it fully settled how one should think about sacrifice. In the *Hom. in Evangelia* (II., xxxvii. 7) he treats of the significance of the sacrifice of the mass for "absolution," for release from the effects of any fault. A "legation" must be sent to God and works of mercy shown to him, but before all "let us offer on his altar the sacrifices [*hostias*] of propitiation; for the sacrifice of the sacred altar, offered with tears and benevolence of mind, pleads especially for our absolution, because he who, having risen from the dead, now no longer dies, still in this dies again for us in his mystery. For as often as we offer to him the sacrifice of his passion, so often do we renew for ourselves his passion for our absolution." Especially celebrated in the Middle Ages were certain remarks of Gregory's in the "Dialogues" (iv. 58, 59). He has been speaking of the efficacy of the sacrifice of the mass for departed souls, prisoners, etc., and says it is better "to die free than to seek freedom after chains." So he commends "the daily sacrifice of tears to God and to offer daily the sacrifice of his flesh and blood. For that victim especially saves the soul from everlasting death which by a mystery renews for us that death of the only begotten, who in himself living immortal and incorruptible is sacrificed again for us in this mystery of the sacred offering. For his body is taken there, his flesh is broken for the salvation of the people, his blood is poured not on the hands of unbelievers but in the mouths of the faithful. So let us appreciate what this sacrifice for us is, which imitates for our absolution the passion of the only begotten son. For who of the faithful can doubt that in the very hour of the sacrifice the heavens are opened to the voice of the priest, that a choir of angels attends that mystery of Jesus Christ, that the lowest are joined with the highest, the earth with the heavens, and that one thing is done by those visible and invisible?"

4. The East. The ideas of the East do not differ essentially from those of the West between 300 and 600. Eusebius of Cæsarea (*Demonstratio evangelica*, i. 10) conceives of the Eucharist as self-evidently a propitiatory sacrificial act. If Christ on the cross was the predicted atoning sacrifice for Jews and Gentiles, then both as Christians attain forgiveness of their sins "by daily making mention of his body and blood." Christ's sacrifice was made once for all, but he has commanded us to "offer a memorial of it to God perpetually." Eusebius's idea of the ceremony as a sacrifice was purely representative. He considers the ritual part as exclusively hierurgic and interprets only the incensing as a sacrifice of Christians. In the Apostolic Constitutions (ii. 25) the "gifts" are fixed requirements for the Eucharist and the support of clergy and widows. The "offering of the Eucharist" (ii. 57) depends on the "gifts," since the "sacrifice" follows after they have been made. Book viii. 12 gives the first complete liturgy. As in Justin, the entire ceremony is thought of as "sacrifice," in which the "offering" has a special place. The offering of the body and blood signifies also "thanks." Cyril of Jerusalem calls the elements a "spiritual sacrifice" and a "sacrifice of propitiation" ("Catechetical Mysteries," v. 8). When "the holy and most awful sacrifice has been made," we offer to God, in prayers for the departed, "Christ slain for our sins, propitiating the benevolent God for them and for us" (v. 9). A definite theory of the manner of the sacrifice is sought in vain in Cyril, Eusebius, and the other Fathers of the time. Evidently the thought of the Supper as a meal counted for more in the speculation of the East than of the West, but perhaps not in popular interest. The recollection of the sacrificial meal seems to have lasted longer than in the West. Little attempt was made to explain what a sacrifice is or what there is sacrificial in the Lord's Supper. The Alexandrian and Antiochian schools are in accord when they come to treat of the doctrine of sacrifice as an act.

Apart from sermons and the productions of the mystagogical literature (see MYSTAGOGIC THEOL-

OGY) neither East nor West produced a special treatise on the Eucharist. Even Chrysostom, who is called *doctor eucharistiæ*, did not write one. His exposition both of sacrifice and the Eucharist is found in his homiletical and exegetical works. He is more occupied with the thought of a "mystery" in general and with that of a "meal" (*trophē*) than with that of sacrifice. His language is baldly realistic—the blood "reddens" the altar or the tongue (cf. *Hom. xxiv., in I Cor.*, no. 1, *MPG*, lxi. 200; *Hom. lxxxii., in Matt.*, no. 5, *MPG*, lviii. 743; *De sacerdotio*, iii. 4, *MPG*, xlviii. 642; *Ad illuminandos catecheses*, ii. 2. *MPG*, xlix. 234)—and he uses the epithets "awful" and "fearful" much more often than his predecessors. He feels fully the horror of the thought that a real body and real blood are present instead of the apparent bread and wine. Reflection on the "horror of the blood" appears first in the East in the pseudo-Ambrosian *De sacramentis* (vi. 3) belonging to the early fifth century (see below, II., 2, § 2). But while here emphasis is put on the supposed benefit to us when the blood is offered in a "similitude," Chrysostom remarks that Christ was the first to drink his blood (*Hom. lxxxii., in Matt.*, no. 1, *MPG*, lviii. 739). Compared with later theories of the "killing" or "destruction" of Christ in the eucharistic sacrifice (see below, 5, § 3) Chrysostom's words are very mild. They express rhetorical pathos more than dogmatic theories. In so far as he considers the sacrifice on Calvary, he makes the eucharistic sacrifice only a "symbol" of it. The "sacrificial act" has only spiritual reference to Calvary. Chrysostom, furthermore, is the first distinct witness to the custom which ultimately led almost to a separation of the "mass" and the "communion." He makes it plain that many came to the service, but went away before the communion, and he condemns the practise in strong terms (*Hom. iii., in Eph.*, no. 4, *MPG*, lxii. 29; *De incomprehensibilitate Dei naturæ*, iii. 6, *MPG*, xlviii. 725-726). That he regarded the "sacrifice" and the communion (*metalēpsis*) as two separable acts and the former as a purely "priestly" function is clear.

5. Chrysostom.

4. Medieval Theories: In the West the theological treatment of the mass underwent no essential change during the Middle Ages. Scholasticism merely systematized the earlier conceptions. But certain practical factors had a greater influence in the West than in the East. It must have lowered the sacrament in the popular estimation when it began to be offered for personal ends. As early as the sacramentary named after Gregory the Great and certainly containing material from him (see below, II., 1, § 3) there are masses for cattle pestilence, droughts and floods, storms, times of war, and sickness. Masses were said for the king, for monasteries, for priests, for travelers, and for the oppressed and troubled. As the number of occasions was multiplied the belief sprang up that there was efficacy in the number of masses. A single mass no longer counted for much. In the ancient Church the Lord's Supper was generally celebrated on Sundays and the anniversaries of martyrs; only in particular places, as North Africa, did the communion take place daily. But the latter custom soon spread. In the fifth century we meet with several masses on the same day. The number increased especially in the eighth and ninth centuries, and chapels and oratories and altars were multiplied indefinitely. At the same time the participation of the people steadily grew less. The private masses of the Roman Church (see below, II., 6) are purely hierurgic. The Greek Church has no private mass, allows only one mass on the same day, and has only one altar in each church. After the twelfth century the Roman Church restricted each priest to one mass a day, except under fixed conditions, and forbade masses after noon. The custom of hearing mass without communicating, however, has continued, and there has even grown up a communion without mass (cf. *KL*, iii. 722). Theological discussion during the Middle Ages always treats sacrifice and communion together and lays stress on the latter, because it is based on the ritual, which has never separated the two notions.

1. Practical Factors.

Peter Lombard treats of the sacrifice of the Eucharist only in barest outline (*Sententiæ*, book iv., dist. 12 and 13). He says that the "sacrament of the Eucharist" is a "sacrifice" and that Christ "is offered repeatedly." The "daily offering" is a "reminiscence [*recordatio*] of the sacrifice which was made" and as such is a "memorial and representation of the true sacrifice." It is difficult to realize what the Scholastics and the Fathers before them mean by "representation" and "memorial." Sometimes they contrast the "representation" and the "truth," sometimes they understand the "representation" as a special part of the "truth." As concerns the efficacy of the sacrifice of the mass, Peter says that it brings about the "remission of venial sins" and the "perfection of virtue." Albertus Magnus follows Peter, but far surpasses him in the subtilty of his questions and answers. Thomas Aquinas assumes that the distinction between sacrifice and sacrament is settled and known to everybody, but in the sense that the Eucharist has two sides, not two parts. He sometimes refers to the distinction to remove difficulties, and when he finds it difficult to distinguish the two sides of the Eucharist he says that they are separated, not actually, but logically.

2. Scholastic Dogmaticians. Thomas Aquinas.

Thomas attempts no systematic exposition of the Eucharist, but in part iii. of the *Summa theologica*, questions 73-83 (Parma ed., vol. iv. 332-403), he considers all queries concerning it, ritual and disciplinary as well as dogmatic, which arose in his own mind, and gives definitions of terms and concepts. He propounds, in question 73, the fundamental question whether the Eucharist is a sacrament. In art. 1 he defines a sacrament as that which contains something sacred. A thing can be sacred either absolutely or in relation to something. The Eucharist contains something sacred absolutely, that is, the body of Christ. Consequently the sign (*res*) of a sacrament is given in its very matter (moreover, that which is the sign merely is in the recipient, that is, the grace which is conferred). In art. 4 the different names of the sacrament are explained. It is called a sacrifice, communion, and viaticum; the first with respect to the past, in that it is commemorative of the Lord's passion, which was a true sacrifice; the second with respect to the present, that is, the unity of the Church, into which men are gathered and united by this sacrament; the third signification has respect to the future, in that it is prefigurative of the enjoyment of God which shall be. He comes to the distinction between sacrament and sacrifice in quest. 79, art. 5. To the query whether all punishment for sin is remitted by this sacrament, he answers: it must be said that this sacrament is both a sacrifice and a sacrament, but it has the character of a sacrifice in that it is offered, the character of a sacrament in that it is received. In art. 7 he adds: in that the passion of Christ, in which Christ offered himself a sacrifice (*hostiam*) to God, is represented in this sacrament, it has the character of a sacrifice, but in that an invisible grace is imparted in this sacrament under a visible form (*species*), it has the character of a sacrament. Clearly the concept of sacrament is the more comprehensive. In part ii, 2, quest. 85, Thomas considers sacrifice. He says (art. 3, end) that things are properly called sacrifices when something is done about things offered to God, as when animals are killed, etc. And the name shows this; for it is called "sacrifice" because man makes something sacred (*sacrum facit*). It is not clear how Thomas applies this thought to the eucharistic sacrifice. In III., lxxvii. 7, he comes to the question of the breaking in the Lord's Supper, and finds it a problem, because only the form of the bread is present and the thought may arise that the breaking of the bread is only according to appearance, not according to real truth. Then the question may arise whether Christ's body itself is not broken. Thomas rejects this as unthinkable, because this body is incorruptible and impassible according to its essence and it is present entire in every part (cf. quest. 73, art. 3, "by concomitance"!). So he shows rather that the form can be really broken, and then it follows for him that the breaking of the form is a sacrament of the Lord's passion, which was truly in the body of Christ. Accordingly the sacrifice of the mass is really a sacrifice, something is done in it about Christ, but to the form. Quest. 83, art. 1, whether Christ is sacrificed in this sacrament, confirms this. Most certainly he is sacrificed, in that celebration of this sacrament is a representative image of the passion of Christ, which is the true sacrifice of him. Quest. 76, art. 2, considers the two forms, bread and wine. Since each of the forms after transubstantiation contains Christ entire, the sacrament in one form would not represent the passion of Christ; the body and the blood would be separated. Therefore the image must present both the body and the blood. Accordingly only the double form, or rather the twofold consecration, presents the passion to view with the separation of body and blood in the true sacrifice. The consecration completes the image of the passion, it is the act of the representation of the passion. In quest. 79 Thomas treats of the effects of the sacrament. He distinguishes between what it effects as sacrifice and what it effects as food. He had already remarked (quest. 74, art. 1) that the body of Christ is offered for the salvation of the body, the blood for that of the soul (cf. the teaching of Ambrose, 3, § 2 above). He recurs to this in 79, 1, to add the qualification that such a distinction is valid only by a sort of assimilation, in reality each effects the salvation of both since Christ is present entire in each. He then explains in detail the effect of the sacrament for the attainment of glory (art. 2), the remission of mortal sin (art 3), and the remission of venial sins (art. 4). In art. 5 he declares that the sacrament, in that it is a sacrifice, has "satisfactive" power, but only according to the quantity of devotion and not in place of all punishment, because, if the latter were true, there would be a defect of human devotion. In art. 7 he asks whether this sacrament profits others than those participating, and answers "yes," but only objectively; whoever is not joined to the passion of Christ by faith and love does not attain the benefits. One mass, according to Thomas, has only one effect. But in many masses the offering of the sacrifice is multiplied and therefore the effect of the sacrifice is multiplied. In quest. 79, art. 1, it is stated incidentally that the effect which the passion of Christ produces in the world, this sacrament produces in man.

5. The Council of Trent and Neoscholastic and Modern Speculations: Luther attacked the doctrine of the sacrifice of the mass on two grounds: because Jesus neither performed nor instituted a sacrifice, and because he thought that it savored of salvation by works. He was preeminently successful in the circles which he influenced directly, and he incited the Roman Church to a new defense and approbation of the doctrine. No earlier synodal gathering had accorded it the consideration which it received from the Council of Trent.

1. The Council of Trent.

The "most holy sacrament of the Eucharist" was treated here in the thirteenth session, Oct. 11, 1551, and the "sacrifice of the mass," as though it were a wholly different thing, in the twenty-second session, more than a decade later, Sept. 17, 1562. The thirteenth session sanctioned a conception which had long prevailed, that the sacrifice was not an act of the congregation, but of the priests for the congregation. In the decree of the twenty-second session it was declared that Christ had performed and instituted a sacrifice to "represent" the sacrifice of the cross, so that the "memory" of the latter should endure "to the end of the world" and its "salutary effect might be applied to the remission of the sins which we commit daily" (canon i.; the thought is explained further in canon ii.). The expressions "sacrifice," "offer," and "represent" are used as equivalent. The sacrifice is not a new suffering of Christ, the "sacrificing" is not renewed, but Christ once sacrificed is daily brought before God as such in his real essence. The "victim" (*hostia*) is "one and the same" on the cross and in the mass, and the "one who offers" is the same, only the "manner" is different, there bloody, here in the form of bread and wine, formerly by Christ without a mediary, now by the mediation of the "ministry of priests." The effect is also the same and the sacrifice of the mass is "truly propitiatory"; those who participate under the necessary conditions (faith, reverence, etc.) draw near to God, receive "mercy and grace," and "great crimes and sins" are remitted to them. A qualification, which has in view the sacrament of penance, is noteworthy here—in giving grace God grants only "the gift of penitence." The necessity for the sacrifice of the mass is based on two principles: first that Christ would not have his "priesthood" terminated "by death" but would "remain" in function what he was, and secondly that the "nature of man" requires a "visible" memorial of the sacrifice on the cross. The catechism ordered by the council and issued by Pius V. in 1506 follows (questions 53 sqq.) the decisions of the Council, but with grosser forms of expression. The sacrifice in the mass appears here less representative of that on the cross than repetitive of it. There were two tendencies at work—one which strove not to obscure the cross; another (Jesuitical) which aimed only to exalt the mass.

The last theologian whose doctrine of the mass merits detailed examination is the Jesuit cardinal, Robert Bellarmine (d. 1621). In his exposition (*Disputationes de controversiis Christianæ fidei*, vol. iii., Cologne, 1628) he bases the distinction between sacrament and sacrifice on transubstantiation.

2. Bellarmine.

The sacrifice is propitiatory, "for the remission of sins," but is also effective for "all sorts of benefits." It has efficacy *ex opere operato*, that is, "in itself"; and the *opus operantis*, that is, "any goodness or devotion in him who works," at the most only strengthens the efficacy of the act. Three classes of persons "work" or "offer" in the mass—Christ, the priest, and the Church or the "Christian people," the last-named in very restricted manner. The sacrament benefits only the recipient, the sacrifice all "for whom it is offered"; it benefits by the mere fact of being offered, wherein it is like prayer, and, indeed, it is a "kind of prayer." It has efficacy only from the sacrifice of the cross; but the latter exists now no longer "in fact" but only "in the mind of God," and so can no longer produce effects "immediately." But if it is the sacrifice of the mass which now "effects" what the sacrifice of the cross founded or "earned," then there is a great difference between its "value" and that of the sacrifice of the cross. For "the value of the sacrifice of the mass is finite. . If its value were infinite, it would be vain to offer many masses." Bellarmine has no doubt about the fact, but "the reason is not so certain." He thinks it strange that the "value" of the sacrifice of the mass is "finite," and the reasons which he adduces therefor he offers only "with deference to better judgment."

After the Council of Trent followed the period of Neoscholasticism, in which speculation about the sacrifice of the mass was active, especially in Spain, and stated problems of which the older Scholasticism had not dreamed. The literature increased enormously. A well-ordered survey of it is given by Renz, who thinks its spirit and tendency were neither progressive nor beneficial. Discussion centered about the thought that there was a renewal of the suffering of Christ in the mass. The older Scholasticism had stood rigidly for merely a "memorial of the passion." The new conception maintained that Christ was actually present suffering and dying, at least "in some sort of manner." The way was prepared for the new idea by Hosius, the Dominican Melchior Cano (professor in Salamanca; d. 1560), and others. Cuesta, bishop of Leon and a member of the Council of Trent (d. 1562), and Gaspar do Casal, bishop of Coimbra (d. 1587), first made it a definite theory. Renz designates the doctrine of Cuesta as the "mactation" theory and that of Casal as the "mortification" theory. The former speaks of a "true separation" of the blood from the body of Christ in the Eucharist. "The mass is a sacrifice for this reason, because Christ in a certain way dies and is sacrificed [*mactatur*] by the priest." He is actually "slaughtered" after the manner of animal sacrifice "by virtue of the sacrament," so far as the consecration of the bread has to do "only" with his body and that of the wine "only" with his blood and thus separates one from the other. According to Casal, Christ is in the bread not in his "natural" form and being. He can exercise spiritual functions in the sacramental form, but not the "bodily" ones of seeing, hearing, etc. In entering the sacrament he destines his body "for consumption." Could he die again he would be killed through being consumed. It is a sort of "killing" that he now, when exalted, subjects himself in the sacrament to limitations of space, which are opposed to his real existence. Cuesta's theory was carried farther by the English Cardinal William Allen (q.v.), and the Jesuits Lessius (d. in Louvain 1623), Hurtado (a member of the Collegium Complutense in the 17th cent.), and Cornelius a Lapide (q.v.; d. in Rome 1637). The Dominicans adopted it, and among them Gonet (d. in Bordeaux 1681), Natalis Alexander (d. in Paris 1724), and Gotti (d. in Faenza 1742) were noteworthy advocates of it. On the other hand it found opponents, like Matthæus Galenus (van der Galen), one of the early teachers in Douai, who declared both Cuesta's and Casal's theories absurdities. For him the chief point was that the bread and the wine are so changed in the consecration that they are better adapted to honor God and express our thanks in the offering. He voices a reaction of the idea of communion against that of sacrifice and represents a tendency which has never wholly died out. Bellarmine brought forward a modification of the mortification (Casal's) theory, which has been called the "destruction" theory. Its essential idea is that the communion of the priest is the real "completion" of the sacrifice. The Carmelites, especially the so-called Salamancans (the authors of a *Cursus theologicus* in fourteen volumes published at long intervals at Salamanca, Lyons, and Madrid from 1631 on), advocated this theory, as did also, with some modifications, Malderus (van Malderen), bishop of Antwerp (d. 1633), and the Jesuit John of Lugo, professor in Valladolid and Rome (d. 1660). No form of destruction-mortification theory, however, attained general acceptance, nor did the mactation theory fare better.

3. Neoscholasticism.

Neoscholasticism flourished at the end of the sixteenth century and in the first half of the seventeenth. Then the Jesuits sought to reconcile the conflicting ideas. Representative theologians of the time and tendency were Jacobus Platel, professor in Douai (d. 1681); Thomas Holzklau, professor at Würzburg (d. 1783); and Honoré Tournely, professor at the Sorbonne (d. 1729). St. Alfonso Liguori (d. 1781) held essentially with Bellarmine. No one attempted an independent theory in the eighteenth century except the Spanish Jesuit, Cardinal Alvarez Cienfuegos (d. 1739), who developed the mortification theory to its most extreme form. The nineteenth century witnessed a revival of the older scholastic ideas, while at the same time the later Scholasticism continued influential. The Roman Church had its period of "enlightenment" and a noteworthy tendency of it is what Renz calls the "theory of the continuance of the sacrificial act on the cross." The "school" which advocates this theory was founded by Jakob Frint, professor in Vienna, afterward bishop of St. Pölten (d. 1834). Its best-known representative was J. A. Möhler (d. 1838), who expounds the theory in his *Symbolik*, § 34 (Eng. transl., pp. 235–249). The Church may be regarded figuratively as the ever living Christ, whose atoning and redemptive work it repeats. Christ himself acts in all sacraments. "If then Christ, hidden behind an earthly veil, develops further to the end of the world his entire activity begun on earth, he necessarily presents himself constantly to the Father as sacrifice for men; and the abiding real representation hereof can not fail in the Church, if the complete

4. Later and Present Theories.

historic Christ is to celebrate in it his constant presence." The Church "substituted" the eucharistic Christ for the historic at his own command; "the former is now taken for the latter, because the latter is also the former." So "the eucharistic Savior" too "is to be regarded as the sacrifice for the sins of the world," and all the more because the sacrifice of Christ on the cross, rightly and exactly expressed, is only a part of an organic whole. It was only one form of his love. "And who will venture the assertion that the eucharistic humiliation of the Son of God is not also a part of the sum total of his merit which is imputed to us?" To the liturgical form of the sacrifice Möhler attached no importance. "Faith in the real presence of Christ in the Eucharist is the foundation of the entire conception of the mass; without that presence the Lord's Supper is a mere memorial of the self-immolating Christ. With faith in the real presence of Christ in the Lord's Supper, on the other hand, the past becomes the present." Christ is present then as "what he actually is and in the full comprehension of his services—in a word, as a real sacrifice." The theory of Frint and Möhler has been accepted, more or less completely, by many eminent Roman Catholic theologians—among others by Hirscher, Klee, Veith, Probst, Döllinger, and especially Professor Thalhofer of Munich. On the other hand, the Jesuits J. Perrone (d. 1876) and J. B. Franzelin follow respectively Vasquez and John of Lugo. Gihr now inclines to the latter, although earlier he preferred Vasquez. The Redemptorist J. Herrmann advocates Bellarmine's theory. M. J. Scheeben, professor in Cologne (d. 1888), revived the Augustinian view of the body of Christ. Schwane, Schell, and Schanz attempt restatements of the Möhler-Thalhofer theory. F. S. Renz, professor at Breslau, the most learned historian of the subject and the latest writer upon it, declares that "the presence of the *res externa*, which represents Christ's death, suffices for the mass, and there is no proper *actio sacrificialis*, because it is not an independent sacrifice, but a function pointing to an independent sacrifice." In the spirit of the Fathers he aims, on the one hand, to simplify the doctrine of the mass, on the other hand, to render it more profound, and in summing up results he ascribes to the thoughts of Augustine an abiding value and truth which he finds elsewhere only in the doctrinal decisions of the Council of Trent. (F. KATTENBUSCH.)

II. The Liturgy.—1. Development of the Roman Mass to Gregory I.: The oldest notices of Christian worship in Rome are found in the First Epistle of Clement. It shows that the service followed the Old-Testament model in having a certain fixed order (xl., xli.), and that the Trisagion from Isa. vi. 3, with introductory formula from Dan. vii. 10, was used in the Eucharist in Rome at the end of the first century (xxxiv.). It may be inferred that a prayer like that known later as the "preface prayer" preceded the act of communicating. The long prayer in chaps. lix.-lxi. is generally assumed to have been the common "church prayer" of Rome, and, in any case, gives a clear conception of the manner of prayer in the Roman

1. The First Three Centuries.

"Word-service" (the morning assembly to hear the Word in distinction from the Eucharist, which took place in the evening; see EUCHARIST, § 1). Both epistles of Clement give substantial hints of the preaching of the time (cf. E. von Dobschütz, *Die urchristlichen Gemeinden*, Leipsic, 1902, p. 147); there is a certain fixation and tendency to formalism, the spirit of order having taken the place of the earlier enthusiasm. Prayers and addresses are ascribed to definite officials. At what point in the service the long prayer was inserted is not known; very possibly it followed the homily. Scripture-reading can not have been lacking. In general the Christian service was alike in the East and the West about 100, and that Rome did not differ from the East fifty years later may, perhaps, be shown by the fact that the Roman Bishop Anicetus allowed Polycarp of Smyrna, who was in Rome in 155, to celebrate the Eucharist. The *Shepherd* of Hermas witnesses to an evening service about 150 (Simil. IX., xi. 7), and seems to know of another in which charismatic revelations were tolerated (cf. Von Dobschütz, ut sup., 23 sqq., 235). It says nothing of the Eucharist. The most important step in the development of the Christian service into the mass had certainly been taken by 150; the Word-service and the celebration of the Eucharist had been combined in Rome at any rate on Sundays (Justin, *I Apol.*, lxv.-lxvii.; see EUCHARIST, § 1). According to Justin this combined service was opened with reading of the Gospels and the Prophets by the lector, lasting while the congregation was assembling. Then the *proestōs* made an address, and the church prayer mentioned above followed, including a petition for the authorities, for enemies, and for all men (*I Apol.*, xiv., xvii.; *Trypho*, cxxxiii., xcvi., xxxv.). The kiss of peace came next, and then bread, wine, and water were brought. The *proestōs* offered a long, free prayer of praise and thanksgiving, which probably included the Trisagion and words of institution, the congregation responded "amen," and the deacon administered the sacrament. The next witness (the Canons of Hippolytus, provided they are genuine), two generations later, shows another step in the development of the mass in that the sermon has been omitted from the introductory Word-service in the combined service (xxxvii., xxvi.). The order of a eucharistic service in the time of Hippolytus may be reconstructed as follows: Scripture-reading by the lectors "till the whole congregation is assembled"; the long church prayer by the bishop (xxxvii., cf. xix.), probably beginning with a general confession (ii.); the kiss of peace (xviii.) and the offertory, the givers being probably named. After the offerings have been blessed the preface begins, introduced by responsory formulas between bishop and congregation. The succeeding prayer probably included the Trisagion and the words of institution, and the Epiklesis (q.v.) can not have been lacking. The presbyter or bishop administered the sacrament, the deacon only exceptionally. The congregation advanced to the "table of the body and blood of the Lord," and the formula of distribution was "this is the body, the blood, of Christ." The recipient answered "amen." The conclusion was doubtless a prayer of thanksgiving for the reception of the holy elements and a blessing of the people. Canon xix. mentions a noteworthy custom, old heathen in character, viz., that at the communion of the neophytes, after the bread and wine, they received a cup containing milk and honey mixed. Later sources and Justin (see above) speak also of a cup of water. The milk and honey disappear about 600. When the water went out of use is not known; the Canons of Hippolytus make no mention of it (for further details concerning the custom of the primitive Church, see EUCHARIST).

2. The Fourth and Fifth Centuries.

The first factor in the development of the mass in the centuries immediately following is the dominance of the Latin tongue in divine service. Opinions differ as to when the Latin displaced the Greek (cf. P. Kleinert, *Zur Kultus- und Kulturgeschichte*, p. 30, Berlin, 1889; F. Probst, *Abendländische Messe vom 5. bis zum 8. Jahrhunderte*, pp. 5–6, Münster, 1896; J. Watterich, *Konsekrationsmoment*, pp. 131–132, 267 sqq., Heidelberg, 1896; F. Kattenbusch, *Symbol*, ii. 131, Leipsic, 1897; G. Rietschel, *Liturgik*, i. pp. 337–38, Berlin, 1900; Steinacker in *Festschrift Theodor Gomperz dargebracht*, pp. 324 sqq., Vienna, 1902). But the Greek certainly lasted into the fourth century, and no doubt there was a time when Greek and Latin services were held side by side in Rome and the two tongues were even employed in the same service. With the use of Latin came a shortening of the prayers corresponding to the more concise character of the Latin language. A second factor was the disappearance of the *arcani disciplina* (q.v.), whereby the fusion of the two forms of service became complete, and a third was the influence of the bishops of Rome. It was they who gave the mass its form. Little is known of the details of their changes in the liturgy, but it is certain that they brought foreign usages to Rome and gave to the prayers of the service a local and incidental character under the influence of the church year. The adaptation of the mass to the church year—a vital deviation from the Eastern liturgy—must have been completed in Rome in the fourth century, although Probst (*Liturgie des 4. Jahrhunderts*, pp. 445 sqq., Münster, 1893) goes too far when he ascribes it to Pope Damasus I. (366–384). A famous letter of Innocent I. to Bishop Decentius of Eugubium (Gubbio) shows that by 416 the kiss of peace had been transposed to the end of the canon, and that the present rubrics xxxiii.–xxxvii. were lacking in the time of Innocent. The same letter also shows that the " names " were now read in Rome in the canon, contrary to the usage of Milan, Spain, Gaul, almost the entire East, and earlier Roman custom. The mass in Rome in the time of Innocent I. (beginning of 5th cent.) may be reconstructed as follows: I. Mass of the catechumens: (1) epistle (rubric viii.); (2) gradual and hallelujah (ix.); (3) gospel (x.); (4) sermon; (5) dismissal; (6) mediatory prayer. II. Mass of the faithful: (1) offertory (rubric xii.); (2) secret (offertory prayer, xvii.); (3) preface with sanctus (xviii.); (4) prayer introductory to the words of institution (xxii. and xxiii.); (5) words of institution (xxiv.); (6) anamnesis (xxv.); (7) epiklesis (in place of xxvi., xxvii., and xixa.); (8) prayer of intercession with reading of the diptychs (xixb, xx., xxi., xxviii., xxix.); (9) kiss of peace; (10) communion (xxxvii.); (11) Lord's prayer (xxxi.); (12) postcommunion (xxxix.); (13) blessing; (14) dismissal (*Ite, missa est*, xxxix.). This mass, differing materially from the present (cf. P. Drews, *Zur Entstehungsgeschichte des Kanons in der römischen Messe*, Tübingen, 1902), is that of the Syrian liturgy (latter part of the fourth century) as it can be reconstructed from Cyril of Jerusalem and Chrysostom (cf. F. E. Brightman, *Liturgies, Eastern and Western*, i., Oxford, 1896, pp. 464 sqq., 470 sqq.), somewhat shortened and slightly transposed. In the fifth century greater changes were made. According to the *Liber pontificalis* (ed. Duchesne, i. 230, 239, 263), Celestine I. (422–432) made the service begin with psalm-singing antiphonally by two choirs, Leo I. (440–61) added the closing words *sanctum sacrificium, immaculatam hostiam* to the prayer in the canon *supra quæ* (rubric xxvi.), and Symmachus (498–514) ordered the daily use of the " Gloria in excelsis." It was certainly in this period that the canon received essentially its present form, probably from Gelasius I. (492–496; cf. Drews, ut sup., 34 sqq.) and perhaps after a Milanese model. After Gelasius the formulas of dismissal were omitted, also the mediatory prayer in the mass of the catechumens, the epiklesis was dropped, and the great prayer of intercession was shortened so that the present rubrics xix.–xxi., xxviii., and xxix. are but remnants. Gregory I. (d. 604) undertook no very important changes apart from his revision and restoration of certain prayers and his reform of the music. The order of the mass in his time was substantially as follows: I. Introduction: (1) introit (rubric ii. in the *Sacramentarium Gregorianum*, iv. of the present mass); (2) kyrie (iii., v.); (3) gloria (iv., vi.); (4) collect (v., viii.). II. Mass of the catechumens: (5) epistle (vi., viii.); (6) psalm with hallelujah (vii., ix.); (7) gospel (viii., x.); (8) exclusion of penitents (*Dialogus* ii., 23); (9) offertory (ix.–x., xii.); (10) secret (xi., xvii.). III. Mass of the faithful: (11) preface with sanctus (xi.–xii., xviii.); (12) canon (xii.–xxiii., xix.–xxx.); (13) Lord's prayer (xxiv., xxxi.); (14) embolism (xxv.–xxvi., xxxvi.); (15) kiss of peace (xxxiv.); (16) communion (xxxviii.); (17) postcommunion and *Oratio super populum* (xxxix.); (18) *Ite, missa est* (xxxix.).

The history of the Roman mass shows that the popes felt themselves in no way bound to the traditional liturgical forms and altered them with great freedom. The changes made in the mass in Rome during the first five or six centuries have no parallel in ancient church history unless it be in similar alterations of the ritual of baptism. The reasons for these changes, unfortunately, are not known.

3. The Sources.

The oldest Roman sacramentaries and ordinaries are: (1) The *Sacramentarium Leonianum* (so called because some of its prayers are evidently modeled after sermons of Leo I.), preserved in a single Veronese manuscript of the seventh century. It appears to be a private collection, made by a layman, not an official or semi-official book. Feltoe (*Sacr. Leon.*, Cambridge, 1896, pp. xv.–xvi.) thinks that it is an original manuscript; Duchesne (*Origines*, p. 132, Paris, 1898) that it is a copy, the original dating between 538 and 590. It certainly contains very old prayers.

(2) The so-called *Sacramentarium Gelasianum*, preserved in several manuscripts, of which the oldest, in the Vatican, belongs to the first half of the eighth century or perhaps to the seventh (cf. A. Ebner, *Missale Romanum*, Freiburg, 1896, pp. 238, 374 sqq.). It contains Gregorian and post-Gregorian elements, hence can not, in its present form, derive from Pope Gelasius I. (d. 496). It was written in Gaul, but, apart from later and Frankish insertions, presents the prayers of the Roman mass of the sixth century. (3) The so-called *Sacramentarium Gregorianum*, extant in many widely variant manuscripts (cf. Ebner, ut sup., 380 sqq.), none of which is older than the ninth century; nevertheless the book contains much material which goes back to Gregory I. (4) Various *ordines* (i.e., complete and exact directions for the conduct of a religious service), of which the most important are: (a) the *Ordo I.* published by Mabillon in his *Museum Italicum* (Paris, 1689; reprinted *MPL*, lxxviii.). Grisar (*ZKT*, ix. 1885, pp. 389 sqq.) and Probst (*Sakramentarien und Ordines*, pp. 386–387, Münster, 1892) assign it to Gregory I.; Duchesne (ut sup., 139–140) denies its pure Roman character and dates it in the ninth century. (b) The first of the *ordines* published by Duchesne (ut sup., 439 sqq.), of the ninth century, from the abbey of St. Amand, and partly Roman. (5) A collection of seventeen collects published by Mercati in the seventh part of his *Studi e Testi* (*Antiche reliquie liturgiche Ambrosiane e Romane*, pp. 35–44, Rome, 1902). It is from Bobbio (now in Milan), the manuscript belongs to the sixth or seventh century, and the prayers were inserted one hundred years later. Thirteen of them are also found in other sacramentaries, four were previously unknown.

2. Liturgies Outside of Rome: Besides the Roman liturgy, those of Africa, South Italy, Milan, Gaul, Spain, and the Celtic-Anglo-Saxon are to be considered. Space forbids here to describe each in detail (cf. the Hauck-Herzog *RE*, xii. 708–712); but a comparison of them with one another and with the liturgy of Rome establishes the following facts: (1) Before Rome began in the third or fourth century to make important changes in the liturgy, all western Churches had substantially one and the same structure of divine service, and, furthermore, it was the same as the East had. (2) So far as is known, the African Church was the only one to keep pace with the Roman development, so that there came to be two types: the Roman-African and that of the other Churches. (3) The latter type in all its changes kept much closer to the original scheme than did Rome. On comparing the two western types with the eastern liturgy, it appears that Rome in the fourth century adopted the Syrian scheme, while the remainder of the West followed the Byzantine development. The point at which this becomes evident is the position of the diptychs. Originally, and in the Byzantine liturgy as late as the seventh century, these had their place in connection with the oblation and before the preface, but the Syrian-Palestinian liturgy put them after the epiklesis as early as the fourth century (Brightman, ut sup., pp. 528, 535–536, 466, 474). Rome and Africa adopted the latter position, while elsewhere in the West the old and Byzantine custom was retained. These facts give, in broad outline, the development of the Western mass-liturgy until about the seventh century. Up to that time a strong influence from the East is evident, which even Rome was not able wholly to withstand. After that, however, this influence ceases and Rome begins to impose its liturgy upon the West. The development here set forth is not in accord with views which have been held up to the present. Some, as Neale, distinguish between a Roman and a Gallic-Spanish type, and regard the liturgy of Milan as a mixed form of these two. Ceriani and Magistretti think that the Roman and Milanese forms belong together. Duchesne accepts the division given in the preceding paragraph, but holds that the eastern liturgy first found entrance in the fourth century through the influence of Bishop Auxentius of Milan (355–374), a Cappadocian, and that from Milan, especially under the authority of Ambrose, it spread over Gaul, Spain, and Britain. English liturgists have asserted that the Gallican liturgy was that of Ephesus, brought to Gaul by the founders of the church of Lyons, whence it spread over the entire transalpine West. All these hypotheses are reconciled if it be admitted that originally everywhere in the West and in the East there was one and the same liturgy, which suffered change more rapidly and radically in Rome than elsewhere.

1. General Character and Relations.

For **Africa** the important witnesses are Tertullian (*Apol.*, xxii., xxx., xxxi., xxxii., xxxix.; *De corona*, iii.; *De exhortatione castitatis*, xi.; *De fuga in persecutione*, ii.; *De jejunio*, xv.; *De monogamia*, x., xii.; *De præscriptione hæreticorum*, xxxvi., xli.; *Ad Scapulam*, iv.; *De oratione*, iii., xi., xviii., xxix.; *Ad uxorem*, ii. 9), Cyprian (*Epist.*, xii. 2, xxxiv. 1; *Ad Demetrium*, xx.; *De oratione domini*, viii., xxxi.), and—150 years later—Augustine (*Confessiones*, ix. 13; *Sermones*, clix., clxxii., ccxxvii.; cf. G. Rietschel, *Liturgik*, i. 299–300, Berlin, 1900). The early mass of **Milan** may be reconstructed from notices in Ambrose (for the passages collected, cf. J. Pamelius, *Liturgica Latinorum*, i. 266 sqq., Cologne, 1571), supplemented by the works mentioned below in the bibliography. The value of the *De sacramentis*, ascribed to Ambrose, is impaired by grave doubts as to its genuineness. Probst (*Liturgie*, pp. 232 sqq., Münster, 1893) and Morin (*Revue bénédictine*, xi. 344 sqq., 1894) think it is a secondary writing based on Ambrose, Rietschel (ut sup., p. 305, note 5) that it is Roman, Ceriani (*Notitia*, pp. 62–63, 65, Milan, 1897) and Magistretti (*Liturgia*, p. 85, Milan, 1899) that it is Gallican, Duchesne (*Origines*, p. 169, Paris, 1898) that it was composed in a North Italian city, perhaps Ravenna, about 400. For **Gaul**, besides scanty notices in *Irenæus* (*Hær.*, iv. 2, 18) and a little fuller information in Hilary of Poitiers (d. 367; *Ad Constantium*, i. 2; *Fragmenta*, viii.; *Contra Constantium*, xxvii.; *De trinitate*, iii. 7) and Sulpicius Severus (d. 410 or 420; *Vita S. Martini*, ix.; *Chron.*, ii. 39), the chief sources are: (1) Eleven masses published by Mone (see bibliography); the manuscript is probably of the seventh century, but the masses are older; Roman influence is not evident. (2) Two letters doubtfully ascribed to Germanus of Paris (d. 576; in *MPL*, lxxii. 89 sqq.); the first, which is purely Gallican and belongs to the sixth century, permits reconstruction of the mass in its essential features (cf. the Hauck-Herzog *RE*, xii. 709–710). (3) The so-called *Missale Gothicum*, probably from Autun; the manuscript is of the late seventh or early eighth century; apart from inserted Roman prayers, the structure of the mass is Gallican and the book gives the liturgy of the sixth or seventh century. (4) The so-called *Missale Gallicanum vetus*, of the seventh or early eighth century, belonging perhaps to the diocese of Besançon; it is probably a composite of two different mass-books (cf. Delisle in *Mémoires de l'Institute de France*, 1886, i. 73 sqq.; F. Kattenbusch, *Apostolisches Symbol*, ii. 774, 776, note 28, Leipsic, 1900); Roman influences are very strong. (5) The so-called *Sacramentarium Gallicanum* (*Missale Vesontiense* or *Bobbiense*), of the seventh century; it has been assigned to Bobbio and Luxeuil, probably belongs to Gaul, and Roman influence is strong. (6) The Lectionary of Luxeuil (*MPL*, lxxii. 171 sqq.), purely Gallican, and containing the lessons for the entire year; it is doubtful if it was used in Luxeuil. (7) The so-called *Missale Francorum*, of the early eighth century or end of the seventh; Roman influence is so strong that Duchesne (ut sup., 128) and Ebner (*Missale Romanum*, p. 364, Freiburg, 1896) class it among Roman mass-books, but it originated and was used in the Frankish realm. (8)

2. The Sources.

The Sacramentary of the abbey of St. Remigius at Relms, written 798–800; the original was burned in 1774, but an incomplete copy is in the Bibliothèque Nationale in Paris (published by Chevalier in the seventh part of the *Bibliothèque liturgique*, pp. 305–357, Paris, 1900); it is essentially Roman. The earliest sources for the liturgy in **Spain** are the acts of certain councils (Gerundia, 517, canon i., cf. H. T. Bruns, *Canones apostolorum et conciliorum*, ii. 18, Berlin, 1839; Valencia, 524, i., in Bruns, ii. 24, cf. the First Toledo, 398, ii., iv., in Bruns, i. 204; Braga, 563, in Bruns, ii. 33; Third Toledo, 589, ii., in Bruns, i. 213; Fourth Toledo, 633, x., xii., xiv., in Bruns, i. 225–226, 227, 228), Isidore of Seville (d. 636; *De officiis ecclesiasticis*, i. 6, 13–18, ii. 5, 7—on the genuineness of the chapter *De acoluthis*, cf. T. Kliefoth, *Liturgische Abhandlungen*, ii. 289, Schwerin, 1859;—*Etymologiæ*, VI., xix. 4; *Epist.*, i. *ad Leudefridum*, ii. *ad Redemptum*), and the so-called *Missale mixtum*, *Goticum*, or *Mozarabicum*. The liturgy published at the instance of Cardinal Ximenes in 1500 (see MOZARABIC LITURGY) contains, it is true, much that is Roman and Gallican, but the original Spanish basis can be separated with some certainty; there are unpublished old Spanish masses still extant in manuscript (cf. Rietschel, ut sup., i. 320). For the sources of the Celtic-Anglo-Saxon and Neapolitan liturgies, see the bibliography below; they are scanty and the Roman coloring is so strong that the original forms can not be recovered.

3. The Supplanting of the non-Roman Liturgies by the Roman: Two factors worked together to bring about general conformity to the Roman ritual—the repute and might of Rome in all things ecclesiastical, and, even more strongly, the desire to make an end of the infinite variety in cultic forms. The popes did not set themselves strenuously to impose Roman usages on other districts, least of all Gregory I.; and the impulse to introduce the cult and order of Rome came from the extra-Roman lands themselves.

1. Africa, Spain, Milan, and Great Britain.

The process doubtless began spontaneously and proceeded at first unnoticed. Africa as a matter of course went with Rome. Elsewhere the first definite fact in the history appears in 538, when Bishop Profuturus of Braga, metropolitan of the kingdom of the Suevi, asked Pope Silverius for advice concerning liturgical questions. Vigilius, successor of Silverius, sent the baptismal liturgy, the canon of the mass, and the Easter prayers to show how things were done in Rome. At a council in Braga in 563 this papal letter was read and it was ordered to conduct the mass after the Roman model (cf. H. T. Bruns, *Canones apostolorum et conciliorum*, ii. 34, Berlin, 1839). But the West Goths established their church in the Spanish peninsula and jealously guarded its independence against Rome, and synods and other assemblies still tried to effect uniformity in worship (e.g., the Fourth Synod of Toledo, 633, canon ii.; Eleventh Provincial Synod of Toledo, 675, iii.; cf. Bruns, ut sup., i. 221, 309). The canon of the *Missale mixtum* (see above, 2, § 2) shows that Rome did not remain wholly without influence, and the Frankish-Germanic Church also made itself felt. Alexander II. introduced the Roman ritual into Aragon (1068), and Gregory VII. induced a synod at Burgos in 1085 to declare the Roman liturgy valid for all Spain. Only Toledo, the former center of the West Gothic Church, retained the old Spanish liturgy till 1285, and Cardinal Ximenes obtained for six churches of Toledo (to which a chapel in Salamanca was afterward added) papal permission to use the old native liturgy, though with many Roman modifications (see MOZARABIC LITURGY); the permission is still valid. Milan probably admitted Roman influence early and all known Milanese liturgies have only the Roman canon. It still had its own (though much romanized) mass as late as the ninth century, which passed for Ambrosian (Walafrid Strabo in *MPL*, cxiv. 944, cxlvii. 583), and it still retains certain peculiarities. The Roman liturgy was doubtless carried to England by Augustine; but the Iro-Scottish missionaries who converted the greater number of the Anglo-Saxons (see ANGLO-SAXONS, CONVERSION OF THE) naturally brought with them their own ritual. Theodore of Tarsus (q.v.), a Greek, appointed archbishop of Canterbury in 668 and the real founder of the English Church, was not strenuous for Roman forms; but others about him were differently minded, and the Council of Clovesho in 747 prescribed the Roman ritual for all England (Haddan and Stubbs, *Councils*, iii. 367). Nevertheless mass-books up to the Norman Conquest (the Leofric Missal, Missal of Robert of Jumièges, Missal of St. Augustine's Abbey of Canterbury, ed. M. L. Rule, Cambridge, 1896) show many non-Roman features, and usage was not uniform. The like is true for Ireland. Adamnan (q.v.) induced the Synod of Tara in 692 to decree that the native usages should be given up, but not until the twelfth century were Roman forms energetically introduced by Malachy of Armagh (see MALACHY O'MORGAIR, SAINT) and Gilbert of Limerick, and, finally, by the Synod of Cashel in 1172. In Scotland the break with the old liturgy was made in the eleventh century (see CELTIC CHURCH IN BRITAIN AND IRELAND).

2. France and Germany.

It is probable that Roman mass-books were brought to Gaul in the time of Cæsarius of Arles (q.v.) and through him (cf. F. J. Mone, *Lateinische und Griechische Messen*, pp. 112 sqq., Frankfort, 1850; Bäumer in *Historisches Jahrbuch*, xiv. 1893, p. 205); but the result at first was merely the substitution of certain prayers for those formerly in use. The structure of the mass was not altered thereby, although the new prayers often did not fit the places in which they were inserted and thus prepared the way for more fundamental changes, which first become evident about the middle of the seventh century. In the time of Gregory I. (d. 604) there was a very manifest difference between the Gallican and the Roman masses (*Epist.*, lvi.*a*, in *MGH*, *Epist.*, ii. 1895, p. 331) and Gregory does not appear as a zealous partizan of the latter. During the sixth century the Roman sacramentary made its way to Gaul and was often copied, and its influence comes to light in the Gallican missals and sacramentaries of the seventh or eighth century—an influence which reached much farther in some places than in others (cf. the *Sacramentarium Gelasianum*, which presents certain Gallican peculiarities with the Roman structure, and the *Sacramentarium Gallicanum*, in which the preface and the mass of the catechumens are essentially Gallican in structure, with some prayers wholly Roman, and the mass of the faithful entirely Roman). The monasteries were probably the chief promoters of changes. In the seventh century they were steadily adopting the Benedictine rule, which had a minute ordering of the hours after Roman models. Thereby the interest of the monks was directed to the Roman mass-liturgy, and the mixed services may have been held first in the monastery chapels. Boniface (q.v.) stood strongly for the Roman liturgy without being able to carry his reforms through in details. What Pepin did for the Roman ritual in his realm (apart from the introduction of the music) is uncertain, but Charlemagne held the Roman forms in the highest esteem and accounted it a sacred duty to introduce them and thereby to make an end of the prevailing confusion in the liturgy. At his request Pope Adrian I. sent him between 784 and 791 a copy of the sacramentary then in use in Rome; but it proved disappointing because of the many departures from the pre-Gregorian form. A compromise was attempted by providing a new mass-book with select prayers and other liturgical forms taken mostly from the pre-Gregorian mass-book (manuscripts of this sort enumerated in A. Ebner, *Missale Romanum*, pp. 383–384, Freiburg, 1896). The selection was probably made by Alcuin, and Amalarius of Metz advocated the Roman liturgy (cf. his *De ecclesiasticis officiis*, *MPL*, cv. 986 sqq.). In time the Roman canon attained general acceptance; but the entire Roman ritual did not become established in either France or Germany during the Middle Ages, nor was a general uniformity reached. During the entire period the mass-liturgy in Frankish-German territory was constantly changing, and, whatever the theory may have been, the practise was far removed from a slavish following of Rome. There was a vigorous liturgical life north of the Alps, having its center in the monasteries, which even reacted on the later Roman development.

4. The Development of the Roman Mass after Gregory I.: The mass of Rome in the time of Innocent III. (d. 1216) is known from that pope's writing *De sacro altaris mysterio* (*MPL*, ccxvii. 773 sqq.). No great changes have taken place in the six hundred years since Gregory I.;

1. Certain Additions.

certain additions have been made, some of them brought in from outside and some devised in Rome. The most noteworthy are a rather elaborate preparation of the priest in the sacristy, the insertion of the *credo* after the Gospel in what was formerly the mass of the catechumens, and ceremonial amplifications—washing of hands, burning of incense, etc.—to fill the gap left by the transposition of the kiss of peace and the commemoration into the canon. The most striking characteristic is the endeavor to treat the holy elements as something superearthly. That the doctrine of the sacrificial character of the mass influenced the development can not be asserted; but the tendency to restrict the active participation of the congregation is much stronger than it is north of the Alps. After Innocent the preparation was simplified, and the old offertory prayers in shorter form and the epiklesis were restored after the offertory—a conformity to German usage. A superstitious practise, the reading of the prologue to John's Gospel, found entrance. This prologue was much used as an amulet during the Middle Ages, and a synod at Seligenstadt in 1022 condemned the reading of it in the mass. Nevertheless the custom spread and Pope Pius V. in 1570 officially sanctioned it in the conclusion after the last salutation. It thus appears that the development after the year 600 brought far fewer and much less important changes than did the first five centuries. Moreover, the changes for the most part were a concession on the part of Rome to extra-Roman usage. That the result is an artistic unity, a well-ordered liturgical structure, can hardly be asserted.

The present Roman missal dates from 1634, all earlier efforts to secure uniformity in the mass of the Church having proved fruitless. The Council of Trent in its session of Dec. 4, 1563, left the issuing of a common mass-book to the pope, a commis-

2. The Roman Missal.

sion entrusted with the task not having completed its work. In consequence the missal of Pius V. appeared on July 14, 1570, with the decree that it alone should be used wherever the Roman rite was followed and there was no local mass-book 200 years old. But differences crept in, and in 1604 Clement VIII. issued a new book thoroughly revised by a commission. Urban VIII. did the like, and the final revision appeared Sept. 2, 1634. This pope made the present division of the entire mass into forty-one rubrics, the first eighteen being counted to the ordinary and the last twenty-three to the canon. The Congregation of Rites, established by Sixtus V. in 1587, safeguards the purity of the ritual (see CURIA). The missal falls into three main divisions: (1) The "Proper of Masses of the Season" (*Proprium missarum de tempore*) contains (a) the services for each day from the First Sunday in Advent to Holy Saturday; (b) the "Ordinary of the Mass" (*Ordo missæ*); (c) the prefaces for the entire year; (d) the "Canon of the Mass" (*Canon missæ*); and (e) the services from Easter to the end of the church year. (2) The "Proper of Masses of the Saints" (*Proprium missarum de sanctis*) gives the services for saints' days and for festivals of mysteries and important events (such as the Transfiguration, the Invention and Elevation of the Cross, etc.), arranged according to months of the civil year. (3) The "Common of Saints" (*Commune sanctorum*) contains the masses for those saints' days which have no mass of their own; it is divided into masses of the apostles, martyrs, confessors, virgins, and women. A sort of supplement gives the mass for church consecrations and their anniversaries, the votive masses in honor of mysteries and for various occasions, the *orationes diversæ*, i.e., prayers for different occasions, and finally the masses for the dead.

[The modern missal begins with a table of movable feasts and the calendar. Then follow the "General Rubrics of the Mass," the "Rite to be Followed in the Celebration of the Mass," and "Defects which may Occur in the Celebration of the Mass," explaining the various kinds of masses, the component parts, the hours of celebration, the kind and color of vestments, the conduct of the priest, and the like. The "Preparation for the Mass," a brief devotional manual, and a collection of prayers and thanksgiving, to be used as occasion offers, come next. Then follow the "Proper of the Season," the "Proper of Saints," the "Common of Saints," etc., as above. An appendix adds "Masses for Certain Places in the United States of America.]

5. The Withholding of the Cup: The Council of Constance in its thirteenth session (June 15, 1415) declared it the law of the Church that the laity should partake of but one element in the communion. The Council of Trent in its twenty-first session (chap. iii., canons i.–iii.) approved the earlier decree. The practise was no innovation and the action at Constance merely gave official sanction to a custom of long standing, which had its roots in the earliest times. The belief that the bread was the more important of the two elements may appear even in the New Testament, where bread is mentioned more frequently than the cup (cf. Luke xxiv. 30). It is more clearly evident in the ancient custom of celebrating the Supper with bread and water instead of wine (Chrysostom, *Hom. in Matt.*, lxxxiii. 4; *Hom. in Gen.*, xxix. 3). To this was added the horror which believers felt if a crumb of the consecrated bread or a drop of the blessed wine fell on the floor (Tertullian, *De corona*, iii.; *Canones Hippolyti*, ccix.; Origen, *Hom. in Exod.*, xiii. 3; Trullan Council of 692, canon ci.; Cæsarius of Arles, *MPL*, xxxix. 2319). Consequently very early the Supper was celebrated with bread alone (*Acta Joannis*, ed. T. Zahn, p. 244, Erlangen, 1880). Pope Gelasius I. (492–496) declared against the practise in Calabria (*MPL*, lix. 141). When it became customary for the communicant to receive the host, not in his own hand, but in open mouth from the hand of the priest, he was freed from all responsibility so far as the one element was concerned. It was natural to seek for a like immunity in case of the other. A means to the end desired was found by dipping the host in the wine and using a spoon (intinction). The custom originated in the East, where it is still followed (see EASTERN CHURCH, III., § 5); the earliest evidence of it in the West belongs to the seventh century. That it originated from the laity is probable, and it is certain that the clergy did not always approve of it (synods at Braga, 675, canon i.; Clermont, 1095, xxviii.; London, 1175, xvi.). Paschal II. calls it a "human and new-fangled institution" (*Epist.* ccclv., *MPL*, clxiii. 442). It spread rapidly in England. Another means to the same end was the use of tubes (*fistulæ, cannæ*, etc.; see FISTULA), which appear from the ninth century. It was not a very far step for the people to renounce the wine altogether, which happened first in the twelfth century and, so far as is known, in England. It is thus a misuse of terms to speak of "withholding" or "withdrawing" the cup; there was a voluntary renunciation, though scarcity of wine in some places may have helped to establish the practise. Later the priests interpreted their partaking of both elements as a prerogative and privilege of their order, though the scholastic theology developed the doctrine that Christ is received whole and entire in each of the elements.

6. Kinds of Masses. The Roman Church classifies masses according to two systems, depending on the time of celebration and the degree of solemnity. From the first point of view masses are either (1) masses of the season (*de tempore*), i.e., masses on Sundays and festivals; (2) masses on saints' days (*missæ de sanctis*); (3) votive masses (*missæ votivæ*, i.e., said by choice—*votum*—of the priest); or (4) masses for the dead (*missæ pro defunctis*) or requiem masses. The votive masses subdivide into (a) those connected with a special exigency or wish concerning the entire Church, single dioceses or congregations (e.g., in times of war and pestilence, in droughts, at church consecrations, for the king, for the sick, at coronations, conclaves, etc.), or individuals (at weddings, birthdays, anniversaries, etc.); and (b) those in honor of certain mysteries (the Trinity, the Holy Spirit, angels, etc.). The proper character of a mass appears in the collects, the antiphons, the lessons, the secrets, etc. This feature is old; the *Sacramentarium Leonianum* contains the most varied kind of collects, secrets, and prefaces and postcommunions. From the second point of view masses are either (1) public or solemn (*missæ publicæ vel solemnes;* high masses) or (2) private (*missæ privatæ*). A public or solemn mass is characterized by a larger number (*frequentia*) of ministrants; that is, deacon, subdeacon, and certain subordinate attendants are present. Incense is burned, the number of altar-lights is greater than on other occasions, and the mass is sung. Such masses are held in parish churches on Sundays and festivals, in collegiate and cathedral churches daily. But since in smaller churches the necessary number of clergy is lacking, a substitute for the *missa solemnis* is provided in the *missa cantata* [or media, which is sung without deacon or subdeacon and the ceremonies proper to high mass]; it is, however, often designated as high mass. A congregation must attend either a *missa solemnis* or *cantata*, as both are "public." The private mass, on the contrary, may be held without the congregation and therefore dispenses with the singing and larger number of ministrants. Only the celebrant and one ministrant are required and the latter in certain cases may be a layman. Since the mass is read it is also called *missa lecta*. Evidently any particular mass may belong to both of the main classifications. A *missa de tempore* may also be *solemnis publica* or *cantata publica;* a *missa votiva* may be private; and a requiem mass may be either solemn or private. (P. DREWS.)

Other names which are given to masses are: pontifical, designating a solemn mass celebrated by a bishop with his insignia; papal, celebrated by the pope on certain great feasts with special rites; low, a mass without music, the priest saying and not singing the mass; capitular, the high mass on Sundays or festivals in collegiate churches; conventual or canonical, the daily mass of cathedral and collegiate churches celebrated solemnly and with music after tierce in memory of the founders. A *missa adventitia* or *manualis* (a "chance" mass, one which "comes to hand") is a mass said for the intention of a person who gives an alms, opposed to a *missa legata*, said for a special intention in consequence of a legacy or foundation. The so-called mass of the presanctified is an office with a communion, but is not a mass in the strict sense of the word, the elements used having been consecrated at a previous occasion (whence the name, *missa præsanctificatorum* [*elementorum*]). It is said in the Greek Church throughout Lent, except Saturdays, Sundays, and the Feast of the Annunciation, and in the Roman Church on Good Friday (see Holy Week). What was known as a dry mass (*missa sicca*), without consecration or communion, was common in the Middle Ages in presence of the sick, at sea, and on other occasions when a real mass could not be said.

7. Modern Procedure in the Mass: The high mass on Sundays is usually preceded by a rite called the *Asperges;* the celebrant goes down the middle aisle, or at least to the sanctuary gates, sprinkling the people with holy water while the choir sings the anthem *Asperges me hyssopo* (Ps. li. 7). The celebrant then changes his cope for the sacrificial vestment, the chasuble (see Vestments and Insignia, Ecclesiastical), and recites the introductory prayers of the mass proper while the choir sings the ninefold *Kyrie eleison*, followed (except in Advent and Lent and at requiem masses) by the *Gloria in excelsis*. Next come the collect, epistle, and gospel, changing with each day; the epistle is sung by the subdeacon at the south end of the altar, as being addressed originally to the faithful, while the deacon sings the gospel, originally proclaimed to an unbelieving world, toward the north, symbolically the quarter of darkness. Lights are carried at the gospel to typify Christ, the light of the world; and the priest kisses the book at the end in token of reverence for the words of the master. The sermon usually comes next, being in most instances an exposition of the gospel for the day. The Nicene creed is then sung, all kneeling at the words "And was incarnate and was made man," in honor of the incarnation. The following section is called the offertory; the priest solemnly offers on the altar first the bread to be consecrated, then the wine mixed with a little water as representing the twofold nature of Christ. Next comes the preface, varying with the feast or mystery commemorated, and leading up to the *Sanctus*. By the time the choir has finished this, the celebrant has already begun the most solemn part of the mass, which he recites in a low, almost inaudible voice—a relic of the days of persecution when the most sacred mysteries had to be kept secret from the heathen world. The bell, which has already been rung three times at the *Sanctus*, is rung once at the beginning of this part (called the canon or prayer of consecration) and three times at the consecration of each of the elements. After the canon the priest sings the Lord's Prayer to a very ancient melody, the final clause coming in as a response by the choir and congregation. The next noticeable ceremony is the "kiss of peace" which in modern usage is reduced to the celebrant's placing his hands on the deacon's shoulders and inclining the head slightly toward him; this ceremonial embrace of Christian brotherhood is then conveyed by the deacon to the subdeacon and by him to any other clergy who happen to be present. Presently follows the consummation of the sacrifice in the priest's communion, preceded by a prayer of humility at which the bell is again rung. As a rule the priest communicates alone at a high mass, the time for general communion, owing to the strict requirement of fasting, being early in the morning. After the ablutions, or cleansing of the sacred vessels, the post-communion prayers are said, and the priest gives the blessing (omitted in masses for the dead). Then, at the north end of the altar, he recites the second gospel, usually John i. 14, while the choir sings a prayer for the state (in monarchical countries for the sovereign) or for the pope. Incense is used at the introit or beginning of the mass, at the gospel, at the *Sanctus*, and at the consecration. The color of the vestments differs with the day or season. White is used on feasts of Christ, the Virgin Mary and other virgins not martyrs, and confessors; red in Whitsuntide and on feasts of martyrs, typifying the fire of the Holy Spirit or the blood of the martyrs; violet in Advent and Lent; black on Good Friday and at masses for the dead; and on ordinary days green, the color of nature or of hope.

Bibliography: On I.: F. S. Renz, *Die Geschichte des Messopfer-Begriffs*, 2 vols., Freising, 1901–02; Bingham, *Origines*, XIII., i. 4–6, XV., iv. 4; J. J. I. von Döllinger, *Die Eucharistie in den ersten drei Jahrhunderten*, Mainz, 1826; J. W. F. Höfling, *Die Lehre der ältesten Kirche vom Opfer im Leben und Cultus der Christen*, Erlangen, 1851; J. N. Diepolder, *Das Wesen des eucharistischen Opfers und der . . Theologen der drei letzten Jahrhunderten*, Augsburg, 1877; J. M. Ragon, *La Messe*, Paris, 1882; C. Rohault de Fleury, *La Messe; études archéologiques sur ses monuments*, 8 vols., ib. 1883–89; J. Schwane, *Die eucharistische Opferhandlung*, Freiburg, 1889; F. Kattenbusch, *Vergleichende Confessionskunde*, i. 414 sqq., Freiburg, 1892; D. Rock, *Hierurgia; or the Holy Sacrifice of the Mass*, 2 vols., London, 1892; J. M. A. Vacant, *Hist. de la conception du sacrifice de la messe dans l'église latine*, Paris, 1894; O. J. Reichel, *Solemn Mass at Rome in the Ninth Century*, London, 1895; N. Gihr, *Die heiligen Sakramente der katholischen Kirche*, 3 vols., Freiburg, 1897; idem, *Das heilige Messopfer, dogmatisch, liturgisch und asketisch erklärt*, 8th ed., ib. 1907, Eng. transl. of sixth ed., *The Holy Sacrifice of the Mass, dogmatically, liturgically and ascetically explained*, St. Louis, 1908; C. H. H. Wright, *The Service of the Mass in the Greek and Roman Churches*, London, 1898; A. Franz, *Die Messe im deutschen Mittelalter*, Freiburg, 1902; W. Götzmann, *Das eucharistische Opfer nach der Lehre der älteren Scholastik*, Freiburg, 1902; A. Baumstark, *Die Messe im Morgenland*, Kempten, 1906; A. Devine, *The Ordinary of the Mass, historically, liturgically and exegetically explained*, New York, 1907; *The Roman Breviary. A Translation by John Marquess of Bute*, Edinburgh, 1908. Incidental topics are discussed in J. H. Matthews, *The Mass and its Folklore*, London, 1903; J. Hunkey, *Two Leading Doctrines of the Catholic Church; Analysis of the Mass*, Atchison, 1904; S. D. Headlam, *The Meaning of the Mass*, London, 1905. On the name consult: Rottmanner, in *TQ*, 1889, pp. 531 sqq.; Kellner, in *TQ*, 1901, pp. 427 sqq.

II. On the liturgical side an immense literature is opened up in the three sections of the *British Museum Catalogue* devoted to Liturgies. Information upon the manuscripts and the earliest printed editions is found in J. Weale, *Bibliographia liturgica. Catalogus missalium ritus Latini*, London, 1886; and in A. Ebner, *Quellen und Forschungen zur Geschichte und Kunstgeschichte des Missale Romanum im Mittelalter*, Freiburg, 1896. The most important collections are: J. Pamelius, *Liturgica Latinorum*, 2 parts, Cologne, 1571, reissued under the title *Rituale patrum Latinorum sive liturgicon Latinum*, ib. 1675; L. Muratori, *Liturgia Romana vetus*, 2 vols., Venice, 1748, Naples, 1776; J. Mabillon, *Museum Italicum*, Paris, 1687–89, 2d ed., 1724; E. Martène, *De antiquis ecclesiæ ritibus*, 3 vols., Rouen, 1700–02 and often; Cabrol and Leclercq, *Monumenta ecclesiæ liturgica*, vol. i., part 1,

Paris, 1902. Special editions of the different sacramentaries are: of the *Sacramentarium Leonianum*, by C. L. Feltoe, Cambridge, 1896; of the *Sacramentarium Gelasianum*, by H. A. Wilson, Oxford, 1894; the *Sacramentarium Gregorianum* is in *MPL*, lxxviii. 25 sqq. For Gallican liturgies consult: J. M. Thomasius (G. M. Tomasi), *Codices sacrament. nongentis annis vetustiores*, Rome, 1680 (first to contain the *Missale Gothicum, Francorum*, and *Gallicanum vetus*); F. J. Mone, *Lateinische und griechische Messen aus dem 2.-6. Jahrhundert*, Frankfort, 1850; J. M. Neale, and G. H. Forbes, *The Ancient Liturgies of the Gallican Church now first Collected*, Burntisland, 1855 (contains the *Missale Gothicum* and *Gallicanum* and the *Sacramentarium Gallicanum*, also the *Missale Richenovense*); U. Chevalier, *Sacramentaire et martyrologe de l'abbaye de S. Remy*, Paris, 1900. Spanish liturgies: the *Missale mixtum* (*Mozarabicum*), ed. P. Hagenbach, first appeared Toledo, 1500, new ed. by Asevedo, Rome, 1755, *MPL*, lxxxv., latest ed., Toledo, 1875. The Milan liturgy was printed Milan, 1499; other editions are: J. Pamelius, *Liturgica Latina*, i. 293–306, Cologne, 1571, reproduced in F. Probst, *Abendländische Messe*, pp. 14 sqq., Münster, 1896; ed. of C. Borromeo, Milan, 1560, and often; cf. E. Martène, *De antiquis ecclesiæ ritibus*, i. 173–176, Bassano, 1787; M. Gerbert, *Monumenta vetera liturgica Alemanniæ*, vol. i., St. Blas, 1777; Berold, *Ecclesiæ Ambrosianæ Mediolanensis kalendarium*, ed. M. Magistretti, Milan, 1894; A. Ceriani, *Notitiæ literariæ Ambrosianæ ante seculum xi. medium*, pp. 2 sqq., Milan, 1895; M. Magistretti, *Pontificale in usum ecclesiæ Mediolani*, ib. 1897. The Neapolitan and Capuan lectionary was edited by Morin in his *Anecdota Maredsolana*, i (1893), 426–435, 436–444. On the Celtic and Anglo-Saxon Liturgy consult: F. E. Warren, *The Liturgy and Ritual of the Celtic Church*, Oxford, 1881; on the Stowe Missal, MacCarthy, in *Transactions of the Royal Irish Academy*, xxvii. 7 (1886); M. L. Rule, *The Missal of St. Augustine's Abbey*, Canterbury, 1896.

For the medieval explanations of the liturgy, important historically, *MPL* is the great source. Individual expositions are found as follows: Isidor of Seville, *MPL*, lxxxiii. 738 sqq.; Rabanus Maurus, ib., cvii. 321 sqq.; Walafrid Strabo, ib., cxiv. 919 sqq.; Amalarius of Metz, ib., cv. 986; Berno of Reichenau, ib., cxlii. 1055 sqq.; Pseudo-Alcuin, ib., ci. 1173 sqq.; Micrologus, ib., cli. 974 sqq. (for a detailed description of the celebration of the mass north of the Alps in the 11th century drawn from the *Micrologus*, cf. Hauck-Herzog, *RE*, xii. 717–718); Hildebert of Tours, ib., clxxi. 1158; Rupert of Deutz, ib., clxx. 13 sqq.; Honorius of Autun, ib., clxxii, 543 sqq., 737 sqq.; Innocent III., ib., ccxvii. 763 sqq. A collection of expositions was made by M. Hittorpius, *De divinis catholicæ ecclesiæ officiis et mysteriis*, Cologne, 1568, ed. G. Ferrarius, Rome, 1591, 3d ed., Paris, 1610.

Noteworthy investigations are: T. Kliefoth, *Liturgische Abhandlungen*, vols. ii., iii., v., vi., Schwerin, 1859; H. A. Köstlin, *Geschichte des christlichen Gottesdienstes*, pp. 91 sqq., Freiburg, 1887; F. Probst, *Liturgie des 4. Jahrhunderts und deren Reform*, Münster, 1893; M. Magistretti, *La Liturgia della chiesa Milanese nel secolo iv.*, Milan, 1899; L. Duchesne, *Origenes du culte chrétien*, Paris, 1902. The literature on the subject treated in II., 5, is collected in J. Smend, *Kelchversagung und Kelchspendung in der abendländischen Kirche*, Göttingen, 1898; cf. Funk, in *Kirchengeschichtlichen Abhandlungen und Untersuchungen*, i (1897), 293–308, and *Zeitschrift für praktische Theologie*, xxi (1899), 82 sqq. Much of the material cited under LITURGICS will be found pertinent and helpful.

MASSALIANS. See MESSALIANS.

MASSILIANS. See SEMI-PELAGIANISM.

MASSILLON, mās″sî″lyōn′, **JEAN BAPTISTE:** French prelate and famous preacher; b. at Hyères (12 m. e. of Toulon) June 24, 1663; d. at Clermont Sept. 18, 1742. He was the son of a notary. In 1681 he entered the Congregation of the Oratory. At first he believed himself fitted rather for the life of a student and teacher than for the pulpit, and taught for some time at Pézenas and then in 1689 at Montbrison. But his superiors divined his talent for preaching, and commissioned him to deliver the funeral orations for Villars, archbishop of Vienne, and Villeroy, archbishop of Lyons (1693) and his Lenten sermons at Montpellier in 1698 attracted general attention. His success drew ill will upon him, and he was obliged for a time to go into retirement; but the dignity and purity of his life silenced those who were envious of him. In 1696 he was called to Paris as superior of the seminary of Saint-Magloire. The Lenten sermons which he preached in 1699 in the church of Saint-Honoré made a deep impression. In the following Advent he was summoned to preach before the king at Versailles, and delivered the Lenten sermons there also in 1701 and 1704. Bourdaloue (q.v.), whose reputation as a preacher then stood highest, is said to have remarked on hearing him, in the words of John the Baptist, "He must increase and I must decrease." Louis XIV. showed him the greatest respect, saying to him, "I have heard more than one great orator in my chapel, and was very well satisfied with them; but whenever I hear you, I am always dissatisfied with myself." Among his funeral orations, besides those mentioned above, special note should be made of those on the Prince de Conti in 1709, on the Dauphin in 1711, and on Louis himself. The simple and impressive beginning of the last is celebrated. Looking over the vast audience in silence, then down at the coffin which held all that was left of the mightiest monarch of his day, he broke the solemn stillness with the words *Dieu seul est grand, mes frères* ("God alone is great, my brethren!"). In 1717 he was named bishop of Clermont, and preached in the following year before the young Louis XV. a course of ten sermons in Lent (commonly known as *Le petit Carême*, and considered as his most finished work), in which he urged upon the youthful monarch and his court the obligations of morality and just government. He became a member of the French Academy in 1719, but from 1720 confined himself to the duties of his episcopate, leaving his diocese only once, to deliver the funeral sermon over Charlotte-Elisabeth, the duchess of Orléans.

Among his contemporaries he was as much regarded as Bossuet (q.v.), whose equal in the pulpit, however, he was not; and his funeral orations mark the point at which this branch of sacred eloquence began to decline. His name was highly honored in the last half of the eighteenth century, thanks to the eulogies of Voltaire and the Encyclopedists, who approved of him because he was more of a moralist than a theologian. In more recent times it has been less prominent, partly owing to the influence of the Jesuits, to whom he was never friendly. His style is not so lofty as that of the brilliant and courtly Bossuet, whom, however, he must be admitted to surpass in sympathy and unction. According to the usage of his time, he takes a text as a matter of form, only to depart from it as freely as he chooses. His structure is lacking in logic and strict order; he loses himself in moral digressions, and has at command an inexhaustible fund of applications to set forth the thoughtlessness of the courtiers, the vices of the great, or the horrors of war. Yet his sermons are characterized by a depth of Christian experience and vital piety which are sometimes absent from the more showy efforts of Bossuet and Bourdaloue. He himself published none of his discourses except that on the Prince de Conti, and the collections which appeared in 1705, 1706, and 1714 were unauthorized and not always correct reports by others. After his death his nephew brought out an edition of his works in 15 vols., Paris, 1745. The most recent collected edition is that of Blampignon, 4 vols., Bar-le-Duc, 1886. English translations of sermons are by Dodd, *Sermons on the Duties of the Great*, London, 1776; *Sermons, with a Life*, by D'Alembert, ib. 1839; a volume of *Sermons*, with *Life*, ib. 1849; and two volumes in the *Ancient and Modern Library of Theological Literature*, London, 1889–90. (J. Viénot.)

Bibliography: The best work on the subject is L. F. F. Theremin, *Demosthenes und Massillon*, Berlin, 1845. Consult the studies by L. Doumergue, Montauban, 1841; R. Labeille, Strasburg, 1857; A. Bayle, Paris, 1867; A. Laurent, Tours, 1870; E. A. Blampignon, *Massillon d'après des documents inédits*, Paris, 1879; idem, *L'Episcopat de Massillon d'après des documents inédits*, ib. 1884; idem, *Supplement à son hist. et à sa correspondance*, ib. 1891; G. Chabert, *Théologie pastorale de Massillon*, Montauban, 1890; E. Chazel, *La Prédication de Massillon*, Paris, 1894; Lichtenberger, *ESR*, viii. 771–774.

MASSUET, RENÉ: French Benedictine of Saint Maur (q.v.); b. at St. Quen, near Bernay (83 m. n.w. of Paris), Aug. 13, 1665 (or 1666?); d. at Paris Jan. 19, 1716. He became a professed on Oct. 20, 1682, and began his literary career by his anonymous *Lettre d'un ecclésiastique au R. P. E. L. J. sur celle qu'il a écrite aux RR. PP. Bénédictins de la Congregation de St. Maur* (Osnabrück, 1699), in which he defended the Maurists against the Jesuit charges that their edition of Augustine was designed to propagate Jansenism. In 1703 he was called to St. Germain des Prés, where he prepared an admirable edition of the *Contra hæreses* of Irenæus (Paris, 1710). In 1713 he edited the fifth volume of the *Annales ordinis S. Benedicti*, which had almost been completed by J. Mabillon, prefixing biographies of Mabillon and T. Ruinart. Five interesting letters of Massuet to B. Pez are contained in J. G. Schelhorn's *Amœnitates literariæ*, xiii. 278–310 (Frankfort, 1725–31); twelve to M. Müller in St. Gall in the *Archives des missions scientifiques et littéraires*, vi. 448–474 (Paris, 1857); a few in E. Gigas' *Lettres inédites de divers savants*, ii. 2 (Copenhagen, 1893); and one to the monastery of St. Emmeran in J. A. Endres' *Korrespondenz der Mauriner* (Stuttgart, 1899, p. 41). His *Mémoire sur l'histoire des patriarcats* still exists in manuscript in the Bibliothèque Nationale, Paris. (G. Laubmann.)

Bibliography: D. Tassin, *Hist. littéraire de la congrégation de Saint Maur*, pp. 304–305, 375–379, Brussels, 1770; J. B. Vanel, *Les Bénédictins de Saint Maur*, pp. 108–111, Paris, 1896; Lichtenberger, *ESR*, viii. 786–787; *KL*, viii. 978–979; Herbst, in *TQ*, 1833, pp. 452 sqq.

MATAMOROS, mat″ɑ-mō′rɑs, **MANUEL:** Spanish Protestant; b. at Lepe (70 m. w. of Seville) Oct. 8, 1835; d. at Lausanne July 31, 1866. He passed his early youth in Malaga, and at the age of fifteen entered the military school at Toledo, but left before the completion of the course and returned to his home. A trip to Gibraltar marked the turning-point of his life, for he there met a Catalan named Francisco de Paula Ruet, who had become a convert to Protestantism, through whose preaching Matamoros abandoned his former faith. He was recalled to Spain to serve his term in the army, and during service in Seville endeavored to make a Protestant propaganda among his comrades. This conduct was brought to the attention of the chaplain of the regiment, and Matamoros found his position so uncomfortable that he was glad to have his mother purchase his discharge. In the service of a Protestant society of Paris Matamoros visited Granada, Seville, and Barcelona. The discovery of letters addressed by him to a Protestant convert caused him to be arrested and brought for trial to Barcelona, where he was imprisoned with some of his coreligionists for more than two years. The efforts of the Evangelical Alliance to secure the release of the prisoners in 1863 were fruitless, but the intervention of the Prussian government resulted in the commutation of the sentence of nine years' labor in the galleys to banishment for an equal length of time. On May 28, 1863, the prisoners were accordingly released and Matamoros went to England, where he was received as a martyr to the Gospel. His stay there was brief, however, and he went to Lausanne to attend the theological lectures of the university. His health soon obliged him to make a long residence in southern France, and at Pau he was instrumental in the foundation of a short-lived Spanish school. In May, 1866, he returned to Lausanne to die. (Fritz Fliedner†.)

Bibliography: H. Dalton, *Die evangelische Bewegung in Spanien*, Wiesbaden, 1872; F. Pressel, *Das Evangelium in Spanien*, Freienwalde, 1877.

MATEER, CALVIN WILSON: Presbyterian missionary; b. in Cumberland Co., near Mechanicsburg, Pa., Jan. 9, 1836; d. at Tsingtau, Shantung Province, China, Sept. 28, 1908. He was graduated at the head of his class in Jefferson College, 1857; was principal of Beaver, Pa., Academy, 1857–59; studied in the Western Theological Seminary (Presbyterian), Allegheny, Pa., in 1859–61, and was graduated with the class of 1861. He had already been accepted as a missionary by the Old School Presbyterian Board of Foreign Missions, but lack of funds preventing the board from sending him out at once he was stated supply of the Presbyterian church at Delaware, O., from 1861 till 1863, when, in company with Hunter Corbett (b. at Leatherwood, Pa., December 8, 1835; graduated at Jefferson College, 1860; studied in Western Theological Seminary 1860–62, graduated at Princeton Theological Seminary 1863, since 1866 missionary at Chefoo, moderator of the General Assembly in 1906), he sailed for China. The voyage was long and the bearing of the captain insulting. He exchanged the ship at Shanghai for a steamer and got into a storm and was wrecked near Chefoo, which happily was their destination, and after a night of suffering they safely arrived there. He was settled at Teng Chow, the port of Shantung, a province as large as the State of Pennsylvania, and remained there till 1904, when he went to live at Wei-Hsien. In 1864 he laid the foundation of a school out of which there was formally organized in 1878 a college, known as The Shantung Union College, which was removed to Wei-Hsien in 1904. He was its president till 1895. He also had a church at Teng Chow down to 1906.

He was a missionary of the grand type, devoted to his work, a master of the language of the people he lived among and for whom he lived, and willing to be spent in their service, for he was home on furlough only three times. He was an extraordinarily versatile man, learning easily whatever he studied and able to impart his knowledge or turn it to practical account. Thus he was very skilful in the use of tools, understood machinery, even the latest application of electricity, and made much of the apparatus used in the college. In 1870 he was superintendent of the American Presbyterian Mission Press in Shanghai. At the same time he was a born teacher, writing text-books in mathematics and the famous "Lessons in Mandarin" which are widely used. Besides administering a college and preaching regularly and eloquently both in Chinese and English he was chairman of the committee for the revision of the Mandarin translation of the Bible, Mandarin being the dialect of Shantung. The New Testament was taken in hand in 1890 and finished in 1906, when the Old Testament was at once taken up but only the book of Genesis and part of the Psalms had been revised at his death. This labor was his last. He had been doing it at Chefoo, where he was spending the summer. As he had been suffering from dysentery he concluded that it would be better on his way back to Wei-Hsien to stop at the German hospital at Tsingtau for treatment. This he did, but his disease had passed beyond cure.

He was twice married, but had no children. His first wife was Miss Julia A. Brown of Delaware, O., whom he married in 1863 and who died in 1898. She was a most efficient coadjutor in educational work. His second wife was Miss Ada Haven, at the time of her marriage in 1900 a missionary of the American Board at Peking. She was equally helpful in his literary work.

MATERIALISM.

By the term materialism is usually meant the metaphysical view that the basis of everything that exists is matter, or that nothing except matter exists. Materialism seems to have been historically earlier than its opposite, spiritualism (see IDEALISM), or than the dualism which recognizes both matter and spirit (see DESCARTES, RENÉ). Thus, in the oldest Greek philosophy is found the assumption that everything originated from a primary matter, and that all phenomena are but transformations of this, and shall one day return to it again, after which new changes will begin, and so on *ad infinitum*. The concept of spirit, as an object of interior perception, and still more of spirit as a cosmic principle, came later. And even where, as with Anaxagoras, spirit appears as the creator of the world, it may be taken as materially conceived. Plato is the first to reach the concept of an absolutely immaterial cosmic principle. With him the spiritual or intelligible world is of a higher order than the world of phenomena cognizable by the senses, which comes into being through the operation of the former. While all true materialism is in a sense monistic, recognizing but a single principle as the essence of the world, this essence may differentiate itself into a finer and a coarser matter, and one of these may influence the other. Greek philosophy begins with a strictly monistic materialism; Thales recognizes water, Anaximenes fire, as the source of all things. But in Heraclitus, although all phenomena are transformations of the principle of fire, and although the Logos which brings harmony out of all is not a second principle but immanent in matter, yet fire itself is opposed, as a finer and more spiritual element, to two coarser ones, water and earth, developed indeed out of itself. This dualistic view was more fully worked out later by the Stoics.

1. Origin in Greek Philosophy.

Speaking generally, the materialism of modern times, descending from Hobbes and winning adherents at first more in France than in England or Germany, has been monistic, in so far as all spiritual processes are conceived merely as functions of matter. This view was set forth by Lamettrie (1709–51), whose best-known work is *L'Homme machine* (Leyden, 1748; new ed., Paris, 1865), and by Holbach in the *Système de la nature* (see DEISM, II., § 3). The great *Encyclopédie* (see ENCYCLOPEDISTS) was to a large extent a product of materialism, although Positivism (q.v.), which is often confused with it, contributes its share. Germany produced many monistic materialists in the nineteenth century. The most heated controversy broke out about the middle of that century owing to the publication of a lecture by the physiologist Rudolf Wagner, *Ueber Menschenschöpfung und Seelensubstanz* (Göttingen, 1854), to which Karl Voigt replied in his once famous satirical pamphlet *Köhlerglaube und Wissenschaft* (ib. 1854). To the further spread of materialistic views the principal contributors were Jakob Moleschott, especially in his *Der Kreislauf des Lebens* (5th ed., Mainz, 1876–1885), and Ludwig Büchner with his popular treatise *Kraft und Stoff* (1855; 21st ed., Leipsic, 1904; Eng. transl., *Force and Matter*, London, 1864). Büchner did more for the spread of this view than Ludwig Feuerbach (q.v.), who is often classed as a materialist, or than David Friedrich Strauss (q.v.), who in *Der alte und der neue Glaube* (Leipsic, 1872; Eng. transl., *The Old Faith and the New*, London and New York, 1873) leans strongly toward materialism without being able wholly to free himself from Hegelian pantheism. Systems more or less akin to materialism have been set forth in more recent times by Heinrich Czolbe and Eugen Dühring, without winning any wide following; and a comparatively moderate essay in the same direction is found in Du Bois-Reymond's well-known lecture *Ueber die Grenzen des Naturerkennens* (Leipsic, 1872) and his book *Die sieben Welträtsel* (ib. 1882). Less moderate is the much-discussed work of Ernst

2. Monistic Materialism.

Häckel, *Die Welträtsel* (Bonn, 1899). All these recent materialistic theories are monistic, and usually more or less connected with the doctrine of evolution. Monistic also is the atomistic materialism, however much its supporters have attempted to give it a dualistic coloring, as may be seen in the teaching of Democritus and of his successors the Epicureans.

In the seventeenth century the Epicurean atomism was revived by Pierre Gassendi (q.v.), who led the way to a mechanical-physical conception of the world and thus to modern materialism.

3. Dualistic Materialism. But whereas Gassendi was unable to include the Deity in his materialistic conception of the universe, placing God rather above this world of phenomena in which only secondary causes are operative, long before his day the Stoics had made their noteworthy attempt to include God as a factor in the material world, thus leading up to a dualistic materialism. Because they emphasized so strongly an ethical idealism which amounts to rigorism, they have been a good deal neglected by historians of materialism; and yet they were thorough-going and logical materialists. All reality to them is corporeal; the Godhead exists, therefore it must be corporeal, i.e., material, and so must the soul, and even the virtues and affections of the soul. It is true they often speak of two principles, thus apparently following Plato or Aristotle; but a closer scrutiny of their views shows that the active formative principle is considered as definitely material. The four elements are not eternal, nor do they spring from different sources, but all come from the one primal matter, which the Stoics, here following Heraclitus, regard as fire. This fire, the artificer of the world, pervades the whole universe and is called God. They also call the Deity *anima mundi*, the world-soul, or Logos; but their Logos is material, not spiritual. In the evolution of the world, the Logos, as *spermatikos*, seminal, is contrasted with the other two coarser elements. It comprehends the single *logoi spermatikoi*, which are also thought of as material substances. But the kind of materialism which commended itself to the Stoics by its logical character found no adherents after the last real Stoic had occupied the imperial throne (see STOICISM). Christian philosophy gave a certain place to *rationes seminales*, but regarded them as rather spiritual than material; there are traces of Stoic materialism in some of the Fathers, but Platonic metaphysics gained the upper hand, as being more in harmony with Christian spiritual ideas. In the Renaissance and later times Stoic philosophy has had more influence than is generally supposed; but its natural system has had but few and unimportant followers, and monism has generally triumphed in the region of materialism.

But besides the distinction already treated between monistic and dualistic materialism, there is another of still deeper significance between organic and mechanical materialism. The latter rejects all teleological considerations, while the former is at least patient of them. The oldest Greek philosophers, materialists as they were, regarded matter as possessing life, if not a soul. Heraclitus may be taken as a type of the older organic materialism, regarding matter as eternally in motion, and moved by certain laws, not from without but according to reason.

4. Mechanical and Organic Materialism. But his Logos is not a conscious, still less a self-conscious agent, and is thus distinguished from the all-knowing, intelligent *nous* of Anaxagoras, which had no slight influence on the Platonic and Aristotelian doctrine of God. The principal representatives of organic as of dualistic materialism were the Stoics, with their decided teleological tendency. In their view the end of all things, of course, is the return into the primary fire; but in the existing world the formative principle is rational. Everything is logically ordained by a provident intelligence. The mechanical materialism of the present day is still based upon the atomistic theory, as laid down by Leucippus and Democritus. The eternal movement of the atoms is not conditioned by any definite cause, and proceeds in no definite order; casually, yet still by necessity, atoms came together from various sides, from one part and another of infinite space, and this brought about a rotary motion out of which the universe ultimately came into being. Since the soul is composed of atoms, its processes also must be purely mechanical. Democritus even considered the perception of the senses to be mechanical, emanations of atoms detaching themselves from objects and affecting the senses. His atomistic system is a strictly logical and scientific one, not depending upon any invisible powers such as the *nous* of Anaxagoras or the love and hate of Empedocles. Sense-perception, indeed, with him is deceptive—a dim knowledge, contrasted with the true, which is to be gained by reason; although according to his whole teaching thought must be based upon sense-perception and can not be independent of it. Epicurus, while as a rule following Democritus, introduced a peculiar variation in teaching, not a primary motion or rotation of atoms, but a mode of motion by which they fell through their own weight and declined a little from a straight line through a sort of self-determination. This declension explains their meeting and permanent combinations, as well as the upward and sidelong motions through which worlds came into being. This element of arbitrary determination helps Epicurus to explain the freedom of the will, which he accepts in a certain sense, but it damages the strict logical consequence of a materialism that denies any freedom or arbitrary determination.

In modern times, without knowing anything of Epicurus, Galileo revived the Democritean mechanical conception of the universe, denying, in opposition to the scholastic-Aristotelian philosophy, any real coming into existence or perishing, and referring all changes to shifting of parts, to quantitative not qualitative relations.

5. Mechanical View in Modern Philosophy. The mechanical view of nature, if not of the universe, was dominant at the beginning of modern philosophy with the most apparently opposite thinkers, with René Descartes (q.v.) as well as with Thomas Hobbes (q.v.), who, regarding philosophy as the science of bodies, considered an incorporeal substance as an absurdity and explained mental processes in a purely mechanical manner. According to Descartes matter consists of corpuscles—not the absolutely indivisible atoms of Democritus, but parts indivisible by us. The mass of matter and motion originally established by God is as a whole incapable of increase or diminution. Equally with Hobbes, Descartes explained mental processes, e.g., the association of ideas, in a purely mechanical way by particular material changes in the brain arising from affection through the senses, and by the generation of new concepts as a result of these changes. Descartes is thus one of the founders of the mechanical-materialistic school as far as anthropology is concerned. It was only necessary to leave out the thinking soul to reach the view of Lamettrie, who believed that the thing to do was not, with Leibnitz (q.v.), to spiritualize matter, but to materialize the soul. For him the soul is the material consciousness; he finds the principle of life not in it but in all the separate parts, since each smallest particle of the organized body is forced to move by an innate principle. Similar views are held by most physiologists and biologists of the present day.

The most obvious justification of materialism lies in the fact that the basis of our knowledge is sense-perception, which shows us the real as having three dimensions; and this leads us to consider these three dimensions as existing outside ourselves and constituting the objects of the intuitive world.

6. Weakness of the Theory.

There is also the experience that mental processes do not occur without a material base. While it may be admitted that as far as our experience goes the material (especially the nerves, and in higher animals the brain) is a *sine qua non* for mental phenomena, no one has ever succeeded in deducing the latter from the former or explaining them by it. In spite of the progress recently made in cerebral anatomy and the success attained in the localization of mental activities, the question is still unanswered, how out of what is visible and tangible, cognizable by the external senses, that which is invisible and intangible, cognizable only by the inner sense, can originate. Moreover, the whole conception of matter is a vague and indeterminate one, resisting exact analysis. What we first get is not matter—that is secondary—but sensations or perceptions. If we try to find external causes for these, we still do not reach matter, as is usually assumed, but forces that work upon us. We are thus driven into a sort of dynamism, according to which matter is a generally operative force, its whole essence being found in operation. This extreme dynamism is represented by Leibnitz and many of his adherents. Another objection to the ordinary materialism is that as far as our perceptions go they present themselves to us as something immanent and spiritual, which is to us the datum, the known, from which we must proceed in all our philosophizing, even to the acceptance of an external world; and it is a complete inversion for materialism to set before us first the external world which is unknown to us and explain what is known to us from that. These and other objections are so conclusive that thoroughgoing materialism may now be considered as philosophically untenable, in spite of the number of physicists who still accept it because it harmonizes with their tendencies or preconceptions.

Theoretical materialism is not, however, inconsistent with strict moral views, and does not necessarily lead to absorption in purely material, i.e., sensual, things. Not only the Stoics but also Democritus and Epicurus may be cited to prove this, as may also Tertullian on the Christian side. And in the most decided materialists of modern times, such as Lamettrie, Holbach, and others, a by no means despicable inculcation is to be found of a virtue which is, indeed, primarily self-love but gives the public interests the preference over the individual. Even Häckel acknowledges as a golden rule "Thou shalt love thy neighbor as thyself." Altruism is so deeply implanted in the mind of humanity that the most extreme theoretical tendencies, even those which assert the most extreme egoism in the region of morals, are forced to give it a predominant place in their practical counsels; and there is scarcely an absolutely egoistic work to be cited, except Max Stirner's *Der Einzige und sein Eigentum* (Leipsic, 1845); but he is not to be classed as a theoretical materialist. (M. HEINZE†.)

BIBLIOGRAPHY: An extensive list of works on the subject, including periodical literature, is given in J. M. Baldwin, *Dictionary of Philosophy and Psychology*, iii. 620–626, New York, 1905. The best history of Materialism is still F. A. Lange, *Geschichte des Materialismus und Kritik seiner Bedeutung in der Gegenwart*, 6th ed., Leipsic, 1896, Eng. transl. of earlier ed., London, 1877. Consult further: T. Hobbes, *Works*, ed. W. Molesworth, 11 vols., London, 1839–45; N. S. Bergier, *Examen du matérialisme*, Paris, 1854; Herbert Spencer, *System of Synthetic Philosophy*, London, 1860–97; P. Janet, *Le Matérialisme contemporain*, Paris, 1864, Eng. transl., London, 1865; F. Westhoff, *Stoff, Kraft und Gedanke*, Münster, 1865; E. Caro, *Le Matérialisme et la science*, Paris, 1868; H. B. Jones, *Croonian Lectures on Matter and Force*, London, 1868; W. Maccall, *The Newest Materialism*, ib. 1873; J. A. Picton, *The Mystery of Matter*, ib. 1873; J. Martineau, *Modern Materialism*, ib. 1876; P. Zimmermann, *Das Räthsel des Lebens und die Rathlosigkeit des Materialismus*, Leipsic, 1877; É. Syffert, *Le Matérialisme*, Paris, 1878; R. Flint, *Antitheistic Theories*, lectures ii.–iv., London, 1879–80; L. Weis, *Idealrealismus und Materialismus*, Berlin, 1879; A. Lefèvre, *La Renaissance du matérialisme*, Paris, 1881; J. Dourif, *Le Matérialisme et l'athéisme*, ib. 1882; G. A. Hirn, *Réflexions critiques sur la théorie cinématique de l'univers*, ib. 1882; M. Berger, *Der Materialismus im Kampfe mit dem Spiritualismus und Idealismus*, Triest, 1883; A. Stadler, *Kant's Theorie der Materie*, Leipsic, 1883; W. F. Wilkinson, *Modern Materialism*, London, 1883; H. Stüven, *Darstellung und Kritik der Grundsätze des Materialismus*, Hamburg, 1885; J. A. Kilb, *Plato's Lehre von der Materie*, Marburg, 1887; P. Ribot, *Spiritualisme et matérialisme*, Paris, 1887; R. Abendroth, *Das Problem der Materie*, 2 vols., Leipsic, 1889–90; W. Strecker, *Welt und Menschheit vom Standpunkte des Materialismus*, ib. 1891; L. Stephen, *An Agnostic's Apology*, London, 1893; G. Plechanow, *Beiträge zur Geschichte des Materialismus*, Stuttgart, 1896; T. Menzi, *Der Materialismus vor dem Richterstuhl der Wissenschaft*, Zurich, 1897; R. C. Shettle, *The Origin of Matter and Force*, London, 1897; L. Büchner, *Kraft und Stoff*, Frankfort, 1898, Eng. transl. of earlier ed., London, 1870; E. Du Bois-Reymond, *Ueber die Grenzen der Naturerkenntnis*, Leipsic, 1898; C. Barbagallo, *Del Materialismo storico*, Rome, 1899; E. Gaynor, *The New Materialism*, Dublin, 1899; W. A. Preuss, *Geist und Stoff*, Oldenburg, 1900; J. Royce, *The World and the Individual*, New York, 1900–01; I. W. Riley, *American Philosophy; the early Schools*, New York, 1907; the works on the history of philosophy; and the literature under IDEALISM.

MATERNUS, ma-ter'nus, **JULIUS FIRMICUS:** Latin apologist of the fourth century. To him is ascribed the authorship of the *De errore profanarum religionum*, a work written between 343 and 348, possibly in 346. Nothing is known concerning Maternus, but in the fourth century a pagan astrological work entitled *Libri octo matheseos* was composed by a certain Julius Firmicus Maternus Junior Siculus, and the identity of name and time, a similarity of style, the Sicilian home of the pagan author and the familiarity with Sicily evinced by the Christian writer give foundation to the supposition that the two are the same. On the other hand, the pagan Maternus is a cosmopolitan and moralistic neo-Platonist, while the Christian author is a fanatic. But since the *Libri matheseos* was composed between Dec. 30, 335, and May 22, 337, it becomes probable that the two books were by the same author and that the neo-Platonist became a Christian.

As the descendant of a senatorial family, Maternus received the customary training in literature and philosophy, while as a Christian he studied the works of Christian authors. Although he cites only Homer and Porphyry, he shows an acquaintance with Plutarch, Cicero, Athenagoras, Minucius Felix, Tertullian, and the writings of Cyprian. The *De errore profanarum religionum*, of which only a single manuscript, that in the Vatican, is known, is incomplete, four folios of the codex being lost. The general plan of the work, however, is clear. It falls into two parts. The first part (chaps. i.-xvii.) treats of the false objects of religious worship, and contains a polemic against the deities of the Greco-Roman state religion and against Oriental cults. The second part (chaps. xviii.-xxix.) seeks to show that the pagan mysteries were a caricature of the words of the Bible and the mystery of salvation. The work closes with an urgent appeal to the emperors to destroy all idols and temples. (A. Hauck.)

Bibliography: The latest ed. of the *De errore* is by C. Halm, in *CSEL*, vol. ii., 1867. It was previously edited by Münter at Copenhagen, 1826, with commentary, reproduced in *MPL*, xii. Consult: Moore, *Julius Firmicus Maternus, der Heide und der Christ*, Munich, 1897; W. S. Teuffel, *Geschichte der römischen Litteratur*, ed. L. Schwabe, ii. 1028 sqq., Leipsic, 1886; A. Ebert, *Geschichte der christlich-lateinischen Litteratur*, pp. 129 sqq., ib. 1889; O. Bardenhewer, *Patrologie*, p. 854, Freiburg, 1901; *DCB*, iii. 862-863.

MATHA, JEAN DE. See Trinitarians.

MATHER: The name of a family of much prominence in the early history of New England.

1. Richard Mather, the ancestor of the family in America, was born at Lowton (14 m. w. of Manchester), parish of Winwick, Lancashire, 1596; d. at Dorchester, Mass., Apr. 22, 1669. He was sent to the Winwick grammar-school, and at fifteen was chosen teacher of a school at Toxteth Park. Here he became acquainted with a branch of the Aspinwall family, by whom he was led to devote himself to the ministry, and went to Brasenose, Oxford, to prepare for the same. But the people at Toxteth were so unwilling to wait for him, that he left the university before taking his degrees, and late in 1618, when only twenty-two, preached his first sermon at Toxteth Park. The Bishop of Chester ordained him; and in Sept., 1624, he married Katherine, daughter of Edmond Holt of Bury. Becoming an earnest Puritan and being for a time suspended, he left—traveling in disguise to Bristol—for New England, May 23, 1635, landing at Boston, after being very nearly shipwrecked, Aug. 17 following. The First Church at Dorchester having emigrated with its pastor, Warham, to Connecticut, Mr. Mather gathered a new (the present First) church there Aug. 23, 1636; he was chosen its teacher and so remained until his death. For his second wife he married the widow of John Cotton (q.v.). By his first wife he left six sons, of whom four—Samuel, Nathaniel, Eleazer, and Increase—followed their father's profession.

Richard Mather was one of the ablest and most influential among the early ministers of New England, a powerful preacher, and a specially wise counselor; he was seized with his mortal illness while moderating that ecclesiastical council in Boston out of whose deliberations the Old South Church was born. He was skilled in the New England plan of church government, wrote three or four of the best early tracts in its exposition and defense, and was the chief composer of the "Cambridge Platform."

2. Samuel Mather, eldest son of Richard Mather, was born at Much Woolton (4 m. s.e. of Liverpool), Lancashire, May 13, 1626; d. in Dublin Oct. 29, 1671. He came to New England with his father in 1635, was graduated at Harvard in 1643, and became fellow; he is said to have been the first fellow who was a Harvard graduate. He returned to England in 1650 and was made a chaplain of Magdalen College, Oxford. He resigned in 1653 to attend the parliamentary commissioners to Scotland. He became an M.A. of Trinity College, Dublin, in 1654, and was one of its senior fellows. He was ordained at Dublin Dec. 5, 1656. At the Restoration he was suspended (Oct., 1660) and then became perpetual curate of Burtonwood, Warrington, Lancashire, whence he was ejected by the Act of Uniformity of 1662. Returning to Dublin he preached there for several years, at first in his own house. He was imprisoned Sept. 20, 1664, for preaching at a private conventicle but was soon released. He declined a call to return to Boston, U. S. A.

3. Nathaniel Mather, third son of Richard Mather, was born at Much Woolton, Lancashire, Mar. 20, 1630; d. in London July 26, 1697. He came to New England with his father in 1635 and was graduated M.A. at Harvard in 1647 He then returned to England and preached at Harberton and at Barnstaple, Devonshire, until ejected by the Act of 1662, when he went to Rotterdam. Here he remained as minister of the English Church until the death of his brother Samuel, when he succeeded him in Dublin. In 1688 he took charge of the Lime Street Church, London, and in 1694 became one of the Merchants' Lecturers at Pinner's Hall. He is interred in Bunhill Fields, London.

4. Eleazer Mather, fifth son of Richard Mather, was born at Dorchester, Mass., May 13, 1637; d. at Northampton, Mass., July 24, 1669. He was graduated at Harvard in 1656. In 1658 he went to

Northampton, gathered the first church there, was ordained in June, 1661, and labored successfully as pastor till his early death.

5. Increase Mather, sixth and youngest son of Richard Mather, was born at Dorchester, Mass., June 21, 1639; d. in Boston Aug. 23, 1723. He was graduated at Harvard in 1656 in the same class with his brother Eleazer, though on account of physical weakness for a time he was a pupil of John Norton. On his nineteenth birthday he preached at Dorchester, and, twelve days later, sailed for England. He took his M.A. at Trinity College, Dublin, and, after preaching in various places, returned to New England in 1661, intending to go back to England when times should be more favorable. He was ordained in New England, however, May 27, 1664, over the Second Church of Boston and remained there till his death. For seventeen years (1685–1701) of this pastorate he was also president of Harvard College; and in 1688 he went to England as special agent of the Massachusetts Colony, where—"his expenses in the mean time greatly exceeding his compensation, and he pledging all his property for money which he borrowed to support himself while he was working for his country"—he remained in this public service about four years.

It is related of Increase Mather that it was his habit to study sixteen hours out of the twenty-four. It is matter of record that he was not merely acceptable, but highly honored, for nearly sixty years, in one of the two most important pulpits on this side of the sea; and he left behind him publications of various sorts to the number of 160. It is in no way strange, therefore, that he should have been almost unanimously held to be the foremost minister of his day in this new country, and that he should have exercised an influence as vast as, in the main, it was salutary. In 1662 he married Maria, daughter of John Cotton, by whom he had three sons and seven daughters. His sons—Cotton, Nathaniel, and Samuel—were graduated at Harvard in 1678, 1685, and 1690 respectively.

6. Cotton Mather, eldest son of Increase Mather, was born in Boston Feb. 12, 1663; d. there Feb. 13, 1728. He became the most renowned of the lineage, although, conceding his omnivorous scholarship and exceptional labors, it may be doubted whether he were even the peer of his father or grandfather in intellectual ability. He took his B.A. at Harvard (1678) when less than fifteen years and six months old; taught for a time; overcame an impediment of speech which had threatened to interfere with his success in the family profession; acted as his father's assistant at the Second Church, Boston; and was ordained, as joint pastor with him, May 13, 1685—a place which he surrendered only at his death. During nearly three and forty years he was indefatigable as a preacher, systematic and thorough as a pastor, eminent as a philanthropist—at great personal risk successfully introducing and defending the inoculative prevention of smallpox—and amazing as an author; being known to have printed 382 separate works, of which several were elaborate volumes, and one a stately folio of 800 pages; while, to his sore and amazed grief, the great work of his life (in his own esteem), his *Biblia Americana*, failed of publication. It remains in manuscript to this day.

It was Cotton Mather's misfortune that the weak and whimsical side of his multiform greatness most impressed itself on many of his generation, and that, for sharing with other good and eminent men of his day in the witchcraft delusion, he has most unfairly been singled out for a specialty of censure and contumely which in no degree fairly belongs to him. He was no more guilty for not being, as to that, in advance of his age, than were Richard Baxter and Sir Matthew Hale in England, or Judge Sewall, or Gov. Stoughton, or Sir William Phips, or scores of others in New England. He married three times.

7. Samuel Mather, fourth son of Cotton Mather (by his second wife) and the only one of his sons who lived to manhood, was born in Boston Oct. 30, 1706; d. there June 27, 1785. He was graduated at Harvard in 1723, before he was seventeen; and four years after his father's death, June 21, 1732, was ordained colleague with Rev. Joshua Gee over that same Boston church which his father and grandfather had served for sixty-four years before him. Of considerable learning and fair abilities, he did not, however, fill the ancient place; and in less than ten years was dismissed, and, with a not very large following, labored with a new church (which did not survive him) until his death. He, too, was an author, of less than a score of books, however, only one of which, *An Apology for the Liberties of the Churches of New England* (Boston, 1738), deserves, or has, remembrance. None of his three sons studied for the ministry.

It may be doubted whether history can parallel this family, of which eleven members were trained for the sacred office in four generations, of whom the seven who wrought in New England expended about 250 years of ministerial labor upon it, besides publishing more than 500 different works, and some of them exerting a popular influence never surpassed, and seldom equalled. For its distinguished services in each of its four generations, in reducing to rigid system, illustrating, defending, and chronicling the way of the churches of New England, if it had done nothing else, this Mather group would deserve, as it will receive, perpetual remembrance.

(HENRY M. DEXTER†.) MORTON DEXTER.

BIBLIOGRAPHY: An excellent edition of Cotton Mather's *Magnalia Christi Americana* (a source for the earlier members of the family), with memoir and transl. of Hebr., Grk. and Lat. quotations, appeared 2 vols., Hartford, 1855. Other early sources are indicated in the series of notices in *DNB*, xxxviii. 27–31. Consult: John Mather, *Genealogy of the Mather Family*, Hartford, 1848; C. Robbins, *Hist. of old North Church in Boston*, Boston, 1852; W. B. Sprague, *Annals of the American Pulpit*, i. 75–80, 151–160, 189–195, 371–375, New York, 1859; B. Wendell, *Cotton Mather*, in *Makers of America Series*, ib. 1891; A. P. Marvin, *Life and Times of Cotton Mather*, Boston, 1892; W Walker, *Influence of the Mathers in New England Religious Development*, New York, 1892; idem, *Hist. of the Congregational Churches in the U. S.*, passim, ib. 1894 (cf. Index); idem, *New England Leaders*, ib. 1901; A. E. Dunning, *Congregationalists in America*, ib. 1894; L. W Bacon, *The Congregationalists*, ib. 1904; J. P. Quincy, *Cotton Mather and the Supernormal in New England Hist.*, in *Proceedings of the Massachusetts Historical Society*, 2d ser., vol. xx., 1907.

MATHESIUS, JOHANNES: German Reformer; b. at Rochlitz (16 m. n.n.w. of Chemnitz) June 24, 1504; d. at Joachimsthal (14 m. n.n.e. of Elbogen), Bohemia, Oct. 7, 1565. He was the first biographer of Luther, the Reformer of Joachimsthal, and one of the most powerful preachers among the Reformers of the second period (1504–65). He studied at Wittenberg, which he gratefully praised as his spiritual home, always regarding himself as a member of the church and school there. In 1532 he became the seventh rector of the Latin school at Joachimsthal, the then new city of northwestern Bohemia which had achieved prosperity by its silver mines and had adopted Lutheranism. In 1540 Mathesius went again to Wittenberg, where he became Luther's table-companion and made notes of his table-talk. In 1542 he was ordained by Luther. In the church at Joachimsthal he labored for nearly a quarter of a century, first as preacher, then as pastor. He was the most famous preacher of that place and of German Bohemia, being distinguished for learning and for spirited and genial eloquence. Under him church affairs became firmly established and protected against disturbances from without and within. Mathesius was so closely bound to his office and position that he refused all offers from abroad, including a call to the University of Leipsic. Against his desire he went to Prague (1546) together with the magistrate and thirty delegates to defend themselves before King Ferdinand I. for their attitude in the Schmalkald war. After that affair, there followed some years of relief, of successful work, of literary activity, and of beneficial intercourse with colleagues in school and church, at home and abroad. But domestic troubles, new political storms, religious persecutions, and physical ailments brought him, prematurely aged, to an early grave. For more than one hundred years the effects of his work remained. The memory of the Joachimsthal "angel of the church," disturbed by the rage of the Jesuits, was renewed there even by Catholics through a memorial tablet. His sermons have been circulated in numerous editions and revisions; some were translated into foreign languages. Best known are two collections of popular yet scientific, instructive yet devotional, lectures delivered in the carnival season, when something amusing was expected. The "Sarepta" was intended to explain sayings, stories, and examples from the Scriptures which mention mining, in order that the Joachimsthal people might have their "mining-book of homilies" as farmers and viticulturists had theirs. In the "Lutherhistorien" Mathesius proved himself a pioneer in the kind of homilies for the church of the Reformation which the Roman Church had given in her "sermons on the saints." They constitute the first real biography of Luther (Nuremberg, 1566). These more than any others carried through the centuries the memory of the Joachimsthal preacher, and in spite of deficiencies, inaccuracies, and mistakes they are still a source of information (last critical edition, Prague, 1906). In Mathesius' sermons seriousness and humor, bluntness and tenderness, go hand in hand. (GEORG LOESCHE.)

BIBLIOGRAPHY: The *Ausgewählte Werke*, 4 vols., are ed. by G. Loesche, with introduction and commentary, Prague, 1896–1908. Extracts are by K. F. Ledderhose, Heidelberg, 1849, in French by L. Schweitzer, 1871. The chief biographical work is by G. Loesche, 2 vols., Gotha, 1895; cf. his *Mathesiana*, in *Jahrbuch für die Geschichte des Protestantismus in Oesterreich*, Vienna, 1904; idem, in *Zeitschrift für deutsche Wortforschung*, i (1900), 235–238. Consult also the works by: Balthasar Mathesius, Dresden, 1705; J. Abraham, Wittenberg, 1883; K. Amelung, Gütersloh, 1894; G. F. Fuchs, in *Halte was du hast*, xxv (1902), 366–373.

MATHESON, GEORGE: Church of Scotland; b. in Glasgow Mar. 27, 1842; d. at North Berwick (19 m. e.s.e. of Edinburgh) Aug. 28, 1906. Although his eyesight gradually failed him until in his eighteenth year he had become blind, he finished his school and university course at Glasgow with high honors (B.A., 1861; M.A., 1862; B.D., 1866) and was licensed to preach in 1866. During the next year he was assistant to John Ross Macduff (q.v.) of the Sandyford Church, Glasgow; from 1868 till 1886 minister of Innellan (35 m. down the Clyde from Glasgow); and from 1886 till his retirement in 1899 minister of St. Bernard's, Edinburgh. Being in easy circumstances he was always able to employ secretaries who read to him and wrote for him, and having an extraordinarily retentive memory and strong literary bent he produced many books which display much reflection and, considering his restrictions, no little learning. He was very broad-minded and saw good in creeds which he rejected. His preaching was of a high order. In consequence of his standing as preacher and author he was the recipient of many honors—D.D. of Edinburgh University, 1879; call to succeed John Cumming (q.v.) as pastor of Crown Court Church, London, 1880; Baird lecturer, 1881; preacher before the queen at Balmoral Oct. 25, 1885; Gifford lecturer, 1899 (declined); fellow of the Royal Society of Edinburgh, 1890; LL.D., Aberdeen, 1902. His books may be divided into three classes: first, those of a philosophical character: *Aids to the Study of German Theology* (Edinburgh, 1874; 3d ed., 1876), issued at first anonymously, a sympathetic study of German theology from Kant to Dorner with a view to relieving it of the charge of "atheism"; *Growth of the Spirit of Christianity from the First Century to the Dawn of the Lutheran Era* (2 vols., 1877), in which he showed his reading in comparative religion, a favorite study, and his acceptance of Hegelian principles as guiding lines in the presentation of church history, but it is not a church history in the ordinary sense; *Natural Elements of Revealed Theology* (1881), his Baird lectures, in which he again utilized his attainments in comparative religion to commend Christianity; *Can the old Faith Live with the New? or, the Problem of Evolution and Revelation* (1885; 3d ed., 1889), an attempt to show that even if evolution be true, and he was non-committal on that point (though afterward he came to the conclusion that it was not true), belief in it is compatible with belief in Christian doctrines; he presented the same idea in more popular form in *The Psalmist and the Scientist, or, Modern Value of the Religious Sentiment* (London, 1886; 3d ed., 1892); *The Distinctive Messages of the Old Religions* (1892; 2d ed., 1893), an attempt to state that for which each of these religions stood. The second class of books was those which are more directly and avowedly preachers' expositions: *The Spiritual Development of St. Paul* (1890; 4th ed., 1897), a study of the thirteen epistles of Paul, but not of the literature on them; *The Lady Ecclesia, an Autobiography* (1896; 2d ed., 1896), an allegory; *Side-lights from Patmos* (1897; 3d ed., 1903); *Studies of the Portrait of Christ* (2 vols., 1899–1900; vol. I., 10th ed., 1907, vol. II., 6th ed., 1907), a very interesting study of the life of Christ as an aid to faith and not as a contribution to scholarship, generally considered his best piece of work; *The Representative Men of the Bible* (2 series, 1902–03; first series, Adam to Job, 6th ed., 1907; second series, Ishmael to Daniel, 3d ed., 1907); *The Representative Men of the New Testament* (1905); and *The Representative Women of the Bible* (1906). But it is likely that he will be longer useful as author of a third class of books, the devotional, for these have had a very wide sale and reached many who were not attracted by his other books: *My Aspirations* (1882); *Moments on the Mount* (1884); *Voices of the Spirit* (1888); *Searchings in the Silence* (1895); *Words by the Wayside* (1896); *Times of Retirement* (1901); *Leaves for Quiet Hours* (1904); *Rests by the River* (1906); *Messages of Hope* (1908); *Thoughts for Life's Journey* (1908); and *Day unto Day* (1908), prayers. He wrote also poetry: *Sacred Songs* (1890; 3d ed., 1904); and one hymn (not in this collection), "O Love that wilt not let me go," will be sung long after all his other compositions are forgotten. It was written at the Innellan manse in five minutes on the evening of June 6, 1882, and only changed in a single word, "trace" for "climbed" in the third stanza. But four other hymns which are in this collection have been incorporated into several hymn-books.

BIBLIOGRAPHY: D. Macmillan, *The Life of George Matheson*, London, 1907.

MATHEW, THEOBALD ("Father Mathew"): Irish temperance advocate; b. at Thomastown (5 m. w. of Cashel), Tipperary, Oct. 10, 1790; d. at Queenstown Dec. 8, 1856. He studied for a year at Maynooth, 1807–08; passed through the novitiate of the Capuchin order and was ordained in 1814. He was then sent to Cork to take charge of a chapel in the destitute portion of the city, where his high personal character and gentle spirit won confidence and affection. He aided in philanthropic and educational enterprises for the uplift of the poorer classes. In 1838 he was impressed with the evils of intemperance and was asked to conduct the total-abstinence crusade. On Apr. 10 of that year, Father Mathew, who was then in his forty-eighth year, definitely committed himself to the work. His success was phenomenal. By January of the next year, two hundred thousand persons, most of whom lived in Cork and its vicinity, had embraced the new gospel. Father Mathew extended his labors over all Ireland, visited Scotland and England (1842–1843), and spent two years in America (1849–51), going as far west as St. Louis, everywhere making converts by the hundreds. His success was due to his exhaustless flow of animal spirits, his humor and wit, his downright earnestness, and, above all, to his ability, courage, and high character.

BIBLIOGRAPHY: The principal life is by J. F. Maguire, London, 1864, abridged ed., 1890. Others are S. R. Wells, New York, 1867; F. J. Mathew, London, 1890; and Katharine Tynan, ib., 1908. Consult also S. H. Burke, *Rise and Progress of Father Mathew's Temperance Mission*, ib. 1885.

MATHEWS, GEORGE DUNCAN: Irish Presbyterian; b. at Kilkenny (73 m. s.s.e. of Dublin), County Kilkenny, Apr. 25, 1828. He was educated at Trinity College, Dublin (B.A., 1848), after which he held successive pastorates at the United Presbyterian Church in Stranraer, Scotland (1854–1868), Westminster Presbyterian Church, New York City (1868–78), and at the Canadian Presbyterian Church, Quebec (1878–88). He was also professor of dogmatic theology in Morrin College, Quebec, from 1880 to his retirement from active life in 1888. He was American secretary of the General Presbyterian Alliance in New York in 1873–88, and since the latter year has been general secretary of the General Presbyterian Alliance at London. He was also a member of the Council of Public Instruction for the Province of Quebec from 1880 to 1888, and in theological position is a liberal conservative. In addition to minor contributions, he was editor of *The Christian Worker* in 1870–74, and associate editor of *Catholic Presbyterianism* in 1879–83 and of *The Quarterly Register* (the official organ of the General Presbyterian Alliance) in 1880–88, of which he has been general editor since the latter year. He likewise edited the *Proceedings of the General Presbyterian Alliance* for 1884, 1892, 1896, 1899, 1904, and 1909.

MATHEWS, SHAILER: Baptist; b. at Portland, Me., May 26, 1863. He was educated at Colby University, Waterville, Me. (A.B., 1884), Newton Theological Institution, from which he was graduated in 1887, and the University of Berlin (1890–91). He was associate professor of rhetoric at Colby University in 1887–89 and professor of history and political economy in the same institution in 1889–94, as well as lecturer in New-Testament literature in Newton Theological Institution in 1888–89, after which he was associate professor of New-Testament history and interpretation at the divinity school of the University of Chicago from 1894 to 1897 and professor from 1897 to 1904. Since the latter year he has been professor of systematic theology in the same seminary, was junior dean of the divinity school 1894–1907, and dean since 1907. In addition to his work as editor of *The World To-day* since 1903 and of the series of *New Testament Handbooks*, as well as associate editor of *The Biblical World* and *The American Journal of Theology*, he has written: *Select Mediæval Documents* (New York, 1891); *The Social Teaching of Jesus* (1897); *A History of New Testament Times in Palestine* (1899); *Constructive Studies in the Life of Christ* (in collaboration with E. D. Burton, Chicago, 1901); *The French Revolution* (New York, 1901); *Principles and Ideals for the Sunday School* (in collaboration with E. D. Burton, Chicago, 1903); *The Messianic Hope in the New Testament* (1905); and *The Church and the Changing Order* (New York, 1907).

MATHIEU, mā"tī"ū', FRANÇOIS DÉSIRÉ: Cardinal; b. at Einville (4½ m. n. of Lunéville), France, May 28, 1839; d. in London Oct. 26, 1908. He was ordained to the priesthood in 1863, after having been professor at the Petit Séminaire of Pont-à-Mousson from 1859, and for ten years was confessor of the Dominican nuns at Nancy. In 1894 he was consecrated bishop of Angers, and two years later was enthroned archbishop of Toulouse. He was created cardinal priest of Santa Sabina in 1899. He wrote *L'Ancien régime dans la province de Lorraine et Barrois d'après des documents inédits* (Paris, 1879) and *Le Concordat de 1801, ses origines, son histoire* (1903).

MATHURINS. See TRINITARIANS.

MATILDA (MECHTILDIS), SAINT, OF HACKEBORN: Benedictine nun of Helfta (Helpede), near Eisleben; b. 1241; d. about 1310. She belonged to the family of the lords of Hackeborn, and was the younger sister of Gertrude, who for forty years stood at the head of the monastery of Helfta (see GERTRUDE). The revelations which she claimed to have here were written down by her sister nuns. The contents of these revelations are visions in which questions were put to Christ and Mary, to which answers were received. For the most part they are questions of the inner life and are sometimes fine and profound. In keeping with the time the holy virgin is worshiped to excess, yet there is a remarkable passage (i. 18, pp. 54 sqq.) in which Mary with all creatures accuse Matilda, but Christ alone has mercy upon her and absolves her. Another passage (ii. 14, p. 148) has secured her a place in the *Catalogus testium veritatis* of Flacius (p. 923 of the editio princeps) because it is shown there how all her imperfection is made perfect by the perfection of the Son of God. It is an undenied truth, though often practically obscured, that in the theology of the Western Church of the Middle Ages all salvation comes finally through the divine mercy in Christ, and in mysticism this is often expressed in the most vivid manner; of this Matilda is a witness. (S. M. DEUTSCH.)

BIBLIOGRAPHY: *Sanctæ Mechthildis liber specialis gratiæ*, in *Revelationes Gertrudianæ ac Mechthildianæ, cura . . Solesmensium O. S. M. monachorum*, ii. 1–421, Paris, 1877; J. Müller, *Leben und Offenbarungen der heiligen Mechthild und der Schwester Mechthild*, Regensburg, 1881; W. Preger, *Geschichte der deutschen Mystik im Mittelalter*, i. 79 sqq., 116 sqq., Leipsic, 1874.

MATILDA (MECHTILDIS) OF MAGDEBURG: Beguine, afterward nun at Helfta (Helpede), near Eisleben; b. 1212 or a year or two later; d. at Helfta c. 1280. In her twelfth year she was "saluted by the Holy Spirit," and thenceforth her spiritual life developed uninterruptedly (Morel, iv. 2, p. 91). At the age of twenty-three she went to Magdeburg and lived there thirty years as Beguine. In her lonely life she had extraordinary experiences which she later wrote down in Low German and thus originated the first six parts of her book; the seventh part she added afterward at Helfta, whither she retired when advanced in years and where she lived for twelve years, highly revered (cf. *Lib. spec. grat.*, ii. 42, v. 7). Her work was translated into High German by Henry of Nördlingen (q.v.) about 1345 (cf. P. Strauch, *Heinrich von Nördlingen*, pp. 246–217, Freiburg, 1882). The first six parts had already been translated into Latin with a wholly different arrangement and in this form are found in the *Revelationes Gertrudinæ ac Mechthildianæ*. Matilda is distinguished from most female mystics by her pronounced individuality. Her spiritual experiences were remarkable and she stands in a firm position from which she can clearly distinguish between the external and internal. Furthermore, she is a real poetess, a true spiritual minnesinger. Her description of Mary and the birth of Jesus (Morel, v. 23) is beautiful, her prayers (v. 35, vii. 41–46) are devout and solemn, and she knows well how to express her thoughts in short sentences. As a faithful daughter of the Church she feels its shortcomings and is not sparing with her censure. To her censures she adds predictions, in which the influence of the writings of Joachim of Fiore (q.v.) is perceptible. But the greater part of her book deals with the inner life, and here Matilda betrays a depth and fulness of understanding which makes its study both attractive and fruitful. On the whole it is one of the most interesting works of mysticism, and a true treasure of medieval German literature. (S. M. DEUTSCH.)

BIBLIOGRAPHY: *Die Offenbarungen der Schwester Mechthild von Magdeburg, oder das fliessende Licht der Gottheit*, ed. G. Morel, Regensburg, 1861; *Sanctæ Mechthildis liber specialis gratiæ* and *Sororis Mechthildis lux divinitatis fluens in corda veritatis*, in *Revelationes Gertrudianæ ac Mechthildianæ, cura . . Solesmensium O. S. M. monachorum*, ii. 1–421 and 435–707, Paris and Poitiers, 1877; W. Preger, *Geschichte der deutschen Mystik im Mittelalter*, i. 70–71, 91 sqq., Leipsic, 1874; C. Greith, *Die deutsche Mystik im Predigerorden*, pp. 207–277, Freiburg, 1861; J. Müller, *Leben und Offenbarungen der heiligen Mechthild und der Schwester Mechthild*, Regensburg, 1881.

MATILDA, COUNTESS OF TUSCANY: Supporter of the papacy; b. 1046; d. in the monastery of Bondeno de' Roncori July 24, 1115. A daughter of Count Boniface of Tuscany and Beatrice of Lorraine, she inherited from her parents, while still a mere child, very extensive possessions in northern and central Italy, through which lay the roads from Germany and France to Rome. They were therefore strategically important in the wars between emperor and pope. Her parentage was German, and her ancestors were adherents of the German emperors; but the treacherous manner in which Henry III. treated her father induced the latter to support the papal position; and during the reigns of Nicholas II., Alexander II., Gregory VII., Victor III., Urban II., and Paschalis II., the Countess Matilda followed their course and was the mainstay of the papacy. Specially intimate were her relations with Gregory VII., whom she sheltered more than once against Henry IV. She continued the war against the emperor, even after Gregory's death. She was twice married, first to Godfrey of Lorraine, then to Duke Guelf of Bavaria; but her first marriage seems never to have been completed, and from her second husband she was divorced. Her enormous wealth, bequeathed to the papal chair, formed part of the so-called "Patrimonium Petri" (see PAPAL STATES).

BIBLIOGRAPHY: The Vita by the monk Donizone (Domnizone) is in best form ed., with two *Epitomes*, L. C. Bethmann in *MGH, Script.*, xii (1856), 348–409; or separately, ed. F. Davoli, Reggio-Emilia, 1888. An excellent list of literature is found in Potthast, *Wegweiser*, p. 1468. Consult: L. Tosti, *La Contessa Matilde*, Florence, 1859, new ed., Rome, 1886; A. Pannenborg, *Studien zur*

Geschichte der Herzogin Matilde von Canossa, Göttingen, 1872; the biographies by Mrs. M. E. Huddy, London, 1905, and Miss Nora Duff, ib., 1909; and the literature under PAPAL STATES, and under the articles on the popes named in the text.

MATINS: The office which, with its complement Lauds (q.v.), forms the nocturnal part of the Breviary (q.v.), and in length amounts to about one-half of that for the whole day. On ordinary week-days and simple feasts it has only one division or nocturn; on Sundays and all feasts above the rank of simple, it has three, corresponding to the ancient Roman division of the night into three watches. After the silent recitation of the Lord's Prayer, Hail Mary, and Creed, it begins with the introductory versicles and responses, and Ps. xcv., interspersed with repetitions of the invitatory, a versicle referring to the day or season; then a hymn, varying with the day, and the psalms, twelve on ordinary week-days, on festivals three to each nocturn. Each psalm or group of psalms has its Antiphon (q.v.) to bring out a special meaning for the day. The psalms are followed by the lessons, each with a short responsory. Those of the first (or on week-days the only) nocturn are taken from the Old Testament; those of the second from the lives of the saints or the writings of the Fathers; those of the third from some patristic exposition of the Gospel for the day. After the last lesson the place of the responsory is taken on Sundays (except in Advent and from Septuagesima to Easter), festivals, and week-days in the Paschal season, by the *Te Deum*.

Before the Reformation, matins, like vespers, was frequently a public service attended by the laity, so that some account was early taken of it in the reorganization of worship. In the *Deutscher Kirchenamt*, probably as early as 1523, there is a reformed vernacular office based upon it. Luther wished to retain matins and vespers, and saw no need of making radical changes in them, since they were mainly taken from Scripture. He wished to shorten matins, and to read the whole Psalter and the rest of the Bible consecutively, adding exposition on Sundays. In the *Formula Missæ* of 1523 and the *Deutsche Messe* of 1526, he sets forth his arrangement at some length. It was not at all universally followed, especially in South Germany. The Reformed Churches knew nothing of it, and even where it was retained among the Lutherans there was no uniformity. In some places it was recited daily, in others on Sundays, and in others again only on great festivals; and the order of the service varied. In the nature of the case it was to be expected that this ancient service should gradually disappear; the last traces of it in Germany were retained on the three great festivals, especially Christmas; but none of the modern *Agenda* make any attempt to reproduce it. [In the Church of England Prayer-book (see COMMON PRAYER, BOOK OF) the vernacular office entitled "Morning Prayer," and colloquially designated as matins to this day, is a fusion of various features of the ancient matins, lauds, and prime.] (P. DREWS.)

BIBLIOGRAPHY: Bingham, *Origines*, XIII., ix. 10; A. J. Binterim, *Denkwurdigkeiten*, iv. 1, pp. 357 sqq., Mainz, 1827; W. Palmer, *Origines liturgicæ*, i. 213, Oxford, 1832; F. Armknecht, *Die alte Matutin- und Vesperordnung in der evangelisch-lutherischen Kirche*, Göttingen, 1856; T. Kliefoth, *Liturgische Abhandlungen*, vi. 185 sqq., vii. 438 sqq., 489 sqq., viii. 164 sqq., Halle, 1859–61; F. X. Kraus, *Real-Encyklopädie des christlichen Altertums*, ii. 530 sqq., Freiburg, 1886; V. Thalhofer, *Handbuch der katholischen Liturgik*, ii. 358, 434 sqq., 450, Freiburg, 1893; *KL*, viii. 1042 sqq.; and much of the literature under BREVIARY.

MATTHEW.

I. The Apostle: In all the lists of the apostles in the New Testament Matthew appears as one of the Twelve, in Mark and Luke occupying the seventh place, in Matthew and the Acts the eighth. By the appellative "publican" (Matt. x. 3) he is to be identified with the Matthew of ix. 9 sqq. and doubtless with the Levi of Mark ii. 14 and Luke v. 27 sqq., Mark adding that his father was Alpheus; possibly Mark and Luke used his earlier name, Matthew being his name after he became a disciple. He was doubtless a Jew, as his name indicates, contrary to the statement of Julius Africanus. Nothing further regarding his life is told in Matthew or the Acts. In tradition his story developed. Thus Clement of Alexandria calls him a vegetarian ("The Instructor," II., i.; *ANF*, ii. 241) and places him in the list of those saints who did not suffer martyrdom; later tradition made him a martyr by fire, beheading, or stoning; he is said to have preached first to his own people, afterward in foreign lands (Eusebius, *Hist. eccl.*, III., xxiv. 6; *NPNF*, 2 ser., i. 152). The stories concerning his grave and his relics may be found in R. A. Lipsius, *Die apokryphen Apostelgeschichten*, p. 217, Brunswick, 1890.

II. The Gospel: In the early Church the authorship of the first Gospel was universally ascribed to Matthew. The tradition of apostolical authorship arose very early, and that Gospel was the chief source used by the Apostolic Fathers, while Papias is expressly quoted as asserting the Matthean origin ("So then Matthew wrote the *logia* in the Hebrew language, and every one interpreted them as he was able," Eusebius, *Hist. eccl.*, III., xxxix. 16; *NPNF*, 2 ser., i. 173). By the assertion that the logia were in the Hebrew was meant not the classical Hebrew of the Old Testament, but the dialect of Syriac which was the mother tongue of Matthew and of Jesus, and he implies that the translations (into Greek) are more numerous than could be desired because inaccurate. With this sentence of Papias, then, begins the external testimony to the authorship of the first Gospel. Later writers never contradict Papias but rather copy or corroborate him (Eusebius, *Hist. eccl.*, III., xxiv. 6, V., viii. 2, VI., xxv. 4). The fact of a Hebrew Matthew receives confirmation from still another source. And by this is meant neither what is related in the Apocryphal Acts of Barnabas (Lipsius, *Die apokryphen Apostelgeschichten*, ii. 2, pp. 270 sqq., 291 sqq.) concerning the finding of an auto-

1. External Testimony.

graph copy of Matthew with the remains of Barnabas, nor a suggestion that eastern Gospels have been thought, contrary to fact, to build upon a Hebrew original. Eusebius reports (*Hist. eccl.*, V., x. 3) that Pantænus, an early apostle to India, found among the Christians a copy of Matthew in Hebrew which had been left by the Apostle Bartholomew and preserved for about a century. Jerome reports (*De vir. ill.*, iii.) that in 392–393 A.D. in the library of Pamphilus at Cæsarea there was a copy of the original Hebrew text, and that he had a rescript of another copy which the Nazarenes of Berea had lent him. But this can be pressed no further than that Pantænus is a witness for the existence of a Gospel in Hebrew letters held to be the Hebrew Matthew, while the Gospel referred to by Jerome is doubtless the Gospel according to the Hebrews so often mentioned by him, reported by Eusebius as used by Hegesippus (*Hist. eccl.*, IV., xxii. 8) and referred to by Clement of Alexandria, Origen, and Epiphanius (cf. Zahn, *Kanon*, ii. 2, pp. 642–723), which diverged widely from the canonical Matthew. Jerome describes this as written "in the Chaldaic and Syriac language but in Hebrew letters," and as the only Gospel used by the Christians of Palestine who spoke Hebrew. It is probable that the Gospel used by the Nazarenes was that by Matthew, that they used this alone and not the fourfold Gospel was due to poverty, and that in accordance with the naiveté of the times they "corrected" it to suit their own doctrinal tendencies. But as a sure witness to the original Hebrew Matthew the Gospel of the Hebrews is not available.

2. Criticism versus Tradition.

Since the Reformation belief in a Hebrew Matthew has been badly shaken. The originality of the Greek was a fundamental proposition with the Reformers. A reaction against this dogmatic assertion came in the seventeenth and eighteenth centuries, when emphasis was laid upon indications of translation in the Greek and attempts were made to reconstruct the Aramaic basis. These attempts were destined to failure for two reasons: (1) the canonical Gospel in its present form can not be the work of an apostle like Matthew who was an eye and ear witness of Jesus, since legend, misunderstanding, and irrelevancy are too prominent; (2) it is too closely dependent upon Mark not merely in choice of matter and arrangement but in verbal detail. Conservative criticism has sought to minimize the weight of these two sets of facts by supposing that the translator of the Hebrew Matthew had the Gospel of Mark before him and was influenced by it in his translation. But the identity of the present Matthew with the assumed Hebrew is no longer maintained, a "relationship" simply is asserted, and this, unfortunately, is no easier to establish than identity. Truly, many foolish arguments against the apostolicity of Matthew have been advanced which it is not necessary to refute, particularly those drawn from comparison with the Fourth Gospel and from the first two chapters and the story of the temptation. But many of the additions to the Synoptic story of the passion bear the marks of invention which in some cases can be traced to a tendency to shift the weight of blame for Christ's death, and other episodes are suspicious, such as the opening of the graves (xxvii. 52–53). Similarly, such passages as xii. 40 are hardly to be attributed to a disciple, and a clear exposition of the consciousness of Jesus might be looked for from an apostle.

3. The Sources.

The relation between Matthew and Mark is totally destructive of tradition. Under the Tübingen hypothesis that Mark was a condensation from Matthew and Luke, both sources of Mark were carried back to apostolic origination. Since that hypothesis has been given up, those who hold the priority of Matthew over Mark do it at the expense of the tradition respecting both, while Zahn supposes that Mark, the disciple of Peter, writing in Greek slavishly used the Hebrew Matthew, while the translator of the latter in turn used the Greek Mark. But comparison of Matthew and Mark and of Luke and Mark show that Mark is the earlier, since Matthew and Luke introduce corrections and explanations. On the other hand, passages show independent treatment by Matthew, as in chap. xiii., where Matthew, though following the thread of the Marcan chain of parables, makes additions. If Matthew, therefore, appears as the work of an author comparatively distant from the events he narrates and also dependent upon Mark for form and content, it can no longer be ascribed to the Apostle Matthew writing in Hebrew. Still, the Papias tradition may have a kernel of fact. For while Matthew is in great part parallel to Mark, it contains large and important portions not derived from the second Gospel. Such are chaps. i.–ii., v.–vii., x., parts of xxiii.–xxv., many of the parables, and bits of history like viii. 5–13; and in these matters Matthew is often in company with Luke. But since this close relationship between Matthew and Luke is limited to definite sections while in other parts the relation of dependence is out of the question, the solution can not be reached by the hypothesis of combination between Matthew and Luke, and there is left the supposition that these two Gospels employed another source besides Mark. It is the misfortune of the two-document theory that it has been bound up with a perverted explanation of Papias and with the supposed tradition that Matthew wrote only the words (*logia*) of Jesus. In fact, it is one of the surest results of a criticism unencumbered by tradition and using internal evidences that it brings into use a lost writing which deals with the words of Jesus. That there were in existence collections of *logia* is shown by the Oxyrhynchus fragments (cf. B. P. Grenfell and A. S. Hunt, *Logia Jesu*, London, 1897). The usage of Paul (I Thess. iv. 15) and of the Gospels themselves in not always giving the historical framework of individual sayings or in differing in the historical setting supports the hypothesis of a logia source, and it is clear from comparison of Matthew and Luke that this source had formulas of introduction which both Gospels have employed. This document may have contained many things which it is now impossible to prove were in it. It can not be decided whether Mark employed it; it is improbable, however, that it was a complete Gospel or that it purposed more than to give an introduction to the teaching of Jesus. Indications do not suggest its attribution to the Apostle Matthew, yet as one of the two sources of the present Matthew Gospel there is the highest probability that an Aramaic collection of the words of Jesus was used, and Matthew's name may have been attached to it. It would be no surprise that such a collection, attributed to this apostle, should bestow its supposed author's name upon the completed Gospel, though this was written by one who was neither an apostle nor the disciple of one. In other words, Matthew is based upon Mark and other sources, one of which was also employed in the Gospel of the Hebrews on other soil, with other helps, and with a different purpose.

4. Content, Structure, and Purpose. An examination of the material does not permit the assertion that the compiler had in mind a sharply defined plan which included division into six or five or three parts, only that he gathered similar materials into great groups and left it to be discovered what was his point of view in the arrangement. The time idea is dominant in chaps. i.-ii., xxvi.-xxviii., and in part also in iii.-xxv. The connectives also give an impression of attention to chronology. But all this is only the employment of a literary form which is merely external. Thus, after a painting of Jesus' deeds (iv. 17-25) the Gospel illustrates his method of teaching (v. 1-7, 27), and then exhibits him as a helper in every kind of need by adducing ten examples of his instruction. It is more difficult to expound the difference between ix. 35 and xx. 34. The apostle shows first how Jesus educated the disciples to assist in his work of evangelization by showing the necessity of help (ix. 35-38), and sketched the plan of operations (x. 5-42), though elsewhere in the Gospel, in spite of these earlier lessons, he is engaged in showing how to do the work; second, Jesus finds himself hindered by the dulness of the masses, for whom he adopts the method of teaching by parables (chaps. xi., xiii., xv., xxi., sqq.); third, he combats Pharisaic obtuseness and prejudice (xii. 1-14, xii. 22 sqq., xv. 1-20). One may say that ix. 35-xviii. 35 (or xx. 34) contains the transition from the first period of success to the turning away of Jesus from the crude people and the fanatical Pharisees to the little flock of devoted and true disciples. Of the purpose of this Gospel two opposing views have been held. One regards it as expressing a narrow type of Jewish Christianity, interested in the Davidic descent of Jesus, in the eternal worth of the law, and in prophecy (v. 17-20, x. 6, xxi. 2-7); the other sees in Matthew an anti-Jewish and anti-Judaistic tendency, especially in viii. 10-12, xii. 41-42, xv. 28, xxvii. 22-23, 25. Zahn thinks that Matthew wished his book to be read especially by Jews as yet unconverted. But this book was intended rather for the faithful, to whom it was meant to prove that in Jesus were realized the prophecies and promises of the Old Testament. It is not a narrative produced for the delights of authorship, nor a polemic writing against unbelieving Israel; it is a positive justification of the Gospel of Christ, the strong apologetics of which is directed less against antagonistic reproach than against particular doubts, and least of all against heretical parties. Thus, the genealogy, arranged in three parts of fourteen steps each, from Abraham to David and then to Jechonias, is intended to prove that with the birth of Jesus a new era had begun. Moreover, in its closing words it is distinctively universalistic; and it recognizes that outside of Christ there is no salvation (xxv. 1-13).

While nothing further can be said of the author than that he was a Jewish Christian, acquainted with both Hebrew and Greek, a resident of Palestine and acquainted with numerous written and oral sources, there yet remains the task of setting his date.

5. Date and Value. If Matthew was the author, the date would be not far from 70 A.D. Passages like x. 23, xvi. 28 echo the earliest period of Christianity, and x. 18 does not contradict this impression. For a time later than 70 A.D. speaks xxii. 7, but how much later? The reign of Trajan (98-117 A.D.) is the latest date allowable because of the testimony of Papias. If Luke is dependent upon Matthew, the date must be put prior to 100 A.D. The trinitarian formula (xxviii. 19) does not presume a very early date; xxiv. 25 does not seem to express immediate expectation of the parousia; the impression of development of the Church is quite marked, suggesting a date later than 75 A.D.; and there is no trace of a conflict such as Paul waged with the idea of the Jewish law as a principle of salvation. Argument as to the date derived from the amount of textual corruption as compared with the other Gospels is inconclusive, because the wide diffusion of the Matthew Gospel in the early Church gave larger opportunities for corruption. Distinction between a proto- and a deutero-Matthew does not seem justified in view of the unity of the book in its dogmatic, literary, and religious characteristics. The regard in which the book was held in the early Church as compared with the popularity of Mark and Luke (the Gospel of John is so different in genius as not to come into comparison) is due to the fact that it expresses the spirit of the early Catholic Church, while the other Synoptics are more individualistic in character. The material is rich, derived from good sources, effectively and strongly presented, and the literary method preserves the mean between inartistic hardness and artificial plainness. And in neither of the other Synoptics does the figure of Jesus so stand out as teacher and helper as in this of Matthew. For the Gospel of Pseudo-Matthew see Apocrypha, B, 1., 2. (A. JÜLICHER.)

BIBLIOGRAPHY: On the apostle the articles in the dictionaries, e.g., *DB*, ii. 295-296; *EB*, iii. 2986-87; E. C. A. Riehm, *Handwörterbuch des biblischen Altertums*, pp. 976-977, Leipsic, 1894; F. Vigouroux, *Dictionnaire de la Bible*, Paris, 1905.

Questions of introduction are treated in the commentaries (below), in the works on New-Testament introduction (see BIBLICAL INTRODUCTION), especially those of Godet, Holtzmann, Jülicher, and Zahn; much of the literature on the life of Christ discusses the subject: the literature on the Synoptic relations is given under GOSPELS. Note may be made here of the following special works: J. H. Scholten, *Das älteste Evangelium*, Elberfeld, 1869; P. Schanz, in *TQ*, lxiv (1882), 517-560; E. Massebieau, *Examen des citations de l'Ancien Testament dans S. Matthieu*, Paris, 1885; A. B. Bruce, *With Open Face*, pp. 1–24, London, 1896; F. P. Badham, *St. Mark's Indebtedness to St. Matthew*, ib. 1897; E. Roehrich, *La Composition des evangiles*, Paris, 1897; P Wernle, *Die synoptische Frage*, Tübingen, 1899; A. Harnack, *Sprüche und Rede Jesu. Die zweite Quelle des Matthäus und Lukas*, Leipsic, 1907; *DB*, iii. 296–305. On the original language consult: D. Gla, *Originalsprache des Matthäus*, Paderborn, 1887; G. Dalman, *Die Worte Jesu*, vol. i., Leipsic, 1898. On the relation to the Gospel of the Hebrews consult: S. Baring-Gould, *Lost and Hostile Gospels*, London, 1874; E. B. Nicholson, *The Gospel according to the Hebrews*, ib. 1879; A. Hilgenfeld, *N. T. extra canonem receptum*, part iv., Leipsic, 1884; R. Handmann, in *TU*, v. 3, 1889; J. A. Robinson, in *Expositor*, 5 ser., v (1897), 194–200; E. Hennecke, *Neutestamentliche Apokryphen*, pp. 11–21, Tübingen, 1904.

Commentaries, outside of patristic and medieval sources, are: P. A. Gratz, 2 vols., Tübingen, 1821; T. J. Conant, New York, 1860; H. Lutteroth, 4 vols., Paris, 1860–76; A. Réville, ib. 1862; W. A. Nast, Cincinnati, 1864; J. P. Lange, New York, 1865; H. T. Adamson, London, 1871; J. A. Alexander, New York, 1873; J. J. Owen, ib. 1873; B. Weiss, Halle, 1876; J. C. F. Keil, Leipsic, 1877; J. L. Sommer, Erlangen, 1877; P. Schaff, New York, 1879; P. Schanz, Freiburg, 1879 (Roman Catholic); E. B. Nicholson, London, 1881; J. Kleutgen, Freiburg, 1882 (Roman Catholic); Juan de Valdes (Eng. transl., London, 1882); E. H. Plumptre, in Ellicott's *Handy Commentary*, New York, 1883; E. W. Rice, Philadelphia, 1886; J. A. Broadus, Philadelphia, 1887; A. Carr, in *Cambridge Bible*, Cambridge, 1879; idem, in *Cambridge Greek Testament*, ib. 1887; J. Maldonatus, Eng. transl., 2 vols., London, 1888–1889 (Roman Catholic, from the 16th century); E. Kübel, Munich, 1889; J. M. Gibson, in *Expositor's Bible*, London, 1890; H. J. Holtzmann, 3d ed., Tübingen, 1901; J. Morison, London, 1895 (one of the best); C. F. Schaefer, in *Lutheran Commentary*, New York, 1895; C. F. Nösgen, Munich, 1897; J. M. S. Baljon, Utrecht, 1900; F. C. Ceulemans, Malines, 1901 (Roman Catholic); F. N. Peloubet, 2 vols., New York, 1901; T. Zahn, Leipsic, 1903; F. S. Gutjahr, Graz, 1904 (Roman Catholic); J. Wellhausen, Berlin, 1904; A. Maclaren, 3 vols., London, 1905–06; W. C. Allen, in *International Critical Commentary*, Edinburgh and New York, 1907; A. Plummer, London, 1909; E. Rice, Philadelphia, 1910.

MATTHEW PARIS: English chronicler; b. in or near St. Albans not much before 1200; d. there, probably in June, 1259. [The origin of the designation "Paris" is questionable. It has been attributed to a supposed (but doubtful) sojourn in the city of Paris during his studies: the claim is also made that it was his family name. The latter supposition is difficult (though not impossible), as the period is early for surnames.] He was educated in the abbey school, and became (Jan. 21, 1217) a monk in this famous monastery, which, founded in 1077, had become a great center of light and learning, and since the time of Abbot Simon (1167–83) had paid special attention to literary and particularly historical production by its monks. Matthew was placed in charge of the *scriptorium* or writing-room in 1236 and retained this office until his death. He frequently visited London, Canterbury, and Winchester, gaining some knowledge of the great world outside his cloister, and made one visit to Norway (1248) to reform the abbey of Niderholm near Trondhjem. He rightly regarded the writing of history, for which he had not only special facilities but special talent, as his life-work. His fame rests principally on his *Chronica majora*, written in the usual form of annals. Up to 1235 it is a recasting and enlargement of the *Flores historiarum* of Roger of Wendover, from that date to 1259 entirely independent. He wrote also a history of the abbey of St. Albans in the form of biographies of the abbots; *Liber additamentorum*, a collection of documents to serve as a supplement to the *Chronica;* lives of the two Offas, kings of Mercia, of Stephen Langton and Edmund Rich, archbishops of Canterbury, and of St. Richard of Chichester. The Chronicle is distinguished by many virtues: an insatiable desire for accurate information, keen realization of the difference between essentials and non-essentials, a broad view of Christianity, outspoken boldness even when dealing with kings and popes, clearness and beauty of style. He is an admirable representative of the English public opinion of his day. Matthew was unusually privileged in having frequent opportunities of intercourse not only with courtiers but with kings, who valued him highly and took a deep interest in his work. But his opportunities would have counted for little if he had not possessed a mind that knew how to search further for any piece of information of value in any part of the civilized world, and to make prompt and systematic use of the knowledge thus gained. He ranks as the first great English historian. (H. Böhmer.)

Bibliography: The *Historia Anglorum*, ed. F. Madden, is no. 44 in *Rolls Series*, 3 vols., London, 1866–69; and the *Chronica majora*, ed. H. R. Luard, is no. 57 of the same, 7 vols., ib. 1872–84 (the prefaces to these works are of especial value); the *Liber additamentorum* is in Luard, ut sup., vol. vi.; excerpts from Matthew's works, ed. F. Liebermann, are in *MGH*, *Script.*, xxviii (1888), 74–455; the *Chronica* in Eng. transl. is in *Bohn's Antiquarian Library*, 3 vols., London, 1852–54. Consult: T. D. Hardy, *Descriptive Catalogue of Materials*, no. 26 in *Rolls Series*, vol. iii., preface, London, 1871; A. Jessop, *Studies by a Recluse*, pp. 1–65, ib. 1893 (an appreciation); H. Plehn, *Der politische Character Matthæus Parisiensis*, Leipsic, 1897; Gross, *Sources*, pp. 299–300; *DNB*, xliii. 203–213, cf. xxxv. 292.

MATTHEW, THOMAS: Pseudonym for John Rogers (q.v.); see also Bible Versions, B, IV., § 4.

MATTHEW, TOBIE (TOBIAS): Anglican prelate and statesman; b. in Bristol 1546; d. at Cawood Castle (9 m. s. of York) March 29, 1628. He was graduated from Oxford (B.A., 1563–64; M.A., 1566; B.D., 1573; D.D., 1574); was chosen public orator of the university, 1569; appointed canon of Christ Church, 1570; archdeacon of Bath, and prebendary of Teynton Regis in the cathedral of Salisbury, 1572; the same year he was made president of St. John's College; dean of Christ Church, 1576; vice-chancellor of the university, 1579; dean of Durham, 1583; vicar of Bishop's Wearmouth, 1590; bishop of Durham, 1595; archbishop of York, 1606. Matthew was in his day a noted orator, a preacher of high repute, faithful even to punctiliousness in the performance of the duties of his bishopric, a diligent guardian of the royal and national interests in the northern counties, and a man of quiet humor and earnest piety. His only publication seems to have been a *Concio apologetica adversus Campianum*, which was circulated in manuscript form some time prior to his death and printed only after his death (London, 1638).

Bibliography: *DNB*, xxxvii. 60–63, where references to other literature are given.

MATTHEW OF WESTMINSTER: The name once given to the supposed author of *Flores Histor-*

iarum, which is now known to be a composite work. A full discussion is to be found in the preface to H. R. Luard's masterly ed. of the *Flores*, no. 95 of *Rolls Series*, London, 1890. See MATTHEW PARIS.

MATTHIAS: According to Acts i. 23, one of the witnesses of the ministry, death, and resurrection of Jesus. He was therefore received among the Twelve, but no traditions have been preserved regarding his activity, although the early Church considered him one of the seventy disciples. The third and fourth centuries possessed a heretical Gospel of Matthias (see APOCRYPHA, B, I., 28). (A. HAUCK.)

MAULBRONN: A little town of Württemberg, 23 m. n.w. of Stuttgart, noteworthy as the seat of a former Cistercian monastery and as the place where a Protestant conference was held in 1564 and a formula drawn up in 1576. The monastery was founded about 1138 by Walter of Lomersheim at a distance of an hour and a half from the present village, whence it was transferred by Bishop Günther of Speyer, between Aug., 1146, and May, 1147, to the valley of the Salzach, where it still forms one of the best-preserved monasteries in Germany. Its daughter abbeys were Bronnbach (1151) and Schönthal (1157). At the beginning of the Reformation it was a center of the monks who remained faithful to the Roman Catholic Church; but in 1557 it received a Protestant abbot, although for a short time during the Thirty Years' War it again came under Roman Catholic control. It is now the seat of a famous theological seminary.

The Monastery.

The Colloquy of Maulbronn arose from the introduction of Calvinism into the Palatinate by the Elector Frederick III., and especially from the formulation of the Heidelberg Catechism in 1563 (see HEIDELBERG CATECHISM; and PHILIPPISTS). The neighboring Lutheran princes, seeking both to unite Protestantism and to maintain pure doctrine, proposed to Frederick (Oct. 4, 1563) to hold a conference of the rival schools in the presence of the princes. Though at first reluctant, Frederick finally consented to a secret "friendly colloquy" to be held at Maulbronn immediately after Easter, the theme to be the meaning of the words of institution. The conference, attended by Frederick and Duke Christopher of Württemberg, with an imposing array of theologians and officials on either side, was accordingly held in ten sessions on Apr. 10-15, 1564. Eight of these were consumed in a debate on the ubiquity of the body of Christ, without reaching any conclusion whatsoever; and the remaining sessions were devoted to an equally useless attempt to reach harmony in Eucharistic doctrine. The princes, hard pressed by affairs of state, put an end to the fruitless debates, and on Apr. 17 the protocols were compared and signed, the two princes exchanging written statements of their several beliefs. Despite the bond of secrecy, the affair leaked out through letters in which the Calvinists boasted that they had triumphed over the Lutherans. The result was a series of publications of the transactions of the conference. These were, on the Lutheran side, J. Brenz, *Wahrhafftiger und gründlicher Bericht von dem Gespräch zwischen des Churfürsten Pfaltzgrafen und des Hertzogen zu Würthemberg Theologen von des Herrn Nachtmahl zu Maulbronn gehalten* (Frankfort, 1564; Lat. ed., 1564); *Protocoll des Gesprechs dem Original gleichförmig, one Zusatz und Abbruch* (Tübingen, 1565); *Erklärung der Württembergischen Theologen Bekanndtnuss der wahrhafftigen Gegenwärtigkeit im heiligen Abendmahl* (1565); and *Letzte Antwort der Wirtembergischen Theologen wider die Heydelbergische* (1566). On the Calvinistic side appeared *Protocoll, das ist, Acta oder Handlungen des Gesprechs zwischen den Pfältzischen und Wirtembergischen Theologen item, der Wirtembergischen Theologen von gemeldtem Gesprech desselben Jares aussgangener Bericht, samt der Pfältzischen Theologen wahrhafftigem und bestendigem Gegenbericht* (Heidelberg, 1565; Lat. ed., 1566); *Solida refutatio sophismatum et cavillationum quibus Würtenbergici totam controversiam incrustarunt* (1565); and *Bestendige Antwort der Pfältzischen Theologen auf der Wirtembergischen Theologen Erklärung und Bekenntniss* (1566). The ensuing controversy involved the theologians of Wittenberg and elsewhere, who decided against the Calvinistic position. Duke Christopher, however, alarmed by the growth of Calvinism in Germany, appealed in addition to the Evangelical princes, and it was only through the energetic intervention of the Elector Frederick at the Diet of Augsburg in 1566 that the threatened storm was averted.

The Colloquy of Maulbronn.

Far more peaceable was the conference held at Maulbronn in 1576, at which theologians from Württemberg, Baden, and Henneberg drew up the "Maulbronn formula," one of the bases of the "Formula of Concord" (q.v.). In conformity with the desire of the Elector August of Saxony to secure doctrinal unity among the Evangelical churches of Germany, a preliminary document was drafted at Stuttgart on Nov. 14, 1575, which formed the basis of the formula adopted at Maulbronn on Jan. 19, 1576 (first printed by T. Pressel in *Jahrbücher für deutsche Theologie*, 1866, 640-711). This was sent to August, who, about the same time, received the Swabo-Saxon formula of Duke Julius of Brunswick. At the Conference of Torgau, opened May 28, 1576, the latter was made the basis of discussion, though with the incorporation of all the essentials of the Maulbronn formula, the result being the "Book of Torgau." In September of the same year a second conference of theologians from Württemberg, Baden, and Henneberg was held at Maulbronn, at which the "Book of Torgau" was ratified in all essentials. (E. NESTLE.)

The "Maulbronn Formula."

BIBLIOGRAPHY: On the monastery, besides the literature under CISTERCIANS, consult: F. Eisenlohr, *Mittelalterliche Bauwerke im südwestlichen Deutschland*, Carlsruhe, 1853-57; J. and P. Hartmann, *Wegweiser durch das Kloster Maulbronn*, Stuttgart, 1875; E. Paulus, *Die Cisterzienserabtei Maulbronn*, Stuttgart, 1889; E. Bassler, *Kleiner Führer durch das Kloster Maulbronn*, Maulbronn, 1902; A. Mettler, *Zur Klosteranlage der Zisterzienser und zur Baugeschichte Maulbronns*, Stuttgart, 1909.

On the Maulbronn Colloquy consult: G. J. Planck, *Geschichte . unsers protestantischen Lehrbegriffs*, v. 2, pp. 487 sqq., 6 vols., Leipsic, 1791-1800; H. L. J. Heppe, *Geschichte des deutschen Protestantismus*, ii. 71 sqq., Frankfort, 1865-66; A. Kluckhohn, *Friedrich der Fromme*, pp. 166 sqq., Nördlingen, 1876-79.

MAUNDY THURSDAY: The day before Easter, also called Holy Thursday. The word "maundy" is derived from the Latin *mandatum* (commandment), referring to John xiii. 34, and the day commemorates the institution of the Lord's Supper and the washing of the disciples' feet. See HOLY WEEK, § 4.

MAUR, mōr (MAURUS), SAINT: A legendary disciple of Benedict of Nursia, who first became famous through the Congregation of St. Maur (q.v.). He is said to have been born at Rome in 511 and died at Glanfeuil in Anjou, 584; also to have introduced the Benedictine rule into France and to have founded at Glanfeuil the first French monastery of his order. His extant biography is ascribed to Faustus, a monk of Monte Cassino and a contemporary of Maurus, but is in reality a forgery of the ninth century. Gregory of Tours does not mention Maur, and the details of his life are doubted not only by Protestants but also by Roman Catholic scholars. (A. HAUCK.)

BIBLIOGRAPHY: For the *Vita*, or other documents, consult *ASB*, Jan., i. 1039, 1051–60; *ASM*, sæc. I., pp. 274–298, IV., 2, pp. 165–183; *MPL*, xciv. 1594–97; and ed. O. Holder-Egger, *MGH*, *Script.*, xv (1887), 462–472. Consult: *S. Maur et le sanctuaire de Glanfeuil en Anjou*, Angers, 1869; A. Ebert, *Allgemeine Geschichte der Literatur des Mittelalters*, ii. 351, Leipsic, 1880; Zeumer, in *NA*, xi. 316; A. Molinier, *Sources de l'hist. de France*, i. 161–162, Paris, 1901.

MAURICE OF HESSE. See VERBESSERUNGSPUNKTE, DIE HESSISCHEN.

MAURICE (MAURITIUS), SAINT: The name of several early Christian martyrs, of whom the most celebrated is the commander (*primicerius*) of the famous Theban Legion (q.v.) which was put to death in a body under the Emperor Maximian for its confession of the Christian faith.

MAURICE OF SAXONY: Elector of Saxony; b. at Freiberg Mar. 21, 1521; d. at Sievershausen (16 m. e. of Hanover) July 11, 1553. He succeeded his father as duke of Saxony in 1541, and obtained the electoral dignity after the battle of Mühlberg, 1547. Though he had embraced the Reformation, and, together with his father, signed the Schmalkald Articles, he refused to join the League, probably because he considered the organization too weak, and his own position in it too subordinate, to form the basis for his ambitious schemes; and at the Diet of Regensburg (q.v.), where he and Duke Eric of Brunswick were the only Protestant princes present, he made a secret alliance with the Emperor Charles V. Accordingly, when the war broke out, he marched his troops into the territory of his cousin, the elector of Saxony, and conquered the country. But as soon as the elector, who stood in Upper Germany with a well-appointed army, heard of this treachery, he hastened back to Saxony, and not only reconquered his own land, but also expelled Maurice from his dukedom. The emperor came to his rescue; and at the Diet of Augsburg (Feb. 24, 1548) he was solemnly invested with a large portion of his cousin's territory and the electoral dignity. He rejected the Augsburg Interim; but the Leipsic Interim, which he substituted after conferring with Melanchthon, Bugenhagen, and others, proved as hateful to his subjects. Realizing that the Reformation would not be kept apart from politics as a purely religious issue, he decided to place himself at the head of the movement, driven onward, no doubt, also by indignation at the emperor's faithlessness toward his father-in-law, Philip of Hesse, and by fear of the intrigues recently set on foot to supersede King Ferdinand, the emperor's brother, and fasten the succession on Don Philip, the emperor's son, but a Spaniard. Concealing his plans with great adroitness, he gathered a great army, formed an alliance with France, and suddenly fell upon the emperor at Innsbruck, and compelled him to fly for his life across the Alps. By the mediation of King Ferdinand, the Treaty of Passau was brought about (1552), and full religious liberty was granted to the Protestants. Maurice now completely regained the confidence of his coreligionists; but he had only a short time to avail himself of the great opportunities thereby offered him. In a feud with the margrave of Brandenburg he was severely wounded, and died a few days after. See INTERIM; and AUGSBURG, RELIGIOUS PEACE OF.

BIBLIOGRAPHY: F. A. von Langenn, *Moritz, Herzog und Churfürst zu Sachsen*, 2 parts, Leipsic, 1841; E. Brandenburg, *Moritz von Sachsen*, Leipsic, 1898. Consult further: O. Winckelmann, *Der schmalkaldischen Bund, 1530–32*, Strasburg, 1892; J. Janssen, *Hist. of the German People*, vi. 308 sqq., St. Louis, 1903.

MAURICE, mō'ris, JOHN FREDERICK DENISON: Church of England theologian, metaphysician, and educator; b. at Normanston near Lowestoft (20 m. s.w. of Norwich), Suffolk, Aug. 29, 1805; d. in London Apr. 1, 1872. He entered Cambridge in 1823, but left in 1827 without taking a degree because he was unable to subscribe; but went to Oxford in 1830, and was ordained to the ministry of the Church of England in 1834. He was chaplain of Guy's Hospital, 1836–46; became professor of English literature and history at King's College, London, 1840; was Boyle lecturer, 1846–47, and Warburton lecturer, 1846; became chaplain of Lincoln's Inn, 1846; assisted in the founding of Queen's College, 1848, and of the College for Working Men, London, 1854, of which latter he became principal; was appointed to St. Peter's, Vere Street, London, 1860; became Knightbridge professor of casuistry, moral theology, and moral philosophy at Cambridge, 1866, retaining charge of St. Peter's till 1869; was appointed to St. Edward's, Cambridge, 1870, and was Cambridge preacher at Whitehall, 1871–72. Maurice came of Unitarian parentage, and his early career was somewhat handicapped by the scruples and limitations involved. But under the influence of the writings of Coleridge he worked his way to an Evangelical position, though the changes in his personal attitude made him ever unwilling to attach himself to any party in the Church. The result was that throughout his life the independence of his thought, sometimes expressed polemically, as well as his dissent from the extremes of the two wings in the Church, brought upon him much of discomfort through the many attacks to which he was subjected. He had a natural aptitude for metaphysics, and in the development of his theology his popularity was often hindered by the profundity of his statements. He was one of the men who profoundly influenced thought both in England and in America. This he did not less by the fact that he was a voluminous writer than by his sincerity and earnestness, being always ready to resign a position rather than to be deemed insincere in holding it, and by his essentially irenic disposition. His industry was remarkable, as is attested by the number of his works (cf. G. J. Gray, *Bibliography of the Writings of F. D. Maurice*, London, 1885). The most important of these are: *The Kingdom of Christ, or Hints to a Quaker Respecting the Principle, Constitution, and Ordinances of the Catholic Church* (3 vols., London, 1837, 3d ed., 1883); *The Epistle to the Hebrews* (Warburtonian Lectures; 1846); *The Religions of the World and their Relations to Christianity* (Boyle Lectures; Cambridge, 1847); *The Old Testament, Nineteen Sermons* (London, 1851; 2d ed. issued as *Patriarchs and Lawgivers of the Old Testament*, Cambridge, 1855); *Theological Essays* (London, 1853); *The Prophets and Kings of the Old Testament* (Cambridge, 1853); *Ecclesiastical History of the First and Second Centuries* (1854); *Claims of the Bible and of Science* (on the Colenso controversy; 1863); *The Gospel of the Kingdom of Heaven; a Course of Lectures on the Gospel of Luke* (1864); *The Conscience; Lectures on Casuistry* (London, 1868); *Moral and Metaphysical Philosophy* (2 vols., 1871-72); and *The Friendship of Books, and Other Lectures*, ed. T. Hughes (1874). Matthew Arnold's remark that Maurice was always beating the bush but never started the hare is accepted as just by many who think that Maurice has been much overrated, and that his "profundity" is frequently allied with obscurity.

BIBLIOGRAPHY: *Life of Frederick Denison Maurice, chiefly told in his own Letters, ed. by his Son, Frederick Maurice*, London, 1884; C. Fox, *Memories of Old Friends*, vol. ii. passim, ib. 1882; C. C. F. Masterman, *Frederick Denison Maurice*, ib. 1907; *DNB*, xxxvii. 97-105.

MAURY, mō″ri′, **JEAN SIFFREIN**: French cardinal; b. at Valréas (78 m. n.n.w. of Marseilles), France, June 26, 1746; d. at Montefiascone (about 50 m. n.n.w. of Rome), Italy, May 11, 1817. He was educated in the seminary of Avignon, but occupied himself more with literature than theology. By his *Oraison funèbre du Dauphin, panégyrique de saint Louis* (Paris, 1766), he attracted great attention as an orator; was made abbot of Frénade, and prior of Lyons, and published his best work *Essai sur l'éloquence de la chaire* (new ed., Paris, 1810, Eng. transl., *Principles of Eloquence*, London, 1793). Elected a member of the States General in 1789, and of the constituent assembly, he played a conspicuous part, defending the prerogatives of the crown, the privileges of the nobility, and the immunities of the church. Compelled to emigrate in 1792, he repaired to Rome, where he was received by Pius VI. with great honor; made archbishop *in partibus* of Nicæa, bishop of Montefiascone, and cardinal 1794. At the instance of Pius VII., it is said, he wrote a humble letter to Napoleon, Aug. 22, 1804, which resulted in his reconciliation with the French Government. In 1806 he returned to Paris; and so absolutely did he devote himself to Napoleon that he became an object of hatred to the legitimists and the ultramontanes. In 1810 Napoleon made him archbishop of Paris; but the chapter protested against the appointment, and the pope refused his sanction. He was expelled from his see as soon as the Bourbons returned, and, when he went to Rome to lay the case before the pope, was imprisoned in the castle of San Angelo until he resigned his see. His *Œuvres choisies* were published by his nephew (5 vols., Paris, 1827); his *Correspondance diplomatique et mémoires inédits* appeared in 2 vols. (Lille, 1891); his *Œuvres oratoires complètes* are in Migne, *Collection des orateurs sacrés*, vol. lxvii.

BIBLIOGRAPHY: J. J. F. Poujoulat, *Le Cardinal Maury, sa vie, ses œuvres*, Paris, 1859; G. Bonet-Maury, *Le Cardinal Maury d'après ses mémoires et sa correspondance inédits, 1746-1817*, ib. 1892.

MAUSBACH, maus′baн, **KARL JOSEPH**: German Roman Catholic; b. at Wipperfeld (a village near Wipperfürth, 23 m. n.e. of Cologne) Feb. 7, 1861. He was educated at the University of Münster (D.D., 1888) and the theological seminary at Eichstätt, having already been a curate in Cologne in 1884. He was teacher of religion in München-Gladbach from 1889 to 1892, and since the latter year has been professor of moral theology and apologetics at the University of Münster. He has written: *D. Thomæ Aquinatis de voluntate et appetitu sensitivo doctrina* (Paderborn, 1888); *Christentum und Weltmoral* (Münster, 1897); *Die katholische Moral, ihre Methoden, Grundsätze und Aufgaben* (Cologne, 1901); *Die ultramontane Moral nach Graf Paul von Hoensbroech* (Berlin, 1902); *Kernfragen christlicher Welt- und Lebensanschauung* (München-Gladbach, 1903-08); *Weltgrund und Menschheitsziel* (1904); *Ausgewählte Texte zur allgemeinen Moral aus Thomas von Aquin* (Münster, 1905); *Die Stellung der Frau im Menschheitsleben* (München-Gladbach, 1906); *Altchristliche und moderne Gedanken über Frauenberuf* (1906); and *Die Ethik des heiligen Augustinus* (2 vols., Freiburg, 1909).

MAXIMIANUS. See DIOCLETIAN.

MAXIMINUS, max″i-mai′nus, **THRAX, CAIUS JULIUS VERUS**: Roman emperor, 235-238; b. of Gothic and Alan parentage in Thrace, probably in 173; d. at Aquileia (the modern Aquileja, 21 m. w.n.w. of Triest) June 17, 238. The first barbarian to occupy the throne of the Cæsars, he was in early life a cowherd and later a cavalryman. Eight feet in height, and powerful and brave in proportion, he gained the favor of Alexander Severus, who made him a senator and the head of a legion, as well as a trainer of the recruits among his compatriots. In the campaign against the Germans, the soldiers proclaimed Maximinus emperor. In terror of the troops, the senate confirmed their choice, but the new emperor never came to Rome, preferring to remain with his soldiers and conquer the Germans, after which he went to Pannonia. But the brutality of his rule, accentuated by his suspicious nature and his knowledge of his lack of culture, resulted in a cruelty and oppression which led to his assassination.

Shortly after his accession to the throne, Maximinus issued an edict against all the Christian clergy, but it was practically disregarded, Sulpicius Severus mentioning only the occasional application of torture during this reign. In Rome the bishop Pontianus and the priest Hippolytus were banished, while Origen, who was a special object of the emperor's hatred on account of his relations with the household of Alexander Severus, found refuge in the home of Juliana, a Christian woman. In Pontus and Cappadocia the persecution was more severe, but there it was inspired rather by popular anger at the Christians because of an earthquake, than by the imperial decree. Although the persecution of Maximinus was in itself unimportant, it was the first systematic, general attack upon the new faith. He was the first to recognize the importance of the Christian hierarchy and to seek to annihilate it, thus furnishing a precedent for Valerian and Diocletian. His precise motive is difficult to determine; he gave no worship to the Greco-Roman deities, and possibly the persecution was due simply to the desire of Maximinus to strengthen his position so far as possible, and to prevent any Christian rebellion against himself. (G. Uhlhorn†.)

Bibliography: The subject is covered from the secular side in the works on the history of Rome of the period, and on the Christian side in those on the history of the Church of that time. See also literature under Persecutions of Christians in the Roman Empire. Reference may be made here to Görres, in *ZWT*, iv., 1876; J. C. L. Gieseler, *Church History*, ed. H. B. Smith, i. 177, New York, 1868; B. Aubé, *Les Chrétiens dans l'empire romain*, pp. 418–460, Paris, 1881; K. J. Neumann, *Der römische Staat und die allgemeine Kirche*, i. 210 sqq., Leipsic, 1890; Schaff, *Christian Church*, ii. 59.

MAXIMUS CONFESSOR.

I. His Life: Maximus, usually known as the Confessor, was the leading representative of the orthodox doctrine against the Monothelites of the seventh century. He was born in Constantinople about 580; d. at Shemari, on the shore of the Black Sea, Aug. 13, 662. He came of a distinguished family, and received an excellent education after the ideals of the time. Of delicate constitution and quiet-loving temperament, he seems at first to have been inclined to a life of contemplation and study, but was called away from it for a time to a political career. The Emperor Heraclius (610–641) summoned him to court and made him his first secretary. When he exchanged this position for the monastic state is uncertain. He entered the monastery of Chrysopolis at what is now Scutari, and before long became abbot. Soon after the beginning of the Monothelite controversy, when the monk Sophronius stood forth as the champion of orthodoxy against Cyrus, patriarch of Alexandria, Maximus was in that city and received the stimulus which led him to devote himself to combating Monothelitism. In a series of treatises and letters he defended the Chalcedonian orthodoxy as to the two natures and the two wills of Christ against both Monophysites and Monothelites, as well as against the imperial efforts at compromise. It was through his influence that North Africa became the headquarters of the orthodox party after the death of Heraclius. On the accession of Constans II. (642-668), the patriarch of Constantinople, Pyrrhus, was forced to flee on account of participation in the intrigues of Martina, the widow of Heraclius, and took refuge in North Africa, where the prefect, Gregory, was a strong supporter of Maximus; and there took place, probably at Carthage in 645, the disputation between Pyrrhus and Maximus which is one of the most remarkable documents in the history of the controversy. Maximus was victorious, and followed up his triumph energetically. The bishops of North Africa and the adjacent islands held a synod in 646 to condemn Monothelitism, and requested Pope Theodore to confirm their decision. Maximus went to Rome with Pyrrhus, who abjured his errors before the pope, and was recognized as rightful patriarch of Constantinople. Maximus was the soul of this apparently formidable coalition, which, however, soon fell to pieces. Gregory fell the next year in battle with the Mohammedans; Pyrrhus retracted his recantation, and made his peace with the emperor. In 648 appeared the *Typus*, a decree of Constans forbidding under heavy penalties any discussion of the question of one or two wills. Maximus, still in Rome, was again the most active spirit in opposition to this, denying the emperor's right to interfere in dogmatic questions and declaring the language of the document irreconcilable with the creeds of the Church. He determined the new pope, Martin I., to call the Lateran synod of 649, and inspired its decision unhesitatingly condemning Monothelitism and the imperial decree.

1. Early Life and Success.

Maximus spent several years in Rome in a monastery, actively engaged in work for his cause, and thoroughly imbued with the hierarchical and dogmatic views of the Roman see.

2. Later Life, Trials, and Death.

He was finally arrested by the emperor's orders and taken to Constantinople where all endeavors were made to induce him to accept the *Typus*, but without avail. In the winter of 654–655 his first formal trial took place before the privy council in the imperial palace. The opening charges were political—of hatred of the emperor, responsibility for the loss to the Mohammedans of Egypt and North Africa, participation in the revolt of Gregory, and the like. There were further charges of Origenistic heresy, and some based on his dealings with Pyrrhus in Africa and Rome. Maximus was able to justify himself on most of the counts, but refused to hold communion with the church of Constantinople as having departed from "the four holy synods." He rejected a compromise formula, and declared that peace could be attained only by the emperor's withdrawing the *Typus*. Fresh proceedings were conducted on May 18, 655, by representatives of

Pyrrhus, and again a few months later by two patriarchs, Peter of Constantinople and Macedonius of Antioch. Maximus refused to make any concessions, and the next day a synod held by the patriarchs recommended that the penalty of banishment be inflicted on him and his disciple Anastasius. Maximus was sent to the fortress of Bizya in Thrace, where he remained for a year amid great discomfort. In August, 656, Bishop Theodosius of Cæsarea and two secular envoys appeared for the purpose of effecting an agreement; but he still firmly declared that nothing would serve but the recall of the *Typus* and the acceptance of the Lateran synod of 649. On Sept. 8 he was transferred to the monastery of St. Theodore near Reggio, where another attempt to win him failed, after which he was subjected to greater severities by the imperial emissaries, and he was removed first to Salembria and then to Berberis, where Anastasius already was. Here the authentic documents of the *Collectio Anastasii* end. According to another account, the historical value of which is disputed, he was brought once more to Constantinople and after a formal discussion solemnly anathematized in a synod, together with all upholders of Dyothelitism; then he and his disciples were delivered to the prefect to be scourged and have their tongues cut out and their hands chopped off. Thus mutilated, they were sent to Lazica on the eastern shore of the Black Sea. They arrived on June 8, 662; Maximus was separated from the others and sent to the fortress of Shemarum (modern Shemari), where he died. Yet his heroic constancy was not without effect. Constans II. fell a victim, only a few years later, to the hatred he had aroused partly by these cruel and arbitrary proceedings, and the faith for which Maximus had suffered was solemnly proclaimed by the sixth ecumenical council in 680.

II. His Writings: In spite of their frequent obscurity, due partly to their technical difficulty and partly to their involved style, his works were highly prized, especially in the Greek monasteries, but also by such keen western philosophers as Scotus Erigena, and by pious and learned women like the Empress Irene and her daughter Anna Comnena. Fabricius enumerates fifty-three different writings, of which five are either lost or still unpublished, while forty-four are printed by the French Dominican Combefis and four elsewhere. Combefis undertook a complete edition, but published only two volumes (Paris, 1675); the third was left unfinished at his death.

1. Exegetical Works on Scripture and the Fathers.

The exegetical writings of Maximus are not so much continuous expositions as theological and mystical excursuses on selected passages, following the anagogical or allegorical method of the Alexandrian school. The most important work in this class is the *Quæstiones ad Thalassium in locos scripturæ difficiles*, addressed to a Roman abbot who has left a collection of moral and ascetic sentences. It begins with a discussion of the problem of evil, and goes on to propound sixty-five questions which Maximus answers, usually taking the text only as a point of departure for rich dogmatic, ethical, or mystical trains of thought. Of a similar nature, though briefer and less original, are the *Quæstiones et dubia*, seventy-nine questions and answers on texts of Scripture and other subjects; *Ad Theopemptum scholasticum*, on three passages of the New Testament; *Expositio in psalmum LIX.*, an allegorical-mystical exposition; *Orationis dominicæ brevis expositio*, rich in mystical ideas. There are also fragments of other exegetical works (on the Psalms, Isaiah, Canticles, Luke, James) in the Greek catenæ. The same kind of treatment is applied by Maximus to patristic texts in his *Scholia* and *Ambigua* on Gregory Nazianzen and Dionysius the Areopagite; he attempts less to explain another man's thoughts than to develop mystical or theological ideas of his own suggested by the text. There are three collections of this sort on the two authors named; the third, *Ambigua in Gregorium Nazianzenum*, was translated into Latin by Erigena about 864, at the instance of Charles the Bald. The unpublished manuscript (at Vienna) *Quæstiones sacræ miscellaneæ* is apparently of a similar nature.

2. Dogmatic and Polemical Writings.

The dogmatic-polemical works treat of Christological, Trinitarian, and anthropological questions. (a) The first class are of the most importance for the history of dogma. In them he defends the doctrine of the two natures against the idea set forth by Philoxenus and Severus in the sixth century, of a single fused or combined nature. To this particular division belong the *Epistola ad Joannem Cubic. de rectis ecclesiæ decretis et adversus Severum hæreticum; Oratio brevis seu liber adversus dogmata Severi*, written before 634; *Epistola dogmatica; De communi et proprio, hoc est de essentia et hypostasi; De duabus Christi naturis; De qualitate, proprio, et differentia; Pro synodo Chalcedonensi ad symbolum additio; Capita de substantia et natura, de hypostasi et persona; De ecclesiastico dogmate quod attinet ad dominicam incarnationem;* and *Ad moniales quæ Alexandriæ a catholica fide discesserant.* Several of these treatises include an attack upon Monothelitism in their opposition to Monophysitism; but a still larger number refer directly to the former, and are among the most valuable documents on the controversy. The most important of these are the following: *Acta disputationis cum Pyrrho; Epistola ad Pyrrhum presbyterum et hegumenum*, written shortly after 633; *Tomus dogmaticus ad Marinum diaconum; Epistola de duabus in Christo voluntatibus; De operationibus et voluntatibus; Ad Marinum Cypri presbyterum responsa*, a reply to the charges of Theodore of Byzantium, written after 642; *Tomus dogmaticus ad Marinum presbyterum; Ad Marinum presbyterum Cypri*, written from Carthage apparently in 645; *Defloratio ex epistola scripta ad Petrum Illustrem*, a fragment of a letter written after 641; *Spiritalis tomus et dogmaticus adversus Heraclii Ecthesin*, written from Rome between 645 and 648; *Hegumenis et monachis ac catholicis populis per Siciliam constitutis*, written probably in Sicily after 646; *De Christi mysterio; De duabus in Christo naturis; De duabus unius Christi dei nostri voluntatibus; Non posse dici unam in Christo voluntatem; De duplici voluntate domini ad orthodoxos; Ex quæstionibus a Theodoro monacho propositis; Adversus eos qui dicunt, dicendam unam Christi operationem,* containing three brief answers to three different assertions of the Monothelites; *Ad illud: Si possibile est, transeat a me calix; Variæ definitiones; Distinctionum et unionum definitiones; Diversæ patrum de duabus operationibus domini Jesu Christi definitiones.* On strictly Trinitarian questions Maximus left a letter to the presbyter Maximus of Cyprus on the procession of the Holy Ghost; and a fragment may be his which is contained in *Ex opere LXIII dubiorum ad Achridæ regem;* but the *Dialogi V de trinitate* attributed to him in the majority of the manuscripts is certainly not his. Anthropological questions are treated in *De animæ natura et affectionibus,* and in two letters, one to John, archbishop of Cyzicus, on the incorporeality of the soul, and one to a presbyter Johannes or Jordanes on its conscious immortality.

3. Ethical, Ascetic, and Other Works.

Another important class of the writings of Maximus is made up of ethical and ascetic treatises. Under the former head may be classed several of the letters, but especially the *Liber ad pietatem exercens,* a dialogue between an abbot and a young monk on the principal duties of the spiritual life, remarkable for its fervor and moral earnestness—an example of the best ascetic literature of the Eastern Church. A sort of supplement to this is the *Capita de caritate,* a collection of four hundred sentences, principally ethical but partly dogmatic and mystical. In another similar collection, the *Capita theologica et œconomica CC,* the mystical predominates. There are two other collections of a similar nature, the *Capita diversa D theologica et œconomica* and *Alia capita* of the same ethical-ascetic bearing; and a still larger collection of passages partly from the Scriptures and partly from all sorts of Christian and pagan authors, known as *Capita theologica* and also as *Sermones per excerpta* or *Loci communes.* Among other works which do not fall under the above classes, the most interesting are the *Mystagogia* and the *Computus ecclesiasticus.* The former contains thoughts on the symbolic-mystical significance of the Church and its ceremonies, of a kind common in later Greek theological writing. The latter, written in 640, is an introduction to the Christian system of reckoning the ecclesiastical seasons and to sacred and profane chronology in general. Of the letters of Maximus forty-two are given by Combefis, and others are extant elsewhere, both published and unpublished; and Daniel gives three of his hymns in the *Thesaurus hymnologicus* (iii. 97 sqq.).

III. His Theology:

1. The Component Elements.

The theological position of Maximus is a combination of various elements—Platonism and Aristotelianism, Scriptural ideas and the orthodoxy of Nicæa and Chalcedon and of the Greek Fathers, and Christian mysticism, especially the mysticism of Dionysius the Areopagite (q.v.). He quotes Dionysius continually, and is responsible for the effect which that author's writings had upon medieval western as well as eastern theology. But since he did not follow him blindly, it is possible with Baur to designate the teaching of Maximus as an ethical or Christian modification of the Dionysian system, or more exactly still as an ethical-theological recasting and continuation of it. The essential character of the Dionysian system lies in a fusion of Neo-Platonism and Christianity, through which the Christian idea of God, the ethical concepts of sin and redemption, and still more the historic reality and specific meaning in the scheme of salvation attached to the person of Christ suffer from the abstract idealism of Platonic speculation. With Maximus, on the other hand, Aristotle supplies a salutary counterpoise, and his theology gains a purer, more fully Christian content by his recourse to Scripture and the older Greek Fathers. Dorner (*Entwickelungsgeschichte der Lehre von der Person Christi,* ii. 283, Stuttgart, 1845–56, Eng. transl., *History of the Development of the Doctrine of the Person of Christ,* Edinburgh, 1861–63) points out the decisive point in which he goes beyond his teacher: "The dialectic element in Maximus seems at strife with the mystical, Areopagitic element, to which he plainly clings with all the fervor of his love. But one gets the impression that it is precisely because he is conscious of the monistic, almost pantheistic strain in his mind that he takes such a strong stand against Monophysitism and Monothelitism. It is the principle of freedom that he strives to incorporate with the Areopagitic system, and through which at least his anthropological teaching is a further development of it."

2. His Christology.

The historical importance of Maximus for his own day lay above all in his firm defense of Dyothelitism. From the double nature of Christ he deduced the twofold character of energy and of will. He is moved by a vivid interest in the real human life of Christ, who without a human will would not be really man. But he is forced to take the same position by his Trinitarian beliefs. If the will of the Savior is a *theandrikon thelēma,* a fused divine-human will, then it would follow that the Father and the Holy Ghost had a similar will, or tritheism would be inevitable. Both wills in Christ are perfectly free, bound together by the same tie which joins the two natures, the union of the single *hypostasis.* In opposition to Nestorianism, he makes it clear that the human will of Christ was not, like ours, fluctuating between moral opposites, but by union with the Logos attained a permanent direction toward good. This direction it affirmed by a multitude of purely human actions; sin, indeed, was excluded—but sin is not an essential characteristic of human nature. The fact is that Maximus saw more keenly and clearly than any of the older Fathers the real centerpoint of the humanity of Christ.

3. His Mysticism.

This alone would be sufficient to make him a notable figure in the history of Christian thought, without the further fact that he furnished the form in which the mysticism of Dionysius exerted its great and far-reaching influence on the later theology of both East and West. How much John of Damascus owes to him has been rather suspected than proved; but the direction given by him is obvious in the later Greek theology of Euthymius Zygabenus, Nicetas Choniates, Nicholas of Methone, and still more in the Greek mysticism of the Hesychasts (q.v.) and of Nicholas Kabasilas. He is yet more important as the connecting link between Dionysius and Scotus Erigena, who depends on him for almost every point of his philosophic system, merely reducing to completer logical form the ideas thrown out as isolated aphorisms by his predecessor. But even more may be said; the "Thomas Aquinas of the Greek Church," as he has been called, may really be considered one of the most important sources and precursors of medieval scholasticism and mysticism in general. Much as he was dependent on those who went before him, and imperfectly as he succeeded in reducing to harmonious unity the rich and many-sided intellectual inheritance he received from them, he is none the less by his intellectual and moral character, by his learning, by his literary and ecclesiastical influence, and by the heroic firmness and patience of his life, entitled to the place of one of the greatest and most venerable of Christian thinkers and confessors. (R. SEEBERG.)

BIBLIOGRAPHY: Sources for a life of Maximus are: *Acta Maximi*, Latin in *Anastasii bibliothecarii collectanea*, ed. J. Sirmond, Paris, 1620, Greek and Latin in the ed. of Maximus by Combefis named in the text (under II.), i., pp. xxix. sqq., and in *MPG*, xc. 109 sqq.; a *Vita* by an unknown author, also in Combefis, i., pp. i. xxviii., in *MPG*, xc. 67 sqq., and in *ASB*, Aug., iii. 118 sqq.; Theophanes, *Chronographia*, ed. C. de Boor, ii. 331–332, 347, 351, Leipsic, 1885.

On his life and activities consult: C. W. F. Walch, *Historie der Ketzereien*, ix. 60, 499 sqq., 11 vols., Leipsic, 1762–85; Neander, *Christian Church*, iii. 171 sqq.; Ceillier, *Auteurs sacrés*, xi. 760–772; Schaff, *Christian Church*, iv. 496–498, 622 sqq.; *DCB*, iii. 884; and literature under MONOPHYSITES; and MONOTHELITES. Particularly on the literary and theological sides consult: J. Bach, *Die Dogmengeschichte des Mittelalters*, i. 15–49, Vienna, 1873–1875; Fabricius-Harles, *Bibliotheca Græca*, ix. 635 sqq., Hamburg, 1804: A. Preuss, *Ad Maximi Confessoris de deo hominisque deificatione doctrinam adnotationes*, Schneeburg, 1894; G. Owsepian, *Die Entstehungsgeschichte des Monotheletismus*, pp. 56 sqq., Leipsic, 1897; O. Bardenhewer, *Patrologie*, pp. 507–511, Freiburg, 1901; Harnack, *Dogma*, iv. passim, v. 274, vi. 30; Krumbacher, *Geschichte*, pp. 61–64; Hefele, *Conciliengeschichte*, iii. 189 sqq., Eng. transl., v. 73 sqq., 126 sqq.

MAXIMUS MARGUNIOS: Greek bishop and theologian; b. in Crete; d. at Venice 1602. In 1579 he became a monk, and later was consecrated bishop of Kythera (the modern Cerigo), but resided chiefly at Venice. He was the most learned theologian of the period, and his life was devoted to the upbuilding of his church and his people. His unionistic tendencies, particularly in his doctrine of the Trinity, occasionally brought him into sharp conflict with Gabriel Severus and even with the ecclesiastical authorities at Constantinople. Nevertheless, he recognized the difficulty of a union under the primacy of the pope, and was, on the other hand, an opponent of Protestantism, being probably the soul of the movement which led Jeremiah to refuse to unite with the Tübingen Lutherans. Margunios was a prolific editor and author, although the majority of his writings are still inedited. His chief published works are: "Manual on the Procession of the Holy Ghost," and a treatise on the divine permission of evil, both contained in his "Two Epistles" (Frankfort, 1591); *Brevis tractatus de consiliis atque præceptis evangelicis* (Venice, 1602); and "Lives of the Saints" (1603). (PHILIPP MEYER.)

BIBLIOGRAPHY: For the best lists of literature and accounts of the man consult: É. Legrand, *Bibliographie hellénique*, ii., pp. xxiii.–lxxvi., Paris, 1885; P. Meyer, *Die theologische Litteratur der griechischen Kirche*, Leipsic, 1899.

MAXIMUS OF TURIN: Bishop of Turin; b., probably in the Rhætian Alps, about 380; d. after 465, although Gennadius states that he died in 420. The only details known concerning his life are that in 451 he attended the Synod of Milan and that in 465 at the Roman synod he signed immediately after Pope Hilarius. He also witnessed the martyrdom of three missionary priests at Anaunia in the Rhætian Alps in 397. He was deeply influenced in his training by Ambrose, whose works include many sermons by Maximus. His numerous writings, 116 sermons, 117 homilies, and 3 tractates on baptism, are important for the history of Christian life while paganism was still strong, especially in the rural districts, and while the migration of peoples was in full course. His ninety-fourth homily alludes to the destruction of Milan by Attila, and he also refers to the cult of "Diana, the divinity of the fields," in whose honor the priests wounded or intoxicated themselves; the games and divination which marked the festival of the new year; and the custom of "helping" the moon by outcries at its eclipse. He sought to calm the terror felt at the barbarian inroads, and urged his people to remain constant in their faith, yet rebuked them sternly for their readiness to profit by the withdrawal of the Huns by purchasing the plunder and even the slaves which the invaders were unable to take away. (R. SCHMID.)

BIBLIOGRAPHY: The extant writings are most conveniently consulted in *MPL*, lvii. For accounts of the man consult: Gennadius, *De vir. ill.*, xl.; O. Bardenhewer, *Patrologie*, p. 497, Freiburg, 1894; and *DCB*, iii. 881–882. The legends collected in *ASB*, June, v. 48 sqq., are without historical value.

MAY LAWS. See ULTRAMONTANISM.

MAY, JOHANN HEINRICH: German Pietist; b. at Pforzheim (16 m. s.e. of Carlsruhe) Feb. 5, 1653; d. at Giessen Sept. 3, 1719. He studied at the University of Wittenberg, which he entered in 1671; while going to Sweden, he made at Hamburg the acquaintance of the Orientalist E. Edzard, with whom he studied the Bible, the Talmud, Arabic, and Syriac. After a winter in Copenhagen, he resumed his studies at Hamburg, but was recalled by his father to southern Germany. At Leipsic he became acquainted with J. B. Carpzov, and at Strasburg with S. Schmidt; but a more profound influence was exerted on him by H. Ludolf, whom he aided in reading the proof of his *Historia Æthiopica* (Frankfort, 1681). From Frankfort, where he had become imbued with the pietism of Spener, he went for a short time to Veldenz as court preacher to the palsgrave, but in 1684 was appointed by the elector professor of Oriental languages at the gymnasium of Durlach, where he was also pastor of St. Stephen's. In 1688 he was called to Giessen as professor of Oriental languages. Here he passed the remainder of his life, becoming second professor of theology, pædagogiarch, bursar, superintendent of Alsfeld, and assessor of the consistory.

Of May's numerous works none has borne the

test of time except his edition of the Hebrew Bible, a revision of the work of his predecessor at Giessen, David Clodius (Frankfort, 1692). His importance lies in the fact that he powerfully influenced the pietistic reformation of the theological faculty at Giessen. When he entered Giessen, he found scant opportunity for a practical propagation of his views; but in 1689 he announced a course of private studies on Romans, in continuation of his confirmation-class, to which both children and adults were invited. This evoked a formal protest to the prince on the part of May's colleague, P L. Hannecken, which led to a controversy which finally caused the retirement of Hannecken in 1693. His successor, Bilefeld, used his influence both as professor and court preacher to break down the opposition of the orthodox party, and by 1695 the pietistic reform was complete. In this latter phase of the conflict May took little public part, but his quiet activity conduced far more to the victory of Pietism than was apparent on the surface. (ERWIN PREUSCHEN.)

BIBLIOGRAPHY: The basal source, apart from the archives at Darmstadt, is the memorial oration by J. G. Schupart, Giessen, 1723. Consult: F. W. Strieder, *Grundlage zu einer hessischen Gelehrten- und Schriftstellergeschichte*, viii. 326 sqq., Cassel, 1788; W. Köhler, *Die Anfänge des Pietismus in Giessen*, vol. i., Giessen, 1907.

MAY, SAMUEL JOSEPH: American Unitarian; b. in Boston, Mass., Sept. 12, 1797; d. at Syracuse, N. Y., July 1, 1871. He was graduated at Harvard College in 1817, attended the divinity school, was ordained in 1822, and was pastor at Brooklyn, Conn. (1822–35), South Scituate, Mass. (1836–42), and Syracuse, N. Y. (1845–68). He was an earnest anti-slavery advocate, and from 1836 to 1854 he was the general agent of the Massachusetts Antislavery Society. He wrote: *Some Recollections of our Anti-Slavery Conflict* (Boston, 1869).

BIBLIOGRAPHY: T. J. Mumford, *Memoir of Samuel Joseph May*, Boston, 1873.

MAYER, EMIL HUGO WALTHER: German Lutheran; b. at Lyons, France, Sept. 9, 1854. He was educated at the Lyons Lyceum and at the University of Berlin, where he studied from 1872 to 1876 (Ph.D., Halle, 1879). He was a teacher at the Königliches Friedrich-Wilhelms-Gymnasium in Berlin from 1880 to 1893, and in the latter year accepted the appointment of associate professor of systematic theology in the University of Strasburg, where he was promoted to his present position of full professor in 1900. In theology he is an adherent of the scientific school, and has written: *Das Verhältnis der Kantischen Religionsphilosophie zum Ganzen des Kantischen Systems* (Berlin, 1879); *Die christliche Moral in ihrem Verhältnis zum staatlichen Recht* (1892); *Das christliche Gottvertrauen und der Glaube an Christus* (Göttingen, 1899); *Ueber die Aufgaben der Dogmatik* (Tübingen, 1902); *Die Aufgabe der innern Mission gegenüber der gegenwärtigen Gefährdung der christlichen Lebensanschauung durch antichristliche Geistesströmungen* (Brunswick, 1903); *Der christliche Gottesglaube und die naturwissenschaftliche Welterklärung* (Strasburg, 1904); *Christentum und Kultur* (Berlin, 1905); *Das psychologische Wesen der Religion* (Strasburg, 1906); and contributed to *Philotesia* (in honor of Paul Kleinert's seventieth birthday; Berlin, 1907).

MAYER, JOHANN FRIEDRICH: German polemical writer and orator; b. in Leipsic Dec. 6, 1650; d. in Stettin March 30, 1712. He studied in Leipsic, taking his master's degree in 1668, and in Strasburg. He was appointed Saturday preacher in Leipsic in 1672, and pastor and superintendent at Leisnig in 1673, whence, in 1678, he was called to Grimma. His one desire was for an academic life, and on April 7, 1684, he accepted the appointment as fourth professor of theology at Wittenberg, becoming at the same time substitute preacher for Quenstedt in the Castle church of the town. It was here that he was awakened to a more earnest understanding of Christianity by Spener (q.v.), whom he praised in his first sermon given before the venerable Calov. Mayer shone in argument and was a very popular preacher and lecturer. In spite of scandal caused by his unhappy marital relations, he was appointed preacher at the St. Jacob's Church in Hamburg, 1686. Although gratified at his promotion, Mayer had no wish to give up his academic vocation, but Spener did not retain him, and his attempt to hold his position as professor and dean of the theological faculty at Wittenberg failed, though he succeeded in obtaining the post of extraordinary professor at the Hamburg Academy, and in addition was made honorary professor of the theological faculty at Kiel in 1687 On Quenstedt's death, May 22, 1688, Mayer made another attempt to be reinstated as professor in Wittenberg University, but in spite of the representations of Johann Winckler (q.v.) Spener was unyielding. From this time, Mayer ranged himself on the side of Spener's opponents.

Among the many religious controversies at that period was one relating to the opera. Mayer and Winckler were opposed to each other on this question, the latter having attacked operatic representations in July, 1686. In the ensuing conflict, Mayer gained a victory over Winckler before the senate and ministry. In the controversy on the "religious oath" Mayer took a prominent part, and appealed for a decision to the theological faculties, while his opponents sought the support of several distinguished theologians outside Hamburg, and in particular of Spener, against whom Mayer vented his personal animosity. Mayer was even more bitter in his controversy with Johann Heinrich Horb (q.v.). He discovered every conceivable heresy—Pelagian, popish, Socinian, quakerish, and Arminian—in a pamphlet put in circulation but not written by Horb, entitled *Klugheit der Gerechten* (Hamburg, 1693), and although Horb explained that it was to be understood only according to the "analogy of faith," Mayer induced the ministers of Hamburg to withhold the sacrament from Horb, who fled the city. Mayer's standing in Hamburg had been greatly injured by the whole controversy, but he was more than ever honored as a theologian and scholar in other countries, and traveled to Sweden and Holland, making the friendship of kings and princes, and receiving titles and honors. He was appointed general superintendent in Pomerania and Rügen, president of the consistory, professor primarius, procancellarius perpetuus, and pastor of St. Nicholas Church in Greifswald. He wished to still retain his Hamburg pastorate, but as this was refused him, he induced his friends to have him recalled to St. Jacob's Church, which, after violent controversy, they did in 1704. But Mayer now wrote to the senate that he had no desire to leave the king's service, and Charles XII. declared that Mayer had no thought of going to Hamburg, and increased his stipend and retained him. Mayer held the theological decanate in Greifswald for eight years. When the Russian General Buck, in January, 1712, requested him to omit the war prayer or give up preaching, he chose the latter and went to Stettin where he died. Before leaving Hamburg he published the first hymn-book for standard use, containing two sacramental hymns by him. The titles of 581 pieces from his pen are given in the sketch found in *Lexikon der hamburgischen Schriftsteller*, v. 89–164, Hamburg, 1870. (CARL BERTHEAU.)

BIBLIOGRAPHY: J. Geffcken, *Johann Winckler und die hamburgische Kirche seiner Zeit*, Hamburg, 1864; idem, in *Zeitschrift des Vereins für hamburgische Geschichte*, i (1841), 567 sqq.; *ADB*, xxi, 99 sqq.; and the literature under HORB, JOHANN HEINRICH.

MAYER, KARL JULIUS: German Roman Catholic; b. at Bühl (26 m. s.w. of Carlsruhe), Baden, Mar. 12, 1857. After completing his education at the University of Freiburg, he was parish priest in Rastatt, Mannheim, and Bruchsal until 1896, when he became director of the archiepiscopal theological seminary at Freiburg, a position which he retained three years. Since 1899 he has been professor of moral theology in the University of Freiburg. Besides editing the new series of the *Freiburger Diözesan-Archiv* (Freiburg, 1900–04), he has written *Geschichte der Benediktiner-Abtei St. Peter auf dem Schwarzwald* (Freiburg, 1893); *Leben des heiligen Ulrichs* (1893); *Die christliche Askese, ihr Wesen und ihre Entfaltung* (1894); and *Der heilige Konrad, Bischof von Konstanz und Patron der Erzdiözese Freiburg* (1898).

MAYHEW, EXPERIENCE: Missionary to the Indians; b. in Martha's Vineyard, Mass., Jan. 27, 1673; d. there Nov. 29, 1758. He came of parentage which for three generations had done missionary work among the Indians, and he himself began to preach to them in 1694, devoting his life to the service. In 1709 he finished a version of the Psalms and of John for the Society for the Propagation of the Gospel in New England (Boston, 1709, cf. C. Evans, *American Bibliography*, i. 198-199, Chicago, 1903). He also published a work upon *Indian Converts* (1727), giving an account of thirty Indian ministers and some eighty other pious Indians (reprinted 1729). In connection with a *Discourse Shewing that God Dealeth with Men as Reasonable Creatures* (Boston, 1720) he gave *A Brief Account of the State of the Indians on Martha's Vineyard . 1694–1720.*

BIBLIOGRAPHY: W. B. Sprague, *Annals of the American Pulpit*, i. 133, New York, 1859.

MAYHEW, JONATHAN: New England minister; b. in Martha's Vineyard, Mass., Oct. 8, 1720; d. in Boston July 9, 1766. He was graduated at Harvard College 1744; entered the ministry, and in 1747 he was called to the West Church, Boston, maintaining the connection throughout his life. He was an earnest preacher and an accomplished controversialist. He was especially noted as a vigorous opponent of the Society for the Propagation of the Gospel in Foreign Parts, because he, in common with intelligent New-Englanders generally, regarded it as a mere disguise for introducing prelacy. He was also an ardent patriot and did much to hasten the Revolution. In this connection he issued a *Discourse concerning unlimited submission and non-resistance to the higher powers: with some reflections on the resistance made to King Charles I., and on the anniversary of his death: in which the mysterious doctrine of that Prince's saintship and martyrdom is unriddled* (Boston, 1750, reprinted there 1818, 1867, 1876, and in Thornton's *Pulpit of the American Revolution*, Boston, 1860). He also published *Observations on the charter and conduct of the Society for the Propagation of the Gospel in Foreign Parts* (1763). Other works by him are cited by full titles in C. Evans, *American Bibliography*, consult index, iii. 424, Boston, 1905.

BIBLIOGRAPHY: A. Bradford, *Memoir of the Life and Writings of Jonathan Mayhew*, Boston, 1838; W. Walker, *Ten New England Leaders*, pp. 293, 298, 333, 339, New York, 1901; F. H. Foster, *Hist. of New England Theology*, pp. 131–133, Chicago, 1907.

MAYNOOTH, mê'nūth, **COLLEGE:** Roman Catholic seminary for candidates for the priesthood, the chief institution of its kind in Ireland, 15 m. n.w. of Dublin. It was established by the Irish parliament in 1765, and received an annual grant originally of £8,000, but after 1845 of over £26,000; after the Union, and especially from 1845 on, it was a constant subject of contention between political and ecclesiastical parties, until the question was settled by the Irish Church Act of 1869, which went into effect in 1871. By this measure, which disestablished the Protestant Church in Ireland, state aid was withdrawn also from the Roman Catholic seminary, on the principle of equal justice. A sum equivalent to fourteen years' purchase of the annual grant was allotted in one payment. Provision was also made for the pensioning of those who at that time formed the teaching staff, and the debt contracted by the making of advance payments through the Commissioners of Public Works was remitted. (C. SCHOELL†.)

BIBLIOGRAPHY: J. Healy, *Maynooth College*, Dublin, 1895.

MAZARIN BIBLE: The first complete book printed in the West from movable type. It receives its name from the fact that "a copy in the library of Cardinal Mazarin first attracted the attention of bibliographers" in 1760 (See BIBLE VERSIONS, A, II., 2, § 4). It was printed by Gutenberg, in Mentz, 1450–55, but is without date or place. There are two sorts of copies of this Bible, that on paper, which is the earlier, and that on vellum.

BIBLIOGRAPHY: S. A. Allibone, in *Literary World*, Boston, Nov. 18, 1882.

MAZARIN, maz″a″rîn′, **JULES** (Guilio Mazzarini): French cardinal and diplomatist; b. at Piscina in the Abruzzi, southern Italy, July 14, 1602; d. at Vincennes Mar. 19, 1661. He studied in the Jesuits College at Rome, then took his degree in law at the University of Alcala in Spain; on his return to

Italy he held a command as captain in the papal army, and finally entered the service of the church. As secretary to Cardinal Sacchetti, he came to France in 1629. His diplomatical ability was immediately recognized; and his partiality to French interests was so pronounced, that in 1639 he was naturalized as a French citizen, and entered the service of the king. In 1641 he was made cardinal, and in 1642 succeeded Richelieu as prime-minister of France, in which position he continued till his death. Partly from religious indifference, and partly from political calculation, he showed great tolerance to the Huguenots. May 21, 1655, he solemnly renewed all edicts in their favor, and at times showed considerable courage in resisting the fanaticism of the Roman-Catholic clergy. Turenne and Gaston retained their positions in the army; and Herworth, a Protestant banker, was made controller-general, in spite of a formidable opposition. The last great favor he showed the Reformed was the permission in 1659 to convoke the synod of Loudun. [Mention should be made of the intervention of France, under Mazarin's guidance, in the Thirty Years' War (q.v.), in pursuance of the purpose to prevent the Hapsburgers from scoring a victory. The Peace of Westphalia (see WESTPHALIA, PEACE OF), with its recognition of the equal rights of Roman Catholics, Lutherans, and Reformed, was in part the result. A. H. N.]

BIBLIOGRAPHY: The first source is the correspondence of Mazarin, ed. A. Chéruel, in *Collection des documents inédits sur l'hist. de France*, Paris, 1872–94. The best modern works on the subject are: A. Chéruel, *Hist. de France pendant la minorité de Louis XIV.*, 4 vols., Paris, 1879–1880; idem, *Hist. de France sous le ministère de Cardinal Mazarin*, 2 vols., ib. 1881–82. Consult further, V. Cousin, *Jeunesse de Mazarin*, ib. 1865; A. Desprez, *Richelieu et Mazarin*, ib. 1883; idem, *Mazarin et son œuvre*, ib. 1883; J. Bourelly, *Cromwell et Mazarin*, ib. 1886; G. Masson, *Mazarin*, London, 1886; J. B. Perkins, *France under Mazarin*, New York, 1886; A. Hassall, *Mazarin*, London, 1903.

MAZDAISM. See ZOROASTER, ZOROASTRIANISM.

MAZDAZNAN. See ZEND FOLK.

MAZZOLINI, SILVESTRO. See PRIERIAS, SILVESTER.

MEAD, CHARLES MARSH: Congregationalist; b. at Cornwall, Vt., Jan. 28, 1836. He was educated at Middlebury College, Middlebury, Vt. (A.B., 1856), after which he taught for two years (1856–58) at Phillips Academy, Andover, Mass., and one year (1858–59) at Middlebury College. He received his theological education at Andover Theological Seminary, from which he was graduated in 1862. He then studied at the universities of Halle and Berlin until 1866 (Ph.D., Tübingen, 1866), and on his return to the United States was appointed professor of Hebrew in Andover Theological Seminary, a position which he held until 1882. He then spent ten years in Germany, and from 1892 until his retirement from active life in 1898 was professor of Christian theology in Hartford Theological Seminary. In 1872 he became a member of the American Bible Revision Committee (Old Testament). In addition to preparing the volume on Exodus for the American edition of J. P. Lange's commentary on the Bible (New York, 1876), and besides translating a portion of I. A. Dorner's "System of Christian Ethics" (in collaboration with R. T. Cunningham; 1887), he has written *The Soul Here and Hereafter: A Biblical Study* (Boston, 1879); *Supernatural Revelation: An Essay concerning the Basis of the Christian Faith* (L. P. Stone lectures at Princeton Theological Seminary; New York, 1889); *Romans Dissected* (under the pseudonym E. D. McRealsham; 1891); *Christ and Criticism* (1893); and *Irenic Theology* (1905).

MEAD (MEDE), JOSEPH: Church of England Biblical scholar; b. at Berden (29 m. n. of London), Essex, Oct., 1586; d. at Cambridge Oct. 1, 1638. He was graduated from the University of Cambridge (M.A., 1610; B.D., 1618), was elected fellow in 1613, and soon after appointed to the Greek lectureship on the Sir Walter Mildmay foundation. He is best known by his *Clavis Apocalyptica* (Cambridge, 1627; Eng. transl. by R. More, *The Key of the Revelation*, London, 1643; new transl. by R. B. Cooper, London, 1833). In this and in his *In sancti Joannis Apocalypsin commentarius* (1632) he advocated the continuistic view of the apocalyptic prophecies. His *Works* were gathered in two parts (London, 1648; enlarged, 1663–64; again enlarged, with a *Life*, 1672).

BIBLIOGRAPHY: J. Hunt, *Hist. of Religious Thought in England*, i. 167–168, London, 1870; *DNB*, xxxvii. 178–180.

MEADE, WILLIAM: Protestant Episcopal bishop; b. near Millwood, Clarke Co., Va., Nov. 11, 1789; d. at Richmond Mar. 14, 1862. He was graduated from Princeton College in 1810; prepared for the ministry under Rev. Walter Addison of Maryland, and was ordained Feb. 24, 1811. He was rector of Christ Church, Alexandria, 1811–13; became curate of Millwood 1813, and afterward rector, and soon was known as an influential leader in his church. In 1823 he was the "Founder of the Protestant-Episcopal Theological Seminary of Virginia," and in 1829 was elected assistant bishop to Bishop Moore of Virginia, succeeding to the charge of the see in 1841. He published *Lectures on the Pastoral Office* (New York, 1849); *Old Churches, Ministers and Families of Virginia* (2 vols., Philadelphia, 1856); *The Bible and the Classics* (New York, 1861).

BIBLIOGRAPHY: J. Johns, *A Memoir of the Life of . . William Meade*, Baltimore, 1867; W. S. Perry, *The Episcopate in America*, p. 51, New York, 1895.

MEADE, WILLIAM EDWARD: Church of Ireland; bishop of Cork, Cloyne, and Ross; b. at Donaghmore, County Cork, Feb. 24, 1832. He was educated at Trinity College, Dublin (B.A., 1857), and was ordered deacon in 1862 and ordained priest in the following year. He was rector of Ardtrea, County Tyrone, from 1864 to 1884, successively prebendary of Armagh (1877–84), treasurer of Armagh Cathedral (1882–85), and archdeacon of Armagh (1885–94). In 1893 he was elected by the Armagh Diocesan Synod as *ad interim* bishop of Armagh, and in the following year was consecrated bishop of Cork, Cloyne, and Ross. He was also a prebendary in St. Patrick's Cathedral, Dublin, in

1882–85, secretary to the General Synod in 1880, a member of the Representative Body in 1883, and examining chaplain to the bishop of Armagh in 1886–93, as well as a diocesan nominator and a member of the diocesan court.

MEALS, HEBREW: The hours for meals among the ancient Israelites and the Orientals of the present day are not as definite or as regular as with modern Europeans. Nevertheless it is probable that they also had their regular time for taking food. The fellah of Palestine eats his bread, perhaps with a little fruit, according to the season, before he goes to work in the fields, or else after having worked for one or two hours. About noon he again takes a little food, some bread and fruit, then enjoying his noonday rest. Neither in the morning nor in the afternoon does he prepare a hot meal, the principal repast being taken in the evening after the day's labor is ended, and consisting usually of a warm dish, even if it be only some onion soup. In general, however, the poor partake of only two meals, one in the late morning and the second in the evening. As these usages are conditioned by the climate which makes the hot noontide an undesirable time for the chief meal, it may be safely assumed that the same custom held in ancient times, although the Old Testament does not say much regarding the hours at which meals were taken. Food was brought to Elijah in the morning and in the evening (I Kings xvii. 6), and the Israelites in the desert had bread in the morning and meat (quails) in the evening (Ex. xvi. 12); the principal meal was in the evening; this was also the case with the servants of Boaz (Ruth iii. 3–7), although the reapers in the field were given food and their hour of repose at noon (Ruth ii. 14; cf. Susanna, 7, 13).

While eating, those Orientals who are not yet influenced by European culture sit cross-legged on the floor, upon mats or carpets, around a low table which consists of a metal sheet or of a large wickerwork plate, resting on a low stand. The larger the board, the greater the hospitality of the host; some are two meters in diameter. Very often the Bedouins use only a round piece of leather spread upon the floor. After its use it is drawn together so as to form a bag, by means of a cord which passes through rings attached at the border. After the Israelites settled in the land, this custom probably changed; chairs and tables existed in ancient times in western Asia (see House, the Hebrew, and its Appointments), and the Old Testament shows that they formed part of the ordinary household furnishings (II Kings iv. 10). Use was also made of the *mittah*, "divan," as a seat during meals (Ezek. xxiii. 41). From a casual remark of Amos it appears that in his time a new fashion arose which he condemned; namely, that of reclining during the repast (Am. ii. 8, vi. 4). In the time of Christ, probably under Greco-Roman influence, this usage was general (Matt. ix. 10, and frequently). The divans, for three or five persons, were covered with costly rugs in the homes of the rich (Prov. vii. 16–17; Ezek. xxiii. 41). The Israelites reclined upon them in such a way as to rest upon the left arm, having the right hand free for use in eating; the one seated at the right might rest the back of his head on the bosom of his left-hand neighbor (cf. John xiii. 23, xxi. 20).

Knives, forks, and spoons were not known as utensils for eating, but were used for cooking purposes; the meat as served was cut into small pieces (Ezek. xxiv. 4). Meat, vegetables, broth, etc., were put together in a large dish that was set on the table; every one had his flat cake of bread, with which he took the broth out of the dish or upon which he put his vegetables, just as on a plate; the meat was taken out with the fingers (Ruth ii. 14; Prov. xxvi. 15; Matt. xxvi. 23). The host himself helped an honored guest to the best pieces (I Sam. i. 4, ix. 23–24). Under these circumstances, washing of the hands before and after meals was necessary; in later times it became even a religious custom.

The usage of praying before a meal is not mentioned in the Old Testament; in the New Testament, however, it appears as a general practise before the meal; at least, Christ as well as his disciples always speak a few words of thanks (*berakah, eulogia, eucharistia;* Matt. xiv. 19 and often; Acts xxvii. 35; cf. I Tim. iv. 3 sqq.). The rabbis also valued praying after meals (cf. Berachoth, 6–8, etc.; see Prayer).

The meal of the common man was very simple, bread formed its most essential part (see Bread and Baking); to this were added milk, butter, and cheese; vegetables and fruit constituted a third indispensable adjunct. Meat was taken only exceptionally on holidays, when a sacrifice was offered, when honored guests arrived, or when a family festival was held. The rich naturally indulged at all seasons in the luxuries of the table (cf. Am. iv. 1, vi. 4–5). When they entertained guests, the guest was honored by the slaughtering of a beast of the herd, otherwise he was principally distinguished by the size of his portion (Gen. xliii. 34; I Sam. ix. 24). I. Benzinger.

Bibliography: An excellent article is found in *EB*, iii. 2989–3002. The subject is discussed in the Bible dictionaries under Food, Meals, Banquets, and like headings; also in the treatises on Biblical archeology.

MEARS, DAVID OTIS: Presbyterian; b. at Essex, Mass., Feb. 22, 1842. He was educated at Amherst College (A.B., 1865), and, after studying theology privately, was ordained to the ministry of his denomination in 1867. He has held successive pastorates at North Avenue Church, Cambridge, Mass. (1867–77), Piedmont Congregational Church, Worcester, Mass. (1877–93), Calvary Presbyterian Church, Cleveland, O. (1893–95), and Fourth Presbyterian Church, Albany, N. Y. (since 1895). He was associate editor of *The Golden Rule* (now *The Christian Endeavor World*) in 1879–80, and besides numerous briefer contributions, sermons, and addresses, and in addition to an edition of E. N. Kirk's *Lectures on Revivals* (Boston, 1875), has written *Life of Edward Norris Kirk* (Boston, 1877); *The Deathless Book* (1888); *The Pulpit and the Pews* (Oberlin, O., 1892); and *Inspired through Suffering* (New York, 1895).

MECCA: The chief holy city of the Mohammedan faith. It is situated in Western Arabia, latitude 21° 30′ north, longitude 40° 8′ east, in a narrow and barren valley in the province of Hedjaz, sixty-five miles east of Jiddah, its port on the Red Sea, and about two hundred and fifty miles south of Medina. It has no manufactures and no commerce. Its inhabitants depend almost entirely on the pilgrims who come to pray in its celebrated mosque, and to kiss the black stone of the Kaaba. See KAABA; and MOHAMMED, MOHAMMEDANISM.

MECKLENBURG-SCHWERIN: A grand-duchy of the German empire; area 5,137 square miles; population (1905) 625,045, of whom 609,914 were Lutherans and Reformed, 12,093 Roman Catholics, 742 Greek Catholics, 810 unclassed Christians, and 1,482 Israelites. Mecklenburg became Christian in the twelfth century and accepted Lutheranism in 1549. The practical administration of the Lutheran State Church was committed in 1571, by statutory regulation, to the polity of Superintendencies and Consistories. The reigning sovereign, along with his territorial *jus circa sacra*, holds the metropolitan *jus in sacra*. Synodical rights are vested in the territorial estates, the representatives of the landed proprietors and of the towns. The sovereign exercises his *jus circa sacra* through the ministry of justice; his metropolitan jurisdiction has been exercised, since 1850, through the Superior Church Council in Schwerin. The ecclesiastical courts are the Consistory and, for cases of appeal, the Superior Ecclesiastical Court, both at Rostock. The church is subdivided into six provincial superintendencies (Doberan, Güstrow, Malchin, Parchim, Schwerin), Wismar, and one town superintendency (Rostock). The provincial superintendencies are further subdivided into thirty-five presidencies, under presiding officers called *præpositi*. There are 308 parishes, and 472 churches, besides 48 chapels. In accordance with the synodical regulation of 1841, the pastors in each presidency hold an annual synod, under the district *præpositus*. There are two general conferences, which alternate in annual sessions, the one consisting of all the pastors, the other of pastors and laymen. With both conferences are associated conventions of the Society for Foreign and Jewish Missions and of the Inner Mission.

The average yearly income of a pastor is approximately 4,000 marks. The superannuating provision of 1900 allows a retirement salary amounting to twenty-five per cent of the stipend after ten years of service, and as high as ninety per cent after fifty years. The widows of pastors, *præpositi*, and superintendents, in addition to their parochial tithe and a residential indemnity from the widows' fund, draw pensions of 750, 850, and 1,200 marks respectively. Ecclesiastical patronage is partly vested in the sovereign (to nearly two-thirds of the cures), and partly proprietary or municipal. Candidates for the spiritual office have to undergo two examinations, *pro licentia concionandi*, and *pro ministerio*. In the way of practical preparation, the candidates attend the theological seminary at Schwerin for the period of a year between the first examination and the second. The duties of sacristans, precentors and organists are fulfilled, in almost every instance, by public-school teachers, in a legally regulated connection with their positions. Church-building expenses are generally so divided that the ecclesiastical patrons furnish the material and half the cash cost of construction; the congregation bearing the remainder of the cost.

In the matter of church doctrine, the clergy stand loyal to the Lutheran Confession, and the congregations are at least externally faithful to ecclesiastical ordinances. Open ecclesiastical enmity is of rare occurrence. Christian benevolence has been on the increase for fifty years past, and yields gratifying fruit in such works as those of the House of Deaconesses at Ludwigslust, with some 300 sisters, laboring in 100 stations, and of the Inner Mission (Rescue House at Gehlersdorf, Infirmary at Schwerin, Home for Cripples, and Magdalen Asylum at Rostock, institutional homes, etc.), as also in the support of the Gotteskasten (q.v.) for helping Lutherans abroad (see DIASPORA) and of missions to the heathen.

The relation between church and schools is close. The direction of schools is constitutionally in the hands of the church superintendents and pastors, under the supervision of the Ministry of Instruction. Rectors of the municipal public schools are certified theological candidates. Common-school teachers obtain their preparation in two seminaries, whose directors and principal teachers must be divines. The Board of Seminary Curators includes (besides a representative of the government) two divines, a superintendent and the resident pastor. Religious instruction in the seven state high schools is likewise in the hands of approved divines. The five theological professors of the state university at Rostock are appointed by the Ministry of Instruction, subject to the approval of the Superior Church Council.

There are no sects in Mecklenburg on any organized footing. Baptists and Irvingites occur sporadically. The Reformed Church has one pastor, the Roman Catholic Church six pastors, with four congregations, belonging to the diocese of Osnabrück.

HEINRICH BEHM.

BIBLIOGRAPHY: J. Wiggers, *Kirchengeschichte Mecklenburgs*, Parchim, 1840; *Mecklenburgische Geschichte in Einzeldarstellung*, parts 5 sqq., Berlin, 1899 sqq.; G. Mau, *Kirchliche Verhältnisse in Mecklenburg*, ib. 1899; E. Millies, *Cirkular-Verordnungen des Oberkirchenrats , aus der Zeit 1849–1894*, Schwerin, 1895; idem, *Die Emertierungs-Ordnung für die evangelisch-lutherischen Geistlichen in . , Mecklenburg-Schwerin*, ib., 1904; *Mecklenburgisches Urkundenbuch*, ib., 1907.

MECKLENBURG-STRELITZ: A grand-duchy of the German empire, separate from Mecklenburg-Schwerin since 1701; area 1,131 square miles; population (1905) 100,451, of whom 100,314 were Lutherans, 2,499 Roman Catholics, 128 Greek Catholics, 212 unclassed Christians, and 298 Israelites.

The church organization is similar to that of Mecklenburg-Schwerin (q.v.). In his metropolitan capacity the sovereign exercises his governing power through the consistory at Neu-Strelitz, which also attends to the ecclesiastical administration of the Ratzeburg district. The *jus circa sacra* is exercised through the state governme t. The consistory at Neu-Strelitz acts as an ecclesiastical court of first instance; appeals lie to the Superior Ecclesiastical Court at Rostock. Mecklenburg-

Strelitz has only one superintendent, under whom are six *præpositi* and the provost at Ratzeburg. There are 153 churches. With reference to other ecclesiastical conditions the statements as to Mecklenburg-Schwerin generally apply here as well.
HEINRICH BEHM.

BIBLIOGRAPHY: Consult the literature under MECKLENBURG-SCHWERIN.

MEDARDUS, SAINT: Missionary bishop in northern France; b. at Salentiacum (Salency) in Picardy, not far from the present St. Quentin, c. 457; d. c. 545. He was educated in the school of his native city where he distinguished himself by his diligence, piety, and charity. He received holy orders at an early age, and about 530 succeeded the bishop of Veromandum (Vermand), but soon removed the see to Noviomagus (Noyon) which, as a fortified place, offered better protection against the barbarians. After the death of Bishop Eleutherius, about 532, he was elected also bishop of Tournay, and for the rest of his life administered both dioceses, being very active and successful in spreading Christianity. By his pure and pious conduct and the enduring steadfastness with which he bore all sufferings and struggles for the advancement of the Christian faith, he occupied a well deserved place among the confessors. He is commemorated by the Roman Catholic Church on June 8, and is considered the patron of horticulture and agriculture, more specifically of haymaking. A church and a monastery were built over his grave at Soissons. Besides this city, the chief seat of devotion to Medardus, Dijon, Jodoigne (Geldonacum) near Louvain, Cologne, Treves, Paris, and Prague boasted the possession of relics of the saint.
(O. ZÖCKLER†.)

BIBLIOGRAPHY: The two early biographies of Medardus were by Fortunatus Venantius and Bishop Radbod, which with other lives, documents and commentary are collected in *ASB*, June, ii. 72–105. Early material is found also in *MPL*, lxxi. 1117–1118, lxxxviii. 533–540, cxxxii. 629–639, and a *Carmen* by Fortunatus Venantius is in *MGH*, *Auct. ant.*, iv. 1 (1881), 44–48. Consult: J. Corblet, *Notice historique sur le culte de S. Médard*, Amiens, 1856; *DCB*, iii. 887 888.

MEDD, PETER GOLDSMITH: Church of England; b. at Leyburn (36 m. n.w. of York) July 18, 1829; d. at North Cerney (near Cirencester, 15 m. s.e. of Gloucester) July 25, 1908. He was educated at King's College, London, and University College, Oxford (B.A., 1852; M.A., 1855). He was ordained deacon in 1853 and priest in 1859. He was curate of St. John Baptist, Oxford (1858–67); rector of Barnes, Surrey (1870–76); and in 1876 became rector of North Cerney, Gloucestershire. He was fellow of University College, Oxford, from 1852 to 1877; lecturer, tutor, bursar, and dean from 1853 to 1870; and Bampton lecturer in 1882. His works include: *The Priest to the Altar, or Aids to the Devout Celebration of Holy Communion* (London, 1865); *Sermons Preached in the Parish Church of Barnes* (1877); and *The One Mediator* (1884), Bampton lectures. Together with W. Bright he edited the Latin version of the Book of Common Prayer (1865).

MEDEBA: A town on the table-land of Moab east of the Jordan. It is situated almost directly east from Bethlehem, about five miles slightly west of south from Heshbon, at an elevation of 2,940 feet, and is the site of a modern town built on a pile of early Christian ruins having a circumference of a mile and a half. New interest attaches to the town because of the discovery there of a mosaic map of Christian Palestine and part of Egypt. The place was anciently of considerable importance and finds frequent mention in the Old Testament (Num. xxi. 30; Josh. xiii. 9, 16; I Chron. xix. 7; Isa. xv. 2; I Macc. ix. 36) and on the Moabite Stone (q.v.). It was originally Moabitic territory, but was taken by the Amorites, then by Israel; in David's time it was an Ammonitic point of defense, was captured by Omri (Moabite Stone, line 8, *Mehedeba*) and recaptured by Mesha, the Moabitic king who indited the Moabite Stone. The place comes into later mention as the home of the robber band which accomplished the death of John the Maccabee; John Hyrcanus took the city after a siege of six months (Josephus, *Ant.*, XIII., ix. 1), and it had to be retaken by Alexander Jannæus. Ptolemy the geographer mentions it (V., xvii. 6) as lying between Bostra and Petra. After the Christian era it appears as the seat of a bishop who attended the Council of Chalcedon (451). After that it was lost to sight until in 1880 a Christian colony, mostly of Greeks, from Kerak settled there, and there is also a Roman Catholic mission. The preparations for building led to a series of discoveries of interesting antiquities. These include a large pool (324 feet by 309, and from 10 to 13 feet deep), ruins of several churches, the remains of a colonnaded street, inscriptions, mosaic pavements, and especially the map referred to above. The character of some of the ruins show that parts of the town had pretensions to elegance.

The story of the mosaic furnishes a lamentable instance of the loss to knowledge and to art which accrues from ignorance or stupidity. The first notice of the map came through a monk belonging to the Christian colony settled at Medeba in 1880, the find having been uncovered in clearing a floor for a new church on the lines of an old one. In 1882 this monk wrote concerning the mosaic to the Greek patriarch of Jerusalem, who simply filed the letter, which remained hidden till the new patriarch, Gerosinos, found it. The latter sent a master-mason (with the title of architect!) to examine the mosaic and with directions to include it in the new church if found worthy. The deputy reported that it was unimportant, and in the building of the church large portions were destroyed, it being calculated that only eighteen square meters remain of an original area of perhaps 280 square meters. In 1896 the patriarch sent Cléopas Koskylides, librarian of the Society of the Holy Sepulcher, to reexamine the map, and he recognized its importance. Large parts had been covered by cement for the flooring of the new church, while nearly all the rest had been destroyed, traces being left, however, which showed how great had been the destruction wrought.

The piece of the map remaining covers the territory from Nablus to the Nile. It is decorative and free in execution, somewhat lacking in perspective, but its location of places is approximately accurate. The East is at the top; the northern portion is nearly all destroyed; the extreme northern part was outside the present church walls, for in the early period the names Ephesus and Smyrna were read on it, showing that it originally included at least the southern part of Asia Minor. The artist accomplished very fair results with the difficult material and subject with which he worked. Mountains are indicated in colored lines, the Dead Sea in blue wavy lines; in the larger cities principal streets are roughly represented, while in Jerusalem appear the principal structures of the period (the Church of the Holy Sepulcher, and at least three other churches, one outside the city), as well as two colonnaded streets which run through the north and south length of the city, and three (or four) gates on north, east, and south. Smaller cities are indicated with walls and round towers. The subdivision of the map was by tribes, with boundaries and chief towns. Nearly 140 names or parts of names can be traced. The territories of six tribes are represented in whole or in part—Dan, Simeon, Judah, Ephraim, Benjamin, and Zebulon. As examples of the places named may be cited: Modein, Nob, Lydda, Gath, Ashdod, Jericho, Ephrata, Ælamon, Bethabara, Ramah (in Benjamin and in Judah), Gibeon, Ænon, Shiloh, Gerizim, Shechem, Gerar, Bethlehem Ephrata, Beth-zur, Ascalon, Gaza, Beersheba, the tomb of Joseph, the well of Jacob, and the oak of Mamre, in Palestine; and in Egypt Pelusium, Tanis, Sais, Hermoopolis, and three arms of the Nile. The date of the map is made out to be probably the middle of the fifth century, since the principal structures of Jerusalem seem to correspond with those of the city of that period. The extant remnant has proved of some service in confirming a number of locations already made out, and in suggesting a few others. Had the entire map been preserved, its value might have been very great. A subject of debate still is whether in the map's composition the *Onomasticon* of Eusebius was employed. GEO. W. GILMORE.

BIBLIOGRAPHY: The principal account of the map is by C. Clermont-Ganneau, in *Recueil d'archeologie orientale*, ii (1897), 161–175, from which is taken the matter in PEF, *Quarterly Statement*, 1897, pp. 213–225, cf. 167, 239, also 1898, pp. 85, 177–183, 251, and 1901, 235–246. Other summaries are to be found in *The* (New York) *Independent*, 1897, p. 1656; *Biblical World*, 1898, pp. 244–250; *Methodist Review*, 1898, 478–480; *Geographical Journal*, 1901, p. 516. Other discussions are: G. Durand, *La Carte mosaique de Madaba*, Paris, 1897; A. Schulten, *Die Mosaikkarte von Madaba*, Berlin, 1900; Kubitschek, in the *Mittheilungen* of the Royal Geographical Society of Vienna, 1900, pp. 335–380; A. Jacoby, *Das geographische Mosaik von Madaba*, Leipsic, 1905. A large and important literature is indicated in Richardson, *Encyclopaedia*, p. 666.

On the town, apart from the map, consult: PEF, *Quarterly Statement*, 1895, July; M. Sejourne, in *Revue biblique internationale*, 1892, 617–644; *DB*, iii. 309–310.

MEDHURST, WALTER HENRY: Missionary, sinologue, and lexicographer; b. in London Apr. 29, 1796; d. there Jan. 24, 1857. He studied at Hackney College; embarked for China as a missionary printer, 1816; was so successful as a student of languages and as a preacher that he was ordained at Malacca, 1819, and labored in Penang and Batavia; returned to England, 1836, but again went out to his work in Java, 1838; on the opening of Shanghai as a treaty port in 1842 he settled there and remained until the year of his death. He was accomplished in the Javanese, Chinese, and Japanese languages. With the cooperation of friends he produced what is known as the "Delegates' Version" of the Bible in Chinese. Among his other works may be noted: *English and Japanese Vocabulary* (Batavia, 1830); *Dictionary of the Hok-Këèn Dialect of the Chinese Language* (Macao, 1832); *China, its State and Prospects* (London, 1838); *Chinese and English Dictionary* (2 vols., Batavia, 1842–43); *Chinese Dialogues* (Shanghai, 1844; new ed. by his son, 1861); and *Dissertation on the Theology of the Chinese* (1847).

BIBLIOGRAPHY: H. O. Dwight, H. A. Tupper, and E. M. Bliss, *Encyclopedia of Missions*, pp. 444–445, New York, 1904; *DNB*, xxxvii, 202–203.

MEDIATOR: A title applied to Jesus Christ in relation to his work as intermediary between God and the world and between man and God. The New Testament presents Christ as mediator in two aspects, the cosmic and the redemptive. The principal passages bearing on the cosmic or universal mediation are I Cor. viii. 6; Col. i. 15–17; Heb. i. 2–3; John i. 3–4. As the image or Logos of God the son is the sole mediator of the divine creative activity. Eternal preexistence is affirmed of him. Through him the universe is a consistent unity, and progressively realizes the divine purpose. In him is seen the rational explanation and final aim of all things. This type of thought has its Jewish as well as Greek background. In the Jewish doctrine of Angels (q.v.), of wisdom (Prov. viii.), and of the Spirit of God (q.v.), the idea of mediatorial agencies between God and the world is made familiar. Greek thought represented the Platonic-Stoic logos both as immanent reason and as expressed will. Josephus described the law as given by angels (*Ant.* XV., v. 3), a view repeated in Acts vii. 53; Gal. iii. 19; and Heb. ii. 2; cf. Jubilees, i. 27–29, and Assumption of Moses, i. 14. Philo gathers up the lines of both Greek and Jewish development in his doctrine of the Logos: the Logos is the mediator between the immortal God and the sinful human race ("Who Is the Heir"). The New-Testament teaching culminates in the unique and unshared mediation of the eternal Christ.

The other aspect of mediation—the redemptive—is more fully represented in the New Testament (Matt. xi. 27–28; Mark viii. 38; Luke ix. 11–27; John, passim; Acts xvii. 31; Eph. i. 10–21; Col. i. 20; I Tim. ii. 5–6; I John ii. 1–2). Mediation before Christ's earthly existence is affirmed in I Cor. x. 4; I Pet. i. 11; and John i. 11–12. For Paul the mediation consists of vicarious suffering and death in behalf of sin, continues after death in his intercession (Rom. viii. 34) and gift of the Spirit (Rom. viii. 8–11), and in manifold saving activities until his return to judgment, the destruction of the last enemy, and the glorification of the saints (I Thess. iv. 16–17; I Cor. xv. 24–28, 50–57; Phil. iii. 20–21). The mediatorship of Jesus is the special theme of the epistle to the Hebrews. He was qualified for this task by the experiences of his earthly life. He was superior to the angels, to Moses, and to the priests. The latter was evinced by the fact that he was appointed not by men but by God, that he offered not an external sacrifice but himself, through the eternal Spirit, the effect of which was spiritual and everlasting. He has opened for men the heavenly world, where as priest-king he continues his mediation of the new covenant.

In successive periods of the Church the Christian doctrine of mediation reflects the changing doctrine of God and of man; it has therefore been identified in part with the various theories of the Atonement (q.v.). By the Church Fathers, Christ is designated as mediator, since he reconciles God and man, by uniting in his own nature the divine and the human which had become mutually estranged through sin (Cyril of Alexandria, *Dial.* i., "Concerning the Trinity"; Theophylact on Gal. iii.; Chrysostom, *Seventh Homily on I Tim.*). Since Gerhard, who followed the lead of many of the Fathers (cf. Eusebius, *Hist. eccl.* I., iii.), Thomas Aquinas, and Calvin, the mediatorship of Christ has been divided into three aspects. (1) The prophetic: during his earthly life Christ revealed God's purpose of redemption. (2) The high-priestly: Christ fulfilled two functions, satisfaction and intercession. He satisfied God's justice through his active and passive obedience in his earthly life and death, to which the worth of his person and the intensity of his suffering lent an infinite value. As exalted he continues his high-priestly work through his intercession for the redeemed. The mediation of Christ was conceived by the Lutherans as meritorious and as related to all men; by the Reformed, as instrumental and as confined to the elect. (3) Christ's royal office, concealed during his earthly life, was assumed at his exaltation; as king he maintains and governs (a) all creatures (*regnum potentiæ*), (b) believers here below (*regnum gratiæ*), and (c) the church triumphant in heaven (*regnum gloriæ*). Ritschl modifies the traditional view by substituting vocation for office in Christ's mediation, by emphasizing the likeness of the community to Christ as respects the vocation, by conceiving of the royal function as fundamental, expressing itself in relation to God in the priestly, in relation to man in the prophetic, activity, and by affirming that the priestly and prophetic vocation extends into the state of exaltation. Christ mediates his forgiveness first to the community and then to individuals according as they become members of the community. The individual believer is brought into communion with God not through the living but through the historical Christ. In many of the popular sermons and hymns of the last two centuries Christ is set forth as mediator between an angry God and the condemned sinner, pleading with God for mercy, at the same time receiving the divine wrath into his own bosom and thus averting from the sinner the consequences of his sin. With the ethicizing of the character of God this view is yielding to a more adequate idea of Christ's mediation, as consisting in the revelation and communication of the life and love of God to men. The intercession of Christ, relieved of its picturesque features, signifies that the relation between God as gracious and man as sinful, established once for all in the life and death of Christ, is permanently valid in the changeless relation of Christ to the Father, and made effective for men through the influence of Christ's Spirit in their lives. C. A. BECKWITH.

BIBLIOGRAPHY: G. Steward, *Mediatorial Sovereignty*, 2 vols., Edinburgh, 1863; W. Symington, *Messiah, the Prince; or, the Mediatorial Dominion of Jesus Christ*, New York, 1881; P. G. Medd, *The One Mediator*, London, 1884; W. Milligan, *The Ascension and Heavenly Priesthood of our Lord*, London, 1892; M. S. Terry, *The Mediation of Jesus Christ*, New York, 1903; and the treatment of Christ as priest and of his offices in the works on dogmatic theology.

MEDICINE. See DISEASES AND THE HEALING ART, HEBREW.

MEDINA: The city next in importance to Mecca, of the holy cities of Islam. It contains a large mosque with the mausoleum of Mohammed, and is annually visited by a great number of pilgrims. It has about 15,000 inhabitants. See MOHAMMED, MOHAMMEDANISM, I.

MEDLER, NICOLAUS: Leader of the Reformation in Naumburg; b. at Hof (72 m. s. of Leipsic) 1502; d. at Bernburg (88 m. s.w. of Berlin) Aug. 24, 1551. His preliminary studies were made in his native town and at the Latin School of Freiberg, after which he attended the universities of Erfurt and Wittenberg. After a brief sojourn as teacher at Arnstadt and Hof, he became rector of the school at Eger, where he caused excitement by his Evangelical sermons, and was obliged to withdraw. Returning to Hof, he took charge of the town school, which flourished under his care from 1527 or 1528 onward, and was associated with the town pastor, Löner, as preacher at St. Michael's. On account of their sharp sermons both were expelled from the town July 13, 1531. Medler removed to Wittenberg, and continued there five years. Provided by the elector of Saxony with an annual stipend, he labored as a private tutor and as assistant preacher to Luther, who was then in poor health, and for some time was chaplain to the exiled Electress Elizabeth of Brandenburg. On Sept. 1, 1536, he removed to Naumburg as pastor and overseer of the Church of St. Wenceslaus, an important post to which he had been nominated by Elector John Frederick on the recommendation of Luther. For the next eight years he was the reformer of the ecclesiastical and educational system of Naumburg. Starting from the existing beginnings he proceeded mainly along the Wittenberg lines. His plan for reorganizing the parish church of St. Wenceslaus was approved Oct. 21, 1537, by Luther, Jonas, and Melanchthon, and was ratified by the elector. It shows not a few distinctive elements. The school prospectus makes provision for Hebrew, Greek, and Latin, and for the mathematical branches. Medler himself gave instruction in Hebrew. In the matter of ceremonial regulation, what is especially to be remarked is the place of the *Confiteor* and its wording, which proved of considerable influence, and the use of Luther's German paraphrase of the *Gloria in excelsis*. The five appendixes, including an order of confirmation, have unfortunately been lost.

By 1540 the victory of Protestantism at Naumburg was assured, and the cathedral alone remained as a citadel of Roman Catholicism. In July, 1541, however, the inhabitants of the cathedral district petitioned the elector for spiritual ministration at the hands of Medler, and John Frederick commanded him forthwith to begin Evangelical worship there, which he did on Sept. 11, 1541. Both Luther and Medler took part officially in the festivities attending the induction of Amsdorf as Evangelical bishop (Jan. 19–20, 1542). Since Amsdorf usually resided at Zeitz, Medler continued to be the leading personality at Naumburg and prosecuted zealously the work of evangelizing the cathedral district. His life, however, became embittered by growing contentions, notably with Georg Mohr, who in 1544 had succeeded Medler's friend, Löner, as cathedral preacher at Naumburg. Even Luther censured Medler's lust of power, and his disposition to treat the new bishop as a nullity. With the council Medler's repeated requests for an increase of salary, and his independence in filling appointments caused manifold frictions. From this situation Medler was released by the elector's command to go to the Electress Elizabeth, his former patroness, who was now seriously ill. He left Naumburg about Apr. 20, 1545, and never returned. About the same time he was confirmed by the elector of Brandenburg in the position of court preacher to the Electress Elizabeth. He declined a professorship at Frankfort-on-the-Oder, but in deference to the wishes of Luther and Melanchthon accepted the superintendency at Brunswick, of which he took charge about Michaelmas, 1545. The agitated state of the times, no less than the wilfulness of his own disposition, prevented any lasting good results. In 1551, on the advice of Melanchthon, he accepted the position of court preacher at Bernburg, but was stricken with paralysis at his first sermon, June 7. Having been conveyed, for better care, to Wittenberg, he had a second stroke, and was brought back to Bernburg to die a few weeks later. His literary works, apart from the Naumburg *Kirchenordnung* and writings against the Interim, are mostly schoolbooks, including revisions of Melanchthon's Latin grammar, rhetoric, and dialectics, and some mathematical works. Luther reckoned him, along with Veit Dietrich and Johann Spangenberg, as one of his three true disciples, because he served school and Church with equal ardor. O. ALBRECHT.

BIBLIOGRAPHY: Sources of knowledge are: The *Oratio de vita . . N. Medleri* by A. Streitberger, Jena, 1591; *Epistolæ Melanchthonis* to Medler, ed. Danz, Jena, 1825; *Briefwechsel des J. Jonas*, ed. G. Kawerau, 2 vols., Halle, 1884–85; *Luthers Briefe*, ed. De Wette, vols. iv.–vi.; *Braunschweigische Schulordnungen*, ed. F. Koldewey, pp. lxix. sqq., 65–97, Berlin, 1886. References to the earlier literature (eighteenth century) will be found in Hauck-Herzog, *RE*, xii. 492. Consult: Riedel, in *Zeitschrift für preussische Geschichte und Landeskirche*, ii (1865), 65–100; Holstein, in the same, iv (1867), 271–287; S. Braun, *Naumburger Annalen*, ed. Köster, Naumburg, 1892; E. Hoffmann, *Naumburg im Zeitalter der Reformation*, Leipsic, 1900; Köster, in *ZKG*, xxii (1901), 145 sqq., 278 sqq.; O. Mertz, *Schulwesen der deutschen Reformation*, Heidelberg, 1902.

MEDLEY, SAMUEL: English Baptist preacher and hymnist; b. at Cheshunt (6 m. s. of Hertford) June 23, 1738; d. at Liverpool July 17, 1799. After serving in the navy (1755–59), he kept school in London (1762–66); entered the ministry and became pastor at Watford, Hertfordshire (1767), being ordained in 1768; and was pastor of the Byrom Street chapel, Liverpool, from 1772 till his death. He is known principally as a hymnist, his best composition being "O could I speak the matchless worth."

BIBLIOGRAPHY: His *Memoirs* were compiled by his son, Samuel, London, 1800; and by his daughter, Sarah, 2 parts, Liverpool, 1833. Consult also: Julian, *Hymnology*, p. 722; S. W. Duffield, *English Hymns*, pp. 51, 402, 623, New York, 1886.

MEDO-PERSIA.

I. The Names: The form of the word Media in the earliest Persian cuneiform texts is *Mâda*, Assyr. and Hebr., *Madai*. The origin of the word, its meaning, and its etymological relationships are entirely unknown. The name Persia, Persian, in the Old Persian inscriptions is *Pârsa*, in Susian *Paršir*, in Babylonian *Parsâ*, in Hebrew *Paras*. The origin, meaning, and relationship of this word are also unknown.

II. The Countries: The geographical boundaries of Media and Persia varied greatly through the centuries, and it is not possible to do more than roughly define them. The earliest knowledge of the geographical situation comes from the Babylonian and Assyrian texts. In these earliest sources the general name for the whole territory afterward known as Media and Persia was, according to Winckler, Anshan, which is usually connected closely with *Suri* ("Syria"). In this double geographical expression the word *Suri* stood for that part of the valley of the Euphrates and Tigris north of Babylonia proper, and extended also northwesterly to Asia Minor. The word Anshan covered the territory east of the Tigris. It was bordered on the northwest by the territory of Man, later Armenia, on the north by the Caspian Sea, on the east by the great desert, and on the south by Elam. This great territory was divided between the complex of peoples known as Medes. The territory originally known as Persia was much smaller, and was located, in general, southeast of the larger Median possessions. Its western and southern border was the Persian Gulf, and its eastern was formed by Carmania. When the Persians rose to supremacy the name Persia was extended to the greater Median territory, and a new geographical signification was acquired by it. This is well

1. Geographical Position and Extent.

expressed in the boasting words of Cyrus the Younger: "My father's kingdom extends so far to the south that men can not live there because of the heat, and northward to where they can not exist because of the cold."

Media and Persia together comprise within their borders temperate, sub-tropical, and tropical conditions. On the extreme northwest the winters are long, and deep snows block the wild and almost trackless mountain-passes. In the neighborhood of the Persian Gulf torrid temperatures prevail, as severe in the plain as those of India. In the immediate neighborhood of the Caspian Sea, the summers are hot and humid, and bear an evil reputation for unhealthiness. The great table-lands have on the whole a temperate climate, but the heat of summer is often very excessive and the presence of deserts, large and small, contributes much sand to the atmosphere when the wind is high. These same table-lands are covered with snows in the winter. The distribution of rain over the entire territory is, even yet, not scientifically known, and estimates of observers vary greatly. In Persia proper ten inches per annum is supposed to represent fairly well the average. Without irrigation, two-thirds of modern Persia would be a desert, and within the historic period the change can not have been great. The remainder of the country includes some of the most fertile portions of the earth, the praises of which poets have sung for centuries. The flora covers a very wide range, from the apple in the northwestern mountain regions to the peaches, figs, pomegranates, and lemons of the warmer sections. Wheat grows on the great steppes, and in the south cotton, opium, tobacco, madder roots, henna, and the mulberry. The fauna is as widely varied as the flora.

2. Climate; Fauna and Flora.

III. Exploration and Excavation: The exploration of the land of Media and Persia falls into two great subdivisions. The former concerns Persia almost exclusively, the latter springs chiefly out of the interest which the discovery and decipherment of the Babylonian and Assyrian inscriptions have awakened (see INSCRIPTIONS, II.). The earliest explorers of Persia were all men engaged in seeking an overland route between Europe and India. The notion that Persia might, in itself, reward the explorer was an afterthought. The story of the earliest explorations may be said to begin with the Italian friar Odoric in 1320, for he saw the ruins of Persepolis and it was from the key afforded by the inscriptions there discovered that all present knowledge of Media and Persia has been derived (see ASSYRIA, III., 1, for the early explorations of Persia). The more recent explorations have been best summed up in the extended tours of George N. Curzon, now Lord Curzon of Kedleston (*Persia and the Persian Question*, 2 vols., London, 1892) and Prof. A. V. Williams Jackson (*Persia Past and Present*, New York, 1906). Both of these had the historical problems in mind, and saw the country in its relations to Babylonia and Assyria as the cuneiform inscriptions have made them known. The former has given a most elaborate review of the work of former explorers, the latter has contributed valuable corrections to the Behistun inscription, first copied and deciphered by Sir Henry Rawlinson and since recopied and perfected by L. W King and R. C. Thompson (*The Sculptures and Inscription of Darius the Great on the Rock of Behistun in Persia*, London, 1907). Persia proper has been much better explored than Media, but in neither land have the known remains of ancient cities been excavated. In some of these it may well be hoped, by analogy with Babylonian, Assyrian, and Elamite mounds, there still lie buried large numbers of inscribed records of the historical events of both the Medes and the Persians. Until this colossal task is begun much of the history of both peoples must be accepted at second hand from allusions in the already discovered records of their neighbors. The sketch of their history which it is now possible to give is but fragmentary, with great gaps, especially in the earlier portions. The interest of the unexplored sites of Media would be scarcely inferior to those of Assyria, surely not inferior to the explored sites of Elam.

IV. Ethnological Data: The peoples of Media and Persia in ancient times afford a very similar set of problems to those which are confronted in Babylonia, Canaan and in Egypt. In all these cases there existed in historic times races, of more or less mixed blood, who may readily be classified among the great ethnological groups or families. The earlier prehistoric inhabitants present the greatest problems of ethnology. The prehistoric populations both of Media and of Persia are of unknown extraction and racial ties. These early inhabitants are called by the Babylonians *Umman Manda*, "the Manda hordes." They were uncivilized and nomadic and, as Winckler has said, fill in the minds of the Babylonians a place somewhat similar to that occupied by the Scythians in the mind of the Greeks. Whence these people came there is at present no knowledge. On the other hand, the peoples of the great historic period, who are known as Medes and Persians, both belonged to the Indo-European race—the great race which in later times has spread all over Europe and America.

V. The History of Medo-Persia: Philological indications would seem to show that in extremely early times there was an invasion of the territory known as Media by a number of people from the Caucasus region, a region once crowded with peoples of Aryan affinities but with much diversity in speech. Into this territory there had previously come a people of dark complexions who may have had some racial ties with the people now called Sumerians, who inhabited Babylonia before the Semitic Babylonians entered it (see BABYLONIA, V., §§ 1, 3–4). The first glimpse of the land and people of Media is secured from an inscription of Anu-banini, king of the Lulubi, in the valleys of the Zagros. The style of this inscription seems to make it contemporaneous with Sargon I. (see BABYLONIA, VI., 3, § 1) about 3750 B.C.; Thureau-Dangin does not venture to place it so early, but classifies it merely as earlier than the first dynasty of Ur (see BABYLONIA, VI., 3, § 3). Whatever the date may be, the people called

1. The Manda Hordes.

Lulubi must have come into the territory from the west or northwest to find it already occupied by the dark-skinned folk, connected above tentatively with the Sumerians, and also by the people from the Caucasus. Their title for "prince" seems to have been "Yanzu." As they entered the land from west or northwest, there came from the east the Kasyapa, or Kasyapi. These may perhaps be all grouped together and called the *Umman Manda*.

2. The Kasshites. After this early period knowledge of Media passes into darkness for many centuries, as the next intelligence comes from the period of the Kasshite dominion in Babylonia when Agum II. (see BABYLONIA, VI., 5, § 1, where this king is registered under the name Agum-kakrime) claimed dominion not only over Babylonia, but also over some Median provinces, from which it may be inferred that the great Kasshite invasion passed also over Media, and conquered portions of its territory. Another long period is to be passed over, of which nothing is known until the reigns of Adad-nirari I. and Shalmaneser I., his son, kings of Assyria about 1300 B.C., who conquered the Lulubi or Lulumi, who were again conquered about two centuries later by Nebuchadrezzar I. of Babylonia. During this entire period there is not a single mention of the people whom the Greeks called Medes. They have not yet appeared in history. All the people who have up to this time attracted attention belonged in some way to the unclassified Manda hordes.

3. The Early Medes. In his twenty-fourth campaign in the year 836 Shalmaneser II., king of Assyria, made an expedition into Namri, and passing on through the country met for the first time the Amadai or Madai, that is, the Medes of the Indo-European family. He claims a great victory over them, carrying away prisoners and devastating their cities. Their recuperative power was great, for during the reign of Adad-nirari V. (formerly known as Ramman-nirari III. or IV. or Adad-nirari III. or IV.; 810–782 B.C.) the eponym canon sets down no less than eight campaigns and still another under Asshur-Dan III. (771–754 B.C.). The Medes seem to have increased in numbers, and then to have mastered more thoroughly the primitive population and to have gained rapidly in power with the passing years in spite of the great efforts of the Assyrians to overcome them. During the next Assyrian reign (Tiglath-Pileser IV.; 745–727 B.C.) two great expeditions were led against the Medes in 744 and in 737, in the former of which the Assyrian king claims to have carried away 60,500 captives, and in the latter 8,650. The king always refers to them as the "dangerous" Medes, and such he doubtless found them to be. There was an almost continuous battery of attacks upon the Medes during the reign of Sargon II., 722–705; and Sennacherib (705–681) received tribute from "the far-away Medes, whose names no one of my predecessors had known."

4. Early Migrations; The Cimmerians. From about 700 B.C. new waves of migration from the neighborhood of Lake Urumiah passed down into the territory once held by the Assyrians and lying east of the Tigris. These were Indo-Europeans, and their names have been preserved in part at least by the Assyrians. The best-known of them are the Cimmerians (the Kimmerioi of the Greeks, the Gomer of the Hebrews). All these peoples were a cause of deep anxiety to the Assyrians during the reign of Esarhaddon (681–668 B.C.), and Asshurbanipal (668–625 B.C.) in vain attempted to hold them in check. In large numbers, and increasing both in power and in daring, they were sweeping all before them. From about the year 640 the native rulers of Elam no longer are mentioned, for the Medes had possessed the land, and very soon after that year there is notice of the kings of Anshan, to whom Cyrus the Great looked back as his ancestors. As Assyrian power dwindled these new invaders east of Assyria were building up a new people, the old Indo-Europeans melting together with the new, and soon this new combination was able to found a kingdom of its own with the capital city Ecbatana.

5. Ecbatana. From many sources there come down memories of that great city. The ancient Persians called it Hagmatana, and the Babylonians Agamatanu, while the Greeks catching a false quantity made it Ecbátana. It is perhaps safe to suppose that it is the city called Amadana by Tiglath-Pileser I., and in this case its origin would go back to the twelfth century before Christ. Herodotus, on the other hand, ascribes its origin to Deioces, whom he regards as the first great ruler of the Median empire about 700 B.C., who is represented as having erected great walls of defense, "the walls being arranged in circles one within another." From this time onward, the stream of Median history is in full flow, and the Greek sources give valuable sidelights upon the native monuments.

6. Deioces and Astyages I. Herodotus makes Deioces the ruler of the Medes 700–647 B.C. The successor of Deioces, according to Herodotus, was Phraortes (646–625), but of him nothing is learned from the inscription material which has come down, and the name is therefore suspect. It has been suggested by Winckler that the real ruler of Media at this time was Astyages I., and that it was he who was first invoked by the Babylonians to lend aid against the Assyrians. There is no solid evidence for this and the statement must suffice that the next king of the Medes, Cyaxares (624–585), is the first really historical monarch of the Median empire. His name is handed down by Darius the Great in the form Uvakshatara, and he it was who broke the Scythian power and formed an alliance with the Babylonians. Urged onward by Nabopolassar, king of Babylon, Cyaxares attacked Nineveh and in the year 606 B.C. laid it waste, and with it the upper part of Mesopotamia and the Babylonian cities which had cast in their lot with the Assyrians. By this one stroke the Medes were enriched through the vast plunder which Nineveh provided, but also they had sprung from insignificance into the position of a world power. The Median armies flushed with victory swept onward into the northwest, conquering as they went, until the river Halys became the western boundary of the new empire which extended eastward to the confines of Elam. It was a vast and powerful empire which Cyaxares left to his son. Astyages (584–550) was not able to keep up the good relations with Babylonia which had continued since the very beginning of his father's reign, and there is evidence of a struggle of some kind with Neriglissar. When Nabonidus became king of Babylon a Median army was besieging Harran, and the Babylonians and Medes were enemies.

While the Medes were thus founding a wide-spread empire, another branch of the Indo-European wanderers was slowly preparing for even greater dominion. The kings who were to lead the new movement are called the Achæmenians or Achæmenides, and three lists of the chief members of this great family have come down, one upon the cylinder of Cyrus, a second upon the great inscription of Darius at Behistun, and the third in Herodotus (vii. 11). The combination of these three sources is by no means easy, but a fair agreement among modern scholars has been achieved, and the following may be regarded as representing the facts as well as they can be made out at present.

7. The Achæmenians.

Hakhamanish (Achæmenes)
|
Ćishpish (Teïspes)
|
Kambuziya (Cambyses)
|
Kurash (Cyrus)
|
Ćishpish

Kurash (Cyrus)	Ariyaramna (Ariaramnes)
Kambuziya (Cambyses)	Arshama (Arsames)
Kurash (Cyrus the Great)	Vishtashpa (Hystaspes)
Kambuziya (Cambyses)	Darayavash (Darius)

8. Cyrus.

In this great family the greatest name is Cyrus, son of Cambyses, grandson of Cyrus. His career was so splendid that the imagination of the whole world of ancient culture was touched, and the writers of Greece and Rome surrounded his personality with legends for which no historical basis is found. When he first appears he is king of Anshan, and his capital was probably Susa. He is also called king of Persia, but the title was not a great one until he made it great, and both as king of Anshan and as king of Persia he was at first more or less subject to the greater kingdom of Media. There was no possibility that a man of his capacity could continue to be a "petty vassal." In 549 B.C. he conquered Astyages, and at one stroke made himself king of the Median empire. The concentration into the hands of one powerful man of three kingdoms, Anshan, Persia, and Media, was a menace to all western Asia, and there was soon a combination arranged in defense. The alliance was formed of Crœsus, king of Lydia, Nabonidus, king of Babylonia, and Amasis, king of Egypt. It must have seemed formidable, but it afforded in reality no defense against Cyrus. He completed the reduction of the whole Median empire and pushed at once into Asia Minor. Crœsus was taken in the autumn of 546, and before the end of 545 the peninsula of Asia Minor had become a part of the new Persian empire and was divided into satrapies and ruled by a strong hand. Cyrus turned next to Babylonia. Nabonidus was busy with temples and restorations, and his son Belshazzar, set to defend the country, went down to defeat before Cyrus at Opis, and Sippar fell without fighting. Gobryas (Gubaru, Ugbaru) entered Babylon without a struggle and on the 3d of Marcheswan (October) 539 Cyrus entered Babylon and was received as a deliverer.

9. Old-Testament Allusions.

It was no wonder that such a career should have captivated the minds of the Hebrews. In Isa. xl.–xlviii. Cyrus is Yahweh's anointed and to him the exiles were looking for the deliverance from Babylonia. In 538 he issued the decree that set the Jews free from their trammels and permitted the beginning of the rebuilding of national and religious life in Jerusalem.

Cyrus built his capital at Pasargadæ, and there also was set his tomb, and in the year 529 his reign, glorious not only in war, but also in peace, came to an end, and Cambyses II. (529–521 B.C.) reigned in his stead.

10. Cambyses; Darius.

Cambyses began his reign by putting to death his brother Smerdis, and a despotic and mad though brief career began. Though far inferior to Cyrus in ability, Cambyses had a daring imagination, and contemplated vast projects of conquest. On slight pretexts he invaded Egypt, captured Memphis, and pushed on victoriously to Thebes. A great expedition sent thence into Nubia met with disaster, and Cambyses set out for home. On the way he learned that a rebellion, serious in extent and dangerous in intensity, had begun in his kingdom. A Magian whose name was Gaumata (Gomates) had put forth a claim to be Smerdis, whom Cambyses had slain, and was ready to seize the supreme power. When this terrible news reached him, he committed suicide. With him ended the elder branch of the Achæmenian line, for his successor Darius, son of Hystaspes, belonged to the younger line. A combination of nobles succeeded in slaying the false Smerdis, and Darius (522–485 B.C.) was made king. His reign began with great works of peace. He reorganized the system of satrap government, giving large autonomy but retaining effective control in all matters of moment to the empire. He dug a canal between the Nile and the Red Sea, established a system of posting over newly built roads covering large portions of his empire, secured a new respect for law and governed by it himself, and even by his enemies seems to have been held in almost universal respect. In war his success was mixed with failure, and his plans were far too great, but the achievements were nevertheless memorable. At one blow he established his dominion over the Punjab in northwestern India, while in the west he conducted a great campaign against the Greeks, only to meet with a decisive defeat at Marathon (490 B.C.). While preparing for another assault he died suddenly, leaving to his son Xerxes a revolt in Egypt, and unfinished preparations against the Greeks.

II. Xerxes, Artaxerxes, and Successors.

Xerxes I. (Khshayarsha), 485–465 B.C., was in no respect the equal of his father, but something of the old military prowess was revealed in his successful suppression of the revolt in Egypt and also of a rebellion in Babylonia. He was then free to attack the Greeks, and with a large army he passed over Asia Minor, crossed the Hellespont, and invaded Europe. But in the naval battle of Salamis his fleet was overwhelmed and he was compelled to return in defeat to his capital. His empire was tottering, but endured with some show of strength a century and a half longer, chiefly because of the organization which it had received at the clever hands of Darius. Xerxes fell a victim at last to intrigue and perished at the hands of assassins. With his end came the beginning of the end of Persian power. The Greeks had cause to remember him, while the Hebrews enshrined a tradition of his court in the book of Esther and called him Ahasuerus.

The next king was Artaxerxes Longimanus (Artakshatsu), 465–424 B.C., in whose reign Nehemiah, his cup-bearer, and Ezra the scribe were permitted to visit Jerusalem and there set in order a new Jewish commonwealth with the organization of a church. His successor Darius II., called Darius Nothus (424–405), had an inglorious reign, suffering not a little at the hands of his sister and Queen Parysatis, who was ambitious to set her beloved son Cyrus on the throne but failed in the effort. The scepter came into the hands of the lazy Artaxerxes I. Mnemon (405–358), under whom the waning power of the empire became a byword. His successor Artaxerxes III. Ochus (358–338) restored for a time the empire, reduced the Egyptians, and put down numerous revolts which had their origin in the laxity of the previous reign. He was murdered at last by Bagoas, who tried to settle upon the throne Arses (338–336), but he proved faithless to his patron, and Bagoas poisoned him and made Darius III. Codomannus (336–331 B.C.), a great-grandson of Darius II., the king. He was unequal to the fearful emergency which came upon him. Alexander the Great, fresh from universal success, met him in battle at Arbela (331) and scattered his hosts, destroyed by fire his palaces at Persepolis, and sent his dead body to his aged mother. The sun of Persian hegemony and independence had set. The history of the Christians under the Sassanidæ is given under Nestorians (q.v.), which involves virtually the history of that period. ROBERT W ROGERS.

BIBLIOGRAPHY: For current bibliography consult E. Wilhelm, "Persien," in *Jahresbericht der Geschichtswissenschaft*, Berlin (an annual). On the explorations and discoveries the literature under Assyria; and the works of Lord Curzon and A. V. W Jackson named in the text. On the inscriptions, besides the works of Jackson, and of King and Thompson, named in the text, consult: H. C. Tolman, *Guide to the Old Persian Inscriptions*, New York, 1902; idem, *Ancient Persian Lexicon and the Texts of the Achæmenian Inscriptions*, ib. 1908; idem, *The Behistun Inscription of King Darius*, ib., 1908; H. C. Rawlinson, *The Persian Cuneiform Inscription at Behistun*, in *JRAS*, 1846–49; F. Spiegel, *Alt-persische Keilinschriften*, Leipsic, 1881; C. Bezold, *Die Achämenideninschriften*, Leipsic, 1882; T. Nöldeke, *Persepolis. Die Achaemenidischen und sasanidischen Denkmäler und Inschriften von Persepolis* . , 2 vols., Berlin, 1882; F. H. Weissbach, *Die Achamenideninschriften zweiter Art*, Leipsic, 1890; F. H. Weissbach and W. Bang, *Die altpersischen Keilinschriften*, Leipsic, 1893–1909; C. Bartholomæ, *Altiranisches Wörterbuch*, Strasburg, 1904. On the history consult: B. Brisson, *De regio Persarum principatu*, ed. J. H. Lederlin, Strasburg, 1710; G. Rawlinson, *Seven Great Monarchies* (many reprints); T. Nöldeke, *Aufsätze zur persischen Geschichte*, Leipsic, 1887; idem, in *Encyclopædia Britannica*, 9th ed., art. Persia; F. Spiegel, *Eranische Alterthumskunde*, ii. 236–581, Leipsic, 1873; E. Meyer, *Geschichte des Altertums*, parts 1–3, Stuttgart, 1884–1901; J. von Prašek, *Medien und das Haus des Kyaxares*, Berlin, 1890; idem, *Die ersten Jahre Dareios des Hystaspiden und der altpersische Kalendar*, Leipsic, 1901; idem, *Geschichte der Meder und Perser bis zur makedonischen Eroberung*, 2 vols., Gotha, 1906–10; F. Justi, *Geschichte Irans von den ältesten Zeiten*, in *Grundriss der iranischen Philologie*, Strasburg, 1895–1904; idem, *Central and Eastern Asia in Antiquity*, London, 1902; idem, *Iranisches Namenbuch*, Marburg, 1895; J. Marquart, *Untersuchungen zur Geschichte von Iran*, Göttingen, 1896–1905; idem, *Eransahr*, Berlin, 1901; P. Kershasp, *Studies in Ancient Persian History*, London, 1905; V. Smith, *Early Hist. of India from 600 B.C. to the Mohammedan Conquest*, pp. 10, 34–35, Oxford, 1908 (deals with the conquest of Northern India, cf. Esther i. 1).

MEGANDER (GROSSMANN), KASPAR: Swiss Reformer; b. at Zürich, 1495; d. there Aug. 18, 1545. He studied at Basel, and in 1518 became a chaplain in his native city. From the beginning he stood unconditionally on the side of Zwingli; after 1525 he was active at the exegetical school founded by Zwingli. In 1528 he was called as professor of theology and preacher to Bern where the foundation for a theological institution was being laid, and the management of ecclesiastical affairs fell into his hands.

The importance of Megander for the history of the church lies in his consistent attitude in the negotiations for union between the Swiss and the German Reformation. Bern formed the center of opposition to the efforts of Butzer, and Megander was the leading spirit of that opposition. At first his older colleagues shared entirely his Zwinglian views, but Sebastian Meyer, the friend of the Strasburg theologians, and Peter Kunz, who for a time had studied at Wittenberg, energetically endeavored to advance the union with the Saxons. Consequently both sides vehemently attacked each other, in colloquies and from the pulpit. A synod held on May 31, 1537, censured the offensive quarreling of both parties and requested silence. Another convention, held in September, gave Butzer an opportunity to defend himself, and declared itself satisfied with his justification. Megander, on the other hand, was asked to revise his catechism because Butzer and Kunz suspected it of heresies in the article on the Lord's Supper. Megander's catechism had appeared in 1536, and although he was not disinclined to make changes, he was so deeply hurt by Butzer's immediate and inconsiderate revision that he refused to acknowledge it. Consequently he was dismissed before the end of 1537, and returned to Zürich where he was made dean at the cathedral. With Leo Jud Megander published "Annotations to Genesis and Exodus" (1527) after Zwingli's oral lectures, also "Annotations to the Epistle to the Hebrews and to I John" (1539). He also wrote short commentaries on Galatians (1533), Ephesians (1534), and Timothy and Titus (1535). See BUTZER, MARTIN. (EMIL EGLI†.)

BIBLIOGRAPHY: The best sources are the letters of Zwingli, in which the activities of Megander often receive notice. The works on the life of Zwingli have also more or less to say of him. Consult: Hundeshagen, *Die Konflikte des Zwinglianismus, Lutherthums, Calvinismus in der bernischen Landeskirche 1532-58*, Bern, 1842.

MEGAPOLENSIS, JOHANNES (Jan van Mekelenburg): Dutch missionary to the American Indians; b. at Koedyck, Holland, 1603; d. in New York City Jan. 24, 1670. He came to America, 1642, on the invitation of the patroon of Rensselaerwyck, and labored as a frontier missionary. He remained until 1649 working among the Mohawk Indians, whose language he learned, many of whom joined his church. He was thus the first missionary among the Indians, preceding John Eliot by three years. From 1649 to his death he was pastor of the Dutch Church in New Amsterdam (New York). His zeal led him into intolerance toward Lutherans and Independents. His valuable "Short Account of the Mohawk Indians, their Country, Language, Figure, Costume, Religion, and Government," written in Dutch and published without his consent (Amsterdam, 1651), is translated in *Historical Collections, State of New York*, vol. iii.

MEGIDDO: A royal Canaanitic city assigned at the conquest to Manasseh, though situated within the borders of Issachar. Apparently it was not occupied at the conquest, though the statement is made that the inhabitants were subjected to tribute (Josh. xvii. 11-13; Judges i. 27-28). It was fortified by Solomon (I Kings ix. 15), and Ahaziah died there (II Kings ix. 27). It is mentioned in connection with Taanach, the modern Tell Ta'anuk (Josh. xii. 21, xvii. 11; Judges v. 19; I Kings iv. 12), on the edge of the plain of Esdraelon about half-way down its southern side. The site is therefore by some recognized in Tell el-Mutasellim, on a spur jutting out from Carmel, not far from Lejjun, which marks the site of the Roman town Legio; others prefer Lejjun itself, the ruins of which lie on both sides of a perennial stream which may well be the "waters of Megiddo" (Judges v. 19). Its situation on the edge of the plain of Esdraelon, a battle-ground of the nations for millenniums (cf. Judges v. 19-21; II Kings xxiii. 29-30; Zech. xii. 11; and the Egyptian inscriptions, e.g., of Thothmes III.), gave it a strategic importance. Accordingly it appears in history as a fortified city (Josh. xii. 21; I Kings ix. 15), and in Rev. xvi. 16 (Har Magedon, i.e., "the mountain [fortress] of Magedon") it figures as the typical fortress about which the final world conflict is to take place. GEO. W. GILMORE.

BIBLIOGRAPHY: Dillmann's commentary on Joshua at xii. 21; G. F. Moore's commentary on Judges, pp. 47, 158; Conder, in the PEF, *Memoirs*, ii. 90-99 (identifies it with Mujedda near Bethshean, unquestionably wrong); G. A. Smith, *Historical Geography of the Holy Land*, pp. 53, 385-387, 406, London, 1896.

MEGILLOTH. See CANON OF SCRIPTURE, I., 6.

MEHLHORN, mêl'hōrn, **PAUL:** German Protestant; b. at Gauern (a village of Saxon Altenburg) Jan. 3, 1851. He was educated at the universities of Jena (1869-72; Ph.D., 1873), Zurich (1872), and Leipsic (1872-73), after which he was successively teacher in a private school for girls in Dresden (1873-74), and at the Nicolai Gymnasium in Leipsic (1875-81), and professor at the gymnasium in Heidelberg (1881-93). He was also a teacher in the theological seminary of Heidelberg from 1883 to 1893 and associate professor of theology at the university of the same city from 1891 to 1893. Since 1893 he has been pastor of the Evangelical Reformed Church in Leipsic. He is a member of the Deutscher Protestantenverein, belongs to the liberal school in theology, and has written, among other works: *Die Bibel, ihr Inhalt und geschichtlicher Boden* (Leipsic, 1877); *Kirchengeschichte für höhere Schulen* (1880); *Grundriss der protestantischen Religionslehre* (1883); *Heidelberger Universitätspredigten* (1891); *Kritisches und Erbauliches* (Berlin, 1891); *Wie ist in unserer Zeit das Christentum zu verteidigen?* (1894); *Aus den Quellen der Kirchengeschichte* (2 parts, 1894-99); *Rechenschaft von unserm Christentum* (Leipsic, 1896); *Aus Höhen und Tiefen* (sermons, 1902); *Der Religionsunterricht in den höheren Schulen* (Heidelberg, 1902); *Die beiden Hauptrichtungen des kirchlichen Protestantismus* (1903); *Wahrheit und Dichtung im Leben Jesu* (Leipsic, 1906); and *Die Blutezeit der deutschen Mystik* (Tübingen, 1907). He has also edited the second part of K. J. Holsten's *Das Evangelium des Paulus* (Berlin, 1898) and the fourteenth and fifteenth editions of J. Hammer's *Leben und Heimat in Gott, eine Sammlung Lieder zur Erbauung und Veredlung* (Leipsic, 1901-05).

MEIDERLIN, PETER. See MELDENIUS, RUPERTUS.

MEIER, mai'er, **ERNST JULIUS:** German Lutheran; b. at Zwickau Sept. 7, 1828; d. at Dresden Oct. 6, 1897 He studied at the University of Leipsic and filled the successive positions of pastor at Flemmingen (1854-64), superintendent at Lössnitz (1864-67), superintendent of the diocese of Dresden (1867-90), and court preacher and vice-president of the national consistory at Dresden (1890-97). By his vigorous personality he exercised a profound influence upon the national church of Saxony and its clergy. His especial gift was preaching. His versatile spiritual interest was coupled with ready command of expression, together with much skill in the way of ingenious coordination of ideas. His sermons stick closely to their text, and his ideas are clearly presented, though their style presupposes a rather high degree of culture in the audience. He published three volumes of sermons (Leipsic, 1871, 1877, 1886), two collections of addresses as superintendent (1871, 1881), and sundry lectures. GEORG RIETSCHEL.

BIBLIOGRAPHY: B. Kühn, in *Beiträge zur sächsischen Kirchengeschichte*, xii. 1 sqq., Leipsic, 1897; C. Mensel, *Kirchliches Handlexikon*, iv. 524-525, Leipsic, 1894.

MEINHOLD, main'hōlt, **JOHANN FRIEDRICH HELLMUT:** German Lutheran; b. at Kammin (40 m. n.n.e. of Stettin), Aug. 12, 1861. He was educated at the universities of Leipsic, Berlin, Greifswald, and Tübingen from 1879 to 1884, and in the latter year became privat-docent for theology at Greifswald, where he was appointed associate professor four years later. In 1889 he went in a similar capacity to Bonn, where he was promoted to his present position of full professor of Old-Testament exegesis and Hebrew in 1903. In addition to briefer contributions, he has written: *Die Composition des Buches Daniel* (Greifswald, 1884); *Beiträge zur Erklärung des Buches Daniel*, i. (Leipsic, 1888); *Die geschichtlichen Hagiographen* (*Chronika, Esra, Nehemia, Ruth, Esther*) *und das Buch Daniel ausgelegt* (in collaboration with S. Oettli; Nördlingen, 1889); *Wider den Kleinglauben, ein ernstes Wort an die evangelischen Christen aller Parteien* (Freiburg, 1895); *Jesus und das Alte Testament, ein zweites ernstes Wort an die evangelischen Christen* (1896); *Jesaja und seine Zeit* (1898); *Die Jesajaerzählungen, Jesaja 36–39* (Göttingen, 1898); *Die Lade Jahves* (Tübingen, 1900); *Studien zur israelitischen Religionsgeschichte*, i. (Bonn, 1903); *Die biblische Urgeschichte in gemeinverständlicher Darstellung* (1904); and *Sabbat und Woche im Alten Testament* (Göttingen, 1905).

MEINHOLD, KARL HEINRICH JOACHIM: German Lutheran; b. at Liepe (on the Island of Usedom in the Baltic) Aug. 21, 1813; d. in Kammin (120 m. n.n.e. of Berlin) July 20, 1888. His father was a pastor and a rationalist, like the clergy of his synod of that time, though his rationalism was not consistent. In 1827 he entered Mary's College at Stettin and in 1831 the University of Greifswald and later that of Halle. Under the influence of Tholuck and of Ullmann, and later of Schleiermacher in Berlin, he severed all relations with rationalism, drawing closer to the Bible. In 1838, he was appointed pastor at Kolzow, in the Island of Wollin, Pomerania, where he succeeded in maintaining Lutheran interests and soon became one of the acknowledged champions of the Lutheran Church. In the later part of the period of organization of Lutheranism within the Prussian state church Meinhold was a prominent worker and influenced the final settlement. The synod of Wollin, to which Kolzow belonged, resolved that their parishioners should take the name of Lutherans officially and that the sacraments should be administered according to the Lutheran rite. In 1846, a general synod petitioned the authorities to guarantee the Lutheran rights, but without success. After 1848, the authorities decided that the Union should become absolute. During the political struggles the Lutheran associations, with headquarters at Naugard, planned for self-defense. In 1851, Meinhold was appointed superintendent at Kammin, where he soon became the leader of the associations in their contest with the authorities. These associations had to contend with two tendencies, first that toward separation, secondly that toward absorption, with the latter of which the authorities sided, and in the contest Meinhold received blame from both parties. In 1869, Superintendent Meinhold was suspended, but he was reinstated in 1874 by order of the ministry. Then supervened the Falk era: the clergy, expecting greater freedom and led by Meinhold, outlined their position at a conference at Gnadau in 1874. However, disciplinary measures were taken against Meinhold. A synodal order was issued, looking to a union between the confessional group and the authorities. In 1875, a general synod assembled and determined upon harmony; the result was that the Lutheran Church gained a right of existence within the Prussian state church. In 1880, Meinhold was reappointed superintendent, then district school inspector, and in 1888 a jubilee was celebrated for his fifty years of active service. (T. MEINHOLD.)

BIBLIOGRAPHY: *Allgemeine evangelisch-lutherische Kirchenzeitung*, 1888, pp. 1107 sqq.

MEINRAD (MEGINHARD), ST. See EINSIEDELN.

MEINWERK, main'vĕrk: Bishop of Paderborn, 1009–1036. He was related to the royal family and received his education in the ecclesiastical schools of Halberstadt and Hildesheim. He was made a canon of Halberstadt; later, in the time of Otto III., court chaplain, and in 1009 Heinrich II. made him bishop of Paderborn. He served faithfully in internal and external affairs the emperor and his country, and was able with great cleverness to assert his influence among kings and nobles, among wealthy clergymen and laymen, obtaining endowments for his diocese or for the monastery of Abdinghofen, built between 1015 and 1031 in the western suburb of Paderborn. (FRANZ GÖRRES.)

BIBLIOGRAPHY: The basal source is an anonymous life written about 1150, ed. G. H. Pertz in *MGH, Script.*, xi (1854), 104–161, and in *ASB*, June, i. 511–553. A very useful bibliography is given in Potthast, *Wegweiser*, pp. 1478–79. Consult: F. X. Schrader, *Leben und Wirken des . Meinwerks, . , 1009–36*, Paderborn, 1895; H. Bresslau, *Jahrbücher des deutschen Reichs unter Konrad II.*, ii. 460 sqq., Leipsic, 1884.

MEISNER, mais'ner, **BALTHAZAR:** German theologian; b. at Dresden Feb. 3, 1587; d. at Wittenberg Dec. 29, 1626; belonged to that circle of theologians in the first decades of the seventeenth century who did not lose sight of the needs of the church. He studied at Wittenberg, Giessen, Strasburg, and Tübingen; was appointed professor in Wittenberg, 1613. He was on intimate terms with B. Mentzer in Giessen and J. Gerhard in Jena, but among them it was he who had the sharpest eye for the deficiencies of the church and made effectual efforts to remedy them. These attempts are evidenced in his publication, *B. Meisneri Pia Desideria*, dictated shortly before his death and published anonymously (Frankfort, 1679). His *Philosophia Sobria* (3 vols., Wittenberg, 1614–23) opposed the prevailing tendencies of logical studies and established his literary fame. (A. HAUCK.)

MEISSEN, mais'sen, **BISHOPRIC OF:** An ancient episcopal see in Germany, founded by the Emperor Henry I. in the sense that it grew out of the fortress which he built at the confluence of the Elbe and the Triebisch. The erection of the bishopric was decided at a synod held at St. Severus in Classe near Ravenna in 972. The first bishop, Burchard, was consecrated at Christmas, 968, and received the largest territory of any of the sees subject to the archbishop of Magdeburg. (A. HAUCK.)

The bishops received the dignity of princes of

the empire, with the right of coinage from the thirteenth century. In the first half of the fifteenth century the Hussites were very strong here, and in the sixteenth Duke Henry of Saxony established Protestantism, the last bishop, John IX. von Haugwitz, resigning the ecclesiastical jurisdiction into the hands of the chapter; his predecessor John VII. von Schleinitz (d. 1537) had already abandoned to the duke all claim to secular jurisdiction. The town of Meissen is fifteen miles northwest of Dresden.

Bibliography: *Codex diplomaticus Saxoniæ*, ed. E. G. Gersdorf, II., i.–iii., Leipsic, 1863 sqq.; E. Machatschek, *Geschichte der Bischöfe des Hochstifts Meissen*, Dresden, 1884; E. O. Schultze, *Die Kolonisierung . der Gebiete zwischen Saale und Elbe*, Leipsic, 1886; *Der Papst, die Regierung und die Verwaltung der heiligen Kirche in Rom*, p. 199, Munich, 1904; J. P. Kirsch, *Illustrierte Geschichte der katholischen Kirche*, p. 262, ib. 1905; *KL*, viii. 1196–1198; Hauck, *KD*, iii. 625–627 et passim.

MEJER, mē'yer, **OTTO KARL ALEXANDER:** German canonist; b. at Zellerfeld (28 m. s.e. of Hildesheim) May 27, 1818; d. at Hanover Dec. 25, 1893; studied jurisprudence at Berlin, Jena, and Göttingen (LL.D., 1841). In 1845 he published his *Institutionen des gemeinen deutschen Kirchenrechts*, containing the elements of canon law. Through this work the Hanoverian government was led to grant him a stipend by means of which he visited Rome, studying the policy of the Roman Church, its power, and its attitude toward Protestants. He officiated as professor at Königsberg and in Greifswald, 1847–50, and was in 1851 appointed consistorial councilor at Rostock, and later librarian of the university there. In Rostock he edited (1854–60), together with Kliefoth, the *Kirchliche Zeitschrift*, and he took a part in the ecclesiastical-political struggles of the time. In 1874 he became professor at Göttingen, and in 1885 president of the ecclesiastical court at Hanover. Of his numerous works may be mentioned: *Die Propaganda, ihre Provinzen, ihr Recht* (2 vols., Göttingen, 1852–53); *Zur Geschichte der römisch-deutschen Frage* (3 vols., Rostock, 1871–85); and *Das Rechtsleben der deutschen evangelischen Landeskirchen. Umrisse zur Orientierung für Geistliche und Gemeindeglieder* (Hanover, 1889). (G. Uhlhorn†.)

MEKHITARISTS: One of the noblest congregations in the Roman Catholic Church, which has developed a literary activity comparable to that of the congregation of St. Maur. Mekhitar, the founder of the order, was born of humble parentage at Sebaste, in Lesser Armenia, Feb. 7, 1676, and died at Venice Apr. 27, 1749. When fourteen years of age he entered the monastery of the Holy Cross near his native place, where in 1691 he was made deacon. He busied himself in study of the Scriptures and patristic writings and developed a talent for hymn-writing. In search of learning he removed to Tokat, and thence to Echmiadzin, the seat of Armenian scholarship. Finding his desires unsatisfied he returned to Sebaste, and in 1693 renewed his study of patristics. In 1695 he set out for Rome, and on the way fell in with the Jesuit missionary Antoine Beauvilliers, who advised him to study in Rome and then diffuse western learning throughout Armemia. His journey was broken, however, by a violent fever which attacked him in Cyprus; he returned to his home in the monastery near Sebaste, and there was made priest, 1696. His ambition had been aroused to accomplish two purposes, the moral and religious uplift of his countrymen and the reconciliation of the Roman Catholic and Armenian Churches. In 1699 he was made doctor of theology at Erzerum, became noted as a teacher, and interested many of his pupils in the missionary work which he had at heart. When his purposes respecting church union became known, he was compelled to move with great circumspection, and engaged a house at Pera, a suburb of Constantinople, where a printing-press was set up in the interest of his propaganda. Then began a persecution that compelled him to take refuge with the French ambassador and in the Capuchin monastery. He was advised to select a site in the peninsula of Morea, now a part of Greece, then a possession of Venice, as the seat of the missionary establishment which he contemplated; in 1703 he settled at Modon, in Morea, and by 1708 a monastery, church, and school had been built and occupied. In 1712 his order was constituted under the rule of St. Anthony and St. Benedict. In consequence of the war between Turkey and Venice, he was compelled to leave Modon; he obtained from Venice the island of San Lazarro, where he settled Sept. 8, 1717. The result of a journey to Rome was the gaining of so complete confidence in him on the part of pope and cardinals that all difficulties were removed, and, aided by rich countrymen, he was permitted to witness the completion of his projected buildings.

Mekhitar sought to improve education among the Armenians not only in secular but in religious instruction. He also attempted to carry further the earlier efforts of Popes Urban VIII., Alexander VII., and Innocent XI. for a union of the Roman Catholic and Armenian Churches. He fostered the study of the old Armenian language, writing *Grammatica Armena* (ed. A. Mekhitar, Venice, 1770) and a lexicon of Armenian (1744). He wrote commentaries on various books of the Bible, e.g., on Matthew (1737); after the translation of individual books, he published a translation of the whole Bible in 1734; he also issued many other works rendered from Latin or Italian, selecting those which he thought would serve the purposes toward which he had worked. After his death the students who had gathered about him, who now called themselves Mekhitarists, took up his work. They and their successors stocked their library with the best treatises and rendered into Armenian the works of the ancient masters in philosophy and theology. Besides this, they were themselves producers, and such works appeared as M. Chamchian's "History of Armenia" (3 vols., Venice, 1784–86, Eng. transl., 2 vols., Calcutta, 1827), L. Indshidshian's "Archeology and Geography" (11 vols., Venice, 1802–16), and the great Armenian lexicon compiled by a number of collaborators (Venice, 1836–37). Contributions to patristics and other branches of learning have resulted, as in the discovery of the thirteen letters of Ignatius in Armenian translation and of the commentary of Ephraem Syrus on the Gospel Harmony (of Tatian?). The institution in Venice has great influence even with Armenians not in the Roman Catholic Church, and branches in other lands—Turkey, Russia, France, Austria, and Hungary—have added to its wealth and prestige. Especially notable among these is the branch in Vienna, planted there in 1810, the printing-department of which has contributed largely to the spread of knowledge in the home country. The mother house is now the goal of all modern scholars who desire an intimate knowledge of Armenian language and literature. (K. Kessler†.)

Bibliography: E. Bore, *Saint Lazare, ou hist. de la société religieuse arménienne de Méchitar*, Venice, 1835; idem, *Le Couvent de S. Lazare à Venise*, Paris, 1837; S. Somalian, *Quadro della storia letteraria di Armenia*, Venice, 1829; C. F. Neumann, *Versuch einer Geschichte der armenischen Litteratur*, Leipsic, 1836; Windischmann, in *TQ*, 1835, part 1, cf. 1846, pp. 527 sqq.; Le Vaillant de Florival, *Les Mékhitaristes de S. Lazare*, Venice, 1856; V. Langlois, *The Armenian Monastery of St. Lazarus—Venice*, Venice, 1874; P. A. Hennemann, *Das Kloster der armenischen Mönche auf der Insel St. Lazzaro*, ib. 1881; A. Mayer, *Die Mechitaristenbuchdruckerei*, Vienna, 1888; F. Scherer, *Die Mechitaristen in Wien*, ib. 1892; K. Kalemkiarian, *Skizze der literarisch-typographischen Thätigkeit der Mechitaristen Congregation in Wien*, ib. 1898; S. Weber, *Die katholische Kirche in Armenien*, Freiburg, 1903; *KL*, viii. 1122–37. Some of the literature given under Armenia will be found pertinent. Consult also Heimbucher, *Orden und Kongregationen*, i. 313–319.

MELANCHTHON, PHILIPP.

I. Life: Philipp Melanchthon, the German humanist and Reformer, was born at Bretten (13 m. e.n.e. of Carlsruhe) Feb. 16, 1497, and died at Wittenberg Apr. 19, 1560. His father, Georg Schwarzerd, was armorer to Count Palatine Philip. Melanchthon received his first instruction in the school of his native city; he then had a private tutor, Johann Unger, in the house of his grandfather. In 1507 he was sent to the Latin school at Pforzheim, the rector of which, Georg Simler of Wimpfen, introduced him to the study of the Latin and Greek poets and of the philosophy of Aristotle. But he was chiefly influenced by his great-uncle, Johann Reuchlin, the great representative of humanism, who advised him to change his family name, Schwarzerd, into the Greek equivalent Melanchthon. Not yet thirteen years old, he entered in 1509 the University of Heidelberg where he studied philosophy, rhetoric, and astronomy, and was known as a good Greek scholar. As the lectures of the university did not satisfy him, he diligently read in private grammar, rhetoric, dialectics, and the ancient poets and historians. Being refused the degree of master in 1512 on account of his youth, he went to Tübingen, where he pursued humanistic and philosophical studies, but devoted himself also to the study of jurisprudence, mathematics, astronomy, and even of medicine. When, having completed his philosophical course, he had taken the degree of master in 1516, he began to study theology. Under the influence of men like Reuchlin and Erasmus he became convinced that true Christianity was something quite different from scholastic theology as it was taught at the university. But at that time he had not yet formed fixed opinions on theology, since later he often called Luther his spiritual father. He became *conventor* (*repetent*) in the *contubernium* and had to instruct younger scholars. He also lectured on oratory, on Vergil and Livy.

1. Education.

His first publications were an edition of Terence (1516) and his Greek grammar (1518), but he had written previously the preface to the *Epistolæ clarorum virorum* of Reuchlin (1514).

The more strongly he felt the opposition of the scholastic party to the reforms instituted by him at the University of Tübingen, the more willingly he followed a call to Wittenberg as professor of Greek, where he aroused great admiration by his inaugural *De corrigendis adolescentiæ studiis*. He lectured before five to six hundred students, afterward to fifteen hundred. He was highly esteemed by Luther, whose influence brought him to the study of Scripture, especially of Paul, and so to a more living knowledge of the Evangelical doctrine of salvation. He was present at the disputation of Leipsic (1519) as a spectator, but influenced the discussion by his comments and suggestions, so that he gave Eck an excuse for an attack. In his *Defensio contra Johannem Eckium* ([Wittenberg,] 1519) he had already clearly developed the principles of the authority of Scripture and its interpretation. On account of the interest in theology shown in his lectures on Matthew and Romans, together with his investigations into the doctrines of Paul, he was granted the degree of bachelor of theology, and was transferred to the theological faculty. Soon he was bound closer than ever to Wittenberg by his marriage to Katharina Krapp, the mayor's daughter, a marriage contracted at his friends' urgent request, and especially Luther's (Nov. 25, 1520).

2. Professor at Wittenberg.

In the beginning of 1521 in his *Didymi Faventini adversus Thomam Placentinum pro M. Luthero oratio* (Wittenberg, n.d.), he defended Luther by proving that Luther rejected only papal and ecclesiastical practises which were at variance with Scripture, but not true philosophy and true Christianity. But while Luther was absent at the Wartburg, during the disturbances caused by the Zwickau

Prophets (q.v.), there appeared for the first time the limitations of Melanchthon's nature, his lack of firmness and his diffidence, and had it not been for the energetic interference of Luther, the prophets would not have been silenced. The appearance of Melanchthon's *Loci communes rerum theologicarum seu hypotyposes theologicæ* (Wittenberg and Basel, 1521) was of great importance for the confirmation and expansion of the reformatory ideas. In close adherence to Luther Melanchthon presented the new doctrine of Christianity under the form of a discussion of the "leading thoughts" of the Epistle to the Romans. His purpose was not to give a systematic exposition of Christian faith, but a key to the right understanding of Scripture. Nevertheless, he continued to lecture on the classics, and, after Luther's return, would have given up his theological work altogether, if it had not been for Luther's urging. On a journey in 1524 to his native town, he was led to treat with the papal legate Campegi who tried to draw him from Luther's cause, but without success both at that time and afterward. In his *Unterricht der Visitatorn an die Pfarherrn im Kurfürstenthumb zu Sachssen* (1528) Melanchthon by establishing a basis for the reform of doctrines as well as regulations for churches and schools, without any direct attack upon the errors of the Roman Church, presented clearly the Evangelical doctrine of salvation. In 1529 he accompanied the elector to the Diet of Speyer (see SPEYER, DIET OF) to represent the Evangelical cause. His hopes of inducing the imperial party to a peaceable recognition of the Reformation were not fulfilled. He later repented of the friendly attitude shown by him toward the Swiss at the diet, calling Zwingli's doctrine of the Lord's Supper "an impious dogma" and confirming Luther in his attitude of non-acceptance.

3. Theological Disputes.

Although based on the Marburg and Schwabach articles of Luther, the Augsburg Confession (q.v.), which was laid before the Diet of Augsburg in 1530, was mainly the work of Melanchthon. It is true, Luther did not conceal the fact that the irenical attitude of the confession was not what he had wished, but neither he nor Melanchthon were conscious of any difference in doctrine, and so the most important Protestant symbol is a monument of the harmony of the two Reformers on Gospel teachings. But at the diet Melanchthon did not show that dignified and firm attitude which faith in the truth and the justice of his cause should have inspired in him, although it is true that he had not sought the part of a political leader, since he lacked the necessary knowledge of human nature, as well as energy and decision. The Apology of the Augsburg Confession, likewise the work of Melanchthon, was also a clear exposition of the disputed doctrines, drawn immediately from experience and Scripture. Now in comparative quiet Melanchthon could devote himself to his academical and literary labors. The most important theological work of this period was the *Commentarii in Epistolam Pauli ad Romanos* (Wittenberg, 1532), a noteworthy book, as it for the first time established the doctrine that "to be justified" means "to be accounted just," while the Apology still placed side by side the two meanings of "to be made just" and "to be accounted just." Melanchthon's increasing fame gave occasion for several honorable calls to Tübingen (Sept., 1534), to France, and to England, but consideration of the elector induced him to refuse them.

4. Augsburg Confession.

He took an important part in the discussions concerning the Lord's Supper which began in 1531. He approved fully of the Formula of Concord sent by Butzer to Wittenberg, and at the instigation of the Landgrave of Hesse discussed the question with Butzer in Cassel, at the end of 1534. He eagerly labored for an agreement, for his patristic studies and the Dialogue (1530) of Œcolampadius had made him doubt the correctness of Luther's doctrine. Moreover, after the death of Zwingli and the change of the political situation his earlier scruples in regard to a union lost their weight. Butzer did not go so far as to believe with Luther that the true body of Christ in the Lord's Supper is bitten by the teeth, but admitted the offering of the body and blood in the symbols of bread and wine (see WITTENBERG, CONCORD OF). Melanchthon discussed Butzer's views with the most prominent adherents of Luther; but Luther himself would not agree to a mere veiling of the dispute. Melanchthon's relation to Luther was not disturbed by his work as a mediator, although Luther for a time suspected that Melanchthon was "almost of the opinion of Zwingli"; nevertheless he desired to "share his heart with him." During his sojourn in Tübingen in 1536 Melanchthon was severely attacked by Cordatus, preacher in Niemeck, because he had taught that works are necessary for salvation. In the second edition of his *Loci* (1535) he abandoned his earlier strict doctrine of determinism which went even beyond that of Augustine, and in its place taught more clearly his so-called Synergism (q.v.). He repulsed the attack of Cordatus in a letter to Luther and his other colleagues by stating that he had never departed from their common teachings on this subject, and in the antinomian controversy of 1537 Melanchthon was in harmony with Luther.

5. Discussions on Lord's Supper and Justification.

It is true, the personal relation of the two great Reformers had to stand many a test in those years, for Amsdorf and others tried to stir up Luther against Melanchthon so that his stay at Wittenberg seemed to Melanchthon at times almost unbearable, and he compared himself to "Prometheus chained to the Caucasus." About this time occurred the notorious case of the second marriage of Philip of Hesse (See LUTHER, MARTIN, § 21). Melanchthon, who, as well as Luther, regarded this as an exceptional case, was present at the marriage, but urged Philip to keep the matter a secret. The publication of the fact so affected Melanchthon, then at Weimar, that he became exceedingly ill. In Oct., 1540, Melanchthon took an important part in the religious colloquy of Worms, where he defended clearly and firmly the doctrines of the Augsburg Confession. It is to be noted that Melanchthon used as a basis of the

6. Relations with Luther.

discussion an edition of the Augsburg Confession which had been revised by him (1540), and later was called *Variata*. Although Eck pointed out the not unessential change of Article X. regarding the Lord's Supper, the Protestants did not then take any offense. The colloquy failed, not because of the obstinacy and irritability of Melanchthon, as has been asserted, but because of the impossibility of making further concessions to the Roman Catholics. The conference at Regensburg in May, 1541, was also fruitless, owing to Melanchthon's firm adherence to the articles on the Church, the sacraments, and auricular confession. His views concerning the Lord's Supper, developed in union with Butzer on the occasion of drawing a draft of reformation for the electorate of Cologne (1543), aroused severe criticism on the part of Luther who wished a clear statement as to "whether the true body and blood were received physically." Luther gave free vent to his displeasure from the pulpit, and Melanchthon expected to be banished from Wittenberg. Further outbreaks of his anger were warded off only by the efforts of Chancellor Brück and the elector; but from that time Melanchthon had to suffer from the ill-temper of Luther, and was besides afflicted by various domestic troubles. The death of Luther, on Feb. 18, 1546, affected him in the most painful manner, not only because of the common course of their lives and struggles, but also because of the great loss that he believed was suffered by the Protestant Church.

7. Controversies with Flacius.

The last eventful and sorrowful period of his life began with controversies over the Interim (q.v.) and the Adiaphora (q.v.; 1547). It is true, Melanchthon rejected the Augsburg Interim, which the emperor tried to force upon the defeated Protestants; but in the negotiations concerning the so-called Leipsic Interim he made concessions which can in no way be justified, even if one considers his difficult position, opposed as he was to the elector and the emperor. In agreeing to various Roman usages, Melanchthon started from the opinion that they are adiaphora if nothing is changed in the pure doctrine and the sacraments which Christ instituted, but he ignored the fact that concessions made under such circumstances have to be regarded as a denial of Evangelical convictions. Melanchthon himself perceived his faults in the course of time and repented of them, having to suffer more than was just in the displeasure of his friends and the hatred of his enemies. From now on until his death he was full of trouble and suffering. After Luther's death he became the "theological leader of the German Reformation," not indisputably, however; for the real Lutherans with Flacius Illyricus at their head accused him and his followers of heresy and apostasy. Melanchthon bore all accusations and calumnies with admirable patience, dignity, and self-control. It can not be denied, on the one hand, that the Lutherans defended themselves against not only supposed but actual deviations from their beliefs, although their zeal sometimes carried them to extremes, nor on the other hand that Melanchthon and his followers represented a justifiable point of view, though they could not always express it within proper limits. In his controversy on justification with Andreas Osiander (q.v.) Melanchthon satisfied all parties.

8. Disputes with Osiander and Flacius.

Melanchthon took part also in a controversy with Stancari, who held that Christ was our justification only according to his human nature. He was also still a strong opponent of the Roman Catholics, for it was by his advice that the elector of Saxony declared himself ready to send deputies to a council to be convened at Trent, but only under the condition that the Protestants should have a share in the discussions, and that the pope should not be considered as the presiding officer and judge. As it was agreed upon to send a confession to Trent, Melanchthon drew up the *Confessio Saxonica* which is a repetition of the Augsburg Confession, discussing, however, in greater detail, but with moderation, the points of controversy with Rome. Melanchthon on his way to Trent at Dresden saw the military preparations of Maurice of Saxony, and after proceeding as far as Nuremberg, returned to Wittenberg (March, 1552); for Maurice had turned against the emperor. Owing to his act, the condition of the Protestants became more favorable and was still more so at the peace of Augsburg (1555), but Melanchthon's labors and sufferings increased from that time. The last years of his life were embittered by the disputes over the Interim and the freshly started controversy on the Lord's Supper. As the statement "good works are necessary for salvation" appeared in the Leipsic Interim, its Lutheran opponents attacked in 1551 Georg Major (q.v.), the friend and disciple of Melanchthon, so Melanchthon dropped the formula altogether, seeing how easily it could be misunderstood. But all his caution and reservation did not hinder his opponents from continually working against him, accusing him of synergism and Zwinglianism. At the conference in Worms in 1557 which he attended only reluctantly, the adherents of Flacius and the Saxon theologians tried to avenge themselves by thoroughly humiliating Melanchthon, in agreement with the malicious desire of the Roman Catholics to condemn all heretics, especially those who had departed from the Augsburg Confession, before the beginning of the conference. As this was directed against Melanchthon himself, he protested, so that his opponents left, greatly to the satisfaction of the Roman Catholics who now broke off the colloquy, throwing all blame upon the Protestants. The Reformation in the sixteenth century did not experience a greater insult, as Nitzsch says. Nevertheless, Melanchthon persevered in his efforts for the peace of the Church, suggesting a synod of the Evangelical party and drawing up for the same purpose the Frankfort Recess (q.v.) which he defended later against the attacks of his enemies. More than anything else the controversies on the Lord's Supper embittered the last years of his life. The renewal of this dispute was due to the victory in the Reformed Church of the Calvinistic doctrine and its influence upon Germany. To its tenets Melanchthon never gave his assent, nor did he use its characteristic formulas. The personal presence and self-impartation of Christ in the Lord's Supper were especially important for Melanchthon; but he did not definitely state how body and blood are related to this. Although rejecting the physical act of mastication, he nevertheless assumed the real presence of the body of Christ and therefore also a real self-impartation. Melanchthon differed from Calvin also in emphasizing the relation of the Lord's Supper to justification.

9. Death. But before these and other theological dissensions were ended, he was at last freed by his death; a few days before this event he committed to writing his reasons for not fearing it. On the left were the words, "Thou shalt be delivered from sins, and be freed from the acrimony and fury of theologians"; on the right, "Thou shalt go to the light, see God, look upon his Son, learn those wonderful mysteries which thou hast not been able to understand in this life." The immediate cause of death was a severe cold which he had contracted on a journey to Leipsic in March, 1560, followed by a fever that consumed his strength, weakened by many sufferings. The only care that occupied him until his last moment, was the desolate condition of the Church. He strengthened himself in almost uninterrupted prayer, and in listening to passages of Scripture. Especially significant did the words seem to him, "His own received him not; but as many as received him, to them gave he power to become the sons of God." When Caspar Peucer (q.v.), his son-in-law, asked him if he wanted anything, he replied, "Nothing but heaven." His body was laid beside Luther's in the Schlosskirche in Wittenberg.

II. Estimate of his Works and Character: Melanchthon's importance for the Reformation lay essentially in the fact that he systematized Luther's ideas, defended them in public, and made them the basis of a religious education. These two, by complementing each other, harmoniously achieved the great results of the Reformation. Only the heroism

1. Luther and Melanchthon. and creative power of a Luther were able to break with the reigning church. Melanchthon was impelled by Luther to work for the Reformation; his own inclinations would have kept him a student. Without Luther's influence Melanchthon would have been "a second Erasmus," although his heart was filled with a deeper religious interest in the Reformation. While Luther scattered the sparks among the people, Melanchthon by his humanistic studies won the sympathy of educated people and scholars for the Reformation. Beside Luther's heroism of faith, Melanchthon's many-sidedness and calmness, his temperance and love of peace, had a share in the success of the movement. Both men had a clear consciousness of their mutual position and the divine necessity of their common calling. Melanchthon wrote in 1520, "I would rather die than be separated from Luther," whom he afterward compared to Elijah, and called "the man full of the Holy Ghost." In spite of the strained relations between them in the last years of Luther's life, Melanchthon exclaimed at Luther's death, "Dead is the horseman and chariot of Israel who ruled the Church in this last age of the world!" On the other hand, Luther wrote of Melanchthon, in the preface to Melanchthon's Commentary on the Colossians (1529), "I had to fight with rabble and devils, for which reason my books are very warlike. I am the rough pioneer who must break the road; but Master Philipp comes along softly and gently, sows and waters heartily, since God has richly endowed him with gifts." Luther also did justice to Melanchthon's teachings, praising one year before his death in the preface to his own writings Melanchthon's revised *Loci* above them and calling Melanchthon "a divine instrument which has achieved the very best in the department of theology to the great rage of the devil and his scabby tribe." It is remarkable that Luther, who vehemently attacked men like Erasmus and Butzer, when he thought that truth was at stake, never spoke directly against Melanchthon, and even during his melancholy last years conquered his temper. The strained relation between these two men never came from external things, such as human rank and fame, much less from other advantages, but always from matters of Church and doctrine, and chiefly from the fundamental difference of their individualities; they repelled and attracted each other "because nature had not formed out of them one man." However, it can not be denied that Luther was the more magnanimous, for however much he was at times dissatisfied with Melanchthon's actions, he never uttered a word against his private character; but Melanchthon, on the other hand, sometimes evinced a lack of confidence in Luther. In a letter to Carlowitz he complained that Luther on account of his polemical nature exercised a personally humiliating pressure upon him. Luther certainly never intended to exercise such a pressure, and if it existed at all, it was Melanchthon's own fault.

As a Reformer Melanchthon was characterized by moderation, conscientiousness, caution, and love of peace; but these qualities were sometimes only lack of decision, consistence, and courage. Often,

2. His Work as Reformer. however, his actions showed not anxiety for his own safety, but regard for the welfare of the community, and for the quiet development of the Church. Melanchthon did not lack personal courage; but it was less of an aggressive than of a passive nature. When he was reminded how much power and strength Luther drew from his trust in God, he answered, "If I myself do not do my part, I can not expect anything from God in prayer." His nature was inclined rather to suffer with faith in God that he would be released from every evil than to act valiantly with his aid. The distinction between Luther and Melanchthon is well brought out in Luther's letters to the latter (June, 1530): "To your great anxiety by which you are made weak, I am a cordial foe; for the cause is not ours. It is your philosophy, and not your theology, which tortures you so,—as though you could accomplish anything by your useless anxieties. So far as the public cause is concerned, I am well content and satisfied; for I know that it is right and true, and, what is more, it is the cause of Christ and God himself. For that reason, I am merely a spectator. If we fall, Christ will likewise fall; and if he fall, I would rather fall with Christ than stand with the emperor." Another trait of his character was his love of peace. He had an innate aversion to quarrels and discord; yet, often he was very irritable. His irenical character often led him to adapt himself to the views of others, as may be seen from his correspondence with Erasmus and from his public attitude from the Diet of Augsburg to the Interim. It was, however, not merely a personal desire for peace, but his conservative religious nature, that guided him in his acts of conciliation. He never could forget that his father on his death-bed had besought his family "never to leave the Church." He stood toward the past history of the Church in an attitude of piety and reverence that made it much more difficult for him than for Luther to be content with the thought of the impossibility of a reconciliation with the Roman Catholic Church. He laid stress upon the authority of the Fathers, not only of Augustine, but also of the Greeks. His attitude in matters of worship was conservative, in the Leipsic Interim even too conservative, though not a Crypto-Catholic, as Cordatus and Schenk said. He never strove for a reconciliation with Roman Catholicism at the price of pure doctrine. He attributed more value to the external appearance and organization of the Church than Luther did, as can be seen from his whole treatment of the "doctrine of the Church." The ideal conception of the Church, which the Reformers opposed to the organization of the Roman Church, which was expressed in his *Loci* of 1535, lost for him after 1537 its former prominence, when he began to emphasize the conception of the true visible Church as it may be found among the Evangelicals. The relation of the Church to God he found in the divinely ordered office, the ministry of the Gospel. The universal priesthood was for Melanchthon as for Luther no principle of an ecclesiastical constitution, but a purely religious principle. In accordance with this idea Melanchthon tried to keep the traditional church constitution and government, including the bishops. He did not want, however, a church altogether independent of the State, but rather, in agreement with Luther, he believed it the duty of the secular authorities to protect religion and the Church. He looked upon the consistories as ecclesiastical courts which therefore should be composed of spiritual and secular judges, for to him the official authority of the Church did not lie in a special class of priests, but rather in the whole congregation, to be represented therefore not only by ecclesiastics, but also by laymen. Melanchthon in advocating church union did not overlook differences in doctrine for the sake of common practical tasks. The older he grew, the less he distinguished between the Gospel as the announcement of the will of God, and right doctrine as the human knowledge of it. Therefore he took pains to safeguard unity in doctrine by theological formulas of union, but these were made as broad as possible and were restricted to the needs of practical religion.

3. As Scholar.

As a scholar Melanchthon embodied the entire spiritual culture of his age. At the same time he found the simplest, clearest, and most suitable form for his knowledge; therefore his manuals, even if they were not always original, were quickly introduced into schools and kept their place for more than a century. Knowledge had for him no purpose of its own; it existed only for the service of moral and religious education, and so the teacher of Germany prepared the way for the religious thoughts of the Reformation. He is the father of Christian Humanism, which has exerted a lasting influence upon scientific life in Germany. His works were not always new and original, but they were clear, intelligible, and answered their purpose. His style is natural and plain, better, however, in Latin and Greek than in German. He was not without natural eloquence, although his voice was weak.

4. As Theologian.

As a theologian, Melanchthon did not show so much creative ability as a genius for collecting and systematizing the ideas of others, especially of Luther, for the purpose of instruction. He kept to the practical, and cared little for a connection of the parts, so his *Loci* were in the form of isolated paragraphs.

The fundamental difference between Luther and Melanchthon lies not so much in the latter's ethical conception, as in his humanistic mode of thought which formed the basis of his theology and made him ready not only to acknowledge moral and religious truths outside of Christianity, but also to bring Christian truth into closer contact with them, and thus to mediate between Christian revelation and ancient philosophy. Melanchthon's views differed from Luther's only in some modifications of ideas. Melanchthon looked upon the law as not only the correlate of the Gospel, by which its effect of salvation is prepared, but as the unchangeable order of the spiritual world which has its basis in God himself. He furthermore reduced Luther's much richer view of redemption to that of legal satisfaction. He did not draw from the vein of mysticism running through Luther's theology, but emphasized the ethical and intellectual elements. After giving up determinism and absolute predestination and ascribing to man a certain moral freedom, he tried to ascertain the share of free will in conversion, naming three causes as concurring in the work of conversion, the Word, the Spirit, and the human will, not passive, but resisting its own weakness. Since 1548 he used the definition of freedom formulated by Erasmus, "the capability of applying oneself to grace." He was certainly right in thinking it impossible to change one's character without surrender of the will; but by correlating the divine and the human will he lost sight of the fundamental religious experience that the desire and realization of good actions is a gift of divine grace. His definition of faith lacks the mystical depth of Luther. In dividing faith into knowledge, assent, and trust, he made the participation of the heart subsequent to that of the intellect, and so gave rise to the view of the later orthodoxy that the establishment and acceptation of pure doctrine should precede the personal attitude of faith. To his intellectual conception of faith corresponded also his view that the Church also is only the communion of those who adhere to the true belief and that her visible existence depends upon the consent of her unregenerated members to her teachings. Finally, Melanchthon's doctrine of the Lord's Supper, lacking the profound mysticism of faith by which Luther united the sensual elements and supersensual realities, demanded at least their formal distinction. The development of Melanchthon's beliefs may be seen from the history of the *Loci*. In the beginning Melanchthon intended only a development of the leading ideas representing the Evangelical conception of salvation, while the later editions approach more and more the plan of a text-book of dogma. At first he uncompromisingly insisted on the necessity of every event, energetically rejected the philosophy of Aristotle, and had not fully developed his doctrine of the sacraments. In 1535 he treated for the first time the doctrine of God and that of the Trinity; rejected the doctrine of the necessity of every event and named free will as a concurring cause in conversion. The doctrine of justification received its forensic form and the necessity of good works was emphasized in the interest of moral discipline. The last editions are distinguished from the earlier ones by the prominence given to the theoretical and rational element.

5. As Moralist.

In ethics Melanchthon preserved and renewed the tradition of ancient morality and represented the Evangelical conception of life. His books bearing directly on morals were chiefly drawn from the classics, and were influenced not so much by Aristotle as by Cicero. His principal works in this line were *Prolegomena* to Cicero's *De officiis* (1525); *Enarrationes librorum Ethicorum Aristotelis* (1529); *Epitome philosophiæ moralis* (1538); and *Ethicæ doctrinæ elementa* (1550). In his *Epitome philosophiæ moralis* Melanchthon treats first the relation of philosophy to the law of God and the Gospel. Moral philosophy, it is true, does not know anything of the promise of grace as revealed in the Gospel, but it is the development of the natural law implanted by God in the heart of man, and therefore representing a part of the divine law. The revealed law, necessitated because of sin, is distinguished from natural law only by its greater completeness and clearness. The fundamental order of moral life can be grasped also by reason; therefore the development of moral philosophy from natural principles must not be neglected. Melanchthon therefore made no sharp distinction between natural and revealed morals. His contribution to Christian ethics in the proper sense must be sought in the Augsburg Confession and its Apology as well as in his *Loci*, where he followed Luther in depicting the Evangelical ideal of life, the free realization of the divine law by a personality blessed in faith and filled with the spirit of God.

6. As Exegete.

Melanchthon's formulation of the authority of Scripture became the norm for the following time. The principle of his hermeneutics is expressed in his words: "Every theologian and faithful interpreter of the heavenly doctrine must necessarily be first a grammarian, then a dialectician, and finally a witness." By "grammarian" he meant the philologist in the modern sense who is master of history, archeology, and ancient geography. As to the method of interpretation, he insisted with great emphasis upon the unity of the sense, upon the literal sense in contrast to the four senses of the scholastics. He further stated that whatever is looked for in the words of Scripture, outside of the literal sense, is only dogmatic or practical application. His commentaries, however, are not grammatical, but are full of theological and practical matter, confirming the doctrines of the Reformation, and edifying believers. The most important of them are those on Genesis, Proverbs, Daniel, the Psalms, and especially those on the New Testament, on Romans (edited in 1522 against his will by Luther), Colossians (1527), and John (1523). Melanchthon was the constant assistant of Luther in his translation of the Bible, and both the books of the Maccabees in Luther's Bible are ascribed to him. A Latin Bible published in 1529 at Wittenberg is designated as a common work of Melanchthon and Luther.

7. As Historian and Preacher.

In the sphere of historical theology the influence of Melanchthon may be traced until the seventeenth century, especially in the method of treating church history in connection with political history. His was the first Protestant attempt at a history of dogma, *Sententiæ veterum aliquot patrum de cœna domini* (1530) and especially *De ecclesia et auctoritate verbi Dei* (1539). Melanchthon exerted a wide influence in the department of homiletics, and has been regarded as the author, in the Protestant Church, of the methodical style of preaching. He himself keeps entirely aloof from all mere dogmatizing or rhetoric in the *Annotationes in Evangelia* (1544), the *Conciones in Evangelium Matthæi* (1558), and in his German sermons prepared for George of Anhalt. He never preached from the pulpit; and his Latin sermons (*Postilla*) were prepared for the Hungarian students at Wittenberg who did not understand German. In this connection may be mentioned also his *Catechesis puerilis* (1532), a religious manual for younger students, and a German catechism (1549), following closely Luther's arrangement. From Melanchthon came also the first Protestant work on the method of theological study, so that it may safely be said that by his influence every department of theology was advanced even if he was not always a pioneer. Rothe did not exaggerate when he said: "Whatever was done in the time of the Reformation for the upbuilding of Evangelical theology in Germany, was his work."

As a philologist and pedagogue Melanchthon was the spiritual heir of the South German Humanists, of men like Reuchlin, Wimpheling, and Rudolf Agricola, who represented an ethical conception of the humanities. The liberal arts and a classical education were for him only a means to an ethical and religious end. The ancient classics were for him in the first place the sources of a purer knowledge, but they were also the best means of educating youth both by their beauty of form and by their ethical content. By his organizing activity in the sphere of educational institutions and by his compilations of Latin and Greek grammars and commentaries, Melanchthon became the founder of the learned schools of Evangelical Germany, a combination of humanistic and Christian ideals. In philosophy also Melanchthon was the teacher of the whole German Protestant world. The influence of his philosophical compendia ended only with the rule of the Leibnitz-Wolff school. He started from scholasticism; but with the contempt of an enthusiastic Humanist he turned away from it and came to Wittenberg with the plan of editing the complete works of Aristotle. Under the dominating religious influence of Luther his interest abated for a time, but in 1519 he edited the "Rhetoric" and in 1520 the "Dialectic." The relation of philosophy to theology is characterized, according to him, by the distinction between law and Gospel. The former, as a light of nature, is innate; it also contains the elements of the natural knowledge of God which, however, have been obscured and weakened by sin. Therefore, renewed promulgation of the law by revelation became necessary and was furnished in the Decalogue; and all law, including that in the scientific form of philosophy, contains only demands, shadowings; its fulfilment is given only in the Gospel, the object of certainty in theology, by which also the philosophical elements of knowledge—experience, principles of reason, and syllogism—receive only their final confirmation. As the law is a divinely ordered pedagogue that leads to Christ, philosophy, its interpreter, is subject to revealed truth as the principal standard of opinions and life. Besides Aristotle's "Rhetoric" and "Dialectic" he published *De dialecta libri iv* (1528); *Erotemata dialectices* (1547); *Liber de anima* (1540); *Initia doctrinæ physicæ* (1549); and *Ethicæ doctrinæ elementa* (1550).

8. As Professor and Philosopher.

There have been preserved original portraits of Melanchthon by three famous painters of his time—by Holbein in the Royal Gallery of Hannover (said to be the best), by Dürer (made in 1526), and by Lukas Cranach. Cranach represented the Melanchthon of later years, worn out, thin, and unsightly, but with a mild and peaceful expression on a highly intellectual face. Melanchthon was small and slight, but of good proportions, and had a bright and sparkling eye, which kept its color till the day of his death. He was never in perfectly sound health, and managed to perform as much work as he did only by reason of the extraordinary regularity of his habits and his great temperance. He set no great value on money and possessions; his liberality and hospitality were often misused in such a way that his old faithful Swabian servant had sometimes difficulty in managing the household. His domestic life was happy. He called his home "a little church of God," always found peace there, and showed a tender solicitude for his wife and children. To his great astonishment a French scholar found him rocking the cradle with one hand, and holding a book in the other. His noble soul showed itself also in his friendship for many of his contemporaries; "there is nothing sweeter nor lovelier than mutual intercourse with friends," he used to say. His most intimate friend was Camerarius, whom he called the half of his soul. His extensive correspondence was for him not only a duty, but a need and an enjoyment. His letters form a valuable commentary on his whole life, as he spoke out his mind in them more unreservedly than he was wont to do in public life. A peculiar example of his sacrificing friendship is furnished by the fact that he wrote speeches and scientific treatises for others, permitting them to use their own signature. But in the kindness of his heart he was ready to serve and assist not only his friends, but everybody. He was an enemy to jealousy, envy, slander, and sarcasm. His whole nature adapted him especially to the intercourse with scholars and men of higher rank, while it was more difficult for him to deal with the people of lower station. He never allowed himself or others to exceed the bounds of nobility, honesty, and decency. He was very sincere in the judgment of his own person, acknowledging his faults even to opponents like Flacius, and was open to the criticism even of such as stood far below him. In his public career he sought not honor or fame, but earnestly endeavored to serve the Church and the cause of truth. His humility and modesty had their root in his personal piety. He laid great stress upon prayer, daily meditation on the Word, and attendance of public service. In Melanchthon is found not a great, impressive personality, winning its way by massive strength of resolution and energy, but a noble character which we can not study without loving and respecting.

9. Personal Appearance and Character.

Estimates of Melanchthon's character and work have undergone radical changes since his death, according to the theological standpoint of those seeking in the representative figures of Luther and Melanchthon their champion or at least their spiritual associate. It is said that Leonhard Hutter (q.v.), the head of the Wittenberg theologians in the beginning of the seventeenth century, on the occasion of a public disputation, when the authority of Melanchthon was invoked, tore down his picture from the wall, and in sight of all trampled it under foot. For more than a hundred years after that, few voices spoke a word in his favor. In 1760 the anniversary of his death was for the first time celebrated, and from that time he began to be regarded in a different light. After this change there was revived not only the interest in his person and works, but even the defects of his rationalism and unionism were defended. Recently, however, these defects have been looked upon again in their true light. The celebration of his four hundredth anniversary in 1897 referred on the whole more to the humanist than to the theologian; but a just opinion will not ignore that Melanchthon rendered great services both to the Church and to theology by his reform of humanistic education. For later followers and their doctrines see PHILIPPISTS. (O. KIRN.)

10. His Fame.

BIBLIOGRAPHY: The *Opera* of Melanchthon, incomplete, appeared in 4 parts, Basel, 1541; ed. C. Peucer, 4 parts,

Wittenberg, 1562-64, in 5 parts, ib. 1601, and in *CR*, vols. i.-xxviii. The *Supplementa Melanchthoniana* to be published in parts, Leipsic, 1910 sqq., will include the works not published in *CR*. The *Loci* in its early form, ed. G. L. Plitt and T. Kolde, appeared Leipsic, 1900. The early *Vita* by J. Camerarius was issued, Leipsic, 1566, ed. A. F. Neander, Berlin, 1841. The most exhaustive life is by K. Schmidt, Elberfeld, 1861, and the best in English is by J. W. Richard, New York, 1898. Other lives are by F. A. Cox, London, 1835; C. F. Ledderhose, Heidelberg, 1847, Eng. transl., Philadelphia, 1854; G. A. Ritter, Berlin, 1860; R. Schaefer, Gütersloh, 1894; G. Ellinger, Berlin, 1902; G. Krüger, Halle, 1906. On Melanchthon's theology and ethics consult: F. Galle, *Versuch einer Charakteristik Melanchthons als Theologen*, Halle, 1840; Herrlinger, *Die Theologie Melanchthons*, Gotha, 1879; C. E. Luthardt, *Die Arbeiten Melanchthons im Gebiete der Moral*, Leipsic, 1884; F. Költzsch, *Melanchthons philosophische Ethik*, Freiburg, 1889; W. H. Rule, *Spirit of the Reformation; Melanchthon*, London, 1856; C. L. T. Henke, *Das Verhältniss Luthers und Melanchthons zu einander*, Marburg, 1860; C. Pansch, *Melanchthon als Schulmann*, Eutin, 1868; A. Richter, *Melanchthons Verdienste um den philosophischen Unterricht*, Leipsic, 1870; T. Brieger, *Die Torgauer Artikel*, ib. 1888; K. Hartfelder, *P. Melanchthon als Præceptor Germaniæ*, Berlin, 1889; W. Bornemann, *Melanchthon als Schulmann*, Magdeburg, 1897; J. Haussleiter, *Aus der Schule Melanchthons*, Greifswald, 1897 (on his disputations); K. Sell, *Melanchthon und die deutsche Reformation bis 1531*, Halle, 1897; P. Tschackert, *Melanchthons Bildungsideale*, Göttingen, 1897; W. Walther, *Melanchthon als Retter des wissenschaftliches Sinnes*, Leipsic, 1897; G. Kawerau, *Die Versuche, Melanchthon zur katholischen Kirche zurückzuführen*, Halle, 1902; *Cambridge Modern History*, vol. ii., passim, London and New York, 1904; W. H. Woodward, *Studies in Education during the Renaissance*, New York, 1907; and, in general, works on the Reformation as well as those which deal with the other leaders of that movement in Germany, especially with Luther.

MELCHIADES, mel-cai'a-dîz (**MILTIADES**): Pope 310-314. According to the *Catalogus Liberianus* he was made bishop in 311, but this contradicts its own dates for his death and the length of his pontificate. The *Liber pontificalis* says that he was an African by birth. He was buried in the cemetery of St. Calixtus, and De Rossi thought he had discovered his grave to the right of the old burial-vault of the popes. In his time fall the edict of toleration by Galerius, the conquest of Rome by Constantine, and the edict of toleration by Constantine and Licinius. Constantine wrote to him from Gaul entrusting the decision in the Donatist question to him and other bishops (cf. Eusebius, *Hist. eccl.*, X., v., in *NPNF*, 2 ser., i. p. 381), and he held a synod in consequence (Oct. 2, 313) in the palace of the Empress Fausta on the Lateran. Its proceedings and decision against Donatus and in favor of Cæcilianus are reported by Optatus (*De schismate Donatistarum*, I., xxii. sqq.). (A. HARNACK.)

BIBLIOGRAPHY: *Liber pontificalis*, ed. Mommsen, in *MGH*, *Gest. pont. Rom.*, i (1898), 46; Jaffé, *Regesta*, i. 28, ii. 732; *DCB*, iii. 917-919 (detailed); B. Platina, *Lives of the Popes*, i. 67, London, n.d.; Milman, *Latin Christianity*, i. 94; Bower, *Popes*, i. 41-45; *KL*, viii. 1523-25.

MELCHITES, mel'choits: The name given to the orthodox Christians in the Roman provinces which had been conquered by the Arabs. It distinguished them from the Monophysites, and, being derived from *melek*, "king," connoted their fidelity to emperor and pope, on account of which they received harsher treatment from the Arabs than did the Monophysites.

MELCHIZEDEK, mel-kiz'e-dek: The king of Salem and priest of El-elyon who met Abraham when returning from his victory over the united kings of the Euphrates valley, brought him bread and wine, blessed him in the name of El-elyon, and received tithes from him. He is mentioned also in an obscure passage, Ps. cx. 4, and in Heb. v.-vii. The data given in these Biblical passages were developed in patristic and pseudepigraphical literature, but without the addition of any historical material. The representation in Gen. xiv. is noteworthy in that, while in general the Canaanites of the Old Testament are regarded as typically heathen, in this passage a Canaanite prince is represented as a worshiper and priest of the Creator of heaven and earth, who is the God of Abraham, while Abraham gives tithes to Melchizedek in recognition of these facts. The discrepancy between these two views is one of which the narrator is entirely unconscious. Historical elements involved are that a Canaanitic deity *Elioun ho hypsistos* ("Elyon the highest") is mentioned by Philo of Byblos (Eusebius, *Preparatio evangelica*, I., x. 11, Eng. transl. by E. H. Gifford, i. 36, Oxford, 1903), while the last element of the name Melchizedek is a Phenician god-name, Ẓidiḳ (W. Baudissin, *Studien zur semitischen Religionsgeschichte*, i. 15, Leipsic, 1876). This still leaves the monotheism of Melchizedek unexplained, since that of the nomadic Jethro is not parallel. An important datum in the narrative is that Melchizedek was king of Salem. Salem has been identified with a place of the same name eight Roman miles south of Scythopolis, and with the Salim of John iii. 23 and the Salem of Judith iv. 4. But these were places of minor importance, while in Ps. lxxvi. 2 Jerusalem is called Salem, in Josh. x. 1 an Adonizedek (a name formed like Melchizedek) is called king of Jersualem, and in the Amarna Tablets (q.v.) "Urusalim" appears as the common name about 1400 B.C. for the city which appears in the David narrative as Jebus. So probably here.

With reference to the historicity of the Melchizedek episode many scholars hold that verses 18-20 seem to be interpolated and that verse 21 continues the narrative in verse 17. The matter of the tithes is difficult to understand, whether regarded as taken from the booty or from Abraham's own property. Similarly, the last part of verse 22, after "Lord," is regarded as an interpolation. It is believed that the compiler used material from various sources, that he was not interested particularly in the historicity of the matter, since for him the importance lay in the significance of Melchizedek as the incarnation of an idea which finds expression in the giving of a tenth by the patriarch. Putting together the facts that the name "Salem" occurs in the late psalm lxxvi., that Ps. cx. is Maccabean, that the name seems to have been "Urusalim" in the time of the Amarna Tablets, and that the Maccabees were called "priests of the most high God," the conclusion might be drawn that the representation of the text is a late creation to exalt the high priests of Jerusalem. On the other hand, such an idea of a Canaanitic personage is not natural for that period. The narrative is best explained as an early remainder of a story of the historical environment of which nothing is now known, and this largely because of the purely religious interest of the compiler. (F. BUHL.)

BIBLIOGRAPHY: H. E. Ryle, *Early Narratives of Genesis*, London, 1892; Rösch, in *TSK*, 1885, pp. 321 sqq.; A. H. Sayce, *"Higher Criticism" and the Monuments*, London, 1894 (to be used with caution); F. Hommel, *Ancient Hebrew Traditions as Illustrated by the Monuments*, ib. 1897; *DB*, iii. 335; *EB*, iii. 3014–16; *JE*, viii. 450; the commentaries on Genesis; the pertinent sections in works on the history of Israel, particularly Kittel's. The *Expository Times*, vols. vii.–viii., contains a series of pertinent articles by Sayce and Hommel.

MELDENIUS, RUPERTUS: The pseudonym of a German Lutheran theologian who, at the time of the Thirty Years' War, wrote a small tract in Latin, admonishing theologians in their disputes not to forget moderation and love. His tract bore the title: *Parænesis votiva pro pace ecclesiæ ad theologos Augustanæ confessionis auctore Ruperto Meldenio Theologo* [Rottenburg, 1626]. The contents indicate that it was written after the death of Johann Arndt (q.v.; d. 1621), when there was a renewal of controversy over his orthodoxy. From the tenor of the closing words: "In a word, were we to observe unity in essentials, liberty in incidentals, and in all things charity, our affairs would be certainly in a most happy situation," Lücke (see bibliography) inferred the author to be the originator of the celebrated phrase *In necessariis unitas, in non necessariis libertas, in utrisque* (or, *in omnibus*) *caritas*. The pseudonym "Rupertus Meldenius" resulted from transposing the letters of Petrus Meuderlinus, the Latinized name of Peter Meiderlin (b. at Oberacker, near Maulbronn, 26 m. n.w. of Heidelberg, in 1582; d. at Augsburg, 1651), ephor of St. Anne's in Augsburg, 1612–50. Meiderlin, in F. A. Veith's *Bibliotheca Augustana* (12 vols., Augsburg, 1785–96), is mentioned as author of the *Parænesis*, hence Meiderlin is to be regarded as the originator of the phrase in question, since so far as is known it occurs nowhere any earlier than in his tract. All else known of him is eminently in accord with that utterance, as with the sentiments manifested in the *Parænesis*. Richard Baxter (q.v.) refers to the phrase in his treatise: *The True and Only Way of Concord of all the Christian Churches* (1680), and speaks of the same as "the Pacificator's old and despised words." CARL BERTHEAU.

BIBLIOGRAPHY: F. Lücke, *Ueber das Alter, den Verfasser, die ursprüngliche Form und den wahren Sinn des kirchlichen Friedenspruches In necessariis unitas, etc.*, Göttingen, 1850; idem, in *TSK*, 1851, pp. 905–938; L. Bauer, *M. Peter Meiderlin*, Augsburg, 1906; *ADB*, xxi. 293.

MELETIUS, me-lî'shî-us, OF ANTIOCH AND THE MELETIAN SCHISM.

Personal History of Meletius (§ 1).
Origin of the Schism (§ 2).
Strengthening of Meletius' Position (§ 3).
Continuance of Schism after his Death (§ 4).

In his personal history Meletius forms a curious complement to Eustathius of Sebaste (q.v.), having come into possession of a large part of the esteem which has been withdrawn from Eustathius. He was spoken of in Rome as an Arian as late as 377, and his first deposition was inflicted on him, according to Philostorgius (v. 5), after conviction of perjury, according to the *Chronicon paschale* (362 A.D.) "for godlessness and other evil deeds"; while to-day he is reckoned as a saint by both the Roman and the Greek Churches. It might be thought that this reversal of judgment was due merely to ecclesiastical policy, if our knowledge of his virtues were confined to the letters of Basil and the pulpit rhetoric of Gregory of Nyssa ("Funeral Oration on Meletius," *NPNF*, 2 ser., v. 514 sqq.) and Chrysostom (*Hom. in S. Meletium*). But fortunately this hypothesis is ruled out by the honorable acknowledgment made by Epiphanius about 376 (*Hær.* lxxiii. 35) in favor of Meletius, with whom he had little dogmatic or partizan sympathy. It is clear that Meletius must have been a man of ascetic strictness of life and generally upright and amiable character, and honored as such widely. He was born at Melitene in the province of Armenia Minor, held property in the northern part of this province at Getasa, and had a good secular education. He makes his first appearance in history soon after 357 as an adherent of the compromise policy of Acacius, with whom he opposed the Homoiousians Basil of Ancyra, George of Laodicea, and Eustathius of Sebaste; and when the last-named was deposed at a synod held in Melitene (probably 358) he became his successor. Possibly on account of the opposition of the followers of Eustathius, he resigned his bishopric and retired to Berœa, then, according to Socrates (*Hist. eccl.* II., xliv., *NPNF*, 2 ser., ii. 73), attended the synod of Seleucia in the autumn of 359 and subscribed an Acacian confession. Even after the synod of Constantinople in the spring of 360, unfavorable as it was to the Homoiousians, he still possessed the confidence of the court party; and when Eudoxius of Antioch was translated to the see of Constantinople (Jan. 27, 360) he was chosen for the vacant bishopric. He was received with enthusiasm in Antioch when he took possession of his new see at the end of the year; but he had occupied it only a month when he lost it. The cause is not certain, but the old tradition asserts that his theological attitude disappointed the party with which he had been acting. Epiphanius indicates, and the orthodox historians of the fifth century say positively, that the special cause was a sermon, the orthodoxy of which embittered the opposite party. It was preached in the emperor's presence and by his command on Prov. viii. 22, after Acacius and a certain George, probably George of Alexandria, not of Laodicea, had already discoursed on the same text. But this was scarcely the cause of his deposition; the most decisive evidence against the tradition is the sermon itself, still extant (in Epiphanius, *Hær.* lxxiii. 29–33), which, while not Arian, is certainly not Homoousian nor even Homoiousian, but just what might have been expected from a Homoian court bishop who was not a crypto-Arian. The conclusion which best satisfies the conflicting authorities is that the first expulsion of Meletius was not on dogmatic grounds, but caused rather by some action of his which embittered opponents could construe as illegal.

1. Personal History of Meletius.

But the origin of the orthodox tradition and the bearing of the faithful followers of Meletius would be alike inexplicable if he had not, before he left Antioch for his home, given a decided anti-Arian impulse to those whom he could influence. The most logical interpretation of the accounts is that when he was replaced by Euzoius, an open Arian, he warned his followers to hold no communion with this man. Part of the Antiochian church followed this admonition, and a state of schism was created. The Meletian party were not the only anti-Arians in Antioch. Ever since the deposition of Eustathius in 330, there had been a small Eustathian party there, whose leader at this time was the presbyter Paulinus. Taking the *homoousios* of the Nicene creed in the sense of *mia hypostasis ē ousia,* they considered the Meletian use of *treis hypostaseis* as Arian; and thus, although the Meletians were more and more inclined to accept the *homoousios* as the later "young Nicene" party held it, the two groups were unable to act together. The accession of Julian made it possible for Meletius, as for Athanasius, to return to his see, but he had apparently not availed himself of the permission when the synod of Alexandria met in the spring of 362. It sent Eusebius of Vercelli and Asterius of Petra to Antioch to arrange a basis of agreement; but their task was rendered more difficult by the fact that Lucifer of Calaris arrived before them and consecrated Paulinus as bishop. There were then three claimants for the see; and the continued antagonism between Eustathians and Meletians may be partly understood from the fact that when (363) Meletius, with a synod at Antioch, accepted the *homoousios* in the sense of *homoios kat' ousian* and condemned the view that the Holy Ghost was a creature, the decree of the synod was signed also by a man so suspected by the whole Nicene party as Acacius. The Eustathians accordingly regarded the synodal decree as a repudiation of the Nicene faith; Athanasius recognized Paulinus, and when he came to Antioch in the end of 363 held communion with him alone. When the Emperor Valens in 365 banished anew from Antioch all who had been exiled under Constantine, Meletius was again driven out, to return on his own responsibility, taking advantage of the political complications of the time, in 367. A third exile began when Valens visited the East in the winter of 371-372, and lasted until the death of Valens (Aug. 9, 378) completely changed the situation. During this third exile Euzoius died (376), but he was immediately succeeded by another Homoian, the Thracian Dorotheus, and the threefold schism continued until Dorotheus was expelled by the government in 380. In fact, there was even a fourth claimant after 375, in which year Vitalius, a former adherent of Paulinus and then converted to Apollinarianism, was consecrated by Apollinaris; some of his followers were still traceable in the time of Sozomen (*Hist. eccl.*, VI., xxv., *NPNF*, 2 ser., ii. 362).

2. Origin of the Schism.

Between his second return and his third exile Meletius had been in correspondence with Basil of Cæsarea, to whose view of him he owes the high position which he takes in the traditions of the "young Nicene" party. Through Basil his position in the controversies of the moment became a decisive one. The West, like Athanasius, had recognized Paulinus, whom the "young Nicene" party suspected, as they did the entire "Old Nicene" view, of Sabellian or Marcellian tendencies. The recognition of Meletius in the West thus became an object of primary importance for the young Nicene party. But though the negotiations brought them a little closer to the West, nothing more could be obtained for Meletius than that the western bishops recognized the orthodoxy of Meletius, saving the rights of Paulinus, and recommended an agreement which would at least provide against the continuance of the schism on the death of either. The renown of Meletius in the East, however, was all the more increased by this, and when he returned from Armenia to Antioch in 379 he was the most prominent of all the eastern orthodox leaders. Under his presidency assembled in Antioch (Sept. or Oct., 379) a synod attended by 153 bishops which attested the doctrinal unity between East and West. He had a hand in the appointment of Gregory Nazianzen to the see of Constantinople, and presided over the ecumenical council of 381, being singled out for special favor by Theodosius, the new ruler of the East. He died, however, soon after the council began its work.

3. Strengthening of Meletius' Position.

The schism would soon have been ended if the Meletians of Antioch and the "young Nicene" party in general would have acknowledged Paulinus, as Gregory Nazianzen warmly urged at the council of Constantinople. But his appeal fell on deaf ears, and the schism was perpetuated by the election of Flavian. The West regarded his position as wholly indefensible; a synod held in Milan (381) under Ambrose's presidency pronounced strongly against him, and another in Rome (382) excommunicated Diodorus of Tarsus and Acacius of Berœa who had consecrated him. Theodosius, who was anxious for an agreement between East and West, apparently did not approve the new election. On the death of Paulinus (c. 388) the Eustathians elected Evagrius, the friend of Jerome, who was recognized scarcely anywhere outside of Antioch, and toward whom the West assumed a friendly but non-committal attitude. Theodosius had a synod called at Capua in the winter of 391-392 to decide the controversy. This gathering committed the question as between Flavian and Evagrius to Theophilus of Alexandria and the Egyptian bishops, hitherto neutral. Flavian won the confidence of the emperor, and made a successful protest against any investigation of his title; and when Evagrius died (c. 393) he succeeded in preventing the election of another contestant. The Eustathians, however, still maintained their schismatic attitude, and Flavian was not recognized by Rome or Alexandria. Peace was finally made by the efforts of Chrysostom, himself a native of Antioch, who on his consecration as bishop of Constantinople (Feb. 26, 398) induced Theophilus of Alexandria to plead for Flavian at

4. Continuance of Schism after His Death.

Rome. The diminishing Eustathian party gradually yielded to Flavian, although they finally disappeared only in the time of Alexander, the second from Flavian, eighty-five years after the outbreak of the schism, or in the year 415. See DAMASUS I. (F. LOOFS.)

BIBLIOGRAPHY: The sources have already been indicated in the text. Consult: C. W. F. Walch, *Historie der Ketzereien*, iv. 410-502, Leipsic, 1768; J. H. Blunt, *Dictionary of Sects, Heresies*, pp. 306-308, Philadelphia, 1874; Neander, *Christian Church*, vol. ii. passim; Hefele, *Conciliengeschichte*, i. 726 sqq., Eng. transl., ii. 275 sqq.; Schaff, *Christian Church*, iii. 372-374; Harnack, *Dogma*, vol. iv. passim; Ceillier, *Auteurs sacrés*, v. 5-12, and consult Index; *DCB*, iii. 891-893; *KL*, viii. 1221-34.

MELETIUS OF LYCOPOLIS: Originator of the so-called Meletian schism in Egypt; d. at Lycopolis between 325 and 326. One account of the events leading to the Meletian schism is contained in *Historiæ fragmentum de schismate Meletiano*, a fragment of an Alexandrian church history. During the persecution of Christians in Lower Egypt, this source relates, four bishops, Phileas of Thmuis, Hesychius, Pachomius, and Theodore, whose sees were in the neighborhood of Alexandria, were removed from their congregations and held in prison in Alexandria, expecting martyrdom or deportation. The spiritual care of the forsaken congregations lay in the hands of itinerant bishops and preachers who did not always perform their duty. Even Alexandria was without a spiritual head, since Peter had forsaken his city. In this time of distress there was only one man who showed himself equal to the occasion, Bishop Meletius of Lycopolis. He not only traveled among the suffering congregations, but at their request instituted new bishops. This action, however, was not consonant with the tradition of the church, both because no bishop had been allowed to take over duties in another see, and because the bishop of Alexandria had for some time claimed to be the spiritual head of the province. Thus the attitude of Meletius was interpreted as a desire to make himself the ecclesiastical primate of Egypt. As it was afterward learned with certainty that the four imprisoned bishops were still alive, there developed in the congregations a party which looked upon them as still their legitimate heads. The bishops related the events to Peter of Alexandria and complained, but Meletius neither excused himself nor did he seek confirmation of his acts from the metropolitan. He even dared to enter Alexandria and to interfere with its ecclesiastical affairs, as he found the city still forsaken by its bishop. He excommunicated two presbyters and ordained two others in their place, thus again meddling with the affairs of another diocese. As a consequence Peter excommunicated him.

According to another source concerning the beginnings of Meletianism, found in Epiphanius (*Hær.* lxviii.), Peter was imprisoned in Alexandria together with Meletius and many other bishops and clergy. The persecution had already lasted for some time; a number of Christians had become martyrs, others had bought their release from prison by sacrifice, thus excluding themselves from the Church, but they repented afterward and endeavored to be received again into the Church through the mediation of the martyrs. The party of the martyrs, headed by Meletius, showed a hesitating attitude, at least for the time of persecution, while another party headed by Peter advocated an immediate rehabilitation. In this way the Meletian schism originated. Meletius together with his adherents founded the "Church of the martyrs." After the return from his deportation to the copper mines of Phaino in Arabia, he did not reoccupy his episcopal seat in Lycopolis, but remained in Alexandria as head of his own church which regarded itself in contradistinction to the Catholic Church as the strict community of pure Christians. The Catholic Church, on the other hand, had no communion with the Meletians, because Peter had excluded Meletius. Owing to the friendly relation of the Meletians to the episcopate of Alexandria, they received a favorable treatment on the part of the members of the Council of Nicæa, especially as the latter hoped to hinder in this way an alliance of Meletianism with Arianism. A document of the council addressed to the bishops of Egypt asked Meletius to return to Lycopolis as bishop, but without the right of ordination. The clericals of his community were to be consecrated anew, and acknowledged in their order, but always as ranking below the Catholic clerics, and in order to suppress all aspirations of the episcopal seat of Lycopolis to the primacy the metropolitan rights of Alexandria over all Egypt were expressly acknowledged. The Meletian party comprised twenty-nine bishops in Egypt, and four presbyters, three deacons, and a military chaplain in Alexandria. Meletius accepted the decree of the synod, delivered his churches to Alexander of Alexandria, and returned to Lycopolis. But there took place a rapid change in the sentiment of the Meletians. The successor of Meletius led an embassy to Constantinople in order to obtain the recognition of the peculiar position of the Meletians, in other words, the annulment of the decree of Nicæa. As they were not admitted, they entered into connection with Eusebius of Nicomedia, who successfully advocated their cause before the emperor, thus obtaining sanction for the union between Meletianism and Arianism. (H. ACHELIS.)

BIBLIOGRAPHY: The "Fragment" cited in the text is in M. J. Routh, *Reliquiæ sacræ*, iv. 91 sqq., Oxford, 1848, and in *MPG*, x. 1565 sqq., xviii. 509-510. Consult on these Hefele, *Conciliengeschichte*, i., § 40 (same in the Eng. transl.). Other sources are: Athanasius, "Apology against the Arians," §§ 11, 59, and his "Letter to the Bishops of Egypt and Libya," chap. xxii.; Socrates, *Hist. eccl.*, i. 6, 9; Sozomen, *Hist. eccl.*, i. 24, ii. 18, 21, 23; Theodoret, *Hist. eccl.* Consult: *DCB*, ii. 890-891; *KL*, viii. 1221 sqq.

MELETIUS PEGAS: Patriarch of Alexandria in the sixteenth century; b. about 1540; d. at Alexandria, 1601 or 1602. He studied at Padua, was employed about 1575 at the courts of the patriarchs of Alexandria and Constantinople, and ascended the patriarchal throne of Alexandria in 1590. His most important work is his "Miscellanies," printed in the "Book of Joy" of the Patriarch Dositheos of Jerusalem (pp. 553-604 [Bucharest], 1705). It treats of the true church and attacks at the same time the primacy of the pope. Against Rome were directed also "An Orthodox Christian Discourse" (Vilna, 1596) and "The Orthodox Doctrine" (1769). Meletius influenced the confessional struggles in Poland by a number of dogmatic epistles, one to King Sigismund III. of Poland, one to Bishop Hypatius Potei of Vladimir and Brest, and a number of letters which were published by Nikodemos Metaxas, "On the Primacy of the Pope, in a Series of Letters" (Constantinople, 1627). Against the Jews he wrote, "Apology of the Christian Religion, Addressed to the Jews" (Greek and Slavonic, Lemberg, 1593) [in catalogue of British Museum, ascribed to another Meletius]. The important part which he took in the synod of 1593 in Constantinople shows that he was active also for the development and expansion of his church. (PHILIPP MEYER.)

BIBLIOGRAPHY: The scattered references are collected in P. Meyer, *Die theologische Litteratur der griechischen Kirche im 16. Jahrhundert*, pp. 53-54, Leipsic, 1899.

MELETIUS SYRIGUS: Greek theologian; b. at Candia 1586; d. at Galata, a suburb of Constantinople, 1664. He studied in Padua and became monk in a monastery of Crete whence he was soon expelled on account of his attacks on the Catholics. After a short stay in Alexandria he turned in 1630 to Constantinople where he received a position as teacher of theology. He was a pronounced opponent of Cyril Lucar (q.v.). In 1642 he cooperated at the synod of Jassy in drawing up the orthodox creed and wrote its Greek translation. In 1644 he was banished from Constantinople by Patriarch Parthenios the Elder, because he had hindered the circulation of the translation of the Bible into modern Greek by Maximos Kalliupolites. Only after the death of Parthenios in 1651 could he safely remain in Constantinople. The only one of his works which has been published is the "Refutation of the Calvinistic Articles and Questions of Cyril Lucar" (Bucharest, 1690). (PHILIPP MEYER.)

BIBLIOGRAPHY: É. Legrand, *Bibliographie hellénique*, ii. 470-472. Paris, 1894: E. a Schelstrate, *Acta orientalis ecclesiæ contra Lutheri hæresim*, i. 393 sqq., Rome, 1739.

MELITO: Bishop of Sardis. He flourished in the reign of Marcus Aurelius (161-180). Of his numerous works in most cases only the titles are known from a list of Eusebius probably copied from a collection in the library of Cæsarea. The list is as follows (*NPNF*, i. 203 sqq.): two books "On the Passover"; "On the Conduct of Life and the Prophets"; "On the Church"; "On the Lord's Day"; "On the Faith of Man"; "On [his] Creation"; "On the Obedience of Faith"; "On the Senses"; "On Soul and Body"; "On Baptism"; "On Truth"; "On Faith"; "On the Birth of Christ"; "On Prophecy"; "On Hospitality"; "The Key"; "On the Devil"; "On the Apocalypse of John"; "On the Corporeality of God"; "Apology to Antoninus"; "Selections"; and perhaps a work "On the Suffering of Christ." There are extant only remnants of the "Selections," of the "Apology," and the works "On Baptism" and "On the Passover." The Greek fragments edited by Anastasius Sinaita are quoted under titles not mentioned by Eusebius. There are also some Syriac fragments which undoubtedly go back to indirect Greek tradition, for probably the Syriac Church never possessed his works complete. Of the works falsely ascribed to him may be mentioned the Syriac Apology, which can not be identical with the Apology mentioned by Eusebius, for the sentences quoted from it are not found in the other, but most probably, as Nöldeke has explained, was a Syriac original work. Under the name of Melito, Pitra published a Latin "Key to the Scripture" which he considered a compilation from the "Key" of Melito; but Steitz and others have proved its spuriousness. From the scantiness of the material it is impossible to estimate justly Melito's importance for the history of church and doctrine. The titles of his works show that he took an interest in the dogmatical questions of his time and participated in the Paschal controversies which preceded the great schism over Easter. He was probably interested in Montanism, as appears from titles like "On the Conduct of Life and the Prophets," "On the Church," or "On Prophecy," yet he can not be called a Montanist (A. Schwegler, *Montanismus*, p. 223, Anm. 5, Tübingen, 1841); for the manner in which Tertullian wrote of him is against such an assumption. His attitude in this matter can be understood if he is compared with Irenæus, whom he resembled also in other ways. His moral strictness, which made him a celibate, and his high regard for prophecy and spiritual matters explain his close relation to Montanism, and still more make clear its spread; for his asceticism showed the universality of the thoughts that it emphasized. In his Christology Melito laid stress on the distinction of both natures. His separating the Apocrypha from the canonical books shows that his theological education surpassed the ordinary standard. A great many surmises have been made in regard to his doctrine of God in connection with his work "On the Corporeality of God," but he probably expressed there the same realism that was represented by Tertullian. (ERWIN PREUSCHEN.)

BIBLIOGRAPHY: The fragments are collected in M. J. Routh, *Reliquiæ sacræ*, i. 115 sqq., Oxford, 1846; J. C. T. Otto, *Corpus apologetarum Christianorum*, ix. 410 sqq., Jena, 1872; and W. Cureton, *Spicilegium Syriacum*, London, 1855. An Eng. transl. is found in *ANF*, viii. 750-762. The earlier literature, named in *ANF*, Bibliography, pp. 110-111, is in the main antiquated. Consult: Harnack, *Litteratur*, i. 246-255, ii. 1, pp. 358 sqq., 517 sqq., 522 sqq., ii. 2 passim; *DCB*, iii. 894-900 (important); A. Ehrhardt, in *Strassburger theologische Studien*, i., Supplement (1900), 258 sqq.; Krüger, *History*, pp. 123-129.

MELIUS, PETER: Hungarian Reformer and author; b. at Horhi 1515; d. at Debreczin (116 m. e. of Budapest) Dec. 15, 1572. His name is a Hellenization of his Hungarian family name Juhász. After three years at the University of Wittenberg (1555-58), he returned as pastor to Debreczin, where he labored till his death. After 1557, only the Lutherans had legally enjoyed religious freedom; but two years later Melius, with his two colleagues, took the first opposing steps in a pastoral conference, clearly stating Calvin's view in a short *Orthodoxa sententia de cœna Domini*. The Transylvanian Lutherans, led by Matthias Hebler, Superintendent of Szeben, both opposed the Reformed party and excluded it from their church. The Reformed joined Melius, who now composed (1562) the comprehensive *Confessio Ecclesiæ Debrecinensis.* The Lutherans appealed to four Lutheran universities in Germany, and accused the men of Debreczin of distorting the Augsburg Confession. Melius replied in two pamphlets (*Refutatio* and *Apologia*), defending the Reformed position, while the Reformed themselves turned to Geneva and Beza at two synods held in 1562–63. New impulse was furnished by this act. The young Prince of Transylvania, John Sigismund, still attempted to hold the Protestants together in a single body, and convened a general synod at Enyed (Apr., 1564); but, after joint debate, the cause of union was lost, and the Diet of Torda (June, 1564) sanctioned equal freedom for the Reformed Church. The matter of organization thus becoming a practical necessity, Melius, as the first Reformed bishop, convoked the first general synod at Debreczin (Feb., 1567), where seventeen presbyteries were represented from both sides of the River Tisza. By adopting the Second Helvetic Confession, they declared themselves an integral part of the Reformed Church in Europe. At the same synod, canons were drawn up, entitled *Articuli majores*, and defining the polity of the synod.

The young Church had hardly been organized when it was destined to encounter a new enemy. The prince's court physician, Georgius Blandrata (q.v.), secretly brought with him from Poland the books of Servetus, and imparted their tenets to the court preacher, Franciscus Davidis (q.v.), who then began to spread the Unitarian doctrines in Transylvania (1566). Melius firmly withstood him, and finally took part in the synod of Csenger (July 26, 1570), but Unitarians who had been invited did not appear. The synod formulated the *Confessio vera*, which was embodied in the *Corpus et syntagma confessionum* (Geneva, 1612) under the incorrect designation *Polonica confessio*. The credit is thus due to Melius and his companions that Hungarian Calvinism was not swallowed up in the Unitarian stream. Melius likewise purposed to oppose the theses of the Jewish rabbis of Paris, assailing the divinity of Christ, but his career was cut short by death.

Melius corresponded with Bullinger, Beza, Thretius, and Dudics, and wrote many books. Among his thirteen Hungarian productions special mention may be made of his *Az egész keresztyén tudomány summája* ("Summary of Christian Doctrine," Debreczin, 1562). He also composed exegetical works, and translated the Books of Samuel and Kings, and the New Testament (1567), the latter version being lost. His nine Latin works are mainly polemical and doctrinal. Of these the most important are *Confessio Ecclesiæ Debrecinensis* (Debreczin, 1562); *Apologia et abstersio Ecclesiæ Debrecinensis a columnis quibus temere apud academias et principes accusatur* (1563); *Refutatio confessionis de cœna Domini Matthiæ Hebler et his coniunctorum* (1564); *Brevis confessio pastorum* (both in Latin and in Hungarian; 1567); and *Articuli ex verbo Dei et lege naturæ compositi* (1567). F. Balogh.

Bibliography: F. A. Lampe, *Hist. ecclesiæ reformatæ in Hungaria*, passim, Utrecht, 1728; E. Budai, *Hist. of Hungary* (in Hungarian), ii. 156–168, Debreczin, 1808; P. Bod, *Hist. eccl. Hungarorum*, ed. Rauwenhoff, i. 256, Leyden, 1888; J. B. Dales and R. M. Patterson, *Report of Proceedings of the Second General Council of the Presbyterian Alliance*, pp. 1099–1120, Philadelphia, 1874; F. Balogh, *Melius Péter hatása*, Debreczin, 1866; idem, *Hist. of the Reformed Church of Hungary*, Lancaster, Pa., 1906.

MELLITUS: First bishop of London and third archbishop of Canterbury; d. at Canterbury Apr. 24, 624. Pope Gregory the Great sent him with Justus, Paulinus, and Rufinianus to join Augustine (q.v.) at Canterbury in 601. Augustine consecrated him bishop of the East Saxons in 604. Ethelbert, king of Kent, with his uncle Sabert, the East Saxon king, built for Mellitus the Church of St. Paul at London, where he established his episcopal see. Mellitus went to Rome in 608 to consult Boniface IV., was present at a synod there, Feb. 27, 610, and brought its decrees, with letters from the pope, to England. Eadbald, son and successor (616) of Ethelbert, as well as the sons of Sabert, adhered to the heathen religion, and Mellitus was driven from London and went to Gaul. After a year, however, he was able to return to Kent (see Laurence of Canterbury), but not to his bishopric. He succeeded Laurence as archbishop in 619, but never received the pallium.

Bibliography: Bede, *Hist. eccl.*, i. 29, 30, ii. 3–7; Haddan and Stubbs, *Councils*, iii. 5 38, 71; *DCB*, iii. 900–901; *DNB*, xxxvii. 221–222.

MELVILL, HENRY: Church of England; b. at Pendennis Castle (2 m. s.w. of Falmouth), Cornwall, Eng., Sept. 14, 1798; d. in London Feb. 9, 1871. He was graduated from the University of Cambridge (B.A., 1821; M.A., 1824; B.D., 1836); was minister of Camden Chapel, Camberwell, London, 1829–43; was appointed chaplain to the Tower of London, 1840; was principal of the East India College, at Haileybury, 1843–59; and held the Golden Lectureship, St. Margaret's Lothbury, 1850–56. In 1853 he was appointed one of her Majesty's chaplains; in 1856 a canon of St. Paul's; in 1863 he was made rector of Barnes, Surrey, and rural dean. He enjoyed a high reputation for pulpit oratory; his style was florid, and his delivery impassioned. Of the twelve volumes published by him, some of them in several editions, all were the results of his pulpit activities. His *Lectures on Practical Subjects* was reprinted in Philadelphia, 1864; and two volumes of his *Sermons*, ed. Bishop McIlvaine, appeared New York, 1870.

Bibliography: J. Grant, *Metropolitan Pulpit*, ii. 1–21, London, 1839; *The Lamps of the Temple*, pp. 210–241, ib. 1856; J. E. Ritchie, *London Pulpit*, pp. 60–68, ib. 1858; *DNB*, xxxvii. 229–230.

MELVILLE, ANDREW: B. at Baldovy, near Montrose (30 m. n.e. of Dundee), Scotland, Aug. 1, 1545; d. at Sedan (130 m. n.e. of Paris), France, in 1622. After preliminary training in Latin, Greek, and French, at Montrose, he entered St. Mary's College, St. Andrews, in 1559; and when he left St. Andrews for the University of Paris, in the autumn of 1564, he was commended as "the best philosopher, poet, and Grecian of anie young maister in the land." In Paris he studied Hebrew as well as Latin, Greek, and philosophy. Two years later he went to Poitiers to master civil law and became a regent in the College of St. Marceon. He afterward traveled to Geneva, where he was speedily appointed to the humanity chair. During his five years' residence there he devoted himself chiefly to the study of theology under Beza, who, at his leaving, wrote that the greatest token of affection the church of Geneva could give, was that it had consented to be deprived of Melville that the church in Scotland might be enriched. Having returned to Scotland, in July, 1574, he accepted the principalship of Glasgow University. He began his work there in Nov., and by his incredible labors and enthusiasm drew students from all quarters; so that the classrooms which for some years before had been literally empty, were soon filled to overflowing. Before Melville's return to Scotland, "Tulchan" episcopacy had been erected; and when John Durie protested in the General Assembly, in Aug., 1575, against the lawfulness of the bishop's office, Melville showed that prelacy was unscriptural, and should be abolished, and parity in rank and authority be restored among the ministers of the church. Five years later, the episcopal office was formally abolished by the assembly, without a dissenting voice. Melville was on all the committees employed in preparing the Second Book of Discipline, took a prominent part in the discussions concerning it, and was moderator of an assembly which approved it, in April, 1578.

In December, 1580, Melville was transferred to the University of St. Andrews; installed as principal of St. Mary's College, which, by act of Parliament, had been appropriated to the study of divinity. Here, at first, he met with much opposition; but in less than two years his learning and zeal wrought a favorable change. The number of students increased; and the cause of religion prospered, both in the city and in the university. This was interrupted only by his being called to defend the polity and liberties of the church. Despite the confession or covenant of 1581, the privy council revived the regulations recognizing episcopacy, framed at Leith in 1572; and Lennox, one of the king's unworthy favorites, had Robert Montgomery presented to the archbishopric of Glasgow. This high-handed procedure of the court was boldly met by the church, and Montgomery was excommunicated. The privy council proclaimed the excommunication null and void, ordered those who refused to pay him the episcopal rents to be imprisoned, and laid Glasgow College under a temporary interdict. In his opening sermon before a special meeting of the assembly, Melville inveighed against those who had introduced "the bludie gullie of absolute power into the country, and who sought to erect a new popedom in the person of the prince." A remonstrance was drawn up, which he and the others presented to the king. In Feb., 1583-84, he was summoned before the privy council for seditious and treasonable preaching. Conscious of his innocence, and furnished with ample proof, he appeared and gave account of his sermon. On the council resolving to proceed with the trial, he maintained that he ought to be tried in the first instance by the church courts. As he would yield neither to entreaties nor threats, he was found guilty of declining the judgment of the council, and was sentenced to imprisonment in Blackness Castle, and further punishment at the king's pleasure; but he escaped to England.

As the court wished to make James absolute by bringing every cause before the privy council, it was necessary to curb the church courts; and accordingly, in 1584, Parliament overthrew presbytery, and laid the liberties of the country at the king's feet. But in 1585, after twenty months' absence, Melville returned with the exiled nobles. Weary of tyranny, their countrymen flocked to their standard, Arran fled, and the king received them into favor. Melville was moderator of the assembly in June, 1587, and was one of its commissioners to the Parliament which annexed the temporal lands of bishoprics, abbacies, and priories to the crown, thus paving the way for the entire abolition of episcopacy. At the coronation of the queen, in May, 1590, he recited a Latin poem entitled *Stephaniskion*, which he composed on two days' notice. Patrick Adamson, who still persevered in opposing presbytery and attacking Melville, having fallen into poverty, addressed "elegant and plaintive verses to his Majesty," who turned a deaf ear to him; but Melville generously supported him for several months, as he himself was afterward aided, when a prisoner in the Tower of London, by Adamson's nephew, Patrick Simpson. In June, 1592, Melville's labors were crowned with success; Parliament having consented to pass an act ratifying the assemblies, synods, presbyteries, and kirk sessions of the church and declaring them, with their jurisdiction and discipline, as agreed to by the king, and embodied in the act, to be, in all time coming "most just, good and godly." This settlement is still the charter of the Church of Scotland's liberties.

Contrary to his promise, James insisted in restoring the popish nobles, and put the ministers on their defense by declaring that state affairs should not be introduced into their sermons, that the assembly should not convene without his command, that its acts should not be valid until ratified by him, and that church courts should not take cognizance of offenses punishable by the criminal law. One minister being dealt with as an example, the others made common cause with him. Soon they were forbidden to speak against the doings of the council, the king, or his progenitors, under the pain of death, and ordered to subscribe a bond, before receiving their stipends, promising to submit to the king and council when accused of seditious or treasonable doctrine. Melville and the other commissioners of assembly were ordered to leave Edinburgh, and their power was declared illegal. Determined to restore episcopacy James, by secret and corrupt influence, secured a vantage-ground for his future plans at an assembly which Melville could not attend. It was with difficulty he carried out his measures, even in a modified form, at next assembly, where Melville was present. The committee of ministers there appointed to advise with the king about church affairs was "the needle which drew in the episcopal thread." In 1597 Melville was deprived of the rectorship of St. Andrew's University after holding it seven years. To get rid of his opposition in the church courts, all doctors or regents teaching theology or philosophy, not being pastors, were forbidden to sit in any of these courts under pain of deprivation and rebellion. Prelates were declared by Parliament to have ever represented an estate of the realm; and, when the assembly met, the king would not allow it to proceed until Melville retired; and ultimately he was forced to quit the town. James protested that he did not intend to restore bishops, but only wished some of the wisest ministers, as commissioners of the kirk, to have a place in the privy council and Parliament to judge in their own affairs. To this the assembly by a small majority agreed. The king would not permit Melville to sit in the assembly of 1600, and, by acceding to many caveats, he induced the members to comply with his plan. When the Scottish Parliament restored the bishops to their ancient privileges, in 1606, Melville, who was sent by St. Andrew's presbytery, protested. As the bishops had as yet no spiritual power, Melville and seven other ministers were summoned to London, nominally to confer with the king on church affairs, really to deprive their brethren of their aid and counsel in opposing the changes contemplated. The English nobles were astonished at Melville's talents and courage. On a highly ritualistic service which he had been made to witness in the Chapel Royal he wrote a Latin epigram, which one of the court spies set to watch him conveyed to the king. For this Melville was tried by the English privy council Nov. 30, and though he had given out no copy, was found guilty of *scandalum magnatum*. In April he was sent to the Tower, where for ten months he was treated with great severity. Pen, ink, and paper were taken from him; and none saw him save the person who brought his food. But his spirit was free and unbroken, and he covered the walls of his cells with verses beautifully engraved with the tongue of his shoe-buckle. By means of packed assemblies and bribery, prelacy was established in Scotland when he and other faithful men were far away. Though the Protestants of Rochelle were eager to have Melville as professor of divinity, James would not consent; but, after four years' captivity, he, at the request of Du Plessis-Mornay (q.v.), allowed him to go to Sedan to share with Tilenus the professorship of divinity. There his last years were spent, the bitterness of his exile being alleviated by the kindness of some Scottish professors and students. Among these last were John Durie (q.v.), and perhaps Alexander Colville, destined so long to carry on his work in St. Mary's College. The contest in which he took so prominent a part affected not only the government of the church but also the cause of civil and religious liberty. "Scotland," says his nephew James, "never received a greater benefit at the hands of God than this man." "If," says Dr. McCrie, "the love of pure religion, rational liberty, and polite letters, forms the basis of national virtue and happiness, I know no individual, after her Reformer, from whom Scotland has received greater benefits, and to whom she owes a deeper debt of gratitude and respect, than Andrew Melville." He was full of spirits, vigorous and courageous, quick-tempered but kindly, of great and varied learning, but more of a scholar than a popular orator. His chief work was in the universities and church courts rather than in the pulpit; and that, perhaps, was the reason why, with all his influence among his brethren, he never gained such sway over the nobles and people as Knox and Henderson attained. The hard measure meted out to him by King James was one of the greatest blots on that reign.

D. HAY FLEMING.

BIBLIOGRAPHY: The principal sources are: J. Melvill, *Autobiography and Diary, with Continuation*, ed. R. Pitcairn, Edinburgh, 1842; J. Row, *Hist. of the Kirk of Scotland*, ed. D. Laing, ib., 1842; W Scot, *An Apologetical Narration of the State and Government of the Kirk of Scotland since the Reformation*, ed. D. Laing, ib. 1846; J. Spottiswoode, *Hist. of the Church of Scotland*, ed. M. Russell, ib. 1851; D. Calderwood, *Hist. of the Kirk of Scotland*, ed. T. Thomson, 8 vols., ib. 1842–49; *Register of the Privy Council of Scotland*, ed. D. Masson, vols. iii.–iv., ib., 1880–81. The one life of importance is by T. McCrie, 2 vols., ib. 1819, also in his works, ed., his son, the younger McCrie, ib. 1856, reissued, 1899. Consult also *DNB*, xxvii. 230; H. Cowan, *Influence of the Scottish Church in Christendom*, London, 1896.

MEMORIALS AND SACRED STONES.

1. Scope of the Subject.

Among cultic objects preserved among practically all primitive peoples and often continued in use in an advanced state of society are pillars and sacred stones. Regard for these objects is in part attributable to fetishistic or animistic concepts (see COMPARATIVE RELIGION, VI., 1, a, 1–3, 7; FETISHISM); in part to superstitious regard of what was, at the time when sacredness first attached to the object, inexplicable or mysterious; and in part to later association with divine powers. Sometimes the reasons for which these objects became sacred have long been lost and are now irrecoverable—such a case is presented by the sacred stone at Delphi, to explain which a myth was invented (see COMPARATIVE RELIGION, VI., 1, a, § 7). For many of the occurrences found in the Semitic field, especially the monoliths regarded as deities, the animistic basis is evident. Other monuments, such as those at crossroads or on boundaries, received their sacred character through being regarded as representing the god of highways or of boundaries. Among the classes of objects to be considered in this article are such reminders of past events as were set up by Jacob (Gen. xxxi. 45 sqq.) and Joshua (Josh. iv., xxiv. 6–7), or such as marked a grave (Gen. xxxv. 20), or which at some time received veneration as embodying a god or as marking the haunt of deity (Gen. xxviii. 18, xxxv. 14; Judges vi. 20). These objects include menhirs (single stones or rude undressed columns), dolmens (stone tables, possibly used as altars, one stone supported by two or more), cromlechs or circles of stones like that at Stonehenge, England, sometimes having a menhir in the center, and cairns or heaps of stones; besides these should be mentioned the figures developed from these originally rough and unshaped forms. These monuments are traceable all the way across the continents of Asia and Europe, and as far west as Ireland.

Because of the abundant remains of Greek

literature, the number of sacred stones in Greece appears to have been exceptionally large; but it may be taken for granted that that country is simply illustrative of a certain stage of civilization. Examples taken from this field are the sacred stone at Hyettos, the thirty stones which the Pharaeans worshiped, that in Bœotia which figured in the sacred festivals, and the image of Artemis in Ephesus. Theophrastus (373–283 B.C.) illustrates the frequency of these monuments when he satirically describes a superstitious Greek performing his devotions before the sacred stones along the road, a part of the worship consisting of anointing them with oil (*Characteres ethici*, xvi.). The form of these early monuments was that of a rough monolith set upright. But it was not to be expected that the artistic Greek would continue to be content with such crude monuments: accordingly the pillar was chiseled into smooth quadrangular form and surmounted later by a sculptured head, originally that of Hermes (whence these pillars bore the name *Hermæ* or *Hermuli*) but later that of other deities. The reference to these in Pausanias is frequent; cf. Frazer's ed. on viii. 34, § 3, x. 24, § 6. The origin of these Hermæ is quite distinctly traced to the rough blocks of stone which marked roads or boundaries and bore the name of *hermeia* or *hermakes;* these in turn may have developed from the cairn, to which respect was shown by the passer-by in the addition of a stone to the heap. The Hermæ passed over to the Romans in the shape of *termini*, having the same general form. Egyptians and Assyrians extended the usage by erecting stelai and pillars to mark the bounds of their conquests. It is noteworthy that this development of the monolith into the statue does not appear among the Semites. Among the sacred places of the Greeks were those known as bætyli (a name formed from the Hebrew Bethel), the center of which were usually sacred stones, some of them meteoric, like that of Artemis mentioned above (cf. Acts xix. 35). There was a sacred meteorite at Tyre (reported by Philo Byblius, q.v.), and one in the temple of Heliogabalus at Emesa. It is probable that in many cases the sanctity of the stone was due to its emblematic character, as when it figured a holy mountain in a Canaanitic high place or a Babylonian ziggurat (see HIGH PLACES). For citations of sacred stones over a larger area and among both primitive and more highly cultured peoples, cf. E. B. Tylor, *Primitive Culture*, chap. xv. (London, 1903), where examples are cited from western Europe as late as the middle of the nineteenth century.

2. In Non-Semitic Territory.

3. Among Semites.

Among Semites the existence of a cult of sacred stones has long been known. The two sacred stones of the Kaaba (q.v.) are merely illustrative of a wealth of sacred objects of this character among pre-Mohammedan Arabs. Lampridius speaks of "stones which were called gods" at Syrian sanctuaries, perhaps the menhirs, dolmens, and the like referred to above. Wüstenfeld (*ZDMG*, xviii. 452, 1864) notes that the Arab geographer Yakut about 1200 A.D. knew of a stone near Aleppo said to mark the tomb of a prophet upon which pilgrims (Moslems, Jews, and Christians) poured rosewater. Renan (*Mission de Phénice*, pp. 399–400, Paris, 1864) speaks of a milestone near Sidon which was anointed with oil. Niebuhr is reported to have heard of a stone venerated by the Jacobite sun-worshipers of Mesopotamia (cf. D. Chwolson, *Die Ssabier*, i. 153, Leipsic, 1856). Among the Arabs sacred pillars (menhirs) were numerous, the most celebrated being the Allat stones (Smith, *Kinship*, pp. 292 sqq.; C. M. Doughty, *Arabia Deserta*, ii. 515 sqq., Cambridge, 1888), looked upon as deities. E. A. T. W. Budge (*Egyptian Magic*, chap. iii., London, 1899) shows that Egyptians believed that the statue of a god contained the deity's spirit; hence the superstitious Christianized Egyptians endeavored to shatter the image in order to make the spirit homeless. In this respect the conceptions of Egyptians and Arabs alike rest upon an animistic basis. For a notice of Canaanitic pillars see GEZER, § 3. The place of such a pillar was a "Bethel" (cf. Gen. xxviii. 18–19), a word which passed over into the Greek *baitylos* or *baitylion* (ut sup.), cf. the Greek *temenos*, Hebr. *'admath ḳodesh*, "holy ground," Arab. *ḥaram*. It implied a manifestation of deity by theophany, vision, dream, release from peril, victory, or the like. Into the idea of such a place there enters the notion of taboo (see COMPARATIVE RELIGION, VI., 1, c) and consecrates the spot to the deity resident or manifest there. Possibly the Hebrew prohibition against using tools on the altar-stones (Ex. xx. 25) was due to this animistic conception and the desire not to disturb the numen in the stone.

4. The Maṣṣebah.

The most general name in the Semitic field for the pillar is derived from a root *nṣb* (Hebr. *maṣṣebah*, pl. *maṣṣeboth*, the most general word, *muṣṣabh*, *neṣibh*, cf. Gen. xix. 26, I Sam. x. 5, xiii. 3–4, where for "garrison" should be read "memorial pillar" as the context clearly implies; Arab. *nuṣub*, *manṣab*, *nuṣb*, pl. *anṣab*, Phenician *maṣṣebeth*, Aramaic *nṣb;* the Hebrew also employs the terms *ammudh*, Gen. xix. 26, Jer. xxvii. 19, rendered by the Greek *stēlē*, *stylos*, *kiōn;* and *ḥamman*, a pillar for sun-worship, Isa. xvii. 8, xxvii. 9; Ezek. vi. 4, 6; Lev. xxvi. 30; II Chron. xiv. 4, 7). The Phenician *maṣṣebeth* usually means a memorial at a grave (as in modern Jewish usage), but is also used of a pillar (not structural) in a temple, as at Sidon, and may possibly refer to a votive tablet. The Aramaic *nṣb* applies to a statue, possibly at a grave. Before Phenician temples twin pillars, not structural, usually stood, as is indicated by coins. Herodotus, ii. 44, describes the two in the temple of Melkart-Heracles at Tyre, one of which he says was of pure gold and the other of emerald (glass? cf. Rawlinson's note on Herodotus, ii. 81, New York, 1875). Bronze pillars were in the temple of Baal-Heracles at Gades. These seem to have been round, though others of the Phenician cult were square with pyramidal tops. Through the spread of Phenician influence along the Mediterranean, the phrase "the pillars of Hercules" came to denote the extreme West, and to be applied to the mountains at the western end of the Mediterranean. The Phenician derivation of the two pillars in Solomon's temple is clear

(I Kings vii. 15–21). At Palmyra votive offerings took the shape of conical terra-cottas, miniature pillars with possibly a phallic reference. Nisibis in Mesopotamia may have derived its name from the word for pillar and the existence there of one of these objects of more than common renown. A stele at Larnaka in Cyprus is called in the inscription a *maẓẓebah*, and has a pyramidal top.

5. Hebrew Usage.

Among the Hebrews the maẓẓebah is clearly distinguished from the Asherah (q.v.), the former being of stone and the latter of wood. Hebrew narratives contain references to the maẓẓebah as the evidence of the presence of deity. Jacob's stone pillow becomes a pillar (Gen. xxviii. 18, xxxv. 14); Joshua's pillar is a hearing witness (Josh. xxiv. 26–27; cf. Judges ix. 6; a thoroughly animistic conception). As a reminder of an event of importance the maẓẓebah is of frequent occurrence. It (or a heap of stones; there are two narratives united in the account in Gen. xxxi. 45–47) marked the compact between Jacob and Laban; twelve pillars at Sinai commemorated the covenant (Ex. xxiv. 4), and Moses commanded to erect monoliths at Mt. Ebal with the words of the law incised in the plaster overlaid on the stones (Deut. xxvii. 2 sqq.); Joshua had twelve pillars set up in the bed of the Jordan and twelve at Gilgal to commemorate the crossing (Josh. iv. 3 sqq., 20 sqq.; the place-name Gilgal, from a word meaning to encircle, may be taken from the existence of cromlechs at the various places bearing that name); in remembrance of the victory over the Philistines Samuel erected a "stone" (Hebr. *ebhen*, not *maẓẓebah*, I Sam. vii. 12), and Saul also set up a monument of victory (Hebr. *yadh*, "hand," I Sam. xv. 12; the verb is to be read *hiẓẓibh*), and a great stone served as an altar (I Sam. xiv. 33; cf. ALTAR, I., §§ 2–3). Absalom reared a pillar (*maẓẓebeth*) to perpetuate his own memory (II Sam. xviii. 18). As a monument to the dead, corresponding to the Phenician and modern Jewish usage, the pillar occurs in Gen. xxxv. 23 (Rachel); II Kings xxiii. 17; Ezek. xxxix. 15 (a temporary sign), and I Macc. xiii. 27. This is parallel with the Arabic usage which applies *nuṣb* to a memorial at a grave (I. Goldziher, *Muhammedanische Studien*, i. 231–238, Halle, 1889; Derenbourg, in *JA*, 8 ser., ii. 245, 1883). Heaps of stones covered the grave of a man executed (Josh. vii. 26, viii. 29; II Sam. xviii. 17). Thus it is seen that memorials at graves were common to Semitic custom, maintained by the Hebrews. Isaiah (xix. 19) predicts that a pillar inscribed "Yahweh's (land)" is to be set up at the border of Egypt as a token that Egypt too is to be a part of God's territory when his kingdom is realized; and Hosea (iii. 4, x. 1–2) mentions pillars as belonging to the Yahweh cult. Other cases of sacred stones to be noted are the stone of Bohan (Josh. xv. 6, xviii. 17), that at Shechem (Josh. xxiv. 26–27), at Ophrah (Judges vi. 20–21), at Gibeon (II Sam. xx. 8), the stone of Ezel (I Sam. xx. 19), and of Zoheleth (I Kings i. 9; a stone of sacrifice). Isa. lvii. 6 may refer to sacred but prohibited stones, cf. lvi. 4 sqq. The *ẓiyyun*, "direction posts," of Jer. xxxi. 21 were not sacred objects in Israel, though they were elsewhere (cf. Ezek. xxi. 21). Maẓẓeboth are prohibited in Deut. xvi. 22, vii. 5, xii. 3; Lev. xxvi. 1; as are the *ḥammanim* (R.V. "sun images") in Lev. xxvi. 30; cf. Ezek. vi. 4, 6; Isa. xxvii. 9; II Chron. xiv. 5, xxxiv. 4, 7; Jehu destroyed the pillars of Baal in Samaria (II Kings x. 26–27), and Josiah broke those of the southern kingdom (II Kings xxiii. 14).

6. Cultic Importance.

The cultic importance of these objects is implicit in what precedes (Gen. xxviii. 22, xxxi. 13, xxxv. 14), and is further supported by the name Bethel (which has the generic signification of "sanctuary") and by the ritual observance of anointing the pillar with oil or performing sacrifice at it or upon it (cf. I Kings i. 9). The maẓẓebah, as a rough unhewn stone, was an accessory of the pre-Deuteronomic sanctuary (see HIGH PLACES), and is unquestionably to be connected with early Semitic stone-worship. Even in Hebrew times the pillar marked the presence of deity (outside of Gen. xxviii. 16 sqq., cf. Josh. xxiv. 26–27, "this stone is a witness, it hath heard"). Accordingly it received the blood or fat of the victim or the oil of the vegetable offering. Thus are to be explained the hollows in many of these objects where the substance of the offering was applied. For the stages in the development of the conception of these objects see the references to ALTAR above. That the Hebrew but followed common Semitic usage is suggested by the fact that in Arabic custom the blood or fat of the sacrificial victim was applied to the stone with the purpose of bringing it into direct contact with deity (cf. the modern custom of stroking with the hand the sacred stones of the Kaaba). Arabs swore by the *anẓab* about a sanctuary (Wellhausen, *Reste*, 2d ed., p. 102), and Herodotus (iii. 8) testifies to the application of the blood directly to the stones. The Hebrew altar of unhewn stones has its analogue in the cairn, which is sometimes an altar, as in the camel sacrifice reported by Nilus, in which case the animal was bound upon a heap of stones (Smith, *Rel. of Sem.*, 2d ed., p. 338). In modern Syria many spots sacred to saints are marked with pillars regarded as sacred, and cultic performances still take place in many respects identical with those noted in earlier times (S. I. Curtiss, *Primitive Semitic Religion To-day*, chap. vii., New York, 1902). The passage in Isa. lvii. 6 might have been written of most primitive peoples. Anointing of stones continued in Norway till the close of the seventeenth century (S. Nilsson, *Primitive Inhabitants of Scandinavia*, p. 241, London, 1868), and the earl of Roden reports a case in which the Irish of Inniskea worshiped a stone kept carefully wrapped in flannel (Tylor, ut sup., ii. 167).

A question yet under debate is the relation to this subject of the use of the Hebr. *ẓur* as applied to Yahweh (Deut. xxxii. 4; I Sam. ii. 2; Ps. xviii. 2, 31; Isa. xvii. 10, xxx. 29). This application occurs only in late passages, never in J or E, and the connection with pillars or stones is not made out. *Ẓur* appears to be used figuratively. On the other hand, analogy seems to give some support for the idea advanced in the fact that *ẓur* occurs as an element in proper names among Sabians, and possibly among place-names in Judea and Midian. On *zur* as a divine name cf. A. Wiegand, in *ZATW*, 1890, pp. 85 sqq. GEO. W. GILMORE.

BIBLIOGRAPHY: Benzinger, *Archäologie*, pp. 314 sqq. et passim; Nowack, *Archäologie*, i. 90–93, ii. 17–21; Smith, *Rel. of Sem.*, passim; idem, *Kinship*, pp. 292 sqq.; G. Baur, *Geschichte der alttestamentliche Weissagung*, i. 128–131, Giessen, 1861; F. Lenormant, in *Comptes rendus de l'académie des inscriptions et belles-lettres*, 1868, pp. 318–322; idem, in *Revue de l'histoire des religions*, iii (1881), 31–53; W. von Baudissin, *Studien zur semitischen Religionsgeschichte*, vol. ii., Leipsic, 1878; Falconnet, in *Mémoires de l'académie des inscriptions et belles-lettres*, vi (1729), 513–532; F. Münter, *Ueber die von Himmel gefallenen Steine*, Leipsic, 1805; F. von Dalberg, *Ueber den Meteor-Cultus der Alten*, Heidelberg, 1811; C. R. Conder, *Heth and Moab*, pp. 190–267, London, 1883; idem, *Syrian Stone Lore*, ib. 1886; R. Pietschmann, *Geschichte der Phönizier*, pp. 205–213, Berlin, 1889; H. Schultz, *O. T. Theology*, i. 209–210, London, 1892; A. von Gall, *Altisraelitische Kultstätten*, Giessen, 1898; A. S. Palmer, *Studies on Biblical Subjects*, no. II., London, 1899; S. I. Curtiss, *Primitive Semitic Religion To-day*, New York, 1902; P. Torge, *Aschera und Astarte*, pp. 29–35, Greifswald, 1902; E. B. Tylor, *Primitive Culture*, chap. xv., London, 1903; J. G. Frazer, *Attis, Adonis and Osiris*, London, 1906; Jane Ellen Harrison, *Prolegomena to the Study of Greek Religion*, Cambridge, 1908; *Folk Lore*, vi. 24 sqq.; Wellhausen, *Heidenthum;* the literature under ALTAR; *DB*, i. 75–77, iv. 289–290, 617–619.

MEMPHIS. See NOPH.

MEN OF UNDERSTANDING. See HOMINES INTELLIGENTIÆ.

MENAHEM: Sixteenth king of Israel, son of Gadi, usurper and successor of Shallum. His dates according to the old chronology are 772–763 B.C.; according to Kamphausen, 740–738; according to Curtis, 741–737 (*DB*, i. 401); according to Kittel, 740–737 The narrative in II Kings xv. 14–22 makes Menahem march from Tirzah and kill Shallum in Samaria, and then waste the region about Tappuah (so the corrected text) because that town had declined to receive him. Tirzah, the old capital of the northern kingdom, was doubtless well fortified, and Menahem was its commandant. He may have been the head of one of the two portions into which the kingdom split after the death of Jeroboam. His victory over Shallum must have been the result of a severe conflict, and Tappuah was doubtless the center of the opposition to Menahem (cf. Isa. ix. 19–20; Hos. vii. 7, viii. 4). The Biblical narrative also states that Pul (Tiglath-Pileser, see ASSYRIA, VI., 3, § 9) came against the land and that Menahem paid him a tribute of 1,000 talents to be recognized as king. This does not involve that it was at Menahem's invitation that Tiglath-Pileser came, but it appears that the Assyrian had been in Syria as early as 740 B.C., that his intervention in Israel was a part of his general plan to reduce that land to a province of his empire, and that Menahem took advantage of the situation. It is hardly possible to allow to Menahem the full ten years assigned to his reign in II Kings xv. 17. His tribute to Pul belongs to the year 738, and he can not have reigned long after this to allow for the other reigns which fell before the destruction of Samaria in 722. (R. KITTEL.)

BIBLIOGRAPHY: The sources are II Kings xv. 14–22. Consult: R. Kittel, *Geschichte der Hebräer*, ii. 468–472, Gotha, 1909; *DB*, iii. 340; *EB*, iii. 3019–20; *JE*, viii. 465–466, and the pertinent sections of the literature given under AHAB; and ISRAEL, HISTORY OF.

MENAION, me-nai′en: The breviary of the later Greek Church. It contains the prayers and hymns appointed for each feast and holy day of the year, together with short lives of the saints and martyrs. When it became too bulky, it was divided into twelve volumes, one for each month (whence the name, Gk. *mēn*, "month"), which are still extant, both in manuscript and in printed editions dating from the sixteenth century to the present time. They were published first at Venice, later elsewhere. (PHILIPP MEYER.)

BIBLIOGRAPHY: Krumbacher, *Geschichte*, pp. 181, 185, 658–659; *Analecta Bollandiana*, xiv (1895), 396–434; P. Meyer, *Die theologische Litteratur der griechischen Kirche*, pp. 148 sqq., Leipsic, 1899; É. Legrand, *Bibliographie hellénique*, Paris, 1894–96.

MENANDER, mê-nān′der: One of the oldest Gnostics. He was, according to Justin (*ANF*, i. 171), born at Capparateia, a village in Samaria, and taught in Antioch. According to Irenæus (*ANF*, i. 348), he was a pupil of Simon Magus. He taught that there was a supreme power unknown to all, and pretended to have been sent from the invisible eons for the salvation of men. The world, according to him, was made by the angels who emanate from Mind. To those baptized by him he promised power over the world—creating angels, immortality, and eternal youth. He was the teacher of Saturninus or Saturnilus and of Basilides. It is not known whether this Samaritan-Syriac gnosis preceded and led to the Hellenistic variety, or whether the Hellenistic developed independently. If the former is the case the importance of Menander would lie in the fact that he formed the transition from Oriental to Hellenistic gnosticism. (G. UHLHORN†.)

BIBLIOGRAPHY: The sources are indicated in the text. Consult *DCB*, iii. 902.

MENDELSSOHN, MOSES: German Jewish philosopher; b. at Dessau (67 m. s.w. of Berlin) Sept. 6, 1729; d. in Berlin Jan. 4, 1786. He came of poor parents and pursued his studies in the Bible, the Talmud, Maimonides, and afterward modern languages and literatures, under great privations. In 1750 he became tutor in the family of a rich Jewish manufacturer in Berlin, in 1754 bookkeeper, and, later, partner in the firm. From about the same time date his intimate acquaintance with Lessing, Nicolai, Abbt, etc., an earnest study of the philosophy of Locke, Shaftesbury, Spinoza, and Wolff, and the beginning of his long and varied literary activity. His *Phädon, oder von der Unsterblichkeit der Seele* (Berlin, 1767; Eng. transl., *Phaedon; or, the Death of Socrates*, London, 1789), and *Morgenstunden* (1786), lectures on the existence of God and immortality, procured for him fame as a philosopher. He also deserves well for his efforts for the elevation, mental and moral, of his coreligionists in Germany, and especially in Berlin. Among his many books may be mentioned: *Pope, ein Metaphysiker* (in collaboration with Lessing; 1755); *Briefe über die Empfindungen* (1755); *Jeru-*

salem, oder über religiöse Macht und Judenthum (2 parts, 1783; Eng. transl., *Jerusalem, a Treatise on Ecclesiastical Authority and Judaism*, 2 vols., London, 1838); and a commentary on Canticles (1772). He also translated the Pentateuch (1783), and the Psalms (1788). The most complete edition of his works is that by his grandson G. B. Mendelssohn (7 vols., Berlin, 1843–45); his philosophical writings were edited by M. Brasch (2 vols., Leipsic, 1880).

BIBLIOGRAPHY: S. Hensel, *Die Familie Mendelssohn*, 9th ed., 1898, Eng. transl., London, 1882; M. Samuels, *Memoirs of Moses Mendelssohn*, London, 1825; J. H. Ritter, *Mendelssohn und Lessing*, Berlin, 1886; M. Kayserling, *Moses Mendelssohn*, Leipsic, 1888; *JE.*, viii. 479–485. An excellent bibliography is furnished in J. M. Baldwin, *Dictionary of Philosophy and Psychology*, iii. 1, pp. 369–370, New York, 1905.

MENDES, FREDERICK DE SOLA: Jewish rabbi; b. at Montego Bay, Jamaica, July 8, 1850. He was educated at Northwick College (1865–68), the University of London (1868–70; B.A., 1869), and the university and Jewish theological seminary of Breslau (1870–73; Ph.D., Jena, 1871). On returning to England, he became rabbi of Great St. Helen's Synagogue, London, in 1873, but within the year accepted a call to the rabbinate of Congregation Shaaray Tefillah (now West End Synagogue), New York City, of which he is still the head. In 1879 he was one of the founders of *The American Hebrew*, which he edited until 1885. In 1900–02 he was likewise associated with the editorial staff of *The Jewish Encyclopedia*, and in 1903 edited the Jewish *Menorah*. He is one of the collaborators in the revision of a new Jewish translation of the Bible, and besides translating the "Jewish Family Papers: Letters of a Missionary" of Gustav Meinhardt (the pseudonym of W Herzberg; New York, 1875), has written *Defense, not Defiance; A Hebrew's Reply to the Missionaries* (1876); *Child's First Bible* (1879); and *Outlines of Bible History* (1886).

MENDICANT MONKS, MENDICANT ORDERS (*Ordines mendicantium*): Those monastic orders which renounce on principle established income and live by the solicitation of alms; such as the Dominicans, Franciscans, Augustinians, Carmelites, and Servites (qq.v.).

MÉNÉGOZ, mê″nê″gōz′, **EUGENE:** French Protestant; b. at Algolsheim (a village near Breisach, 40 m. s.s.w. of Strasburg), Alsace, Sept. 25, 1838. He was educated at the gymnasium of Strasburg and the faculty of Protestant theology in the same city. After being subdirector of the preparatory school of Lutheran theology in Paris for four months in 1866, he was assistant pastor of the Église des Billettes, Paris, until 1877. Since the latter year he has been professor at the faculty of Protestant theology, Paris, and director of the seminary of the same faculty. He was likewise a member of the Council of the University of Paris in 1895–1906 and of the Upper Council of Public Instruction in 1901–05. In theology he is a "symbolo-fidéiste," seeking "a middle way between rationalism and orthodoxy." He has written *Étude dogmatique sur l'idée de l'église* (Strasburg, 1862); *Réflexions sur l'Évangile du Salut* (Paris, 1879); *Le Péché et la rédemption d'après Saint Paul* (1882); *Quid de catechismo sentiendum sit* (1882); *La Notion du catéchisme* (1882); *Luther considéré comme théologien* (1883); *La Prédestination dans la théologie paulinienne* (1884); *L'Autorité de Dieu* (1892); *La Théologie de l'épître aux Hébreux* (1894); *La Notion biblique du miracle* (1894); *Étude sur le dogme de la Trinité* (1898); *Du Rapport entre l'histoire sainte et la foi religieuse* (1899); *Le Salut d'après l'enseignement de Jésus-Christ* (1899); *La Justification par la foi d'après Saint Paul et Saint Jacques* (1901); *Aperçu de la théologie d'Auguste Sabatier* (1901); *Le Fidéisme et la notion de la foi* (1905); *La Religion et la vie sociale* (1905); *La Mort de Jésus et le dogme de l'expiation* (1905); *L'Anti-fidéisme* (1906); and *Une triple distinction théologique. Observations sur le rapport de la foi religieuse avec la science, l'histoire et la philosophie* (1908). He was also one of the founders of the *Annales de bibliographie théologique.*

MENI: A deity named in the Old Testament only in Isa. lxv. 11 (A.V. "that number," margin "Meni"; R.V. "Destiny," margin "Meni") as worshiped by idolatrous Israelites. Light is thrown on the subject by the etymology (Hebr. *manah*, "to number," Arab. "to apportion"), by the occurrence in Arabic of the feminine form *Manat*, one of the daughters of Allah (Koran, liii. 20), and by the use of the Arabic *maniyya*, "fate" (cf. the Nabatæan *Manawat*, "Fates," Wellhausen, *Heidentum*, pp. 25–29). The word *ebedhmeni*, "servant of Meni," occurs on Achæmenian coins, and *Meni(s)* is found as a parallel to *Belus fortunæ rector*, "Bel, controller of fortune," on an altar at Vaison in Provence, in which there seems to be present a reminiscence of the Biblical passage. It is unlikely that Meni is of Babylonian origin, the name not having been found as a god name in the cuneiform inscriptions. He was probably introduced into Palestine by Aramæans or by the Arabs who began to press in soon after the exile. The plausible suggestion has been made that as Gad was the deity of (good) fortune, Meni is the controller of misfortune. The equation Meni-Ishtar-Venus is probably ruled out by the sex of Meni. The name was misunderstood by Aquila, Symmachus, Theodotion, and Jerome. GEO. W. GILMORE.

MENIUS, mê′ni-us, **JUSTUS (JODOCUS MENIG):** German Reformer; b. at Fulda Dec. 13, 1499; d. at Leipsic Aug. 11, 1558. In 1514, at the age of fifteen, he entered the University of Erfurt, where he cemented friendship with such humanists as Mutianus, Crotus, Eoban Hess, and others. Joachim Camerarius taught him Greek. At the suggestion of Melanchthon, whose pupil he became, he went in 1519 to Wittenberg. After Luther's return from the Wartburg he enjoyed his personal friendship. In 1523 he was appointed vicar at Mühlberg near Erfurt, but in 1525 resigned his position and went to Erfurt to teach. In the same year he became pastor of the Church of St. Thomas in Erfurt. But soon the council of the town changed its attitude toward the Reformation. In 1525, after the end of the Peasants' War, Roman Catholic clergymen and monks were allowed to return. Their most prominent spokesman was Konrad Kling, a Franciscan monk, against whom Menius directed his polemical treatise, *Wider den hochberühmten Barfüsser zu Erfurt, D. Conrad Kling, Schutzrede* (Wittenberg, 1527) and his sermon, *Etlicher Gottlosen und Widerchristlichen Lehre von der papistischen Messe* (1527). Luther wrote a preface for both of these works, but in spite of his assistance and intercession the council of the town did not change its position. Under those circumstances Menius removed in 1528 with his family to Gotha where he became intimately acquainted with Friedrich Myconius. He wrote and instructed the youth, but his chief activity was the visitation of Thuringia, jointly with Christof von der Planitz, Melanchthon, and Myconius. After his return from this visitation he was appointed in 1529 pastor and superintendent at Eisenach where he labored eighteen years. He became one of the chief champions in the fight against Anabaptism, was active as a reformer, and took part in several other visitations, in 1533 and 1539 in Thuringia, subsequently in Schwarzburg, and in 1545 in the bishopric of Naumburg. In 1542 he introduced the Reformation in the imperial city of Mühlhausen. He took part in the religious colloquy of Marburg (1529), in the Wittenberg *Concordia* (1538), and in the meeting at Schmalkald (1537). Upon the death of his faithful friend Myconius in 1546 he became his successor in Gotha. After the unfavorable termination of the Schmalkald War he was compelled to leave Gotha for some time, but was soon able to return. Like his colleagues he protested against the Augsburg *Interim*. The propagandism of the Anabaptists which threatened to invade Thuringia from Hesse and Mühlhausen induced him to resume his polemical activity against them, especially against their antinomian doctrine, according to which it is impossible for man to sin if he is born of God. [Antinomianism was not characteristic of the Anabaptists. A. H. N.] In 1552 Menius was involved in the Osiandrian controversy. Elector John Frederic sent an embassy to Prussia for the purpose of allaying the dissensions caused by Osiander's teachings. Beside two of his councilors he sent Menius and Johann Stolz to Königsberg in 1553. The duke of Prussia commissioned Funck to transmit to them a confession of faith in accordance with Osiander's views, which was answered by Menius and Stolz. Funck replied shortly afterward. As Menius was taken ill, the negotiations were delayed. A later conference between Menius and Stolz, Funck and Sciurus led to no agreement, and the delegates returned without having attained their object. A few months afterward, on the occasion of the Thuringian visitations, Amsdorf found an opportunity to involve Menius intimately in the Majoristic Controversy (q.v.). Menius returned from Eisenach to Gotha, full of the hope to resume his duties; but Amsdorf, Ratzeberger, Aurifaber, and others continued their calumnies, denouncing him as an Adiaphorist and Majorist. The ungracious attitude of the court induced him to resign his position. By the intercession of Melanchthon and Camerarius, Menius received a position at the Church of St. Thomas in Leipsic. There he defended himself against further assaults of Flacius and Amsdorf, who did not cease their polemical attacks until his death. It is owing to the conditions of the time that Menius' literary activity was chiefly polemical. He published *Œconomia Christiana* (1529) which was prefaced by Luther, and against the Anabaptists he wrote, *Der Wiedertäufer Lehre und Geheimniss aus heiliger Schrift widerlegt* (1530) and *Von dem Geist der Wiedertäufer* (1544). He also published a somewhat modified edition of Luther's Small Catechism under the title, *Catechismus Justi Menii* (1532), a copy of which is preserved in the town library of Breslau. The manual continued in use till the 19th century. Menius also wrote *De usu historiæ sacrarum literarum* (1532) which is an exposition of I Sam.; a translation of Luther's large commentary on the Galatians (1535) and *Wie ein jeglicher Christ gegen allerlei Lehre, gute und böse, nach Gottes Befehl sich gebührlich halten soll* (1538). His treatise, *Von der Notwehr Unterricht, nützlich zu lesen* (1547) was occasioned by the war of Schmalkald. The aggressive attitude of the Anabaptists induced him once more to write against them a polemical treatise, *Von den Blutsfreunden aus der Wiedertaufe* (1551). Against Osiander he wrote, *Erkenntnis aus Gottes Wort und heiliger Schrift über die Bekenntnis A. Osiandri* (1552), and *Von der Gerechtigkeit, die für Gott gilt: Wider die neue alcumistische Theologiam A. Osiandri* (1552). (G. KAWERAU.)

BIBLIOGRAPHY: Thirteen letters are to be found in *Zeitschrift des Vereins für thüring. Geschichte*, x (1882), 243 sqq., and others are among the correspondence of Luther, Melanchthon, Jonas, Mutianus, and Eobanus Hess. Autobiographic material is communicated in *ZHT*, 1865, pp. 303 sqq. The one biography is G. L. Schmidt, *Justus Menius, der Reformator Thüringens*, Gotha, 1867. Material will be found in the literature dealing with the Reformers with whom he came into touch (e.g., J. W. Richard, *Philip Melanchthon*, pp. 159, 185, 254, New York, 1898), and in that on the Reformation and on the Anabaptists.

MENKEN, GOTTFRIED: German Reformed pastor; b. at Bremen May 29, 1768; d. there June 1, 1831. In the house of his parents he imbibed a Biblical piety which was, however, free from all narrowness though consciously opposed to rationalism. While still in the gymnasium he preached, and when he entered the University of Jena in 1788 his theological convictions had already assumed definite form. The rationalism of the university induced him to devote himself wholly to the Bible, to which the mysticism of his earlier days gave way. In 1790 he went to the University of Duisburg where he found a more sympathetic atmosphere in the circle of F. A. Hasenkamp and others whose study of the Bible was governed by the spirit of Bengel and Collenbusch. In 1791 he passed his theological examination, but stayed two years longer at Duisburg. He was assistant preacher in Uedem near Cleve (1793–94), for the German Reformed congregation in Frankfort-on-the-Main (1794–96), pastor of the Reformed congregation in Wetzlar (1796–1802), second preacher of St. Paul in Bremen (1802–11), and first preacher of St. Martin (1811–25).

The theology of Menken was not original with him; but the vigor of his expressions gave him a far-reaching influence, especially upon Bible students. The immovable center of his theology was the Bible, which he looked upon as the divine testimony of the past, present, and future history of salvation in the center of which stood Christ. From Collenbusch Menken acquired his views on the ethical relation of God to humanity, the atonement, and salvation. The divine nature is love, of which holiness and justice are only phases. These fundamental attributes of God are revealed in the order of his kingdom, which is never based upon an unfathomable decree, but always upon foreseen worthiness. In order to assure this worthiness, every reasonable creature is in need of a test; if in this way sin comes into the world, it serves only a good purpose that there may come into existence a more perfect and blessed creation. If Adam fell, death was for him not a punishment, but a natural consequence of sin, and if his heirs are overcome by sin, this also is not a punishment, but a suffering of injustice, since they are personally innocent of the sinfulness and mortality of their being. Christ delivered human nature from that unjust imposition, by assuming it not as it was originally, but as it was after the fall. This was not intended to assail the divinity or personal sinlessness of Christ, but only to emphasize his humanity. So it follows that in no way is there a compensation of the claims of divine holiness or of the law by the death of Christ. The sinlessness acquired by Christ can be appropriated by faith in him. Faith in Christ is a divine power producing that holiness and glory in man, and on this depends the main interest of the whole doctrine, and consequently the worthiness of man is in no way a divine gift, but the chief demand of God, for the sake of which he imparts to man his grace. All predestinarian ideas are combated from this standpoint. It is only consistent with this whole conception, which lacks a clear estimate of sin as positive opposition to God, that sanctification can be completed upon earth. As justification or forgiveness of sins in no way necessarily results from this doctrine, they really have no place in it, and the fact that Menken nevertheless used these conceptions shows that the Biblical vein in him was stronger than the influence of Collenbusch.

His chief works are: *Christliche Homilien* (Frankfort, 1797); *Neue Sammlung christlicher Homilien* (1801); *Christliche Homilien über Stellen an die Geschichte des Propheten Elias* (1804); *Versuch einer Anleitung zum eignen Unterricht in die Warhheiten der heiligen Schrift* (an exposition of his system; 1805); *Betrachtungen über das Evangelium Matthäi* (only one volume published; 1809); *Das Glaubensbekenntnis der christlichen Kirche* (1816); *Erklärung des elften Kapitels des Briefes an die Hebräer* (1821); *Predigten* (1825); *Blicke in das Leben des Apostel Paulus und der ersten Christengemeinen* (1828); and *Homilien über das neunte und zehnte Kapitel des Briefes an die Hebräer* (1831). His works have been collected in seven volumes (Bremen, 1858–65; new edition, 8 vols. 1894–95). (E. F. KARL MÜLLER.)

BIBLIOGRAPHY: C. H. Gildemeister, *Leben und Wirken des Gottfried Menken*, 2 vols., Bremen, 1861. E. C. Achelis published a selection of Menken's *Homilien*, to which he prefixed an introduction dealing with the life, Gotha, 1888. Consult also A. Ritschl, *Geschichte des Pietismus*, i. 566 sqq., Bonn, 1880.

MENNAS: Patriarch of Constantinople 536–552; d. at Constantinople Aug. 5, 552. Nothing is known of his early life. He was a priest and president of the Hospice Samson when he was appointed to the patriarchate at the desire of Justinian in the place of Anthimus (who had been deposed by a synod at Constantinople in 535), and was consecrated by Agapetus, being the first Eastern patriarch to receive consecration from a pope. He presided at a synod held at Constantinople in 536, called to finish the case of Anthimus, left uncompleted by the death of Agapetus. His administration is marked by ability and a regard for the peace of the Church. He is commemorated by the Greek Church on Aug. 24, and by the Latin on Aug. 25.

BIBLIOGRAPHY: *ASB*, Aug., v. 164 165; Hefele, *Conciliengeschichte*, ii. 571, 763 sqq., 787 sqq., 812 sqq., 855–856, Eng. transl., iv. 193–194, 218, 285–286; *DCB*, iii. 902–903.

MENNO SIMONS. See SIMONS, MENNO.

MENNONITES.

I. Origins: The Mennonites form a number of religious bodies which originated on the continent in the sixteenth century, where they were characterized by antipedobaptist and antisacerdotal doctrines. Since the seventeenth century their chief center has been Holland. They must be sharply distinguished from the Baptists, for though the General Baptists were developed from the Mennonites, 1609 onward, their distinctive tenet of immersion was both late and infrequent among the older body. As early as the sixteenth century the term Anabaptists [used opprobriously of Antipedobaptists of all types. A.H.N.] did not connote any special church, but was applied to an entire tendency which developed in western and central Europe between 1521 and 1550 from the popular side of the German Reformation, from which it borrowed form and coloring. Under the influence of the newly discovered "Gospel," it rejected the Christianity received through infant baptism on the ground that it did not effect regeneration. It therefore required not only adult baptism, but also a Christianity based upon personal faith, and awaited the coming of the regeneration of the heart and of all Christendom, or rather the establishment of a living church of Christ within the world. As the representative of voluntary, or even of subjective Christianity, moreover, it taught the absolute separation of religious and secular life, thus advocating freedom of conscience. After the middle of the sixteenth century some churches, especially those of a unitarian trend, came into close connection with the Mennonites. The adherents and the spirit of these became in later years, subsequent to 1640, an independent force in England among such bodies as the Quakers. About a century earlier, however, it had received a permanent organization in communities which have continued to the present time and are still called Mennonites.

The term *Wiedertäufer* (" Re-baptizers ") may be employed to connote that faction of the Anabaptists which aimed to establish the kingdom of Christ on earth through temporal force, and did not seek to reform social conditions simply by the regeneration of individuals. The type of this faction was the kingdom of Münster and its plans of social revolution (see MÜNSTER, ANABAPTISTS IN). The only party of antipedobaptists which has preserved a historic continuity until the present day is the Mennonites, who now have some 250,000 members, divided both historically and geographically into (1) Swiss and South German; (2) the Dutch, who form the basis of the West and North German, and these, in their turn, of the Russian; and (3) the American. [The remnant of the Huterites that settled in South Dakota in 1874, who have never been identified with the Mennonites, constitutes at least one exception. A. H. N.]

II. Swiss and South German Antipedobaptists: The first independent church within the general Anabaptist movement was formed at Zurich in 1523. On Jan. 18, 1525, the church began to baptize on profession of faith, despite the efforts of the authorities to suppress it by force, and about the same time kindred societies were founded at Augsburg, Nuremberg, and Worms. The plan of forming churches of pious Christians separated from the world originated in the Unitas Fratrum, and was not unknown to Luther, while at first infant baptism was not regarded as obligatory by Zwingli, Butzer, Farel, Erasmus, Capito, Schwenckfeld, Billican, Hübmaier, or Brunner. Although Anabaptism was no baseless phenomenon, suddenly evolved from the Reformation, there seems to be little evidence to show that it was derived from older religious bodies. Anabaptists denied the doctrine of a grace which was decreed from without, and which was, therefore, independent of personal piety and devoid of influence on life. Faith, they declared, must be personal, and they were, accordingly, influenced by the same spirit which led Michael Sattler to reject infant baptism simply because " piety and salvation are sought through it," and because they " would not abandon their separation from the world " (i.e., the worldly churches). The doctrine that the grace of God must be regained by man, however, has been common among Protestants from the earliest times, while the monastic ideals of poverty and celibacy, attributed to the Anabaptists, were in reality antipodal to their real tenets. Nor did they consider themselves without sin, although they held that a Christian might have a good conscience and live blamelessly.

Immediately after the Peasants' War, Anabaptist communities sprang up throughout Germany in Strasburg, Augsburg, Salzburg, and elsewhere, headed by Denk, Gross, and Kautz. As early as Feb. 24, 1527, an assembly was convened at Schlatten near Schaffhausen by Sattler, who had founded the communities of Horb and Rottenburg-on-the Neckar. Throughout the Palatinate of the Rhine and Swabia many deserted both the Roman Catholics and the Protestants for the Anabaptists, even though the itinerant preachers, controlling neither the press nor large congregations, could only urge individuals to repentance and baptism. Communities also existed in St. Gall, Bern, and Basel, while in 1526 the Anabaptists entered the Tyrol and Moravia. After the spring of 1527, the extension of the movement was attended, except in Moravia, by bitter persecutions. According to the government records of Innsbruck, 700 persons were executed, banished, or otherwise punished in the Tyrol in 1530, while 600 were put to death in Ensisheim before 1535. Only Strasburg, Nuremberg, and Philip of Hesse refrained from the effusion of blood, and in Augsburg, which was protected by imperial privilege and the edict of Worms, Hut barely escaped the stake (see HUT, HANS). [But Hans Leupold, the minister of the antipedobaptists of Augsburg, was beheaded (cf. F. Roth, *Augsburgs Reformationsgeschichte, 1517–30,* p. 251, Munich, 1901). J. HORSCH.] The Evangelical authorities at the Diet of Speyer concurred in the imperial decision of 1529 that all Anabaptists should be executed without a trial before ecclesiastical judges, their motive probably being their fear that the separatistic tendency of the body would destroy all civil and social institutions.

The erroneous opinion has long existed that antipedobaptism involved communism and the abolishment of private property. These were practised, however, only in Moravia, and even there surrender of private rights was purely voluntary and confined to members of that church. It is clear, on the other hand, that they denied the State the right to compel belief and to regulate religion, or to expel from home on account of belief, for " the earth is the Lord's "; yet, though " in the perfection of Christ " there was neither magistracy nor sword, they rendered obedience to the temporal authorities. It was an exception that Hut and some others taught the speedy coming both of the day of judgment and of the condemnation of the wicked by the righteous. Although Zwingli constantly charged the Anabaptists with immorality, there is no basis for his assertions, nor is it known that there were cases of polygamy among them, as there were later in Münster. This does not imply, however, that no discordant elements entered into Anabaptism, or that their persecutions, in particular, did not lead them to excesses. The position of the majority of the martyrs, as well as the wealthy members of the communities of the Tyrol, the writings of Denk, the Worms translation of the Prophets, and the rich hymnology, render it certain that the Anabaptists did not belong to the lowest grades of society.

All those, however, who might have given a theological formulation of their doctrines and have become leaders of distinction were soon snatched away by death. It is impossible to speak, therefore, of uniformity in their dogmas, especially as their doctrinal interests paled before their enthusiasm for practical Christianity. Their hymns, the treatises of Denk and Hübmaier, the letters of Sattler, and other memorials of the martyrs all breathe the same spirit; love of Jesus and the Bible; the cross as the token of the Christian; the joy of the consciousness of salvation; gratitude for safety from this evil world and horror of it; brotherly love; and full freedom of conscience. In all else there was the widest divergency. Denk, Kautz, and Hetzer regarded Christ as their predecessor and example, not as the mediator in the presence of God; but in their *Getrewe Warnung* the Strasburgers "know not why Anabaptists call Our Lord 'Jesus Christ of Nazareth,' since he is of heaven." On the one hand, their baptismal hymn runs:

"I am alone the only God,
I am alone, I am not three";

while Hoffmann, on the other, was an avowed Trinitarian. The inner word interpreted the Scriptures to Denk, others based their exegesis on the literal meaning, and some Anabaptists laid special stress on revelations, visions, and dreams. The pantheistic trend of Denk was offset by the deep pietistic morality of Sattler and the chiliasm of Hut. Some regarded baptism as indifferent, and the washing of feet was practised but rarely, as in Zurich and the Harz. All, however, followed Zwingli in the breaking of bread in the Lord's Supper, as a witness of unity, while Arianism, sleep of the soul, and universal salvation were here and there taught among them. Their unifying bond was the belief that by the baptism of repentance and by the individual fear of God and love to him they were members of the church of Jesus Christ, separated from the world and purified by the power of the ban. Their creed, which was not dogmatic, but practical, was the "Brotherly Union of some Children of God," formulated at the conference of Schlatten. This confession was known at Zurich as early as 1527 and was attacked by Zwingli in that year and by Calvin in 1541. In its articles some of their teachers united concerning seven points: baptism of repentance and change of life, the ban, the breaking of bread, separation, pastoral care, the sword, and the prohibition of oaths—all practical problems, rather than doctrinal. Over the questions of private property and the paying of taxes levied for purposes of war a schism arose in Moravia in 1528.

About 1530 not only did the extension and the persecutions of the Anabaptists enter upon a new stage, but the obscurity which had thus far enveloped them was dissipated, and in the previous year the man was found and baptized at Strasburg who was to give the church a new home in the north, Melchior Hoffmann (q.v.). The same period was the beginning of the two tendencies which have continued side by side among the Mennonites to the present time, although both are equally opposed to an official church which teaches faith and salvation by means of dogma and sacrament. The one body (Swiss, Moravian), founded by Hoffmann, lays stress on personal piety and the formation of a church which is to have sharp external delimitations. The other party (Denk, Hübmaier) regards Christianity as a sum total of inner feelings and as a spiritual tendency in the world, having no earthly church, yet retaining the ban.

After 1530 the outward condition of the Anabaptists gradually altered. Although many, including Luther and Melanchthon, still regarded them as rebels, they were free from peril of death in some districts, and they might live there in comparative quiet, despite occasional oppression, imprisonment, and banishment. Their numbers also increased in the Palatinate, Alsace, Hesse, the eastern part of the Canton of Bern, the bishopric of Basel, and especially in Moravia. Elsewhere, however, they were exposed to constant persecution, and every trace of them disappeared, the few survivors either dying out or fleeing to Moravia, this being the case especially in Bavaria, the Tyrol, Austria and Silesia, and eastern Switzerland. Despite many vicissitudes and even banishment in 1535, Anabaptists from Austria, Carinthia, and Silesia sought refuge in Moravia, whence some of them later emigrated to Poland, Hungary, and Transylvania, while about 1550 and after 1561 the Venetian Anabaptists came into relation with their Tyrolese brethren. Many of these churches became very important. In 1537 the one at Lorsch contained some 240 adults; there were 250 at Grünberg (Hesse) in 1538; between 1,400 and 1,500 were at the controversy of Rhenish Anabaptists held at Worms in 1556; and in the great Strasburg congress of 1557 representatives were present from nearly fifty churches in Moravia, Swabia, Switzerland, Württemberg, Breisgau, and Alsace. In 1545, according to a moderate estimate, the Moravian Anabaptists numbered but 2,000; exact historians show that at a later time the church had increased considerably. Elsewhere, however, the persecutions continued with unremitting severity. In 1581, the Anabaptists knew of executions in South Germany and Austria to the number of 2,169, and many executions are not reported.

In the sixteenth century the Anabaptists remained closely united, but at the close of this period the intercommunication diminished, partly in consequence of the disappearance of many Anabaptists through persecution, and partly because the condition of the others had become more settled and quiet. Simultaneously with this new security, on the other hand, came differentiations and even dissensions. The communistic followers of the Tyrolese Jacob Hutter separated from the other Germans, whom they called "Swiss Brethren." In 1533 he succeeded in organizing the great majority of Moravian Anabaptists into a communistic body which remained unshaken for a century and a half, inspiring it with his spirit and giving it his name when he died at the stake in Innsbruck in 1536. During the administration of the active and talented elders who succeeded him, the Bavarian Hans Amon (d. 1542), the Silesian Peter Riedemann (1532–56), the Tyrolese Peter Walpot (1565–78), and Claus Braidl or Schuster (1585–1611), Hutter's followers received continual accessions of men of means, industry, and economy from other lands. Their watchword was separation from the world, but there was no trace of asceticism; while their entire interest was devoted to a moral life, the organization of the church, and economic and industrial development, so that they neglected theology entirely. They published but few works, which now have almost vanished, such as Peter Riedemann's *Rechenschaft unserer Religion, Lehre und Glaubens* (Brünn, 1565; reprinted by the Huterites of South Dakota in 1902); but a number of treatises and a mass of hymns are extant only in manuscript. The followers of Hutter sent out many missionaries, including Hans Raiffer, or Schmidt (burned at the stake in Aachen, 1558), who were indefatigable in urging the faithful to go to Moravia and be received into the church. They were hostile, on the other hand, to the "Swiss" Anabaptists, among whom, in their turn, divergencies arose which were laid before congresses in the course of the century, although only the conferences of Strasburg are known.

The letters of these assemblies are among the best products of the non-Hutterian Anabaptists of the sixteenth century. On Aug. 24, 1555, at the instance of the Dutch brethren and the followers of Hoffmann, the first convention was held, and the doctrines of the incarnation and the Trinity were considered. Believing that their dissensions were, perhaps, a punishment for their endeavor to gain a higher knowledge than God has made attainable for man, they declared that all should be content henceforth to follow the commandments of God with a pure and humble heart and in a life dead to the world. In a second conference, held two years later, the greatest moderation was enjoined, especially in the use of the ban, nor, in case one of a married pair had fallen under excommunication, was the other required to avoid him or her. Thus they deviate sharply from the view of Menno and the majority of Dutch Anabaptists.

The cleavage between the disciples of Hutter and the Roman Catholics was far wider than between the German Anabaptists and the Reformed churches, although the latter could not accept the Mennonite insistence on the ban, nor agree that neither the sacraments nor obedience to the Church, but only inner and experimental faith, constituted a Christian. Gradually it came about that Lutherans and Calvinists no longer regarded Anabaptists as heretics and opponents of all ordinances, human and divine, who should be destroyed with fire and sword, but rather as erring souls who were to be won by gentle means to renounce their separatism and unite with the Church. This was the attitude of the diplomatic Butzer, who, at the request of the landgrave, held a conference of the Hessian brethren at Marburg in 1538. The controverted problems were the equality of the Old Testament with the New, which the Anabaptists denied, the atonement of Christ and his death, the incarnation, the necessity of works, Christian baptism, the oath and magistracy, and the ban. The refusal of the Anabaptists to submit to the organized state church roused the hostility of the authorities rather than their doctrinal heresy. It was contrary to the interest of the state, however, to expel the Mennonites by harshness, so that, while both in Hesse and in Bern all severity was exercised against the envoys of Hutter with their advocacy of emigration, provision was made for the property of the children of Mennonites who had been banished or punished. This explains the efforts of the authorities to induce the Anabaptists to enter the Church by means of religious conferences, as at Marburg, Pfeddersheim, and especially at Frankenthal (1571), while pleas for freedom of conscience for the Mennonites were made at Zurich and Bern as early as 1558.

The pressure of authority, wielded with mercy and even with recognition, gradually induced many to unite with the Church, so that by 1600 the Hessian communities, still flourishing after the Marburg conference of 1538, had almost disappeared. The Anabaptists no longer regarded the state church as anti-Christian in itself, but rejected it solely on account of its lack of spiritual fruits. Some even granted that infant baptism was not really ungodly, so that although it was not Biblical, it might be advantageous, in case it was followed by a Christian education. From this point of view it was indeed possible to organize a church of the pious which should be separated by means of the ban, but it gave equal scope to the opposite tendency by which each one might join a visible church. There were, moreover, many elements peculiar to the Anabaptists which could scarcely tend to strengthen the community: the lack of a formulated theology, the absence of dogmatism, their exclusion from the universities and all higher social culture, and the oppression and opposition of the churches. These disadvantages were augmented by the lack of organization, common to all similar bodies. In the period of their early enthusiasm this was no disadvantage, but with the waning of their zeal little was left to sustain the church, so that the south was not the district where the Mennonites could survive and preserve an active spiritual life; this land was Holland, especially the province of Friesland and the towns of Amsterdam and Haarlem.

III. Mennonites in Holland Prior to 1536: Such Evangelical views as the denial of transubstantiation had long been current in the Netherlands, although the fact that Holland formed an imperial inheritance made it impossible for them to gain open acknowledgment until about 1530, when the Anabaptists from the Lower Rhine and East Friesland became influential among the Dutch. In that year the eloquent apocalyptic lay-preacher Melchior Hoffmann worked and baptized at Emden, teaching the Bible and the community of believers as opposed to the Church, yet inculcating obedience to the magistracy, non-resistance, and moral purity. Returning to Strasburg, he appointed Jan Volkerts Trijpmaker bishop, and the latter soon went to Amsterdam, where he founded the first Dutch community, but was beheaded, with nine others, Dec. 5, 1531. At Emden, on Dec. 10 of the previous year, he had baptized Sicke Freerks Snyder, who was beheaded at Leeuwarden on Mar. 20, 1531. Within an incredibly short time "covenanters" were found in large numbers throughout Holland, Zeeland, and Friesland, so that the testimonies of prisoners speak of 3,500 in Amsterdam, and 400 in Kampen. The converts were all adherents of Hoffmann, regarding baptism as the token of the covenant through which they were to share in the coming kingdom of Christ. Many of them were gentle, righteous pietists, even after Nov., 1533, when Jan Matthysen proclaimed himself Elijah, the immediate precursor of the kingdom of Christ, and when passive expectancy became active aggression. A minority endeavored from Nov., 1533, to May, 1535, to gain fortified positions. That this was but a small group is clear both from the trials and from the fact that only forty or fifty of the many Anabaptists took part in the attack on Amsterdam, May 11, 1535, while their bishop, Jacob of Kampen, condemned all violence. After 1534, pure and impure elements alike, chiefly from Holland and Friesland, but also from the Rhine and Westphalia, united to seek Münster, the city chosen by God as the New Jerusalem, where they were carried away by John of Leyden (see MÜNSTER, ANABAPTISTS IN). With the fall of Münster, June 2 [24-25], 1535, the hopes of temporal power, held by a faction, vanished. The conference in a village near Bockholt (Westphalia) marked the amicable separation between those who were unwilling to renounce the expectation of an earthly kingdom (which was not, however, to be established by force), and those who found the kingdom in the hearts of the regenerate, the latter party being in harmony with Obbe and Dirk Philips, and obtaining a leader in Dec., 1536, in Menno Simons. Persecutions in Holland drove the Anabaptists into exile in Holstein, Mecklenburg, England, and Prussia. They found many sympathizers in the country last named, especially among the followers of Schwenckfeld, and succeeded in remaining there, despite some official expulsions up to this time. There were also French-speaking Mennonites about 1536, probably in Walloon Belgium, Ghent, and Strasburg, while Anabaptists were even found in Sweden. Representatives from various countries were either present or expected in Bockholt. In 1540 all the Mennonites formed a single, though loosely organized, "church of Christ."

IV. In the North.—1. In Holland 1536-80 (1640): After 1536 the elders (Menno Simons, Dirk Philips, Adam Pastor, Gillis of Aachen, Lenaert Bouwens, and others) toiled to bring order out of the confusion. Their crucial task was the maintenance of the true church of Christ, as opposed both to the national church in East Friesland and Prussia on the one hand, and to the teachings of David Joris (see JORIS, JAN DAVID) on the other, who refused to form openly a congregation, and exposed his followers to excessive moral perils. Menno and his successors continually warned their disciples not to form a sect, but rather to establish the true church of Christ. The Mennonites are important, therefore, as being the only body in the sixteenth century who did not seek to reform the Church, but believed themselves justified in reestablishing beside it the ancient apostolic teachings, and appealed diligently to the Church Fathers, desiring to revivify the church of the apostles, which had been obscured for a time, rather than to continue the medieval secularized ecclesiasticism. The unremitting toil of the elders and, in still greater degree, the charm exerted by the piety of the brethren brought success, and neither the persecutions of the Roman Catholics nor the later oppression of the Evangelical authorities were able to check the growth of the Mennonites. Probably 5,000 Protestants were executed by the Roman Catholic authorities in the Netherlands after 1530. Of these 3,700 were Mennonites; of the Lutherans and others six per cent and of the Mennonites thirty per cent were women. In the north the last to die was burned at the stake in 1574, and in the south a young woman was buried alive in 1597.

The persecutions, especially after 1550, drove hundreds from the south of Holland to the north, whence they were expelled to other countries, where they found an abode both on account of former immigrations and because of independent Anabaptist movements. Their safest refuge was East Friesland. After 1550, organized congregations existed in close contact with Holland, in Westphalia, Oldenburg, Cleves, Jülich, Berg, Cologne, Aachen, and Odenkirchen. New circles or churches likewise arose in Holstein, Wismar, and Rostock, although, next to Emden, their chief center was Schottland, the suburb of Danzig, where Dirk Philips lived. Anabaptist congregations existed in Elbing and Montau near Graudenz as early as 1552, and even in Wisby, Gothland.

Since Reformed Protestantism prevailed in nearly all these lands, the Mennonites were obliged to protect themselves against it, while the Reformed, in their turn, felt threatened by Anabaptism. The claims of the churches, their preachers, and their baptism to exclusive control over the people and to validity among them, as well as the official character of religion and the Church, were never recognized by the Mennonites, while their opponents assailed the Anabaptist views of the State, war, oaths, and similar tenets, but reserved their chief polemics for their doctrine of the incarnation. This dogma continued to be, as Hoffmann had taught, that the Son of God is man, and "was made flesh" (John i. 14), being transformed into man. Jesus received nothing in his conception by Mary, nor did he have a unity of two natures. The Reformed not unjustly charged the Mennonites with unitarianism. When the Dutch magistracy and church were reformed after the revolution of 1572, William of Orange protected the Anabaptists both in their civil and in their religious rights, although they were frequently assailed by the Reformed Church and its preachers. The communities and their doctrines thus gained safety in Holland, and enjoyed freedom of conscience after the Union of Utrecht in 1579.

As the Mennonites had saved their concept of a free church by bitter struggle from 1530 to 1580, so they were forced to endure internal strife for almost a century before their democracy could become independency. These problems found expression in the controversies over the ban and the avoidance of the faithful who had lapsed, as well as of everything connected with the secular church and religion. Their other characteristics were denial of original sin and emphasis of the freedom of the will, with a consequent standard of measurement in terms of morality, so that regeneration was the improvement of life, while they remained indifferent to all scholastic dogmas. It was doubtless from fear of exclusion from Christendom that Adam Pastor was attacked by Menno and banned by Dirk Philips for denying the Trinity, and asserting that Christ was one with the Father in works and purpose, but not in essence, else he could not have prayed to God in Gethsemane. In the eyes of the Mennonites neither baptism nor the Lord's Supper was, strictly speaking, a sacrament. In their gatherings only the Germans prayed audibly, which usage gradually permeated Holland also after the seventeenth century.

In 1555 the "Waterlanders" seceded from the strict Mennonites, rejecting the ban without previous warning, as well as avoidance of the lapsed in any relations except those of religion, and opposing patience and adaptability to the rigor of the elders. Between 1566 and 1567 the church was divided into the Frisians and the Flemings, the latter permitting themselves greater luxury in clothing, insisting on a more friendly attitude toward the world, and opposing certain organizing and centralizing measures of the elders. The result was unending division and subdivision, until after 1600 many adopted the point of view of the "Waterlanders," who regarded the church as an ordinance of man and granted the individual local congregations a considerable degree of self-government. In Holland, the government by elders was retained, however, by the "Old Frisians" and the "Old Flemings," who adhered most closely to tradition, until the end of the eighteenth century, while in Prussia and Russia it has survived until the present time, like rebaptism and the washing of feet, both of which disappeared in Holland about 1780.

2. In Holland and North Germany 1580 (1640)–1700: After the "Waterlanders" and their leader Hans de Ries (1553–1638) had striven from 1577 on to unite their own communities, and all others which were available, into an organic union free from a rigorous application of the ban, the milder Mennonites grew closer and closer together. Many "Waterlanders" attended the Frisian and High German conference at Cologne, May 1, 1591. Conventions of that sort were held occasionally until 1640. The conferences gave rise to the first symbolic writings of the Mennonites, such as the creed of Hans de Ries and Lubbert Gerrit at Cologne (1591), the symbol adopted at a conference between "Waterlanders" and a community of English Brownists or Independents (1615; see BROWNE, ROBERT; and CONGREGATIONALISM, I., 1, §§ 1–2), the creed of the olive-tree (1627) and of Jan Cents (1630) and the Dort symbol of Adrian Cornelisz (1632). All these symbolical statements were formulas of union, not of government in dogmatics.

A new factor had meanwhile entered the church. Since 1580 the unitarian tendency of the Mennonites had received fresh life from the Socinians, despite the opposition of Hans de Ries and others. The "Old Flemings," most strict in regard to the community and practical life, were the most liberal in doctrine. Many Mennonites stood in equally close relations with the Remonstrants, and sought their theological training in the Remonstrant seminary. Both parties furnished recruits for the Collegians or Rhynsburgers, who in 1622 borrowed from the Socinians baptism by immersion. This entire Socinian and anti-ecclesiastical rationalistic tendency was blended with pietistic elements, but an intense opposition developed, which led at Amsterdam in 1664 to a division between the liberals and the conservatives. Almost without exception the Dutch churches took sides with one faction or the other, but the controversy was of short duration, and the two parties were working together in brotherly harmony in 1672, although the dual administration continued in Amsterdam until 1801.

Throughout the seventeenth century the Mennonites were opposed by the Reformed as despising the Church and denying Christian doctrines, original sin, predestination, and the divinity of Christ, although their principle of non-resistance and their refusal to take oaths were respected. They were debarred, however, like all the non-Reformed, from official positions. Notwithstanding this, their numbers and their wealth rendered them an influential body. Between 1580 and 1600 they counted at least 200,000 adherents, more than a tenth of the population, and they included some of the greatest artists, poets, and engineers of Holland's prime. Since the Reformed theological faculties were closed to them, they devoted themselves chiefly to medicine and science. It was not until the eighteenth century that they had salaried pastors who did not occupy themselves with other callings.

3. In Holland 1700–1909: The Mennonites and the Remonstrants were the most zealous adherents and propagandists of the scientific and philosophical doctrines of the illumination which made headway in Holland in the eighteenth century. They grudged neither financial nor diplomatic aid in behalf of their oppressed coreligionists in Switzerland, the Palatinate, Jülich, Poland, and Lithuania, while they became more and more convinced that all ecclesiastical distinction was antiquated. Additional elements of dissolution were the sympathy felt for the Moravians by the pietistic party among them, the restriction of public office to those who belonged to the Reformed Church, and the frequent lack of preachers in the country districts. Increasing numbers joined the established church, and neither the theological seminary founded by the community at Amsterdam in 1735 nor the unions of congregations for mutual financial and spiritual support could check the movement. In 1808 the Mennonites numbered but 28,000. This decline was ended, however, by the foundation of the *Algemeene Doopsgezinde Sociëteit* at Amsterdam in 1811, which took charge of the theological seminary and the care of needy communities. Now all congregations have ministers who have received academic training. The Mennonites now have 134 communities with 126 preachers and 60,000 adherents, almost 10,000 being in Amsterdam. The other Protestants are no longer hostile to them; their pastors frequently officiate in the churches of other denominations, and *vice versa*, and the teachers in their theological seminary rank as professors of the University of Amsterdam. The fact that some of them represent orthodoxy in opposition to the prevalent rationalism does not destroy their inherent unity. They are associated with their coreligionists outside of Holland chiefly by their board of foreign missions which works in Java and Sumatra. Their hostility to the State has disappeared, many of the congregations receive state aid, and Mennonites now take part in public office. Their distinctive features are abstinence from taking oaths, adult baptism, and the substitution of moral earnestness and piety for dogma. The congregations possess full autonomy, and are directed by the preacher, who need have no official authorization or qualification, and by the deacons, who are chosen by all members, male and female.

V. On the Lower Rhine, and in North Germany and Russia 1700-1909: During the period of oppression, which lasted until 1720, the majority of the Mennonites in Jülich, Berg, Cleves, and neighboring districts emigrated to Holland, while many settled in Crefeld, where they came in contact with such pietists as Hochmann and Tersteegen. This community still flourishes, like that in Altona and the congregations in East Friesland. The chief Mennonite center of Germany, however, is West Prussia, where the body numbers 11,000 out of a total in Germany of 18,000. All these communities have passed through the same stages as their Dutch coreligionists, although the two bodies have been far less closely associated since 1780. They maintained their doctrine of non-resistance until 1868, when political equality and the growth of culture put an end to their isolation from their fellow citizens. To avert the danger of absorption into larger religious bodies, the Vereinigung der Mennonitengemeinden im deutschen Reiche was founded at Hamburg in 1884. The chief organ of the German Mennonites is the *Mennonitische Blätter*, established in 1854.

The Russian grant of large territories and the unrestricted right of religious freedom led a few thousand Mennonites to emigrate from Prussia to Russia in 1788, where they received numerous accessions until 1824. They now have, together with the followers of Hutter, who in 1874 emigrated from Hungary to the United States, 70,000 members, and are settled in the governments of Yekaterinoslav, Taurida, Warsaw, the Crimea, Saratof, Samara, the Caucasus, and Khiva. In their communities, which are sharply defined socially and economically, the churches and schools are excellently organized, the former being rigidly controlled, as in the rural congregations of Prussia, by elders and by preachers chosen from among the brethren and exercising their office in addition to their civil calling. They are noteworthy, moreover, for their industry, especially in agriculture. Thousands emigrated to America when military service was forced upon them. Immigrant Prussians have also founded communities in Galicia. All these congregations have been affected by the activity of Baptist and Methodist missionaries, and are characterized by a liberal spirit, although they are tenacious of their ancient customs and still faithful to their old doctrines of sobriety, independence, and separation of Church and State.

VI. The South German and Swiss Mennonites 1600-1909: Throughout the seventeenth century the Mennonites were subject to oppression from the Swiss governments, nor was it until 1715 that imprisonment and deportation to the Italian galleys ceased at Zurich. In Bern, on the other hand, the emigration, with the financial assistance of the Dutch, of all Mennonites whom the government could seize, that they might seek new homes in America, was powerless to prevent the continuance of churches in the Emmenthal, the bishopric of Basel, and Neuenburg, which have survived to the present day. Their organ is the *Zionspilger*. After 1600 a large number of Mennonites was settled by Alsacian nobles on their estates, where they amalgamated with older Anabaptist communities and still exist, like their French-speaking coreligionists in eastern France. In the nineteenth century their numbers were much diminished by emigration to America. Many also entered the Palatinate, and thence sought America, after accepting the rigid teachings of Jacob Amman, who, about 1690, introduced into the highlands of Bern the doctrines of avoidance of all under the ban, the washing of feet, and the condemnation of such luxuries as the use of buttons on clothing, thus founding the "Amish" sect. The fate of the followers of Hutter was most pathetic. Driven from Moravia in 1622, they settled in Hungary and Transylvania, where they renounced their communism in 1685. They were unable, however, to make headway against the Jesuits after 1680, and entered the Roman Catholic Church in increasing numbers subsequent to 1762.

VII. In the United States and Canada 1683-1909: Mennonites from the Netherlands and Holstein settled in New Amsterdam (New York) as early as 1650, and on Oct. 6, 1683, thirteen families from Crefeld occupied the territory on the Delaware which they had purchased from Penn, and founded Germantown, now a part of Philadelphia. In 1688 their numbers were augmented by coreligionists from the Palatinate and Crefeld, and they began an emigration which lasted throughout the eighteenth and nineteenth centuries. After 1820 they received new additions from Switzerland and South Germany, while they were joined by entire communities of Russians subsequent to 1870. Many American Mennonites stood in close relations with the Quakers, the Schwenkfeldians, and other bodies. Others, however, maintained their individuality, usually separating themselves rigidly from all others. These still retain the washing of feet and excommunication in case of mixed marriage. Only after long deliberation did they permit elders who had not received the laying on of hands in Europe to administer baptism and the Lord's Supper. The majority of Mennonites cling to their past, remembering with pride their protest against slavery as early as 1688, and still retaining, after the lapse of two centuries, their Anglicized Rhenish German dialect ("Pennsylvania Dutch"). As in the case of the Quakers, their principle of non-resistance was respected both in the Revolution and in the Civil War, although in 1786 many, disapproving of the resistance to England, emigrated to Canada, where their numbers were much increased especially by Russian immigrants to Manitoba in 1874.

The Mennonites now number some 250,000, of whom 60,000 are in Holland, 18,000 in Germany, 1,500 in Switzerland, 800 in France, 800 in Poland and Galicia, 70,000 in Russia, 20,000 in Canada, and more than 80,000 in the United States. In Germany their numbers are decreasing, but in Holland they remain stationary, while they are increasing in Russia and the United States. In Holland and North Germany they possess no unifying doctrine, the most rationalistic unitarianism existing side by side with pietistic orthodoxy. Their distinguishing characteristics are their doctrines of opposition to all ecclesiastical control, personal responsibility, autonomy of the churches, freedom of conscience, separation of Church and State, and a practical piety, devoid of dogma but manifested in domestic and economic virtues. Their external tokens are adult baptism, avoidance of taking oaths, non-resistance, and, with some, the washing of feet as a symbol of the equality of all in ministering love. Their churches are essentially voluntary and family organizations, and this fact explains even more than the long periods of persecution which they have endured, and their resultant caution, their reluctance to receive new members. Although they defend their own doctrines, they do not polemize against others. S. CRAMER.

VIII. In America.—1. Antecedents: Of the various bodies of Mennonites in America some represent schisms and subdivisions from the church in which Menno Simons was the most prominent leader, while others antedate Menno's renunciation of the Church of Rome. The modern Mennonites are the direct successors of three distinct Anabaptist denominations of the Reformation time—the Swiss Brethren, Obbenites, and Hutterites.

1. Swiss Brethren.

The Swiss Brethren, the leading Anabaptist denomination of Switzerland and southern Germany, were first organized at Zurich, in Jan., 1525. Their first leaders were Conrad Grebel, Felix Manz, Georg Blaurock, Michael Sattler, and Pilgram Marbeck (q.v.). The Swiss Brethren were the only Anabaptist body in South Germany and Switzerland that survived the relentless persecution of the dissenters. Their principal stronghold was Strasburg, where their sufferings stopped short with banishment, confiscation, and imprisonment. As to their doctrinal position there are extant various reliable sources, such as the confession of Schlatten (1527, republished by W. Köhler, Giessen, 1908; cf. the articles of Kautz in *Selected Works of Huldreich Zwingli*, ed. S. M. Jackson, pp. 177 sqq., Philadelphia, 1901); the protocols of the disputations of Zofingen (1532), St. Gall (1532), and Frankenthal (1571); the proceedings of a number of conferences, held at or near Strasburg, in 1555, 1557, 1568, and 1607, at Obersülzen (exact date unknown) and at Offstein in 1688; also numerous epistles and the *Ausbund*, the hymnal of this denomination, published for the first time in 1570 or 1571 (R. Wolkan, *Die Lieder der Wiedertäufer*, p. 122, Berlin, 1903), which has been reprinted for the tenth time, Lancaster, Pa., 1908, besides editions published at Elkhart, Ind. From Menno Simons the Swiss Brethren differed on certain points to which Menno ascribed great importance. Between 1693 and 1700 Jacob Amann, a Swiss minister, began to insist on the avoidance of the excommunicated, as taught by Menno; his agitation resulted in a schism which has continued to this day. The followers of Amann, called Amannite or Amish Brethren, number now over 15,000 in America, although only the Old Order Amish have retained all their former peculiarities. After the secession of the Amish from the Swiss Brethren, the latter were sometimes named Reist Brethren, from Hans Reist, their leading minister at the time of the schism. The largest Mennonite body in America, known in some states as "Old Mennonite," descends from the Swiss (Reist) Brethren, whom they follow in doctrine and practise. Both the Reist and Amish Brethren, with the exception of the Old Order Amish, have in South Germany and America adopted the name Mennonite; in Switzerland and France this name is not officially used by them.

2. Obbenites.

On the relation of the Swiss Brethren to Menno Simons, it is first of all to be said that Menno's sphere of influence was confined to the Netherlands and northern Germany where Dutch or Low German was the vernacular. In 1536 Menno Simons (see SIMONS, MENNO), until then a Roman Catholic priest, united with a sect called Obbenites, from Obbe Philips. These people had only a few years prior renounced Romanism to become adherents of Melchior Hoffmann (q.v.). For a short time Hoffmann practised the baptism of adults only and rejected infant baptism, hence he is generally considered an Anabaptist; but he soon suspended this practise and a few years later expressly sanctioned the baptism of infants, while refusing to recant other teachings upon which he placed greater importance (Hulshof, *Geschiedenis van de Doopsgezinden te Straatsburg*, p. 180, Amsterdam, 1905). Offensive to Lutherans and Swiss Brethren alike was his faith in the prophecies of Ursula Jost of Strasburg, whose visions date from the year 1524. Hoffmann accepted her dreams as divinely inspired and consequently believed great changes in Church and State to be imminent, and that a wonderful period of liberty of conscience and missionary activity (not the millennium) was close at hand. Hoffmann developed a peculiar doctrine on the incarnation—that Christ's human nature as well as his divine nature was of heaven. He also taught the sinlessness of believers and other doctrines that were regarded as unscriptural by the Swiss Brethren, whom he considered outside of true spiritual enlightenment. His followers were known as the Melchiorites. After Hoffmann's imprisonment in Strasburg in 1533, Jan Matthysen, a baker of Haarlem, the founder of the sect of the Münsterites, arose among his followers, proclaiming, on the ground of revelations with which he had been favored, that the time when the persecution was to cease was now at hand and the saints themselves were to be used of God to inaugurate a new order of things. A new state church was to be established, not like the Roman Catholic and Protestant state churches, in which saint and sinner alike were compelled by the State to hold membership, but one which should be truly the communion of the saints and used of God to bring judgment upon those who had deserved it. It is worthy of notice that some of the most offensive teachings and appalling excesses of the Münsterites are of later date (see MUENSTER, ANABAPTISTS IN). Matthysen's principal opponent from the ranks of the Melchiorites was Obbe Philips, who, with his brother Dirk, not only saw in him a wolf in sheep's clothing and a fanatic, but also realized that some of Melchior Hoffmann's ideas and teachings were unsound. Obbe and his friends became strict Biblicists; the Word of God was the only standard of doctrine and the New Testament the rule of life and practise; special revelations were considered dangerous and unnecessary. Christian believers must bear the cross and follow the lowly and non-resistant Nazarene; they must suffer with him if they would reign with him in the world which is to come. Only those who are willing to follow in the footsteps of the Savior and have been baptized upon the confession of their faith may be members of Christ's church. Without fear or favor Obbe Philips excommunicated all who yielded to Münsterite influences, no one being permitted to keep company with them or eat with them (according to I Cor. v. 11). This was the beginning of the practise of the avoidance of the excommunicated which was destined to lead to endless disputes and various schisms among the Mennonites. The latter name superseded the designation Obbenites after Obbe Philips had (in 1540) withdrawn from that body and Menno Simons had become their principal leader. Menno's writings afford thorough information regarding the doctrines, practises and aims of the Obbenites. Menno testifies that the Obbenites, when he identified himself with them, were "unblamable in doctrine and life," in other words, their characteristics did not undergo a change through his influence. This statement is corroborated by other evidence and is entirely trustworthy. Hoffmann's doctrine of the perfection of believers and of the impossibility of obtaining forgiveness for sins that have been knowingly committed after regeneration was rejected by the Obbenites. They insisted on the strict avoidance of the excommunicated except in cases of emergency; even the marital relation must, in a given case, be suspended. The refusal of the Waterlander churches, in Holland, to sanction marital avoidance led to the first schism among the followers of Menno, in 1555. It was on "avoidance" and on the incarnation that the Swiss Brethren differed from Menno and his friends. The former held a conference at Strasburg in South Germany in 1555 and again in 1557 and stated their position on these points. The conference of 1557 wrote a friendly letter to Menno Simons pleading for union and brotherhood notwithstanding the prevailing differences. But Menno held that a doctrine of the Scriptures was at stake. In his opinion the rejection of "avoidance" was a matter of grave importance. At the disputation of Frankenthal in the Palatinate, in 1571, the Swiss Brethren declared that "Menno is not and never has been of one mind with us." They never accepted his teaching on the points in question, although some of them, at a much later date, adopted the name Mennonites, recognizing in Menno Simons the principal representative and expositor of their fundamental teachings.

3. Two Groups of Churches.

Among those Mennonites whose ancestors were the followers of Menno Simons two great groups are to be distinguished: (1) The churches of Holland and of northwestern Germany; (2) the churches of West Preussen, a province of Prussia, including their descendants in Russia and America. All Mennonites of South Russia, as well as those who emigrated from Russia and Prussia to America are the descendants of the churches of West Preussen. They are principally of Dutch ancestry. About the middle of the sixteenth century a number of Netherlandish families fled to what is now West Preussen, but was then a part of Poland. The majority of the Mennonites of this group, numbering not less than 110,000 souls of whom at least 30,000 are found in America, descended from those Dutch fugitives. They continued to use the Dutch language in worship until after the middle of the eighteenth century. The fact deserves notice that the number of family names in this group is surprisingly small; most of the names are represented by a large number of families; and the names found in the Russian Mennonite settlements in America are the same as those of the Mennonites of West Preussen and Russia. Emigration from Prussia to Russia began in 1788, and from both these countries to America in 1874. The language of all Mennonites of this group, including those of Russia, is German. While the churches of this group, as well as those who are the descendants of the Swiss Brethren, are thoroughly and conservatively orthodox on such leading doctrines as the Trinity, the deity of Christ, the atonement, the inerrancy of the Scriptures, the resurrection, etc., the Mennonites of Holland and northwestern Germany are of a decidedly liberal, rationalistic type. The supposition advanced by some of them that early Mennonite teaching had a liberalistic tendency has never been established by evidence. The more liberal wing of the early Mennonites, the Waterlanders who seceded from the main body in 1555, accepted unreservedly orthodox doctrines, as is established by their comprehensive confession of 1577. The confessions of all other Mennonite factions teach the same doctrines. Menno Simons, as well as Dirk Philips, a coworker with Menno, was orthodox on the preexistence and deity of Christ. It was at a much later date that the churches of Holland and northwestern Germany accepted rationalistic views. These churches are to-day scarcely holding their own as far as numbers are concerned. The *Vereinigung der Mennonitengemeinden im deutschen Reiche,* comprising a minority only of the Mennonites of the fatherland, is dominated by rationalistic influences, and consequently the churches of West Preussen, Baden, Württemberg, Alsace-Lorraine and most of those of Bavaria are holding aloof from this body. The organ of the "evangelical" Mennonites of Germany is *Das Gemeindeblatt*, Reihen, Baden. The principles of non-resistance and the rejection of the oath are upheld by well-nigh all American Mennonites. In Russia Mennonites are required, instead of serving in the army, to labor in the forestry work of the State. In Prussia they have the privilege of serving as nurses or drivers in the army.

In some of the Mennonite bodies in America various practises are in vogue which can be explained only from their history; particularly is this true of the Old Order Amish. It is improbable that any other denomination was called upon to endure so relentless persecution as the Swiss Brethren in the cantons of Zurich and Bern (cf. E. Müller, *Geschichte der bernischen Täufer*, Frauenfeld, 1895). In consequence of their principle of non-resistance to which they strictly adhered, they were truly "as sheep for the slaughter." The severest persecution notwithstanding, extending over a period of over two hundred years, small churches continued to exist in the mountains of the canton Bern. When some of the oppressed found it possible to assemble for worship, the services were several hours in length. The members were scattered over a large territory and the paths over the mountains were difficult at best, consequently it was found necessary to provide a meal for the worshipers. This meal, coming after the services, attained a semi-religious significance which it retains among the Old Order Amish Brethren, the brother in whose house the meeting is held being the host of the congregation. The custom of the ministers to enter the audience room after the congregation has sung some hymns, dates from the time when oppression had taken the place of bloody persecution, and orders were to apprehend the ministers only.

2. Doctrinal and Statistical Description: The Mennonites in America are divided in general into Old Mennonites, General Conference, Mennonite Brethren in Christ, Mennoniten Brüder Gemeinde, Reformed Mennonites, and Old Order Amish.

The **Old Mennonites** are of "Pennsylvania Dutch" stock and of Swiss descent. They have an actual membership of about 29,000 in the United States and Canada (about 8,000 in Lancaster County, Pa.). They observe as ordinances, besides baptism of believers only (by affusion) and the Lord's Supper, feet-washing, the anointing of the sick, the kiss of charity, and the literal application of I Cor. xi. 5. Their meeting-houses are quite plain; instrumental music is not tolerated in worship. The churches are, as a rule, well supplied with ministers who are chosen from the brotherhood, special preparation not being considered essential for candidates. In case of more than one receiving the votes of the congregation, decision is obtained by lot. Few of the ministers receive financial support. Stipulated ministerial salaries are considered unscriptural. Discipline is strictly enforced. Prior to every communion service a "counsel meeting" is held to ascertain whether any member who has given offense has refused to make amends after brotherly reminder by one or two other members. In case of serious offense a public confession by the offender is asked. Only those at peace with the church and who confess peace with God may partake of the Lord's Supper. Simplicity of attire, as opposed to the ever-changing whims of fashion, is held to be a Scriptural requirement. Titles, such as Mr. or Rev., are not in use. Members of secret societies are excluded. Oaths are forbidden, as well as suits at law. Non-resistance and the condemnation of war are emphatically insisted upon. This branch of the denomination has a flourishing mission with asylums for orphans and lepers in India, home missions in various cities (three in Chicago), also orphans' homes, homes for the aged, and a sanitarium. Their church organ is the *Gospel Herald*, published at Scottdale, Pa., by the Mennonite Publishing House, which is owned and controlled by the church. Books and tracts on the doctrine and history of the church are also published. The works of Menno Simons and of his coworker Dirk Philips, as well as the comprehensive work on the martyrs of the church by Braght, are common possessions. Goshen College, Goshen, Ind., their largest institution of higher education in America, also Hesston Academy, Hesston, Kans., belong to this branch of Mennonites.

The **General Conference Mennonites,** the most progressive branch of the denomination, consisting principally of German congregations which have immigrated to the western states from Russia and Prussia, have over 13,000 members. They have abandoned most of the former peculiarities. Bethel College, Newton, Kans., is their most prominent institution of learning, besides Bluffton College, Bluffton, Ohio. They have prosperous missions among the Indians of Oklahoma and in India. Their organs are *Der Bundesbote* and *The Mennonite*, both published by the Mennonite Book Concern, Berne, Ind.

The **Mennonite Brethren in Christ,** numbering about 6,000 members, form a very active church. They baptize by immersion, have open communion and practise feet-washing as an ordinance. Their camp and revival meetings are conducted after the fashion of the early Methodists. They support about thirty foreign missionaries. Their organ is *The Gospel Banner*, of Cleveland, O.

The **Mennoniten Brüdergemeinde** consists of German colonists who immigrated to the western states from Russia. They do not agree among themselves on the administration of baptism. The larger branch (with nearly 5,000 members), having been under English Baptist influence in Russia, immerse the applicant for baptism forward while the Crimean branch insist on backward immersion. The latter have nearly 1,000 members. The organ of the former body is *Der Zionsbote*, published at McPherson, Kans. Tabor College, Hillsboro, Kans., belongs to this branch. They have mission stations in India and Oklahoma.

The **Reformed Mennonites,** called also Herrites after their founder John Herr (who in 1812 seceded from the Old Mennonites), have about 1,700 members, living mostly in Pennsylvania. Considered even from the view-point of Menno Simons, they are ultraconservative. The well-known novel, *Tillie, a Mennonite Maid* (New York, 1904), by H. R. Martin, is designed to portray life among them.

The **Old Order Amish,** who about 1690 seceded from the Mennonites in Switzerland and Alsace, have about 4,500 members. Their congregations are necessarily small, owing to the fact that they do not build meeting-houses. They meet for worship in dwelling-houses or barns. In their opinion, under the Christian dispensation one place can not surpass another in sanctity. There must be no other house of God than his true spiritual house, the church. The fact that Solomon, at God's command, built a temple is to be considered in the same light as the sacrificial offerings under the old covenant. The principal purpose of the Mosaic ceremonies and law was to typify Christ and the New Covenant. Various usages that were permitted under the old covenant, such as resistance by force, the taking of human life, the swearing of oaths, and divorce, were abolished by Christ, who fulfilled the whole law. The Old Testament is to be interpreted in the light of the New which alone is the Christian's rule of life and worship. Building church-houses would be the first step toward ritualism, which is utterly foreign to New-Testament teaching and would mean death to true Christian piety. Among the Old Order Amish services are conducted exclusively in the German language and ordinarily require about four hours, while on communion Sunday they are continued from morning till dusk without intermission, there being always a number of ministers present. No text is taken on such occasions; the sermon begins, after introductory remarks, with the first parents of the human race and covers the content of Scripture. The subject may be said to be the wickedness of sin and the faithfulness of God toward those who love him and keep his commandments. Their hymnal is still the *Ausbund*, the old hymn-book of the Anabaptist Swiss Brethren, which was published for the first time in 1571 and reprinted at least twelve times in America. The hymns are sung to what are supposed to be the original tunes, which have never been written in musical notation. After meeting, dinner is served for the whole congregation by the family with whom the meeting convenes. There is no church property except hymnbooks, plain benches, and the utensils necessary to prepare a plain dinner for the worshipers. They may be said to live in a voluntary semi-communism. Their apparel and houses are kept exceedingly plain and unassuming. Carpets, curtains and wall pictures are forbidden, as is also property insurance. Their largest settlements are found in Pennsylvania, Ohio, Indiana, and Ontario.

Besides these divisions there are a number of smaller Mennonite bodies.

The **Hutterites** have about fourteen prosperous churches or communities in South Dakota, whither they immigrated from South Russia in 1874. They name themselves "Hutterite Brethren" from Jacob Hutter who was burned at the stake at Innsbruck in the Tyrol in Feb., 1536. Their organization dates from the year 1533. Although never in any sense identified with or influenced by Mennonites, they hold the same doctrines and principles excepting on one point: they are strict communists—the oldest communistic society in the United States. Their communism is based entirely upon religious principles. It is to be noted, however, that one of these congregations has discarded the doctrine of community of goods. By this denominational body the principle of non-resistance is carried to the extent of disapproval of the payment of war taxes. From the fact that their communities in Dakota are known as Bruderhöfe they received in the United States census bulletins the name **Bruderhof Mennonites,** which, as already indicated, is not the name by which they prefer to be known. More than usual interest attaches to them because of their possession of numerous early documents of considerable historic value. Among these is the important and comprehensive confession of faith by Peter Riedemann (d. 1566), which was reprinted, *Rechenschaft unserer Religion* , n.p., 1902; also some valuable "chronicles" which have been collected and published by Joseph Beck, *Die Geschichtsbücher der Wiedertäufer*, Vienna, 1883. Their hymns have been collected but not published by R. Wolkan.

The **Old Colony Churches** (a name given to them in Russia), a body which has never deviated in doctrine or practise (including "avoidance") from the early Mennonites, are in Manitoba and Saskatchewan. They constitute a distinct body numbering a few thousand members. Their recent elder Johann Wiebe was a man of extraordinary abilities as a preacher and leader. Another small body of the same descent, known as **Die kleine Gemeinde,** has also perpetuated old Mennonite customs and usages. They have a few hundred members in Manitoba and Kansas.

Among the most conservative descendants of the Swiss (Reist) Brethren is a small body, called the **Old Swiss,** which has a few congregations in Ohio and Indiana. The **Conservative Amish Mennonites** differ from the Old Order Amish in that they have meeting-houses and are somewhat less strict in discipline. They have about 2,000 members. The most progressive body of Amish Mennonites, the **Independent Mennonites** of Illinois, have a number of churches and about 1,000 members. The **Defenseless Mennonites** date from the year 1866 when Jacob Egli, of Indiana, seceded from the Old Order Amish on the ground that definite conversion and religious experience had not a sufficiently prominent place in Amish teaching. They have a number of congregations. Their English organ is *Zion's Call* (Gridley, Ill.). The **Wisler Mennonites** represent a schism from the Old Mennonites, from whom they seceded in 1870, believing them to be too progressive in such innovations as continued meetings and general aggressiveness. They have a few thousand members in the United States and Canada. JOHN HORSCH.

BIBLIOGRAPHY: The reader should consult the literature under ANABAPTISTS, while part of that under BAPTISTS contains pertinent matter. The articles on the leaders named in the text and that on SIMONS, MENNO, also contain references to a rich literature. Consult further: S. Blaupot ten Cate, *Geschiedenis der Doopsgezinden*, 5 parts, Leeuwarden and Amsterdam, 1839–47; R. Baird, *Religion in U. S. A.*, pp. 593–594, Glasgow, 1844; B. Ely, *Kurzgefasste Kirchen-Geschichte und Glaubenslehre der taufgesinnten Christen und Menoniten*, n.d., Lancaster, Pa.; the periodical *Doopsgezinde Bijdragen*, 1860 sqq.; J. F. Funk, *The Mennonite Church and her Accusers*, Elkhart, Ind., 1878; D. Musser, *The Reformed Mennonite Church*, Lancaster, 1878; F. Ellis and S. Evans, *Hist. of Lancaster Co., Pa.*, chap. xxvii., Lancaster, n.d.; A. Brons, *Ursprung und Schicksale der Taufgesinnten oder Mennoniten*, Norden, 1884; M. Schoen, *Das Mennonitenthum in Westpreussen*, Berlin, 1886; B. C. Roosen, *Geschichte der Mennoniten-Gemeinde zu Hamburg und Altona*, 2 parts, Hamburg, 1886–87; A. Klaus, *Unsere Kolonien in Russland*, Odessa, 1887; J. P. Müller, *Die Mennoniten in Ostfriesland*, Emden, 1887; H. C. Vedder, *Short Hist. of the Baptists*, pp. 103–106, Philadelphia, 1891; idem, *The Baptists*, pp. 24 sqq., New York, 1903; T. Armitage, *Hist. of the Baptists*, pp. 51, 366, New York, 1893; J. Loserth, *Anabaptismus in Tirol*, Vienna, 1892; idem, *Communismus der mährischen Wiedertäufer*, ib. 1894; A. H. Newman, in *American Church History Series*, vol. ii. passim, New York, 1894; idem, *Hist. of Anti-Pedobaptism*, pp. 296 sqq., Philadelphia, 1897; C. H. A. Smissen, *Kurzgefasste Geschichte der Täufer*, Summerfield, Ill., 1895; H. P. Krehbiel, *Hist. of the General Conference of the Mennonites of North America*, Canton, Ohio, 1898; G. Tumbült, *Die Wiedertäufer*, Bielefeld, 1899; Wedel, *Geschichte der Mennoniten*, 4 vols., Newton, Kans., 1900–02; E. C. Pike, *The Story of the Anabaptists*, London, 1904; C. H. Smith, *The Mennonites of America*, Goshen, Ind., 1909.

MENOLOGION: The equivalent in the Greek Church of the *Calendarium* and *Martyrologium* of the Latin Church. It contains a list of the festivals in honor of the saints and martyrs, together with short notices of the life and death of the saint or martyr celebrated. It is not to be confused with the Menaion (q.v.), which contains the offices for the day as well as the "Acts" of the saint. The basis of the present Menologion was laid in 886 under the Emperor Basil. See ACTA MARTYRUM, ACTA SANCTORUM, II., § 1.

MENSES PAPALES ("PAPAL MONTHS"): A term applied to the pope's right of making appointments to certain benefices falling vacant in certain specified months, while the bishops and other patrons appointed in the remaining months. The arrangement is set down in the Roman chancery regulations, under No. IX. The point should be particularly noted that in common parlance the expression "papal months" is incorrectly supposed to mean the same as odd months, alternating months, *alternativa mensium*, while in fact the papal months are January, February, April, May, July, August, October, and November. There is one defined exception to the rule as stated, and this is specifically laid down in the chancery regulations, namely, that in favor of the patriarchs, archbishops, and bishops who contemplate personal residence in their sees, the eight papal months are reduced to six, and in such fashion that the pope has reserved for himself only the six odd months (January, March, May, July, September, November).

The origin of the papal months rests on the following facts. From the twelfth century, the popes began to recommend incumbents for vacant benefices in case of particular churches, at first through the channel of written requests (*preces*); and if this proved ineffectual, they would then supply the place with the designated incumbent, by a mandatory rescript (*mandatum de providendo*). When the mandate itself was not observed, it was customary to issue, in due succession, *literæ monitoriæ, præceptoriæ* and *executoriæ* (briefs of admonition, injunction, and execution); and then, if necessary, the "execution" followed. Since these mandates came to be issued, for the most part, in favor of indigent petitioners, such concessions were styled *per formam communem*, or *in forma pauperum*. Before long, however, the issue of *mandata de providendo* was applied to benefices not only actually but also prospectively vacant, which involved a violation of a provision of the Lateran Council of 1179, forbidding the bestowal of a contingent incumbency. A regulation of the practise was undertaken by the Council of Basel (1418) and by the Concordat of Vienna 1448; though it came to be much modified later by custom and by special indults.

The right of the papal months is still in existence, although with fresh modifications in modern times, or under special agreements. Thus the Bavarian concordat of 1817 provides that the king shall appoint two canonries in the six apostolic or papal months. In the case of Prussia, the bull *De salute animarum* (1821) decrees "from this time forth, canonries falling vacant in the months of January, March, May, July, September and November, shall be bestowed in the manner hitherto observed in the Chapter of Breslau." In Breslau, by virtue of his title as sovereign duke of Silesia, the king had exercised the right of nomination to vacant canonries in the odd months, the bishop supplying credentials as to canonical fitness, whereupon the papal brief of provision was issued. In various other countries, the papal months have lapsed along with other curial reservations; as in Hanover, the territories belonging to the ecclesiastical province of the Upper Rhine, etc. E. SEHLING.

MENTAL HEALING. See PSYCHOTHERAPY.

MENTZER, BALTHASAR: The name of four German scholars.

1. **Balthasar the Elder:** Theologian; b. at Allendorf (11 m. e. of Marburg) Feb. 27, 1565; d. at Marburg Jan. 6, 1627. After preliminary studies at the gymnasium at Hersfeld, he entered the University of Marburg in 1583; became pastor at Kirtorf in 1589; and professor at Marburg in 1596, enjoying the friendship of Ludwig III., landgrave of Hesse, until the latter's death in 1604. Mentzer was a strict adherent of Lutheran orthodoxy; the course of the new landgrave of Hesse-Cassel, Maurice, in favoring the Reformed type of doctrine was therefore a severe blow, intensified by the prohibition of discussions which involved the points at issue between Lutherans and Reformed and by the sending of advocates of the Reformed teachings to preach in Marburg. This gave an opportunity to the landgrave of Hesse-Darmstadt to interfere in the affairs of Hesse. He therefore, in 1605, invited Mentzer and two other professors to establish a gymnasium at Giessen for the protection of Lutheranism. The new institution was a success from the first, and this led to the founding

of the University of Giessen (1607), and Mentzer was one of the first professors chosen. When the political difficulties between the two landgraves ended in 1625, the university was transferred back to Marburg, and Mentzer was elected its first rector. In his new office he showed great zeal and ability, introducing new studies, taking great interest in the moral improvement of the students, and advising the theologians to refrain from mere scholasticism and to base their studies upon the Bible. He was an earnest, sincere, and devoted, if somewhat narrow, theologian. Practically all his writings were polemical, and had value only for his contemporaries. They were aimed in part at Johann Pistorius, Johann and Ludwig Crocius (qq.v.), and Anton Sadeel. Even his *Exegesis Augustanæ Confessionis* (Giessen, 1613) had a polemical purpose.

2. Balthasar II.: Theologian and diplomatist; son of the preceding; b. at Giessen May 14, 1614; d. at Darmstadt July 28, 1679. He was educated at the University of Marburg; accompanied Landgrave George II. on a journey to Saxony in 1631, and on his return finished his studies at Jena and Strasburg. He was appointed extraordinary professor at Marburg in 1640, and at the University of Rinteln in 1646; when the University of Giessen was reestablished in 1650, he was made professor of Hebrew and theology. He was, however, more at home in diplomacy and the landgrave made use of his talents in this direction. In 1652 Mentzer was appointed court preacher and superintendent at Darmstadt, and had ample opportunity for displaying his administrative talents. He was the constant companion of the landgrave in the latter's travels, and proved himself a capable diplomat. Several religious difficulties were settled satisfactorily through his skill and tact.

3. Balthasar III.: Mathematician, son of the preceding; b. at Rinteln Feb. 21, 1651; d. at Hamburg Mar. 8, 1727. In his sixteenth year he was elected professor of mathematics at the University of Giessen. He was a member of the orthodox party, and opposed the pietistic movement so energetically that he lost his position in 1693. A few years later he was chosen professor of mathematics at the Johanneum of Hamburg (a private institution).

4. Balthasar IV.: Theologian, son of the preceding; b. at Giessen Jan. 12, 1679; d. at Hanover Dec. 20, 1741. He studied philosophy and oriental languages at Leipsic and Wittenberg; spent some time in travel, then became pastor of the German Church in London in 1714; court preacher at Hanover, 1722; superintendent at Calenberg in 1726, and at Hanover, 1732. (Erwin Preuschen.)

Bibliography: The *Opera Latina* of Balthasar I. were published Frankfort, 1669, and contain a brief account of his life by his son-in-law, M. Hannecken; consult further for his life: F. W Strieder, *Hessische Gelehrten- und Schriftstellergeschichte*, viii. 418 sqq., Cassel, 1788 (contains on p. 424 a list of Balthasar's writings). On 2 consult: E. F. Neubauer, *Hessische Hebopfer*, i. 379 sqq., Giessen, 1734; F. W. Strieder, ut sup., viii. 442 sqq.; W. M. Becker, *Geschichte der Universität Giessen*, Giessen, 1907.

MENZIES, men'zez, ALLAN: Church of Scotland; b. at Edinburgh Jan. 23, 1845. He was educated at St. Andrews (M.A., 1864) and the universities of Edinburgh (B.D., 1868) and Erlangen. From 1873 to 1890 he was minister of the parish of Abernyte, Perthshire, and was also examiner in classics at St. Andrews from 1881 to 1884. Since 1889 he has been professor of divinity and Biblical criticism at St. Mary's College, St. Andrews. In 1897 he was elected president of the National Church Union, a position which he held for a number of years. He has translated F. C. von Baur's *Paulus, der Apostel Jesu Christi* (2d ed., 2 vols., Leipsic, 1866–67) and *Das Christentum und die christliche Kirche der drei ersten Jahrhunderte* (3d ed., Tübingen, 1863) under the titles *Paul, the Apostle of Jesus Christ* (London, 1876) and *The Church History of the First Three Centuries* (1879); J. Wellhausen's *Prolegomena zur Geschichte Israels* (2d ed., Berlin, 1883) under the title *Prolegomena to the History of Israel* (in collaboration with J. S. Black, Edinburgh, 1885); and also O. Pfleiderer's *Religionsphilosophie auf geschichtlicher Grundlage* (2d ed., 2 vols., Berlin, 1883–84) under the title *Philosophy of Religion* (in collaboration with A. Stewart; 4 vols., London, 1886–88), and has likewise edited the supplementary volume of the *Ante-Nicene Fathers* (New York, 1896) and the *Journal of Theology and Philosophy* since 1905. As independent works he has written, in addition to briefer contributions, *National Religion* (London, 1888); *The History of Religion* (1895); and *The Earliest Gospel* (1902).

MERCERSBURG THEOLOGY: A school of philosophy and theology which took its rise about 1836 in Marshall College and in the Theological Seminary of the German Reformed Church, then located at Mercersburg, Pa. It grew out of the contact between the modern Evangelical theology of Germany and Anglo-American church life, and quickened the German Reformed Church to new activity. It produced considerable fermentation and controversy, which affected also the Lutheran and other neighboring churches, but is now a matter of history, though its fruits remain. The movement had three phases. The first was philosophical (1836–43); the second was theological, and turned chiefly on the church question (1843–58); the third was liturgical (1858–66).

The leaders of this school of thought were F. A. Rauch, J. W. Nevin, and Philip Schaff (qq.v.), though Rauch's plans were frustrated by his premature death. Complementing each other reciprocally, Nevin and Schaff developed the ideas of Mercersburg theology in different ways. Nevin discussed the questions concerning the Church and the sacraments. Turning to Cyprian and the Nicene age, he represented the contrast between the church idea then extant and the sect system of the nineteenth century, but aimed chiefly to show that the Oxford Tractarian theory of repristination was historically untenable, and would lead logically to the whole system of the papacy. On the nature of the sacraments he reproduced the anti-Zwinglian and anti-Lutheran conception of John Calvin, which he held to be the true Reformed doctrine. Schaff, in his *Principle of Protestantism*, vindicated the doctrines of the Reformation on the basis of historical development, in decided opposition to Romanism and Puseyism on the one hand, and also to rationalism and sectarianism on the other. The Mercersburg school was charged with transcendentalism, mysticism, and Romanizing tendencies, but all these charges gradually subsided. A regular heresy trial was held at the synod of York in 1845, and again at two subsequent synods; but in each case the Mercersburg professors were acquitted by an almost unanimous vote.

Mercersburg theology taught that the divine-human person of Jesus Christ is the primordial truth of Christianity, both of revelation and redemption. From the Christ-idea, as the fundamental principle, are to be developed all scriptural doctrines. Issue was taken with the high Calvinistic principle of a twofold unconditional predestination, as well as with the contrary Arminian principle of free will, and no less decidedly, also, with the Roman system, which starts from the idea of the Church as a visible and centralized organization. Mercersburg was the first theological school in America to propound and vindicate what has since been called the "Christocentric" idea of Christianity. Jesus Christ, the incarnate Son of God, is the second Adam, the head of a regenerate human race. Born in him and of him, by the Holy Spirit, believers are his members. He, glorified in heaven, and they, though still in the flesh on earth, together constitute one mystical body, a spiritual organism. This is the Christian Church, holy, catholic, and apostolic. Of supernatural origin, invested with divine authority, possessing spiritual powers adequate to the fulfilment of her mission, instinct with heavenly life, and destined to overcome her enemies, she is the communion in which men may obtain salvation and eternal life. The Church, extending through all ages, and destined to embrace all nations, is ever identical with herself, having one Lord, one faith, one baptism; yet different phases of the fulness of her spiritual life, including doctrine and morals, cultus and ecclesiastical polity, appear at different epochs in her history. Hence no statements of doctrine formulated in any past age need be final, and no form of organization can be fixed and unchangeable. The Church modifies doctrinal formulas according to her progress in the knowledge of Christian truth, and adjusts her organization to the advanced status of her life and to her altered connections with the world. Christ perpetuates his mediatorial office by an order of chosen men, who, by the laying-on of hands, are duly invested with divine authority to speak in his name, to dispense the sacraments, and to bear rule as undershepherds over the flock. At the same time, Mercersburg always taught the general priesthood of the laity and the equality of ministers.

The sacraments of baptism and the Lord's Supper are not empty forms, but the significant signs and seals of God's covenant with us. They are means of grace which become efficacious by faith alone. By baptism, the subject is received into the covenant. The Lord's Supper is the commemoration of the once crucified but now glorified Christ, and the communion of his body and blood, wherein, by the impartation of his own divine-human fulness, he nourishes his people unto everlasting life. The contrary opinion, which then largely prevailed in the American churches, that baptism is only the empty symbol of forgiveness and of the new birth, and the Lord's Supper merely a celebration of the crucifixion of Christ, was sharply criticized. Mercersburg found fault with the common style of extemporaneous public prayer, and advocated a revival, in a modernized form, of the liturgical church-service of the Reformation period. The result was, *A Liturgy, or Order of Christian Worship* (Philadelphia, 1858), prepared by Schaff, Nevin, Harbaugh, Gerhart, and others, and a book of common prayer, entitled *An Order of Worship for the Reformed Church* (1866). Both, however, were merely optional, and not intended to supersede free prayer. A new German hymn-book was also prepared by Dr. Schaff (1859), which is now generally used in the German congregations of the Reformed Church.

The Mercersburg movement was Christological, and in close sympathy with the positive Evangelical theology of Protestant Germany, though necessarily modified by American surroundings and wants.

At present, the peculiar characteristics of the Mercersburg school are no longer distinctive, because similar Christological tendencies have since sprung up, and taken root in other denominations; hence former issues have been superseded. The formation of the General Synod in 1863 settled the doctrinal differences which had divided the church into two parties. See REFORMED CHURCH.

E. V GERHART†.

BIBLIOGRAPHY: F. A. Rauch, *Psychology*, New York, 1846; J. W. Nevin, *The Anxious Bench*, Chambersburg, 1843; *The Mystical Presence, a Vindication of the Reformed or Calvinistic Doctrine of the Holy Eucharist*, Philadelphia, 1846; idem, *The History and Genius of the Heidelberg Catechism*, Chambersburg, 1847, and his Introduction to the triglot tercentenary ed. of the *Heidelberg Catechism*, New York, 1863; idem, *Antichrist; or, the Spirit of Sect and Schism*, New York, 1848; P. Schaff, *The Principle of Protestantism as Related to the Present State of the Church*, Chambersburg, 1845; idem, *What is Church History? A Vindication of the Idea of Historical Development*, Philadelphia, 1846; E. V. Gerhart, in *Bibliotheca Sacra*, Jan., 1863, pp. 1–78; idem, *Institutes of the Christian Religion*, New York, 1891; H. Harbaugh, *Christological Theology*, Philadelphia, 1864; T. G. Apple, *The Theology of the German Reformed Church*, in the *Proceedings of the Second General Council of the Presbyterian Church, held in Philadelphia, 1880*, Philadelphia, pp. 484–497. Consult also *The Mercersburg Review*, vols. i.–xii., 1849–60; *Der deutsche Kirchenfreund*, 1848–54; *German Reformed Messenger; Minutes of the German Reformed Synod*, from 1843 to 1866; *The Provisional Liturgy*, Philadelphia, 1858; *The Order of Worship for the Reformed Church*, ib. 1867.

MERCY, SISTERS OF: The name of several religious congregations of women in the Roman Catholic Church.

1. Institute of Our Blessed Lady of Mercy: A congregation founded by Catherine Elizabeth McAuley (q.v.). The beginnings of this order go back to 1827 when the founder, then forty years of age, and having recently inherited a large fortune, established in Dublin (on the feast of Our Lady of Mercy, Sept. 24) an institution for the harboring of destitute women and orphans and for the aid of poor schools. The house was placed in charge of Miss Anna M. Doyle who was assisted in the school work by Miss Katherine Byrne. At that period there was no intention of founding a religious order, but rather of organizing a society of secular ladies who, between the period of leaving school and settling in life, might devote a portion of their time to the instruction of the poor and to other works of charity. But as several of her associates evinced a desire to make this a life-work and become sisters, Miss McAuley was led to establish, with the permission of the archbishop, a religious community under the title: "Institute of Our Blessed Lady of Mercy." In 1828 the members adopted a distinctive costume, but it was not until Dec. 12, 1831, after a year's novitiate in the Presentation Monastery of George's Hill, that they made their religious profession, taking the three vows according to the presentation form. Returning to their convent, Sister Mary Katherine was appointed superior by Dr. Murray, archbishop of Dublin, but for several years the institute had no written rule. The costume adopted by the foundress consists of a habit of coarse black serge, or cashmere, falling in folds from the throat to the feet in front, and lengthened into a train behind. It is confined to the waist by a leathern girdle, or cincture, on which the beads and cross of the order are suspended. The sleeves are long and wide, falling in plaits from the shoulders, with tight undersleeves. The habit and veil are very ample: the guimp is a deep linen collar, worn in front, and the coif, an envelop of the same material, covers the head, partly concealing the face. The rule of the institute, based on that of St. Augustine, was approved by Pope Gregory XVI. June 8, 1841. The specific objects of the order are the education of the poor, the visitation of the sick, and the protection of distressed women of good character. Besides the three ordinary vows of religion the sisters bind themselves to the service of the sick, the poor, and the ignorant, and they also take a vow of stability or perseverance in the institute. The order comprises two classes of sisters, choir and lay religious, and each separate community is subject canonically to the bishop of the diocese in which it is situated. Forty-three convents of the order were established before the death of the founder in 1841. There are houses of the order also in England, Scotland, Australia, and the United States. The Sisters of Mercy were first introduced into the United States in 1843 by Bishop O'Connor of Pittsburg, where the beginnings of the American foundation were materially furthered by the generosity of Miss Eliza Jane Tiernan who, on joining the community, bestowed upon it a large fortune inherited from her father. The development of the order in the United States was quite rapid, and it had in 1909 about forty mother houses in various cities from Maine to California. The sisters conduct schools, academies, hospitals, asylums, etc. The number of pupils under their charge is about 80,000, and the total number of professed sisters is about 4,500.

2. Sisters of Mercy of Seez, France: A congregation founded in 1823 in the diocese of Seez, France, by five pious women under the direction of a zealous priest, M. Bazin. They first took the name "Sisters of Charity," but in 1825 it was changed to "Sisters of Mercy" in order that the new community might be distinguished from that of the Sisters of Charity founded by St. Vincent de Paul. The object of the order is to minister to the spiritual and temporal needs of the sick, and especially of the poor in their homes. There are foundations of the order in England as well as in France.

3. Sisters of Mercy of Montreal (*Sœurs de la miséricorde*): A congregation established in Montreal, Quebec (where the mother house is located), by Bishop Ignatius Bourget in 1848. The foundress was Madame Rosalie Jetté (in religion, Mother Mary of the Nativity), but from the beginning she declined to accept the office of superior, and Sister St. Jane de Chantal was placed in charge. The specific object of the institute is to assist women in labor, both rich and poor, especially the latter, whom the sisters receive in their institutions or visit in their homes. In receiving patients no discrimination is made in respect to religion, color, nationality, or place of residence. No questions are asked, and all precautions are taken to protect the honor of patients and avert the crime of infanticide. The children are cared for both in the main institutions and in homes established especially for the purpose. Patients who desire to remain in the institution for a time after their convalescence are placed in charge of a sister. They follow a certain rule of life, without, however, contracting any religious obligation, and are known as "consecrated" (*consacrées*). If they choose to remain in the convent permanently and show the proper dispositions, they are allowed, after a period of probation, to become "Magdalens," and after a further probationary period they are admitted to take the vows of the subsidiary Magdalen order. The congregation is governed by a mother general who is elected every six years. The institute was approved by Pope Pius IX., June 7, 1867. These sisters have establishments not only in Canada, but also in New York, Chicago, Milwaukee, and Green Bay. JAMES F. DRISCOLL.

BIBLIOGRAPHY: Heimbucher, *Orden und Kongregationen*, iii. 386–387, 554; Currier, *Religious Orders*, pp. 576–578, 595; *Official Catholic Directory*, New York, 1909.

MERIBAH, mer'i-bā: A Hebrew word meaning "strife," apparently given as a name to two places where water was miraculously provided through Moses for the wandering Israelites. A critical problem is raised by the fact that two accounts are given in the Pentateuch of events closely resembling each other but apparently at different places. One account is in Ex. xvii. of occurrences at Horeb (verse 6), and to the place the name Massah was also given; another account is in Num. xx. 1–13 of occurrences apparently connected with Kadesh (cf. Num. xxvii. 14; Deut. xxxii. 51; Ezek. xlvii. 19, xlviii. 28). The Septuagint and Vulgate generally translate the word by expressions which mean "railing, reproach, irritation" (so the English A.V. of Ps. xcv. 8, "in the provocation"), a sense which would fit the context in Num. xx. 13, 24, xxvii. 14; Deut. xxxii. 51, xxxiii. 8; Ps. lxxxi.

7, xcv. 8, cvi. 32 (in the last two cases the English R.V margin explains "strife"). Ezekiel's mention implicitly connects the occurrence with Kadesh, and does not oppose the rendering of the word by "striving"; his mention does not even necessitate that such a place as Meriboth-kadesh or Meribath-kadesh (note the two forms!) existed in his day, since his scheme of the land and its partition is ideal. Attempts to locate the places serve only by the variance between scholars to emphasize the conclusion that the word is probably an appellative, not a proper name. GEO. W. GILMORE.

MERICI, ANGELA, SAINT: Founder of the Ursuline nuns (see URSULINES); b. at Desenzano (20 m. w. of Verona) Mar. 21, 1474; d. at Brescia Jan. 27, 1540. In early youth she became a Franciscan tertiary, and devoted herself to works of piety and charity while still living in the world. She was already fifty-six, however, before she was convinced by a vision that the time had come to carry out a long-cherished plan by founding an order of women devoted to works of mercy. She took a house in Brescia with twelve companions, and the order was formally established on Nov. 25, 1535. According to Angela's plan the members were not to leave the world but to live with their parents or other relatives, assembling for conference at stated times and observing various rules of conduct, though without the requirement of vows. At a chapter held in March, 1537, attended by fifty-nine out of the seventy-six sisters, Angela was unanimously elected mother superior, and by the influence of her holy life did much to strengthen the order in her few remaining years. She was buried in the church of St. Afra at Brescia; beatified in 1768; and canonized in 1807.

BIBLIOGRAPHY: *Das Leben der heiligen Angela Merici*, Augsburg, 1811; M. Sintzel, *Leben der heiligen Angela*, Regensburg, 1842; W. E. Hubert, *Die heilige Angela Merici*, Mainz, 1891; *Geschichte der heiligen Angela Merici und des . . . Ordens der Ursulinen*, Innsbruck, 1892; *Lebensgeschichte der heiligen Angela Merici*, Paderborn, 1892.

MERIT.

The conception "merit," in a religious-ethical sense, points to a fundamental opposition between Roman Catholicism and Protestantism. While the former recognizes merit as establishing a relation between man and God, the latter denies this absolutely. In the Roman Catholic view, religion is concerned with man's securing after his death eternal salvation from God as a reward for his merits; and under "merit" is understood works done voluntarily in the service of God constituting a claim on a reward from God. Connected with this is the narrower conception of merit as something done beyond the normal measure of ordinary duty. The origin of the religious conception of merit is to be found in Jewish practical piety, in the thought of a legal relation between God and mankind. But in post-exilic Judaism the idea became more usual that there was to be a retribution for service of God after death, limited, however, to the good and the pious. The classical example of this view is found in the book of Tobit: "If thou servest God it will be requited thee" (iv. 14). God's service consists chiefly in prayer and almsgiving. The main principle of the religious relation of man to God was that he wins from the divine judge a reward, first of all by keeping the commandments, second by good works not involved in the performance of the Law. It was implied that enough could be done to satisfy God's demands and that therefore a claim of reward was legitimate. An atomistic weighing and counting of separate performances, good as well as evil, from the human as well as the divine side was in order and was a characteristic feature of Pharisaic piety. A similar view is found in the works of Philo of Alexandria, intermingled there with strains of Platonism, for Plato in many places speaks of rewards given to the good and punishment of evil deeds. In the early Christian view these Judaistic conceptions were not received, for man's salvation goes back to God's grace in Christ; despite the paradoxical character of Jesus' teaching in several places his clearest statements tend to reject the thought of any human claim of merit from God (Matt. xx. 1 sqq.; Luke xv. 17 sqq.). The kingdom of heaven is not built on the right of men but on the grace of God. Paul's position was naturally entirely in line with this, for he was occupied in many places in showing that God did not reward man according to his merit but according to free grace.

1. Definition; Origin of the Conception.

Although Pharisaical Jewish Christianity was so directly opposed by Paul as a perversion of a fundamental idea of the Gospel, yet the earliest works of the Apostolic Fathers and of the apologists show the introduction of the merit idea into the church system. The sins of past life are forgiven in baptism (Hermas, *Mandates*, IV., iii.; Justin, *I Apol.*, lxi.; Tertullian, *De baptismo*, i.). In this and in the promise of future blessings the grace of God is exhausted (cf. Clement, I., vii. 4). The baptized has now the duty of avoiding sins and fulfilling God's commandments, observing the new law of Christ in order that in the retribution at the resurrection of the dead he may inherit eternal life (Hermas, *Vision*, I., iii. 4a; Clement II., viii. 4). Of course the condition of this is man's freedom of will by which he can choose the good and fulfil God's law (Hermas, *Mandates* XII., iii.-v.; Justin, *II Apol.*, vii. 14; Tertullian, *De Anima*, xxi.). In Hermas (*Similitude*, V., iii. 3) the conception of merit also appears as an act going beyond what is commanded: "If thou doest anything good outside of the commandments of God thou wilt gain for thyself more abundant glory and thou wilt be of more repute with God than thou wert about to be." It was Tertullian who introduced the strict juristic conception of merit: "From the beginning he [God] sent into the world messengers endowed with the Holy Spirit . . . to preach that there is only one God . . . to declare the rules appointed by him for

2. Views of Apostolic Fathers.

securing his favor, and what rewards he had destined for those who ignore, forsake, or keep them" (*Apol.* xviii.). Tertullian brought the whole of Christianity into a scheme of works and rewards that became characteristic of occidental Catholicism. Cyprian follows closely in the steps of his teacher: "There is need of justice that any one may secure merit with God our judge: his precepts and warnings must be obeyed that our merits may receive reward" (*De ecclesiæ unitate*, xv.). Again, "What will be the glory of those who work—how great and exalted the joy when the Lord will begin to number his people and distribute the promised rewards to our merits and works, giving heavenly things for earthly, eternal things for temporal, great things for small A mighty and divine thing a salutary operation a thing placed in the power of him who acts . the true and greatest gift of God, necessary for the weak, glorious for the strong, by which the Christian who is aided shows a spiritual grace, deserves merit from Christ the judge, accounts God his debtor The Lord will never fail to give a reward for our merits" (*De opere et eleemos.*, xxvi.). The works of Christians deserving such merits are, in general, alms, fasting, celibacy, but particularly martyrdom. Occidental thought was not strictly logical, for both Cyprian and Ambrose state that the life marked by virtues is possible only through the Holy Spirit. Augustine was the first to cast aside this prevalent teaching of merit.

3. Augustine and Others. He denied that the grounds of merit lay in the freedom of the will (*Enchiridion*, xxxii.), holding that divine grace calls forth a good will without any previous works of merit. The process is founded on the inspiration of love, which is synonymous with grace. This is needed not only for the beginning but in separate acts (*De gestis Pel.*, lvi.). Related to the rejection of merit was Augustine's teaching of an absolute predestination, of the irresistibility of God's grace, and of the gift of perseverance received by the elect. Yet he shows tendencies to relapse into the old teaching that God crowns man's merits, "but God does not crown thy merits as thy merits but rather as his gifts" (*De gratia et libero arbitrio*, VI., xv.; cf. *Enchiridion*, cvii.). Later on Catholic theological development by its adoption of a conditional instead of an absolute predestination ("For those whose merits he foresaw he predestined rewards," Ambrose, *De fide*, V., vi. 83) returned in principle to the older theory. Gregory the Great adheres to the Augustinian predestination but recognizes merit: "Grace preceding and good will following, that which is of God becomes merit in us" (*Hom. in Ezek.*, I., ix. 2). Grace is conceived of not as salvation but as clearing the ground for the successful operation of free will. The great scholastic philosophers of the Middle Ages systematically worked up this semi-Augustinian tendency, Peter Lombard (q.v.) laying the foundation with his theory of the cooperation of grace and will in the production of good works. He plainly declares that there is no merit in man that is not through free will, and makes the hope of future depend on God's grace and preceding merits, "For without merits to hope for anything can not be called hope but presumption" ("Sentences," IV., xxvi. 1).

Thomas Aquinas makes merit the end of religion, yet in appearance holds to the Augustinian teaching (cf. *Summa*, II., i. 109–114). He distinguishes two kinds of grace, one belonging to the sphere of salvation, the other extending over the whole field of God's activity.

4. Thomas Aquinas. This second type of grace does not give man's acts meritorious character, although through it he may love God above all things. To inherit eternal life man, who is not able to produce merits proportioned to it, requires a higher virtue, the virtue of grace. As his nature is corrupt it must be healed by grace. This grace is called operative, inasmuch as it heals or justifies the soul, and from the other point of view cooperative, inasmuch as it marks the beginning of meritorious action which proceeds from free will. The merit produced by operative grace is the motion of free will by which we accede to God's righteousness in making us righteous. Strictly speaking, merit can not be predicated of man in relation to God, but according to the prearrangement of the divine ordinance so established that man may attain it from God through his own operation, a reward, as it were, for what God bestowed on him, viz., the virtue of acting. In relation to free will he distinguishes a congruous merit from the condign merit which comes from the grace of the Holy Spirit. Man can prepare himself to receive grace through the action of his free will, not, however, without the aid of God who moves it. Its action is imperfect compared with what it can do when it is infused with grace, but the infusion of grace necessarily follows this cooperation between man's free will and God's motion.

The nominalists criticized this theory of merit, yet the tendency has been since the Middle Ages to stress congruous merit and moreover to confer merit only on those works which have the stamp of churchliness, introducing as chief factors the sacraments of baptism and the Eucharist.

5. Later Roman Catholic Views. The scholastics also introduced the thought of the supererogatory merits of the saints (see SUPEREROGATION, WORKS OF). At the time of the Reformation the Roman Catholic position on merit was intensified through the conflict with Protestantism. This is seen in confessional documents even before the time of the Council of Trent. Its decrees (Session VI.) laid down the position that through the righteousness of Christ all deserve the grace of justification. This is given to each individual. Justification comes through the sacraments and reward is given to good works, for God is so good to man that he wills that what are really his gifts should be their merits. Yet the essential spirit of merit remains. Bellarmine states plainly that the good works of the just are properly and truly merits and deserve eternal life (*Disputationes*, V., i. 6). Present-day Roman Catholic teaching distinguishes between auxiliary or actual grace and sanctifying or habitual grace. The first is imparted temporarily to man but is necessary to every good work. The second is given through the sacraments, baptism, penance, but is lost through mortal sin. A meritorious work requires the cooperation of both. Among good works especially meritorious are prayer, fasting, and almsgiving. The grace that is lost through deadly sin is restored by penance. The general idea is that the church system acts as a factor along with human free will in the attainment of salvation.

6. Protestant Views.

The Reformation was especially a conflict against the theory of merit, but Luther's final position on this question was the result of a development. In his earlier years he talked of congruous merit and accepted the terms "preparation" and "disposition" for salvation. Later on he still continued to use the word merit, but evacuated it of its meaning. He recognized nothing in man to increase the value of human works. There is no longer any room for merit, since all are made just by the justness of Christ. The works do not deserve heaven, but men, receiving heaven, through faith do good works. Melanchthon incorporated in the Augsburg Confession and Apology (cf. Apology, lxii. 17 sqq.) a clear-cut definition of Luther's position where he attacks the distinction between congruous and condign merit and develops the Reformed justification-teaching in opposition to the whole merit theory, especially denying the possibility of the transference of the merits of the saints. Christ's merits are given us in order that we may be reputed just by our faith in the merits of Christ when we believe in him, just as if we had our own proper merits (Apology, ccv. 14 sqq.). The use of the word merit in Protestant theology is associated with the satisfaction of Christ, not with individual deserts enabling man to appear before God. Kant discussed the question of merit, but in an unfavorable sense, saying the impulse to it was due to self-love and that it had some relation to sensuousness. Paulsen approximates to Roman Catholic ethics by distinguishing between actions which are in accordance with duty and others which deserve merit. Stange opposes this classification of an ordinary and extraordinary morality, as if there was something higher than duty. The deficient element in Roman Catholic teaching is that it makes the essence of morality depend on the separate act rather than on the whole atmosphere and direction of the personal will. See ATONEMENT; GRACE; GOOD WORKS; and SATISFACTION.

(JOHANNES KUNZE.)

BIBLIOGRAPHY: The subject is treated usually in the works on systematic theology, e.g., W. G. T. Shedd, *Dogmatic Theology*, i. 366 sqq., New York, 1891; C. Hodge, *Systematic Theology*, ii. 308–311, New York, 1871–73; and in the theological dictionaries, e.g., J. H. Blunt, pp. 139–141, 145, 805–808. Consult further: K. H. Wirth, *Der Begriff des meritum bei Tertullian*, Leipsic, 1892; idem, *Der Verdienstbegriff bei Cyprian*, ib. 1901; K. R. Hagenbach, *Hist. of Christian Doctrines*, ii. 308–311, Edinburgh, 1880; H. Schultz, in *TSK*, lxvii (1894), 1–50, 245–314; C. Stange, *Einleitung in die Ethik*, vol. ii., Leipsic, 1901; *KL*, xii. 690–694; Harnack, *Dogma*, consult Index.

MERKLE, SEBASTIAN: German Roman Catholic; b. at Ellwangen (45 m. e.n.e. of Stuttgart) Aug. 28, 1862. He was educated at the University of Tübingen from 1882 to 1886, and after being a teacher at Rottenburg in 1887–88, was a lecturer at the Wilhelmsstift, Tübingen, from 1888 to 1898. Since the latter year he has been professor of church history, dogmatics, and Christian archeology in the University of Würzburg, of which he was rector in 1904–05. In 1894 he visited Italy, where he became a member of the historical institute of the Görres-Gesellschaft, under whose auspices he visited Spain and France in 1896 and Austria, Hungary, and South Germany in 1897. He has written, *Giovanni Dominici und seine Lucula noctis* (Tübingen, 1892); *Die ambrosianischen Tituli* (Rome, 1896); *Kardinal Gabriel Paleotti* (1897); *Zur Quellenkunde des Trienter Konzils* (Tübingen, 1898); *Concilium Tridentinum, i.* (Freiburg, 1901); *Gutachten im Prozess Berlichingen* (Munich, 1904); *Die theologischen Fakultäten und die religiöse Friede* (Berlin, 1905); *Das Konzil von Trient und die Universitäten* (Würzburg, 1905); and *Die katholische Beurteilung des Aufklärungszeitalters* (Berlin, 1909).

MERLE D'AUBIGNÉ, märl dō″bī″nyē′, **JEAN HENRI:** Swiss Protestant; b., of French family exiled during the religious disturbances, at Eaux Vives (now a part of Geneva) Aug. 16, 1794; d. at Geneva Oct. 21, 1872. His father, though a citizen of Geneva, was a merchant in Marseilles, and it was intended that the son should follow a like career;

Life.

but a strong personal inclination led the latter to the ministry. He was a student at the University of Geneva when the religious movement known as "the Awakening" (*le réveil*) began, and in 1816, when the pastors of the city were accused of rejecting the divinity of Christ, he led his fellow students in a public expression of confidence in their spiritual superiors. Early in the following year, however, he came fully under the influence of Robert Haldane (q.v.), the leading spirit of the awakening. It was not without hesitation that he subscribed to the edict issued by the Venerable Company of Pastors May 3, 1817, forbidding preachers to speak in the pulpit on doctrines in dispute (see MALAN, CÉSAR HENRI ABRAHAM); but the edict was interpreted liberally, and Merle d'Aubigné was ordained July 3, 1817. He almost immediately went to Germany, where he busied himself with literary studies, translating Ariosto and Schiller, and intending to devote his life to literature. But the celebration of the three-hundredth anniversary of the Reformation at Eisenach in October gave his ambition a new direction and suggested to him the idea of writing an exhaustive history of the Reformation. He went to Berlin, heard Schleiermacher, DeWette, and Neander, and became the warm friend of Neander, whose influence remained with him permanently. Appointed pastor of the Reformed congregation in Hamburg in 1818 and court preacher in Brussels in 1824, he exercised great influence in both places, although opposition in Hamburg at one time induced the consistory to attempt to secure his recall. The revolution of 1830 drove him from Belgium. He was offered a professorship at Montauban and a church in Paris, but, although it involved some pecuniary sacrifice, decided to return to his native city. The Evangelical Society of Geneva (q.v.) had been formed during his absence, and for the rest of his life he labored as professor in the theological school which it founded, lecturing chiefly on church history and doctrine, but also on symbolics, homiletics, catechetics, ecclesiology, and pastoral duties. In 1832 he founded the weekly *Gazette évangélique* and, with Gaussen and Galland, he preached for the congregation of the Society in the Chapelle de l'Oratoire. The Genevan Church naturally looked with suspicion on the new society, and the Company of Pastors forbade the pulpit to Merle d'Aubigné and his associates. The former had Christian unity deeply at heart, but he felt that he could not allow any external authority to interfere with his office as a preacher of the Gospel. So, reluctantly and under compulsion, as he believed, in 1835 he consented that the Lord's Supper should be administered in the Oratoire, thereby making the congregation independent of the State Church. The final step was taken in 1849 when the Oratoire was united with the old separated church of the Bourg-de-Four and the Evangelical Church (Église Évangélique) was formed. Two years later, when changes in the constitution of the national church were under consideration, he published *La Liberté des cultes* (Geneva, 1851; Eng. transl., *The Separation of Church and State*, published by the British Anti-State Church Association, London, 1851) and other tracts, demanding more power for the laity and that the congregations should have a voice in the choice of pastors, and herein his plea was successful. His contention that the constitution should not emanate from a political body which counted Roman Catholics among its members, but from a synod representing the Protestant citizens was not listened to. His view of the proper relations of Church and State did not exclude all power of the latter in certain external and secular matters. He would not have the Church receive its material support from the State; nor would he have a hard and fast compact, but an understanding limiting the sphere of each by mutual agreement. Concerning the form of church government, he held the presbyterial most Scriptural; but refused to condemn Episcopalians or Congregationalists because of their preference.

Writings. The first volume of the history of the Reformation appeared in 1835, the thirteenth and last in 1878 (the last three volumes published posthumously). The entire work comprises two parts, the first (*La Réformation du seizième siècle*, 5 vols., Paris, 1835–53; Eng. transl. by D. Walther, 3 vols., London, 1838–1841, by H. White, 5 vols., Edinburgh, 1846–53, and others) treating of the time of Luther, about whom are grouped Zwingli and Farel in Switzerland and the predecessors of the Reformation in France and England (vol. v.=*La Réformation d'Angleterre*). In the second part (*La Réformation en Europe au temps de Calvin*, 8 vols., Paris, 1863–78; Eng. transl., 8 vols., London, 1863–78) Geneva is made the central point of the narrative. The author's chief merit is the patient search for the sources and penetrating study of them. He writes with zeal and learning, earnestness, and charm of style. His defects are an inclination toward pathos, and such a use of the sources as results in a partizan and prejudiced coloring of the narrative. The work appeared at a favorable time, and its success was remarkable, particularly in English-speaking lands.

The more noteworthy of Merle d'Aubigné's other publications, omitting numerous occasional sermons, are the following: *Le Cult domestique* (Paris, 1827; Eng. transl. London, 1846); *Le Christianisme et le Protestantisme, sont-ils deux choses distinctes?* (Paris, 1828); *Discours sur l'étude de l'histoire du Christianisme* (Geneva, 1832); *La Voix de l'Église une sous toutes les formes successives* (Geneva, 1834); *Foi et science* (Geneva, 1835); *Les Miracles ou deux erreurs* (Geneva, 1840); *Genève et Oxford* (Geneva, 1842; Eng. transl., London, 1843); *Le Lutheranisme et la Réforme* (Geneva, 1844; Eng. transl., *Luther and Calvin*, Glasgow, 1844); *Rome and the Reformation* (London, 1844); *Le Protecteur ou la république d'Angleterre aux jours de Cromwell* (Paris, 1848; Eng. transl., Edinburgh, 1847), a somewhat overdrawn apology for the English leader; *Trois siècles de lutter en Écosse* (Geneva, 1850), a narrative of the struggle for religious liberty in Scotland from John Knox to the founding of the Free Church in 1843; *L'Authorité des écritures inspirées de Dieu* (Geneva, 1850); *Le Témoinage de la théologie ou le biblicisme de Néander* (Geneva, 1850); *Deux discours prononcés à Londres, exposition universelle* (London, 1851); *Quelle est la théologie propre à guérir les maux du temps actuel?* (Geneva, 1852; Eng. transl., *What is the Theology Fitted to Cure the Evils of the Present Time?* Glasgow, 1853); *L'Église et la diète de l'Église* (Berlin, 1853; Eng. transl., *The Church and the Church Diet* (London, 1854); *Du caractère nécessaire au théologien et au chrétien dans l'époque actuelle* (Paris, 1845); *Faith and Criticism . Address Delivered at the Opening of the Presbyterian College, Belfast* (Belfast, 1853; French ed., Geneva, 1854); *Jean Chrysostôme* (Geneva, 1854); *Souvenir des derniers jours de Marianne Merle d'Aubigné née Brélaz*, his first wife (Geneva, 1855); *L'Ancien et le ministre* (Paris, 1857); *L'Assemblée de Berlin ou unité et diversité dans l'église* (Geneva, 1857); *L'Orient ou Origène et la science—L'Occident ou Cyprien et la pratique* (Geneva, 1857; Eng. transl. in *Christianity in the First Three Centuries*, Edinburgh, 1858); *Vie et doctrine* (Geneva, 1858); *Il y a un ministre de la parole* (Paris, 1858); *La Pierre sur laquelle l'Académie de Genève fert posée en Juin, 1559* (Geneva, 1850); *Le Réveil de l'église contemporaine* (Toulouse, 1860); *Septembre, 1861, ou l'Alliance Evangélique à Genève* (Geneva, 1861); *Caractère du Réformateur et de la Réformation du Genève* (Geneva, 1862); *Enseignement de Calvin: glorifier Christ*, address at the three-hundredth anniversary of Calvin's death (Geneva, 1864; Eng. transl., *Calvin's Teaching for the Present Day*, London, 1864); *Les Coups et les enseignements de Dieu* (Geneva, 1865); *L'Expiation de la croix* (Geneva, 1867; Eng. transl., *The Expiatory Sacrifice of the Cross*, London, 1868); *Jean Calvin un de fondateurs des libertés modernes* (Geneva, 1868); *Le Comité et l'infallibilité* (Geneva, 1870).

(Duchemin.)

Bibliography: J. Bonnet, *Notice sur la vie et les écrits de Merle d'Aubigné*, Paris, 1874.

MERODACH, mer'o-dac (Hebr. *Merodak*; Assyr. *Marduk* or *Maruduk*): The god of light of Babylonia who revealed himself in the beneficent appearance of the sun of the morning and of spring time. Long before the time of Hammurabi Merodach was brought, as son of Ea, into connection with the cult of healing in Eridu (see Babylonia, IV., § 2, VII., 2, §§ 3, 10), in the inscriptions is often sent as a messenger of good by his father, and is by him recognized as equal in knowledge, all of which is in accordance with his nature as a light deity and as the dispeller of the shadows of night and cold of winter. After Babylonia had been unified under Hammurabi, the priests of his temple based their claim for the rulership of the world by Babylon upon the alleged creation of the world by Merodach. To Merodach they applied the story of creation previously told of Bel of Nippur (see BABYLONIA, VII., 1, § 1, 2, § 2), and he became "king of the gods, king of heaven and earth, lord of lords and king of kings." His seven-storied temple in Babylon bore the name *E-temen-anki*, "House of the foundation of heaven and earth." His cultus lived on in the religion of the Mandæans (q.v.).

It is important for the understanding of the use of his name in the Bible to remember that in the time when it was written Merodach was called Bel (from Bel of Nippur). These two names enter as elements into personal names, as in Belshazzar and Merodach-baladan. Merodach is also brought into close connection with Nebo, god of the sister city of Borsippa (Isa. xlvi. 1; so also in the inscriptions). A close relationship existed between the New Year's feast of Merodach and the Purim of the Jews ("the day of Mordecai," II Macc. xv. 36; H. Winckler, *Altorientalische Forschungen*, iii. 1 sqq., Leipsic, 1895). Indeed, a thoroughgoing influence upon Biblical conceptions, especially as to the relations of God and man, is ascribed by H. Zimmern to the Babylonian Merodach. Babylonians and Hebrews were united by a threefold bond of relationship in speech, ideas, and mythological expression, though this does not necessarily involve literary dependence. Moreover, where both peoples have used material in common, the Biblical narratives are incomparably higher in religious content than the Babylonian. Indeed, it may be asked in some cases whether the Babylonian expressions have not been influenced toward their best form by Hebrew thought and personalities. At any rate, the religion which centered in Merodach, at least in its latest phases as shown in the development of the Mandæans, contained the idea of salvation.

(A. JEREMIAS.)

BIBLIOGRAPHY: A full list of literature is given under BABYLONIA. Consult particularly *DB*, iii. 347, and extra vol., p. 545; A. Jeremias, in W. H. Roscher, *Lexikon der griechischen und römischen Mythologie*, ii. 2340–72, Leipsic, 1896; H. Gunkel, *Schöpfung und Chaos*, Göttingen, 1895; M. Jastrow, *Religion of Babylonia and Assyria*, Boston, 1898, and the German ed., Giessen, 1902 sqq.; H. Zimmern, in Schrader, *KAT*, ii. 370 sqq.; P. D. Chantepie de la Saussaye, *Lehrbuch der Religionsgeschichte*, i. 294–299, Tübingen, 1905; F. Martin, in Vigouroux, *Dictionnaire*, part xxvi. 997–1001.

MERODACH-BALADAN: The Babylonian king mentioned in Isa. xxxix. as sending an embassy to Hezekiah, in the parallel passage, II Kings xx. 12–19, appearing either by mistake or change of consonants as Berodach-baladan. He was the second of the name on the throne of Babylon, the first being a member of the Kasshite dynasty and ruling 1129–17 B.C. The sources of information about him, outside of Biblical sources and the Ptolemaic Canon, are the cuneiform inscriptions, particularly the king-lists, the inscriptions of Tiglath-Pileser, Sargon and Sennacherib, and two inscriptions of Merodach-baladan himself. The mention in the inscriptions involves the period 729–700 B.C. as that of his activity. Variations in the way in which he is mentioned in the inscriptions of Sennacherib, as compared with those of Tiglath-Pileser and Sargon, were supposed to indicate that two persons of the name were referred to, but recent research has made it more probable that all the passages deal with the same man. The Biblical narrative calls him "son of Baladan," possibly through a misunderstanding of the relation of the two elements in his name; Tiglath-Pileser and Sargon call him "son of Yakin"; he speaks of himself as a descendant of Erba-Marduk (an early king of Babylon) but does not give his father's name. He was king of Bit-Yakin, one of the Chaldean states on the lower course of the Tigris and Euphrates, but became a vassal of Tiglath-Pileser in 729. In 722 he utilized the confused condition of affairs to make himself king of Babylon, after forming an anti-Assyrian alliance with Elam, succeeding in 721 in his effort and holding the position till 709, when he was driven out by Sargon and his paternal kingdom ravaged. After the death of Sargon, Merodach-baladan renewed his activity against Babylon and in 703 [704] once more sat on the throne of that city, only to be driven out within a year by Sennacherib and compelled to hide in the marshes near the sea. In 701–700 he again attempted to make headway against the Assyrian, but the vigorous measures of Sennacherib foiled his efforts. After that he disappears from the Assyrian annals.

There is no reason to doubt the historicity of the Old-Testament account of the embassy sent to Hezekiah, though the purpose was doubtless not that of sympathy and congratulation, but rather to involve the Judean king in an anti-Assyrian league. The time when this took place is not definitely indicated in the Biblical narrative, and has been variously placed by students, with the probabilities in favor of the time 721–709 when Merodach-baladan was first king of Babylon [more probably in 704 when Merodach-baladan was again king of Babylon, about fifteen years before the death of Hezekiah; Isa. xxxviii. 5, xxxix. 1]. (See ASSYRIA, VI., 3, §§ 11–12; and BABYLONIA, VI., 7, § 1.)

(R. KRAETZSCHMAR†.)

BIBLIOGRAPHY: Schrader, *KAT*, pp. 72–73, 79–80 et passim; idem, *KB*, vols. ii.–iii.; idem, in E. C. A. Riehm, *Handwörterbuch des biblischen Altertums*, pp. 997–998, Leipsic, 1894; the pertinent sections in the works on the history mentioned under ASSYRIA, especially those of Rogers, Hommel, and Tiele; H. Winckler, *Die Keilschrifttexte Sargons*, i., pp. xv. sqq., xxxi. sqq., Leipsic, 1889; idem, *Untersuchungen zur altorientalischen Geschichte*, pp. 54 sqq., ib. 1889; idem, *Alttestamentliche Untersuchungen*, pp. 138 sqq., ib. 1892; J. F. McCurdy, *History, Prophecy and the Monuments*, §§ 340, 621, 637–638, 660–672, 3 vols., New York, 1894–1901; F. Martin, in Vigouroux, *Dictionnaire*, part xxvi. 1001–04; the later commentaries on II Kings and Isaiah; *DB*, iii. 347; *EB*, iii. 3037–38.

MERRIAM, ALEXANDER ROSS: Congregationalist; b. at Goshen, N. Y., Jan. 20, 1849. He was educated at Yale College (A.B., 1872), and after teaching at the Hartford High School for two years (1872–74) he entered Andover Theological Seminary, from which he was graduated in 1877. He was pastor of Payson Congregational Church, Easthampton, Mass., from 1877 to 1884, when he accepted a call to the pastorate of the First Congregational Church, Grand Rapids, Mich., which pulpit he filled until 1891. Retiring from the ministry on account of ill-health, he then resided at Brattleboro, Vt., for two years, and since 1893 has been professor of homiletics, pastoral care, and sociology at Hartford Theological Seminary.

MERRICK, JAMES: Church of England Biblical scholar and poet; b. at Reading Jan. 8, 1720; d. there Jan. 5, 1769. He was graduated from the University of Oxford (B.A., 1739; M.A., 1742); became a fellow, 1745; was ordained, but owing to ill-health never took a charge. His earlier productions were on the Greek classics. He issued among other works a *Dissertation on Proverbs ix. 1-6* (Oxford, 1744); *Poems on Sacred Subjects* (1763); *Annotations, Critical and Grammatical*, on John i. 1-14 (Reading, 1764); and on John i. 15-iii (1767); *The Psalms Translated or Paraphrased in English Verse* (1765); *Annotations on the Psalms* (1768). His paraphrases of the Psalms were often reproduced, and some of them are found in modern hymn-books, though in general his poetical work is severely criticized as too verbose for profitable employment in church hymnody.

Bibliography: S. W. Duffield, *English Hymns*, pp. 576-578, New York, 1886; Julian, *Hymnology*, pp. 725-726; *DNB*, xxxvii. 289-291.

MERRILL, SELAH: Congregationalist; b. at Canton Center, Conn., May 2, 1837; d. at Fruitvale, Cal., Jan. 22, 1909. He was educated at Yale College, but left before graduation. He then studied at Yale Divinity School, from which he was graduated in 1864; chaplain of the Forty-ninth (colored) Infantry at Vicksburg, Miss., 1864-65; pastor at Chester, Mass., 1865-66; First Congregational Church, Le Roy, N. Y., 1867; and stated supply at the Third Congregational Church, San Francisco, Cal., 1867-68. In 1868-70 he studied in Germany, and was pastor at Salmon Falls, N. H., in 1871-72, and taught Hebrew at Andover Theological Seminary in 1872 and again in 1879. He was archeologist of the American Palestine Exploration Society from 1875 to 1877 He was United States consul at Jerusalem in 1882-86, 1891-94, and 1898-1907, and honorary curator of the Biblical museum of Andover Theological Seminary. He was well and favorably known for his contributions to Biblical archeology, especially in connection with excavations in and about Jerusalem, especially those which disclosed the second wall. He made collections dealing with the coins, implements, and fauna of Palestine. In theology he was orthodox and approved critical methods so long as they remained reverent. In addition to a large number of contributions to theological and Oriental periodicals, he wrote *East of the Jordan: A Record of Exploration carried on in 1875-77* (New York, 1881); *Galilee in the Time of Christ* (Boston, 1881); *Greek Inscriptions collected in the Years 1875-77 in the Country east of the Jordan* (New York, 1885); *The Site of Calvary* (Jerusalem, 1885); and *Ancient Jerusalem, Topography and Archæology* (New York, 1908).

MERRY, WILLIAM WALTER: Church of England; b. at Evesham (15 m. s.e. of Worcester), Worcestershire, Sept. 6, 1835. He was educated at Balliol College, Oxford (B.A. 1857; M.A., Lincoln College, 1860), and was ordered deacon in 1860 and ordained priest in the following year. He was a fellow and lecturer in Lincoln College from 1859 to 1884, and was also vicar of All Souls, Oxford, from 1862 to the same year. He was classical moderator at Oxford in 1863-64, 1869-71, 1874, 1877, and 1883-84, select preacher at the university in 1878-79 and 1889-90, and Whitehall preacher in 1883-84. He was likewise a member of the Hebdomadal Council, pro-vice-chancellor in 1902-1904, and vice-chancellor in 1904-06. His literary work has dealt with editions of classical authors: the "Odyssey" (2 vols., Oxford, 1870-78); *Specimens of Greek Dialects* (London, 1875); the "Clouds" (Oxford, 1879), "Acharnians" (1880), "Frogs" (1884), "Knights" (1887), "Birds" (1889), "Wasps" (1893), and "Peace" (1900) of Aristophanes; and *Selected Fragments of Roman Poetry* (1891).

MERRY DEL VAL, RAPHAEL: Cardinal; b. in London (of a Spanish father and an English mother) Oct. 10, 1865. He was educated successively at Brussels, St. Cuthbert's, England, and the Accademia dei nobili ecclesiastici, Rome, and was ordained to the priesthood in 1889, after having already been made privy chamberlain to the pope in the previous year. In 1892 he became "guardaroba" to the pope, and in 1897 was appointed domestic prelate. He was then entrusted with a mission to Canada, and on his return was made president of the Accademia dei nobili ecclesiastici in 1899. In the following year he was consecrated titular archbishop of Nicea. He was the envoy of Leo XIII. to congratulate King Edward on his accession to the English throne, and was also secretary of the conclave which elected the present pope. On the accession of Pius X., Merry del Val was appointed pro-secretary of state, and in 1903 was created cardinal priest of Santa Prasede, his promotion to full secretary of state following two days later.

MERSEBURG, mer'se-burg, **BISHOPRIC OF:** A former episcopal see in Saxony, founded at the same time and in the same manner as those of Meissen and Zeitz, as part of the plan for binding more closely to the empire the territory of the Wends on the right bank of the Saale (967). The first bishop was Boso, a monk of Ratisbon, distinguished by his missionary labors among the Wends. His successor Gisiler procured the suppression of the see through Otto II.'s power over Benedict VII. in 981; but this step was so clearly against the interests of the Church that it was revoked in 998 or early in 999 at a Roman synod. The diocese did not, however, recover all its former territory, and was now almost exclusively a missionary jurisdiction among the Wends, who were not wholly converted to Christianity until the middle of the twelfth century (see Wends, Conversion of). (A. Hauck.)

The Reformation was forcibly established here during the episcopate of Sigismund von Lindenau (d. 1544) after his protector, Henry of Brunswick-Wolfenbüttel, had been driven out by the Schmalkald League in 1542. The electors of Saxony thereafter put in members of their own house with the title of administrator, and from 1652 to 1738 with that of duke of Saxony-Merseburg. By the decision of the Congress of Vienna three-fourths of the diocesan territory was assigned to Prussia, the rest remaining Saxon; the religious attitude of the people was by that time almost entirely Protestant.

BIBLIOGRAPHY: Gams, *Series episcoporum*, pp. 291–292; *Chronicon episcoporum Merseburg*, ed. R. Wilmans in *MGH, Script.*, x (1852), 163–212; cf. Wilmans in *Archiv der Gesellschaft für ältere deutsche Geschichtskunde*, xi. 146–211; Hauck, *KD*, ii. 130 sqq., 142 sqq., et passim.

MERSWIN, RULMAN. See FRIENDS OF GOD.

MERULA, ANGELUS (Engel de Merle): Early Dutch Protestant; b. at Briel (14 m. w. of Rotterdam) 1482 or 1487; d. at Bergen (34 m. s.s.e. of Brussels) July 26, 1557. He studied four years at the University of Paris (M.A., 1507; Lic. theol., 1508), was ordained priest at Utrecht, 1511, and became preacher in Briel. In 1530 he removed to Heenvliet. Before 1540 he came under suspicion of heresy, but was not molested till 1553, when he was arrested at The Hague. In 1554 the authorities claimed that he retracted, but it is probable that, being deaf, he did not understand the document which was read to him. He was not released and was finally condemned to death at Bergen, but died while kneeling in prayer at the place of execution. He was a learned scholar and his convictions were the fruit of his study. His view of the Lord's Supper was the same as Zwingli's, but was not borrowed from him. He wished to reform the Church from within by the pure preaching of God's Word, which he made the sole authority; to church tradition he attached no worth. Each one must follow his own conscience, since without freedom no faith is possible. Unbelief is the chief sin. Christ alone is savior, and the invocation of the saints is fruitless. Baptism and the Lord's Supper are the only sacraments. All Christians are priests. The Roman Church is but one branch of the Church catholic and the pope is antichrist. He rejected purgatory, transubstantiation, and the church doctrine of absolution and indulgences. He is described as an amiable, discreet, and good-hearted man, who loved to do good. An orphan asylum founded by him in Briel is still in existence.

(S. D. VAN VEEN.)

BIBLIOGRAPHY: W. Moll, *Angelus Merula, de hervormer en martelaar des geloofs*, Amsterdam, 1855 (cf. on this H. de Jager, in *Archief voor Nederlandsche Kerkgeschiedenis*, vi. 1–44, and A. H. L. Hensen, in *De Katholiek*, cxi., 1897, 43–68); I. M. J. Hoog, *De Verantwoording van Angelus Merula*, Leyden, 1897.

MERX, ERNST OTTO ADALBERT: German Protestant; b. at Bleicherode (10 m. s.w. of Nordhausen), Prussian Saxony, Nov. 2, 1838; d. at Heidelberg Aug. 4, 1909. He was educated at the universities of Marburg, Halle, and Berlin, 1857–61 (Ph.D., Breslau, 1861); became privat-docent at the University of Jena, 1865, and associate professor, 1869; professor of Oriental languages at Tübingen, 1869; of theology at Giessen, 1873; and of Old-Testament exegesis at Heidelberg, 1875. He was the author of *Meletemata Ignatiana* (Halle, 1861); *Bardesanes von Edessa* (1863); *Cur in libro Danielis juxta Hebræam Aramæa adhibita sit dialectus* (1865); *Grammatica Syriaca* (1867); *Das Gedicht von Hiob* (Jena, 1871); *Neusyrisches Lesebuch* (Tübingen, 1873); *Türkische Sprichwörter ins Deutsche übersetzt* (Venice, 1877); *Die Prophetie des Joel und ihre Ausleger von den ältesten Zeiten bis zu den Reformatoren* (Halle, 1879); *Die saadjanische Uebersetzung des Hohen Liedes ins Arabische* (Heidelberg, 1882); *Chrestomathia Targumica* (1887); *Idee und Grundlinien der allgemeinen Geschichte der Mysterien* (Heidelberg, 1892); *Documents de paléographie hébreue et arabe* (Leyden, 1894); *Ueber die heutigen Aufgaben des evangelischen Bundes* (Leipsic, 1892); *Die vier kanonischen Evangelien nach ihrem ältesten bekannten Texte* (3 vols., Berlin, 1897–1905); *Aus Muallim Nadschis Sünbule* (1898); *Die morgenländischen Studien und Professoren an der Universität Heidelberg* (Heidelberg, 1903); and *Die Bücher Moses und Josua . für Laien* (Tübingen, 1907). He edited the *Archiv für wissenschaftliche Erforschung des Alten Testaments* since 1871, as well as *Vocabulary of the Tigré Language written down by Moritz von Beurmann* (Halle, 1868); and the second edition of F. Tuch's *Commentar über die Genesis* (1871).

MERZ, GEORG HEINRICH: German Lutheran; b. at Crailsheim (46 m. n.e. of Stuttgart) Aug. 8, 1816; d. at Stuttgart Dec. 31, 1893. At Maulbronn and Tübingen he came under the influence of Strauss and Baur, only to turn from them to a more positive faith. Schelling's lectures at Berlin (1841–42) suggested to him the possibility of apprehending historic revelation as the pivotal center for a philosophic system; while Kugler inspired him to a concrete historical understanding of medieval art, a study promoted by his extensive travels in Germany, Belgium, France, England, and Austria. On his return to Germany, he began a careful study of German art, and his *Uebersichten* took up the cause of ancient German and Evangelical art.

From 1846 to 1850 Merz was deacon at Neustadt-on-the-Kocher, while during the years that marked the frustration of national hopes he was pastor of St. Catherine's in Hall, Swabia (1850–63). His most effective literary work was his *Armut und Christentum* (Stuttgart, 1848), in which he advocated not merely "Christian communism," as practised by open-handed Pietism, but rather "Christian socialism," or the corporate application of personal assistance, and the enlistment of women in forms of Christian activity. Pursuing a popular vein, he now wrote his most widely circulated book, the *Christlichen Frauenbilder* (Stuttgart, 1851; Eng. transl. by S. Jackson, "*Eminent Women of the German Reformation*," London, 1856), presenting a collection of biographies of Christian women of all eras of the Christian Church. Meanwhile, he further cultivated the study and practise of art, restoring his own church with very modest means and writing the text for J. Schnorr von Carolsfeld's *Bibel in Bildern* (Leipsic, 1852–60; Eng. transl., *The Bible in Pictures*, 2 vols., London, 1869). His main object, however, was to reach a scientific ground of harmony with the practical church problems of the present; and his results were set forth in his *Die innere Mission in ihrem Verhältnis zu den wissenschaftlichen und kirchlichen Richtungen der Gegenwart* (*TSK*, 1854), in which he explained the significance and status of the Innere Mission in both actual and ideal relation to the German Church.

Merz now became successively dean and circuit school-inspector at Marbach (1863), supreme consistorial councilor at Stuttgart (1869), and prelate and general superintendent of Reutlingen (1873). With these positions was also associated his entrance into the house of deputies, in which capacity he was a member of the state synod. His own distinctive province, however, was the cultivation of Christian art, in which field he succeeded Grüneisen as director of the Verein für christliche Kunst in der evangelischen Kirche Württembergs and as editor of the *Christliches Kunstblatt* from 1878 onward. He gave the impulse, counsel, and ready assistance toward furnishing and renovating many churches in Württemberg, and also took a leading part in all the more important enterprises in the domain of church art in his time, both in and beyond Württemberg proper. J. MERZ.

BIBLIOGRAPHY: *Lutheranische Kirchenzeitung*, xxviii. 473 sqq.

MESHECH. See GOG AND MAGOG; and TABLE OF THE NATIONS.

MESOPOTAMIA, mes″o-po-tê′mi-a: The name applied by the Greeks after the time of Alexander and by the Romans to the region between the Tigris and the Euphrates (cf. Acts ii. 9). In earlier times the equivalent term applied only to the region northwest of Babylonia through which the Balich and the Chabur flowed. Before the Assyrian period the district was the locus of independent states, one of which was Kisshati, capital Haran, the title of whose king was assumed by early Babylonian monarchs. Of the history of this region before 1500 B.C little is known. About 2000 B.C. it was settled by the peoples of the branch of Semites to which Canaanites, Phenicians, and Hyksos belonged. The Egyptian wars of the eighteenth and nineteenth dynasties, following the expulsion of the Hyksos, were in part directed against Nahrina (see below), "land of the rivers," which was Mesopotamia in its proper sense (cf. W. M. Müller, *Asien und Europa*, pp. 144, 249 sqq., Leipsic, 1893), and reports of these wars give the earliest information of the region. The next news comes from the Amarna Tablets, which speak of non-Semitic conquerors, the Mitanni (see ASSYRIA, VI., 2, § 1), under a King Tushratta (see AMARNA TABLETS, III.), whose father and grandfather had had diplomatic relations with Egypt, while his own kingdom had a considerable area. Shortly afterward, the region belonged to Assyria, the kings of which assumed the title "king of Kisshati," and Shalmaneser II. (see ASSYRIA, VI., 3, § 7) extinguished the remains of the independence of its princes. Much of the culture, especially on its linguistic side, which came to be known as Assyrian, was due to the influence of this region of Kisshati. After the subjection of the Mitanni, the Arameans overran the region (cf. A. Sanda, *Die Aramäer*, Leipsic, 1902). A result of this migration was the establishment of the kingdom of Bit-Adini (the "children of Eden" of Isa. xxxvii. 12), which reached from the Balich to the Euphrates and was destroyed by the Assyrians (see ASSYRIA, VI., 2; 3, § 7).

Acts vii. 2 refers to a command received by Abraham "when he was in Mesopotamia, before he dwelt in Charran." The common explanation that by Mesopotamia is here meant the entire region between the Euphrates and the Tigris is untenable. Winckler would read the passage "when he was (once) in Mesopotamia, before he (finally) came to dwell in Charran," and refer it to a legendary missionary journey of Abraham, mention of which occurs in the pseudepigraphic Apocalypse of Abraham (ed. N. Bonwetsch, in *Studien zur Geschichte der Theologie und Kirche*, i. 1, Leipsic, 1897; see PSEUDEPIGRAPHA, II., 21). The history of Jacob is also connected with Mesopotamia proper (Gen. xxix. 1). The narrator in Gen. xxiv. 10 calls the region Aram-naharaim (cf. R. V. margin), the Nahrina of the Egyptian inscriptions and the Narima of the Amarna Tablets, and in Gen. xxv. 20 it appears as Padan-aram ("plain of Aram," cf. Hos. xii. 12, R. V.). See ARAM, ARAMEANS. (A. JEREMIAS.)

BIBLIOGRAPHY: On the geography: C. Chesney, *The Expedition of the Survey of the Rivers Euphrates and Tigris*, vol. i., London, 1850; J. C. F. Hoefer, *Chaldée, Assyrie, Médie, Babylonie, Mésopotamie*, pp. 151-192, Paris, 1852; W. K. Loftus, *Travels and Researches in Chaldea and Susiana*, London, 1859; H. Kiepert, *Lehrbuch der alten Geographie*, Berlin, 1878, Eng. transl., *Manual of Ancient Geography*, London, 1881. On the history: H. Winckler, in Schrader, *KAT*, i. 26-32 et passim; F. Vigouroux, *La Bible et les découvertes modernes*, vol. iii., 4 vols., Paris, 1881-82; G. Maspero, *Hist. ancienne des peuples de l'orient classique*, i. 551-564, ib. 1895; L. B. Paton, *Early Hist. of Syria and Palestine*, New York, 1901.

MESROB (MESROP, MASHTOZ): The inventor of the Armenian alphabet, founder of Armenian literature, and one of the original translators of the Bible into that language; b. at Hazegaz (Hatzik) in the province of Taron, Armenia, c. 350; d. at Valarsabad Feb. 19, 441. He was a son of a certain Wardan, and studied Greek, Persian, and Syriac under the Catholicos Nerses I. the Great (see ARMENIA, III., § 3), whose secretary he became. After the death of Nerses, he was for seven years a royal secretary under King Vramshapuh, having under his charge matters concerned with the Persian tongue. He then followed his bent for the ascetic life and entered a monastery, but very soon from the Catholicos Sahag (Isaac) the Great, successor of Nerses, he received the commission to preach the Gospel, which he did in various parts of the country. In this work his attention was called to the lack of Armenian Christian literature and indeed of a vehicle for it, since Syriac and Persian were used respectively in the churches and at court. He set himself to supply the need of an Armenian script and provided an alphabet. His important work for Armenia having become known in Georgia and Albania, he was invited thither by Bakur, the ruler of Georgia, and by the Archbishop Moses, and created the Georgian and later the Albanian alphabet, one result of which was the foundation of schools in Albania for the teaching of Christianity under the patronage of King Arswagh and Bishop Jeremiah. Returning then to Armenia, Mesrob assisted Sahag in translating the entire Bible into Armenian (see BIBLE VERSIONS, A, VI.).

The political and religious persecutions set in motion by the Persian king after the death of Vramshapuh drove Sahag and Mesrob for a time into Grecian Armenia. After the subsidence of these disturbances, both returned to their own region and engaged in translating into Armenian Syriac and Greek patristic work. Pupils were sent to Alexandria and Athens to lay a foundation in accurate knowledge of Greek for correct translation of works into Armenian.

Mesrob was a zealous opponent of heresy, and brought about the exile of the heretical teachers Barbarianus and Theodius. He was also active in promoting the monastic life, and many monasteries were built on his initiative. The Armenian alphabet invented by him has thirty-six characters, arranged in general after the order of the Greek alphabet with signs peculiar to the Armenian inserted. It was based neither on the Syriac nor on the Middle Persian, but on the Greek. The script is written from left to right. See ARMENIA, II., §§ 1-3. (K. KESSLER.)

BIBLIOGRAPHY: The Life by Gorium exists in Germ. transl. by Welte, Tübingen, 1841 (weighted with legend). The "History of Armenia" by Moses of Chorene (a pupil of Mesrob), printed often (e.g., Venice, 1827), is found in translations—Latin by Whiston, London, 1736; French (with Armenian text) by Le Vaillant de Florival, Venice, 1842; German by Lauer, Regensburg, 1842. Consult: E. Boré, *Saint Lazare*, pp. 90 sqq., Venice, 1835; V. Langlois, *Notice sur le convent arménien de l'île S. Lazare à Venise*, Venice, 1869; J. Nirschl, *Patrologie*, iii. 215-262, Mainz, 1885; *KL*, i. 1347-48, viii. 1305-09; and the literature under ARMENIA, especially the works by P. Lukias Somal, M. Patcanian, V. Langlois, and F. Nève.

MESSALIANS, mes-sê'li-anz (from Aram. *meẓallin*, participle of *ẓela*, "to pray"): A Syrian sect of the fourth century, also called *Euchites*, *Euphēmites* or *Choreutes*.

Epiphanius tells of assemblies of pagans who were neither Jews nor Christians but were strongly influenced by both. They worshiped only one God, the Almighty, meeting for this purpose in the evening and at dawn and directing their prayers and hymns to God. On this account they suffered persecutions and therefore called themselves Martyrians. A close connection between these pagan Euchites and the Christian Messalians can not be shown. From the name Messalians it is plain that the Christian sect arose in Mesopotamia, which sect Epiphanius is the first to mention, their heresy being the last described in his *Panarion*. He knows nothing of their origin and affirms that they can not be called a definitely organized sect. They declared themselves to be Christians in the fullest sense since they had renounced the world and forsworn the possession of private property. They had no scruples in calling themselves prophets, patriarchs, angels; they even applied to themselves the name of Christ. They considered it fitting to their perfection as Christians to abjure all work and to live wholly upon alms. They did not fast, but devoted themselves to constant prayer. The men and the women slept in the same apartment, during the summer in the open air.

Later Theodoret and Timotheus give an account of them. Amphilochius, who presided at the Synod of Side, convicted them of heresy on account of their writings, and Theodoret relates that Flavian, the patriarch of Antioch, induced them to expound their views on religious themes. Evidently they were a sect of enthusiastic mystics, who had, however, no intention of separating themselves from the Church. They believed they could attain to a perfect realization of Christianity, without reliance on the Church's means of grace, though still within her fold. They taught that through Adam's fall human nature acquired such a strong bent toward evil, that every one from his very birth is the dwelling-place of a devil. Baptism removes former sins, but it can not destroy the root of sin. That can be done only by constant prayer. Through prayer, to which therefore they devoted themselves, especially at night, they believed they could drive out the devil, and Augustine tells of their assertion that they saw swine issuing from their mouths and instead shining unconsuming fire entering. In perceptible fashion did the Holy Spirit enter the worshipers and accomplish the betrothal of their souls with the heavenly bridegroom. Thereby they were enabled to become prophets not only of the future but also of the secrets of the Trinity. Even the body of Christ had to be purified from devils by the Logos, but through its glorification he became like unto the Father. So the man who has been united to God needs no longer ascetic practises nor instruction, but assumes the divine nature. No longer is it necessary for him to partake of communion; he can sin no more. Women were teachers among them.

Their origin was certainly in Mesopotamia, whence they spread to Syria. Their progress may be followed in the acts of several synods. Flavian brought them from Edessa to Antioch and gained in an underhand way the confidence of their leader Adelphius. When from him he had learned their teachings, he condemned them, and refused to receive them again into the Church. From Antioch they removed to Pamphylia. Some decades later the Synod at Ephesus condemned their writings and threatened them with excommunication. Later still Lampetius was accused of heresy and was removed from office by Hormisdas, and two bishops, both named Alphæus, who defended him were likewise degraded. In the fifth century in Armenia proceedings were instituted against the sect. Priests and deacons who were convicted of this heresy were branded and forced to become hermits in expiation. Those who fell into their errors a second time were hamstrung, even the laity being treated in this way. In Greece in the time of Justinian a certain Marcian became their leader whence they were called Marcianites, just as before they had been called Adelphians and Lampetians. Gregory the Great vindicated an elder, accused of being a follower of Marcian, from the charge of heresy. As time went on their doctrines became more spiritual and less purely ascetic. On the Messalians of a later time see PAULICIANS; NEW-MANICHEANS.

(N. BONWETSCH.)

BIBLIOGRAPHY: The sources are Epiphanius, *Hær.*, lxxx.; Cyril of Alexandria, *De adoratione*, in *MPG*, lxviii. 282; Theodoret, *Hist. eccl.*, v. 10; Augustine, *De hæresibus*, lvii. Consult: *DCB*, ii. 258-261 (best); J. H. Blunt, *Dictionary of Sects and Heresies*, pp. 150-151, Philadelphia, 1874; Karapet Ter-Mkrttschian, *Die Paulikianer im byzantinischen Kaiserreiche*, Leipsic, 1893; F. C. Conybeare, *The Key of Truth*, Oxford, 1898; H. Achelis, *Virgines subintroductæ*, Leipsic, 1902; K. Holl, *Amphilochius von Ikonium in seinem Verhältnis zu den griechischen Kappadoziern*, pp. 30 sqq., Tübingen, 1904.

MESSIAH, MESSIANISM.

I. In the Old Testament: In the Old Testament the word "Messiah" is not used alone as an absolute title, but is usually met in the phrase "the anointed of Yahweh," meaning Yahweh's consecrated king. It is a title of honor of the reigning king of Israel from the time of Saul and David (I Sam. xxiv. 6, 10, and often). Once Yahweh applies the term to the Persian King Cyrus, because he had appointed him to carry out his designs (cf. also I Kings xix. 15, where a heathen is to be anointed king over Syria because Yahweh intends to use him as an instrument of punishment).

1. The Original Signification.

The implication of the term was that something of the sublimity and sacredness of his God had been communicated to the king, and he stood before the people as the representative of Yahweh, governing in his place. The relationship of Yahweh to the people of his covenant became in the case of the king a personal relationship. The religion of Yahweh, which had originated in individual revelations of God to a few, tended, after it had assumed a national form, toward the concentration of this relationship to God in a person. The king was the natural focus for this tendency. He was placed by the word of the prophet in that filial relation to God in which the whole people had long been conscious of standing (II Sam. vii. 14; Ex. iv. 22; Deut. xxxii. 6; Hos. xi. 1; see KINGSHIP IN ISRAEL). The relationship became in this way a more lifelike and intimate one. This religious idealization of royalty had already attained a high development in the period of the united kingdom, especially under David. As Yahweh had been from of old the king of Israel, so David, who had brought the ark of the covenant to Zion, endeavored to realize the ideal. Psalms ii., lxxii., cx., state the consequences of such a rule: Yahweh rules from Zion over the whole world, and his anointed is unconquerable and virtually Lord of all the earth. This induced the prophets Amos, Hosea, Isaiah, Micah, and others to take their stand upon the synthesis of Yahweh's residence in Zion and his establishment there of a kingdom of the house of David which was never to be overthrown (cf. Joel iii. 16; Amos i. 2; Isa. ii. 2 sqq., iv. 2 sqq.).

But the actuality in the royal person and in his government never corresponded to the lofty ideal of the prophets. Even in the time of David this fact appears, and consequently the consummation of this kingdom was postponed to the future. Thus according to the "last words" of David (II Sam. xxiii. 1 sqq.), the full glory of this kingdom had as yet only dawned, although with great promise; but under Solomon there was brought about the destruction of those beginnings which had been so full of promise. Only a poor remnant of David's kingdom remained for his heirs; nevertheless, the kings of the divided kingdom held firmly to their Messianic relationship to Yahweh, as is shown by the royal psalms, and the spiritual inheritance from the time of David remained a nourishing soil, whence new hope in a greater future would arise spontaneously or could be evoked by the words of the prophets.

2. Failure to Realize the Ideal.

Indeed, the less actualities in the kingdom of Judah corresponded to the sublimity of the ideal, the more probable it appeared that they would be fully and completely realized in the consummation of the kingdom of Yahweh. It is true that this consummation was to be preceded by the judgment of the Day of Yahweh (q.v.). This is the hope which is in a broader sense Messianic. The whole of God's activity in judgment and in mercy, to which the prophets bear witness, points toward such a consummation; but they do not always speak of such a personal Messiah in the language which later Judaism and the New Testament employed in describing the new king from the house of David, in whom the prophetic ideal of a divine and human king was to be fully realized. Some of the prophets are entirely silent regarding this organ of divine rule and speak only of Yahweh as the one to whom will belong universal dominion, while others describe as the Messiah the human bearer of the divine power and mediator of the divine mercy to his people. Indeed, some prophets recognize the Davidic king as the central point of the future kingdom of God, yet in other descriptions of the future speak solely of the coming of Yahweh and of his future residence in the midst of his people.

It was the firm conviction of the prophets of the northern kingdom that the royal house of David, in spite of its political insignificance, had an indestructible support in God's settlement upon Zion and his covenant with David; and Amos and Hosea discerned there the point of crystallization for the future kingdom of Yahweh.

3. Early Prophetic Doctrine.

Amos, however, alludes in more general terms to the reestablishment of the tabernacle of David, whose rule is again to be extended over the lands promised to him (Amos ix. 11 sqq.). Hosea speaks more individually of "the king, David" of the future (iii. 5) under whose rule the whole people will unite (i. 11) and around whom will gather those scattered and driven from the land by the judgment. In Hosea preparation is made for the portrayal of a Messiah in the later sense of the word, that is, of an ideal future king who will fully realize the sublime assurances of grace because he will be entirely worthy of them. [The passages referred to above are thought by most recent interpreters to be additions by later hands. If so, they illustrate the stages described in the sequel.] Subsequent prophets have drawn the picture with great individuality, for example, Zech. ix. 9 sqq., where the Messiah is praised as a king of peace, bringing salvation and help to his city and people. Similarly Isaiah's expectations were founded upon the house of David. For this reason they revolve about a double center, Yahweh's seat in Zion and a particular king, who, endowed with all the gracious gifts of a ruler blessed by God, is to reestablish the throne of his father. This ruler appears vaguely to the prophet in Isa. vii.; he will be born in the deepest humiliation of the royal house of David, for Immanuel is not some undetermined child who was then to be born, but the future possessor of the land (viii. 8; cf. viii. 10 with ix. 6). From this time, the figure of the descendant of David becomes continually clearer and larger to the prophet. The superhuman attributes which are heaped upon this king in ix. 6–7 should not be taken as mere hyperbole, for nothing was farther from Isaiah's mind than excessive exaltation of human greatness. The prophet would have sternly rejected any mixture of human and divine honors, such as was habitual with Assyrians, Babylonians and Egyptians. The sublime predicates applied to the scion of David can be understood only as meaning that he recognized in this future ruler a wonderful in-dwelling of God, and this affords the answer to the question as to how the texts regarding the heir to Davidic dignity can agree with the sayings of the same prophet wherein there is no mention of this human king, but only of Yahweh's sublime self-manifestation in Zion. This rule of Yahweh in Zion is the essential and most intimate part of the divine plan for the future. The son of David is only the organ, though a pure and worthy organ, of the invisible ruler. Micah, the contemporary of Isaiah, also described the coming son of David as a mysterious, sublime figure, full of the divine, ruling with infinite beatitude and peace. He, too, makes this ruler in his lofty majesty proceed from humble surroundings in David's ancestral home at Bethlehem. Micah, also, prophecies concerning Zion as God's seat, where Yahweh will reveal himself to all nations. In the prophecies of Isaiah regarding foreign nations there is again a remarkable confirmation of this universal rule of Yahweh from Zion as well as of the idealized human kingship there; Egypt and Ethiopia (Cush) and Tyre will do homage to the God of Israel, and the Moabites will seek protection and justice at the gracious throne of David.

4. Doctrine of the Later Prophets.

The utterances of Obadiah and Joel (which are here placed before those of Amos and Hosea) belong to the prophecies which do not treat of the Messiah, but of the consummation of the rule of Yahweh over Israel and over the nations; later come those of Nahum, Habakkuk (cf., however, iii. 13) and Zephaniah. In Jeremiah and Ezekiel, also, the promises which refer in general terms to God's kingdom are preponderant. The nearer the political rule of the house of David approached its fall, the more definitely did the prophets claim that to no one but to him would belong the rule over the earth, and that the remnant of his people would be distinguished before the whole world by his self-manifestation in his holy dwelling-place. However, the hope of a vicegerent of God, who will procure salvation and blessings for his people, often appears as an accompanying factor of this expectation (cf. Jer. xxiii. 5–6 with xxxiii. 1 sqq., 15 sqq.; also, Jer. xxx. 9; Ezek. xvii. 22 sqq., xxxvii. 23–24; against the attacks of those who deny the existence of Messianic prophecies in the pre-exilic period, or are at most willing to admit them after the time of Josiah, cf. W. Moeller, *Die messianische Erwartung der vorexilischen Propheten*, Gütersloh, 1906). In the "servant of Yahweh" of Deutero-Isaiah, instead of the Davidic king there appears another human figure as the medium of the consummation of the divine plan of salvation for Israel and for humanity. By his designation, he realizes fully and purely the ideal which should constitute the vocation of the whole people: to serve Yahweh in intelligent and willing obedience. Submission to the will of God is with him so complete and so thoroughly unselfish in contradistinction to the obstinacy of the people, that he endures without resistance the extreme of humiliation, the bitterest suffering and death, although he has in no wise deserved it. Precisely through such patient endurance of the unbearable does he fulfil his all-embracing mission and move onward to his exaltation. Whatever may be the difference between the appearance of this generally rejected and despised "servant of Yahweh" and the glorious king whose picture has been drawn in Isa. ix., xi.; Micah iv., etc., there exists an intimate relationship between them; Delitzsch, therefore, is quite right in calling this servant "the mediator of salvation as prophet, priest, and king in the same person." It is also true that there is no lack of testimony in favor of the external lowliness of the God-chosen prince in the earlier Messianic utterances. In Isa. xi. and elsewhere, the Messiah grows up in the lowliest surroundings. If Zech. xii.–xiv. was composed before the exile, not only was the synthesis between the royal and the prophetic vocation already completed, but the chastisement and the death of the trusted companion of God, of the true shepherd of his people, had also been predicted. It is the bitter sorrow over his death which brings the saving change of heart among the people. After the Babylonian exile Messianic prophecy revives both in a narrower and a broader sense. Haggai and Zechariah at first had in view the rebuilding of the temple as the place where Yahweh would reveal himself more sublimely than ever before. But this future revelation of the invisible God can not be separated from the elevation of the house of David (Hag. ii. 20 sqq.), nor from the appearance of the "sprout" of this race, which, springing from such small beginnings, is to complete the divine structure on Zion and unite the royal with the priestly dignity for the blessing of his people (Zechariah). Malachi, without alluding to this personality, speaks of the coming "angel of Yahweh" who will sit in judgment on his people; and, as regards human instruments, he thinks only of an "Elias," who will prepare the way for him. Finally, in the book of Daniel, the kingdom of God appears and is to triumph over the successive empires through the "people of the saints," i.e., Israel, which has remained faithful. But this people is to have a human chief who is designated as the "son of Man," vii., 13. Here the Messiah acquires a universal designation which Jesus assumes in the New Testament.

5. Individualization of the Messianic Idea.

When, however, the figure of the great future king had become rooted in the hope of the community, prophecies concerning him were found not only in such utterances as expressly mentioned him, but passages which referred in the first place to the living and ruling kings of Israel and Judah were also brought into relationship with him. His figure was embellished from Psalms such as ii., xlv., lxxii., cx., and, indeed, from the royal psalms in general, and words which were used in regard to the rise or glorification of royalty in Israel were referred to the Messiah personally (as Num. xxiv. 15-19). Even such passages as Gen. ix. 25-27, xii. 1-3, and the analagous sayings of the patriarchs were interpreted in the same way; more especially Gen. xlix. 10 and similar texts were conceived in a directly Messianic sense. Later the Church placed Gen. iii. 14-15 at the head as the protevangelium, since it announced the victory of the seed of the woman (which was taken in an individual sense) over the power of evil. The words of Deut. xviii. 15, also, were interpreted to signify an individual prophet, and he was partially identified with the Messiah. The tendency to interpret many passages as Messianic had become habitual in the Jewish community before Christ. In the so-called apocryphal writings of the Old Testament the Messianic hope is not prominent. The reason for this is to be sought partly in the historical and didactic character of the class of writings to which these books belong, partly in the fact that expectations regarding the future were not so much in the foreground in the circles in which these writings originated. On the other hand, the Pseudepigrapha (q.v.) prove that after the Maccabean period the Messianic hope, both in a wider and in a narrower sense, awakened to new life. As long as it seemed that the honored Hasmoneans (q.v.) would be able to lead the people to a new and happy future, the parties attached to them had no longing for the dynasty of David. It was rather a subject of satisfaction that the theocratic offices were united in them, as when John Hyrcanus, in addition to his princely dignity, was also endowed with that of high priest and was even regarded as a prophet with whom God communicated (Josephus, *Ant.* XIII., x. 7; *War* I., ii. 8). Prophecies such as Ob. 19 sqq. and Amos ix. 11-12, seemed to be fulfilled by him when he conquered Samaria and Idumæa, destroyed the temple on Gerizim, and forced circumcision upon the Edomites. The narrow and formal spirit which reigned among the devotees of the law was as little favorable to the comprehension of the prophecies regarding the future salvation of the people as was Philonic Hellenism.

II. In the Pseudepigrapha: In the mean time eschatology, which had been neglected by the teachers of the law and by the philosophers, found all the more zealous adherents in certain circles and was brought into connection with the general historical interests of the time, resulting in the production of apocalyptic writings.

1. Influence of Eschatology.

The newly won and often quite modern conceptions were put in the mouth of some seer or sage of primitive times, Enoch, Abraham, Moses, Elias, Ezra, Baruch, or Solomon. Whether this was understood by contemporaries as being only a disguise, or whether it was taken in earnest, the trivial origin and character of these apocalyptic books, as compared with those of former times, was well understood in the higher circles of Judaism, and the pseudepigrapha were not read in the synagogue. Nevertheless, in a more private way they were widely circulated, and exercised a potent influence upon the religious conceptions of the people and upon their hopes. These aspirations regarding the future were even placed in the mouths of the heathen Sibyls by Hellenistic Jews. The mystic tendencies of Greek civilization were appealed to by Jews who were in touch with the Greeks, and they presented these mysterious prophetesses, in whom the old heathen oracles were personified, as the bearers of Jewish ideas, above all of the belief in one God in contrast with idolatry. This was done in such a way, however, that the general history of the peoples as well as heathen mythology, which was treated in a euhemeristic manner, were freely interwoven with these sayings. The Sibylline Books (q.v.) arose in this way, and their beginnings should be placed not long after the time of the Maccabees. Of the collection of Sibylline Books extant, the larger part of book iii. comes from the period of Ptolemy VII. Physkon (145-117), probably from the time after 140 B.C. In this writing, the history of the world is passed in review from the building of the tower of Babel until the period of the author; then the end of the world is predicted as imminent, coming to pass through the manifestation of the God of Israel and of his Messiah (verse 652 sqq.: "Then will God send a king from where the sun rises" in agreement with the passage Isa. xli. 25, which was used in a Messianic sense) who will make an end of wicked war over the whole earth, by killing some and making binding treaties with the others" (cf. Isa. xi. 4 with ii. 2 sqq.), etc.

2. Messianism of Earlier Part of Enoch.

The eschatological hope was, however, even more frequently and exhaustively treated in an esoteric form, as is shown above all in the Book of Enoch (see PSEUDEPIGRAPHA), the original version of which, chaps. i.-xxxvi., lxxii.-cv., may probably be referred to about 110 B.C. The Messiah appears in chaps. lxxxv.-xc. For the period between the destruction of Jerusalem and the erection of the Messianic kingdom, Israel will be placed by God under seventy shepherds (lxxxix. 59). The seventy years of servitude of Jeremiah become seventy heathen rulers, who each reign for one hour, as in Daniel for seventy weeks of years. The shepherds are not human kings but angels of the peoples (Von Hofmann, Schürer), each feeds his flock for one hour. The first (Assyrio-Babylonian) period comprises twelve hours (lxxxix. 72), the second twenty-three hours (Cyrus to Alexander; the reading of the text, "thirty-five," includes the preceding twelve); this is the central point of the era (xc. 1). After this follow other twenty-three hours (Alexander to Antiochus Epiphanes, xc. 5) and twelve still remain from Antiochus to the time of the writer (xc. 17). If the great horn (xc. 9) refers to Hyrcanus, then the time of this ruler must be looked upon as that of the author. After this goat with the great horn has been sorely beset by all nations, the saving angel appears and causes the destruction of the enemies. The nations fall beneath the sword of the obedient sheep, that is, the faithful Israelites. God sets up his throne in the holy land and holds his judgment there over the fallen angels, and also over the seventy shepherds; they are found guilty and cast into a fiery abyss. Into a similar fiery pit, which opens up at the right of the house of God (Gehinnom), come the blinded sheep, that is, the apostate Jews. Thereupon God erects a new temple wherein he dwells in the midst of the good sheep, before whom the remaining nations bow down in adoration. The scattered and slain sheep are also gathered together again in this house. Then a white steer is born, the Messiah, to whom all nations do homage, and thereupon all the sheep change into white steers, that is to say, into men resembling patriarchs (for the first men from Adam on have appeared to the seer as white and black steers, lxxxv. 3 sqq.). This first-born steer of the new race, however, the Messiah, changes into a buffalo [wild ox] with large black horns. Since then the tried companions of the kingdom become like the Messiah, he himself is exalted and becomes a superior being. The vision closes harmoniously with the untroubled joy of God in all men. Here the Messiah does not erect the kingdom of God on earth and also does not hold the last judgment, but only appears at the end, after the earth has been purified and subjected to God, as the keystone of the edifice.

3. The Psalms of Solomon.

It is otherwise in the Psalms of Solomon (see PSEUDEPIGRAPHA), which show that in the middle of the last century before Christ a vigorous interposition in history for the salvation of his people was expected from the Messiah. These Psalms may be more exactly assigned to about the period 63–45 B.C. The Messianic hope must have penetrated deeply into the popular mind at that period, especially among the Pharisees (cf., e.g., iii. 8 sqq.), and the idea that eternal salvation was promised to Israel was firmly held (xi. 7, xii. 6, xiv. 4–5, 9–10, xv. 12–13). More definitely, a salutary action was awaited from the "Son of David," the "anointed of the Lord," whom God will raise up, that he may conquer the heathen rulers, purify the desecrated land of the Lord, gather together the members of his people and reestablish their nationality, while the heathen do homage to him (xvii. 21 sqq.). He is just and sinless and brings to his people eternal peace and eternal salvation, so that to live beneath his rule will be a blessed condition.

4. The Later Part of Enoch.

Much more highly developed is the conception of the Messiah contained in the later portion of the Book of Enoch, chaps. xxxvii.–lxxi., written after 38 B.C. While in the older book the perfect just live upon the earth, in the spacious and new house of God, in the later writing the abode of the blessed is celestial (xxxix. 4 sqq.), and they will also inhabit the new earth when the evil-doers have been rooted out (xlv. 5). The kingdom of God as described by the later writer is conceived in a more transcendental manner. Heaven is the home of holy men where they live forever like the angels of God; among them there the Messiah dwells eternally (xxxix. 6 sqq.), is called the "chosen one" (xxxix. 6, xl. 5, xlv. 3), the just one (xxxviii. 2), the anointed (lii. 4), the son of man (xlvi. 1 sqq.); in one passage God himself calls him "my son" (cv. 2, cf. Ps. ii. 7). He is the possessor of all justice and wisdom (xlix. 3); from him proceeds intelligence and power, he is the staff of the just and the holy, the light of the nations, and the hope of those whose heart is troubled (xlviii. 4); he leads all the inhabitants of the earth to sing the praises of the true God (xlviii. 5); in him dwells the spirit of those who have fallen asleep in righteousness (xlix. 3). Through his wisdom the resurrection takes place, and through his unfailing justice the last judgment (li.–liv., lxi. 7 sqq.). With him the just will enjoy a glorified existence for eternity; the unjust, on the other hand, and especially the kings, the high and mighty ones of the earth, will languish in hell (lxii. 13 sqq., lxiii. 10). In chap. lxxi. Enoch himself is declared to be the son of man and by his translation from the earth is established in heaven in this character, and the later rabbinical theologians make him the equal of the *Metatron*, that is, the highest spirit, who stands nearest to God and serves him and governs with him. This section was not written by a Christian, since the human personality of the Messiah conceived by Christians as a living reality is entirely lacking in this writing. Even a Christian "reviser" would assuredly have introduced something of this and especially of Christ's sufferings, death, and resurrection. In favor of the opinion that the book was written after the time of Christ is the circumstance that, according to the Gospels, the expression "son of man" was in no wise so common a designation of the Messiah among the contemporaries of Jesus as it must have become after this work was generally known.

5. The Apocalypse of Baruch.

Baruch and the Apocalypse of Ezra (IV Ezra), which have been preserved in a Syriac version, belong to the period after the destruction of Jerusalem by the Romans. Baruch seems to have been composed not long after that event. It proves that the longing for the splendid future promised by the prophets had been newly and powerfully stimulated by the destruction of Jerusalem and of its sanctuary, and that the people, by manifold explanations and embellishments of these promises, consoled themselves in their unhappy situation. Bitter oppression, devastations, wars, and unrest were expected in the immediate future as precursors of the end (xxvii., cf. lxix.–lxx.). Then the Messiah will reveal himself and will shield the remnant of his people in his land (lxxi.). He will usher in a period of great prosperity (xxix. 5 sqq., cf. lxxiii.–lxxiv.), and the earth will give forth her fruits a thousand fold. Then he will return to heaven (xxx. 1), whereupon the resurrection of the dead and the last judgment will take place. The four kingdoms of Daniel appear in chaps. xxxv. sqq., wherein the Roman empire is explained to be the fourth kingdom. Under this rule the Messiah appears; he uproots this kingdom (xxxix. 7), kills the unjust ruler of the world (xli.–xlii.), and the nations are delivered into "the hands of my servant," the Messiah (lxx. 9, lxxi. 1). Some of the nations will be destroyed, while others will be spared, according to their conduct toward Israel, to whom those that are spared shall be subject (lxxii. 2 sqq.). At the resurrection the dead are given up by the earth in the form in which it received them; then, however, the corporeal form changes according to the conduct shown in life. The just receive an ethereal body, which can not age and resembles that of the angels, with whom they live in the heavenly paradise (xlix. sqq.). According to this book, therefore, the kingdom of the Messiah precedes the end of the world; it belongs to "this eon" and constitutes its last period. On the other hand, the future life of the just in the coming eon is described as transcendental and heavenly.

6. The Apocalypse of Ezra.

Related to the Apocalypse of Baruch is the Apocalypse of Ezra, commonly called IV. Ezra, which is probably of somewhat later date. Chaps iii.–xiv. were written under Domitian, about 96 A.D., chaps. i., ii., xv. and xvi. are additions by a Christian writer. This book is a species of theodicy in apocalyptic garb. It is revealed to the Jewish author that the eon approaches its end (iv. 26); the world has grown old (v. 50 sqq.); wonderful signs of the last revelations will be manifest on earth (vi. 11 sqq., cf. ix. 1 sqq.). The men who have been translated without enduring death (Enoch, Elias, Ezra) will show themselves, evil will be rooted out, faith will flourish, and truth will be manifested (vi. 25 sqq.). Since the world was created for the Jews (vi. 55), they will rule over it after the godless have been swept away by plagues. Then the Messiah (vii. 28) will appear and will for 400 years give joy to all who have survived; then he will die and all men with him (vii. 29). After seven days of silence, there follow the resurrection of the dead and the day of judgment, lasting a week of years, when the Most High will sit upon the throne. The conception of the Messiah appears in the vision of the eagle, by which the Roman empire up to the time of Domitian is represented (xi. 1 sqq.). Against this eagle (the fourth world-kingdom of Daniel, xii. 11 sqq.) there finally comes a lion speaking with the voice of a man (xi. 36 sqq.). He is a symbol of the Messiah (xii. 32) whom the Most High has reserved for the end of days. He will then arise from the seed of David and will pass judgment on mankind. He will redeem the remnant of his people and give them joy until, after 400 years, the final judgment occurs. In the following vision (xiii. 1 sqq.) a man appears from the sea and flies upon the clouds of heaven; he sends from his mouth a stream of fire against all who oppose him, while God calls him "my Son" (xiii. 32). He will judge and destroy the froward by his word alone (cf. Isa. xi. 4), and then will lead back to their native land the ten exiled tribes.

III. Late Jewish Messianism:

1. General Characteristics.

Apocalyptic literature was far from being exhausted in this period and continued to be cultivated in Jewish (cf. M. Buttenwieser, *Outlines of the Neo-Hebraic Apocalyptic Literature*, Cincinnati, 1901) and Christian circles for several centuries. The Christians as a rule only elaborated Jewish originals and sometimes simply provided them with annotations. These writings offer fantastic pictures of future conditions, since in the domain of eschatology a large field was left open to the imagination of the individual writer. From the first century before Christ, the Messianic hope was drawn only partly from the writings of the Old Testament. It is, then, very easy to understand that although this hope was very wide-spread and held powerful sway over religious sentiment and expectation, it had neither clear outlines nor a well-defined unity. It had a popular side, promising material blessings, and also a more spiritual side, which is found in the Gospels and in Jewish writings after the time of Christ. The rabbinical view of the Messiah runs in the following manner:

2. In the First Christian Century.

That, in the time of Jesus, the hope of a proximate appearance of the Messiah was part and parcel of the Jewish common belief, is apparent in the Gospels. Naturally this hope was most stedfastly maintained and faithfully cherished among such faithful Israelites as Simeon and Anna (Luke ii. 25–26, 36–37), John the Baptist and his followers, and the disciples of Jesus. Even the Pharisees, the opponents of Jesus, expected the coming of the son of David who was to bring about the realization of the kingdom of God. The common people also held so firmly to this conviction that they were more than once tempted to make Jesus king, and for this very reason he exercised extreme caution and self-restraint in the revelation of his Messianic character. Even the ill-fated insurrection that led to the destruction of the temple in the year 70 was caused in part by Messianic expectations of a political character (Josephus, *War*, VI., v. 4, probably based on Dan. ix. 24–27, viii. 13–14). Josephus luminously refers to false prophets and seducers (*War*, II., xiii. 4), and says that till the end of the siege the zealots hoped that salvation would suddenly be accorded from above (*War*, VI., v. 2). Once again did the Messianic hope, attaching itself to Bar Kokba (q.v.), animate the people to a daring struggle for freedom in spite of warnings on the part of some teachers. Against this expectation a few voiced their dissent, as in the case of Rabbi Hillel, to whom the celebrated Rabbi Joseph of Pumbedita replied.

3. Early Rabbinic Ideals.

The rabbis usually placed the coming of the Messiah in the age then present. The "days of the Messiah" was an indefinite period, which, however, was to form the transition to that state of perfect retribution which begins with the resurrection of the dead (cf. Luke xx. 34–35, xviii. 30; Matt. xii. 32). Sometimes the age of the Messiah was placed in the future. After the temporally limited Messianic kingdom, the destruction of this world and the creation of a new world were to follow. In the future world there is neither eating nor drinking nor procreation. Messianic times would be preceded by a great humiliation of the Jews and a war of all kingdoms against each other, which would mark the birth-pangs of the Messiah. All manner of plagues, the sword, hunger, pestilence, earthquakes, are to occur. Israel will find rescue from these tribulations by holding fast to the Torah and by works of mercy. But the Jewish nation will have been reduced to extremities. Nevertheless, the belief is not lacking that the Messiah would find a people worthily prepared.

4. The Functions of Elias.

As a rule, the preparation of the nation for the coming of the Messiah was expected through Elias, whose reappearance was awaited by the scribes (Ecclus. xlviii. 1–10, on the basis of Mal. iii. 1 sqq.; cf. Matt. xvii. 10–11, xi. 14). This is indeed usually understood in a purely material sense; however, Malachi did not exclude a spiritual purification and unity. According to rabbinic teaching, Elias was to purify the law from spurious intrusions, and restore clauses wrongly excluded, to decide questions under debate, bring about the final atonement for Israel, and even cause the resurrection of the dead (cf. C. Schöttgen, *Horæ Ebraicæ*, pp. 533 sqq., Leipsic, 1733–42; J. Lightfoot, *Horæ Hebraicæ*, ii. 384, 609, 965, Leipsic, 1679). Other great prophets, as Moses and Jeremiah, were expected to arise from the dead at the beginning of the Messianic epoch and aid the Messiah in his work.

5. Duration of Messianic Rule.

The duration of the Messianic kingdom was expected to be limited (cf. *Baba Sanhedrin*, 97 sqq.: "It is a tradition of the school of Elias that the world will last 6,000 years: 2,000 tohu, 2,000 torah, 2,000 days of the Messiah; but, because of our sins, which are many, a part of this time has elapsed"). In another view the duration of the world is placed at eighty-five jubilee periods, in the last of which the son of David comes, "whether at the beginning or at the end of it, no one knows." Others, on the contrary, reject any chronological calculation regarding the coming of the Messiah. When calculation is made, the duration of the days of the Messiah rests upon many different methods and reaches divergent results. Some reckon it at forty years (cf. Ps. xcv. 10); others, again, conjecture seventy years (Isa. xxiii. 15); R. Akiba, forty years, from the forty years in the wilderness; in *Sifre*, 134a, the Messianic period is extended to three generations (cf. Ps. lxxii. 5, where, however, the duration is not given). Still others discover 100, 365, 1,000, 2,000, or even 7,000 years.

6. The Person of the Messiah.

The person of the Messiah, the son of David, is usually conceived as human, and this is more and more sharply insisted on in contradistinction to Christianity. The strongest statement of this kind is that in Justin Martyr, *Trypho*, xlix., *ANF*, i. 219: "We all expect that Christ will be a man." The passage *Taanith*, ii. 1, is also sharply polemical: R. Abbahu spoke: "If a man say to you, 'I am God'—he lies; 'I am the Son of Man'—he will repent it at the end; 'I shall ascend to heaven'—he will not prove it." In general, the mysterious quality of the prophetic utterances is reduced to the standard of common humanity. The names of the Messiah in Isa. ix. 6 are for the most part attributed to God, even though this requires arbitrary exegesis. Hence the Messiah comes like others of the race of David. The assertion that the Targums sometimes identify the Messiah with the *memra de Yahweh* ("word of Yahweh") is incorrect. On the contrary, this divine word is expressly distinguished from the Messiah, as in *Targum Jonathan* to Isa. ix. 6–7, where the concluding sentence is rendered: "through the memra of Yahweh will this be performed." It is, however, quite true that a kind of preexistence of the Messiah in heaven was taught. Thus his name was pronounced by God even before the creation (*Bereshith rabba*, chap. i.), though this signifies merely that he was from the beginning an object of the divine plans of salvation. A more real preexistence is implied in the Book of Enoch and the related apocalyptic writings, and even in some Midrashim appears the doctrine that the Messiah is a superior being who existed before all time. Still, such passages as *Bereshith rabba* to Gen. i. 2 do not prove that the Messiah was regarded as a divine being in the metaphysical sense.

7. The Messiah's Activities.

The Messiah was to appear suddenly (*Baba Sanhedrin* 97: "Three things come unexpectedly: the Messiah, a thing that is found, and a scorpion"), though the exact time is a subject of dispute. A period of concealment on earth, however, precedes his appearance (Justin Martyr, *Trypho*, viii.). Christ when he comes is unknown, does not even know himself (as Messiah) until the prophet Elias comes, anoints him, and reveals everything (*Trypho*, cx.). In the mean time, he perfects himself in the knowledge of God and of the Law, instructed by God as were Abraham, Job, and Hezekiah (*Bammidbar rabba*, xiv.), and submits to discipline in good works. According to *Sanhedrin*, 98a, he sits in Rome at the gate, surrounded by the wretched and the sick, whose wounds he binds, waiting for that "to-day" (Ps. xcv. 7) when the conversion of his people will allow him to come to them. By this recognition of a state of lowliness and disesteem an effort was made to do some slight justice to the picture of the suffering Messiah in Isa. lii., liii., recognized as Messianic by the Targum, although with a weakening of the vicarious expiatory sufferings and death there portrayed. Later, this suffering figure, if it were at all accepted, was referred to another and subordinate Messiah (see below). Regarding the form in which the son of

David was to appear, there was never a very clear idea. The distinction between Dan. vii. 13 and Zech. ix. 9 presented an enigma to the rabbis. His work consists in breaking the foreign yoke (*Targum Jonathan* to Isa. x. 27) and bringing his people back from captivity. In order to erect his kingdom (*Targum Onkelos* to Num. xxiv. 17; *Targum Jonathan* to Amos ix. 11; Origen, *Contra Celsum*, ii. 29) he endures mighty struggles with the nations (*Targum Jonathan* to Zech. x. 4). The principal enemy is the Roman empire, whose leader Armilius, who is the anti-Messiah, will be killed by the breath from the lips of the Messiah (cf. II Thess. ii. 8, and J. A. Eisenmenger, *Entdecktes Judenthum*, ii. 705 sqq., Frankfort, 1700). The dispute whether the ten tribes are or are not included in this bringing back of the exiles was decided in later times by assuming the coming of a second, subordinate Messiah, the son of Joseph, to be the precursor of the son of David (*Baba Sukkah*, 52a). This Messiah is to be a descendant of Ephraim; he will lead back the ten tribes from their exile and subject them to the son of David, and will then be killed in the war with Gog and Magog. His death, according to a later conception, will serve as an expiation for the sins of Jeroboam (cf. Eisenmenger, ut sup., ii. 720 sqq.). By this assumption of two Messiahs a place was sought for those features of the suffering and murdered Messiah which are present in Isa. liii. and Zech. xii. 10, yet were not easily included in the usual conception of the Messiah. At an earlier period, however, the rabbis knew of only one Messiah, and while they often acknowledge the prophecies concerning his sufferings, they attenuate them by saying that the Messiah is at first to work in lowliness among the poor and wretched and to suffer because of the sins of his people, which delay his revelation (so *Targum Jonathan* to Isa. liii.). The suffering servant of Yahweh is an especially favorite theme. Later Judaism with its ceremonial righteousness was little inclined to receive the more earnest Biblical promise of a complete atonement. The activity of the Messiah will, therefore, consist in bringing about the universal rule of the Jewish theocracy. He will rebuild the temple in Jerusalem and establish the authority of the Torah.

8. Accompaniments of the Messiah's Coming.

The fruitfulness of the land and the prosperity of the nation are described in glowing terms, and in these blessings the repatriated exiles and even the departed just will also share, since a first resurrection of the dead takes place in the land of Israel, the faithful who have died in other lands being transported thither beneath the surface of the earth (Eisenmenger, ut sup., ii. 893 sqq.). The reawakening of the dead is sometimes ascribed to God and sometimes to the Messiah; it occurs at the sound of a trumpet, but the Samaritans will be excluded from it. *Kethubot* (111b) says that even the unlearned will have no part in it. The living heathen will offer homage to the Messiah and to the sanctuary at Jerusalem, though there will be a great difference and a strict barrier between them and Israel. Following the order of events as given in Ezekiel, at the end of the Messianic epoch, there will again ensue a general uprising of the heathen nations against the rule of the Messiah, the originators and leaders of which will be Gog and Magog, though according to other views they are the bitterest enemies of the Messiah at the beginning of the Messianic era. This uprising is succeeded by a final and universal judgment of the world, with the resurrection of all the dead to eternal happiness or to condemnation. Then begins the state of perfection, for which a new heaven and a new earth are created. The just enter into paradise, the godless into the pains of hell. Still, it must be admitted that this distinction is not always maintained, and the two epochs often run into one another. In one particular, however, there is agreement: the Messiah brings about the consummation of all things and the resurrection of the just to new and eternal life precedes the state of final retribution.

C. VON ORELLI.

BIBLIOGRAPHY: The material on Messianism is abundant. The reader is referred to the commentaries on the Biblical books containing passages regarded as Messianic, to works on Biblical theology, especially those of Schultz and Dillmann: the subject is also treated more or less fully in the literature given under APOCRYPHA; ISRAEL, HISTORY OF; PROPHECY; and PSEUDEPIGRAPHA. On the Messianism of the Bible there is nothing better than the works of C. A. Briggs on the subject: *Messianic Prophecy*, New York, 1886; and *Messiah of the Gospels*, 3 series, New York, 1893–95. A thoroughly worthy book on Old-Testament Messianism is F. H. Woods, *The Hope of Israel*, ib. 1896. Considerably broader in scope, but based on what used to be called rationalistic exegesis, is the scholarly work by J. Drummond, *The Jewish Messiah*, London, 1877, covering the period down to the close of the Talmud. A book which has caused much debate from its extreme positions is A. Kuenen, *Prophets and Prophecy in Israel*, ib. 1877. Consult further: J. C. K. Hofmann, *Weissagung und Erfüllung*, Nördlingen, 1841–44; J. J. Stähelin, *Die messianischen Weissagungen des A. T.*, Berlin, 1847; E. W. Hengstenberg, *Christologie des A. T.*, 3 vols., Berlin, 1854–57, Eng. transl., *Christology of the O. T.*, Edinburgh, 1854–1858; A. Tholuck, *Die Propheten und ihre Weissagungen*, Gotha, 1867; R. Anger, *Geschichte der messianischen Idee*, Berlin, 1873; E. C. A. Riehm, *Die messianische Weissagung*, Gotha, 1875, Eng. transl., *Messianic Prophecy*; Edinburgh, 1891; E. Böhl, *Christologie des A. T.*, Vienna, 1882; W. F. Adeney, *The Hebrew Utopia; a Study of Messianic Prophecy*, London, 1879; P. J. Gloag, *Messianic Prophecies*, Edinburgh, 1879 (conservative); C. von Orelli, *Die alttestamentliche Weissagung*, Vienna, 1882, Eng. transl., *Old Testament Prophecy of Consummation of God's Kingdom*, Edinburgh, 1885; B. W. Saville, *Fulfilled Prophecy*, London, 1882; A. Edersheim, *Prophecy and History in Relation to the Messiah*, ib. 1885; E. H. Dewart, *Jesus the Messiah in Prophecy and Fulfillment*, Cincinnati, 1891; G. S. Goodspeed, *Israel's Messianic Hope*, New York, 1900; F. Delitzsch, *Die messianische Weissagungen*, Berlin, 1899, Eng. transl. of earlier ed., *Messianic Prophecies in Historical Succession*, Edinburgh, 1891; J. Richter, *Die messianischen Weissagungen und ihre Erfüllung*, Giessen, 1905; J. H. Greenstone, *The Messiah Idea in Jewish History*, Philadelphia, 1907; W. O. Oesterley, *The Evolution of the Messianic Idea*, London, 1908; Lagrange, *Le Messianisme chez les Juifs*, Paris, 1908; E. P. Berg, *Our Lord's Preparation for Messiahship*, London, 1909; A. Causse, *L'Evolution de l'espérance messianique dans le christianisme primitif*, Paris, 1909.

On the late Jewish ideas the works of Eisenmenger and Schöttgen mentioned in the text are to be placed among the important contributions. Consult further. R. Young, *Christology of the Targums*, Edinburgh, 1853; A. Hilgenfeld, *Die jüdische Apokalyptik, in ihrer geschichtlichen Entwickelung*, Jena, 1857; T. Colani, *Jésus Christ et les croyances messianiques de son temps*, Strasburg, 1864; Holtzmann, in *Jahrbücher für deutsche Theologie*, 1867, pp. 389 sqq.; A. Wünsche, *Die Leiden des Messias*, Leipsic, 1870; M. Vernes, *Hist. des idées messianiques*, Paris, 1874; F. Weber, *System der altsynagogalen palästinischen Theologie*, Leipsic, 1880; J. Hamburger, *Realencyklopädie für Bibel und Talmud*, vol. ii., Strelitz, 1883; G. Dalman, *Der leidende und sterbende Messias der Synagoge*, Berlin, 1888; J. Wellhausen, *Skizzen und Vorarbeiten*, part vi., Berlin, 1899; E. Huhn, *Die messianischen Weissagungen*, Tübingen, 1899; W. Wrede, *Das Messiahgeheimniss in den Evangelien*, Göttingen, 1901; Schürer, *Geschichte*, vols. ii.–iii., and the Eng. transl. The articles in *DB*, *EB*, and *JE* are also to be used on the Biblical side.

MESTREZAT, mes″tre″zā′, **JEAN**: French Reformed; b. in Geneva 1592; d. in Paris May 2, 1657. He studied in Saumur, then accepted a call from the church at Charenton, and remained there till his death. He was a learned theologian, a distinguished preacher, and one of the main supports of the French Reformed Church in the seventeenth century. He was active in its synods, in its disputations with the Jesuits, and in its negotiations with the court. He published many sermons, which are interesting to the historian of the Reformed preaching because of their expository character (e.g., *Exposition de l'epître aux Hebreux*, 5 parts, Geneva, 1653–55). His other writings are polemical; a treatise, *De la communion à Jesu Christ au sacrement de l'eucharistie* (Sedan, 1624), was translated into German (Frankfort, 1624), English (1631), and Italian (Geneva, 1638).

(C. Schmidt†.)

Bibliography: André, *Essai sur les œuvres de J. Mestrezat*, Strasburg, 1847; A. Archimard, in *Mémoires et documents*, xv. 29–72, published by the Society of History, Geneva; Lichtenberger, *ESR*, ix. 113–121.

METALS, HEBREW USE OF.

The mountains of Palestine show strata of the Upper Cretaceous formation, older deposits occur only sporadically, and the coast plains and valley of the Jordan contain fluvial deposits; all these formations are notably poor in metals. The reference in the latter part of Deut. viii. 9, where the Holy Land is extolled as a "land whose stones are iron, and out of whose hills thou mayest dig copper," can not be to [modern] oreless Palestine; while in the first clause the author may have had in mind the black basaltic rocks east of the Jordan. It is furthermore probable that he consolidates with the promised land a large portion of Lebanon, where mining was practised. The neighboring regions are in this respect more favorably endowed. On Mt. Sinai, mining (of copper) dates back into the fourth dynasty (c. 3000 B.C.). And in the north, Lebanon yields ore, though in small quantities. Traces of old copper mines and iron mines occur north of Beirut in the Kesravan range, described in the annals of Sargon as one that contains mines. The Septuagint of I Kings ii. 46c of Swete's ed. (= ii. 48 of Lagarde) has a passage bearing on this point, which is wanting in the Hebrew and reads: "And Solomon began to open up the mighty riches of Lebanon." Jeremiah (xv. 12) also speaks of "iron from the north." On the other hand, the mines which so strongly impress the poetical Job should be sought in the Sinaitic peninsula or in Nubia. At all events the Israelites for the most part derived their metals from the neighboring peoples, but they soon learned the art of working them. It was known that the ores must be cleansed of their impure ingredients, a result mainly achieved by the smelting-process. In order to accelerate the separation of metals in fusion, they added some such vegetable alkaline salt (*bōr*) as the carbonate of potash obtained from wood ashes, or a mineral alkaline salt (*nete;* cf. Isa. i. 25; Ezek. xxii. 18–22).

1. Mineral Poverty of Palestine.

Gold (*zahabh*, *paz*, "fine gold," Ps. xix. 10, xxi. 3; Isa. xiii. 12; chiefly in poetical passages; *kethem* and *haruṣ* almost exclusively in poetic style; Isa. xiii. 12; Job xxviii. 16, etc.; Zech. ix. 3; Ps. lxviii. 13; Prov. iii. 14), according to the Old Testament, comes principally from Ophir (I Kings ix. 26 sqq.), Havilah (Gen. ii. 11) and Sheba (I Kings x. 2). The gold of Ophir was deemed peculiarly fine (Job xxviii. 16; Ps. xlv. 9). During Solomon's reign, the gold from those countries reached the Israelites in course of the king's direct mercantile operations; otherwise through the Phenicians. Early narratives ascribe wealth in gold to the patriarchs (Gen. xiii. 2, xxiv. 22, 53). Solomon's ships are supposed to have brought from Ophir gold to the amount of 420 talents (about $25,000,000)—an enormous sum for those times, yet consistent with legendary embellishment (cf. I Kings x. 21). It was the Phenicians, recognized as expert goldsmiths, who served as guides to the Israelites in the goldsmith's art, and from them the Israelites obtained the finer products of the metal. Nevertheless, the goldsmith's craft was early plied among the Israelites (cf. Judges viii. 27, xvii. 4). For gold as a medium of exchange see Money of the Bible. The earliest gold coin in Palestine was the daric. Yet even in early times the gold employed as money had its fixed forms in the shape of bars ["wedges" or "tongues"; see Gezer] and rings of defined weight. Otherwise, gold was chiefly wrought into objects of adornment—rings, chains, jewels, drinking-vessels, cups (see Dress and Ornament, Hebrew). The account of the building of the Temple says much of the golden utensils for use there (I Kings x. 21) and of overlaying the walls and doors with gold-leaf (I Kings vi. and vii.). Possibly this belongs to the later legend (cf. Benzinger on I Kings vii. 48 sqq.); the Temple in later times had great treasures, which in seasons of necessity served as a state reserve (cf. II Kings xii. 14; Ezra i. 7 sqq.; I Macc. i. 21 sqq.). In special favor stood the art of inlaying with gold-leaf; idolatrous images were overlaid with gold (Judges viii. 27; Isa. xxx. 22); Solomon's throne was of ivory, "overlaid with the finest gold" (I Kings x. 18); and his officers had "targets of beaten gold" (I Kings x. 16; cf. I Macc. vi. 2). Textures interwoven with gold threads were much esteemed (Ps. xlv. 13; Judith x. 21; Ecclus. xlv. 10).

2. Gold.

Silver (*keseph*) also came to the Israelites by way of the Phenicians, and principally from Tarshish

(Jer. x. 9; Ezek. xxvii. 12). Pliny reports that when the Phenicians made their first voyage to Spain, they had silver anchors cast in that country. Unfortunately it is not stated where Solomon obtained his abundant silver (I Kings x. 27). The practical uses of silver answered in general to those of gold; for current exchange (Gen. xxiii. 16, xliii. 21), for utensils and ornament (Gen. xliv. 2; Ex. xxviii. 27 sqq.; I Chron. xxii. 14). [In the earliest times gold was more plentiful and less precious than silver, which had to be purified by smelting. But after the Phenicians had utilized the great deposits of Spain, the abundance of silver caused its relative deterioration in value, and it has ever since been worth less than gold.] The ratio of value between silver and gold was constant throughout the East, one to thirteen and one-half, the ratio between the moon's revolution and that of the sun, silver being "moon metal" and gold belonging to the sun. Copper, however, belongs to Venus-Ishtar, and its ratio to silver is as one to sixty. It has been known in the East from very remote times; and it was known there at a very early period that the combination of copper with tin, or bronze, shows a much greater degree of hardness than pure copper. Reference has been made to the ancient copper mines on Sinai, and in Babylonia the copper utensils of Telloh date from about the same era, c. 3000 B.C. In Canaan copper was known long before the incursion of the Israelites. The specimens discovered in Tell Hesy (probably Lachish) date from about 1500 B.C. Bronze appears in that country from c. 1250, and from c. 800 B.C. was more and more supplanted by iron. Goliath had bronze weapons, and his spear's head alone is iron (I Sam. xvii. 5). In Jericho, the Israelites acquired copper and bronze vessels. Because the Phenicians fetched their material from Cyprus, a principal mart of native copper, it came to be termed "Cyprian ore," or *cyprium, cuprum.* Many objects were wrought of bronze; bow, shield, spear, greaves (II Sam. xxi. 16, xxii. 35); all sorts of household and cooking utensils (cf. I Kings vii.), mirrors (Ex. xxxviii. 8; Job. xxvii. 18), chains, bars, and doors (II Sam. iii. 34; Deut. xxxiii. 25; Ps. cvii. 16; Isa. xlv. 2); also sacred images (Num. xxi. 9); in the Temple the utensils of the court and for sacrifices—the altar, the "sea," the pillars Jachin and Boaz, the basins, etc. (I Kings vii. 13-46). That the Israelites, even though not strangers to bronze-casting, were not equipped for elaborate and artistic achievements in Solomon's time is plain from the circumstance that Solomon had the Temple utensils designed by Hiram of Tyre (I Kings vii. 13 sqq.). The imagery of the Bible makes bronze the symbol of hardness and stability (Deut. xxviii. 23; Lev. xxvi. 19; Job. vi. 12, xl. 18; Isa. xlviii. 4).

3. Silver and Copper.

Iron is of considerably later date in Palestine than copper. To the Babylonians it came to be more generally accessible in the period between Tiglath-Pileser I. (1100) and Asshurnasirpal (886). Under the latter, iron weapons were already in use; for other implements, iron was employed along with bronze. After 800 B.C., iron displaced bronze as a metal for practical use; and in Khorsabad there was discovered a great iron couch of Sargon's (722-705). In Canaan iron begins to appear about the same time as in Babylon; in Tell Hesy, from 1100 B.C.; in Gezer (q.v.), it was of rare employment prior to Solomon's time, but it seems to have been earlier in use there for implements of husbandry than for weapons, since coincidently with iron hooks and sickles there appear bronze knives, daggers, and arrow-heads. Hence the introduction of iron was contemporaneous with the colonization of the Israelites. The statement that the war chariots of the Canaanites were tired with iron (Judges i. 19; cf. iv. 3; Josh. xvii. 18) is an anachronism, since bronze was the metal thus employed. The various discoveries through excavations and from the reports of the Old Testament during the royal period show that bronze long remained predominant over iron. Weapons are of bronze, while the earliest use of iron was for implements in the time of David (II Sam. xii. 31; cf. Amos i. 3). Subsequently, iron is mentioned more frequently; doors with iron bars (Isa. xlv. 2), coat of mail (Job xx. 24), chains (Ps. cxlix. 8), ax-heads and hatchets (II Kings vi. 5; Deut. xix. 5, xxvii. 5), nails and "styles" (Jer. xvii. 1; Job xix. 24). Deut. xxvii. 5 assumes that stone-cutting instruments are of iron as a rule. The Israelites had knowledge of iron furnaces for smelting the ores (Deut. iv. 20; Jer. xi. 4; I Kings viii. 16), but did not cast iron; for skilled craftsmen the metal used was always bronze, not iron. The widely current assumption that they knew how to harden iron into steel is erroneous. Hebrew imagery frequently made use of iron in similes and the like.

4. Iron.

Tin (*bedhīl*), which is mentioned in the Old Testament among the metals of which utensils were made (Num. xxxi. 22; Ezek. xxii. 18, 20), appears rarely to have been employed by itself alone. In one instance a tin plummet is mentioned (Zech. iv. 10); otherwise, the plummet is of lead. Tin is ordinarily employed as an adjunct with other metals (Ezek. xxii. 18, 20). *Bedhil* also designates the baser elements of silver ore (Isa. i. 25). The Phenicians imported tin from Tarshish (Ezek. xxvii. 12). Lead (*'ophereth*) is seldom mentioned; it came from Tarshish by way of Phenicia (Ezek. xxvii. 12; cf. Pliny, III., vii.). It ranked as a base metal (Jer. vi. 28 sqq.). Its gravity rendered it suitable for the plummet of carpenters and masons (Amos vii. 7 sqq.), and the "lead" of ships (Acts xxvii. 28). There were leaden tablets for writing (cf. Job xix. 23 sqq.; Pliny, XIII., ii.). It was also employed as an adjunct with certain alloys (Ezek. xxii. 18-22), and in the refining of silver from other mineral ingredients (Jer. vi. 29). Antimony (*stibium, pukh*) is employed by the Hebrews in preparing the black powder that was used by the women for painting their eyelids and eyebrows, and is still used in the East (Jer. iv. 30; Ezek. xxiii. 40; Job xlii. 14; II Kings ix. 30; Josephus, *Wars*, IV., ix. 10). Since it was rare and costly, substitutes were used in preparing the paint. The Hebrew word *pukh* is used to denote in general paints of this

5. Other Metals.

character, hence the term is not to be construed as everywhere identical with stibium. Whether the Hebrew *ḥashmal* (Ezek. i. 4, 27; viii. 2) is to be identified with the *elektron*, "amber," of the ancients, and whether "amber" is the designation of a metallic substance are matters of debate. Neither is it certain that the "fine brass" of Rev. i. 15, ii. 18, and the "burnished brass" of Ezek. i. 7; Dan. x. 6; the "bright brass" in Ezra viii. 27, should be interpreted to mean the "Corinthian brass," an alloy of gold, silver and copper, although in these instances the reference is to an alloy more valuable and finer than ordinary brass. I. BENZINGER.

BIBLIOGRAPHY: K. C. W. Bähr, *Symbolik des mosaischen Cultus*, i. 258–295, Heidelberg, 1837; R. F. Burton, *Gold Mines of Midian*, London, 1878; Benzinger, *Archäologie*, pp. 148–149; Nowack, *Archäologie*, pp. 243 sqq.; J. P. A. Erman, *Life in Ancient Egypt*, New York, 1894; G. Maspero, *Hist. ancienne des peuples de l'orient*, i. 756–757, ii. 534, Paris, 1896, Eng. transl., *Passing of the Empires*, and *Dawn of Civilization*, London, 1899–1902; F. Vigouroux, *Dictionnaire*, part xxvi. columns 1045–47; idem, *La Bible et les découvertes modernes*, iv. 299–302, Paris, 1896; *JE*, viii. 513–515; the articles in *DB* and *EB* on the individual metals (gold, silver, iron, etc.), and *EB*, iii. 3097–98, with the references to other articles there indicated.

METCALFE, WILLIAM MUSHAM: Church of Scotland; b. at York, England, Sept. 14, 1840. He was educated at New College, London, and after being minister of Tigh-na-bruaich, Argyllshire, from 1873 to 1878, became minister of South Parish, Paisley, which position he still retains. He was likewise assessor to the lord rector of St. Andrews University from 1892 to 1898, and is chairman of the Local Endowment Educational Trust, and a governor of the Paisley Technical College and School of Arts. In theological position he is liberal. Besides editing the quarterly *Scottish Review* from 1882 to 1900, he has written or edited *The Natural Truth of Christianity* (Paisley, 1880); *The Reasonableness of Christianity* (1882); *Pinkerton's Vitæ Antiquæ Sanctorum Scotiæ* (2 vols., 1889); *Ancient Lives of Scottish Saints from the Latin and Icelandic* (1895); *Scottish Legends of the Saints* (3 vols., Edinburgh, 1896); *Charters and Documents relating to the Burgh of Paisley* (Paisley, 1902); *The Legends of Saints Ninian and Machor in the Scottish Dialect of the Fourteenth Century* (1904); and *History of the County of Renfrew* (1905).

METEMPSYCHOSIS. See COMPARATIVE RELIGION, VI., 1, a, § 6.

METH, EZEKIEL: German mystic and leader of a band of enthusiasts; b. in Langensalza (19 m. n.w. of Erfurt) late in the sixteenth century; d. at Erfurt Oct. 26, 1640. The founder of the sect was Meth's uncle, Esaias Stiefel, but Meth appears to have been the real leader. For the characteristics of the sect, which entertained beliefs partaking of the peculiarities of those of the Quakers, Anabaptists, and Schwenckfeldians, see STIEFEL, ESAIAS. Stiefel was supposed to be immortal, and after his death in 1627 proved this supposition to be mistaken, Meth returned to the Lutheran Church.

BIBLIOGRAPHY: B. F. Göschel, *Chronik der Stadt Langensalza*, ii. 310, Leipsic, 1820; G. Arnold, *Unparteyische Kirchen- und Ketzer-Historie*, Theil III., cap. iv., 4 vols., Frankfort, 1700–15.

METHODIST NEW CONNECTION. See METHODISTS, I., 3.

METHODIST PROTESTANT CHURCH. See METHODISTS, IV., 3.

METHODISTS.

I. In England. 1. **Wesleyan Methodists:** John Wesley, in his *Short History of Methodism*, gives the names of four Oxford students who, in Nov., 1729, began to spend certain evenings in a week in reading together, chiefly the New Testament in Greek. The number slowly increased and, in 1735, George Whitefield affiliated with them. "The exact regularity of their lives and studies occasioned a gentleman of Christ Church to say, 'Here is sprung up a new sect of Methodists.'"

The undisputed founder of Wesleyan Methodism, John Wesley (q.v.), was the great-grandson of Bartholomew Wesley, a clergyman educated at Oxford, and one of 2,000 ministers ejected from their pulpits in 1662 under the Act of Uniformity (see UNIFORMITY, ACTS OF). His son John also studied in Oxford, became a clergyman, and, like his father, for being true to his principles, was expelled from his parish.

1. John Wesley; Early Life.

He was the father of Samuel Wesley, also an Oxford scholar, and the father of a large and notable family, including John and Charles Wesley. Their mother came of an intellectual, devout, and non-conformist ancestry. The spirit of independence was hereditary, and the environment was favorable to its expression. During the childhood and youth of John Wesley everything relating to religion "except morals" received attention in England, and from early manhood his life was a continual protest against the prevailing religious laxity and immorality. He took his master's degree Feb. 14, 1727; and from August of that year to Nov., 1729, having been ordained deacon and priest, officiated as his father's curate at Epworth. Soon after his father's death Wesley became a missionary to Georgia, and, accompanied by his brother Charles, who was secretary to James Oglethorpe, founder of the colony, arrived Feb. 5, 1736, expecting to be pastor to the English and missionary to the Indians. Upon the ship were certain devout Moravians, who, during a fearsome storm, manifested a degree of calmness and faith in the face of death beyond that possessed by Wesley, and he ever after acknowledged his indebtedness to them. In Georgia he met a Moravian, Peter Bohler, who told him to preach faith until he experienced it. His career in Georgia was disappointing. The whites in that colony would not endure his asceticism. His government of the parish was imperious, though none impeached his motives. Social relations impeded his work; a combination was formed to drive him from the colony; the civil law was invoked against him, and he determined to return to London and submit his grievances to the authorities. On the voyage homeward his mind was wholly occupied in the search for a self-sustaining faith, fortified by the witness of the Spirit. After his return to England he spoke frequently in small societies, consisting chiefly of members of the Established Church seeking for clearer spiritual life. The crisis came on the evening of May 24, 1738, while he was listening to the reading of Luther's preface to the epistle to the Romans. His own account is: "I felt my heart strangely warmed, I felt I did trust in Christ, Christ alone, for salvation; and an assurance was given me that he had taken away my sins, even mine, and saved me from the law of sin and death." In that moment Evangelical Methodism was born.

When George Whitefield (q.v.) returned from America he promptly visited Wesley. The reputation of Whitefield as the greatest of pulpit orators had spread on both continents; and as

2. Early Associations.

no building could contain the number who desired to hear him he resorted to the fields. Wesley found it difficult to approve this; but as he continued to preach with the terrible energy and unction of a first believer, he was not usually allowed to speak a second time in the churches; on this account and because of the crowds, he also was led to preach in the open air. For doing the same thing the archbishop of Canterbury threatened Charles Wesley with excommunication. Wesley's Arminianism caused an estrangement from the uncompromising Calvinist Whitefield. When controversy had become intense, Wesley summed up by saying that "those who believed in universal redemption had no desire to separate, but that those who held particular redemption would not hear of any accommodation, being determined to have no fellowship with men who were in such dangerous errors; so there were now two sorts of Methodists—those for particular and those for general redemption." The break between Wesley and Whitefield lasted but a short time, but the result was the formation of two sorts of organized Methodists, "Wesleyan Methodists" and "Calvinistic Methodists." Before this separation numerous societies had been formed, but, not having proper supervision, most of them dissolved. Peter Bohler suggested to Wesley the formation of another in London, and it was established in Fetter Lane, conducted in connection with the Moravian Church. In the summer of the same year, several small companies in Bristol united under the name of the Methodist society; a similar union took place in Kingswood, and another in Bath. These received the name of "United Societies." Wesley places the time when the first of these was formed toward the close of the year 1739.* Dissensions arose in the Fetter Lane society. Errors were so strongly advocated that on Sunday, July 6, 1740, Wesley read to the society his objections to them. The principal heresies were "denunciation of the Christian ministry as an institution"; "opposition to all ordinances"; and the affirmation that "silence is the best substitute for the means of grace." Wesley repelled these views, and he and about seventy-five seceding members met at the Foundry instead of at Fetter Lane; and thus, on July 23, 1740, "the Methodist Society in London" was founded.

While affiliating with the Moravians, Wesley's followers had instituted "Men's Bands" and "Women's Bands," which were to meet at least once a week to sing, pray, and exhort. They were expected to reveal the true state of

3. Bands; Class Meetings.

their souls as they understood it, and confess their faults one to another. Wesley met the men every Wednesday evening, and the women on Sunday. Some objected on the ground that the Bands were "man-made." Wesley replied: "They are prudential helps, grounded on reason and experience, in order to apply the general rules given in Scripture according to particular circumstances." Others stigmatized them as "mere popery." Wesley answered: "Do they not yet know that the only popish confession is the confession made by a single person to a priest? Whereas what we practise is the confession of several conjointly, not to a priest, but to each other." Members of the "Bands" were selected from the united societies. The united

* Thomas Jackson, author of *The Centenary of Wesleyan Methodism* (London, 1839), says: "From that time Wesley distinguishes what he sometimes designates the United Societies, and at other times the United Society, from all religious associations with which he had been previously connected."

societies consisted of the awakened, but the "Bands" of those only who were supposed to have received remission of sins. Later there were select societies composed of those who were believed to walk in the light of God's countenance. Members were bound "to abstain from evil, especially buying or selling on the sabbath; tasting spirituous liquors; pawning; backbiting; wearing needless ornaments, as rings, earrings, necklaces, laces and ruffles; taking snuff or tobacco; to maintain good works, especially alms-giving and reproving sin, to attend the service at church, to receive the sacrament once a week, and to observe Fridays as days of fasting or abstinence." Wesley had built a meeting-house in Bristol, but though subscriptions and collections were made to pay the debt, a large amount remained due. On Feb. 15, 1742, the principal members of the Bristol Society met to devise measures whereby the debt might be discharged. One said: "Put eleven of the poorest with me, and if they can give nothing, well; I will give for them as well as for myself. And each of you call on eleven of your neighbors weekly, and do the same." This was done. Wesley had instructed the collectors to inquire into the conduct of the members, and after a while some of these informed him that "such and such did not live as he ought." It struck him immediately, "this is the thing, the very thing, we wanted so long." From this sprung the class-meeting. Six weeks afterward Wesley instituted it in London, where it had long been difficult to become acquainted with the members personally. They divided the society into classes like those at Bristol, Wesley appointing as leaders those in whom he could confide. In process of time the class-meeting incorporated all the elements in the Bands found to be useful, and the Bands were discontinued.

Love Feasts originated in the proposal that, on one evening in the quarter, the men, and on the next, the women, in the Bands should meet, and on a third day they should meet together. The latter Wesley called a Love Feast. In these assemblies bread and water, partaken of by all present, are the symbols of fellowship. Prayer, singing of hymns, and testifying to experimental religion succeed each other, and in the early period of Methodism developed the greatest enthusiasm.

4. Love Feasts, Prayer-Meetings, Lay Preaching.

Public prayer-meetings were established in 1763 by two young men who introduced them in places where there was no Methodist preaching. They soon became general, for it was found that they exercised the talents of young men, training them in the various services of the church. When Wesley visited the Germans he heard Christian David (see UNITY OF THE BRETHREN) preach, was deeply impressed, and was prepared by David's career to establish lay preaching, when a suitable person should appear. John Cennick, a spiritual, and intellectually capable man, was invited to hear a brother read a sermon to the colliers, but, the reader not arriving, Cennick was requested to speak to the people; he reluctantly complied, and "the Lord bore witness with his words in so much that many believed in that hour." When Wesley came many desired him to forbid Cennick to preach, instead of which he gave encouragement, and for the next eighteen months Cennick preached constantly, sometimes supplying Wesley's place in Bristol. Writers before Tyerman assumed that Thomas Maxfield was the first lay preacher; Tyerman maintains that John Cennick preceded him.

As unity, direction, and instruction of the lay preachers and actively sympathizing clergymen who affiliated with Wesleyan Methodism were essential to the integrity and spirit of the movement, they were assembled for consultation. The first conference was in the Foundry in London on June 25, 1744. John and Charles Wesley, John Hodges, Henry Piers, Samuel Taylor and John Meriton, clergymen of the Church of England, were present; and four lay preachers, Thomas Rogers, Thomas Maxfield, John Bennett, and John Downs. They evolved a system of doctrine, discipline, and practise. At the third conference the country was divided into seven circuits. Copies of the minutes of the conference were to be given to those who were present, but were ordered read to the stewards and leaders of Bands the Sunday and Thursday following each conference. At the conferences the preachers were stationed at the various circuits: the result of their systematic and energetic labors amazed the United Kingdom. The most distinguished clergyman in sympathy with the work of Wesley, and for many years the most useful to him next to his own brother Charles, was John Fletcher (q.v.), vicar of Madeley. A Swiss by birth, a man of culture and rare gifts in speech and literary composition, he had been converted by Methodists. As in the apostolic era and in every religious movement since, excess of enthusiasm turned the heads of some, so George Bell, one of Wesley's local preachers, became a fanatic, believing that he could work miraculous cures. He became almost if not actually insane. Wesley bore with him long, Methodism suffering in reputation thereby. To the grief and astonishment of Wesley, Bell secured the support of Thomas Maxfield, who had been converted under Wesley's preaching during his first visit to Bristol, and had been ordained by the bishop of Londonderry who, in laying hands upon him, said, "Sir, I ordain you to assist that good man, John Wesley, that he may not work himself to death." Bell, whose fanaticism daily intensified, caused a panic by prophesying that the world would end on a given day, and Wesley was obliged to expel him. Many in London withdrew from the societies, exclaiming, "Blind John is incapable of teaching us; we will keep to Mr. Maxfield." Subsequently Bell lost his religious ardor, became a skeptic, and then a politician, "as ultra in his political opinions as he had been in religion." Maxfield opened an independent chapel (A. Stevens, *History of Methodism*, i. 409, New York, 1858).

5. Origin of Conferences: George Bell.

It was not wonderful that thousands flocked to Wesley's standard, that many societies were established and chapels reared, since he was apparently ubiquitous, traveling constantly and preaching often ten times in a week, inspiring the people by his sermons, the immortal hymns of his brother Charles, and his ability to converse in the German, Spanish, and Italian tongues. Many clergymen of the Church of England secretly, and not a few openly, sympathized with the apostolic brothers. The growth by the year 1767 is shown by the following table.

	Circuits.	Preachers.	Members.
England	26	75	22,410
Ireland	9	19	2,801
Scotland	5	7	468
Wales	1	3	232
	41	104	25,911

These had endured the scrutiny and discipline of Wesley. As Wesley advanced in years the necessity for measures to prevent the dissolution of the societies became obvious, not only to the magician who had wrought such marvelous results, but to leading minds among the clergymen who affiliated with him, lay preachers, and the more astute members of the society.

6. The Deed of Declaration. To meet the emergency, in the year 1784 Wesley gave to the conference "a legal settlement." From an early period the deeds of chapels and preachers' houses or parsonages had conveyed the said buildings to trustees for the use of such preachers as John or Charles Wesley should send, and, after their death, as the conference should appoint. Thomas Coke, a wealthy clergyman, educated for the bar, who had devoted his time and possessions to Methodism, advised Wesley to consult the civil authorities; and he ascertained that the conference could not be recognized unless more precisely defined, and that, as things then were, it could not claim control over the pulpits. Wesley reported this to the conference, which requested him to "draw up a definition of its character and powers." Under the guidance of the best legal counsel he executed a deed of declaration, in which the names of one hundred preachers were recorded, to constitute a legal conference after his death. He deemed this number sufficient to secure the property and insure the unity of the body, and also as many as could wisely be withdrawn annually for a week or more from pastoral work. Wesley recorded that "in naming these preachers, as he had no advisers he had no respect to persons, but simply set down those which according to the best of his judgment were most proper." The deed provides that the conference meet once a year at London, Bristol, Leeds, or any other place which the members should select. The sessions were never to last over three weeks, nor less than five days, and the conference was empowered to fill vacancies. To give validity to any act or vote, forty members must be present, with the exception that if the legal hundred should by death or other cause be reduced, those present might conduct business. In order to secure attendance, any member who should remain away from two successive annual sessions forfeited membership, unless he appeared on the first day of the third session, or was voted exemption. It was forbidden to appoint to any of the chapels a preacher not a member of the Methodist connection. "No appointment could be made for a longer term than three years, except in the cases of ordained clergymen of the Church of England." The conference had power to commission members of the body to represent it in any part of the earth, their "official acts being recognized as acts of the conference." The life estate of John and Charles Wesley in the houses and chapels of the connection was not to be affected by this deed. As there were 191 members of conference, the names of ninety-one were not included in the deed and they were not allowed to participate in the conference on equal terms with their brethren. Controversy ensued, and several preachers left the connection. Those who remained were permitted to vote, and such as had been members a given number of years were allowed to vote for the president in nomination, for the confirmation of the legal hundred.

7. Events after Wesley's Death. After the death of Wesley serious contests arose and continued for several years. Influential laymen and ministers proposed to adhere to the Church of England, and a few attached themselves to various dissenting bodies. The conference of 1791 expressed its views equivocally, and that of 1792 cast lots to determine whether the sacraments should be administered in the ensuing year. Eventually the following rules were enacted:

"No ordination shall take place in the Methodist Connection without the consent of the Conference.

"If any brother break the above-mentioned rule by ordaining or being ordained without the consent of the conference, the brother so breaking the rule does thereby exclude himself. The Lord's Supper shall not be administered by any person among our societies in England and Ireland for the ensuing year on any consideration whatever except in London."

In 1793 the conference resolved that:

"Where the Societies desired it they should have it, and that there should no longer be any distinction between ordained and unordained preachers, that no gowns, cassocks, bands nor surplices, nor the title of Reverend should be used."

Neither party was satisfied. The substance of the plan adopted in 1795 was that where the sacraments were being peaceably administered they should be continued; but that they should not be administered elsewhere unless a majority of the trustees and of the leaders and stewards concurred in desiring it; not for many years was the practise of laying-on of hands in ordination adopted.

8. Polity. Wesleyan Methodism is a form of Presbyterianism, yet, "strictly speaking, it is neither Episcopal, Presbyterian, nor Congregational," but has characteristics of each. Wesleyan Methodism denies a radical distinction between teaching and ruling presbyters, but reserves for the presbyters or pastors the determination of questions of doctrine and discipline. When the society developed into a church, the leaders and stewards became the local church council. There is a distinct local preachers' quarterly meeting, over which the superintendent minister of each circuit presides. There are also lay officials, formerly called general, but now circuit stewards; these receive the moneys from stewards of the societies in the circuit. Such society and circuit officers are appointed to office by the ministers, and chosen by the members of the meeting into which they are to be introduced. The administration of the spiritual affairs of each society or local church is vested in the leaders' meeting; and that of the general business of the circuit in the quarterly meeting or collective assembly of the lay officers of the circuit. These invite ministers, determine their allowances, review all interests of the circuit, and send resolutions to the district synod or memorials to conference. A peculiar feature of the polity of Wesleyan Methodism is that in case of the enactment of a new law intended to be binding in the circuits and societies, each quarterly meeting has the right to suspend the operation of the law for one year, until reconsidered by the conference. Subject to the conditions laid down in the deed of declaration as constituted and defined by Wesley, the conference rules the whole body. At the present time it is an annual assembly of copastors, meeting to exercise mutual discipline and take mutual counsel in regard to specifically pastoral subjects; and in part it is a conjoint assembly of ministers and lay brethren convened to receive reports, deliberate and determine in regard to the general interests of the connection. At the close the "Legal Conference" "as a matter of necessary legal form and solemnity" adopts what has been done in the sessions of the general conference. Between the conference and circuits are district meetings, which are practically provincial "synods," so called since 1893. These were originally organized as committees of the conference. During the transaction of pastoral business they are assemblies of pastors only; for other business, they are lay and clerical assemblies; the circuit stewards, the specially elected representatives of the circuit quarterly meetings, district treasurers of connectional funds, lay members of district committees of "Sunday and day school affairs" and of the district organization of the Foreign Missionary Society. At the pastoral sessions of the synod ministers exercise discipline, counsel concerning spiritual interests, candidates for the ministry, and the like. The conference receives recommendations from the synod, and remits questions to it. The synod is also a court of appeal; nor can legislation adopted by the conference become binding law till it has been ratified by a majority of the synod.

9. Eminent Officers and Representatives.

The conference confers great power on its president; but, in general, the presidents have been both defenders and guides. The most dominating ruler was Jabez Bunting (q.v.), four times president, and, whether in or out of that office, for more than a third of a century the controlling spirit. Robert Newton, a chaste orator, was also four times president. Adam Clarke (q.v.), oriental scholar, vigorous preacher and Biblical commentator, three times; and Thomas Coke (q.v.), Joseph Bradford, John Pawson, Thomas Taylor, Thomas Jackson, historical and connectional book editor; John Hannah, John Scott, Richard Reece, Joseph Entwisle, Henry Moore, one of the appointed biographers of Wesley; John Barber, James Wood, George Marsden, John Farrar, George Osborne, and James Harrison Rigg (q.v.) each twice filled the chair. The last-named was one of the most eminent in the list, in force of character and clearness of mind, who was long connected officially with public education. There is one living ex-president, who has served twice, Charles H. Kelly, beloved as a personality, and useful in high connectional offices. Several of the most notable men in the presidency served but once. Of these, perhaps the greatest was William Arthur (q.v.), conspicuous for fifty years throughout the religious world. Hugh Price Hughes (q.v.), of the modern type, was known as an evangelist and promoter of enterprises for uplifting the submerged classes and popularizing the Christian religion and church. Among the noteworthy men that Wesleyan Methodism has produced are Richard Watson, William B. Pope, theologians, and William Morley Punshon (qq.v.), the orator; from the beginning laymen have increased in influence, many being as well known and as useful as the most distinguished of the clergy.

10. Educational and Missionary Agencies.

Wesleyan Methodism has always placed a high estimate upon education. The views of Wesley on this subject were in some particulars unendurably ascetic, but mingled with these were principles of permanent value. In 1836 the conference took up the subject of education in general and a Wesleyan Educational Committee was appointed. Week-day and infant schools were established in 1843. In 1851 a training-college at Westminster was opened, and in 1872 a second training-college for female teachers. Houses for the Wesleyan schools are held in trust for the connection. The conference of 1875 approved the Education Committee's plan for establishing middle-class schools, of which there are ten or more. The first great movement in the direction of higher education was the establishment of Wesley College, Sheffield; the next, the institution now known as Queen's College, Taunton. A theological institution was established in 1834, and there are four branches, situated respectively at Richmond, Didsbury, Headingley, and Handsworth. Besides these are the Methodist College at Belfast, Ireland, the Westminster Training School and the Leys School at Cambridge. Missions to the heathen were not undertaken until 1786, when Thomas Coke started a mission to negro slaves in the British West Indies. At his instigation a mission to West Africa was begun in 1811, and in 1813 another in Ceylon. In 1815 missions were opened in Australasia, in Germany in 1830, in Switzerland in 1839, in Italy in 1860. Many of the missions established are now independent. The missions under the immediate direction of the British conference are: in Europe: Italy, Spain, Portugal, Gibraltar, and Malta; in Africa, Cairo; in South Africa, Transvaal, Swaziland, Rhodesia; in West Africa, Sierre Leone, Gold Coast, Lagos; in Asia, Ceylon, India (north and south), and China; in the western hemisphere, the Bahamas, Honduras, and the West Indies. In general, Wesleyan Methodist foreign missions have prospered greatly. Home missions are reduced to a most efficient system. The Wesleyan Methodists report for 1909 in Great Britain, 520,868 communicants; foreign missions, 143,467; French conference, 1,675; South African, including English and native, 117,146.

11. Wesleyan Methodism in Ireland. Methodism was introduced into Ireland in 1747 by Thomas Williams. In the same year Wesley visited that country, and on his return to England sent back his brother Charles and Charles Perronet, who remained six months preaching and organizing societies. As Methodism increased so did the efforts of the Roman Catholic Church to crush it. Mobs attacked the "Swaddlers," as Methodists were called, but Wesleyan Methodism gained many converts from the Roman Catholics, as well as from the unattached peasantry, whatever their belief or non-belief. Wesley visited Ireland more than twenty times, and after his death Coke became the apostle of Ireland, visiting it twenty-five times, at his own charge, giving freely to needy preachers and for the erection of chapels. In 1782, when he presided at the Irish conference, there were fifteen circuits and 6,000 members. In 1813 there were fifty-six circuits and 28,770 members. Among the untiring laborers Gideon Ouseley was foremost. Disputes arose concerning the sacraments, which, after the death of Coke, the people received from Presbyterians or the Established Church, according to the tendency of the Methodist preacher. In 1816 a large number seceded, claiming to be members of the Established Church of Ireland, and organized the Primitive Methodist Society of Ireland; but in 1878, after serious vicissitudes, they reunited with the Wesleyan Church of Ireland. A permanent difficulty in the way of retaining a large number of Methodist communicants in the Emerald Isle has been the constant emigration to America; by this means the church for years lost more than 1,000 members per annum. Yet in the centennial year 1839, the 26,000 members contributed $75,000 to the fund, established schools in Dublin and Cork, and, with the aid of friends in the United States and Canada, founded in 1868, and have since maintained, a college of high repute in Belfast. Prominent laymen and ministers have been converted and developed in the Irish Wesleyan Methodist Church; among the ministers, William Arthur, Adam Clarke and Henry Moore, the more distinguished. In 1877 laymen were admitted to the conference. The acts of the Wesleyan conference in Ireland, in accordance with the provision in the conference deed-poll, are made valid by the official concurrence with the said acts of a delegate from the British conference, which concurrence is to the Irish conference what the legal hundred is to the British conference. Ten ministers of the Irish conference are members of the legal hundred of the British, and the ex-president of the British conference presides in the sessions of the Irish conference.

The report for 1909 is 246 ministers, 621 lay preachers, 421 church buildings, 1,606 other preaching-places, 25,969 communicants.

2. Calvinistic Methodists: After the death of Whitefield, the Calvinistic Methodists divided into three sects. The first, known as Lady Huntingdon's Connection (see HUNTINGDON, SELINA HASTINGS, COUNTESS OF), observed strictly the liturgical forms of the Church of England, and instead of an itinerant ministry instituted a settled pastorate. As practically a congregational polity was adopted, many of the congregations became associated with the collection of Congregational churches. The second division was the Tabernacle Connection, or Whitefield Methodists. As each society considered itself independent, they soon disappeared as a distinctive denomination, most of them affiliating with the Congregationalists or Independents. The third was the Welsh Calvinistic Methodists (see PRESBYTERIANS), organized in 1743. They have prospered, extending principally in Wales and reaching the United States by way of immigration. They are influential and vigorous, at times experiencing revivals of such intensity as to attract the attention of the Christian world. After contributing for many years to the London Missionary Society, the Welsh Calvinistic Methodist Foreign Missionary Society was founded in Liverpool in 1840. Its first attempts were in India, where persevering faith has been rewarded. There are more than 500 preaching-places, 450 day schools, 6,000 communicants, and nearly 20,000 attendants.

3. The Methodist New Connection: Alexander Kilham, born in Epworth, 1762, of Methodist parents, became a local preacher, and in 1785 Wesley received him into the regular itinerant ministry. As he grew in influence he proposed various alterations. Three years before the death of Wesley, Kilham made known his design of petitioning the conference "to let us have the liberty of Englishmen, and to give the Lord's Supper to our societies." He sent petitions to the conference of 1791, and submitted a new system of government for the connection. As discussion progressed he grew more determined, appealing to God "to destroy everything that belongs to despotism wherever it appears." At the conference of 1796 he was put upon trial. After hot debate the conference unanimously adjudged him "unworthy of being a member of the Methodist Connection." Soon afterward he began the formation of the Methodist New Connection. In places where the Wesleyans would not allow him to preach in their chapels, dissenters opened their houses of worship. To disseminate his views he established, at Leeds, a periodical called *The Monitor*. In Leeds 167 class-leaders and other officers, and sixty-seven delegates from the trustees of the connection appeared at the conference of 1797, calling for changes in the government. The spread of sympathy with Kilham's projects within the pale of the Wesleyan connection caused alarm.

The conference of the Methodist New Connection was constituted upon the representative system, laymen having an equal voice with the clergy in the government of the church; while in doctrine and general usages they did not differ from the old connection. This church at first gained rapidly, and later at a slow but steady pace. At the first ecumenical conference, held in London, 1881, it was reported to have 31,652 members. It took the first step in mission work in 1824, and soon after established missions in Ireland. It began a mission in Canada in 1837, and thirty-eight years after, when it united with other Methodist bodies in that province, it contributed 7,661 members. In 1859 this church began mission work in China, and in 1862 in Australia. This mission affiliated with other Methodisms. The China mission prospered, having more than 4,466 communicants, 100 churches, and many chapels. In 1907, it reported 41,875 communicants in the United Kingdom.

4. Primitive Methodists: The Primitive Methodists arose in 1810. Lorenzo Dow (q.v.), an eccentric American Methodist preacher, with a spark of genius, visited England and Ireland and there introduced camp-meetings. The story of the remarkable meetings in the western forests of the United States recalled to older members the marvelous open-air triumphs of Wesley and Whitefield. Dow was master of a weird eloquence and absorbed by his conviction that the Lord had sent him to England to revive the spirit of the ancient days. A few regular Wesleyan preachers permitted the camp-meetings to be held within the bounds of their circuits, and attended them; but the conference denounced this as highly improper. About this time young Hugh Bourne was passing through an experience in some respects similar to that of John Wesley. When he was twenty-seven years of age he read *The Life of Fletcher*, several of Wesley's sermons, Alleine's *Alarm*, and Baxter's *Call to the Unconverted*, and these works seemed to meet his spiritual needs. He joined the Wesleyans and zealously sought the salvation of certain rough lumbermen in his employment. In May, 1807, assisted by several Wesleyans, especially by William Clowes and Thomas Cotton, he held a camp-meeting at Mow Cap, " a border-line between Staffordshire and Cheshire." The next summer special meetings of like character were held. The Wesleyan preachers of the circuits adjacent to Mow Hill, fearing the spread of a fanaticism which might bring scorn upon true religion, issued hand-bills repudiating the movement. At the next session of the Wesleyan Methodist conference the following resolution was passed: " It is our judgment that even supposing such meetings to be allowed in America, they are highly improper in England and likely to be productive of mischief; and we disclaim all connection with them." Thereafter, most of the leading Methodists held aloof from the camp-meeting. Bourne and a few others persisted and, securing recognition of their meeting by the civil authorities, were enabled to preserve order. The Wesleyan conference would not endure what it described as Bourne's " insufferable contumacy." Bourne and Thomas Clowes were expelled from the connection, which naturally made them yet more zealous. In 1809 Hugh Bourne and his brother James hired James Crawfoot, noted for piety, to preach in neglected places for three months, the salary being ten shillings per week. " This is generally looked on as the commencement of the Primitive Methodist ministry." In the spring of 1810 those converted in meetings held by Hugh Bourne were formed into a class, which was offered to the Burslem circuit (Wesleyan), but the authorities declined to accept its members " unless they pledged to sever their connection with Hugh Bourne." Bourne took the class under his personal charge as a distinct society, Sept., 1810; and this is considered to be the birth of the connection. The name " Primitive Methodist " was formally assumed in 1812. Two years later a comprehensive body of laws was adopted. The form of church government is in substance Presbyterian, but with a larger mixture of the lay element than is found in Presbyterian, or, even at this day, in other Methodist denominations. The general conference convenes yearly, and consists of twelve " deed poll " members, four persons elected by the previous conference, and delegates chosen by the district meetings, in the unusual proportion of two laymen to one traveling preacher. In 1829 a deed poll was " enrolled in chancery " to make more effectual the deeds, leases, etc., and to render donations and trusts secure; it was also valued as a permanent statement for the settling of controversy. An appeal is allowed from court to court to the final arbiter, the conference. This communion has paid much attention to education. One of the foremost scholars of to-day, Arthur Samuel Peake (q.v.), is associated with other accomplished persons on the staff of the Hartley College of this church, located at Manchester, England, and named after the philanthropist, W. P. Hartley, who has given munificently for its endowment. Famous preachers such as James Macpherson, William Antliff, Samuel Antliff, James Travis, and John Flanagan have been among the leaders of this enterprising and growing section of the Church of Christ. The Primitive Methodist Church is by far the largest of those which follow Wesley in Great Britain, with the exception of the original Wesleyan body. It has constantly grown; in 1881 it had 185,316 communicants, 1,150 ministers and more than twelve times as many local preachers, the majority preaching every Sunday. This denomination formed a foreign Missionary Society in 1844, opening missions in Canada, New Zealand, and Australia. These missions were affiliated with the other Methodist bodies of those countries. It also carries on energetic missions in Africa among the natives. Statistics for 1909 show 212,168 members, 5,148 church buildings at home and 5,018 members and probationers in foreign missions.

5. The Protestant Methodists: The Protestant Methodists, who in 1828 organized themselves into a separate body, resulted from irreconcilable differences of opinion in the society over the introduction of an organ into the largest chapel in Leeds. Until 1820 trustees of chapels could obtain this " risky innovation " only by direct application to the conference. In this case the conference had prematurely consented, and a local preacher convoked unauthorized assemblies for the purpose of agitation. When, at the appeal of the superintendent, he would not desist, the latter sentenced him to three months' suspension from his office. Thereupon seventy local preachers made common cause, and refused to preach, affirming that they would sit in silence with him. He was expelled, and a futile attempt made to secure pacification. A large number seceded, assuming the name of non-Conformist Methodists (popularly called " Non-Cons."). This name they changed for that of Protestant Methodists. In Leeds alone 1,040 members were lost, and elsewhere the depletion was even more serious. As a separate body they have long ceased to exist.

6. The Wesleyan Methodist Association: The Wesleyan Methodist Association began in the determination of the Wesleyan conference to establish a theological seminary. Two days before the conference of 1834, a number of ministers and laymen met to discuss the project of such an institution, to be presided over by Dr. Jabez Bunting. In the progress of the controversy, Samuel Warren found himself in a minority; and as soon as the conference adjourned he began a general agitation. The Manchester district meeting suspended him, and Robert Newton was requested to undertake the superintendency. Warren applied to the court of chancery for an injunction against Newton and the trustees of the Oldham Street Chapel. The vice-chancellor sustaining the district meeting, Warren appealed to Lyndhurst, the lord chancellor, who, after a thorough review of the Methodist polity, as established by Wesley's deed of declaration, and of the chief events in the history of the conference, affirmed the decision of the vice-chancellor. Warren was expelled, as were two others on charges of lawlessly abetting him. Circulars had been distributed denouncing the action of the conference, as well as the leaders who directed the acts. All who had anything to do with the distribution were under censure, and others under suspicion. The disruption of 1849 began with the expulsion of James Everett, Samuel Dunn, William Griffith, James Bromley, and Thomas Rowland, suspected of connection with the "fly-sheets." No formal and general secession took place until after the conference of 1850. Within five years after that date the original Wesleyan connection was depleted by 100,469, and "some of the fairest and most fruitful circuits in Methodism were laid waste." But, less than half of those who left the Wesleyan connection entered the new denomination.

7. The United Free Churches: The Protestant Methodists, the Wesleyan Methodist Association, and the "Wesleyan Reformers" (the title taken by those who organized after the expulsion of Everett and his companions), certain societies calling themselves "Arminian" Methodists, and others styling themselves Welsh Independent Methodists, united in the year 1857 under the name of the United Free Churches. This body at once became the third in numerical importance of the Methodist denominations in England. When consolidated it had 39,986 members and 2,152 probationers. At the end of twenty years the church included 72,997 members and 6,984 on probation. The government is democratic. The home circuits are divided into districts, but district meetings are not possessed of remarkable powers; the annual assembly controls only matters of connectional interest. The connectional officers are the president of the assembly, elected annually, the connectional secretary, treasurer, and the corresponding secretary. The church has shown commendable interest in foreign missions, continuing those which came in with the union, and establishing others in the West Indies, Africa, and China. Among the most eminent of British Methodists in his day was Marmaduke Miller, heard on religious and civic questions with great interest. At the end of 1907 it had 84,464 members and probationers at home, and in the foreign field 18,739 members and probationers.

8. Bible Christians: The denomination known as "Bible Christians" originated in Cornwall. William O'Bryan was one of its founders, and in May, 1810, was formally excluded from the Methodist society, "in the chapel of which he had given the freehold beside one-half the cost of the building, for no crime except irregular attempts to save souls." In 1814 he retired from business in order "to be ready to go whithersoever providence directed his steps." He sought out parishes in which there was no evangelical preaching and wrought much good. After a few years of independent action he reunited with the Methodist society, but subsequently his "ticket" was withheld on the ground that he had not been excluded, but that he had excluded himself. He then began to form his own plan of appointments, and a new society resulted. James Thorne was an associate founder of the "Bible Christians." During 1815 and 1816 throngs were converted, O'Bryan being so active that the converts were characterized as "Bryanites." Societies were formed in various parts of England and adjacent islands. The first conference consisted of twelve of the itinerant brethren. Every circuit was empowered to send one of its stewards to the annual district meeting, "and, to prevent priestly domination, every fifth year additional representatives were to be so appointed as to make the number of the itinerant preachers and representatives equal." A contention began in 1827 as to the authority of conference, and O'Bryan developed a spirit similar to that of those Wesleyans who had disfellowshiped him. In the struggle both O'Bryan and those who formulated their demands used the iron hand without the velvet glove. In the end O'Bryan migrated to America and had no further connection with the Bible Christians. The work had spread throughout the outlying provinces of England. The first chapel was built in 1818; in 1859 the connection occupied 453 chapels at home, and in 1900 the number had increased to 607. Between the years 1851 and 1860 separate conferences were established in Canada, South Australia, and Victoria. The enterprising spirit of the society was apparent in the fact that, in 1821, a missionary society was established for sending missionaries into dark parts of the United Kingdom and other countries, "as divine providence might open the way." In 1831 two missionaries were sent to British North America; and in 1850 James Rowe and the devout James Way were set apart to open a mission in South Australia, which prospered exceedingly and extended into the neighboring colony of Victoria. Missions were established later in New Zealand, Queensland, and China. In the report to the ecumenical conference in 1881 its number of communicants had reached 31,542. At home it had long maintained a force of missionaries working among the lowest stratum of London's population, and in other parts of England. See BIBLE CHRISTIANS.

9. The United Methodist Church: In 1902 the United Free Churches had 83,803 members, and raised more than £104,000 for the twentieth-century fund. The organization declared that its denomination was a practical illustration of the advantages of union, and that it believed that those who are nearest to each other in their foundation principles should unite. The United Free Churches, the Methodist New Connection, and the Bible Christians in 1905 prepared a basis of union. Substantial agreement was reached; and in Sept., 1907, at Wesley's Chapel, City Road, London, the adjourned conferences of these three churches met as a "uniting conference," and by permission of an act of parliament formed the United Methodist Church. The total membership of the three amalgamating bodies is 186,905.

Methodism in Great Britain and Ireland now consists of three large bodies, Wesleyan Methodists, the Primitive Methodist Church, and the United Methodist Church.

Besides these are two smaller societies, the Wesleyan Reform Union, 8,489, and the Independent Methodist Churches, 9,442. There are in all these bodies 969,078 members, exclusive of members of the foreign missions.

II. In Australasia: The Rev. Samuel Leigh, the first Methodist preacher to go to Australia, arrived in Aug., 1815, and began his work in New South Wales. By Mar., 1816, an address of the Methodist societies in New South Wales was sent to the Wesleyan mission committee in London. The history of his subsequent work and that of his successors is as interesting as the civil and personal history of the country and its inhabitants. Thirty years after Mr. Leigh began his work, the Primitive Methodists appeared; and later the Bible Christians, United Methodist Free Churches, and the Methodist New Connection planted missions. The Wesleyan spread among the English in the seven colonies, and established missions in Fiji, Tonga, and New Guinea. The Primitive Methodists were also at work in all the colonies save West Australia. The Bible Christians labored in South Australia, Victoria, and New Zealand, maintaining a few circuits in New South Wales. The United Free Methodists were represented in Victoria, New South Wales, Queensland, and New Zealand. The Methodist New Connection had established but two circuits in Australia. About 1888 these circuits were incorporated with the Wesleyan and Bible Christian churches. In 1895 the Wesleyan Methodists had in Australasia 51,702 members, and there were in the missions 34,691 members. According to the number of members at that time the Bible Christian denomination was twice the size of the United Methodist Free Churches, and the Primitive Methodist body double the size of the Bible Christians. These smaller bodies were two-fifths the size of the Wesleyan Church in Australia, New Zealand, and Tasmania, and one-fourth that of Wesleyan Methodism in the whole southern world. Methodist union in Australasia was agitated for a long time before effective steps were taken. In New Zealand, after prolonged negotiation, the ministers and members included in the Wesleyan conference, the United Free Methodist Churches, and the Bible Christians formed a union in the year 1896. The only section of Methodism in that island which declined to enter into the union was the Primitive Methodist. Two years later a union of the denominations was effected in Queensland. The Primitive Methodists and the Bible Christians in South Australia came together, and later the Methodist New Connection; and in 1900 the Wesleyan Methodists, the Primitive Methodists, and the Bible Christians, joined by the United Free Church, were consolidated into one body in South and West Australia. By this time preparations for the complete union of all Methodists in Australia reached a culmination, and from Dec. 31, 1902, Methodism became one in Australia, a continent nearly as large as Europe, and almost one in New Zealand, about as large as the British Isles; there was, therefore, a united Methodism throughout Australasia, except the Primitive Methodists in New Zealand, who represented only one-eightieth in numbers of the Methodism of Australia.

1. History.

The Methodist Missionary Society of Australasia supports missions in Samoa, Fiji, and New Britain. Tonga was formerly connected with the board of missions. The latest mission is that to Solomon Islands. The list of native ministers is long, and includes such names as Philemon Waqaniveitagavi, Ananias Tagavi, Tychicus Noke, Moses Mamafainoa, and Zephaniah Bilavucu. The Fiji district synod has reached such a degree of development that the conference resolved that the principle of lay representation be brought into operation in 1908. It is also under contract to accept from the Wesleyan Missionary Society of England a definite field of work in India, and a complete plant in one of the presidencies in that country. A recent conference recorded its gratitude to God for the signal success which he has given to its missions in the South Seas; for the islands which have been won from savagery and cannibalism and that are now Christian; for the thousands of men and women savingly converted to God, and for the native ministers, local preachers, and teachers raised up, by whose labors, in conjunction with those of the missionaries sent from England and Australia, so great a work has been done. These incontestable statements constitute a pillar of defense against attacks upon missionary effort in behalf of the uncivilized races. The Australasian Methodist Church is devoting itself to education. It supports a theological college and other institutions for training-purposes and a number of high and village schools. The progress of Australasia, though unequally distributed in the various colonies, of recent years has been extraordinary, and not only the British Empire but all leading nations have watched with interest its various experiments in legislation which have dealt with the burning questions of the age. As in other continents Methodism has shown in Australasia its ability to stem a dangerous tide or swell a beneficent one. Many able ministers and

2. Agencies and Activities.

laymen have been developed and some of them sent abroad as fraternal delegates. Their communications, no less than the indications of a vigorous church life, attested by the comments of the secular press, give good ground to believe that Australasian Methodism is, and is to continue, a powerful civilizing and Christianizing factor. The total number of ministers is 1,820, of whom 77 are of native races. The total number of members is 150,-751, of whom one-third are natives. Besides these are 10,465 on probation. The attendance on preaching services reaches the great number of 644,183.

III. In **Japan**: The Methodist Episcopal Church established a mission in Japan in the year 1873. In the same year the Canadian Methodist Church began a similar work in that country. Twelve years later, the Methodist Episcopal Church South also sent missionaries there. The work of the Methodist Episcopal Church has expanded into two annual conferences, and that of the Canadian Church and the Methodist Episcopal Church South into two more. As the same doctrines were taught, and the same spirit infused, a sentiment arose in favor of a union of the Methodist Churches in Japan. The churches in America appointed commissioners to effect a union and, in July, 1906, they unanimously agreed upon a plan. In accordance therewith, a general conference was convened in Tokyo, Japan, on May 22, 1907, composed of delegates, previously elected by the four annual conferences of the three uniting churches in Japan, and the Nippon Methodist Kyokwai was formally organized. A system of government was adopted, and went at once into effect, the first general conference under the same being held in June, 1907. The relation of the churches in the United States and Canada to the Methodist Church of Japan is cooperative. The missionaries from America hold their conference relation in their home conferences, and are supported by them; but they are entitled to the rights and privileges of membership in the annual conference to which their work of the preceding year has been related, except when the character or relations of Japanese preachers are under consideration.

IV. In **America.–1. Methodist Episcopal Church:** Philip Embury (q.v.), an Irish Methodist local preacher, accompanied by his wife, Paul Heck, Barbara, his wife, and several others, emigrated in 1760 from Limerick to New York. Five years later came five families, some of whom were related to Embury. In 1766 Barbara Heck, finding several of them engaged in card-playing, expostulated, and begged Embury to sound a note of warning. He opened his house for a meeting, preaching there to Mrs. Heck and four others who had responded to her invitation. Those present at this first service were enrolled in a class. Numerous conversions followed and additional classes were formed. Embury was strongly reinforced by Thomas Webb (q.v.), a Wesleyan local preacher and captain in the British army, and soon it was necessary to build a church. While Embury and Webb were preaching in New York, a similar awakening was creating excitement in Maryland. Robert Strawbridge (q.v.), an Irishman, had emigrated to Maryland, and, as he was persuasive in private, convincing in public, and ever active, many accessions resulted from his labors. The society in New York continued to prosper, and Thomas Taylor, a layman, besought Wesley to send over a preacher of wisdom, sound in faith, and a good disciplinarian. The twenty-sixth annual British conference, held in 1768, sent to the church in New York City fifty pounds, also passage money for two missionaries, Richard Boardman and Joseph Pilmoor. In 1771 came Francis Asbury (q.v.), as devoted and untiring as Wesley, who, in Oct., 1772, appointed him "assistant superintendent." Pilmoor and others objecting to his methods as a disciplinarian, Wesley appointed Thomas Rankin (q.v.) "superintendent of the entire work of Methodism in America"; and with him sent George Shadford, who received a letter from Wesley which reveals the vastness of his imagination and expectations, all of which have been more than fulfilled. " I let you loose, George, on the great continent of America. Publish your message in the open face of the sun, and do all the good you can. I am, dear George, Yours affectionately, John Wesley." Asbury came to America to stay, determined to identify himself fully with its people and their institutions; Rankin was full of notions and emotions of loyalty and government, and so magnified authority that those who had thought Asbury's hand iron found that of Rankin to be of steel. The first American conference was held in Philadelphia in 1773; ten preachers were present. It acknowledged the authority of Wesley and the Wesleyan conference; resolved that the doctrine and discipline of Methodism, as contained in the minutes, should be the sole rule of conduct; and that the members of the conference should "strictly avoid administering baptism and the Lord's Supper." Strawbridge had administered the sacraments before any of Wesley's regular missionaries arrived, and would not comply. Asbury explained that the rule was adopted with the understanding that "no brother in our connection shall be permitted to administer the ordinances at this time except Mr. Strawbridge, and he under the particular direction of the assistant." But Strawbridge refused to administer under such direction. At the second conference there was sharp conflict between Rankin and Asbury. The latter records, "My judgment was stubbornly opposed for a while, but at last submitted to." Unable to take the test-oaths or to sympathize with the colonies, Rankin left the country, and Rodda, another English preacher, also fled. Finally, Asbury of all the European Wesleyan preachers was left alone. The conference of 1778 showed a loss of 873 members; but in 1779, extensive revivals having occurred in those parts of the connection not directly affected by the war of the Revolution, the loss was made up with a gain of 1,600.

1. Beginnings.

The first serious controversy occurred in 1779, the preachers in the South having determined to secure authority to administer baptism and the holy communion. A committee was chosen by those thus minded, who ordained themselves and others, and to the satisfaction of most of the Methodists in that region began at once to administer the sacraments. The preachers north of Virginia opposed the step, and the conference of 1780 took harsh measures. The members declared their unanimous disapproval of the step of the brethren in Virginia, and declared that, until retracted, they would not consider them as Methodists in connection with Wesley and the conference. The question was temporarily settled by an agreement to refrain until Wesley should be heard from. At the close of 1783 Asbury received directions from Wesley to act as general superintendent, to receive no preachers from Europe not recommended by him, and neither to accept nor to retain any in America who would not submit to the minutes of the conference. Wesley perceived that unity upon the subject of administration of the sacraments had not been reached; that the truce would be but temporary, and that the societies would disintegrate unless relief should be speedily given. To meet the emergency he performed an act unparalleled in the history of organized Protestantism. In Feb., 1784, he proposed to Thomas Coke to receive ordination from him and go to America to ordain others and establish an adequate system of church government. In July Wesley adopted the measure. Richard Whatcoat and Thomas Vasey offered to accompany Coke as missionaries, and at Bristol, Wesley, assisted by Coke and James Creighton, presbyters of the Church of England, ordained them as presbyters for America. Coke was ordained as a superintendent; Wesley accredited him by a document explaining the grounds for the step, the substance of which was that Lord King's account of the primitive church and the *Irenicum* (London, 1661) of Bishop Stillingfleet, which maintained that neither Christ nor his apostles prescribed any particular form of church government, had convinced him (Wesley) "that bishops and presbyters are the same order, and consequently have the same right to ordain"; that he had been "importuned from time to time to exercise his right by ordaining part of the traveling preachers, but had refused, not only for the sake of peace, but because he was determined to violate as little as possible the established order of the national church," to which he belonged. The case was different between England and North America, as in the latter no bishops have legal jurisdiction. The closing words of this letter were: "They [the Methodists in the United States] are now at full liberty simply to follow the Scriptures and the primitive Church. And we judge it best that they should stand fast in that liberty wherewith God has so strangely made them free."

2. Dissensions; Wesley's Device.

Coke and his companions landed in New York on Nov. 3, 1784. On Sunday the 14th, by appointment, he met Freeborn Garrettson at the residence of Judge Bassett of Delaware, and in a neighboring chapel preached to a multitude, administering the Lord's Supper to more than 500. At this service sixteen preachers, including Asbury, learned the purpose of the commissioners in coming to this country. A special conference was opened Dec. 24 of the same year, and about sixty preachers agreed to organize themselves into a Methodist Episcopal Church "in which the liturgy (as presented by the Rev. John Wesley) should be read, and the sacraments administered by a superintendent, elders and deacons, who shall be ordained by a presbytery, using the Episcopal form, as prescribed in the Rev. Mr. Wesley's prayer-book." Asbury was ordained deacon by Coke, assisted by Vasey and Whatcoat; on the following Sunday was ordained an elder, and on Monday consecrated superintendent. Before receiving ordination Asbury was unanimously elected superintendent, having stated that he could not serve as he had hitherto done, merely by Mr. Wesley's appointment. Coke also was elected superintendent. Several days were spent in perfecting a code of rules, selecting preachers to receive orders, and in ordinations. The first *Discipline* of the Methodist Episcopal Church was adopted by this convention. The prayer-book which Wesley had prepared and printed for the use of the church in America was entitled, *A Sunday Service of the Methodists in North America, with Other Occasional Services.* The articles of religion of the Church of England were reduced from thirty-nine to twenty-four, and those retained were so altered as "to eradicate all traces of Romanism, High-church ritualism, and the distinctive points of Calvinism." The church now formed consisted of 18,000 members, 104 traveling preachers, as many local preachers, and twice as many licensed exhorters. There were sixty chapels and 800 recognized preaching-places. Coke went everywhere baptizing children and administering the Lord's Supper, as did Asbury wherever opportunity offered. In the mean time the general superintendents at their own initiative assumed the title of bishop, asking the conference to approve it, not to the exclusion of the name general superintendent under which they were ordained, but for brevity's sake, as its equivalent and alternative.

3. The New Organization.

By the year 1789 it became necessary to hold eleven conferences. A plan was devised by Bishops Coke and Asbury, which involved the establishment of a council to be invested with extraordinary powers, and to consist of general superintendents (i.e., bishops) and presiding elders. The council met that year, and a second was convened in 1790, which boldly claimed additional power. Its proceedings created such dissatisfaction that the plan was abandoned, and it was decided to provide for a general conference. The annual conferences unanimously authorized the bishops to call such an assembly to meet in Baltimore the first of Nov., 1792. The most important event was a conflict between Bishop Asbury and James O'Kelly (q.v.), a strenuous elder, who presided over a wide district. He proposed that preachers not satisfied with their appointments might appeal to the conference. The motion was lost by a large majority and O'Kelly and several other preachers seceded. The second general conference met in Baltimore in 1796, and the subject of slavery was discussed at length. An earnest debate, concerning the relations of Coke to the Methodist Episcopal Church, occupied two days. Jesse Lee—a powerful debater and preacher—and others, who opposed

4. The General Conference.

a conditional offer by Coke, were rapidly gaining adherents, until Bishop Asbury intervened. Coke himself made a conciliatory speech, and Lee's party lost the day. Coke, while remaining a member of the Wesleyan conference, continued to perform the duties of general superintendent when in America. The general conference of 1800 from the beginning took on a radical form, but conservative views prevailed. Richard Whatcoat was elected to the episcopacy by only four majority, his competitor being Jesse Lee. The general conference of 1804 is celebrated for the enactment of the rule forbidding bishops "to allow any preacher to remain in the same station or circuit more than two consecutive years," except presiding elders. In 1807, the New York conference adopted a memorial expressing its conviction that a representative or delegated general conference, composed of a specific number, on principles of equal representation, from the several annual conferences, was essential to unity. This was submitted to the other conferences, and presented to the conference of 1808, in which the proposition was launched by a motion to proceed to "the business relative to regulating and perpetuating general conferences." A committee was formed of two members from each annual conference, who agreed upon a plan, the first provision of which was: "The General Conference shall be composed of delegates from the annual conferences." This was lost by a majority of seven in 121 votes. Confusion reigned, and various members from distant conferences began preparations to return home, but unanimity being attained, the conference provided for a delegated general conference to have full powers to make rules and regulations for the church under six restrictions. At this conference William McKendree was elected bishop, the first of American birth to be invested with that responsibility. The membership was now 144,590 laymen and 516 preachers. There were more than four times as many adherents. The general conference of 1812, the first delegated body in the history of the church, gave attention to the operation of the restrictive rules, and it was soon seen that in McKendree a will as firm as that of Asbury was being rapidly developed. In 1820 the conference enacted that the bishop should nominate three times the number of presiding elders needed and the conference, without debate, should elect from those thus nominated the number desired, and that presiding elders should become the advisory council of the bishop or president of the conference in stationing the preachers. The passage of these resolutions caused Joshua Soule, who had been elected—but not consecrated—to the episcopacy, to state that he considered them unconstitutional, and that he would not be governed by them. The conference was equally divided, and Soule resigned; but action on the resolutions was by vote "suspended" for four years. After adjournment McKendree wrote a circular letter to the annual conferences protesting against the suspended resolutions as unconstitutional. Seven conferences voted them to be so, but six of these recommended their legalization by a change in the constitution. The remaining conferences, indignant at what they considered the dominating manner of the senior bishop and the obstructive attitude of Soule, refused to pay any attention to McKendree's letter. In 1824 these resolutions were pronounced void, and Soule and Elijah Hedding, representing opposite sides on the presiding-elder question, were elected bishops.

By 1828 the astonishing increase in members became a topic of public discussion. The increase in the next quadrennium was thirty-three per cent., and placed the membership more than 13,000 beyond the half-million mark. In 1836 the church established an annual conference in Africa, and plans were made to enter China.

5. Slavery and the Church in the South.

Notwithstanding several petitions, the conference refused to change the section on slavery, or to countenance the agitation on the slavery question then assuming the aspect of a crisis. Perplexing questions presented themselves in 1840. A resolution was adopted "that it is inexpedient and unjustifiable for any preacher among us to permit colored persons to give testimony against white persons in any state where they are denied that privilege in trials at law." To quell the commotion which this created, explanatory resolutions were passed. The material and spiritual progress of the denomination is indicated in part by the election of four book-agents, editors of the *Quarterly Review, Christian Advocate, Western Advocate, Christian Apologist, Ladies' Repository, Southern Christian Advocate, Richmond Advocate*, and the *South-Western Advocate;* and the fact that, in addition to the main centers, depositories were appointed at Charleston, Pittsburg and Boston. The subject of slavery came up with explosive force in the conference of 1844. The Baltimore conference had expelled a member for holding slaves through his wife. He appealed to the general conference, which affirmed the expulsion by 117 to 56. The numerous petitions for the enactment of laws to exclude slave-holders from the church might have been dealt with to the pacification of a majority; but a fatal element entered with the knowledge that Bishop James O. Andrew had become a slave-owner by inheritance and marriage. A motion was made that he be asked to resign. Efforts to reach a peaceable solution were futile, and the conference finally declared, by a vote of 111 against 61, "That it is the sense of this conference that Bishop Andrew desist from the exercise of his office so long as this impediment remains." The southern delegates presented a protest "in behalf of thirteen annual conferences of the Methodist Episcopal Church, and portions of the ministry and membership of several other conferences, embracing nearly 5,000 ministers, and a membership of nearly 500,000 constitutionally represented in this general conference." A plan of separation was passed, and a prominent member, Leonidas Lent Hamline, educated to the law, maintained that the only point in it which touched the constitution related to the division of the funds of the Book Concern, and that was the only one to be sent to the annual conferences. On a test resolution there were 135 votes in the affirmative, and fifteen in the negative. After ten months of excited discussion throughout the country, the protesting conferences elected delegates to a convention which met May 1, 1845, in Louisville, Ky., and organized the Methodist Episcopal Church South. The general conference of 1844 elected Edmund S. Janes and Leonidas Lent Hamline to the episcopacy—the last to be chosen by the undivided Methodist Episcopal Church. A portentous reaction soon began in the Methodist Episcopal Church. The annual conferences declined to grant the request for a division of the property of the Book Concern. The general conference of 1848 would not receive, in an official capacity, a fraternal delegate from the Methodist Episcopal Church South. It maintained that the plan of separation was unconstitutional, if not that the Southern conference had not acted in harmony with it. It replied to the commissioners of the Southern body that it had no power to negotiate a division of the property with the Southern church without the concurrent vote of the annual conferences, which had been refused. This led to legal proceedings in state and federal courts. The general conference of 1856 contended over several aspects of the slavery question, particularly the church membership of slave-holders. This conference began a movement which, when perfected, altered the constitution so as to permit the election of missionary bishops, the exercise of whose functions should be restricted to a definite territory. Slavery, in 1860, was still a thorn in the church. The general conference of that year, responding to many petitions, replaced, by one more radical, the chapter on slavery, which had come down from 1780. A plan for the introduction of lay representatives included an informal vote of male members over twenty-one years of age, to be followed by a vote by the members of the annual conferences. Two of the border conferences practically repudiated the new chapter on slavery, and, as the civil war was imminent, excitement on that subject was heightened by the rancor prevailing in both the body politic and the body ecclesiastic. The Baltimore, Pittsburg, Philadelphia, and Ohio conferences, Maryland, Delaware, and a part of Virginia, became centers of competition for members between the two Episcopal Methodisms. Before 1864 the Baltimore annual conference had lost more than sixty members, and five of its districts had become incorporated with the Methodist Episcopal Church South. The general conference of that year took a constitutional vote so as to make the rule on slavery read, "slaveholding, buying, or selling slaves." The informal vote of the laity on lay representation gave a majority against the proposition. A deputation of laymen addressed the conference, criticizing the method of taking the vote, and plans were made to reballot. This conference lengthened the possible duration of pastorates from two years to three, and passed a rule on class-meetings unintentionally so framed as in practise to make attendance voluntary. When the general conference of 1868 convened, the war was over and slavery abolished. The reports justified the claim of 1,146,081 members, with an increase of 222,687 during the past four years. With the exception of the gain of the last quadrennium of the undivided church, this was the largest in the history of the denomination; of this gain 117,326 were in the southern states.

6. Lay Representation.

The second vote for lay representation had failed, but in the interim the Methodist Episcopal Church South had admitted lay delegates, and sentiment speedily changed throughout the whole church. Nearly all the members of this conference were ready to concede this long-deferred boon, but there were differences of opinion concerning the *modus operandi*. The plan adopted provided for a lay vote, and, should there be a majority for the innovation, the annual conferences were to vote to change the constitution so as to enable the ensuing general conference, after ratifying that action by a vote of two-thirds, to admit laymen provisionally elected. The required three-fourths were obtained, and on the first day of the general conference of 1872, the lay representatives were seated. The conference selected episcopal residences, and prescribed a method of residential assignment. A law was passed, that the general conference should declare "who of the bishops are effective, and who are non-effective." In 1876 the election of presiding elders was strongly advocated, but being opposed on the grounds of unconstitutionality and inexpediency, the proposition was lost. The body also refused to approve the licensing of women to preach, and allowed conferences having both white and colored members to be divided on race lines "when it shall be requested by a majority of the white and also a majority of the colored members; but in no case where it is not clearly to be seen that such division would improve the work," etc. When the general conference of 1848 refused to receive Lovick Pierce as delegate from the Methodist Episcopal Church South, he announced that, should there ever be official fraternal relation, the Methodist Episcopal Church would be obliged to initiate it. Such preliminary steps having been taken by the Methodist Episcopal Church, the first fraternal delegates from the Methodist Episcopal Church South were welcomed with every demonstration of satisfaction, and their message augmented the spirit of fraternity. From that time the relations between the two churches have been increasingly friendly. The conference of 1880 is notable for having revised the ecclesiastical code. In 1884 William Taylor (q.v.), already the most renowned world-exploring voluntary missionary, was elected missionary bishop for Africa. The general conference also adopted and ordered inserted as a preface to the "Form of Consecrating Bishops," the following:

"This service is not to be understood as an ordination to a higher Order in the Christian Ministry, beyond and above that of Elders or Presbyters, but as a solemn and fitting Consecration for the special and most sacred duties of Superintendency in the Church."

At the conference of 1888 several women presented credentials of election, but their right to seats was challenged on the ground of sex, and by a small majority they were denied admission. It was maintained that the constitution did not allow women to act as representatives; therefore the conference sent the issue to the annual conferences that there might be a lay and clerical vote as to such a change in the constitution. James M. Thoburn (q.v.) was elected a missionary bishop for India.

7. Female Representation.

This conference lengthened the possible pastoral term from three years to five. The conference of 1892 dealt chiefly with matters relating to the ordinary work of the church and did not add to the number of bishops. In 1896 two bishops were consecrated and a missionary bishop for Africa to succeed William Taylor, retired on account of declining health. Four women were elected to the general conference, and the usual debate arose, but this compromise was reached, that the claimants might remain, but under a title in dispute, and that the conference should adopt an amendment to the constitution legalizing the admission of women to the body, to be ratified by the annual conferences. Under the circumstances the women preferred not to remain. The annual conferences failed to adopt the amendment. During the next four years the church was agitated by a controversy concerning the inequality of clerical and lay representation. The annual conferences having given a constitutional majority for doing away with this inequality, the general conference of 1900, after completing the action, admitted the needed number of delegates, who had been provisionally elected. It also removed the time limit of the pastorate, leaving the appointments entirely to the judgment of the bishops. The same conference amended the draft of a revised constitution then pending by substituting "lay members" for "laymen." The annual and lay electoral conferences confirmed the constitution; thus the struggle of twelve years ended. In the succeeding conferences the few women elected have performed the duties of their office creditably. The constitution as revised contains several regulations long in the discipline, the constitutionality of which some disputed, and also some recognized essentials, which were before but rules. The most important change was in the number of votes of ministers in the annual conferences necessary to a vote to initiate or confirm a change of the constitution. Formerly it was three-fourths, now but two-thirds. The lay electoral conferences were invested with the same power, conditional on two-thirds of their members. The conference of 1908 substituted the title "district superintendent" for that of "presiding elder," and removed the time limit upon probation for membership in the church, placing the responsibility jointly upon the pastor and the official board, who must concur as to the fitness of a candidate and the time when he may be received into full membership.

8. Government.

The general conference is the supreme legislative, judicial, and executive body, having "full power to make rules and regulations for the church," with certain constitutional restrictions. It can not do away with episcopacy, nor destroy the plan of itinerant general superintendency. This plan excludes diocesan bishops, gives the power of ordination to the bishops, makes them presidents in the annual conferences, and gives them authority to decide questions of law when presiding there, subject to appeal to the general conference. To them belong the power and duty of appointing the preachers and district superintendents, and to transfer pastors. Each annual conference is divided into districts, of which, in the absence of a bishop, the district superintendent has the charge. The quarterly conference is the ultimate body in the local church. The annual conference has substantially the function of a Presbyterian synod, except that, as a conference, it has no legislative function. It is the sole decider whether candidates for the ministry shall be received on trial, and, if so, who among them shall be ordained deacons and elders. Appointments are in the power of the bishop in charge and of his agents the district superintendents. Deeds to church property contain the provision that the pastors sent by the general conference through a bishop (and such only) shall be received. A bishop presides in the general conference, but in the absence of a bishop, the conference can elect one of its members president *pro tempore*. As an appeal can be taken from the presiding officer's decisions on parliamentary law direct to the conference, and he has no right to make decisions of law or interpret the constitution before the general conference, his functions are strictly those of a moderator. But the veneration felt for his office as bishop adds moral influence to his office as president, and it is rarely that his parliamentary decisions are contested. The bishop is amenable to the general conference. It can superannuate him, as annual conferences do their members, and can order the manner of his trial, and expel him if, in its judgment, this be just and necessary. From its decision there is no appeal. The rights of members and ministers to trial before a committee and to an appeal are guarded. The profits of the Book Concern and chartered fund are restricted to the purposes specified in the constitution. The general rules can be changed only as the constitution provides, and the ratio of representation is to be determined in the same manner. The doctrines of the church are protected by a double constitutional guard. They can not be changed by the general conference, nor by the constitutional methods which apply to other protected subjects. The method of change must itself be revoked before the doctrines, as embodied in the "Articles of Religion," the *Sermons* of Wesley, and his *Notes on the New Testament*, can be modified in the least degree.

9. Missions.

The Missionary Society was founded in 1819, having the compound title of "The Bible and Missionary Society." The next year the title of "Bible" was eliminated, and the society made entirely missionary. It was adopted by the church in 1820, and dealt at first strictly with the home field. Foreign fields were entered in the following order: Africa, in 1833; South America, 1836; China, 1847; India, 1856; Bulgaria, 1857; Japan, 1872; Mexico, 1873; Korea, 1885; Malaysia, 1885; Germany, 1849; Norway, 1853; Sweden, 1854; Switzerland, 1856; Denmark, 1857; Italy, 1871; Finland, 1884; France, 1906; Russia at St. Petersburg, 1907. The missions in Scandinavia, Germany, and Switzerland received their initial impulse by citizens of those countries migrating to the United States, coming there under the influence of Methodism and reporting doctrinal and spiritual transition to their friends in the Fatherland. In 1906 the missions of the Methodist Episcopal Church in Japan and the missions of the Methodist Episcopal Church South and the Methodist Church of Canada, with the consent and under the direction of their respective churches, united to form the Japan Methodist Church; and the first general conference of that church was convened in Tokyo on May 22, 1907. The Woman's Foreign Missionary Society, founded in 1869, succeeded a number of other organizations of limited scope. As an adjunct to the "parent" society, and as an independent missionary force, it has been of incalculable value. Within thirty-eight years it has raised and expended in foreign lands $9,244,187, of which $984,975 was collected in the year 1908-9. The Woman's Home Missionary Society was organized in 1880. It has accumulated $1,250,000 in property, invested in industrial homes for girls; others for children, deaconesses, and training-schools for missionaries, deaconesses, and nurses for hospitals. Its annual income is about $200,000. In the general missionary work of the church, until 1907, domestic or home missions were dealt with by the Missionary Society and included under the general term of missions. This included mission conferences and missions to the English-speaking churches needing help in the annual conferences, and non-English-speaking citizens of the United States, such as Germans, Scandinavians, Chinese, Finns, and Italians. In conformity with action taken by the general conference of 1904, and consummated by a commission appointed for the purpose, all such domestic missions were transferred to the care of the Board of Church Extension; and in conformity with the action in and by the states of New York and Pennsylvania, the title was changed to the Board of Home Missions and Church Extension. This board is located in Philadelphia. The name of the original society was changed to the Board of Foreign Missions, its headquarters remaining in New York.

10. Brotherhoods.

The origin and organization of the Methodist Brotherhood is as follows: In 1877 Dr. A. B. Kendig organized a group of men in the church of which he was pastor, which he styled the Mizpah Brotherhood. He continued to organize such societies until 1898. Bishop T. B. Neely, independently of this movement, organized in the churches of which he was successively pastor what was termed a Wesley Brotherhood. The first of these was organized in 1890. Meanwhile societies of men in local churches had been springing up. Some of these were called the International Brotherhood of St. Andrew and Philip (see ANDREW AND PHILIP, BROTHERHOOD OF). Besides these there were Oxford Clubs and Brotherhoods, Embury Brotherhoods, etc. In 1896 Dr. F. D. Leete organized in his church the Brotherhood of St. Paul. In the succeeding two years the Wesley Brotherhood and the Brotherhood of St. Paul began to spread. In 1898 Dr. Neely invited representatives of all local and general brotherhoods to a convention. There was a union of several, and those bodies that united took the name, first, of the Brotherhood of the Methodist Episcopal Church, which later was changed to "The Wesley Brotherhood—the Brotherhood of the Methodist Episcopal Church." This was its legal title. As the Brotherhood of St. Paul had not affiliated with this body, there arose in the church two distinct movements, and this brought about the wide-spread organization of independent brotherhoods. In Nov., 1907, the first real convention of the Wesley organization was held at Louisville, Ky. At the convention of the Brotherhood of St. Paul, and at the instance of Bishop Berry, a resolution was adopted calling for union with the Wesley Brotherhood. Commissions were appointed by each body and the joint commission of unification met in Buffalo Mar. 11, 1908. The two brotherhoods then went out of existence and the Methodist Brotherhood was formed. The Methodist Brotherhood memorialized the general conference of 1908 for recognition and adoption, which was granted. In these later movements from the year 1905 Mr. William B. Patterson, corresponding secretary of the Wesley Brotherhood, was very influential, and he was elected general secretary and still holds that position.

11. Other Agencies.

In the Methodist Episcopal Church, almost from the beginning, education has been in the front rank of denominational enterprise. The official list shows that the church sustains 173 institutions of learning: 26 of these are theological institutions; 54 universities and colleges; 27 classical seminaries; 8 institutions exclusively for women; 55 foreign-mission schools; and 4 missionary institutes and Bible training-schools. Wesleyan University was founded in 1831. It is the first institution of its grade established under distinctively Methodist auspices. The Northwestern, Syracuse, Boston, and Wesleyan universities have the largest endowments; and the first three the largest number of students.

The first theological institution established by American Methodists was located at Concord, N. H., in 1847. Its corporate name was the Methodist General Biblical Institute. After Boston University was established, the Institute was transferred from Concord, and became in 1871 The Boston University School of Theology. The Garrett Biblical Institute, incorporated by the legislature of Illinois in 1855, situated in Evanston, Ill., was endowed by the philanthropic woman whose name it bears. Drew Theological Seminary, formally opened in 1867, at Madison, N. J., was made possible, furnished with buildings, and endowed by Daniel Drew. The value of the property held for the church by the trustees of these institutions is twenty-six million dollars, and the sum total of the endowment twenty-four million dollars. In addition to the Missionary and Church Extension societies, the church supports a Board of Education, a Board of Sunday-schools, and a peculiarly interesting Board of Freedmen's Aid. It has, in the southern and neighboring states, 217,011 communicants of African descent. Vast sums have been expended in aiding them to maintain churches and schools. To an intelligent and sympathetic appreciation, the results appear commensurate with the expenditures and efforts. These members have every ecclesiastical right and privilege, including representation in the general conference and eligibility to all offices. Methodism has always made extensive use of the press. Nearly all the churches bearing that name have Book Concerns and *Advocates*. Hospitals were introduced in 1880. The first is the Methodist Episcopal in Brooklyn, N. Y., founded by George I. Seney; and the second, in Philadelphia, was founded by Scott Stewart, M.D., who provided for it in his will. Twenty-six hospitals are now directly under the care of the church. Deaconesses were authorized in 1888. More than sixty institutions are now managed by them, including training-schools, hospitals, and homes, and they are numerous and increasingly useful in the foreign mission fields. Children's institutions are growing in numbers, proportions, and endowment. Homes for the aged are not yet in sufficient numbers, but some of the few that exist are models for those that should be built. That phenomenon of growth—the Epworth League, was the result of a union of several Young People's Societies. Though founded only in 1889, its membership long since passed the million line. At all times, local preachers, in every denomination of Methodism, have been most efficient helpers of the regular ministry, maintaining worship and raising up societies where traveling preachers were not available, and, usually supporting themselves, have been true builders of the church.

12. Notable Representatives. The episcopacy has been the most potent personal force in the development of those bodies in which it exists. After Coke and Asbury, the most representative directing and constructive bishops were William McKendree, Joshua Soule (q.v.), and Elijah Hedding. Since 1844, Edmund S. Janes (q.v.), who was most efficient for more than thirty years, Edward R. Ames, who was a dominant factor for a quarter of a century, and Matthew Simpson (q.v.), who combined administrative skill with unsurpassed persuasive oratory, were the most notable. The last-named probably did more to popularize his denomination in the United States, and other countries, than any other of its bishops. In higher education, Wilbur Fisk (q.v.) occupies the first place in time and value of influence. In the organization and promotion of foreign missions, John Price Durbin (q.v.) stands forth most clearly; and among the missionaries whose work is done William Butler, William Taylor, and Robert Samuel Maclay (qq.v.) will be recognized as leaders. The relation of William Nast to his countrymen in Germany, and in this country, is similar to that of the men who, having migrated from Sweden, Norway, and Denmark to this country and falling under the influence of Methodism, have returned and laid the foundations of that form of Christianity in those countries.

The whole number of communicants in the United States at the close of 1909 was 3,159,913; and the number of communicants in the foreign missions of the church, 313,618—a total of 3,473,531 members.

2. The Methodist Episcopal Church South: The separate history of this body, the second in number of communicants in the Methodist world, begins with the close of the fourteenth general conference of the Methodist Episcopal Church. The momentous proceedings of that body are recorded above. It adjourned at midnight June 10, 1844. The next day the southern delegates met to determine what course should be pursued.

1. Organization. Wisely they suggested to their constituents that nothing be done till " all the conferences represented " could assemble in a general convention. It was decided to meet in Louisville, Ky., May, 1845. In the interim the quarterly conferences, stations and circuits, and annual conferences discussed the subject and concluded that " dire necessity " was upon them to be freed from the jurisdiction of the northern conferences. All recommended strict adherence to the Plan of Separation adopted by the general conference. The convention assembled, and a committee on organization was instructed to consider events and influences which had a bearing on the possibility of maintaining the " unity of Methodism under one General Conference jurisdiction, without the ruin of Southern Methodism." It reported that ninety-five per cent of the ministry and membership in the south deemed a division of jurisdiction indispensable, and on May 17, by a vote of ninety-four to three, the convention adopted a report which declared:

> " The jurisdiction hitherto exercised over said Annual Conferences by the General Conference of the Methodist Episcopal Church entirely dissolved; and that said Annual Conferences shall be, and hereby are, constituted a separate ecclesiastical connection under the provisional Plan of Separation aforesaid, and based upon the Discipline of the Methodist Episcopal Church, comprehending the doctrines and entire moral, ecclesiastical, and canonical rules and regulations of said discipline, except only in so far as verbal alterations may be necessary to a distinct organization, and to be known by the style and title of the Methodist Episcopal Church South."

The first general conference (under this plan of withdrawal and organization) met in May, 1846, in Petersburg, Va., and its successors were to convene in the month of April or May, once in four years successively. There Bishop Soule formally declared his adherence to the Methodist Episcopal Church South, upon which, by a unanimous rising vote, he was received as one of the bishops of that church. A permanent Board of Missions was organized, and an agent chosen to establish a Book Concern. Three commissioners were elected to confer with a similar body from the Methodist Episcopal Church concerning the division of the property of the Book Concern. Lovick Pierce (q.v.) was elected fraternal delegate to the ensuing general conference of the Methodist Episcopal Church. William Capers and Robert Paine were elected bishops, and ordained by Bishops Soule and Andrew. The pastoral address, sent out to the conferences, declared:

> " No recognized principle of the Methodism of our fathers has been in any way affected by these changes. All the doctrines, duties, and usages, the entire creed and ritual of the Church before the separation, remain without change of any kind."

The report to this first conference showed the following constituency:

Traveling preachers	1,519
Local preachers	2,833
White members	327,284
Colored members	124,961
Indian members	2,972
Total	459,569

2. Property and Development.

In 1849 the Methodist Episcopal Church South entered suit, in the United States courts of New York and Ohio, for a *pro rata* part of the property of the Book Concern. That brought in New York was decided in 1851 in favor of the claimants on every material point; that in Ohio was, in 1852, decided adversely to them and the commissioners appealed to the supreme court of the United States, when the judgment was reversed by a unanimous decision. The conclusions of the court are thus stated:

"The division of the Church as originally constituted, thus became complete; and from this time two separate and distinct organizations have taken the place of the one previously existing. . . We entertain no doubt that the General Conference of 1844 was competent to make it; and that each division of the Church, under the separate organization, is just as legitimate, and can claim as high a sanction, ecclesiastical and temporal, as the Methodist Episcopal Church first founded in the United States. The authority, which founded that Church in 1784, has divided it, and established two separate and independent organizations, occupying the place of the old one. . As a division of the common property followed, as matter of law, a division of the Church organization, nothing short of an agreement or stipulation of the Church South to give up their share of it, could preclude the assertion of their right; and it is quite clear no such agreement or stipulation is to be found in the Plan of Separation."

By this decision the Methodist Episcopal Church South secured the printing-establishments in Richmond, Charleston, and Nashville. "To them were transferred the debts due from persons residing within the limits of their annual conferences, and in addition $270,000, in cash, the defendant also paying the cost of the suit." The second general conference, held in 1850, showed an increase of 60,000, of which four-fifths were white. Two years before the meeting of this conference, California was ceded to the United States. The bishops, urged by southern emigrants, sent missionaries "to unfurl their banner in that distant and interesting portion of the great republic." Another large increase of membership was noted when the general conference of 1854 convened. New conferences were required, and Drs. Pierce, Early, and Kavanaugh were added to the episcopacy. The general conference of 1858, in session at Nashville, Tenn., permanently located the publishing-house in that city. This "determined the future rank of Nashville as the ecclesiastical center of Southern Methodism." The general conference provided the organization of the Rio Grande Mission Conference, recommended the establishment of a mission in Central America, and requested the bishops and Board of Missions to organize a mission at such point in Africa as should be deemed expedient. New Orleans was chosen as the place for the conference of 1862. The historian Gross Alexander says, "Little did the delegates dream of the events and changes that were to take place in the interval." During the war "halls were vacated, schools deserted, endowments swept away, hundreds of schools as well as churches burned or dismantled by use as hospitals, warehouses, or stables; mills destroyed, plantations and farms laid waste." "In April, 1862, New Orleans was in the possession of the Federal Government, which was represented there by General Butler." Delegates were appointed, but it was impracticable to hold a conference at that time and place. Not till 1866 was a general conference held, which met in New Orleans. The Baltimore conference of the Methodist Episcopal Church at the time of the separation had adhered to that church, but in 1861 a large part of it withdrew from its jurisdiction and maintained a separate existence. Now it was received into the Methodist Episcopal Church South. The statistics showed a loss of 246,044 members during the Civil War, "practically a threefold decimation." The Missionary Society of the church was $60,000 in debt, and the publishing-house practically in ruins. Of the 207,776 colored members in 1860, in the southern body, there remained at the close of the war only 48,742. Attendance upon class-meeting was made voluntary, and the rule requiring a probation of six months before membership, set aside. The pastoral term was extended from two to four years. The reconstructive spirit of this conference and the statesmanship manifested in the introduction of equal lay and clerical representation into the general conference, and a limited representation of the laity in the annual conferences, was a prophecy that the ravages of war would soon be repaired.

3. Government and Activities.

The government of the Methodist Episcopal Church South is still, in most respects, in agreement with that of the undivided church, but the general conference of 1870 initiated a constitutional change of vital import, which the annual conferences confirmed. It was, that when any rule is adopted by the conference which, in the opinion of the bishops, is unconstitutional, they may present their objections in writing, and if the general conference shall by a two-thirds vote adhere to its action, the rule shall take the course prescribed for altering a restrictive rule. The bishops' veto, therefore, in any case, delays the consummation for four years. In the first instance, if the conference should not by a two-thirds vote adhere to its action, it is made by the objection of the bishops null and void. Another feature of the government is that when a bishop decides a question of law in an annual conference, it controls for that time and place; but is not binding elsewhere unless the college of bishops approves it. The making of and dealing in intoxicants is treated unequivocally and laconically as follows: "If any preacher or member shall engage in the manufacture or sale of intoxicating liquors to be used as a beverage, let the discipline be administered as in cases of immorality." From 1845 to 1860 the church, as its members had been from the beginning, was much occupied with the instruction and conversion of the slaves. When the Civil War began, there were "207,776 negro members with 180,000 children under regular catechetical instruction." In 1848 the church organized a mission in China. About thirty missionaries, exclusive of those connected with the Women's Foreign Missionary department, were sent to China before 1890. At present there are 21 missionaries and their wives, 22 native preachers, 1,883 members. The Mexican mission, founded in 1873, has been successful, having at present 6,405 members, 16 missionaries and 63 native preachers. The Brazilian mission, dating from 1875, shows the largest increase in membership, the largest collections in the field, and more self-supporting churches than any other. The Japan mission, together with the Methodist Episcopal and the Canadian Methodist missions, has become an integral part of the Japan Methodist Church (see JAPAN). There were included in this mission of the Methodist Episcopal Church South 26 missionaries and 1,573 members. The missionaries are still under the final control of the church which sent them out. The Korean mission (see KOREA), but 12 years old, has 15 workers and has gathered 1,600 members. Prior to the Spanish War, mission work was done in Cuba. After independence was achieved, the mission was reorganized, and has already, resident in five cities, about 2,500 communicants. The Methodist Episcopal Church South sustains many schools and colleges, the most important being Vanderbilt University, Nashville, founded in 1872, largely endowed by members of the family whose name it bears. Its theological department is steadily advancing in reputation and efficiency. Altogether there are 175 institutions, the titles to which are held by the Methodist Episcopal Church South. These institutions, of every grade, with the exception of perhaps fifteen, have been founded since the organization of the Methodist Episcopal Church South. The church supports twelve orphanages in as many states.

No small elected body has included a larger majority of competent men of different types than the college of bishops of the Methodist Episcopal Church South. In its early period Bishops Soule and Andrew and William Capers and Robert Paine were the most revered. H. B. Bascom, already renowned, died less than six months after he was elected. The oratorical fame of Bishop George Foster Pierce spread throughout the United States, and he lived to diffuse it more than thirty years after his election. No more potential bishop arose in that body than Holland Nimmons McTyeire (q.v.), legislator, administrator, historian. John Christian Keener (q.v.) was for half a century unusually influential in several spheres. The sage Lovick Pierce, who survived to be appointed fraternal delegate to the general conference of the Methodist Episcopal Church, the Nathaniel of the church, and John Berry McFerrin, the rejuvenator of every embarrassed enterprise, were pillars amidst the changes of their times. In all the diverse and increasing modes of Christian effort upon which Methodism, in Europe and America, has been so ready to enter, the Methodist Episcopal Church South is energetically working, being rewarded by a constant increase of members and liberality. The tendency to federation, if not to union, between the two great divisions of Episcopal Methodism is shown in their copartnership in the publishing-work in China, a common catechism, and a common hymnal, compiled by joint commissioners, authorized by the general conferences and introduced to the congregations by the signatures of the bishops of both communions.

4. Representatives and Results.

The membership of the Methodist Episcopal Church South was computed at the end of 1909 to be 1,780,778, and in the foreign missions over 15,000, making a total membership of about 1,800,000.

3. The Methodist Protestant Church: William S. Stockton, an influential layman of the Methodist Episcopal Church, began, in 1821, the publication of the *Wesleyan Repository*, its contributors being ministers and members of the Methodist Episcopal Church. "Church polity" was criticized in successive numbers by Nicholas Snethen (q.v). As its circulation increased, its utterances became more aggressive, and it encountered wide opposition, but on account of an announcement in the *Methodist Magazine* of 1823 that its editors would not admit "subjects of controversy which act to disturb the peace and harmony of the church," the *Wesleyan Repository* gained a large patronage.

While the general conference of 1824 was in session in Baltimore a convention of reformers was held there. It consisted of local and itinerant ministers, several of whom were members of the general conference, and numerous laymen. To take the place of the *Wesleyan Repository* this convention established a periodical entitled *The Mutual Rights of the Ministers and Members of the Methodist Episcopal Church*, and made preparations to organize union societies in various parts of the country. The Methodist Episcopal Church, considering this movement revolutionary, took steps to suppress it. Dennis B. Dorsey, a member of the Baltimore conference, was excluded from the church for refusing to pledge himself to desist from "spreading incendiary publications." W C. Pool was similarly dealt with, and within thirty days eleven local preachers and twenty-two laymen were expelled in Baltimore; they took an appeal. When the general conference of 1828 drew nigh, the reformers adopted a memorial to be presented to that body and also issued an address to the public. Thomas Emerson Bond, a physician of Baltimore and a local preacher, issued a powerful appeal to Methodists in opposition to the changes proposed by the reformers; these were the elimination of the episcopacy and the presiding eldership, and the admission of laymen to the general and annual conferences. The general conference confirmed the expulsion of Dorsey and Pool. Prior to this a number of expelled members and their sympathizers formed themselves into a society named Associate Methodist Reformers. Its members were most numerous in New York, Baltimore, Philadelphia, Pittsburg, and Cincinnati. A book issued by one of their number, Alexander McCaine, which proved peculiarly irritating, was chiefly devoted to attacks upon episcopacy as a form of government, and upon the personal administration of the bishops. Continual secessions from the church followed and local combinations were made. A general convention of such was assembled, which framed a constitution and discipline; this was amended and adopted, and a new denomination formed, The Methodist Protestant Church. According to its last analysis, the reformers declared the point of controversy to be an unmixed question of representation of the laity. In twelve years the Methodist Protestant Church included eighteen conferences and 50,000 members. The Methodist Protestant Church included, among those who formed it, many whom the Methodist Episcopal Church could ill afford to lose, such as Asa Shinn, orator, debater, and powerful preacher, and Nicholas Snethen, seldom equaled as a polemic speaker and author. The Methodist Episcopal Church South and the Methodist Episcopal Church have fulfilled the prediction of Snethen made in 1864:

"If we are true to it [the pure, unmixed question of representation], if we are not ashamed of it, if we glory in it, it must finally prevail, and proselyte every Methodist in the United States. They may, indeed, remain episcopal Methodists, but so sure as we are not moved away from our high calling, the whole lump will be leavened into representative Methodists."

Its government is the embodiment of the representative principles for which it contended. In no period of its existence has it failed to be represented by men of rare ability. Among those of the middle period was Thomas Hewlings Stockton (q.v.), who had few if any superiors as a preacher. Another was Dr. Alexander Clark, orator, author, editor, traveler, no mean poet, and the principal compiler of the *Voice of Praise*, the hymn-book of the denomination. This communion has always been interested in education, and maintained useful institutions. For many years it aided the foreign mission work of other denominations. The Woman's Foreign Missionary Society was formed in 1879, and the Board of Foreign Missions in 1882. Its work has been chiefly in Japan and China.

The membership in 1909 numbered 188,806, a gain of over sixty per cent since 1892.

4. Wesleyan Methodist Connection or Church of America: Divers uncompromising abolitionists conferred together in 1842 as to the wisdom of secession from the Methodist Episcopal Church. In that year Orange Scott, Jotham Horton, and Leroy Sunderland announced, in a paper called the *True Wesleyan*, their withdrawal, and issued a call for a convention of all who agreed with them to prepare a plan of government and to organize a church which should be non-episcopal and anti-slavery. The convention met May 31, 1843, at Utica, N. Y., and founded the Wesleyan Methodist Connection of America. About 6,000 joined, twenty-two of whom were traveling ministers of the Methodist Episcopal Church, and as many more from the Methodist Protestant and Reformed Methodists. To these were added forty-four who reported by letter. The discipline of the Wesleyan Methodist Connection of America differs in various particulars from that of other sections of the Methodist family. Members are forbidden to join any secret society, and if any break this rule and refuse to withdraw "they shall without trial be declared withdrawn from the church." Unstationed ministers are allowed to speak in the conference but not to vote. In less than eighteen months after it was founded the membership increased from 6,000 to 15,000; but thirty-two years later it had no more. Its rigid condemnation of secret societies repelled many, and after slavery was destroyed, nearly one hundred ministers, accompanied by thousands of communicants, returned to the Methodist Episcopal Church. This denomination of Christians strives faithfully to convert men, and to enforce the stringent rules which it conscientiously holds to be just—to be Christian. Its present roster shows 19,485 members.

5. The Free Methodist Church: This church was organized in 1860 at a convention of ministers and laymen. The action was the culmination of an agitation in the Genesee conference of the Methodist Episcopal Church. Certain ministers in that body had, for several years, been declaring that the church was tolerating worldly practises, and contradictory teachings on entire sanctification; that primitive Methodist simplicity was disappearing, unconverted persons being received into the church; that little attention was paid to discipline, and that many Methodists were allowed to belong to secret societies. They condemned the renting of pews, choir-singing, all worldly amusements, and the building of costly churches. In 1858 B. T. Roberts and Joseph McCreary were expelled from the Methodist Episcopal Church on charges of contumacy and alleged immoral and unchristian conduct. The charge of contumacy was based upon Roberts' publishing and circulating a second edition of *New School Methodism* and a pamphlet giving a short account of his previous trial. Many considered the expulsion of these ministers as persecution. Several ministers of the conference publicly expressed their sympathy, and four of them were expelled on similar charges, and two others were retired from the itinerant ministry to the local. At the general conference of 1860 the cases were taken up and the appeal of Roberts was not allowed. The conference affirmed that an unendurable spirit of censoriousness and insubordination was the cause of the action against them, and that their expulsion was in harmony with the regular forms. In the government of the Free Methodist Church a general superintendent, elected quadrennially, was substituted for the episcopacy. In all church courts the number of laymen was made equal to the ministry. The office of presiding elder was retained, but the officer is entitled district chairman. Two articles of faith were added to those of the Methodist Episcopal Church. The first is on entire sanctification, and the second on future reward and punishment. B. T. Roberts, who was long general superintendent of the body, having been reelected several times, was an alumnus of Wesleyan University, a good writer, and in private intercourse a man of both commanding and persuasive ability. The Free Methodist Church has furnished many illustrations of heroic self-denial. Limited as are the resources of the body, it has small missions in Africa, India, San Domingo, and

Japan, and maintains a large number of schools and seminaries, and one college. In recent years it has made some modifications. The general conference of Aug., 1907, by a vote of seventy-eight to forty, changed the title of their presiding officer from superintendent to bishop. It now reports 1,132 ministers and 32,166 communicants.

6. The African Methodist Episcopal Church: Early in the history of American Methodism there was dissatisfaction in the colored membership, who were aroused by Question 25 in the minutes of the conference of 1780: "Ought not the assistant to meet the colored people himself, and appoint as helpers in his absence proper white persons, and not suffer them to stay late and meet by themselves? Ans. Yes." In Philadelphia, in 1787, certain colored people belonging to the Methodist Church met to consider their condition. When their ideas were opposed, they withdrew from the church, and Bishop William White (q.v.), of the Protestant Episcopal Church, ordained a colored preacher for them. Asbury, in 1799, ordained Richard Allen (a slave who had bought his freedom, grown rich, and erected on his own land a church for the people of his race) a deacon, he being the first colored preacher ordained by the Methodist Episcopal Church. The African Methodist Episcopal Church sprang from the relations between the white and colored Methodists of Philadelphia. John Emory (q.v.), representing the Methodist Episcopal Church, sent a letter to them stating that the white preachers could no longer maintain pastoral responsibility over them. On account of this they considered themselves disowned by the Methodists, but an attempt was made to regain them. The case was taken into the courts, and was decided in favor of Bethel Church, with the result that the colored people in 1816 organized themselves into an independent body, adopting as its standards the doctrines of the Methodist Episcopal Church, and, with a few modifications, its form of government. Richard Allen was elected bishop. The church steadily prospered, but not proportionately in education. In 1843 a controversy arose on the subject of the qualifications for ministers, led by Daniel Alexander Payne (q.v.), who had been trained as a theologian in the Gettysburg Theological Seminary, and to him is due a large part of the intellectual progress of the church. In 1863 the church purchased Wilberforce University in Ohio. This institution has been successfully conducted. After the Civil War, the church increased steadily. Educational work is carried on with intelligence and enthusiasm. The African Methodist Episcopal Church and the British African Methodist Episcopal Church of the Dominion of Canada were united as a result of negotiations begun in 1880. A peculiarity of this body is that it makes the bishops members of the general conference. The African Methodist Episcopal Church has been devoted to missions. Before it was sixteen years old it established a mission in Hayti. In 1847 it founded The Parent Home and Foreign Missionary Society. It carries on missions in Africa, South America, West Indies, and Hawaii, and in Africa its missions have about 12,000 members. This body has produced notable orators, such as Bishops Campbell and Arnett, who have elicited admiration and respect for themselves, their race, and their denomination. The government of the body resembles that of other Methodist Episcopal Churches in most respects, but includes special differences of its own origination. The corrected returns by Dr. Carroll give the membership at 452,126.

7. The African Methodist Episcopal Zion Church: The colored people of the City of New York resented caste prejudice, which "forbade their taking the sacrament until white members were served." This, and the desire for other church privileges denied them, induced them to organize among themselves, which they did in 1796, and in the year 1800 they built a church and called it "Zion." A contract was made between that body and the Methodist Episcopal Church of the United States of America, that, as they had no ordained ministers of their own race, the Methodist Episcopal Church should provide them. Under this arrangement "Zion" received the services of preachers of that church for "about twenty years." In the end, a minister, who had been sent to "Zion Colored Church," having seceded from the Methodist Episcopal Church, the trustees of "Zion" invited him to finish out the year, and, when this was done, the members induced him to ordain as elders three of their brethren, already ordained as deacons. These proceeded to ordain others. These elders, following the example of Wesley, ordained one of the number a bishop. During 1820 churches were organized in Philadelphia and New Hampshire. An eight years' controversy began in 1848, which finally reached the civil courts. The laity were admitted to representation in the annual and general conferences in 1851, and by 1858 the spirit of unity in the church had gained the ascendency. As late as 1865 the church had but 92 ministers and 5,000 members; but between 1864 and 1876 it doubled its membership more than five times. This body eliminated the word "male" from the discipline so that the sexes are equally eligible to all positions, lay and clerical. In 1868 an unsuccessful attempt was made by Gilbert Haven (q.v.) and others to promote the union of the Zion Church with the Methodist Episcopal Church. Negotiations for union between the African Methodist Episcopal Zion Church and the African Methodist Church have also proved abortive. In 1868 the episcopacy was made technically a life office; nevertheless the bishop was to be elected quadrennially; if not reelected, he was considered to be "retired," but could retain the title of bishop. This rule, in practise, created dissatisfaction, and in 1880 it was enacted that, without reelection, the bishop should be certain of tenure during good behavior. This church early espoused education, but for a long while its enterprises to promote it were unsuccessful; at last, however, Livingstone College was firmly established under the presidency of Dr. Joseph C. Price, whose abilities were extraordinary. On the platform and in conversation he was irresistible; anywhere in England or America he could secure money for the institution, which became famous. The church publishes weekly periodicals and a *Quarterly Review*, and is endeavoring to secure the best modern equipment for extension. Foreign missions were made a separate department in 1884. The home membership (1909) is 545,681.

8. The Colored Methodist Episcopal Church: In 1866 the conference of the Methodist Episcopal Church South authorized the bishops to organize its colored members "into an independent ecclesiastical body," if it should appear that the members desired it. The bishops then formed a number of annual conferences, consisting wholly of colored preachers. These requested in 1870 the appointment of five as a commission to meet five of their own number to create an independent church. The convention chose as the name of the body "The Colored Methodist Episcopal Church." Two bishops of the Methodist Episcopal Church South presided and ordained to the episcopacy two colored elders, W. H. Miles and R. H. Vanderhorst, selected by the eight colored conferences. The total value of church property then made over by the Methodist Episcopal Church South to the Colored Methodist Episcopal Church was $1,500,000. Members of the Methodist Episcopal Church South have given them plots of ground and aided them in building churches. Paine College, Augusta, Ga., (with an enrolment of 300 in 1907), and Lane College, Jackson, Tenn., are carried on by the Colored Methodist Episcopal Church in connection with the Methodist Episcopal Church South. This church took over, from the body that had nourished it, the articles of religion and the forms of government. Its rules will not allow any others than negroes the privilege of membership. At the outset there were but little more than 60,000 members; in 1909 it had 233,911, shepherded by 2,809 ministers and housed in 2,619 churches.

9. Minor Methodist Churches: The Primitive Methodist Church, as it exists in the United States, came from England. It has three annual conferences subdivided into districts and maintaining itinerant and local ministers and class-leaders. They are slowly growing, having had 4,764 communicants in 1890 and 7,295 in 1909. **The Independent Methodist Churches** are composed of congregations in Maryland, Tennessee, and the District of Columbia. Their statistics are inaccessible. **The Evangelist Missionary Church** comprises ministers and members in Ohio, who in 1886 withdrew from the African Methodist Episcopal Zion Church. They have now about 5,000 members. They have one bishop and profess to have no creed but the Bible. **The New Congregational Methodists** withdrew in 1881 from the Methodist Episcopal Church South in Georgia on account of alleged arbitrary action. Seven years later a number of its churches united with the Congregationalists. At the present time they report 1,782 members. **The Congregational Methodists** originated in Georgia in 1852. When the Congregational body began to establish congregations in the South after the war many of the churches and ministers that organized the Congregational Methodist Church went over to them. In doctrine, the Congregational Methodists agree with other Methodist bodies; and in polity they are not strictly Congregational. Appeals from the decision of the lower church may be taken to a district conference, thence to the state conference, and ultimately to the general conference. This church has 15,529 members, chiefly in the southern states. **The African Union Methodist Protestant Church** dates from 1816, and differs from the African Methodist Episcopal Church in opposing itinerancy, paid ministers, and episcopacy. It has 3,867 members in eight states. **The Union American Methodist Episcopal Church** agrees in doctrines and usages with other Methodist bodies. It antedates the African Methodist Episcopal Church, being organized in 1813 in Wilmington, Del., is divided into conferences, and elects its bishops for life. In 1890 it had 2,279 members, and now reports 18,500. **The Zion Union Apostolic Church** was organized in 1869 in Virginia. It was reported in 1890 to have 2,346 communicants, and at the end of 1909 reports 3,059.

10. In Canada and the Maritime Provinces: Methodism was introduced into Newfoundland in 1765 by Lawrence Coughland, who was admitted as a traveling preacher by John Wesley in 1755.

1. Beginnings.

Coughland preached there until 1773, his work being strengthened by local preachers. In 1785 Wesley sent John McGeary especially to that colony. Methodism came into being in Nova Scotia in 1779 by the conversion of William Black through the influence of Wesley's sermons, and the efforts of newly arrived Methodists. Black in 1784, seeking for reinforcements, visited the conference called at Baltimore, Md., to receive Dr. Coke and form the Methodist Episcopal Church. By 1791 the work had so prospered in Nova Scotia as to demand a district with Black as elder, to act as superintendent of six stations, manned by as many preachers from the United States. Other preachers had been sent to various parts of the provinces. Methodism reached New Brunswick by way of Nova Scotia and the United States. In the Province of Canada local preachers had been working before the year 1790, but to William Losee, a preacher on trial without a definite appointment, belongs the honor of being the first missionary to Canada. His experiment proving successful, the next year he was regularly appointed. By 1799 a flourishing, presiding elder's district existed. In 1810 the Genesee conference was organized, and preachers in Canada for the most part assumed relations with that body. Until 1812 they had been associated with the Methodist Episcopal Church. From the beginning there had been steady advance till the war between the United States and Great Britain; but during that conflict the members were dispersed, and at its close only 1,785 could be found. The Methodists of Lower Canada, having no preacher competent to administer the ordinances, applied to Nova Scotia for aid, and a regular minister was sent from the British conference. This created confusion, which continued till 1820, when the upper province was allotted to the American preachers, and the lower to the British. In 1824 Methodism in Upper Canada, then comprising thirty-five ministers and preachers on trial and 6,150 members, was organized into a single annual conference, and during the next four years increase was encouraging. At the conference of 1828 the Methodist churches located in Canada, by the consent of the general conference of the Methodist Episcopal Church, were formed into an independent denomination, and William Case was appointed its general superintendent until the ensuing annual conference. That conference was visited by Bishop Hedding, under whose counsel the organization was perfected.

2. Division and Denominations. In 1833 the Methodist Episcopal Church of Canada had three annual conferences, 197 effective ministers, 25,000 members, and a polity practically the same as that of the Methodist Episcopal Church in the United States. In that year it unified with the British conference, changing its name and form of government. When the conference agreed to this union it did so without formal consultation with the laity. The majority both of ministers and laymen acquiesced, but certain dissentients declared that, as it had not been submitted to the societies, the act was unconstitutional, and that it infringed upon the agreement made between the church in Canada and the Methodist Episcopal Church in the United States. These organized a new Methodist Episcopal Church of Canada, more than one-thirteenth of the membership, declining to affiliate with the British conference, associating with them. Being without schools, parsonages, and churches, they began litigation to secure a pro rata part of the property. The lower courts decided in their favor, but on appeal the higher court recognized the Wesleyan Methodists of Canada as the rightful owners. After this question was settled the Wesleyan Methodist Church of Canada entered on a career of prosperity, and the Methodist Episcopal Church, thrown wholly on its own resources, made every sacrifice in order to succeed. Four Primitive Methodist ministers had been sent in 1829 from England because of the number of that sect emigrating to the United States. Three years later the Hull circuit in England decided to take the Canadian societies under its immediate charge. A general missionary committee was formed by the home church and under its management the increase of members was such that in 1854 the Canadian annual conference of Primitive Methodists was established. In 1831 the Bible Christians sent two missionaries to the British dominions in America, one to West Canada and the other to Prince Edward Island. In 1855 the society was strong, and held its first conference in Columbus. It then had 51 churches, 21 regular preachers and many lay helpers, and 2,200 members. Ten years afterward the union with it of the Prince Edward Island churches, together with local growth, raised its membership to 5,000. The Canadian Wesleyan Methodist Church was formed in 1829. It was founded principally by Henry Ryan and introduced lay representation in all its courts. Ryan died in 1833, but the little church struggled on, and in 1841 united with the Methodist New Connection. The Methodist New Connection of England, with the consent of the parent society, established a mission in Canada in 1837 The mission, enlarged by admitting a small denomination, assumed the title "Canadian Methodist New Connection." In 1840 the British conference "withdrew from its cooperation" with the Canada conference, which acted independently for seven years, but during that period the form and name of the Wesleyan Methodist Church remained unchanged. In 1847 the union was restored, and in 1854, by special arrangement, the Lower Canada and the Hudson Bay missionary districts, both of which had stood in immediate connection with the British Wesleyan conference, became incorporated with the Wesleyan church in Canada. In 1857 the Methodist Episcopal Church founded an educational institution at Bellville, which was incorporated as Bellville Seminary; three years later it was affiliated with the Toronto University as Bellville College, the ladies' department taking the designation of Alexandria College, and later the remaining part of the institution being known as Albert University.

3. Unification. For years a yearning existed in many hearts for organic union of Methodist bodies. This first bore fruit in the union of the Wesleyan Methodist Church in Canada, the Eastern British American conferences, and the Methodist New Connection Church, proposed in 1872, and consummated in Toronto in 1874, the uniting bodies adopting the all-inclusive name of the Methodist Church of Canada. Its first census reported 1,031 ministers, and 101,946 members, two universities, three theological schools, and several colleges and secondary schools. Yet something still greater awaited Canadian Methodism. The first Ecumenical Conference of Methodism, which convened in Wesley Chapel, London, in 1881, gave such impulse to fraternity as to extend the horizon till glimpses of complete Methodist unity could be perceived in the not distant future. Canada was the first to know its visitation. In Bellville, in 1883, was accomplished the formal and actual union of the Methodist Church of Canada, the Methodist Episcopal Church in Canada, the Primitive Methodist Church in Canada, and the Bible Christian Church of Canada. The body thus formed was in the possession of seven colleges, having 100 professors and 5,068 students. The Methodist Church of Canada contributed to the union 128,337 members; the Methodist Episcopal Church in Canada, 25,678 members; the Primitive Methodists, 8,000; and the Bible Christians, 6,800—a sum total of 168,815 members. The itinerant general superintendents hold office for the term of eight years, and are eligible to reelection. The annual conferences are composed of ministers and an equal number of laymen, a president being selected from among the ministerial members. The president of the annual conference is the superintendent of the district in which he may be stationed. The annual conference elects superintendents for each district. There are now six departments of mission work, home, Indian, French, Chinese and Japanese in British Columbia, and foreign. The home work embraces needy fields in the dominion, Newfoundland, and Bermuda. These include more than 35,000 communicants. The French missions are in Quebec. The foreign missions are in China and

Japan. That in Japan has been affiliated with the missions of the two Episcopal Methodist Churches which have formed the Methodist Church of Japan (ut sup., I). The connectional educational institutions are: Victoria University, Toronto, the germ of which was planted in 1837, and it was incorporated in 1841; Mount Allison College, founded in 1840 at Sackville, N. B.; Wesleyan Theological College, Montreal; Wesley College, Winnipeg; Albert College, Bellville, Ont.; Alma College, St. Thomas; Methodist College, St. Johns, Newfoundland; Columbian College, New Westminister, British Columbia; Ontario Ladies' College, Whitby, incorporated in 1874; and the Stanstead Wesleyan College, Stanstead, Quebec, established in 1873. Long is the list of able and devoted men who have built up this noble structure. Among those who have finished their course can be mentioned, without exciting jealousy, Egerton Ryerson (q.v.), the renowned educator, George Douglas, whose memory is ever green, Samuel S. Nelles (q.v.), so long president of Victoria University, and William Morley Punshon (q.v.), whose preaching, administration, and guidance promoted every interest of the advancing church and country. To-day the vastness of the territory of the Methodist Church of Canada is suggested by the names of its conferences on the continent of North America: Toronto, London, Hamilton, Bay of Quinte, Montreal, Nova Scotia, New Brunswick, and Prince Edward Island, Newfoundland, Manitoba, Alberta, and British Columbia. Distributed over this immense area are its 2,476 ministers and 334,637 members.

V. The Doctrinal Standards of Methodism: John Wesley was a clergyman of the Church of England. The societies which he formed were organizations for the conversion of men and their religious development.

1. Doctrinal Bases.

He aimed to retain his converts within the pale of that great national church, and from its clergymen the majority of Methodists received the sacraments. He and they believed the fundamental doctrines of universal Christendom, as contained in the articles, homilies, and ritual to which they had been accustomed from childhood. Nevertheless, in the judgment of Wesley, certain doctrines of the New Testament were neglected by the clergy or robbed of their true proportion and emphasis. These doctrines were by him considered vital to the spread of pure Christianity. Accordingly he expounded them in his conferences, published them with comments in the *Minutes* and preached upon them. Also he found it necessary to write and publish sermons upon the doctrines which Methodism emphasized; for his preaching excited vehement opposition from unsympathetic Anglican clergymen, and from Presbyterian, Independent, and Baptist ministers. The Baptists differed from him on the method and subjects of baptism and its relation to the reception of the Lord's Supper. To preserve unity of belief among the preachers and members of his societies, he prepared *Notes on the New Testament,* wherein are clear explanations of the pivotal passages upon which he based the views he so firmly believed and fervently preached. To render impossible the preaching of heretical doctrines in the chapels, the deeds by which they were held contained a limitation of the powers of trustees in the following words: "Provided always, that the persons preach no other doctrine than is contained in Mr. Wesley's '*Notes on the New Testament,*' and four volumes of '*Sermons.*'" The same provision subsists in the model deed of the Wesleyan Methodist Church (in England, Ireland, etc.) in the following words: "No person shall be allowed to preach, who shall maintain, promulgate, or teach any Doctrine or Practise contrary to what is contained in certain Notes on the New Testament, commonly reputed to be the Notes of the said John Wesley, and in the first four volumes of Sermons, commonly reputed to be written and published by him."

When introducing these *Sermons* to the public, Wesley said,

> "The following sermons contain the substance of what I have been preaching for eight or nine years past. During that time, I have frequently spoken in public on every subject in the ensuing collection, and I am not conscious that there is any one point of doctrine, on which I am accustomed to speak in public, which is not incidentally, if not professedly, laid before every Christian reader. Every serious man, who peruses these, will, therefore, see in the clearest manner what these doctrines are, which I embrace and teach as the essentials of true religion."

It was for this purpose that Wesley made these *Sermons* so large and vital a part of his doctrinal standards. Certain discrepancies have been alleged with respect to the number of these *Sermons.* The Wesleyan Methodist Church of Great Britain and Ireland and the Methodist Episcopal Church in the United States recognize fifty-three; the Methodist Church of Canada and the Methodist Episcopal Church South but fifty-two, and certain critics but forty-three. The discrepancies are of no significance, as all agree on the smallest number, stated in the model deed, and all essential truths of the system of doctrine on which Methodism depends are discussed in the forty-three, and nothing additional of doctrinal value is contained in the nine or ten added by Wesley after he had made the others a standard.

2. Distinctive Doctrinal Features.

The distinctive doctrinal features of Methodism are suggested by the titles of these *Sermons*: "Scriptural Christianity," "The Almost Christian," "Awake thou that sleepest," "The Way to the Kingdom," "Salvation by Faith," "Justification by Faith," "The Righteousness of Faith," "The First Fruits of the Spirit," "The Spirit of Bondage and Adoption," "The Master of the New Birth," "The Witness of our own Spirit," two sermons on the "Witness of the Spirit," "Sin in Believers," thirteen sermons on the Sermon on the Mount, "The Nature of Enthusiasm," "A Caution against Bigotry," "Christian Perfection," "The Judgment." Incidental to the direct exposition of these topics the distinction between Wesley's Arminian theology and that of Calvin is pointed out; and the dangerous license of Antinomianism condemned. Wesley emphasized foreknowledge, but opposed the doctrines of election and reprobation as taught by Calvin. Magnifying free will and resultant responsibility, he acknowledged natural depravity, yet held that the Spirit of God so counteracts its effects that every man is capable of surrendering himself to him through Christ by faith. He taught Christian perfection as the consummation of the work of salvation; and that it is subsequent to regeneration, so that, while believers may grow in grace daily, perfection is reached by faith. By subtle distinctions he met successfully the current attacks upon his view. Upon this subject his writings were voluminous, and have occasioned controversy within as well as without Methodist circles.

3. American Position.

Until 1784 Methodism in America was under the control of Wesley; it was in fact the extension of his societies. In that year it devolved upon him to superintend its transformation into a church. Before his plan had fully matured or any American had anticipated it, the American conferences asked, and by vote answered, a peculiar question.

Q. "How shall we conduct ourselves toward European preachers?" Answer: "If they are recommended by Mr. Wesley, will be subject to the American conference, preach the doctrine taught in the four volumes of Sermons, and Notes on the New Testament, we will receive them; but if they walk contrary to the above directions, no ancient right or appointment shall prevent their being excluded from our connection."

Wesley sent to America a series of articles of religion, selected from the Thirty-nine of the Church of England. The following were adopted, with slight verbal changes and minor omissions: "Of Faith in the Holy Trinity," "Of the Word, or the Son of God, who was made very Man," "Of the Resurrection of Christ," "Of the Holy Ghost," "Of the Old Testament," "Of Free Will," "Of the Justification of Man," "Of Good Works," "Of Works of Supererogation," "Of Sin after Justification," "Of the Church," "Of Purgatory," "Of Speaking in the Congregation in such tongue as the People understand," "Of the Sacraments," "Of the Lord's Supper," "Of both Kinds," "Of the one Oblation of Christ, finished upon the Cross," "Of the Marriage of Ministers," "Of the Rites and Ceremonies of Churches," "Of Christian Men's Goods" and "Of a Christian Man's Oath." The following were retained with important omissions: "The Sufficiency of the Holy Scriptures for Salvation," "Of Original or Birth Sin," "Of the Church," and "Of Baptism." The following were rejected: "Of the Going down of Christ into Hell," "Of the Three Creeds," "Of Works before Justification," "Of Christ alone without Sin," "Of Predestination and Election," "Of Obtaining Eternal Salvation only by the Name of Christ," "Of the Authority of the Church," "Of the Authority of General Councils," "Of Ministering in the Congregation," "Of the Unworthiness of the Ministers which Hinders not the effect of the Sacrament," "Of the Wicked which eat not the Body of Christ in the Use of the Lord's Supper," "Of Excommunicate Persons, how they are to be avoided," "Of the Homilies," "Of Consecration of Bishops and Ministers," "Of the Civil Magistrates."

4. Purpose and Results.

A comparison between the English Articles as they were originally and as they were transmitted to the American conference reveals that the guiding purpose of Wesley, in altering and omitting, was to expurgate the leaven of ritualism, Calvinism, and Romanism. These articles, however, do not contain special reference to some of the most precious doctrines held by the founder of Methodism and by the churches that derived preaching, teaching, and example from those whom he instructed. But Wesley knew that the American Methodists had incorporated in their standards all that he had imposed upon English Methodism. Episcopal Methodist Churches, including the Canadian Methodist Church, accepted the articles sent by Wesley. The Methodist Episcopal Church of America is in harmony with these facts. The rule on the subject is as follows:

"The General Conference shall not revoke, alter or change our Articles of Religion, nor establish any new standard or rules of doctrine contrary to our present, existing, and established standards of doctrine."

The unparalleled unity in belief among the various Methodist bodies is the fruit of Wesley's method of conserving doctrines. Had he expressed them in confessions or even creeds, they would have been centers of controversy. His followers in every land concur with the Canadian Methodist theologian, Burwash:

"It is to the spirit and type of this preaching that our obligations bind us. There may be in the Notes and Sermons things incidental, accidental and personal, to which no Methodist minister or layman would feel bound to profess assent; but Methodism demands that in all its pulpits we should preach this Gospel and expound the word of God according to this analogy of Faith."

The Calvinistic Methodists signify their doctrines by their name. In Evangelical spirit they are similar, but in the doctrines on which Wesley took the Arminian position they adhere to the Calvinist standards.

J. M. Buckley.

Bibliography: The fundamental sources are the Works of John Wesley, the best ed. for this purpose being that issued as standard by the Methodist Book Concern, New York, in 7 vols., including in vols. i.–ii. his Sermons, in vols. iii.–iv. his Journals, and in vols. v.–vii. his miscellaneous works; his *Explanatory Notes upon the New Testament*, issued by the same house as a standard (the recently deciphered diaries from which the Journals were written, containing a considerable amount of new material, are in course of publication in London, and will be available at the principal repositories for Methodist literature in the United States); the *Lives* and other literature given under the articles on the Wesleys in the last volume of this work; the Books of Discipline of the various Methodist bodies; the *Journals* of the Methodist Episcopal Church and of the Methodist Episcopal Church South; the *Minutes* of the annual conferences; the *Proceedings* of the Ecumenical Methodist Conferences, held in London, 1881, Washington, 1891, and London, 1901; the *Records* of the Centennial Convention in Baltimore, 1884; the *Year Books* of the various bodies; and the early periodicals to which reference is made in the text. Consult also the numerous sketches of Methodist worthies in this work, and the literature given there.

Treatises of a general character are: A. Stevens, *Hist. of the Religious Movement . Called Methodism*, 3 vols., New York, 1858–61; H. S. Skeats, *Hist. of the Free Churches of England, 1688–1851*, London, 1859; G. Smith, *Hist. of Wesleyan Methodism*, 3 vols., ib. 1865; L. S. Jacoby, *Geschichte des Methodismus, seiner Entstehung und Ausbreitung*, 2 vols., Bremen, 1870; W. H. Daniels, *Illustrated Hist. of Methodism in Great Britain and America from the Wesleys to the Present Time*, New York, 1880; J. Atkinson, *Centennial Hist. of American Methodism*, ib. 1884; idem, *Beginnings of the Wesleyan Movement in*

America, ib. 1896; J. W. Lee, N. Luccock, and J. M. Dixon, *Illustrated Hist. of Methodism*, St. Louis, 1900; J. F. Hurst, *British Methodism*, 3 vols., London, 1909; W. J. Townsend, *A New Hist. of Methodism*, 2 vols., ib., 1901.

Works on various Methodist bodies are: G. Smith, *Hist. of Wesleyan Methodists*, 3 vols., London, 1857–61; H. Smith, *Sketches of Methodist New Connexion Ministers*, ib. 1893; G. Packer, *The Centenary of the Methodist New Connexion 1797–1897*, ib. 1897; T. Colhouer, *Sketches of the Founders of the Methodist Protestant Church and its Bibliography*, Pittsburg, 1880; A. H. Bassett, *Concise Hist. of the Methodist Protestant Church*, Baltimore, 1882; E. J. Drinkhouse, *Hist. of Methodist Reform and the Methodist Protestant Church*, 2 vols., Baltimore, 1899; E. Bowen, *Hist. of the Origin of the Free Methodist Church*, North Chili, New York, n.d.; F. W. Bourne, *The Bible Christians: Origin and History*, London, 1905; J. Petty, *Hist. of the Primitive Methodist Connexion*, ib. 1861; W. Williams, *Welsh Calvinistic Methodism. A Historical Sketch*, ib. 1884; D. Young, *The Origin and Hist. of Methodism in Wales and the Borders*, ib. 1893; J. S. MacGeary, *The Free Methodist Church*, Chicago, 1909.

For the Methodist Episcopal Church North and South consult: *Hist. of the Organization of the Methodist Episcopal Church South. Comprehending all the Official Proceedings of the General Conferences*, etc., Nashville, 1845; A. Stevens, *Memorials of the Introduction of Methodism into the Eastern States*, 2 vols., Boston, 1848–52; idem, *Hist. of the M. E. Church in U. S. A.*, 4 vols., New York, 1864; idem, *Centenary of American Methodism*, ib. 1866; C. Elliott, *History of the Great Secession from the Methodist Episcopal Church in the year 1845, Eventuating in the Organization of the New Church Entitled "The Methodist Episcopal Church South,"* Cincinnati, 1855; J. Lednum, *A History of the Rise of Methodism in America. Containing Sketches of Methodist itinerant Preachers, 1736–85*, Philadelphia, 1859; N. Bangs, *Hist. of the Methodist Episcopal Church*, 4 vols., New York, 1860; L. C. Matlack, *Antislavery Struggle and Triumph in the M. E. Church*, ib. 1881; H. N. McTyeire, *Hist. of Methodism*, Nashville, 1886; J. G. Jones, *A Complete Hist. of Methodism as Connected with the Mississippi Conference of the Methodist Episcopal Church South*, Vol. i., *1799–1817*, Nashville, 1887; G. Alexander, in *American History Series*, vol. xi., New York, 1894; J. M. Buckley, in *American Church History Series*, vol. v., New York, 1897.

For Methodism among the African races consult: J. B. Wakeley, *Lost Chapters Recovered from the Early History of African Methodism*, New York, 1889; L. M. Hagood, *The Colored Man in the Methodist Episcopal Church*, Cincinnati, 1890; D. A. Payne, *Hist. of the A. M. E. Church*, Nashville, 1891; J. W. Hood, *One Hundred Years of the African M. E. Zion Church*, New York, 1895; I. L. Butt, *Hist. of African Methodism in Virginia; or, four Decades in the Old Dominion*, Eastville, Va., 1908.

Books dealing with special topics are: J. Emory, *Defense of Our Fathers*, New York, 1827; D. W. Clark, *Life and Times of Elijah Hedding*, ib. 1855; R. Paine, *Life of W. McKendree*, 2 vols., Nashville, 1869; E. H. Myers, *Description of the M. E. Church, 1844–46: comprising a 30 Years' History of the Relations of the two Methodisms*, Nashville, Tenn., 1875; T. L. Flood and J. W. Hamilton, *Lives of Methodist Bishops*, New York, 1882; F. A. Archibald, *Methodism and Literature*, Cincinnati, 1883; A. W. Cummings, *Early Schools of Methodism*, New York, 1886; W. J. Townsend, *The Story of Methodist Union*, London, 1906; D. B. Brummitt, *Epworth League Methods*, Cincinnati, 1906; H. K. Carroll, *Missionary Growth of the M. E. Church*, Cincinnati, 1907; J. Telford, *Wesley's Veterans. Lives of Early Methodist Preachers told by Themselves. With Additions and Annotations*, London, 1909.

On Methodism in various countries consult: G. H. Cornish, *Cyclopedia of Methodism in Canada*, Toronto, 1881; E. Ryerson, *Canadian Methodism; its Epochs and Characteristics*, ib. 1882; A. Sutherland, *Methodism in Canada*, London, 1903; J. E. Sanderson, *First Century of Methodism in Canada*, vol. i., Toronto, 1908; C. H. Crookshank, *History of Methodism in Ireland*, vol. i., *Wesley and his Time*, vol. ii., *The Middle Age*, Belfast, 1885–1886; E. Thomas, *Irish Methodist Reminiscences*, London, 1889; R. C. Phillips, *Irish Methodism*, ib. 1897; H. B. Foster, *Wesleyan Methodism in Jamaica*, ib. 1881; J. Colwell, *Illustrated Hist. of Methodism in Australia, New South Wales, and Polynesia*, Sydney, 1904; H. Adams, *Methodism in the West Indies*, London, 1908; J. M. Erikson, *Metodismen i Sverige*, Stockholm, 1895; J. Jüngst, *Der Methodismus in Deutschland*, Giessen, 1906.

On the polity, constitution, doctrines, and discipline of Methodism consult: R. Emory, *Hist. of the Discipline of the M. E. Church*, New York, 1843; T. E. Bond, *The Economy of Methodism Illustrated and Defended*, ib. 1852; T. E. Bond, *Economy of Methodism*, ib. 1852; E. Grindrod, *A Compendium of the Laws and Regulations of Wesleyan Methodism*, London, 1858; B. Hawley, *Manual of Methodism; or the Doctrines, General Rules and Usages of the Methodist Episcopal Church*, New York, 1868; J. H. Rigg, *Connexional Economy of Wesleyan Methodism*, London, 1879; idem, *Church Organizations*, ib. 1896; H. W. Williams, *Constitution and Polity of Wesleyan Methodism*, London, 1881; S. M. Merrill, *A Digest of Methodist Law; or, Helps in the Administration of the Discipline of the M. E. Church*, Cincinnati, 1885; D. Sherman, *Hist. of the Revisions of the Discipline of the M. E. Church*, New York, 1890; T. B. Neely, *Evolution of Episcopacy and Organic Methodism*, ib. 1888; idem, *Hist. of the Origin and Development of the Governing Conference in Methodism*, Cincinnati, 1892; B. Gregory, *Side Lights on the Conflicts of Methodism, 1827–52*, London, 1898; D. J. Waller, *Constitution and Polity of the Wesleyan Methodist Church*, ib. 1898; W. F. Barclay, *Constitution of Methodist Episcopal Churches in America*, Nashville, Tenn., 1902; G. F. Oliver, *Our Lay Office Bearers*, Cincinnati, 1902; J. J. Tigert, *Doctrines of M. E. Church in America*, ib. 1902; idem, *Constitutional Hist. of American Episcopal Methodism*, Nashville, 1903; *Doctrines and Discipline of the M. E. Church South*, ed. Alexander, ib. 1906; D. A. Goodsell, J. B. Hingeley and J. M. Buckley, *The Doctrines and Discipline of the Methodist Episcopal Church*, Cincinnati, 1908; H. Wheeler, *Hist. and Exposition of the Twenty-five Articles of Religion of the M. E. Church*, New York, 1908; H. T. Hudson, *Methodist Armor; or, A Popular Exposition of the Doctrines, Peculiar Usages and Ecclesiastical Machinery of the M. E. Church South*, Nashville, n.d.

METHODIUS: Greek Church Father and bishop of Olympus, in Lycia; probably martyred by Maximinus, 311. The only one of his works preserved entire in Greek is the "Symposium," which, as its name implies, forms a counterpart to Plato's "Symposium." Ten maidens, invited to the "garden of virtue," are the speakers, their themes being the following: (1) the praise of virginity as the essence of the likeness to God brought by Christ; (2) the divine ordinance of marriage; (3) virginity preferable to the married state; (4) virginity the best medicament to immortality; (5) virginity the great vow; (6) virgins keep themselves undefiled for the marriage with the Logos; (7) they are equal to the martyrs and are meant by Cant. ii. 2, iv. 9 sqq., vi. 7 sqq.; (8) the woman of Rev. xii. 1 sqq. is the Church, and the human will is free; (9) with her we must adorn ourselves for the Feast of Tabernacles, which is the Resurrection; (10) perfect righteousness (cf. Judges ix. 8 sqq.) first came into the world through Christ. The maidens close with a hymn to the heavenly bridegroom. The *De Autexusio* is preserved independently in Greek only in the portion i.–vii. 5, but considerable fragments are given by Eusebius, but under the name of Maximus (*Præparatio evangelica*, vii. 22; Eng. transl., ii. 366 sqq., 2 vols., Oxford, 1903), Photius (*Bibliotheca*, 236), the *Sacra Parallela;* while it is fully reproduced in an Old Church Slavic translation of the eleventh century. Its theme is the origin of evil, which arose from Satan's disobedience to God. In his *Peri genētōn*, of which only a few fragments have been preserved by Photius (*Bibliotheca*, 235), Methodius assails Origen's doctrine of an eternal cre-

Works.

ation of the world. The same opposition is maintained in his most important work next to the "Symposium," the *De resurrectione*, in which, at Patara, with one Theophilus presiding, the physician Aglaophon and Proclus plead for Origen against Eubulius (Methodius) and Memian. As the angels prove, things created are not necessarily mortal; and since the soul is immortal, while only the dead can rise, the body becomes mortal that the sin which dwells in it may be removed by death, the resurrection of the body being everywhere taught by the Scriptures. The work is extant only in an Old Church Slavic translation, though the Greek text of i. 20–ii. 8 is given by Epiphanius (*Hær.*, lxiv. 12 sqq.), and fragments are found in Photius (*Bibliotheca*, 234), the *Sacra Parallela*, the Syriac florilegia, the *Catena* of Procopius, Justinian (*Ad Menam*), Œcumenius, Eustratius, and others. The three fragments of his polemic against Porphyry are valuable for a knowledge of Methodius' theory of salvation; while those of his exegesis of Job ix., xxv., xxvii.–xxix., xxxviii., xl., are important for his doctrine of grace. Of his *De martyribus* scant fragments have been preserved by Theodoret and the *Sacra Parallela*. His other works are preserved almost exclusively in abbreviated Old Church Slavic translations, such as that "On Life and Reason" and "On Foods and the Red Heifer," the latter treating also of the blessings of suffering, true purity, and the spiritual understanding of the Scriptures. In the "To Sistelius, On Leprosy" (a few fragments also in manuscript in Greek), he connects the legal rules for leprosy with Christian penance; and in his "On the Horseleach of Proverbs, and 'The Heavens Declare the Glory of God'" he interprets the horseleach as the serpent of lust. His treatises "On the Body," and *De Pythonyssa*, as well as his exegeses of Genesis and Canticles, and, possibly, a dialogue *Xenon*, are lost; while the orations *De Symeone et Anna* and *In ramos palmarum*, like the Armenian fragments in the *In ascensionem Domini nostri Jesu Christi*, are spurious. Nor were the *Revelationes*, ascribed to him under various names and forming in various languages one of the favorite books of the Middle Ages, written by him. Their origin doubtless dates from the seventh century, although they appeared in Latin translation as early as the century following.

Doctrine. Deeply influenced by Platonism and Stoicism, and strongly allegorical in interpretation, Methodius is at once an advocate of early Christian realism and of the ascetic and contemplative life. The main points of his constant opposition to Origen have already been noted. His concept of God was characterized by the attributes of non-becoming, power, and exemption from all need. If the Father is the essential principle of all being, the Son is the external effective force; yet Methodius stresses the divine nature of the Son, who was the means of all revelation of salvation, even in the Old Testament. The world was created for the microcosm man, whose will is absolutely free, and who is progressively taught by God to conquer the devil. The Logos necessarily became incarnate to bring man into harmony with the Divine, and, bringing "knowledge of the Father of all," he stripped off the old man, which he replaced "with his own flesh." This is done through the Church, for whom the Logos left the Father in heaven; and the souls betrothed to him are "helps meet for him," thus realizing the "deep sleep" of Adam (Gen. ii. 21). Nevertheless, outward membership is no guaranty of salvation, which is the work of grace that rewards longing with fulfilment. Yet even the Christian does not entirely extirpate sin in this life, and the forgiveness of sins and deeper recognition of the divine will only strengthen the natural good in him; while the birth of Christ in the faithful, transforming them into Christs, is essentially a spiritual growth, though coming to pass on principle in baptism. The cure for all evils and the root of true morality is the spiritual understanding of the Scriptures, wisdom blooming in the desert, where dwells the bride of the Logos. The progress in the Christian life here outlined, however, finds its culmination, as implied above, in perfect virginity of both body and soul. The ideal of Methodius is that of the ascetic sage. In accordance with the tradition of the Church, moreover, Methodius was inclined toward a moderate chiliasm, holding that in the seventh millennium the faithful would celebrate the true sabbaths and the real Feast of Tabernacles with Christ, this millennium being the rest preliminary to endless eternity.

(N. BONWETSCH.)

For Methodius the apostle to the Slavs see CYRIL AND METHODIUS.

BIBLIOGRAPHY: The first complete ed. of the "Banquet" was by Allatius, Rome, 1656. An incomplete collection of the works was made by F. Combefis, Paris, 1644, enlarged, 1672. The works are also in A. Gallandi, *Bibliotheca veterum patrum*, iii. 670 sqq., Venice, 1767; in *MPG*, xviii. 27–408; and an edition is by A. Jahn, Halle, 1865. There is an Eng. transl. with introduction in *ANF*, vi. 307–402. The earlier literature on the subject is given very completely in *ANF*, Bibliography, pp. 75–76. Consult: Jerome, *De vir. ill.*, lxxxiii.; Socrates, *Hist. eccl.*, vi. 13; A. Pankau, *Methodius, Bischof von Olympus*, Mainz, 1888; N. Bonwetsch, *Methodius von Olympus*, Leipsic, 1891; idem, *Die Theologie des Methodius von Olympus*, Berlin, 1903; O. Bardenhewer, *Patrologie*, pp. 154 sqq., Freiburg, 1894; Ehrhard, *Die altchristliche Litteratur und ihre Erforschung*, 1884–1900, pp. 363 sqq., ib. 1900; Harnack, *Litteratur*, i. 468–478, 786, 929–930, ii. 2, pp. 147 sqq., 150–151; idem, *Dogma*, vols. i.–v. passim; Krüger, *History*, pp. 235–242; Schaff, *Christian Church*, ii. 309–312; Ceillier, *Auteurs sacrés*, iii. 62–73; *DCB*, iii. 909–911.

METHURGEMAN ("Interpreter"): The title given to the Palestinian official who in the synagogue service translated into the vernacular (Aramaic) the lesson read in Hebrew from the law verse by verse, and the lesson read from the prophets three verses at a time. See SYNAGOGUE, I.; and TALMUD.

METROPHANES, mê"tref'a-niz, **CRITOPULUS**, crai'tep-u-lus: Patriarch of Alexandria; b. at Berrhœa, Macedonia, probably in 1589; d. at Alexandria, probably in 1639. After entering a monastery at an early age and becoming the protosyncellus of the patriarch of Constantinople, he was sent to England by Cyril Lucar (q.v.) and studied at Oxford until 1623. He then went to Helmstedt, and, after visiting other German cities, was an associate of the Reformed at Geneva in 1627. In 1631 he signed himself at Alexandria as

Metropolitan of Memphis and Egypt; and in 1637 he was enthroned as patriarch, signing the synod's condemnation of Lucar's teachings in 1638.

His most important work is his "Confession of the Catholic and Apostolic Eastern Church," written at Helmstedt (given in full by J. Michaelcescu, *Die Bekenntnisse der griechisch-orientalischen Kirche*, Leipsic, 1904). This is a clear presentation of Greek doctrine and worship with sharp criticism of Roman Catholic tenets. Dividing theology into "simple" and "economic," he treats under the former head the doctrine of God and the Trinity, showing that each of the Persons sustains a definite relation to the other two, and defending the single procession of the Holy Ghost. In the "economic" section he seeks to show that man, deprived of the light of the Spirit by his fall (but not bereft of free will), and long condemned by the law, could best be reconciled with God only through the Incarnation in sinful flesh, mankind both being reconciled through the sacrifice of Christ, and being renewed and pardoned by immediate participation in the Divine. He cautiously defines the Church as possessing the marks of catholic and apostolic holiness and doctrine, though making little mention of hierarchic organization. The sacraments are reduced to three: baptism, representing reconciliation with the Father; the Eucharist, incorporation with the Son; and penance, the perseverance of the Holy Ghost. The remainder of the work is devoted chiefly to the rites of the Greek Church.

In his "Panegyric on the Incarnation" (ed. G. Queccius, Altdorf, 1626) he polemizes against those who deny the divinity of Christ, besides treating of redemption and emphasizing the true humanity of Christ. In his "Answer to the Inquiry . . on Gal. v. 16" (Nuremberg, 1626), moreover, he explains the opposition between flesh and spirit, in genuine Greek fashion, as that between body and soul. He also wrote an *Epistula . . . de vocibus in musica liturgica Græcorum usitatis* in 1626 (ed. J. J. Crudelius, probably in 1737), as well as letters, sermons, the polemic *Antipanoplia* against the Uniate Rhodinus, and a large work still preserved in manuscript in Cod. Harl. 5059.

Considered by some a Greek Lutheran, by others a Calvinist, and by others still a friend of the Roman Catholics, Metrophanes seems to have been willing to enjoy the favor of the powerful without regard to creed. Herein may lie the reason why he was not polemic against other communions, and was relatively indifferent to his own.

(PHILIPP MEYER.)

BIBLIOGRAPHY: Lives have been written by J. A. Dietelmair, Altdorf, 1769; A. C. Demetracopulos, Leipsic, 1870; and G. G. Mazarakis, Cairo, 1884. Consult further: Fabricius-Harles, *Bibliotheca Græca*, xi. 597 sqq., Hamburg, 1808; A. H. Hore, *Eighteen Centuries of the Orthodox Greek Church*, pp. 560–561, New York, 1899; *KL*, viii. 1444–46.

METROPOLITAN: The title of the bishop of the provincial capital, who possesses provincial as opposed to merely diocesan rights, including jurisdiction over (neighboring) suffragan bishops. See ARCHBISHOP; EXARCH; PATRIARCH, and cf. Bingham, *Origines*, II., xvi., where synodal and other references are given.

METROPOLITAN CHURCH ASSOCIATION. See MISCELLANEOUS RELIGIOUS BODIES, 18.

METZ, BISHOPRIC OF: An ancient episcopal see in Lorraine, founded according to unhistorical tradition by disciples of the apostles, probably in fact during the Roman domination. The town, known as Divodurum when it was the old capital of the Celtic tribe of the Mediomatrici, survived the fall of the empire and appears under the name of Mettis in the Frankish era as the seat of a bishop. The first certain occupant of the see is Hesperius, whose name is attached to the proceedings of the Synod of Clermont in 535. The diocese was of considerable extent in the Middle Ages, and contained a mixed population, though more German than French. (A. HAUCK.)

Angilram or Engelram (bishop 768–791), a Benedictine, was *archicapellanus* to Charlemagne and *apocrisiarius* under Adrian I. From 823 to 855 the see was occupied by Drogo, a brother of Louis I. Bishop Theodoric I. of Hamaland (964–984), one of the most influential counselors of Otto I. and Otto II., secured from the latter (977) the insignia and title of a prince of the empire for himself and his successors. With the next bishop, Adalbero II. of Bar (984–1005), a son of Duke Frederick I. of Upper Lorraine, begins a new period of nearly six centuries, during which the see is no longer involved in the affairs of the court and develops a strong ecclesiastical life, though troubled frequently by conflicts between the citizens of Metz and the bishops as secular lords. With the election of Henry II. of Lorraine-Vaudemont (1484–1505) the see became for over a century an appanage of the house of Lorraine—a relation which helped materially to retard the progress of the Reformation. The peace of Cateau-Cambrésis (1559) gave the king of France a protectorate over his "allies" of the districts of Metz, Toul, and Verdun, without altering their fundamental relations to the empire. Charles IX. attempted to suppress the Protestant religion, but Henry IV. permitted it to be practised in 1592 and 1597, and this liberty continued until the revocation of the Edict of Nantes in 1685, after Metz had become part of France by the Peace of Westphalia (1648). The last prince-bishop, Louis-Joseph de Montmorency-Laval (1761–1802), was driven out by the Revolution, and even the "constitutional bishop of the department of the Moselle," Nicolas Francin, was imprisoned in 1793, while the cathedral was turned into a Temple of Reason and all church property confiscated. By the Concordat of 1801 the bishopric was restored and made subject to the archbishop of Besançon, although with somewhat altered limits, which were reduced to about one-third of the former extent by the agreement of Louis XVIII. with Rome (1817–21). When Lorraine was annexed to Germany in 1871, the diocese was removed by Pius IX. from the metropolitan jurisdiction of Besançon and made immediately subject to the Holy See, with a further readjustment of boundaries.

BIBLIOGRAPHY: Sources for the early history are found in *MGH*, *Script.*, ii (1829), 260–270, iv (1841), 426 sqq., 461 sqq., 658 sqq., 696–700, x (1852), 531–572, xii (1856), 450–479, xiii (1881), 303 sqq. Consult: Gams, *Series episcoporum*, pp. 292–293, supplement, pp. 75, 77; J. F. and N. Tabouillet, *Hist. de Metz*, 6 vols., Metz, 1769–90; *Gallia Christiana*, xiii. 677–805, 987, Paris, 1785; Clouet, *Hist. ecclésiastique de la province de Trèves*, 2 vols., Verdun, 1844–51; Hauck, *KD*, vols. i.–iv., passim; Rettberg, *KD*, i. 90 sqq., 484 sqq.

MEURER, mei'rer, MORITZ: German Lutheran; b. at Pretzsch (13 m. s.w. of Wittenberg) Aug. 3, 1806; d. at Callenberg, near Chemnitz, May 10, 1877. He studied theology at the University of Leipsic (1825–28), and then spent four years as private tutor in the house of H. L. Heubner, superintendent at Wittenberg. After temporary service in a Prussian normal school, he obtained his first pastoral appointment at Waldenburg in Saxony. In 1841 he removed to the neighboring Callenberg, where he spent the rest of his life. His industrious spirit manifested itself in frequent participation in the proceedings of the provincial synod, and in the issue of church periodicals. He was the author of numerous larger and smaller works, mainly on the Reformation era. Among these are: *Luthers Leben, aus den Quellen erzählt* (3 vols., Leipsic, 1845–46; Eng. transl., New York, 1848); *Katharina Luther* (Dresden, 1854); and *Philipp Melanchthon* (1860). In connection with the collective work entitled *Altväter der lutherischen Kirche*, Meurer contributed volumes ii.–iv., including the biographies of Bugenhagen, Myconius, and Hausmann. He was a distinguished writer also in the field of ecclesiastical art, and gladly promoted the study of it. Meurer set forth his general views on the subject in two valuable writings: *Der Altarschmuck, ein Beitrag zur Paramentik in der evangelischen Kirche* (Leipsic, 1867) and *Der Kirchenbau vom Standpunkt und nach dem Brauche der lutherischen Kirche* (1877).

THEODOR FICKER.

MEXICO: A republic in the southern part of North America, having an area of 767,005 square miles. Out of a population (1900) of 13,600,000, about 2,500,000 were of pure, or nearly pure, white race; 5,800,000 of mixed race; and 5,200,000 of Indian race. Of these latter about 1,300,000 are of the most ignorant savage type, knowing practically no Spanish and having not the merest rudiments of civilization. Even of the mixed or better class of Indian races, few can be considered civilized, so that the Mexico known to the world includes probably not more than one-third of the entire population. Of that third only a little over a third (1,800,000) could, in 1895, both read and write, while about 325,000 more could read but not write. Since then the proportion has undoubtedly increased under the free and compulsory system of state education, assisted by beneficent societies. In 1904 there were 9,194 elementary, 36 secondary, 20 normal, and 45 professional schools, with 18,310 teachers and 634,136 enrolled pupils. There were also private clerical and association schools to the number of 2,281, with 135,838 pupils.

From the time of the conquest by the Spaniards to 1810 the country was absolutely under the power of the Roman Catholic Church and the Spanish government. Then came a revolt, headed by a priest, and in 1821 independence of Spain was achieved; the Church, however, still reigned supreme. In 1857 the Liberal party drew up a program of religious liberty, which was not carried into effect till 1867, when the French rule of Maximilian was overthrown and Juarez established the present republic. Roman Catholic religious houses were closed, church property confiscated, ecclesiastical buildings assigned for the use of schools, libraries, hospitals, etc., and a law passed forbidding any ecclesiastical body to acquire landed property. The era of Protestant influence dates from the entrance of a large number of Bibles carried by General Scott's army in the war of 1846. Gradually little companies were formed which met in private houses; these received help from Miss Melinda Rankin's school, first at Brownsville, Tex., and then at Monterey, and from an agent of the Bible Society. A number of similar individual enterprises were started, and a Baptist Church was organized in Monterey in 1864. With the establishment of the new republic Protestant missionaries went into the country until at least seventeen societies are represented there. At first they were bitterly opposed not merely by the Roman Catholic Church authorities but by the strongest elements among the Mexican people. Gradually this opposition has weakened until the best people of the nation and even of the Roman Catholic Church to a certain degree manifest their interest in and approval of the work done by the Protestant evangelists and in the Protestant schools. The latest missionary statistics show 227 missionaries, 491 native workers, 133 schools with 10,447 pupils, 39,838 professing Christians connected with the mission churches. As the number of Protestants reported in 1895 was about 40,000, the total number must on this basis be much larger. The Protestant influence is augmented by four printing-presses issuing annually a great amount of literature; Young Men's Christian Associations and Christian Endeavor Societies are exerting a mighty influence, and the whole tone of Mexican life is changing, even within the bounds of the Roman Catholic Church, with its more than 12,000,000 communicants and its full hierarchy.

EDWIN MUNSELL BLISS.

BIBLIOGRAPHY: F. H. Vera, *Colleccion de documentos eclesiásticos de Mexico*, 3 vols., Amecameca, 1887; *Concilio provincial Mexicano IV., 1771*, Querétaro, 1898; *Acta et decreta concilii provincialis Mexicani quinti, 1896*, Mexico, 1899; W. Butler, *Mexico in Transition*, New York, 1892; C. F. Lummis, *Awakening of a Nation; Mexico of To-day*, ib. 1898; P. F. Martin, *Mexico of the 20th Century*, 2 vols., ib. 1907; C. R. Enock, *Mexico; its ancient and modern Civilization, Hist., and political Conditions*, ib., 1909.

MEYER, FREDERICK BROTHERTON: English Baptist; b. at London Apr. 8, 1847. He was educated at Brighton College and Regent's Park Baptist College (B.A., London University, 1869), and held successive pastorates at Pembroke Baptist Chapel, Liverpool, in 1870–72, York, in 1872–1874, Victoria Road Church, Leicester, in 1874–78, Melbourne Hall, Leicester, in 1878–88, Regent's Park Chapel, London, in 1888–92, and Christ Church, Westminster Bridge Road, Lambeth, in 1892–95. He was president of the National Federation of Free Churches 1904–05. Since that time, as general evangelist of the Federation of Free Churches, he has conducted missions in South Africa and the far

East, returning to England in the spring of 1909. In theology he is a liberal Evangelical. Among his numerous works, special mention may be made of his *Elijah and the Secret of his Power* (London, 1887); *Israel a Prince with God* (1887); *Abraham; or, the Obedience of Faith* (1888); *Christian Living* (1888); *Present Tenses of the Blessed Life* (1888); *Shepherd Psalm* (1889); *Joseph, Beloved, Hated, Exalted* (1890); *Tried by Fire* (1890); *Life and Light of Men* (1891); *Moses, the Servant of God* (1892); *Joshua and the Land of Promise* (1893); *Way into the Holiest* (1893); *Jeremiah, Priest and Prophet* (1894); *Prayers for Heart and Home* (1894); *Christ in Isaiah* (1895); *David, Shepherd, Psalmist, King* (1895); *Reveries and Realities* (1896); *Through Fire and Flood* (1896); *Paul, a Servant of Jesus Christ* (1897); *Saved and Kept* (1897); *Statutes and Songs* (1897); *Work-a-day Sermons* (1897); *Blessed are Ye* (1898); *Our Daily Homily* (5 vols., 1898–99); *Love to the Uttermost* (1898); *Love, Courtship, Marriage* (1899); *John the Baptist* (1900); *The Prophet of Hope* (1900); *The Soul's Ascent* (1901); *Art of Life* (1903); *Jottings and Hints for Lay Preachers* (1903); *Religion in Homespun* (1903); *Some Deeper Things* (1903); *Directory of a Devout Life* (1904); *In the Beginning God!* (1904); *Epistle to the Philippians* (1905); *The Soul's Wrestle with Doubt* (1905); *In Defence of the Faith* (1907); *The Soul's Pure Intention* (1907); and *A Winter in South Africa* (1908).

MEYER, moi'er, **HEINRICH AUGUST WILHELM:** German Lutheran; b. at Gotha Jan. 10, 1800; d. at Hanover June 21, 1873. He received his theological training at Jena (1818–20). After teaching for a time in a private school at Grone, near Göttingen, he was pastor successively at Osthausen (1822–26), Meiningen (1826–31), and Harste (1831–37). In 1837 he was called to Hoya as superintendent and pastor; and in 1841, declining a professorial appointment at Giessen, he was made consistorial councilor, superintendent, and pastor at Neustadt, Hanover. Here he was the sole pastor of a community of some 5,000, and to his threefold task was added the ever-increasing burden of his labor on the New Testament. After 1848 he restricted himself to his consistorial and exegetical duties, residing at Hanover. In 1861 he was created a councilor of the supreme consistory, but in 1865 he requested and obtained honorable retirement. He regarded his Latin edition of the Lutheran symbolic books (Göttingen, 1830) as an episode in his life-work. His great work was *Das Neue Testament griechisch nach den besten Hülfsmitteln kritisch revidiert mit einer neuen deutschen Uebersetzung und einem kritischen und exegetischen Kommentar*, of which the first eleven volumes were prepared by himself (Göttingen, 1829–47; text and translation of the New Testament, and commentary on Matthew-Philemon), the remaining volumes being necessarily entrusted to younger collaborators, all Meyer's strength being needed in the preparation of new editions of the parts already issued by him. His original plan had been to divide the work into three parts: text and translation; commentary on the Gospels and Acts; commentary on the other books and a handbook containing isagogic investigations, the history of exegesis (especially from the Church Fathers), and his own methods. He likewise planned to write a system of Biblical rationalism, which was to give a summary of exegetical results. His work was translated into English (20 vols., Edinburgh, 1873–85; American ed., New York, 1884 sqq). In his lifetime he employed as collaborators J. E. Huther (the Pastoral, Petrine, and Johannine Epistles, Jude and James; Göttingen, 1850–52), G. Lünemann (I and II Thessalonians and Hebrews, 1850), and F. Düsterdieck (Apocalypse, 1865). Since his death later editions have been prepared by B. Weiss (Matthew, John, Romans, the Pastoral and Johannine Epistles, and Hebrews; 7th ed., Göttingen, 1901–02), B. and J. Weiss (Mark and Luke; 9th ed., 1901), H. H. Wendt (Acts, 8th ed., 1899), C. F. G. Heinrici (I and II Corinthians; 8th ed., 1896–1900), F. Sieffert (Galatians; 9th ed., 1899), E. Haupt (Ephesians, Philippians, Colossians, and Philemon; 8th ed., 1902), W. Bornemann (I and II Thessalonians; 6th ed., 1894), E. Kühl (Petrine Epistles and Jude; 6th ed., 1897), W. Beyschlag (James; 6th ed., 1897), and W. Bousset (Apocalypse; 6th ed., 1906). (F. Düsterdieck.)

Bibliography: A. H. Newman, in *Baptist Quarterly*, viii (1874), 438 sqq.; H. S. Burrage, in *Bibliotheca Sacra*, xxxii (1875), 438 sqq.

MEYER, JOHANN FRIEDRICH VON: German theologian, jurist and statesman; b. at Frankfort Sept. 12, 1772; d. there Jan. 28, 1849. In his earlier youth he studied classics, drawing, painting, and music; from 1789 he studied law and philology at Göttingen, and from 1793 philosophy and natural science at Leipsic. After a term of practise at the imperial chamber at Wetzlar, he settled down in 1802 in his native city where he served as president of the court of appeals, member of the senate, and mayor. In 1816 he became president of the Bible Society in Frankfort. The first period of his literary activity was influenced by the rationalism of the age, seen in his essays in Wieland's *Merkur*, his romance *Kallias*, and his epic *Tobias*. He then began serious study of the Bible, recognized the necessity of revelation and saw in redemption the center and essence of Christianity; all this without contemning science, but employing it in the service of God. In his thirty-fifth year (1807) he learned Hebrew, making use of old and new translations and commentaries. His comprehensive knowledge, especially in the field of archeology and jurisprudence, enabled him to form his own exegesis. In 1812 he published his *Bibeldeutungen*, a sharp attack upon the theological conceptions of the time. In 1819 appeared his annotated revision of Luther's translation of the Bible, which had a wide circulation (3d ed., 1855). Meyer was not only a theologian, but also a mystic and theosophist, and emphasized theosophy in the third period of his literary activity. The mechanical conception of transcendental supernaturalism and orthodoxy satisfied him as little as rationalism. Nature and the Bible he regarded as supplementary documents, the key to which was in symbols—numbers and figures. He was intent upon fathoming the fundamental sense of the divine Word which he held to lie beyond the grammatical sense. Eschatological and apocalyptical studies had great attraction for him. From this period originated such works as *Schlüssel zur Offenbarung Johannis von einem Kreuzritter* (1833) and *Blicke in den Spiegel des prophetischen Wortes* (1847). Meyer's predilection for symbolism led him to study not only old-world mysteries, but also the higher degrees of freemasonry. Results of this are his works, *Das Buch Jezira, die älteste, kabbalistische Urkunde der Hebräer* (1831); *Zur Aegyptologie* (1840) and his eleven collections of *Blätter für höhere Wahrheit* (1819 to 1832) to which he added *Inbegriff der Glaubenslehre* (1832). He wrote also some poems and a number of criticisms for the *Heidelberger Jahrbücher*, 1811-18.

(G. E. Steitz†.)

Bibliography: There is a biographical introduction to *Auswahl aus den Blättern für höhere Wahrheit*, pp. v.-xl., Stuttgart, 1853. Consult also *ADB*, xxi. 597.

MEYFART (MAYFART), JOHANN MATTHAEUS: German Lutheran theologian; b. at Jena Nov. 9, 1590; d. at Erfurt Jan. 26, 1642. He was the son of a clergyman of Walwinkel in the Thuringian forest; studied at Gotha, Jena, and Wittenberg. In 1616 he was called to Coburg as professor at the newly founded Gymnasium Casimirianum which distinguished itself by its strict discipline in morals, and in 1623 became its head. In 1631 or 1633 he was appointed professor of theology at the university of Erfurt. Of his Latin works, some are dogmatic: *Prodromus elucidarii theologici sive distinctionum theologicarum centuriæ duæ, ex omnium prope theologorum, qui post exhibitam A. C. floruerunt, scriptis collectæ*, etc. (1620, unfinished); others are polemic: *Grawerus continuatus* (Coburg, 1623); *Anti-Becanus sive manualis controversiarum theol., a Becano collecti, Confutatio* (2 vols., Leipsic, 1627) and *Nodus Gordius sophistarum solutus* (Coburg, 1627), an original attempt to reconcile Aristotle and Petrus Ramus. But his independent activity, awakened by the philosophy as well as the history and poetry of antiquity, united itself with a deep longing for the highest ideals, with an experience of the love of Christ, and with an enthusiastic absorption in subjective experiences of supernatural perfection. At the same time, however, Meyfart had a keen eye for corruption in the Church, for the dead mechanicalism of traditional theology, and for the moral defects of his age. This is shown, furthermore, by his German works, which fall into two groups, speculative-eschatological and practical-reformatory. To the first group belong *Tuba novissima* (Coburg, 1626), four sermons on Death, the Last Judgment, Eternal Life, and Damnation. There followed *Von dem himmlischen Jerusalem* (2 vols., Coburg, 1627), which contained his celebrated hymn, "Jerusalem, du hochgebaute Stadt" (several English translations, e.g., Miss Winkworth's "Jerusalem, thou city fair and high"); *Das höllische Sodoma* (2 vols., ib. 1630), and *Das jüngste Gericht* (Nuremberg, 1632). To the second group belong his *Christliche Erinnerung*, concerning witchcraft (1636), and *Christliche Erinnerung*, concerning the German universities (1636), a striking description of life among theological students. Meyfart also attempted in several of his works to reform the clergy, the church service, church discipline and service of prayer, and to counteract the ecclesiastical dissensions and the hatred of the theologians. He was one of the best of the precursors of Spener, a learned but enthusiastic mystic, and yet had his eyes fully open to the deficiencies of his times.

(E. Henke†.)

Bibliography: H. Witten, *Memoria theologorum nostri sæculi*, Frankfort, 1685; G. Ludewig, *Ehre des Casimiriani academici*, ii. 261 262, Coburg, 1729; A. F. W. Fischer, *Kirchenlieder-Lexicon*, vol. ii., Gotha, 1879; Julian, *Hymnology*, pp. 732-733; *ADB*, xxi. 646.

MEYRICK, FREDERICK: Church of England; b. at Ramsbury (27 m. w. of Reading), Wiltshire, Jan. 28, 1827; d. at Blickling (13 m. n.n.w. of Norwich), Norfolkshire, Jan. 3, 1906. He was educated at Trinity College, Oxford (B.A., 1847), where he was fellow, 1847-60, and tutor, 1851-1859. He was tutor to the Marquis of Lothian, 1847-53; was ordered deacon in 1850 and ordained priest in 1852; was an inspector of schools 1859-1868; examining chaplain to the bishop of Lincoln 1868-85; principal of Codrington College, Barbados, 1886-87; rector of Blickling, Norfolk, from 1868 till his death, and also non-resident canon of Lincoln after 1869. He was Whitehall preacher in 1856-57 and select preacher at Oxford in 1856, 1866, and 1876. He took an active part in the Old Catholic movement and attended the Bonn conference of 1875. Among his numerous writings mention may be made of his *Practical Working of the Church of Spain* (London, 1851); *Clerical Tenure of Fellowships* (Oxford, 1854); *Moral and Devotional Theology of the Church of Rome* (London, 1856); *The Outcast and the Poor of London* (1858); *The Wisdom of Piety* (1859); *Correspondence with Old Catholics and Orientals* (4 series, 1877-78); *Is Dogma a Necessity?* (1883); *The Doctrine of the Church of England on the Holy Communion Restated* (1885); *The Church of England, A.D. 597-1887* (1887); *The History of the Church in Spain* (1892); *Scriptural and Catholic Truth and Worship* (1901); *Old Anglicanism and Modern Ritualism* (1901); *Sunday Observance* (1902); *Appeal to the Primitive Centuries* (1904); *Appeal to the Sixteenth and Seventeenth Centuries* (1905); *Memories of Life at Oxford and Elsewhere* (1905). He contributed to the *Speaker's Commentary* the parts on Obadiah (London, 1876) and Ephesians (1880), and to the *Pulpit Commentary* the sections on Leviticus (1882) and Joshua and Judges (1895).

MEZUZAH: A rectangular piece of inscribed parchment enclosed in a wooden or metal case and attached by Jews to the upper part of the right-hand door post of a dwelling. The inscription consists of Deut. vi. 4-9, xi. 13-21, and is written in twenty-two lines according to the rules made for copying the Torah. The parchment is rolled with the writing inside, on the outside at the upper end the divine name Shaddai is written, and a glass-covered aperture in the case leaves this visible. The Mezuzah is by the pious touched with the hand as they enter or leave the house, and a short prayer is recited at the same time. The practise is founded on the injunction in Deut. vi. 9.

Bibliography: Dassorius, *De ritibus Mezuzæ*, in B. Ugolinus, *Thesaurus antiquitatum sacrarum*, vol. xxi., 34 vols., Venice, 1744–69; *JE*, viii. 531–532.

MEZZOFANTI, met"so-fān'tī, **GIUSEPPE GASPARD:** Italian cardinal; b. at Bologna Sept. 17, 1774; d. in Rome Mar. 15, 1849. He was educated in the archiepiscopal seminary of his native city and was ordained priest in 1797. He held various professorial positions in the University of Bologna until 1831, when he removed to Rome, where he succeeded Mai as librarian of the Vatican. In 1838 Gregory XVI. created him cardinal-priest. He was said to have been the greatest linguist of ancient or modern times. According to his biographer Russell he spoke with uncommon fluency thirty-eight languages; less perfectly, eleven; imperfectly, seven; and could read, but not speak, twelve others. He was acquainted besides with at least fifty dialects of those languages.

Bibliography: C. W. Russell, *Life of Cardinal Mezzofanti*, London, 1858, cf. T. Watts, *On Dr. Russell's Life of Cardinal Mezzofanti*, ib. 1860; A. Manavit, *Esquisse historique sur le Cardinal Mezzofanti*, Paris, 1854; A. Bellesheim, *Giuseppe, Cardinal Mezzofanti*, Würzburg, 1880.

MIANI, GIROLAMO. See Somaschians.

MICAH (Hebr. *Miykayah*, "Who is like Yahweh?"): The prophet whose book is sixth among the Minor Prophets. From his home in Moresheth-gath (i. 14) he is called the Morasthite (i. 1) and is so distinguished (e.g., Jer. xxvi. 18) from other men of the name, notably from Micah, son of Imlah (I Kings xxii. 8). He belonged to the southern kingdom, where he exercised his office (Jer. xxvi. 18), though the range of his prophecies covered Samaria. The superscription (i. 1) places his activity in the reigns of Jotham, Ahaz, and Hezekiah, all kings of Judah. This fact has been questioned, and the attempt made to date his work wholly under Hezekiah. But chaps. i.–iii. echo the period of Ahaz, and if iv. 1–5 (cf. Isa. ii. 2–5) is original with Micah, he may be placed also under Jotham. But his greatest activity is to be placed under Hezekiah.

Chap. i. deals with the imminent judgment of God first on Israel (Samaria) and then on Judah; chaps. ii.–iii. lay the blame upon the sins of the upper classes, including the false prophets; in chaps. iv.–v., in which the high point of Micah's oracles is reached, the author has alternately in view an immediate and a remoter future of Judah, in which it is to be wasted by Babylon and Assyria and then restored (these alternations have led to much discussion concerning the date and genuineness of the prophecies here collected); chaps. vi.–vii. start from a new point of view, since in them the guilt of the whole people is discussed. In these last chapters the literary form of dialogue appears, in which Yahweh, the people, and the prophet are the speakers; Yahweh states his ground of action against his people (vi. 1–5) and is answered with contrition by the people (vi. 6–7), to whom the prophet replies (vi. 8); Yahweh denounces the sins of the capital (vi. 9–16); vii. 1–13 is a dialogue between prophet and people; vii. 15 is Yahweh's encouragement continued by the prophet in verses 16–20.

The genuineness of parts of the book of Micah has been violently assailed. Thus the presence of ii. 12–13 has been justified by some only as the (quoted) words of a lying prophet like the one implied in verse 11, in which case a connection between verses 11–12 is made by supposing a suppressed "saying" at the end of verse 11. But it is best understood as a genuine promise of restoration following the denunciation which had just been pronounced. Stade makes iv. 1–4, 11–14, v. 1–3, 6–14 exilic and iv. 5–10, v. 4–5 still later interpolations, and sees in them inconsistencies and differences of standpoint. Ryssel combats this view, assigns the whole to Micah or at least to the time of Hezekiah, and regards it as in vital connection with chaps. i.–iii. The difficulty arose in the mention of Babylon as the place of exile (iv. 10) in a time when Assyria was the world power and Nineveh the world capital. The solution is to be found in the great significance and importance of Babylon, even in the Assyrian period, as the historic seat of world empire (Gen. x. 10–11) and so essentially and typically antagonistic to the city of God. Similarly, from the time of Ewald, the genuineness of chaps. vi.–vii. has been assailed. Ewald dated them in Manasseh's time; Wellhausen and Stade followed him in so dating vi. 1–vii. 6, putting vii. 7–20 in the exile; Cornill sees in vii. 7 sqq. references to the second temple; and other scholars take positions essentially in agreement with these. But when it is noted that in vii. 7–20 the exile lies still in the future and that between this part and chaps. i.–v. there are numerous coincidences and points of contact, the conclusion will follow that this part has the same author as the rest of the book. The impression the book makes is that of a unit, with fuller reports of the deliverances in chaps. i.–ii., more condensed and fragmentary reports in the other chapters.

Chap. vi. has a special interest in that the scheme of history which it assumes as that known by those to whom it is addressed is that found in Numbers and Joshua, showing that at least the writing of J lay before the prophet. Another point of interest in this chapter has to do with Micah's position as to sacrifice (vi. 6–8). Some have inferred that Micah did not regard sacrifice as demanded by the divine law. But the words of the prophet necessarily imply sacrifice as a legal requirement, which is met by the people, however, in a formal manner which deprives it of its quality as a God-pleasing service.

The language is purely classical. In point of rhetorical peculiarity, Micah stands between his contemporaries, Hosea and Isaiah, but nearer to the latter than the former; for although, like the former, he is abrupt, abounding in sudden and quick changes, in depth of spirituality he is the worthy companion of Isaiah, sharing with him a mingling of mildness and strength, of gentleness and elevation, together with great vigor and an artistic turn of expression. (W. Volck†.)

Of the prophecies placed under the name of Micah in the Hebrew text it is not certain that anything except chaps. i.–iii. proceed from Micah the Morasthite. These, with the possible exception of ii. 12, 13, which have no obvious relation to the context, and contain an indefinite and unmotived promise of a return from exile, are an important supplement to the genuine discourses of Isa. i.–v., and are especially interesting as showing the bitter feeling of a small landholder in a country village arising from the treatment of the poorer classes by the rapacious nobles and office-holders of the capital. The natural climax of the prophecy, iii. 12, is quoted as a memorable saying a century later (Jer. xxvi. 18).

The remainder of the book as we now have it is apparently composed of several unclassified discourses or fragments of discourses of dates later than Micah. Chap. iv. describes a great deliverance and restoration of Israel after it has been punished for its sins with exile and disintegration, and chap. v. announces the deliverer as a descendant of the princely house of David and a native of Bethlehem, and pictures the results of the reclamation as a triumph over the national enemies followed by the abolition of all forms of idolatry. These two chapters, which form a unit, were presumably written under the influence of Isa. vii. 14 sqq., and are perhaps exilic (see the reference to Babylon in iv. 10). Chap. vi. 1–vii. 6 was composed by a great prophet living in Jerusalem, presumably in the earlier days of Manasseh. Of chap. vii. 7–20 it can only be said that it is a cento of unconnected fragments which give no clue to the time or circumstances of their author or authors. They are, if possible, still less relevant to the conditions of Micah's time than are the three preceding chapters.

For the reason that the several divisions of the book differ greatly in subject-matter, style, and outlook, it is not possible to describe it in any terms that will apply to the collection as a whole. Of most significance and permanent value are chaps. iii. and vi., the latter being especially memorable as containing the classical definition of the religion of Yahweh (verse 8). J. F. McCurdy.

Bibliography: The most thorough investigation is B. Ryssel, *Untersuchungen über die Textgestalt und die Echtheit des Buches Micha*, Leipsic, 1887. Still valuable are the older commentaries by E. Pocock, Oxford, 1677; C. W. Justi, Leipsic, 1799, and A. T. Hartmann, Lemgo, 1800. More recent works are by C. P. Caspari, 2 parts, Christiania, 1851–52 (elaborate); E. B. Pusey, Oxford, 1862; C. F. Keil, Eng. transl., Edinburgh, 1868; T. Roorda, Leyden, 1869; L. Reinke, Giessen, 1874; P. Kleinert, in Lange, Eng. transl., New York, 1875; S. Clark, in *Bible Commentary*, London, 1876; T. K. Cheyne, in *Cambridge Bible*, Cambridge, 1887; H. J. Elhorst, Arnheim, 1891; C. von Orelli, Eng. transl., *The Twelve Minor Prophets*, New York, 1893; J. Wellhausen, *Kleinen Propheten*, Berlin, 1893; G. A. Smith, *The Book of the Twelve*, in *Expositor's Commentary*, London, 1896; J. T. Beck, Gütersloh, 1898; W. Nowack, in *Handkommentar*, Göttingen, 1903; M. L. Margolis, Philadelphia, 1908–09.

On questions of introduction consult: B. Stade, in *ZATW*. i (1881), 161 sqq.; W. Nowack, in *ZATW*, iv (1884), 288–290; J. Taylor, *The Massoretic Text and the Ancient Versions of . . Micah*, London, 1891; W. H. Kosters, in *ThT*, 1893, pp. 249 sqq.; V. Ermoni, in F. Vigouroux, *Dictionnaire de la Bible*, part xxv., pp. 1064–1067, Paris, 1905; Smith, *Prophets*, pp. 287 sqq.; *DB*, iii. 358–360; *EB*, iii. 3067–74; *JE*, viii. 533–535; the pertinent sections in the works on introduction to the Old Testament, particularly those by Driver, Cornill, W. Baudissin (*Einleitung in die Bücher des Alten Testamentes*, Leipsic, 1901), and Wellhausen, in Bleek (*Einleitung in das Alte Testament*, Berlin, 1886).

MICHAEL: One of the four (or seven) archangels of Jewish post-exilic angelology. His name occurs in the Bible only in Dan. x. 13, 21, xii. 1; Jude 9; Rev. xii. 7 The conception in Daniel is that of the guardian angel of Israel (see Angel, II., §§ 1–2), with which the New-Testament passages accord. The passage in Jude is a quotation from the Ascension of Moses (see Pseudepigrapha, Old Testament, III., 6). In the pseudepigraphic literature Michael's figure looms large, and he often appears as the first of the archangels. In rabbinical writings his part is still further expanded. From Judaism he passed over into the Christian Church as the guardian angel of all Christians, and is celebrated in the Roman calendar on Sept. 29 (see Michaelmas), and in the Greek on Nov. 9. Two military orders took his name—the French order founded in 1469 by Louis XI., and the Bavarian order founded in 1721 by Elector Joseph Clemens of Cologne—as did a number of congregations. A song said to have been sung by Michael and the good angels in triumph over Lucifer and the fallen angels and revealed to St. Amadeus is given in J. A. Fabricius, *Codex pseudepigraphus Veteris Testamenti*, i. 26–27 (Hamburg, 1723), and a partial translation is in S. Baring-Gould, *Legends of the Patriarchs and Prophets*, p. 16 (New York, 1872).

Bibliography: A. Kohut, *Jüdische Angelologie*, Leipsic, 1866; W Lueken, *Michael*, Göttingen, 1898; F. J. Peters, *St. Michael und seine Verehrung*, Cologne, 1902; A. Butler, *Lives of the Fathers, Martyrs, and Saints*, Sept. 29, vol. ii., London, 1860.

MICHAEL, EMIL THEODOR RICHARD: Austrian Roman Catholic; b. at Reichenbach (32 m. s.w. of Breslau), Prussian Silesia, Sept. 20, 1852. He was admitted to the Society of Jesus in 1874 and was educated at the universities of Innsbruck and Breslau (Ph.D., 1884; D.D., 1888). In 1888 he became privat-docent for church history at the former institution, and three years later he was appointed associate professor of the same subject, being promoted to the rank of full professor in 1895. Since 1906 he has been professor of Christian art at Innsbruck. In addition to numerous contributions to theological periodicals, he has written *Salimbene und seine Chronik* (Innsbruck, 1889); *Rankes Weltgeschichte, eine kritische Studie* (Paderborn, 1890); *Ignaz von Döllinger* (Innsbruck, 1892); *Geschichte des deutschen Volkes* (4 vols., Freiburg, 1897–1906); and *Kritik und Antikritik in Sachen meiner Geschichte des deutschen Volkes* (2 parts, 1899–1902).

MICHAELIS: A family of German Lutheran exegetes of the seventeenth and eighteenth centuries.

1. Johann Heinrich: b. at Klettenberg (20 m. s.w. of Blankenburg), Brunswick, July 26, 1668; d. at Halle Mar. 10, 1738. Educated in theology, philosophy, and orientalia at Frankfort-on-the-Oder, he began to lecture in Halle in 1698, becoming successively associate professor of oriental languages (1699), full professor in the theological faculty (1709), and senior and inspector of the theological seminary (1732). He was important primarily as representing the critical school in the midst of Pietism, then centering in Halle. He was in great part the author of the plan for the Collegium Orientale Theologicum established there by A. H. Francke. He was likewise distinguished for his partial edition of the Old Testament (Halle, 1720), based on five Erfurt manuscripts and nineteen printed editions, the variants also being given. The edition was, however, too hastily done, and proved unreliable, though it is still not without value. He also prepared for it his *Uberiores annotationes* (3 vols., Halle, 1720), in which he diligently consulted the earlier versions. Some of the exegetical material here contained, like several of his dissertations and his *Sonderbarer Lebenslauf P. Heylings aus Lübeck und dessen Reise nach Ethiopien* (Halle, 1724), is still noteworthy.

2. Christian Benedikt (nephew of the preceding): b. at Elrich (8 m. n.w. of Nordhausen) Jan. 26, 1680; d. at Halle Feb. 22, 1764. He was educated at Halle, where he was successively associate (1713–1714) and full (1714–31) professor of philosophy, professor of theology (1731–38) and of Greek and Oriental languages (1738–64). Besides contributing to his uncle's edition of the Hebrew Old Testament and *Uberiores annotationes*, he wrote *Dissertatio de antiquitatibus œconomiæ patriarchalis* (Halle, 1728) and *Tractatus criticus de variis lectionibus Novi Testamenti caute colligendis et diiudicandis* (1749), in addition to an edition of the Hebrew Bible (with the Apocrypha and New Testament in Greek; Halle, 1741), based on H. Opitz's edition of 1709.

3. Johann David (son of the preceding): b. at Halle Feb. 27, 1717; d. at Göttingen Aug. 22, 1791. After completing his studies at Halle and traveling in England and Holland he went in 1745 to Göttingen, where he was professor of philosophy (1746–50) and of Oriental languages (1750–91). He was a prolific author, as is evidenced by his writing the entire periodical *Orientalische und exegetische Bibliothek* (later the *Neue orientalische und exegetische Bibliothek*; 35 parts, Frankfort and Göttingen, 1771–91). Moreover, he was the first to give to the cultured public the results of scientific views of the Bible as divorced from dogmatic assumptions in his annotated translation of the Old (13 vols., Göttingen, 1769–86) and New (2 vols., 1790) Testaments, these following his exegeses of some of the Messianic psalms (Frankfort, 1759), Ecclesiastes (Bremen, 1762), and I Maccabees (Frankfort, 1778). He gained equal favor, though more slowly, with his *Einleitung in das Neue Testament* (Göttingen, 2d ed., 1788; Eng. transl., *Introduction to the New Testament*, 4 vols., Cambridge, 1793–1801), which was followed by the less popular and uncompleted *Einleitung in das Alte Testament* (Hamburg, 1787).

The chief services of Michaelis were rendered in the domain of Biblical ancillary sciences, especially with regard to the Old Testament. Here belongs his *Supplementa ad lexica Hebraica* (6 vols., Göttingen, 1784–92), in which he sought primarily to free Hebrew lexicography from rabbinical tradition and to operate with the kindred languages, especially Arabic. At the same time he carefully studied the early versions, and such was his attention to the Peshito that he may be considered one of the founders of Syriac philology. Note should be made here of his *Grammatica Chaldaica* (Leipsic, 1771) and *Grammatica Syriaca*. He also made valuable contributions to Biblical antiquities, especially in his *Mosaisches Recht* (6 vols., 2d ed., Frankfort, 1771–75; Eng. transl. by A. Smith, *Commentaries on the Laws of Moses*, 4 vols., London, 1814), in which he advanced the view, then new, that the Pentateuchal laws were a product of the statesmanship of Moses, who aimed at the separation of Israel from the heathen [involving denial of the directly divine character and universal validity of the laws], thus judging antiquity by the standards of its own time, instead of by the criterion of the Christian Church; as well as in his *Abhandlung von den Ehegesetzen Mosis* (Göttingen, 1755). His geographical and archeological interests, already evinced by his securing from Frederick V. of Denmark the sending of an expedition to Arabia in 1761 (for which he wrote his *Fragen an eine Gesellschaft reisender Gelehrten*, Frankfort, 1762), found expression in his *Spicilegium geographiæ exterorum* (2 vols., Göttingen, 1769–80) and in many places in his *Syntagma commentationum* (2 parts, 1759–67) and *Vermischte Schriften* (2 parts, Frankfort, 1766–69).

Although never a member of the theological faculty, Michaelis lectured on systematic, dogmatic, and moral theology, writing in these departments his *Gedanken über die Lehre der heiligen Schrift von Sünde und Genugthuung* (Bremen, 1748); *Compendium theologiæ dogmaticæ* (Göttingen, 1760; German ed., 1787); and *Entwurf einer typischen Gottesgelehrtheit* (Göttingen, 1753). These works, inferior to the rest, were weakened by his attempt not to break with external orthodoxy, though secretly he had renounced it, thus leading him to an attitude of untenable compromises. At the same time, this position gained him great popularity with both pupils and the Government, besides winning him the title of "regent of Göttingen" and the posts of secretary, director, and editor of the Göttingen Academy of Sciences. In the last two decades of his life, however, his prestige declined. (R. KITTEL.)

BIBLIOGRAPHY: 1, L. Diestel, *Geschichte des A. T. in der christlichen Kirche*, pp. 415 sqq., Jena, 1868. 3. His *Briefwechsel*, ed. Buhle, is in 3 vols., Leipsic, 1794–96, and his autobiography, ed. E. R. Hessenkamp, appeared at Rinteln, 1793. Consult further: L. Diestel, ut sup., pp. 583 sqq., 683 sqq., 745 sqq.; R. Smend, *Johann David Michaelis*, Göttingen, 1898; and especially Roethe, *Johann David Michaelis*, in the *Festschrift der Göttinger Gelehrten Gesellschaft*, Berlin, 1901.

MICHAELMAS: A festival celebrated Sept. 29, not only in the Roman Catholic Church, but also in the Greek and various Protestant churches in honor of the archangel Michael (q.v.), not with reference to any particular apparition of his, but generally commemorating the benefits which mankind have received from the angels. The festival seems to have been Roman in origin, and it is very old. In the eighth century the celebration was quite common in the Church. The Roman Catholic Church celebrates three special apparitions of the archangel, viz., May 8, Sept. 6, and Oct. 16. Michaelmas is also known as the Festival of St. Michael and All the Holy Angels. In England Michaelmas day is one of the four quarter-days, on which rents are paid, burghal councils elected, etc. Here, and also in other countries, it marks the beginning of the autumn term at schools and universities.

BIBLIOGRAPHY: A. Butler, *Lives of the Fathers, Martyrs and Other Principal Saints*, on Sept. 29; J. C. W Augusti, *Denkwürdigkeiten*, iii. 281 sqq., Leipsic, 1820; A. J. Binterim, *Denkwürdigkeiten*, v., i., pp. 465 sqq., Mainz, 1829; *DCA*, ii. 1177–79.

MICHELET, SIMON TEMSTRUP: Norwegian theologian; b. at Trondhjem Feb. 8, 1863. He was graduated from the University of Christiania (B.A., 1881; medalist, 1885; candidate in theology, 1887); studied at German universities, particularly at Leipsic, for several years, devoting himself to the history of religion, Semitic languages, and the Old Testament; received ordination and pastorates at Trondhjem and Christiania, 1894–96; was appointed professor of theology at the University of Christiania, 1896. He is a representative of the higher criticism, aiming through his publications to interest not merely academic circles, but also the Norwegian public. In his dogmatics he has been influenced by F. Petersen (q.v.), and in his exegesis by Frants Buhl (q.v.). He has argued in favor of retaining the ancient languages in the curricula of the gymnasia, and is a leader in the Norwegian student world. He has published *Amos, oversat og fortolket* *Med en udsigt over de samtidige tilstande i Israel* (1893); *Det gamle testamentes syn paa synden* (1899); *Gamle Helligdomme i nyt Lys* (1902); and *Aandens Tjenere, ikke Bogstavens* (1907), on the confessional question. JOHN O. EVJEN.

MICHELIANS. See HAHN, JOHANN MICHAEL.

MICRONIUS, MARTINUS (Marten de Cleyne): Dutch Protestant; b. probably at Ghent 1522 or 1523; d. at Norden (17 m. n. of Emden) Sept. 12, 1559. He studied at Basel and Zurich, and early in 1550 went to London as pastor of the Flemish congregation there. After the death of Edward VI. (1553), Mary forbade the preaching of Protestantism, and on Sept. 17 Micronius left England. He went to Denmark, but Lutheran opposition prevented him from the peaceable conduct of worship and he finally reached Emden. Meanwhile some of the London exiles had come into conflict with the Mennonites at Wismar, and Micronius, called from Emden, held a disputation with Menno Simons (q.v.) on Feb. 6 and 15, 1554. Lutheran hostility now drove him successively from Wismar, Lübeck, and Hamburg, but after a brief period of repose at Emden, he was called to the pastorate at Norden, where he remained until his death, except for a short visit to Frankfort in 1555, at Lasco's request, to organize the congregations of Dutch exiles settled there.

Micronius was a master of disputation. His writings show him to have been somewhat Nestorian in Christology and quite Zwinglian in Eucharistic doctrine, but universalistic in his concept of salvation. He was deeply influenced by his teacher and friend Bullinger, but his importance lay less in his theology than in the services he rendered the religious exiles from Holland. His chief works were: *De kleyne Catechismus oft kinderleere der Duytscher Ghemeynte van London* (ed. 1552 and often; Eng. transl., London, 1552); *Een corte undersouckinge des gheloofs* (1553); *Een claer bewijs van het recht gebruyck des Nachtmaals Christi ende wat men van de miss houden sal* (Buyten, London, 1554); and *Christlicke Ordinancien*, etc. (1554). Among his polemics mention may be made of his *Een waerachtig verhaal*, etc. (Emden, 1556), on his disputations with Menno Simons; *Apologeticum scriptum* (3 parts, 1557), against Joachim Westphal; and *Een Apologie of verandtwoordinghe* (Emden, 1558), against Menno Simons. (S. D. VAN VEEN.)

BIBLIOGRAPHY: J. H. Gerretsen, *Micronius, Zijn leven, zijn geschriften, zijn geestesrichting*, Nijmegen, 1895 (cf. S. Cramer, in *ThT*, 1896, pp. 304–317); Menno Simons, *Opera omnia Theologica*, pp. 545–618, Amsterdam, 1681.

MIDDLETON, CONYERS: English controversialist and author of the famous *Life of Cicero;* b. at York Dec. 27, 1683; d. at Hildersham (8 m. s.e. of Cambridge) July 28, 1750. He was graduated from the University of Cambridge (B.A., 1702–03; M.A., 1707; D.D., 1717). He was elected fellow of Trinity College, and was for a short time curate of Trumpington, near Cambridge. He won for himself a wide reputation by his caustic attacks on Bentley, the master of Trinity, who, in spite of his great scholarship, was very unpopular on account of his harsh personalities. In one of these (1720) Middleton assailed Bentley's proposal to issue an edition of the Greek Testament, discovering some errors in the advance sheets, and to this attack Bentley's retirement from that field has been wrongly attributed. Middleton was chosen principal librarian of Trinity College, 1721. See DEISM, I., § 7.

In 1724 he visited Rome, and later wrote *A Letter from Rome, showing an Exact Conformity between Popery and Paganism* (London, 1729, republished 1868), in which he attempted to prove that the religion of the Roman Church was a continuation of the heathenism of ancient Rome. Middleton's controversies were not confined to Bentley, but extended to Daniel Waterland, Thomas Sherlock, and others. He assailed the medical profession in his *De medicorum apud veteres Romanos degentium conditione dissertatio* (Cambridge, 1726). His controversy with Waterland originated with the latter's attack upon Middleton's assertion that there were "contradictions in the evangelists which could not be reconciled," and that "the story of the fall of man was a fable or allegory." In 1741 he published the great work of his life, the *History of the Life of M. Tullius Cicero* (2 vols., London, best ed., ib. 1848), written after the labors of six years, though the charge is made that it is plagiarized from a rare book by William Bellenden. This biography has been condemned as being too partial, and praising as "wise, virtuous, and heroic" acts which Cicero himself condemned. In his *Free Inquiry into the Miraculous Powers which are Supposed to have Subsisted in the Christian Church from the Earliest Ages through Several Successive Centuries* (London, 1749), he denies the continuance of miraculous powers in the Church after the apostolic age. He attacked Sherlock in *An Examination of the Lord-Bishop of London's Discourses concerning the*

Use and Intent of Prophecy (London, 1750). His *Miscellaneous Tracts* (London, 1752) collect a number of Middleton's shorter writings. His *Miscellaneous Works*, not including Cicero's Life, appeared 4 vols., London, 1752, 5 vols., 1755.

BIBLIOGRAPHY: The literature under BENTLEY, RICHARD; SHERLOCK, THOMAS; and WATERLAND, DANIEL. Consult also: John Nichols, *Literary Anecdotes of the 18th Century*, v. 405-423, 9 vols., London, 1812-15; *DNB*, xxxvii. 343-348.

MIDDLETON, THOMAS FANSHAW: Church of England bishop of Calcutta; b. in Kedleston (4 m. n.w. of Derby) Jan. 26, 1769; d. in Calcutta July 8, 1822. He was graduated with honors from the University of Cambridge (B.A., 1792; M.A., 1795; D.D., 1808); was appointed curate of Gainsborough, Lincolnshire, 1792; rector of Tansor, Northamptonshire, 1795; of Little and Castle Bytham, Lincolnshire, 1802; a prebend at Lincoln, 1809; vicar of St. Pancras, London, 1811; archdeacon of Huntingdon, 1812; and was consecrated first bishop of Calcutta, 1814. At Calcutta he founded in 1820 the Bishops' College, for the training of missionaries and clergymen for Asia. Dr. Middleton is justly famed for his *Doctrine of the Greek Article applied to the Criticism and Illustration of the New Testament* (London, 1808; 2d ed. by Rev. James Scholefield, 1828, 5th ed., 1855). A posthumous volume of *Sermons, Charges*, etc., with *Memoir*, was issued by H. K. Bonney (London, 1824).

BIBLIOGRAPHY: Besides the *Memoir* in his *Sermons*, ut sup., consult: C. W. Le Bas, *Life of T. F. Middleton*, 2 vols., London, 1831; C. M. Yonge, *Pioneers and Founders; or, recent Workers in the Mission Field*, ib. 1871; *DNB*, xxxvii. 363-365.

MIDIAN: The name of a people or stock (not of a country) which comes into especial prominence in the story of Gideon (Judges vi.-viii.). In the Old Testament the relations between them and Israel are in part friendly, though more often they are hostile. In the time of Gideon Midianites appear as ravaging nomads who cross the Jordan from the east and seize the produce and cattle of the Hebrews. They seem to be a belated part of the same migration as that to which the Israelites belonged, and Judges viii. 11 indicates that their home was the desert. The narrative in chap. viii. belongs in the main to a different narrator (J) from that in vi.-vii., and gives a slightly different view. When Ex. ii. 15 speaks of a "land of Midian," the reference is not to a region generally so named, but to a district named after a definite tribe which lived there. From Ex. ii.-iv. (and perhaps Num. x. 29-32) all that can be gathered of the region is that it was east of Egypt and south of the Jordan. Ptolemy (*Geographike*, vi. 7), and Eusebius and Jerome (*Onomastica*, 136, 276) knew of a Madiama or Madiam, east of the Red Sea and south of the Roman province of Arabia, mentioned by Arab geographers as Madyan, identified by R. F. Burton in 1878 with the region about the ruins of Magha'ir shu'aib, or "caves of Jethro"—a region called by its present inhabitants *arḍ madyan*, "land of Midian," having its northern boundary not far from the site of Elath and its southern near the coast fortress al-Muwelih. This modern district is about 45 miles from north to south and from twenty-three to thirty-four miles in width. There are still traces of mining operations for copper, silver, and gold.

The relation of friendship between the two peoples is illustrated by the case of Moses, who fled to the country and entered the family of "Hobab son of Raguel" (Num. x. 29, cf. Judges iv. 11, and "Reuel" Ex. ii. 18) or Jethro (Ex. iii.1, xviii. 1, cf. "Jether" Ex. iv. 18, margin). Hobab is called a Kenite in Judges iv. 11, and Stade suspects that the Kenites were in early times associated with the Midianites (see CAIN, KENITES). Num. x. 29-32 suggests not a settled people but a nomadic tribe. Other Old-Testament passages raise the question whether settled, semi-nomadic, or nomadic peoples were in mind. Gen. (xxxvii. 28, 36) implies not Bedouin but a settled people carrying wares to the north and in the contrary direction, Isa. lx. 6 must refer to nomads; Num. xxii., xxv. and xxxi. are not clear on the point, though Winckler, relying on Gen. xxxvi. 35 (cf. I Kings xi. 14-22), looks on these chapters as implying a pre-Moabitic and abiding possession of the region, a conclusion not wholly warranted by the text. The narrative in Num. xxxi. is not so reliable as to permit from the mention of "kings of Midian" (verse 8) the deduction that the Midianites were a settled people.

Genealogical details concerning the Midianites are not easy to interpret, partly because only a few names are given, partly because the nomadic tribes were so mobile that the same names appear from the Euphrates to the Red Sea. Gen. xxv. 1-6 derives them from Keturah and gives five branches of the stock. Of these Ephah is by Delitzsch placed in North Arabia as known to Tiglath-Pileser III. Knobel equates Epher with the Ghifar of Mohammed's age, who tented near Medina. For the time when they came into contact with Israel they are to be regarded as Aramaic nomads. With Israel's regal period they vanish from history; the Ishmaelites of Judges viii. 24 may be the same people (see ISHMAEL). From the occurrence of Jether, Jethro, and Raguel among Hebrew names, a coalescence with the Hebrews has been suspected.

(H. GUTHE.)

BIBLIOGRAPHY: T. Nöldeke, *Die Amalakiter und . . andere Nachbarvölker der Israeliten*, Göttingen, 1864; R. F. Burton, *The Land of Midian*, 2 vols., London, 1878-79 (contains collections of ancient materials); F. Delitzsch, *Wo lag das Paradies?* Leipsic, 1881; E. Glaser, *Skizze der Geschichte und Geographie Arabiens*, ii. 445 sqq., Berlin, 1890; H. Winckler, *Geschichte Israels*, i. 47 sqq. et passim, Leipsic, 1895; *Schrader, KAT*, i. 143, 145; *DB*, iii. 365-366; *EB*, iii. 3079-82; *JE*, viii. 547-548.

MIDRASH.

The word *midrash* occurs in II Chron. xiii. 22, xxiv. 27 (A. V. "story," margin "commentary," R. V. "commentary"), but the meaning in both passages is doubtful. In post-Biblical usage, the verb from which the noun is derived means "to examine, to elucidate," while the noun expresses "interpretation," especially the interpretation of Scripture, and then comes to mean the haggadic (i.e., illustrative and practical) or, sometimes, the halachic (i.e., exegetical) commentaries on the Old Testament, especially such works as the Mishna, Tosephta, and Talmud (q.v.; cf. W Bacher, *Die älteste Terminologie der jüdischen Schriftauslegung*, pp. 25 sqq., 103 sqq., Leipsic, 1899). The period of the kingdom in Israel was followed not by a hierocracy but by a rule under the Law (nomocracy), which more and more controlled the common external life and also the spiritual life of Israel. This is indicated by Haggai (ii. 10 sqq.), who makes the priests the recognized teachers of the law, while Ezra's whole striving was to bring the law of Moses into relation with common life. It is no wonder, in view of the changed conditions, that when other institutions were lost the Jews clung fondly to the written law, their only possession from the past. Yet this law was not a complete code; it hardly sufficed for the period immediately following the exile, still less could it supply the need when a fuller development of national life had bloomed. It had to be fitted to these later times and to be expanded, and this was done by the process of midrash. The name given to this activity was halachic, a collection of the results being called halakoth. The first authoritative collection of this material is that of Judah ha-Nasi, another is the Tosephta, while very early halachic material is found in the Baraithoth, in the midrashim Mekhilta, Siphra, Siphre, etc. Since the Old Testament was for the Jews the sum total of all that is good, beautiful, and worthful, it followed that it was regarded as the sufficient norm for all purposes of life. The application of this norm to practical purposes was brought about through midrash, but in this relation it was usually called haggada. Haggada sometimes adheres closely to the Scriptural text, sometimes takes it as a starting-point for varied expositions, which latter might be given in the synagogue or at private homes, in public observances as the Sabbath or festival occasions, or at important events of public or private life. (For the rules of halachic and haggadic interpretation, consult H. L. Strack, *Einleitung in den Thalmud*, VII., § 2, Leipsic, 1900).

1. Meaning and Essence of Midrash.

In spite of regulations once existent against reducing haggada and halacha to writing, it is abundantly evident that this material did exist in written form as early as the first part of the third century, though the purely haggadic midrashim now extant date from a later time. The time when this reduction to writing took place is difficult to ascertain because of the frequent redactions to which the material at hand has been subjected and because the text has not been carefully transmitted, (cf. L. Zunz, *Die gottesdienstlichen Vorträge der Juden*, Berlin, 1832). Much arduous work upon the manuscripts is necessary before a history of midrashic literature can be written. The most productive midrashic activity dates immediately after the close of the Babylonian Talmud and ends about 1040 A.D., being supplanted by philosophical studies. Many midrashim contain consecutive exposition of some book of the Old Testament, e.g., *Genesis rabba;* others consist of homilies based either on the cycle of synagogue readings or on the cycle of feasts. The homilies are usually the development of a theme on the basis of a text or verse of Scripture, and in the homiletic midrashim the compilers have been at pains to collect proems of various kinds to the themes (cf. S. Maybaum, *Die ältesten Phasen in der Entwickelung der jüdischen Predigt*, i. 14–27, Berlin, 1901). Thus it is reported of Rabbi Meir that his lectures were composed of halachic, haggadic, and illustrative materials, and of Rabbi Thanchum that he prefixed to a halachic lecture a haggadic introduction. The later midrashim often introduce a haggadic lecture by discussion of a halachic problem. The discussion which follows the proem is usually concerned with only a few verses, is often concentrated into a single verse or part of one, for the rest of the section chosen the exposition being rather cursory in character.

2. Date and Structure.

In the midrashim *Mekhilta* (on Exodus), *Siphre* (on Numbers and Deuteronomy), and *Siphra* (on Leviticus) two tendencies are discerned, that of the school of Rabbi Akiba and that of the school of his contemporary and opponent Rabbi Ishmael. The second is easily recognized by the learned by the names of the teachers which are given and also by certain technical expressions which appear. Mekhilta was in earlier times included under the term *Siphre;* it treats of Ex. xii. 1–xxiii. 19, xxxi. 12–17, xxxv. 1–3. Originally this was only halachic in character, the more strictly exegetical material being of later date. Many traces indicate that it covered a larger part of the book than the material which has survived. Editions are: Constantinople, 1515; Venice, 1545; Vienna, 1865; ib. 1870. "Siphre" (a Talmudic plural meaning "books") was originally a collective designation of the Tannaitic midrashim on Exodus, Numbers, and Deuteronomy; when "Mekhilta" was applied to the midrash on Exodus, "Siphre" was applied only to the midrash on Numbers and Deuteronomy. The extant Siphre on Numbers arose in the school of Ishmael, though it is of diverse authorship; the haggadic parts on Deuteronomy also are of that school, but in the legal portions (on chaps. xii.–xxvi.) it suggests the school of Akiba. Editions are: Venice, 1545; Vienna, 1864 (part 1 only). Siphra ("the book") is halachic and of the school of Akiba, except in viii. 1–x. 8, xviii. 1–5, xxvi. 3–46. It takes its name from the fact that instruction began not with the first book of the Pentateuch, but with the third. The basis is the teaching of Rabbi Judah, a pupil of Akiba; the final redactor was Chiyya the elder, pupil and friend of Judah ha-Nasi. The midrash of Ishmael's school is used only indirectly (cf. Z. Frankel, *Hodogetica in Mischnam*, pp. 307–311, Leipsic, 1859; D. Hoffmann, *Zur Einleitung in die halachischen Midraschim*, Berlin, 1887). Editions of Siphra are: Venice, 1545, 1609–11; Bucharest, 1860; Vienna, 1862; Warsaw, 1866.

3. Three Tannaitic Midrashim.

Genesis rabba, or *Bereshith rabba*, the larger midrash on Genesis, is probably so called in distinction from a smaller and shorter midrash based upon Rabbi Oshaya's work. The term *rabba*, "large," was in late times applied to the most common haggadic midrash on the Pentateuch and even to that on the Rolls. This midrash on Genesis is an explanation both of words and of things, taking fully the character of public lectures. Halachic exposition is rare in it. The range of interpretation is large; the basis is traceable to Rabbi Oshaya; though the artistic working-out of the plan is later, it is still not subsequent to the time of the redaction of the Palestinian Talmud, and intrusions of later matter occur. From xxxii. 4 on, the materials have the stamp of the later haggada, and the later manuscripts add many details. Apparently this midrash was never fully completed, for after xliv. 18 the progress is no longer verse by verse; chap. xlviii. is lacking in the manuscripts, and chap. xlix. in the codices has the earmarks of a late recension. The view that it was first edited as a whole between 650 and 750 A.D. does not seem well supported. In most editions this midrash is in 100 chapters; the manuscripts vary between 97 and 101 chapters, though all agree in their limits as far as chap. xcvi., beginning with Gen. xlvii. 28. The basis of the chapter division is not consistent or uniform. Editions are: the midrash on the Pentateuch, Constantinople, 1512; on the Rolls, Pesaro (?), 1519, Constantinople, 1520; of the whole, Venice, 1545; with commentary of Issachar Baer Kohen, Cracow, 1587–88; of Samuel Japheh Ashkenazi on Genesis, Venice, 1597 sqq., on Exodus, ib. 1657, on Leviticus, Constantinople, 1648; of David Luria and Samuel Straschun, Vilna, 1843–1845. Other editions are: Berlin, 1866; Vilna, 1878. The midrash on Lamentations (*Midrash Eykah*) is one of the oldest of Palestinian origin. It is exceedingly rich in proems owing to the fact that the celebration of the destruction of Jerusalem was accompanied by lectures on that book. These lectures are the source of a great part of the expositions of which the midrash is composed. The redaction is later than that of the Palestinian Talmud, though very early materials are used. The exposition is of the same character as that of Genesis rabba—smooth comment with interspersed haggadic pieces that are only loosely attached to their context. The redaction is prior to 650 A.D. An old midrash of the name *Pesiḳta* was long known through citations. Its recovery shows that it consists of thirty-two homilies delivered on specified festivals or Sabbaths, and that it was composed of two collections, one beginning with New Year's day, the other with Tammuz 17. The manuscripts show considerable variations in contents, especially at the beginning. The question of the date depends upon literary relations—it is a question whether Pesiḳta is dependent upon Genesis rabba and the midrash on Lamentations, or whether it is older than these. In the first case its date would be about 700 A.D.; in the second case it would be earlier than this. It is no longer in its original form, but has undergone many alterations and has received many additions. The name means "section," and is derived from the fact that each chapter was entitled "Section of ". It was edited by S. Buber (Lyck, 1868), but unfortunately not on the basis of the Oxford manuscript. The *Midrash Yelamdenu* or *Tanḥuma* covers the entire Pentateuch. Originally it contained only one homily for each Sabbath reading; in its present shape each homily has a halachic exordium, several introductions, exposition of the first verse of the lesson, Messianic conclusion. This formed the model of many collections. Editions are: Constantinople, 1520–22; Venice, 1545; Mantua, 1563; Verona, 1595; with commentaries, Vilna-Grodno, 1831; Stettin, 1864.

4. Genesis Rabba, Midrashim on Lamentations, Pesiḳta, and Tanḥuma.

The *Exodus rabba* or *Shemoth rabba* is in fifty-two sections, of which the first fourteen are continuous expositions of the verses in each Sabbath lesson, while the rest have introductions and treatment of the first verse only. This indicates that two parts are to be distinguished, the first of which is derived from an early exegetical midrash, while the second is dependent upon Tanḥuma. Its date is probably the eleventh or the twelfth century. *Leviticus rabba* or *Vayyikra rabba* is made up of thirty-seven homilies on the sections appointed for festival readings. It appears to belong to the seventh century. *Numeri rabba* or *Bemidhbar rabba* or *Bemidhbar Sinai rabba*, in twenty-three sections, is in two very different parts. The first (sections 1–14, about one-third of the whole) is a late haggadic exposition of Num. i.–vii., of which Num. i.–iv. are expansions of Tanḥuma, while in Num. v.–vii. there is an effort to discuss the entire text by compilations from halachic and haggadic works. This part is not earlier than the twelfth century. The second part is essentially Tanḥuma to the eight sections beginning with Num. viii., but with a different introductory formula. The nine chief sections correspond to as many Sabbath readings in the single-year cycle; but thirty homilies are distinguishable. *Deuteronomium rabba* or *Debarim rabba* follows generally in the printed editions the single-year cycle in eleven sections. But in fact there are twenty-seven separate homilies which are related to the three-year cycle of reading. These homilies begin with a halachic exordium, then one or more introductions of quite independent homiletical character, exposition of the beginning of the Scripture lesson, and a hortatory or comforting conclusion. The time of compilation of this mishna is about 900 A.D. The authors of the thirteenth and later centuries often refer sections of this collection to Tanḥuma, though there is little in common between them in the printed text. There are in this mishna only three homilies completed according to the rules for such discourse. It was published by S. Buber (Vienna, 1885) from a Munich manuscript. *Aggadath Bereshith*, consisting of homilies, is later than the close of Genesis rabba. A late edition is by B. Epstein (Shitomir, 1899). *Pesiḳta rabbathi* is a collection of homilies for festivals, and is not earlier than 850 A.D., though it is claimed that the details on which this dating depends are glosses. It is believed to have been the work of at least four authors. A critical edi-

5. Homiletic Midrashim.

encouraging. At the conference of 1828 the Methodist churches located in Canada, by the consent of the general conference of the Methodist Episcopal Church, were formed into an independent denomination, and William Case was appointed its general superintendent until the ensuing annual conference. That conference was visited by Bishop Hedding, under whose counsel the organization was perfected.

2. Division and Denominations. In 1833 the Methodist Episcopal Church of Canada had three annual conferences, 197 effective ministers, 25,000 members, and a polity practically the same as that of the Methodist Episcopal Church in the United States. In that year it unified with the British conference, changing its name and form of government. When the conference agreed to this union it did so without formal consultation with the laity. The majority both of ministers and laymen acquiesced, but certain dissentients declared that, as it had not been submitted to the societies, the act was unconstitutional, and that it infringed upon the agreement made between the church in Canada and the Methodist Episcopal Church in the United States. These organized a new Methodist Episcopal Church of Canada, more than one-thirteenth of the membership, declining to affiliate with the British conference, associating with them. Being without schools, parsonages, and churches, they began litigation to secure a pro rata part of the property. The lower courts decided in their favor, but on appeal the higher court recognized the Wesleyan Methodists of Canada as the rightful owners. After this question was settled the Wesleyan Methodist Church of Canada entered on a career of prosperity, and the Methodist Episcopal Church, thrown wholly on its own resources, made every sacrifice in order to succeed. Four Primitive Methodist ministers had been sent in 1829 from England because of the number of that sect emigrating to the United States. Three years later the Hull circuit in England decided to take the Canadian societies under its immediate charge. A general missionary committee was formed by the home church and under its management the increase of members was such that in 1854 the Canadian annual conference of Primitive Methodists was established. In 1831 the Bible Christians sent two missionaries to the British dominions in America, one to West Canada and the other to Prince Edward Island. In 1855 the society was strong, and held its first conference in Columbus. It then had 51 churches, 21 regular preachers and many lay helpers, and 2,200 members. Ten years afterward the union with it of the Prince Edward Island churches, together with local growth, raised its membership to 5,000. The Canadian Wesleyan Methodist Church was formed in 1829. It was founded principally by Henry Ryan and introduced lay representation in all its courts. Ryan died in 1833, but the little church struggled on, and in 1841 united with the Methodist New Connection. The Methodist New Connection of England, with the consent of the parent society, established a mission in Canada in 1837. The mission, enlarged by admitting a small denomination, assumed the title "Canadian Methodist New Connection." In 1840 the British conference "withdrew from its cooperation" with the Canada conference, which acted independently for seven years, but during that period the form and name of the Wesleyan Methodist Church remained unchanged. In 1847 the union was restored, and in 1854, by special arrangement, the Lower Canada and the Hudson Bay missionary districts, both of which had stood in immediate connection with the British Wesleyan conference, became incorporated with the Wesleyan church in Canada. In 1857 the Methodist Episcopal Church founded an educational institution at Bellville, which was incorporated as Bellville Seminary; three years later it was affiliated with the Toronto University as Bellville College, the ladies' department taking the designation of Alexandria College, and later the remaining part of the institution being known as Albert University.

3. Unification. For years a yearning existed in many hearts for organic union of Methodist bodies. This first bore fruit in the union of the Wesleyan Methodist Church in Canada, the Eastern British American conferences, and the Methodist New Connection Church, proposed in 1872, and consummated in Toronto in 1874, the uniting bodies adopting the all-inclusive name of the Methodist Church of Canada. Its first census reported 1,031 ministers, and 101,946 members, two universities, three theological schools, and several colleges and secondary schools. Yet something still greater awaited Canadian Methodism. The first Ecumenical Conference of Methodism, which convened in Wesley Chapel, London, in 1881, gave such impulse to fraternity as to extend the horizon till glimpses of complete Methodist unity could be perceived in the not distant future. Canada was the first to know its visitation. In Bellville, in 1883, was accomplished the formal and actual union of the Methodist Church of Canada, the Methodist Episcopal Church in Canada, the Primitive Methodist Church in Canada, and the Bible Christian Church of Canada. The body thus formed was in the possession of seven colleges, having 100 professors and 5,068 students. The Methodist Church of Canada contributed to the union 128,337 members; the Methodist Episcopal Church in Canada, 25,678 members; the Primitive Methodists, 8,000; and the Bible Christians, 6,800—a sum total of 168,815 members. The itinerant general superintendents hold office for the term of eight years, and are eligible to reelection. The annual conferences are composed of ministers and an equal number of laymen, a president being selected from among the ministerial members. The president of the annual conference is the superintendent of the district in which he may be stationed. The annual conference elects superintendents for each district. There are now six departments of mission work, home, Indian, French, Chinese and Japanese in British Columbia, and foreign. The home work embraces needy fields in the dominion, Newfoundland, and Bermuda. These include more than 35,000 communicants. The French missions are in Quebec. The foreign missions are in China and

Japan. That in Japan has been affiliated with the missions of the two Episcopal Methodist Churches which have formed the Methodist Church of Japan (ut sup., I). The connectional educational institutions are: Victoria University, Toronto, the germ of which was planted in 1837, and it was incorporated in 1841; Mount Allison College, founded in 1840 at Sackville, N. B.; Wesleyan Theological College, Montreal; Wesley College, Winnipeg; Albert College, Bellville, Ont.; Alma College, St. Thomas; Methodist College, St. Johns, Newfoundland; Columbian College, New Westminister, British Columbia; Ontario Ladies' College, Whitby, incorporated in 1874; and the Stanstead Wesleyan College, Stanstead, Quebec, established in 1873. Long is the list of able and devoted men who have built up this noble structure. Among those who have finished their course can be mentioned, without exciting jealousy, Egerton Ryerson (q.v.), the renowned educator, George Douglas, whose memory is ever green, Samuel S. Nelles (q.v.), so long president of Victoria University, and William Morley Punshon (q.v.), whose preaching, administration, and guidance promoted every interest of the advancing church and country. To-day the vastness of the territory of the Methodist Church of Canada is suggested by the names of its conferences on the continent of North America: Toronto, London, Hamilton, Bay of Quinte, Montreal, Nova Scotia, New Brunswick, and Prince Edward Island, Newfoundland, Manitoba, Alberta, and British Columbia. Distributed over this immense area are its 2,476 ministers and 334,637 members.

V. The Doctrinal Standards of Methodism: John Wesley was a clergyman of the Church of England. The societies which he formed were organizations for the conversion of men and their religious development. He aimed to retain his converts within the pale of that great national church, and from its clergymen the majority of Methodists received the sacraments. He and they believed the fundamental doctrines of universal Christendom, as contained in the articles, homilies, and ritual to which they had been accustomed from childhood. Nevertheless, in the judgment of Wesley, certain doctrines of the New Testament were neglected by the clergy or robbed of their true proportion and emphasis. These doctrines were by him considered vital to the spread of pure Christianity. Accordingly he expounded them in his conferences, published them with comments in the *Minutes* and preached upon them. Also he found it necessary to write and publish sermons upon the doctrines which Methodism emphasized; for his preaching excited vehement opposition from unsympathetic Anglican clergymen, and from Presbyterian, Independent, and Baptist ministers. The Baptists differed from him on the method and subjects of baptism and its relation to the reception of the Lord's Supper. To preserve unity of belief among the preachers and members of his societies, he prepared *Notes on the New Testament*, wherein are clear explanations of the pivotal passages upon which he based the views he so firmly believed and fervently preached. To render impossible the preaching of heretical doctrines in the chapels, the deeds by which they were held contained a limitation of the powers of trustees in the following words: "Provided always, that the persons preach no other doctrine than is contained in Mr. Wesley's '*Notes on the New Testament*,' and four volumes of '*Sermons*.'" The same provision subsists in the model deed of the Wesleyan Methodist Church (in England, Ireland, etc.) in the following words: "No person shall be allowed to preach, who shall maintain, promulgate, or teach any Doctrine or Practise contrary to what is contained in certain Notes on the New Testament, commonly reputed to be the Notes of the said John Wesley, and in the first four volumes of Sermons, commonly reputed to be written and published by him."

1. Doctrinal Bases.

When introducing these *Sermons* to the public, Wesley said,

> "The following sermons contain the substance of what I have been preaching for eight or nine years past. During that time, I have frequently spoken in public on every subject in the ensuing collection, and I am not conscious that there is any one point of doctrine, on which I am accustomed to speak in public, which is not incidentally, if not professedly, laid before every Christian reader. Every serious man, who peruses these, will, therefore, see in the clearest manner what these doctrines are, which I embrace and teach as the essentials of true religion."

It was for this purpose that Wesley made these *Sermons* so large and vital a part of his doctrinal standards. Certain discrepancies have been alleged with respect to the number of these *Sermons*. The Wesleyan Methodist Church of Great Britain and Ireland and the Methodist Episcopal Church in the United States recognize fifty-three; the Methodist Church of Canada and the Methodist Episcopal Church South but fifty-two, and certain critics but forty-three. The discrepancies are of no significance, as all agree on the smallest number, stated in the model deed, and all essential truths of the system of doctrine on which Methodism depends are discussed in the forty-three, and nothing additional of doctrinal value is contained in the nine or ten added by Wesley after he had made the others a standard.

2. Distinctive Doctrinal Features.

The distinctive doctrinal features of Methodism are suggested by the titles of these *Sermons*: "Scriptural Christianity," "The Almost Christian," "Awake thou that sleepest," "The Way to the Kingdom," "Salvation by Faith," "Justification by Faith," "The Righteousness of Faith," "The First Fruits of the Spirit," "The Spirit of Bondage and Adoption," "The Master of the New Birth," "The Witness of our own Spirit," two sermons on the "Witness of the Spirit," "Sin in Believers," thirteen sermons on the Sermon on the Mount, "The Nature of Enthusiasm," "A Caution against Bigotry," "Christian Perfection," "The Judgment." Incidental to the direct exposition of these topics the distinction between Wesley's Arminian theology and that of Calvin is pointed out; and the dangerous license of Antinomianism condemned. Wesley emphasized foreknowledge, but opposed the doctrines of election and reprobation as taught by Calvin. Magnifying free will and resultant responsibility, he acknowledged natural depravity, yet held that the Spirit of God so counteracts its effects that every man is capable of surrendering himself to him through Christ by faith. He taught Christian perfection as the consummation of the work of salvation; and that it is subsequent to regeneration, so that, while believers may grow in grace daily, perfection is reached by faith. By subtle distinctions he met successfully the current attacks upon his view. Upon this subject his writings were voluminous, and have occasioned controversy within as well as without Methodist circles.

3. American Position. Until 1784 Methodism in America was under the control of Wesley; it was in fact the extension of his societies. In that year it devolved upon him to superintend its transformation into a church. Before his plan had fully matured or any American had anticipated it, the American conferences asked, and by vote answered, a peculiar question.

Q. "How shall we conduct ourselves toward European preachers?" Answer: "If they are recommended by Mr. Wesley, will be subject to the American conference, preach the doctrine taught in the four volumes of Sermons, and Notes on the New Testament, we will receive them; but if they walk contrary to the above directions, no ancient right or appointment shall prevent their being excluded from our connection."

Wesley sent to America a series of articles of religion, selected from the Thirty-nine of the Church of England. The following were adopted, with slight verbal changes and minor omissions: "Of Faith in the Holy Trinity," "Of the Word, or the Son of God, who was made very Man," "Of the Resurrection of Christ," "Of the Holy Ghost," "Of the Old Testament," "Of Free Will," "Of the Justification of Man," "Of Good Works," "Of Works of Supererogation," "Of Sin after Justification," "Of the Church," "Of Purgatory," "Of Speaking in the Congregation in such tongue as the People understand," "Of the Sacraments," "Of the Lord's Supper," "Of both Kinds," "Of the one Oblation of Christ, finished upon the Cross," "Of the Marriage of Ministers," "Of the Rites and Ceremonies of Churches," "Of Christian Men's Goods" and "Of a Christian Man's Oath." The following were retained with important omissions: "The Sufficiency of the Holy Scriptures for Salvation," "Of Original or Birth Sin," "Of the Church," and "Of Baptism." The following were rejected: "Of the Going down of Christ into Hell," "Of the Three Creeds," "Of Works before Justification," "Of Christ alone without Sin," "Of Predestination and Election," "Of Obtaining Eternal Salvation only by the Name of Christ," "Of the Authority of the Church," "Of the Authority of General Councils," "Of Ministering in the Congregation," "Of the Unworthiness of the Ministers which Hinders not the effect of the Sacrament," "Of the Wicked which eat not the Body of Christ in the Use of the Lord's Supper," "Of Excommunicate Persons, how they are to be avoided," "Of the Homilies," "Of Consecration of Bishops and Ministers," "Of the Civil Magistrates."

A comparison between the English Articles as they were originally and as they were transmitted to the American conference reveals that the guiding purpose of Wesley, in altering and omitting, was to expurgate the leaven of ritual- **4. Purpose and Results.** ism, Calvinism, and Romanism. These articles, however, do not contain special reference to some of the most precious doctrines held by the founder of Methodism and by the churches that derived preaching, teaching, and example from those whom he instructed. But Wesley knew that the American Methodists had incorporated in their standards all that he had imposed upon English Methodism. Episcopal Methodist Churches, including the Canadian Methodist Church, accepted the articles sent by Wesley. The Methodist Episcopal Church of America is in harmony with these facts. The rule on the subject is as follows:

"The General Conference shall not revoke, alter or change our Articles of Religion, nor establish any new standard or rules of doctrine contrary to our present, existing, and established standards of doctrine."

The unparalleled unity in belief among the various Methodist bodies is the fruit of Wesley's method of conserving doctrines. Had he expressed them in confessions or even creeds, they would have been centers of controversy. His followers in every land concur with the Canadian Methodist theologian, Burwash:

"It is to the spirit and type of this preaching that our obligations bind us. There may be in the Notes and Sermons things incidental, accidental and personal, to which no Methodist minister or layman would feel bound to profess assent; but Methodism demands that in all its pulpits we should preach this Gospel and expound the word of God according to this analogy of Faith."

The Calvinistic Methodists signify their doctrines by their name. In Evangelical spirit they are similar, but in the doctrines on which Wesley took the Arminian position they adhere to the Calvinist standards. J. M. Buckley.

Bibliography: The fundamental sources are the Works of John Wesley, the best ed. for this purpose being that issued as standard by the Methodist Book Concern, New York, in 7 vols., including in vols. i.–ii. his Sermons, in vols. iii.–iv. his Journals, and in vols. v.–vii. his miscellaneous works; his *Explanatory Notes upon the New Testament*, issued by the same house as a standard (the recently deciphered diaries from which the Journals were written, containing a considerable amount of new material, are in course of publication in London, and will be available at the principal repositories for Methodist literature in the United States); the *Lives* and other literature given under the articles on the Wesleys in the last volume of this work; the Books of Discipline of the various Methodist bodies; the *Journals* of the Methodist Episcopal Church and of the Methodist Episcopal Church South; the *Minutes* of the annual conferences; the *Proceedings* of the Ecumenical Methodist Conferences, held in London, 1881, Washington, 1891, and London, 1901; the *Records* of the Centennial Convention in Baltimore, 1884; the *Year Books* of the various bodies; and the early periodicals to which reference is made in the text. Consult also the numerous sketches of Methodist worthies in this work, and the literature given there.

Treatises of a general character are: A. Stevens, *Hist. of the Religious Movement . Called Methodism*, 3 vols., New York, 1858–61; H. S. Skeats, *Hist. of the Free Churches of England, 1688–1851*, London, 1859; G. Smith, *Hist. of Wesleyan Methodism*, 3 vols., ib. 1865; L. S. Jacoby, *Geschichte des Methodismus, seiner Entstehung und Ausbreitung*, 2 vols., Bremen, 1870; W. H. Daniels, *Illustrated Hist. of Methodism in Great Britain and America from the Wesleys to the Present Time*, New York, 1880; J. Atkinson, *Centennial Hist. of American Methodism*, ib. 1884; idem, *Beginnings of the Wesleyan Movement in*

America, ib. 1896; J. W. Lee, N. Luccock, and J. M. Dixon, *Illustrated Hist. of Methodism*, St. Louis, 1900; J. F. Hurst, *British Methodism*, 3 vols., London, 1909; W. J. Townsend, *A New Hist. of Methodism*, 2 vols., ib., 1901.

Works on various Methodist bodies are: G. Smith, *Hist. of Wesleyan Methodists*, 3 vols., London, 1857–61; H. Smith, *Sketches of Methodist New Connexion Ministers*, ib. 1893; G. Packer, *The Centenary of the Methodist New Connexion 1797–1897*, ib. 1897; T. Colhouer, *Sketches of the Founders of the Methodist Protestant Church and its Bibliography*, Pittsburg, 1880; A. H. Bassett, *Concise Hist. of the Methodist Protestant Church*, Baltimore, 1882; E. J. Drinkhouse, *Hist. of Methodist Reform and the Methodist Protestant Church*, 2 vols., Baltimore, 1899; E. Bowen, *Hist. of the Origin of the Free Methodist Church*, North Chili, New York, n.d.; F. W. Bourne, *The Bible Christians: Origin and History*, London, 1905; J. Petty, *Hist. of the Primitive Methodist Connexion*, ib. 1861; W. Williams, *Welsh Calvinistic Methodism. A Historical Sketch*, ib. 1884; D. Young, *The Origin and Hist. of Methodism in Wales and the Borders*, ib. 1893; J. S. MacGeary, *The Free Methodist Church*, Chicago, 1909.

For the Methodist Episcopal Church North and South consult: *Hist. of the Organization of the Methodist Episcopal Church South. Comprehending all the Official Proceedings of the General Conferences*, etc., Nashville, 1845; A. Stevens, *Memorials of the Introduction of Methodism into the Eastern States*, 2 vols., Boston, 1848–52; idem, *Hist. of the M. E. Church in U. S. A.*, 4 vols., New York, 1864; idem, *Centenary of American Methodism*, ib. 1866; C. Elliott, *History of the Great Secession from the Methodist Episcopal Church in the year 1845, Eventuating in the Organization of the New Church Entitled "The Methodist Episcopal Church South,"* Cincinnati, 1855; J. Lednum, *A History of the Rise of Methodism in America. Containing Sketches of Methodist itinerant Preachers, 1736–85*, Philadelphia, 1859; N. Bangs, *Hist. of the Methodist Episcopal Church*, 4 vols., New York, 1860; L. C. Matlack, *Antislavery Struggle and Triumph in the M. E. Church*, ib. 1881; H. N. McTyeire, *Hist. of Methodism*, Nashville, 1886; J. G. Jones, *A Complete Hist. of Methodism as Connected with the Mississippi Conference of the Methodist Episcopal Church South*, Vol. i., *1799–1817*, Nashville, 1887; G. Alexander, in *American History Series*, vol. xi., New York, 1894; J. M. Buckley, in *American Church History Series*, vol. v., New York, 1897.

For Methodism among the African races consult: J. B. Wakeley, *Lost Chapters Recovered from the Early History of African Methodism*, New York, 1889; L. M. Hagood, *The Colored Man in the Methodist Episcopal Church*, Cincinnati, 1890; D. A. Payne, *Hist. of the A. M. E. Church*, Nashville, 1891; J. W. Hood, *One Hundred Years of the African M. E. Zion Church*, New York, 1895; I. L. Butt, *Hist. of African Methodism in Virginia; or, four Decades in the Old Dominion*, Eastville, Va., 1908.

Books dealing with special topics are: J. Emory, *Defense of Our Fathers*, New York, 1827; D. W. Clark, *Life and Times of Elijah Hedding*, ib. 1855; R. Paine, *Life of W. McKendree*, 2 vols., Nashville, 1869; E. H. Myers, *Description of the M. E. Church, 1844–46: comprising a 30 Years' History of the Relations of the two Methodisms*, Nashville, Tenn., 1875; T. L. Flood and J. W. Hamilton, *Lives of Methodist Bishops*, New York, 1882; F. A. Archibald, *Methodism and Literature*, Cincinnati, 1883; A. W. Cummings, *Early Schools of Methodism*, New York, 1886; W. J. Townsend, *The Story of Methodist Union*, London, 1906; D. B. Brummitt, *Epworth League Methods*, Cincinnati, 1906; H. K. Carroll, *Missionary Growth of the M. E. Church*, Cincinnati, 1907; J. Telford, *Wesley's Veterans. Lives of Early Methodist Preachers told by Themselves. With Additions and Annotations*, London, 1909.

On Methodism in various countries consult: G. H. Cornish, *Cyclopedia of Methodism in Canada*, Toronto, 1881; E. Ryerson, *Canadian Methodism; its Epochs and Characteristics*, ib. 1882; A. Sutherland, *Methodism in Canada*, London, 1903; J. E. Sanderson, *First Century of Methodism in Canada*, vol. i., Toronto, 1908; C. H. Crookshank, *History of Methodism in Ireland*, vol. i., *Wesley and his Time*, vol. ii., *The Middle Age*, Belfast, 1885–1886; E. Thomas, *Irish Methodist Reminiscences*, London, 1889; R. C. Phillips, *Irish Methodism*, ib. 1897; H. B. Foster, *Wesleyan Methodism in Jamaica*, ib. 1881; J. Colwell, *Illustrated Hist. of Methodism in Australia, New South Wales, and Polynesia*, Sydney, 1904; H. Adams, *Methodism in the West Indies*, London, 1908; J. M. Erikson, *Metodismen i Sverige*, Stockholm, 1895; J. Jüngst, *Der Methodismus in Deutschland*, Giessen, 1906.

On the polity, constitution, doctrines, and discipline of Methodism consult: R. Emory, *Hist. of the Discipline of the M. E. Church*, New York, 1843; T. E. Bond, *The Economy of Methodism Illustrated and Defended*, ib. 1852; T. E. Bond, *Economy of Methodism*, ib. 1852; E. Grindrod, *A Compendium of the Laws and Regulations of Wesleyan Methodism*, London, 1858; B. Hawley, *Manual of Methodism; or the Doctrines, General Rules and Usages of the Methodist Episcopal Church*, New York, 1868; J. H. Rigg, *Connexional Economy of Wesleyan Methodism*, London, 1879; idem, *Church Organisations*, ib. 1896; H. W. Williams, *Constitution and Polity of Wesleyan Methodism*, London, 1881; S. M. Merrill, *A Digest of Methodist Law; or, Helps in the Administration of the Discipline of the M. E. Church*, Cincinnati, 1885; D. Sherman, *Hist. of the Revisions of the Discipline of the M. E. Church*, New York, 1890; T. B. Neely, *Evolution of Episcopacy and Organic Methodism*, ib. 1888; idem, *Hist. of the Origin and Development of the Governing Conference in Methodism*, Cincinnati, 1892; B. Gregory, *Side Lights on the Conflicts of Methodism, 1827–52*, London, 1898; D. J. Waller, *Constitution and Polity of the Wesleyan Methodist Church*, ib. 1898; W. F. Barclay, *Constitution of Methodist Episcopal Churches in America*, Nashville, Tenn., 1902; G. F. Oliver, *Our Lay Office Bearers*, Cincinnati, 1902; J. J. Tigert, *Doctrines of M. E. Church in America*, ib. 1902; idem, *Constitutional Hist. of American Episcopal Methodism*, Nashville, 1903; *Doctrines and Discipline of the M. E. Church South*, ed. Alexander, ib. 1906; D. A. Goodsell, J. B. Hingeley and J. M. Buckley, *The Doctrines and Discipline of the Methodist Episcopal Church*, Cincinnati, 1908; H. Wheeler, *Hist. and Exposition of the Twenty-five Articles of Religion of the M. E. Church*, New York, 1908; H. T. Hudson, *Methodist Armor; or, A Popular Exposition of the Doctrines, Peculiar Usages and Ecclesiastical Machinery of the M. E. Church South*, Nashville, n.d.

METHODIUS: Greek Church Father and bishop of Olympus, in Lycia; probably martyred by Maximinus, 311. The only one of his works preserved entire in Greek is the "Symposium," which, as its name implies, forms a counterpart to Plato's "Symposium." Ten maidens, invited to the "garden of virtue," are the speakers, their themes being the following: (1) the praise of virginity as the essence of the likeness to God brought by Christ; (2) the divine ordinance of marriage; (3) virginity preferable to the married state; (4) virginity the best medicament to immortality; (5) virginity the great vow; (6) virgins keep themselves undefiled for the marriage with the Logos; (7) they are equal to the martyrs and are meant by Cant. ii. 2, iv. 9 sqq., vi. 7 sqq.; (8) the woman of Rev. xii. 1 sqq. is the Church, and the human will is free; (9) with her we must adorn ourselves for the Feast of Tabernacles, which is the Resurrection; (10) perfect righteousness (cf. Judges ix. 8 sqq.) first came into the world through Christ. The maidens close with a hymn to the heavenly bridegroom. The *De Autexusio* is preserved independently in Greek only in the portion i.–vii. 5, but considerable fragments are given by Eusebius, but under the name of Maximus (*Præparatio evangelica*, vii. 22; Eng. transl., ii. 366 sqq., 2 vols., Oxford, 1903), Photius (*Bibliotheca*, 236), the *Sacra Parallela;* while it is fully reproduced in an Old Church Slavic translation of the eleventh century. Its theme is the origin of evil, which arose from Satan's disobedience to God. In his *Peri genētōn*, of which only a few fragments have been preserved by Photius (*Bibliotheca*, 235), Methodius assails Origen's doctrine of an eternal cre-

Works.

ation of the world. The same opposition is maintained in his most important work next to the "Symposium," the *De resurrectione*, in which, at Patara, with one Theophilus presiding, the physician Aglaophon and Proclus plead for Origen against Eubulius (Methodius) and Memian. As the angels prove, things created are not necessarily mortal; and since the soul is immortal, while only the dead can rise, the body becomes mortal that the sin which dwells in it may be removed by death, the resurrection of the body being everywhere taught by the Scriptures. The work is extant only in an Old Church Slavic translation, though the Greek text of i. 20–ii. 8 is given by Epiphanius (*Hær.*, lxiv. 12 sqq.), and fragments are found in Photius (*Bibliotheca*, 234), the *Sacra Parallela*, the Syriac florilegia, the *Catena* of Procopius, Justinian (*Ad Menam*), Œcumenius, Eustratius, and others. The three fragments of his polemic against Porphyry are valuable for a knowledge of Methodius' theory of salvation; while those of his exegesis of Job ix., xxv., xxvii.–xxix., xxxviii., xl., are important for his doctrine of grace. Of his *De martyribus* scant fragments have been preserved by Theodoret and the *Sacra Parallela*. His other works are preserved almost exclusively in abbreviated Old Church Slavic translations, such as that "On Life and Reason" and "On Foods and the Red Heifer," the latter treating also of the blessings of suffering, true purity, and the spiritual understanding of the Scriptures. In the "To Sistelius, On Leprosy" (a few fragments also in manuscript in Greek), he connects the legal rules for leprosy with Christian penance; and in his "On the Horseleach of Proverbs, and 'The Heavens Declare the Glory of God'" he interprets the horseleach as the serpent of lust. His treatises "On the Body," and *De Pythonyssa*, as well as his exegeses of Genesis and Canticles, and, possibly, a dialogue *Xenon*, are lost; while the orations *De Symeone et Anna* and *In ramos palmarum*, like the Armenian fragments in the *In ascensionem Domini nostri Jesu Christi*, are spurious. Nor were the *Revelationes*, ascribed to him under various names and forming in various languages one of the favorite books of the Middle Ages, written by him. Their origin doubtless dates from the seventh century, although they appeared in Latin translation as early as the century following.

Doctrine.

Deeply influenced by Platonism and Stoicism, and strongly allegorical in interpretation, Methodius is at once an advocate of early Christian realism and of the ascetic and contemplative life. The main points of his constant opposition to Origen have already been noted. His concept of God was characterized by the attributes of non-becoming, power, and exemption from all need. If the Father is the essential principle of all being, the Son is the external effective force; yet Methodius stresses the divine nature of the Son, who was the means of all revelation of salvation, even in the Old Testament. The world was created for the microcosm man, whose will is absolutely free, and who is progressively taught by God to conquer the devil. The Logos necessarily became incarnate to bring man into harmony with the Divine, and, bringing "knowledge of the Father of all," he stripped off the old man, which he replaced "with his own flesh." This is done through the Church, for whom the Logos left the Father in heaven; and the souls betrothed to him are "helps meet for him," thus realizing the "deep sleep" of Adam (Gen. ii. 21). Nevertheless, outward membership is no guaranty of salvation, which is the work of grace that rewards longing with fulfilment. Yet even the Christian does not entirely extirpate sin in this life, and the forgiveness of sins and deeper recognition of the divine will only strengthen the natural good in him; while the birth of Christ in the faithful, transforming them into Christs, is essentially a spiritual growth, though coming to pass on principle in baptism. The cure for all evils and the root of true morality is the spiritual understanding of the Scriptures, wisdom blooming in the desert, where dwells the bride of the Logos. The progress in the Christian life here outlined, however, finds its culmination, as implied above, in perfect virginity of both body and soul. The ideal of Methodius is that of the ascetic sage. In accordance with the tradition of the Church, moreover, Methodius was inclined toward a moderate chiliasm, holding that in the seventh millennium the faithful would celebrate the true sabbaths and the real Feast of Tabernacles with Christ, this millennium being the rest preliminary to endless eternity.

(N. Bonwetsch.)

For Methodius the apostle to the Slavs see Cyril and Methodius.

Bibliography: The first complete ed. of the "Banquet" was by Allatius, Rome, 1656. An incomplete collection of the works was made by F. Combefis, Paris, 1644, enlarged, 1672. The works are also in A. Gallandi, *Bibliotheca veterum patrum*, iii. 670 sqq., Venice, 1767; in *MPG*, xviii. 27–408; and an edition is by A. Jahn, Halle, 1865. There is an Eng. transl. with introduction in *ANF*, vi. 307–402. The earlier literature on the subject is given very completely in *ANF*, Bibliography, pp. 75–76. Consult: Jerome, *De vir. ill.*, lxxxiii.; Socrates, *Hist. eccl.*, vi. 13; A. Pankau, *Methodius, Bischof von Olympus*, Mainz, 1888; N. Bonwetsch, *Methodius von Olympus*, Leipsic, 1891; idem, *Die Theologie des Methodius von Olympus*, Berlin, 1903; O. Bardenhewer, *Patrologie*, pp. 154 sqq., Freiburg, 1894; Ehrhard, *Die altchristliche Litteratur und ihre Erforschung*, 1884–1900, pp. 363 sqq., ib. 1900; Harnack, *Litteratur*, i. 468–478, 786, 929–930, ii. 2, pp. 147 sqq., 150–151; idem, *Dogma*, vols. i.–v. passim; Krüger, *History*, pp. 235–242; Schaff, *Christian Church*, ii. 309–312; Ceillier, *Auteurs sacrés*, iii. 62–73; *DCB*, iii. 909–911.

METHURGEMAN ("Interpreter"): The title given to the Palestinian official who in the synagogue service translated into the vernacular (Aramaic) the lesson read in Hebrew from the law verse by verse, and the lesson read from the prophets three verses at a time. See Synagogue, I.; and Talmud.

METROPHANES, mê″trof′a-nîz, **CRITOPULUS**, crai′tep-u-lus: Patriarch of Alexandria; b. at Berrhœa, Macedonia, probably in 1589; d. at Alexandria, probably in 1639. After entering a monastery at an early age and becoming the protosyncellus of the patriarch of Constantinople, he was sent to England by Cyril Lucar (q.v.) and studied at Oxford until 1623. He then went to Helmstedt, and, after visiting other German cities, was an associate of the Reformed at Geneva in 1627. In 1631 he signed himself at Alexandria as

Metropolitan of Memphis and Egypt; and in 1637 he was enthroned as patriarch, signing the synod's condemnation of Lucar's teachings in 1638.

His most important work is his "Confession of the Catholic and Apostolic Eastern Church," written at Helmstedt (given in full by J. Michaelcescu, *Die Bekenntnisse der griechisch-orientalischen Kirche*, Leipsic, 1904). This is a clear presentation of Greek doctrine and worship with sharp criticism of Roman Catholic tenets. Dividing theology into "simple" and "economic," he treats under the former head the doctrine of God and the Trinity, showing that each of the Persons sustains a definite relation to the other two, and defending the single procession of the Holy Ghost. In the "economic" section he seeks to show that man, deprived of the light of the Spirit by his fall (but not bereft of free will), and long condemned by the law, could best be reconciled with God only through the Incarnation in sinful flesh, mankind both being reconciled through the sacrifice of Christ, and being renewed and pardoned by immediate participation in the Divine. He cautiously defines the Church as possessing the marks of catholic and apostolic holiness and doctrine, though making little mention of hierarchic organization. The sacraments are reduced to three: baptism, representing reconciliation with the Father; the Eucharist, incorporation with the Son; and penance, the perseverance of the Holy Ghost. The remainder of the work is devoted chiefly to the rites of the Greek Church.

In his "Panegyric on the Incarnation" (ed. G. Queccius, Altdorf, 1626) he polemizes against those who deny the divinity of Christ, besides treating of redemption and emphasizing the true humanity of Christ. In his "Answer to the Inquiry . . on Gal. v. 16" (Nuremberg, 1626), moreover, he explains the opposition between flesh and spirit, in genuine Greek fashion, as that between body and soul. He also wrote an *Epistula de vocibus in musica liturgica Græcorum usitatis* in 1626 (ed. J. J. Crudelius, probably in 1737), as well as letters, sermons, the polemic *Antipanoplia* against the Uniate Rhodinus, and a large work still preserved in manuscript in Cod. Harl. 5059.

Considered by some a Greek Lutheran, by others a Calvinist, and by others still a friend of the Roman Catholics, Metrophanes seems to have been willing to enjoy the favor of the powerful without regard to creed. Herein may lie the reason why he was not polemic against other communions, and was relatively indifferent to his own.

(PHILIPP MEYER.)

BIBLIOGRAPHY: Lives have been written by J. A. Dietelmair, Altdorf, 1769; A. C. Demetracopulos, Leipsic, 1870; and G. G. Mazarakis, Cairo, 1884. Consult further: Fabricius-Harles, *Bibliotheca Græca*, xi. 597 sqq., Hamburg, 1808; A. H. Hore, *Eighteen Centuries of the Orthodox Greek Church*, pp. 560–561, New York, 1899; *KL*, viii. 1444–46.

METROPOLITAN: The title of the bishop of the provincial capital, who possesses provincial as opposed to merely diocesan rights, including jurisdiction over (neighboring) suffragan bishops. See ARCHBISHOP; EXARCH; PATRIARCH, and cf. Bingham, *Origines*, II., xvi., where synodal and other references are given.

METROPOLITAN CHURCH ASSOCIATION. See MISCELLANEOUS RELIGIOUS BODIES, 18.

METZ, BISHOPRIC OF: An ancient episcopal see in Lorraine, founded according to unhistorical tradition by disciples of the apostles, probably in fact during the Roman domination. The town, known as Divodurum when it was the old capital of the Celtic tribe of the Mediomatrici, survived the fall of the empire and appears under the name of Mettis in the Frankish era as the seat of a bishop. The first certain occupant of the see is Hesperius, whose name is attached to the proceedings of the Synod of Clermont in 535. The diocese was of considerable extent in the Middle Ages, and contained a mixed population, though more German than French. (A. HAUCK.)

Angilram or Engelram (bishop 768–791), a Benedictine, was *archicapellanus* to Charlemagne and *apocrisiarius* under Adrian I. From 823 to 855 the see was occupied by Drogo, a brother of Louis I. Bishop Theodoric I. of Hamaland (964–984), one of the most influential counselors of Otto I. and Otto II., secured from the latter (977) the insignia and title of a prince of the empire for himself and his successors. With the next bishop, Adalbero II. of Bar (984–1005), a son of Duke Frederick I. of Upper Lorraine, begins a new period of nearly six centuries, during which the see is no longer involved in the affairs of the court and develops a strong ecclesiastical life, though troubled frequently by conflicts between the citizens of Metz and the bishops as secular lords. With the election of Henry II. of Lorraine-Vaudemont (1484–1505) the see became for over a century an appanage of the house of Lorraine—a relation which helped materially to retard the progress of the Reformation. The peace of Cateau-Cambrésis (1559) gave the king of France a protectorate over his "allies" of the districts of Metz, Toul, and Verdun, without altering their fundamental relations to the empire. Charles IX. attempted to suppress the Protestant religion, but Henry IV permitted it to be practised in 1592 and 1597, and this liberty continued until the revocation of the Edict of Nantes in 1685, after Metz had become part of France by the Peace of Westphalia (1648). The last prince-bishop, Louis-Joseph de Montmorency-Laval (1761–1802), was driven out by the Revolution, and even the "constitutional bishop of the department of the Moselle," Nicolas Francin, was imprisoned in 1793, while the cathedral was turned into a Temple of Reason and all church property confiscated. By the Concordat of 1801 the bishopric was restored and made subject to the archbishop of Besançon, although with somewhat altered limits, which were reduced to about one-third of the former extent by the agreement of Louis XVIII. with Rome (1817–21). When Lorraine was annexed to Germany in 1871, the diocese was removed by Pius IX. from the metropolitan jurisdiction of Besançon and made immediately subject to the Holy See, with a further readjustment of boundaries.

BIBLIOGRAPHY: Sources for the early history are found in *MGH, Script.*, ii (1829), 260–270, iv (1841), 426 sqq., 461 sqq., 658 sqq., 696–700, x (1852), 531–572, xii (1856), 450–479, xiii (1881), 303 sqq. Consult: Gams, *Series episcoporum*, pp. 292–293, supplement, pp. 75, 77; J. F. and N. Tabouillet, *Hist. de Metz*, 6 vols., Metz, 1769–90; *Gallia Christiana*, xiii. 677–805, 987, Paris, 1785; Clouet, *Hist. ecclésiastique de la province de Trèves*, 2 vols., Verdun, 1844–51; Hauck, *KD*, vols. i.–iv., passim; Rettberg, *KD*, i. 90 sqq., 484 sqq.

MEURER, mei'rer, MORITZ: German Lutheran; b. at Pretzsch (13 m. s.w. of Wittenberg) Aug. 3, 1806; d. at Callenberg, near Chemnitz, May 10, 1877. He studied theology at the University of Leipsic (1825–28), and then spent four years as private tutor in the house of H. L. Heubner, superintendent at Wittenberg. After temporary service in a Prussian normal school, he obtained his first pastoral appointment at Waldenburg in Saxony. In 1841 he removed to the neighboring Callenberg, where he spent the rest of his life. His industrious spirit manifested itself in frequent participation in the proceedings of the provincial synod, and in the issue of church periodicals. He was the author of numerous larger and smaller works, mainly on the Reformation era. Among these are: *Luthers Leben, aus den Quellen erzählt* (3 vols., Leipsic, 1845–46; Eng. transl., New York, 1848); *Katharina Luther* (Dresden, 1854); and *Philipp Melanchthon* (1860). In connection with the collective work entitled *Altväter der lutherischen Kirche*, Meurer contributed volumes ii.–iv., including the biographies of Bugenhagen, Myconius, and Hausmann. He was a distinguished writer also in the field of ecclesiastical art, and gladly promoted the study of it. Meurer set forth his general views on the subject in two valuable writings: *Der Altarschmuck, ein Beitrag zur Paramentik in der evangelischen Kirche* (Leipsic, 1867) and *Der Kirchenbau vom Standpunkt und nach dem Brauche der lutherischen Kirche* (1877).

THEODOR FICKER.

MEXICO: A republic in the southern part of North America, having an area of 767,005 square miles. Out of a population (1900) of 13,600,000, about 2,500,000 were of pure, or nearly pure, white race; 5,800,000 of mixed race; and 5,200,000 of Indian race. Of these latter about 1,300,000 are of the most ignorant savage type, knowing practically no Spanish and having not the merest rudiments of civilization. Even of the mixed or better class of Indian races, few can be considered civilized, so that the Mexico known to the world includes probably not more than one-third of the entire population. Of that third only a little over a third (1,800,000) could, in 1895, both read and write, while about 325,000 more could read but not write. Since then the proportion has undoubtedly increased under the free and compulsory system of state education, assisted by beneficent societies. In 1904 there were 9,194 elementary, 36 secondary, 20 normal, and 45 professional schools, with 18,310 teachers and 634,136 enrolled pupils. There were also private clerical and association schools to the number of 2,281, with 135,838 pupils.

From the time of the conquest by the Spaniards to 1810 the country was absolutely under the power of the Roman Catholic Church and the Spanish government. Then came a revolt, headed by a priest, and in 1821 independence of Spain was achieved; the Church, however, still reigned supreme. In 1857 the Liberal party drew up a program of religious liberty, which was not carried into effect till 1867, when the French rule of Maximilian was overthrown and Juarez established the present republic. Roman Catholic religious houses were closed, church property confiscated, ecclesiastical buildings assigned for the use of schools, libraries, hospitals, etc., and a law passed forbidding any ecclesiastical body to acquire landed property. The era of Protestant influence dates from the entrance of a large number of Bibles carried by General Scott's army in the war of 1846. Gradually little companies were formed which met in private houses; these received help from Miss Melinda Rankin's school, first at Brownsville, Tex., and then at Monterey, and from an agent of the Bible Society. A number of similar individual enterprises were started, and a Baptist Church was organized in Monterey in 1864. With the establishment of the new republic Protestant missionaries went into the country until at least seventeen societies are represented there. At first they were bitterly opposed not merely by the Roman Catholic Church authorities but by the strongest elements among the Mexican people. Gradually this opposition has weakened until the best people of the nation and even of the Roman Catholic Church to a certain degree manifest their interest in and approval of the work done by the Protestant evangelists and in the Protestant schools. The latest missionary statistics show 227 missionaries, 491 native workers, 133 schools with 10,447 pupils, 39,838 professing Christians connected with the mission churches. As the number of Protestants reported in 1895 was about 40,000, the total number must on this basis be much larger. The Protestant influence is augmented by four printing-presses issuing annually a great amount of literature; Young Men's Christian Associations and Christian Endeavor Societies are exerting a mighty influence, and the whole tone of Mexican life is changing, even within the bounds of the Roman Catholic Church, with its more than 12,000,000 communicants and its full hierarchy.

EDWIN MUNSELL BLISS.

BIBLIOGRAPHY: F. H. Vera, *Colleccion de documentos ecclesiásticos de Mexico*, 3 vols., Amecameca, 1887; *Concilio provincial Mexicano IV., 1771*, Querétaro, 1898; *Acta et decreta concilii provincialis Mexicani quinti, 1896*, Mexico, 1899; W. Butler, *Mexico in Transition*, New York, 1892; C. F. Lummis, *Awakening of a Nation; Mexico of To-day*, ib. 1898; P. P. Martin, *Mexico of the 20th Century*, 2 vols., ib. 1907; C. R. Enock, *Mexico; its ancient and modern Civilization, Hist., and political Conditions*, ib., 1909.

MEYER, FREDERICK BROTHERTON: English Baptist; b. at London Apr. 8, 1847. He was educated at Brighton College and Regent's Park Baptist College (B.A., London University, 1869), and held successive pastorates at Pembroke Baptist Chapel, Liverpool, in 1870–72, York, in 1872–1874, Victoria Road Church, Leicester, in 1874–78, Melbourne Hall, Leicester, in 1878–88, Regent's Park Chapel, London, in 1888–92, and Christ Church, Westminster Bridge Road, Lambeth, in 1892–95. He was president of the National Federation of Free Churches 1904–05. Since that time, as general evangelist of the Federation of Free Churches, he has conducted missions in South Africa and the far

East, returning to England in the spring of 1909. In theology he is a liberal Evangelical. Among his numerous works, special mention may be made of his *Elijah and the Secret of his Power* (London, 1887); *Israel a Prince with God* (1887); *Abraham; or, the Obedience of Faith* (1888); *Christian Living* (1888); *Present Tenses of the Blessed Life* (1888); *Shepherd Psalm* (1889); *Joseph, Beloved, Hated, Exalted* (1890); *Tried by Fire* (1890); *Life and Light of Men* (1891); *Moses, the Servant of God* (1892); *Joshua and the Land of Promise* (1893); *Way into the Holiest* (1893); *Jeremiah, Priest and Prophet* (1894); *Prayers for Heart and Home* (1894); *Christ in Isaiah* (1895); *David, Shepherd, Psalmist, King* (1895); *Reveries and Realities* (1896); *Through Fire and Flood* (1896); *Paul, a Servant of Jesus Christ* (1897); *Saved and Kept* (1897); *Statutes and Songs* (1897); *Work-a-day Sermons* (1897); *Blessed are Ye* (1898); *Our Daily Homily* (5 vols., 1898–99); *Love to the Uttermost* (1898); *Love, Courtship, Marriage* (1899); *John the Baptist* (1900); *The Prophet of Hope* (1900); *The Soul's Ascent* (1901); *Art of Life* (1903); *Jottings and Hints for Lay Preachers* (1903); *Religion in Homespun* (1903); *Some Deeper Things* (1903); *Directory of a Devout Life* (1904); *In the Beginning God!* (1904); *Epistle to the Philippians* (1905); *The Soul's Wrestle with Doubt* (1905); *In Defence of the Faith* (1907); *The Soul's Pure Intention* (1907); and *A Winter in South Africa* (1908).

MEYER, mai'er, **HEINRICH AUGUST WILHELM:** German Lutheran; b. at Gotha Jan. 10, 1800; d. at Hanover June 21, 1873. He received his theological training at Jena (1818–20). After teaching for a time in a private school at Grone, near Göttingen, he was pastor successively at Osthausen (1822–26), Meiningen (1826–31), and Harste (1831–37). In 1837 he was called to Hoya as superintendent and pastor; and in 1841, declining a professorial appointment at Giessen, he was made consistorial councilor, superintendent, and pastor at Neustadt, Hanover. Here he was the sole pastor of a community of some 5,000, and to his threefold task was added the ever-increasing burden of his labor on the New Testament. After 1848 he restricted himself to his consistorial and exegetical duties, residing at Hanover. In 1861 he was created a councilor of the supreme consistory, but in 1865 he requested and obtained honorable retirement. He regarded his Latin edition of the Lutheran symbolic books (Göttingen, 1830) as an episode in his life-work. His great work was *Das Neue Testament griechisch nach den besten Hülfsmitteln kritisch revidiert mit einer neuen deutschen Uebersetzung und einem kritischen und exegetischen Kommentar*, of which the first eleven volumes were prepared by himself (Göttingen, 1829–47; text and translation of the New Testament, and commentary on Matthew-Philemon), the remaining volumes being necessarily entrusted to younger collaborators, all Meyer's strength being needed in the preparation of new editions of the parts already issued by him. His original plan had been to divide the work into three parts: text and translation; commentary on the Gospels and Acts; commentary on the other books and a handbook containing isagogic investigations, the history of exegesis (especially from the Church Fathers), and his own methods. He likewise planned to write a system of Biblical rationalism, which was to give a summary of exegetical results. His work was translated into English (20 vols., Edinburgh, 1873–85; American ed., New York, 1884 sqq). In his lifetime he employed as collaborators J. E. Huther (the Pastoral, Petrine, and Johannine Epistles, Jude and James; Göttingen, 1850–52), G. Lünemann (I and II Thessalonians and Hebrews, 1850), and F. Düsterdieck (Apocalypse, 1865). Since his death later editions have been prepared by B. Weiss (Matthew, John, Romans, the Pastoral and Johannine Epistles, and Hebrews; 7th ed., Göttingen, 1901–02), B. and J. Weiss (Mark and Luke; 9th ed., 1901), H. H. Wendt (Acts; 8th ed., 1899), C. F. G. Heinrici (I and II Corinthians; 8th ed., 1896–1900), F. Sieffert (Galatians; 9th ed., 1899), E. Haupt (Ephesians, Philippians, Colossians, and Philemon; 8th ed., 1902), W. Bornemann (I and II Thessalonians; 6th ed., 1894), E. Kühl (Petrine Epistles and Jude; 6th ed., 1897), W. Beyschlag (James; 6th ed., 1897), and W. Bousset (Apocalypse; 6th ed., 1906). (F. DÜSTERDIECK.)

BIBLIOGRAPHY: A. H. Newman, in *Baptist Quarterly*, viii (1874), 438 sqq.; H. S. Burrage, in *Bibliotheca Sacra*, xxxii (1875), 438 sqq.

MEYER, JOHANN FRIEDRICH VON: German theologian, jurist and statesman; b. at Frankfort Sept. 12, 1772; d. there Jan. 28, 1849. In his earlier youth he studied classics, drawing, painting, and music; from 1789 he studied law and philology at Göttingen, and from 1793 philosophy and natural science at Leipsic. After a term of practise at the imperial chamber at Wetzlar, he settled down in 1802 in his native city where he served as president of the court of appeals, member of the senate, and mayor. In 1816 he became president of the Bible Society in Frankfort. The first period of his literary activity was influenced by the rationalism of the age, seen in his essays in Wieland's *Merkur*, his romance *Kallias*, and his epic *Tobias*. He then began serious study of the Bible, recognized the necessity of revelation and saw in redemption the center and essence of Christianity; all this without contemning science, but employing it in the service of God. In his thirty-fifth year (1807) he learned Hebrew, making use of old and new translations and commentaries. His comprehensive knowledge, especially in the field of archeology and jurisprudence, enabled him to form his own exegesis. In 1812 he published his *Bibeldeutungen*, a sharp attack upon the theological conceptions of the time. In 1819 appeared his annotated revision of Luther's translation of the Bible, which had a wide circulation (3d ed., 1855). Meyer was not only a theologian, but also a mystic and theosophist, and emphasized theosophy in the third period of his literary activity. The mechanical conception of transcendental supernaturalism and orthodoxy satisfied him as little as rationalism. Nature and the Bible he regarded as supplementary documents, the key to which was in symbols—numbers and figures. He was intent upon fathoming the fundamental sense of the divine Word which he held to lie beyond the grammatical sense. Eschatological and apocalyptical studies had great attraction for him. From this period originated such works as *Schlüssel zur Offenbarung Johannis von einem Kreuzritter* (1833) and *Blicke in den Spiegel des prophetischen Wortes* (1847). Meyer's predilection for symbolism led him to study not only old-world mysteries, but also the higher degrees of freemasonry. Results of this are his works, *Das Buch Jezira, die älteste, kabbalistische Urkunde der Hebräer* (1831); *Zur Aegyptologie* (1840) and his eleven collections of *Blätter für höhere Wahrheit* (1819 to 1832) to which he added *Inbegriff der Glaubenslehre* (1832). He wrote also some poems and a number of criticisms for the *Heidelberger Jahrbücher*, 1811–18.

(G. E. Steitz†.)

Bibliography: There is a biographical introduction to *Auswahl aus den Blättern für höhere Wahrheit*, pp. v.–xl., Stuttgart, 1853. Consult also *ADB*, xxi. 597.

MEYFART (MAYFART), JOHANN MATTHAEUS: German Lutheran theologian; b. at Jena Nov. 9, 1590; d. at Erfurt Jan. 26, 1642. He was the son of a clergyman of Walwinkel in the Thuringian forest; studied at Gotha, Jena, and Wittenberg. In 1616 he was called to Coburg as professor at the newly founded Gymnasium Casimirianum which distinguished itself by its strict discipline in morals, and in 1623 became its head. In 1631 or 1633 he was appointed professor of theology at the university of Erfurt. Of his Latin works, some are dogmatic: *Prodromus elucidarii theologici sive distinctionum theologicarum centuriæ duæ, ex omnium prope theologorum, qui post exhibitam A. C. floruerunt, scriptis collectæ*, etc. (1620, unfinished); others are polemic: *Grawerus continuatus* (Coburg, 1623); *Anti-Becanus sive manualis controversiarum theol., a Becano collecti, Confutatio* (2 vols., Leipsic, 1627) and *Nodus Gordius sophistarum solutus* (Coburg, 1627), an original attempt to reconcile Aristotle and Petrus Ramus. But his independent activity, awakened by the philosophy as well as the history and poetry of antiquity, united itself with a deep longing for the highest ideals, with an experience of the love of Christ, and with an enthusiastic absorption in subjective experiences of supernatural perfection. At the same time, however, Meyfart had a keen eye for corruption in the Church, for the dead mechanicalism of traditional theology, and for the moral defects of his age. This is shown, furthermore, by his German works, which fall into two groups, speculative-eschatological and practical-reformatory. To the first group belong *Tuba novissima* (Coburg, 1626), four sermons on Death, the Last Judgment, Eternal Life, and Damnation. There followed *Von dem himmlischen Jerusalem* (2 vols., Coburg, 1627), which contained his celebrated hymn, "Jerusalem, du hochgebaute Stadt" (several English translations, e.g., Miss Winkworth's "Jerusalem, thou city fair and high"); *Das höllische Sodoma* (2 vols., ib. 1630), and *Das jüngste Gericht* (Nuremberg, 1632). To the second group belong his *Christliche Erinnerung*, concerning witchcraft (1636), and *Christliche Erinnerung*, concerning the German universities (1636), a striking description of life among theological students. Meyfart also attempted in several of his works to reform the clergy, the church service, church discipline and service of prayer, and to counteract the ecclesiastical dissensions and the hatred of the theologians. He was one of the best of the precursors of Spener, a learned but enthusiastic mystic, and yet had his eyes fully open to the deficiencies of his times.

(E. Henke†.)

Bibliography: H. Witten, *Memoria theologorum nostri seculi*, Frankfort, 1685; G. Ludewig, *Ehre des Casimiriani academici*, ii. 261–262, Coburg, 1729; A. F. W. Fischer, *Kirchenlieder-Lexicon*, vol. ii., Gotha, 1879; Julian, *Hymnology*, pp. 732–733; *ADB*, xxi. 646.

MEYRICK, FREDERICK: Church of England; b. at Ramsbury (27 m. w. of Reading), Wiltshire, Jan. 28, 1827; d. at Blickling (13 m. n.n.w. of Norwich), Norfolkshire, Jan. 3, 1906. He was educated at Trinity College, Oxford (B.A., 1847), where he was fellow, 1847–60, and tutor, 1851–1859. He was tutor to the Marquis of Lothian, 1847–53; was ordered deacon in 1850 and ordained priest in 1852; was an inspector of schools 1859–1868; examining chaplain to the bishop of Lincoln 1868–85; principal of Codrington College, Barbados, 1886–87; rector of Blickling, Norfolk, from 1868 till his death, and also non-resident canon of Lincoln after 1869. He was Whitehall preacher in 1856–57 and select preacher at Oxford in 1856, 1866, and 1876. He took an active part in the Old Catholic movement and attended the Bonn conference of 1875. Among his numerous writings mention may be made of his *Practical Working of the Church of Spain* (London, 1851); *Clerical Tenure of Fellowships* (Oxford, 1854); *Moral and Devotional Theology of the Church of Rome* (London, 1856); *The Outcast and the Poor of London* (1858); *The Wisdom of Piety* (1859); *Correspondence with Old Catholics and Orientals* (4 series, 1877–78); *Is Dogma a Necessity?* (1883); *The Doctrine of the Church of England on the Holy Communion Restated* (1885); *The Church of England, A.D. 597–1887* (1887); *The History of the Church in Spain* (1892); *Scriptural and Catholic Truth and Worship* (1901); *Old Anglicanism and Modern Ritualism* (1901); *Sunday Observance* (1902); *Appeal to the Primitive Centuries* (1904); *Appeal to the Sixteenth and Seventeenth Centuries* (1905); *Memories of Life at Oxford and Elsewhere* (1905). He contributed to the *Speaker's Commentary* the parts on Obadiah (London, 1876) and Ephesians (1880), and to the *Pulpit Commentary* the sections on Leviticus (1882) and Joshua and Judges (1895).

MEZUZAH: A rectangular piece of inscribed parchment enclosed in a wooden or metal case and attached by Jews to the upper part of the right-hand door post of a dwelling. The inscription consists of Deut. vi. 4–9, xi. 13–21, and is written in twenty-two lines according to the rules made for copying the Torah. The parchment is rolled with the writing inside, on the outside at the upper end the divine name Shaddai is written, and a glass-covered aperture in the case leaves this visible. The Mezuzah is by the pious touched with the hand as they enter or leave the house, and a short prayer is recited at the same time. The practise is founded on the injunction in Deut. vi. 9.

Bibliography: Dassorius, *De ritibus Mesuzæ*, in B. Ugolinus, *Thesaurus antiquitatum sacrarum*, vol. xxi., 34 vols., Venice. 1744–69; *JE*, viii. 531–532.

MEZZOFANTI, met"so-fān'tī, **GIUSEPPE GASPARD**: Italian cardinal; b. at Bologna Sept. 17, 1774; d. in Rome Mar. 15, 1849. He was educated in the archiepiscopal seminary of his native city and was ordained priest in 1797. He held various professorial positions in the University of Bologna until 1831, when he removed to Rome, where he succeeded Mai as librarian of the Vatican. In 1838 Gregory XVI. created him cardinal-priest. He was said to have been the greatest linguist of ancient or modern times. According to his biographer Russell he spoke with uncommon fluency thirty-eight languages; less perfectly, eleven; imperfectly, seven; and could read, but not speak, twelve others. He was acquainted besides with at least fifty dialects of those languages.

Bibliography: C. W. Russell, *Life of Cardinal Mezzofanti*, London, 1858, cf. T. Watts, *On Dr. Russell's Life of Cardinal Mezzofanti*, ib. 1860; A. Manavit, *Esquisse historique sur le Cardinal Mezzofanti*, Paris, 1854; A. Bellesheim, *Giuseppe, Cardinal Mezzofanti*, Würzburg, 1880.

MIANI, GIROLAMO. See Somaschians.

MICAH (Hebr. *Miykayah*, "Who is like Yahweh?"): The prophet whose book is sixth among the Minor Prophets. From his home in Moresheth-gath (i. 14) he is called the Morasthite (i. 1) and is so distinguished (e.g., Jer. xxvi. 18) from other men of the name, notably from Micah, son of Imlah (I Kings xxii. 8). He belonged to the southern kingdom, where he exercised his office (Jer. xxvi. 18), though the range of his prophecies covered Samaria. The superscription (i. 1) places his activity in the reigns of Jotham, Ahaz, and Hezekiah, all kings of Judah. This fact has been questioned, and the attempt made to date his work wholly under Hezekiah. But chaps. i.–iii. echo the period of Ahaz, and if iv. 1–5 (cf. Isa. ii. 2–5) is original with Micah, he may be placed also under Jotham. But his greatest activity is to be placed under Hezekiah.

Chap. i. deals with the imminent judgment of God first on Israel (Samaria) and then on Judah; chaps. ii.–iii. lay the blame upon the sins of the upper classes, including the false prophets; in chaps. iv.–v., in which the high point of Micah's oracles is reached, the author has alternately in view an immediate and a remoter future of Judah, in which it is to be wasted by Babylon and Assyria and then restored (these alternations have led to much discussion concerning the date and genuineness of the prophecies here collected); chaps. vi.–vii. start from a new point of view, since in them the guilt of the whole people is discussed. In these last chapters the literary form of dialogue appears, in which Yahweh, the people, and the prophet are the speakers; Yahweh states his ground of action against his people (vi. 1–5) and is answered with contrition by the people (vi. 6–7), to whom the prophet replies (vi. 8); Yahweh denounces the sins of the capital (vi. 9–16); vii. 1–13 is a dialogue between prophet and people; vii. 15 is Yahweh's encouragement continued by the prophet in verses 16–20.

The genuineness of parts of the book of Micah has been violently assailed. Thus the presence of ii. 12–13 has been justified by some only as the (quoted) words of a lying prophet like the one implied in verse 11, in which case a connection between verses 11–12 is made by supposing a suppressed "saying" at the end of verse 11. But it is best understood as a genuine promise of restoration following the denunciation which had just been pronounced. Stade makes iv. 1–4, 11–14, v. 1–3, 6–14 exilic and iv. 5–10, v. 4–5 still later interpolations, and sees in them inconsistencies and differences of standpoint. Ryssel combats this view, assigns the whole to Micah or at least to the time of Hezekiah, and regards it as in vital connection with chaps. i.–iii. The difficulty arose in the mention of Babylon as the place of exile (iv. 10) in a time when Assyria was the world power and Nineveh the world capital. The solution is to be found in the great significance and importance of Babylon, even in the Assyrian period, as the historic seat of world empire (Gen. x. 10–11) and so essentially and typically antagonistic to the city of God. Similarly, from the time of Ewald, the genuineness of chaps. vi.–vii. has been assailed. Ewald dated them in Manasseh's time; Wellhausen and Stade followed him in so dating vi. 1–vii. 6, putting vii. 7–20 in the exile; Cornill sees in vii. 7 sqq. references to the second temple; and other scholars take positions essentially in agreement with these. But when it is noted that in vii. 7–20 the exile lies still in the future and that between this part and chaps. i.–v. there are numerous coincidences and points of contact, the conclusion will follow that this part has the same author as the rest of the book. The impression the book makes is that of a unit, with fuller reports of the deliverances in chaps. i.–ii., more condensed and fragmentary reports in the other chapters.

Chap. vi. has a special interest in that the scheme of history which it assumes as that known by those to whom it is addressed is that found in Numbers and Joshua, showing that at least the writing of J lay before the prophet. Another point of interest in this chapter has to do with Micah's position as to sacrifice (vi. 6–8). Some have inferred that Micah did not regard sacrifice as demanded by the divine law. But the words of the prophet necessarily imply sacrifice as a legal requirement, which is met by the people, however, in a formal manner which deprives it of its quality as a God-pleasing service.

The language is purely classical. In point of rhetorical peculiarity, Micah stands between his contemporaries, Hosea and Isaiah, but nearer to the latter than the former; for although, like the former, he is abrupt, abounding in sudden and quick changes, in depth of spirituality he is the worthy companion of Isaiah, sharing with him a mingling of mildness and strength, of gentleness and elevation, together with great vigor and an artistic turn of expression. (W. Volck†.)

Of the prophecies placed under the name of Micah in the Hebrew text it is not certain that anything except chaps. i.-iii. proceed from Micah the Morasthite. These, with the possible exception of ii. 12, 13, which have no obvious relation to the context, and contain an indefinite and unmotived promise of a return from exile, are an important supplement to the genuine discourses of Isa. i.-v., and are especially interesting as showing the bitter feeling of a small landholder in a country village arising from the treatment of the poorer classes by the rapacious nobles and office-holders of the capital. The natural climax of the prophecy, iii. 12, is quoted as a memorable saying a century later (Jer. xxvi. 18).

The remainder of the book as we now have it is apparently composed of several unclassified discourses or fragments of discourses of dates later than Micah. Chap. iv. describes a great deliverance and restoration of Israel after it has been punished for its sins with exile and disintegration, and chap. v. announces the deliverer as a descendant of the princely house of David and a native of Bethlehem, and pictures the results of the reclamation as a triumph over the national enemies followed by the abolition of all forms of idolatry. These two chapters, which form a unit, were presumably written under the influence of Isa. vii. 14 sqq., and are perhaps exilic (see the reference to Babylon in iv. 10). Chap. vi. 1-vii. 6 was composed by a great prophet living in Jerusalem, presumably in the earlier days of Manasseh. Of chap. vii. 7-20 it can only be said that it is a cento of unconnected fragments which give no clue to the time or circumstances of their author or authors. They are, if possible, still less relevant to the conditions of Micah's time than are the three preceding chapters.

For the reason that the several divisions of the book differ greatly in subject-matter, style, and outlook, it is not possible to describe it in any terms that will apply to the collection as a whole. Of most significance and permanent value are chaps. iii. and vi., the latter being especially memorable as containing the classical definition of the religion of Yahweh (verse 8). J. F. McCurdy.

Bibliography: The most thorough investigation is B. Ryssel, *Untersuchungen über die Textgestalt und die Echtheit des Buches Micha*, Leipsic, 1887. Still valuable are the older commentaries by E. Pocock, Oxford, 1677; C. W. Justi, Leipsic, 1799, and A. T. Hartmann, Lemgo, 1800. More recent works are by C. P. Caspari, 2 parts, Christiania, 1851-52 (elaborate); E. B. Pusey, Oxford, 1862; C. F. Keil, Eng. transl., Edinburgh, 1868; T. Roorda, Leyden, 1869; L. Reinke, Giessen, 1874; P. Kleinert, in Lange, Eng. transl., New York, 1875; S. Clark, in *Bible Commentary*, London, 1876; T. K. Cheyne, in *Cambridge Bible*, Cambridge, 1887; H. J. Elhorst, Arnheim, 1891; C. von Orelli, Eng. transl., *The Twelve Minor Prophets*, New York, 1893; J. Wellhausen, *Kleinen Propheten*, Berlin, 1893; G. A. Smith, *The Book of the Twelve*, in *Expositor's Commentary*, London, 1896; J. T. Beck, Gütersloh, 1898; W. Nowack, in *Handkommentar*, Göttingen, 1903; M. L. Margolis, Philadelphia, 1908-09.

On questions of introduction consult: B. Stade, in *ZATW*, i (1881), 161 sqq.; W. Nowack, in *ZATW*, iv (1884), 288-290; J. Taylor, *The Massoretic Text and the Ancient Versions of . . Micah*, London, 1891; W. H. Kosters, in *ThT*, 1893, pp. 249 sqq.; V. Ermoni, in F. Vigouroux, *Dictionnaire de la Bible*, part xxv., pp. 1064-1067, Paris, 1905; Smith, *Prophets*, pp. 287 sqq.; *DB*, iii. 358-360; *EB*, iii. 3067-74; *JE*, viii. 533-535; the pertinent sections in the works on introduction to the Old Testament, particularly those by Driver, Cornill, W. Baudissin (*Einleitung in die Bücher des Alten Testamentes*, Leipsic, 1901), and Wellhausen, in Bleek (*Einleitung in das Alte Testament*, Berlin, 1886).

MICHAEL: One of the four (or seven) archangels of Jewish post-exilic angelology. His name occurs in the Bible only in Dan. x. 13, 21, xii. 1; Jude 9; Rev. xii. 7. The conception in Daniel is that of the guardian angel of Israel (see Angel, II., §§ 1-2), with which the New-Testament passages accord. The passage in Jude is a quotation from the Ascension of Moses (see Pseudepigrapha, Old Testament, III., 6). In the pseudepigraphic literature Michael's figure looms large, and he often appears as the first of the archangels. In rabbinical writings his part is still further expanded. From Judaism he passed over into the Christian Church as the guardian angel of all Christians, and is celebrated in the Roman calendar on Sept. 29 (see Michaelmas), and in the Greek on Nov. 9. Two military orders took his name—the French order founded in 1469 by Louis XI., and the Bavarian order founded in 1721 by Elector Joseph Clemens of Cologne—as did a number of congregations. A song said to have been sung by Michael and the good angels in triumph over Lucifer and the fallen angels and revealed to St. Amadeus is given in J. A. Fabricius, *Codex pseudepigraphus Veteris Testamenti*, i. 26-27 (Hamburg, 1723), and a partial translation is in S. Baring-Gould, *Legends of the Patriarchs and Prophets*, p. 16 (New York, 1872).

Bibliography: A. Kohut, *Jüdische Angelologie*, Leipsic, 1866; W. Lueken, *Michael*, Göttingen, 1898; F. J. Peters, *St. Michael und seine Verehrung*, Cologne, 1902; A. Butler, *Lives of the Fathers, Martyrs, and Saints*, Sept. 29, vol. ii., London, 1860.

MICHAEL, EMIL THEODOR RICHARD: Austrian Roman Catholic; b. at Reichenbach (32 m. s.w. of Breslau), Prussian Silesia, Sept. 20, 1852. He was admitted to the Society of Jesus in 1874 and was educated at the universities of Innsbruck and Breslau (Ph.D., 1884; D.D., 1888). In 1888 he became privat-docent for church history at the former institution, and three years later he was appointed associate professor of the same subject, being promoted to the rank of full professor in 1895. Since 1906 he has been professor of Christian art at Innsbruck. In addition to numerous contributions to theological periodicals, he has written *Salimbene und seine Chronik* (Innsbruck, 1889); *Rankes Weltgeschichte, eine kritische Studie* (Paderborn, 1890); *Ignaz von Döllinger* (Innsbruck, 1892); *Geschichte des deutschen Volkes* (4 vols., Freiburg, 1897-1906); and *Kritik und Antikritik in Sachen meiner Geschichte des deutschen Volkes* (2 parts, 1899-1902).

MICHAELIS: A family of German Lutheran exegetes of the seventeenth and eighteenth centuries.

1. Johann Heinrich: b. at Klettenberg (20 m. s.w. of Blankenburg), Brunswick, July 26, 1668; d. at Halle Mar. 10, 1738. Educated in theology, philosophy, and orientalia at Frankfort-on-the-Oder, he began to lecture in Halle in 1698, becoming successively associate professor of oriental languages (1699), full professor in the theological faculty (1709), and senior and inspector of the theological seminary (1732). He was important primarily as representing the critical school in the midst of Pietism, then centering in Halle. He was in great part the author of the plan for the Collegium Orientale Theologicum established there by A. H. Francke. He was likewise distinguished for his partial edition of the Old Testament (Halle, 1720), based on five Erfurt manuscripts and nineteen printed editions, the variants also being given. The edition was, however, too hastily done, and proved unreliable, though it is still not without value. He also prepared for it his *Uberiores annotationes* (3 vols., Halle, 1720), in which he diligently consulted the earlier versions. Some of the exegetical material here contained, like several of his dissertations and his *Sonderbarer Lebenslauf P. Heylings aus Lübeck und dessen Reise nach Ethiopien* (Halle, 1724), is still noteworthy.

2. **Christian Benedikt** (nephew of the preceding): b. at Elrich (8 m. n.w. of Nordhausen) Jan. 26, 1680; d. at Halle Feb. 22, 1764. He was educated at Halle, where he was successively associate (1713–1714) and full (1714–31) professor of philosophy, professor of theology (1731–38) and of Greek and Oriental languages (1738–64). Besides contributing to his uncle's edition of the Hebrew Old Testament and *Uberiores annotationes*, he wrote *Dissertatio de antiquitatibus œconomiæ patriarchalis* (Halle, 1728) and *Tractatus criticus de variis lectionibus Novi Testamenti caute colligendis et diiudicandis* (1749), in addition to an edition of the Hebrew Bible (with the Apocrypha and New Testament in Greek; Halle, 1741), based on H. Opitz's edition of 1709.

3. **Johann David** (son of the preceding): b. at Halle Feb. 27, 1717; d. at Göttingen Aug. 22, 1791. After completing his studies at Halle and traveling in England and Holland he went in 1745 to Göttingen, where he was professor of philosophy (1746–50) and of Oriental languages (1750–91). He was a prolific author, as is evidenced by his writing the entire periodical *Orientalische und exegetische Bibliothek* (later the *Neue orientalische und exegetische Bibliothek;* 35 parts, Frankfort and Göttingen, 1771–91). Moreover, he was the first to give to the cultured public the results of scientific views of the Bible as divorced from dogmatic assumptions in his annotated translation of the Old (13 vols., Göttingen, 1769–86) and New (2 vols., 1790) Testaments, these following his exegeses of some of the Messianic psalms (Frankfort, 1759), Ecclesiastes (Bremen, 1762), and I Maccabees (Frankfort, 1778). He gained equal favor, though more slowly, with his *Einleitung in das Neue Testament* (Göttingen, 2d ed., 1788; Eng. transl., *Introduction to the New Testament*, 4 vols., Cambridge, 1793–1801), which was followed by the less popular and uncompleted *Einleitung in das Alte Testament* (Hamburg, 1787).

The chief services of Michaelis were rendered in the domain of Biblical ancillary sciences, especially with regard to the Old Testament. Here belongs his *Supplementa ad lexica Hebraica* (6 vols., Göttingen, 1784–92), in which he sought primarily to free Hebrew lexicography from rabbinical tradition and to operate with the kindred languages, especially Arabic. At the same time he carefully studied the early versions, and such was his attention to the Peshito that he may be considered one of the founders of Syriac philology. Note should be made here of his *Grammatica Chaldaica* (Leipsic, 1771) and *Grammatica Syriaca*. He also made valuable contributions to Biblical antiquities, especially in his *Mosaisches Recht* (6 vols., 2d ed., Frankfort, 1771–75; Eng. transl. by A. Smith, *Commentaries on the Laws of Moses*, 4 vols., London, 1814), in which he advanced the view, then new, that the Pentateuchal laws were a product of the statesmanship of Moses, who aimed at the separation of Israel from the heathen [involving denial of the directly divine character and universal validity of the laws], thus judging antiquity by the standards of its own time, instead of by the criterion of the Christian Church; as well as in his *Abhandlung von den Ehegesetzen Mosis* (Göttingen, 1755). His geographical and archeological interests, already evinced by his securing from Frederick V of Denmark the sending of an expedition to Arabia in 1761 (for which he wrote his *Fragen an eine Gesellschaft reisender Gelehrten*, Frankfort, 1762), found expression in his *Spicilegium geographiæ exterorum* (2 vols., Göttingen, 1769–80) and in many places in his *Syntagma commentationum* (2 parts, 1759–67) and *Vermischte Schriften* (2 parts, Frankfort, 1766–69).

Although never a member of the theological faculty, Michaelis lectured on systematic, dogmatic, and moral theology, writing in these departments his *Gedanken über die Lehre der heiligen Schrift von Sünde und Genugthuung* (Bremen, 1748); *Compendium theologiæ dogmaticæ* (Göttingen, 1760; German ed., 1787); and *Entwurf einer typischen Gottesgelehrtheit* (Göttingen, 1753). These works, inferior to the rest, were weakened by his attempt not to break with external orthodoxy, though secretly he had renounced it, thus leading him to an attitude of untenable compromises. At the same time, this position gained him great popularity with both pupils and the Government, besides winning him the title of "regent of Göttingen" and the posts of secretary, director, and editor of the Göttingen Academy of Sciences. In the last two decades of his life, however, his prestige declined. (R. Kittel.)

Bibliography: 1. L. Diestel, *Geschichte des A. T. in der christlichen Kirche*, pp. 415 sqq., Jena, 1868. 3. His *Briefwechsel*, ed. Buhle, is in 3 vols., Leipsic, 1794–96, and his autobiography, ed. E. R. Hessenkamp, appeared at Rinteln, 1793. Consult further: L. Diestel, ut sup., pp. 583 sqq., 683 sqq., 745 sqq.; R. Smend, *Johann David Michaelis*, Göttingen, 1898; and especially Roethe, *Johann David Michaelis*, in the *Festschrift der Göttinger Gelehrten Gesellschaft*, Berlin, 1901.

MICHAELMAS: A festival celebrated Sept. 29, not only in the Roman Catholic Church, but also in the Greek and various Protestant churches in honor of the archangel Michael (q.v.), not with reference to any particular apparition of his, but generally commemorating the benefits which mankind have received from the angels. The festival seems to have been Roman in origin, and it is very old. In the eighth century the celebration was quite common in the Church. The Roman Catholic Church celebrates three special apparitions of the archangel, viz., May 8, Sept. 6, and Oct. 16. Michaelmas is also known as the Festival of St. Michael and All the Holy Angels. In England Michaelmas day is one of the four quarter-days, on which rents are paid, burghal councils elected, etc. Here, and also in other countries, it marks the beginning of the autumn term at schools and universities.

BIBLIOGRAPHY: A. Butler, *Lives of the Fathers, Martyrs and Other Principal Saints*, on Sept. 29; J. C. W. Augusti, *Denkwürdigkeiten*, iii. 281 sqq., Leipsic, 1820; A. J. Binterim, *Denkwürdigkeiten*, v., i., pp. 465 sqq., Mainz, 1829; *DCA*, ii. 1177–79.

MICHELET, SIMON TEMSTRUP: Norwegian theologian; b. at Trondhjem Feb. 8, 1863. He was graduated from the University of Christiania (B.A., 1881; medalist, 1885; candidate in theology, 1887); studied at German universities, particularly at Leipsic, for several years, devoting himself to the history of religion, Semitic languages, and the Old Testament; received ordination and pastorates at Trondhjem and Christiania, 1894–96; was appointed professor of theology at the University of Christiania, 1896. He is a representative of the higher criticism, aiming through his publications to interest not merely academic circles, but also the Norwegian public. In his dogmatics he has been influenced by F. Petersen (q.v.), and in his exegesis by Frants Buhl (q.v.). He has argued in favor of retaining the ancient languages in the curricula of the gymnasia, and is a leader in the Norwegian student world. He has published *Amos, oversat og fortolket Med en udsigt over de samtidige tilstande i Israel* (1893); *Det gamle testamentes syn paa synden* (1899); *Gamle Helligdomme i nyt Lys* (1902); and *Aandens Tjenere, ikke Bogstavens* (1907), on the confessional question. JOHN O. EVJEN.

MICHELIANS. See HAHN, JOHANN MICHAEL.

MICRONIUS, MARTINUS (Marten de Cleyne): Dutch Protestant; b. probably at Ghent 1522 or 1523; d. at Norden (17 m. n. of Emden) Sept. 12, 1559. He studied at Basel and Zurich, and early in 1550 went to London as pastor of the Flemish congregation there. After the death of Edward VI. (1553), Mary forbade the preaching of Protestantism, and on Sept. 17 Micronius left England. He went to Denmark, but Lutheran opposition prevented him from the peaceable conduct of worship and he finally reached Emden. Meanwhile some of the London exiles had come into conflict with the Mennonites at Wismar, and Micronius, called from Emden, held a disputation with Menno Simons (q.v.) on Feb. 6 and 15, 1554. Lutheran hostility now drove him successively from Wismar, Lübeck, and Hamburg, but after a brief period of repose at Emden, he was called to the pastorate at Norden, where he remained until his death, except for a short visit to Frankfort in 1555, at Lasco's request, to organize the congregations of Dutch exiles settled there.

Micronius was a master of disputation. His writings show him to have been somewhat Nestorian in Christology and quite Zwinglian in Eucharistic doctrine, but universalistic in his concept of salvation. He was deeply influenced by his teacher and friend Bullinger, but his importance lay less in his theology than in the services he rendered the religious exiles from Holland. His chief works were: *De kleyne Catechismus oft kinderleere der Duytscher Ghemeynte van London* (ed. 1552 and often; Eng. transl., London, 1552); *Een corte undersouckinge des gheloofs* (1553); *Een claer bewijs van het recht gebruyck des Nachtmaals Christi ende wat men van de misse houden sal* (Buyten, London, 1554); and *Christlicke Ordinancien*, etc. (1554). Among his polemics mention may be made of his *Een waerachtig verhaal*, etc. (Emden, 1556), on his disputations with Menno Simons; *Apologeticum scriptum* (3 parts, 1557), against Joachim Westphal; and *Een Apologie of verandtwoordinghe* (Emden, 1558), against Menno Simons. (S. D. VAN VEEN.)

BIBLIOGRAPHY: J. H. Gerretsen, *Micronius, Zijn leven, zijn geschriften, zijn geestesrichting*, Nijmegen, 1895 (cf. S. Cramer, in *ThT*, 1896, pp. 304–317); Menno Simons, *Opera omnia Theologica*, pp. 545–618, Amsterdam, 1681.

MIDDLETON, CONYERS: English controversialist and author of the famous *Life of Cicero;* b. at York Dec. 27, 1683; d. at Hildersham (8 m. s.e. of Cambridge) July 28, 1750. He was graduated from the University of Cambridge (B.A., 1702–03; M.A., 1707; D.D., 1717). He was elected fellow of Trinity College, and was for a short time curate of Trumpington, near Cambridge. He won for himself a wide reputation by his caustic attacks on Bentley, the master of Trinity, who, in spite of his great scholarship, was very unpopular on account of his harsh personalities. In one of these (1720) Middleton assailed Bentley's proposal to issue an edition of the Greek Testament, discovering some errors in the advance sheets, and to this attack Bentley's retirement from that field has been wrongly attributed. Middleton was chosen principal librarian of Trinity College, 1721. See DEISM, I., § 7.

In 1724 he visited Rome, and later wrote *A Letter from Rome, showing an Exact Conformity between Popery and Paganism* (London, 1729, republished 1868), in which he attempted to prove that the religion of the Roman Church was a continuation of the heathenism of ancient Rome. Middleton's controversies were not confined to Bentley, but extended to Daniel Waterland, Thomas Sherlock, and others. He assailed the medical profession in his *De medicorum apud veteres Romanos degentium conditione dissertatio* (Cambridge, 1726). His controversy with Waterland originated with the latter's attack upon Middleton's assertion that there were "contradictions in the evangelists which could not be reconciled," and that "the story of the fall of man was a fable or allegory." In 1741 he published the great work of his life, the *History of the Life of M. Tullius Cicero* (2 vols., London, best ed., ib. 1848), written after the labors of six years, though the charge is made that it is plagiarized from a rare book by William Bellenden. This biography has been condemned as being too partial, and praising as "wise, virtuous, and heroic" acts which Cicero himself condemned. In his *Free Inquiry into the Miraculous Powers which are Supposed to have Subsisted in the Christian Church from the Earliest Ages through Several Successive Centuries* (London, 1749), he denies the continuance of miraculous powers in the Church after the apostolic age. He attacked Sherlock in *An Examination of the Lord-Bishop of London's Discourses concerning the*

Use and Intent of Prophecy (London, 1750). His *Miscellaneous Tracts* (London, 1752) collect a number of Middleton's shorter writings. His *Miscellaneous Works*, not including Cicero's Life, appeared 4 vols., London, 1752, 5 vols., 1755.

Bibliography: The literature under Bentley, Richard; Sherlock, Thomas; and Waterland, Daniel. Consult also: John Nichols, *Literary Anecdotes of the 18th Century*, v. 405–423, 9 vols., London, 1812–15; *DNB*, xxxvii. 343–348.

MIDDLETON, THOMAS FANSHAW: Church of England bishop of Calcutta; b. in Kedleston (4 m. n.w. of Derby) Jan. 26, 1769; d. in Calcutta July 8, 1822. He was graduated with honors from the University of Cambridge (B.A., 1792; M.A., 1795; D.D., 1808); was appointed curate of Gainsborough, Lincolnshire, 1792; rector of Tansor, Northamptonshire, 1795; of Little and Castle Bytham, Lincolnshire, 1802; a prebend at Lincoln, 1809; vicar of St. Pancras, London, 1811; archdeacon of Huntingdon, 1812; and was consecrated first bishop of Calcutta, 1814. At Calcutta he founded in 1820 the Bishops' College, for the training of missionaries and clergymen for Asia. Dr. Middleton is justly famed for his *Doctrine of the Greek Article applied to the Criticism and Illustration of the New Testament* (London, 1808; 2d ed. by Rev. James Scholefield, 1828, 5th ed., 1855). A posthumous volume of *Sermons, Charges*, etc., with *Memoir*, was issued by H. K. Bonney (London, 1824).

Bibliography: Besides the *Memoir* in his *Sermons*, ut sup., consult: C. W. Le Bas, *Life of T. F. Middleton*, 2 vols., London, 1831; C. M. Yonge, *Pioneers and Founders; or, recent Workers in the Mission Field*, ib. 1871; *DNB*, xxxvii. 363–365.

MIDIAN: The name of a people or stock (not of a country) which comes into especial prominence in the story of Gideon (Judges vi.–viii.). In the Old Testament the relations between them and Israel are in part friendly, though more often they are hostile. In the time of Gideon Midianites appear as ravaging nomads who cross the Jordan from the east and seize the produce and cattle of the Hebrews. They seem to be a belated part of the same migration as that to which the Israelites belonged, and Judges viii. 11 indicates that their home was the desert. The narrative in chap. viii. belongs in the main to a different narrator (J) from that in vi.–vii., and gives a slightly different view. When Ex. ii. 15 speaks of a "land of Midian," the reference is not to a region generally so named, but to a district named after a definite tribe which lived there. From Ex. ii.–iv. (and perhaps Num. x. 29–32) all that can be gathered of the region is that it was east of Egypt and south of the Jordan. Ptolemy (*Geographike*, vi. 7), and Eusebius and Jerome (*Onomastica*, 136, 276) knew of a Madiama or Madiam, east of the Red Sea and south of the Roman province of Arabia, mentioned by Arab geographers as Madyan, identified by R. F. Burton in 1878 with the region about the ruins of Magha'ir shu'aib, or "caves of Jethro"—a region called by its present inhabitants *arḍ madyan*, "land of Midian," having its northern boundary not far from the site of Elath and its southern near the coast fortress al-Muwelih. This modern district is about 45 miles from north to south and from twenty-three to thirty-four miles in width. There are still traces of mining operations for copper, silver, and gold.

The relation of friendship between the two peoples is illustrated by the case of Moses, who fled to the country and entered the family of "Hobab son of Raguel" (Num. x. 29, cf. Judges iv. 11, and "Reuel" Ex. ii. 18) or Jethro (Ex. iii.1, xviii. 1, cf. "Jether" Ex. iv. 18, margin). Hobab is called a Kenite in Judges iv. 11, and Stade suspects that the Kenites were in early times associated with the Midianites (see Cain, Kenites). Num. x. 29–32 suggests not a settled people but a nomadic tribe. Other Old-Testament passages raise the question whether settled, semi-nomadic, or nomadic peoples were in mind. Gen. (xxxvii. 28, 36) implies not Bedouin but a settled people carrying wares to the north and in the contrary direction; Isa. lx. 6 must refer to nomads; Num. xxii., xxv. and xxxi. are not clear on the point, though Winckler, relying on Gen. xxxvi. 35 (cf. I Kings xi. 14–22), looks on these chapters as implying a pre-Moabitic and abiding possession of the region, a conclusion not wholly warranted by the text. The narrative in Num. xxxi. is not so reliable as to permit from the mention of "kings of Midian" (verse 8) the deduction that the Midianites were a settled people.

Genealogical details concerning the Midianites are not easy to interpret, partly because only a few names are given, partly because the nomadic tribes were so mobile that the same names appear from the Euphrates to the Red Sea. Gen. xxv. 1–6 derives them from Keturah and gives five branches of the stock. Of these Ephah is by Delitzsch placed in North Arabia as known to Tiglath-Pileser III. Knobel equates Epher with the Ghifar of Mohammed's age, who tented near Medina. For the time when they came into contact with Israel they are to be regarded as Aramaic nomads. With Israel's regal period they vanish from history; the Ishmaelites of Judges viii. 24 may be the same people (see Ishmael). From the occurrence of Jether, Jethro, and Raguel among Hebrew names, a coalescence with the Hebrews has been suspected.

(H. Guthe.)

Bibliography: T. Nöldeke, *Die Amalakiter und . . andere Nachbarvölker der Israeliten*, Göttingen, 1864; R. F. Burton, *The Land of Midian*, 2 vols., London, 1878–79 (contains collections of ancient materials); F. Delitzsch, *Wo lag das Paradies?* Leipsic, 1881; E. Glaser, *Skizze der Geschichte und Geographie Arabiens*, ii. 445 sqq., Berlin, 1890; H. Winckler, *Geschichte Israels*, i. 47 sqq. et passim, Leipsic, 1895; *Schrader, KAT*, i. 143, 145; *DB*, iii. 365–366; *EB*, iii. 3079–82; *JE*, viii. 547–548.

MIDRASH.

Meaning and Essence of Midrash (§ 1).
Date and Structure (§ 2).
Three Tannaitic Midrashim (§ 3).
Genesis Rabba, Midrashim on Lamentations, Pesiḳta, and Tanḥuma (§ 4).
Homiletic Midrashim (§ 5).
Other Exegetical Midrashim (§ 6).
Compilations (§ 7).
Narrative, Ethical, and Esoteric Midrashim (§ 8).

The word *midrash* occurs in II Chron. xiii. 22, xxiv. 27 (A. V. "story," margin "commentary," R. V. "commentary"), but the meaning in both passages is doubtful. In post-Biblical usage, the verb from which the noun is derived means "to examine, to elucidate," while the noun expresses "interpretation," especially the interpretation of Scripture, and then comes to mean the haggadic (i.e., illustrative and practical) or, sometimes, the halachic (i.e., exegetical) commentaries on the Old Testament, especially such works as the Mishna, Tosephta, and Talmud (q.v.; cf. W. Bacher, *Die älteste Terminologie der jüdischen Schriftauslegung*, pp. 25 sqq., 103 sqq., Leipsic, 1899). The period of the kingdom in Israel was followed not by a hierocracy but by a rule under the Law (nomocracy), which more and more controlled the common external life and also the spiritual life of Israel. This is indicated by Haggai (ii. 10 sqq.), who makes the priests the recognized teachers of the law, while Ezra's whole striving was to bring the law of Moses into relation with common life. It is no wonder, in view of the changed conditions, that when other institutions were lost the Jews clung fondly to the written law, their only possession from the past. Yet this law was not a complete code; it hardly sufficed for the period immediately following the exile, still less could it supply the need when a fuller development of national life had bloomed. It had to be fitted to these later times and to be expanded, and this was done by the process of midrash. The name given to this activity was halachic, a collection of the results being called halakoth. The first authoritative collection of this material is that of Judah ha-Nasi, another is the Tosephta, while very early halachic material is found in the Baraithoth, in the midrashim Mekhilta, Siphra, Siphre, etc. Since the Old Testament was for the Jews the sum total of all that is good, beautiful, and worthful, it followed that it was regarded as the sufficient norm for all purposes of life. The application of this norm to practical purposes was brought about through midrash, but in this relation it was usually called haggada. Haggada sometimes adheres closely to the Scriptural text, sometimes takes it as a starting-point for varied expositions, which latter might be given in the synagogue or at private homes, in public observances as the Sabbath or festival occasions, or at important events of public or private life. (For the rules of halachic and haggadic interpretation, consult H. L. Strack, *Einleitung in den Thalmud*, VII., § 2, Leipsic, 1900).

1. Meaning and Essence of Midrash.

In spite of regulations once existent against reducing haggada and halacha to writing, it is abundantly evident that this material did exist in written form as early as the first part of the third century, though the purely haggadic midrashim now extant date from a later time. The time when this reduction to writing took place is difficult to ascertain because of the frequent redactions to which the material at hand has been subjected and because the text has not been carefully transmitted, (cf. L. Zunz, *Die gottesdienstlichen Vorträge der Juden*, Berlin, 1832). Much arduous work upon the manuscripts is necessary before a history of midrashic literature can be written. The most productive midrashic activity dates immediately after the close of the Babylonian Talmud and ends about 1040 A.D., being supplanted by philosophical studies. Many midrashim contain consecutive exposition of some book of the Old Testament, e.g., *Genesis rabba;* others consist of homilies based either on the cycle of synagogue readings or on the cycle of feasts. The homilies are usually the development of a theme on the basis of a text or verse of Scripture, and in the homiletic midrashim the compilers have been at pains to collect proems of various kinds to the themes (cf. S. Maybaum, *Die ältesten Phasen in der Entwickelung der jüdischen Predigt*, i. 14–27, Berlin, 1901). Thus it is reported of Rabbi Meir that his lectures were composed of halachic, haggadic, and illustrative materials, and of Rabbi Thanchum that he prefixed to a halachic lecture a haggadic introduction. The later midrashim often introduce a haggadic lecture by discussion of a halachic problem. The discussion which follows the proem is usually concerned with only a few verses, is often concentrated into a single verse or part of one, for the rest of the section chosen the exposition being rather cursory in character.

2. Date and Structure.

In the midrashim *Mekhilta* (on Exodus), *Siphre* (on Numbers and Deuteronomy), and *Siphra* (on Leviticus) two tendencies are discerned, that of the school of Rabbi Akiba and that of the school of his contemporary and opponent Rabbi Ishmael. The second is easily recognized by the learned by the names of the teachers which are given and also by certain technical expressions which appear. Mekhilta was in earlier times included under the term *Siphre;* it treats of Ex. xii. 1–xxiii. 19, xxxi. 12–17, xxxv. 1–3. Originally this was only halachic in character, the more strictly exegetical material being of later date. Many traces indicate that it covered a larger part of the book than the material which has survived. Editions are: Constantinople, 1515; Venice, 1545; Vienna, 1865; ib. 1870. "Siphre" (a Talmudic plural meaning "books") was originally a collective designation of the Tannaitic midrashim on Exodus, Numbers, and Deuteronomy; when "Mekhilta" was applied to the midrash on Exodus, "Siphre" was applied only to the midrash on Numbers and Deuteronomy. The extant Siphre on Numbers arose in the school of Ishmael, though it is of diverse authorship; the haggadic parts on Deuteronomy also are of that school, but in the legal portions (on chaps. xii.–xxvi.) it suggests the school of Akiba. Editions are: Venice, 1545; Vienna, 1864 (part 1 only). Siphra ("the book") is halachic and of the school of Akiba, except in viii. 1–x. 8, xviii. 1–5, xxvi. 3–46. It takes its name from the fact that instruction began not with the first book of the Pentateuch, but with the third. The basis is the teaching of Rabbi Judah, a pupil of Akiba; the final redactor was Chiyya the elder, pupil and friend of Judah ha-Nasi. The midrash of Ishmael's school is used only indirectly (cf. Z. Frankel, *Hodogetica in Mischnam*, pp. 307–311, Leipsic, 1859; D. Hoffmann, *Zur Einleitung in die halachischen Midraschim*, Berlin, 1887). Editions of Siphra are: Venice, 1545, 1609–11; Bucharest, 1860; Vienna, 1862; Warsaw, 1866.

3. Three Tannaitic Midrashim.

Genesis rabba, or *Bereshith rabba*, the larger midrash on Genesis, is probably so called in distinction from a smaller and shorter midrash based upon Rabbi Oshaya's work. The term *rabba*, "large," was in late times applied to the most common haggadic midrash on the Pentateuch and even to that on the Rolls. This midrash on Genesis is an explanation both of words and of things, taking fully the character of public lectures. Halachic exposition is rare in it. The range of interpretation is large; the basis is traceable to Rabbi Oshaya; though the artistic working-out of the plan is later, it is still not subsequent to the time of the redaction of the Palestinian Talmud, and intrusions of later matter occur. From xxxii. 4 on, the materials have the stamp of the later haggada, and the later manuscripts add many details. Apparently this midrash was never fully completed, for after xliv. 18 the progress is no longer verse by verse; chap. xlviii. is lacking in the manuscripts, and chap. xlix. in the codices has the earmarks of a late recension. The view that it was first edited as a whole between 650 and 750 A.D. does not seem well supported. In most editions this midrash is in 100 chapters; the manuscripts vary between 97 and 101 chapters, though all agree in their limits as far as chap. xcvi., beginning with Gen. xlvii. 28. The basis of the chapter division is not consistent or uniform. Editions are: the midrash on the Pentateuch, Constantinople, 1512; on the Rolls, Pesaro (?), 1519, Constantinople, 1520; of the whole, Venice, 1545; with commentary of Issachar Baer Kohen, Cracow, 1587–88; of Samuel Japheh Ashkenazi on Genesis, Venice, 1597 sqq., on Exodus, ib. 1657, on Leviticus, Constantinople, 1648; of David Luria and Samuel Straschun, Vilna, 1843–1845. Other editions are: Berlin, 1866; Vilna, 1878. The midrash on Lamentations (*Midrash Eykah*) is one of the oldest of Palestinian origin. It is exceedingly rich in proems owing to the fact that the celebration of the destruction of Jerusalem was accompanied by lectures on that book. These lectures are the source of a great part of the expositions of which the midrash is composed. The redaction is later than that of the Palestinian Talmud, though very early materials are used. The exposition is of the same character as that of Genesis rabba—smooth comment with interspersed haggadic pieces that are only loosely attached to their context. The redaction is prior to 650 A.D. An old midrash of the name *Pesiḳta* was long known through citations. Its recovery shows that it consists of thirty-two homilies delivered on specified festivals or Sabbaths, and that it was composed of two collections, one beginning with New Year's day, the other with Tammuz 17. The manuscripts show considerable variations in contents, especially at the beginning. The question of the date depends upon literary relations—it is a question whether Pesiḳta is dependent upon Genesis rabba and the midrash on Lamentations, or whether it is older than these. In the first case its date would be about 700 A.D.; in the second case it would be earlier than this. It is no longer in its original form, but has undergone many alterations and has received many additions. The name means "section," and is derived from the fact that each chapter was entitled "Section of ". It was edited by S. Buber (Lyck, 1868), but unfortunately not on the basis of the Oxford manuscript. The *Midrash Yelamdenu* or *Tanḥuma* covers the entire Pentateuch. Originally it contained only one homily for each Sabbath reading; in its present shape each homily has a halachic exordium, several introductions, exposition of the first verse of the lesson, Messianic conclusion. This formed the model of many collections. Editions are: Constantinople, 1520–22; Venice, 1545; Mantua, 1563; Verona, 1595; with commentaries, Vilna-Grodno, 1831; Stettin, 1864.

4. Genesis Rabba, Midrashim on Lamentations, Pesiḳta, and Tanḥuma.

The *Exodus rabba* or *Shemoth rabba* is in fifty-two sections, of which the first fourteen are continuous expositions of the verses in each Sabbath lesson, while the rest have introductions and treatment of the first verse only. This indicates that two parts are to be distinguished, the first of which is derived from an early exegetical midrash, while the second is dependent upon Tanḥuma. Its date is probably the eleventh or the twelfth century. *Leviticus rabba* or *Vayyikra rabba* is made up of thirty-seven homilies on the sections appointed for festival readings. It appears to belong to the seventh century. *Numeri rabba* or *Bemidhbar rabba* or *Bemidhbar Sinai rabba*, in twenty-three sections, is in two very different parts. The first (sections 1–14, about one-third of the whole) is a late haggadic exposition of Num. i.–vii., of which Num. i.–iv. are expansions of Tanḥuma, while in Num. v.–vii. there is an effort to discuss the entire text by compilations from halachic and haggadic works. This part is not earlier than the twelfth century. The second part is essentially Tanḥuma to the eight sections beginning with Num. viii., but with a different introductory formula. The nine chief sections correspond to as many Sabbath readings in the single-year cycle; but thirty homilies are distinguishable. *Deuteronomium rabba* or *Debarim rabba* follows generally in the printed editions the single-year cycle in eleven sections. But in fact there are twenty-seven separate homilies which are related to the three-year cycle of reading. These homilies begin with a halachic exordium, then one or more introductions of quite independent homiletical character, exposition of the beginning of the Scripture lesson, and a hortatory or comforting conclusion. The time of compilation of this mishna is about 900 A.D. The authors of the thirteenth and later centuries often refer sections of this collection to Tanḥuma, though there is little in common between them in the printed text. There are in this mishna only three homilies completed according to the rules for such discourse. It was published by S. Buber (Vienna, 1885) from a Munich manuscript. *Aggadath Bereshith*, consisting of homilies, is later than the close of Genesis rabba. A late edition is by B. Epstein (Shitomir, 1899). *Pesiḳta rabbathi* is a collection of homilies for festivals, and is not earlier than 850 A.D., though it is claimed that the details on which this dating depends are glosses. It is believed to have been the work of at least four authors. A critical edi-

5. Homiletic Midrashim.

authors of everything evil. They, too, had caused hatred and persecutions against Christianity, circulating all those rumors and reproaches more justly applying to the heathen service of idols. With moral indignation Octavius paid ample tribute to the purity of the Christians' manner of life, divine worship and faith; and spoke of the righteousness and goodness of God. Their doctrine of the end of all things contradicted neither the laws of nature nor the teachings of the philosophers. Christians welcomed adversity as a school for virtue; the prosperity in which the heathen rejoiced was transitory and fallacious and heathens' pleasures were censurable and indecent. This discourse made a powerful impression upon Cæcilius, who admitted his defeat, and the three returned to the city.

So it is plain that the colloquy did not turn upon the fundamental doctrines of Christianity, neither is it an apology in the proper sense. Attempts at explanation are widely divergent, although the difficulties are not to be waived. Some have sought to prove the dialogue a polemic against Crescentius the Cynic or the Epicurean Celsus, or, finally, against Cornelius Fronto, the rhetorician.

4. Purpose and Structure of Dialogue.

The most natural explanation, however, lies in the author's purpose of disarming the prejudices then current against Christianity in cultured circles by proving that the views of the philosophers coincided essentially with the faith of the Christians; that the heathen mythology was shameless, whereas the new faith was pure and lofty. Hence, in the work of Minucius Felix, Christianity appears wholly as a moral and philosophic religion. Minucius, frequently finding himself obliged to meet attacks against his religion, had to examine them carefully and confute them. The structure of the dialogue is so excellent that even to-day certain critics regard it as having actually taken place. The introduction especially has a poetic charm, and likewise worthy of praise is the drawing of the leading characters. Minucius was well read in the poetic works of the Greeks and Romans, and had a good knowledge of the works of Cicero, whom he adopted as his model. Traces of decadent Latinity appear nevertheless; still the language of Minucius is comparatively pure for that age.

The repeated attempts to discover whether the dialogue of Octavius was influenced by any other apologetic have led to no generally recognized result, for he does not mention his sources. There undoubtedly exists a dependent relation between Minucius, Tertullian, and Cyprian. The latter, in his treatise "On the Vanity of Idols" (c. 245), copied Minucius and Tertullian. The priority of Tertullian's "Apology" (c. 200), which has various points of contact with "Octavius," was long held to be incontestable, but now, especially since Ebert's investigations, Minucius is rated the earlier. He wrote between 150 and 245, probably before 200. The "Octavius" is appended to the seven books of Arnobius "Against the Heathen" in a manuscript dating from the ninth century preserved in Paris. There is a transcript in Brussels. From the former there was printed the first edition of Arnobius (Rome, 1543), wherein the "Octavius" appeared as the eighth book. It was first edited separately by Francis Baldwin (Heidelberg, 1560). Since then, the dialogue has been frequently published (e.g., ed. C. Halm, in *CSEL*, Vienna, 1867; in *MPL*, iii. 239–276; ed. J. J. Cornelissen, Leyden, 1882; ed. A. Bährens, Leipsic, 1886). Eng. transls. are by D. Dalrymple (Edinburgh, 1781; new ed., Cambridge, 1854); in *ANF*, iv. 173–198; and in A. A. Brodribb, *Pagan and Puritan; The Octavius of Minucius, freely translated*, London, 1903. H. Boenig.

5. Sources and Manuscripts of Minucius.

Bibliography: Lists of literature are to be found in *Le Musée Belge*, xvi (1892), nos. 2–3, and in *ANF*, Bibliography, pp. 47–50. Consult: C. Rören, *Minuciana*, part i., Bedburg, 1859, part ii., Brilon, 1877; A. Soulet, *Essai sur l'Octavius de Minucius Felix*, Strasburg, 1867; T. Keim, *Celsus*, pp. 151–168, Zurich, 1873; idem, *Rom und das Christenthum*, pp. 383–384, 468–486, Berlin, 1881; P. de Félice, *Étude sur l'Octavius de Minucius Felix*, Blois, 1880; V. Schultze, in *JPT*, vii (1881), 485–506; R. Kühn, *Der Octavius des Minucius Felix*, Leipsic, 1882; R. Schwenke, in *JPT*, ix (1883), 263–294; M. L. Massebieau, in *Revue de l'hist. des religions*, xv (1887), 316–346; F. Wilhelm, *De Minucii Felicis Octavio*, Breslau, 1887; E. Kurz, *Ueber den Octavius des Minucius Felix*, Burgdorf, 1888; B. Seiller, *De sermone Minuciano*, Augsburg, 1893; M. Schanz, in *Rheinisches Museum*, l (1895), 114–137; H. Boenig, *Marcus Minucius Felix; ein Beitrag zur Geschichte der altchristlichen Litteratur*, Königsberg, 1897; E. Norden, *De Minucii Felicis ætate et genere dicendi*, Greifswald, 1897; Ceillier, *Auteurs sacrés*, i. 550–557; Krüger, *History*, pp. 138–142; Schaff, *Christian Church*, ii. 833 sqq.; Harnack, *Litteratur*, i. 647, 743, ii. 2, pp. 324–330, 408; idem, *Dogma*, ii. 196 sqq.; *DCB*, iii. 920–924; A. Elter, *Prolegomena zu Minucius Felix*, Bonn, 1909.

MIRACLE PLAYS. See Religious Dramas.

MIRACLES.

The concept of miracles, found in nearly all religions, is due to the belief in the power of the supernatural over the world, either in whole or in part. The types of miracles are as manifold as the religions themselves, ranging from cosmic phenomena (especially of creation and eschatology) and divine manifestations to the founders of religions, to omens and warnings, rewards and punishments, and responses to prayer and priestly power.

The Bible bears witness to the general belief in miracles, although here, in contradistinction to other oriental religions, miracles are, in general, fewer in number and more religious in character. This is in keeping with the spirituality of the Biblical concept of God, who, though omnipotent (Gen. xviii. 14; Job xlii. 2; Ps. lxxvii. 14), is regarded as acting only in accordance with his nature. Creation and rain, comfort to the sorrowing and thwarting of the wicked are all miracles (Job. v. 9 sqq.). The concept of the orderly progress of all natural phenomena is extremely firm in the Old Testament (cf. Gen. viii. 22; Ps. cxlviii. 5–6; Jer. xxxi. 35–36), and this same concept prevails in the New Testament, where the religious character of miracles is even more marked since phenomenal miracles are here combined with spiritual miracles.

1. Biblical Data.

Accordingly, the miracles of Christ are intended to prove that the time of redemption or of the kingdom of God is come (Matt. xi. 5, xii. 28; Mark ii. 10–11). Not only did Christ work no miracles for his own benefit (Matt. iv. 4, 7, xxvi. 53), but he refused miracles to those who asked unworthily (Matt. xvi. 1 sqq.). His miracles were wrought through his word or in virtue of the spirit of God that dwelt within him (Matt. viii. 16, xii. 28, xv. 28; Mark i. 25, ii. 11; John iv. 50; Acts x. 38), and although later in his career external miracles became less numerous, yet he promised his disciples that they would do greater miracles than he (John xiv. 12 sqq.). This implies, however, simply the greater miracles of the operations of the Spirit upon the heart; and when Paul concentrates the operation of the Spirit on the Gospel and prefers love to all external marvels (I Cor. xiii.), he followed the thoughts of Christ himself, the concept of the New Testament which through the Spirit writes the will of God upon the heart of man (Jer. xxxi. 33; Ezek. xxxvi. 26–27; Joel ii. 28). While, moreover, individual miracles are less important and striking than in other religions, it must be borne in mind that in Christianity religion itself bears an essentially miraculous character, seen not only in every event in the life of Christ and in the experiences of the apostles, but in the religious life of the Christian.

2. Patristic and Scholastic Views.

In the centuries following primitive Christianity the miracles of the Spirit came gradually to be depreciated, while the inner transformation of the Christian received an interpretation of mere psychology. The desire for miracles was gratified by legends of the apostles, martyrs, and confessors, or, still later, of hermits and monks; Jewish eschatology was adopted with all its marvels; and even a series of demoniac miracles was taken from early folklore. Side by side with this practical belief in miracles was evolved the theory regarding them. The basis for this was laid by Augustine. Holding that the world is full of miracles and is itself the greatest of all miracles, yet realizing that the marvels of creation become commonplace, he taught that God, who alone can create, caused new miracles to appear, though he had possessed them from all eternity. While these miracles apparently contradict the laws of nature, they do not really do so, since God, being the creator of nature, can create nothing opposed to it. The elements of the world contain, in addition to their "visible seeds," certain "hidden seeds," which are the source of miracles. There is, therefore, a hidden and inner operation of God in addition to the operation of natural causes. In themselves both these operations are equally marvelous and are simply different components of one and the same creation. The difference between miraculous and natural events is, therefore, not objective but subjective—"the miracle does not violate nature, but only nature as now known" (*De civitate Dei*, XXI., viii. 2). The Neo-Platonic theory of Augustine never vanished, though the Aristotelian causal theory of the universe maintained by Thomas Aquinas contested its supremacy in the Church. Nothing can happen outside the sum total of the system of divine governance, and in the great systematized order called the world God works as the first cause which simply determines a long chain of causes. In this sum total God can make no change, but he both can and does substitute some individual secondary causes for others. The result is a miracle, and God accordingly created cosmic order with the condition that he himself might be directly operative in it otherwise than through the usual and regularly operative causes. Miracles are accordingly defined as "those things which are done by God contrary to causes known to us" (*Summa* I., quæst. cv. art. 6). Miracles are thus placed within the sphere of divine governance, the sole difference between them and ordinary natural phenomena being that in the latter God is the first in a causal series, while in the case of miracles he directly intervenes. Not all direct intervention of God, however, is to be considered a miracle, this category including only deviations from the course of nature, whereas justification and creation are not miracles.

3. Post-Reformation Theories.

Luther held that God had caused visible miracles in the early stages of Christianity to foster belief in it and that these, subsequently proving unnecessary, were replaced by the far greater invisible spiritual miracles wrought by the Word and the sacraments. Other early Protestants considered miracles as divine suspensions of the ordinary course of nature, while Leibnitz maintained that miracles, like the hearing of prayer, were components of the original plan of the cosmos which must necessarily be realized. Spinoza, on the other hand, denied the possibility of miracles, except on the impossible hypothesis that the will of God and the law of nature, although identical, are different. The term miracle can, therefore, be applied only relatively to a phenomenon the cause of which is unknown. Hume made a still more vital attack on miracles by declaring the testimony for them too feeble to make them credible. During the period of the Enlightenment belief in miracles was gradually surrendered, and they were explained either as natural phenomena or as adapted to the views of their time, very much as Spinoza had explained them as projections of the mental processes of those who recorded them or as making God the first cause to the exclusion of mediate causes. Like Strauss, many modern theologians discredit miracles in the strict sense of the term, though positing the operation of marvelous powers of a higher order. Even though the great religious revival early in the nineteenth century rehabilitated belief in miracles, opposition to this belief has never disappeared, and still constitutes to many the great barrier to faith in Christianity. Once the foundation of all apologetics, miracles have now become the great apologetic crux.

A study in the concept of miracles can not begin with a general discussion of their possibility or impossibility, but with the problem whether the assertion of their existence is essential to the religious life of the Christian. The authority of the Bible, which affirms miracles, can not be appealed to, for this depends solely on religious experience, which is not concerned with historic events, natural phenomena, or Biblical cosmology. The investigator must pass thus from the Bible to immediate religious experience where, through the preaching of the Word, the Christian experiences a non-naturalistic power of an almighty will which, continuing and ever increasing, in itself constitutes a miracle in that it is by no means identical with the earthly agency through which it works, and reveals a power exalted above its surroundings. This coexistence of divine operation and natural phenomenon must be considered the chief characteristic of every sort of miracle. Revelation thus becomes a miracle, and miracle becomes revelation. Accordingly, in all the phases of life the Christian is convinced that God orders the world for the good of them that believe on him, and this in the smallest as in the greatest details. Even events which may be explained on purely natural grounds—as when Augustine heard the words *Tolle, lege* (see AUGUSTINE, I., 1, § 9)—may be considered miracles in so far as God is regarded as operating through them. From this point of view any event may be regarded as either miraculous or natural, according to the sensations which it evokes. If the experience of the revelation of God is thus experience of the miraculous, the divine revelation in question, operative through previous ages in a complex of concepts, naturally entered at a definite point in history. If, moreover, these concepts were permanent vehicles of the marvelous operation of God, those who first advanced them could form them only on the basis of their experience of the miraculous works of God. In confirmation of this, history shows that the Gospel bears witness to great historic facts judged from a specific point of view. In other words, the Gospel arose from witnessing miraculous facts, and is simply a record and explanation of these facts. Therefore the Christian takes a very different attitude toward them than toward other ancient religious records. The miracles here considered are almost invariably phenomena diverging from the regular course of nature. While it may be denied that some of the recorded miracles actually occurred, while it may be supposed that circumstances attending some of them were not quite those which were described, and while it may be alleged that they have been more or less modified involuntarily in transmission, it must be remembered that they were all wrought to proclaim knowledge of God or of Christ. Herein they were successful. The critic, on the other hand, has merely a report of an external event and of the impression upon the witness that this event was divine. The actual processes which led these witnesses to adjudge the events in question to be miraculous the critic can never know with certainty, and this lack of knowledge must be reckoned as a factor in the criticism of miracles. If, however, the uniform impression received by Christ's disciples from his many miracles be considered, it may be regarded as certain that this impression represents the true understanding of the miraculous works of Christ.

4. Theory and Proof of Miracles.

Two general objections may be alleged against the historicity of the miracles recorded in the Bible: their violation of natural law; and the fact that they occurred in a credulous age. Considering the latter objection first, it is true that the ancients, including the Jews, not only did not consider divine intervention of the deity to be suspicious or impossible, but they absolutely required such visible divine manifestations. Especially was this the case if they were to believe that Christ was really divine. Again, the history of divine revelation shows that God has always given it the forms best adapted to the requirements of the age. The fact, therefore, that external miracles no longer occur implies simply that they are no longer needed for faith; but this does not militate in the least against the occurrence of miracles in periods of an entirely different character. Neither does the theory that miracles were merely types of attitude molded by the needs of ancient gods disprove the actuality of miracles. All these hypotheses are based on the unhistorical rationalistic notion that things must always have been as it is now thought they should be. It is also alleged that miracles are contrary to the law of nature. The laws of nature, however, are nothing but formulas describing the regular operations of natural phenomena; but if the concept of God be introduced, they may then be regarded as expressing the divine will, so that the course of the world in conformity with the laws of nature is in no way opposed to the will of God. Yet even as man, by attentively studying the laws of nature, is enabled to rise above nature and to produce results which nature itself can not produce, since he unites regular processes of nature in new combinations for the attainment of the end which he desires without annulling or impairing the original potencies or laws of nature, so miracles should not be construed as abrogations or violations of the laws of nature, but as special adaptation of the forces of nature for a specific and divine purpose.

5. Arguments against Miracles.

In the present article three classes of miracles have been postulated: the constant miracle of the revelation of God; the operation of God in purely natural and orderly events of human life; and the revelation of God by irregular natural phenomena at a specific period. The question now arises as to the relation between these three classes, the first of which is usually ignored, while the second and the third are distinguished as subjectively and objectively miraculous respectively. At the same time, the great characteristic of a miracle, the arousing of consciousness of an external process, is common to all three classes, so that they all share in miraculousness. In the first and second class the miraculous process is in accordance with natural law, while in the third class it is irregular. Since, however, it can not be shown that the abnormal events in question are either opposed to nature or subversive of cosmic order, it follows that a miracle is not the producing of a more or less regular phenomenon, but the divine adaptation of an earthly event to make the presence of God immediately operative or to convince man of the divine presence in the event in question. The

6. Classification of Miracles.

essential difference between the third class of miracles and the other two classes can not, therefore, be maintained. A distinction may, however, be drawn between the miracles of the period of divine revelation and the later miracles manifested in the outworking of this revelation in the history of the human race. From this point of view there are four classes of miracles, the first two comprising immediate revelation and the last two mediate revelation; the spiritual miracle of the revelation which produced the Word of God (inspiration); the miracles manifested in history and nature to bring forth the Word of God; the miracles of the spiritual operation of the Word of God; and the miracles of faith worked by the divine guidance of the life of man.

(R. Seeberg.)

7. Present Tendencies.

Aside from the Ritschlian conception of miracles as striking occurrences with which the experience of God's special help is connected, are two other positions, not wholly to be distinguished from each other, by which miracles are explained. (1) They are regarded as extraordinary events coincident with a religious message, the events being of such a character as to justify the conviction that God wrought them in attestation of the message. This view, suggested by J. B. Mozley (*Miracles*, pp. 5–6, 168, London, 1886), finds many adherents (cf. W. N. Clarke, *Outline of Christian Theology*, p. 133, New York, 1898; G. P. Fisher, *Grounds of Theistic and Christian Belief*, pp. 163 sqq., New York, 1902; E. Y. Mullins, *Why Is Christianity True?* pp. 170–179, Chicago, 1905; G. F. Wright, *Scripture Confirmations of Old Testament History*, pp. 87 sqq., "mediate miracles," Oberlin, 1906; A. H. Strong, *Systematic Theology*, i. 118–119, Philadelphia, 1907). According to this view, miracles are extraordinary events in nature wrought by the same God who is everywhere present and active. They may be traced to natural causes and thus be naturally explained: miracles and natural causes are only different names for the one will of God. All sorts of physical antecedents of miracles are possible; and these antecedents, as well as the miracles, are themselves signs of the authorization of the commission of the leader or teacher. The essential element here is the coincidence. In this way it is supposed that the claims of science and religion are fully acknowledged. (2) The other explanation, akin to the Ritschlian, distinguishes between two aspects of events, according as they occur in a system of law conditioned by antecedent causes—the how; and as they reveal purpose—the wherefore; the causal and the teleological aspect of reality. (a) From the causal point of view, two affirmations are made: first, that of a uniform and comcomitant variation among phenomena; secondly, that of the origination of all phenomena in the immanent activity of God. All events are both natural and supernatural—natural in the mode of their appearance, supernatural in their ultimate ground. Thus a metaphysical basis is laid for the manifestation of free intelligence in the order of the world, and for uniformity in nature which includes even the alleged miracle. If law is the expression of the divine purpose, then no interference from beyond the law is possible. If all the antecedents of an event were known, even the miracle would be explained; for the "all" contains not only the phenomenal antecedents but also the divine will and purpose (cf. B. P. Bowne, *Theism*, pp. 199–247, New York, 1902). (b) Thus the teleological point of view is reached, which admits a different interpretation of events from that offered by the causal relation. Here the question is that of meaning or end. The interest centers in the significance of the event for the religious life. The degree of the significance will determine whether it shall be regarded as a miraculous or as a common event.

The present-day emphasis on the ethical and religious content of Christianity is withdrawing attention from the aspect of miraculousness long associated with it. Irrespective of the difficulties concerning miracles which have arisen from the side of history, science, philosophy, and comparative religion, the tendency is to find what is essential to Christianity in the type and power of the life which Christ both initiates and completes. Hence, it is affirmed that forgiveness of sins, comfort in sorrow, hope in eternal life, impulse to social service, and communion with God are in no way dependent on the common doctrine of miracles as interruptions of the order of nature, or interventions or suspensions of the laws of nature (cf. G. A. Gordon, *Religion and Miracle*, Boston, 1909). C. A. B.

Bibliography: Besides the literature on the life of Christ, in which generally the subject of miracles is fully discussed, and the works on dogmatic theology and Biblical theology, consult: G. Campbell, *A Dissertation on the Miracles*, London, 1846; R. Wardlaw, *On Miracles*, New York, 1853; F. De Quincey, *Hume's Argument against Miracles*, in *Theological Essays*, vol. i., Boston, 1854; B. Powell, *The Order of Nature Considered in Reference to the Claims of Revelation*, London, 1859; B. F. Westcott, *Characteristics of the Gospel Miracles. Sermons preached before the University of Cambridge*, Cambridge, 1859; W. Beyschlag, *Die Bedeutung des Wunders im Christentum*, Berlin, 1863; A. Harvey, *The Miracles of Christ as Attested by the Evangelists*, Boston, 1864; W. M. Taylor, *The Miracles, Helps to Faith, not Hinderances*, Edinburgh, 1865; F. L. Steinmeyer, *Die Wunderthaten des Herrn*, Berlin, 1866, Eng. transl., *The Miracles of Our Lord in Relation to Modern Criticism*, Edinburgh, 1875; J. B Mozley, *Eight Lectures on Miracles*, London, 1867; E. A. Litton, *Miracles*, London, 1868; O. Flügel, *Das Wunder und die Erkennbarkeit Gottes*, Leipsic, 1869; W. Mountford, *Miracles, Past and Present*, Boston, 1870; John H. Newman, *Two Essays on Scripture Miracles, and on Ecclesiastical*, London, 1870; W. Bender, *Der Wunderbegriff des N. T.*, Frankfort, 1871; J. H. Newman, *Two Essays on Miracles*, London, 1873; J. S. Mill, *Nature, the Utility of Religion, Theism; Being Three Essays on Religion*, London, 1874 (against miracles); R. C. Trench, *Notes on the Miracles of Our Lord*, London and New York, 1874; W. R. Cassels, *Supernatural Religion*, 3 vols., London, 1879 (against miracles); W. M. Taylor, *The Gospel Miracles in their Relation to Christ and Christianity*, New York, 1880; J. W. Reynolds, *The Mystery of Miracles*, London, 1881; D. Hume, *An Essay on Miracles*, republished, London, 1882; R. Kübel, *Ueber den christlichen Wunderglauben*, Stuttgart, 1883; J. J. Lias, *Are Miracles Credible?* London, 1883; E. C. Brewer, *A Dictionary of Miracles: Imitative, Realistic and Dogmatic*, Philadelphia, 1884; S. Cox, *Miracles: an Argument*, London, 1884; A. B. Bruce, *The Miraculous Element in the Gospels*, New York, 1886; B. Maitland, *Miracles*, London, 1886; T. W. Belcher, *Our Lord's Miracles of Healing Considered in Relation to Some Modern Objections and to Medical Science, with Preface by Archbishop Trench*, London, 1890; E. A. Abbott, *Philomythus*, London, 1891 (a reply to Newman); G. Stokes, *Natural Theology*, Edinburgh, 1891; J. Hutchinson, *Our Lord's Signs in St. John's Gospel. Discussions chiefly exegetical and doctrinal on the eight Miracles in the Fourth Gospel*, New York, 1892; E. Ménégoz, *La Notion biblique du miracle*, Paris, 1894; A. M. Lépicier, *Del Miracolo, sua natura, sue leggi*, Rome, 1897; F. Barth, *Die Hauptprobleme des Lebens Jesu*, pp. 103 sqq., Gütersloh, 1899; A. T. Lyttelton, *The Place of Miracles in Religion*, London, 1899; J. M. Whiton, *Miracles and Supernatural Religion*, New York, 1903; K. Beth, *Die Wunder Jesu*, Lichterfeld, 1905; J. O. F. Murray, *Spiritual and Historical Evidence for Miracles*, in *Essays on Some Theological Questions*, ed. H. B. Swete, London, 1905; G. Traub, *Die Wunder im N. T.*, Tübingen, 1905; P. Saintyves, *La Miracle et la critique historique*, Paris, 1907; idem, *Le Discernment du miracle*, ib., 1909; A. A. Brockington, *Old Testament Miracles in the Light of the Gospel*, New York, 1907; L. von Gerdtell, *De urchristlichen Wunder vor dem Forum der modernen Weltanschauung*, Stuttgart, 1907; *The Miracles of Jesus, A Series of Expositions*, Manchester, 1907; G. Wobbermin, *Der christliche Gottesglaube*, Berlin, 1907; F. J. Lamb, *Miracle and Science; Bible Miracles examined by the Methods, Rules and Tests of the Science of Jurisprudence as administered in Courts of Justice*, Oberlin, 1909; *DB*, iii. 379–396; *DCG*, 186–191; Vigouroux, *Dictionnaire*, part xxvi. cols. 1110–22.

MIRAMIONES. See Genevieve, Saint, Orders of, 2.

MIRANDOLA, GIOVANNI PICO DELLA. See Pico della Mirandola, Giovanni.

MIRBT, CARL THEODOR: German Lutheran; b. at Gnadenfrei (32 m. s. of Breslau) July 21, 1860. He was educated at the universities of Halle, Erlangen, and Göttingen (Lic. Theol., 1888), and, after a year as privat-docent at the latter institution, was called to Marburg in 1889 as associate professor of church history, being promoted to his present position of full professor of the same subject in the following year. In 1903 he was made a consistorial councilor and a member of the Cassel consistory. He has written *Die Stellung Augustins in der Publizistik des gregorianischen Kirchenstreits* (Leipsic, 1888); *Die Absetzung Heinrichs IV durch Gregor VII.* (1890); *Die Wahl Gregors VII.* (Marburg, 1892); *Die Publizistik im Zeitalter Gregors VII.* (Leipsic, 1894); *Quellen zur Geschichte des Papsttums und des römischen Katholizismus* (Freiburg, 1895; 2d. ed., 1901); *Die preussische Gesandtschaft am Hofe des Papstes* (1899); and *Die katholisch-theologische Fakultät zu Marburg* (Marburg, 1905). He is likewise an associate editor of the *Deutsch-Evangelische Zeitschrift für die Kenntnis und Förderung der deutschen evangelischen Diaspora im Ausland.*

MIRRORS, HEBREW: The use of mirrors among the Hebrews is proved by some late and somewhat enigmatic passages. It can not be held that the context of Isa. iii. 23 forbids the translation of *gilyonim* by "mirrors," since articles of clothing and of mere adornment are mentioned without separation into classes. The singular *gillayon* (Isa. viii. 1) signifies the uncovered, that is, the smoothed, tablet (A. V. "roll"), cf. *galah*, "shear," "shave." Ex. xxxviii. 8, a passage of late date, states that the laver of the tabernacle was made from the looking-glasses of the women who served (A. V. "assembled") in the sanctuary (cf. I Sam. ii. 22). The Targum renders the *re'i* of Job xxxvii. 18 by *ispaklarya*, the Latin *specularia;* the translation "molten mirror" is correctly given by three late commentators on Job (K. Budde, Giessen, 1900; B. Duhm, Tübingen, 1897; and F. Delitzsch, Leipsic, 1902). Mirrors are alluded to in Ecclus. xii. 11, dated about 200 B.C. In the Hebrew text of Ecclesiasticus (ed. H. L. Strack, Leipsic, 1903), mirror is rendered by *raz*, probably a corrupted *re'i;* the Greek version gives *eisoptron.* It may be deduced from the passages cited that mirrors were exclusively or at least usually hand-mirrors for women. They are designated as polished plates in Isa. iii. 23. According to Ex. xxxviii. 8, they were of metal (the Jerusalem Targum translates expressly "*ispaklarya* of brass" and Job xxxvii. 18 asserts that they were "molten." These Old-Testament data are confirmed by other ancient sources, for even in the luxurious homes of the later Romans and Greeks, there were rarely pier-glasses but usually only hand-glasses; and that, even toward the end of antiquity, polished metal plates were still used can be inferred from their liability to become dull (Ecclus. xii. 11; Wisdom, vii. 26, "an unspotted mirror") and also from their imperfect reflection (I Cor. xiii. 12). In Egypt the mirrors were of tin; with the Greeks of brass, silver, gold, etc.; among the Romans commonly of copper, mixed with tin, zinc, and other materials. The Talmud knew only of metal mirrors. Pliny asserts that glass mirrors (unsilvered) were invented in Sidon, but the first certain testimony comes from Alexander Aphrodisiensis at the beginning of the third century. It may be assumed that some of the Hebrew mirrors were fabricated by Hebrew metal-workers while others were imported; for both the Assyrians and the Egyptians used them and Corinth was especially renowned for the manufacture of these articles. (E. König.)

Bibliography: F. Vigouroux, *Dictionnaire de la Bible*, fasc. xxvi., cols. 1123–26, Paris, 1905; E. Gerhard, *Etruskische Spiegel*, 5 vols., Berlin, 1843–67; J. de Witte, *Les Miroirs chez les anciens*, Brussels, 1872; H. J. Van Lennep, *Bible Lands*, ii. 536–537, London, 1875; M. Collignon, *Manuel d'archéologie grecque*, pp. 346 sqq., Paris, 1881; Guhl and Koner, *Leben der Griechen und Römer*, ed. R. Engelmann, pp. 317, 746, 747, Berlin, 1893; *DB*, iii. 396–397; *EB*, iii. 3153; *JE*, viii. 609.

MISCELLANEOUS RELIGIOUS BODIES.

1. Apostolic Christian Church: An organization started about 1850 by a Swiss preacher, S. H. Froelich, who came to the United States and gathered a small company of churches, chiefly among German Swiss immigrants, emphasizing especially the doctrine of entire sanctification. Under the general name of the Apostolic Christian Church, though with no definite ecclesiastical organization, they have grown in numbers until in 1906 there were reported 42 organizations in 11 states, 19 ministers and 69 licentiates, 4,558 members, 44 church edifices with a seating capacity of 11,475, and church property valued at $141,550.

2. Apostolic Faith Movement: A movement originated in the year 1900 by Charles F. Parham and other evangelists, who, after conducting revival services in Topeka, Kan., felt the need of some organization for the securing of the best results and organized the Apostolic Faith Movement. The headquarters are at Los Angeles, Cal., but there are a number of centers from which revival enterprises are started, among them being Houston, Tex., where there is a camp-meeting ground, and at Spokane, Wash. The object of the movement is "the restoration of the faith once delivered to the saints, the old-time religion, camp-meetings, revivals, missions, street and prison work, and Christian unity everywhere." Special attention is paid to "salvation and healing." There is no definite organization, but individuals, preachers, evangelists, and special workers devote their time to the work without salaries or collections of any kind. Foreign missionary work is carried on in Japan, Korea, China, the Philippines, India, Africa, and South America, and in some European countries, by individuals under the supervision of committees which have charge of distributing and forwarding such funds as are committed to them. Their figures are very incomplete. In only a few instances is there any regular membership reported, while no account of funds contributed or expended is given. The statistics of 1906 show 350 members in Washington, 48 in Texas, and 140 in Kansas; 1 church edifice, and property valued at $450.

3. The Armenian Church in the United States: Armenian immigration to the United States can scarcely be said to have commenced before the Russo-Turkish war of 1877 With the failure of the European powers to enforce the conditions of the treaty of Berlin, so far at least as the Armenians were concerned, they began to come in larger numbers, and by 1889 there were several small colonies, mostly in Massachusetts (see ARMENIA, III., § 9). These belonged for the most part to the National or Gregorian Church, as it is often called from the name of Gregory the Illuminator (see ARMENIA, III., § 2), although some identified themselves with the Congregational or Presbyterian churches. For the benefit of the Gregorian communities the patriarch in Constantinople in 1889 sent Rev. Hovsep Sarajian to Worcester, Mass., and a church was built which became the ecclesiastical headquarters for America. Other priests followed as the communities increased in number and size, and in 1906 the catholicos of Echmiadzin, the ecclesiastical head of the Armenian Church, made the United States a missionary diocese, and Father Sarajian was consecrated bishop. In 1902 a special constitution was granted, the bishop was invested with archiepiscopal authority, and seven pastorates were formed, the nuclei of future dioceses. For some time the question of provision for church services was a most difficult one. The Armenian communities were both small and poor, and unable to build church edifices. In 1906 there were three edifices, in Worcester, Mass., New York City, and Fresno, Cal., and plans were being made for other buildings. In other places services have been held in rented halls or private houses, except when churches of other bodies, particularly of the Protestant Episcopal Church, have been placed at the disposal of the priests.

In doctrine and polity the Armenian Church in the United States is in entire accord with the National Church. It accepts the Nicene Creed, without the "filioque," and the canons of the three councils of Nice, Constantinople, and Ephesus, and has a longer creed of its own, in which it makes it clear that while not accepting the formulas of the Council of Chalcedon, as to the two natures of Christ, it believes that he was "perfect God" as well as "perfect man." Seven sacraments are accepted, as in the Greek and Roman Catholic churches. Baptism is by immersion, generally soon after birth, and is followed immediately by confirmation and the administering of the communion in both kinds. All baptized persons, including infants, are then registered as communicants. The Virgin and the saints are venerated.

The government of the Armenian Church centers in the catholicos of Echmiadzin, who is elected by the ecclesiastical and lay representatives of all the Armenian dioceses in the world. In America, besides the archbishop and the resident pastors, subordinate to the catholicos, there are missionary priests and deacons, who have no fixed appointments but care for numerous missionary stations. The principal service is the mass, performed on Sundays and holy days in the classical Armenian language, which differs somewhat in construction from the colloquial language, though so similar in its vocabulary as to be readily understood by educated persons. The church year follows the Julian rather than the Gregorian calendar.

According to the figures furnished at the close of 1906 there were 73 organizations, 19,889 communicants, 3 church edifices, and 60 halls or other buildings. The church edifices seat 1,300 persons, and are valued at $38,000, one of them reporting a debt of $4,000. One church has a parsonage valued at $2,500. Four organizations have Sunday-schools, with 9 officers and teachers and 340 scholars.

4. Christian Congregation: An organization formed in 1899, at Kokomo, Ind., by a company of Christian workers representing different bodies, but predominantly Methodists, for the purpose of securing a broader Christian fellowship and a better system of Christian charity. In general type of doctrine and church organization it is in accord with the Methodist Episcopal Church. In 1906 there were 9 organizations, 395 members, 5 church edifices with a seating capacity of 1,550, church property valued at $7,200, and 7 Sunday-schools with 73 officers and teachers and 332 scholars.

5. Christian Israelite Church: An organization whose principal object is the ingathering of the twelve tribes of Israel, started by John Wroe, of Bowling, Yorkshire, England, in 1822. He taught that the Hebrews of to-day constitute two tribes, that the other ten are scattered among all races, creeds, and nations, being found among the Methodists, Baptists, Lutherans, etc., and that they should all be gathered into one body. A branch was started in New York in 1844. The members believe that the law of Moses should be reestablished, and that by obeying this law men will be made immortal so that their mortal bodies will never see death. All mankind will be saved, but will attain to different degrees of blessedness. They subscribe to the "four books of Moses and the four books of the Gospel," observe the Jewish Sabbath as well as the Christian Sunday, and other Jewish festivals, do not cut either hair or beard, and are opposed to pictures and images. They have preachers but no ordained ministry. In 1906 there were 5 organizations, with 78 members, of whom 45 were males; 1 church edifice in New York City valued at $30,000, 1 Sunday-school with 2 teachers and 12 scholars.

6. Church of Daniel's Band: An organization which includes 4 churches in Michigan and a few in Canada that lay special emphasis on evangelistic work, fellowship, abstinence from excesses, and liberty in the exercise of faith. Organized at Marine City, St. Clair county, Mich., in 1893, they reported, in 1906, 92 church members, 2 church edifices valued at $2,400, 15 ministers, and 1 Sunday-school with 3 teachers and 50 scholars.

7. Colored Primitive Baptists in America: With the reorganization manifest in all departments in the South after the Civil War, the colored Primitive Baptist churches were gathered in separate associations, retaining, however, the same general type of doctrine and church life. Toward the close of the last century a revival movement developed, which resulted in gathering these associations into the body named above, and in infusing into the churches a new life. The older opposition to an educated ministry, to Sunday-schools, missionary societies, state conventions, ministerial support, and the like was broken down, and the motto has been "union, peace, and progress." The doctrinal basis is the Philadelphia Confession of the northern Baptists. In polity also they are in accord with the northern Baptists rather than with the Primitive Baptists. The national convention is an administrative body, having special reference to the varied departments of church, educational, benevolent, and other activity. The young people are organized in the Primitive Baptist Young People's Volunteer Band, which conducts a Young People's and Sunday-school Congress. They have two weekly religious journals published at Huntsville, Ala., and Mexia, Tex., and a Sunday-school paper published at Jacksonville, Fla.

They report for 1906, 797 organizations with 35,076 members, of whom about 12,500 were males. Reports on church buildings, etc., were not complete, only 501 church edifices and 44 halls being given, with a value of $296,539, and indebtedness on 34 edifices to the amount of $6,968. There were 166 Sunday-schools with 911 officers and teachers and 6,224 scholars.

8. Duck River Association of Baptists: An organization arising from a division of the Elk River Association, founded in 1808 in Tennessee, Kentucky, Georgia, and Alabama, and strongly Calvinistic in character. As Methodism and the revival influences which resulted in the organization of the Cumberland Presbyterian Church and the Disciples of Christ spread through the same section, there developed a counter-movement for a stricter discipline and more rigid theology. In this controversy the Elk River Association divided and a minority more in sympathy with milder doctrine organized the Duck River Association. Subsequently other similar associations were formed, each with its own creed, yet so far recognizing their mutual fellowship as to send messengers to the annual meetings. The single churches call themselves Baptist Churches of Christ, and in the report for 1890 a number of these associations were grouped under the head Baptist Church of Christ. As some of them expressed unwillingness to be classed under a definite denominational name, the heading Duck River and Kindred Associations of Baptists was adopted. The other associations are East Union, Ebenezer, Liberty, Mount Pleasant, Mount Zion, and Union. Attempts have been made to bring about union between these associations and the associations of Separate Baptists.

The total number of organizations reported in 1906 by the 7 associations was 93; of these, 92 reported 6,416 members; there were 86 church edifices besides 2 halls, and the seating capacity was 27,508; the total value of church property reported was $44,321, and 3 organizations showed a total debt of $107; there were 9 Sunday-schools with 37 officers and teachers and 402 scholars.

9. Evangelical Union of Bohemian and Moravian Brethren: A small body of churches, most of them in Texas, representing in the United States the Evangelical Union of Bohemian and Moravian Brethren in Austria, the lineal successor of the church of John Huss and Jerome of Prague (see Bohemian Brethren; Unity of the Brethren; Zinzendorf, Nikolaus Ludwig). Only scattered communities held the faith and the name; one of these founded the Unity of the Brethren. After the revolution of 1848 they began to look to America. Some from Bohemia and western Moravia settled in the northern and western states and identified themselves with other bodies. Those from eastern Moravia settled in Texas and preferred to retain the old name for its historic interest as well as because it helped them to preserve their identity. In 1906 there were 15 organizations, 771 members, under the general care of 3 ordained ministers, worshiping in 6 church edifices and 7 halls, church property valued at $13,750, 2 Sunday-schools with 6 officers and teachers and 97 scholars, and 2 parsonages valued at $700. The churches maintain friendly relations with the German Evangelical Synod (q.v.), especially in the use of the educational privileges of that body.

10. Free Christian Zion Church of Christ: A body organized at Redemption, Ark., in 1905, by a small number of colored ministers, chiefly Methodists, in protest against the attempt to tax church members for the support of an ecclesiastical system. Coordinate with this was the feeling that the church itself should care for its poor and needy. The doctrine and polity accord with those of the Methodist churches, the laity having a large share in the general ecclesiastical system. As reported in 1906, there were 15 organizations, 1,835 members, 20 ministers and 10 licentiates, 14 church edifices and 1 hall, church property valued at $5,975, and 7 Sunday-schools with 63 officers and teachers and 340 scholars.

11. Gospel Mission: An association of eight churches in Pennsylvania, organized especially for evangelistic work and the development of Christian fellowship. They have no special system of doctrine or form of church polity. The communities vary in size and are principally evangelistic in their services. The number of members as reported in 1906 was 196; there were 4 church edifices valued at $3,100, 10 ministers, and 9 Sunday-schools with 34 officers and teachers and 245 scholars.

12. Heavenly Recruit Church: A body derived from the Heavenly Recruit Association, organized in 1885 as the result of revival work commenced in 1882 and carried on chiefly by members of Methodist churches. The association grew and a number of churches were formed in other states. Subsequently, dissatisfaction arose and there was division, a part of the churches taking the name Holiness Christian Association, while those in Indiana organized as the Heavenly Recruit Church. In doctrine and polity they are in general accord with the Methodist Episcopal Church, emphasizing especially the doctrine of complete sanctification. In 1906 the church reported 27 organizations, 938 members, 8 church edifices and 15 halls for worship, value of church property $8,950, with a debt of $700 on 3 of the churches, 14 Sunday-schools with 116 teachers and 527 scholars.

13. Hephzibah Faith Missionary Association: An organization formed in 1892, at Glenwood, Ia., by a number of independent churches primarily for the purpose of preaching the doctrine of holiness, but also to carry on general missionary and philanthropic work more efficiently than was possible for them acting separately. They are not an ecclesiastical body, and have no creed. Each local church, usually called an assembly, keeps its own records, but acts in matters affecting all the churches through a central committee located at Tabor, Ia. In 1906 they reported 10 organizations with 293 members; 9 church edifices valued at $11,300; 36 ministers and 39 licentiates; and 9 Sunday-schools with 75 teachers and 402 scholars. Their missionary work was carried on in this country by about 60 persons, including ordained and licensed ministers, evangelists, and deaconesses. They have a missionary training-home with 70 students, and an orphanage with 23 inmates. The association is represented in India, China, Japan, and Africa, where 7 stations are occupied by 24 missionaries. The total amount contributed through the association for the home work is not given; that for the foreign work amounts to about $5,200. There are churches or local organizations using the name but not identified with this association.

14. Holiness Churches: In addition to the Pentecostal Church of the Nazarene (q.v.) there are various small bodies and individual churches which make prominent the doctrine of entire sanctification. Methodist bodies give this point of belief a place in their doctrinal system, holding not to an absolute and sinless perfection, but "a freedom from sin, from evil desires and evil tempers, and from pride." Some, feeling that this doctrine was not sufficiently emphasized, sought those of their own way of thinking and held separate meetings for the promotion of holiness. Some added other peculiarities and stood for the "Fourfold Gospel" or the "Full Gospel," which has been stated as "regeneration for the sinner; sanctification as a second work of grace for the believer; the healing of the bodies of believers in answer to prayer; and the premillennial coming of Jesus Christ as King of this earth." Among those proclaiming the fourfold Gospel is the Christian and Missionary Alliance (q.v.). Single churches also adopted the four principles and then either joined forces in such bodies as the International Apostolic Holiness Union (see below), and various evangelistic associations, or remained ecclesiastically independent. The Pentecostal Church of the Nazarene takes a very moderate position on the last two points. Besides these, however, there is a large number of local organizations popularly designated as Holiness Churches, and known by a great variety of names, such as Holiness Church of God, Apostolic Holiness, Sanctified Church, Fire Baptized Holiness, etc. In general doctrine they are Methodistic, and are active in evangelistic, missionary, and charitable work. On account of the varied forms of organization even an estimate as to their number is scarcely possible, though some place it among the thousands, including not merely the Independent Holiness Churches, but several of the smaller denominations, and a large number of churches which, while not severing their ecclesiastical relations with regular denominations, emphasize the "Fourfold Gospel." It is to be noted that the Independent Holiness Churches are chiefly in the southern states.

15. Independent Congregations: Independent or unattached congregations were first reported in the United States by the census of 1890. There were then 156 independent congregations, besides 231 independent Lutheran organizations. When plans were being formed for getting statistics for the census of 1906 there were many indications that the practise, if not the principle, of independency had gained a still stronger foothold. Special efforts were made to secure returns for all such organizations, with the result that 1,079 such churches were registered, besides a considerable number that were loosely organized in evangelistic associations, and such organizations as the Nonsectarian Churches of Bible Faith, which is practically merely the gathering under one head of organizations which have little more in common than similarity of worship and opposition to ecclesiastical rule. Taking these together there were in 1906 not far from 1,500 local churches which refused to recognize ecclesiastical connection with any regular denomination.

While, in general, this is their chief characteristic, it is possible to arrange them in four classes: (1) churches originally established in newly settled or outlying districts as mission or union Sunday-schools, and which have developed a church life, but on account of the heterogenous component elements have declined to enter any one denomination; (2) churches which use a denominational name, Congregational, Lutheran, etc., but refuse to be included in denominational lists; (3) union churches in which representatives of two or more denominations unite, independently of their denominational relations; (4) churches which are absolutely opposed to any denominational bonds lest the development of their distinctive ideas of church life be hindered. This last is by far the largest class and includes most of the so-called Holiness Churches (see above). While the list of independent congregations includes some of very broad doctrinal views, the great majority appear to be distinctly conservative. Their local organization is very simple, as is also generally their form of worship. In a number of cases their members are largely interested in various missionary and philanthropic movements, but as individuals rather than as organizations. The 1,079 churches reported 73,673 members. Of these, 10,029 were in New York state; 9,431 in Illinois, and 7,586 in Pennsylvania. The number of their church edifices was 812, besides 229 halls, and the value of their church property was $3,934,267.

16. International Apostolic Holiness Union: A body founded by Martin W Knapp, at Cincinnati, O., in 1897, for the purpose of emphasizing the doctrine of holiness, which, in his view, had gradually dropped out of the Methodist Church. The form of organization includes both regular churches and local bands or unions, and corresponds in general to that of the Methodist Episcopal Church. Very few of the ministers have regular salaries, the greater number being supported by free-will offerings. The body emphasizes missionary work at home (in the mountain regions of West Virginia, North Carolina, and Kentucky, and in Oklahoma), and abroad (India, Japan, Korea, South Africa, and China, where there were in 1906 twenty-five missionaries). There are two Bible schools, in North Carolina and Kansas, and a school in Ohio. Three rescue homes and an orphanage are also conducted at an annual cost of about $3,600. As reported in 1906, there were 74 organizations, 2,774 church members, 178 ministers, 44 church edifices and 31 halls, church property valued at $80,150, against which a debt is reported by 23 of the organizations of $13,246, and 68 Sunday-schools with 503 officers and teachers and 3,276 scholars.

17. Lumber River Mission: An organization of five churches in North Carolina, which call themselves Holiness Methodist churches, but do not affiliate with other Methodist bodies. The special purpose is to carry on evangelistic work in the lumber section of the state. In 1906 they reported 265 members, 5 ministers and 3 licentiates, 5 church edifices valued at $3,000, and 5 Sunday-schools with 28 teachers and 256 scholars.

18. Metropolitan Church Association: An organization developed from the Metropolitan Methodist church, which was itself the result of revival meetings held in 1894 on a vacant lot in the densely populated district of Chicago. Emphasizing the doctrine of holiness, the workers did not find the most cordial welcome in the churches, and rented halls, theaters, and other buildings; at last a somewhat famous resort at Waukesha, Wis., was purchased and made the headquarters for the movement, which came to be known as the "Burning Bush." The special feature of the association is its revival work, which extends all over the United States and into foreign lands; it also has a number of departments of educational and philanthropic character in the establishment at Waukesha. No salaries are paid to workers in any department, whether at home or abroad, the entire enterprise being conducted on the "faith" basis. Foreign work is carried on in India, Africa, and Wales; the number of missionaries being reported as 15. During 1906 some $30,000 was expended for the development of the work. The statistics for 1906 were: 6 organizations, 466 members, 19 ministers, 4 church edifices with a seating capacity of 2,025, church property valued at $118,300; 4 Sunday-schools with 29 officers and teachers and 360 scholars.

19. Missionary Church Association: An organization formed in 1898 by a number of persons resident in Berne, Ind., who desired to emphasize their belief in the "Fourfold Gospel" (i.e., "regeneration for the sinner, sanctification as a second work of grace for the believer, the healing of the bodies of the believers as an answer to prayer, and the premillennial coming of Jesus Christ as king of this earth"), to reach neglected parts of the home field with this gospel, and to carry it to foreign fields. Its general doctrinal status is essentially that of the Christian and Missionary Alliance (q.v.), and it carries on some of its work through that society. It differs from it, however, in having a regular church organization, which the Alliance has not. The headquarters are at Berne, Ind., and the 32 churches reported in 1906 were chiefly in Indiana and adjoining states. The total number of members given was 1,256; there were 19 church edifices and 12 halls, a seating capacity in churches of 4,735, church property $33,135; 34 Sunday-schools with 271 officers and teachers and 1,916 scholars.

20. New Apostolic Church: An organization of essentially the same type, with the same doctrine and in all respects but one the same polity, as the Catholic Apostolic Church (q.v.). The difference between the two lies in the interpretation of the apostleship, the New Apostolic Church holding that there may be any number of apostles (i.e., more than twelve), that there should always be an apostleship among men, and to this end the living apostles may and should select bearers to the title according to their needs. As the apostles of the Catholic Apostolic Church diminished in numbers, a bishop in Germany named Schwarz consulted in regard to their successors, claiming that the spirit of the apostles had often incited new selections. He was excommunicated, but subsequently a priest named Preuss was selected "through the spirit of prophecy" in 1862, and with him the New Apostolic Church commenced. Schwarz was afterward selected as apostle. The first church in the United States was organized in 1897, and in 1906 there were 13 organizations in 8 states, 19 ministers, 2 church edifices valued at $8,500, and 3 Sunday-schools with 10 officers and teachers and 150 scholars.

21. The Servian Orthodox Church. See Servian Orthodox Churches in America.

22. United American Free-will Baptists, Colored: A denomination organized in 1900. Previous to that date the churches were included in the general reports for the Free Baptists or Free-will Baptists, but within recent years there has been a desire for a separate organization. In general they accord with the Free-will Baptists, but in polity are more closely organized, somewhat after the Methodist type, having a system of quarterly, annual, and general conferences, with a graded authority. The conferences have no jurisdiction over individual church members, but if upon investigation it appears that a church has failed to accord with the standards, it may be dropped from the conference. It is undertaking educational work, and has a college at Kinston, N. C., and another at Dawson, Ga. There were, in 1906, 251 organizations with a membership of 14,489, 560 ministers, a considerable number of whom were engaged in general evangelistic work, 149 church edifices, and 8 halls, church property valued at $79,278, with a small amount of indebtedness, 100 Sunday-schools with 382 officers and teachers and 2,207 scholars.

23. Vedanta Society: An organization which is the outcome of a series of lectures on Vedanta philosophy in New York in 1894 by Swami Vivekananda (q.v.). It was first organized in 1898, and gradually became strong enough to have centers in other cities, Pittsburg, San Francisco, and Los Angeles, besides various retreats. Without attempting to form a new sect or creed, the society aims to set forth the end of wisdom, how it is attained, and give to religion a scientific and philosophic basis. It publishes works on religious philosophy and furnishes lectures by various Vedantists.

24. Voluntary Missionary Society in America: A body organized in 1900 by a few colored churches in Alabama, representing different denominations, as a protest against the principle of financial assessments for the support of the ministry, which had been so generally adopted. In doctrine and local church government they differ in no respect from the Methodist or Baptist churches about them, but insist on absolutely free-will offerings for their church work. In 1906 the society reported 3 organizations with 425 members; 3 church edifices, 2 of which were valued at $2,400, while 1 showed a debt of $1,000; 11 ministers and 18 licentiates; 3 Sunday-schools with 21 teachers and 390 scholars.

E. M. BLISS.

MISERERE: Designation of Psalm l. as a liturgically chanted prayer, the name being taken from the first word in the Latin translation. The Greek Church employs this psalm in the midnight office, following vespers, in the third of the canonical hours; at confession, unction, and burial of the dead. The Roman Church uses it at matins and lauds, during Sundays of the Septuagesimal season, and on all week-days except at Eastertide and in the office of the dead. But some churches also use it in the latter office and at vespers, and in the hours from Maundy Thursday to Easter Saturday. Furthermore, at the laying of the corner-stone of a church, consecration of an altar, cemetery, or house, it is used as choral chant. It likewise ushers in the consecration of a bell; and in the rite of blessing the fields it follows immediately the introductory public *confiteor*. In connection with the reconciliation of penitents it was recited over them by the bishop, along with two other psalms (lvi., lvii.).

In the Evangelical Church, the *miserere* has survived as a liturgical prayer where the old liturgic tradition is fostered; and its more general restoration is desired. Its normal rendering is that of psalmody; although from of old it has been likewise an object of artistic elaboration. Masters of all times and schools have written beautiful musical settings for the *miserere*. On the one hand, these compositions more or less closely adhere to the psalmodic standard of presentation; on the other hand, their sole aim is to give musical expression to the fundamental tone and thoughts of the text. Especially famous is its use in the pope's chapel at Rome in connection with the offices of Holy Week. Of twelve compositions preserved for this purpose, the three nowadays usually rendered are those of Gregorio Allegri, Tommaso Bay, and Giuseppi Baini.

H. A. KÖSTLIN†.

BIBLIOGRAPHY: J. G. Mettenleiter, *Enchiridion chorale*, pp. clxxvii. sqq., 74 sqq., Regensburg, 1853; L. Spohr, *Selbstbiographie*, ii. 37 sqq., Cassel, 1861; P. Mendelssohn-Bartholdy, *Reisebriefe von Felix Mendelssohn-Bartholdy*, pp. 122 sqq., 163 sqq., Leipsic, 1862; C. Proske, *Musica divina*, iv. 209 sqq., Berlin, 1863; G. Grove, *Dictionary of Music and Musicians*, vol. ii., s.v., London, 1880; F. X. Haberl, *Officium hebdomadis sanctæ*, Regensburg, 1887; V. Thalhofer, *Handbuch der katholischen Liturgik*, ii. 370, 373, 424, 453, Freiburg, 1890; *KL*, viii. 1555-59; and the literature under BREVIARY; and PENITENTIAL PSALMS.

MISHNA. See TALMUD.

MISSA. See MASS.

MISSAL (Lat. *Missalis [Liber]*, *Missale*): The office-book of the Roman Catholic Church, containing the liturgy of the Mass (q.v.). The name came into use in the eighth century, superseding the earlier term "sacramentary," which was applied to a book giving the rites and prayers for all the sacraments. At first other books also had to be used for a proper celebration of the Eucharist, such as the antiphonary, lectionary, evangelistary, etc. A missal containing all the forms of the mass was called complete or plenary (*missale plenarium*). Of course the missal for many centuries was only in manuscript and, as was inevitable, these manuscripts differed more or less. But when printing was discovered there was opportunity to produce a standard and uniform text. So the Council of Trent decreed such an edition, and the pope appointed a commission to prepare it and when it appeared accompanied it by a bull dated July 14, 1570. This edition has undergone revision in 1604, 1634 (see MASS, II., 4, § 2) and 1884. (Cf. W. H. J. Weale, *Bibliographia liturgica. Catalogus missalium ritus Latini ab anno M. CCCC. LXXV impressorum*, London, 1886; A. Ebner, *Quellen und Forschungen zur Geschichte und Kunstgeschichte des Missale Romanum im Mittelalter*, Freiburg, 1896). Latin editions of the missal are numerous (e.g., F. Pustet, 9th ed., Regensburg, 1904), as well as translations into the modern languages—e.g., *The Roman Missal for the Use of the Laity* (London, 1806, 1852), and *The Missal for the Use of the Laity* by F. C. Husenbeth (London, 1853, 1903).

MISSION: The term used by Roman Catholics to express what Protestants style revival services, in which the principal appeal is to the emotions.

MISSIONARY CHURCH ASSOCIATION. See MISCELLANEOUS RELIGIOUS BODIES, 19.

MISSIONS TO THE HEATHEN.

[The present article deals with missions, Catholic and Protestant, to non-Christian peoples, considering especially the basis, history, results, and methods of this work. Various aspects of missions, especially of home missions, are treated in the articles CITY MISSIONS; EMIGRANTS AND IMMIGRANTS, MISSION WORK AMONG; HARMS, GEORG LUDWIG DETLEV THEODOR; HOME MISSIONS; INDIANS OF NORTH AMERICA, MISSIONS TO; INNERE MISSION; JEWS, MISSIONS TO THE; and SLAVIC MISSIONS IN THE UNITED STATES; and in the biographical articles on the missionaries who gave their efforts to the Church.]

A. Roman Catholic Missions.

[The figures enclosed in parentheses in the following summaries give for purposes of comparison the corresponding data of the Protestant Missions, or, as the author prefers to designate them, "Evangelical," an objectionable term in its implications, though frequently used and appropriate if properly defined.]

I. Introduction: According to the Roman Catholic conception, the missionary task consists in the Catholicizing of non-Catholic peoples, while Protestants understand by it the Christianizing of non-Christians. In conformity with this view, this treatment will deal with the work of Roman Catholics among the heathen. It is, however, difficult to carry out this distinction, since efforts are made in the missionary fields not only occasionally to convert Europeans, but also to draw over native Evangelical converts to the Roman Catholic Church [the counterpart to the Protestant propaganda]. Those who are expelled or are dissatisfied furnish a welcome excuse for this work, and an excessive lenity toward unchristian customs serves as a temptation. It therefore happens that among the Roman Catholic converts from heathenism, many are counted who are gathered from Evangelical missions. Besides the Congregation de propaganda fide in Rome, where all the threads of the widely diffused Roman missions are brought together, there are in the different Roman Catholic countries missionary societies. Thus there is the Xavier Society or Society for the Propagation of Faith, founded in 1822 in Lyons; branch societies exist in most Roman Catholic countries. The journal of the society, the "Year Book," appears in various languages. The contributions reach the sum of from one and a quarter to one and a half million dollars annually. Others are the Society of Foreign Missions (Paris, 1820); the Leopoldinische Stiftung (Vienna, 1829); the Society of Holy Childhood (Paris, 1843) for the rescue of heathen children, who are baptized when in danger of death. In fifty years, twelve million children were baptized (mostly in China) and sixteen and one-half million dollars were expended by the society. Missionary seminaries exist in Paris, Lyons, Milan, Verona and Rome. England also has one: St. Joseph of Mill Hill. The seminary at Steyl, Holland, is principally for the education of German missionaries. Recently several mission homes have been founded in Germany to provide for the German colonies. The greater number of missionaries come, however, from the congregations, many of which serve the heathen mission exclusively; for instance, the Congregation of the Sacred Heart of Mary (1841; later combined with that of the Holy Spirit); the Marists in Lyons and Paris; the Congregation of Picpus (Congregation of the Sacred Heart of Jesus and Mary); the order of the Oblates of the Immaculate Conception of Mary; in Algiers, the Fathers of the Holy Spirit (called the White Fathers); in Paris, the Lazarists. The old orders also—Dominicans, Franciscans (Minorites), Capuchins, Carmelites, and others—share in the work. Many of these orders have special missionary fields assigned to them, and have their procurators with the Propaganda. Others assume an auxiliary position, in that they supply the missions with lay brothers in great numbers for teaching, the care of the sick, work of civilization, and similar tasks. Many female orders work in this manner and send out hosts of sisters as missionaries.

II. Separate Fields of Labor. 1. **Africa:** The Christianity which was planted in the fifteenth century in the coast region by the Portuguese through the Dominicans and Franciscans rapidly declined with the downfall of the Portuguese power, and only slight traces remain of it, obscurely intermixed with the older heathenism. In the eighteenth century, in connection with the French possessions in Senegambia, the Roman Catholic mission was resumed. It first became active when the Congregation of the Immaculate Heart of Mary (founded by Father Liebermann, who was stimulated by the success of the Evangelical mission) took up the work in the apostolic vicariate constituted in 1842.

1. West Africa.

In the apostolic vicariate of **Senegambia,** with the apostolic prefecture of Senegal, the preparatory work of teaching and the care of orphans occupied the leading place. In one seminary, natives are educated as priests; besides this, some translations are made into the languages of the country and the institution does its own printing. The results seem slight, since in 1886 the number of Roman Catholics was given at a higher figure (12,000) than at present. The apostolic prefecture of **Guinea,** in the south, was established in 1897. For a long time previous the Evangelical mission on the Rio Pongas had worked in this field. In the vicariate of **Sierra Leone** the converts are mostly from the already evangelized population of the English colony. The vicariate of the **Ivory Coast,** founded in 1895 by separation from the foregoing, is still in its beginnings. The prefecture of the **Gold Coast** has been for a long time a successful Evangelical mission field. In 1879 the Fathers of the Holy Spirit entered it and later it was ceded to the Lyons Seminary. The prefecture of **Togo,** in the German protectorate, is an old Evangelical missionary field, but since 1892 the Steyl Mission House has sent missionaries there. The prefecture of **Dahomey** embraces the French protectorate, and was founded in 1882. The vicariate of **Benin** includes, since 1889, Lagos and the hinterland, where from the middle of the nineteenth century the Church Missionary Society has been very successful. The prefecture on the **Lower Niger** and that on the **Upper Niger** (Lokoja) are both in older English fields of labor. The prefecture of **Kamerun** was founded in 1890 in the German protectorate, where was an old field of the English Baptists, which was transferred to the Basel Mission. The totals for this region are: 73 stations (237), 185 priests (216), 7 native priests (252), 112 lay brothers, 226 sisters, 169 schools (729), 11,687 scholars (42,869), among these about 3,000 girls (15,440), 51,725 Roman Catholics (170,705 Christians). In 37 orphan asylums and 24 other institutions, there are over 1,300 children, many of whom have been freed by purchase.

Through the favor of the king of Portugal and the ardent zeal of the Inquisition, the old mission had great apparent success in the kingdom of the Kongo; this, however, was followed in the eighteenth century by a complete reversion to heathenism, with the retention of Christian forms, as soon as the Portuguese withdrew. In 1865, the Roman mission was taken up again by the Congregation of the Holy Spirit. On the **Gabun,** a countermission to that of the American Protestants was started in 1842.

2. Western Central Africa.

The vicariate of Gabun, on the boundary of Kamerun, has its most successful station in the model colony of Libreville. Of the other nine stations, some are far in the interior, where they compete with the Protestant mission which has been taken over by the Paris society. It has 34 priests, 20 lay brothers, 27 sisters, 12,000 Roman Catholics. The vicariates of the **Lower French Kongo** and of the **Upper French Kongo** are both entrusted to the Congregation of the Holy Spirit. From Brazzaville, the seat of the vicar of the Upper Kongo, the work is carried on among the cannibal tribes living on the Ubanghi. They report 14 scholars, 50 priests, 3,500 Catholics. The vicariate of the **Belgian Kongo** (northern part) has 15 stations of the Congregation Scheutveld on the great river up to Stanley Falls, with 62 priests and 3,516 Catholics. The vicariate of the **Upper Kongo** (eastern part of Kongo Free State) is assigned to the White Fathers who work with 16 priests in 5 stations and have, in addition to 2,371 converts, over 5,000 candidates for baptism (1901). The prefecture **Uelle,** on the river of the same name, founded in 1898, has 2 stations of the Belgian Premonstrants with 12 priests and 600 converts. The prefecture on the **Lower Kongo** embraces the region of the old Kongo Mission, with 9 stations, 21 priests, and 5,689 Catholics. The prefecture of **Upper Cimbebasia** in Benguella is under the Fathers of the Holy Spirit, and has 6 stations with 16 priests and 5,000 converts. The totals are 67 stations (67), 204 priests (167), 4,070 scholars (6,737), among these 948 girls (2,845), 39,015 Roman Catholics (11,354).

The prefecture of **Lower Cimbebasia** in the northern part of German Southwest Africa has been since 1892 a field of the Oblates of the Immaculate Conception, as is also the vicariate of the **Orange River.** In **Cape Colony** there are the vicariates of the western and eastern districts between which lies the prefecture of the central district. The results, since 1837, appear to be slight. After completing the imperfect returns, the number of colored Roman Catholics may be estimated at 2,400. The propaganda here seems to be carried on principally among the whites, besides which there is great activity in education. The vicariate of **Natal** has been since 1850 in the hands of the Oblates of the Immaculate Conception, and the German Trappists have extensive agricultural and industrial enterprises. The vicariate of the **Orange Free State** (now East Colony) has been assigned, since 1884, to the above-named, as has the prefecture of **Basutoland,** where a successful French Protestant mission has operated since 1883; the greater part of the 6,000 Catholics now counted were probably derived from its adherents. The prefecture of the **Transvaal** has been under the same congregation since 1886. How many Europeans are among the 6,200 Roman Catholics is not apparent.

3. South and East Africa.

Totals for South Africa are: 82 stations (580), 174 priests (574), 161 schools (1,400), 7,493 scholars (87,421)*, among these 3,565 girls (36,333), 12,200 colored Roman Catholics (333,984). In East Africa, with eastern Central Africa, is the **Zambesi** mission of the Jesuits (since 1879), bounded by the Transvaal and by the Kongo Free State, with 3 stations and 1,200 converts. The number of native converts is unknown. The prefecture of **Nyassa,** west of the lake, has been a field of the White Fathers since 1897. The prefecture of **Southern Zanzibar,** in the southeastern part of German East Africa, is under the German Benedictines. In the vicariate of **Tanganyika,** on the eastern shore of the lake, the White Fathers have their seminary. It reports 2,436 catechumens. The vicariate of **Northern Zanzibar** embraces the northeastern part of German East Africa and the eastern portion of the British sphere of influence, and is worked by the Congregation of the Holy Spirit and the Trappists. There is great activity in education, and the number of Roman Catholics increased rapidly from their 5,000 scholars. On the west this vicariate is bounded by **Uganda,** where there are the following missionary districts: The vicariate of the **Upper Nile** under the English Brotherhood of Mill Hill; the vicariate of the **Northern Victoria Nyanza,** under the White Fathers; and the vicariate of the **Southern Victoria Nyanza.** The Roman mission had reaped a rich harvest from the remarkable movement of Christianization initiated by the older Protestant mission among the Baganda, and they have also made a clever use of the political conditions. The statistics give, for North-

* Statistics are lacking in reference to the former Boer Republics.

ern Victoria **Nyanza** alone, 39,586 Roman Catholics and 166,150 catechumens. The vicariate of **Unianyembe** in German East Africa is under the White Fathers, with 1,133 converts, 6,755 catechumens. For East Africa the totals are: 63 stations (128), 162 priests (239), 89 lay brothers, 64 sisters, 107 schools (227), 7,771 scholars (33,050), among these 3,578 girls (11,852), 69,288 adherents (46,639 Christians).

4. North Africa, African Islands.

The vicariate of the **Galla** regions is bounded by that of North Zanzibar. The Capuchins have been at work there since 1846. The vicar has his seat in Harrar, and reports one seminary, 7,000 converts. The prefecture of **Erythræa,** in the Italian protectorate, was transferred in 1894 to the Capuchins as a branch of the vicariate of **Abyssinia.** There the Lazarists have worked since 1838 under serious difficulties. During the conflicts with the Italians, the mission was interrupted. The Ethiopic ritual is permitted here.

After the separation from Erythræa (with 7,900 adherents) there remain 4,000 converts; formerly 30,000 were counted. The vicariate of **Egypt** has a Roman Catholic population of 78,580, of whom 56,000 follow the Coptic rite and 20,500 the Latin. There are numerous stations of various congregations. The vicariate of the **Nile Delta** is especially in the charge of the Lyons mission. The vicariate of **Tripoli** has been since 1654 a missionary field of the Franciscans, and reports 7,450 adherents. In the vicariate of **Morocco** the Franciscans were active in the Middle Ages. The mission was renewed in 1859, and reports 6,260 converts.

In the prefecture of the **Sudan** Austrian priests began the work about the middle of the last century on the White Nile; the task was transferred to the missionary seminary of Verona in 1872. Because of the war with the Mahdi the work was abandoned for a long period, and it was resumed only in 1898 with the occupation of **Omdurman.** The vicariate of the **Sahara** has been occupied since 1868 by the White Fathers, whose work is largely preparatory. Of all the Roman Catholic missions in North Africa only the last-named and those to the Galla can be looked upon as real missions (among non-Christians). On this basis there are reckoned 15 stations, 45 priests, 14 lay brothers, 24 sisters, 18 schools, 574 scholars, 175 girls (?), and 7,000 converts. The *Missiones Catholicæ* report 108,930 of whom the greater part by far did not come from heathenism but represent those drawn from other Christian confessions and their descendants. In the African Islands the prefecture of **Annobom, Corisko and Fernando Po** is worked by Spanish missionaries who report 3,400 converts. The vicariate of **North Madagascar** is occupied by priests of the Holy Spirit. The vicariate of **South Madagascar** affords work for the Lazarists. In the vicariate of **Central Madagascar** the Jesuits have worked for a long time as competitors of the Evangelical mission. As early as 1886, 84,000 Roman Catholics were reported there, later only 41,135. Since the French conquest the communities have grown considerably, as the Evangelical Christians, threatened with severe pressure from without, were led in great numbers to Catholicism. The last statement of the *Missiones Catholicæ* gives 61,500 communicants and 258,956 catechumens. Recently the civil authorities have given less aid to the mission. In the prefecture of **Mayotta Nossibé** and the **Comores** there are many colored Christians from Réunion, who can not be regarded as fruits of the mission of to-day and are therefore not counted here.

The totals for the islands are: 28 stations (85), 90 priests (88), 82 lay brothers, 61 sisters, 863 schools (2,247), 148,503 scholars (136,980), among these 68,509 girls (34,201), 64,900 Roman Catholics (138,216); and for all Africa 328 stations (1,070), 833 priests (1,275 ordained Evangelical missionaries), 13 native priests * (890), 796 lay brothers, 927 sisters, 1,382 schools (4,718); 187,105 scholars (307,357), among these 80,981 girls (98,766), 242,136 Roman Catholics (699,899).

2. Asia: The Roman Catholic mission in Asia Minor, Mesopotamia, Syria, Palestine, Arabia, and Persia (with 145,580 adherents) is here omitted on the ground that the work in these countries is directed only to the winning of Christians from other confessions (Syrians, Chaldeans, Armenians), as is done in part by the Protestants who work there.

1. Eastern and Southern India.

With the Portuguese colonization in the sixteenth century, a mission of the Franciscans and Dominicans was immediately combined, but proved unsuccessful. When, in 1534, the bishopric of Goa was erected but few communities existed in spite of the efforts of the Inquisition. Francis Xavier (q.v.), who arrived here in 1542 with two Jesuits, worked chiefly among the degenerate and coarsely immoral white population. It was only in the southeastern region of India, Tinnevelli, whither the Portuguese had gone to give aid against the Mohammedan conquerors, that Xavier succeeded in baptizing great numbers of heathen from among the lower castes—10,000 in one month. He had similar success in Madura and Travancore. It is, however, characteristic that Xavier left this field at the end of a few years in order to labor elsewhere, and begged the king of Portugal to transfer the work of spreading Christianity to the secular officials. Other Jesuits came, however, but their work led to the planting of only the outward forms of the Roman Catholic Church. When Goa was raised to an archbishopric in 1557, 300,000 Catholics were counted in the Portuguese colony, and this number was notably increased in 1599 by the incorporation of a number of Christians of St. Thomas of Melapur (see NESTORIANS). Up to this time the converts had come from the lowest castes; but after 1606, Roberto de' Nobili was able to bring the Brahmins into the Roman Catholic Church. As was the case with Hindu founders of sects, he gained followers (30,000). It is true that his policy of compromise was condemned by the pope, but it was abandoned only after a long resistance on the part of the Jesuits. In northern India they gained influence with the Grand Mogul Akbar, but had no permanent success. With the founding of the Propaganda (q. v.), the work was taken up in many other parts of India and to a certain extent by other congregations (Carmelites and Capuchins). In the eighteenth century, the political conditions were unfavorable to the mission. With the suppression of the order of Jesus it nearly died out and there were few conversions. The masses of the Roman Catholics were neglected and constituted only a caste among the others. In the nineteenth century the mission was

* The statistics appear to be incomplete.

indeed revived, but the conflicts of the papacy with the Portuguese crown were for a long time a great hindrance to its success, until these disputes were settled by the concordat of 1886. The archdiocese of Goa, as well as the dioceses of Daman, Kotchin, and St. Thomas of Melapur, with 534,000 souls under the primate of Goa (patriarch of India), have remained under Portuguese jurisdiction. The other regions of British India are now subject to the Curia. The earlier apostolic vicariates have been changed into bishoprics, a few into archbishoprics. The largest number of Roman Catholics is found in the diocese of Madura, which stretches from Cape Comorin nearly to the river Cavery. More than four per cent of the Tamil population are Roman Catholics; the episcopal seat is Trichinopoli. In fifteen years, the number of converts had increased by twenty-five per cent. On the northern boundary is the archdiocese of Pondicherry, where adherents come principally from the French colonies. The southern portion was detached in 1899 as the diocese of Kumbakonam. The archdiocese of Madras embraces the northern part of the land of the Tamils and the southern part of that of the Telugus, while the diocese of Koimbatur includes the western portion of the land of the Tamils and is bounded by Madras. Nearly half of the Hindu Roman Catholics (forty-one per cent) belong to the above-mentioned dioceses, although the number of stations and priests is only a quarter of the aggregate.

On the west coast of India the Roman Catholics of Goa predominate. There are, however, in this region the following dioceses directly depending from Rome: Quilon in Travancore; on its northern boundary the archdiocese of Verapoli, which extends into Malabar. In both the United Syrians predominate. The entire coast region up to the territory of Goa is included in the diocese of Mangalur, in which the Jesuits are zealous rivals of the Evangelical Basel Mission. Beyond the Ghats lies the bishopric of Mysore, which, extending beyond the state of the same name, embraces peoples of various languages. Hyderabad is the last diocese in the region of the Dravidic peoples.

2. Western and Northern India.

Among the Arian population, the archdiocese of Calcutta stands out as the most successful. Above all, great numbers of the hill people of Chota Nagpur, among whom the Evangelical Gossner Mission has worked for many years, have been won for Rome, principally by means of promises touching their social standing. The greater laxity permitted has also drawn many from the Evangelical Christians to the Roman Catholics. As suffragan bishoprics Dacca and Krishnagar are detached from the archbishopric. The latter includes Lower Bengal as well as the eastern coast region of the Bay of Bengal as far as Akyab, with a Burmese population, and also extends up into the mountains, where dwell various aboriginal tribes. The greater number of stations are in places where Baptists had already been active at an earlier time. Krishnagar, on the other hand, is a district north of Calcutta where, in 1839, thousands joined the Evangelical Church as a result of a remarkable movement. Later, many fell away, and this brought considerable accessions to the Roman Catholic mission. Assam is, since 1889, an apostolic vicariate; here the Roman mission has been less successful in its appeals to converts of the Evangelical missions here. The bishopric of Allahabad embraces the southeastern half of the United Provinces and Oudh. The Hindus and Mohammedans are unreceptive.

Population in thousands.	Missionary Field.	Cath.	St.	Ch.	Sch.	Sem.	P.	N.P.	O.A.	Congregation.
5,000	1. D. Madura	206,000	37	980	239		51	24	10	Jesuits
5,000	2. Ad. Pondicherry	133,770	51	275	80	1	77	27	19	Paris Seminary
3,000	3. D. Kumbakonam	85,000	27	502	45		19	17	4	Paris Seminary
7,076	4. Ad. Madras	44,870	29	142	76	1	23	22	6	Secular priests and Brothers of Mill Hill
2,028	5. D. Coimbatore	35,870	22	114	59	1	36	8	8	Paris Seminary
1,210	6. D. Quilon	87,000	29	167	?	1	16	28	3	Bare-footed Carmelites
1,200	7. Ad. Verapoli	59,700	41	53	149	1	13	32	5	Bare-footed Carmelites
3,709	8. D. Mangalore	83,690	34	73	64	1	34	47	15	Jesuits
5,500	9. D. Mysore	41,170	27	97	71	1	47	10	15	Paris Seminary
11,054	10. D. Hyderabad	12,590	11	45	30		19		5	Milan Seminary
21,000	11. Ad. Calcutta	45,290	32	290	127		77	27	7	Jesuits
17,000	12. D. Dacca	11,000	6	22	15		8		8	Brothers of the Holy Cross
15,000	13. D. Krishnagar	4,050	6	43	18		8		6	Milan Seminary
7,000	14. D. Assam	1,340	7	9	9		9			Soc. of the Divine Redeemer
38,147	15. D. Allahabad	6,420	15	32	27		19	5	6	Capuchins
13,000	16. Pf. Bettiah	4,025	11	11	13		15		11	Capuchins
25,000	17. Ad. Agra	8,095	24	36	19	1	35		12	Capuchins
14,200	18. Pf. Rajputana	3,650	9	14	5	1	12	2	5	Capuchins
13,600	19. D. Lahore	3,590	13	20	22		23		4	Capuchins
2,000	20. Pf. Kafiristan and Kashmir.	3,000	10	11	4		14		6	St. Joseph's of Mill Hill
12,380	21. Ad. Bombay	16,160	27	46	23		51	22	2	Jesuits
7,000	22. D. Puna	13,000	22	38	98		21	10	2	Jesuits
15,500	23. D. Nagpur	8,000	10	28	15		20	5	11	Salesians
9,000	24. D. Vizagapatam	12,915	14	59	25		18			Salesians
254,604		930,195	514	3,107	1,233	9	665	286	174	
	Under Portuguese jurisdiction	534,000								
	Catholics in Western India	1,464,195								
	Evangelical	776,562	719		6,866		1,057	884		

Cath. = Roman Catholics, St. = stations, Ch. = churches, Sch. = schools, Sem. = seminaries, P. = priests, N.P. = native priests, O.A. = orphan asylums, D. = diocese, Ad. = archdiocese, Pf. = prefecture.

A detached prefecture is that of Bettiah, named after a successful station with extensive benevolent institutions. To it three districts and even Nepal are assigned. The northwestern half of the United Provinces includes the bishopric of Agra, where the Roman mission was active two and a half centuries ago, but had small success. The prefecture of Rajputana, with its seat in Ajmir, was separated in 1892. The diocese of Lahore also, formerly the vicariate of the Punjab, has been detached from Agra, from which the prefectures Kafiristan and Kashmir were separated later. The archdiocese of Bombay embraces Sindh, the northern Mahratta country and the intervening region. The rest of the Mahratta country has been detached as the diocese of Puna. To the east of this are the dioceses of Nagpur and Vizagapatam. In Nagpur, where 8,000 Roman Catholics were counted, there were, in 1900, no less than 30,827 baptisms. It is true that 28,930 baptisms, administered to children in peril of death, are included.

The statistical summary, on p. 398, of the missions in India is taken from the *Missiones Catholicæ*. It should be remarked that among Roman Catholics, Europeans and Eurasians are included; their number is placed at 79,661, according to the census of 1901. In this way the number of native-born Roman Catholics is reduced to 805,534. The Roman Catholics under Portuguese jurisdiction are given in the same source at 534,000. This statement can not be checked, nor can any figures be obtained in regard to other missionary work in the various fields. In all, the separate reports account for 398 lay brothers and 1873 sisters; among the latter are many native nuns.

3. Ceylon. Ceylon, as a British Crown Colony, is not connected with the Empire of India. Roman Catholicism gained much ground here under the Portuguese rule (1517–1658); during the Dutch sovereignty (until 1796), the Reformed religion was introduced by pressure from without. When the English brought religious freedom, it was not difficult to lead back great numbers of these migratory Christians to the Roman Catholic Church. Therefore, the Roman Catholics who are to-day in Ceylon are only to a small extent the result of modern Roman missions. There are the following dioceses:

Diocese.	Population in thousands.	Cath.	St.	Ch.	Sch.	Sem.	P.	N.P.	O.A.	Congregation
Ad. Colombo	1,083	198,120	46	271	661	2	80	14	10	Of the Immaculate Conception
D. Jaffna	392	42,500	23	202	108	1	34	10	2	Of the Immaculate Conception
D. Kandy	633	21,150	11	60	24	1	10	19	5	Benedictines
D. Galle	748	6,300	5	37	34		12			Jesuits
D. Trinkomallie ...	159	7,150	3	22	20		8			Jesuits
	2,015	275,220	88	592	847	4	144	43	17	
Evangel. mission ..		31,953	45		861		49	95		

In addition there are 70 lay brothers and 308 sisters, the latter principally natives. The number of Roman Catholics has especially increased in the archdiocese of Colombo, where in 1889 there were 139,978, and in 1868, 102,222.

4. Eastern Asia. In **Burma**, where formerly different congregations had worked, without noteworthy success, Romanism was first able to record important results under English rule.

There are here three vicariates: **North Burma** (6,000 converts), **South Burma** (41,000 converts, among these not a few formerly Evangelical Karens), and **East Burma** (9,600 converts). The two former are assigned to the Paris Seminary and the last to the Milanese. But of a population of 9,930,000 there are 56,600 Roman Catholics, 46 stations, 154 schools, 3 seminaries, 70 priests, 13 native priests, 42 lay brothers, and 62 sisters. **Siam** had, in the eighteenth century, a flourishing Roman Catholic mission, which died out under the Burmese rule, but was revived in 1840. Now it is a vicariate under the care of the Paris Seminary, with 22,000 Roman Catholics (out of five million inhabitants), 27 stations, 41 schools, 1 seminary, 36 priests, 14 native priests. The diocese of Laos, detached in 1888, has 9,430 Roman Catholics, 12 stations, 30 schools, 21 priests, and 4 native priests.

In the French possessions of to-day in Eastern India, the Jesuits (especially Alexander of Rhodes) had already won a great number of adherents at an earlier time by skilful use of the political conditions. Bitter persecution of the Christians induced France to intervene and to found its colonial domain, in which the Roman Catholic mission exerts a wide-reaching influence. In the eighteenth century Spanish Dominicans worked alongside of the Jesuits. This resulted in troublesome conflicts between them. Instead of the former, missionaries of the Paris Seminary have recently entered this field in Cambodia and Cochin China.

There are 10 apostolic vicariates, one in Cambodia, three in Cochin China, and six in Tonkin. Altogether, there are 840,760 Roman Catholics, out of twenty-three million inhabitants, with 370 stations, 353 priests, 494 native priests, 2,068 schools. The diocese of **Malacca** (under the Paris Seminary) has, out of 1,200,000 inhabitants, 19,830 Roman Catholics (among these some Chinese), 26 stations, 32 priests, 2 native priests, and 25 schools. All Eastern Asia has, out of a population of forty-one millions, 948,650 Roman Catholics, and 481 stations, 512 priests, 527 native priests, 2,318 schools, about 134 lay brothers and 541 sisters, among these some natives. (Evangelical: 127,707 Christians, 46 stations, 94 missionaries, 299 ordained natives, 599 schools.)

5. Dutch East Indies; Philippines. In the **Dutch East** Indies the Roman mission has only the prefecture of North Borneo, with Labuan (St. Joseph's Brotherhood of Mill Hill) and the vicariate of Batavia (Jesuits). The former compete with the Anglicans in Sarawak (1,200 Roman Catholics), the latter have 10 stations in Java, 4 in Sumatra, 3 in Celebes (where they work among the Evangelical population of the Minahassa—5,974 Roman Catholics), and 7 in Flores and Timor. The *Missiones Catholicæ* reports 49,831 converts. According to *Die katholische Kirche* there are among them only 22,382 Asiatics, 40 stations, 63 priests, 48 schools, 28 lay brothers, and 259 sisters. The **Philippines** are not in the charge of the Propaganda. *Die katholische Kirche* states that many different orders work here with a smaller number of secular priests. In 736 parishes and 105 missionary parishes, there were in round numbers 6,560,000 converts and 957 priests. According to this there would be only 590,000 heathen, with whom it is likely that the Roman Catholic Church has little to do. Since the American conquest, several Evangelical missionary societies have taken up the work here (see PHILIPPINE ISLANDS).

It is well known that in the seventeenth century the Jesuits, through a clever use of political conditions, and through a complacent attitude regarding heathen customs, enjoyed considerable success.

6. China.

It is said that there were at that time 300,000 Roman Catholics in the empire. Against the Jesuits, because of their methods of compromise, accusations were made by the Dominicans and Franciscans, who entered the field in 1630; the Jesuits, however, persisted and abused their influence as favorites of the emperor so far as to cause the imprisonment of a papal legate. To the young heir apparent, Yung Ching, the intervention of the pope seemed to portend danger to the State, and he interdicted Christianity. This resulted in persecution and the number of Christians rapidly dwindled away. In spite of all, the Jesuits maintained themselves for a long time; even the repeated condemnation of their practises by the pope did not shake them. However, with the suppression of the order, the Roman Catholic mission in China became reduced to a small remnant. Only by the Peace of Nanking (1842) did the Roman Catholics secure an edict of toleration, and by the Peace of Peking the restoration of all the former church property was accorded. Under the protection of France, the Roman Catholic mission has much increased since that time; in cases of local persecution, heavy pecuniary indemnities were enforced. Externally also the cause is favored in that the dignitaries of the church are accorded the rank of mandarins, so that the native converts are withdrawn from Chinese jurisdiction. For this very reason, however, many doubtful characters are drawn to the Roman Catholic Church.

There are in China, according to *Die katholische Kirche*, p. 256, 39 vicariates and 2 prefectures, in the five following groups: (1) Pechili (1. North, 2. East, 3. Southwest, 4. Southeast); Manchuria (5. South, 6. North, 7. East); Mongolia (8. East, 9. Central, 10. Southwest) and 11. North Honan. (2) 12. Kulja; 13. Kansu; Shensi (14. North and 15. South); 16. Shansi (according to *Missiones Catholicæ* there are two vicariates, North and South, both under Franciscans); and Shantung (17. North, 18. East, 19. South). (3) 20. Che-Kiang; 21. South Honan; Hunan (22. North, 23. South); Hupe (24. Northwest, 25. East, 26. Southwest); 27. Kiangnan; Kiangsi (28. North, 29. South, 30. East). (4) 31. Kweichow; Szechuen (32. Northwest, 33. East, 34. South); 35. Yunnan; 36. Tibet. (5) 37. Fukhien; 38. Amoy; 39. Hongkong; and the prefectures 40. Kwangsi and 41. Kwangtung. The missions are carried on by the following organizations, whose fields are indicated by the affixed numbers.

	Priests.	Converts.
1. Paris Seminary (5, 6, 31–36, 40, 41)...	313	235,973
2. Lazarists (1–3, 20, 28–30)	115	128,563
3. Jesuits (4, 27)	168	188,921
4. Franciscans (14, 16–18, 23–26)	126	109,428
5. Dominicans (37, 38)	43	42,684
6. Augustinians (22).	8	215
7. Milanese Seminary (11, 21, 39)	39	22,200
8. Roman Seminary (15).	13	9,1[illegible]0
9. Scheutvold Congregation (8–10, 12, 13).	84	30,3[illegible]2
10. Steyl Seminary (19)...	33	15,[illegible]2
Total....................	942	7[illegible]

The *Missiones Catholicæ* gives the following figures: 7[illegible]-540 converts, 734 stations, 904 priests, 471 native priest[illegible], 3,584 schools, 65,990 scholars, 239 sisters. (Evangelic[illegible]: 205,747 converts, 478 stations, 973 missionaries, 297 nati[illegible] pastors, 1,823 schools, 37,057 scholars.)

Korea (q.v.) received, in 1784, the first missionaries, who soon obtained numerous adherents. Bitter persecution, in which three bishops and eleven priests were martyred, hindered all

7. Korea and Japan.

further development. In 1831 the vicariate was founded and assigned to the Paris Seminary. Since Japanese influence has supplanted that of China and there is greater security in the land, the Roman Catholic mission is rapidly spreading. The *Missiones Catholicæ* gives the following figures: 35 stations, 39 priests, 9 native priests, 59 schools, 481 scholars.

Francis Xavier began the mission in Japan in 1549, but had little success. His followers were able to connect their interests with those of a political party, whose victory they shared. Numerous missionaries came to the land and gained as many as 600,000 converts. A change in the political situation resulted in severe persecutions, and in 1641 the last missionaries were removed from the country. Only after America had brought about the opening of the empire was the mission renewed. The missionaries of the Paris Seminary work in four dioceses: the archdiocese of Tokyo and the dioceses of Osaka, Nagasaki, and Hakodate.

Out of a population of 47,812,138 there are 55,453 Roman Catholics, 86 stations, 115 priests, 32 native priests, 36 schools, 2,826 scholars (among these 2,041 girls), 35 lay brothers, and 109 sisters are reported. (Evangelical: 145 stations, 237 missionaries, 297 native pastors, 85,715 Christians, 104 schools, 7,141 scholars—among these 851 girls.)

For all Asia: 2,966,142 Roman Catholics * (1,583,796 Evangelical Christians), 1,930 stations (1,632), 2,348 priests (2,632), 1,368 native priests (5,809), 8,358 schools (10,768), —scholars † (413,428).

3. America: In this treatment account is taken only of missions to Negroes and Indians; no consideration is given to the growth of the Church among the white population, of which *Missiones Catholicæ* reports a membership of 10,309,970.

The Roman mission to the Indians, according to the reports of the *Missiones Catholicæ*, must be a very limited one. From many regions once belonging to Spain, a number of Roman

1. United States and British North America.

Catholics from an earlier period are noted, with the remark that they have entirely relapsed into barbarism. Concerning other regions see the appended tables; *Die katholische Kirche* counts 98,638; the Year Book treating of the Indian regions, 74,468. These later figures can be reached only by including the older adherents who have relapsed into barbarism (the Evangelical Indians number 74,468). Little can be learned regarding the success of the mission among the Negroes; the *Missiones Catholicæ* contains only isolated statements. According to *Die katholische Kirche*, in 25 dioceses, out of 4,914,000 Negroes there are 145,000 Roman Catholics, with 46 churches, 48 priests, 111 schools, and 8,533 scholars. At an early period Jesuits from the French colony did zealous mission work among the Indians of British North America (see INDIANS OF NORTH AMERICA,

* The 534,000 Roman Catholics who are not subject to the Propaganda, but under Portuguese jurisdiction, and the 6,560,000 said to be in the Philippines are omitted.

† The statistics regarding scholars are so imperfect that they can not be reckoned.

Missions to); under English rule the work was paralyzed, but it was taken up again in the nineteenth century by oblates of the Immaculate Conception, who followed the Canadian fur-hunters on their extensive journeys, and were spurred on by the growing Evangelical mission. While in the archdioceses of Quebec and Toronto most of the Indians were already Roman Catholics, to the wild tribes in the icy West the Gospel was carried. On the Red River, the Roman Catholic and Evangelical missions worked side by side. There is now the flourishing province of Manitoba, with 400,000 inhabitants. Statistics do not show how many of the 35,000 Indians are Roman Catholics. Besides the archdiocese of St. Bonifacius, the diocese of St. Albert and the vicariate of Saskatchewan and Athabasca-Mackenzie have been formed in the West—the last-named reaches up to the Polar Sea. Beyond the Rocky Mountains the diocese of New Westminster has been founded. Among its 30,000 Roman Catholics there are, according to the *Missiones Catholicæ*, 15,000 Indians. Oblates of the Immaculate Conception work everywhere, but accurate statistics in regard to their activity are not to be had.

The following table is taken from the *Official Catholic Directory* for 1908:

Archdioceses, Dioceses and Vicariates.	Indian Population.	Catholic Indians.	Churches.	Priests.	Schools.	Pupils.	Religious Order.
Alaska	29,000	5,000	13	10	6	184	Jesuits, Lay Bros.
Baker City ...	3,200	1,000	1	1	2	95	Jesuits, Lay Bros.
Boisé	4,500	1,400	4	4	3	188	Jesuits, Lay Bros.
Brownsville .							
Fargo							
Grand Rapids	2,950	2,150	7	6	2	125	
Green Bay ...	3,100	1,400	5	4	1	190	Franciscans
Oklahoma ...	96,000	3,400	13	6	14	819	Benedictine, Bros. Sacred Heart
Omaha							
Lead City ...	18,000	6,000	18	11	3	630	Jesuits, Benedictine
Marquette....	1,500	1,040	5	1	1	48	Jesuits
Nesqually ...	10,000	3,500	1	8	4	364	Jesuits
Oregon City .	1,300	2	1			795	.
San Francisco	626	626	4	5	3		
Santa Fé ...		18,000			2	220	
Superior		2,676	16	4	6	401	Franciscans
Tucson	32,000	3,000	8	5	3	371	Franciscans
Totals	202,176	49,194	96	65	50	4,430	

2. Latin America and the West Indies.

The regions colonized by the Spaniards and Portuguese were won at that time for Roman Catholic Christianity through the labors of the Franciscans and Dominicans. Later came the Jesuits, who had in many cases great apparent success. With the suppression of the order, their institutions decayed and the converts were scattered and lapsed into heathenism. However, in course of time, a portion of the Indians in this region gained a certain civilization and at the same time adopted the Roman Catholic forms. On the whole, the region appears to be Christianized, but the conditions are entirely unsound. The educational level of the clergy is incredibly low and the general morality is degraded. In many of these lands nothing is done for those who are still heathen. In **Mexico,** there are now more than 12,000,000 Roman Catholics, namely, 2,000,000 Spanish Creoles, 4,000,000 Indians, and 70,000 Negroes, the remainder being half-breeds; only 200,000 Indians are still heathen, and apparently no mission work is done among them. On the other hand, it may be remarked that several Protestant denominations in the United States carry on a successful work of propagandism among the Roman Catholic population. In **Central America** there are said to be still 1,200,000 Indians out of a population of 3,000,000. They are for the most part Roman Catholics; but here also there are uncivilized Indians, among whom mission work is apparently not carried on. Although the whole region is under the Propaganda, only Honduras is noted in the *Missiones Catholicæ*. Here Jesuits report 19,000 Roman Catholics; whether work is done among the heathen is not stated. In the church provinces of the **Antilles,** missions to the heathen can hardly be expected. The *Missiones Catholicæ* gives the following statistics:

	Inhabitants.	Roman Catholics.
Vicariate of Jamaica................	727,630	13,000
Ad. Port of Spain (Trinidad, Tobago, Grenada, St. Vincent and Sta. Lucia)	394,000	180,340
D. Roseau (Dominica, Antigua, Barbuda, St. Thomas, St. Croix, etc.)	146,000	50,000
Vicariate of Curaçao	46,190	38,200

Besides the Jesuits, Dominicans and Redemptionists labor there. The principal activity is in the direction of making conversions among the Evangelical Negro population. The other islands of the Greater Antilles are not noted in the *Missiones Catholicæ*. In South America, the same source reports for Guiana and Patagonia the following statistics:

	Inhabitants.	Roman Catholics.
1. Vicariate of Demerara (with the Barbados).......................	200,000	500
On the mainland.............	260,000	23,500
2. Vicariate Surinam (Redemptionists).	64,000	17,000
3. Prefecture of Cayenne.	31,000	29,000

Patagonia has the two apostolic vicariates, North and South Patagonia, in which the Salesians work. Beside 103,000 Roman Catholics and 5,700 Protestants there are here 1,500 Indians; nothing is said regarding a mission to them. Franciscans and Capuchins do mission work among the Indians of South America. In Chili there are stations in Chillan and in the island of Chiloe, whence work is done among the Araucanians of the mainland. The Capuchins have in Arauco, Valdivia, and Llanquihue 26,700 converts. In Bolivia an Indian mission is mentioned (Tarija, La Paz, Tarata, Sucre and Potosi, the last with 4,000 adherents). In Brazil, the mission undertaken in 1870 was almost destroyed by the downfall of the empire, but recently it has been actively pushed. Here the Capuchins work and they have 20,350 converts among 500,000 heathen. The number of heathen Indians in South America is estimated at two millions. The statistics regarding Roman missions in America are so incomplete and inexact that a statistical summary, similar to that given for other parts of the world, is impossible. All that can be said is that in America, according to attainable information, there are 544,402 Roman Catholic converts from heathenism

(Evangelicals, 813,700, excluding the Negroes of the United States).

4. Australia and Oceania: (1) The Roman mission in **Australia** among aborigines is of slight moment. In New Nursia, in West Australia, four priests (Spanish Benedictines) and 43 lay brothers, with 2 sisters, care for the 100 (according to *Die Katholische Kirche*, 140) surviving aborigines. In the north, on Beagle Bay, the Trappists labor with 8 priests and 10 lay brothers, since 1890, among 350 natives. They had 60 converts, but abandoned their task, which was then taken up by the Pallottinians (see PALLOTTI, VINCENZO, PALLOTTINIANS). In the diocese of Victoria and Palmerston several thousand natives are known, but nothing is said of a mission among them. In Queensland a vicariate was erected in 1887 for the aborigines; but there is no report of missionary work there (the Evangelical mission has 23 stations with 1,100 native Christians, 11 stations for Chinese with 700 Christians, and 8 stations for natives who have been brought in from the islands, with 2,000 converts. (2) In **New Zealand** the Roman Catholic missionaries established themselves in 1838, when the Evangelical mission was already flourishing. They succeeded in gathering 5,000 Maoris. During the insurrections which followed, these were scattered and in 1870 the complaint was made that there was no longer a Maori mission. In the archdiocese of Wellington are 4 stations with 1,500 Roman Catholics; for the diocese of Auckland 5,000 are given (according to *Die Katholische Kirche*, 5,700), in charge of eight priests of Mill Hill. (3) In **New Caledonia**, where the first efforts of the London Mission were rendered vain by the Marists, the Roman mission was soon very successful; it was, however, destroyed by a revolt of the natives, but was resumed under the protection of the French. Since the founding of the colony, the aborigines have rapidly died out; of 100,000 but 25,000 remain. The neighboring Loyalty Islands, whose inhabitants at the time of the seizure of these islands were for the most part evangelized, are incorporated in the vicariate of New Caledonia. The London Mission which was working there was forced out and the remaining heathen islanders were easily won for the Roman Catholic mission; the remainder continued true to their faith in spite of oppression. The vicariate, which includes also the northern **New Hebrides**, has 36 stations and 11,500 Roman Catholics. Of this number, 18 stations are on the mainland, but the number of converts there is not given; in any case, the majority of the aborigines have not yet been won for the Roman Catholic Church. Native Evangelical teachers from the Loyalty Islands have undertaken independent missionary work in New Caledonia; recently the Paris Evangelical Mission has entered this field as well as the Loyalty Islands.

The *Missiones Catholicæ* gives the following figures: 63 priests, 23 schools (19 boarding-schools with 1,500 scholars), 52 lay brothers and 54 sisters (Evangelical mission in the Loyalty Islands: 3 stations, 2 missionaries, 34 native pastors, 10,195 Christians). (4) Prefecture of the **New Hebrides.** This was separated from the above-mentioned vicariate in 1901. Here too the Marists entered the field of the Evangelical mission, worthily founded here by the blood of the martyrs which was freely shed in Erromanga. There are 16 priests, 7 schools, and, according to *Die katholische Kirche*, 1,200 converts. (Evangelical mission: 9 stations, 37 missionaries, 1 ordained native, 8,995 Christians, and 234 schools with 4,000–5,000 scholars.) (5) Vicariate of **Central Oceania**: Futuna and Wallis Islands form the chief seat of the Marists who, starting from here, placed missions in the Evangelical missionary fields on the neighboring island-groups. They were brought into Tonga, by the military occupation of the French, but have won only 1,890 of the 22,000 islanders. The entire vicariate counts 15 stations, 18 priests, 2 lay brothers, 59 sisters, 9,450 converts, 44 schools and 2,000 scholars. (6) Vicariate of the **Samoan Islands.** Here too the Marists have established work in a field already evangelized. As a result of the confessional divisions, old tribal feuds broke out anew in bloody conflicts. The Roman Catholic mission makes every effort to profit by the new political situation. There are 15 stations (25), 18 priests (10 missionaries), 1 native priest (181), 3 lay brothers, 10 sisters, 6,000 converts (33,310), 67 schools (261), 758 scholars (8,783). (7) The vicariate of the **Viti Islands** was detached from the prefecture of Central Oceania in 1844. At first the efforts of the Marists had but little success in comparison with the earlier work of the English Methodists. Only when the colonisation from Australia increased did larger Roman Catholic communities arise among the natives. There are 17 stations (10), 32 priests (11), 11 lay brothers, 28 sisters, 9,848 converts (97,254), 31 schools, 2,471 scholars (34,966). The statistics relating to Rotuma are here included. (8) The vicariate of **New Guinea** embraces the English part of the island besides the Louisiade and Torres Islands, and was in 1887 assigned to the Congregation of the Sacred Heart at Issoudun. The London Mission had already opened up this field after overcoming great difficulties: 8 stations (10), 18 priests (10 missionaries and 104 native pastors), 22 lay brothers, 37 sisters, 4,000 converts (6,492), 29 schools (45), 1,084 scholars (2,011). (9) The vicariate of **New Pomerania** was assigned in 1889 to the same congregation. It embraces the whole Bismarck Archipelago. The Roman mission came here also into a successful Evangelical missionary field, that of the Australian Methodists, from whose communities the greater number of Roman Catholics were won. There are 11 stations (3), 20 priests (3, besides 4 ordained natives and 98 assistants), 29 lay brothers, 17 sisters, 13 schools (101), 600 scholars (3,000), 6,600 converts (7,962). In the prefecture of **Kaiser Wilhelmsland** are 3 Roman Catholic stations of the Steyl Society of the Divine Word, situated in the western part of the German protectorate (7 Evangelical in the East), 7 priests (13), 9 lay brothers, 4 schools. (4) *Die katholische Kirche* reports 400 converts. (11) and (12) The prefectures of the **Solomon Islands** were founded in 1897 and 1898, and entrusted to the Marists. In the two 7 priests are active. (13) In the vicariate of the **Caroline Islands,** after the group was awarded to Spain, the Carmelites in Ponape sought with the aid of the military power to suppress the Evangelical mission. In spite of their bloody defeats, they finally succeeded in drawing over to their church the Christians, who were at last intimidated. The same congregation had already worked at an earlier period in the West Carolines. They report 4 stations (3, with the Marshall Islands), 12 priests (7 missionaries, besides 22 native pastors), 14 lay brothers, 16 schools (120), 900 scholars (5,587), 1,400 converts (18,115). (14) The vicariate of the **Gilbert Islands** includes the Ellice Islands. Here the missionaries from Issoudun compete with the English and American missions. There are 11 stations, 11 priests (27 native pastors, including the Tokelon Islands), 12 lay brothers, 9 sisters, 67 schools (27), 1,220 scholars (3,357), 11,000 converts (10,734, including the Tokelon Islands). (15) The vicariate of **Tahiti** has existed since 1844, when the Evangelical mission was forced out by French arms. On the principal island, the Roman mission, carried on by the congregation of Picpus, has had but little success. The natives have remained true to their confession. The same holds good of the western islands of the group. The Roman Catholics had greater success with the still heathen population of the Pamnotu Islands and recently they have won converts in great numbers in the Harvey Islands also, which belong to the same apostolic vicariate. Of the 32,000 inhabitants of the regions here noticed, 7,230 are Roman Catholics (18,470); there are 26 stations (7), 18 priests (8), 12 lay brothers, 24 sisters, 32 schools (46?) and 1,800 scholars (3,389). (16) In the vicariate of the **Marquesas Islands,** among the savage and rapidly diminishing population, the Congregation of Picpus has after long-continued efforts at last succeeded in winning the greater number. Of 4,000 natives 3,150 are Roman Catholics; there are 8 stations, 7 priests, 10 lay brothers, 10 sisters, 660 scholars. (17) The vicariate of **Hawaii** is also in the hands of the Picpus Society. Nearly half of the islanders, who were long before evangelized, have been converted, resulting in 14,000 Roman Catholics (14,922). Almost as many have been won among the Chinese and Japanese immigrants, with whom the Roman Catholic Portuguese are counted. There are reported 15 stations (1), 24 priests (3), 33 lay brothers, 48 sisters, 17 schools (507), 1,943 scholars (5,599).

Die katholische Kirche gives the following statistics in regard to the whole Catholic mission in the Pacific: 205 stations (207), 268 priests (122), 219 lay brothers, 452 sisters, 126,032 converts (278,000), 426 schools (2,917), 19,927 scholars (71,437). The corresponding figures in regard to the aborigines on the mainlands could not be obtained. The whole Roman Catholic mission to the heathen can be summarized as follows: 2,870 stations (3,790), 4,009 priests (4,485), 1,954 lay brothers, 4,937 sisters (3,119 unmarried female missionaries, according to J. S. Dennis, *Centennial Survey of Foreign Missions*, New York, 1902), 10,494 schools (18,921), 700,000 scholars (867,370), 3,878,712 converts (3,371,588 excluding the Negroes in the United States).

R. Grundemann.

B. Protestant Missions.

I. Introduction: Christianity being the one world religion, it alone has the vocation for a world mission. It is the world religion, because it is both universal and absolute. It is the universal religion; for it offers to all humanity, without difference of sex, age, education, rank, civilization, nationality, color, or race, that assured salvation which is needed by all, and imposes a condition of salvation which can be realized by all. It is the absolute religion; for it differs from all other religions through the assurance of the objective truth of its faith, warranted by the sacred person of Jesus Christ. It therefore differs not only in degree but in kind in that it substitutes (1) an objective true knowledge of God for purely subjective human conceptions of him, and (2) the divine act of deliverance for human attempts at self-deliverance. As God has prepared in Christ the salvation of the world, so he wills that this salvation should be offered to all men, at all times, and in all places; and since this can be accomplished only by the orderly sending forth of messengers of salvation, so God wills the world mission. The whole history and doctrine of Christian salvation is so penetrated by thought of universal salvation that the world mission is a simple and natural consequence. But, outside this logical obligation, there is a direct mission command which, like a categorical imperative, compels obedience from every one who wishes to be a disciple of Jesus. Tradition declares that the risen Christ gave the command to his apostles to go forth and, by proclaiming his Gospel to the whole world, to bring all nations to him. The mission command is as much the logical result of the human personality of Jesus and of the universalistic quality of his teachings as the fruit of his death. Altogether the instrument of God, Jesus made salvation a reality at first in the most modest sphere; from the holy seed in Israel he raised his instruments, and only when everything was accomplished he gave them the royal command to conquer the world. He first familiarized them with the great idea of the universality of his kingdom, and then drew the practical consequences; he sowed one missionary seed after the other, until, with the growing understanding of his life-work, the understanding of the missionary task was ripened. And only after he had fulfilled everything, and as the Crucified and Risen One went unto his Father, he promised to his disciples strength from above enabling them to do greater works than he had done. To these great works especially belongs the preaching of the kingdom beyond the bounds of Israel over the whole world.

1. The Basis of Christian Missions.

A great world movement was produced by the marching order of Jesus, so majestic in its simplicity: "Go forth." Innumerable armies of messengers have "gone forth"—first to the Greco-Roman world, then to the German-Slavonic world, and lastly over all parts of the earth since the age of great discoveries, the fifteenth and nineteenth centuries. The whole history of the Christian Church has become mission history, and if now and then there have been periods of quiescence, that marching order has nevertheless always produced a renewal of missionary work. Nineteen hundred years after its issuance, it has become again so vital that Christian nations and churches have started a missionary movement which has no parallel in either of the two former periods. The words of Jesus demonstrate their truth by their effect. The mission command of Jesus has revolutionized the history of the world. Of the about 1,540 millions of human beings who inhabit the earth today, 550 millions are Christians at least in name. This status of Christendom is the fruit of missions, for to each of the Christian peoples of the present era the Gospel has been brought by missionaries. This great Christianity gathered in by missions is composed both of peoples who already possessed a civilization before they were Christianized, and of those who lacked this possession; and it is striking that the barbarian nations since their conversion to Christianity have become the standard-bearers of civilization and the leaders in history. So the mission history of the past has proved that neither race nor civilization constitutes a difference; salvation in Christ is for all men, all are in need of it, all may gain it, and in all it has proved its strength. This fact of missionary history is a proof of so much greater force for the vocation of Christianity as a world religion and a world mission in that it is not confined to the closed missionary periods of the past. There is a modern missionary period in which this fact is being repeated, and this phase is the subject of this article. Unfortunately it is not a united Christianity which carries on the mission of the present day—a circumstance which constitutes one of its dark sides and causes many impediments and disagreements.

2. General Results.

This section will treat of Protestant missions in two principal divisions: (1) a general view of the history of colonial missions, by which is meant Christian work carried on by different nations within the limits of Christendom or of the territories acquired by them; and (2) of the separate fields of foreign missions.

II. Colonial Missions. **1. The Period of the Reformation and of the Old Protestant Orthodoxy;** It was long before a mission era dawned in Evangelical Christendom, although a great era of discovery and conquest preceded and accompanied the Reformation which inspired the Roman Catholic Church to extended mission work in Africa, America, and Asia.

1. Attitude of the Reformers.

But the great fact of the opening of the New World had scarcely any marked effect upon the Reformed churches; principally because the new discoveries were made by the Roman Catholic powers which took possession of the transatlantic countries. Therefore the young Protestantism lacked any direct connection with the heathen lands which then became attainable, and even had it wished to enter those fields, Spain and Portugal would certainly have been hostile. Besides this, the conflict with the degenerate Christianity of the older Christian nations, the struggle for self-preservation against papal and imperial aggression, the necessity of consolidating its own life and government, and the general confusion and wars which followed the era of the Reformation laid claim to all the strength of Protestantism. Moreover, the missionary idea was lacking because the comprehension of a continuous missionary duty of the Church was limited among the Reformers and their successors by a narrow-minded dogmatism combined with a lack of historical sense. They knew of the great missions of the past, but according to their ideas the apostles had already gone forth to the whole world and they and their disciples had essentially accomplished the missionary task. Christianity, therefore, had already proved its universal vocation as a world religion and the missionary promises had been met. The Christianity of that time was considered by them to be the Church which had been gathered together from the heathen. When Luther spoke of the heathen, he meant those who were not Israelites, but were formerly heathen and had come to constitute Christendom. Very rarely did his outlook go beyond these; but even when this happened, he never thought of sending a mission to the heathen of his time. The thought of missions was in a sense precluded both by the doctrine of predestination, according to which it is left to the sovereign grace of God to lead the heathen unto Christ, and by the eschatology of the time, which looked upon the end of the world as fast approaching. Calvin regarded the apostolate as a *munus extraordinarium*, while a special effort of man, that is to say, the establishment of a mission for the heathen, was not necessary. Even Zwingli and Butzer do not recognize continuous mission work as a duty of the Church.

Only one theologian of the Reformation, and he was of the second rank, raised himself above this narrow view. This was Adrian Saravia, whose importance has been discovered quite recently.

2. Adrian Saravia.

He was pastor in Antwerp and Brussels and also professor in Leyden; later he went to England, where he died in 1613. Saravia published in 1590 an essay, *De diversis ministrorum gradibus sic ut a domino fuerunt instituti*, to defend the episcopal form of church government, in which he emphasized the necessity of an episcopate clothed with apostolic authority by referring among other things to the planting of new churches. In this connection Saravia devotes a special chapter (xvii.) to missions, under the title: The command to preach the Gospel to all peoples has become an obligation of the Church since the apostles entered into heaven. He proves in this chapter that the command to preach the Gospel to the whole world and the duty of spreading it among all peoples refer to all times until the end of the world. Even to-day, Saravia continues, the Gospel is not yet proclaimed to all peoples, and it is the duty of the Church to obey that command, which was first given to the apostles alone. The Church has therefore not only the duty but also the authority for this great work. It is true that those who undertake this work must be well equipped mentally, and since individuals may easily deceive themselves as to their vocation for the task, the authorization of the Church is necessary. But in this sane understanding of the mission command Saravia stood alone. Beza and Johann Gerhard of Jena opposed Saravia, the former as early as 1592, the latter twenty-five years later. Beza did this in a special polemical work: *Ad tratationem de ministrorum gradibus ab Adriano Saravia Belga editam, Theo. Bezæ responsio*, and Gerhard, in locus xxiii. of his *Loci theologici*.

Nevertheless in the years 1555 and 1559 two enterprises were initiated which were designated missions, one of the Reformed and the other of the Lutheran Church.

3. Two Early Attempts.

One of these was established in Brazil in order to found there a French colony by a French adventurer, Durand de Villegaignon, who, however, turned out later to be a traitor to Protestantism. The colonists were accompanied by four pastors from Geneva, who were also to preach the Gospel to the native heathen; but the whole enterprise was a failure, and a mission was never established. A similar fate befell the attempt of the Swedish King Gustavus Vasa when, in the sixteenth century, he tried to bring into the Evangelical church the nominal Roman Catholics among the Laplanders. This was an attempt at reformation by the exercise of the territorial authority of the Church, and it consisted only in the sending of priests (little qualified for the task) and the building of parsonages. The undertaking failed and a real mission to the Laplanders was first realized by Thomas von Westen and Nils Joachim Christian Stockfleth (qq.v.).

Still more decidedly than the Reformers, the representatives of the old Protestant orthodoxy, Lutheran as well as Reformed, denied the continuous missionary duty of the Church

4. Reformed and Lutheran Opposition.

in spite of the charge repeatedly brought in the Roman Catholic polemics of the time that the Church of the Reformation could not be the true Church because it did no mission work among the heathen. The chief leaders of the opposition to missions were the great dogmatician Johann Gerhard (q.v.) and the Wittenberg theological faculty. Their argument is essentially twofold: (1) The apostles have already proclaimed the Gospel throughout the whole world; (2) the missionary vocation of the Church became extinct with the death of the apostles. Accompanying this polemic against missions, a few voices began to be raised in their favor, especially in Germany, Holland, and Denmark. One can divide these advocates into three groups: (1) those who, though not recognizing the duty of the Church to send out missions, still admitted the duty of the Christian powers to Christianize their heathen subjects; (2) those who in principle believed in a mission duty of the Church, but for reasons of expediency did not think it should be fulfilled at this time; and (3) those who without any reservations required obedience to the missionary command. However, they all lacked practical energy and they attained no positive results whatever. Only one enterprise can be noted and this bears a thoroughly individualistic stamp. It was the journey to Abyssinia of Peter Heiling, a lawyer of Lübeck who, probably influenced by Hugo Grotius, went thither to restore to life the moribund Abyssinian Church (see ABYSSINIA AND THE ABYSSINIAN CHURCH; and AFRICA, II., Abyssinia). Outside of the translation of the New Testament into the Amharic language, the twenty years' stay of Heiling in Abyssinia had no results and no one continued his work. German Lutheran Christianity was for the first time earnestly reminded of its missionary duty by Baron Justinian von Weltz, who was born in 1621 in Chemnitz, educated in Ulm, and descended from an old and noble Austrian house. He was an ardent Pietist, and demanded the founding of a missionary society in connection with the efforts for spiritual regeneration. He urged this in three tractates issued in 1664–66, of which the first was the most important. It contains questions and appeals to all those addressed, and then is divided into three principal divisions: (1) the reasons which prove the necessity for the founding of a mission; (2) a refutation of the objections made by orthodox theologians to the continuous missionary obligation, as stated above, and (3) definite propositions as to the way in which a mission should be instituted. This tractate, as well as the second similar one, Weltz presented at the *corpus evangelicorum* at Regensburg, where, however, no action was taken. Disappointed, he wrote a third essay, went to Holland and, after being ordained there, departed as a missionary to Surinam, where this prophet of missions, who had been denounced as a fanatic and dreamer, soon found a lonely grave. For a time this appeal for an awakening remained the voice of one crying in the wilderness. Johannes Heinrich Ursinus, the superintendent of Regensburg, issued a tract opposing Weltz, but the tone adopted in this writing is rather violent than cordial, and the argumentation is exceedingly weak; naturally the author does not defend the assumption of Gerhard, but he declares a mission to be inexpedient because of the obstacles on the part of the Christians, the heathen, and God himself which hinder its realization.

It was in Holland after the deliverance from the Spanish yoke and when it became a colonial power that the first missionary activity was developed among the Protestants. However, considerations of colonial politics rather than of religion were the cause of this movement in 1602. The Dutch East India Company, which at that time had authority over the colonies, sent out missionaries and supported missions; the clerical convocations and synods participated only by providing colonial pastors who were at the same time missionaries. A seminary for the education of these missionaries opened by Professor Waläus in Leyden existed only during 1622–34. The theory of the missionary duty of the colonial government was here first put into practise on a large scale. It is true that there was no lack of excellent, spiritual-minded colonial pastors in the mission, which gradually extended over the whole Malay Archipelago, but most of them performed their duties in a formal manner and soon returned to their homes. Although hundreds of thousands were baptized, Christianity was little more than a veneer. The rather degenerate remnants of this old Dutch mission became, however, once more the object of special pastoral care in connection with the missionary revival in the nineteenth century.

5. Dutch Work in East Indies.

In England, which, after the destruction of the Spanish Armada (1588), also became a sea-power, the long-continued political and religious struggle was the principal hindrance to the awakening of an interest in missions. This struggle, however, led to the first attempt at missionary work among the Indians of North America, and it was then that the first interest in missions was aroused in England. After the so-called Cavaliers had founded the first English colony in North America (Virginia), in 1584, there occurred, in 1620, under the religious oppression of the Stuarts, the second and larger Puritan emigration, that of the so-called Pilgrims who settled in Massachusetts, and in 1682 there followed a third headed by William Penn (q.v.), who settled in Pennsylvania. The Puritans immediately included the conversion of the Indians in their colonial program. But it was not till 1646 that the missionary task was pursued in a really Evangelical spirit by John Eliot (q.v.). He succeeded in establishing thirteen communities of "praying Indians"; unfortunately, at the end of his self-sacrificing life he experienced the sorrow of seeing most of these communities destroyed by the dreadful Indian wars which had meanwhile broken out. The heroic and successful missionary activity of Eliot aroused attention in England and a general collection was resolved by the Long Parliament, and in 1649 a Society for the Propagation of the Gospel in New England was founded which was, however, essentially confined to the collection of donations. Only in 1695 and 1701 were two societies founded which gradually attained importance for missions: The Society for Promoting Christian Knowledge, which was especially helpful to the Danish and Halle mission in India, and the Society for the Propagation of the Gospel in Foreign Parts, which, however, confined

6. Work of English Colonists.

its activity for the first century of its existence principally to the religious care of the colonists. The powerful East-India Company, which received its charter in 1600 from Queen Elizabeth, gave no thought to missions.

Denmark also possessed colonies after 1620 in the East Indies and after 1672 in the West Indies. The first Lutheran mission started from Denmark in 1705, on the initiative of King Frederick IV But as no missionaries could be found in Denmark, the court preacher Luetkens of Copenhagen, who had been called from Berlin, turned to his pietistic friends in Germany. In this way the Danish mission came into relationship with the German Pietists and soon also with August Hermann Francke (q.v.). Two of his pupils, Bartholomäus Ziegenbalg (q.v.) and Heinrich Plütschau, went as "royal missionaries" to East India (Tranquebar), where they opened the way for an Evangelical mission. In Copenhagen there was founded a royal "College for Advancing the Cause of the Gospel," but Francke was the effective leader. Through him Pietism was combined with the mission and this combination kept the latter alive. Still another mission was established by Denmark, namely in Greenland, not however by the king but by a pastor of the Lofoden, Hans Egede (q.v.), who succeeded in reaching the land for which he longed only in 1721, after unspeakable efforts and only by connecting himself with a commercial company enjoying a royal privilege.

7. Early Danish Missions.

2. The Era of Pietism and Rationalism: Pietism (q.v.), the first great reform movement inside the churches of the Reformation, insisted upon personal Christianity instead of mere submission to external authority, upon a Christianity of deeds instead of a Christianity of words; upon Bible Christianity instead of dogmatism; and upon the general priesthood instead of adherence to a rigid rule of office. Its insistence upon an active faith qualified Pietism for the mission task as soon as its attention was directed to the non-Christian world. Pietism was the father of the heathen mission as of all the institutions for rescue work, a combination which was illustrated by Francke, who became the standard-bearer of the missionary movement emanating from Pietism. By his far-reaching pedagogical plans, by his correspondence with Leibnitz, and by the call of two of his pupils to aid in the Danish mission, he was led to mission work to the heathen. His chief services in the field are: (1) that he provided it with workers. A pedagogue of great talent, he was able to make his orphan asylum a means of education of workers of all descriptions in the service of the kingdom of God; (2) that he awoke in Evangelical Christendom the consciousness that it should itself carry on the mission task by sustaining the missionaries with its prayers and gifts; (3) that by a periodical publication he diffused knowledge and understanding of mission work. Francke was the first to collect a praying, giving, and striving missionary society, and so began to lift from missions the ban of being merely the official duty of the Christian colonial government.

1. Francke's Services.

Naturally, for the time being, it was only the Pietists of North and South Germany who took part in the work; orthodoxy still fought it bitterly. The institutions of Francke graduated in the course of the eighteenth century about sixty missionaries, among them, besides Ziegenbalg, Fabricius, and Christian Friedrich Schwartz (q.v.), so that the Tranquebar mission is rightly called the Danish-Halle Mission. Amid much trouble caused by petty annoyances from colonial officials, by war and disputes of various kinds, this mission endured until the last quarter of the eighteenth century, when it was undermined by rationalism at home. English aid saved it from entire destruction; later, the Leipsic Lutheran Mission entered into the old inheritance, so far as it had not already been absorbed by Anglican societies.

A thoroughly new life came into the missionary movement by the entrance of the United Brethren into the field. Count Nikolaus Ludwig von Zinzendorf (q.v.) was the instrument whom God used to raise the missions to a higher plane. Zinzendorf can well be called a missionary genius. His first impulses to mission work were received in the house of Francke, and the last impulse to the practical realization of his missionary plans was given by the sojourn in Copenhagen, 1731, where he became acquainted with a negro from St. Thomas, West Indies, and with Greenlanders. But the inclination toward the mission was implied in the whole quality of his religious nature. He was full of Christian zeal which animated him to collect around him and to organize coworkers, for whose sphere of activity he recognized no local limits. In the winning of these coworkers, the Providence of God is unmistakable. Zinzendorf found them among those heroic Moravians who were driven from their fatherland because of their faith and were ripened by suffering and persecution. From them and certain pilgrims who came to Herrnhut, the organizing genius of the count formed a community which became in the highest degree a mission church. That a community was then established which put all its energy into the heathen mission, so that its very existence became identified with this work and has remained so to this day, is the great achievement of Zinzendorf in the history of missions. At the death of the count (1760), the missionary success of the Moravian Church surpassed everything that had been done by the Protestant world for the conversion of the heathen. They had sent out 226 missionaries to all parts of the earth, except Australia, and not alone to Protestant colonial possessions. In this business-like haste, the restless genius of the count shows itself, but, nevertheless, there is something heroic in the fact that such a small community could operate enterprises which extended over nearly the whole world.

2. Zinzendorf and the United Brethren.

Nevertheless the missionary activity, till then unheard of, developed by this community, failed to inspire the Protestantism of the eighteenth century to missionary effort. The missionary era of Zinzendorf fell in the transition period between the decline of orthodoxy and the rise of rationalism, and neither of these had any comprehension of the missionary task. The dislike nourished by orthodoxy for the Pietist mission was also felt toward that of Herrnhut; the rationalistic spirit, however, which soon spread over the whole Christian world, had for all missions the same contemptuous dislike, since toleration was its chief glory. But since the Moravian brotherhood cherished Zinzendorf's inheritance faithfully and bravely, even in such an unfortunate time it came to form a living bond with the great missionary movement of Germany and England in the nineteenth century; a movement that owed more of its inspiration to Herrnhut than isolated facts prove. As in Germany Rationalism dug the grave of the Danish and Halle mission, so in Holland, also, it proved destructive. Under its baleful influence, the Dutch Colonial Mission, which had grown more and more mechanical and feeble, became nearly extinct. Besides this, the colonial government changed its policy, considering it wiser to favor Mohammedanism, and this attitude was maintained until the latter half of the nineteenth century. In England from 1698 and 1701 existed the two societies already mentioned. In Scotland, also, a Society for the Promotion of Christian Knowledge was founded, which from 1740 sent some missionaries to the North American Indians, among them David Brainerd (q.v.). Otherwise there was but little interest and no activity in missions up to the last decade of the eighteenth century, although Great Britain had in the mean while become the foremost sea-power. The cause lay in the low level of moral and religious life which obtained after the Restoration (1660). In the fifth decade of the eighteenth century an awakening took place which did not immediately develop a missionary activity, but in which lay hidden the motive power that, in the following generation, caused the great mission movement with which the present missionary era began. John Wesley and George Whitefield (qq.v.) were the instruments of the impressive awakening which extended to the following generation and from it to the European countries and North America. It was the great importance of the English revival that, accompanied as it was by a series of great events in the world's history, it opened the ears of the awakened part of Evangelical Christianity to the voice of the Holy Ghost, reminding it of the nearly forgotten missionary command and rendering it both capable and willing to obey this command.

3. Apathy under Rationalistic Influences.

3. The Present Mission Era: The modern missionary movement was not due solely to the religious revival just mentioned; a series of secular facts of historical importance contributed. Among these, four play the principal part: (1) the great geographical discoveries which began with Captain Cook and the extension of the world's commerce which ensued; (2) the struggles against the slave-trade and slavery; (3) the awakening of the national conscience of England against the arbitrary rule of the East India Company; and (4) the growth of colonial conquest.

1. Events Leading to Renewed Effort.

To what a degree earnest Christians, especially in England, were aroused by the discoveries of Cook, appears clearly in a number of tracts, issued in the last decades of the eighteenth century, which sought to arouse enthusiasm for the missionary cause by reference to these discoveries; in the great influence which they exerted on William Carey (q.v.), the great pioneer of the missionary movement and the founder of the first modern missionary society, and in the choice of a group of South Sea Islands (Tahiti) as the first field of labor of the second modern missionary society, that of London. The discoveries of Cook were followed by others which continually attained greater proportions, especially in Africa, and the fact always repeated itself that, as Livingstone said: "The end of the geographical act is the beginning of missionary enterprise." The agitation for the abolition of the slave-trade and of slavery, carried on in connection with the ideas of political liberty and philanthropy, also drew the attention of Christians to the heathen world. The leader in this agitation was William Wilberforce (q.v.). After a struggle of nineteen years, the slave-trade was at last, in 1807, declared illegal, and in 1834 slavery itself was abolished in the English colonies. Already in 1791, a philanthropic society was formed, which transported liberated English and American slaves to Sierra Leone and made their civilization its exclusive task. The experiment was unsuccessful, but it helped the foundation of the Missionary Society of the English Church (1799), in which Wilberforce took an active part. England had in the mean time become a great colonial power, but the old colonial history of England was full of bloodshed, treachery, injustice and harshness against the subject peoples, especially those of India. Since 1600 a company of merchant princes, who had little by little become a conquering power, had possessed a monopoly of the commerce with India. It had but one aim: to enrich itself. Besides this, its officials led godless lives, kept large harems, and looked upon it as an amusing spectacle when their concubines paid worship to their idols. The rule of this company lasted for more than eighty years in India without the erection of a single church for their officials, and of the few chaplains who from 1698 were sent out as a result of the renewal of the charter, a governor-general said: "Their black garb offers no protection against the general moral corruption." In the beginning the company was religiously indifferent, and afterward it was bitterly hostile to all missionary endeavor. Therefore, when the unjust wars which it waged, the violation of treaties which was a part of its policy, and the oppressive taxation which impoverished the people became known at home, there began a struggle in 1783 against this misgovernment, which lasted for thirty years and ended in the legally enforced opening of India to the missionaries. In these struggles, the recognition of the sins of omission of the government toward its heathen subjects grew in England, so that the missionary duty came to be regarded as a national obligation.

2. Carey and the English Missionary Societies.

It is true that the missionary idea had at this time found entrance into a restricted circle. The primal impulse came from William Carey, a self-taught but gifted man of remarkable linguistic capacity. By three different means he set in motion the missionary movement in 1792: (1) by a tract: *An Enquiry into the Obligations of Christians to use Means for the Conversion of the Heathen;* (2) by a powerful sermon on Isa. liv. 2, 3; and (3) by the foundation of the Baptist Missionary Society, as whose first messenger he went himself to India, where he developed a powerful activity, especially of a literary sort, which opened up the way for the modern missions. This had a stimulating effect far beyond the Baptist denomination. Already in 1794 an appeal for missions was made to all Evangelical pedobaptist dissenters, and it was heartily approved, even by the bishops, of whom Dr. Haweis was the leader. As a result of this beginning, the London Missionary Society, in which great numbers participated, was founded, which in the course of time became essentially an organ of the Independents. Partly shamed by these enterprises of the dissenters, and partly hindered by their Anglican conceptions from joining with them, such members of the Evangelical party in the Established Church as came together under the leadership of John Venn, Charles Simeon, William Wilberforce, and others, united for the founding of an Anglican missionary society, the Church Missionary Society for Africa and the East, in 1799. In the beginning, it had a thorny path to travel; the bishops held back and the first missionaries had to be drawn from Germany; but after its great secretary Henry Venn succeeded, in 1841, in establishing a *modus vivendi* with the episcopate, and it was found that the society became more and more the backbone of the Evangelical tendency in the Established Church in its struggle against ritualism, it developed little by little into the greatest of all Evangelical missionary societies.

3. Results on the Continent.

So, in the course of scarcely seven years, three epoch-making missionary organizations were called into existence, and with them the missionary activity of Protestantism entered not only into an entirely new phase, but also obtained the firm foundation which was an assurance of healthy progress. This was at first apparent in the fact that the new missionary movement spread also on the continent of Europe and in North America. This had already been the case with the English revival movement, which had exercised a vivifying influence on Germany, Holland, France, and the United States, rejuvenating the older Pietism which had found a new guardian in the German Christian Society founded in 1780 and having its home in Basel. Between these circles and the English missionary organizations an earnest accord was established, which resulted not only in awakening a lively interest in missions, but also led to the founding of independent missionary organizations, first in Holland, through the instrumentality of John van der Kemp (1747–1811), who at the age of fifty went to South Africa as the pioneer of the London Missionary Society. Then occurred the founding of the Dutch Missionary Society (1797); and later, in Germany, the establishment of the first missionary school by the Berlin Pastor Johann Jänicke (1800); this, however, confined itself to sending educated missionaries to the missions already established. In 1815 occurred the founding in Basel of what was also at first only a missionary school, but in 1822 became an independent missionary institution. Only in 1824 did France enter the modern missionary movement by the founding of missionary societies, while such organizations had been formed in North America as early as 1810.

4. Missionary Organizations: Not only in England but on the continent the State churches held aloof from the missionary movement and even assumed an attitude of hostility. This trying situation left two alternatives open to the friends of missions: either to refrain from missionary activity or to call into being organizations independent of the State churches, and they naturally decided upon the latter course; and since the new missions received no support from the colonial governments, but rather encountered open hostility, they were dependent upon the voluntary service of Christians. The independent societies were recognized as new corporate bodies which, through the organization of Christian endeavor, had brought about an intensified activity in the churches; so that, at the present time, the most friendly relations of mutual assistance exist between the State churches and the independent missionary organizations. Apart from the small Moravian church, it is only in the Scotch churches and in certain of the American denominations that missions were from the beginning the care of the churches as such. But even when they formed a part of the church activity, the expenses of maintenance were covered by voluntary contributions. These have grown from very small sums to very considerable ones, and they now reach the amount of nearly $20,000,000 yearly in all Evangelical Christendom.

1. Ecclesiastical Attitude toward Missions. (side heading of the preceding paragraph)

2. The Training of Missionaries.

When the State churches refused this task, a second difficulty arose; no theological graduates could be found for mission work. The old Dutch and the Danish-Halle missions had employed only theological graduates in the missionary service; when these were lacking, it became necessary to follow the example of the United Brethren and to send out lay missionaries. At first but little stress was laid upon education; soon, however, missionary schools were established whose course of four to six years became gradually more thorough and systematic. Excepting in America and Scotland, where it was from the beginning the rule to draw the missionaries from the theological seminaries or from the universities, the missionary societies in Protestant countries have founded schools for their missionaries. Only from the last third of the nineteenth century has the percentage of theological graduates who have entered the missionary field become considerable, especially in England; on the continent it is still quite small, although it is increasing. From about the middle of the last century and to an ever-increasing extent, qualified physicians and unmarried women have been sent out, the latter principally to be active as teachers, physicians, and deaconesses among the heathen and convert women.

3. Rise of Missionary Organizations.

In the course of the nineteenth century the missionary organizations have increased so greatly that now it is scarcely possible to give a complete list of them. This increase has its root, in the first place, in the great variety of church forms among Protestants. To an ever-increasing extent each denomination took up the mission work independently, and, in this way, because of the multitude of sects, in England and North America especially, there arose a great number of missionary organizations; but the various theological tendencies and schools within the State churches also led to the founding of separate missions. In addition to this, new missionary societies have been called into being by different theories as to missions, and, usually in connection with such views, by the individual characteristics of potent personalities, and finally by motives touching political divisions at home or colonial policy. On the one hand, the great number of missionary organizations that arose in this way unquestionably augmented missionary zeal, but, on the other hand, it resulted in a division of strength, caused much friction, and increased the cost of mission work, so that at present a concentration of the existing missionary societies is rather to be desired than the founding of new ones. Unfortunately, the efforts tending toward a combination of the missionary organizations is accompanied by an individualistic tendency, the extreme expression of which are so-called free missionaries, who pursue the work of evangelization on their own account, without belonging to any society. Their numbers as well as their very doubtful success can not well be estimated.

Protestantism in all its various denominations is strongly represented in the field of missionary labor.

4. Survey of Missionary Organizations.

In view of the fact that it is impossible in this article to sketch the foundation and development of the nearly 185 missionary organizations, the following statistical summary is offered, arranged according to countries.

(1) **Great Britain** has the greatest number of missionaries; in round numbers 3,550 ordained and lay missionaries, in addition to 1,970 unmarried women workers; and she contributes, annually, about eight and one-half million dollars for mission work among the heathen, this amount being almost evenly distributed between the Church of England and the Dissenters. Of the forty or more missionary societies nine belong to the English Church, the others either belong to various free churches or are interdenominational. Prominent among the former are the Church Missionary Society, the Society for the Propagation of the Gospel, and the Universities' Mission; and among the latter, the London Missionary Society, the Baptist and the Wesleyan societies, and that of the United Free Church of Scotland; among the interdenominational should be named the China Inland Mission. (2) **North America** (United States and Canada) counts over 50 missionary societies, nearly all denominational with about 2,290 ordained and lay missionaries, besides 1,580 unmarried women workers, and it raises for foreign missions from six and one-half to seven million dollars annually.* The most important societies are the American Board of Commissioners for Foreign Missions, the American Baptist Missionary Union, the Missionary Boards of the Methodist Episcopal Church North and South, and of both General Assemblies of the Presbyterian Church in the United States of America, each of which supports from 100 to over 200 male missionaries in foreign lands. Of great importance for the increase of American missionary activity are the Student Volunteer Movement, and the Young Men's Christian Association (q.v.). (3) **Holland** has 8 quite small missionary societies, no one of which supports more than 15 missionaries; in all they have 65. The revenue is $150,000; but several old fields of mission work, especially in Celebes, have been ceded to the Colonial Dutch Church, which cares for them by means of 26 "auxiliary preachers." (4) **Germany** with German Switzerland counts 25 missionary societies, the 8 oldest of which, those of the United Brethren, Basel, Berlin, Rhenish, North German, Gossner, Leipsic, and Hermannsburg, are the largest. All told, Germany provides 1,120 missionaries, nearly all ordained, and about 150 women workers. The receipts in Germany amount to over $1,750,000 and in the missionary fields to over $500,000. (5) **France** and **French Switzerland** support two missionary societies, that of Paris, with 120, and the Mission Renaude with 22 male and 20 female missionaries. The total annual income is about $250,000. (6) **Scandinavia** has in Denmark, Norway, Sweden, and Finland twelve missionary societies, the most important of which are the Norwegian Society, the Swedish Vaterlandsstiftung and the Swedish Missionary Union. All together they support 230 male and 100 female missionaries and have a total income of $750,000. (7) Finally there are independent missionary societies in the colonies of these nations, in all probably 26, and four which belong to the native Christian churches. The 5 largest are in South Africa with about 180 missionaries; in Oceania are 10 with 75; in Dutch India, 2 with 12; in British India, 5 with 35; and in the West Indies, 4 with 45 missionaries, not counting native assistants. The total income is perhaps $950,000.

5. Summary.

Altogether, therefore, Protestantism has (including those not ordained) 7,940 male and 4,010 unmarried female missionaries to the heathen, and raises at home about $20,000,000 annually for their support. To what extent the 614 male and 308 female missionary physicians are included in these figures can not be certainly determined on account of the inexactness of the statistics of many societies. A very essential aid is given to the different Evangelical missions of all denominations by a number of Bible and Tract Societies which, at their own expense, care for the printing and also to a certain extent for the distribution of translations of the Bible and other books (see Bible Societies). Of the Tract Societies (q.v.), the principal are the London (1799) and the American Tract Society (1825) and the Society for the Promotion of Christian Knowledge (1698). Worthy of mention beside these, among the thirty in the missionary fields, are the Christian Literature Society for India (1859) and the Society for the Promotion of Christian and General Knowledge among the Chinese (1887). The ever-increasing need for mutual understanding has led to the institution of general missionary conferences, as well as those which were assembled by the united missionary organizations of a special territory (India, China, Japan, South Africa), as those called together by the missionary organizations of all Protestantism for general consultation.

* Since the majority of these societies carry on an extensive work among Roman Catholics in the West Indies and in Central and South America, and frequently do not clearly separate this work from the work among the heathen, it is possible to give only approximate data.

The ecumenical conferences have now become a permanent institution; they are held every ten years and constitute not only a bond of fraternal unity among the often widely differing missionary bodies, but they also offer in their voluminous reports very valuable material for the study of the theory and history of missions.

III. The Evangelical Missionary Fields. 1. America: The objects of missionary activity in America are (1) the aborigines; (2) the Africans who have been brought there as slaves and their descendants; (3) Asiatic immigrants. The aborigines fall into two main groups: the Eskimos in the northern arctic regions, and the Indians, who, from Alaska and Canada, are spread in numerous tribes over this quarter of the globe. The imported population consists partly of Negroes, who have settled principally in the United States and the West Indies, but are also found in Central America and in Guiana; and partly of Hindu and Chinese coolies who have been introduced as laborers into the West Indies and the colonial possessions in the northern part of South America. The other Asiatics, Chinese and Japanese, are found almost exclusively in the United States and in the western part of Canada. See HOME MISSIONS.

1. The Arctic Regions. The population of **Greenland,** consisting of about 10,500 Eskimos, is entirely Christianized; this occurred as well through the Danish mission begun in 1721 by Hans Egede (q.v.) as through that of the United Brethren, begun by Matthæus Stach in 1733. Since the specific mission work has been completed the United Brethren ceded in 1900 its six stations to the Danish Church and withdrew from this, its second oldest missionary field. In the neighboring **Labrador,** also inhabited by about 1,500 Eskimos, the United Brethren have worked exclusively since 1771. In six stations they have, with unspeakable patience, collected 1,300 Christians. The third compact Eskimo population, numbering about 1,500—already much intermixed with the Indians, who number about 19,000—is found in **Alaska.** The mission here was begun only in 1877 by the Presbyterian Church in the United States under the leadership of Sheldon Jackson (q.v.). There are now ten American missions in operation, including that of the United Brethren, reporting in thirty-one stations about 8,500 Eskimos and Indians under their care. One of the most noteworthy is that of the independent lay missionary, William Duncan; b. at Beverley, Yorkshire, England, April, 1832; determined to be a foreign missionary in Dec., 1853; went to Highbury College for two years, and in 1856 to British Columbia for his life-work among the Tsimshian Indians, living at Metlakahtla (17 m. s.e. of Fort Simpson, of the Hudson's Bay Company, on the border of Alaska). He reduced their language to writing, preached religion in it, and so was the means of Christianizing and civilizing the tribe. The zeal of Bishop William Ridley, who made Metlakahtla the seat of his diocese in 1879, was unfortunately in the direction of vestments and ritual to the amazement and misunderstanding of the simple-minded Indians, and as the bishop and Duncan could not agree, he sought from Congress "the Annette Islands, in Alexander Archipelago, Southeastern Alaska, as a reservation for the use of the Metlakahtla Indians and such other of the Alaska nations as may join them," and on Aug. 7, 1887, he transferred his converts to New Metlakahtla. The official name of the church is "The Christian Church of Metlakahtla." It belongs to no denomination. No part of the Bible has been translated into their language, though the preaching is done in it. There is, however, a translation of the Book of Common Prayer by Bishop Ridley.

2. British North America. British North America has a population of about 120,000 Eskimos and Indians, almost a third of whom are Evangelical Christians, a twelfth part being incorporated in the colonial churches. Although the English, through the Hudson Bay Company, controlled the northeastern part of the land from 1669, and in 1763 conquered the southern part or French Canada, it was only in 1820 that John West, a pious chaplain of the Hudson Bay Company, succeeded in starting a mission among the Indians. This mission, taken up by the Church Missionary Society, spread in the course of eighty years from Lake Superior, on the southwest, to the Herschel Islands at the boundary of Alaska, on the northwest, and has now, in forty-one principal stations, divided into ten episcopal dioceses, 15,000 Christian Indians and Eskimos, many of them living in well-ordered and flourishing communities. The Society for the Propagation of the Gospel and the Canadian Methodists and Presbyterians, with their forty stations, are also engaged in this work. In the near future the Christianization of the Indians will have been accomplished in the entire Dominion of Canada. Mission work is also carried on, but with little success, among the Chinese in British Columbia.

3. United States. The remnant of the aboriginal **Indian** population, now reduced to about 237,224 (census of 1900) and scattered over a great part of the Union, are a living reproach to the Christian white settlers, who by their shameful conduct have been the essential cause of the ever-recurring failure of Indian missions so hopefully begun by John Eliot (q.v.) in 1646, and continued with great fidelity by the Mayhew family for five generations (see MAYHEW, JONATHAN; MAYHEW, EXPERIENCE), by David Brainerd (q.v.), Eleazer Wheelock (q.v.) and his Indian preachers, Sampson Occum and Samuel Kirkland (qq.v.), principally, however, by the United Brethren, under the heroic and devoted David Zeisberger (q.v.). Even in the nineteenth century, when a number of North American denominations again took up the abandoned work among the Indians, the land hunger of the settlers greatly impeded success by the dishonesty and harshness and the unjust wars which it involved. It is not surprising, therefore, that the Christianizing of the Indians has not been crowned with complete success. Only about 95,000 are Evangelical Christians. Much more numerous than the Indian is the **Negro** population of the United States, which has to-day increased to over nine millions. Exact data of the work among Negroes are singularly lacking. The work was in progress long before the emancipation. In 1866 Baptists and Methodists alone counted 525,000 communicants among the Negro population, which was then 5,000,000. The work entered upon a phase of great activity after the Civil War, especially through the great development of the school system, in which almost all denominations took part. The Negroes themselves have been, however, the most zealous workers for the uplifting of their race, and have since emancipation raised for school purposes about $28,000,000 and for the building of churches $40,000,000. As a result of these energetic efforts, almost the whole of the Negro population is now under Christian influences, thirteen-fifteenths being Protestant. The great majority have formed independent churches, of the members of which 1,865,000 are Baptists, 1,412,000 Methodists, and about 100,000 are Presbyterians or Congregationalists. Although the Christianity of the majority may still be at a low level, especially in the matter of morality, it is nevertheless an important fact that here the Christianization of a whole people has taken place on a grand scale. The Chinese, numbering about 100,000, and the Japanese, with about 40,000, form a fluctuating element of the population, since they remain only temporarily in the United States, principally in the West. Of the 4,000-6,000 Chinese who are charges of the missions, many return as Christians to China, and of the Japanese more than 1,500 were baptized in the United States during the seven years 1893–1900. See Home Missions, § 1–3, 11; Negro Education and Evangelization.

4. West Indies. Of the Greater Antilles, **Cuba, Hayti,** and **Porto Rico** are nominally Catholic, and in the other West Indian islands there is also a considerable Catholic population. More especially since the cession of the Spanish possessions to the United States, an increasingly active Evangelical propaganda is carried on in Cuba and Porto Rico, as already at an earlier period in Hayti. The principal missionary fields are Jamaica, the English and Danish Lesser Antilles, and the Bahama Islands. In the Danish islands of the Lesser Antilles (St. Thomas, etc.), the United Brethren began work in 1732, and soon embraced Jamaica and the British Lesser Antilles within their sphere. Their entire West Indian field shows 39,000 baptized Christians and is in process of development into a condition of independence. In 1786 the Methodists entered the field, at first through the individual effort of the fervent but restless Thomas Coke (q.v.), and in 1813 as an organized work. Gradually the four principal districts, **Antigua, St. Vincent, Jamaica,** and the **Bahamas,** were included, where there are to-day 160,000 Christians. The first three districts have for a long time formed an independent West Indian district. In 1813 the Baptists also sent their workers; and as early as 1872 they formed, with about 100,000 Christians, a Baptist Union of Jamaica, and to-day their adherents in all the West Indies number more than 165,000. The largest number of adherents belong to the English Church, which has developed great activity, especially since the emancipation. It has placed the mission in the hands of the church organizations and has educated a capable body of native teachers. There are 380,000 Christian Negroes belonging to this church. Not very wide-spread but distinguished by its stability is the Scotch Presbyterian Church mission in Jamaica, with its Christian community of 21,000. Altogether in the West Indies there are about 840,000 Evangelical Christians.

5. Central and South America. Central America (q.v.) with its five small states has an entirely Catholic population of about 5,000,000, composed of Indian aborigines, half-breeds, and Negroes, among whom an Evangelical propaganda is carried on from the United States; besides this the Society for the Propagation of the Gospel, the English Wesleyan Methodists, and the United Brethren work among the heathen on the Mosquito Coast belonging to **Nicaragua.** There are about 1,300 Evangelical converts. The great South American continent is a field of Evangelical missionary effort both in its extreme northern edge, that is, in **Dutch** and **British Guiana** (see Guiana), and at its southern extremity. Since a certain degree of religious liberty was accorded, a great number of North American denominations have undertaken mission work among the nominally Roman Catholic population. Also the Presbyterians of the United States have lately started a mission to the Indians, along the Amazon in **Brazil,** and in **Paraguay, Argentina,** and **Chili** (qq.v.); this work is also pursued by the English South American Missionary Society. In **Dutch Guiana** (Surinam), it is again the United Brethren, who have from 1738, although with interruptions, carried on a mission which shows to-day, grouped about twenty principal stations, a body of Christians numbering 30,000, composed in the main of former slaves; more than half of these are inhabitants of the capital Paramaribo. More extensive and richer in results is the Evangelical mission in the neighboring **British Guiana.** Here the way was opened in 1807 by the London Missionary Society. The society's zeal for independence induced it, in 1838, to render self-governing the 18,000 converts it had made up to that date; about 6,000 formed a Congregational Union, the others joined the English Church which, entering this work in 1839, has gained a following of 130,000. The English Wesleyan Methodists as well as the Plymouth Brethren and the United Brethren have gathered together here 20,000 Christians from among the heathen. The southern missionary field consists of **Tierra del Fuego** and the **Falkland Islands,** sparsely inhabited by a population in the lowest grade of civilization. From 1844-1860, unavailing attempts were made to establish a mission here, three by Allen Gardiner, formerly an officer in the English navy; another attempt by the South American Missionary Society ended in the murder of all the participants. In 1862 a courageous missionary, Bishop Waite Hocking Stirling, at last succeeded in founding two settlements, where up to the present day 200 Christians have been gathered by heroic efforts.

SUMMARY OF THE RESULTS OF THE AMERICAN MISSIONS.

	Christians.
Greenland, Labrador, Alaska	20,500
Canada	43,500
Indians of the United States	95,000
Negroes of the United States	7,500,000
Chinese and Japanese of the United States.	4,000
West India	845,000
Central and South America	195,000
Total	8,703,000

2. Africa*: The African fields of labor occupied by the Evangelical missions include five principal regions: (1) The west coast of Senegal, which embraces Senegambia, Sierra Leone, Liberia, the Gold and Slave Coasts, Yoruba, Nigeria, Kamerun, Kongo, Angola. (2) South Africa, embracing German Southwest Africa, Cape Colony, Natal and Zululand, the former Boer Republics, Basutoland, Matabeleland, Mashonaland, and Gasaland. (3) The East African Islands, Madagascar, Mauritius, and the Seychelles. (4) East and Central Africa, embracing the kingdom of Basuto, the Lake Region, and German and British East Africa. (5) North Africa, with the Italian Erythræa, Egypt and, to a very moderate degree, Tripoli, Algeria, and Morocco. For the details of missionary operations and for statement of results, see AFRICA, I., 4.

SUMMARY OF THE RESULTS OF AFRICAN MISSIONS.

	Christians.
West Africa	208,000
Cape Colony	600,000
Remaining South Africa.	301,500
African Islands	295,000
East and Central Africa	107,000
Total	1,511,500

3. Central Asia: In contrast with the American and African mission fields, in Asia missions have to do principally with compact masses of peoples, united by political, ethnographic, linguistic, and religious bonds, and possessing a historical past as well as an old civilization and literature. They form, therefore, much more important subjects for the world mission than do primitive peoples, without political unity, civilization, or literature, and with a low grade of religion. For this reason much greater obstacles are encountered in the attempt to Christianize the former than the latter. The extensive efforts for evangelization and education made in western Asia, with its old Christian and Mohammedan population, by American Congregationalists and Presbyterians and Episcopalians, reporting about 101,000 Christians and about 62,000 pupils, need not here be noted, because this is no heathen mission; and the Mohammedan Mission of the Church Missionary Society in Persia and the missions of the Free Church of Scotland and the Reformed Church of America in Arabia have had but small success. The present outlook is, however, very bright.

4. British India: The Evangelical Danish-Halle Mission began in Tranquebar in 1706, but it was strictly localized through the entire eighteenth century and its results were small, about 20,000 converts. Only in the second period, beginning with the entrance of William Carey (q.v.) into this field in 1793, and the opening of India to missionaries in 1813, enforced by an Act of Parliament, a slow expansion took place. The Anglican Mission, the London, the Baptist, the Wesleyan Methodist, and the American Independent Missions, and the Basel, Leipsic, and Gossner Missions, were most active. Especially the entrance of the Scotch missions of the Established Church as well as of the Free Church was of prime importance because this gave quite an impulse to the establishment of schools through the prominent missionaries John Wilson, Alexander Duff (q.v.), and John Anderson, and extended this activity to the upper classes. Even this second period bears essentially the character of foundation work and experiment; the numerical result is in round numbers about 130,000 Evangelical Christians. The third period, from the great rebellion in 1857 to the present day, is marked by the unhindered expansion of the mission over all the provinces of this vast empire, reaching far up into Afghanistan and to the doors of Tibet; by the organization of churches; by the increase of the number of societies to about seventy, and of the Occidental and native ordained workers to 1,000 of the former, and 900 of the latter; by the improvement of missionary methods; by an augmented activity in education and literature as well as by an increase in the number of women and physicians. In this period belongs also the great native movements both of reform and reaction (Brahmo Somaj, q.v., and the like), which partly prepared the way for Christianity and partly opposed it; in any case they give proof that the preaching of the Gospel has produced a fermentation showing that Christianity has begun to influence the religious atmosphere of the land. The growing female and medical mission, which has already numerous native women in its service, has gained great importance; among these the work of the Brahmin widow, Pandita Ramabai (q.v.), a deaconess of a superior kind, with her influential institutions in and near Poona, merits special mention. While in the second missionary period the prevailing form was individual mission work, in the third compact masses of Christians gathered from which sprang church organizations. This concentration is most marked in the south in the country of the Tamils, especially in Tinnevelli, the Anglican field of labor in the north in the region of the Telugus, the field of the American Baptists; and in the southwest, in Cochin and Travancore, the field of the London Missionary Society; in the presidency of Bengal, the field of the Gossner-Kols Mission, and in the northwest provinces in Oudh, the sphere of the American Methodist Episcopalians; and, lastly, in Lower Burma, in the Karen mission of the American Baptists. The great majority of Hindu Christians belong to the lower castes or to the casteless tribes, and their religious and moral quality is still elementary. But it is an important fact in the defense of missions, that precisely through the religious, moral, social, and even economic elevation of these down-trodden peoples, Christianity has shown a saving power which has been acknowledged even by the Brahmins. It is true that, while no general Christian movement has reached the higher castes, there are also converts from them; among the native government officials, lawyers, physicians, and others, a considerable per-

*Supplementary or confirmatory data will be found for these fields in AFRICA, II.

centage are Christians, and of the native pastors, the most eminent are from the higher castes. There are, moreover, among them not a few secret Christians who lack the courage for open adherence. It must be admitted, nevertheless, that the number of the religiously indifferent is growing among them, and even of the entirely unbelieving, and these are more difficult to reach than orthodox Hindus. In British Ceylon, whose population follow either a corrupt Hinduism or Buddhism or a barbarous demon worship, the old Dutch Mission has scarcely left a trace, and it is only since the second decade of the nineteenth century that a genuine Evangelical mission has been established under the auspices of the Anglicans, Wesleyan Methodists, Baptists, and of the American Board, and these are active in educational work. The labor is concentrated about the district of Jaffna in the north, Candy in the center, and Colombo and Galle in the southwest and south, and there are about 36,000 Christians.

5. Non-British Upper India: This is but little occupied by the Evangelical mission. That part of Indo-China which is under French control is exclusively a field of the French missions. In Siam and Laos the Americans and Presbyterians have succeeded in gathering in this very difficult field a few small communities with altogether perhaps 15,000 Christians. In Malacca, where Singapore is the principal station, the Anglicans, the English Presbyterians and Methodists, as well as different independent missionaries, have assembled about 2,500 Christians. For a review of India, statistics, and other important matter, see INDIA.

6. Malay Archipelago: The Malay Archipelago in the possession of Holland is for the greater part Mohammedan and is the field of labor of the Dutch and of the Rhenish and Neukirchen missionary societies. While these prosecute mission work proper among the heathen and Mohammedan population, the Protestant Church in Dutch India has undertaken the charge of the already established communities, partly derived from the old colonial mission and partly ceded to the Church by the missionary societies; they number together 274,000 Christians. On the Talaut and Sanjir Islands 55,000 have been gathered by missionaries of the Gossner Society, while the Dutch missionary societies show about 24,000, and the Neukirchen mission in central Java has gathered 1,000 Christians. The results of the Rhenish Mission among the Batak in Sumatra are very important—about 90,000 baptized. Here an excellently organized Christian Church is in process of growth; it has numerous native teachers and ordained pastors in its service and is nearly self-supporting. The arch enemy is Islam, but from its followers also a few thousands have been won. On Nias, where the Rhenish Mission has been settled since 1865, there is now a great Christian movement, nearly 11,000 are baptized and 4,000 are among the catechumens. In Borneo, on the contrary, which was taken possession of in 1835 by the Rhenish Mission, and where seven missionaries were murdered in a bloody insurrection in 1859, the results up to date have been very slight; the number of the baptized has just passed 2,000 in British North Borneo; the Society for the Propagation of the Gospel has worked since 1848 not without success among the Jaks, reporting 3,000 baptized. The total number of Evangelical Christians in the Malay Archipelago is 472,000.

7. China: See CHINA, II., 3, §§ 1–7.

8. Korea: See the article KOREA.

9. Japan: See the article JAPAN.

SUMMARY OF THE RESULTS OF THE ASIATIC MISSIONS.

	Christians.
British India and Ceylon	1,195,000
Non-British Upper-India	9,500
Malay Archipelago	472,000
China, with Korea	398,500
Japan	71,800
Total	2,146,800

10. Oceania: The South Sea Missions, inspired by Cook's discoveries, have extended gradually over all the South Sea Islands, starting from Tahiti, where the London Missionary Society established itself in 1797. The American Board, the Church Missionary Society, the Melanesian, the Wesleyan Methodists, the Scotch and Canadian Presbyterians, the Paris and some German missionary societies also occupy the field. Polynesia is for the most part already Christianized. In the **Hawaiian Islands** (q.v.), the American Board began in 1820 its work of Christianization and in 1870 the work was declared completed. Hurried away by its zeal for doctrinal independence, the American Board left the young mission church to itself, although it was not yet ripe for self-government, and the consequence was a reaction, both within and without. Of 38,000 Christians, full-blooded and half-breed natives, scarcely 15,000 remained in that Church; others went over to the Anglican Mission, which later entered this field, or became Catholics; a part may also have relapsed to heathenism. Among the numerous Japanese and Chinese immigrants some conversions have been made. The Evangelical mission had an eventful history in the three groups of the **Society Islands,** especially in Tahiti. In 1815 the complete victory of King Pomare helped the Christian party to power; in 1826 the conversion *en masse* began; in 1836, the Catholic propaganda forced its way into the field; in 1842, a French protectorate was proclaimed, and lastly, in 1863, the Paris Missionary Society in Tahiti had to relieve the London Missionary Society, and in 1887 also in Rajatea. The former has now in its care all the 11,000 converted natives. The whole English **Hervey Archipelago,** of which Raratonga was made widely known by John Williams (q.v.), has been Christianized by the London Missionary Society, with its 9,000 church members. The same is the case with the Samoan group, now mostly German; but here, besides the London Missionary Society, the Wesleyan Methodists were also active, reporting 32,000 converts. Principally by native teachers from Raratonga and Samoa, the **Takelan,** the **Ellice** and southern **Gilbert Islands** are all, at least for the greater part, Christianized. The London Missionary Society counts here about 11,000 Christians. By the Wesleyan Methodists, the neighboring **Tonga Islands** have also been thoroughly Christianized, with their 17,000 converts. In the **Witi Archipelago** Wesleyan Methodists gathered 98,000 converts. Much more recent than in Polynesia is the mission in **Melanesia,** which lies to the west and is inhabited by a half-savage population. Here the most successful and best occupied field is in the **New Hebrides,** which are divided into three groups. With the Melanesian Missionary Society, the Scotch, Canadian, and Australian Presbyterians do nearly all the work which has resulted in gathering about 20,000 Christians among 85,000 inhabitants. Here John G. Paton (q.v.) did his heroic work. The Melanesian mission extends to the **Santa Cruz** and **Solomon Islands.** On the Nickapu Island, belonging to the former group, Bishop John Coleridge Patteson (q.v.) died a martyr to his cause. Altogether the Melanesian mission carried on by the colonial church of New Zealand counts, on twenty-six islands of the three above-named groups, 12,000 converts. In the **Bismark Archipelago,** under the German protectorate since 1884, the Australian Wesleyans have established in New Pomerania, New Lauenburg, and New Mecklenburg a mission chiefly under the care of native Polynesian evangelists; it counts about 8,000 converts. In British New Guinea, the London Missionary Society and the Wesleyan Methodist and Anglican missions have gathered together about 18,000 Christian adherents; in Dutch New Guinea, where the Utrecht Mission has worked since 1885, and in the German Kaiser Wilhelmsland, where the New Dettlesau and Rhenish Missionary Societies have labored since 1886–87, they count 2,000 converts. In **Micronesia,** the English Gilbert Archipelago, and the German Marshall and Caroline Islands have been cared for since 1852 by the London Missionary Society and the American Board, mostly by means of native teachers. Altogether Micronesia counts 13,700 Evangelical Christians. In Australia among the Papuans, a dying race, consisting at most of 55,000 souls, widely scattered and of the lowest civilization, the United Brethren, the German Lutherans, and the Anglicans work with patient endurance but with little success; 4,000 to 5,000 are in the care of the missions. In New Zealand, the Church Missionary Society in 1814 took up the task, the Wesleyan Methodists in 1822; they soon had a surprising success, which unfortunately was much interfered with by the growing white immigration and the agitating land question resulting from the English occupation, which led to a bloody war with the Maoris. The number of Maori Christians is to-day 27,000.

General Summary of Results of Evangelical Missions.

	Christians.
America	8,708,000
Africa	1,511,500
Asia	2,146,300
Oceania	292,500
Total	12,658,300*

11. Conclusions: Against one thousand millions of non-Christians and considering the immense missionary apparatus of the present, the 12,658,300 heathen converts do not seem a great success. But (1) this is the fruit of a foundation work, very slowly extended, opposed by innumerable difficulties and forced to pay dearly for lack of knowledge and experience; and (2) it is the beginning of a harvest which will produce new seed. Missionary success increases in growing proportion with the duration of the work and the number of the workers; in the last twenty-five years, it has been greater than in the preceding three-quarters of a century. Besides this, missionary success in religion, morals, and civilization far surpasses the results registered by statistics. The past must be compared with the present in order to estimate rightly in the separate missionary fields the progress due to missions. The comparison between what they have been and what they have become gives also the just measure for determining the quality of heathen converts. The Christianity of the majority of these converts may be very elementary, but in comparison with the darkness of the heathenism whence they came, it is a dawn which promises the beginning of a new day. In spite of all its faults, the heathen mission of the present day is a work wherein God's greatness is manifested.

IV. Methodology of Missions: The methodology of missions also has its history. It is true that it has not yet been unified, and the diverse characteristics of the various missionary organizations, national, ecclesiastical, and pedagogical, scarcely permit unification; nevertheless, essential agreement regarding the fundamental principles has been gradually attained, even though in the practical application of these principles there are always variations, conditioned by the quality of the missionary organizations. Little by little a clearer view has been gained of the great problems, which became more and more apparent in the course of the work; and if these problems are not all solved as yet, they are at least apprehended.

1. The Purpose of Missions.

According to the idea held by almost the whole of the older generation of missionaries, the task of the mission was considered to be: (1) to convert individual heathen and give them the blessing of faith, and (2) to gather these heathen converts into *ecclesiolæ*, which were formed entirely after the pattern of those in the home lands. Against this individualistic tendency of the missions, by which they hoped to form select "communities," there gradually arose a sober second thought, and the fact could no longer be ignored that the assembled communities did not consist exclusively of real converts, but were rather fragments of a species of native church with embryo Christians, the level of whose religious and moral life never rose above that of the average Christians at home, and often stood lower. The better this fact was understood the more the conviction grew that developed Christians could be the result only of a longer Christian education, not confined to individuals but directed toward the moral, spiritual, and social elevation of the whole life of the people, and toward a leavening of all the natural conditions of the people with the leaven of the Gospel. In this way the broader view of the missionary task prevailed against the merely individual one, and it was realized that in combination with the work of salvation dealing exclusively with the individual, there must be a missionary education of the people directed to the formation of a genuinely native Christianity. In the

* Without the Negroes of the United States, 5,158,300.

closest connection with this broader conception of the missionary task, stands the clearer recognition of the missionary aim, namely, the founding of self-supporting churches, independent of the organization in the home land. This aim calls up one of the most difficult missionary problems, the solution of which is not yet reached. But the fact that this problem is recognized, while the earlier missionaries did not know its existence, is an important advance. All the larger missionary enterprises are now working to educate the convert churches to become independent, only some do this more hastily and others more thoroughly.

A number of important consequences for the methodology of missions result from the greater missionary task imposed by this education leading to ecclesiastical independence:

2. Ends to be Attained.

(1) A rational cultivation of the native character. Only when Christianity is implanted in the soil of the heathen nation in such a way that it becomes naturalized as a native growth can a really independent Christian church among the heathen be realized. This naturalization requires an adaptation of the process of Christianization to all the phases of native life, extending to the language, the morals, and the social relations of the people. This is a task which offers an abundance of the most complicated problems. Two principal dangers are especially to be avoided: the treatment of foreign customs with religious rigorism and a confusion of Christianizing with Europeanizing or Americanizing. The first of these dangers was a fruit of sectarian narrowness, the second lies in the superior civilization and the national pride of the missionaries; both are fostered by a lack of pedagogic tact toward the objects of the mission. (2) The development of a body of native teachers. While much was done in this direction in earlier missionary effort, especially by the free church missions, the effective manner in which this is accomplished to-day is a result of the later historical development of missions, though improvement in this respect is still a desideratum. Evangelical missions, as a whole, have in their service to-day 4,170 ordained pastors and 75,000 teachers and evangelists from among the natives, and it maintains for their education 375 schools attended by 12,000 scholars. In connection with this increase of native workers there is not only an extension of the field of labor and a general systematization, there is also an increase in the financial contributions of the communities, and a continuous development of church organization, so that by this means progress is made in various directions in preparation for ecclesiastical independence. (3) There is an enrichment of missionary resources. Naturally the preaching of the Gospel was from the beginning the principal instrument of the missions, but alongside of this an even greater and more independent place was taken first by educational and literary work and then by the labors of physicians and women. It is true that the educational and literary activities were not entirely lacking from the beginning; but a systematically ordered school organization suited to insure not only a religious but also a general culture for all classes of the people, from the primary school up to the high schools and sometimes even up to the universities, and a literary activity in connection with this general intellectual elevation of the people, have been interwoven with the mission work only since the middle of the past century.

3. Auxiliaries Employed.

In this matter statistics are eloquent. In addition to 26,000 primary schools with over 1,150,000 scholars, —and, what is of importance, over 300,000 girls—there are 1,500 high schools, with 130,000 scholars. In literary enterprise, the Bible translations occupy the foremost place. There are to-day 105 translations of the whole Bible prepared by missionaries, 100 of the New Testament and 224 of separate parts of the Bible, not reckoning those in the dead languages. The rest of missionary literature, which from small tracts up to scientific works covers nearly all the fields of knowledge besides that of religion, is so extensive that it can no longer be recapitulated. In the various missionary fields there are 159 book stores and publishing-houses in operation. In connection with the work of the female missionaries and the physicians, statistics regarding which have been given, there are a great number of benevolent institutions: 379 hospitals, 783 polyclinics, 247 orphan asylums, 100 leper asylums, 30 institutions for the blind and the deaf and dumb, and 156 other refuges, with tens of thousands of inmates. All this is putting word into action, and does an effective pioneer service for the missions. Lastly, when it is noted that, besides the indirect civilizing education which is pursued by the missionaries, there are not only 180 industrial schools, but by a great number of missions, industrial and agricultural instruction is systematically combined with religious teaching, it is apparent to what an extent the work of Christianization influences the whole life of the people. The longer the mission has been at work, the more manifold and powerful a factor does it become in the general education of non-Christian peoples (cf. J. S. Dennis, *Christian Mission and Social Progress*, 3 vols., New York, 1897–1906).

4. The Movement for Immediate Evangelization.

Nevertheless a counter-movement against this conception of the missionary task has been started during the last few decades, emanating from the founder of the China Inland Mission, John Hudson Taylor, and such supporters as Arthur Tappan Pierson, Albert B. Simpson, founder of the Christian Missionary Alliance, and John Robert Mott of the Student Volunteer Movement (qq.v.). It characterizes the missionary task as being "the evangelization of the world" and the section of this opposition represented by the Student Volunteer Movement has accepted as its watchword the addition "in this generation." It is difficult in view of the varying definitions which have been and still are given of the watchword "evangelization," to say precisely what it really means. John R. Mott, in *The Evangelization of the World in this Generation* (London, 1900), declares it to signify "to give to all men an adequate opportunity to know Jesus Christ as their Savior and to become his real disciples," but not "Christianization of the world, if by that is meant the permeating of the world with Christian ideas," although educational, literary, and medical activity are not excluded. Pierson understands it only as "preaching and witness; these two words include everything that is meant by evangelization." Whatever these definitions lack in clearness is supplied by the methodical principles which the movement aims to put in practise. They are as follows: (1) The sending of great hosts of evangelists in order to give all men, in the shortest possible time, the opportunity to hear the Gospel. (2) The greatest haste as well in the sending of missionaries as in the preaching of the Gospel; for this reason preaching becomes the essential missionary duty. Schools, literary activity, and church organization are regarded as of secondary importance. (3) World-wide spread of the preaching; therefore, a scattering of the resources, according to the motto "diffusion, not concentration." These principles are said to be founded on the command of Christ (Matt. xxiv. 14), which ordered preaching to all the world; on the example of the apostles, who as itinerant preachers went rapidly from place to place; and on the connection of the mission with the second coming of Christ which is to be hastened by the speedy proclamation of the Gospel among all peoples. As this view is one-sided and exegetically untenable, ignores the difference between the conditions in the age of the apostles and in the present, and rests upon fond expectations and impatience, so its methodical principles contradict the experience of a century of missions, lack the assurance for the maintenance of the results attained, and leave entirely out of account the grave difficulties which rational mission work must overcome in order to realize even a comprehensible preaching of the Gospel, to say nothing of establishing a firmly founded Christian Church.

This last is the missionary task; the limitation of the task to mere evangelization confuses the means with the end. Established settlements, patient endurance in thorough instruction, faithful care of souls, earnest church discipline and wise organization are indispensable, and solid work can not be accomplished hastily over the whole world, certainly not in one generation. The mighty missionary movement, carried forward by sincerely pious men under the motto "evangelization of the world in this generation," has often been a powerful stimulus and contains in many respects much that is encouraging for all missionary workers, but as a reform movement in missionary methods it will have no permanent value. If all signs are not deceptive, a sober second thought has already begun to prevail; after much dearly bought experience, which could have been avoided, the leaders of this movement will accept the principles of missionary methodology which rest upon the experience of a century of mission work. But see MOVEMENT, LAYMEN'S MISSIONARY.

5. The True Method.

G. WARNECK.

BIBLIOGRAPHY: The literature of missions is enormous; titles can be given here only of books which cover more or less suggestively the different fields. Lists of literature are found in great richness in the subject indexes to the general catalogues named on pp. xii.–xiii. of vol. i. of this work, especially in the *Subject Index* of Fortescue and in the *Schlagwort Catalog* of Karl Georg. A feature of the *Encylopedia of Missions* by Dwight et al. (ut inf.) is the bibliography appended to each article, usually short, but good and recent. Further literature is to be found under the various geographical articles in this work, e.g., AFRICA, and under the biographical articles on various missionaries. For statistics the reader is referred to the reports issued by the various missionary societies, the year-books of the denominations, to the journals devoted to missionary interests, to the articles in this work on the separate denominations, and to such works as: *Kirchliches Jahrbuch*, Gütersloh (an annual); *Ecumenical Missionary Conference, Report on Foreign Missions*, 2 vols., New York, 1900; H. P. Beach, *Geography and Atlas of Protestant Missions*, 2 vols., New York, 1902; J. S. Dennis, *Centennial Survey of Foreign Missions*, New York, 1901; H. P. Beach, *Missionary Literature of the 19th Century; Character and Uses of recent Books on Foreign Missions*, in *Missionary Review of the World*, Feb., 1902; H. O. Dwight, H. A. Tupper, and E. M. Bliss, *The Encyclopedia of Missions*, New York, 1904; H. O. Dwight, *The Blue Book of Missions for 1907*, New York, 1907; H. A. Krose, *Katholische Missionsstatistik. Mit einer Darstellung des gegenwärtigen Standes der katholischen Heidenmission*, Freiburg, 1908.

For Roman Catholic missions in general, consult: *Collectanea constitutionum, ac instructionum sanctæ sedis ad usum operariorum apostolicorum societatis missionum ad exteros*, Hongkong, 1905; A. Huonder, *Deutsche Jesuitenmissionäre des 17. und 18. Jahrhunderts*, in *Stimmen aus Maria-Laach*, heft lxxiv., 1871; R. de Martins, *La Propaganda Cattolica al secolo xix.*, Napoli, 1884; A. Pieper, *Die Propaganda-Congregation und die nordischen Missionen im xvii. Jahrhundert*, Bonn, 1886; A. Launay, *Histoire de la société des missions étrangères*, Paris, 1894; idem, *Société des missions étrangères; histoire de la mission du Thibet*, Paris, 1903; idem, *Société des missions étrangères: documents historiques relatifs à la société*, Vannes, 1905; L. E. Louvet, *Les Missions catholiques au xix. siècle*, Lyons, 1894; *Catholic Missions: Record in Connection with the Society of the Propagation of the Faith*, London, 1900; J. B. Piolet, *Les Missions catholiques françaises aux xix. siècle*, 6 vols., Paris, 1900; P. Peeters, *Les Missions catholiques et les langues indigènes*, Brussels, 1905; A. Huonder, *Der einheimische Klerus in den Heidenländern*, Freiburg, 1909.

Literature on the separate continents is as follows: For **America** of first importance is the massive collection, *Jesuit Relations and Allied Documents*, ed. R. G. Thwaites, 73 vols. and index, Cleveland, 1896 sqq.; J. G. Shea, *History of Catholic Missions among the Indian Tribes of the United States from 1529 A.D. to 1854 A.D.*, New York, 1857; W. I. Kip, *The Early Jesuit Missions in North America*, Albany, 1873; C. Hawley, *Early Chapters in Cayuga History, Jesuit Missions in Goi-o-Gouen, 1656–84; also Sulpitian Mission among Cayugas about Quinte Bay 1668*, Auburn, N.Y., 1879; J. Cardus, *Las Misiones franciscanas entre los infideles de Bolivia, 1883–84*, Barcelona, 1886; S. R. Monner, *Misiones guaraniticas 1607–1800*, Buenos Ayres, 1892; A. Coll, *Segunda memoria de las Misiones de Fernando Poo*, Madrid, 1899; G. W. James, *In and out of the Old Missions of California; an Account of the Franciscan Missions*, Boston, 1905. For **Africa** consult: L. Bethune, *Les Missions catholiques d'Afrique*, Lille, 1889; F. Klein, *Le Cardinal Lavigerie et ses œuvres d'Afrique*, Paris, 1890; M. J., *L'Ouganda; la mission catholique et les agents de la compagnie anglaise*, Paris, 1893; E. Colin and P. Suau, *Madagascar et la mission catholique*, Paris, 1895; *Société des missionaires d'Afrique, Pères Blancs memento chronologique*, Paris, 1900; A. de Carouge, *Une Mission en Ethiopie d'après les mémoires du Cardinal Massaja*, Paris, 1902; M. M. Mulhall, *Explorers in the New World before and after Columbus, and the Story of the Jesuit Missions of Paraguay*, London, 1909. For **Asia** consult: C. M. Caddell, *History of Roman Catholic Missions in Japan and Paraguay*, London and New York, 1856; W. Strickland, *Catholic Missions in Southern India to 1865*, London, 1865; Berthold-Ignace, *Histoire de la mission de Perse par les pères Carmes-Déchaussés, 1604–18*, Brussels, 1887; L. de Guzman, *Historia de la misiones de la Compania de Jesus en l'India y China*, Bilbao, 1891; L. Guiot, *La Mission du Su-Tchuen au xviii. siècle*, Paris, 1892; A. F. Cardim, *Batalhas da Companhia de Jesus na sua provincia do Japao*, Lisbon, 1894; M. Jullien, *La Nouvelle Mission* *de la Compagnie de Jesus en Syrie, 1831–95*, Tours, 1898; A. Launay, *Les Missionaires français au Tonkin*, Paris, 1900; idem, *Histoire des missions de l'Indie*, 4 vols., ib. 1898; B. A. H. Wilberforce, *Dominican Missions and Martyrs in Japan*, London, 1897; C. M. Caddell, *The Cross in Japan; a History of the Missions of St. Francis Xavier and the early Jesuits*, ib. 1904; A. Ligneul, *L'Évangile au Japon au xx. siècle*, Paris, 1904; M. Steichen, *Les Daimyo chrétiens; un siècle de l'histoire du Japon 1529–1650*, Hongkong, 1904. For **New Zealand**: A. Monfat, *Les Origines de la foi catholique dans la Nouvelle-Zelande; les Maoris; étude historique*, Lyons, 1896.

On the philosophy, methods, and economics of Protestant missions consult: W. P. Walsh, *Christian Missions*, London, 1862; D. Dorchester, *The Problem of Religious Progress*, New York, 1881; T. E. Slater, *The Philosophy of Missions*, London, 1882; G. Warneck, *Modern Missions and Culture*, Edinburgh, 1883; C. H. Carpenter, *Studies in Mission Economics*, Philadelphia, 1886; J. Liggins, *The Great Value and Success of Foreign Missions; with an Introduction by Arthur T. Pierson*, New York, 1889; B. Broomhall, *Evangelization of the World*, London, 1894; R. N. Cust, *Essay on the Prevailing Methods of the Evangelization of the non-Christian World*, ib. 1894; idem, *The Gospel Message, or Essays on the different Aspects of Christian Missions*, ib. 1896; S. L. Baldwin, *Foreign Missions of the Protestant Churches*, New York, 1900; J. R. Mott, *The Evangelization of the World in this Generation*, ib. 1900; C. M. Yonge, *The Making of a Missionary*, London, 1900; E. T. Churton, *Foreign Missions*, New York, 1901; J. C. Gibson, *Mission Problems and Methods in S. China*, Edinburgh, 1901; V. F. Penrose, *Opportunities in the Path of the Great Physician*, Philadelphia, 1902; H. H. Montgomery, *Foreign Missions*, London, 1902; idem, *Principles and Problems of Foreign Missions*, Westminster, 1904; A. Murray, *The Key to the Missionary Problem*, New York, 1902; R. E. Speer, *Missionary Principles and Practices*, ib. 1902; idem, *Missions and Modern History*, 2 vols., ib. 1904; Bryan F. Clinch, *California and its Missions*, 2 vols., San Francisco, 1904; J. R. Mott, *The Home Ministry and Modern Missions*, London, 1905; R. A. Hume, *Missions from the Modern View*, New York, 1905; J. L. Barton, *The Missionary and his Critics*, ib. 1906; J. S. Dennis, *Christian Missions and Social Progress*, 3 vols., ib. 1897, 1902, 1906; idem, *The New Horoscope of Missions*, ib. 1908; A. J. Brown, *The Foreign Missionary: An Incarnation of a World Movement*, ib. 1907; J. H. J. Ellison and G. H. S. Walpole, *Church and Empire: Essays on the Responsibilities of Empire*, London, 1907 (not on Church and State, but on coordinating Christian efforts); L. G. Mylne, *Mission to Hindus; A Contribution to the Study of Missionary Methods*, London, 1908; E. M. Bliss, *The Missionary Enterprise*, New York, 1908; W. Owen Carver, *Missions in the Plan of the Ages*, ib. 1909.

For early missions consult the various church histories, and the following special works: C. Merivale (editor), *Conversion of the West*, 5 vols. (I. *The Continental Teutons*, by C. Merivale; II. *The Celts*, by G. F. Maclear; III. *The English*, by G. F. Maclear; IV. *The Northmen*, by G. F. Maclear; V. *The Slavs*, by G. F. Maclear), London, 1878, New York, 1879; J. Wyse, *A Thousand Years, or, The Missionary Centers of the Middle Ages*, London, 1872; L. C. Barnes, *Two Thousand Years of Missions before Carey*, Chicago, 1901; A. Harnack, *Die Mission und Ausbreitung des Christentums in der ersten drei Jahrhunderten*, Leipsic, 1902, 2d ed., 1906, Eng. transl., *Expansion of Christianity*, 2 vols., New York, 1904–05, 2d ed., 1909; G. Smith, *Short History of Christian Missions; from Abraham and Paul to Carey*, Edinburgh, 1904; Schaff, *Christian Church*, V., 1, chap. ix.

For the missionary societies consult: J. M. Reid, *Missions and Missionary Society of the Methodist Episcopal Church*, 2 vols., New York, 1879; *Society for the Propagation of the Gospel; Digest of the Records of the Society*, London, 1893; idem, *Results of 180 Years of Work*, London, 1887; N. Landmark, *Det Norske Missionsselskab*, Christiania, 1889; C. S. Horne, *Story of the London Missionary Society*, London, 1894; E. F. Kruijf, *Geschiedenis van het Nederlandsche Zendelingsgenootschap*, Groningen, 1894; C. Hole, *Early History of the Church Missionary Society to the End of 1814 A.D.*, London, 1896; W. O. B. Allen and E. McClure, *Two Hundred Years: the History of the Society for Promoting Christian Knowledge, 1698–1898*, London, 1898; R. Lovett, *History of the London Missionary Society, 1795–1895*, 2 vols., ib. 1899; E. Stock, *The History of the Church Missionary Society*, ib. 1899; P. Eppler, *Geschichte der Basler Mission, 1815–99*, Basel, 1900; J. T. Hamilton, *History of the Missions of the Moravian Church during the 18th and 19th Centuries*, Bethlehem, 1901; C. F. Pascoe, *200 Years of the Society for the Propagation of the Gospel 1701–1900*, London, 1901; W. Bornemann, *Einführung in die evangelische Missionskunde im Anschluss an die Basler Mission*, Tübingen, 1902; E. F. Merriam, *History of the American Baptist Missions*, Philadelphia, 1902; *Centenary Volume of the Church Missionary Society 1799–1899*, London, 1902; W. H. Eaton, *Historical Sketch of the Massachusetts Baptist Missionary Society, 1802–1902*, Boston, 1903; R. Clark, *Missions of the Church Missionary Society and the Church of England Zenana Missionary Society in the Punjab and Sindh*, London, 1904; J. T. N. Løgstrup, *Det danske Missionsselskabs Historie*, Copenhagen, 1905; I. H. Barnes, *In Salisbury Square, An Account of the Church Missionary House*, London, 1905; A. F. Beard, *A Crusade of Brotherhood: a Hist. of the American Missionary Association*, Boston, 1909.

More or less general surveys of mission work are furnished by: F. E. A. Forster, *Heralds of the Cross*, London, 1882; A. C. Thompson, *Moravian Missions*, London, 1883; A. H. de Wandelbourg, *Études sur l'Orient et ses missions*, Paris, 1883; James Croil, *The Missionary Problem; a History of Protestant Missions in some of the principal Fields of Missionary Enterprise; with a historical and statistical Account of the Rise and Progress of Missionary Societies in the 19th Century*, Toronto, 1884; G. W. Hervey, *Story of Baptist Missions in Foreign Lands*, ib. 1884; E. Hodder, *Conquests of the Cross*, 3 vols., London, 1890; R. Young, *Success of Christian Missions*, ib. 1890; *Centenary Celebration of the Baptist Missionary Society*, ib. 1893, and *Centenary Volume of the Society*, ib. 1892; J. S. Dennis, *Foreign Missions after a Century*, Edinburgh, 1894; A. T. Pierson, *The New Acts of the Apostles*, London, 1894; idem, *Modern Mission Century*, New York, 1901; E. A. Lawrence, *Modern Missions in the East*, ib. 1895; D. L. Leonard, *A Hundred Years of Missions*, ib. 1895; idem, *Missionary Annals of the Nineteenth Century*, Cleveland, 1899; P. Barclay, *A Survey of Foreign Missions*, Edinburgh, 1897; E. M. Bliss, *History of Missions*, New York, 1897; A. H. Japp, *Master Missionaries, Chapters in Pioneer Effort throughout the World*, London, 1905; G. Warneck, *Outlines of a History of Protestant Missions*, London, 1906; E. Stock, *The Story of Church Missions*, London, 1907; *Methods of Mission Work among Moslems. By various Authors*, New York, 1908; H. C. Vedder, *Christian Epoch-makers: The Story of the great missionary Eras in the Hist. of Christianity*, Philadelphia, 1908; W. T. Whitley, *Missionary Achievement*, London and New York, 1908; J. L. Warneck, *The Living Christ and Dying Heathenism*, ib. 1909.

On **Africa**, besides the literature under AFRICA, consult: G. E. Beskow, *Den Svenska Missionen i Ost-Afrika*, Stockholm, 1884; A. E. M. A. Morshead, *History of the Universities' Mission to Central Africa, 1859–96*, London, 1897; S. G. Stock, *The Story of Uganda*, ib. 1894; W. L. Elmslie, *Among the Wild Ngoni; Chapters in the History of the Livingstonia Mission in British Central Africa*, Edinburgh, 1899; F. E. Guinness, *The New World of Central Africa. With History of the first Mission in the Congo*, London, 1890; J. Spillman, *Vom Cap zum Sambesi. Die Anfänge der Sambesi Mission*, Freiburg, 1882; H. Goldie, *Calabar and its Mission*, Edinburgh, 1901; M. Genischen, *Bilder von unserem Missionsfelde in Süd-Afrika*, Berlin, 1902; M. C. Gollock, *River, Sand, and Sun; Sketches of the C. M. S. Mission*, London, 1905; J. Rutherford, *The Gospel in North Africa*, ib. 1900; J. J. K. Fletcher, *The Sign of the Cross in Madagascar*, Edinburgh, 1901; A. Karlgren, *Svenska Kyrkans Mission i Sydafrika*, Upsala, 1909.

For **America**, besides the literature under INDIANS OF NORTH AMERICA, MISSIONS TO THE, consult: W. H. Brett, *Mission Work among the Indian tribes in Guiana*, London, 1881; M. Eels, *Ten Years' Missionary Work among the Indians*, Boston, 1886; E. F. Wilson, *Missionary Work among the Ojibway Indians*, London, 1886; E. C. Millard and L. E. Guinness, *South America, the Neglected Continent*, ib. 1894; H. Dykstra, *Het Evangelie in onze Oost, De Protestansche zending in het tegenwoordige Nederlandsche Indie*, Leyden, 1900; H. P. Beach et al., *Protestant Mis-*

sions in South America, New York, 1900; H. Lawaetz, *Brødremenighedens Mission i Dansk Vestindien, 1769–1848*, Copenhagen, 1902.

For **Asia** consult: James Hough, *The History of Christianity in India from the Commencement of the Christian Era*, London, 1839; C. H. Carpenter, *Self-Support; History of the Bassein Karen Mission*, Boston, 1883; L. Hertel, *Den Nordiske Santhalmission*, Copenhagen, 1884; M. A. Sherring, *History of Protestant Missions in India, 1706–1881*, London, 1884; *Missionary Conference, Statistical tables of Protestant Missions in India, Burma and Ceylon*, Calcutta, 1892; L. B. Wolfe, *After Fifty Years, Historical Sketch of the Gunthur Mission of the Lutheran Church of the United States of America*, Philadelphia, 1896; J. Johnston, *China and Formosa: Story of the Mission of the Presbyterian Church of England*, New York, 1897; H. Ritter, *A History of Protestant Missions in Japan*, Tokyo, 1898; M. G. Guinness, *The Story of the China Inland Mission*, 2 vols., London, 1900; E. Chatterton, *Story of Fifty Years' Mission Work in Chhota-Nagpur*, ib. 1901; S. Coolsma, *De Zendingseeuw voor Nederlandsche Oost-Indie*, Utrecht, 1901; E. A. Lawrence, *Modern Missions in the East*, Chicago, 1901; F. Penny, *The Church in Madras: the History of the ecclesiastical and missionary Action of the East India Company in Madras*, London, 1904; H. K. Miller, *History of the Japan Mission of the Reformed Church, 1879–1904*, Philadelphia, 1905; J. Jackson, *Lepers, 31 Years' Work among them: Hist. of the Missions to Lepers in India and the East 1874–1905*, London, 1906; D. MacGillivray, *A Century of Protestant Missions in China, 1807–1907*, London, 1908; *Centenary Missionary Conference Records; Report of the great Shanghai Conference held April 25 to May 2, 1907*, New York, 1908; A. Lloyd, *The Wheat among the Tares . . . Exposition of . . . missionary Problems of the Far East*, ib. 1908; L. G. Mylne, *Missions to Hindus*, London, 1908; J. Gindraux, *Hist. du christianisme dans le monde païen. Les Missions en Asie*, Geneva, 1909.

Special works on parts of **Oceania** are: J. Williams, *Missionary Enterprises in the South Sea Islands*, Philadelphia, 1889; *London Missionary Society; Ten Decades, Australian Centenary Story*, London, 1895; F. Awdry, *In the Isles of the Sea; The Story of fifty Years in Melanesia*, London, 1902; J. Chalmers, *Work and Adventure in New Guinea*, London, 1902; H. A. Robertson, *Erromanga, the Martyr Isle*, London, 1902; H. H. Montgomery, *The Light of Melanesia*, London, 1904; R. L. Lamb, *Saints and Savages: Five years in the New Hebrides*, Edinburgh, 1905.

Hints on medical missions may be gained from: V. F. Penrose, *Opportunities in the Path of the Great Physician*, Philadelphia, 1902; G. Saunders, *The Healer Preacher*, London, 1884; J. Lowe, *Medical Missions, their Place and Power*, New York, 1891; W. B. Thompson, *Reminiscences of Medical Missionary Work*, London, 1895; J. R. Williamson, *The Healing of the Nations*, New York, 1899.

MITCHELL, ALEXANDER FERRIER: Church of Scotland; b. at Brechin Sept. 10, 1822; d. at St. Andrews Mar. 22, 1899. He studied literature, philosophy, and theology at the University of St. Andrews (M.A., 1841), became minister of the parish of Dunnichen, in the presbytery and county of Forfar, in 1847, professor of Hebrew and Oriental languages in the College of St. Mary in the University of St. Andrews in 1848, and was transferred to the chair of ecclesiastical history and divinity in the same college in 1868. He retired in 1894. From 1856 to 1874 he was convener (chairman) of the Church of Scotland's Jewish Mission, visited the stations of the mission in Turkey, and recommended the occupation of Alexandria, Beirut, and Constantinople. He was first convener of the Assembly's committee on the minutes of the Westminster Assembly, one of the Church of Scotland's representatives at all the general councils of the Reformed Churches, convener of its committee on the *desiderata* of Presbyterian history, and moderator of the General Assembly of the Church of Scotland in 1885. He was an authority on all matters connected with Scottish ecclesiastical history, and the author of *The Westminster Confession of Faith, a Contribution to the Study of its History and the Defence of its Teaching* (Edinburgh, 1866; 3d ed., 1867); *The Wedderburns and their Work, or the Sacred Poetry of the Scottish Reformation in its Relation to that of Germany* (1867); *Minutes of the Westminster Assembly from November, 1644, to March, 1649* (ed. John Struthers), *with Historical Introduction* (1874); *Historical Notice of Archbishop Hamilton's Catechism* (prefixed to black-letter reprint of the same, 1882); *The Westminster Assembly, its History and Standards* (Baird Lecture for 1882, London, 1883); *The Catechisms of the Second Reformation* (1886); and *The Scottish Reformation; Its Epochs, Episodes, Leaders and Distinctive Characteristics* (Baird lecture for 1899; ed. D. Hay Fleming, 1900). He edited in 1860 the *Sum of Saving Knowledge, Translated into Modern Greek* by the late Prof. Edward Masson; in 1876 the late Prof. Thomas Jackson Crawford's *The Preaching of the Cross and other Sermons;* in 1888 John Gau's *The Richt Vey to Heuine;* and in 1897 *The Gude and Godlie Ballatis* from the edition of 1567, both for the Scottish Text Society; in 1892 for the Scottish History Society (with James Christie), *The Records of the Commissions of the General Assemblies of the Church of Scotland, holden in Edinburgh in the years 1646 and 1647;* and for the same and with the same in 1896 the *Records* of the same in 1648 and 1649. He was a frequent contributor to the periodic press and to encyclopedias.

Bibliography: A biographical sketch by James Christie is prefixed to his *Scottish Reformation*, ut sup., London, 1900.

MITCHELL, EDWARD CUSHING: Baptist; b. at East Bridgewater, Mass., Sept. 20, 1829; d. at New Orleans Mar. 2, 1900. He was graduated from Waterville College (now Colby University), Me., 1849, and Newton, Mass., Theological Institution, 1853; was resident graduate for a year; pastor at Calais, Me., 1854–56; Brockport, N. Y., 1857–58; Rockford, Ill., 1858–63; professor of Biblical interpretation, Alton, Ill., 1863–70; of Hebrew and Old-Testament literature, Baptist Union Seminary, Chicago, 1870–77; of Hebrew, Regent's Park College, London, Eng., 1877; president Baptist Theological School, Paris, France, 1878–82; president Roger Williams University, Nashville, Tenn., 1884-1885. He wrote: *A Critical Handbook: a Guide to the Authenticity, Canon, and Text of the New Testament* (Andover, 1880); *Les sources du Nouveau Testament, recherches sur l'authenticité, le canon, et le texte du Nouveau Testament*, Paris, 1882; *Hebrew Introduction, An Elementary Hebrew Grammar and Reading Book*, Andover, 1883. He also edited and enlarged Benjamin Davies' *Hebrew Lexicon* (Andover, 1880); revised and reedited Davies' *Gesenius' Hebrew Grammar* (1881); and edited *The Present Age* (Chicago, 1883–84). He also delivered the Lowell Institute lectures for 1884 upon *Biblical Science and Modern Discovery*.

MITCHELL, HINCKLEY GILBERT: Methodist Episcopalian; b. at Lee, N. Y., Feb. 22, 1846. He was educated at Wesleyan University, Middletown, Conn. (A.B., 1873), the school of theology attached to Boston University (B.D., 1876), and the University of Leipsic (Ph.D., 1879). He was then pastor of the church of his denomination at Fayette, N. Y., for a year (1879-80), after which he was tutor in Latin and Hebrew at Wesleyan University for three years (1880-83). Since 1883 he has been connected with Boston University, first as instructor in Hebrew and Old-Testament exegesis (1883-84) and later as professor of the same subjects (since 1884). In 1901-02 he was director of the American School for Oriental Study and Research in Palestine. In addition to translating C. H. Piepenbring's "Theology of the Old Testament" (New York, 1893), he has written *Final Constructions of Biblical Hebrew* (Leipsic, 1879); *Hebrew Lessons* (Boston, 1885); *Amos, an Essay in Exegesis* (1893); *Isaiah, a Study of Chapters i.-xii.* (New York, 1897); *The World before Abraham* (Boston, 1901); *Tales told in Palestine* (in collaboration with J. E. Hanauer, Cincinnati, 1904); and the volume for Genesis in *The Bible for Home and School* (New York, 1909).

MITHRA, MITHRAISM.

1. Mithraism and Christianity.

Interest in Mithraism is not attributable merely to the fact that it is a rediscovery of comparatively recent date. Two other reasons give the subject importance: (1) This religion contested with Christianity for the religious hegemony of the Roman world more closely than any other of the pagan cults in the syncretism which marked the religious practise of the later Roman empire. Renan says of it, and without exaggeration: "We may say that if Christianity had been arrested in its growth by some mortal malady, the world would have been Mithraistic. It needed to destroy it the terrible blows struck at it by the Christian empire" (*Marcus Aurelius*, p. 332, London, n.d.). (2) The causes for this able rivalry furnish the second reason. The diffusion of Mithraism and of Christianity in the Roman world was from the same direction, at about the same time, and its propaganda, popular rather than philosophic, was carried to the same class of people. In theory, ritual, and practise Mithraism parodied or duplicated, after a fashion, the central ideas of Christianity. The birth of Mithra and of Christ were celebrated on the same day; tradition placed the birth of both in a cave; both regarded Sunday as sacred; in both the central figure was a mediator (*mesitēs*) who was one of a triad or trinity; in both there was a sacrifice for the benefit of the race, and the purifying power of blood from the sacrifice was, though in different ways, a prime motive; regeneration or the second birth was a fundamental tenet in both; the conception of the relationship of the worshipers to each other was the same—they were all brothers; both had sacraments, in which baptism and a communion meal of bread and the cup were included; both had mysteries from which the lower orders of initiates were excluded; ascetic ideals were common to both; the ideas of man, the soul and its immortality, heaven and hell, the resurrection from the dead, judgment after death, the final conflagration by which the world is to be consumed, the final conquest of evil, were quite similar. Of course the rationale behind these conceptions and the ways in which they were carried out were very different, but the general effect is almost startling. The Church Fathers were themselves astounded at the resemblances, and could explain them only by the theory which has so often been applied in the history of the contact of Christianity in its missions to the pagan world—the observances of Mithraism were the cunning parodies devised by Satan to discredit the holy things of God and to seduce the souls of men from the true faith by a false and insidious imitation of it (Tertullian, *De corona*, xv.; *De præscriptione*, xl.; Justin Martyr, *I Apol.* lxvi.; *Trypho*, lxxviii.). There were, however, two very important differences between the two faiths: Christianity had as its nucleating point a historic personage; Mithra came out of a distant past with all its accretion of myth and fancy. In the second place, Mithraism, like Buddhism and Brahmanism, was syncretistic, was tolerant of the practises of other cults. Where it could not supplant, it assimilated or adopted. As Renan says, once more (ut sup.): "Mithra lent himself to all the confusions, with Attis, with Adonis, with Salazius, with Men, who had already been in possession for a long time back, to make the tears of women flow." Christianity, on the other hand, was intolerant; its teachers were confident that they alone had the whole and only truth, that all else was error with which there could be no compromise. It would brook no rival; Mithraism, like all else pagan, was ruthlessly and completely crushed when the empire became Christian.

2. Mithra as an Indo-Iranian Deity.

Mithra was originally an Indo-Iranian deity. In the Vedas he appears as one of the Adityas, a light-deity commonly invoked with Varuna, but later giving way to Savitar. He was a guardian of truth, fidelity, and justice. In Zoroastrianism Mithra was very important. He was one of the Yazatas or lofty genii of the religion, second in age and honor only to Ahura Mazda the Supreme, and is often put on an equality with him. How prominent his part was in Mazdaism may be seen from the fact that in the Avesta the second longest of the Yasts, the Mihir Yast, is in his praise, and to him the Mihir Nyayis is dedicated (*SBE*, xxiii. 119-158, 353-355). Here, too, he is a light-god, while his attributes appear in the Avesta as follows (a single passage only for each attribute is cited). He is lord of the country side (*Fargard*, i. 1) and of wide pastures (*Sirozah*, i. 7), having 100 ears and 10,000 eyes (*Sirozah*, i. 16); his club strikes the demons (*Khorshad Yast*, 5); he makes the world grow (*Farvardin Yast*, 18); has piercing rays (*Afrin Paighambar Zartust*, 6), possesses full knowledge, is strong, sleepless, was made by Ahura the most glorious of all gods, "Mithra and Ahura, the two great gods" (*Khorshed Nyayis*, 6–7). In his own (Mihir) Yast Mithra appears as god of the heavenly light, who sees all and therefore knows the truth, of which he is therefore a witness and the preserver of oaths and of good faith, chastising liars and those who break promises, destroying their homes and smiting them in battle, but protecting those who keep faith. Ahura Mazda created Mithra as worthy of sacrifice and prayer as himself (§ 1); to him the chiefs sacrifice as they go to battle (§ 8); he precedes the sun over the hills (§ 13); is the invincible director of the fortunes of battle (§§ 35–43). He is the warrior and chief helper of Ahura in his contest with Ahriman, the giver to men of gifts both material and spiritual. Yet it is curious to note that in spite of the exalted position thus conceded in the documents of the religion as thus cited and in the worship accorded him by the princes and nobles of Persia (see below), there appears an effort to reduce him in rank in that he was not given a place with the six Amshaspands who are closely associated with Ahura as the seven great spirits, but is relegated to the position of Yazata or genius. Significant for the future is his association with Sraosha ("Obedience") and Rashnu ("Justice") in the protection of the soul from demons, from which develops the doctrine of redemption in the later mysteries. It may be noted in passing that the rites of these mysteries find their beginning in the Zoroastrian literature; baptism goes back to the purificatory aspersion of the Avesta; while the trials of the mysteries are implicit in the flagellations; and both of these were preliminary to the sacrifice (*Mihir Yast*, § 122). While the theoretical and documentary position of Mithra in Persia was as here described, he was if anything more prominent in the cult. He was a favorite with the Persian monarchs, consequently also with the nobility, and was regarded as the especial protector of this order. This continued after the spread of the cult into the West, the royal favor being shown later by the frequency with which his name enters as an element into royal names in Asia Minor, while Roman emperors see reason to regard him as their protector. The Achæmenidæ worshiped him as making the great triad with Ahura and Anahita. His great festival on the sixteenth day of the seventh month (possibly the entire seventh month was sacred to him) was of especial moment in the royal calendar. Sacrifices were offered in his worship, consisting of cattle, great and small, and birds, and the preliminary to sacrifice consisted of ablutions and flagellations. As a consequence of the royal favor, the worship of Mithra spread throughout the empire. Moreover, Mithra was notably a deity with masculine characteristics; he appealed to the soldierly and the virile. It is hardly a wonder then that in its diffusion the Mithraic cult took on the character of an independent religion, and was promulgated no more as an element of Zoroastrianism, the intolerance of which unfitted it for a propaganda in contest with other religions as haughty as itself.

3. Development and Diffusion of Mithraism.

The first step in the development of Mithraism as an independent religion was the carrying of the cult to Babylon, the winter capital of the empire. It there encountered the philosophical theologizing of the Babylonian priests, who identified Mithra with Shamash (see BABYLONIA, VII., 2, § 4), and welded to Mithra's story the mythology in which Babylonia was so rich. In addition to this there was ingrafted the mythology of the zodiac and shreds of Babylonian astrolatry, and this all came to have a large part in the symbolism of Mithraism. Into Armenia the faith was carried, and thence into Asia Minor, where, after the division of the empire of Alexander, Mithra became the favorite deity. It was probably at this period, 250–100 B.C., that the Mithraic system of ritual and doctrine took the form which it afterward retained. Here it came into contact with the mysteries, of which there were many varieties, among which the most notable were those of Cybele. Cumont attributes the development of the mysteries to the habit in Persia of transmitting from father to son the essentials and secrets of ritual. But if this be the origin, there is left unaccounted for the markedly sodalistic or fraternity character of the Mithraic communities. The worshipers in each mithræum were a small body, limited in membership, and the ensemble was much like that of a modern lodge. When it is remembered that the period 300 B.C.–100 A.D. was the one marked by a renascence of that curious feature of savage life, the mysteries, and that Asia Minor was the source from which the movement in the Roman and Greek world emanated, it seems more probable that the new cult took this form under the influences then and there so active, and that in this way the then fluent mass of Mithraic belief and practise took permanent form. The spirit of identification which had helped so in Babylon was employed in the new home. Mithra and Helios were identified, while Anahita, the Persian companion of Mithra, to whom the bull was sacred, was regarded as Artemis Tauropolos. These facile accommodations conciliated the populace, the element of secrecy and the grades or orders of the initiates added to the charm, while the belief that in the mysteries access was granted to the fabled wisdom of the East was one more element in favor of the religion. But the great triumphs of Mithraism were not won east of the Ægean, even Greece was wholly inhospitable; it was in the Roman world where success was to be gained. The story of the transition thither is almost that of romance. Among the people of Asia Minor the Cilicians were possibly the most devoted Mithraists. In their ambition they presumed to dispute with the Romans the control of the seas, and this brought upon them the force of Roman arms and the consequent conquest by the Romans of the "Cilician pirates." Among the immediate results of this was the initiation of Roman soldiers into the mysteries—it must not be forgotten that the cult of Mithra appealed especially to the soldier, and one of the ranks in the mysteries was that of *miles* or "soldier." To this was due the introduction of the mysteries into the army, and the army was the principal of three methods by which Mithraism passed into the Roman world. The successive wars of the Romans in the East brought the

Roman soldiers into ever renewed touch with this cult, and the first Christian century was the period of the energetic propaganda, though as early as 70 B.C. Mithraism was known to the Roman world. It must not be forgotten also, in accounting for the spread of the religion, that orientals formed very largely the personnel of the Roman army; and as these forces were drafted to distant posts in Africa and Europe, even as far west as Scotland, the ardent faith of the initiates in the ranks and among the officers made each post the center of a new propaganda. The Roman roads and waterways were dotted with Mithraic sanctuaries, a fact attested by inscriptions and votive offerings *Soli invicto Mithræ*, "to the sun, invincible Mithra," bearing the names of officers and soldiers. These are, as a rule, where they would be expected—on the outskirts of the empire, along the frontier. But the existence of mithræums in the great cities and centers of trade, Alexandria, Syracuse, Carthage, and Rome, point to a different agency for the propaganda; to these places the Syrian merchants brought their wares and their religion. Also in the rural districts the cult of Mithra flourished, and this points to a third agency. Rome in its wars captured slaves by the thousands, who were distributed to the hamlets and the mines. So thus post and city and village and mountain valley hymned their praises to Mithra. Moreover, the votaries entered the civil service of Rome, and in their transfers carried their faith with them and as devoted missionaries established new centers. In the first Christian century there were at Rome associations of the followers of Mithra, probably organized as burial associations, in accordance with a common device of that period employed to acquire a legal status. The growth and importance of the cult in the second century are marked by the literary notices; Celsus opposed it to Christianity, Lucian made it the object of his wit. Nero desired to be initiated; Commodus (180–192) was received into the brotherhood; in the third century the emperors had a Mithraic chaplain; Aurelian (270–275) made the cult official; Diocletian, with Galerius and Licinius, in 307 dedicated a temple to Mithra; and Julian was a devotee. Indeed, the un-Roman cult of the worship of the emperors is a direct reflection of the oriental cults in which the sun was the attendant and patron of the ruler.

The four elements, fire, water, earth, and air—the first and third typified by the lion and the serpent—were deified and worshiped. So, too, the sun, moon and planets were objects of regard. Babylonian influence wove into Mithraism its theories of the control by each of the planets of one day in the week, and with each a metal was associated, while the signs of the zodiac, which take creation under their influence, marked the devotions of the months in their turn.

4. Mythology and Theology.

In the background as the primal cause which created and governed all things was Kronos, Unending Time, figured as a lion-headed human figure with four wings, sexless and passionless, his legs and body in the embrace (sometimes sixfold) of a serpent (representing the motion of the sun in the ecliptic), the head of which rested on his head. The figure carried a key, a scepter, and a torch, while the insignia of other deities (the thunderbolt of Zeus, the hammer and tongs of Hephæstus, the cock and cone of Æsculapius) were arranged about it to indicate that Kronos embodied the qualities of all the gods. He was fate, destiny, supreme cause, the ultimate creator. The dualism inherent in the parent religion continued its theoretic influence, leading to constant need for interposition by the savior, the part assumed by Mithra, who was called *mesitēs*, "mediator," first because he inhabited the air, midway between heaven and earth, on account of which the sixteenth of each month was sacred to him; and, second, because he was middleman between the ineffable, unknowable, and unapproachable god and the race of men. In many of the monuments of Mithraism appear two torch-bearers, interpreted as the double incarnation of Mithra, with himself forming a triad or triple Mithra. One of these, with torch erect, symbolized the growing sun and life; Mithra himself, in the center, was the sun at noon and the vigor of life; the other torch-bearer, with torch inverted, was the declining sun and death. Mithra himself is pictured in the mythology as born of the rock, and the sculptured representation of this event, common in the mithræums, showed him issuing from the living rock with knife and torch in his hands. It was then his task to demonstrate his invincible strength, and his first trial was against the sun, whom he vanquished, then crowned with the rayed crown and made his faithful ally. His next labor was with the bull, and this became the central point in the Mithraic myth, the portrayal of which furnished the set piece in Mithraic art which corresponds to the cross or the crucifix in Christian art. The bull was the first creature made by Ormuzd. It was caught and mastered after a severe struggle, and dragged by Mithra to his cave, whence it escaped. But Mithra was commanded to pursue and sacrifice it, which the pitying god reluctantly did; then from its body sprang all useful herbs, from its spinal marrow wheat, from its blood the grape which furnished the wine used in the mysteries, and from the seminal fluid all useful animals, while its soul became Silvanus, guardian of herds, also a great figure in the mysteries. Thus the death of the bull was the birth of life, and for this reason took its high place in the ceremonial and art of the Mithraic cultus. Meanwhile the first pair had been created and were put under the protection of Mithra. This was necessary because Ahriman was assailing humanity; drought, flood, conflagration, pestilence, and other dangers were met and conquered by Mithra, and then his labors were ended, the conclusion of which was celebrated by a last supper, after which he retired to heaven, whence he still protects his worshipers.

But the battle between Ormuzd and Ahriman continues, so far as humanity is concerned. Life is a warfare, and to win, the faithful must ever obey the commands of Ormuzd. What the explicit commands were is not known, but that the Persian ethics persisted is clear. Purity was the end set before man, sensuality was to be avoided; lustrations and ablutions were therefore frequent. Philosophic speculation was at a minimum, practical effort at a premium. In this contest Mithra ever helps the devout, ever conquers the powers of darkness, and on this account he bears the Persian epithet *nabarze*, Gk. *anikētos*, Lat. *invictus*, "victorious."

5. Anthropology, Eschatology. The psychology of man is as follows: An infinite multitude of souls preexisted in the ethereal heavens, and these descend to inhabit the bodies of men. As they descend, they pass through the realms governed by the planets and receive from them certain qualities, the proportion of which determines the character of the man. Thus from Saturn was received the determining dispositions, from Jupiter ambition, from Venus sensual appetite, from Mercury other desires, from Mars combativeness, from the moon vital energy, and from the sun intellectual powers. At death judgment by Mithra decided the soul's fate. If it was to return to heaven, it was enabled by the savior Mithra to satisfy the guardian of the gate to each sphere, where it gave up the qualities received on its descent, and so passed to the eighth sphere to enjoy life with Mithra. It is almost certain that the dogma of the resurrection of the flesh was a later addition to the eschatology. The final consummation will be the destruction of the world, a wonderful bull like the pristine bull will appear, Mithra will descend, waken all men to life, separate the good and the bad, will sacrifice the bull and give the fat mixed with wine to the good and thus immortalize them, while a fire will consume the wicked, including Ahriman and his demons.

That the doctrine always remained pure is of course unlikely. The syncretism has been sufficiently indicated, and it is not unlikely that each district had its own coloring—in Rome Jupiter, Juno, and Minerva were spoken of in the religion, while in Celtic regions Celtic deities appear in the Mithraic crypts. But while syncretism existed, Persian conceptions were the guiding principles.

The Mithraic liturgy is probably wholly lost, the *Mithraic Ritual* (London, 1907) issued by G. R. S. Mead being almost certainly Gnostic and not Mithraic. Indications are clear that at least part of the ritual was in Persian. There were seven degrees of initiation, in which the mystic assumed the names successively of raven, griffin, soldier, lion, Persian, courier of the sun, and father; on certain occasions a garb suggesting the name was put on and the actions of the bird or animal were simulated, in this way recalling the mimetic action common in the other mysteries of the period.

6. The Mysteries. The original number of degrees was probably only two—raven and lion, the subsequent increase being due to development in doctrine, perhaps to a desire to increase the awe and mystery, and also to the sacredness of the number seven. The first three degrees were preparatory only, and did not admit to the mysteries proper. The real initiation was called *sacramentum*, possibly from the oath not to divulge the doctrine and rites of which the initiate gained knowledge. The various steps were accompanied by ablutions and aspersions, signifying the purging away of sins. It would seem that on attaining the rank of soldier, the candidate was branded with a hot iron. In the grade of lion, typical of fire, water, the enemy of fire, was not used, and purification was with honey. Those who had passed the grade of lion were called participants, because to them was administered a sacrament of bread and water or wine commemorative of Mithra's banquet after he had finished his labors. Participation in this was supposed to impart immortality. Before partaking, the initiate underwent severe trials, physical and mental, endured prolonged fasting, and had part in dramatic representations which approached the terrible. Above these seven grades was a priesthood (*sacerdos, antistes*) which had charge of the ritual, conducted the threefold daily worship at morning, noon, and evening (toward the east, south, and west respectively), also the worship of the planet which governed each day, and replenished the ever-burning sacred fire. The sixteenth day of each month was a Mithraic festival, and Dec. 25 was probably a great feast. Initiations were probably at the vernal equinox. The sodalities were twofold, spiritual brotherhoods and legal associations. In the latter capacity they elected officials not spiritual in function, who conducted the secular and property affairs. The expenses were met by voluntary contributions, and the conduct of modern church life was anticipated in practically every respect in these directions. The progress of a mithræum and its community from indigence to affluence is sometimes clearly marked in the change from a rude chapel to a costly temple. The communities of each temple must have been small, possibly not largely exceeding one hundred. Thus the conception of brotherhood was fostered, as also an intensity of loyalty which well accounts for the tenacity of the cult. Conditions inside, where all met on the ground of equality, furnished a strong contrast with the social conditions in the empire, where extremes so great were furnished between the masses and the classes. Yet women were not admitted; Cumont affirms that not a single inscription occurs out of the hundreds known which implies a female initiate or even one who made a gift. This deficiency may have been supplied by the quasi alliance with the cult of the Mater Magna, who in the West took the place of Anahita in the East; and under still other influences there was introduced the blood bath in which a bull was slain over a lattice and the blood was allowed to flow upon a person beneath. This was connected with the Mazdian belief, and was thought to effect the renewal of life to the soul.

The Mithraism of the barbaric world no doubt celebrated its mysteries in caves, and this memory was preserved in the fact that the mithræum continued to be an underground structure, in a crypt so fitted up as to be susceptible of an illumination throwing into strong relief the cultic objects.

7. Art and Architecture. The central representation was the tauroctonous Mithra. The torch-bearers might guard the approach, the lion of Mithra was there, two altars, the lion-headed Kronos, the zodiacal signs, the symbols of the different grades—all these were the adornments of the mithræum, while the illumination was probably so arranged as to impress the neophyte during the initiation. Along the sides, at least in some cases, were the benches at which the assistants knelt and prayed. In general, there is reason to suppose that as great differences existed between the Mithraic temples as between Christian churches, due to the resources, taste, and ambition of the communities which they served. The art of Mithraism is original neither in *motif* nor execution. The central figure of the tauroctonous Mithra goes back to a group by a sculptor of the school of Pergamon made in imitation of the sacrificing Victory of the temple of Athena Nike, while the dying Alexander furnished the type of the Mithra of this group. In general, the figures used in the West were derived from the current types of Greco-Roman art; Kronos, however, in the main kept his Asiatic form, the ugly leontocephalous figure entwined with the serpent, though at least one example exists where the head and face are rendered human with a cold calm countenance, while the lion's head is placed as a sort of medallion on the breast. In most cases the objects have little artistic value; by far the greater number of Mithraic objects known are either votive offerings—crude and formless—or such as were made to serve in the humble homes of the devotees in the same way as crucifixes now serve to fix at home the attention of devout Roman Catholics. But the Phrygian cap and robes bear witness still to the eastern origin and Asiatic content of the teaching. Cumont claims that Mithraic art influenced strongly Christian art, that Mithra shooting at the rock became Moses smiting the rock; the sun raising Mithra from the ocean became the ascension of Elijah in the chariot of fire; the tauroctonous Mithra became Samson rending the lion; while the figures of heaven, earth, ocean, sun, moon, planets, the zodiacal signs, the winds, the seasons, and the like, found on Christian sarcophagi and in mosaics and miniatures are claimed by Cumont as adaptations of Mithraic models.

8. The Decay. The decay of Mithraism was begun by the attack of the barbarians on the Roman empire, and naturally fell first where Mithraism was strongest, on the outposts. Diocletian favored the religion because it opposed Christianity. Under Constantine imperial favor was withdrawn, and Christianity demanded the repression of the cult. A Roman panegyric of the year 362 says that under Constantius no one dared to look at the rising or setting sun, and that farmers and sailors were afraid to observe the stars, and this very vividly suggests not only active persecution of the Mithraic religion, but also implies that those objects were regarded with worship in the way which the cultic objects suggests. Julian's short reign was a time of favor to this cult, for that prince regarded himself as under the favor of Mithra and introduced the practise of the worship at Constantinople. When George, patriarch of Alexandria, was slain by a mob roused to fury by his attempt to build a church on the site of a ruined mithræum, the emperor addressed a comparatively mild remonstrance to the city. After Julian's death, the attack of Christianity was definite and furious. But the contest was no local nor easy matter. Mithraism had its temples from India to Scotland, its devotees in families of senatorial rank, among the merchants, in the ranks of laborers and slaves, and especially in the military camps, and these devotees were inspired with sincerity in worship, and were governed to no small degree by a real nobility of teaching, and uplifted by the hope of immortality which was a fundamental tenet of the cult. At times the persecution was bloody, and the remains prove that the priests were sometimes slain and their corpses were buried in the mithræums in order to desecrate the site. A feeble period of revival took place under Eugenius, but Theodosius ended the prospects of the cult.

GEO. W. GILMORE.

BIBLIOGRAPHY: The one book on the subject, gathering up what little is known both from patristic and classical authors and from art objects and excavations, is F. Cumont, *Textes et monuments figurés relatifs aux mystères de Mithra*, Brussels, 2 vols., 1896–99. The conclusions and part of the discussion are available for readers of English in the *Open Court*, xvi (1902), passim, cf. xvii (1903), and in F. Cumont, *The Mysteries of Mithra*, Chicago, 1903. Consult further: E. Renan, *Marc-Aurèle*, pp. 579–580, Paris, 1882, Eng. transl., p. 332, London, n.d.; W. H. Roscher, *Lexikon der griechischen und römischen Mythologie*, ii. 3028 sqq., Leipsic, 1896; S. Dill, *Roman Society in the Last Century of the Western Empire*, London, 1898; idem, *Roman Society from Nero to Marcus Aurelius*, ib. 1904; M. Bossuet, in *Archiv für Religionswissenschaft*, iv (1901), 160 sqq.; J. von Grill, *Die persische Mysterienreligion im römischen Reiche und das Christentum*, Tübingen, 1903; J. G. Frazer, *Adonis, Attis, Osiris*, pp. 195 sqq., London, 1906; G. R. S. Mead, *The Mysteries of Mithra*, London, 1907; F. Passauer, *Die Saalburg und der Mithraskult*, Frankfort, 1907. Magazine literature of some importance is indicated in Richardson, *Encyclopædia*, p. 738.

MITER. See VESTMENTS AND INSIGNIA, ECCLESIASTICAL.

MIXED MARRIAGES. See MARRIAGE.

MOAB.

Moab is the name of a people dwelling east of the Dead Sea and of the land which they inhabited, in Greek times called Moabitis. The modern Arabic name of the land north of Wadi Mojib is el-Belḳa, of the part south of that wadi, Kerak. The western boundary is the Dead Sea, the

1. Geography and Topography. eastern is the desert; on the south Wadi el-Ḥasa separates it from Edom. The northern boundary changed with the history of the people, but the Wadi Ḥesban is probably the extreme northern limit. Moab is a high plateau, which continues eastward into the desert with little change of altitude. The western boundary is an abrupt line of cliffs, with a somewhat broad shore at their foot in the south which grows narrower toward the north until the cliffs rise directly from the water. At the mouths of the Wadi bani Hammad and Wadi Kerak a tongue-shaped sandy peninsula stretches out into the Dead Sea and bears the name *al-Lisan*, "the Tongue." The geological formation of the region is at the base Nubian sandstone, covered with hard limestone on which rests a softer limestone. In various places there are outcroppings of basalt which has broken through the limestone, often accompanied with hot springs. The altitude of the plain is 2,500–3,800 feet. The region presents evidences of having been the seat of great convulsions which have made deep rents in its surface. Especially important are the three great wadis, generally beginning in slight depressions in the eastern part of the land, but rapidly sinking into deep but narrow chasms debouching into the Dead Sea. These are: (1) the Wadi Kerak on the south (the Zared of Num. xxi. 12, the Zered of Deut. ii. 13), called the Wadi Ain Franji in its upper course. (2) The Wadi al-Mojib (the Arnon of the Old Testament), formed by the union of several tributaries (cf. "the brooks of the Arnon," Num. xxi. 14), the chief of which, Rash Mojib, rises not far from Kerak and in its northerly course becomes the Wadi Lejjun, later uniting with the Wadi al-Sultan, Wadi Balna, Wadi Saida, and finally with the Wadi Heidan. The third great valley is Wadi Zerka Ma'in, known in the time of Josephus as the Kallirrhoe. An hour from its mouth is the celebrated hot sulphur spring visited by Herod the Great. Besides the three great wadis, a number of smaller ones issue from the western portion of the plain. The northeastern part of the region forms a rolling plain called in the Hebrew *mishor* (Deut. iii. 10, iv. 43). Southwest from Hesban rises a range of hills, the western sides of which form the abrupt drop to the coast beneath, the extreme projection being Rash Siyaja. To the east is a hill still called Neba, and the Nebo of Deut. xxxiv. 1 should be sought either in this or in Rash Siyaja, both of which afford an extensive view to the west and north. Pisgah (Num. xxi. 20), a name in use as late as the time of Eusebius, seems to mean a definite region in the northwestern part of Moab. Peor (Num. xxiii. 28) was not far distant, possibly the present al-Mushakkar. The fortress Machaerus is recalled by the hill Mkaur, the "mount of the valley" of Josh. xiii. 19. Kerak is a fortress on a mountain lying entirely within Wadi Kerak. The plateau is almost treeless, yet the soil is rich and suitable for pasturage or agriculture, especially the region south of Kerak, and many springs are found. A semi-tropical vegetation clothes the wadis as they approach the sea. The sheep is the animal most kept by the present as by the early inhabitants. Wild animals are the bear, wolf, and rock badger, on the steppe the gazelle and ostrich, while of rodents the rat is especially abundant. The streams abound in fish. The range of temperature is great, the summer heat being excessive and the winter being cold.

2. Cities.

The Old Testament and the Moabite Stone (q.v.) mention a great number of Moabitic cities. Many ruins are to be seen, but the most of them point to Roman occupation. Beth-jeshimoth (Ezek. xxv. 9) is located at Suweme; neither Beth-peor nor Sibma (Isa. xvi. 8) have been identified; Elealeh is located at El-'al, east of upper Wadi Hesban; to the south of this is Heshbon (Isa. xv. 4), which still retains its name Hesban; if Neba is the Biblical Nebo, the city of that name must be sought in one of the numerous masses of ruins discovered there; southeast from Neba are the ruins of Madeba, the Medeba (q.v.) of Isa. xv. 2, where ruins of several churches exist and an inscription of the year 362 was found; southwest of this the name Ma'in recalls the Baal-meon of Ezek. xxv. 9, and of the Moabite Stone. Between Wadi Zerka Ma'in and Wadi Wa'le are ruins on Mt. Attarus which mark the site of the old 'Ataroth of the Moabite Stone; Kureyat, to the south, locates the Kiriathaim of Gen. xiv. 5 (R. V. margin); to the west is a tower with a cistern which marks the celebrated fortress of Machairus, near which must be sought Zereth-shahar (Josh. xiii. 19). Between Wadi Wa'le and Wadi al-Mojib is Dhiban, where the Moabite Stone was found; the excavation of this site is very desirable, since it indicates the Biblical Dibon (Jer. xlviii. 18); to the north al-Jumeil is provisionally identified with Beth-gamul of Jer. xlviii. 23); Ara'ir, on the north side of Wadi el-Mojib, suggests the Aroer of Jer. xlviii. 19. Along the main road from the Arnon are the important ruins of Rabbath Moab, named by Eusebius. Kir-hareseth (Isa. xvi. 7) is probably to be sought in Kerak (compare, however, the "Kir of Moab" of Isa. xv. 1). Eastward from Rabba there are many ruins dating from the Roman period. Southeast from the Dead Sea is to be sought Zoar (Isa. xv. 5). Many other places are named in the Old Testament and on the Moabite Stone the locations of which are not yet found.

The many dolmens and cromlechs point back to a very early period in the history of the land, but no certain knowledge exists of the early population. The Old Testament speaks of the Emim as early inhabitants (Gen. xiv. 5) whom the Moabites superseded.

3. History Prior to 586 B.C.

Gen. xix. 30 sqq. preserves a tradition which represents a historical fact, namely, the close relationship of both Moabites and Ammonites to the Hebrews, though the history of the wandering in the desert implies that the Moabites were already settled when the Hebrews came upon them, but had lost the territory north of the Arnon to the Amorites, who had established there a rich kingdom. The Hebrews were at first regarded as friends by the Moabites, but after the former had retained the district conquered from the Ammonites, this sentiment changed. Of the settlement of Gadites and Reubenites in the region two accounts exist, not entirely concordant (Num. xxxii. 34–36; Josh. xiii. 15). Various accounts in the history of Israel, such as the episode of Ehud (Judges iii.), of Jephtha (Judges xi.), and of Saul (I Sam. xiv. 47), imply vigorous contests between the two peoples, though the details are obscure. David's war against Moab (II Sam. viii. 2) is historical, though Moab had been a refuge for his family in his time of distress (I Sam. xxii. 3–4). The Book of Ruth can hardly be regarded as a basis for historical conclusions, especially since the passage in Samuel says nothing of relationship with the Moabites. Moab was not made a province of David's kingdom, but tribute was required. Moab's subjection to Israel ceased either under Solomon or under his successor until the time of

Omri, when the northern kingdom began to reconquer the territory north of the Arnon, and the Moabite Stone tells of the progressive success of Israel until the time of Mesha, who recovered his territory with considerable losses to the Hebrews (cf. II Kings i. 1, iii. 5). The story is told in II Kings iii. of a new attempt to subject Moab made by Jehoram of Israel and Jehoshaphat of Judah, which was brought to an end by the sacrifice of the Moabitic king's eldest son upon the walls of the stronghold into which the Moabites had retreated, this bringing about the retirement of the allied forces, though the exact way in which this operated is not told (cf. MOLOCH, MELECH, § 7). It is debated whether II Chron. xx. details an independent event or is a restatement of II Kings iii. II Kings xiv. 25 (cf. Amos vi. 14) does not necessitate the renewal of Israel's hegemony over Moab, and Amos ii. 1 implies the independence of Moab. During the Assyrian period Moab figures in the cuneiform inscriptions, sometimes as bringing tribute to the Assyrians (so in the time of Tiglath-Pileser III.), as contributing to the materials being gathered for the erection of Assyrian palaces (so under Esarhaddon), as joining in combinations against the Assyrian power (as under Sargon), at another time as relying upon Assyrian help to repulse the attacks of nomadic Arabs. The hostility of Moab to Judah is stated in II Kings xxiv. 2; Jer. xxvii. 2 involves projected common action by Moab, Ammon, Phenicia, and Judah against the Babylonians; Ezek. xxv. 8 suggests national hostility against Judah on the part of Moab, though Jer. xl. 11 involves that in Moab fugitives from Judah found refuge.

4. History after 586 B.C.

In postexilic times little is heard of the Moabites. Among the foreign wives of the people whose children did not speak pure Hebrew Moabites are mentioned (Neh. xiii. 23; cf. Ezra ix. 1-2), though whether Nehemiah's foe Sanballat was a Moabite is not satisfactorily made out. Quiet possession by the Moabites of their land was disturbed by the Nabatæan migration in the period between Nehemiah and the Maccabean rising. By the time of Josephus the occupation by the Nabatæans of the territory of Moab and the whole district across the Jordan was so complete that he regarded Moabites and Gileadites as Arabs, and cities once deemed Moabitic were said to be in Arabia. A Nabatæan kingdom was founded with capital at Petra, and to this the greater part of the territory east of the Jordan was subject. No important conclusions can be drawn from Dan. xi. 41 or Ps. lxxxiii. 6, since these passages employ the old prophetic terminology. John Hyrcanus appears as the friend of the Nabatæans and as the foe of "children of Bæan" and "children of Jambri" (I Macc. v. 4-5, ix. 35 sqq.), and this shows a disintegration of the old national forces in the region. Alexander Jannæus fought against the Nabatæans and took the old Moabitic fortresses of Medeba, Horonaim, Eglaim and Soar, also Heshbon, which by this time was a Hellenistic city. Nabatæan kings contemporary with Alexander were Obodas I. and Rabilos I., both of whom fought Antiochus Dionysius of Antioch. Hyrcanus, son of Alexander, promised to restore to the Nabatæan Aretas I., the cities captured by Alexander, but Heshbon must have remained Judaic, since it belonged to Herod the Great. The district of Moabitis, with the Arnon as the northern boundary, remained in the possession of the Nabatæans till their rule was overthrown in 106 A.D., when it became a part of the province of Arabia. Later it belonged to *Palæstina tertia*. Under Roman rule the land must have become quite populous, as is attested by the large number of Roman ruins and the remains of Roman roads. Christianity entered later, and among the ruins are those of a considerable number of churches. The first assault of the Mohammedans upon the region was repulsed, but soon after Mohammed's death the old land of Moab became Mohammedan territory. See NABATÆANS.

5. Products, Culture, and Religion.

The beginnings of Moabitic national life were doubtless not unlike those of their neighbors across the Jordan. The people came in from the desert and settled and developed in general along lines like the Hebrews. One important difference, however, was that the latter were shielded from the inroads of Arabs, to which the Moabites were constantly exposed. The history of the land reflects this condition, since there were recurrent periods when it sank into the position of the resort of Bedouins. On the other hand, the native productivity of the soil made it natural to develop a settled population and the culture which goes with it. The Moabite Stone and II Kings iii. 4 imply rich results from pasturage, and this is corroborated by the reports of Doughty in modern times; II Kings iii. 25 and Ezek. xxvii. 17 involve also abundant returns from agricultural pursuits; similarly Isa. xvi. 8 implies a celebrated wine as one of the products. Though small in extent, the land must have had a considerable population. This fact is corroborated by the large number of cities mentioned as Moabitic in the Old Testament. The existence of the Moabitic Stone is rich in implications respecting the cultural development of the people. The art of writing must have been advanced before they could use a material so refractory as basalt, and culture sufficient to permit the reading of it by at least a part of the people is also a postulate. Moabites knew well how to build fortresses; commerce was cared for, and provision made for water supply. Light is thrown upon the religion both by the Old Testament and the Moabite Stone. The chief deity of the land was Chemosh (q.v.), and the Moabites ascribed to his anger with his people their subjection to the Israelites. He was a war deity, before whose altar the foes were slain. He had high places in at least two cities, and Mesha's language in the Moabite Stone involves also an oracle which was consulted. The inscription speaks also of a deity who must have been feminine (the form corresponds to Ashtar or Ishtar) whose character must have been similar to that of Chemosh. A Baal-peor, "Lord of Peor," is mentioned (Num. xxv. 1-5), who may have been identical with Chemosh or with some other deity. The name of Nebo attached to a mountain in Moabitic territory involves also the cult of that deity in this region. All that is known of the Moabitic religion implies that it did not rise above the usual nature religion of the Semites, but the inscription mentions an Israelitic sanctuary in the land in the shape of an *'Arel* (cf. Ezek. xliii. 15, margin).

6. Relations between Moab and Israel. The Old Testament concerns itself not only with the relations between Israel and Moab, but it deals also with the attitude of Moab in universal ethics. Amos condemned Moab for its breaches of the common laws of morality. On the other hand, Isa. xv.–xvi., xxv. 9–12; Jer. xlviii.; Zeph. ii. 8–9 speak from a national point of view, though the date of these pieces is not entirely settled. That the attitude toward the Moabites in the Old Testament is not uniformly hostile is shown by the fact that David had a Moabite in his train (I Chron. xi. 46). The background of Deut. xxiii. 4 is intense hostility toward the Moabites, since admission of a Moabite to the congregation is forbidden to the tenth generation (cf. Neh. xiii. 1), while the Edomites and Egyptians of the third generation are admitted. On the other hand, the whole atmosphere of the book of Ruth is one of kindly complaisance toward Moabites—a book which may have been written late. The general attitude of the Chronicler is unfriendly (II Chron. xx., xxiv. 26). Rabbi Joshua is reported as pronouncing favorably upon the admission of an Ammonitic proselyte on the ground that the Ammonites had long ceased to exist, a fact which applies equally to the Moabites. (F. BUHL.)

BIBLIOGRAPHY: Honoré T. P. J. d'Albert, Duke de Luynes, *Voyage d'exploration à la mer morte, à Petra*, i. 23–182, ii. 81–140, iii. passim, 3 vols., Paris, 1871–76; C. Ritter, *Comparative Geography of Palestine*, ii. 148–156, Edinburgh, 1866; H. B. Tristram, *Land of Moab*, New York, 1873; S. Merrill, *East of the Jordan*, ib. 1881; C. R. Conder, *Heth and Moab*, London, 1883; C. M. Doughty, *Travels in Arabia Deserta*, i. 18–127, ib. 1888; PEF, *Survey of Eastern Palestine, Memoirs*, vol. i., ib. 1889; F. Buhl, *Geographie des alten Palästina*, Tübingen, 1896; G. A. Smith, *Historical Geography of the Holy Land*, chap. xxvi., London, 1897; C. Clermont-Ganneau, *Recueil d'archéologie orientale*, ii. 185–234, Paris, 1898; L. Gautier, *Autour de la mer morte*, pp. 48–122, Geneva, 1901; R. E. Brünnow and A. Domaszewski, *Die Provincia Arabia*, i. 1–110, Strassburg, 1904; Vigouroux, *Dictionnaire*, parts xxvi.–xxvii., Paris, 1905–06; A. Musil, *Arabia petræa*, i., *Moab*, Vienna, 1907; G. Dalman, *Petra und seine Felsheiligtümer*, Leipsic, 1908; PEF, *Quarterly Statement* 1871, pp. 40–73 (by E. Palmer), 1895, pp. 203–235, 332–373 (by E. Bliss), 1896, pp. 24–47 (by G. Hill); *ZDPV*, ii. 2 (1879), 1–12 (by Schick), pp. 124 sqq. (by Klein), pp. 201 sqq. (by Kersten), xvi (1893), 162 sqq. (by Schumacher); *DB*, iii. 402–413; *EB*, iii. 3160–3179.

MOABITE STONE, THE: A slab of black basalt containing an inscription in the Moabitic language by Mesha, king of Moab, who is probably the Mesha of II Kings iii. 4. It was discovered at Dhiban, the ancient Dibon (Num. xxi. 30), by F. A. Klein, a German missionary, in 1868. Attempts were made by the discoverer to secure it for the Berlin Museum, and at the same time by C. Clermont-Ganneau, then of the French consulate in Jerusalem, for the Louvre. This rivalry of interests made the Arabs suppose the stone to be of very great value, while the interposition of the Turkish authorities led them to fear its entire loss. They therefore broke it into fragments. Fortunately a squeeze had been obtained by Clermont-Ganneau through a friendly Arab, so that when piecemeal large fragments were recovered, the reconstruction was made possible and nearly all of the inscription was in the possession of scholars, two-thirds of it on the reconstructed stone. The slab is forty-four and a half inches high, twenty-seven and a half inches wide, and thirteen and three-quarter inches thick, and contains thirty-four lines of writing. The indistinctness and strangeness of form of some of the characters, and the lacunæ, especially in the last lines, at first caused differences of rendering of the inscription. But the researches of Smend, Socin, Clermont-Ganneau, Nordlander, Holzinger, and Lidsbarski (see below, the bibliography) have resulted in practical agreement in the reading and meaning of the entire text.

The stele records the thanks of the king to the Moabite deity Chemosh, who had helped him against his enemies, so that he had extended and strengthened his kingdom. In return, Mesha had built " this sanctuary," i.e., where the stone was erected. He seized the occasion to tell what he had done in peace and war for his people. Among the foes of Moab he named Omri of Israel, and referred to Omri's son and successor, his own contemporary, Omri having oppressed Moab because Chemosh was angry, and his son having vainly desired to do so. Mesha recovered Medeba, for forty years in Israel's possession, took Ataroth where the Gadites had dwelt and destroyed the population as a " spectacle " for Chemosh and Moab, and settled other people there, while the altar-hearth (?) he placed in the sanctuary in Kerioth. He also took Nebo from Israel, destroying all its population and removing the Yahweh altar to Chemosh's sanctuary. He captured Jahaz and Horonayin and added them to his realm. He restored and fortified a number of cities, especially the chief city Dibon, and took thought for the water supply.

The stone affords a glance at the political and religious conditions in Moab and shows the national expansion under this vigorous king. The chief interest is in the relations between Moab and Israel, though it is not easy to bring the inscription and the Old Testament into harmony. Of Omri's conquest of Moab the Bible says nothing (cf. I Kings xvi. 27), though II Kings i. 1, iii. 4–5 records a rebellion of Mesha after Ahab's death, in consequence of which Jehoram of Israel and Jehoshaphat of Judah undertook a campaign which succeeded until the besieged Moabite king offered up his eldest son, in consequence of which the allies abandoned the war (II Kings iii.). The silence of the inscription as to this episode and the reference to Omri's son make it probable that Mesha's rebellion and the events he narrates took place in Ahab's reign and not after his death, and so far appear to correct the Biblical narrative. The stone also introduces chronological difficulties, since it implies that Omri's reign and half of Ahab's made up forty years, while the Biblical account would make this only twenty-three. Possibly Mesha ignored the reigns of Ahab and Ahaziah, which would make the Biblical and Mesha's accounts approximately the same; but the inscription itself seems against this solution. On the other hand, the stone implies a long activity. Not only are important wars but considerable building activities referred to. It is possible, therefore, that the period of the inscription is that of Jehu's reign, after he had overthrown the dynasty of Omri, when Israel (the house of Omri) might seem to have "perished for ever" (line 7 of the inscription).

The inscription has great value for the history of Semitic writing, orthography, and linguistics. The characters are like the Phenician and early Hebrew, but more archaic in form. In the written form the Moabitic language was essentially the same as the Hebrew, though the vocalization might have been different. Numerous verbal and syntactical agreements between the two languages appear. On the other hand there are variations which appear dialectal in character, covering vocabulary, accidence, and syntax. The orthography is nearer to the Hebrew than to the Phenician, but is more archaic.

(F. Buhl.)

A translation of the inscription follows; the figures on the left refer to the lines of the inscription:

1. I am Mesha, son of Kemosh , king of Moab, the D
2. aibonite. My father was king over Moab thirty years, and I reign
3. ed after my father and made this high place for Kemosh in *Krḥh* for
4. . . , for he saved me from all the (k)ings (?) and because he made me to see (my desire) on all who hated me. Omr
5. i was king of Israel and afflicted Moab many days, for Kemosh was (a)ngry with his la
6. nd. And his son succeeded him, and he too said: I will afflict Moab, in my days he said (it)
7. But I saw (my desire) on him and his house, and Israel surely perished for ever. And Omri seized . .
8. . Mehedeba and inhabited it (his?) day and half his son's days, forty yea(rs) . . .
9. it Kemosh in my days. And I built Ba'al,-Me'on, and made in it the (reservoir?) and . .
10. Kiryathen. And the men of Gad had inhabited the land of th from of old, and for himself had built the king of . .
11. srael 'Ataroth. And I fought against the city and took it, and I slew all the . .
12. city, a spectacle for Kemosh and for Moab. And I brought back thence the altar-hearth of *Dudh* and [it] I (dr)
13. agged (?) before Kemosh in Keryoth, and I caused to dwell there the men of Shrn and the m . .
14. (of) *Mḥrt.* And Kemosh said to me: Go, take Nebo against Israel, and .
15. went by night and fought against it from break of dawn till noon, and I . (to)
16. ok it and slew all , seven thousand , and women, and .
17. and maid servants, for to Ashtor-Kemosh had I devoted it. And I took thence . .
18. of Yahweh and dragged them before Kemosh. And the king of Israel had built . .
19. Yahaṣ and inhabited it while he warred with me. But Kemosh drove him out before . .
20. I took from Moab 200 men, all chiefs, and led them up against Yahaṣ and took it
21. to add to Daibon. I built *Krḥh*, the wall of Yearim [i.e., Jearim] and the wall of
22. the Mound. And I built its gates and I built its towers, and I
23. built the house of the king, and I made the two reser-(voirs [?] tow)ers (?) in the mid(st)
24. of the city. And there was no cistern in the midst of the city in *Krḥh*, so I said to all the people: Make .
25. for you each man a cistern in his house. And I cut the cutting of *Krḥh* with the help of prisoner(s)
26. . Israel. And I built 'Aro'er and I made the highway by the Arn(on),
27. and I built Beth-Bamoth, for it was pulled down. And I built Beṣer, for
28. . of Daibon were fifty, for all Daibon was obedient. And I reig(ned)
29. . a hundred in the cities which I added to the land. And I bui(lt)
30. . b. . a and Beth-Diblathen and Beth-Ba'al-Me'on and took there the .
31. sheep of the land. And Horonen—there dwelt therein
32. . Kemosh said to me: Go down, fight with Horonen; so I we(nt down) .
33. Kemosh it in my days. And I we(nt up?) thence
34. and I

Bibliography: C. Clermont-Ganneau, *La Stèle du Dhiban*, Paris, 1870; idem, *Revue archéologique*, 1870, pp. 184 sqq., 357 sqq.; idem, *Revue critique*, 1875, pp. 166 sqq.; idem, *La Stèle de Mésa*, Paris, 1887, cf. *JA*, 8 ser., ix (1887), 72 sqq.; T. Nöldeke, *Die Inschrift des Königs Mesa*, Kiel, 1870; F. Hitzig, *Die Inschrift des Mesha*, Heidelberg, 1870; Petermann, in *ZDMG*, 1870, pp. 640 sqq.; R. Smend and A. Socin, *Die Inschrift des Königs Mesa*, Freiburg, 1886; E. Rénan, in *Journal des savans*, 1887; S. R. Driver, *Hebrew Text of Samuel*, pp. lxxxv. sqq., London, 1890; A. Nordlander, *Die Inschrift des Königs Mesa*, Leipsic, 1896; A. Socin and H. Holzinger, in *Berichte der sächsischen Gesellschaft der Wissenschaft*, 1897; M. Lidzbarski, in *Handbuch der nordsemitischen Epigraphik*, i (1898), 103–104, 415–416; idem, in *Ephemeris für semitische Epigraphik*, i (1900), 1 sqq. (Lidzbarski's researches are practically conclusive); Halévy, in *Revue sémitique*, viii (1900), 236 sqq., 289 sqq., ix (1901), 297 sqq.; J. Lagrange, in *Revue biblique*, x (1901), 522 sqq.; A. Loewy, *Critical Examination of the Moabite Inscription*, London, 1903 (attacks the genuineness); F. Vigouroux, *Dictionnaire de la Bible*, part xxvi (1905), 1014–21, xxvii (1906), 1168–69; *DB*, iii. 403–408; *EB*, iii. 3040–48; *JE*, viii. 634–636; and the pertinent sections in the later works on the history of Israel.

MOBERLY, GEORGE: Church of England bishop; b. in St. Petersburg Oct 10, 1803; d. at Salisbury July 6, 1885. Studied at Winchester and Balliol colleges, Oxford (B.A., 1825; fellow, 1826; M.A., 1828; D.C.L., 1836). He was select preacher before the university in 1833, 1858, and 1863, and Bampton lecturer in 1868; was public examiner in 1830, 1833, 1834, and 1835; as a tutor he had Manning and Tait as pupils; he vacated his fellowship 1834; was appointed head-master of Winchester 1835; became rector of Brightstone, Isle of Wight, in 1868, and a canon of Chester Cathedral in the same year; and was appointed bishop of Salisbury by Gladstone 1869. His sympathies were with the High-church party. In 1872 he appealed to churchmen to consent to an omission of the damnatory clauses from the Athanasian Creed, and in 1877 spoke strongly against the use of the confessional, especially in schools. He was the author of: *Practical Sermons* (London, 1838); *Sermons Preached at Winchester College* (two series, 1844, 1848); *The Sayings of the Great Forty Days between the Resurrection and Ascension, Regarded as the Outlines of the Kingdom of God* (five sermons; 1844); *All Saints, Kings and Priests* (two sermons; Winchester, 1850); *The Law of the Love of God, an Essay on the Commandments of the First Table of the Decalogue* (Winchester, 1854); *Sermons on the Beatitudes, with Others mostly Preached before the University of Oxford, with Preface Relating to a Recent Volume of "Essays and Reviews"* (London, 1860); *Five Short Letters to Sir W. Heathcote on Studies and Discipline of Public Schools* (1861); *The Administration of the Holy Spirit in the Body of Christ* (Bampton lectures; Oxford, 1868); *The Bright-*

stone Sermons (London, 1869). He was one of the "five clergymen" (Henry Alford, G. Moberly, John Barrow, Charles J. Ellicott, and William G. Humphry), who published a revised version of John, Romans, Corinthians, Galatians, Ephesians, Philippians and Colossians (London, 1857, 1858, and 1861).

BIBLIOGRAPHY: *DNB*, xxxviii. 87–88.

MODALISM: The doctrine, first set forth by Sabellius, that the Father, the Son, and the Holy Spirit were not three distinct personalities, but only three different modes of manifestation. See ANTI-TRINITARIANISM; CHRISTOLOGY; MONARCHIANISM; SABELLIANISM; and TRINITY.

MODERATES: The name given to a party in the Established Church of Scotland during the eighteenth century, because of its alleged laxity in doctrine. Their principal members were Hugh Blair and William Robertson (qq.v.). In general they preached morals rather than doctrines. Opposition to them resulted in the formation of the Secession and Relief Synods, and finally in the Free Church. See PRESBYTERIANS, I.

MODERATOR: The title given to the presiding officer of Presbyterian courts (session, presbytery, synod, general assembly). Perpetual moderators for presbyteries were proposed at the introduction of episcopacy into Scotland.

MODERNISM: The name applied to a movement loosely defined but widely extended in the Roman communion, intended, as the name indicates, to bring that communion into contact with methods of thought as developed chiefly by modern philosophic and critical scholarship. The word "modernist" first appears in English in Dean Swift's writings. In its Latin form it was used in late scholastic writers. Contrasted with the other nineteenth-century anti-official movements in Roman communion, it has two characteristic marks: (1) It is international. This can not be said of either Guntherism or Herrmanism, both of which are markedly German. Its international character is much more striking than was the case in the Old-Catholic movement (see OLD CATHOLICS). Modernism has representatives in America, England, France, Italy, Germany, and even in Spain. (2) It is especially difficult to summarize in a series of principles abstractly stated the standpoint of the modernistic school. When Pope Pius X. did this in his encyclical and syllabus of 1907, the modernists united in protesting that not only were they misrepresented by these particular propositions supposed to have been extracted from their writings, but they were equally unanimous in objecting that no such series of formulas could adequately represent what they stood for. The modernist movement may therefore be said to represent a temperamental or intellectual attitude rather than a series of propositions. It is plain that the opposition between the modernists and the official position of the Roman Church was made acute by the attempt of Pius X. to carry out concretely and in detail the principle theoretically set forth by Leo XIII. when he laid down the philosophic and theological system of St. Thomas Aquinas as the norm of church teaching. This direction had been disregarded in practise by many Roman Catholic professors in Italy, France, and Germany. Reviews, dissertations, and books were published, all showing that the scholastic system was being quietly passed over and relegated to the background. Roman Catholic scholars were using in their investigations the methods of research followed by modern scholarship in general. In addition to the introduction of modern systems of philosophy and theology, many Roman Catholics were devoting themselves to Biblical criticism along non-traditional lines. In both these respects, the antagonism between the new methods and new teaching and the traditions of the Roman system on its intellectual side became acute. Loisy (q.v.), the most eminent of French Biblical critics, who in his methods practically agreed with Wellhausen, Schmiedel, and Van Manen, was excommunicated. The papal encyclical is largely directed against his position. For in addition to being a critic, Loisy also in several works attempted a synthesis dealing with the history of dogma and the principles of religious psychology. The case of Father Tyrrell (q.v.), a member of the Jesuit order, who was unquestionably the leader of the modernistic movement in England, is somewhat different, for his variation from the official teaching can not be so definitely determined as in the case of Loisy. Father Tyrrell's books, published with the official sanction, were of a popular religious character, and although they were obviously incompatible with the strict scholastic system, they were published with the official sanction of the church authorities, and the immediate cause of the excommunication of Father Tyrrell was a personal letter, afterward printed under the title of *The much Abused Letter*, written to an Italian professor to urge him to remain in the Roman communion even if many items in the teaching and practise of the Church seemed contrary to his convictions and distasteful to his feelings. It was plain here that Father Tyrrell's point of view was not that of his correspondent; apparently, therefore, Tyrrell's condemnation was brought upon him because he spoke in a slighting way of the administration of the Church, and failed to hold that scholasticism was absolutely involved in the Roman Catholic system of belief. It has been noted that Father Minocchi, the Italian Biblical scholar, was admonished because he ventured in the field of Biblical criticism to speak of the mythical character of the narrative in the first chapters of Genesis. Indeed, in the recent campaign against modernism it has often been hard to decide exactly upon what principle the official condemnations were made. Individual priests were disciplined in France and Italy, after the papal encyclical had been published, who were not known to have written or spoken anything resembling the tenets condemned in the papal documents. The leaders of the Christian Democratic movement in France and Italy have been especially singled out for this treatment. There is apparently a kind of unofficial political and social modernism as distasteful to the authorities at Rome as the critical and philosophical type. Papal pronouncements have taken no account specifically of this development, but the social modernist appears to be in an even more precarious position than the philosophical modernists. Laberthonniere who, as the editor of the *Annuale de la philosophie chrétienne*, has been especially active in substituting a newly modeled Christian system of philosophy in place of scholasticism, and his review, though it has been a clearing-house for many French modernistic writers, has escaped excommunication. But several of the French clergy who edited Christian Democratic newspapers favorable to the republic and loyally accepting disestablishment have been disciplined.

Modernism has had few victims in Germany and Austria, not because the movement has not many sympathizers there, but largely because the critics of the traditional system of the Roman Catholic Church are professors in Roman Catholic universities where they have the protection of the State. There have been some cases of attempted interference on the part of the authorities at Rome, but it appears as if the Roman Catholic bishops in Germany are buffers between the scholars of the Church and those Roman Catholics who have professorial chairs. The Roman Catholics in Germany have been more stirred by the case of Hermann Schell (q.v.), a Roman Catholic professor at Würzburg, who was disciplined from Rome because of his non-scholastic system of theology; but his case occurred several years before the encyclical was published and before the modernistic agitation commenced. Indeed, the genesis of the present policy of the Roman Church may be studied in these separate cases of official condemnation, some going back almost ten years, where what is now called modernism is foreshadowed vaguely both as regards the teaching held and the condemnations issued from Rome. In this connection there deserve to be mentioned the condemnation of Father Zahm, an American Roman Catholic professor, who was excommunicated because of his reinterpretation of several theoretical dogmas in the light of modern evolutionary science; the condemnation of Father Duggan, the English Roman Catholic parish priest who published a widely circulated work on the reunion of Christendom ten years ago; and the long discussion over the condemnation of the so-called Americanism in the Roman Church, which grew out of the biography of Father Hecker, which was translated into French and has had a wide influence on the French school of modernism. See ULTRAMONTANISM.

W. L. BEVAN.

BIBLIOGRAPHY: The encyclical of Pius X., Latin and English, is in *Am. Cath. Quarterly Review*, Oct., 1907, and English in *Programme of Modernism*, below; a defense of the encyclical by Canon J. Moyes is in *The Nineteenth Century*, Dec., 1907. An excellent and informing brochure, by L. H. Jordan, *Modernism in Italy; its Origin, its Incentive, its Leaders and its Aims*, Oxford and New York, 1909, is broader than its title indicates and besides is invaluable for its bibliography. Consult: *What we Want, An open Letter to Pius X. from a Group of Priests. Transl. from the Italian by A. L. Lilley*, London, 1907; E. Barbier, *Les Democrates chrétiens et le modernisme. Histoire documentaire*, Paris, 1908; R. H. Benson, *Lord of the World*, New York, 1908 (pictures the downfall of modernism and the return of Christendom to the pope, "the lord of the world"); *Berliner internationale Wochenschrift*, Nov., 1907–Feb., 1908 (a symposium); J. Godrycz, *The Doctrine of Modernism and its Refutation*, Philadelphia, 1908; P. Kneib, *Wesen und Bedeutung der Enzyklika gegen den Modernismus*, Mainz, 1908; J. Lebreton, *L'Encyclique et la théologie moderniste*, Paris, 1908; E. T. O'Dwyer, *Cardinal Newman and the Encyclical Pascendi Domini gregis*, New York, 1908; *The Programme of Modernism; a Reply to the Encyclical of Pius X. with the Text of the Encyclical in an English Version, transl. from the Italian by Father G. Tyrrell, with Introduction by A. L. Lilley*, New York, 1908; H. B. Swete, in *The Guardian*, Jan. 28, 1908; C. Beauredon, *Le Modernisme, ou les bases de la foi*, Paris, 1908; J. Bourdeau, *Pragmatisme et modernisme*, ib. 1908; P. Kneib, *Wesen und Bedeutung der Enzyklika gegen den Modernismus*, Mainz, 1908; K. Kübel, *Geschichte des katholischen Modernismus in Amerika, Deutschland, England, Frankreich, und Italien*, Tübingen, 1908; A. L. Lilley, *Modernism; a Record and a Review*, New York, 1908; P. Sabatier, *Modernism*, London, 1908; idem, *Les Modernistes. Notes d'hist. religieuse contemporaine*, Paris, 1909; Delmont, *Modernisme et modernistes en Italie, en Allemagne, en Angleterre, et en France*, ib. 1909; Maumus, *Les Modernistes*, ib. 1909; G. Weill, *Histoire du catholicisme libéral en France*, ib. 1909.

MODESTUS: Anti-Gnostic writer. According to Eusebius (*Hist. eccl.*, IV., xxv., cf. xxi.), an otherwise unknown Modestus, contemporary of Philip of Gortyna and Irenæus, wrote an impressive, but no longer extant, tract against Marcion. Jerome (*De vir. ill.*, xxxii.) refers to other syntagmata by Modestus, which "are regarded as spurious by the learned." The source of this intelligence is no longer ascertainable.

G. KRÜGER.

MOEHLER, mū'ler, JOHANN ADAM: Roman Catholic historian; b. at Igersheim (37 m. s.s.w. of Würzburg), Württemberg, May 6, 1796; d. at Würzburg Apr. 12, 1838. In 1814 he entered the lyceum of Ellwangen, devoting himself to the study of philosophy and theology, and, in 1817, removed with the Roman Catholic faculty to Tübingen. He was ordained priest in 1819, and became vicar at Weilerstadt and Riedlingen, but soon returned to Tübingen to prepare himself for academic activity; in 1820 he became repetent, and was invited by the theological faculty to become privatdocent in church history and its related branches (1822). After visiting various universities he began in 1823 to lecture on church history, patrology, and church polity. A series of essays written at that time for the *Tübinger Quartalschrift* (after his death collected and published by Döllinger, in *Gesammelte Schriften und Aufsätze*, 2 vols., Regensburg, 1839–40) reveals an almost Protestant standpoint. Among other abuses of the Roman Catholic Church he attacked the withholding of the cup from the laity and the use of the Latin language in worship. His first larger work, *Die Einheit der Kirche oder das Prinzip des Katholicismus, dargestellt im Geiste der Kirchenväter der drei ersten Jahrhunderte* (Tübingen, 1825, 2d ed., 1843), attracted considerable attention among scholars. Möhler distinguishes between the mystical unity of the Holy Spirit, which unites all believers in a spiritual community, and the rational unity, which unites them in the doctrine of the Church as the intellectual expression of the Christian spirit, in opposition to the heresies as the plurality without a unity; and finally between the unity in the plurality, that is, the preservation of the individuality in the unity of believers. In the second part of the work the bishop is considered as forming the center of the unity of the congregation. A higher ecclesiastical unity is concentrated in the metropolitan and the synod, a still higher in the entire episcopate and the highest in the Roman primacy, the development of which by gradual steps is proved from the historical conditions of antiquity and Medievalism. The work did not escape giving offense in Roman Catholic circles, but it established the fame of the young man. It was followed in the next year by another large work, *Athanasius der Grosse und die Kirche seiner Zeit, besonders im Kampf mit dem Arianismus* (Mainz, 1827; 2d ed., 1844), which proved to be in perfect harmony with the views of the Roman Catholic Church, offering a picture of the labors and struggles of the Church in the fourth century. In 1827 the author was appointed professor of church history at Tübingen. His lectures drew large audiences, and exercised great influence. Nevertheless, his *Kirchengeschichte* (published by P. B. Gams, 3 vols., Regensburg, 1867–70) is not his chief work. He felt that Roman Catholic theology was sorely in need of a deeper and more comprehensive understanding of the principles of the Reformation, and of the divergencies between Romanism and Protestantism, and after an exhaustive study of the symbolical books of the two confessions, he published his *Symbolik oder Darstellung der dogmatischen Gegensätze der Katholiken und Protestanten* (Mainz, 1832; 5th ed., enlarged and improved by Reithmayer, 1838; 7th ed., 1864, Eng. transl. by J. R. Robertson, *Symbolism, or Exposition of the Doctrinal Differences between Catholics and Protestants as evidenced by their Symbolical Writings*, 2 vols., London, 1843; 5th ed., 1 vol., 1906). There is considerable idealization in his representation of Romanism; and his representation of Protestantism is not altogether free from caricature. The sensation which the work produced was great, even among Protestants. F. C. Baur wrote against it (*Der Gegensatz des Katholicismus und Protestantismus*, Tübingen, 1834), as well as C. I. Nitzsch (*Eine protestantische Beantwortung der Symbolik Möhlers*, Hamburg, 1835), and others. Möhler answered in *Neue Untersuchungen der Lehrgegensätze zwischen Katholiken und Protestanten* (Mainz, 1834); and a protracted controversy began. This controversy, especially with his colleague, F. C. Baur, made his stay in Tübingen unpleasant, and in 1835 he accepted a call to Munich. The climate of that place did not agree with his constitution, and his health failed. Shortly before his death he retired to Würzburg as dean of the chapter.

(A. Hauck.)

Bibliography: A life by Reithmayer was prefixed to the 5th ed. of the *Symbolik*, Mainz, 1838, and a sketch by the same author is in *KL*, viii. 1677–1689. Other lives are by B. Wörmer, Regensburg, 1866; J. Friedrich, Munich, 1894; A. Knöpfer, ib. 1896; L. Monastier, Lausanne, 1897.

MOELLER, mŭl'er, **CHRISTEN VILHELM VICTOR:** Danish bishop; b. in Copenhagen May 29, 1845. He was educated at the Aalborg Skole (B.A., 1863) and the University of Copenhagen (candidate in theology, 1868); became chaplain in Ringsted and Benlöse, 1869, and in Copenhagen, 1874, in the latter place instituting services for children at Bethesda, 1877; was made censor, 1883, and later became examiner in religious branches at teachers' examinations; edited the weekly *Saedemanden*, 1879–83; became provost at Copenhagen, 1883, in Gamborg on Fünen, 1891, at Slagelse, 1896; was appointed bishop of Aalborg, 1905. His most important works (text-books) are: *Bibelhistorie for Seminarier og höjere Skoler* (1891); *Bibelhistorie for Folkeskolen* (1892); *Lärebog i Bibelhistorien for Elementarskoler* (5th ed., 1896); *Den förste Vejledning i Luthers lille Katekismus* (1897). Along exegetical lines mention may be made of *Salomos Höjsang i bibelsk Sammenhäng forklaret* (1896); *Guds Oprindelige Aabenbaring. En Fortolkning for läge Kristne til förste Mosebogs tre förste Kapitler, särlig afpasset efter Läreres og Lärerinders Tarv i Folkeskolen* (1892). John O. Evjen.

MOELLER, ERNST WILHELM: German church historian, son of Johann Friedrich Möller (q.v.); b. at Erfurt Oct. 1, 1827; d. at Kiel Jan. 8, 1892. He studied at the cathedral gymnasium in Magdeburg, at the University of Berlin, at Halle, and at Bonn. Returning home, he preached, held Bible classes in the Young Men's Association, and occupied himself with a thorough study of Origen and Gregory of Nyssa. For the continuation of these studies he returned to Halle, where he published *Gregorii Nysseni doctrina de hominis natura et illustravit et cum Origeniana comparavit* (Halle, 1854), on the basis of which he established himself in 1854 as privat-docent in Halle, just at the time when Baur and Zeller had started their revolutionary methods in theological science, and he was led to oppose their methods and conclusions. He lectured on the New Testament, on the early history of the Church, on the history of dogma, and later also on the church history of the Middle Ages. In 1862 he was called to the congregation of Grumbach, a little village in the ecclesiastical district of Langensalza, and about 1869 he received a similar position in Oppin near Halle. In 1873 he was appointed professor of church history in Kiel, where he lectured on church history and the history of dogmas for almost twenty years. He distinguished himself not so much by special researches in church history as by a comprehensive grasp of its whole sphere, which enabled him to become one of the most efficient and many-sided collaborators on the second edition of the Herzog Realencyklopädie (for which he wrote sixty-three articles, mainly on the history of dogma in the early Church), and one of the most respected contributors to theological periodicals. Theologically and ecclesiastically he was a representative of the German "mediating theology." His first comprehensive work was *Geschichte der Kosmologie in der griechischen Kirche bis auf Origenes* (Halle, 1860). But his principal work is his thorough and scholarly life of Osiander which appeared as the fifth part in *Leben und ausgewählte Schriften der Väter und Begründer der lutherischen Kirche* (Elberfeld, 1870). In the later years of his life he published his *Lehrbuch der Kirchengeschichte* (vol. i., *Die alte Kirche*, 1889, 2d ed., by H. von Schubert, 1902; vol. ii., *Das Mittelalter*, 1891, 2d ed., 1893; vol. iii., *Reformation und Ge-*

genreformation, ed., G. Kawerau, 1894, 3d ed., 1907. These new editions of vols. i. and ii. render partly obsolete the Eng. transl., London, 1892–1893, but not so much as that of vol. iii., 1900) which unites a lucid representation with a continual reference to sources. He also revised De Wette's commentaries on Galatians and Thessalonians (1864) and on the Pastoral Epistles and the Epistle to the Hebrews (1867). (G. Kawerau).

Bibliography: *ZKG*, xiii (1892), 484 sqq.

MOELLER, JOHANN FRIEDRICH: German Lutheran theologian; b. at Erfurt Nov. 13, 1789; d. at Magdeburg Apr. 20, 1861. He was educated at the gymnasium in Erfurt and the University of Göttingen. In 1814 he became teacher of catechetics and methods at the teachers' seminary of Erfurt, in the following year also deacon of the Barfüsser-Kirche, in 1829 regular pastor, in 1831 senior of the Evangelical ministry, and in 1832 councilor of the consistory. By the publication of religious poems, *Christenglück und Christenwandel in religiösen Gesängen* (Erfurt, 1817), he attracted the attention of Claus Harms (q.v.) with whom he came into personal relation. His activity at Erfurt, though successful, was hampered by the hostile attitude of the so-called Old Lutherans, who resisted all attempts at conformity with the Prussian Union. In 1843 he was appointed general superintendent of Magdeburg, and here, too, had to face struggles with rationalistic elements such as the Friends of Light (q.v.), and with the ecclesiastical administration of the province. His failing health compelled him in 1857 to lay down his office as general superintendent, but he still remained for some time first preacher of the cathedral church in Magdeburg. During his activity at Erfurt, in the interest of religious instruction in the public schools, he published *Ueber die erste Behandlung des Religionsunterrichts in den unteren Klassen der Volksschule, i., Die eigentliche Gotteslehre* (Erfurt, 1824); and *Unterlagen der Gotteserkenntnis in der christlichen Volksschule* (2 ed., 1836). Other publications, prompted by the same tendency, are: *Leitfaden und Spruchbuch zum Konfirmandenunterricht nach dem Katechismus Luthers* (Magdeburg, 1850); *Handreichung der Kirche an die Schule zum Eingang in die heiligen zehn Gebote Gottes* (1850); *Katechetisch-evangelische Unterweisung in den heiligen zehn Geboten Gottes nach dem Katechismus Lutheri* (1854). His first collection of spiritual poems was followed by *Der christliche Glaube und das christliche Leben; geistliche Lieder und Gesänge für Kirche, Schule, und Haus* (Erfurt, 1822) from which Harms made a number of selections for his hymn-book; toward the close of his life Möller published another collection, *Geistliche Dichtungen und Gesänge auf Unterlage der heiligen Schrift* (Magdeburg, 1852). (W. Möller†.)

MOELLER, LARS OTTO: Danish pastor and author; b. in Taarup parish, Denmark, Feb. 20, 1831. He received his education at Horsens' Skole (B.A., 1852), and at the University of Copenhagen (candidate in theology, 1858); became chaplain at Gylling in 1860, and provost in 1870. He is justly renowned for his original contributions to Danish theology, grounded in the school of Nicolai Grundtvig (q.v.), but original and independent and opposed to the "new Grundtvig school." His chief work is *Genlösningen eller Jesu Christi Liv, Död og Opstandelse til Verdens Frelse* (1884). In defense of Grundtvig's ideas he has written *Smaabidrag til at oplyse den kirkelige Anskuelses Berettigelse* (1866); *Det faldne Menneskes Genfödelse og Fornyelse ved Daab og Nadver* (2d ed., 1872); *Det gjenoprejste Menneskes Tjeneste i Ordets Forkyndelse og Bekendelse* (1877). Other works are: *Til Forstaaelse og Bedömmelse af Nutidens Fritänkeri* (1881; a vigorous attack on infidelity); *Den kristelige Vished eller Troens fulde Forvisning* (1892); *Noget om Determinisme og Frihed* (1893). His attitude to the New Testament is shown in: *Den Evangeliske Historie eller Herrens Liv paa Jorden* (2d ed., 1892); *Forsög til en kort Forklaring over St. Joh. Aabenbaring* (1888); and to the Old Testament in: *En Opdrager til Christus for dem "som ikke have Loven"*; *En Betragtning af de 10 Buds Forhold til Hedningernes Sandhedslov . .* (1899); *Nogle Stöttepunkter under Bedömmelsen af det gl. Test.* (1893). His ability as a preacher was made known to wide circles by *Fra Gylling Kirke. En Aargang Prädikener* (1899).

John O. Evjen.

MOERIKOFER, mœr″i-kef′er, **JOHANN KASPAR:** Swiss Protestant; b. at Frauenfeld (22 m. n.e. of Zurich) Oct. 11, 1799; d. at Riesbach (a village near Zurich) Oct. 17, 1877. After the completion of his theological education in Zurich in 1822 he was a teacher and gymnasial director in his native city for many years, but in 1851 was called to the pastorate of the church at Gottlieben, in the vicinity of Constance. In 1869 he retired from active life, living first at Winterthur and later at Zurich, receiving honorary citizenship from the latter. He actively promoted an institution founded in 1845 at Bernrain for the education of the poor, acted as a member of the cantonal synod, dean of the Steckborn chapter, president of the cantonal Gesellschaft zur Beförderung des Guten und Gemeinnützigen, and was one of the founders of the historical society of his canton of Torgau and contributed much to its journal. With equal versatility he sought to preserve the scientific and artistic treasures of the Torgau monasteries suppressed in 1848, and wrote: *Die schweizerische Mundart im Verhältniss zur hochdeutschen Schriftsprache* (1838). The significance of these interests, however, was overshadowed by his *Die schweizerische Litteratur des achtzehnten Jahrhunderts* (Leipsic, 1861) and by the theme which had attracted him even as a student in 1819—the history of the Reformation in Switzerland. After a preliminary *Bilder aus dem kirchlichen Leben der Schweiz* (Leipsic, 1861), he published the first comprehensive biography of the Swiss Reformer in his *Ulrich Zwingli nach den urkundlichen Quellen* (2 vols., 1867–69); and also wrote *J. J. Breitinger und Zurich* (1873); and *Geschichte der evangelischen Flüchtlinge in der Schweiz* (1876). (G. Meyer von Knonau.)

Bibliography: Autobiographic material, ed. H. G. Sulzberger, appeared in *Thurgauischen Beiträge zur vaterländischen Geschichte*, heft xxv., pp. 2–155; *ADB*, xxii. 260.

MOERLIN, mūr'lin (**MOEHRLE, MOEHRLEIN,** Lat. **MORLINUS**), **JOACHIM.**

Joachim Mörlin, who was an important figure in the controversies following Luther's death, was born at Wittenberg Apr. 5, 1514, and d. at Königsberg May 29, 1571. He studied at Wittenberg under Luther, Melanchthon, Jonas, and Cruciger from 1532 to 1536. After a brief residence at Coburg, he returned to Wittenberg and in 1539 became Luther's chaplain, declining a call to succeed Poliander at Königsberg. While a true pupil of Luther, Mörlin was more influenced by the dogmatics of Melanchthon, though devoid of sympathy with the Philippistic efforts for union with the Reformed. On Sept. 22, 1540, he left Wittenberg to become superintendent at Arnstadt, where, until deposed in Mar., 1543, for his rigid discipline and opposition to union, he displayed great activity, moral earnestness, and courage. But neither the appeal of his congregation nor the sympathy of Luther could overcome the hostility of the count of Schwartzburg, and on May 10, 1544, Mörlin became superintendent at Göttingen. Here he was equally firm in insistence on purity of life and doctrine, and wrote his *Enchiridion catecheticum* (1544), taught rhetoric in the Latin school, and lectured on Erasmus and the *Loci* of Melanchthon. Mörlin's activity in Göttingen came to an end with his uncompromising resistance to the union advocated by the Interim (q.v.), and on Jan. 17, 1550, after vain protests by both council and congregation to Duke Erich, he was dismissed from office. Mörlin went to Erfurt, thence to Arnstadt, and finally to Schleusingen, where he lived and preached in the castle of the count of Henneberg. Yet even here he was not altogether safe, and on Aug. 25, 1550, he left Schleusingen, arriving at Königsberg on Sept. 13. There, since Prussia did not belong constitutionally to the empire, he could not be molested, and was appointed, on Sept. 27, 1550, pastor at the Kneiphöfer Dom and inspector.

1. Early Life.

There Mörlin became involved in the Osiandrian controversy (see OSIANDER, ANDREAS), for it was not in his nature to remain neutral. The break, however, between Mörlin and Osiander was gradual. When the latter defended his view of justification (Oct. 24, 1550), Mörlin remained a silent witness; but Osiander's work on the incarnation and the image of God, and still more his *Bericht und Trostschrift*, with its savage attack on Melanchthon, led Mörlin to complain on Feb. 7, 1551, to Albert of Prussia (q.v.), though he did this so delicately that the duke commissioned him and Aurifaber, Osiander's son-in-law, to assemble the theologians for the conference which was held Feb. 13–17. Here Morlin's sincere desire for peace was evident, but his suspicion of Osiander increased, even though the latter claimed to be in harmony with Luther, denying the truth of Mörlin's *Antilogia seu contraria doctrina inter Lutherum et Osiandrum.* On Apr. 19 Mörlin preached against those who depreciated the merits of Christ, and Osiander rightly took this as directed against himself. The breach was now complete, and after an interchange of recriminations, Mörlin was replaced by Stancarus, professor of Hebrew. Before a new colloquy could be held, however, the duke directed (May 8) first Osiander and then his opponents to present their views in writing. Osiander hesitated, and Mörlin attacked him coarsely from the pulpit (May 27). The duke now forced Mörlin to defend his tenets in writing, and further roused him and his followers to passionate resistance by appointing Osiander to administer the bishopric of Samland, and by requiring Mörlin and others to submit to the decision of the church. The characteristic reply (July 21) was that Mörlin and his adherents refused to recognize Osiander's jurisdiction, since he was a heretic, and they appealed to a free synod. Osiander's opponents now continued their attacks and virtually set up a separate church. This was forbidden by the duke (Aug. 12), who sent them Osiander's confession of faith, which was returned unread. The polemics still continued, and Albert in despair sent Osiander's confession to the princes and cities of Germany, urging a synod. Mörlin's position was gaining strength in Prussia, and the majority of the opinions of the churches outside Prussia were also favorable to him. The very refusal of the duke to publish these condemnations of Osiander aided Mörlin, who, on May 23, 1552, published a polemic defending the doctrine of justification against his opponent, in which he clearly set forth the orthodox Wittenberg position, and emphasized the difference between it and Osiander's teaching. Besides continuing to urge the publication of the opinions just mentioned, Mörlin preached a sermon (June, 1552) directed against Osiander, deprecating speculations on the inscrutable essence of God; and Osiander replied with his impassioned *Schmeckbier*, in which he arraigned Mörlin and his friends. The controversy increased in pettiness and coarseness, until Albert threatened (July 15, 1552) to depose Mörlin, only to receive the respectful but firm reply that Mörlin held it his divinely commissioned duty to polemize against Osiander. Meanwhile a second opinion came from Württemberg, and from it both Osiander and Mörlin claimed the support of Johann Brenz (q.v.), but on Oct. 17, 1552, the weary struggle found its end in the death of Osiander, a defeated man.

2. Controversy with Osiander.

The peace-loving policy of Albert was still to demonstrate its futility. The ambiguity of the Württemberg declaration seemed to him to constitute a good formula of union, and on Jan. 24, 1553, he required that sermons on justification should be preached according to the six Württemberg articles, and that all coarseness should be avoided. This was tantamount to a defense of Osiandrianism, but the great majority of the duke's subjects were opposed, while Mörlin declared himself unable to obey the ducal mandate when contrary to the obligations of religion. This was the only course open to him, but the duke's

3. Driven from Königsberg.

displeasure was now finally incurred, and on Feb. 16, 1553, he presented his resignation. Three days later he sought refuge in Danzig, where he awaited an expected recall, supported as he was by the council and the citizens. But all appeals to the duke were in vain; and the exile at last resigned himself to his punishment and sought for a new field of activity. Mörlin had not long to wait. Brunswick and Lübeck were rivals for his services; the former won by right of priority, and he entered Brunswick on July 25, 1553. In the following year he received an assistant in the Melanchthonian Martin Chemnitz (q.v.), and developed a powerful activity, strengthening the Lutheran cause with the aid of the religious peace of Augsburg (see AUGSBURG, RELIGIOUS PEACE OF), and preparing, in 1577, his *Leges pro ministerio Brunsvicensi*, which all the clergy of his superintendency were required to subscribe when entering upon office. He assailed the Reformed as bitterly as the Roman Catholics. Again, in 1564, the council of Brunswick enacted that the *Corpus doctrinæ* should be subscribed by all theologians, a rule which remained in force until 1672. And this was no dead letter, for in 1566 Johannes Becker, a pastor in Brunswick who had subscribed to the *Corpus* but become a Calvinist, was forced to resign and ultimately was banished from the city. Meanwhile Mörlin and Chemnitz were active in other inter-Lutheran controversies and in warding off Calvinistic attacks; and the former was the prime mover in the rejection, by the Brunswick clergy, of the doctrines of Schwenckfeld, besides being one of those asked by the council of Bremen to settle the dispute between Johann Timann and Albert Hardenberg (qq.v.). He furthermore defended Hesshusen in his pamphlet *Wider die Landlügen der heidelbergischen Theologen* (1565).

4. Efforts for Theological Reconciliation.

In the struggle with Calvinism Mörlin supported Westphal, and to this end wrote his *Confessio fidei de eucharistiæ sacramento ministrorum ecclesiarum Saxonicarum* (Magdeburg, 1557). At Coswik he sought to mediate between Melanchthon and Flacius (qq.v.), and in his eagerness for peace, when the delegates of the Hanseatic League assembled at Brunswick, he held a conference with Chemnitz, Westphal, and others (Jan. 14, 1557), and reached an agreement on articles tending to reconcile the adiaphorists (see ADIAPHORA) and those holding to the true Gospel. Mörlin then took these articles to Flacius at Magdeburg, after which he conferred with Melanchthon at Wittenberg, but returned to Brunswick unsuccessful (Jan. 28, 1557). Eight months later he went to the Colloquy of Worms (see WORMS), but by his opposition to the Philippists (q.v.) and by his withdrawal helped render the conference resultless. In Dec., 1558, he visited Weimar and Jena to reconcile Flacius and Strigel, and in 1560 he signed the petition of the Jena theologians to the princes to call a Lutheran synod to combat Calvinism. Mörlin was also a prominent figure at the conference of theologians from Lower Saxony held at Lüneburg in July, 1561, and wrote the confession of faith there drawn up, *Erklärung aus Gottes Wort und kurzer Bericht der Artikel*, etc. (Magdeburg, Jena, and Regensburg, 1561), which became binding on all pastors in Brunswick; and he again showed his Wittenberg orthodoxy in his *Verantwortung der Präfation so für die lüneburgischen Artikel* (1562). In 1563 the Council of Wesel asked the opinion of the Brunswick theologians for a ruling on the admission of Reformed refugees from England, and the decision was that the immigrants should be received and instructed; but, should they propagate their erroneous views, they should be expelled. In 1566 and 1567 Mörlin found himself compelled to break with his old friend Flacius because of the latter's teaching on original sin; and at the same time he wrote against the Antinomians his *Tres disputationes de tertio usu legis*.

5. Recalled to Königsberg.

Meanwhile, inspired partly by him, the struggle had continued in Prussia between the Melanchthonians and the Osiandrian peace-policy of the court. Well informed of all that went on in Königsberg, Mörlin strengthened his sympathizers with his *Historia welcher Gestalt sich die osiandrische Schwärmerei im Lande zu Preussen erhoben* (Brunswick, 1554). In 1555 he published two other pamphlets on the course of events in Prussia; and finally Albert found himself obliged to yield. On Nov. 30, 1566, Mörlin was invited to return to Prussia, but he declined to leave Brunswick. The invitation was repeated, however (Jan. 31, 1567), and after much persuasion Mörlin accepted and obtained leave of absence from the reluctant Council of Brunswick. On Apr. 9, 1567, he and Chemnitz were joyfully welcomed in Königsberg, and at once began the restoration of Melanchthonian orthodoxy. After much consideration it was decided that the confessional bases should remain the Augsburg Confession, the Apology, and the Schmalkald Articles, the only change being the correction of certain false doctrines which had crept in since the formulation of the Augsburg Confession. The duke, assenting to the rejection of Osiandrianism, readily agreed, and on May 6 Mörlin and Chemnitz gave him their *Repetitio corporis doctrinæ Christianæ*, refuting Osiandrianism, Synergism, Antinomianism, Majorism, and similar teachings. Accepted by the synod and the estates, the *Repetitio* was proclaimed by Albert on July 8, 1567, and Prussia was at last free from theological rancor.

6. Becomes Bishop of Samland.

Though offered the bishopric of Samland, and though urged by clergy and laity alike to remain in Prussia, Mörlin still felt bound to Brunswick. Accordingly, promised by the estates (June 8, 1567) that no Calvinists should be allowed at court, he returned to Brunswick. But his stay there was brief, and he was unexpectedly released. Learning that a patricide had been let go free, both he and Chemnitz sharply upbraided the magistracy in a sermon on July 13, and were cited to appear before the court. Under these circumstances the envoys of Albert succeeded in inducing the council, unwilling though it was even then, to let Mörlin go (Sept. 24, 1567). He was now declared bishop of Samland, while Chemnitz was made superintendent. Henceforth until his death, in his new office, he was active in preaching and catechizing, never ceasing to polemize against Philippists, Synergists, and, above all, Calvinists.

(F. Lezius.)

Bibliography: Important from a biographical point of view and for a review of his opinions are two posthumous works, *Postilla*, Erfurt, 1587, and *Psalterpredigten*, 3 vols., Königsberg, 1576–80; also Koch, *Briefwechsel Mörlins mit Herzog Albrecht*, in *Altpreussische Monatsschrift*, xxxix., parts 7–8; and two lives by J. Wigand and S. Göbel, in *Acta Borussica*, i. 149 sqq., ii. 477 sqq., 3 vols., Königsberg, 1730–32. Consult also the *Lebensbild* by Walther Arnstadt, 1856; and G. J. Planck, *Geschichte des protestantischen Lehrbegriffs*, vols. iv.–vi., 6 vols., Leipsic, 1781–1800.

MOERLIN, MAXIMILIAN: German Lutheran, brother of Joachim Mörlin; b. at Wittenberg Oct. 14, 1516; d. at Coburg Apr. 20, 1584. He studied theology at Wittenberg under Luther and Melanchthon, and, after being active for a time in churches at Pegau and Zeitz, was called in 1543 to the pastorate of Schalkau. In 1544 he accepted a call to Coburg as court preacher, and in 1546 he became superintendent. Like his brother, he remained throughout his life a Melanchthonian Lutheran, and like him he was for a time under the influence of Flacius. During his brother's controversy with Osiander, moreover, he wrote a polemic against Osiander, though its title is no longer known. He subscribed to the strictures of the Weimar and Coburg theologians on Osiander, and made a zealous, though fruitless, effort at the Synod of Eisenach to secure the condemnation of Menius; while he also took part in the futile colloquy at Worms. With Musæus and Stössel, though inspired rather by Flacius, he compiled the *Konfutationsbuch* (1557–58), which was made the norm for the churches of Coburg. In 1560, when the Elector Palatine Frederick contemplated introducing Reformed doctrines into his territories, his son-in law, John Frederick of Coburg, sought to dissuade him, and went for that purpose to Heidelberg with Mörlin and Stössel. The ensuing disputation between Mörlin and Stössel for the Lutherans and Bouquin for the Calvinists, which lasted five days, was without result, but in any case the triumph of Reformed doctrines in the Palatinate was almost inevitable. But though, like his brother, breaking with Flacius, Mörlin was ever inclined to moderation and peace, and these qualities gained his appointment to the consistory of Weimar. Here, in the interests of peace and of Melanchthonian dogmatics, he advocated the deposition of Flacius and the expulsion of his adherents, and with a like irenic spirit he sought to have all pastors subscribe the somewhat Philippistic Declaration of Strigel (Mar. 3, 1562).

With the regency of Flacius' sympathizer, John William, in Coburg, Mörlin was deposed, but was appointed court preacher by Count John of Nassau-Dillenburg. This position, however, was brief, for the count was Calvinistically inclined, while Mörlin was as decidedly opposed to Reformed tenets. Meanwhile John Frederick, from his prison in Thuringia, had induced his brother, John William, to recall Mörlin, who accordingly returned to Coburg in the winter of 1572, only to find it held by the partizans of Flacius. In 1573, under the new regent, Elector August, he was reinstated in all his former positions and his chief antagonist, Musæus, was expelled. Mörlin now removed all clergy whom he suspected of the slightest taint of Flacianism. His mediating tendency carried the day in the Formula of Concord, and he also took part in the conferences of Lichtenberg and Torgau. Besides the lost work mentioned above, Mörlin wrote: *Apophtegmata collecta ex Eusebii Historia Ecclesiastica et Tripartita* (Nuremberg, 1552); *Lazarus resuscitatus* (Frankfort, 1572); and *Trostschrift von den Kindlein die nicht können zur Tauf gebracht werden* (Nuremberg, 1575). (F. Lezius.)

Bibliography: A. Beck, *Johann Friedrich der Mittlere*, 2 vols., Gotha, 1858; W. Preger, *Matthias Flaccius*, 2 vols., Erlangen, 1859–61; G. C. B. Berbig, *Aus der Gefangenschaft Johann Friedrich des Mittleren*, Gotha, 1898.

MOFFAT, JAMES: United Free Church of Scotland; b. at Glasgow July 4, 1870. He was educated at the University of Glasgow (M.A., 1890) and the Free Church College in the same city (B.D., 1894). After the completion of his post-graduate studies, he was chosen minister of Dundonald Church, Ayrshire, a position which he left in 1907 to go to Broughty Ferry. He was also Bruce lecturer in the United Free Church College, Glasgow, in 1906, and Jowett lecturer in London in 1907, and has been a member of the Oxford Historical Society and a member of the editorial board of the *Hibbert Journal* since 1903. In addition to translating A. Harnack's *Die Mission und Ausbreitung des Urchristentums* (Leipsic, 1902; 2d ed., 1906) under the title *Expansion of Christianity in the first three Centuries* (2 vols., London, 1904–05, 2d ed., 1908), he has written *The Historical New Testament* (Edinburgh, 1901); *The Golden Book of John Owen* (London, 1904); *Literary Illustrations of the Bible, Epistle of St. James* (1906); and *George Meredith; a Primer to the Novels* (1909); and has in preparation *An Introduction to the Literature of the New Testament* and the Epistles to the Thessalonians and Revelation for *The Expositor's Greek Testament*.

MOFFAT, JAMES DAVID: Presbyterian; b. at New Lisbon, O., Mar. 15, 1846. He was educated at Washington and Jefferson College (A.B., 1869) and at Princeton Theological Seminary (1869–71). He was then stated supply of the Second Presbyterian Church, Wheeling, W. Va., in 1871–73, and pastor of the same church from 1873 to 1882. Since the latter year he has been president of Washington and Jefferson College. He was also associate editor of *The Presbyterian Banner* from 1894 to 1906, and was moderator of the Presbyterian General Assembly at Winona Lake, Ind., in 1905. In theology he describes himself as "a Presbyterian who advocated revision of the Westminster Confession of Faith, and now advocates the union of all Presbyterian churches in the United States."

MOFFAT, ROBERT: African missionary; b. at Ormiston (9 m. s.e. of Edinburgh), Scotland, Dec. 21, 1795; d. at Leigh (25 m. s.e. of London) Aug. 9, 1883. From a boy he was religiously inclined, and after offering himself for mission work to the London Missionary Society he was accepted and sent to South Africa, 1816. He went first to Namaqua Land, where he was assisted by Afrikauer, a native chief converted by him. From there he went to Lattakoo in 1820, then on to Kuruman in 1825. From 1839 to 1843 he was in London lecturing for the Missionary Society, and translating the Psalms. He met Livingstone at this time, and secured his services for the Bechuana mission. In 1843 he resumed his work in Kuruman, and in 1857 finished his translation of the Bible. In 1870 he returned to England permanently. In 1872 he was honored with a doctorate in divinity from Edinburgh, and a testimonial of £5,000 from his friends. He and Mrs. Moffat, who shared his labors and dangers, were pioneers in South African mission work, and stanch friends of the natives, while he proved himself a skilful organizer, teacher, and translator. During his work in South Africa he labored at intervals on a translation of the Bible into Chuana (Bechuana, Sechuana), which was published London, 1872, revised 1890. He was the author of "A Book of Hymns in Chuana" (Mission Press, Kuruman, 1838); *Missionary Labours and Scenes in Southern Africa* (London, 1842); *Rivers of Water in a Dry Place, Being an Account of the Introduction of Christianity into South Africa, and of Mr. Moffat's Missionary Labours* (1863).

BIBLIOGRAPHY: Lives were written by his son, J. S. Moffat, latest ed., London, 1904 (includes life of Mary Moffat); W. Walters, New York, 1882; J. D. Marrat, London, 1884; D. J. Deane, ib. 1887; M. E. Wilder, Chicago, 1887; and in *DNB*, xxxviii. 97–101. Consult also: *Robert Moffat, an Example of Missionary Heroism*, London, 1878; Miss A. Manning, *Heroes of the Desert*, ib. 1885.

MOGILAS, mo-hī'lās, **PETRUS**: Metropolitan of Kief and author of the Greek "Orthodox Confession"; b. of a Wallachian family c. 1597; d. 1647. He was elevated to the metropolitanate in 1632 by Theophanes, patriarch of Jerusalem, and had already published several liturgical works when, in 1638, he prepared the first draft of his "Confession" with the aid of three of his bishops. The work, originally written in Latin, with a Romaic Greek version by Meletius Syrigus, was amended and approved by the Synod of Kief in 1640, and by that of Jassy in Moldavia in 1642. With an introduction by Nectarius of Jerusalem (1642) and the approbation of Parthenius (1643) this "Orthodox Confession of the Catholic and Apostolic Church of the East" was first printed at Amsterdam in 1667. Several editions followed, the best that of E. J. Kimmel, in his *Libri symbolici* (Jena, 1843). The "Confession" was translated into Rumanian in 1691 and into Russian in 1696.

The situation of the period was one of struggle for the Greek Church to preserve her individuality between Roman Catholicism, working vigorously in Russia and Poland, on the one hand, and Protestantism, to which individual Greeks (notably Cyril Lucar, q.v.) felt themselves drawn, on the other. As the patriarchate at Constantinople was far too weak to take any step decisive for the Church at large, the overthrow of Cyril's creed by another based upon Greek tradition naturally proceeded from the younger, but more independent, Russian Church. The immediate cause of the "Confession" was a Roman Catholic catechism printed at Kief, in 1632. The "Confession" is a comprehensive summary of the doctrines of the Greek Church, and its substance is given in its declaration that the requisites of the Catholic Christian for eternal life are "orthodox faith and good works." This twofold division is obscured by Mogilas' basal arrangement according to faith, hope, and love, comprised in exegesis of the Creed, the Lord's Prayer and the Sermon on the Mount, and the Decalogue. A further twofold division is into the Bible and tradition, the latter leading to numerous patristic citations, especially from Gregory, Athanasius, Basil, Dionysius, and John of Damascus. In the doctrine of the Trinity a distinction is drawn, though not too subtilely, between the essential and hypostatic *idiomata*. The controversy on the procession of the Holy Ghost is decided chiefly because of the lack of the *Filioque* in the oldest text of the Creed. The creation is traced in Greek fashion, through nine classes of angels to man, who is termed a microcosm. The omnipresence of God is reconciled with his exaltation by the statement that, "himself being his own place," he at once controls and excludes all limitations of space. The definitions of original sin lack Roman Catholic and Protestant definiteness. Through disobedience Adam lost his perfect reason, righteousness, and ignorance of sin, and his nature became exceedingly inclined to evil. But he was only weakened, not destroyed, so that the spirit and grace of God might freely operate upon him—a synergism which is indispensable to Greek theology. In his discussion of foreknowledge, foreordination, and providence, Mogilas makes the second conditioned by the first, while the third combines the other two, controls them, and thus guides all earthly things in the best possible way. The sole head of the Church is Christ, and the mother Church is Jerusalem. The traditional seven sacraments are defended, though the influence of non-Greek developments may here be discerned.

The second section of the "Confession" is on hope, or the grace partly given and partly promised by Christ. The exegesis is conditioned by ecclesiastical and ascetic points of view, while parallels and lists of analogies take the place of inner development. Rev. iv. 5 and Isa. xi. 2 afford bases for the theory of the seven graces, and Gal. v. 22 for the doctrine of the nine fruits of the Spirit. There are likewise nine rules of the Church (including confession, fasting, and avoidance of heretical books) and seven works of mercy each for the body and the soul, the number nine corresponding to the angels and seven to the sacraments and their effects. In the third part of the "Confession," with its theme of love and its exegesis of the Decalogue, the same themes are further developed under the captions of the seven virtues of prayer, fasting, benevolence, understanding, righteousness, bravery, and moderation. The first two commandments give rise to a justification of the invocation of the saints and the use of icons. The saints are invoked, but not prayed to, as the friends of God; while icons are considered representations of actual persons and things, and hence fitted to raise the thought from the material to the celestial, and so to God. The worship, therefore, is not received by the icons, but by the divinity or the saint represented. The "Confession" of Mogilas, accordingly, reproduces the point of view of ancient Catholicism, as maintained by the Eastern Church (q.v.) in opposition to Rome; nor can it be said, as is sometimes thought, that it is either Roman Catholic or Lutheran in tendency.

(PHILIPP MEYER.)

BIBLIOGRAPHY: E. Legrand, *Bibliographie hellénique*, particularly ii. 202 sqq., iv. 104–159, 4 vols., Paris, 1894–1896. For the "Confession," its history and contents, consult the works of Kimmel, Gass, Kattenbusch, and Michalcescu named under EASTERN CHURCH, and the Eng. transl. by P. Lodvill, London, 1898; and Schaff, *Creeds*, i. 58–61 (history and summary of contents), ii. 275–400 (Gk. text and Lat. transl. of part i. only).

MOHAMMED, MOHAMMEDANISM.

I. Introduction: Mohammedanism has unique claims upon the interest of the student of religions. (1) It is one of the three great monotheistic faiths (its followers would say one of the two, since to them Christianity is tritheistic), and its fundamental tenet is essentially the same as that given in the *Shema'* of Israel: "Hear, O Israel; Yahweh thy God is one" (Deut. vi. 4). (2) It is not, like Judaism or Shinto, a national but a world religion. Sprung, like Judaism and Christianity, from Semitic origins, it claims its followers also among Arian and Turanian peoples and has proved its adaptability to the needs of them all. (3) It is, therefore, one of the missionary religions, and with Buddhism and Christianity, it is contesting, not unsuccessfully, for the religious leadership of mankind. It confronts the Christian missionary in the great fields of missionary effort in Asia and Africa and presents knotty problems for him and for the Christian apologist. (4) It is the one world religion outside of Christianity the origins of which lie open in the light of history. It arose in one man's lifetime, was shaped by one hand and directed by a single mentality. It is a religion in which the miraculous is minimized, yet within eighty years it won an empire as great as Christianity's in the time of Constantine, and it is still extending its influence. The initial success of Islam was due not simply to its own power, but in large part to the conditions of the times and to the effects of surprise. A unified Arabia was the world's astonishment. The peninsula was outside the track of world movements, its forces were unknown. Moreover, Rome and Persia had exhausted each the other's strength by centuries of warfare. Besides this, the Christian Church was divided, and neither branch was loath to see the other crippled by a third power. The onset of the Arabs, inspired by the certainty of conquest and the assurance of paradise if they fell, was irresistible till 732, when their progress was checked in the West by Charles Martel, and 740, when they met defeat in the East by Leo III. at Acroinon. The present strength of Mohammedanism can only be estimated, since an Eastern census is not exact. Estimates for 1909 place the number of adherents in Europe at 6,000,000, in Africa at 72,000,000, in Asia at 192,000,000, or about 270,000,000 in all.

II. Mohammed: Mohammed, "The Praised," the posthumous son of Abdu Allah, a member of the Koraish tribe, by Aminah, was born at Mecca Aug. 20, 570, and died at Medina June 8, 632. His grandfather, Abdu al-Muttalib, took charge of him when at the age of six he lost his mother, and his foster mother gave him additional protectors by the fact that she belonged to the Bani Saad. He was again bereaved at the age of eight by the death of his grandfather, and he then entered the family of his uncle, Abu Talib. From his mother he inherited a nervous, excitable temperament and a tendency to epilepsy, manifested by a fit when he was four years old, again when he was six, and later in life by relapses into the cataleptic state, the latter at that time apparently under control. He was melancholy in disposition, easily depressed, exceedingly sensitive to disagreeable odors, superstitious, a believer in jinn, omens, dreams and charms, vivid in imagination, and with a taste for the sublime. In maturity he was of medium height, of large but somewhat stooping frame. He had a large head covered with long wavy hair, an oval face, bloodshot but keen black eyes with shifty gaze, a prominent nose, and a large mouth with well separated teeth. A fleshy tumor surrounded with moles on his back was claimed by him as a sign of his prophetic mission. He was careful in habit, fond of the bath and of perfumes, amorous in disposition, and exceedingly fond of the delights of the table. His spiritual development began at the age of twelve, when his uncle took him to Syria and he came into closer touch with both Jews and Christians than he had so far experienced. It was possibly at that time that he gained his first insight by contrast into the enormities of Arabic idolatry and immorality. When he was twenty-five he entered the service of Ḥadijah, a rich Meccan widow, was entrusted with the charge of her trading ventures, and again visited Syria, where he gained new insight into Judaism and Christianity. Probably at the initiative of Ḥadijah, he married her, though she was fifteen years his senior, and while she lived he married no other. Meanwhile, by the exercise of native sagacity he had obtained a reputation for practical wisdom and was frequently appealed to as the arbiter of disputes. When thirty-five years of age he settled in characteristic fashion a hot religious quarrel among four parties at Mecca, each of which claimed the right to replace in its niche the Black Stone of Mecca—representatives of the four parties raised it to the level of its position by lifting the four corners of a cloth placed beneath it, and then Mohammed himself put the stone in place. It was at this period that he began to feel his mission; he became more highly contemplative, used to retire to a mountain cave for meditation, and finally, in 609, in consequence of a vision in which Gabriel commanded him (though illiterate)

1. Early Life, Physique, Temperament.

to read what appears in the Koran as Surah xcvi. 1-5, he began to preach.

His earliest labors were in his family and among his intimates. Ḥadijah was his first convert, Ali and Zaid, his adopted children, were next, and then his friend Abu Bekr. Three years of preaching gained him about fifty followers, and then (612) he began to teach in public, using a house opposite the Kaaba. His points were three: (1) the oneness and absoluteness of Allah who (2) revealed his will to men (3) by chosen men who were prophets (cf. the beginning of Surah xcvi.). By this time he had abandoned idolatry in consequence of his first principle. Part of the period following the beginning of his work was marked by intervals of depression during which Ḥadijah alone could comfort him. His hearers demanded credentials of his mission in the shape of miracles. But he disclaimed the power to produce these: his claim was that his witness was his preaching, in which he resembled his predecessors Adam, Abraham, Moses, David, and Jesus; and that since he was sent to preach, his hearers would reject him at their peril. When his audience became indifferent, he used invective, and this in turn evoked insult and persecution, so that his followers fled to Abyssinia. At this time he compromised with idolatry, having been misled, as he claimed, by Satan. The Meccans urged that if one revelation was Satanic, others might be, to which Mohammed could reply only by passionate oratory. Avoided by the Meccans, he began to preach to strangers visiting Mecca, among them some from Yathrib (soon to be known as Medinat al-Nabi, "City of the Prophet," or simply as Medina), who carried his story home and sent others and still more to hear him. The Medinans urged him to leave Mecca and adopt their city as his home, promising him protection there. The rancorous opposition of Meccans continuing and extending even to the point of banning him and his supporters, he exiled himself, and in the Hejira, "Flight," to Medina he took the step which made the Mohammedan era, June 16, 622 A.D. This was the turning-point in his career, the beginning of success.

2. Second Period.

Mohammedanism owes much to the differences between Mecca (q.v.) and Medina. The former, gathered about the Kaaba (q.v.), in which were collected about the Black Stone more than 300 idols representative of the gods of the tribes, made trade of religion then as now, and was the seat of such fanaticism as perhaps only Arabs could show. Mohammed's propaganda seemed to strike at the very foundations of the city's trade and preeminence, and its present prestige and future prospects seemed menaced when Mohammed attacked idolatry. Medina, 250 miles north, was a center of traffic, open therefore to the civilizing influences of the empires of Rome and Persia, consequently more cosmopolitan and tolerant. Idolatry was already under suspicion, and there was consequently an opening for the prophet's resolute preaching. Mohammed's repute for wisdom grew with the frequency with which he was called upon to act as arbiter; his decisions he claimed not as his own but as the dictates of Allah, and his position soon came to be practically that of city judge and dictator. Ordinances for practise were soon formulated by the prophet; prayer was directed toward Mecca (not Jerusalem, which, in the endeavor to conciliate the Jews and gain their support, he had formerly adopted), the fast of Tisri was changed for that of Ramadan. The five fundamentals of Islam (see below, IV.) were conceived and formulated at Medina. Most important of all, citizenship was made dependent not on family but on faith, preparing the way for a united Arabia and a world religion. For the triumph of the faith the bonds of kinship had to yield if they stood in its way—Mohammed did not blanch at fratricidal war. The idolater, even though a brother, was doomed unless he gave up this practise, and to the believer belonged the idolater's goods. In this last was manifested Mohammed's shrewdness, making capital of the Arab's lust for plunder. Mecca was idolatrous, therefore its caravans were fair booty. When the Meccans retaliated, they were defeated by the appalling fury of the Moslems' attack. Thus the battle of Bedr (Jan. 13, 624) was the result of a raid in which Mohammed hoped to capture a rich Meccan caravan, but instead he found himself confronted by an unencumbered armed force of twice his own strength, over whom he won a decisive victory. Yet the Medina period was not one of unvarying success. Mohammed lost heavily in the battle of Ohod (Jan. 625), when the Koraish defeated the Moslems, and in some minor affairs his followers lost. This period was marked also by many assassinations instigated or sanctioned by the leader and by wholesale slaughter of those opposed to him or whose wealth he coveted for his followers, including that of the Jews. These latter looked with scorn upon Mohammed's claim that he was reinstating the religion of Abraham, while in retaliation for treachery he had the men of a whole tribe, 800 in number, slaughtered in cold blood and their women and children sold into slavery, while the proceeds were divided among his followers. In self-interest Arabs flocked to him, and he was soon ready to march upon Mecca, which he had already fixed upon as the center of the faith. In thus deciding, he was doubtless influenced by his kinship with the Koraish, also doubtless by the fact that in this method he was following the lines of least resistance and would eventually conciliate the Meccans.

3. The Medina Period.

The start for Mecca was made early in Jan., 630. The city fell easily, doubtless because of an arrangement with some inside who favored Mohammed, and in part because his force was too great to be resisted. A general amnesty was proclaimed from which ten persons were excluded, though of these, through the intercession of persons in Mohammed's own circle, only four were put to death. The Kaaba was swept of all idols except the Black Stone. The Koraish were conciliated and the traditional privileges of the city as a religious center were retained. The Medinans, to whose fidelity so much was due, were disappointed, but were reconciled by Mohammed's impassioned appeals to their

4. Final Period.

loyalty and by his promise still to make his home with them. As master of Mecca, the center of pilgrimage and the sanctuary of all the Arabs, the prophet was able to dictate the terms on which the tribes might worship there. Taif, a rival stronghold of idolatry, submitted in Dec., 630, and its idol was destroyed. A last attempt to overturn the new religion, made by a confederation of tribes, was defeated with comparative ease. The tribes soon accepted Islam, since Mohammed's policy toward Arabs was—conciliation if possible, but at any cost submission. In 631 the Kaaba was closed to all but Moslems. This act marked the peninsula as Mohammedan. Before the prophet's death all Arabia was at his feet; Christians and Jewish tribes were permitted to exist, but only upon condition of paying a heavy tribute.

5. Character. The non-Mohammedan estimates of the founder vary in all possible ways, some classing him among the most highly endowed prophets and others placing him with rank impostors. Of his mental abilities there can be no doubt—the Koran is incontestable testimony to his powers as poet and orator, organizer and statesman; and this book, chronologically arranged, affords an index to his character and is the chart of his development from the time when he began to write. His courage was magnificent and seems to have failed him but once (when he compromised temporarily with idolatry). To preach against idolatry in its home and under such circumstances to incur persecution for what had become conviction, later to prohibit wine to wine-loving Arabs, still later to refuse compromise when that seemed an easy way out of an apparent *impasse*, to insist upon the absolute submission which eventually unified Arabia—these are marks of a courage almost sublime paralleled, indeed, perhaps often in the history of Christian religion, yet none the less worthy of acknowledgment when found in Mohammed. Not the least eminent of his characteristics was his faith in himself and his mission. Two meritorious qualities, aside from what have been mentioned, were enthusiasm and patriotism. Once more, the loyalty which he inspired among men of worth such as Abu Bekr is absolute proof of his deep sincerity. Of his spiritual nature his abhorrence of idolatry and lofty doctrine of God are sufficient evidence. On the other hand, Mohammed had many of the vices of his age and surroundings. He showed often a cold vindictiveness, a savage insistence upon vengeance, and a severe ruthlessness in procuring or permitting the wholesale slaughter of his foes or of those whose property he needed for his followers. His lenience after the taking of Mecca was due not to motives of mercy but to policy. Those who escaped the proscription at that time owed their lives to the urgent intercession of Mohammed's trustiest friends, not to his clemency. Of his early sincerity as a reformer there can be as little doubt as of his courage. But he failed under the test of success. His decline began with the Medina period. The early Surahs of the Koran, long after they pass the period of inquiry, bear well the test of examination. But after success seemed assured, they show advancing deterioration in the prophet's character. Revelations thereafter were not always in the interest of the faith, they pandered often to Mohammed's desires. When he wished another wife, a revelation was forthcoming to sanction it. If former utterances stood in the path of present wish, the doctrine of abrogation permitted removal of the obstacle. When he desired the wife of his adopted son Zaid—among Arabs a scandalous thing—Surah xxxiii. sanctioned the divorce by Zaid of his wife that she might be free to marry the prophet. Four was the legal limit of wives for a believer, but the same Surah gave the prophet all license. And when old age and approaching death aroused his uxorious jealousy, though by Arab law a widow not only may but rather must marry, it was revealed for his comfort that his wives were to remain bereaved.

III. The Koran: There is no room to question that the Bible of Islam is the work of one man and that man Mohammed. The speaker, except in the prayer in the opening Surah and in a few scattered passages, is Allah. But as he is too exalted to speak directly even with his prophet, Gabriel is the medium of communication. The book, the claim runs, is not a new creation, but exists in archetype in heaven, fixed in the very essence of God, and was delivered piecemeal to the prophet. But the arrangement is due to the editor. Mohammed had not only memorized his own deliverances but had taught them to his followers. Necessarily many knew parts of the Koran, none knew all. When the prophet died, the utterances existed on scattered bits of leather, ribs of palm leaf, even on stones, and in the memory of the faithful. In the wars of revolt which followed the path of Mohammed, many who knew parts of the Koran perished, and Omar began to fear that it would be wholly lost. He therefore begged Caliph Abu Bekr to have it collected. From all the sources named Zaid of Medina, who was made editor, gathered it. But variant texts existed. A second edition was therefore made by Zaid with the help of three members of the Koraish tribe; this was made canonical, and all variants obtainable were destroyed. In the editing no principle was thoroughly carried out, the one that is partly observable being to place the longer Surahs first. The immediate acceptance of this text by those who had heard the original is fairly presumptive of its fidelity, especially in view of the antagonisms of the times. The claim is made by Mohammedans that its contents evince its entire and complete inspiration. Since it is spoken by Allah, it is absolutely and wholly true. As a historical monument the Koran is valuable for the light it throws upon the mentality of the prophet. Significant is the diffuse and prosaic character of the latest Surahs as compared with the concise, exalted, and poetic style exhibited by the earlier ones. As to the order in which the Surahs were delivered, it must be said that of five authorities, Jajalu al-Din, Rodwell, Muir, Nöldeke, and Hughes, no two agree and Palmer favors a still different order. As to the originality it displays, there is now no doubt that while most of the matter is new, Mohammed wove into his deliverances bits of tribal tradition, popular sayings, legends beloved by the people, and much that he had gathered from his converse with Jews and Christians, though in the latter case the real origin was apocryphal rather than canonical, while the Jewish matter was haggadic rather than derived from the Old Testament.

IV. The Religion: The coming of Mohammed was in a sense opportune. The local religions of the Arabs were growing effete. Allah was already known, but much in the same way as Baal was in pre-Israelitic Canaan—each tribe might call its own deity Allah, and a process of unification had already begun. That this was due in part to the influence of Judaism and Christianity is very probable. There were a number of Jewish tribes in Arabia, and to Arabs Jews were "the people of the book." Jewish accounts of Arab origins were accepted, and both peoples claimed Abraham as the common ancestor. That from the Jews in his early journeys the founder derived his tendency toward a rigid monotheism is at least possible; and Mohammedanism employs many Jewish theological terms. Christianity also, through two channels, affected Islam: (1) through the hermits whose huts and caves dotted the desert, while they themselves were respected by the nomads; (2) through the faith of the Abyssinians, whose country was the refuge of Mohammed's followers in the stormy times of the close of the first Meccan period. By Mohammed and his followers Jesus was recognized as a prophet second in honor only to Mohammed, while the devout Moslem never speaks of him without uttering the benediction "on whom be peace." But the complexion Christianity takes on as reflected in Islam is, like that of Judaism, apocryphal rather than as portrayed in the Gospels. A third source of Mohammed's inspiration was the Hanifs—a discovery comparatively recent. Hanif probably means "penitent," and the name was applied to men who, not constituting a sect, were scattered through Arabia as recluses, individual seekers after God. Among these men had developed belief in a deity like Allah, who was rising into lofty superiority above the idols of the tribes. The problems of sin and judgment were real to these Hanifs, and the practise of austerity and penitence were parts of their solution of the question. Through a cousin of Ḥadijah Mohammed came into contact with these men and their developing monotheism; and the light gained from Judaism and Christianity doubtless illumined for him the meditations of the Hanifs as communicated to him. His own rapid logic and invincible spirit conducted him to his own absolute monotheism, and the later steps followed as already indicated: instruction of his friends, public preaching, intensification of purpose through opposition, development at Medina, assimilation of elements not absolutely incompatible with the system, break with Judaism, politicalization of the faith, and the submission of Arabia.

1. The Background.

The fundamental theological doctrine of Islam is the unity of God, whose will, declared by the prophet Mohammed, is law for man. The doctrine of God is intensely and baldly unitarian. Special points antagonized were the Christian trinity and the deity of Christ. Emphasis was laid upon the sovereignty of Allah and his omnipotence. Allah was not a philosophic first cause, but a present active agency ever working in his world and accomplishing his purposes. In other words, Mohammed's was a practical, not a speculative monotheism. Allah was sharply distinguished from his creation, and the latter included evil as well as good. From no logical consequences of this doctrine did the founder shrink. Right is right not because of its essence but because Allah decrees it. Hence Mohammedan predestination is arbitrary in its absoluteness, acquiring the force of fatalism. The practical result was the inspiration of a magnificent but terrible courage. Arab warriors went into battle convinced that their life-span was so definitely determined that whether they stayed at home or went to the fight their hap would surely overtake them. This fanaticism was intensified by the eschatology of the faith, which is gross, crude, and vivid. Both heaven and hell are material, both are preceded by resurrection and judgment, through which all Moslems pass with success—though some may have to be purified in purgatory. But the warrior who dies in battle is sure of paradise. It is to these facts that the dread of a jehad or holy war is due. Hell is in seven regions, of which the first is purgatory; to hell all infidels (non-Mohammedans) are destined. Heaven is across a chasm over which is a bridge broad and easy for the believer, but shrinking to the width of a razor's edge when infidels attempt its passage, and they then fall from it into the fire which for them is eternal. While the delights of the Moslem heaven as portrayed in the Koran are sensual, there can be no doubt that, as in other religions, the idea conveyed depends upon the mental and spiritual culture of the individual. One may well compare the conceptions inspired in Christians by the reading of the Book of Revelation, though the adjectives sensuous and sensual well distinguish the views held by Christian and Mohammedans respectively. Surah xiii. proves that the prophet's heaven was not bounded by the delights of the senses. Another consequence of the doctrine of the unity of God was the prohibition of idolatry, both of the making and worshiping of images. The only inconsistency is the retention of the Black Stone of the Kaaba—an inconsistency recognized and denounced by some of the sects of the religion. Equally a corollary of the doctrine of the absoluteness of deity is the angelology of Islam. Angels are a postulate of the faith. They are required as ministers of Allah, who is too exalted to accomplish his ends by personal ministrations. The angelology is elaborate, the angelic beings are arranged in order of rank, with the archangels Gabriel, Michael, Israfil, and Asrael at the head, each of whom has duties here or hereafter in relation to mankind. There are also recording angels whose records appear as testimony at the judgment. Of angels of lesser rank there are hosts; besides these there are genii, good and bad. The devil is a fallen angel named Iblis.

2. The Theology and its Implicates.

Briefly, the four practical points of the Mohammedan creed are: (1) prayer five times a day; directed toward Mecca; (2) almsgiving on a fixed scale at least, above that scale according to one's inclination; (3) fasting in the daytime during Ramadan; (4) pilgrimage to Mecca at least once in a lifetime. These things are regarded as most firmly binding on all Moslems. By prayer, in Arabic, five times a day facing Mecca, the day is mortgaged to God. Yet the prayers are short, therefore soon over, and consequently not burdensome. On Friday, in addition to the prayers, brief hortatory addresses or sermons are delivered in the mosques. But Friday is not a day of cessation from labor. There can be little doubt that the injunction to turn toward Mecca at prayer does much to support the observance of the injunction to make the pilgrimage. Equally faithful are Mohammedans in observing the command to bestow alms, a consequence of which is the large proportion of beggars found in most Mohammedan centers. In its social system Islam lags centuries behind because of its legitimation of polygamy, of divorce by the husband at will, and of slavery. The charter of Islam is the Surah numbered ix. by Sale, cxiii. by Rodwell, and cxiv. by Muir, and believed to be the last but one delivered. Moslems are to enforce conversion of idolaters with the alternative of death, while to Jews and Christians the alternative is payment of heavy tribute. Force became the basis of the propaganda, the sword was the instrument. Hence the two characteristics which obtrude themselves in contact of Mohammedanism with other faiths are fanaticism and intolerance. Yet it is not improbable that modern Mohammedan success in Africa is not wholly due to the sword. The function of this religion in world history seems to be that of disciplining peoples in a low stage of culture. Its fault is that it is an insuperable obstacle to progress beyond a certain stage. Christianity makes relatively few converts from its adherents.

3. System of Practise.

V. Developments after Mohammed: While the primitive doctrine of Islam was as thus stated, that the Koran would continue alone to be the norm of action was not to be expected. This work summed up merely the phenomena within the founder's horizon. Consequently, just as in Christianity there grew up in the ecumenical councils and in the life of the Church norms as really authoritative in belief and practise as the New Testament itself, so in Islam there came to recognition four bases of authority, the Koran, *sunnah*, *ijma*, and *kiyas*. Sunnah, "custom, usage," sums up the doctrine that so far as practicable not only the injunctions but the practise of the founder is to be followed. This led to a collection of traditions respecting Mohammed, made in the third Mohammedan century, which were compared with the Koran, and this body of tradition, thus sifted, became equally authoritative with the Koran. Ijma is a word which is the Islamic equivalent of the Christian *semper, ubique, et ab omnibus*, or "universal assent." It is the collection of legal and doctrinal decisions made by the prophet, his companions, and their immediate successors. It is of three kinds, unanimity in opinion, in practise, and by tacit consent. Where this unanimity exists with reference to any doctrine, that doctrine is as binding as any explicitly taught in Koran or sunnah. Kiyas is the Mohammedan equivalent of the Jewish Talmud. It is a collection of inferences drawn from the more general pronouncements of Koran, sunnah, and ijma, meant to be applied to special cases such as may at any moment arise. It is therefore the interpretation of the other three collections applied to practical life. It will at once be noticed that these three additions to the Koran added immensely to the elasticity of the system.

1. The Four Bases of Doctrine and Practise.

At the death of Mohammed there were three possible candidates for leadership: Ali, nephew and son-in-law of the prophet, of whom it is said that Mohammed indicated him as leader before his death, but that the pronouncement was suppressed by Ayesha because Ali had accused her of unchastity; Omar, a father-in-law of Mohammed; and Abu Bekr, father of Ayesha. Omar refused to stand, and Abu Bekr was elected. The partizans of Ali were prevented from contesting the election with arms only by the general revolt of the tribes which left Mecca, Medina, and Taif the only faithful centers, while the revolt was quelled only on the return of the army then operating in southern Palestine. Under the first caliph ("successor") Arabia was once more united, and Persia, Palestine, Syria, Mesopotamia, Babylonia, and Egypt came in large part under Moslem rule. Before Abu Bekr died (634) he nominated Omar, who was elected, the conquest of the countries named was nearly completed, and the erection of a Moslem state proceeded under the able administration of Omar. At his death in 644, Ali was again a candidate, but was defeated by Othman supported by the Koraish, against whom uprisings at once began, and Othman, detected in double-dealing, was slain (655). Ali was then elected, and his two rivals fled to Persia and raised a revolt, but this was suppressed, Ayesha was captured and the two rivals killed (656). The governor of Syria at this time was Mu'awiya, holding a strong position because of the better discipline of the Arabs who formed his army. He espoused the cause of Othman, refused to acknowledge Ali as caliph, and an attempt was made to arbitrate the dispute. Meanwhile Ali's following became divided and a part deserted him, while a conspiracy was formed to murder both parties to the dispute and also the General Amr, who was acting as arbitrator. Ali alone was killed, though Mu'awiya was wounded. Ali's brother Husain went to Mecca to assume the caliphate, but he was slain and Mu'awiya was acknowledged in his place. Thus Mu'awiya became the first of the Ummayad caliphs (so named from Ummaya, great-grandfather of Mu'awiya), fourteen in number, who ruled at Damascus till 750, and were succeeded by the Abbasids (claiming descent from Abbas, uncle of the prophet). Out of this contest, which involved the first five caliphs, sprang the prime distinction in Islam between Sunnah and Shiah, two forms of doctrine which comprise between them all the lesser distinctions or sects into which Islam has been and is still divided. The Sunnah doctrine is that all

2. The Early Caliphate.

four of the first caliphs were legitimate; Shiah holds that the office of caliph is not elective and not usurpable, that it comes by divine right and is spiritual, and that Ali was the first caliph or Imam, kept from his own by Ayesha, and finally dislodged by Mu'awiya.

Possibly the tradition is apocryphal which attributes to Mohammed the prediction that Islam would split into seventy-two divisions, but for a man who knew his people as did the prophet the prediction is not improbable. Within his own lifetime the seeds of division were sown in the honor paid to the Muhajirs, "companions in the Hegira," who went with him from Mecca to Medina (together with the Ansar, "helpers," who invited him thither), and in the distinction of these from the converts who accepted Islam because they must, among whom developed the Ummayads, so important in the very near future of Mohammed's time. The events of the succession created a party to whom the name "legitimists" may be applied, because they held that succession was through appointment by Allah and not through election by men. The election of the third caliph was a triumph for the Ummayads, his assassination and the election of the fourth caliph (Ali) was a triumph for the legitimists. The contest between Ali and Mu'awiya was fruitful in divisions. Thus the promise by Ali given to Mu'awiya, to submit his right to the caliphate to arbitration, evoked the active disapproval of a large party of his followers on the ground that the duly elected caliph had no right to submit to question his unquestionable right. These were the Kharijites, "seceders," who differed from the legitimists in that they held election to give an undisputed title. The Kharijites in turn continued for centuries to split into factions, each of which differed from the others on various counts, practical or theoretical, and their survivors in the present are the sect of Ibadites. But the great division was between Shiah and Sunnah, already defined. Shiah started as a political tenet, concerned primarily with the succession to the caliphate; but this had a theological basis, and naturally the distinction between Shiites and Sunnites became essentially theological. From the Shiah doctrine of the inherent right of Ali developed divisions in the body of Shiites according as the conception of Ali's personality varied—Ali being regarded at one time as an incarnation of deity, at another as an Imam in whom the heavenly light existed (see BABISM), and so on—or as opinions varied concerning the line through which legitimacy flowed, whether through descendants of Ali by his wife Fatima, the daughter of Mohammed, or through some other of Ali's descendants. The great freedom in speculation which has always characterized Shiah contributed further to division into sects as pantheism and mysticism and rationalism evolved positions around which those to whom the variant doctrines appealed easily gathered. Especially fruitful of divisions was the doctrine of the Imamate, the two great parties of the "Seveners" and the "Twelvers" differing on the question whether the Imamate descended to the twelfth or only to the seventh generation from Ali before it suffered occultation. The Druses (q.v.) and the Assassins are but extreme developments in the circle of Shiah. The distinction between Shiites and Sunnites in its total intra-Islamic effect is that between the heterodox and the orthodox, the latter term being applicable to Sunnah doctrine alone. The Sunnites were, so to speak, driven into existence by the necessity of opposing Shiah tenets and their developments. Hence Sunnites are the traditionalists of Mohammedanism, whose central position is that in the four bases of authority named above all necessary guidance is contained. But even while they thus explicitly disavowed philosophizing, this activity claimed its workers among them, and as differences of theory and practise grew up in the larger life opened up by Islamic conquests, discord arose, and the history of Sunnah is no less a story of division than is that of Shiah. But the Sunnites are by far the more numerous, constituting nine-tenths of Mohammedan religionists.

3. Shiites and Sunnites.

The reasons for this great diversity of sects in a system theoretically so rigid as Mohammedanism may be given as follows: (1) Advance in culture through contact with the peoples of the world brought its immediate consequences in an acquired bent for speculative and analytical philosophizing—not a native trait in Semites (see ARABIA). Thus the implicit contradictions in the Koran respecting predestination and free will, the interpretation and methods of interpreting that book, difficulties in eschatology—all these challenged individual opinion, prejudice, and passion, and opened chasms between bodies of believers. (2) The diversity in the human make-up of the great realm covered by the faith had its influence. Peoples as diverse as the Negro races of Africa, the Aryans and native races of India and Persia, Malays and Mongolians own its sway. Peoples so different could not be expected to hold the faith in the same way. An illustration of the modifications thus brought in is furnished by Persia, where the decided trend of the mind of the Eastern Aryan toward pantheism and the liking for the theory of reincarnation have compelled Islam to include within its fold believers in both these originally un-Mohammedan principles. (3) The fanaticism which Mohammed evoked and fostered contributed to the ardor with which any tenet once enunciated and received with any degree of favor was embraced and its propaganda carried on. (4) Coordinate elements were the Semitic tendency to segregation and the hugeness of the Mohammedan realm. Arabs of unnumbered clans, Babylonians, Assyrians, Syrians, Arameans, Copts—indeed the whole Semitic world except the Jews—accepted the faith. Scission was in the very material of which the fabric was built, even if no account be taken of the alien races, each with its own psychological history and categories of religious intuitions. The mystery is not that sects developed, but rather that the religion has held together the hordes of Semites, not to mention the swarms of other peoples whom it dominates. From these roots therefore sprang division. Scholasticism developed, and logical, theological, and

4. Causes of Sectarianism.

metaphysical discussion proved an orchard which bore apples of discord. Mutazilites denied in deity the existence of attributes and did not allow the truth of predestination; Jabarites were content to deny predestination; Sifatites maintained the existence of attributes and through it became the supporters of the rankest of anthropomorphic doctrines. Some sects, again, would interpret the Koran literally; others insist upon a thoroughgoing metaphorical exegesis; some again use here the literal, there the metaphorical, and are by both the others charged with inconsistency. The literalists descended to anthropomorphism; the metaphorists read Allah out of the world except as pantheism makes room for him. And yet the marvel is, that while a deadly hatred exists between Shiite and Sunnite, both unite in even a bitterer hostility to the "infidel" who denies the tenets of Islam. From the standpoints of Christianity and of missions, Islam presents perhaps the most difficult problem which they have to meet.

GEO. W. GILMORE.

BIBLIOGRAPHY: The literature on the subject is enormous. An authoritative bibliography of some of the phases is given in the indispensable volume of D. B. Macdonald, *Development of Muslim Theology, Jurisprudence and Constitutional Theory*, pp. 358-367, New York, 1903. On the founder consult: the lives by W. Muir, 4 vols., London, 1858-61 (the classic; contains valuable introduction and notes; an abridged ed., *Life of Mohammed from Original Sources*, appeared, ib. 1877, and still further abridged, 1887); Syed Ameer Ali, London, 1873, cf. his *Life and Teachings of Mohammed*, ib. 1881; A. Sprenger, 3 vols., Berlin, 1861-69; T. Nöldeke, Hanover, 1863, cf. his *Sketches from Eastern History*, chap. ii., London, 1892; W Irving, under title *Lives of Mahomet and his Successors*, New York, 1849-50, often reissued. The preceding are of importance. Further literature on Mohammed is: G. Weil, *Mohammed der Prophet*, Stuttgart, 1844; B. Saint-Hilaire, *Mahomet et le Coran*, Paris, 1865; R. B. Smith, *Mohammed and Mohammedanism*, London, 1874; J. Wellhausen, *Muhammad in Medina*, Berlin, 1882; R. Krehl, *Das Leben und die Lehre des Mohammeds*, Leipsic, 1884; W. Koelle, *Mohammed and Mohammedanism*, London, 1889; H. P. Smith, *The Bible and Islam*, chap. i., New York, 1897; H. Grimme, *Mohammed*, new ed., Münster, 1904; D. S. Margoliouth, *Mahomet and the Rise of Islam*, London, 1905; R. Ducasse, *Mahomet dans son temps*, Geneva, 1909; Ibn Saad, *Biographien Muhammads*, ed. E. Sachau, vols. i.-ii., Leyden, 1905-09. The works on the Koran and on the religion usually contain sketches of the life of the founder.

Of the Koran the best ed. is that by G. Fluegel, Leipsic, 1834, often reprinted. Of English translations the best are by E. H. Palmer, in *SBE*, vols. vi., ix., and by J. M. Rodwell, London, 1879. Still of high value for its notes is the rendering of G. Sale, London, 1734, and often, e.g., 1882; valuable also is E. Lane, *Selections from the Koran*, ib. 1879. For introduction consult: G. Weil, *Einleitung in den Koran*, Bielefeld, 1878; E. Sell, *Historical Development of the Quran*, London, 1905; and for exegesis, E. M. Wherry, *Comprehensive Commentary on the Qur'an*, 4 vols., London, 1882-86. Consult further: T. Nöldeke, *Geschichte des Qorans*, Göttingen, 1860, 2d ed., ed. F. Schwally, part 1, Leipsic, 1909; W. St. C. Tisdall, *Original Sources of the Quran*, London, 1904; H. Hirschfeld, *Beiträge zur Erklärung des Korans*, Leipsic, 1886.

On the religion: T. Nöldeke, *Orientalische Skizzen*, Berlin, 1892, Eng. transl., London, 1892; I. Goldziher, *Muhammedanische Studien*, 2 parts, Leipsic, 1889-90; J. W. H. Stobart, *Islam and its Founder*, ib. 1878; T. P. Hughes, *Dictionary of Islam*, ib. 1885; W St. C. Tisdall, *The Religion of the Crescent*, ib. 1895, new ed., 1906; T. W. Arnold, *The Preaching of Islam*, ib. 1896; R. F. Burton, *Personal Narrative of a Pilgrimage to al-Madinah and Mecca*, 2 vols., London, 1898 (indispensable for insight into the character and psychology of the Arabs); E. Sell, *The Faith of Islam*, ib. 1908; idem, *Essays on Islam*, Madras, 1901 (Sell's attitude is polemical); idem, *The Religious Orders of Islam*, ib. 1908; P. D. Chantepie de la Saussaye, *Lehrbuch der Religionsgeschichte*, i. 438-538, Tübingen, 1905 (contains sketch of Mohammed's life and a treatment of the Koran); A. N. Wollaston, *The Sword of Islam*, London, 1905; *Die Kultur der Gegenwart*, I., iii. 87-135, Berlin, 1906; F. A. Klein, *Religion of Islam*, London, 1906. Special topics are discussed in: M. Wolff, *Muhammedanische Eschatologie*, Leipsic, 1872 (giving the ideas of the populace); C. Brockelmann, *Geschichte der arabischen Litteratur*, Weimar, 1898-99; T. J. De Boer, *Geschichte der Philosophie in Islam*, Stuttgart, 1901, Eng. transl., London, 1903; D. B. Macdonald, ut sup.; E. M. Wherry, *The Muslim Controversy*, London, 1905; H. Galland, *Essai sur les Motazelites*, Paris, 1906; E. Herzfeld, *Samarra. Aufnahmen und Untersuchungen zum islamischen Archäologie*, Berlin, 1907; L. Caetani, *Annali dell' Islam*, 2 vols., Milan, 1907; W. Eickmann, *Die Angelologie und Dämonologie des Korans im Vergleich zu der Engel- und Geisterlehre der heiligen Schrift*, Leipsic, 1908; T. N. Juynboll, *Handbuch des islamischen Gesetzes nach der Lehre der schafi'itischen Schule, nebst einer allgemeinen Einleitung*, ib. 1908; W. Niekrens, *Die Engel- und Geister-vorstellungen des Korans*, Rostock, 1908; H. Saladin, *Manuel d'art musulman*, Paris, 1908; A. G. Leonard, *Islam: her moral and spiritual Value*, London, 1909; D. B. Macdonald, *The Religious Attitude and Life in Islam*, Chicago, 1909; H. R. Sayani, *Hasan, Ibn Adham, and Junaid*, in *Saints of Islam*, London, 1909; Carra de Vaux, *La Doctrine de l'Islam*, Paris, 1909. Consult further: H. P. Smith, *The Bible and Islam*, ut sup.; T. Nöldeke, *Sketches*, ut sup., chap. iii.; Gibbon, *Decline and Fall*, chap. l.; Smith, *Rel. of Sem*, and *Kinship*; and the literature under ARABIA, especially Doughty. The new *Enzyklopädie des Islam* (in English, *Encyclopedia of Islam*, London) begun by T. Houtsma and A. Schaade, Leyden and Leipsic, 1908, part 5, 1910.

MOHAMMEDAN PROPAGANDISM AND OPPOSITION TO CHRISTIANITY: Two features distinguish Mohammedanism from all other non-Christian religions, its bitter opposition to Christian teaching and its active missionary spirit. Islam is one of the great missionary religions of the world, and its spread may be divided chronologically into three periods. The first period was from the death of Mohammed, 632-800; the second under the Ottomans and Moguls, 1280-1480; and, lastly, the modern period from 1780 on. During the first period Islam triumphed in western Asia, North Africa, and western China. During the second it extended into Central Asia, India, Malay Archipelago, and southeastern Europe. Recent advance has taken place in Africa, Russia, Malaysia, and India. Islam is still aggressive and is overrunning districts once pagan. Its numbers are increasing in Bengal, Burma, South India, the East Indies, West Africa, Uganda, the Congo Basin, Abyssinia, and on the Red Sea coast. In West Africa and Nigeria missionaries know of a "Mohammedan peril."

To the modern Christian world, missions imply organization, societies, paid agents, subscriptions, reports, and the like. All this is absent from the present Moslem idea of propagation, and yet the spread of Islam continues. With loss of political power, the zeal of Islam seems to increase, for Egypt and India are more active in propagating the faith than are Turkey or Morocco. The three currents of present progress in Africa are along the Upper Nile from Zanzibar into the Congo Region, and up the Niger Basin. Five factors favor the spread of Islam in Africa: the strategical geographical position, the advantage of higher culture over paganism, the favor of European colonial governments, the growth of race-hatred against Europeans, and the low moral standards and pagan elements in Islam. All this applies, although to a less extent, to the spread of Islam in other parts of the world.

Mohammedan opposition and objections to Christianity either arise from unregenerate human nature, in common with all other religions, or spring from belief in Islam and ignorance of the true nature of Christian faith. The latter are by far the stronger obstacles, and include: objections assailing the genuineness of the Bible and its present authority, those directed against leading Christian doctrines, especially the Trinity and the need of the atonement; and objections based on the claim that Mohammed succeeded Christ as Christ did Moses. Nine out of ten of objections by Mohammedans come from the ineradicable tendency to look upon everything and interpret everything carnally. It is the task of the missionary to meet these objections, since they are not only urged orally by individuals, but are the basis of an immense anti-Christian literature, which, although constantly shifting its ground of attack and defense, continues to spread in the Moslem world, chiefly from Cairo, Delhi, Constantinople, and Calcutta, as centers.

S. M. ZWEMER.

BIBLIOGRAPHY: T. W. Arnold, *The Preaching of Islam*, Westminster, 1896 (a history of the propagation of the Moslem faith); W. St. Clair Tisdall, *A Manual of the Leading Muhammadan Objections to Christianity*, 2d ed., London, 1909; E. M. Wherry, *Islam and Christianity in India and the Far East*, New York, 1907; S. M. Zwemer, *Islam. A Challenge to Faith*, ib., 1907; F. Würz, *Die Ausbreitung des Islam in Afrika*, in *Allgemeine Missionszeitschrift*, Jan. 1910; *Azhar-ul-Hak* (an Arabic work against Christianity in 2 vols., published at Cairo, of which there are Persian and Urdi translations, and one in French issued at Paris); *Al Hidayah* (an Arabic work in 4 vols. issued at Cairo, replying to Arabic polemics, especially to the *Azhar-ul-Hak*).

MOHAMMEDANS, MISSIONS TO: The long-standing neglect of the Mohammedan world by those engaged in Christian work is explained by the mutual hostility of the two religions (see COMPARATIVE RELIGION, II., § 1). Yet the names of John of Damascus and Peter the Venerable (qq.v.) are memorable for the double fact that they studied Mohammedanism sympathetically and wrote against it in defense of Christianity. The former's "Conversation between a Saracen and a Christian" (*MPG*, xciv. 1585 sqq.) was long the armory in the Eastern Church for controversial writings against Islam; while Peter was the first to translate the Koran into Latin, and he advocated the translation of the Scriptures into the language of the Saracens, treating also in his two books against Mohammedanism (ed. J. Thomä, Leipsic, 1896) the questions of the inspiration of the Koran and the prophetship of Mohammed with true insight. Raymond Lully (q.v.) was the first to attempt actual missionary operations among Mohammedans; he devised a philosophical system to show to them the truth of Christianity, and established missionary colleges for the study of oriental languages. Five centuries of inactivity followed, and then came Henry Martyn (q.v.) as the leader of a band of missionary pioneers in this field, among whom Karl Gottlieb Pfander (q.v.) is especially worthy of mention not only for his personal efforts, but for his "Balance of Truth" which impressed not merely Persia but the whole Mohammedan world. Operations have been carried on since Martyn's day by the Church Missionary Society, the Society for the Propagation of the Gospel in Foreign Parts, the London Missionary Society, the Church of Scotland Mission, by American Presbyterians and Methodists, and English and Australian Baptists, the fields being India, Persia, Turkey, Africa, Arabia, and the East Indies.

General Survey of Missionary Effort.

In **Persia** (q.v.) work was attempted prematurely in 1834 by the American Board of Commissioners for Foreign Missions, and in 1871 the work was taken up by the Presbyterians with some success, converts having been gained, with also the result of some martyrdoms (cf. the story of Mirza Ibrahim in R. E. Speer, *Young Men who Overcame*, New York, 1905). In 1875 the Church Missionary Society opened work at Ispahan for Moslems, and Yezd, Kirman, and Shirza have been occupied with large results. In **Arabia** (q.v.) the pioneer missionary was Ion Grant Neville Keith-Falconer (q.v.), whose work has been continued by the United Free Church of Scotland at Aden. The American Arabian Mission (organized 1889) has opened stations at Busrah, Bahrein, and Muscat, and is working directly for Mohammedans, reaching far inland by tours and hospital service. It has twenty-five missionaries on the field, three hospitals and three outstations. The Danish Church has also opened work in this field. In the **Turkish Empire** (see TURKEY), the American Board occupies European Turkey, Asia Minor, and eastern Turkey; the Presbyterian Church, Syria; the Reformed Presbyterians, northern Syria; and the Church Missionary Society, Palestine. These together count a total of nearly 700 missionaries, but until recent years the difficulties of the problem and the terror of the Turk prevented direct work for Moslems, although by printing-presses, schools, colleges, and hospitals they have been reached indirectly and a great work of preparation has been accomplished. The entire population has the Bible in the vernacular. Hundreds of thousands have been taught to read; the spirit of inquiry has been awakened, and educational institutions have broken the fetters of superstition and ignorance and to a degree emancipated womanhood. The proclamation of a constitution and the deposition of the late sultan have completely changed the attitude of the government, and by freedom of the press and religious liberty made possible work which was forbidden for centuries. The translation of the Scriptures into Arabic, begun in 1848 and completed in 1865, together with the Turkish and Persian versions, marked an epoch in missions to the Mohammedan world. Work in **North Africa** among Mohammedans was attempted but abandoned by the Moravians and the Church Missionary Society as early as 1825. The American United Presbyterian Church missionaries reached Egypt in 1854, and their work has spread along the entire Nile Valley with results

Special Fields.

chiefly among the Copts, but also among Moslems. Over 3,000 Moslem pupils attend their schools, and special literature for Moslems has been printed and distributed. In 1882 the Church Missionary Society resumed its work in Egypt directly among Mohammedans and has met with encouraging results. In 1880 work was begun at Algiers. It now has eighteen stations in Egypt, Tunis, Tripoli, Algiers, and Morocco, with nearly a hundred missionaries. The American Methodist Episcopal Church opened work in 1909 at Algiers. There are also smaller independent missions, and recently work has begun in the Sudan.

In **Malaysia** Sumatra and Java are the principal typical fields of work for Moslems. The Rhenish mission entered in 1861, and with other societies from the Netherlands has gained over 30,000 living converts from Islam.

No direct missionary work has yet been carried on for the Mohammedans of Afghanistan and central Asia, western China, the Russian empire, central and western Arabia, and the central Sudan. In western Africa and in Nigeria every effort should be made to forestall the entrance of Islam into the pagan border-lands before this religion renders evangelization tenfold more difficult. The situation is alarming, and every mission north of the equator in Africa will sooner or later be compelled to do direct work for Moslems or imperil its very existence.

From the standpoint of missions, Islam is unique (see MOHAMMED, MOHAMMEDANISM, I.). Consequently missions to Moslems have a special character and require special methods and trained workers who have knowledge of the vernacular, Arabic, the Koran, the traditions, and the doctrine and ritual of Islam. While, because of the extent of the Mohammedan world, Moslem mission fields differ vastly one from another, yet in all the difficulties are practically the same. These may be enumerated as: (1) the utter divorce between morality and religion; (2) the intolerance and pride of the Moslem creed which stands diametrically opposed to the spirit and teaching of the Gospel; (3) the almost universal hostile attitude of the Moslems toward a convert from their religion to Christianity, making it almost impossible for Moslems to confess Christ without serious risks; (4) the intellectual difficulties and popular objections to Christianity, nine-tenths of which are due to the ineradicable tendency on the part of Moslems to look upon everything carnally (they misunderstand the Bible, misinterpret its spiritual symbolism, and stumble at the doctrine of the Trinity, the incarnation, and the atonement); (5) finally, in Turkey, Morocco, Persia, Tripoli, Afghanistan, and parts of Arabia, the union between the temporal and spiritual power blocks effort. Apostasy in Turkey until the proclamation of the constitution was treason to the State. As regards methods, the distribution of God's Word is efficient, inoffensive, strikes at the root of Islam, and is possible nearly everywhere. Medical missions overcome prejudice and have been fruitful in results as no other agency. Educational institutions disintegrate Islam. From the kindergarten to the university, all educational forces help to undermine that stupendous rock of ignorance and superstition, Moslem tradition. Street preaching is seldom possible, but the door of access to individual Mohammedans is open, and women missionaries find ready entrance into Moslem homes.

Difficulties and Methods.

In spite of long neglect and feebleness of effort, the results direct and indirect have not been inconsiderable. The latter have been far greater than the former and have in God's providence prepared the way for final victory. Much preliminary work has been accomplished; nearly every strategic center has been occupied; the Bible has been translated into every language spoken by Moslems and has a constantly increasing circulation among them. An important apologetic literature has been prepared in the chief literary languages; the attitude of the learned classes has changed for the better, and the number of inquirers and converts is steadily increasing. In North India there are at least 200 preachers who were once followers of the prophet. A special conference of missionaries from every part of the Moslem world met at Cairo in 1906, and from this conference dates a revival of interest in the study of the subject, the reports and literature of the conference calling attention to the greatness and difficulty of this work. A similar conference is to meet at Lucknow in January, 1911. S. M. ZWEMER.

Results.

BIBLIOGRAPHY: M. Steinschneider, *Polemische und apologetische Litteratur in arabischer Sprache zwischen Muslimen, Christen und Juden*, Leipsic, 1877; A. Keller, *Der Geisteskampf des Christentums gegen den Islam bis zur Zeit der Kreuzzüge*, ib. 1896; W. Muir, *The Mohammedan Controversy*, Edinburgh, 1897; idem, *The Old and New Testaments . . Moslems invited to see and read them*, ib. 1899; H. H. Jessup, *The Setting of the Crescent and the Rising of the Cross; or, Kamil Abdul Messiah*, Philadelphia, 1898; Imad-ud-Din, *A Mohammedan Brought to Christ: an Autobiography . from the Hindustani, by the late Rev. R. Clark*, London, 1900; J. Rutherford and E. H. Glenny, *The Gospel in North Africa*, ib. 1900; S. M. Zwemer, *Arabia, the Cradle of Islam*, New York, 1900; idem, *Islam, a Challenge to Faith*, ib. 1907; idem and others, *Mohammedan World of Today: Papers read at the . Conference . . at Cairo, . . . , 1906*, ib. 1906; J. Awetaranian, *Geschichte eines Muhammedaners der Christ wurde*, Grosslichterfeld, 1905; J. L. Barton, *Daybreak in Turkey*, Boston, 1908; *Our Moslem Sisters: a Symposium*, New York, 1906; C. R. Watson, *Egypt and the Christian Crusade*, Philadelphia, 1907; and the literature under LULLY, RAYMOND; MARTYN, HENRY; PFANDER, KARL GOTTLIEB; and also under MISSIONS TO THE HEATHEN; and MOHAMMED, MOHAMMEDANISM.

MOLANUS, mo-lā'nus, **GERHARD,** ger'hārd, **WALTER:** Lutheran theologian; b. at Hamelin (25 m. s.w. of Hanover) Nov. 1, 1633; d. at Loccum (26 m. w.n.w. of Hanover) Sept. 7, 1722. He studied theology at Helmstädt; and in 1659 was appointed professor of mathematics and theology in the University of Rinteln. In 1674 Duke John Frederick called him to Hanover as director of the consistory, and in 1677 he became abbot of Loccum, one of the most influential offices in the duchy. As a disciple of Calixtus, Molanus used his power to abolish the hostility which prevailed between the Lutherans and the Reformed. He was very active in aiding the Reformed, who after their expulsion from France by the revocation of the edict of Nantes (1685) found a refuge in the country of

Hanover. Molanus was also commissioned by the duke to bring about a reconciliation between Protestants and Roman Catholics. The Roman Catholic representative was Christoph Rojas de Spinola (q.v.), who appeared in Hanover in 1676 and then in 1683. These discussions were followed in 1691, 1692, and 1693 by negotiations between Bossuet and Molanus, but no agreement resulted. Molanus found himself in agreement with Bossuet in regarding most of the differences between the Catholics and the Lutherans as misunderstandings or as different designations of the same content. But he did not regard the Council of Trent legitimate because the Protestants had been condemned without being heard, and because it had not been accepted by the entire Catholic Church. Molanus considered further negotiations in vain, as the Protestants would never concede the matter of communion under both species. On account of the spirit of conciliation which Molanus manifested in these negotiations, it was rumored that he had become Roman Catholic, and he had to defend himself publicly in letters and treatises. (A. HAUCK.)

BIBLIOGRAPHY: The correspondence between Molanus and Bossuet is in Migne's ed. of Bossuet, ix. 809–1070, Paris, 1856. A life of Molanus was written by J. J. von Einem, Magdeburg, 1734; a sketch is also given in K. A. Dolle, *Lebensbeschreibung aller Professorum theologiæ zu Rinteln*, ii. 331–338, Hanover, 1752; and by Wagenmann in *ADB*, xxii. 86 sqq.

MOLINA, LUIS, MOLINISM: A Spanish Jesuit, and his doctrine of the relation of divine grace to the human will. Two efforts had already been made to reconcile the teachings of Augustine with the Semipelagianism dominating the moral tradition of the Church—by the Spanish Thomist Didacus Deza (bishop successively of Salamanca and Valencia), and by the Belgian Michael Bajus (q.v.). A new phase of the controversy began with the appearance of the *Liberi arbitrii cum gratiæ donis, divina præscientia, providentia, prædestinatione, et reprobatione concordia* (Lisbon, 1588) of the Jesuit Luis Molina. Born at Cuenca (100 m. n.w. of Valencia) in 1535, Molina entered the Society of Jesus in early life, studied theology with distinction at Coimbra, and became professor there. He taught Thomistic philosophy at Evora twenty years, and finally was called to Madrid, where he was professor of moral theology until his death, Oct. 12, 1600. He wrote many works, including *De justitia et jure* (6 vols., Mainz and Antwerp, 1593–1609), and a commentary on the first part of the *Summa* of Thomas Aquinas (Cuenca, 1592, and often), but his greatest fame was won by the *Liberi arbitrii*, which ran through repeated editions (e.g., Cuenca, 1592; Lyons, 1593; Venice, 1594, 1602; Antwerp, 1595, 1609, 1715; Paris, 1876). Strictly speaking, the work is a commentary on certain sections of the *Summa* of Thomas Aquinas, through which Molina endeavors to harmonize Augustine and Semipelagianism.

God's knowledge determined by his will, being the source of all things, is also the basis of the free acts of man. Through the cooperation of God (see CONCURSUS DIVINUS) man, even though not in a special state of grace, can accomplish some moral good; and when the free will is prepared by its natural faculties to accept all that appertains to faith, repentance, and justification, the necessary grace and aid for immortal life are given by God. This aid, however, is not the result of any human merit, but only of the merit of Christ, for whose sake God gives man grace whereby he may experience the supernatural working of salvation. Nevertheless, the free will is unceasingly active even with this gift and growth of grace; and it is in human power to render the help of God effective or noneffective. Justification, moreover, depends on the union of will and grace.

The doctrine here sketched was a distinct modification of the unconditional predestination taught by Augustine and Thomas Aquinas, since it holds that God has given the power of cooperating freely in their own salvation to all those who he foresaw would surrender their will to his grace. In this theory Molina was aided by the hypothesis, known by his name and developed and applied by him, though borrowed from his teacher Fonseca, of "intermediate knowledge." According to this, God perceived, from his inscrutable survey of every free will in his essence, what each one would do of his own free will. God, therefore, saves or condemns men according as he knows that under their conditions they will be good or evil. Predestination thus becomes the gracious will of God, which is conditioned by the divine foreknowledge, and thus takes into consideration the free will of man.

While the attempt was thus made to blend strict Augustinianism with popular Roman Catholic synergism, and while the new doctrine gained favor by its antitheses to the views of Calvin and Luther, its Semipelagianism was attacked, not only by such Jesuits as Henriquez of Salamanca and Mariana of Toledo, but especially by the Dominicans. A public disputation was held at Valladolid, and complaints of the book were even lodged with the Holy Office. In 1594 all controversy on the subject was forbidden until the Church should decide, and in 1596 all documents were submitted to Clement VIII. So difficult was the problem, however, that in 1598 a special *Congregatio de auxiliis gratiæ* was appointed, before which Jesuits and Dominicans pleaded in countless sessions in the interests of their orders. The congregation came to an end in 1607, but since it did not give the decision which it had promised, Paul V., in 1611, absolutely forbade all further discussion of the theme. The controversy was revived by the works of Hyacinthe Serry and Gerhard Schneemann (see bibliography).

(O. ZÖCKLER†.)

BIBLIOGRAPHY: K. Werner, *Thomas von Aquin*, iii. 378 sqq., Regensburg, 1858; idem, *Franz Suarez und die Scholastik der letzten Jahrhunderte*, i. 244 sqq., Vienna, 1861; Augustin le Blanc (pseudonym for Hyacinthe Serry), *Historia congregationis de auxiliis gratiæ*, Louvain, 1700; G. Schneemann, *Die Entstehung und Entwickelung der thomistisch-molinistischen Kontroversie*, Freiburg, 1879–80; T. de Regnon, *Bannes und Molina*, Paris, 1883; idem, *Bannesianisme et Molinisme*, vol. i., ib. 1890; P. Schanz, in *TQ*, 1885, i. 141 sqq.; F. H. Reusch, *Der Index der verbotenen Bücher*, ii. 45–46, 298–309, Bonn, 1885; H. Gayraud, *Thomisme et molinisme*, Paris, 1890; Feldner, in *Jahrbuch für Philosophie und speculative Theologie*, v (1889), 282–332; Ranke, *Popes*, ii. 89 sqq.; *KL*, viii. 1731–50.

MOLINOS, MIGUEL DE: The founder of Spanish quietism; b. at Saragossa Dec. 25, 1640; d. at Rome Dec. 28, 1697. The son of noble parents and educated at Coimbra, where he received his doctorate in 1669 or 1670, he settled at Rome, where he gained the friendship of distinguished ecclesiastics, through his personal piety. Among his patrons was Benedetto Odeschalchi, who ascended the papal throne as Innocent XI. in 1676. In the previous year Molinos had published the work on which his fame rests—the *Guida spirituale, che disinvolge l'anima e la conduce per l'interior camino all aquisto della perfetta contemplazione e del ricco tesoro della pace interiore* (Rome, 1675; Eng. transl., *The Spiritual Guide which Disentangles the Soul, and Brings it by the Inward Way to the Getting of Perfect Contemplation, and Internal Peace*, London, 1688, and often; reprint, Glasgow, 1885; *Golden Thoughts from the Spiritual Guide*, Glasgow, 1883). To this was usually appended (after 1687) the *Breve trattato della cottidiana communione.* Though published with reluctance by Molinos, both works proved most popular among Protestants as well as Roman Catholics. Long before the appearance of the "Spiritual Guide" the Jesuits had begun their propaganda in France against Jansenism and mysticism as well as against Protestantism. Even Molinos' favor with the pope and the esteem in which he was held as a priest and confessor in Rome could not prevent the Jesuits from regarding his concentration on inward piety to the neglect of outward religion as perilous. The first formal attack was by the Jesuit Paolo Segneri, in his *Concordia tra la fatica e la quiete nell' oratione* (Bologna, 1681). Feeling ran high in favor of Molinos, and the Inquisition appointed a committee to investigate the writings of Molinos and the *Contemplasione mistica acquistata* of his friend Petrucci, bishop of Jesi. The result was a complete approval of the writings of Molinos and Petrucci (1682) and the more or less complete condemnation of the polemics against them.

Life and Writings.

The struggle was now transferred from literature to the political arena. In 1585, at the instance of Père La Chaise, Louis XIV urged the pope to proceed against Molinos' doctrines, which were endangering the Church. At first referring the matter to the tribunal of the Holy Office, Innocent soon found that his favor to Molinos gave rise to suspicions of himself, and felt himself obliged to change his course. In 1685, accordingly, Molinos was placed under arrest. His position was rendered still more grave by the revelations of some 20,000 letters from all parts of the Roman Catholic world, showing not only the wide diffusion of his mystical teachings, but also their danger for the Church and even for morality. Molinos was now kept in confinement until he should recant, and in Feb., 1687, about 200 persons, some of high rank, were suddenly arrested by the Inquisition for "Quietism." In August of the same year the Inquisition pronounced its condemnation, and three months later the verdict was confirmed by the pope. Molinos escaped the stake by recantation, probably in harmony with his own teachings of submission, but was confined in a Dominican monastery until his death. While the records of the trial have never been published, though preserved in manuscript at Munich, the nineteen articles of accusation issued by the Inquisition (*La Condemnation du Docteur Molinos et de la secte des Quiétistes*, Cologne [?], 1687), and the sixty-eight propositions on which the condemnation was based (reprinted from the decree of the Holy Office as an appendix to A. H. Francke's Latin translation of the *Guida spirituale, Manductio spiritualis*, Leipsic, 1687, and repeatedly since, e.g., in H. Denzinger's *Enchiridion symbolorum*, pp. 266-274, Würzburg, 1888), suffice to show that the unfavorable verdict was rendered partly because of unhappy expressions and partly because of passages where misinterpretation might readily have been distinguished from true opinion. In any case a man who declared that meditation, confession, and outward mortifications were only for tyros, and who counseled monks and nuns to discard their rosaries and relics to serve God inwardly, could only have been regarded by the Jesuits as perilous to the traditions of the Church and as opening the way for the inroads of Protestantism. The excitement roused by his trial at a time when the continued triumph of the Jesuits and the still undecided struggle between papal authority and the Gallican Church formed the center of attention, was intense among both clergy and laity. In Germany this interest was heightened by the affinity between Molinos and the Pietists, who, feeling the common bond of inward piety, saw in Molinos an innocent victim of Jesuit intrigue. The persecution of his adherents lasted into the eighteenth century.

Teachings Condemned.

The teachings developed by Molinos in his *Guida spirituale* are based on principles adopted (on a Neo-Platonic basis) by the Church, developed by Dionysius the Areopagite, and maintained more or less by the foremost ecclesiastical authorities. Mystical phenomena and testimonies were especially rich in Spain in the sixteenth and seventeenth centuries; and Molinos himself was deeply influenced by St. Theresa (q.v.), St. John of the Cross, the Mexican hermit Gregorio Lopez (d. 1596), and Madame de Chantal. Otherwise his sources were such fathers and mystics as Augustine, Thomas Aquinas, Bernard, Dionysius the Areopagite, and Bonaventura; and the true bases of his doctrines were simple experiences of Christian piety. Endeavoring to reconcile the life of active service with the life of contemplation, Molinos seeks in his "Spiritual Guide" to show the way to inward peace. This way is fourfold: prayer, obedience, frequent communions, and inward mortification. Yet he is so far from urging abstraction from external affairs of life, that he characterizes the exercise of one's ordinary calling, provided it be done with true inward concentration and devotion to the divine will, as "virtual prayer." At the same time, he is in harmony with those who see the highest degree of mysticism in an inward abstraction which even excludes either theoretical speculations on the Godhead or practical longing for it. From meditation, necessary for the beginner, the mystic must pro-

His Doctrines.

ceed to contemplation. As a practical counterpart to this, there must be a progressive resignation to the divine will. Thus there is an earthly counterpart to the bliss of the saints in heaven, " the only difference being that they see face to face, we in dim faith." In this way the requirement to abstain from speculation on, or longing for, the Godhead looses its harshness, and at the same time Molinos gives a rational basis to hypermysticism. Finally, the author advances to the still more abstruse height of " passive infused contemplation," a state of complete quietism and resignation in which contemplation has become habitual. At the same time Molinos clearly sees the dangers that beset the contemplative life—aridity, dim faith, and the temptations of the world. In obedience, absolute subjection to the father confessor and subjection of self-will are required by Molinos as by many others. External mortifications, being too often mixed with this self-will, and even confession are enjoined by him only for beginners, the latter being merely a preparation for inward peace. Frequent communion, on the other hand, is recommended, because of the ineffable mystery in which the infinite God becomes incarnate in the finite creature.

(O. ZÖCKLER†.)

BIBLIOGRAPHY: J. Bigelow, *Molinos the Quietist*, New York, 1882; G. Burnet, *Three Letters concerning the Present State of Italy, Written . . . in 1687 Relating to the Affair of Molinos, and the Quietists* (London?), 1688; J. M. Guyon, *The Life of Lady Guyon, to which are added . . the Lives of Worthy Persons*, 2 vols., Bristol, 1772; J. B. Bossuet, *Instruction sur les états d'oraison*, Paris, 1687; idem, *Œuvres*, xxvii. 493 sqq., Versailles, 1817; C. E. Weismann, *Memorabilia ecclesiastica*, vol. ii., Stuttgart, 1745; K. E. Scharling, *M. de Molinos*, Gotha, 1855; H. Heppe, *Geschichte der quietistischen Mystik in der katholischen Kirche*, pp. 110–135, 260–282, Berlin, 1875; Menendez Pelayo, *Hist. de los heterodoxos Españolas*, vols. iii.-iv., Madrid, 1880; F. H. Reusch, *Index der verbotenen Bücher*, ii. 610–619, Bonn, 1885; E. de Broglie, *J. Mabillon et la société de l'abbaye de St. Germain*, i. 397 sqq., Paris, 1888; J. Köhler, in *ZKG*, 1898, pp. 572–595; R. A. Vaughan, *Hours with the Mystics*, ii. 171, 180, 242, 245, 8th ed., London, n.d.; *KL*, viii. 1750–57.

MOLL, WILLEM: Dutch Protestant; b. at Dort Feb. 28, 1812; d. at Amsterdam Aug. 16, 1879. After completing his theological education at the University of Leyden in 1836, he was pastor at De Vuursche, Utrecht, from 1830 to 1839, when illness forced him to retire. A few months later, however, he was able to go to Heidelberg, where he studied until the autumn, when he returned to De Vuursche and resumed his charge. Here he wrote his *Geschiedenis van het kerkelijke leven der Christenen gedurende de zes eerste eeuwen* (2 vols., Amsterdam, 1844–46); but his intention to continue the work to modern times was never carried out. After a brief pastorate at Arnheim in 1845–46, Moll was appointed professor of theology at the Athenæum Illustre at Amsterdam, where he remained until his death, declining a call to Leyden in 1860. Although lecturing for many years on exegesis and dogmatics, his favorite subject was church history, and as an author he devoted himself almost exclusively to the pre-Reformation period in Holland. Here belong his *Johannes Brugman en het godsdienstig leven onzer vaderen in de vijftiende eeuw* (2 parts, Amsterdam, 1854) and his *Kerkgeschiedenis van Nederland voor de Herforming* (6 vols., Arnheim, 1864–71), both of which consider not merely the external course of events, but also take into account the development of spiritual life, motives, and other phases of internal history. Deserving mention are two essays in the publications of the Amsterdam Academy of Sciences, of which Moll was a member and vice-president twenty-four years, *Gozewijn Comhaer, een Nederlander aan het hoofd der kerk van Ysland* (1877) and *Geert Groote's dietsche vertalingen* (1880). Moll was also the author of *De musica sacra in ecclesia Protestantium ad exemplum veterum Christianorum emendanda* (Leyden, 1834) and *Angelus Merula, de hervormer en martelaar des geloofs* (Amsterdam, 1851). Together with some of his pupils, he founded, in 1853, a society for the study of the church history of the Netherlands, which lasted until 1868, and published, under his guidance, *Kalender voor de Protestanten in Nederland* (8 vols., Amsterdam, 1856–63) and *Kerkhistorische jaarboekje* (2 vols., Schoonhoven, 1864–65).

(J. G. R. ACQUOY†.)

BIBLIOGRAPHY: J. G. R. Acquoy, in the *Jaarboek van de koninklijke Akademie van wetenschappen* for 1879, pp. 66–137; F. Nippold, *Die römisch-katholische Kirche im Königreich der Nederlanden*, pp. 486–489, Leipsic, 1877; Rogge, in *Mannen van beteekenis in onze dagen*, Haarlem, 1879.

MOLLER (MOELLER, MUELLER), HEINRICH: Supposed formerly to be the proper name of Henry of Zütphen. Accordingly Henry was credited with the authorship of the hymn, " Hilf Gott dass mir gelinge," as the initial letters of the lines spell Heinrich Muler, and the song closes with " has Heinrich Möller sung in his prison." As Moller was not the name of Henry of Zütphen, Henry could not have composed this song, or the two others attributed to him by Wackernagel, which are written in high German. For further treatment see ZÜTPHEN, HENRY OF.

The authorship of the above-mentioned poem was attributed by Johann Christoph Olearius to Heinrich Moller, professor of Hebrew at Wittenberg, 1560–1574, who died in Hamburg, 1589, as a result of imprisonment during the crypto-calvinistic controversy (see PHILIPPISTS); but as the poem was printed in 1527 and this Heinrich Moller was born in 1530, the conjecture is not tenable, and the authorship of the poem is still undetermined.

(CARL BERTHEAU.)

BIBLIOGRAPHY: J. F. Iken, *Heinrich von Zütphen*, Halle, 1886; *ADB*, xxii. 554, 758 sqq.

MOLOCH, MOLECH.

According to the common conception, Moloch (Hebr. *Molek*) is the name of a West-Semitic deity whose cult was introduced into Israel between the time of Solomon and Ahaz and was practised by both king and people. The existence of this deity has been universally assumed from early Christian times, probably even from the period of the Greek translators of the Old Testament, down to a very recent date. But in the present century mainly, close study of the Old-Testament text and of the cults of peoples into connection with whom the Hebrews came has raised the question whether a deity of that name existed or whether a rite involving human sacrifice from a source not hitherto understood was superposed upon the worship of Yahweh in much the same manner as the Baal cults were associated with it (cf. Jer. xix. 5, which asserts that the Hebrews "burnt their sons with fire for burnt offerings unto Baal"). In the latter case, this rite was imported from abroad from the worship of some deity (or deities) whose proper name was not Moloch or Molech, but one to whom the title "king" was applied much as "Baal" was applied to different local deities.

1. The Problem.

An examination of the passages in which the name occurs or in which there is mention of the rites belonging to this worship is necessary. As a preliminary it is to be remarked (1) that the consonants of the word rendered "Moloch" are those which compose the word for "king," and (2) that the article is attached in every case where "Moloch" is read except one (I Kings xi. 7), where it is practically certain that the reading should be *Milkom*, "Milcom," and not *Molek*, "Moloch" (Septuagint, A, *Melcho;* Lucian, *Melchom*). The only textual differentiation between the Hebrew word for "king" and "Moloch" is the pronunciation, concerning which it is to be remembered that the punctuation of the Hebrew text is at best as late as the sixth Christian century (see BIBLE TEXT, I., 2, § 2). In the following passages the reading in the Hebrew is *molek* with the article: Lev. xviii. 21, xx. 2, 3, 4, 5 (Gk. *archon*, "ruler," "king"); I Kings xi. 7 (see above); II Kings xxiii. 10 (Lucian, *Melchom*); Jer. xxxii. 35 (Septuagint conflate reading *tōi Moloch basilei* "to Moloch king"). In these passages the characteristic practise associated with the name which is forbidden or denounced is the "giving of one's seed to Molech (Moloch)" or "making one's son or daughter to pass through the fire (i.e., offering by fire) to Molech." With the preceding eight passages are to be taken the numerous places which refer to offering son or daughter by fire without stating specifically to which deity the offering is made. The representative passages are Deut. xii. 31, xviii. 10; Ps. cxxxvi. 37; Isa. lvii. 5; Jer. vii. 31, xix. 4–6; Ezek. xvi. 21, xx. 26, 31; cf. II Kings xvii. 31. In many of these the rites are localized in "the valley of Ben-hinnom," or at "Tophet (Topheth) in the valley of the son (sons) of Hinnom." In all probability the early name of this place was *Tapheth*, the vocalization coming from the Jewish practise of reading *bosheth*, "shame," wherever the word occurs. The meaning of Tophet is uncertain, but the rendering "fireplace" is provisionally proposed (cf. Isa. xxx. 33). It is conjectured that the name Benhinnom is connected with the rites performed there, and that the element *hinnom* is derived from the root *naham*, "to groan." The later name of the locality was Gehenna (q.v.), distinctively a "place of burning," which with Tophet came to be applied figuratively to the place of eternal punishment. Certain passages other than those quoted are read in the light of these as referring to the same cult. Thus, Isa. xxx. 33, where Tophet is mentioned, is regarded as referring to the cult elsewhere associated with Moloch, but the word is pointed so as to read "the king." There is some question as to Isa. lvii. 9. The chapter is one in which various forms of idolatry are mentioned, and "the king" probably refers to the deity with whom the sacrifice of children is associated (cf. verse 5). Amos v. 26 is difficult; the Hebrew reads *malkekem*, "your king," Septuagint *Moloch* (the first appearance of this form, quoted by Stephen in Acts vii. 43); A. V., "ye have borne the tabernacle of your Moloch," margin and R. V., "Siccuth your king." Another verse concerning which two opinions are possible is Zeph. i. 5, where the Hebrew text reads *malkam* (Septuagint *Moloch*, *Melchom*, thus showing a wavering between Moloch and Milcom; A. V., R. V., "Malcham," R. V. margin "their king"). The Hebrew here is susceptible of the pointing which makes of it the name of the Ammonite deity Milcom (q.v.)—not an impossibility, but it is better, considering the date of Zephaniah (q.v.), viz., in the period when this form of sacrifice was prominent (see below), to render the last part of the verse "which swear to Yahweh and swear by their (divine) king," or, still better, to read "which swear (we are) Yahweh's (people), and swear by their (divine) king." In this case, the reference would be to the practise under consideration in combination with the worship of Yahweh.

2. Old-Testament Mention.

According to the above, in eight passages the Hebrew is vocalized *Molek*. Outside of the Hebrew Old Testament, the versions, the quotation in Acts vii. 43, and writings based upon these sources, this pronunciation or that rendered "Moloch" has not been found. Moreover, the versions are discrepant in their renderings, the Septuagint in particular showing a confusion and an uncertainty between a form corresponding to Moloch and one corresponding to Milcom. Accordingly it has by critical scholars been accepted that the pointing of the Masoretic text has arisen from an understood Keri (see KERI AND KETHIBH) by which, in place of the textual *mlk* (however it was pronounced), there was read the word *bosheth*, "shame," to recall the idolatry of the cult; and then the vowels of the Keri were used by the Masoretes to point the consonants of the text. This is supported by several considerations: (1) by the known usage of the Hebrews in such cases. (2) By the fact that Tophet is similarly pointed, though both Septuagint (*Thapheth, Tapeth, Thaphpheth*) and Syriac (*Tappath*) suggest a different vocalization. In other words, both to the name of the assumed deity and to the chief place of his cult the vowels of the word *bosheth* were applied. (3) By the conjunction of the article with the word in all the undoubted cases of its occurrence, while it is against the genius of the Hebrew to employ the article with proper names. If this reasoning be correct, the above facts reduce to the statement

3. Pronunciation of the Word.

that the practise in question was one in honor of a deity one of whose titles was *hammelek*, " the king," whoever this deity was. Several considerations point to the application of this title to a number of West-Semitic deities, one of which is the case of Milcom (q.v.), whose name appears to be formed from the word, while a salient case, to be discussed later, is that of Melkarth (" king of the city ") of Tyre; and the method was not dissimilar from that by which Baal was applied to these and other gods.

4. Compounds of Mlk. Much stress has been laid upon the fact that the word, the consonants of which form the assumed god-name Moloch and the word for " king," is a frequent element in names, some of them divine, among the West Semites. Thus it appears in the Palmyrene *Mlk-'el*, " *Mlk* is god," or " a king is god " (M. Lidzbarski, *Nordsemitische Epigraphik*, Berlin, 1898); among the West Syrians occurred the names Adrammelech, " Adar is king " and Anammelech, " Anu is king " (II Kings xvii. 31); in early Canaanitic history and among the Philistines were such names as Abimelech (Gen. xx., xxi., xxvi.), as also among the Hebrews (Judges viii. 31, ix.; I Chron. xviii. 16); kings of Byblos are known with the names *Mlkshp'* and *Adarmlk*, while other names from the same locality are *Urumlk* and the Grecized form *Melkarthos* (which gives a clue to the pronunciation and is against the pronunciation Moloch or Molech). The Tyrian Melkarth (*melek ḳarath*, " king of the city," Gk. *Melkarthos*) is of great importance here, not only because it was probably from his worship that the cult was imported into Israel (see below) but because of the light which the formation of his name throws on the use of *mlk* as a divine name or as an element in such names. *Mlk* does not occur among Phenicians as in itself a divine or human name, only as an element in compound names; an instance of the occurrence alone as a proper name is found in the Hebrew in I Chron. viii. 35. In this usage *mlk* is to be compared with Baal, which was not originally a proper name (see Baal, § 2) but came to be applied to the local divinity in many places as his name. It is inherently probable that the same process was carried out with *melek*, " king," so that it, too, in conjunction with a further element, became practically a proper name. The forms *Baalmlk*, " Baal is king," Melchizedek, " a king is (the god) Ẓedeḳ "(?) or " Melek is righteous " (cf. Zedekiah, " Yah[weh] is righteous "), *Ẓdḳmlk*, " (the god) Ẓedeḳ is king," *Mlkythn*, " *Mlk* has given," or " the king has given," *Gdmlk*, " Gad is king "(?), *Malik-rammu*, the name of an Edomitic king given on the Taylor prism of Sennacherib, *Mlkb'l*, a deity of Palmyra, *'bdmlk*, " servant of *Mlk* " (quite decisive of *mlk* as a divine name), and *'ḥthmlk*, " sister of *mlk*," from a (Phenician?) seal of the seventh century, are excellent examples from West Semitic sources and finely illustrate the use as a divine name or title of the word under consideration. It is pertinent that Malik is the Islamic name for the watchman of the lower regions. An array of names partly inclusive of the foregoing has been supposed to show that a deity Moloch or Molech was widely worshiped among the West Semites. But the argument fails for three reasons: First, the pronunciation of that element in the names cited is seldom known. In cases where these names are cited as compounded with Moloch, the pronunciation is assumed. Two excellent examples of this are given in Vigouroux, *Dictionnaire*, fasc. xxvii., col. 1226, where " Moloch-Baal " is twice given as the reading, though the text is unpointed and only *mlkb'l* appears in the inscription. Second, where the pronunciation is given at all, it does not appear in the form *molok* or *molek*, but in a form which suggests the local pronunciation of the word for " king," as in Melkarth; in the absence of definite knowledge of such a deity, the probabilities are against the vocalization assumed. Third, compounds apparently of the form cited above appear in the early periods of Hebrew history, though no trace appears of such a cult as that under discussion. Thus there are Melchishua, " king of help " or " Melek is help " (I Sam. xiv. 49); Abimelech (cited above). They exist also in the later periods, when there are met Nathan-melech, " a king has given " (II Kings xxiii. 11); Malchiram, " my king is exalted " or " Melek is exalted " (I Chron. iii. 18); The Ebedmelech of Jer. xxxviii. 7, xxxix. 16 is a Cushite (" Ethiopian "), whatever that may mean (see Cush), and so can not be counted to Israel; but his name extends perhaps the area in which this form was used; and in this particular it is to be put with Regemmelech (Zech. vii. 2). But Malchiah or Malchijah (I Chron. vi. 40, ix. 12; Ezra x. 25 and elsewhere) is Jewish. These are possibly to be brought into connection with the application of the honorific title of king applied to Yahweh (see below, § 8). The sum of the foregoing discussion is therefore adverse to a vocalization of the word in the form Moloch or Molech, and implicitly against the existence of a deity known by that name.

5. The Cult. The cult in Israel, it is clear, was the sacrifice of children, often if not invariably the first-born, by fire. Ezek. xvi. 20–21, xxiii. 29 (cf. Isa. lvii. 5) seem to imply that the victims were killed before being placed in the fire; and the verb *saraph* in passages like Jer. vii. 31, xix. 5; cf. Deut. xii. 31 would indicate merely the characteristic method of completing the offering. Closer description of the method of making the offering as practised among the Hebrews is not obtainable, and the Christian and rabbinic accounts lack historical basis. At Carthage, a Phenician colony, according to Diodorus Siculus (*Bibliothēkē historikē*, xx. 14) the method was to place the victim on the hands of a colossal image, whence it rolled into a furnace of fire beneath. The Hebrew accounts furnish no basis for the supposition of such a method in Israel, and so notable an image could hardly have escaped description by the prophets. If the derivation of the practise was from Melkarth's worship (see below, § 7), it is to be noted that this deity was probably a sun god and that therefore his worship by fire was natural and appropriate. His symbols appear to have been two pillars, and he is reported to have been represented by the bull. Dr. William Hayes Ward knows of a representation of a bull with pyramidal or pointed back, from the breast of which two arms stretch out; and there are representations of bull-headed deities in the Semitic region. But these can not be identified securely with Melkarth or with a "melek-deity." Diodorus Siculus describes the statue of the Carthaginian Kronos as human in form with the arms outstretched—a feature used in the rabbinic descriptions already alluded to. Yet Melkarth is not to be conceived wholly as a malign divinity, since compounds such as "Melkarth is gracious," "Melkarth saves," "Melkarth hears (answers)" are known. Human sacrifice seems rather abnormal among the Semites. There are traces or direct testimony for it among Aramæans (Palmyrenes) and Phenicians, and it appears as a phenomenon of a decadent stage in religious development. Such a feature is not unusual in the development of a religion when distrust of ordinary means of obtaining divine favor has entered. It must be noted, however, that human sacrifice does not imply a special divinity to whom it is offered; emergency may be conceived to warrant it as a present to any god. In such a case it is the result of a common anthropopathism—what is of highest value to mortals is held in the same estimate by the gods. Attempts have been made by Jewish interpreters and others to minimize the worship by reducing the practise to the simple custom of passing children through the fire for purposes of purification and not as sacrificial victims. This custom is one widely prevalent among primitive peoples, fire and water being recognized as the two purgative elements. Such a practise is described by Theodoret (on II Kings, quest. xlvii.), and was forbidden by the Trullan Synod of 692 (canon 65; Hefele, *Conciliengeschichte*, iii. 338, Eng. transl., v. 232). But the passages cited above are decisive of the fact of sacrifice. [Indeed the descriptive phrase does not mean "to pass through" but "to pass over," "to transfer," i.e., "to dedicate or offer," as is shown by its use in Ex. xiii. 12, where Yahweh is the object of worship and there is no allusion to fire. J. F. M.] The attempt to minimize the wickedness is no more successful here than in the case of Jephthah's daughter.

6. Date of Introduction into Israel.

A factor in the question of the date of the introduction of this practise among the Hebrews has been the assumption of the practical identity of Moloch and Milcom (q.v.). The basis for this is the linguistic fact that the same word "king" is at the root of both forms. Were the identity of the two established, supposing always that there were a deity Moloch, the date of the introduction of the cult into Israel would be fixed by I Kings xi. in the time of Solomon. But several sets of data are against this. (1) The sacrifice of children is not in the Old Testament associated with Milcom. (2) The place of worship of the two cults was different. (3) In the category of the sins of Solomon in the chapter cited the sacrifice of children does not appear; he burned incense and sacrificed to the gods of the peoples, but there is silence as to human sacrifice. (4) The condemnation of this sin by the prophets is not in evidence till a late period, and it is inconceivable that such a practise could have escaped the denunciation of early prophets had it existed. The cases of human sacrifice in Israel prior to Solomon do not suggest a custom of offering children. The case of Abraham and Isaac is altogether individual, the instance being quite exceptional; that of Jephthah was emergential in nature and appears also as unusual. It is true that something sacrificial is imported into the killing of Agag, whom Samuel hewed to pieces "before the Lord" (I Sam. xv. 33), but there is no connection between this example and the offering of children by fire. II Sam. xii. 31 can not be adduced, since the corrected Hebrew text affords the reading "made them labor at the brick kiln" for "made them pass through the brick kiln" (S. R. Driver, *Notes on the Hebrew Text of Samuel*, pp. 226–229, Oxford, 1890). The age of Solomon as the period of the introduction of the cult may be dismissed. There is nothing at all to connect Ahab or Jezebel with the cult except inference based on Jezebel's derivation from Tyre where it was known to exist. The earliest definite statement of this practise is in connection with Ahaz (II Kings xvi. 3; cf. II Chron. xxviii. 3). The historicity of the passage is questioned on the ground of the silence of the prophets of his own and the immediately following period. That the objection is not insuperable in this instance is shown by those who defend the historicity by supposing that the sacrifice (the case is singular, "his son") was emergential and in some measure like that of Mesha (II Kings iii. 26). Further, that Ahaz was inclined to syncretism, or at least to following fashions of worship, is shown by the passage II Kings xvi. 10–13. Moreover, Isa. xxx. 33 plays suggestively upon the words Tophet and *melek* (Driver regards the passage as Isaianic, but Guthe, Cheyne, and others refer verses 27–33 to the exilic period). Isa. viii. 21 (which should read: "curse the house of their king and their God," see ISAIAH, II., 2, § 2) can not be brought into this connection since "their king" refers to Yahweh, cf. Isa. vi. 5—unless the cult was one imposed upon his worship and "their king" refers to him (cf. Isa. vi. 5 and see below, § 8). Manasseh is the next king connected with the sacrifice of children (II Kings xxi. 6; cf. II Chron. xxxiii. 6, where Tophet is mentioned). To the extension of the practise under Manasseh may be due the passages in Deuteronomy (xii. 31, xviii. 10), the one denunciatory and the other prohibitory. They seem to show that just before the time of Jeremiah the practise had become one of which it was necessary that the legislators take note—the cult had become prominent with a definite locus. It is not surprising therefore that Josiah "defiled Topheth" (II Kings xxiii. 10) so as to make it a place unfit for sacrificial purposes. The passages cited from Jeremiah (xix. 5, xxxii. 35) and Ezekiel show a renewed prevalence during the last days of the Judaic kingdom. Lev. xviii. 21, xx. 2 belong to an early stratum of the priest code, while Isa. lvii. 5, 9 look back on preexilic or early exilic practise. The indications therefore are that it was introduced and in force under Manasseh.

It was long the custom, in this as in other matters, on account of inexact knowledge of Assyrian and Babylonian practises, to refer the origin of the

"Moloch" cult to the Assyrian-Babylonian religion. But as already noted, the traces of human sacrifice in that region are few and faint. II Kings used to be advanced in favor of this theory, as Sepharvaim was identified with Sippara (see BABYLONIA, IV., § 11). But it is now known that Sepharvaim was a town in western Syria, and this location falls in with the testimony yet to be adduced. In this connection it is noteworthy that Deut. xii. 29–31 regards the practise as Canaanitic. The practise of offering children has been shown not to be early Hebraic, and this is corroborated by the excavations at Gezer (q.v.), where the foundation sacrifice, common and quite normal in the prehebraic period, as is usual among civilizations of a low grade, disappears in the Hebraic period. The case of Hiel the Bethelite (I Kings xvi. 34) has often been explained as a case of "foundation" and "completion" sacrifice. While this interpretation may be correct, since the period as a whole is one of adoption of Canaanitic cults by the Hebrews, the data are too incomplete to permit of dogmatizing, and another explanation, that of accidental fatality coincident with beginning and end of the building operations, is at least possible. II Kings iii. 27, R. V. margin, "there came great wrath upon Israel," is explained by many facts revealed by comparative religion as the common fallacy of *post hoc propter hoc,* associating an Israelitic disaster with the sacrifice, and shows the practise in the Canaanitic region to have been sometimes one of emergency. But this feature of the case argues against the Moabitic origin for the cult as practised by the Hebrews. The most likely and almost certain fountain of the Hebrew practise is the Phenician cult. Abundant testimony is extant from Greek and Roman authors, agreeing therefore with the passages in Deuteronomy and Leviticus, that in Phenicia and in Phenician colonies, notably at Carthage, the sacrifice of children was a prominent rite in the public religious services. The Greeks, following the common custom of identifying the gods of other peoples with their own, called the deity to whom these offerings were made Kronos, to whom, it is relevant to note, Greek writers applied the term *basileus,* "king." Pliny (*Nat. hist.,* XXXVI., v. 12) states that to Melkarth, god of Tyre, identified by the Greeks with Herakles, child sacrifices were offered; a fragment of Philo of Byblos asserts that sacrifices of this type were offered to "El," which, however, is not necessarily a proper name. Other Greek writers call the god of this cult Zeus. For the references to Greek and Roman writers cf. F. C. C. H. Münter, *Religion der Karthager* (Copenhagen, 1816). Melkarth and cognate deities appear to have been sun-gods, to whom sacrifice by fire was normal and natural. The connection between Phenicians and Hebrews was sufficiently close to make this derivation easy.

7. Source of the Cult.

If, then, as the facts seem to justify, it may be concluded that the rite was one imposed upon the worship of Yahweh and was in his honor and imitation of a foreign cult, can a motive be found? This can be done, and the indirect testimony is rather strong. The codes (e.g., Ex. xiii. 11–15) demanded the consecration of the first-born to Yahweh, with, however, the option of redemption (in the ethnic history of sacrifice a late device; see COMPARATIVE RELIGION, VI., 1, d, § 4). Under the principle already enunciated, that in times of trouble nations not infrequently resort to human sacrifice, though it is not a usual habit, it is not impossible that the Hebrews followed the stress of feeling in the later days of their kingdom under accumulated disaster and decay of power. There seem to be hints that their logic led them to the conclusion that their law demanded this form of worship, that they had long been remiss in not paying what was due, and that their cumulative distress was due to this. Jer. xix. 5, "to burn their sons with fire for burnt offerings unto Baal, which I commanded not, nor spake it, neither came it into my mind," reads like a disavowal of such an interpretation as is here suggested. It is an explicit disclaimer by Yahweh that he had ordered such a cult, together with the statement that it is really an offering to Baal. The two motives—*dernier resort* in time of trouble, and, in view of this, a not impossible construction of a well-known legal provision—are sufficient to explain such an importation into the Yahweh worship. This appears the easier since to Yahweh the title and attributes of king were often attributed. He is called king in Num. xxiii. 21; Deut. xxxiii. 5; Isa. vi. 5, xxxiii. 17, 22, xli. 25, xliv. 6; Jer. viii. 19; Micah ii. 13; and often in the Psalms; the use of the verb "reign" is also frequent in connection with his relation to Israel (e.g., Ex. xv. 18; Isa. lii. 7; Micah iv. 7); while the mention of him on his throne appears in such passages as I Kings xxii. 19; Isa. vi. 1. If there were a *melek* cult of human sacrifice among the surrounding nations, the fact that this epithet was applied to Yahweh would make the cult more feasible. The one difficulty is that the rite does not appear to have been practised in the Temple or inside Jerusalem. Ezek. xxiii. 38 sqq. appears to make a distinction between the worship of Yahweh and this rite. The passage states that the rite was performed on the sabbath, and that on the same day the worshipers went into Yahweh's sanctuary and thus defiled it. The answer of course is that this is the view of one who condemns the cult, and would not be held by those who employed it, who would not jeopardize success by alienating the deity. It is well known that a deity may have offered to him sacrifices differing essentially in character. Thus to Zeus it is known that the pig was offered, though this animal was appropriate as an offering only to chthonic deities (cf. Jane Ellen Harrison, *Prolegomena to the Study of Greek Religion,* pp. 13 sqq., Cambridge, 1908). The cult in Tophet may have been in honor of Yahweh, and the following of a double cultus may have been regarded as doubly efficacious.

8. Basis in National Conscience.

GEO. W. GILMORE.

BIBLIOGRAPHY: The earlier literature, from the modern point of view for the most part antiquated, is given in Hauck-Herzog, *RE,* xiii. 269–270; much of it is collected in Ugolini, *Thesaurus antiquitatum sacrarum,* vol. xxiii., Venice, 1760. Consult: J. Selden, *De dis Syris,* London, 1617; F. C. Movers, *Die Religion der Phönizier,* pp. 322–498, Bonn, 1841; C. Schwenck, *Die Mythologie der Semi-*

ten, Frankfort, 1849; A. Kuenen, in *ThT*, ii (1868), 551-598; idem, *De Godsdienst van Israel*, chap. iv., Eng. transl., *Religion of Israel*, i. 249–252, London, 1873; H. Oort, in *Waarheid in Liefde*, 1868, pp. 1–31, 81–108, 161 173; W. von Baudissin, *Jahve et Moloch*, Leipsic, 1874; E. Nestle, *Die israelitischen Eigennamen*, pp. 174–182, Haarlem, 1876; P. Scholtz, *Götzendienst und Zauberwesen bei den alten Hebräern*, pp. 182–217, Regensburg, 1877; C. P. Tiele, *Hist. comparée des anciennes religions de l'Égypte et des peuples sémitiques*, 281 sqq., 311 sqq., 435 sqq., Paris, 1882; idem, *Geschichte der Religion im Altertum*, i. 240 244, 343–344, 349–352, Gotha, 1896; Hoffman, *ZATW*, iii (1883), 124; idem, in *GGA*, xxxvi (1890), 25; B. D. Eerdmans, *Melekdienst en vereering van hemellichamen in Israel's assyrische periode*, Leyden, 1891; G. B. Gray, *Studies in Hebrew Proper Names*, pp. 115–120, 138, 148, London, 1896; A. Kamphausen, *Das Verhältnis des Menschenopfers zur israelitischen Religion*, Bonn, 1896; G. F. Moore, in *JBL*, pp. 161–165, and in *EB*, iii. 3183–3191; M. J. Lagrange, *Études sur les religions sémitiques*, pp. 99, 109, Paris, 1903; Schrader, *KAT*, pp. 469–472; Smith, *Rel. of Sem.*, pp. 372 sqq.; *DB*, iii. 415–417; *JE*, 650–654; Vigouroux, *Dictionnaire*, fasc. xxvii., cols. 1224–1230.

MOLOKANI. See RUSSIA, III., § 6.

MOLTHER, mel'tăr, MENRAD: Humanist and Reformer; b. at Augsburg in 1500; d. at Heilbronn Apr. 8, 1558. He received his first education in the school of Johann Pinicianus; went to Heidelberg in 1526, where he became a tutor for young noblemen, and also edited several works, some of which had been recently recovered, e.g., those of Alcuin, Avitus, Christian Drutmar, and Willimar Ebersbergiensis; he directed the Realistenburse, 1532; was called as preacher to Heilbronn to assist Johann Lachmann (q.v.) 1533, whom he succeeded in 1539; and in 1543 he arranged the church rules according to the pattern of Hall. Because of the threatening presence of the imperial troops, he advised, in 1548, the acceptance of the Interim (q.v.); but he continued to preach in a strictly Evangelical and anti-Roman spirit, without, however, being able to persuade the council to abolish the mass. His successor was Jacob Ratz (q.v.). G. BOSSERT.

BIBLIOGRAPHY: G. Bossert, in *Blätter für württembergische Kirchengeschichte*, 1887, pp. 57–61.

MOMBERT, JACOB ISIDOR: Protestant Episcopalian; b. at Cassel, Germany, Nov. 6, 1829. In early life he went to England, where he was engaged in business for a number of years, after which he studied both in England and at the universities of Leipsic and Heidelberg. He was ordered deacon in 1856 and in the following year went to Canada, where he was ordained priest. He was then curate of Trinity, Quebec (1857–59), curate (1859–60) and rector (1860–70) of St. James', Lancaster, Pa., and rector of St. John's, Dresden, Germany (1870–76), Christ Church, Jersey City, N. J. (1877–79), and St. John's, Passaic, N. J. (1879–82). In 1882 he retired from active parochial work, and since that time has been engaged in literary pursuits. He has translated F. A. Tholuck's "Commentary on the Psalms" (London, 1856) and the commentary on the Catholic Epistles for the American Lange series (New York, 1867), edited William Tyndale's *Five Books of Moses* (1884), and has written: *Faith Victorious: Account of the Venerable Dr. Johann Ebel, Late Archdeacon of the Old Town Church of Königsberg in Prussia* (1882); *Handbook of the English Versions of the Bible* (1883; new ed., 1907); *Great Lives: A Course of History in Biographies* (Boston, 1886); *History of Charles the Great* (New York, 1888); *Short History of the Crusades* (1894); and *Raphael's Sistine Madonna* (1895).

MOMERIE, ALFRED WILLIAMS: Church of England; b. in London Mar. 22, 1848; d. there Dec. 6, 1900. He was of Huguenot stock and restored his name from its phonetic form of Mummery. His father was a Congregational minister, who, after sending him to the City of London School, sent him to the University of Edinburgh (M.A., 1875; Sc.D., 1876). But to his Scotch training he added English, for he went through another university course in Cambridge (M.A., 1881). Previously he had been admitted to holy orders in the Church of England, becoming deacon in 1878 and priest in 1879. In 1879 he was elected fellow of St. John's College, Cambridge, and in 1880 professor of logic and mental philosophy at King's College, London. He was curate of Leigh in Lancashire from 1878 to 1880. In 1883 he became morning preacher at the Foundling Hospital in London. His sermons and his teaching attracted great attention, but their outspoken "Broad Churchism" brought him into trouble, and he was forced to retire from his preachership and professorship in 1891. After that he preached at the Portman Rooms, London. In 1896 he married. The number and sale of his publications attest the interest in his teachings. Mention may be made of: *Personality the Beginning and End of Metaphysics* (London, 1879, 4th ed., 1889); *The Basis of Religion* (Edinburgh, 1883, 2d ed., 1886), a criticism of J. R. Seeley's *Natural Religion*; *The Religion of the Future, and other Essays* (1893); *The English Church and the Romish Schism* (1896); and *Essays on the Bible*, ed. J. Nield (1909).

BIBLIOGRAPHY: *Alfred Williams Momerie: his Life and Work, written by his Wife*, Edinburgh, 1905; *DNB*, Supplement, iii. 183.

MOMIERS, MUMMERS: The contemptuous name, meaning "hypocrites," given to certain strict Calvinists in the two French cantons of Switzerland, Geneva and Vaud, because of their fervent acceptance of the doctrines of the Trinity, the divinity of Christ, and of total depravity, which had been denied by the great majority of the pastors of the State Church, and because of their practise of holding meetings in which these and similar so-called "pietistic" views found expression. In Geneva the party was started in 1813 by Henri Louis Empaytaz, a theological student; in 1820 their most distinguished leader, Rev. Cesar Malan (q.v.), organized them into a church. In 1831 a theological seminary was started, and in 1848 the party declared themselves free altogether of the State Church. In Vaud they ran a similar course. They started about the same time and were ignored by the authorities till, on Dec. 24, 1823, three of the cantonal clergy, who had been prominent members, resigned from the State Church. Four others followed them the next month. The authorities condemned this action and so the meetings held henceforth were subjected to some petty persecution.

BIBLIOGRAPHY: G. B., *Geschichte der sogenannten Momiers, einer in einigen Schweizer-Cantonen sich ausbreitenden Secte*, 2 parts, Basel, 1825.

MONARCHIANISM.

I. The Beginnings of Monarchianism: Up to the end of the second century the doctrine of the Logos had by no means been definitely fixed, despite the statements of the apologists, Irenæus, Tertullian, and Clement, and despite the general recognition that Christ must be thought of in the same way as God. There was, therefore, no strict formulation of the nature and dignity of the Redeemer or of the being of God. Nor was a comparison of the two persons even contemplated, for the recognition of the preexistence of the Son had influence on the concept of the Godhead so long as this preexistent Son was considered a creature, and so long as a plurality of heavenly spirits and personified powers was assumed. The points regarding the personality of the Redeemer generally established and defended between 140 and 180 were derived from the short creed based on Matt. xxviii. 19: the Son of God, the Lord and Savior, born of the Holy Ghost and the virgin. The recognition of the supernatural birth (itself assuming preexistence) marked the delimitation between the strict Judæo-Christians and those who would merely admire Christ as a second Socrates; while the recognition of his physical birth and true human life formed a barrier against the Gnostics. Even at this early period there existed side by side Christologies which were to form the bases of the Monarchian, Arian, Athanasian, and even Docetic and Gnostic systems; and the same writer uses formulas in which the divinity of the Son is ascribed in one place to special election and endowment by the deity, in a second to the actual indwelling of the Holy Ghost, and in a third to a celestial hypostasis or an incarnation of the Godhead. There is nothing to show, however, that at that time Christ was regarded as the actual Godhead. He was rather deemed either as the man in whom the Godhead or the Spirit of God dwelt, or—this being doubtless the more general view—as the heavenly Spirit which had become incarnate and manifest. Those who maintained the latter view held that Christ became what he is before his miraculous birth; while those who adhered to the former hypothesis believed that the indwelling of the divine Spirit had taken place at his baptism, it being also possible to assume a progressive filling of the Son of Man with the Holy Ghost.

1. The Christology of the Early Church.

To the two views here set forth may be referred the various Christologies of the second century; and, although the distinction between them might be glossed over in public worship, the theological discrepancy was still felt, and even the laity came to take part in the ensuing controversy.

2. Discrepancies in Primitive Christologies.

The Bible was cited in support of both views, although the conditions of the time favored belief in the incarnation of a special divine being in Christ. This was confirmed by the interpretation of the theophanies of the Old Testament as explained by the Alexandrine school, by the testimony of St. Paul and a series of ancient writings, and by the cosmological and theological principles borrowed from the religious philosophy of the period to serve as the basis of a rational Christian philosophy. Assuming the theory of the divine Logos to explain the origin and history of the world, the establishment of the divine dignity and the divine sonship of the Redeemer was already fixed. Nor did this involve any peril to monotheism even when the Logos was allowed to be more than a procession from the creative will of God, since the infinite substance of the Godhead might be developed in various subjects and be communicated to various persons without being emptied or divided in essence. Neither was the divinity of Christ imperiled by the doctrine that he was the incarnation of the Logos, for the Logos-concept was capable of the most varied interpretation and lent itself to each new development of speculation and exegesis. It accordingly developed finally into the very antithesis of its original concept, but until this happened, and so long as the Logos connoted either the archetype of the world or the rational law of the universe, it was somewhat mistrusted as a means for establishing the divinity of Christ, for the pious would see in Christ nothing less than the Godhead itself. Athanasius was the first to render this possible by his interpretation of the Logos, though he practically put the Logos-doctrine into the background; so that from him to Augustine the history of Christology became the history of the replacement of the concept of the Logos by that of the sonship of Christ. The first formal protest against the Logos-Christology in the second century was prompted by a desire to preserve strict monotheism—primarily by the interest in the humanity of the Redeemer—combined with a repugnance to the employment of Platonic and Stoic philosophy in Christian doctrine. The primary concern of the Monarchians, who were at first charged with lowering (if not destroying) the dignity of the Redeemer —a charge they later turned against their opponents—was the man Jesus, and then monotheism and the divine dignity of Christ. Hence gradually developed a controversy on the entire theological implication of the first two articles of the rule of faith, which were suspected of both ditheism and reminiscences of Gnosticism. The beginnings of the struggle, which lasted more than a century and a half, are wrapped in obscurity. It may be regarded as the history of the substitution of the preexistent for the historic Christ and as the replacement of the person of Christ by the mystery of the person, or as the victory of Platonism over Aristotelianism in Christian theology.

3. Meaning of "Monarchian." The term "Monarchians," coined by Tertullian, denotes the representatives of strict monotheism in the early Church. This definition, however, is too narrow, for some, if not all, of the older dynamistic Monarchians assumed two hypostases, recognizing the Holy Ghost as the eternal Son of God. Since, on the other hand, these binitarians did not consider Jesus as the real incarnation of this Holy Ghost, they were, Christologically, neither trinitarian nor binitarian, but Monarchian. But the term was restricted in the early Church to those who recognized in Christ an incarnation of God the Father; and while the Arians and all who held the acknowledged independence of a divine element in Christ to be a product of the creative activity of the Father may be considered in a sense Monarchians, such an application of the term would lead too far from the ancient connotation and would fail to recognize the limitation of rigid monotheism among even the most radical Arians. It is best, therefore, to apply the term only to those who regarded Jesus either as the man filled with the Holy Ghost and called to be the Son of God (though some considered the Holy Ghost a second hypostasis), or as an incarnation of God the Father.

4. Relations to the Catholics. The Monarchians, arising, as implied above, after the establishment of the anti-Gnostic interpretation of the rule of faith in the Church, must be considered as Catholic. They accordingly were in harmony with their opponents except in the points in controversy; and even had traces of pre-Catholic (but not non-Catholic) characteristics, so that their deviations from the Catholic canon point to the period before the formation of this canon, while other "heresies" of the older group must be referred to the formative age of the Catholic Church. The history of the movement is as obscure as its origin. Even the current distinction between dynamistic (or rather adoptian) and modalistic Monarchianism—the former regarding the power or Spirit of God as indwelling in the man Jesus, and the latter considering Jesus as the incarnation of the Godhead—is not free from objections. Though the common bond between the Monarchian systems was their concept of God, and their differences concerned revelation, no strict classification is possible on the basis of the sources thus far known, which consist almost entirely of the accounts of opponents, who garbled, distorted, and misrepresented the doctrines of their antagonists. Both the history and the geography, moreover, of Monarchianism are uncertain, nor are definite dates yet determined for the Alogi, Artemas, Praxeas, Sabellius, or the synods at Antioch against Paul of Samosata.

II. The Alogi (q.v.) **of Asia Minor:** Hippolytus (quoted by Epiphanius, *Hist. eccl.*, li., and others) and Philastrius (*Hær.*, lx.) recognize the existence of a sect in Asia Minor to which the former applied the name Alogi (perhaps designedly ambiguous, meaning both "without the Logos" and "irrational"). Hippolytus also says that they rejected the Gospel of John and the Apocalypse, ascribing them to Cerinthus; of their views on the Johannine Epistles nothing is certainly known, although they probably rejected them also. Besides his *Syntagma*, Hippolytus wrote a work in defense of the Johannine writings, and apparently a special polemic against the Monarchians, probably in 204–205. It is clear, from the statements of Hippolytus and Irenæus (*Hist. eccl.*, III., xi. 9) that the sect existed in Asia Minor between 170 and 180. Belonging to the radical anti-Montanistic party, they sought to exclude all prophecy from the Church, thus proceeding to reject the Gospel of John (and consequently the Logos which it postulates—whence their name) as containing Christ's prophecy of the Paraclete, and the Apocalypse because of its prophetic revelations. They likewise alleged internal evidence, discrepancy with the other Gospels, absurdity, and untruthfulness against the two books; and they regarded the Gospel of John as tending to Docetism because of its abrupt transition from the Logos to the ministry of Jesus. They objected to the use of the term Logos, in which they saw Gnosticism, to denote Christ, and to the statement in John they opposed the natural origin given by Mark. Nevertheless, both Hippolytus and Irenæus considered the Alogi schismatics rather than heretics, the former expressly emphasizing their orthodoxy, except on the points in controversy. Of their Christology nothing is known except that they rejected the concept of the Logos and the birth "from on high," and that, from their antipathy to Gnosticism, their chief interest lay in the human life of Christ. It is also probable that they laid special stress on the events at the baptism of Christ, though this can not be demonstrated. They seem to have been the first within the Church to apply historical criticism to Christian writings and tradition; but how long they existed, or when, how, or by whom they were excluded from the Church in Asia Minor, are all unknown.

III. Adoptionism in the West: Toward the end of the pontificate of Eleutherus or at the beginning of that of Victor (d. 190), Theodotus the tanner went from Byzantium to Rome, and became the founder of dynamistic Monarchianism.

1. Theodotus and His Teachings. He had probably come into contact with the Alogi of Asia Minor, and was a man of thorough education and highly esteemed. All that is certainly known of him, however, is that he was excommunicated by Victor between 189 and 199 because of the Christology which he taught at Rome. The *Philosophumena* explicitly affirms Theodotus' orthodoxy in theology and cosmology. In Christology he taught that Jesus was a man born of a virgin through the operation of the Holy Ghost in accordance with a special decree of God; but that he received no specifically divine essence until, after a life of perfect purity, the Holy Ghost descended on him at baptism, so that he became Christ and received the power for his mission and the righteousness which rendered him preeminent above all mankind. Nevertheless, even the descent of the Spirit did not entitle Jesus to be considered God. Some of Theodotus' followers asserted that Jesus became God through his resurrection, but others denied this. Theodotus and his school sought to base their Christology on the Bible, and his citations, as preserved by Epiphanius through the *Syntagma* of Hippolytus, show that the canon of Scripture was now established and that the Gospel of John was recognized. His exegesis is of interest as representing the same sober system as that of the Alogi. Epiphanius mentions the appeal of the Theodotians to Deut. xviii. 15; Jer. xvii. 9; Isa. liii. 2–3; Matt. xii. 32; Luke i. 35; John viii. 40; Acts ii. 22; and I Tim. ii. 5. From Matt. xii. 32, they deduced that the Holy Ghost is superior to the Son of Man; while from Deut. xviii. 15 they argued that even the risen Christ was not God. In Luke i. 35, Theodotus stressed the phrase, "The Holy Ghost shall come upon thee," and, if Epiphanius may be believed, misread the remainder of the verse, besides interpreting the "Word" of John i. 14, as "Spirit" (cf. II Clement, ix. 5).

2. Successors of Theodotus and Their Exegesis.

The circle which gathered around Theodotus at Rome seems to have been small, nor did he found a separate sect there. His most important scholar, Theodotus the money-changer, and a certain Asclepiodotus (both apparently Greeks), after being excommunicated by Pope Zephyrinus (199–218), made a fruitless attempt to found a church of their own in Rome, and persuaded the confessor Natalius of Rome, who soon deserted them, to become their bishop at a monthly salary of 150 *denarii*. This abortive attempt in itself shows the wide cleft between the Catholics and the Monarchians at Rome about 210; while the author of the "Little Labyrinth" (preserved in extracts by Eusebius, *Hist. eccl.*, v. 28) charges the leaders of the sect with shameless perversions and falsifications of Scripture, in which they were not even consistent with each other; and also accuses them of rejecting the law and the prophets altogether, and seeking support for their allegations in the writings of Euclid, Aristotle, Theophrastus, and Galen. It is clear, from the very statements of the author of the "Little Labyrinth," that the Monarchians, adopting the same methods as were doubtless followed by the Alogi and the older Theodotus, pursued their system of exegesis, text-criticism, and the study of logic, mathematics, and natural science entirely in the cause of their theology; and he was also obliged to acknowledge that they assailed neither the inspiration nor the canon of the Scriptures. This implies, as contrasted with orthodox Catholicism, the substitution of the Empiricists for Plato and Zeno, grammatical for allegorical exegesis, and a more original for the traditional text. But the distinction, in the theology of the time, was more than one of method. They remained, therefore, outside the Church, though they considered themselves Catholics. Of their works all traces have vanished, but their researches confirmed them in their concept of Christ as the man in whom the Spirit of God was peculiarly operative, and made them opponents of the Logos Christology.

3. Melchisedicians.

It is not clear wherein the tenets of the younger Theodotus differed from those of the older, though it is evident from the *Philosophumena* that there was a controversy among the Monarchians whether Christ could be called God after the resurrection. On the other hand, they recognized the miraculous birth. Later writers, however, following Hippolytus' interpretation of Theodotus the younger's exegesis of Heb. v., vi. 20–vii. 3, 17, ascribed to him the foundation of a sect of Melchisedicians. Theodotus is said to have taught (Epiphanius, *Hist. eccl.*, lv.) that Melchizedek was "a very great power" and more exalted than Christ, the relation between the two being that of copy and original. Melchizedek was considered the advocate of the heavenly powers before God and as the high priest of mankind. Jesus is a priest a degree lower and born of Mary, while the origin of Melchizedek is hidden because heavenly (cf. Heb. vii. 3). Epiphanius likewise adds that the sect offered their oblations "in the name of Melchizedek," since he was the "guide to God," "the king of righteousness," and "the true Son of God." It would seem, however, that Theodotus here played an exegetical joke on his opponents, showing that by their arguments a preexistent Melchizedek could be deduced from Heb. v.–vii., a sarcasm the more biting since the Catholics themselves were involved in controversy on the signification of Melchizedek. Nevertheless, the explanation can not be so simple, for the statements of the *Syntagma* and *Philosophumena* are obviously based on written sources and stand in close proximity to assertions which are clearly Theodotian, but which at the same time show an exact parallelism with a concept long current in the Catholic community at Rome (cf. the Shepherd of Hermas, Similitude V., especially vi. 3). As is clear from their exegesis of I Cor. viii. 6, where "Christ" was made to connote "Holy Ghost" (the name of Jesus being here stricken out), these Theodotians maintained that the sole divine essence besides the Father was the Holy Ghost, who was identical with the Son of God (thus agreeing with Hermas). This Holy Ghost accordingly appeared to Abraham as the "King of righteousness." They further maintained that Jesus was a man anointed with the power of the Holy Ghost; and they were thus in accord with Catholic teaching when they held that prayers and oblations were due the true, eternal Son of God, the King of righteousness that had appeared to Abraham, who had blessed him and his descendants, i.e., the Christians. Furthermore, according to both Theodotus and Hermas, Jesus, the chosen and anointed Son of God by adoption, was inferior to and not to be compared with the Holy Ghost as the true Son. It must be borne in mind, however, that there was a wide divergency between the Theodotians and Hermas in that the former designed their speculations to discard the historic Jesus in favor of the metaphysical. Views closely resembling those of the Theodotians are repeated by Origen in elevating the eternal Son of God above the crucified; while a like tendency is found with Hieracas and his monks, as well as among the Origenistic monks in Egypt in the fourth and fifth centuries. It is evident, therefore, that these theologians retained the old Roman Christology, though they revised its theology and changed its purport.

The question arises whether the doctrine of the Theodotians was really Monarchian, since a special and apparently independent place was given the Holy Ghost beside the Father. Although it is not clear how the hypostasis of the Holy Ghost was reconciled with the unity of the Godhead, it is at least certain that in the Theodotian Christology the Spirit was regarded merely as a "power." They differed from their opponents not in their concept of God, but in their views of Christ. For if an eternal Son of God, or anything resembling that Son, appeared in the Old Testament, then the traditional estimate of Jesus could no longer be retained; nor would the theory of the Man anointed by the Spirit suffice to establish the preeminent magnitude of the revelation of God in Christ. It thus becomes clear why, under the spur of theological speculation, the old Christology gave place at a comparatively early date to the complete and essential apotheosis of Jesus.

5. Theodotian Concept of Christ.

Twenty or thirty years later another attempt was made by Artemas to revive the early Christology, apparently at Rome. The sources here are scanty, for Eusebius confined his excerpts from the work against Artemas and its appendix, the "Little Labyrinth," almost exclusively to the Theodotians. It is plain, however, that the followers of Artemas claimed that the ancient Christology which they defended had been distorted by Zephyrinus. Wherein they differed from the Theodotians is uncertain, and they clearly agreed with them in denying the epithet "God" to Jesus. Artemas was still living in excommunication at Rome about 270, as is shown by the condemnation of Paul of Samosata by the Synod of Antioch (Eusebius, *Hist. eccl.*, vii. 30). It is evident, moreover, that he must be considered a dynamistic Monarchian; while by his association with Paul of Samosata he eclipsed the fame of Theodotus in the East. In him dynamistic Monarchianism exhausted itself at Rome without ever gaining importance in the Church. The adherents of Artemas are probably implied by Novatian when, in his *De trinitate*, he speaks of those who considered Jesus simply as a man, and he is also mentioned by Methodius (*Symposium*, viii. 10). Hilary of Poitiers, in his *De trinitate* (especially x. 18 sqq., 50 sqq.), shows how various were the Christologies existing in the West in the middle of the fourth century. Even as late as the beginning of the fifth a certain Marcus was expelled from Rome for maintaining Photinian views and founded a community in Dalmatia. Though there is no evidence that Photinus' doctrines ever gained much following in the West, it is noteworthy that Augustine, even when preparing to enter the Catholic Church, entertained a Christology essentially Photinian (*Conf.*, vii. 19 [25]).

6. Artemas; Decay of Western Dynamistic Monarchianism.

IV. Suppression of Adoptionism in the East: It is plain from the writings of Origen that there were many in the East who rejected the Logos-Christology. The majority of these were modalists, but there were also those who ascribed to the Son merely a human nature, and others still who regarded Christ as a man filled with the Godhead but not specifically different from the prophets. Origen did not brand those who held these tenets as heretics, but considered them misguided or simple, reclaimable by a friendly attitude. Origen's own complicated Christology was unjustly considered by some to be adoptionistic. Dynamistic Monarchianism seems to have been taught by Beryllus of Bostra (Eusebius, *Hist. eccl.*, vi. 33; Socrates, *Hist. eccl.*, iii. 7), who, probably in 244, was convinced of his error in a disputation by Eusebius, who had been sent to Arabia for that purpose.

1. Opponents of Logos-Christology in the East.

The wide dissemination of dynamistic Christology in the Semitic and Hellenistic East is shown by the fact that Paul of Samosata, bishop of Antioch, the most important see of the East, began expressly to promulgate it about 260 and opposed the doctrine of the essential divinity of Christ. The result was the great Eastern controversy which ended with the downfall of adoptionism. The Alexandrine theology of the third century had made the terms *logos, ousios, prosōpon*, and the like current and indispensable in dogmatics; and at the same time the belief had become widely prevalent that the original nature of the Redeemer was not human but divine, and that he did not first come into existence with his birth on earth. These tenets were opposed by Paul, and—though little is known of the beginning of the controversy—there is reason to suppose that he, as the viceroy of Zenobia, was opposed by the Roman party in Syria. His fall, therefore, meant their triumph, and behind the theological controversy there lay political strife. But Paul proved a doughty antagonist. A great synod was convened at Antioch in 264, attended by bishops from the most various parts of the East, but their debates, like those of a second synod, came to no result. It was not until a third synod, held at Antioch between 266 and 269 (probably in 268), that the metropolitan was excommunicated and succeeded by Domnus. The proceedings of the synod were sent by its members to Rome and Antioch and to all the Catholic churches. Nevertheless, Paul remained in office with Zenobia for four years, while the church in Antioch was divided. In 272, however, Antioch was taken by Aurelian, who, when appealed to, decided that the church edifice should be given to him with whom the Christian bishops of Italy and the city of Rome were in correspondence. The teaching of Paul of Samosata was as follows: The Father, Son, and Holy Ghost

2. Paul of Samosata.

are one person; and though in God the Logos (Son) and "Wisdom" (Holy Ghost; elsewhere in Paul Logos is identical with "Wisdom") may be distinguished, they nevertheless remain qualities of God. God sent forth the Logos from himself from eternity and even begat him, so that the Logos may be termed "Son" and have a being ascribed to him, though he remains an impersonal power. The Logos, which can not be made manifest, worked in the prophets, still more in Moses, and most of all in the son of David born of the Holy Ghost by the Virgin. The Redeemer is, therefore, human in essence and comes "from hence," while the Logos works in him "from above." The union of the Logos with the man Jesus is to be considered an indwelling (with an appeal by Paul to John xiv. 10), so that the Logos is in Jesus what the apostle called the "inner man" in the Christian. On the other hand, since the Logos does not dwell essentially in Jesus, the two are to be distinguished, the Logos being the greater. Mary did not give birth to the Logos, but to a man essentially like other men; and the man, not the Logos, was anointed with the Spirit in baptism. On the other hand, Jesus was made peculiarly worthy of the divine grace, and was correspondingly preserved from sin. In consequence of his mental endowment and his will, Jesus was like God and became one with him, not only being without sin himself, but also overcoming by his toil and struggle the sin of the first parent of mankind. As Jesus steadily progressed ethically, the Father endowed him with miraculous powers; so that he became the redeemer and savior of mankind, and finally became inseparably united with God forever, receiving as the reward of his love a "name which is above every name" and the power of judgment. He is, moreover, enthroned in divine honor, so that he may be termed "God from the Virgin." His preexistence may, therefore, be postulated on the basis of foreknowledge and prophecy; and in like manner he may be regarded as born through the grace of God. Doubtless Paul of Samosata, in his view of the baptism, recognized a special degree of the indwelling of the Logos in the man Jesus; and he seems to have held that Jesus did not become Christ until his baptism. In his polemics Paul sought to show that the belief that Jesus was by nature the son of God led to ditheism; he openly opposed the Alexandrine exegetes; and he banished from the liturgy all psalms of the Church in which the essential divinity of Christ was maintained. While the doctrines of Paul of Samosata clearly mark a continuation of those of Hermas and Theodotus, he not only adopted the current theological terminology of his time, but also gave a philosophical, ethical, and Biblical foundation to the old heterodox type of doctrine. While in certain respects he was foreshadowed by the complicated theology of Origen—and also perhaps by the Alogi of Asia Minor and the Theodotians of Rome—his development of the nature and the will in the persons, the character and power of love, and the recognizability of Christ's divinity solely from his activity as being one with the divine will—these stand almost alone in the entire dogmatic literature of the oriental churches of the first three centuries. He is especially characterized, however, by his conscious substitution of history and ethics for metaphysics, as in his rejection of Platonizing dogmatics. While, moreover, he considered the peculiar divinity of Jesus to consist in his attitude and his will rather than in his nature, he held that the spirit and the grace of God rested in special measure (in accord with the divine promises) on Christ as the peculiar object of the predestination of God, Christ's activity and his life in and with God thus becoming unique. By this theory room was left for a human life.

3. Paul's Homoousianism and Influence.

Yet Paul taught an eternal son of God, and an indwelling of that son in Jesus; he proclaimed the divinity of Christ, held the doctrine of two persons (God and Jesus); and, like the Alexandrine theologians, rejected Sabellianism. The very synod of Antioch which condemned him apparently rejected the term *homoousios* in deference to him, on the ground that (according to the conjecture of Athanasius), if Christ was of the same nature as the Father, the latter was not the ultimate source of divinity, but both the Father and the Son must be derived from a primordial substance, and thus be in the relation of brothers. The possibility must also be borne in mind, however, that, as Hilary says, the synod rejected the term *homoousios* because Paul himself had declared God and the (impersonal) Logos (the Son) to be of the same substance. At all events, the majority of the synod considered the doctrines of Paul extremely heterodox, and, with all their own uncertainty on the precise character of the essentially divine element in Christ, they picked a very real flaw in Paul's Christology—his practical teaching of two sons of God, though the actual difference between the two parties lay in the problem of the divine nature of the Redeemer. With the deposition of Paul of Samosata it was no longer possible to gain a hearing for a Christology which denied the personal, independent preexistence of the Redeemer. It was no longer sufficient to interpret his theanthropic life from his deeds, but it was necessary to believe in his divine nature. Nevertheless Paul's school lingered on for a time, giving inspiration to the tenets of Lucian of Samosata (q.v.) and his followers, who ultimately developed into the Arians. In the fourth century Photinus approximated the teachings of Paul, whose affinity with the great Antiochian theologians is also clear, independent though the tenets of the latter school were in their origin. Among the great Antiochians Paul of Samosata was again condemned, and his name was used a third time in the Monothelite controversy (see MONOTHELITES). Even in the early fourth century the *Acta Archelai* show that in easternmost Christendom there was a Christology untouched by Alexandrine teachings and to be ranked with Adoptionism. Here it is clearly evident that as late as this period the Logos-Christology had not overpassed the boundaries of the Christianity confederated in the empire.

[The influence of Paul of Samosata was probably perpetuated in the Paulicians of Armenia (q.v.), and his name appears in their denominational epithet. It is highly probable that adoptionist Christology widely prevailed in Armenia until the triumph of Greek influence and continued to be zealously maintained by a persecuted minority until its adherents crystallized into the Paulicianism the chief peculiarities of which were the uncompromising rejection of infant baptism and the maintenance of adoptionist Christology. "The Key of Truth" (edited and translated by F. C. Conybeare, Oxford, 1896), probably written in the ninth century, but representing the doctrines and practises of a much earlier time, is outspoken in its adoptionism. In the section on the baptism of Christ it is said: "So then it was in the season of his maturity that he received baptism; then it was that he received authority, received the high-priesthood, received the kingdom and the office of chief shepherd. Moreover he was then chosen, then he won lordship, then he became resplendent, then he was strengthened, then he was revered, then he was appointed to guard us, then he was glorified, then he was praised, then he was made glad, then he shone forth, then he was pleased, and then he rejoiced. It was then he became chief of beings heavenly and earthly, then he became light of the world, then he became the way, the truth, and the life. Then he became the door of heaven, then he became the rock impregnable at the gate of hell; then he became the foundation of our faith; then he became savior of us sinners; then he was filled with the Godhead. Furthermore, he then put on the primal raiment of light which Adam lost in the garden. Then accordingly it was that he was invited by the Spirit of God to converse with the heavenly Father," etc. A. H. N.]

V. Modalistic Monarchianism in Asia Minor, Rome, and Carthage: The real peril to the Logos-Christology between 180 and 240 was not the dynamistic Monarchianism thus far discussed, but the view which regarded Christ as God in person, and as the Father incarnate. Called Monarchians and Patripassians in the West, and Sabellians in the East, they were combated by Tertullian, Origen, Novatian, and, above all, Hippolytus. According to the latter, the Monarchian controversy disturbed the entire Church; while Tertullian and Origen declare that in their day the "economic" Trinity and the application of the concept of the Logos to Christ were regarded with suspicion by the majority of Christians. The popularity of modalism, especially in the East, is reflected in the multitude of apocryphal acts of the apostles (see APOCRYPHA, B, II.), which almost invariably represent or approximate modalistic Christology. Here, too, falls the Christology of Irenæus, with its strange attempt to blend the Logos-Christology with modalism. In Rome Monarchianism had been the official teaching for nearly a generation; and that it was no new thing in the Church is clear from the presence of a Monarchian faction among the Montanists and Marcionites. The predominance of Monarchianism in the Church was due primarily to the struggle with Gnosticism; and though its adherents were mostly not professed theologians, adherents of scientific training were not lacking. The modalists claimed by their doctrines to obviate ditheism, to assert the complete divinity of Christ, and to cut the ground from under Gnosticism. But the weakness of its cardinal hypothesis was too evident, and it was lost as soon as it saw itself obliged to assume either the defensive or offensive. Its contest with orthodoxy was strikingly reminiscent of the controversy between the genuine and the Platonizing Stoics on the concept of God. As the latter subordinated Plato's transcendental, dispassionate God to the Logos (God) of Heraclitus and the Stoics, so Origen reproached the Monarchians with remaining content with the visible God operating in the world, instead of proceeding to the "ultimate" God. It is not surprising, therefore, that when once modalistic Monarchianism had invoked the aid of science (i.e., of Stoicism), it was on the road to a pantheistic concept of God. Nevertheless, the earliest literary representatives of Monarchianism had a distinctly monotheistic interest which centered in Biblical Christianity.

1. Wide Popularity of Modalistic Monarchianism.

2. Rise of Patripassianism at Rome.

As dynamistic Monarchianism first gained vogue in Asia Minor, the Church of this same region seems to have been the scene of the earliest Patripassian controversy; and in both instances Asia Minor may be regarded as having transplanted the strife to Rome. Noetus, who seems to have been excommunicated about 230, doubtless first attracted attention as a Monarchian, probably in the last fifth of the second century, either at his native city Smyrna, or at Ephesus. His excommunication in Asia Minor seems to have taken place after the entire controversy had been settled at Rome. Epigonus (d. 200), a pupil of Noetus, came to Rome during the pontificate of Zephyrinus, and is said there to have promulgated the teachings of his master and to have founded a separate Patripassian party. The first head of the faction was Cleomenes, the pupil of Epigonus, and in 215 he was succeeded by Sabellius. Although they were opposed at Rome especially by Hippolytus, the sympathy of the majority of the Roman Christians was Monarchian. Even Zephyrinus, like his predecessor Victor, was inclined toward modalism, though his chief endeavor seems to have been to avoid schism at any cost. His policy was followed by his successor Calixtus (217–222); but when the struggle only became intensified, he resolved to excommunicate both Sabellius and Hippolytus, though it is not impossible that Hippolytus and his minority had already broken with Calixtus. The moderates of both parties seem to have been satisfied with the Christological formula proposed by Calixtus, and formed the bridge by which the Roman Christians passed from Monarchian to hypostatic Christology. The small faction of Hippolytus maintained an existence in Rome for some fifteen years; the Sabellians survived still longer. The scantiness of the sources for the history of Monarchianism in Rome—to say nothing of other cities—despite the discovery of the *Philosophumena*, is exemplified in the fact that Tertullian never mentions Noetus, Epigonus, Cleomenes, or Calixtus, but mentions a Monarchian in Rome ignored entirely by Hippolytus, Praxeas. He probably came to Rome during the pontificate of Victor, but remained there only a short time. Fifteen years later, when the controversy was in full course at Rome and Carthage, his name was forgotten. Notwithstanding this, Tertullian polemized against him as the first to arouse controversy in Carthage, although in his attacks he regarded the conditions of about 210, with reference, apparently, to the Roman Monarchians. Praxeas was a confessor of Asia Minor, the first to bring the Christological controversy to Rome, and a man filled with zeal against the rising prophetic school. Not only did he find no opposition at Rome, but he even induced the pontiff (either Eleutherus or Victor) to retract the "letters of peace" which he had bestowed on the new prophets and their communities in Asia. But the presence of Praxeas in Rome caused no lasting strife. From Rome he went to Carthage, where he opposed the hypostatic Christology, only to be silenced and forced to a written retraction by Tertullian. Thus ended the first phase of the controversy, and the name of Praxeas vanished; nor is anything certainly known of the downfall of Monarchianism in Carthage.

3. Doctrines of the Early Modalists.

The sources are too scanty for a complete presentment of the tenets of the earlier modalistic Monarchianism. Yet the sources are not alone to blame; for the theory that in Christ God himself had become incarnate might lead to wild hypotheses of transformation or approximate dynamistic Monarchianism. Again, so soon as the indwelling of the "divinity of the Father" in Jesus was not regarded strictly as an incarnation, the way was open for the Artemonite heresy (see ARTEMON). In the writings of Origen are many passages which may refer to either modalists or Artemonites, especially as the two were united by their opposition to the Logos-Christology. The best account of the older modalists is contained in the polemic of Hippolytus against Noetus. His followers held that Christ was the Father, and that the Father himself had been born, had suffered, and died. If Christ is God, he is surely the Father, or else not God; and therefore, if Christ suffered, then God suffered. Yet it was not only their decided monotheism, which made them term their opponents ditheists, that led them on; they were impelled, besides this, by their interest in the divinity of Jesus, which, in their opinion, could be maintained solely by their teachings, in support of which they appealed to such passages as Ex. iii. 6, xx. 2–3; Isa. xliv. 6, xlv. 5, 14–15; Bar. iii. 36; John x. 30, xiv. 8–9; Rom. ix. 5. While they thus recognized the Gospel of John, they explained away its allusions to the Logos allegorically. In his *Philosophumena* Hippolytus asserts that the Noetians maintained that the distinction between the Father and the Son was merely nominal (except in so far as it was redemptorial), since the one God, when born as man, appeared as the Son. God is invisible when he will, and visible when he will (this being based on an appeal to the Old-Testament theophanies); and in like manner he is both incomprehensible and comprehensible, unconquerable and conquerable, unbegotten and begotten, immortal and mortal. In so far as the Father suffered himself to be born of the virgin, he is the son of himself, and not of another, and he who suffered the passion and rose on the third day was the God and Father of all. While Stoic influence can not be denied in the Noetian system, the basis is certain ancient quasi-liturgical formulas as used by Ignatius, the author of II Clement, and Melito, and of similar purport with the views just cited.

4. Later Modalism and Catholic Compromise.

The concept and importance of the human "flesh" of Jesus, according to these Monarchians, is uncertain (see FLESH). More complicated are the Monarchianistic formulas attacked by Tertullian in the *Adversus Praxeam* and ascribed by Hippolytus to Calixtus. Tertullian's Monarchians maintain the complete identity of the Father and the Son, and had no place for the Logos in their Christology, regarding the word as empty sound. Like the Noetians, they were intensely monotheistic and feared the recrudescence of Gnosticism in hypostatic Christology. Obliged to explain the Biblical passages in which the Son appears as distinct from the Father, they asserted that the flesh made the Father the Son, or that in the person of the Redeemer the flesh (the man, Jesus) was the Son, and the spirit (God, Christ) was the Father, appealing, in support of their view, to Luke i. 35. Since God is spirit only, he could not suffer; but by assuming human flesh, he could be a fellow sufferer. It is at once evident that as soon as the distinction between flesh (the Son) and spirit (the Father) was taken seriously, the doctrine approached the Artemonite teaching. Yet such a distinction could not satisfy the advocates of the Logos Christology, since it maintained the identity of the Father with the spirit in Christ. Any attempt to recognize the Logos Christology on the basis of modalism necessarily led to dynamistic Monarchianism; yet the formulas of both Zephyrinus and Calixtus had arisen from efforts at compromise. In the formula of the latter—that God (the Logos, both Father and Son) was an indivisible spirit filling all things, the incarnate spirit being identical with the Father, so that the human manifestation was the Son and the indwelling spirit the Father, the Father suffering with the Son—Origen rightly recognized a mixture of Sabellian and Theodotian views. The adoption of this formula in Rome, except by a few extremists of either party, was due not only to its admission of the Logos-concept, but to its declaration that, at the incarnation, God had deified the flesh; and that the Son, as representing the essentially deified flesh, should be regarded as a second person, though truly one with God. The formula was, moreover, admirably adapted, by its ambiguity, to establish among the faithful the mystery under whose protection hypostatic Christology gradually gained entrance.

Hypostatic Christology, as opposed to modalism, was evolved between 200 and 250 on the basis of the theology of the apologists. It easily refuted, by arguments from the Bible, the Monarchian identification of the Father with the Son, and rejected as an innovation the Patripassian doctrine.

5. Struggle between Hypostatism and Modalism. In their concept of God, on the other hand, the Monarchians were generally supported by the earliest Christian tradition. Their opponents, well aware of the difficulties confronting them, plunged into speculation, even at the risk of approximating Gnosticism. Yet in their Christology Tertullian and his disciples were unable either to satisfy the Christian views or to silence their opponents; for though their Logos was essentially one with God, yet in origin he is an inferior divine being. This view, moreover, conflicted with liturgical tradition, which taught that God himself must be seen in Christ; while the attempt to deduce the appellation of Son of God for Christ from an act before the creation of the world, instead of from his miraculous birth, was opposed by dogmatic tradition. The final conquest of Monarchianism, impossible for Tertullian and Hippolytus, was achieved by Origen and the Alexandrine theologians. In the Logos-doctrine of the third century, there was no positive answer to the problem whether the divine which was manifest on earth in Christ was identical with the Godhead. Athanasius was the first to make certain reply on the basis of the Logos-doctrine; but until his time the modalistic Monarchians represented a primitive and valuable movement in the Church. After Calixtus' formula of compromise and the excommunication of Sabellius (see CALIXTUS I.), aggressive modalism, as well as Hippolytus' sect, declined in the West. Nevertheless, sporadic modalistic tendencies, formulas, and doctrines still survived, as assailed by the Creed of Aquileia, by Cyprian, and by Dionysius of Rome, and as shown by numerous passages in the writings of Commodian. There were Sabellians at Rome as late as the fourth century. The true cause of the downfall of western modalism lay in the firm attitude assumed by the West in the Roman struggle, in the energetic defense of the *homoousia*, and in the rejection of the formula of three hypostases.

VI. Modalistic Monarchians in the East; Sabellianism: **1. Sabellius; Obscurity of the Sources.** The term "Sabellians" was applied in the East, after the beginning of the third century, to the modalistic Monarchians, and occurs sporadically in the West in the fourth and fifth centuries. The data concerning the teaching of Sabellius himself and of his immediate successors, however, is very confused. Not only have the doctrines of Marcellus of Ancyra (q.v.) been confounded with those of Sabellius—especially as Monarchianism assumed various forms in the century between Hippolytus and Athanasius—but philosophical speculation also entered in, and Kenotic (see KENOSIS) and transformation theories were developed; besides which, deductions were drawn and consequent tenets assigned by the sources which probably never existed in the form described. It is, therefore, impossible to write a history of Monarchianism from Calixtus to Marcellus, no matter how carefully all available material be studied. Nevertheless, it is clear that, at least between 220 and 270, the battle against Monarchianism must have been bitter in the East, and that the development of the Logos Christology was there directly influenced by this opposition. The very fact that in the East Monarchianism was almost exclusively known as "Sabellianism" shows that schisms first arose there through the activity of Sabellius, that is, after the fourth decade of the third century. Apparently during the pontificate of Zephyrinus, Sabellius, who was probably born in the Pentapolis in Libya, became the successor of Cleomenes as the head of the Monarchians at Rome. With his excommunication by Calixtus, he became the leader of a Monarchian sect which branded Calixtus as an apostate. He was still in Rome when Hippolytus wrote the *Philosophumena*, and there developed far-reaching relations, especially with the East. His doctrines, which were evidently unknown to Origen, were closely akin to those of Noetus, from which they differed, however, both in their more exact theology and in their recognition of the Holy Ghost. The cardinal tenet of Sabellius was that the Father, the Son, and the Holy Ghost are identical, but with three names. Ever inspired by a rigid monotheism, Sabellius also termed the one God the "Son-Father," evidently to avoid all suspicion of ditheism, meaning hereby the final designation of God himself, and not any manifestations of a monad remaining in the background. At the same time, he taught that God is not the Father and the Son simultaneously; but that he became operative in three successive energies: first, as the person ("manifestation," not "hypostasis") of the Father, the creator and legislator; then as the person of the Son as the Redeemer (this period extending from the incarnation to the assumption); and finally as the person of the Holy Ghost as the maker and giver of life. It is improbable, however, that he was able to make a strict delimitation of these successive persons, for he can scarcely have avoided the recognition of the continuous activity of God the Father in nature.

While both Sabellius and his followers acknowledged the catholic canon, Epiphanius states that they derived their entire heresy from certain apocryphal books, especially from the Gospel of the Egyptians. It is thus evident that the Sabellian Christology was not essentially different from the older Patripassian system.

2. Relations and Decay of Sabellianism. The only noteworthy points of divergence were the attempt to demonstrate the succession of the persons; the recognition of the Holy Ghost; and the formal parallelization of the person of the Father with the two other persons. The first point may be regarded as a harking back to rigid modalism, while the second was in keeping with the new theological school. The most important point was the third, since by paralleling the person and the energy of the Father with the other two persons, not only was cosmology introduced into modalism as a parallel to soteriology, but the preeminence of the Father over the Son and the Holy Ghost was broken. Thus the way was prepared for Athanasian and Augustinian Christology —Sabellius was the forerunner of the exclusive *homoousios*. The doctrines of Sabellius were rejected by Marcellus of Ancyra (q.v.), who found no recognition of the Logos in Sabellianism, and consequently deemed that his fellow Monarchian had formed an incorrect concept of God. But his Monarchianism won few adherents. The times had changed; the consubstantiality of the Father and the Logos had been enunciated; and Monarchianism had become superfluous in the Church. The controversy of the two Dionysii, though properly a preliminary to Arianism, must be mentioned here, since the Sabellian tendencies in the Pentapolis led Dionysius of Alexandria to a rigid statement of his doctrine. The ambiguity of Origen's Christological terminology, however, is revealed in the formulas of his disciples Dionysius and Gregory Thaumaturgus, which contain passages susceptible of Monarchianistic interpretation, though, like Origen, both were bitter opponents of the Monarchian system. It must be borne in mind, however, that in the period between 250 and 320 there was a frequent tendency toward tritheism, while, on the other hand, there was a deep-seated mistrust of the Logos Christology as imperiling Monarchianism, so that Origen's followers felt themselves obliged to emphasize Monarchianistic tenets. In the second half of the third century the fluidity of all dogmatic concepts thus led to a condition of theological confusion. What Athanasius and later writers called Sabellianism was a comprehensive term for various doctrinal systems, modified by philosophical concepts and the influence of Alexandrine theology. The bold attempt of Paul of Samosata to return to primitive tradition came too late; and the same judgment holds of the effort of Marcellus of Ancyra to abandon Alexandrine speculation as a whole and to solve the Christological problem by again taking up Biblical concepts and the theology of Irenæus. The problem remained confined to the limits of Origen's theology, and here it met its fate. See ANTITRINITARIANISM, § 2.

(ADOLF HARNACK.)

BIBLIOGRAPHY: Consult the literature under ALOGI, and under the sketches of the leaders named in the text, especially Epiphanius, Hippolytus, Irenæus, and Philaster. Important are the works on the history of doctrine, especially: Harnack, *Dogma*, i. 196, 331, ii. passim, iii. 8–88, 93; K. R. Hagenbach, *History of Christian Doctrines*, i. 74, 160, 178, Edinburgh, 1880; I. A. Dorner, *Die Lehre von der Person Christi*, 4 vols., Stuttgart, 1846–56, Eng. transl., *History of the Development of the Doctrine of the Person of Christ*, 5 vols., Edinburgh, 1861–1863. Also the works on the church history of the period, e.g., Schaff, *Christian Church*, ii. 571–583; and Neander, *Christian Church*, i. 575 sqq., ii. passim. Consult also: L. Lange, *Geschichte und Lehrbegriff der Unitarier vor der nicänischen Synode*, Leipsic, 1831; F. D. E. Schleiermacher, *Sämmtliche Werke—Zur Theologie*, vol. ii., 30 vols., Berlin, 1835–1864; J. Schwane, *Dogmengeschichte der vornicänischen Zeit*, pp. 142–156, 199–203, Münster, 1862; H. Hagemann, *Die römische Kirche in den ersten drei Jahrhunderten*, Freiburg, 1864; J. Bornemann, *Die Taufe Christi*, Leipsic, 1896; Hefele, *Conciliengeschichte*, vols. i.–ii., Eng. transl., vols. i.–iii.

MONASTICISM.

I. Monasticism in the East: Monasticism is a general term for the system of renunciation of life in the world for that of devotion and asceticism. A trace of the attitude which later characterized this system may be found in the preference given by Paul to the unmarried over the married state (I Cor. vii. 38, 40) and in his counsel not to marry on account of the expected return of the Lord (verse 26).

1. Ante-Nicene Practise.

In the Roman church of the apostolic period there appeared an Encratite tendency which taught abstinence from meat and wine (Rom. xiv. 2, 21). The Acts, too, characterize the four daughters of Philip the deacon as virgins; and the book of Revelation designates as the "first-fruits unto God and to the Lamb" the hundred and forty-four thousand "which were not defiled with women" (xiv. 4). Hegesippus states that James, the Lord's brother, lived as a Nazarite in complete abstinence from meat and wine (Eusebius, *Hist. eccl.*, II., xxiii.). The works of the apostolic fathers and apologists are full of references to both men and women who lived an ascetic life. Ignatius names as their motive for renunciation of marriage "respect for the body which is the Lord's," Athenagoras the hope of a higher reward in heaven. The claim of the ascetics to the first rank in the church on earth, as the most perfect Christians, is early heard. Clement of Rome warns them not to boast, and Ignatius rebukes some who thought themselves more than the bishops. There was perfect freedom in the ascetic life in this early period. Some merely abstained from marriage, others from meat and wine as well. The renunciation of property did not always go with that of marriage; Cyprian (*De habitu virginum*, vii.) knew some consecrated virgins who still retained their own property. Some of them continued to live in their own houses, others lived in common in special dwellings called *parthenones*. The same is true of the male ascetics. Origen lived unmarried, without property, in constant prayer and meditation, abstaining from meat and wine and imposing the severest penances on himself; in fact, his life differed from that of later monks only in being passed in the midst of the world. A strict cloistral separation is not found in early asceticism, though a certain degree of retirement was required from women who adopted this life. The male ascetics passed from place to place after the manner of the apostles, "confirming the churches." Their self-denying activity and care for the sick and friendless during the persecution of Diocletian is lauded by Eusebius (*De martyribus Palæstinæ*, x., xi.).

2. Official Status.

The first witness for a public vow of virginity for women is Tertullian (*De virgine velanda*, xiv.). This vow, however, had no legal force; a marriage contracted by one who had made it was valid (Cyprian, *Epist.*, lxii.). But penalties were early decreed for a breach of such a vow; thus the Spanish Council of Elvira (306) imposed lifelong excommunication, while that of Ancyra (314) only required the same penance as for bigamy, or excommunication for a year. About the middle of the fourth century the custom seems to have been introduced of the priest before whom the vow was pronounced giving the virgin a veil and a special robe (Ambrose, *De virginibus*, I., xi.). Men, on the other hand, as late as the time of Basil made no public vow and were distinguished by no special costume. In spite of the high regard felt for the ascetics, the church of the first centuries was forced by its opposition to Gnostics, Encratites, and Montanists into a certain reserve on the subject. While some of these sects required from their adherents complete abstinence from meat and wine, and even from marriage, in the Church only tentative efforts were made to enforce the ascetic ideal on all its members in regard to food (see FASTING, II.). Origen, indeed, exhorted Christian priests to perpetual continence, and the Council of Elvira threatened with deposition bishops, priests, and deacons who did not abstain from intercourse with their wives; but the first Council of Nicæa (325) declared against the enforcement of clerical celibacy (see CELIBACY). At the end of the third century for the first time is mentioned the foundation of an association of ascetics (Epiphanius, *Hær.*, lxvii.). It originated with Heraclas, a disciple of Origen, who came from Leontopolis in Egypt. It embraced both men and women, who lived in perpetual abstinence from marriage, from meat, and from wine (see HERACLAS).

3. The Motive.

It was in this second half of the third century that monasticism properly so called originated and the ideal of an entire separation from the world was realized. The cause of the new movement, which made large numbers desert the world in order to live an ascetic and contemplative life in the desert, has been sought, on Jerome's authority (*Vita Pauli*, i.), in the Decian persecution; but historical proof is lacking (for origins see below, § 4). The same lack of evidence weakens the theory of imitation of non-Christian practise, as of Buddhism (Hilgenfeld) or the Egyptian cult of Serapis (Weingarten). Keim's theory of the influence of Neo-Platonism is equally untenable; though this system undoubtedly affected the Church, it can not possibly have been a determining factor in the growth of monasticism, and it could not have had a specially strong influence upon the rural population of the Thebaid. The real source of the monastic movement is to be sought in the development of the Christian ideal. In the picture which Clement of Alexandria draws of "the true Gnostic," and still more clearly in Origen, may be traced the conception of the perfect Christian as one who lives remote from the world and its passions. It is true, of course, that the distressing social and political circumstances of Egypt later in the third century contributed to the increase of Christian heroism and of the tendency to fly from the world, just as similar conditions farther west called forth the movement of the Circumcelliones (q.v.) in connection with the Donatist controversy (see DONATISM). But the principal motive of Christian monasticism was the desire to attain everlasting happiness and moral perfection by escape from the world.*

4. Egyptian Origins; Anthony and Ammonius.

Some individual instances of this flight may have existed as early as the beginning of the third century. In connection with Jerome's *Vita Pauli* (ut sup.) it was formerly the custom to find the origin of Christian monasticism in Paul of Thebes as a result of the Decian persecution. This was thought to be substantiated by the account in Eusebius (*Hist. eccl.*, VI., xlii.) of "flight into deserts and mountain regions" at this time. But the historicity of the *Vita Pauli* is now not recognized. As a consequence, if satisfactory historical evidence alone be considered, the title of the first hermit must be assigned to Anthony, whose life was written, from knowledge based on close personal relationship, by Athanasius (soon after Anthony's death, or between 356 and 362; Eng. transl. in *NPNF*, 2 ser., iv. 188–221). St. Anthony was born of wealthy Christian parents at Coma, on the borders of Upper Egypt, c. 250, lost his parents when he was in his eighteenth year, six months later gave all his goods to the poor, leaving his sister to the care of a pious woman, and retired first to a tomb and then to a ruined castle near the Nile, where he lived alone for twenty years. He issued from his retirement at times to instruct the multitudes who came to hear him, and sometimes visited the Christians of Alexandria to comfort them in times of stress. Eventually he retired still farther into the solitude near the Red Sea, where he died at the age of 105, attended only by the two disciples Amathas and Macarius (q.v.). He seems to have created no regular organization; the colonies of hermits which were known as *monastēria* were united only by ties of free fellowship under his spiritual direction. The "Rule" ascribed to him is not his, though it is of Egyptian origin and very old. Tracing the further develop-

* While in the text the proximate cause of monasticism is probably correctly given, and "imitation" of non-Christian practise is rightly rejected, the more fundamental cause is passed over. This is the belief, common to most advanced and to some primitive religions, that "the world" or "the flesh" is an evil, and that consequently perfection in the religious life is soonest and best attained by retirement from the world and mortification of the flesh. This was the motive in the asceticism of Brahmanism and Buddhism (qq.v.), of Greece, and of the Hanifs of Arabia (see MOHAMMED, MOHAMMEDANISM, IV., 1). It is one of the curious facts of history and of logic that the subduing of the flesh was attempted in either of two forms—total abstention from indulgence in sensual pleasures and denial of the demands of appetite or extreme indulgence. In the Christian sphere this latter appeared in certain of the Gnostic outgrowths, and a sporadic case was the Christian-Philadelphia Society (see BUTTLAR, EVA VON). G. W. G.

ment of Egyptian monasticism, especially in the *Historia Lausiaca* of Palladius and the *Historia monachorum* of Rufinus, during Anthony's lifetime independent colonies of hermits appear to have been established in Lower Egypt by Ammonius or Amun, the father of Nitrian monasticism. He had been married against his will; after a life of continence lasting eighteen years, his wife turned their house into a home for consecrated virgins, while he went out into the desert, forty Roman miles to the south of Alexandria, and gathered (according to Palladius) not less than 500 disciples around him. They lived either solitary or in small communities, and assembled every Saturday and Sunday in the church, served by eight priests, for common worship. The day was divided between work and prayer; the strictest discipline prevailed. After twenty-two years of this life, Ammonius died some time before 356, while Anthony was yet living. Among his disciples were Arsisius, Serapion, Cronius, Putubastus, Asion, and Didymus, while the younger generation of the Nitrian colony included Pambo, Benjamin, Apollonius, and the four "Long Brothers," Ammonius, Dioscurus, Eusebius, and Euthymius. The Nitrian monks were especially devoted to the theology of Origen, and when he was declared a heretic by Theophilus of Alexandria in 399, they had their share of persecution.

Twenty-four hours' journey to the southward, in the Scetic desert near a place called Cellia, another famous colony had its abode. The cells were even more primitive than the Nitrian, and perpetual silence was the rule, except when the monks came together on Saturdays and Sundays for public worship. According to Cassian, Macarius, called "the Great," was the first to settle here (see MACARIUS, 1). Palladius asserts that this was at the age of thirteen, and that he possessed the gifts of healing and prophecy. His sayings in the *Apophthegmata* and the fifty homilies still preserved give the idea of a pious and humble character and an important representative of primitive Christian mysticism. He died at the age of ninety, either in 387 or in 383. His principal associates were the Ethiopian Moses, Pachon, and Macarius the Younger. Two of his disciples, Evagrius Ponticus (q.v.) and Marcus Eremita (q.v.), attained some importance as writers. By the end of the fourth century Egypt was full of hermits, living either solitary or in communities. The numbers attributed to them may be exaggerated (e.g., 20,000 women and 10,000 men at Oxyrhynchus in central Egypt); but the extent of the movement is attested not only by Athanasius in more than one passage, but by the edict of the Emperor Valens in 365, and by his drafting 5,000 Nitrian monks as soldiers in 375. The loose fellowship of the Egyptian hermits was organized by Pachomius (q.v.), who surrounded the scattered cells by a wall and gave the monks a common rule of life. This earliest monastic rule is primitive and incomplete; but it enforces the duty of labor, makes an effort to systematize the devotional life, contains provisions concerning clothing, food, and hours of sleep, and by forbidding the reception of strangers attempts to shut off the monastery from the world. While the older sort of hermit colonies still maintained their existence, the cenobitic system spread rapidly throughout Egypt. The hermit life was less adapted for women. Pachomius founded the first convent for his sister Mary, and the cloistered life was adopted by a constantly increasing number of female ascetics. At the same time a number of communities of women continued to exist in which a less strict rule of asceticism and seclusion from the world prevailed.

5. Other Egyptian Settlements.

From Egypt monasticism spread to the peninsula of Sinai, which produced two important ascetic writers in Nilus Sinaita (see NILUS, 1) and Johannes Climacus (q.v.), and to Palestine, in the southern part of which Hilarion (q.v.) of Gaza, a disciple of Anthony, introduced the hermit life in the latter half of the fourth century. Sozomen and Palladius mention a number of Palestinian hermits, and numerous monasteries arose here about the middle of the fourth century. Melania, a rich Roman woman and a friend of Rufinus, founded a convent on the Mount of Olives, and another Roman, Paula (d. 404), houses for both monks and nuns at Bethlehem. A younger Melania (d. 439) was also a noted founder. The western monks and nuns lived here in the spirit of their Egyptian models, and Jerome translated the rule of Pachomius for Paula's convent. Syria was, however, after Egypt, the country in which early monasticism flourished most remarkably. The men and women who were associated with Aphraates did not leave the world, and were "solitary" (as he calls them in the sixth homily, of 337) only in the sense of having taken a vow of celibacy. But Jacob of Nisibis (q.v.) seems to have led a hermit's life with Eugenius, the founder of Persian monasticism, before he became bishop of Nisibis in 309. According to the account which he wrote of Eugenius (published in P. Bedjan, *Acta martyrum Syriace*, iii. 376–380, 7 vols., Paris, 1890–97), the latter seems to have come from Egypt, bringing with him the cenobitic tradition of the monasteries of Pachomius. He is perhaps to be identified with the Aones whom Sozomen calls (VI., xxxiii. 4) the founder in Syria of the strict hermit life, as Anthony was in Egypt. Among the monastic pioneers of Edessa and Osrhoene, Jerome names as the first a certain Julian, a contemporary of Julian the Apostate; Ephraem Syrus (q.v.) was one of the celebrated ascetics of this region. In eastern Cilicia and in the neighborhood of Antioch flourishing colonies of hermits existed from the middle of the fourth century in the desert of Chalcis, which acquired the name of the Syrian Thebaid. Here Jerome lived as a hermit from 373 to 380. In northern Syria the peculiar form of asceticism represented by the "pillar-saints" became common in the fifth century. Its earliest example is supposed to have been Simeon, who abode on the top of a column near Antioch, gradually increasing its height, and after thirty-six years died about 460. This form of mortification is apparently connected with pagan Syrian prototypes. Scattered practitioners of it were found in the east until the fifteenth century. The

6. In Palestine and Syria.

most famous of them was the younger Simeon (d. 596), who lived for sixty-eight years on top of a pillar near Antioch. See STYLITES.

Information as to Galatia comes from Palladius, a native of that region. In Roman Armenia, Paphlagonia, and Pontus, monasticism owed its origin to Eustathius of Sebaste (q.v.), whose semi-Arian associates, like the bishops Marathonius and Macedonius (q.v.), were zealous supporters of the movement. It assumed a fanatical character in Armenia, and conflicts resulted with the hierarchy; the Council of Gangra (? 343) was obliged to take action against the exaggerated asceticism of the Eustathians. A cognate phenomenon is the party of the Euchites or Messalians (q.v.) in northern Syria and Pamphylia in the latter half of the fourth century. They were still more radical in their insistence on a life of unbroken prayer, rejected the sacraments and fasts of the Church, and displayed distinctly Manichean tendencies. Repressed by the bishops, they disappeared for the time, to come up again in the medieval sects of the Bogomiles (see NEW MANICHEANS, I.) and Paulicians (q.v.). [The Paulicians had scarcely anything in common with Manicheans or Messalians, and their origin can be otherwise accounted for. A. H. N.] Monasticism was domesticated in Cappadocia first by Basil the Great and then by Gregory Nazianzen and Gregory of Nyssa (qq.v.). The work of Basil was epoch-making. The two rules, a longer and a shorter one, which bear his name, while they are rather catechisms on monastic virtues and duties than formal rules, are to-day the only standard of Greek monasticism. His ideal is essentially identical with that of Anthony. The monk is the perfect Christian; the ascetic life consists not in specific practises of self-denial but in the sanctification of the whole personality; the monk must exercise, next to the love of God, that of his neighbor, though practically this was confined to his fellow monks and contemplated no far-reaching influence on the Church at large or on society. According to Basil, the monastic life meant not a suppression of nature but the return to it, not opposition to but the completion of ancient wisdom. As to the life in detail, the candidate for admission to a monastery was required to renounce his property and go through a period of probation. No binding vows were made; the *apotagē* was a renunciation of all relations with the world, but not an external act. The *proestōs* or head of the monastery had full disciplinary powers. The daily life of the monks was divided between prayer, for which there were six fixed hours, and work, especially agriculture. There was no prescription as to food except that it should be taken in moderation and not serve to pamper the palate; the use of wine was prohibited. No special costume was prescribed.

7. In Asia Minor.

In spite of Basil's influence in favor of a cenobitic system, the hermit life continued to be held in the highest esteem. It seemed to many that the monastic ideal of uninterrupted devotion could be attained only by the anchorite. But the two classes of monks lived peaceably together, the cloister being regarded as a training-school for the higher stage. During the fifth and sixth centuries, Palestine was the special home of monachism, partly on account of its associations, which brought thither an increasing number of devout pilgrims. Soon after the beginning of the fifth century an attempt was made to link together the various monasteries and colonies of hermits in a common organization. Each of these classes now had an archimandrite of its own, chosen by the whole body and confirmed by the patriarch of Jerusalem. These offices assumed considerable importance when the Cappadocian Theodosius (414–519), head of the monastery founded by him and named after him at Jerusalem, became archimandrite of the monasteries, and another Cappadocian, Sabas (q.v.; 439–532), held the corresponding position among the hermits. Sabas founded seven lauras (see ABBEY) or colonies of hermits in Palestine, of which that at Jerusalem, under his own guidance, was the principal one. Even after the Mohammedan conquest in the seventh century, monasticism maintained its footing in Palestine; but its consequent isolation caused it gradually to decline. After Egypt and Palestine had ceased to be the centers of eastern monasticism, this place was taken by Constantinople. About 430 the system of the *akoimetæ* (monks who kept up an unbroken prayer day and night in three divisions which relieved each other) was introduced there by Alexander, an abbot from a monastery on the Euphrates. The monastery of this kind founded about 460 by the Roman consular Studius and known from him as Studion attained special importance in the epoch of the iconoclastic controversy through the work of its abbot Theodore (see THEODORE THE STUDITE), who reformed Byzantine monasticism by adapting the Basilian rule to altered conditions. His "Constitutions," which, if not drawn up by him, represent his work, give precise information as to the life of his own house, and were accepted by many others. The reception of a monk, with the binding vow which had been required since the Council of Chalcedon, was a solemn act, considered almost as a second baptism in its power to cleanse from sin. It was made at the foot of the altar during the liturgy and in the presence of all the brethren. After receiving the tonsure and habit, the new monk then partook of the communion. Besides domestic economy and agriculture the monks were occupied in theology, philosophy, and grammar, so that their houses became nurseries of orthodox divinity. The abbot was required to give a catechetical lecture three times a week to the monks. They were to live simply and temperately, but the use of meat was allowed. The distinction between *makroschēmoi* and *mikroschēmoi* seems to have been introduced about the time of the iconoclastic controversy. The latter, answering to the lay brothers in the West, performed the household duties; the former, the western choir-brothers, lived in complete abstraction from worldly things, devoted wholly to contemplation and study. This gradation, though it weakened the sense of unity, served to facilitate the entrance into the monastery of those who did not feel called to take upon themselves the extremer obligations. The

8. Later History of Oriental Monasticism.

next great center was Mount Athos (see ATHOS), which was inhabited by hermits from the middle of the ninth century, though the first regular monastery was not founded until 963. In the Hesychastic controversy (see HESYCHASTS) the fanatical element in eastern monachism once more found expression. The monks regarded themselves as inspired and endowed with the gifts of miracles and of prophecy in order to make what amounted to a new development of revelation. The colonies on Mount Athos increased in number until in 1045 there were 180. With its numerous hermits and monasteries of combined aristocratic and democratic constitution, Athos is still the most famous seat of Greek monasticism.

9. Relation to Church and State.

Although monasticism stood out originally in sharp contrast to the Church in the midst of the world, open conflict was avoided. The bishops, especially Athanasius, succeeded in abating the anticlerical tendencies of monasticism, which on its side preserved an abiding respect for the Church and its institutions, so that the relations between secular and regular clergy in the East finally became a very friendly one, until by the increasing enforcement of celibacy and the choosing of dignitaries from the monastic ranks the opposition was almost entirely removed. The trouble which the Church had in the fifth century with monastic fanaticism led to strict regulation by the Council of Chalcedon (canons iv., viii., xxiii., xxiv.). The monasteries and all the monks of a diocese were to be subject to the bishop, without whose leave no new monasteries might be erected; slaves were not to be received without the consent of their masters; to the ordinary vows was added the obligation of "stability" or continuance in one fixed residence, to prevent disorderly roving. The same line was followed by Justinian in his monastic legislation, which became the model for all subsequent state regulations in the East. The second Trullan synod of 692 increased the freedom of entrance into the monastic state, which Justinian had facilitated for slaves, ordered wandering hermits either to allow themselves to be gathered into monasteries or to retire into the desert (see GYROVAGI), and laid down the principle that only he who had approved himself as a cenobite should become a hermit. Under the iconoclastic emperors the monks led the defense of images, with John of Damascus (q.v.), who belonged to the monastery of St. Sabas on the Dead Sea, at their head. The monasteries underwent great trials during this period, and there is some reason to think that the emperors contemplated their total suppression. The Second Council of Nicæa (787) allowed the unrestricted foundation of monasteries (though that of Constantinople, 861, restored the requirement of episcopal permission), and reiterated the prohibition of monks and nuns leaving their convents. Since the Trullan synod of 692 had confined the requirement of celibacy to the bishops, they were thereafter usually taken from the monasteries, which gave great power to monasticism. This was increased by the fact that the monks, who had given to the practise of confession its systematic development, were long its chief ministers. The main service of Greek monasticism as a whole was the awakening of the Church to the consciousness of practical needs. The monks' constant effort for the sanctification of their own hearts had given them a deep insight into the inner life, and the great preachers of the East, such as Basil, Chrysostom, and Gregory Nazianzen, had learned to know human nature through monasticism, while its influence may be traced also in the attention paid to psychological problems in the dogmatic theology of John of Damascus.

II. Monasticism in the West: This was wholly of eastern origin. In his Roman exile (341–343) Athanasius spread the news of the work of Anthony and Pachomius, and according to Palladius (*Historia Lausiaca*, i.), a monk named Isi-

1. Beginnings in Italy, Gaul, and Germany.

dore visited Rome about 350. Peter, the successor of Athanasius, who took refuge in Rome in 373, perhaps determined the movement of ascetics toward the East already noted. The first western monasteries seem to have originated between 370 and 380; but the movement made slow progress, and was hindered rather than helped by the older institution of communities of consecrated virgins. During his Roman sojourn (382–385), Jerome labored for the promotion of monasticism; but when the daughter of his pupil Paula died in 385 as a result of her extreme asceticism, the populace broke out in violent opposition, and he was forced to leave Rome, Paula and her other daughter Eustochium following him to the East to end their lives in a convent at Bethlehem. Nevertheless, when Augustine was in Rome in 388, he found a number of monastic "abodes of the saints" there, and he states that the inmates of the Roman convents procured their livelihood by spinning and weaving. In northern Italy Ambrose was the most prominent promoter of monasticism; he founded in the suburbs of Milan a monastery modeled on the eastern type, though he maintained it from his own resources, which was a departure from the model. Eusebius of Vercellæ deserves special mention as being, with Augustine, the first to organize a community life of a more or less monastic kind for the clergy (see CHAPTER). In southern Italy, Paulinus (q.v.), later bishop of Nola, was a pioneer of the new movement. It was for the monastery of Pinetum, probably near Terracina, that Rufinus translated the rule of Basil. By 412 Jerome was able to boast of "many convents of virgins and an innumerable multitude of monks" in Italy. In Gaul Martin of Tours (q.v.) forwarded the movement by founding, soon after 360, the monasteries of Ligugé near Poitiers and Marmoutiers near Tours. In the south an association of hermits was founded at the beginning of the fifth century by Honoratus on the island of Lerins, and two others in Marseilles by Cassian about the same time (see CASSIANUS, JOHANNES), followed by a large number of others in the course of the century. The new institution soon took root in German soil, possibly owing to an impulse given by Athanasius during his exile at Treves. When the officer Pontitianus came from that city to Milan in 387, he told Augustine of the

Vita Antonii, which he had come to know there, and of the hermits who lived in the vicinity of the city. It seems to have been planted in Spain by one Donatus from North Africa, where Augustine had been its most influential promoter, but where, as in Italy, it had encountered strong opposition.

In spite of the desire to imitate Egyptian and Palestinian models, divergences from them soon appear in western monastic institutions. Great freedom prevailed; each monastery followed its own rule; in some more than one was observed, in others the directions of the abbot took the place of a written rule. Cassian, who was the first to undertake (in his *De institutis cœnobiorum*) the codification of these diverse systems, speaks strongly in favor of independent development in the West, on the ground of differences of climate, surroundings, and social order. The costume of the eastern monks he considered unsuitable to the West, and he opposed the use of the hair-shirt as both hindering the monks in their work and tempting them to spiritual pride. He mitigated the rule as to food by allowing two meals, one at three o'clock and the other in the evening. He had the ancient eremitical character of monasticism in mind, as is shown by his enjoining the monks to work alone in their cells and to avoid as far as possible all intercourse with the outside world. In a condensation by a later hand of the first four books of the *Instituta*, the so-called "Rule of Cassian" served as a standard down to the ninth century; other rules employed were that of Basil in Rufinus' translation, that of Pachomius as rendered by Jerome, and that of Macarius. Convents of women frequently followed the so-called "Rule of St. Augustine"—really a treatise written by him on a special occasion for a community of African nuns. This was used by Cæsarius of Arles (q.v.; d. 542) as a basis for his own *Regula ad virgines*. We have several others of the sixth and seventh centuries which are independent of the Benedictine rule; but they were only local in their authority, while Benedict's spread far and wide from Monte Cassino (q.v.) until it drove out all the others. The Benedictine rule (see BENEDICT OF NURSIA AND THE BENEDICTINE ORDER) was marked not so much by originality as by reasonable moderation and wise elasticity. It was intended to educate the monks in the principles of strict obedience, stability, and ordered work. It was due to Magnus Aurelius Cassiodorus (q.v.) that systematic study formed a part of the plan. The most serious obstacle to its general adoption was found in the competition of the rule of the Celtic missionary Columban (q.v.), the founder of the abbeys of Luxeuil and Bobbio, which was used in many monasteries of France and northern Italy. But the stern rigorism of this rule could not stand against the greater mildness of Benedict's, which Gregory II., Gregory III., and Boniface made the standard for the Frankish empire. Their work was continued by Charlemagne and Louis the Pious, with the help of Alcuin and Benedict of Aniane. As the number and importance of the monasteries increased, it became the interest of the bishops to see that they were brought under episcopal jurisdiction. The clerical character of the abbot made him in a sense dependent on the bishop, who, however, on his side, could not ordain any monk without the abbot's consent. Though the Benedictine rule prescribed the election of abbots by the monks, founders frequently reserved to themselves a right of nomination. From the sixth century the abbot was installed in his office by episcopal benediction. By the end of that century many monasteries sought to oppose a barrier to the encroachments of the bishops by placing themselves under the special protection of kings or of the pope (see EXEMPTION).

2. The Rules.

From the time of Boniface, western monasticism stood forth as the standard-bearer of civilization. Benedictine monks turned the forests into ploughed fields, brought the message of Christianity to the north of Europe, and handed down the ancient theology and some part of ancient civilization. Monasteries were the central points of the religious life of the day, and schools everywhere arose in connection with them. Yet the assumption of the work of general civilization, together with the growth of possessions which made it possible for them to do so much, tended to secularize the monastic life. The first of many attempts to restore the ancient strictness is connected with the name of Benedict of Aniane (q.v.); for some that succeeded see BENEDICT OF NURSIA. Special notice must be given here to the reform of Cluny in the tenth and eleventh centuries, to which the cooperation of temporal princes and the patronage of popes gave a universal significance, and enabled it to reform not only its order but the Church at large (see CLUNY, ABBEY AND CONGREGATION OF). The Cluniac reform, however, by the foundation of a separate congregation with the abbot of Cluny at its head, began the process of disintegration of western monasticism, which had been everywhere united under the rule of Benedict, first into congregations and then into separate orders. In the twelfth century the greatest influence was exercised by the new congregation of the Cistercians (q.v.), which took up the task of reform when the Cluniac congregation had been infected in its turn by worldliness. Their success was due in no small measure to their abandonment of the antiquated economic system of the older monasticism. They farmed their own land, and combined industrial activity with agriculture. While all these congregations still adhered to the rule of Benedict as a basis and merely developed it by their particular constitutions, the Premonstratensians (q.v.) were an order of clerics living by the rule of St. Augustine and attempting to combine monastic strictness with the duties of secular clergy. The reform movement of the eleventh century gave a powerful impulse to the crusades, and created, as a product of these, the knightly orders in which the temporal and spiritual ideals of the Middle Ages were singularly united. New orders and congregations multiplied to such an extent that a check was finally put upon their further increase by the (fourth) Lateran council of 1215 (canon xiv.).

3. Relation to Civilization.

Monasticism took a novel form in the work of Francis of Assisi (q.v.). The old vow of poverty became an absolute renunciation of all possessions not only by the individual but by the order. The cloistered retirement of the existing orders gave place to a vigorous attempt to influence the life of the day through preaching and the confessional. Western monasticism had been aristocratic down to the end of the twelfth century; it now became popular. A mighty spirit of new devotion went out from Assisi and took possession of the Church, breathing a fresh life into preaching, church music, art, and learning. Side by side with the Franciscan order arose the Dominican (see DOMINIC, SAINT, AND THE DOMINICAN ORDER), destined originally for the conversion of heretics, but soon conforming to the spirit of the Franciscan and becoming like it a mendicant order. These two associations, in the later Middle Ages, produced the chief representatives of scholastic theology, while the mysticism which flourished among them awoke the religious spirit of the individual and recast the ideal of the Christian life in a new form, which amounted to a reformation. The thirteenth century saw the development as mendicant orders of two communities which had begun as associations of anchorites, the Carmelites (q.v.) and the hermits of St. Augustine (see AUGUSTINIANS). They were followed by other mendicant orders—the Servites, Hieronymites, Minims, Trinitarians, and the Order of Our Lady of Mercy. Worldliness, however, crept into these as it had into the cloister. The Franciscans were rent asunder by the controversy regarding the vow of poverty, and the breach between the extreme or "spiritual" party with the pope displayed once more the old antinomy between monasticism and the Church in the world. The attempts at reform in the fifteenth century had only a temporary success, and in spite of the vast number of monasteries and religious brotherhoods of all sorts, monasticism seemed doomed to fall into a state of idle unprofitableness.

4. The Mendicant Orders.

The age of the Counter-Reformation, however, brought new life to some of the older orders in the work of the Theatines and Capuchins (qq.v.), the Discalced Carmelites, and the French Cistercian reform of the Feuillants. But more importance attached to the new foundations, especially the Jesuits (q.v.), who developed a wholly new phase of monasticism. Standing between the secular clergy and monasticism, they considered ascetic practises and renunciation of the world only means for the spread of the Church's dominion. This purpose is expressed in a new fourth vow, "to devote the life to perpetual service of our Lord Jesus Christ and the Roman pontiff." A number of other new orders now arose which replaced the old monastic ideal of perfection and retirement from the world by adaptation to a variety of practical ends such as the education of the clergy, that of the laity in the confessional, the pulpit, and the school, and the care of the sick. The services of women were especially organized for the work of the Church. Most of these new foundations took the freer and more elastic form of congregations; in some the vow was only for a time, or was simple instead of solemn. Only a few of these can be named here, such as the Ursulines (1535), the Piarists (1600), Vincent de Paul's great foundations of the Lazarists and Sisters of Mercy, and the Brothers of the Christian Schools (1681). Theological learning and popular devotion were promoted by the Oratory of Philip Neri (q.v.), and the French Oratory (1611). In the Trappists (q.v.) the old spirit of severe asceticism revived, on the basis of the Benedictine rule. The order of the Visitation (1610) is the only important foundation of the seventeenth century. The Jesuits found several imitators, of which the most prominent is the Redemptorist order founded by Alfonso Liguori (q.v.). The Reformation had largely diminished the sphere of influence of monasticism; but the effect of the French Revolution was still more radical. Its work was foreshadowed by that of Joseph II., who in 1782 suppressed in his dominions a number of contemplative orders and greatly reduced the numbers of the others, and was followed by the secularization of the German monasteries in 1803. With the revival of the Jesuits in 1814 began the restoration of Roman Catholic monasticism, pervaded, however, whether in the old orders as restored or in the new foundations, by the spirit of the Jesuits. The Benedictine order alone has been able to preserve an independent adherence to the ancient ideals, and at Solesmes (restored 1833), Beuron (1863), and Maredsous (1872) to achieve a remarkable work in many departments of learning.

5. Later Orders.

According to the careful statistics of the Benedictine Baumgarten, which are in most cases brought down to 1901, the membership of the following orders may be given: Christian Brothers, 20,457; Franciscans, 16,458; Jesuits, 15,073; Capuchins, 9,464; Marists, 6,000; Benedictines, 4,565; Trappists, 4,538; Dominicans, 4,350; Lazarists, 3,304; Fathers of the Holy Ghost, 2,149; Carmelites, 2,000; Augustinians, 1,858.

In the Protestant churches, before the nineteenth century, ascetic zeal was strong enough to impel their members to a formal monastic life only among the so-called "Precisians" of the Reformed Church. Thus Johannes Gennuvit, of Vennigen on the Ruhr (d. 1699), attempted to restore the cloistered life. In 1728 John Conrad Beissel (see COMMUNISM, II., 5; DUNKERS, I., 2), a German Pietist, who had emigrated to America and had joined the Dunkers (q.v.) in 1724, withdrew to live in solitude, and was joined by others who formed a community and adopted a habit something like that of the Capuchins. In the latter half of the nineteenth century the High-church movement in the Anglican communion brought about the foundation of a large number of quasi-monastic communities for both men and women. Most of them are modeled in their organization on the type of Roman Catholic monasticism, though as a rule without binding vows; and the main purpose of nearly all of them is missionary or charitable work, at home or abroad. See ABBEY;

6. Monastic Attempts under Protestantism.

ANDREW AND PHILIP, BROTHERHOOD OF; ASCETICISM; METHODISTS; PROTESTANT EPISCOPALIANS.

(G. GRÜTZMACHER.)

BIBLIOGRAPHY: A large part of the story of Monasticism is told in the literature under the articles referred to in the text dealing with the persons there mentioned and with the different orders. Consult also the literature under ASCETICISM. A small group of books of first importance consists of: C. F. de Montalembert, *Les Moines de l'occident*, 7 vols., Paris, 1860 sqq., Eng. transl., *Monks of the West from St. Benedict to St. Bernard*, 6 vols., London, 1895; Helyot, *Ordres monastiques;* O. Zöckler, *Askese und Mönchtum*, 2 vols., Frankfort, 1897; J. S. Assemani, *Bibliotheca orientalis*, vol. iii., Rome, 1728; and Heimbucher, *Orden und Kongregationen.* Consult further: M. R. A. Henrion, *Histoire des ordres religieux*, 2 vols., Paris, 1835; T. D. Fosbrooke, *British Monachism; or, Manners and Customs of the Monks and Nuns of England*, London, 1843; S. Fox, *Monks and Monasteries: an Account of English Monasticism*, ib. 1845; W. Dugdale, *Monasticon Anglicanum*, 8 vols., London, 1849; F. S. Merryweather, *Bibliomania in the Middle Ages, with Anecdotes Illustrating the Hist. of the Monastic Libraries of Great Britain*, ib. 1849; W. J. Mangold, *De monachatus originibus et causis*, Marburg, 1852; S. P. Day, *Monastic Institutions: their Origin, Progress, Nature, and Tendency*, London, 1855; W. Reeves, *The Culdees of the British Islands*, Dublin, 1873 (contains many documents); O. D. T. Hill, *English Monasticism*, London, 1867 (deals particularly with Benedictine and Franciscan influence on art, literature, and common life); M. E. C. Walcott, *Church Life and Work in English Minsters*, vol. ii., ib. 1879; P. Ladewig, *Poppo von Stablo und die Klosterreformen unter den ersten Saliern*, Berlin, 1883; F. Suarez, *The Religious State*, 3 vols., London, 1884; C. Kingsley, *The Hermits: their Lives and Works*, London, 1885; A. Lindner, *Die Aufhebung der Klöster in Deutschtirol*, Innsbruck, 1886; E. Amélineau, *Étude sur le cénobitisme primitif dans la Haute-Égypte*, Cairo, 1887; idem, *Histoire des monastères de la Basse-Égypte*, Cairo, 1894; E. von Bertouch, *Geschichte der Genossenschaften*, Wiesbaden, 1888; F. Herve-Bazin, *Les Grandes Ordres des femmes*, Paris, 1889; F. C. Doyle, *Principles of Religious Life*, London, 1890; A. Harnack, in *GBA*, 1891; I. G. Smith, *Christian Monasticism from the Fourth to the Ninth Centuries*, London, 1892; H. D. M. Spence, *Cloister Life in the Days of Cœur de Lion*, London, 1892; J. Berthier, *L'État religieux*, La Salette, 1893; J. Sokolow, *Zustand des Klosterwesens in der byzantinischen Kirche (824–1204)*, Kasan, 1894; E. Spreitzenhofer, *Die Entwicklung des alten Mönchtums in Italien bis auf Benedikt*, Vienna, 1894; T. Kolde, *Die kirchlichen Bruderschaften und das religiöse Leben im modernen Katholizismus*, Erlangen, 1895; L. Eckenstein, *Woman under Monasticism*, Cambridge, 1896; Mrs. A. Jameson, *Legends of the Monastic Orders*, many editions, e.g., Boston, 1896; T. W. Allies, *The Monastic Life from the Fathers of the Desert to Charlemagne*, London, 1896; F. C. Woodhouse, *Monasticism, Ancient and Modern, its Principles, Origin, Development, Triumphs, Decadence, and Suppression*, London, 1896; E. Marin, *De studio cœnobio Constantinopolitano*, Paris, 1897; idem, *Les Moines de Constantinople (330–898)*, ib. 1897; U. Berlière, *Monasticon belge*, 2 vols., Bruges, 1897; W. Nissen, *Die Regelung des Klosterwesens im Romäerreiche bis zum Ende des 9. Jahrhunderts*, Hamburg, 1897; E. Preuschen, *Palladinus und Rufinus. Ein Beitrag zur Quellenkunde des ältesten Mönchtums*, Giessen, 1897; K. Holl, *Enthusiasmus und Bussgewalt beim griechischen Mönchtum*, Leipsic, 1898; D. Bolter, *Der Ursprung des Mönchtums*, Freiburg, 1900; A. Harnack, *Monasticism: its Ideals and History*, London, 1901; F. M. Keele, *The Convents of Great Britain*, London, 1902; H. J. Feasey, *Monasticism: what is it?* St. Louis, 1902; A. W Wishart, *A Short History of Monks and Monasteries*, Trenton, 1902; J. O. Hannay, *Spirit and Origin of Christian Monasticism*, London, 1903; idem, *The Wisdom of the Desert*, London, 1904; J. Hocart, *Le Monachisme. Ses origines païennes*, Paris, 1903; W. Humphrey, *Elements of Religious Life*, London, 1903; J. Jaeger, *Klosterleben im Mittelalter*, Würzburg, 1903; F. M. Steele, *Anchoresses in the West*, London, 1903; F. A. Gasquet, *The Old English Bibles and Other Essays*, London, 1897; idem, *English Monastic Life*, London, 1904; idem, *Henry VIII. and the English Monasteries*, new ed., New York, 1906; C. E. Hooykaas, *Oud christelijke Ascese*, Leyden, 1905; J. von Walter, *Die ersten Wanderprediger Frankreichs. Studien zur Geschichte des Mönchtums*, Leipsic, 1906; E. A. W. Budge, *The Paradise or Garden of the Holy Fathers: being Histories of the Anchorites, Recluses, Monks, Cœnobites, and ascetic Fathers of the Deserts of Egypt 250–400, compiled by Athanasius . , Palladius . . , St. Jerome and Others*, 2 vols., London and New York, 1909; A. Savine, *English Monasteries on the Eve of the Dissolution*, New York, 1910; S. Schiwietz, *Das morgenländische Mönchtum*, Mainz, 1904; Schaff, *Christian Church*, v. i., pp. 308–426; and, in general, the works on the history of the Church in all periods.

MONEY OF THE BIBLE.

Standardized Forms Anterior to Coinage (§ 1).
The Unit of Value. Ratio of Gold to Silver (§ 2).
The Earliest Coins (§ 3).
Maccabean Coins (§ 4).
The Roman Time (§ 5).
Coins of the New Testament (§ 6).
Value of the Coins (§ 7).

1. Standardized Forms Anterior to Coinage.

Even prior to the Israelites' occupation of Canaan, gold and silver were standards of value and mediums of exchange in that country. In the Old Testament no other metals are named in this connection. The word *keseph*, "silver," is the usual Hebrew term for money in general (cf. the Latin *argentum*), showing the influence of Babylonia, where silver, the "moon metal," was the basis of the fiscal system. Coined money was not known before the Exile; in making payments the gold or silver was weighed (Gen. xxiii. 16; II Sam. xviii. 12; I Kings xx. 39; cf. the marginal readings). The scales and appertaining weights were carried in a bag at the girdle (Deut. xxv. 13; Isa. xlvi. 6; Prov. xvi. 11). This does not exclude the probability, of course, that these "pieces of money" were used mostly in prescribed forms, the weight of which was known, and which, accordingly, it was not always necessary to weigh out expressly. In the Egyptian tribute-lists and paintings, gold appears in the shape of bars (cf. Polybius, x., xxvii. 12; Pliny, *Hist. nat.*, XXXIII., iii. 17) and especially rings. The ring form is perhaps indicated by the use of the Hebrew *kikkar* ("circle") for talent. Since in I Sam. ix. 8 the fourth part of a shekel of silver is mentioned, inference points to a silver piece of definite form. Whether *ḳesiṭah* (Gen. xxxiii. 19; Josh. xxiv. 32; Job xlii. 11) denotes a definite piece of money, or is an otherwise unknown designation of weight, remains uncertain; and it is likewise uncertain whether the golden "wedge" or "tongue" of Josh. vii. 21 was a species of gold bar or an ornament (but see GEZER, § 5). These rings or bars were proportioned according to divisions or multiples of the unit of weight; the gold rings discovered in Egypt weigh $\frac{2}{60}$, $\frac{3}{60}$, $\frac{4}{60}$, $\frac{5}{60}$ of the standard mina, that is, 2, 3, 4, 5 standard shekels.

The shekel, the unit of weight, was also the unit of value (cf. the terms *lira*, *livre*, pound, as applied to coins). In the course of time, however, this occasioned practical difficulties in connection with the conventional ratio of gold to silver. In all western Asia, this was the standing ratio of $1 : 13\frac{1}{3}$, assumed under the influence of astral mythology, wherein each planet has its own metal. Silver is moon metal; gold, sun metal; the lunar and solar revolutions bear the proportion of 27 : 360 = 1 : $13\frac{1}{3}$. From this it resulted that 1 standard gold shekel = $13\frac{1}{3}$ standard silver shekels, which, however, was not a ratio that found practical currency in the circulation of gold and silver money. If the gold shekel were made the base of comparison, then the silver unit had to be so modified that it both stood in a convenient ratio to the gold shekel and yet aptly coincided with the weight system. This was done by making the silver shekel either $\frac{1}{10}$ or $\frac{1}{15}$ (in value) of the gold shekel; that is, $\frac{1}{10}$ or $\frac{1}{15}$ of $\frac{13\frac{1}{3}}{60}$ of a mina (1 gold shekel = $\frac{13\frac{1}{3}}{60}$ of a silver mina). In the former case the result was a piece weighing $\frac{1}{45}$ of a mina = 10.913 gr., or $\frac{1}{10}$ of a gold shekel in value; in the latter case $\frac{2}{135}$ of a mina = 7.275 gr., or $\frac{1}{15}$ of a gold shekel in value. Both silver units are found in use; and they both alike bear the name of "shekel," though having nothing to do with the shekel of weight. The fifteen-shekel basis was in use prior to the Persian era; and this lesser shekel is halved and quartered (Ex. xxx. 13; I Sam. ix. 8). A half shekel ($\frac{1}{2}$ of $\frac{2}{135}$ of a mina), in terms of this lesser shekel,—$\frac{1}{3}$ of the greater shekel ($\frac{1}{3} \times \frac{1}{45} = \frac{1}{135}$ of a mina). The greater shekel (= $\frac{1}{10}$ of a gold shekel) then came to have currency through the Persian monetary system. It is subdivided into thirds, for at this period the temple assessment is one-third of a shekel (Neh. x. 32). The Persian monetary system had for its basis the smaller talent; and the Persian shekel was half the Babylonian. In the Maccabean period, the fifteen-shekel basis again came into current use. In the time of Christ, the temple tribute was a half-shekel (=2 drachmæ, according to Josephus, *Ant.* III., viii. 2; Matt. xvii. 24, 27). The Maccabean coins are a determining factor in these questions; the shekels vary in weight from 14.50 to 14.65 gr.; an amount or value corresponding to $\frac{2}{135}$ of the great Babylonian mina (14.55 gr.). So the entire scheme of minas and talents was once more adjusted to this twofold basis of the silver shekel; and specifically the mina to the equivalent of 50 shekels (see WEIGHTS AND MEASURES).

2. The Unit of Value. Ratio of Gold to Silver.

Stamped coins did not begin to circulate among the Jews until the Persian period. The earliest ones named in the Old Testament are the darics (Ezra viii. 27, R. V.; I Chron. xxix. 7, R. V.), by which name is also designated the gold stater of Crœsus (Ezra ii. 69, R. V.; the A. V reads "drams" in the three passages; Heb. *adharkon* = daric, *darkemon* = drachma). The real darics, i.e., the gold piece which Darius Hystaspes made a national coin, weighed 8.40 gr., or very nearly $\frac{1}{60}$ of the lighter Babylonian mina. The corresponding silver coin (Gk. *siglos Mēdikos*) is mentioned in Neh. v. 15, and x. 33, under the ancient name, shekel. Subsequently, too, Alexander's coins (gold staters and silver coins) were current in Palestine, and some of Alexander's tetradrachmæ have been discovered. They were succeeded, as rulers changed, by the coins of the Ptolemies and Seleucidæ.

3. The Earliest Coins.

By the terms of an edict of Antiochus VII. in the year 174 of the Seleucidan era (139–138 B.C.; I Macc. xv. 6), Simon Maccabeus was authorized to stamp coins of his own. But whether the coins that are so frequently ascribed to him, dated in the years 1 to 5, belong to him and to the era of Jerusalem beginning in 143–142 B.C. (170 of the Seleucidan era), or whether they did not rather originate in the years 66–70 A.D., is doubtful (cf. Schürer, *Geschichte*, i. 192). There are silver shekels and half-shekels; on one side is a lily, with the inscription "Jerusalem the Holy"; on the other, a cup and the inscription "shekel of Israel," with no mention of the ruling prince, though the year is given. Some copper coins of Simon's successors are known with various designs. The first prince who had his name stamped on these coins was John Hyrcanus. The Greek language was first utilized by Alexander Jannæus, the Hebrew for "King Jonathan" appearing with the Greek translation, *BASILEOS ALEXANDROU*, on his coins.

4. Maccabean Coins.

In the Roman period the provinces were licensed to issue none but copper coins under their own stamp; so that copper coins are the only ones known prior to the Herodian line. The designs vary,—cups (or vases), anchors, tripods, three ears (of wheat), etc. No silver coins were struck again till during the two insurrections under Vespasian and Hadrian. The coins of Eleazar, during the first insurrection, bear on the obverse a pitcher, on the reverse a cluster of grapes, and are dated according to the "Years of Israel's Liberation." Bar-Kokba's coins show similar notation of date, and bear the name "Simon." In many instances the new Jewish stamp is simply imprinted upon old Roman denarii. Even down to the latest period the larger places of Palestine retained the right to stamp small coin (cf. the coins of Hadrian's time with the inscription *Ælia Capitolina*, i.e., Jerusalem).

5. The Roman Time.

Collaterally with the Jewish, the Greek and Roman coins were continually in use. The New Testament mentions the *drachma* (= $\frac{1}{4}$ shekel; Luke xv. 8); the double drachma or *didrachma* (Matt. xvii. 24); the *statēr* (according to Matt. xvii. 27, where it is made the temple tax for two persons, =4 Attic drachmæ = 1 shekel); the *lepton* (= $\frac{1}{2}$ the Roman *quadrans*, Mark xii. 42; Luke xii. 59); and, of Roman coins, the *denarius* (Matt. xxii. 19; Mark xii. 15), the universal monetary unit in the Roman Empire, a silver coin of 3.898 gr., which was made legally equivalent in value to the Attic drachma; the *as* or *assarion* (Matt. x. 29; Luke xii. 6), a copper coin = $\frac{1}{16}$ of a denarius; and the *quadrans* (Matt. v. 26; Mark xii. 42) = $\frac{1}{4}$ of an assarion.

6. Coins of the New Testament.

The bullion value of all these coins may easily be calculated, but this tells nothing in respect to the money's purchasing-power. Nor do many data of comparison exist to determine the latter factor. Joseph was sold for twenty shekels, and in other cases a slave is valued at thirty shekels (Ex. xxi. 32; cf. Hos. iii. 2; Matt. xxvi. 15); at a later time, slaves were considerably dearer (II Macc. viii. 11).

A vineyard, inferentially of great value, is assessed at a thousand shekels for a thousand vines (Isa. vii. 23). Ten shekels of silver, with "a suit of apparel and victuals," were the hire of a household priest in ancient times (Judges xvii. 10). The companion of Tobias received "a drachma a day." In the time of Christ the usual day's hire was a denarius. Unfortunately, however, there is no knowledge of the most important item, namely, the cost of living.

7. Value of Coins.

I. Benzinger.

Bibliography: T. E. Mionnet, *Description de medailles antiques*, vol. v., supplement vol. viii., Paris, 1811, 1837; A. Böckh, *Untersuchungen über Gewichte, Münzfüsse, und Masse des Altertums*, Berlin, 1838; M. A. Levy, *Geschichte der jüdischen Münzen*, Breslau, 1862; B. Zuckermann, *Talmudische Gewichte und Münzen*, ib. 1862; J. Brandis, *Das Münz-, Mass-, und Gewichtssystem in Vorderasien*, Berlin, 1866; C. W. King, *Early Christian Numismatics*, London, 1873; F. de Saulcy, *Numismatique de la terre sainte*, Paris, 1874; F. W. Madden, *Coins of the Jews*, London, 1881 (authoritative); T. Reinach, *Les Monnaies juives*, Paris, 1887; F. Friedensburg, *Die Münze in der Kulturgeschichte*, Berlin, 1909; Benzinger, *Archäologie*, pp. 196–204; Nowack, *Archäologie*, i. 209–213; C. W. Johns, in *Expositor*, Nov., 1899; Schürer, *Geschichte*, and Eng. transl., consult the Indexes (exceedingly full); *DB*, iii. 417–432 (highly valuable); *EB*, iv. 4442–47.

MONGOLS, CHRISTIANITY AMONG THE.

1. Religious Toleration among Early Mongols.

The Mongols were an important stock of Central Asia. In their original home, south of Lake Baikal, they were shamanists, and even when Genghis Khan was preparing for his great invasion, Christianity seems to have numbered no converts among them, though it had been brought by Nestorian missionaries to their neighbors the Keraits and Uigurs. These latter tribes had been among the first to affiliate with the Mongols, and the resultant matrimonial alliance between Mongols and Keraits exercised considerable influence on the treatment of Christians in many parts of the Mongol empire. The expeditions of Genghis Khan, moreover, brought his people into contact with the Lamaists, Confucians, and Taoists of China and with the Mohammedans of Turkestan and Persia, as well as with scattered but well-organized and influential communities of Nestorian, Jacobite, and Greek Christians; while still further westward, in Armenia, Georgia, and Russia, entire nations had long professed the Christian faith. The Mongol empire was essentially political, not religious. Genghis Khan himself, like his grandsons Mangu and Kublai, is reported to have held that there was one God, but that creeds and rituals were immaterial. So long as such views prevailed, the priests and monks of the various creeds of the East were able to worship freely and were even welcomed for their prayers and blessings. Mohammedan mullahs, Buddhist bonzes, and Nestorian priests were almost entirely untaxed and were exempt from military service. Khan Kuyuk (1246–48) permitted a Christian chapel with daily services near his tent, while Mangu (1251–59), together with his son and daughter, fasted with the Christians and kissed the crucifix. Yet all this marked no real conversion, and it was frequently the case that a khan, after being brought up as a Christian, renounced this faith for the religion which happened at the time to be in the ascendent. The treatment of religions other than the one professed by the khan varied according to his disposition and the conditions of the time.

2. Christianity in Mongolia and China.

In the ancient Mongolian capital Karakorum, where the monk Rubruk spent Easter, 1254, there were twelve temples, two mosques, and a church with Nestorian clergy. The fame of Kuyuk as a friend of the Christians attracted to the capital monks from Asia Minor, Syria, Bagdad, and Russia, while Christians of various nations were brought thither as prisoners of war. A like policy of toleration was pursued by Kublai at Peking after 1264, when he showed equal favor to priests of all religions. Rubruk reports that Nestorians resided in fifteen cities of Cathay and that they had a bishop in "Segin" (probably Singan-fu); while Marco Polo, who resided in the country in 1275–92, records a church at Kinsai (Hang-chau), three at Kenchu (the capital of Kan-su), and two at Chingiansu, built by Sarghis in 1278. When the Venetian brothers Niccolo and Massio Polo were about to return home from Khanbaligh (Peking), the great khan requested that the pope send a hundred scholars to China to give instruction and to demonstrate the superiority of Christianity to other religions. The pope accordingly sent the Franciscan John of Montecorvino (q.v.), and as a result three churches were built in Peking between 1299 and 1307. In a letter of 1305 John complained of the antagonism of the Nestorians, but lauded Khan Togan Temur (1294–1307). In 1307 John was consecrated archbishop of Khanbaligh in recognition of his conversions in the East, which were estimated at between 5,000 and 6,000, and suffragan sees were erected. In 1342 a second papal legate appeared in Peking in the person of the Franciscan Giovanni de Marignola, who three or four years after was able to report a cathedral and several churches in Peking, and three churches in Chuan-chi-fu. With the fall of the Mongols, however, Christian missions in China came to an abrupt end, and all traces of them vanished with the accession of the Ming dynasty.

3. Christianity in Mongolian Persia.

The first khan of Persia, Hulagu, the grandson of Genghis Khan, was the more favorable to Christianity since it was the religion of both his mother and his wife. His successor, Abaka (1265–82), followed a similar course, and the Curia availed itself of this opportunity both to thank the khan for his kindness to his Christian subjects, and to make a vain effort for his own conversion. After a brief period of persecution under the Mohammedan Sultan Ahmad (1282–84), Khan Argun (1286–91) again favored the Christians and expressed willingness to engage in a crusade, promising to be baptized if Jerusalem should be taken. With the death of Argun, however, it became clear that the rising power of Mohammedanism in Persia rendered it impossible for a prince favorable to Christianity to mount the throne. The victorious candidate, Gasan (1295–1304), embraced Islam, and as his first royal act ordered the destruction of the sacred edifices of idolaters, Christians, Jews, and Zoroastrians. Buddhist priests were put to death unless they renounced their faith, and Christians were treated with ignominy, though the intercession of Hethum II. of Armenia secured the rescinding of the edict to destroy the churches. The succeeding reigns of Uljaitu (1304–16) and Abu Said brought the Christians no relief. The Persian Christians, who were Nestorians, Jacobites, and other schismatics, despite all persecution preserved their organization through their patriarchs, whose seat was at Bagdad and who controlled over twenty metropolitan sees. At this same period, moreover, the Roman Catholic Church established dioceses, orders, and lay communities in Persia in answer to the request of some of the khans to the popes, who gladly sent many mendicant monks. The majority of these wandering missionaries were more interested in the reclamation of schismatics to the Roman Catholic Church than in making new converts. Their most important colonies were at Tauris and Sultanieh, especially as in the former city many Fraticelli had settled. At Sultanieh John XXII. erected an archiepiscopal see with six dioceses, while others were afterward created for a bishop of Tauris. The speedy dissolution of the khanate, however, rendered these archdioceses and their dependent sees short-lived.

East Turkestan and southern Siberia had passed, on the division of Genghis Khan's dominions, to his third son Ogotai; while his second son, Jagatai, had received western Turkestan. Here the great majority of the inhabitants were Mohammedans, and desperate efforts were made to extirpate the Christians. Nevertheless, two papal briefs of the first half of the fourteenth century are extant which thank a Tatar prince of the region and two of his court for their protection of the Christians under their sway and for the building and the repair of churches. The Franciscans had settled at Jagatai's capital, Almaligh on the Ili, but in 1338 a persecution there brought a martyr's death both to their bishop and to a visiting Franciscan from Spain. On the other hand, Giovanni de Marignola, when on his way to China, was able, two years later, to build a church in Almaligh and preach and baptize in public. West of Jagatai's dominions lay the khanate of Kipchak, its center on the lower stretches of the Volga. The population was mixed, the invading Mongols being settled among Ossetes, Kipchaks, Cherkesses, Russians, and Greeks. Between the Mohammedan Bulgarians and Kipchaks were Christian Armenians and Ruthenians. The rulers must, therefore, be either Christian or Mohammedan. Berke, the brother of Batu, the founder of the capital, Sarai, was a zealous Mohammedan; but Sortak, Berke's son, was rumored to be a Christian. The monk Rubruk was accordingly sent to the land, only to find that the rumor was false. Mohammedanism took firm root in this branch of Genghis Khan's family. Usbek Khan (1313–41),

4. Christianity in Turkestan and Kipchak.

while a firm follower of Mohammed, in 1813 granted the Metropolitan Peter a patent of protection and exemption from taxes to the Russian Church in his archdiocese. This policy of Usbek's was dictated by political expediency; but the patent was respected by his successors, though some of them again imposed taxes on the Christians. In 1261 the Greek Church received a further concession when Berke permitted the erection of a bishopric in Sarai. Pope John XXII., in 1318, made Kassa the see city of a diocese extending from Sarai to Varna, the first bishop being a Franciscan named Hieronymus. Other Latin bishoprics were established in Soldaia, Cembalo (Balaklava), and Kertsch, often side by side with Greek sees. The Franciscans, moreover, had two dioceses, one with ten stations in the province of Sarai, and the other with seven in the province of Gazaria (Crimea). These monks developed great activity, and frequently converted to Christianity members of the Mongol royal family. For more recent missions see China; Missions to the Heathen. (W. Heyd†.)

Bibliography: H. Howorth, *Hist. of the Mongols*, 3 vols., London, 1881–88; W. W. Rockhill, *Land of the Lamas: Notes of a Journey through China, Mongolia and Tibet*, New York, 1891; J. C. Hannah, *Brief Hist. of Eastern Asia*, London, 1900; J. Curtin, *The Mongols*, Boston, 1907; idem, *A Journey in Southern Siberia; the Mongols, their Religion and their Myths*, ib., 1909.

MONHEIM, mon'haim, JOHANN: German Roman Catholic, evangelical in type; b. at or near Elberfeld 1509 (?); d. at Düsseldorf Sept. 9, 1564. Educated at Münster and the University of Cologne, he was rector of the cathedral school at Essen in 1532–36, then in like position at Cologne until 1545, when he became rector of an institution founded by his patron, Duke William of Jülich-Cleve-Berg, at Düsseldorf, where he remained until his death. Under his guidance the school attained high prestige and an attendance surpassing that of most universities. As an author Monheim showed his pedagogical devotion by restricting himself to educational themes. After revising a catechism of C. Hegendorfer (Wesel, 1547), he published (Cologne, 1551) two catechisms based on Erasmus. The point of view is essentially Roman Catholic, the doctrines of purgatory and the seven sacraments being maintained, although communion in both kinds is advocated for the laity. After his death appeared his commentary on the Gospel and epistle for each day of the year (Cologne, 1569), the translation used being that of Erasmus.

The most noteworthy work of Monheim, however, was his *Catechismus in quo christianæ religionis elementa syncere simpliciterque explicantur* (Düsseldorf, 1560), which was momentous for the ecclesiastical development of western Germany in that it was the first catechism of Evangelical spirit to appear on the lower Rhine. Deviating from its author's former Erasmian position, in its eleven dialogues it treats of God, man, the law (exegesis of the Decalogue), faith (exegesis of the Apostles' Creed), justification, prayer (exegesis of the Lord's Prayer), the sacraments in general, baptism, the Eucharist, penance, and the other sacraments. The material is borrowed largely from Calvin's "Institutes," with reminiscences of the Geneva catechism and of Luther's smaller catechism. In the section on the Eucharist there is an unmistakable effort to preserve a middle course between Geneva and Wittenberg, and in the dialogues on the Church and the sacraments the author endeavors to retain certain Roman Catholic traditions with a Protestant basis. The work is, therefore, unionistic in spirit.

It was, accordingly, not surprising that Monheim incurred the displeasure of the Jesuits, and the *Censura et docta explicatio errorum catechismi Joannis Monhemii* (Cologne, 1560), inspired by them, marks the first noteworthy Jesuit polemics against Protestantism in Germany. Attack after attack was made on Monheim. The papal nuncio Commendone implored the duke to remove him, the cardinal legates of the Council of Trent were invoked, and the Jesuits persuaded the emperor to request the duke to banish Monheim. But all was in vain; the duke at most forbade his protegé to defend himself publicly and prohibited the use of the catechism. Monheim was also defended in J. Anastasius' *Bekenntnis von dem wahren Leibe Christi gegen der Papisten abgottische Messe* (1561), H. Hamelmann's *Resolutio duodecimi articuli in censura theologorum Coloniensium de catechismo M. Johannis Monhemii* (1561), H. Artopœus's *Ad theologastrorum Coloniensium censuram responsio pro defensione catechismi Johannis Monhemii* (Grenoble, 1561), and, above all, in Martin Chemnitz's *Theologiæ Jesuitarum præcipua capita* (1562). Polemics for and against him continued after his death, the chief work being Chemnitz's monumental *Examen concilii Tridentini* (1565–73).

(E. Simons.)

Bibliography: F. E. Koldewey, in *ZWT*, 1899; C. W. Kortüm, *Nachricht über das Gymnasium zu Düsseldorf im 16 Jahrhundert*, Düsseldorf, 1819; C. Krafft, *Die gelehrte Schule zu Düsseldorf*, ib. 1853. A sketch of Monheim's life appears in C. H. Sack's ed. of the Catechism, Bonn, 1847.

MONNICA (MONICA), SAINT: Mother of Augustine; b. of Christian parents possibly at Tagaste (60 m. w. by s. of Carthage) c. 332; d. at Ostia, at the mouth of the Tiber, May 4, 387. She was married at an early age to Patricius of Tagaste, to whom she bore three children, Augustine (q.v.), Navigius, and an unnamed daughter. Her husband was apparently coarse, unsympathetic, choleric, and unfaithful; but such was her beautiful Christian life, that she was the means of his conversion. He was baptized in 371, and shortly thereafter died. Monnica shared Patricius' ambition respecting Augustine's career as a scholar, but was deeply grieved when he abandoned the catholic faith. For many years she followed him with her prayers, and at last made the journey to Milan to be with him. There the one wish of her life was met. Augustine was converted 386, and was baptized by Ambrose, Easter (Apr. 25), 387. Monnica shared the society of the little company of friends Augustine had gathered around him immediately before and after his baptism, and added much to the spiritual value of their intercourse. After the purpose of their meeting was accomplished, viz., his conversion and baptism, they set out for Africa. On the way, Monnica fell sick and died. As the mother of the greatest of the Latin Church Fathers, and as herself a wise, loving, and Christian woman, she will always be remembered.

In 1430 her remains were removed by Pope Martin V. from Ostia to Rome, and buried in the Church of St. Augustine. Her most imperishable monument, however, is the *Confessions* of her illustrious son, who has written of his unfilial conduct with a candor unsurpassed, and who ends his biography of his mother with an outburst of sorrow over her death, and a prayer for her eternal welfare.

Bibliography: Early lives and collections from the "Confessions" of Augustine (the one source) are brought together in *ASB*, May, i. 474–492. Consult C. Braune, *Monnika und Augustinus*, Grimma, 1846; P. Schaff, *Life and Labors of St. Augustine*, New York, 1854; idem, *Saint Augustine, Melanchthon, Neander*, ib. 1886; A. le Goupils, *S. Monique, modèle et patronne des mères chrétiennes*, Tours, 1878; E. Bougaud, *Hist. de S. Monique*, Paris, 1887; A. Vivoli, *Vita di S. Monica*, Bologna, 1888; Mrs. A. Jameson, *Sacred and Legendary Art*, i. 324 sqq., Boston, 1893; *DCB*, iii. 932–934; and, in general, the literature dealing with Augustine's life.

MONOD, ADOLPHE (LOUIS FRÉDÉRIC THÉODORE): French Protestant; b. at Copenhagen Jan. 21, 1802; d. at Paris Apr. 6, 1856. The son of a distinguished pastor first at Copenhagen and then, after 1808, at Paris, he was educated at the Collège Bourbon at Paris, and in 1820–24 studied theology at Geneva. In 1825 he visited Italy and soon founded a Protestant congregation at Naples, where he was pastor until 1827. Returning to France, he became pastor of the Reformed church at Lyons, but was deposed in 1831 because of the opposition aroused by his orthodoxy, the ostensible cause being a sermon in which he sought to restrict participation in the communion to worthy recipients. He then founded a free church at Lyons which still exists, but in 1836 he was called to a theological professorship at Montauban, where he taught and preached till 1847, when he was called by the Reformed Consistory to Paris. Here he labored, especially at the Oratoire, until his death. The secrets of Monod's success were not only his clear intellect, his deep sympathy, and his thorough training both in literature and theology, but also his absolute insistence on the Bible, his unwavering adherence to the Reformed principles of the sixteenth century, and, above all, his Christian character. He was unquestionably the foremost pulpit orator of the French Reformed Church in the nineteenth century. The one purpose of his sermons was to rescue immortal souls from destruction, and to this one theme were devoted his merciless logic, his intense earnestness, his almost exclusive selection of the weightiest questions of salvation for his themes, his glowing eloquence, and his confessions of his own difficulties, doubts, and struggles.

In 1830 Monod published three sermons in which he sharply controverted the Pelagian views which had crept into the Reformed Church in the course of the eighteenth century, declaring that man can be saved only by the truths of the Gospel. From this time on he frequently published individual sermons and collections of addresses which ran through repeated editions. Among these special mention must be made of his *Sermons* (Paris, 1844;

Eng. transl., London, 1849); *La Femme* (1848; Eng. transl., London, 1851), and *Saint Paul* (1851; Eng. transl., London, 1853). He was likewise the author of *Lucile, ou la lecture de la Bible* (Paris, 1841; Eng. transl., *Lucilla; or Reading of the Bible*, London, 1842) and *Explication de l'epître aux Ephésiens* (1866). An edition of his sermons in commemoration of the centenary of his birth appeared Paris, 1902. Even in his last illness he continued to preach to his friends in his sick-room, these addresses appearing posthumously under the title *Adieux d'Adolphe Monod à ses amis et à l'église* (Paris, 1856; Eng. transl., *The Parting Words of Monod to his Friends and the Church*, London, 1857, New York, 1873). (C. PFENDER.)

BIBLIOGRAPHY: Of the first importance is *Adolphe Monod: Souvenirs de la vie, extraites de la correspondance, choix de lettres*, 2 vols., Paris, 1885–1902. Consult further: A. Richardot, *A. Monod considéré comme prédicateur*, Strasburg, 1863; A. J. Vabre, *Étude sur la prédication d'A. Monod*, ib. 1865; E. de Pressensé, *Contemporary Portraits*, London, 1880; L. Comte, *Étude homilétique sur la prédication contemporaine; A. Monod et Lacordaire*, Paris, 1882; P. Stapfer, *La Grande Prédication chrétienne en France; Bossuet, Adolphe Monod*, ib. 1898; Lichtenberger, *ESR*, ix. 317–325.

MONOD, mō″nō′, FRÉDÉRIC: French Protestant, brother of Adolphe Monod (q.v.); b. at Monnaz, near Morges (7 m. w. of Lausanne), Switzerland, May 17, 1794; d. at Paris Dec. 30, 1863. He received his education at Geneva, but was more influenced by Robert Haldane (q.v.) than by his Unitarian teachers. Ordained at Geneva in 1818, he went to Paris, where he was active for a time in the Bible society there. He was then a private tutor in Jena for a brief period, but in 1820 he returned to Paris, being at first assistant to his father, and after 1832 titular pastor of the Oratoire. In the early years of this period he assumed the editorship of the *Archives du christianisme au dixneuvième siècle*, which he conducted for forty-three years as a bold and uncompromising advocate of Calvinistic orthodoxy. His editorial position brought him into prominence in 1848, when the revolution began to affect religious conditions. Here he was eager both for the separation of Church and State and for the formulation of a creed for the Reformed Church. In Sept., 1848, a general synod of the Reformed Church was held in Paris without governmental recognition. But though Monod delivered the opening sermon in the Oratoire, his motion for the formulation of a creed was voted down and it was held that questions of dogma should not be considered by the synod. Monod, convinced that he could no longer remain in a creedless Church, resolved to form a free church on an orthodox basis, even hoping that such a step would lead to a union of all the orthodox who had hitherto been divided into Reformed and Lutherans, free churches and State churches. The synod, the Paris Consistory, and his brother Adolphe urged him to reconsider his decision, but their efforts were in vain; and on Jan. 8, 1849, he resigned his pastorate of the Oratoire. A few months later he opened in Paris a small chapel, where he gathered the first members of the future Église Libre; and a synod to form a constitution of the union of " free evangelical churches " was held Aug. 20–Sept. 1, 1849. Monod thus succeeded in welding together the scattered Protestant communities which had broken off from the State Church or had been constituted as a result of the " awakening," the characteristics of their organization being their separation from the State and their mutual creed. The first sentence of the constitution which he proposed for the new church declared: " We believe that the entire Scripture of the Old and New Testament is inspired by God, and thus constitutes the sole and infallible rule of faith and life." See FRANCE, II., 1.

Monod remained pastor of his free church until his death, aided by generous contributions from America, England, and Scotland. He forms one of the most striking figures of modern French Protestantism. Yet he was no learned theologian, though he had the knack of skilfully presenting his dogmatic and ecclesiastical views in journalistic form. He was, moreover, a clever administrator, and as president of the synodical committee of the Union des Églises évangéliques libres he guided the alliance of French free churches with consummate skill.

The Union celebrated its fiftieth anniversary Oct. 25, 1899. It has sought from the first to leave problems of organization, liturgy, discipline, and even the mode and time of baptism to the discretion of the individual communities. A synod is held biennially. At the third (1852) a committee of evangelization was formed which now has twenty-two posts with numerous affiliations; the fifth (1856) established a committee to supervise the education of ministers; and the ordination of pastors was regulated at the ninth (1864). The external development, however, has not kept pace with its internal organization. Up to 1873 new congregations were formed until they numbered seventy-three; now there are but thirty-six. This decrease is due primarily to the changed conditions in the Reformed Church of France, for with the adoption of a creed by the older body the younger has lost its reason for existence. Many accordingly returned to the Reformed Church, among them Monod's own son Théodore (q.v.). (EUGEN LACHENMANN.)

BIBLIOGRAPHY: G. Monod, *La Famille Monod*, Paris, 1890; J. Pédezert, *Cinquante ans de souvenirs religieux*, Paris, 1896; the work on the jubilee of the French Church, *L'Union des églises évangéliques libres de France*, Paris, 1899; Lichtenberger, *ESR*, ix. 316–317.

MONOD, THÉODORE: French Reformed, son of the preceding; b. in Paris Nov. 6, 1836. He studied law 1855–58; accompanied his father to the United States, and was converted in New York Apr., 1858; studied theology in the Western Theological Seminary, Allegheny, Pa., 1858–60; preached among the French Canadians in Illinois, 1860–63; was his father's successor at the Chapelle du Nord, Paris, 1864–75; traveling agent for home mission work in France, 1875–78; and became pastor of the Église Reformée, Paris, in 1878. From 1875 to 1879 he edited *Le Libérateur*, later absorbed in the *Bulletin de la mission intérieure*. His writings embrace: *Regardant à Jésus* (Paris, 1862; Eng. transl., *Looking to Jesus*, New York, 1864); *Le Chrétien et sa croix* (Lausanne, 1865); *The Gift of God* (London, 1876; French, *Le Don de Dieu*, Paris, 1877); *Life*

More Abundant (London, 1881); *Loin du Nid, poésies* (Paris, 1882); *Crucefiés avec Christ* (1883); *Au vent la voile, poésies* (1898).

MONOGRAM OF CHRIST. See JESUS CHRIST, MONOGRAM OF.

MONOÏMOS: Arabian Gnostic; known only from the *Refutatio* of Hippolytus (VIII., v.-viii., X., xiii.; Eng. transl. in *ANF*, v. 120-122, 146). His system, in so far as it is determined, is a mixture of Pythagorism and Biblical conceptions. The Supreme Being is the unborn and perfect "Man"; and from him the Son of Man proceeded, not in the way of procreation, but as light proceeds from fire. The perfect Man has for his symbol the "one iota"; and is, therefore, a monad. But as *iota* is the Greek numerical symbol for 10, he is likewise *dekas*, a decad. Men imagine, indeed, that the Son of Man is born of woman; but all who are involved in this error are powerless to apprehend his beauty. (The argument of Monoïmos reflects an acute phase of docetism, if it be not an utter rejection of the historic Christ.) The world is created not by the Son of Man, but by the *hexad*, contained in the decad. This thought is based upon the Mosaic narrative of the six days of labor, and is an obvious attempt to derive the world otherwise than from the Supreme Being, yet it does not attempt to offset him dualistically. Monoïmos construed the Old Testament allegorically. His use of the New Testament appears from the circumstance that he cites Matt. v. 18. R. LIECHTENHAN.

MONOPHYSITES, men-ef'i-saits.

1. The Chalcedonian Decree.

On Oct. 25, 451, the Council of Chalcedon proclaimed a new dogmatic definition, requiring all the faithful to acknowledge "our one Lord Jesus Christ, perfect God and perfect man ... of one substance with the Father as touching his Godhead, of one substance with us as touching his manhood ... in two natures without confusion, without change, without distinction, without separation," in such a way that "the difference of natures is in no way abolished by the union, but rather the properties of each nature are preserved and united in one person and one mode of being." The politicians agreed to this definition in the hope of securing peace. The edict of Feb. 7, 452, issued jointly by Marcian and Valentinian III., imposed severe penalties on all who should thenceforth publicly discuss the points of controversy. But this could be enforced only in the neighborhood of the court.

2. Outbreak in Palestine.

The first signs of the coming trouble appeared in Palestine, where a positive revolution broke out under the leadership of fanatical monks. Bishop Juvenal of Jerusalem (q.v.), who at Ephesus had been an active partizan of Dioscurus (see EUTYCHIANISM), had been induced at Chalcedon by the fear of danger to his ecclesiastical position not merely to break away from the Alexandrians and their *protégé* Eutyches, but to support the definition, in the final formulation of which he had a hand. This change of front cost him the confidence of the monks, who were specially numerous and influential in Palestine. When after his return he declared his adhesion to the decrees of the council, a monk named Theodosius was set up as a rival bishop, and Juvenal was obliged to flee. A similar course was followed in other places; bishops of the orthodox party were driven out, sometimes with bloodshed, and their places filled by their opponents. The most noted intellectually of these was Peter the Iberian, who, brought up at the court of Theodosius II., had become a monk and was now made bishop of Majuma. They were supported by the widow of the Emperor Theodosius, Eudocia, who was then living in Jerusalem. Cyril asserts that almost all Palestine was carried away by the movement. Juvenal returned to Constantinople to ask for aid. Marcian, underestimating the force of the revolt, sought to suppress it by simple edicts, but when they went unheeded took stronger measures. The *comes* Dorotheus was sent with troops, who, after an attempt at compromise had failed, sternly put down the insurrection. Among the monks who took flight was Theodosius, who was afterward captured, suffered a long imprisonment in Constantinople, and was set free under Leo I. only to die as a result of the treatment he had received. Peter the Iberian escaped to Alexandria; but the movement was not even provisionally suppressed before July, 453.

3. Events in Egypt.

Still more significant was the course of events in Egypt, where an irreconcilable conflict broke out. A large part of the people, apparently the monks and the lower classes, held to Dioscurus after his deposition; the other party elected Proterius, who seems to have been personally and intellectually allied to Dioscurus until the decision of the council caused him to change his attitude. Supported by the civil authorities, he enforced these decisions by means of confiscation and banishment, which led to riots and excesses. An imperial edict of July 28, 452, condemned in the sternest language those who held to the Eutychian errors and refused to acknowledge Proterius. Two thousand soldiers were ordered to Alexandria, and peace seemed likely to follow upon their vigorous repressive measures. But the death of Dioscurus in his exile at Gangra in Paphlagonia (Sept., 454) stirred up fresh excitement. There was a powerful party at court indisposed to harsh measures; and this tendency gained strength at the death of Marcian and the succession of Leo I. (Feb., 457). The party of Dioscurus in Alexandria took courage and elected as patriarch Timotheus Ælurus, who had followed Dioscurus into banishment. He was consecrated in a tumultuous and irregular manner. Military aid enabled Proterius to expel him; but after bloody riots his partizans gained the upper hand, when he returned, and Proterius was murdered by the mob at Easter, 457. Timotheus now took energetic measures to confirm his power, and drove out a number of orthodox bishops, who appealed to the pope and the emperor. Leo ordered an investigation of the murder of Proterius and inflicted severe penalties on those who were found responsible; but he did not at once move against Timotheus, in spite of urgent requests from Rome. He thought of calling another council, but was persuaded out of the notion by Anatolius, who suggested a circular letter asking all the bishops of the empire their opinion on the decrees of Chalcedon. Such a letter was sent out, probably in Oct., 457, and the replies, as was to be expected, were for the most part unfavorable to Timotheus, even where a certain lack of enthusiasm for the decrees of Chalcedon may be read between the lines. Pope Leo answered on Aug. 17, 458, in a long letter (*Epist.*, clxv.) which should be read in connection with his famous "Tome." Meantime Anatolius had died (July 3, 458) and been succeeded by the learned Gennadius (q.v.), a determined adherent of the definition of Chalcedon. He did not, however, accomplish the banishment of Timotheus Ælurus until the beginning of 460, when another Timotheus, known as Salophaciolus, was chosen in his place.

Even in Antioch, the place where in general Alexandrian theology was most unfavorably received, trouble was now made by the instigation of Peter the Fuller, a presbyter of Chalcedon, who was supported by the emperor's son-in-law Zeno. He was zealous for the proposition that "God was crucified," and for the insertion in the *Trisagion* of the words "Who was crucified for us," in such a way as to make it appear that the Son of God in his deity suffered for us. He intruded into the see, driving out the legitimate Bishop Martyrius, but was himself expelled by the emperor on the advice of Gennadius not long afterward. Meantime political intrigue had been busy at the court, and after the death of Leo I. (Feb. 3, 474) and his seven-year-old grandson Leo II. (Nov., 474), Zeno secured the throne for himself, having practically held the power for some time. Only a few weeks later, however, he was overthrown in his turn by Basiliscus, another son-in-law of Leo I. In the train of the usurper, Timotheus Ælurus held a prominent place, and in spite of the efforts of the patriarch of Constantinople, Acacius, who had succeeded Gennadius in Sept. (?), 471, he persuaded Basiliscus to send out a circular letter or encyclical condemning the "Tome" of Leo and the definition of Chalcedon, and threatening their adherents with the severest penalties. The weakness of the eastern bishops is shown by the fact that at least five hundred of them accepted this pronouncement. Timotheus Ælurus was now able to return to Alexandria, from which see his namesake had already been removed. On the way he consecrated a bishop of his own party for Ephesus and presided at a synod which sent a solemn admonition to the emperor, exhorting him to remain constant in the good work and to remove Acacius, as unworthy, from the patriarchate of Constantinople.

4. At Antioch and Constantinople.

But the day of Timotheus was nearly over, although Antioch and Jerusalem were occupied by Monophysite bishops. Acacius was absolutely firm, and did all he could to arouse the capital against the usurper. The populace responded to his efforts; a great ecclesiastical demonstration was arranged, and Daniel the Stylite came down from his pillar to bear witness to the orthodox faith. Basiliscus was forced to abandon the city, and Zeno, gathering strength as he came, approached. A last means of averting the counter-revolution was tried in the recall of the encyclical; but it was of no avail, and Zeno, resuming the throne, annulled the acts of his opponent (Dec. 17, 476). The bishops of Asia Minor made haste to declare with the utmost penitence that their assent to the encyclical had been extorted from them by force. Pope Simplicius had already written to Basiliscus, and now wrote again to Zeno, to demand the deposition of Timotheus Ælurus; but Timothy died July 31, 477. The Monophysite party elected Petrus Mongus, then archdeacon, to succeed him, but the government restored Timotheus Salophaciolus by military force. Feeling his end approaching, he was urgent with the emperor that only an orthodox bishop should be chosen to succeed him. When he died (probably in June, 482) his *œconomus* John Talaja contrived to secure the succession; but it was not long before Zeno saw fit to restore Petrus Mongus, on condition of his assenting to the document (afterward so famous under the name of *Henoticon*) put forth by Acacius with the view of securing peace.

5. Attempts at Peace.

Acacius was an accomplished politician, as is sufficiently proved by his ability to maintain himself for eighteen years (471–489) amid all the changes and conflicts of the times. Unfortunately the sources are unsatisfying on the preliminaries to the issue of the *Henoticon;* but there must have been negotiations in which Acacius endeavored to secure the good-will of Petrus Mongus, evidently his candidate for Alexandria and like himself a politician. The formula of union, addressed to the bishops, clergy, monks, and people of Alexandria, Egypt, Libya, and Pentapolis, is a masterpiece of tactical skill. It is avowedly based on the faith of Nicæa, Constantinople, and Ephesus, condemns Nestorius and Eutyches, adopting the twelve articles of Cyril against the latter, and while not expressly repudiating the decisions of Chalcedon, rejects the statements of "anyone who now or at any time, in Chalcedon or elsewhere, has thought or thinks otherwise." On the positive side, it asserts the consubstantiality of the Son of God with both the Father and man, going on to insist that it was one and the same person who wrought wonders and endured suffering—thus virtually accepting the "God crucified" of the Monophysites. It repudiated all separation as confusion (of the natures, although the term is carefully avoided), as well as anything like

6. The Henoticon.

Docetism. The first result was the settlement of the Alexandrian difficulties, as far as could be expected in the heated state of the popular mind. Petrus's position was not an easy one, and he got through only by some very adroit juggling with terms. Even then an irreconcilable party remained, led by a certain Nephelius, who did all possible to keep up the disturbance; but the majority were content, and, what was of greatest importance, Constantinople and Alexandria were once more on good terms. In Antioch also the situation seemed to improve. Peter the Fuller had been deposed after the downfall of Basiliscus; and when the next incumbent but one, Stephen, had been assassinated, Acacius availed himself of the opportunity to appoint of his own motion a certain Calandion as patriarch (probably at the end of 481). Calandion soon entered into an alliance with the Chalcedonian opponents of the *Henoticon* and with Rome. He was in consequence deposed in 485, and Petrus returned for the third time, it is said amid great enthusiasm, accepting the *Henoticon*, as did also Martyrius of Jerusalem—so that the leading rulers of the Eastern Church seemed now to be at one.

7. The Breach with Rome.

But they were reckoning without Rome. The pope was offended not only by the disregard of his wishes in Alexandria but by the arbitrary action of Acacius in the appointment of Calandion. In the latter case, he was appeased by the assurance that it had been done merely out of necessity, by the subsequent calling of a synod, and by the formal notification of the choice on the part of Calandion and his suffragans. It is uncertain whether Simplicius had heard of the *Henoticon*; his last extant letter complains merely of Acacius' silence in regard to what was happening in Alexandria. He died Mar. 10, 483, and was succeeded by the more determined and successful Felix III., who at once sent two long epistles to Constantinople. He warned Zeno not to lay rash hands on the faith of Peter and to bear in mind the fate of Basiliscus; he admonished Acacius in the tone of a superior not to remain recalcitrant but to atone for past misdeeds by redoubled zeal. The letters, however, had scarcely been despatched when he learned through John Talaja, who on his expulsion had finally come to seek support in Rome, more of the Eastern situation. In great displeasure he sent off fresh letters citing Acacius to appear in Rome and informing the emperor of this proceeding. But Acacius got hold of the papal envoys and either overawed or cajoled them. Felix made haste to call a synod in which he deposed his untrustworthy legates, excommunicated Acacius, and notified the people of Constantinople on July 28, 484, as well as the emperor on Aug. 1. Acacius took no notice of the sentence except to retaliate by striking out the name of Felix from the diptychs, and the breach was complete between Rome and so much of the Eastern Church as remained in communion with him. It is usual to represent this breach and the thirty-five-year schism which followed as the result of the *Henoticon*, and this document as a thoroughly harmful measure. Superficially, of course, this view is correct; if the decrees of Chalcedon had been adhered to and submission had been rendered to the directions of Rome, there would have been no schism. But it is by no means certain that such an unconditional surrender to the will of Rome would have been either possible or desirable. It is evident from Felix's letters that he held a startling conviction of the supremacy of the pope which was in irreconcilable conflict with the solution of the Eastern precedence question set forth in canon xxviii. of Chalcedon and Zeno's edict of 476, in which he had strongly confirmed the prerogatives of the patriarch of Constantinople. The development of this prelate's power had been accepted with complacency in the East, and a patriarch who attached so much importance to it as did Acacius was likely to regard it as more vital than the maintenance of a good understanding with Rome. He was in a position to carry his point as long as the government of Constantinople was absorbed in securing its position in the East; it was only when, a generation later, the imperial ambition attempted to embrace the whole known world that the question of reunion with Rome became pressing—for whoever wished to rule in the West was obliged to take the pope into account. In the mean time, however, the main thing was to establish ecclesiastical and dogmatic unity between the great sees of the East. This could be done neither by a formula which should center around the definition of Chalcedon, nor by an absolute rejection of the definition and the council. The method adopted in the *Henoticon* was thus the only practicable one, although not without its difficulties; it was no use trying to reconcile the fanatical extreme Monophysites, and on the other wing the orthodox opposition in Constantinople was kept in line by the monasteries, accessible to Roman influence and supplying the pope constantly with information on current events; while the successors of Acacius were not equal to their task, and threw many obstacles in the way of the imperial union policy.

8. Eastern Support of the Henoticon.

Acacius died probably at the end of 489. His successor Fravitas (probably a Goth) notified Petrus Mongus of his election in a letter which definitely adheres to the *status quo*, and wrote to Felix in the usual way, although, it appears from Felix's answer, without making any distinct pledges as to his future conduct. His incumbency of the patriarchal see, however, lasted but four months. His successor was Euphemius, who took his stand outspokenly among those who wished to place as orthodox a construction as possible upon the *Henoticon*, if not to drop it altogether. This brought him into conflict with Petrus Mongus, whom he was apparently preparing to depose in a synod when Petrus died, being succeeded by Athanasius II. Euphemius announced his elevation to the pope, who refused recognition on the ground that he had not struck the names of Acacius and Fravitas out of the diptychs. About a year later (Apr. 9, 491) the Emperor Zeno died, and the throne was occupied by the former *silentiarius* Anastasius, who set out to follow in Zeno's path and maintain the *Henoticon* and the same unyielding attitude toward Rome. Personally a convinced Monophysite, he was led, especially toward the end of his reign, into unreasoning subjection to the extreme wing of the party. But at first Euphemius opposed his elevation to the imperial throne, and succeeded in forcing him to sign an undertaking to introduce no innovations and to recognize the decisions of Chalcedon. During the Isaurian war, the patriarch entered into treasonable communications with the enemy, and thus gave the emperor an excuse to depose him and banish him to Euchaita in Pontus (probably in the summer of 496). The new patriarch was Macedonius, a grandson of Gennadius. He was compelled to sign the *Henoticon*, but his heart was on the other side, and it took only a little pressure from the orthodox monks to range him definitely with them.

9. Radical Monophysitism. The struggle entered a new stage when, about the same time, the Syrian Monophysites attempted to go beyond the *Henoticon* as an inadequate concession. Flavian, bishop of Antioch from 498 (or 499), had been approved by the emperor and had signed the *Henoticon*, while apparently at heart favoring the orthodox creed. The Monophysites of his province rose in revolt against him under the leadership of Philoxenus (q.v.), made bishop of Hierapolis by Peter the Fuller, and succeeded in inducing him to condemn (in a synod at Antioch 508–509) Diodorus, Theodore, and others of the same group, and to express his own belief in four distinctly Monophysite propositions. Not contented even with this, in a synod held at Sidon, 511–512, Philoxenus demanded the explicit repudiation of the Council of Chalcedon. Flavian, however, strengthened by the presence of the less flexible Elias, patriarch of Jerusalem, refused to do this in the synod, but later yielded to imperial and popular pressure and anathematized the Council of Chalcedon. His submission profited him little, for in 512 he was banished by the emperor to Petra in Arabia. The change in the policy of Anastasius is assigned by Theodorus Lector (ii. 20) to the period following the end of the Persian war in 506, by which time he had come under the personal influence not only of Philoxenus but of John III. (Niceta), patriarch of Alexandria 505–515, and still more of the clever Severus, who from 510, with many other monks of Palestine, was present in the capital. The position of Macedonius became increasingly difficult; his opponents were continually finding new causes of complaint against him, and the end was that he was banished (Aug. 7, 511) to Euchaita, like his predecessor. His place was taken by Timotheus Litrobulbes or Celon, who interpreted the *Henoticon* in a Monophysite sense; but the unrest was not appeased, and finally a fierce revolt broke out over the Monophysite interpolation into the *Trisagion*, when Anastasius grew timid. Yet the Monophysite party in the East was on the eve of its triumph. Flavian was succeeded by Severus on Nov. 6, 512. He called a synod at Tyre in 513 (or 515, according to Diekamp), at which Chalcedon was repudiated and the *Henoticon*, with the Monophysite exposition of Philoxenus and himself, affirmed. Soon afterward (in 514 according to the usually accepted chronology; in Aug., 516, according to Diekamp), Elias of Jerusalem was banished to Aïla on the Red Sea, where he died in 518; and his successor, John, was kept in check by the work of Sabas, the pillar of Palestinian orthodoxy. In Egypt, under the illegally chosen Patriarch Dioscurus II., Monophysitism kept the upper hand; and at the death of Anastasius (July 9, 518) the moderate party of the strict adherents of the *Henoticon* had practically disappeared.

10. Attempts at Reconciliation. No real change took place in the relations with the Roman see under Anastasius. Pope Gelasius I. (492–496) had been known before his elevation as a determined opponent of Monophysitism and of the policy of Acacius, and as pope he maintained the same attitude. His successor Anastasius II. (496–498) was a man of a different temper. He notified the emperor of his election, which Gelasius had neglected to do, and he must in other ways have shown a desire for reconciliation, or the *patricius* Festus could not have sent an embassy to the emperor hinting at the possibility of winning his assent to the *Henoticon*. His pontificate was too short for the development of these hopes; but in spite of the efforts of Festus to secure the election of his candidate, the orthodox majority chose Symmachus (498–514), who wrote to the emperor in energetically uncompromising terms. That it was too late for any thought of subjecting the papacy to the ideals of eastern imperialism is shown very plainly by the first proceedings in the pontificate of Hormisdas (514–523). At this time the position of Anastasius was seriously endangered by the revolt of Vitalian, who put forward the protection of the orthodox faith as a pretext for his movement. In the negotiations between them, the emperor expressed his readiness to seek the mediation of the pope with a view to the termination of religious controversy. In two letters (Dec. 28, 514, and Jan. 12, 515) he formally invited Hormisdas to a synod to be held at Heraclea. Hormisdas returned a courteous answer, expressing his benevolent interest in the proposal, but instructed his envoys to do nothing which might seem to involve a resumption of communion. He required a full recognition of the Council of Chalcedon and a repudiation of Acacius; on these conditions he was willing to attend in person. Anastasius was not, however, prepared to go so far in the direction of submission, and sent the legates back with a letter denying that he had ever repudiated the decrees of Chalcedon, but saying that he was unable to give way on the question of Acacius, since to do so would be to provoke serious trouble among his subjects. In two other letters he expressed a wish for reconciliation, but Hormisdas remained firm, and the emperor broke off the negotiations in a letter of July 11, 517

On the death of the emperor a year later, the throne was seized by Justin, captain of the guard, a rough, uneducated man, full of zeal for orthodoxy, and from the beginning a mere tool in the hands of his clever and ambitious nephew Justinian. The orthodox throughout the East began to rise against their late oppressors. Five days after Justin's accession, a mob entered the cathedral, and the Patriarch John II. (the Cappadocian, who had succeeded Timothy on Apr. 17) was compelled to anathematize the "Manichean," the "new Judas," Severus of Antioch (q.v.), and promise the people that he would solemnly confirm the decrees of Chalcedon, which he did the next day. Four days later a synod met and made formal request to the emperor and empress for the restoration of orthodoxy. This was echoed from Jerusalem on Aug. 6, and from Tyre on Sept. 16. In the province of Antioch, where Monophysitism had held undisputed sway, Severus was banished in September, and fled to Alexandria, where Timothy IV., patriarch since the previous October, received him and still supported him. Justin, who had already notified the pope of his accession, wrote again on Sept. 7 to express his willingness and that of the Synod of Constantinople to resume negotiations. Hormisdas first sent a formal acknowledgment, and then despatched legates with detailed instructions, directing them to avoid holding intercourse with the patriarch until he should have signed a formula condemning the Monophysite leaders with Acacius and his "followers," apparently meaning Euphemius and Macedonius—although they were allowed in case of necessity to let the last condition drop. On Mar. 28, 519, the patriarch signed the formula, and in presence of the legates struck out the names of Anastasius and Zeno from the diptychs. Promises of submission were freely made; but the execution was somewhat disappointing. At Thessalonica the metropolitan Dorotheus opposed the union, supported by the people who murdered the host of a Roman legate; another legate was dangerously wounded. Hormisdas demanded that Dorotheus should be sent to Rome for judgment; but he was set at liberty. There was also some delay in filling the see of Antioch with an orthodox candidate, although finally the choice fell on Paul, a presbyter of Constantinople, who proceeded with such severity against the Monophysites that he was forced to resign in two years. His successor Euphrasius had been on the Monophysite side but returned to the faith and apparently continued to persecute his former associates, while the next patriarch, Ephraem (526–545), came out also in support of the official orthodoxy. The same policy ruled at Constantinople, where Epiphanius was patriarch from 520 to 535; and the capital witnessed an unprecedented sight when the successor of Hormisdas, John I. (523–526), assisted in person at the Easter mass of 525, side by side with the local patriarch but on a more elevated throne.

11. Beginning of Victory for Orthodoxy.

Justinian (q.v.) was proclaimed co-emperor on Apr. 1, 527, and when his uncle died, exactly four months later, began his absolute rule. For his attitude toward the West and Rome see THREE CHAPTER CONTROVERSY; THEOPASCHITES; VIGILIUS. He was probably more anxious to restore unity to the Church than to give the victory to any particular phase of doctrine, while his wife Theodora, a woman of great force of character and influence, was believed to favor the Monophysites. He caused conferences to be held between Catholic and Monophysite bishops, but without result. On Mar. 15, 533, he issued an edict declaring Chalcedon to be, with the three earlier councils, the standard of orthodoxy. Negotiations still proceeded with the Monophysites; a long correspondence was held with Severus, the real head of the party, who, however, declined to come to Constantinople until 535. Anthimus, who became patriarch about the same time, was a favorite of Theodora, and, though of a devout and ascetic life, strongly inclined to agree with Severus, who announced the fact with joy to his friends in Alexandria. Their joy was shortlived; Ephraem of Antioch, who knew Anthimus of old, made haste to lay the matter before Pope Agapetus, and he, coming to Constantinople to plead for the Gothic King Theodahad, then hard pressed by Belisarius, had sufficient influence to bring about the disgrace of Anthimus. Mennas was raised to the vacant throne (Mar. 13, 536), and was consecrated by the pope himself, who died in Constantinople a month later. In May and June Mennas held an important synod at which Anthimus, Severus, and their principal partizans were excommunicated. Another, held at Jerusalem in September, approved the deposition of Anthimus, without apparently touching the case of the others; and Ephraem of Antioch subjected the Monophysites of his jurisdiction to a severe persecution. In Alexandria, during the episcopate of Timothy IV., the Monophysites had split up into the conflicting parties of Severians and Julianists, each of whom set up a candidate for the vacant see on Timothy's death (Feb. 8, 535). Ultimately both were put down, and Paul, an abbot from Tabennæ, was consecrated by Mennas in Constantinople and entrusted with far-reaching powers by Justinian. He seems to have been unsuccessful in his use of them, and it is possible that his dogmatic position was not wholly satisfactory. At any rate, he fell into disfavor with the court, and Justinian, through the papal legate Pelagius (later pope himself) brought about his deposition by the other eastern patriarchs at a synod held at Gaza not later than Easter, 542.

12. Events Under Justinian.

But Theodora had been busy in the direction of Rome also. She had gained influence over the deacon Vigilius, who had come to Constantinople with Agapetus, and he is said to have promised her that if he were elected pope he would set aside the Constantinopolitan Synod and hold communion with Anthimus and Severus. In his absence Silverius had been chosen pope in Rome; but at Theodora's bidding Belisarius, then all-powerful in Italy, imprisoned and banished him on a charge of treasonable intercourse with the Goths, and procured the election of Vigilius (Mar. 29, 537). Vigilius now sent to Theodosius, Anthimus, and Severus a confession of faith which rejected the two natures and condemned the Antiochian theology, requesting

13. Theodora's Efforts for Monophysitism.

them, however, to keep it secret that he might the more effectively work for their cause. At the same time he was officially declaring his adherence to the faith of Chalcedon, and in his letters to Justinian and Mennas (Sept. 17, 540) he formally approved the anathemas of the synod of 536 against the three Monophysite patriarchs. The Monophysites maintained their existence as a party in Constantinople to the end of Justinian's reign, and had a preponderating influence in Syria and Egypt. At Theodora's bidding Jacobus Baradæus was consecrated bishop in Constantinople by Theodosius, the Severian patriarch of Alexandria at the time of the conflict with the Julianists, and set out to begin his career as organizer of eastern Monophysitism (see JACOBITES). Justinian himself became increasingly interested in theological discussions, and toward the end of his life gave fresh offense to the orthodox by his support of the Aphthartodocetæ (see JULIAN OF HALICARNASSUS). Eutychius (q.v.), patriarch of Constantinople from 552, was deposed and banished for refusing to agree to this (Jan. 22, 565), and Anastasius Sinaita, patriarch of Antioch, escaped a similar fate only by the emperor's death (Nov. 13, 565).

Justinian's nephew Justin II., who succeeded him (565–578), was a tool in the hands of the patriarch Johannes III. Scholasticus (q.v.), and from 571 there were severe persecutions of the Monophysites in the capital. There were, however, long-continued negotiations with the party leaders, of whom the principal ones were now John of Ephesus (q.v.) and Paul "the Black," nominal bishop of Antioch. A diplomatic appeal was made to the union formula of 433 (see NESTORIUS) and the authority of Cyril in its favor. The Monophysite bishops were distrustful and hesitated a long time; they were just on the point of avowing their readiness to reenter the communion of the Church when the patriarch startled them by saying that the matter must first be referred to Rome. Feeling that they had been deceived and regretting their concessions, they drew back, and after being summoned before the emperor were banished. Few of the Egyptians accepted the patriarch of Alexandria who had been appointed under the influence of Justinian; the great majority chose a patriarch of their own, and formed a schismatic church which was never reconciled, and the Ethiopian church cast in its lot with the Alexandrian. In Armenia also the Monophysite party, favored by the Persian rulers of the country, gained the upper hand toward the end of the fifth century. Early in the sixth the Synod of Theoria declared in favor of Monophysite views, and about 600 the Armenian church ceased to be in communion with the Iberian, which held to the decrees of Chalcedon. In Syria and Mesopotamia the Monophysites, persecuted and forsaken, seemed to be on the point of disappearing altogether, when they were revived by the extraordinary zeal and energy of Jacobus Baradæus, after whom they were called Jacobites (q.v.).

14. Final Schism of Monophysite Churches.

As was the case with other opposition parties in the Church, the Monophysites were united only in their repudiation of the orthodox formula; among themselves they differed widely and fiercely. The party whose most prominent representative was Severus always protested energetically against the imputation of Eutychianism and Apollinarianism; in fact, they accused the adherents of Chalcedon of being Nestorians, and called themselves the orthodox; they emphasized the view that their faith was that of the fathers of Nicæa, which was confirmed at Constantinople and Ephesus, and made the rejection of the definition of Chalcedon and the Tome of Leo a matter of principle, while they could accept the *Henoticon* of Zeno only by putting their own interpretation on the passage relating to Chalcedon. Severus and other like-minded theologians were far from wishing to reduce the human element in the Logos to mere appearance, nor did they entertain the idea of a mixture or transubstantiation. According to them, the Christ came into being by the junction of two natures, whose attributes were in the abstract distinguishable; but they refused to speak of two natures after the incarnation, because the conception of two independent factors seemed necessarily to involve that of two subjects or individual beings. Following the phraseology of Cyril and of the Areopagite, Severus spoke of a divine nature and person of the Logos complete in itself, which by the assumption of flesh, together with a reasonable soul, became flesh and man; the united elements form one nature and divine-human hypostasis to which all the activities of the Savior are to be referred. The radical Monophysites, on the other hand, adhering to an expression of Eutyches, refused to speak of the body of Christ as consubstantial with us; nothing merely human was to cling about the person of the Incarnate Word. This fanatical party of extremists was always powerful in Alexandria, and was constantly receiving accessions from the lower clergy and the monks. It was out of such elements that the faction of Julianists or Gaianites grew up there in contradistinction from the Theodosians (see above). Julian's doctrine of *aphtharsia* (see JULIAN OF HALICARNASSUS), that the human nature of Christ was so absorbed in the divine that he was not subject to the accidents of humanity or to corruption, from which his party gained the name of Aphthartodocetæ or Phantasiasts, had nothing in common with the assertion of consubstantiality by the orthodox and the Severians alike, although Severus was forced by the need of support against the upholders of Chalcedon to make common cause with him. A section of the Julianists even went so far as to say that the body of Christ, from the moment of the incarnation, was actually uncreated, whence they got the name of Actistetæ. There was division, too, among the Severians. Against the Patriarch Timothy IV. of Alexandria arose a deacon Themistius with the assertion (supported by passages like Mark xiii. 22; John xi. 34) that as the body of Christ was subject to natural conditions, so also he could not be conceived as omniscient. The doctrine of the Themistians, or Ag-

15. Various Aspects of Monophysitism.

noetæ, must have caused no little excitement, for even toward the end of the sixth century the orthodox monks in Palestine are found communicating on the subject with the papal legate in Constantinople, who not only reported the matter to Gregory I., but requested a formal pronouncement from Eulogius, the orthodox patriarch of Alexandria. It was going wholly beyond the bounds of Monophysitism in the strict sense when Stephen Niobes, an Alexandrian sophist, was driven by his feeling of the contradiction between the asserted unity of nature and the attempted maintenance of natural differences between the divine and human to say that after the incarnation there was in Christ no distinction of natures whatever. Against him and his followers, called Niobites, the Patriarch Damianus and Peter of Antioch (Peter of Callinicus) came forward decidedly. Besides all these differences, the Monophysite party was disturbed also by the Tritheistic Controversy (q.v.).

For convenience in following the course of the developments, the following dates of the patriarchs of Constantinople, Alexandria, Antioch, and Jerusalem are given. Constantinople: Anatolius, Aug. (?), 449–July 3, 458; Gennadius to Sept. (?), 471; Acacius to the end (?) of 489; Fravitas till spring, 490; Euphemius probably till the summer of 496; Macedonius II. till Aug. 7, 511; Timothy I. till Apr. 5 (?), 518; John II. of Cappadocia, Apr. 17–Feb., 520; Epiphanius Feb. 25, 520–June 5, 535; Anthimus to Mar., 536; Mennas Mar. 13, 536–August, 552; Eutychius till Jan. 22, 565; John III. Scholasticus till probably Aug. 31, 577; Eutychius till Apr. 12, 582; John the Faster till Sept. 2, 595.

Alexandria: Proterius Nov., 451– (probably) Mar. 28, 457; Timotheus Ælurus till the beginning of 460; Timotheus Salophakiolus, June, 460–Nov., 475; Timotheus Ælurus till July 31, 477; Petrus Mongus till Sept. 4, 477; Timotheus Salophaciolus till probably June, 482; John I. Tabennesiotes till the end of 482; Petrus Mongus till May, 490; Athanasius II. May, 490–Sept. 17, 496; John II. Hemula, 496–Apr. 29, 505; John III. Nikiotes till May 22, 515 (516); Dioscurus II. till Oct. 14, 517 (518); Timothy IV. till Feb. 8, 535 (536); Theodosius I. Feb., 10–11, 535 (536); Gaian, Feb. 10–May 23, 535 (536); Theodosius I. July, 535– (probably) 537 or 538 (Jan., 540); Paul, 539? (541)–Easter, 542 (543 at the latest); Zoilus till 551 (550); Apollinarius, 551 (550)–569; Peter IV., 576–Jan. 19, 578; Damianus, July, 578–June 12, 605.

Antioch: Maximus 449–Mar., 455(?); Basil 456(?)–458; Acacius 458–459(?); Martyrius 460(?)–470(?); Peter the Fuller 468 (? 470)–471; Julian 471–475–476; Peter the Fuller 475–6–476–7 (477–8); John 477 (478); Stephen 478–481 (?); Calandion 481–2–485; Peter the Fuller 485–488 (?); Palladius 488 (?)–498; Flavian 498 (499)–512; Severus Nov. 6, 512–Sept. 29 (?), 518; Paul II. end of May, 519–May 1, 521; Euphrasius 521–May 29, 526; Ephraem 526–545; Domnus III. 545–559.

Jerusalem, according to Diekamp: Juvenal 422–458; Anastasius beginning of July, 458–beginning of Jan., 478; Martyrius 478–Apr. 13, 486; Sallust Apr., 486–July 23, 494; Elias 494–Aug., 516; John I. Sept., 516–Apr. 20, 524; Peter 524–beginning of Oct., 532; Macarius Oct.–Dec., 552; Eustochius Dec., 552–563 (564); Macarius 563 (564)–c. 575.

(G. KRÜGER.)

BIBLIOGRAPHY: The principal sources are: (1) The acts of the synods named in the text, to be consulted in the works of Mansi and Hefele (the latter is available here in Eng. and Fr. transls.). (2) The letters and deliverances of the popes, such as are collected in A. Theil, *Epistolæ Romanorum pontificum vitæ*, vol. i., Brunsberg, 1868; Jaffé, *Regesta*, vol. i. (3) Histories: Evagrius, *Hist. eccl.*, Eng. transl., London, 1898; John of Antioch, in C. Muller's *Fragmenta*, Paris, 1870; John of Nijion, in H. Zotenberg's article in *JA*, 7 ser., xii (1878), 245–347; John Malalas, *Chronographia*, xiv.–xviii.; Nicephorus Callistus, *Hist. eccl.*; Procopius, *Hist. arcana*, in *CSHB*, 1833; *Theodore Lector*, in *MPG*, lxxxvi. 1, pp. 165–228; Liberatus, in *MPL*, lxviii. 963–1096; Marcellinus Comes in T. Mommsen, *MGH*, *Chron. min.*, ii (1894). *The Syrian Chronicle of Zachariah of Mitylene*, London, 1899; the "Commentary" of John of Ephesus, in Latin, Amsterdam, 1889; *The Chronicle of Joshua Stylite*, text and Eng. transl., ed. W. Wright, Cambridge, 1882; John of Majuma (cf. F. Nau, in *Revue de l'orient chrétien*, iii. 232–259, 337–392); Timothy the Presbyter, in *MPG*, lxxxvi. 1, pp. 11–74; *Select Letters of Severus, Patriarch of Antioch, 508–518*, 4 parts, London, 1902–04; *Corpus scriptorum Christianorum orientalium*, note especially vol. xxv., *Vitæ virorum apud Monophysitas celeberrimorum*, part 1, text, ed. E. W. Brooks, and vol. xxxvii., *Documenta ad origines Monophysitarum illustrandos*, ed. J. B. Chabot, Paris and Leipsic, 1907–08; Timotheus Ælurus, *Widerlegung der auf der Synode zu Chalcedon festgesetzten Lehre*, Armenian text with preface, ed. K. Ter-Mekrttschian and E. Ter-Minassiantz, Leipsic, 1908.

The subject is treated in the works on the history of doctrine, see DOCTRINE, HISTORY OF; in the literature under ALEXANDRIA, SCHOOL OF; ANTIOCH, SCHOOL OF; and in the works on the church history of the period. Consult further: G. Krüger, *Monophysitische Streitigkeiten*, Leipsic, 1884; S. A. Assemani, *Bibliotheca orientalis*, vols. i.–ii., Rome, 1719–21 (valuable); M. Le Quien, *Oriens Christianus*, 3 vols., Paris, 1762–65; F. C. Baur, *Die christliche Lehre von der Dreieinigkeit*, ii. 37–96, Tübingen, 1842; I. A. Dorner, *Person Christi*, ii. 150–193, 5 parts, Berlin, 1845–63, Eng. transl., 5 vols., Edinburgh, 1861–63; H. G. Kleyn, *Het leven van Johannes van Tella door Elias*, Leyden, 1882; idem, *Bijdrage tot de Kerkgeschiedenis van het Oosten durende de 6. eeuw*, Utrecht, 1891; J. C. L. Gieseler, *Commentatio: Monophysitarum veterum variæ . opiniones*, 2 vols., Göttingen, 1835–38; J. Langen, *Geschichte der römischen Kirche von Leo I. bis Nikolaus I.*, Bonn, 1885; G. A. Rose, *Kaiser Anastasius I.*, vol. i., Halle, 1882, vol. ii., Wohlau, 1888; J. B. Bury, *Hist. of the Later Roman Empire*, 2 vols., London, 1889; A. von Gutschmid, *Kleine Schriften*, ii. 395–525, Leipsic, 1890; H. Gelzer, in *Byzantinische Zeitschrift*, i (1892), 34–49; idem, in Krumbacher, *Geschichte*, pp. 911 sqq.; A. Knecht, *Die Religionspolitik Justinians*, i., Würzburg, 1896; W. H. Hutton, *The Church of the Sixth Century*, London, 1897; F. Diekamp, *Die origenistischen Streitigkeiten und das 5. ökumenische Konzil*, Münster, 1899; O. Baumstark, in *Oriens Christianus*, ii (1902), 151–169, 358–389; F. Schmid, in *ZKT*, xxx. 2 (1902); J. Pargoire, *L'Église byzantine 527–847*, Paris, 1905; Gibbon, *Decline and Fall*, chap. xlvii.; *DCB*, iii. 308–320; *KL*, viii. 1781–1797.

MONOTHELITES, mon'eth-el-aits.

Rise under Sergius (§ 1).
Union of Monophysites and Monothelites (§ 2).
The Statement of Sophronius; the Ekthesis (§ 3).
Rising Opposition to the Doctrine (§ 4).
The Trullan Councils (§ 5).
Basis in Patristic Dogmatics (§ 6).
Relation to New-Testament Statements (§ 7).

1. Rise under Sergius.

The Monothelites owe their origin to an attempt to bridge over the difference between the orthodox position based on the decrees of the Council of Chalcedon and the Monophysite principles (see MONOPHYSITES), which had caused a schism in the Eastern Church. The impulse to this reconciliation was twofold. During the age of Justinian the development of theology had tended toward the Christology of Cyril to whom the Monophysites had always appealed. The Emperor Heraclius (610–641) had political reasons for encouraging the movement. The Asiatic provinces of the empire were being invaded both by the Persians and the Arabs, and it was necessary to consolidate the population for defense. The emperor was powerfully supported by the Patriarch Sergius (q.v.), whose sympathies were with the program of union from the first. It was theological discussion in Alexandria that first brought to the front the terms "one energy" and "one will" or at least "one state of will" as descriptive of Monophysite views. This teaching had been opposed by the Patriarch Eulogius (q.v.), but Sergius was not prevented by this from establishing relations with the Alexandrian adherents of "one energy" and "one will." He requested a Monophysite leader, Georgius Arsas, to supply him with the proofs to which he appealed for the teaching of "one will." His conciliatory letter excited the displeasure of the Patriarch Johannes Eleemon (q.v.), who was prevented only by the capture of Alexandria by the Persians from taking steps to protest against Sergius' scheme (Maximus Confessor, in *MPG*, xci. 333). During the next few years Sergius won over the emperor to his plan of union based on the teaching of "one energy"; more than once during his residence in the East, Heraclius attempted to secure prominent bishops as adherents for the new teaching. Later, the Metropolitan Cyrus of Phasis is found corresponding with Sergius and asking for further information on this subject (Mansi, *Concilia*, xii. 525 sqq., 560–661). He was referred by the patriarch to the letter of Pope Leo I. as bearing witness to the fact that the teaching of two "energies" had not formed a part of orthodox dogma. He also cited a letter not now extant from the Patriarch Mennas of Constantinople to Pope Vigilius, which contained the expression "one will of Christ" and "one life-making energy." He used the same arguments with several other bishops to win them over to his plan.

For some years there is obscurity about the success of the movement. But in 631, Cyrus was appointed patriarch of Alexandria under the distinct condition that he would work for reunion with the Monophysites. The conditions were carried out, for on June 3, 633, the principles of union were formulated on the basis that the one Lord Jesus Christ acts in a human and divine way with one human-divine energy (Mansi, *Concilia*, xi. 564 sqq.). The teaching of Cyril was appealed to concerning the one incarnate nature; the recognized theopaschite principles of the Church were especially stressed. The result was that Cyrus reported the adherence of thousands of Monophysites. About the same time the Armenians united with the orthodox Church at a synod at Karim at which the emperor was present. In 634 Heraclius was arranging a union with the Monophysite patriarch of Antioch, Athanasius, whom he agreed to appoint orthodox patriarch on condition that he accepted the Council of Chalcedon with the Monothelite interpretation (*Vita Maximi*, *MPG*, xc. 76–77). At this point a new difficulty arose through the interference of the monk Sophronius (q.v.), who came from Palestine to Egypt to protest against the terms of union with the Monophysites (Mansi, xi. 532–533, x. 690–691). The Patriarch Cyrus defended his conciliatory policy, appealing in its defense to historic precedents. Sophronius, still discontented, proceeded to Constantinople and attempted to induce Sergius to remove the expression "one energy" from the act of union. Sergius refused, but he directed Cyrus not to allow any dispute over the one or two energies, but to insist on the fact that the one and same incarnate Logos was the source of each divine and human action. Especially to be avoided was the teaching of two wills. In 634 the patriarch of Constantinople was directed to furnish to the emperor passages from the writing of Mennas to prove the position as to the single energy. Sergius advised that speculation on this subject be dropped. He placed the situation before Pope Honorius, who, in a writing now extant only in a Greek translation, agreed with the patriarch's position, accused Sophronius of bringing up idle questions, and expressed the opinion that the controversy over one or two energies should be abandoned or left to logicians; the use of either expression, he declared, savored either of Nestorianism or Eutychianism. On one point he was perfectly definite: "We confess one will of the Lord Jesus Christ." "There can be no question," he said, "of a second different or opposing will." Even passages like John v. 30 and Matt. xxvi. 39, where Christ seems to set his own and the divine will in contrast, do not really prove a different will but refer only to the "economy" of the assumed manhood. In these places, he argues, Christ is speaking as our example, that we may follow his footsteps and that each may choose not his own will but the will of God.

2. Union of Monophysites and Monothelites.

In the mean time Sophronius had been elevated to the patriarchal see of Jerusalem. He took occasion immediately to issue the so-called *Synodikon* (*MPG*, lxxxvii. 3, cols. 3148–3200), in which he laid down the following principles: that from the two natures, divine and human, two energies proceed; the human conditions of the life of the Son of God were real. Room was given to human nature to do and to suffer what is peculiar to human nature. This was voluntary, but the process took place after a natural way. All of the words and works of both natures are to be referred to the one person of the God-man, but the unity is not a simple one. Sophronius applies to it the expression of Dionysius "a new and divine-human energy"; he makes no mention of two wills. He attempted to get Honorius' support against the Monothelites. The pope tried to quiet his difficulties by appealing to the Scriptures where nothing is said about one or two energies, stating that both natures were naturally united in the one Christ (Mansi, xi. 579–581). Sophronius agreed to reject the expression "two energies" and Cyrus of Alexandria consented to give up speaking of "one energy." It is on this basis that Sergius in the year 636 prepared the so-called *Ekthesis* (Mansi, *Concilia*, x. 991–998), which was signed by the emperor in 638. This stated that neither one nor two energies are to be spoken of. Although there was precedent for the use of "one energy" in the writings of the Fathers, the term might be considered to be a denial of the two natures; "two energies" was not supported by authority and might be interpreted as establishing two contradictory wills. There is one will in Christ; at no point of time does his body, endowed with reason and soul, fulfil separately its own natural motion contrary to the impulse of the divine Logos

3. The Statement of Sophronius; the Ekthesis.

united hypostatically with it, but only at what time and in what way and in what degree the Logos himself wills it. This amounted to a practical abandonment of monergism, but was an emphatic statement of Monothelitism.

Sergius was succeeded by a patriarch of like views, Pyrrhus (638–641). In Italy the emperor's religious policy met with great disfavor. Severinus, who followed Honorius as pope (638), and his successor John IV. led the opposition.

4. Rising Opposition to the Doctrine.

The *Ekthesis* was condemned at a Roman synod (641; Mansi, x. 607). John asked the new emperors, the sons of Heraclius, Constantine and Heracleon, to withdraw the document, and wrote explaining and apologizing for Honorius' acceptance of the one-will theory (Mansi, *Concilia*, x. 682–686). Political changes led to the fall of Pyrrhus, who took refuge in North Africa after a celebrated disputation with Maximus the Confessor, the records of which are most important for this controversy—giving up his Monothelite views. The African churches warmly seconded the papal protest against Monothelitism, and appealed to the emperor to abandon the false teaching. Pyrrhus, now in Ravenna, was induced by court influence to return to the Monothelite position. The pope excommunicated him and declared his successor, Paul, patriarch of Constantinople, deposed. Paul attempted to settle the difficulty by abandoning the *Ekthesis* and by inducing the emperor to publish a new religious document called the *Typus* (648), which forbade, under severe penalties, discussion of the question as to whether Christ had one or two wills (Mansi, x. 1029–32). The question came up in an acute form in a widely attended Roman synod held in 649 under Martin I. (Mansi, x. 863–1188). It specially added to the Chalcedonian creed the doctrine of two natural wills and two natural energies, explaining as a deduction from Cyril's teaching on the incarnation that there is one nature of the God-Logos incarnated, and that the word "incarnated" indicates a full and undiminished human nature apart from sin. The unity of the closely united wills is made dependent on the operation of a nature willing man's salvation. Martin sent the decrees to Constantinople and took active steps in Gaul, North Africa, and even in the East to bring support to them. He was accused of treasonable relations with the exarch of Ravenna, was taken forcibly to Constantinople, and from there sent into exile where he died (655). His successor, Eugenius (654), was inclined to compromise on the basis of allowing the conception of two wills as well as of one will, the terms to be interpreted from different points of view. The hypostatic union constituted one, but the fact of the conjunction of the two natures made it allowable to speak of two. Maximus the Confessor, who has been already mentioned as taking a prominent part in the controversy from the first, was appealed to as an authority for this last declaration (*MPG*, xci. 229c), but he denied in several public letters that he had ever held such teaching and was active in raising public opinion in the West against it. But for a while communion between Rome and Constantinople was restored; Vitalian worked in harmony with the Emperor Constans, who was loyally received in Rome in 663. While the Eastern Empire was resisting the attacks of the Avars, Bulgarians, and Saracens, difficulties again rose between the two sees. The understanding between Rome and Constantinople was interrupted, and Adeodatus (q.v.) declined the *Synodikon* of Constantine I. of Constantinople (Mansi, *Concilia*, xi. 576). The name of Pope Vitalian (657–672) was stricken from the diptychs in Constantinople. The Emperor Constantine Pogonatus (668–685) tried to arrange a reconciliation. Pope Agatho (678–681) took occasion to rally about him the support of the Western Church, and proclaimed himself the representative of orthodox teaching, declaring that the patriarchs of Constantinople had introduced heretical tendencies into the church. As the patriarch, Theodore (676–678), resisted the emperor's conciliatory policy, he was deposed and Georgius was appointed in his place, who carried out imperial directions to summon and consult the metropolitans and bishops of his patriarchate.

This gathering became the sixth Ecumenical Council, called Trullan because it met in the domed hall (*troullos*) of the imperial palace. It lasted from Nov. 7, 680, to Sept. 16, 681 (Mansi, *Concilia*, xi. 189–922).

5. The Trullan Councils.

Macarius of Antioch defended the Monothelite standpoint. He appealed to the letter of Mennas to Vigilius, to Vigilius's letters to Justinian and Theodore, all of which were declared by the Roman representatives to be fabricated by the Monothelites. The patriarch of Constantinople, supported by his bishops, was openly in favor of the views of Agatho. Pope Vitalian's name was restored to the diptychs, Macarius and his supporter Stephanus were deposed for falsification of documents and for heresy. In the thirteenth session, on Mar. 28, Pope Honorius, along with several of the recent patriarchs of Constantinople, all of whom had been condemned in a letter from Agatho, were anathematized by the council. Honorius was placed with the other Monothelite leaders, because the council considered that his letter to Sergius proved that he was a Monothelite himself and established his godless teaching. All compromise plans were rejected, and the synod would hear nothing of the patriarch's attempts to save the reputations of his predecessors. In the eighteenth session, a dogmatic decree was accepted, acknowledging the teaching of two natural wills and two natural energies, but stating that the two natural wills are not opposed. Rather the human will follows and is subordinate to the divine will. In accordance with the doctrine of Athanasius, that Christ's body is called and is the body of the divine Logos, the natural will of his body is called and is the proper will of the Logos; just as his holy, sinless, rational body is not done away with by the deification, but continues in its own proper limitations and relations, so by the deification the human will is not destroyed but preserved. Agatho died before the council concluded its sessions. Macarius, who was sent to Rome for instruction, refused to retract, and with his adherents was imprisoned in a monastery. The second Trullan Council of 692 accepted the acts of the first. One emperor, Philippicus Bardanes (711–713), attempted to reestablish Monothelitism, but unsuccessfully.

The Monothelite discussion may be considered a sequence of the Monophysite controversy. An important point, however, to notice is that correct diphysite opinion had not previously led to diothelite consequences. Sergius in his letter to Cyrus of Phasis makes a good deal of this fact and insists that no evidence for the expression "two energies" can be found in earlier teachers. Although this statement is not true, as several authorities used it (Eustathius, *MPG*, lxxxvi. 1, 909 B; Justinian, ib. 1149A), yet Sergius was correct in pointing out the lack of recognized patristic examples. His case is still better as concerns the use of the term "two wills." Apparently it had not been a matter of debate to any considerable extent; Eulogius of Alexandria is the only writer who made the question the subject of polemical discussion (*MPG*, lxxxvi. 2, 2939–44). Interest in it seems to have been limited to Alexandria. Sergius was not aware of the existence of this work of Eulogius and it escaped the notice even of Photius. It can not be said that the monergistic question was decided in the time of Justinian along lines identical with those of its latest settlement. It is true, though, that the Leonine teaching concerning the dual nature logically admits of two natural energies. Indeed Sergius may be accused of quibbling when he appeals to Leo for support, since that pope had never used the expression "two energies." It must be allowed, though, that the point of departure for the monergistic view was in no way unorthodox. It is fair to contend that as from the moment of the Incarnation the personal center in which the human nature subsists and grows is the person of the Logos, all that Christ says or does can be ascribed to the one energy of the God-man. Good patristic precedent is found for this position, especially the passage appealed to by Sergius and his supporters from Dionysius, where the expression "one theandric energy" is used (*MPG*, iii. 1072C), and the passage from Cyril, where, in commenting on Luke viii. 54, he had spoken of Christ's "showing through both, namely, the commanding word and the touch with the hand, one correlated energy" (*MPG*, lxxiii. 577C). The idea of the monergists was that there is one sole source for all the actions of the God-man, that is, the divine nature. The impulses of this source are carried out through the rational human soul and through the human body. The acts and activities of Christ, they claimed, do not have their origin in the human nature, as this does not subsist for itself. There is one energy, its creator God, its instrument humanity; there is one will and that divine. Sergius could claim orthodoxy for his statement that the body of the Lord, endowed with soul and spirit, carried out its natural motions according to the measure of the divine will. And he could say that as man's body is controlled by his rational soul, so with Christ the whole complex of his human nature is always under the control of the Godhead.

6. Basis in Patristic Dogmatics.

The objections to the unity of the "energy" are concerned with the involved necessity that the distinctively human element with its self-determined activity would be done away; human nature would be reduced to a dead organ, without soul, or, at least, without reason. On this account the Monothelites were affirmed to be followers of Apollinaris. On account of the obscurities and ambiguities involved in the term "energy," Sergius and his school abandoned its use, and concentrated their attention on the kernel of the whole question, the unity of the will. For two wills seem to call for two willing subjects. When passages like Matt. xxvi. 39, with their contrast of the human and divine will, were appealed to, they argued against the two-will theory on the basis that with the appropriation of human nature through the personal Logos, a will that makes itself known in the personal subject of the God-man, in distinction from his divine will, must be due to an undivine direction in the nature which has been assumed. They appealed to Gregory of Nyssa's statement (*Oratio* ii., *De filio*) "for his act of will is in no way contrary to God, it is wholly from God." They insisted on the impossibility of two mutually distinct wills even if they had the same content, and quoted the dictum of Macarius: "For it is impossible that there be in one and the same Christ, our God, two wills together and at the same time contrary, even if they are alike." More ancient patristic authorities in their comments on this passage of St. Matthew treat it as if the God-man, in conditioning himself to a human will, assumed as it were voluntarily a special character in this as a distinct act of salvation. The Monothelites made use of this explanation, for they did not deny a human operation, they only affirm that it was called forth by the divine will. Accordingly, in relation to the divine energy, the human manifestation of it is passive rather than active. When Gregory of Nyssa (*MPG*, xlvi. 616D), speaking of Christ, says, the soul wills, he means, according, to Monothelite explanation, that the willing of the soul takes place through the divine willing of the Godhead, which is personally united with it. It is, therefore, divine willing in human form. The Monothelite conception, therefore, was not far removed from the position of the Church on the teaching of the incarnation. Even Maximus himself, after the term "one energy" had been abandoned, made no essential objection to the standpoint of Pyrrhus. But through the efforts of Maximus, the logical consequences of the Chalcedonian decrees were drawn. The will was treated as an essential and characteristic part of human nature. He who denies the human will in Christ, denies the human soul in him. If Christ did not take a human will, but only adopted one, he placed himself in the relation of a willing human subject; the taking of all the other characteristics of humanity must be placed in the same class and the whole incarnation becomes docetic. Yet the opponents of Monothelitism were careful not to allow to Christ a gnomic will, that is, he did not decide for the good through weighing arguments for and against it; unity of the human nature with the

7. Relation to New-Testament Statements.

divine Logos directed necessarily the decision toward the selection of the good. Maximus was not afraid of saying that the God-man had, according to his nature, a human will, but according to his essence, a divine one. This statement is hard to reconcile with the Scriptural passages adduced to prove the duality of the will (John i. 43, v. 21, xvii. 24, xix. 28; Matt. xxvii. 34; Luke xiii. 24); it shows how close Maximus approached Monothelite terminology. See CHRISTOLOGY, V., § 2. (G. KRÜGER.)

BIBLIOGRAPHY: Sources are: The acts of the Lateran and other synods and councils mentioned in the text, for which consult Mansi, *Concilia*, vols. x.–xi., and Hefele, *Conciliengeschichte*, books xvi.–xvii. in the Ger. and Fr. (vol. iii.) and in Eng. (vol. v.); *Collectanea ad Joannem diaconum*, most convenient in *MPL*, cxxix. 561–690; the *Opera* of Maximus the Confessor, also convenient in *MPG*, xc.–xci.; the *Chronikon paschale*, in *MPG*, xcvii.; the *Historia syntomos* of the Patriarch Nicephorus, ed. C. de Boor, Leipsic, 1880; the *Chronographia* of Theophanes, ed. De Boor, ib. 1883–85; the *Vita Maximi Confessoris*, in *MPG*, xc. 67–110. Earlier discussions of note are: F. Combefis, *Auctarium novum*, ii. 1–198, Paris, 1648; J. B. Tamagnini, *Hist. Monotheletarum*, ib. 1678; C. W. F. Walch, *Historie der Ketzereien*, ix. 1–666, Leipsic, 1780. Of modern discussions not to be overlooked is G. Owsepian, *Die Entstehungsgeschichte des Monothelitismus*, Leipsic, 1897. Consult further: F. C. Baur, *Die christliche Lehre von der Dreieinigkeit und Menschwerdung Gottes*, ii. 96–128, Tübingen, 1842; I. A. Dorner, *Development of the Doctrine of the Person of Christ*, 5 vols., Edinburgh, 1862; O. Bardenhewer, in *TQ*, lxxviii (1896), 353–401; Krumbacher, *Geschichte*, pp. 946–959; F. Gregorovius, *Hist. of the City of Rome*, vol. ii., chap. v., London, 1894. The subject is, of course, treated in the works on the church history of the period, e.g., Schaff, *Christian Church*, iv. 489–511; Neander, *Christian Church*, iii. 175–197; and in those on the history of dogma, e.g., Harnack, *Dogma*, vols. iii.–v. Note also the works given under CHRISTOLOGY.

For the relation of Honorius to the discussion and the consequent debate in its bearing upon infallibility see the literature under HONORIUS, and P. Bottata, *Pope Honorius before the Tribunal of Reason and History*, London, 1868; G. Schneemann, *Studien über die Honoriusfrage*, Freiburg, 1868; J. von Hefele, *Honorius und das sechste allgemeine Concil*, Tübingen, 1870, Eng. transl., in *Presbyterian Quarterly and Presbyterian Review*, Apr., 1872; J. Pennachi, *De Honorii I. . . causa in concilio VI.*, Rome, 1870; P. Le P. Renouf, *The Condemnation of Pope Honorius*, London, 1868; idem, *The Case of Honorius Reconsidered*, ib. 1870; J. J. I. von Döllinger, *Fables Respecting the Popes in the Middle Ages*, pp. 223–248, New York, 1872.

MONSELL, JOHN SAMUEL BEWLEY: English hymnist; b. at St. Columb's (1 m. n.e. of Londonderry), Ireland, Mar. 2, 1811; d. at Guildford, Surrey, England, Apr. 9, 1875. He graduated from Trinity College, Dublin (B.A., 1832; LL.B. and LL.D., 1856); was ordained deacon in 1834, and priest 1835; was successively chaplain to Bishop Mant, chancellor of the diocese of Connor, and rector of Ramoan; and became vicar of Egham, Surrey, 1853, and rural dean; then rector of St. Nicholas, Guildford, 1870. His verse has been drawn upon largely for hymnological collections. He was the author of *Hymns and Miscellaneous Poems* (Dublin, 1837); *Parish Musings, in Verse* (London, 1850); *Verses Addressed to the Cross* (1854); *His Presence, not his Memory* (1855); *Spiritual Songs for Sundays and Holidays throughout the Year* (1857); *The Beatitudes, Sermons* (1861); *Hymns of Love and Praise for the Church's Year* (1863); *The Passing Bell and Other Poems* (1866); *Our New Vicar, or Plain Words on Ritual and Parish Work* (1867); *Lights and Shadows* (1868); *Teachings of the Epiphany* (1871); *Watches by the Cross* (1874); *Simon the Cyrenian, and Other Poems* (1876). He edited also *The Parish Hymnal* (1873). Among his individual hymns are "Earth below is teeming" and "Holy offerings rich and rare."

BIBLIOGRAPHY: *DNB*, xxxviii. 192–193; S. W. Duffield, *English Hymns*, p. 235 et passim, New York, 1886; Julian, *Hymnology*, pp. 762–763, 1673–74.

MONSTRANCE. See VESSELS, SACRED, § 3.

MONTAGU (MOUNTAGUE), RICHARD: Church of England bishop; b. at Dorney (26 m. w. of London) in Buckinghamshire, during Christmastide, 1577; d. at Norwich Apr. 13, 1641. He was educated at Eton and King's College, Cambridge (B.A., 1598; M.A., 1602; and B.D., 1609). He received the living at Wooton Courtney, 1610; was made rector at Stanford Rivers, Essex, and fellow of Eton, 1611; dean of Hereford, 1616; canon of Windsor, 1617; and archdeacon of Hereford the same year. Throughout life Montagu was continuously active as pamphleteer and controversialist, aiming, as he professed, to support the Church of England against its enemies on both sides. His *Diatribæ* (London, 1621) in defense of tithes threw him into the brunt of popular controversy. The *Immediate Address unto God Alone* (1624) brought upon him the charge of advocating prayer to saints and angels. This he answered with his *Apello Cæsarem* (1625) in which he sought to vindicate himself against the charge of Arminianism and popery. It was issued without license; and in 1626 the House of Commons petitioned the king that the book be burned and the author fitly punished. In 1628 he was elected bishop of Chichester. He was strenuously opposed by the Presbyterian tendency, but applied himself assiduously to the promotion of his diocese and, in 1638, was elected bishop of Norwich. He bore the reputation of great scholarship and left besides his controversial works: *Eusebii de demonstratione evangelica* (Paris, 1628); *Apparatus ad origines ecclesiasticas* (Oxford, 1635); *De originibus ecclesiasticis* (London, 1636, 1640); and *The Acts and Monuments of the Church before Christ Incarnate* (1642).

BIBLIOGRAPHY: J. H. Overton, *The Church in England*, ii. 43–56, 59, London, 1897; W. A. Shaw, *Hist. of the English Church, 1640–60*, i. 323, ii. 412, 430, New York, 1900; W. H. Hutton, *The English Church (1625–1714)*, London, 1903; *DNB*, xxxviii. 266–270.

MONTALEMBERT, mōn″tā″lān″bār′, **CHARLES FORBES RENÉ, COUNT DE TRYON:** French Roman Catholic; b. at London Apr. 15, 1810; d. at Paris Mar. 12, 1870. After receiving his education at the Collège Sainte Barbe, already imbued with liberal Roman Catholic principles, he became associated with Lamennais and Lacordaire (qq.v.) in Paris about 1830; in 1832, when the encyclical of Aug. 15 condemned Lamennais and his friends, Montalembert reluctantly parted company with him, and made his formal submission to Cardinal Pacca Dec. 8, 1834. He then spent several years in Italy and Germany, devoting himself particularly to the study of early legend and religious art, primarily of the medieval period. The results were his *Histoire de Sainte Elisabeth d'Hongrie* (Paris,

1836) and *Du vandelisme et du catholicisme dans l'art* (1839). He lived in Madeira, 1842–44, but still continued his political activity, writing several pamphlets on questions of the day. In the house of peers, which he had entered in 1835, Montalembert championed Roman Catholicism, for which he sought to regain temporal power; but his wish to found an organized Roman Catholic party gained little favor among the bishops, who feared lay participation in ecclesiastical and religious affairs. When Pius IX. ascended the papal throne, Montalembert hoped for a triumph of liberal Roman Catholicism; elected representative for the department of Doubs, he continued his defense of the Church; while on the *coup d'état* of Dec. 2, 1851, he became a member of the commission consultatif, and from 1852 to 1857 was a member of the corps legislatif. At last, hopeless of his cause, he retired from public life, representing liberal Roman Catholicism only in *Le Correspondant*, and expressed his fear of the approaching downfall of the temporal power of the Church in his *Pie IX. et la France en 1849 et en 1859* (Paris, 1860; Eng. transl., *Pius the IX. and France in 1849 and 1859*, Boston, 1861). The encyclical of 1864 was a severe blow to his liberalistic hopes; he sought consolation in writing his *Les Moines d'occident* (5 vols., Paris, 1860–1867; Eng. transl., 7 vols., *The Monks of the West*, London, 1861–79). He died before the proclamation of the infallibility of the pope, yet his letters show that, much as he deprecated the doctrine, he would, had he lived, have assented to the will of the Church. A few other noteworthy books are: *Des Intérêts catholiques au XIXe siècle* (Paris, 1852; Eng. transl., *Catholic Interests in the Nineteenth Century*, London, 1852); *De l'avenir de l'Angleterre* (Paris, 1856; Eng. transl., *The Political Future of England*, London, 1856); *Un débat sur l'Inde au parlement anglais* (Brussels, 1858; Eng. transl., *Montalembert on Constitutional Liberty*, London, 1858); and *L'Insurrection polonaise* (Paris, 1863; Eng. transl., *The Insurrection in Poland*, London, 1863). His works were collected in 9 vols., Paris, 1861–68. (C. Pfender.)

Bibliography: The main biography in English is by Mrs. M. O. Oliphant, 2 vols., Edinburgh, 1872; in French the notable work is by E. Lecanuet, 3 vols., Paris, 1895–1901. Briefer notices and estimates are: A. Cochin, Paris, 1870; A. L. A. Perraud, ib. 1870; G. White, London, 1870; J. T. Foisset, Lyons, 1877; L. Bouthors, Abbeville, 1896; C. de Meaux, Paris, 1897; and E. Lecanuet, *L'Église et le second empire*, vol. iii., Paris, 1902. His *Correspondance* with the Abbé Texier (1835–59) was published, Paris, 1899, and that with Cornudet in 1905.

MONTANUS, mon-tê'nus, **MONTANISM**, mon'-ta-nizm.

The chronology of the Montanistic movement has as its starting-point the remark of its anonymous opponent in Eusebius (*Hist. eccl.*, V., xvii. 4) that thirteen years of peace had passed since the death of the Montanistic prophetess Maximilla. This anonymous author must have written about 192–193, and Maximilla must accordingly have died in 179. The year of her death is likewise mentioned by Epiphanius (*Hær.*, xlviii. 2), especially as she had associated that event with the end of the world. In the same year that she died, according to Epiphanius, Montanus began his activity. The latter event is placed by the anonymous writer (Eusebius, *Hist. eccl.*, V., xvi. 7) in the proconsulate of Gratus, this name evidently being corrupted from *Kodratos* (Quadratus). Since a Quadratus was proconsul of Asia Minor in 155 and another in 166, the Montanistic movement must have originated in one of these two years. By 177 the movement must have had a long development behind it; and even in the writings of Apollinaris the tenets of Montanism seem to have been condemned. Moreover, Maximilla died not long after Montanus and Prisca, and it is noteworthy that the prophecies lamenting persecutions by the Church are ascribed to her alone. A fruitless effort to convict Maximilla is mentioned both by the anonymous writer and by the anti-Montanist Apollonius (Eusebius, *Hist. eccl.*, V., xvi. 17–18, xviii. 13) in connection with the probably contemporary martyrdom of Thraseas. The latter event, according to Rufinus, took place under Sergius Paulus, who was apparently proconsul in Asia Minor about 166–167. In addition to all this, the antipathy of the Alogi (q.v.; see also Monarchianism) to the Johannine writings seems to have been evoked by the appeal of the Montanists to them; and since the Montanistic prophets claimed to have received their prophetic powers from Quadratus and Ammia, the latter two can not have been long previous to the former. The account of the martyrdom of Polycarp, finally, shows that at that time tendencies existed in Phrygia which corresponded to the Montanistic views. It is evident, therefore, that the Montanistic movement must have arisen after the middle of the second century. About this same time a transformation began in the life of the Church. As in the early period the prophets had exercised the first authority in the churches (cf. Acts xiii. 1 sqq., and the *Didache*), so now those who were vested with the administration of the organized communities were termed "gifted with the Spirit." The Church now felt herself to be catholic as opposed to the heretics; but with the increase in her membership there came an accession of earthly interests; the lively expectation of the last day (I Clement, lix. 4; II Clement xx. 2–3; Barnabas iv. 3, 9, xv. 5 sqq.; *Didache* ix. 3, x. 5–6, xvi.) gave place to other views. A conservative reaction was the natural result. The struggle was most intense in Asia Minor; and here, where the Church could already point to lights of prophecy (Eusebius, *Hist. eccl.*, III., xxxi., V., i. 49, iii. 2), there was a peculiar inspiration for the revival of prophecy.

1. The Origin of Montanism.

Montanus, but recently become a Christian, appeared in a village of Phrygia as such a prophet. He is said by Jerome to have been formerly a priest of Cybele, and the "new prophecy" was doubtless influenced by the wild enthusiasm of the Phrygian religious nature. The very names applied to the

Montanists—Phrygians and Cataphrygians—imply that the movement had a quasi-national character.

2. Montanus; His Mode of Prophecy. Voluntarily placing himself in a state of abstraction, Montanus is said to have proceeded to involuntary ecstacy, seeing in this suppression of self-consciousness, and in his submission to the Godhead as a will-less instrument the proof of his perfect prophecy (see ECSTASY). This form of prophesying, however, was regarded as contrary to the custom of the Church, essentially different as it was from the prophecies recorded in the New Testament and the writings of the early Church. Moreover, the ecstatic utterances of Montanus must gradually have changed from what was customary in the Church. The Montanists appealed in support of their form of prophecy to the examples of ecstacy recorded in the Bible, yet at the same time claimed that their mode was a proof of the magnitude of the new revelation. It was, indeed, the completion of the law of Christ, and in it the promised Paraclete had appeared, since the time of full maturity had now replaced childhood (I Cor. xiii. 11). The new prophecy, therefore, not only was a protest against suppression, but also claimed the right, in view of the approaching end of all things, to regulate life in the Church.

On the other hand, Montanistic prophecy made no claim to reveal further the truths of salvation. Whenever it touched on dogmatic problems, its utterances were designed only to support the Church's tradition.

3. Characteristics of Early Montanism. The practical trend of Montanism led it to defend the doctrine of the resurrection of the dead and to develop a rich eschatology. The entire purpose, in fact, of the new prophecy was preparation for the approaching end, and expectation of this great event should determine the entire life of the Christian. Yet the new prophecy was seldom introduced by new forms; what had hitherto been voluntary now became duty. Thus, if the Church approved only first marriage and virginity, the Montanists regarded second marriages as impure and excluded those who contracted them. Sexual purity was a necessary condition for receiving revelations, and the voluntary fasts on the "station days" were extended from three to six in the afternoon and made obligatory. There were likewise *zerophagia*, or half fasts, consisting in abstinence from meat, soups, and juicy fruits, and "fasts proper," apparently kept at the same time as the public celebrations peculiar to the Montanists. Again, wherever the Church permitted a distinction between a laxer and a stricter rule, the Montanists invariably allowed only the latter, so that, for example, flight in persecution was forbidden and martyrdom was encouraged. All these requirements were made by the Paraclete because the last day was nigh, and marriage should no longer be contracted. Because of the shortness of the time, the Paraclete could annul the words of Paul as Christ had abrogated those of Moses. Even fasting was advocated by Tertullian (*De jejunio*, xii.) not for ascetic reasons, but as a preparation for the last day; while sinners must be excluded from the Church that, as the pure bride of Christ, she might prepare to receive the bridegroom. In its consistency Montanism urged its followers to withdraw from their churches and assemble at Pepuza in Phrygia, which Montanus plainly considered the "wilderness" of Rev. xii. 14, that they might await the second advent. At the same time he arranged for a propaganda. As prophetesses he had Prisca (or Priscilla) and Maximilla, whose sayings, like those of Montanus himself, were collected by their followers into quasi-Gospels, even though such a proceeding was a deviation from the fundamental concepts of Montanism. Montanus also found valuable support in one Alcibiades (Miltiades?) and Theodotus, the latter being mockingly designated the first steward of the new prophecy (Eusebius, *Hist. eccl.*, V., xvi. 14). A similar position was held somewhat later by a certain Themistion, while a martyr Alexander was also highly honored by the sect. The prophets were succeeded in the development of organized Montanism by the *Cenones*, who assumed a place immediately after the patriarchs and above the bishops. While only a portion of the followers of Montanus could be emancipated from all their previous associations, all retained a close connection with Pepuza, where they sent representatives at the feast of the Paraclete (probably Whitsuntide), while those who could not attend took part in spirit by a common fast.

The precise date of the formal organization of the Montanists as a distinct sect is uncertain. The adherents of the new prophecy sought to remain members of the Catholic Church, and

4. Catholic Opposition. the Church hesitated long before she definitely decided against them. There was much in common in Catholic and Montanist teaching—the ethical ideals of marital life, fasting, martyrdom, and the expectation of the last day—while a hasty rejection of prophecy was regarded as sin against the Holy Ghost (*Didache*, xi. 7). Nevertheless, sharp opposition to the new prophecy soon arose, first headed by Apollonius (q.v., 2), and attempts were also made to exorcise both Prisca and Maximilla. Various synods of Asia Minor discussed the problem, filled with a vague dread of the new movement. The ecstatic aspect of the sect seems first to have aroused suspicion, and was attacked in a special polemic by Miltiades (q.v.), while the Alogi (q.v.) went to the extreme of denying the authenticity of all the Johannine writings because of the Montanist appeal to the Apocalypse and to the promise of the Paraclete in the Gospel of John. Yet even the antagonists of the Alogi assumed a position of hostility toward the new prophecy, and by the seventh decade of the second century the opposition to Montanism was evidently general. In the lifetime of Maximilla the antagonism had become intense, for she makes the Spirit lament that he was driven away like a wolf. For the ecstasy of the prophets the Montanists appealed to Gen. ii. 7 sqq.; Ps. cxvi. 11; and Acts x. 10, as well as to the prophecies recorded in Acts xv. 32, xxi. 11; and I Cor. xii. 28, and to John, the daughter of Philip, Ammia, and Quadratus, while they based the right of prophetesses on Miriam and Deborah. Their opponents, on the other hand, declared that prophecy ended with John the Baptist and was sealed by the passion of Christ, also urging the words of Christ and the apostles against false prophets (Matt. vii. 15; II Thess. ii. 9; I John iv. 1–3; and especially I Tim. iv. 1–3). The doctrine that the Paraclete had not come until now was an insult to the apostles; the legalistic requirements of the Montanists destroyed Christian freedom, and directly contravened such passages of the Bible as Isa. lviii. 4–5; Ps. li. 16; Jer. viii. 4; Ezek. xviii. 23; Mark vii. 15; and Matt. xi. 19.

5. Decline of the System.

About 177 the confessors and the church at Lyons sought, without sharing Montanistic views, to plead for a certain recognition of the prophetic gift and to effect a peaceable understanding, writing both to the churches in Asia Minor and to Eleutherus at Rome. Nevertheless, the latter (or possibly Victor) seems to have decided adversely to Montanism; yet the slow exclusion of the sect from the Catholic Church is clear from the fact that about 192 the church at Ancyra was filled with the new prophecy, while forty years after the appearance of Montanus Apollonius had to battle against his teachings, and about 200 Serapion of Antioch had to demonstrate the untenability of Montanistic doctrines. About 230 the Synod of Iconium refused to recognize Montanistic baptism; yet they themselves declared that the Christian faith had arisen with them, and in the eyes of outsiders they were the "Christians of the ancient faith." The Montanists deviated from the Catholic Church in several other respects. They reckoned Easter by the sun and celebrated it on the eighth before the ides of April or on the following Sunday; women might be deacons (on the basis of I Tim. iii. 11), or even priests and deacons (appealing to Gal. iii. 28); they had either three or four seasons of fasting; their doctrine of eight heavens and their accounts of the tortures of the damned point to the use of apocalyptic writings among them. Beginning with the reign of Constantine imperial edicts were issued against them, though these were at first dead letters, at least in Phrygia and its vicinity. Finally, however, Montanism could preserve its existence only in secret. [It is reported that in 550 John of Ephesus had the remains of Montanus and three prophetesses exhumed and burned (J. S. Assemani, *Bibliotheca orientalis*, ii. 88, 3 vols., Rome, 1719–28)].

6. Western Montanism; Tertullian.

Though primarily a phenomenon of the Church of Asia Minor, Montanism spread to the West with a suppression of its ecstatic features and emphasis on its ethical requirements. In Rome it was represented by Proclus, who debated with Caius between 200 and 215. But the great Montanist of the West was Tertullian (q.v.). Led on by its moral earnestness, and predisposed against any conformity with the world, Tertullian saw in the new prophecy the divine seal of his endeavors. In his *Passio Perpetuæ* Montanistic tendencies may already be recognized, and are more strongly expressed in his *De corona* and *De fuga*. As a Montanist he was the protagonist of the Church against Gnosticism; and in his *De ecstasi* he definitely defended the Montanistic revelations, polemizing in part directly against Apollonius. Tertullian's final, though gradual, break with the Church seems to have resulted primarily from its opposition to Callixtus, exemplified in his indignant rejection, in the *De pudicitia*, of the declaration of the pontiff regarding the return to the Church of those guilty of carnal sins, since Tertullian affirmed that only the Spirit in the "pneumatic" could decide in matters of discipline. In his *De monogamia* and *De jejunio* he combated the Catholics as harshly as the "psychics" for their rejection of the things of the Spirit. How ineffectual was the suppression of all revelations by the rejection of Montanism is evident from the case of Cyprian. The followers of Tertullian were won back to the Church by Augustine, although an attempt was made to found a Tertullianistic community at Rome (Prædestinatus, *Hær.*, lxxxvi.). (N. BONWETSCH.)

BIBLIOGRAPHY: The prophetic utterances of the founders of Montanism are collected in F. Münter, *Effata et oracula Montanistarum*, Copenhagen, 1829; in G. N. Bonwetsch, *Die Geschichte des Montanismus*, Erlangen, 1881; and in A. Hilgenfeld, *Die Ketzergeschichte des Urchristenthums*, Leipsic, 1884. Further sources are: the Montanistic writings of Tertullian (Eng. transl. in *ANF*, vol. iii.); Irenæus, *Hær*, III., xi. 9, IV., xxxiii. 6–7; Epiphanius, *Hær*, xlviii.–xlix.; and the passages in Eusebius named in the text. The best single work is that of Bonwetsch, named above. Consult further: C. W. F. Walch, *Historie der Ketzereien*, i. 611–666, Leipsic, 1762; A. Schwegler, *Der Montanismus*, Tübingen, 1841; A. Short, *The Heresies of Montanus, Pelagius*, etc., Oxford, 1846; A. Hilgenfeld, *Glossolalie in der alten Kirche*, pp. 115 sqq., Leipsic, 1850; A. Ritschl, *Entstehung der altkatholischen Kirche*, pp. 402–550, Bonn, 1857; A. Reville, in *Nouvelle revue de théologie*, 1858, and in *Revue des deux mondes*, Nov., 1864; F. C. Baur, *Geschichte der christlichen Kirche*, i. 235–245, 288–295, Leipsic, 1863; E. Ströhlin, *Essai sur le montanisme*, Strasburg, 1870; J. de Soyres, *Montanism and the Primitive Church*, Cambridge, 1878; W. Cunningham, *The Churches of Asia*, London, 1880; W. Belck, *Geschichte des Montanismus*, Leipsic, 1883; H. Weinel, *Die Wirkungen des Geistes und der Geister im nachapostolischen Zeitalter*, Freiburg, 1899; E. C. Selwyn, *The Christian Prophets and the Prophetical Apocalypse*, London, 1900; Harnack, *Dogma*, vols., i.–iii.; idem, *Litteratur*, ii. 363 sqq.; idem, *Expansion of Christianity*, 2 vols., London, 1904–05; Neander, *Christian Church*, i. 206, 508–527, 715, et passim; Schaff, *Christian Church*, ii. chap. x.; *DCB*, iii. 935–945; *KL*, vii. 252–268; and the literature under TERTULLIAN.

MONTE CASSINO: The mother house of the Benedictine order (50 m. n.w. of Naples). For the story of the foundation see BENEDICT OF NURSIA, I., § 3. Though repeatedly disturbed by barbarian hordes during the rule of the three abbots following Benedict (d. 543)—Constantius, Simplicius, and Vitalis—it was first destroyed by the Lombards in 589, when Bonitus was abbot. The monks escaped to Rome, and Pelagius II. permitted them to build a monastery beside the Lateran, where they remained almost a century and a half, enjoying the special favor of Gregory the Great. Meanwhile only a few hermits remained at Monte Cassino, and about 653 it was alleged that the bones of Benedict and his sister Scolastica had been translated to Fleury in France (hence called St. Benoît sur Loire) by Aigulf and his companions. A long controversy consequently arose between the monks of the restored monastery of Monte Cassino and those of Fleury, and a bull of Pope Zacharias implies that the bones in question were in their original grave at Monte

Cassino about 742. The explanation seems to be that merely certain portions of the remains were taken to Fleury.

The monastery of Monte Cassino was restored about 720, during the pontificate of Gregory II., by Abbot Petronax of Brescia (d. 750). During his rule, the autograph copy of Benedict's rule, brought to Rome when the monastery was destroyed, is said to have been returned to Monte Cassino in 748 by Zacharias, who also granted the monastery special privileges and enriched its library. At this same period, too, began the literary fame of Monte Cassino, and here Paul the Deacon (q.v.), ex-chancellor of the last Lombard King Desiderius, wrote his *Historia Longobardorum* and *Expositio in regulam Sancti Benedicti*. The monastery was further enlarged and beautified during the abbacy of Gisolfus (797–817), and was enriched by princely gifts in the period immediately following. Abbot Bertharius (856–884) was a distinguished scholar, both as exegete, grammarian, and physician, and his writings on the latter theme make the beginning of Monte Cassino's services to medical science. The monastery possessed an excellent hospital, and thus influenced the Benedictine monastery of Salerno and its medical school.

A second period of devastation and of seventy years' exile was caused in 884 by the Saracens, who murdered Abbot Bertharius at the altar. The surviving monks fled to Teano, where they remained thirty years, after which they went to Capua. Here they degenerated, but, returning to Monte Cassino, Abbot Aligernus (949–985) began a rigid reform and a restoration of the former grandeur of the monastery. Nevertheless, a new period of degeneration came under Abbots Manso (985–996) and Atenulf (1011–1022), until Theobald (1022–35), aided by Odilo of Cluny, restored strict discipline. Under Desiderius (1059–87; later Pope Victor III.) Monte Cassino reached its zenith. Desiderius turned all his influence to the advantage of the monastery, increasing the number of the monks, restoring the buildings, and beautifying the basilica with the aid of artists from Upper Italy, Amalfi, and Constantinople. He fostered the progress of learning by obtaining valuable liturgical books, and enlarged the monastery hospital.

The policy of Desiderius was continued by his successors Oderisius I. (1087–1105) and Bruno (1107–23). Although Monte Cassino's temporal power declined in the twelfth and thirteenth centuries through the hostility of feudal lords and Hohenstaufen emperors, the monastery was still adorned by noteworthy authors, such as Peter the Deacon, and by artists, especially painters on glass. In 1240 the monks were expelled by Frederick II. The decline of discipline, moreover, had become so pronounced that it could not be permanently restored even by the efforts of Abbot Bernardus Ayglerius (1263–82), who prepared a new rule, nor by Celestine V., who sought to change the Benedictines into Celestines (1294), nor by John XXII., who made the abbey a bishopric and its monks cathedral clergy (1331). In 1349 an earthquake almost annihilated its buildings, and during the pontificate of Urban V. Abbot Andreas of Faenza again made a transitory reform of discipline. After the middle of the fifteenth century Monte Cassino was ruled by secular abbots *in commendam*, who shamelessly robbed it and impaired its discipline. Julius II., in 1504, forced it to accept the reform of St. Justina, and in 1515 Abbot Squarcialupi began an extensive renovation of its buildings.

Throughout the sixteenth century Monte Cassino controlled four bishoprics, two principalities, twenty counties, 1,662 churches, and much besides, while its income was reckoned at half a million ducats. Still more important were its spiritual, artistic, and literary treasures. In 1645 its library was the most important in Italy and one of the most valuable in Europe, containing over 1,000 documents from popes, emperors, kings, and princes, and more than 800 manuscripts earlier than the fourteenth century. In 1866 the monastery was made a national monument of the kingdom of Italy and became an educational institution under clerical control, while at the same time its literary treasures became more generally accessible than had been possible previously. [The monastery of Monte Cassino is a fortress-like structure with a commanding location, 1,715 feet elevation, overlooking the town of Cassino, 85½ m. s.s.e. of Rome. In it are forty monks and some 200 pupils. The buildings are on different levels. Lowest is that in which is shown the cell of St. Benedict; highest is the church, which is richly adorned. The noteworthy frescoes in its subterranean chapels are by German Benedictines. Among the objects shown is a figure of the Virgin Mary which is reported to have once spoken. The library is rich in beautifully written manuscripts.] (O. Zöckler†.)

Bibliography: Sources are to be found in Leo of Ostia, *Chronicon Casinense*, ed. Wattenbach in *MGH, Script.*, vii (1846), 551–727; Peter the Deacon, *De vir. ill.*, in Angelus de Nuce, *Chronica . . monasterii Casinensis*, Paris, 1668, cf. Alfani Versus, *De situ . . monasterii Casinensis*, in A. F. Ozanam, *Documents inédits*, Paris, 1850; and C. Margarini, *Bullarium Casinense*, 2 vols., Venice and Todi, 1750–70. Consult further: E. Gattola, *Historia abbatiæ Casinensis . .*, Venice, 1733–34; W. Giesebrecht, *De litterarum studiis apud Italos*, Berlin, 1844; A. Dentier, *Monastères d'Italie*, 2 vols., Paris, 1866; G. Krätzinger, *Der Benediktinerorden und die Kultur*, Heidelberg, 1876; J. Peter, in *Revue chrétienne*, July, 1881; H. Rickenbach, *Monte Cassino von seiner Gründung bis zu seiner höchsten Blüte . . .*, Einsiedeln, 1884–85; *Tabularium Casinense*, *Spicilegium Casinense*, and *Miscellanea Casinense*, 3 vols., Monte Cassino, 1887–97; L. Tosti, in his *Opera*, vols. xiv.–xvi., Rome, 1888–89; G. Grützmacher, *Die Bedeutung Benedikts von Nursia*, Berlin, 1892; G. Clausse, *Les Origines bénédictines*, pp. 81–110, Paris, 1899; O. Kaemmel, *Herbstbilder aus Italien und Sizilien*, pp. 135–183, Leipsic, 1900; E. Caspar, *Petrus Diaconus und die Monte Cassineser Fälschungen*, Berlin, 1909; Heimbucher, *Orden und Kongregationen*, i. 209 sqq., et passim; *KL*, viii. 1842–47; and also the literature under Benedict of Nursia and the Benedictine Order.

MONTENEGRO: A principality of Europe bounded by Dalmatia, Herzegovina, Rascia (Novi-Bazaar), Albania, and the Adriatic Sea; the estimated area is 3,486 square miles and the population is estimated at 225,000, nine-tenths being Montenegrins, and members of the Orthodox Greek Church, whose metropolitan obtains his commissions from the Holy Synod in Russia, while 13,000 are Mohammedans and 14,000 Roman Catholics, these being Albanians or Serbs. From 1516 to 1852, the bishop or metropolitan held the additional title of prince, there being at the same time a governor of temporal and military affairs. The bishop was long elected by popular vote; but from the time of Daniel I. (1697–1737) the office has been hereditary, needing, however, the confirmation of the Servian patriarch at Ipek, later at Carlovitz, while beginning with the eighteenth century the Czar of Russia became the recognized head. The metropolitan of the capital city, Cetinje, retains a merely qualified influence. As supreme head of the ninety parishes of the land, whose precincts chiefly coincide with those of the temporal districts, he controls most of the parochial clergy as priests; but there are also thirteen small cloisters, whose monks also exercise pastoral duties. The popular education is backward; even the regulation as to a general four years' course of obligatory schooling is far from thoroughly carried out. There are three intermediate schools, and a girls' seminary and boarding-school at Cetinje, established by Russian contributions. The Roman Catholic faith has a considerable following in the southern districts, where they number about 8,000. The Roman Catholics are affiliated, in the main, to the archbishop of Antivari; save the more scattered ones northward, to the bishop of Cattaro. Their pastoral care is committed almost entirely to Franciscans. The Catholic Church became a nationally recognized religious community in Montenegro by the Concordat of 1886 (see CONCORDATS AND DELIMITING BULLS, VI., 2, § 8, 4), and Catholics again enjoy the advantages of the civil code of 1888. The Mohammedans, since conditions are less favorable to them, emigrate more and more to Turkey. W GÖTZ.

BIBLIOGRAPHY: W. Denton, *Montenegro, its People and their History*, London, 1877; P. Coquelle, *Hist. du Monténégro*, Paris, 1895; W. Miller, *The Balkans*, New York, 1898; L. Passarge, *Dalmatien und Montenegro*, Leipsic, 1904; R. Wyon, *The Balkans from within*, London, 1904.

MONTES PIETATIS: Institutions for the relief of the poor on the principle of the pawnshop, but designed to protect their patrons against usury, though a certain interest was charged to cover expenses. Primarily religious institutions, the *montes pietatis* later became secularized. They originated in Italy, where the cardinal of Ostia established one at Orvieto in 1463, which was confirmed by Pius II. Leo X., by the constitution *Inter multiplices* at the tenth session of the fifth Lateran Council (May 4, 1515), gave general approval to the *montes pietatis* and declared their opponents excommunicated. They soon spread to Lombardy and the continental possessions of Venice, and thence reached France, Germany, Holland, England, and other countries. [In New York these institutions are represented by the Provident Loan Society, which has been very successful.] (A. HAUCK.)

BIBLIOGRAPHY: H. Holzapfel, *Die Anfänge der Montes pietatis*, Munich, 1903; W. Endemann, in *Jahrbücher für Nationalökonomie*, i (1863), 324 sqq.; idem, *Studien in der romanisch-kanonistischen Wirtschafts- und Rechtslehre*, i. 460 sqq., Berlin, 1874.

MONTFAUCON, mēn"fō"cōn', BERNARD DE: French Maurist; b. at Soulatge (department of Aude, just east of Toulouse, France) Jan. 16, 1655; d. at Paris Dec. 21, 1741. A scion of a noble family, he entered the army in 1672, serving in Turenne's campaign against Germany until 1674. Resuming his studies, he made his profession in the Maurist congregation on May 13, 1676, and after being stationed at Sorèze, La Grasse, and Bordeaux, he was sent, in 1687, to Saint-Germain des Prés, the scientific center of his order, where he devoted himself primarily to editing Greek Church Fathers. He published, with the collaboration of J. Lopin and A. Pouget, a single volume of a projected *Analecta Græca sive varia opuscula Græca hactenus non edita* (Paris, 1688), which he followed by his *La Verité de l'histoire de Judith* (1690). After publishing the best edition of Athanasius thus far made—*Athanasii archiepiscopi Alexandrini opera omnia* (3 vols., Paris, 1698), he went, with his fellow Maurist Paul Briois, to Italy, since the manuscripts at Paris were inadequate for his plans. While at Rome, and being for a period the administrator of his congregation, he wrote his anonymous *Vindiciæ editionis Sancti Augustini a Benedictinis adornatæ* (Rome, 1699) in answer to Jesuit critics. In 1701 he returned to Paris, where his interests ranged over the literature and all other remains of classical antiquity, as evinced by his *Diarium Italicum, sive monumentorum veterum, bibliothecarum, musæorum, etc. Notitiæ singulares* (Paris, 1702; Eng. transl., *The Travels of Father Montfaucon from Paris through Italy* , London, 1712). In his *Palæographia Græca* (Paris, 1708) he laid the foundations of the science of paleography, while in his *Bibliotheca Coisliniana olim Segueriana* (1715) and his *Bibliotheca bibliothecarum manuscriptorum nova* (1739) he proved his ability as a bibliographer. In his *Collectio nova patrum et scriptorum Græcorum* (2 vols., Paris, 1706) he published much unedited material, including the commentaries of Eusebius on the Psalms and Isaiah, minor writings of Athanasius, and the Christian geography of Cosmas Indicopleustes. This was followed by an edition of the fragments of the *Hexapla—Hexaplorum Origenis quæ supersunt* (2 vols., Paris, 1713; superseded by the work of Frederick Field, q.v.); as well as by a complete edition of Chrysostom (*Joannis Chrysostomi opera omnia*, 13 vols., Paris, 1734–41). Montfaucon's classical interests found expression in his *L'Antiquité expliquée et représentée en figures* (10 vols., Paris, 1719; 5 supplementary vols., 1724; Eng. transl., *Antiquity Explained and Represented in Sculptures*, 10 vols., London, 1821–25), in which he considered the mythology, religion, and private and social life of the Greeks and Romans, with an account of the religious monuments of the Egyptians, Arabs, Syrians, Persians, Scythians, Germans, Gauls, Spaniards, and Carthaginians. The work was continued for France in his *Les Monumens de la monarchie françoise* (5 vols., Paris, 1729–33; partial Eng. transl., *A Description of the Basso Relievos* , London, 1767), of which only the first section, comprising the dynastic monuments to Henry IV., appeared. Among the other works of Montfaucon, who became a member of the Académie des inscriptions et belles lettres in 1719, special mention may be made of his *Le Livre de Philon de la* *vie contemplative avec des observations où l'on fait voir que les Thérapeutes dont il parle étoient Chrétiens* (Paris, 1709); and *Lettres pour et contre sur la fameuse question si les solitaires appellez Thérapeutes . étoient Chrétiens* (1712). Many of his letters, which are preserved in the Bibliothèque Nationale and elsewhere, have been published in Valery's *Correspondance inédite de Mabillon et de Montfaucon avec l'Italie* (3 vols., Paris, 1846); U. Capitaine's *Correspondance de Bernard de Montfaucon avec le baron G. de Crassier* (Liège, 1855); and E. Gigas's *Lettres inédites de divers savants*, vol. ii (Copenhagen, 1892–93). (G. LAUBMANN.)

BIBLIOGRAPHY: E. de Broglie, *La Société de l'abbaye de Saint-Germain des Prés au 18. siècle*, especially ii. 311 323, Paris, 1891; R. P. Tassin, *Hist. littéraire de la congrégation de S. Maur*, pp. 585–616, Brussels, 1770; H. Omont, *Bernard de Montfaucon*, in *Annales du midi*, 1892, pp. 84–90; J. B. Vanel, *Les Bénédictins de S. Maur*, pp. 112 115, Paris, 1896.

MONTGOMERY, mont-gum'e-ri, **HENRY:** Founder of the Remonstrant Synod of Ulster in Ireland; b. in the parish of Killead (on Lough Neagh, 4 m. s. of Antrim), County Antrim, Jan. 16, 1788; d. at Dunmurray (4 m. s.w. of Belfast) Dec. 18, 1865. He studied at Glasgow College (M.A., 1807); was ordained minister of Dunmurray, 1809, and spent his life there. He combined teaching with his pastoral duties, from 1817 to 1839 was head master of the English school in the Belfast Academical Institution, gave lectures to divinity students from 1832, and in 1838 was appointed professor of ecclesiastical history and pastoral theology at Belfast for the association of Irish non-subscribing Presbyterians. During the greater part of his life he was the antagonist of Henry Cooke (q.v.), whose strenuous advocacy of orthodoxy drove him and his associates from the Synod of Ulster in 1829; as an orator and thinker he was Cooke's equal, but he lacked his power to persuade the majority. He was liberal in politics and his views of religious liberty were in advance of his time. His publications were sermons, speeches, and magazine articles.

BIBLIOGRAPHY: J. A. Crozier, *Life of . Henry Montgomery . with Selections from his Speeches and Writings*, vol. i (no more published), London, 1875; idem, *Henry Montgomery*, ib. 1888; the literature under COOKE, HENRY; *DNB*, xxxviii. 313–315.

MONTGOMERY, JAMES: English religious poet and hymn-writer; b. at Irvine (25 m. s.w. of Glasgow), Scotland, Nov. 4, 1771; d. at Sheffield, England, Apr. 30, 1854. After attending school in Fulneck, the chief Moravian settlement in England, he settled at Sheffield (1792), where he became proprietor and editor of *The Iris*. In 1789 he was sentenced to three months' imprisonment and a fine of twenty pounds for having printed *The Bastile*, a poem surmounted by a woodcut representing liberty and the British lion. A little later he was sentenced to six months' imprisonment because of reflections upon a colonel of militia, published in his paper. In spite of these judicial condemnations his name was unaffected, and when he retired from the editorship of his paper, in 1825, he received public favors, and at his death had the honor of a public funeral. In 1830–31 he delivered a series of lectures on poetry and literature before the Royal Institution; and in 1846 a life pension was settled upon him of a hundred and fifty pounds. He made no public profession of religion till his forty-third year, when he united with the Moravians; but ever afterward, eminent for his piety, he was most active in furthering all philanthropic and religious work.

He was one of the best sacred poets of his day. Among his works may be named: *The Wanderer of Switzerland, and Other Poems* (London, 1806); *Poems on the Abolition of the Slave Trade* (in collaboration with J. Grahame and E. Benger, 1809); *The West Indies* (1810); *The World before the Flood* (1813); *Greenland* (1819); *The Songs of Zion, being Imitations of the Psalms* (1822); *The Christian Psalmist, or Hymns, Selected and Original* (Glasgow, 1825); *The Pelican Island, and Other Poems* (London, 1827); *The Christian Poet; or, Selections in Verse on Sacred Subjects* (Glasgow, 1827); *Journal of Voyages and Travels by the Rev. D. Tyerman and G. Bennet Esq., compiled by J. Montgomery* (London, 1831); *Lectures on Poetry and General Literature Delivered at the Royal Institution in 1830 and 1831* (1833); *A Poet's Portfolio: or, Minor Poems* (1835); *Lines of the Most Eminent Literary and Scientific Men of Italy, Spain and Portugal* (in collaboration with Mrs. Shelley and others, 3 vols., 1835–37); *Our Savior's Miracles. Six Original Sketches in Verse* (Bristol, 1840); *The Poetical Works of J. M., Collected by himself* (4 vols., London, 1841); and *Original Hymns for Public, Private, and Social Devotion* (1853). He was a favorite lyric poet, and many of his works went through numerous editions. He was known chiefly for his hymns, of which the favorites are the missionary hymns, "O Spirit of the living God," "Hail to the Lord's Anointed," the fine advent hymn, "Angels from the realms of glory," and "Forever with the Lord."

BIBLIOGRAPHY: The main biography is by J. Holland and J. Everett, 7 vols., London, 1854–56 (expanded to a tedious degree). Others are by J. W. King, ib. 1858; A. S. Patterson, in *Poets and Preachers of the 19th Century*, Glasgow, 1862; S. Ellis, ib. 1864; S. C. Hall, in *Book of Memories of Great Men and Women*, pp. 81–93, ib. 1883; S. W Duffield, *English Hymns*, pp. 481–483, New York, 1886; G. W. Tallent-Bateman, in *Papers of the Manchester Club*, 1889, pp. 385 392, 435 440; Julian, *Hymnology*, pp. 763–764.

MONTH, THE HEBREW. See MOON; and YEAR.

MONUMENTAL THEOLOGY: That branch of Christian archeology which deals with monuments of various descriptions, inscriptions, coins, medals, statuaries, paintings, and architectural constructions so far as they are expressive of theological ideas. Comparison of the medieval cathedral of Europe with the modern meeting-house of America shows that, though in the congregations which built those houses of worship the piety may have been the same, the theology was different; and further comparison can not fail to lead to a definite conception of the theological differences, since the very outlines of the structures show that they were built to realize different ideas. Thus, the study of the literary monuments of theology may at every point be aided by the study of the corresponding archeological monuments. In some cases it will be supplemented (a great portion of the history of the church of Rome during its first centuries has been dug out of the catacombs); in others it will be strikingly illustrated. See ARCHEOLOGY, CHRISTIAN; ARCHITECTURE; ART AND CHURCH; SCULPTURE, CHRISTIAN USE OF.

BIBLIOGRAPHY: F. Piper, *Einleitung in die monumentale Theologie*, Gotha, 1867; J. P. Lundy, *Monumental Christianity*, New York, 1881; H. D. M. Spence, *The White Robe of Churches*, ib. 1900; and the literature in and under the three articles referred to above.

MOODY, DWIGHT LYMAN (RYTHER): Evangelist; b. at Northfield, Mass., Feb. 5, 1837; d. there Dec. 22, 1899. He was the sixth of the nine children of Edwin and Betsy Moody (née Holton). His father, who was a mason, died in 1841 (aged 41) and the family was in very straitened circumstances for years. His mother died in 1895, aged ninety. Moody received his first religious impressions in the village Unitarian church and his first missionary work was in getting pupils for its Sunday-school, which he attended. His schooling was carried only as far as the district school could take him, and while a young boy he had to earn his living. In 1854 he resolved to try his fortunes in Boston, and there was hired by his uncle, Samuel Holton, as a clerk in his boot and shoe store. One of the conditions of his engagement was that he should regularly attend his uncle's church, the Mount Vernon (Orthodox) Congregational Church, and also its Sunday-school. This promise he faithfully kept and was so much impressed by the truths he heard taught that in 1855 he applied for admission into the church. But his examination was not considered satisfactory and his application was held over for a year when he was thought to have made sufficient attainments in theology for church membership. In Sept., 1856, he went to Chicago and quickly found a more lucrative position than his uncle could offer him, and made a reputation as a salesman and traveler in the shoe trade. He also accumulated $7,000 toward the $100,000 upon which he had set his heart. But while diligent in his business and uncommonly successful he became absorbed more and more in religious work. His energies were first spent upon the Sunday-school as teacher, as gatherer-in of new pupils, and most unpromising ones, who under his instruction improved marvelously, and then as superintendent of the North Market Hall Sunday-school which he built up until it had a membership of 1,500 and out of it in 1863 the Illinois Street Church was formed. He thus was well known in the state as a Sunday-school worker. From the time of his coming to Chicago he had entered heartily into the work of the Young Mens' Christian Association, and he raised a large part of the money for its building, not once but twice, for the first was burned in 1867, and the second in 1871. In 1861 he gave up business and was an independent city missionary, then agent of the Christian Commission in the Civil War, and after that again in Sunday-school work and the secretary of the Chicago Young Men's Christian Association. But as yet he had done nothing to give him international fame.

In 1867 he made a visit to Great Britain on account of his wife's health—he had married in 1862. He made some valuable acquaintances and did a little evangelistic work. One of his converts was John Kenneth Mackenzie (q.v.). In 1872 he was again in Great Britain, held numerous meetings and won the esteem of prominent Evangelicals. From these he received an invitation to return for general revival work. He came the next year, bringing with him Ira David Sankey (q.v.), who was henceforth to be linked with him in fame as a revivalist. They landed at Liverpool on June 17, 1873, and held their first services in York. Moody's downright preaching and Sankey's simple but soul-stirring singing won attention, and as they passed from city to city they were heard by great crowds. They spent two years in this arduous labor, and then returned to America. Their fame was now in all the churches and invitations poured in upon them to do at home what they had done abroad, so they repeated these services and duplicated their successes, and that in all parts of the country. In 1881 and again in 1891 and 1892 they were in the United Kingdom. One of their most loyal supporters was Henry Drummond, who owed to them the quickening of his religious life in 1874.

In 1892 Moody by invitation of friends made a brief visit to the Holy Land. It was on his return to London that autumn that he first knew of the heart difficulty which ultimately caused his death. It may have been this knowledge that induced him during his remaining years to seek rather to deepen the spiritual life of professing Christians through church services of the ordinary quiet type, than to address the enormous miscellaneous crowds in all kinds of buildings as he did in earlier days. It was while holding services in Kansas City, Mo., on Nov. 16, 1899, that he broke down, and, although he was able to reach home, he was fatally stricken and soon after died.

Moody had "consecrated common sense." He was honest, preached a Calvinistic creed which he accepted with all his heart, and was master of an effective style. His sermons and shorter addresses abound in personal allusions, in shrewd remarks and home thrusts. He had a hatred of shams and scant respect for persons who had only place to recommend them. He was often abrupt, sometimes brusk. He had no polish, small education, but he knew the English Bible and accepted it literally. He was fond of treating Bible characters very familiarly and enlivening his sermons by imaginary conversations with and between them. But that he was truly bent upon promoting the kingdom of God by the ways he thought most helpful there is no doubt. Like other great revivalists he had much praise which was undesirable, but he never lost his head. He also never allowed excitement to carry his audiences off their feet. For sanity, sincerity, spirituality, and success Moody goes into the very first rank of revival preachers.

During Moody's and Sankey's mission at Newcastle, England, in 1873, the first form of the familiar hymn-book which bears their name appeared in response to the necessity of having a book which was adapted to their needs. This book was originally little better than a small pamphlet, but it was enlarged and has taken on various shapes and had varied contents while preserving its main features. The sale of the book in its different forms has been enormous. Up to 1900 more than a million and a quarter of dollars had been paid its compilers in royalties. Of his share in this money Moody made noble use, and thus opened a chapter in his life which is less known to the public, but will have more permanent interest than his preaching. For with it he founded, or helped to found, the chain of educational institutions which does not bear his name but which is his greatest monument. The first was the Northfield Seminary for Young Women, erected and carried on in his native town. It dates from 1879. This is a school which trains girls for college, if they go so far, but in any case gives them good instruction permeated with religion. All the work of the house is done by the students. In 1881 Mount Hermon School for Young Men was started. The two schools are only a few miles apart. The students are taken at very low rates, combine manual training with the usual school courses, and are under strong religious influences. The Bible Institute for Home and Foreign Missions in Chicago, open to both sexes, is another of the educational aids which owe their origin to him. The Students' Conferences and the Northfield Christian Workers' Conference, both of which meet annually at Northfield, were inaugurated by him. They have exerted a great influence, and of a very sane and thoughtful type.

In church connection Moody belonged to the independent Chicago Avenue Church. In his activities he belonged to the Church universal.

Bibliography: The principal biography is by his son, W. R. Moody, New York, 1900. Others are by H. Drummond, New York, 1900; J. S. Ogilvie, ib. 1900; and A. W. Williams, Philadelphia, 1900. Phases of Moody's life and work are treated in: T. S. J., *D. L. Moody at Home*, New York, 1886; H. M. Wharton, *A Month with Moody in Chicago*, Baltimore, 1894; H. B. Hartzler, *Moody in Chicago*, New York, 1894.

MOON, HEBREW CONCEPTIONS OF THE.

Names; Relation to Time (§ 1).
Conception of the Moon and its Functions (§ 2).
Worship of the Moon (§ 3).
The New Moon (§ 4).

1. Names; Relation to Time.

The usual Hebrew name for the moon (*yareaḥ*; cf. Assyr. *iriḫu, arḫu*, "month"; Ethiopic *wareḥ;* Palmyrene *yrḥ*) is evidently to be connected with a root *yaraḥ* or *waraḥ*, cognate with *'araḥ*, "to wander," cf. Assyr. *urḫu*, "road," connoting the moon's motion among the stars. With this Semitic root meaning is to be contrasted the Aryan idea of the moon as "the measurer (of time)." While the moon did not among the Semites receive its name from its function as a marker of time periods, the regularity of its phases made its use general as a fixer of times and periods, as with other peoples, and with this were connoted other related conceptions. Thus in Egypt the moon-god Thoth was god of measures, then of knowledge and wisdom in general (with which cf. the Assyrian Sin, explained as *zu-en*, "knowledge-lord," and the Greek ideas associated with Hermes). The Mandæans (q.v.), who derived a large part of their system from Babylonian sources, made the demiurge Ptahil say: "I gave the moon as time-measurer for the world" (A. J. H. W. Brandt, *Die mandäische Religion*, p. 61, Leipsic, 1889). Similarly among the Hebrews the idea of the moon as a divider of time was predominant, and its measuring-function is strikingly expressed in Ps. civ. 19: "He appointed the moon for seasons." The Hebrews and Phenicians called the new moon *hodesh*, "new," the former called the new moon *kese'* (cf. Assyr. *kuse'u*, "cap," connected with the idea that the moon-god wore a cap when the moon was full). A Hebrew poetic name for the moon is *lebhenah*, "white"; and in Gen. i. the terminology used is "the lesser light." The Assyrians and Babylonians called the moon-god Sin (see above; from him the Sinaitic peninsula drew its name), while other names in the Semitic region were Aku (Elamitic?), Nannar, Aa (consort of Shamash; also frequently rendered "queen"), and the Phenician Ashtaroth-Karnaim. The importance of the moon to the Hebrews is seen when it is noted how fundamental a division of time the month was for them. The date of the new moon as marking the beginning of a new reckoning of time was by them not calculated but observed. The length of a month, twenty-nine or thirty days, depended, therefore, upon the day when the moon was first seen, except that in cloudy weather the thirtieth day was reckoned to the preceding month. That this basis of reckoning determined the custom of counting the day, not from morning till morning or midnight to midnight, but from evening to evening can not be proved; but it may be confidently assumed, since in general peoples who have only lunar months use this method of defining the day. It is equally difficult to be assured that the week was derived from the month by division of the latter into four parts (see Week). There is general agreement that the seven-day period was derived from Babylonia, where it was employed in pre-Semitic times—this is confirmed by the fact that not only were the seventh, fourteenth, twenty-first, and twenty-eighth days of the month observed, but that the nineteenth was also a special day, the reason being apparently that thirty plus nineteen are forty-nine, this number making up a week of weeks. The union of the planetary bodies with the names of the days of the week seems to have been a very late phase, probably not completed till the Greek period. While the sacred seasons of the Hebrews were fixed by reference to lunar reckoning, there is a suggestion of solar reference in the Old Testament. It may be mere coincidence that Gen. viii. 14, cf. vii. 11, apparently makes the length of the flood a year and eleven days, i.e., a lunar year of 354 days plus eleven, or 365 days. The circumstances of husbandry necessitated regard for the solar year, but the adjustment of the solar and the lunar periods by intercalation was probably not made in the Hebrew region till after Old-Testament times (see Time, Biblical Reckoning of).

There are a number of indications that the pre-Canaanitic relations of the Hebrews with the moon-cult were close. Abraham is traced back to Haran (q.v.) and Ur (see Babylonia, IV., § 3), two noted centers of moon-worship. Moreover, in the Abrahamic family names and genealogies the moon has left its mark. Thus with Terah may be compared Assyr. *tarahu*, "gazelle" (sacred to Ishtar); Nahor is connected with Nannar, the name of a moon-god; Abram recalls *aburammu*, "exalted father," a frequent title of the moon-deity; Sarah ("princess") and Milcah ("queen") are titles of the moon-goddess; Laban is to be connected with *labanu*, "the white one," cf. *lebhenah* above; while Lamech may be brought into relations with Assyr. *Lamgu*, a name of Sin. Yet with the Hebrews the moon was subordinate and secondary to the sun. Whether this represents the original Semitic conception is uncertain, since it is held, though not demonstrated, that the moon-cult represented an earlier Semitic stage of culture. The age of the worship of Sin is not determined; the Aramean cult at Haran was of great antiquity and persisted into the Roman period. Sahar, the name of a moon-god, is probably to be seen in the Mandæan Sauriel, while the Palmyrene deities Yarhibaal and Aglibaal were moon-deities. The Hebrews were, therefore, in the provenance of the moon-cult, and their conceptions of this body were in general agreement with those of their neighbors. The idea that the moon influenced the earth and its products was practically universal, and this influence was conceived as either malign or benign. This body was thought to be an agent in the production of crops, perhaps through its supposed function as a creator of dew (W. von Baudissin, *Jahve et Moloch*, p. 24, Leipsic, 1874; W. H. Roscher, *Ueber Selene*, pp. 49–99, ib. 1890). The Aryans went further than this and attributed to the moon the growth of animals (*Avesta*, Mah Yast, Mah Nyayis, *SBE*, xxiii. 88–91, 355); the Indo-Iranians connected the moon with the primeval bull, itself a symbol of fertility; Pliny (*Hist. nat.*, ii. 221) associated growth with the moon; Macrobius ("On the Dream of Scipio," I., xi. 7) attributes to the moon power over terrestrial objects for increase or decline; while it is a world-wide superstition that a waxing moon brings increase of crops, and occasionally even the power of impregnation is attributed to that body. The Old-Testament references to this notion are necessarily scanty, yet beyond question Deut. xxxiii. 14, "the precious things put forth by the moon," is to be brought into relationship with this idea. In the Assyrian hymns the moon is called "the mighty bull, with large horns, perfect form, and flowing beard, bright as crystal" (the bull is also a Semitic symbol of fertility); the supposed beard in seals is probably the effect of a necklace with pendants. On the malign side pestilence was associated with the moon (Ps. cxxi. 6), while the Greek notion of the lunar origin of epilepsy (cf. the Greek verb *seleniazesthai*, "to be struck with epilepsy," from *selēnē*, "moon") is shown to be held by Jews (Matt. iv. 24, xvii. 15). With this may be connected the name of the Mandæan angel of death, Sauriel, as well as such passages in the Old Testament as Gen. xxxi. 40 and Jer. xxxvi. 30. In the imagery of the Day of Yahweh (q.v.) the moon was to participate with the other heavenly bodies in the cataclysmic phenomena of that time (Isa. xiii. 10; Ezek. xxxii. 7; Joel ii. 10, iii. 4, 15; Matt. xxiv. 29; Acts ii. 20; Rev. vi. 12); also in the repair and glorifying of all nature (Isa. xxx. 26), though in the new era there will be no need for its light, since God is to be the light of his people (Isa. lx. 19; cf. Rev. xxi. 23, xxii. 5). Yet its stability is one of the images of eternal duration (Ps. lxxii. 5, 7, lxxxix. 37), and it is also a synonym of beauty (Job xxxi. 26; Cant. vi. 9; Ecclus. l. 6).

2. Conception of the Moon and Its Functions.

Worship of the moon appears to have been native with the Semites. Wadd in Arabia, Sin and Nannar in Babylonia, Sahar in Mesopotamia (appearing on Aramaic steles at Merab near Aleppo; cf. C. Clermont-Ganneau, in *Bibliothèque de l'école des hautes études*, fasc. 113, pp. 193–195, 211–215, Paris, 1897) are but a few of the examples which might be cited, the moon being representative of both male and female deities. Apart, however, from the suggestions contained in the tracing of Abraham to centers of moon-worship and in the connections of names in the Abrahamic family with names or titles of moon-deities, there is little or nothing in the early history of the Hebrews to connect them with worship of the moon (cf. Smith, *Rel. of Sem.*, 2d ed., p. 135). It was only toward the end of the monarchy, in the period of declension and of eclectic religious practises, that the worship of this body appears among them, when it is registered by the denunciation of the prophets (Jer. viii. 2, xix. 3; Zeph. i. 5), by prohibition through legislation (Deut. iv. 9, xvii. 3), by the repressive measures of Josiah (II Kings xxiii. 5), and later by the disavowal of participation in the cult by the righteous sufferer (Job xxxi. 26–27). In general the worship of the moon was associated with that of other heavenly bodies, and the method was by prostration, and by kissing of the hands (Job. xxxi. 26–27), the latter a custom mentioned by Pliny (*Hist. nat.*, XXVIII., ii. 25). In Jer. vii. 18, xliv. 17–19, 25, there is mention of the "queen of heaven" in which a distinct cult is evidently distinguished, and its peculiarities in part given, as in the offering by fire of special cakes in the preparation of which men, women, and children united. The prophet in chap. xliv. represents the people as arguing for this worship on the experiential ground that its practise was attended with prosperity and the cessation of it was contemporaneous with disaster. It has been the custom since Jerome to identify this "queen of heaven" with the moon, though from the time of Isaac of Antioch (c. 450) she was also identified with Venus. The concrete deity with whom identification was made, however, was Ishtar, whose most intimate connection was with Venus and not with the moon (see Ashtoreth, § 5); accordingly later scholars are disposed to see in the cult under question the Ishtar-Venus type and to disconnect it from the moon. Perhaps the last word has not been said on the subject. As cults passed from the East to the West, Ishtar was associated with the moon, and this association registered itself in the Greek religion as well as in the Sidonian conception of Astarte as the moon. It is not beside the mark to note that cakes were offered in Athens to Artemis (the moon-

3. Worship of the Moon.

goddess), a practise which may be the analogue of that noted in Jeremiah. On the other hand, offerings like these were made in Arabia to the sun and to Venus. Other indications of worship in the Hebrew region are seen in Isa. iii. 18, in the ornaments "round like the moon," R. V., "crescents" (Hebr. *saharonim;* cf. the proper name Sahar for the moon-god in the vicinity of Aleppo, mentioned above), which seem to be referred to in Judges viii. 21–26, A. V margin "ornaments like the moon," R. V "crescents," and are by the commentators associated with worship of the moon.

The new-moon festival as an occasion of joyous character seems to belong to the oldest stratum of Hebrew observance. I Sam. xx. 5–6 shows it in connection with clan celebrations, and this implies antiquity In II Kings iv. 23; Isa. i. 13; Hos. ii. 11; and Amos viii. 5 it is placed apparently on an equal footing with the sabbath, and the passage last named involves cessation from work on that day, while it was in popular practise a day of assembling at the sanctuaries with offerings. It is, therefore, a peculiar phenomenon that JE and D are silent regarding the festival, which reappears in Ezekiel and the priestly legislation. Various explanations have been offered for the silence noted. Dillmann (in his commentary on Exodus-Leviticus, p. 635, Leipsic, 1897) supposes that the observance was so common and such a fixture that provision for it was unnecessary; in that case it is difficult to account for other provisions covering matters known to be no less firmly fixed (cf. Ex. xxi.–xxiii.). Benzinger (*EB*, iii. 3402) thinks that the increasing importance of the sabbath "forced the new-moon festival into the background"; if this be true, it is difficult to say what brought it into notice in the later codes, though it is not impossible that popular insistence made its demands felt. Wellhausen (*Prolegomena*, p. 118, Berlin, 1883) makes the ignoring in the JE and D legislation purposive, the intent being to wean the people away from an observance in which the Canaanitic rites were an especial feature. Whatever the reason for this silence, later popularity of the festival is evinced by the fact that the prophets dated their oracles by it (Ezek. xxvi. 1, xxix. 17, xxxi. 1, xxxii. 1; Hag. i. 1), and this further implies actual gatherings of the people at which the prophecies were delivered, while it is known that at this time the people also visited the prophets (II Kings iv. 23). In the newer legislation the day was not one of rest (except the new moon of the seventh month, Lev. xxiii. 24) but of extraordinary sacrifices, surpassing in richness those of the sabbath. Thus in Ezekiel (xlvi. 4–6) for the new moon there were prescribed a bullock, six lambs, and a ram; for the sabbath, six lambs and a ram. In Num. xxviii. 9–13 (which prescribes from a national standpoint) for the sabbath were prescribed two lambs with one-tenth deal of flour for each; for the new moon, two bullocks with three-tenths deal of flour for each, a ram with two-tenths deal of flour, and seven lambs with one-tenth deal for each. To the daily burnt offering there was added a festal offering. For notes of the observance cf. I Chron. xxiii. 31; II Chron. ii. 4, viii. 13, xxxi. 3; Ezra iii. 5; Neh. x. 33, which regard the offerings as fixed and normal. Further, that the new moon was regarded as one of high observance is shown by the directions to blow the trumpets. The new moon of the seventh month has a sabbatical character in that cessation from labor is directed together with assemblage at the sanctuary, and possibly after the exile this took the character of a New Year's festival (Ezra iii. 6; Neh. viii. 1 sqq.). Judith viii. 6 shows the observance still later, while Gal. iv. 10 and Col. ii. 16 indicate that Jewish Christians were inclined to lay stress upon the observance. See FEASTS AND FESTIVALS, I.; SYNAGOGUE, II. GEO. W. GILMORE.

4. The New Moon.

BIBLIOGRAPHY: C. L. Ideler, *Handbuch der Chronologie*, Berlin, 1831; D. Chwolsohn, *Die Ssabier*, pp. 399–443, Leipsic, 1856; R. Pietschmann, *Hermes Trismegistos*, Leipsic, 1875; F. Baethgen, *Beiträge zur semitischen Religionsgeschichte*, Berlin, 1887; A. Kuenen, *De Godsdienst van Israel*, Haarlem, 1889, Eng. transl., *The Religion of Israel*, London, 1897; P. de Lagarde, in *GGA*, xxxv (1889), 46; P. Jensen, *Die Kosmologie der Babylonier*, pp. 101–108, Strasburg, 1890; W. H. Roscher, *Ueber Selene und Verwandtes*, Leipsic, 1890; E. Sachau, in *Sitzungsberichte der Berliner Akademie*, 1895, pp. 119–122; F. X. Kugler, *Die babylonische Mondrechnung*, Freiburg, 1900; E. Maass, *Die Tagesgötter in Rom und den Provinzen*, Berlin, 1902; W. St. C. Boscawen, *First of Empires*, pp. 31, 80–81, 306, London, 1906; J. G. Frazer, *Adonis, Attis, Osiris*, pp. 295 sqq., London, 1906 (for ethnic notions regarding the moon); Schrader, *KAT*, pp. 361–367; Benzinger, *Archäologie*, passim; Nowack, *Archäologie*, ii. 138–144; *DB*, iii. 433–435, 521–523; *EB*, iii. 3192–97, 3401–04; *JE*, viii. 678–679, ix. 243–244.

MOORE, CLEMENT CLARKE: Protestant Episcopal; b. in New York July 15, 1779; d. in Newport, R. I., July 10, 1863. He was graduated from Columbia College, 1798; though prepared for the ministry he never took orders, but devoted himself to literature; and from 1821 to 1850 he was professor, first of Hebrew and Greek, then of Oriental and Greek literature, in the General Theological Seminary, New York. The ground on which the seminary now stands was his gift. He was the pioneer in America of Hebrew lexicography, for his *Hebrew and Greek Lexicon* (2 vols., New York, 1809) was the first Hebrew lexicon published in the United States. He wrote also: *Poems* (1844); *George Castriot, Surnamed Scanderbeg, King of Albania* (1850); and the favorite *A Visit from St. Nicholas* (1848; a story for children in verse), beginning "'Twas the night before Christmas."

MOORE, DUNLOP: Presbyterian; b. at Lurgan (19 m. s.w. of Belfast), County Armagh, Ireland, July 25, 1830; d. at Pittsburg, Pa., Nov. 14, 1905. He was educated at Edinburgh and Belfast, being graduated in 1854. He was next a missionary of the Irish Presbyterian Church in Gujarat, India (1855–67), and to the Viennese Jews (1869–1874). From 1875 to 1891 he was pastor of the Presbyterian church at New Brighton, Pa., but after the latter year was without charge, engaged in evangelistic and literary work. After a year at Lansdowne, Pa., he made his home in Pittsburg. While in India he aided in preparing the Gujarati translation of the Bible and wrote treatises on Jainism and Mohammedanism in the same language. He likewise edited the Gujarati monthly *Jñānadīpaka*, and besides a number of contributions to the periodical press, collaborated with S. T. Lowrie in translating C. W. E. Nägelsbach's *Isaiah* for the American Lange series (New York, 1878).

MOORE, EDWARD: Church of England; b. at Cardiff, Wales, Feb. 28, 1835. He was educated at Pembroke College, Cambridge (B.A., 1857), and was ordered deacon in 1859 and ordained priest two years later. From 1858 to 1864 he was fellow and tutor of Queen's College, Oxford, and since the latter year has been principal of St. Edmund Hall, Oxford. He has been honorary fellow of Pembroke College since 1899 and of Queen's College since 1902, as well as canon of Canterbury and librarian of Canterbury Cathedral since 1903. He is best known as a Dante scholar, and has written or edited *Introduction to Aristotle's Ethics*, i.–iv. (London, 1871); *Aristotle's Poetics, with Notes* (Oxford, 1875); *Time References in the Divina Commedia* (London, 1887); *Textual Criticism of the Divina Commedia* (Oxford, 1889); *Dante and his Early Biographers* (London, 1890); *Tutte le opere di Dante Alighieri nouvamente rivedute nel testo* (Oxford, 1894, 1904); *Studies in Dante* (3 series, 1896–1903); *L'Autenticità della Quæstio de aqua et terra* (London, 1899); and *Gli Accenni al tempo nella Divina Commedia* (Florence, 1900).

MOORE, EDWARD CALDWELL: Congregationalist; b. at West Chester, Pa., Sept. 1, 1857 He was graduated from Marietta College, Marietta, O. (A.B., 1877), Union Theological Seminary (1884), and studied at the universities of Berlin, Göttingen, and Giessen (1884–86). He was pastor of the Westminster Presbyterian Church, Yonkers, N. Y. (1886–1889) and of the Central Congregational Church at Providence, R. I. (1889–1902). He was appointed to his present position of Parkman professor of theology at Harvard University in 1902. He was Lowell lecturer in 1903 and chairman of the Board of Preachers of Harvard University in 1905, and has also been a member of the Prudential Committee of the American Board of Commissioners for Foreign Missions since 1899, being chairman since 1905. He has written *The New Testament in the Christian Church* (New York, 1903).

MOORE, GEORGE FOOTE: Congregationalist; b. at West Chester, Pa., Oct. 15, 1851. He was educated at Yale (A.B., 1872) and Union Theological Seminary (1877), after having taught in the Hopkins Grammar School, New Haven, and privately in Columbus, O. (1872–74), and after having been principal of the High School at Lancaster, O. (1874–1875). He was then pastor of the Presbyterian Church at Bloomingburg, O., in 1877–78, and of the Putnam Presbyterian Church, Zanesville, O. (1878–1883), and Hitchcock professor of the Hebrew language and literature in Andover Theological Seminary (1883–1902). Since 1902 he has been professor of the history of religion in Harvard University. In theology he belongs to the critical school, and is a member of the Deutsche morgenländische Gesellschaft and the Society of Biblical Literature and Exegesis, and recording secretary of the American Oriental Society. Besides articles in the *Encyclopædia Biblica*, he has written *Commentary on Judges* (New York, 1895); translated and edited Judges for the *Polychrome Bible* (2 vols., 1898–1900); and assisted in editing *Old Testament and Semitic Studies in Memory of William Rainey Harper*, 2 vols., Chicago, 1908, to which he also contributed.

MOORE, HENRY: Wesleyan Methodist; b. in Dublin Dec. 21, 1751; d. in London Apr. 27, 1844. In 1780 he became an itinerant on the Londonderry circuit; later as the constant companion of John Wesley in London he did most efficient service. After Wesley's death he figured prominently in the discussions from 1791 to 1797 concerning the permanent ecclesiastical organization of the Methodists, personally favoring the Episcopal form. He was a stanch upholder of the authority of the conference, even though disagreeing with its policy in certain matters. He opposed the movement to found a theological institute for training men for the ministry, and as the last survivor of those ordained by John Wesley he championed the right of the Wesleyan ministers to administer the sacraments. He was active in the itinerant ministry till 1833, when he became a supernumerary. His works of significance are: *The Life of the Rev. John Wesley, Including an Account of the Great Revival of Religion of which he was the . Instrument* (in collaboration with T. Coke, London, 1792); *Thoughts on the Eternal Sonship of the Second Person of the Holy Trinity. Addressed to the People Called Methodists,* . (Birmingham, 1817); *The Life of Mrs. M. Fletcher Compiled from her Journal* (2 vols., London, 1817); *The Life of the Rev. J. Wesley in which are Included, the Life of his Brother the Rev. C. Wesley, and Memoirs of their Family, Comprehending an Account of the Great Revival of Religion in which they were the Chief Instruments* (2 vols., 1824–25); *Sermons Held on General Occasions . With a Brief Memoir (by the Author) of his Life and Christian Experience from his Birth to the First Conference Held after the Death of Mr. Wesley* (1830).

Bibliography: Mrs. R. Smith, *The Life of Rev. H. Moore, . Including the Autobiography*, London, 1844; and the literature under Methodists dealing with the early history of that people.

MOORE, JOHN HENRY: Dunker; b. at Salem, Va., Apr. 8, 1846. He was educated in the Illinois public schools, and in 1868 entered the ministry of his denomination, of which he was chosen bishop in 1879. In 1876 he became editor of *The Brethren at Work*, a Dunker weekly published at Lanark, Ill., but later merged with others and removed to Elgin, Ill., and renamed *The Gospel Messenger*. Of this he is still editor. In theology he is strongly Puritan, being opposed to war and intemperance in all forms. Like his denomination, he accepts only the New Testament as his creed. He has written: *Trine Immersion Traced to the Apostles* (Elgin, Ill., 1872); *The Perfect Plan of Salvation* (1874); and *One Baptism* (1876).

MOORE, WALTER WILLIAM: Presbyterian (Southern assembly); b. at Charlotte, N. C., June 14, 1857. He was educated at Davidson College, N. C. (A.B., 1878), and Union Theological Seminary, Va. (1881). He was an evangelist in Buncombe County, N. C. (1881–82) and pastor at Millersburg, Ky. (1882–83). Since 1883 he has been professor of the Hebrew language and literature in Union Theological Seminary, Va., of which he has also been president since 1904. He is a member of the Richmond Education Association and has been a trustee of Hampden-Sidney College since 1905. He has written *A Year in Europe* (Richmond, Va., 1904).

MOORE, WILLIAM EVES: Presbyterian; b. at Strasburg, Pa., Apr. 1, 1823; d. at Columbus, O., June 5, 1899. He graduated from Yale College, New Haven, Conn., 1847; studied theology under Dr. Lyman H. Atwater at Fairfield, Conn.; became pastor at West Chester, Pa., 1850; and at Columbus, O., 1872. From 1884 he was permanent clerk of the General Assembly of the Presbyterian Church. He was the author of *The New Digest of the Acts and Deliverances of the Presbyterian Church, New School* (Philadelphia, 1861); and *The Presbyterian Digest, United Church* (1873).

MOORHOUSE, JAMES: Church of England, former bishop; b. at Sheffield Nov. 19, 1826. He was educated at St. John's College, Cambridge (B.A., 1853), and was ordered deacon in 1853 and ordained priest in the following year. He was curate of St. Neots (1853–55), Sheffield (1855–59), and Hornsey (1859–61), and perpetual curate of St. John's, Fitzroy Square, London (1861–67). From 1867 to 1876 he was vicar and rural dean of Paddington, London, and in 1876 was consecrated bishop of Melbourne, Australia. In 1886 he was translated to the see of Manchester, which he resigned in 1903. He was Hulsean lecturer in 1865 and Warburtonian lecturer in 1874 and chaplain in ordinary to the queen and prebendary of Caddington Major in St. Paul's Cathedral (1874–76). He has written *Nature and Revelation* (London, 1861); *Our Lord Jesus Christ the Subject of Growth in Wisdom* (Hulsean lectures; 1866); *Jacob* (three sermons before the University of Cambridge; 1870); *The Expectation of the Christ* (1889); *The Dangers of the Apostolic Age* (Manchester, 1891); *The Teaching of Christ* (London, 1891); *Church Work* (1894); and *The Roman Claim to Supremacy* (Manchester, 1894).

MOORS. See SPAIN.

MORAL THEOLOGY. See THEOLOGY, MORAL.

MORALISTS, BRITISH.

I. Introduction: The British moralists of the seventeenth and eighteenth centuries accomplished for ethics what the English deists of the same period accomplished for the science of religion. The deists cut loose from the ideal conception of religion founded on psychology and metaphysics, and established an analysis of religion founded on the psychological study of its phenomena. The British moralists cut loose from a dogmatically founded system of ethics, controlling the State, the Church, and private life, and founded an autonomous system of modern scientific ethics. In neither case were these movements isolated, they were a part of the social phenomena of an age which, among other things, tended to build up independent treatment of the various sciences. Specifically the work of the British moralists may be distinguished as follows. First they gave a scientific form to the practical material furnished them by Christian ethics, to which they stood sometimes in a hostile relation, sometimes enlarging its conceptions, sometimes incorporating with it purely secular interests and aims. Second, in place of deriving morality from dogmatic authoritative teaching and from the supernatural dualistic system of salvation and grace, they introduced the method of psychological analysis.

II. Development of the Autonomy of Ethics: The first stage of the discussion concerns itself with the ethical ideas of Roman Catholicism. The combination of Christianity with the culture of the ancient world drove into the background the primitive system of Christian ethic, which concerned itself with the end of the world and a life of complete divine indwelling. The great process of amalgamation resulted in the objectification of Christianity, with the Church conceived as a supernatural institution of grace. Various elements were taken up in the process of combination. Participation in the divine was secured through neo-Platonic theories, by which the interval between the natural and supernatural was bridged. As each of these two spheres had its legitimate existence, a place was made for an ethical system resting largely upon the traditional law of nature as found in the philosophy of the Stoics, while the Aristotelian conception of the State was also wrought into the scheme. The esthetic ethics of antiquity completely disappeared. The law of nature was made identical with the decalogue, hence the sphere of a real political and civil ethics was very limited. Ecclesiastical ethics had the predominance. A different value was given to the morality of the layman from that of the clergy. As time went on, the weak points of this system were criticized and the secular element accentuated, and at the same time direct protests were heard against the prevailing conception of ethics as a system of laws and regulations enforced by the objectively divine institution of the Church.

1. The Roman Catholic Theory.

The Protestant movement accomplished much in minimizing the dualism between natural and supernatural factors. But the distinction between natural powers weakened by original sin and the supernatural morality of grace still remained.

2. The Protestant Position.

It is true that from the Protestant standpoint religious perfection could be attained in the world. Normal man, not the ascetic, is the object of saving grace. The State with its various functions is allowed to be free of ecclesiastical prescriptions; although it represents fallen human nature, it can be inspired by a real Christianity. So the Christian as a citizen can live as a Christian without performing some specially divine works at the bidding of his ecclesiastical superiors. Calvin took an optimistic view of the possibility of living a Christian life according to Christian rules in the State. The primary authority was founded on the identity of the law of nature with the decalogue, of which the first table contained the demands of a spiritual character and the second controlled the natural forms of life in a civilized state. The object of Christianity is to restore the law of nature in this form, for heathendom was supposed to have been forgetful of the natural law in both directions. Protestants avoided adding to this scripturally contained law of nature by the so-called Evangelical Counsels (see CONSILIA EVANGELICA). But the idea of secular law was to be accepted as a guide only for the unregenerate. The Christian could not accept it as a standard of conduct; it stood only for a natural form of life. Its prescriptions and indeed all of the forms and activities of the State were regarded as a species of discipline prepared and ordained by God as a part of that earthly system through which the Christian had to go as a pilgrim in his journey to heaven. As to the right of resistance to the prescriptions of the State, Lutheranism and Calvinism differed. Both united, however, in denying any proper ethical aim to the State and to civilized society *per se*. All its rights in this sphere came through the divine ordinance as laid down in the second table of the decalogue. (On this cf. H. Wiskemann, *Darstellung der in Deutschland zur Zeit der Reformation herrschenden nationalökonomischen Ansichten*, Leipsic, 1861; P. Lobstein, *Ethik Calvins*, Strasburg, 1877; E. Troeltsch, *Vernunft und Offenbarung bei . Gerhard und Melanchthon*, Göttingen, 1891; C. Thieme, *Sittliche Triebkraft des Glaubens*, Leipsic, 1895; E. Brandenburg, *Luthers Anschauung von Staat und der Gesellschaft*, Halle, 1901; M. Schulze, *Meditatio futuræ vitæ in System Calvins*, Leipsic, 1901; G. Hönnicke, *Studien zur altprotestantischen Ethik*, Berlin, 1902.)

What had been repressed by Roman Catholicism, viz., the free sphere and subjectivity of the Christian idea of ethics, was more fully developed, but in neither aspect can the development be called complete. The existence of the State and the value of the State's activity as a religious entity, not in opposition to spiritual concerns, was acknowledged. What was omitted was the recognition that the State and social institutions were derivations from the Christian idea. A necessarily ethical aim was

not allowed to the State. The State was permitted as a part of a natural order, with the duty laid upon it of providing for the supremacy of Biblical truth and Biblical moral law.

3. The State and the Law of Nature.

On this ground its special forms of activity were acknowledged as legitimate. Secular ends alone, such as the laying-down of systems of law, and the provisions for economic prosperity, were assigned to it. A further stage in the emancipation of the State came from the conception of the law of nature that had been made a part of the religious system by both Roman Catholics and Reformers. This conception of natural law can take on a thoroughly conservative color if it is made a mere abstraction from existing political ordinances and from commonly acknowledged legal and ethical principles. These are assumed to be a natural divinely created system, the postulates of all social life. This was the point of view taken in the ethics of the Reformers, and on it was built the political system and the theoretical ethical system of the Reformation. But the law of nature is capable of being handled as an instrument of criticism of the actual and the existent. In this fashion it is used by Grotius, who gives it a free sphere, apart from the decalogue or any other theological sanction. Its power would come from reason even if there were no God, and it is to be referred to God only because he is the source of human activity in which the ideas of reason work themselves out. In this way a path is made for the ethical idea of the State and of law. Grotius wished to preserve this idea on a sound basis, independent of confessional contests and unmoved by theological subtleties. Indeed his law of nations is the opponent of confessionalism and religious warfare. The idea as developed by Grotius strengthened the unity and sovereignty of the State, gave ethical and legal independence to the individual, and aimed at a rational derivation of political and social conditions in the State, making legitimate its care for the welfare of the citizens, and also constituting its ideal aim, the realization of the idea of law. Yet even here the profounder ethical tasks of State life are left out of consideration. Non-ecclesiastical morality still has limitations, but the system performed good service as being the kernel of ethical independence from which modern civilization is derived. The emancipation of the State through the discussion and supporters of the theory of natural law became complete. Along with the full recognition of the sovereignty of the State as an end in itself comes also the recognition of the right of the individual citizen in the State to share in the aims of the State's life. The result of the English political movements of the seventeenth century was a definite separation between political freedom and theology. On this ground, England became a model, furnishing practical ideas and political theories to the Continent. (Cf. C. Kaltenborn, *Vorläufer des Hugo Grotius*, Leipsic, 1848; O. Gierke, *Johann Althusius*, Breslau, 1880; G. Jellinek, *Das Recht des modernen Staates*, i. 288–301, 399–424, Berlin, 1900.)

Less important to the question under consideration is the influence of the Renaissance. It is true

4. Influence of the Renaissance.

it proclaimed the independence of secular morality from the traditional transcendent ethical theories of the Middle Ages, and produced a sharp-cut expression of individualism. But the leaders in the Renaissance lacked system; they were inclined to skepticism and anarchy and represented an exclusive and aristocratic type of thought. Through its great representative Machiavelli, the Renaissance exercised strong influence over Hobbes and his critics. The ethical analysis of the Renaissance with its dependence on a psychological treatment of ethics is of importance, but on the whole the ethical ideas of the Renaissance had slight impelling power and were too esthetic in character to admit of wide application. In this way the influence of the Renaissance remained indirect and of minor importance.

5. Importance of Reformed Protestant Ethics.

Of really decisive importance was Protestant ethics in the particular form assumed by it in the Reformed Church in Geneva, France, Holland, and England, where the supremacy of the Calvinistic system of predestination worked out a complete civil order. It recognized political, economic, and social elements, but its science was theology, while it left art altogether out of account. The law of nature was made identical with the revealed law; the State was to aid the Church to advance pure teaching and establish a civil life corresponding to Christian ideals. On the one hand, there was the external discipline keeping citizens in subjection to those ideals and, on the other hand, the so-called "guardianship of both tables" by which civil discipline and the purity of church teaching were maintained, a combination of the law of nature and the proclamation of salvation. Calvin's position on this point was much more thoroughgoing than Luther's, who left to the State a large sphere of activity for its natural functions and assigned to it considerable control in Church administration (see POLITY, IV., § 3). Calvin provided for a theocracy by which the demands and forms of civil life should be brought into harmony with the exact standards of Christian ethics, proclaimed by an independently organized Church acting as the interpreter of the Bible. The various elements of Calvinistic theology, its theory of predestination and grace, were brought into practical application in the life of the individual and the State. But the political conception of Calvinism was aristocratic. It thought of the Church as the fellowship of the predestinated who were to bear sway over the whole sphere of life; the Bible in all its details was the standard of ethical conduct, not simply a source of grace and guide to penitence. Calvinism was not content with the small sphere of Lutheranism in directing the moral conduct and ethical aspirations of the individual citizen, it attacked also directly the control of important ecclesiastical functions by the State authorities. The State indeed was bound to maintain order and execute law, and also by divine and natural right it had to maintain Biblical truth and Scriptural ordinances within its territory. If it failed to do this the society of the elect had the right of revolt, and this right was exercised in the wars of the Huguenots and of the Netherland Reformers. The Christian people were sovereign, and the Christian democracy was the supreme court of appeal. This was a very different principle from the Lutheran conservatism with its principles of practical passive obedience and its inconsistent distinction between the Church with its guidance of the individual and the State with its right to carry out measures of general utility. With Calvin Church and State worked together to establish the Scriptural social order. So one of the crucial stages in the spiritual development of modern times is reformed teaching and practise in ethics and politics and in the construction of state and society. (Cf. M. Schneckenburger, *Vergleichende Darstellung des lutherischen und reformierten Lehrbegriffes*, Stuttgart, 1855; Elster, *Calvin als Staatsmann, Gesetzgeber und Nationalökonom*, in *Jahrbücher für Nationalökonomie und Statistik*, 1878; W. Walker, *John Calvin*, chap. x., New York, 1906.)

6. English Ethics Under Puritanism.

This system found realization in England on a different ground from that in any other country, for there was a monarchy struggling for absolutism, a church catholicizing in tendency, both set over against a parliamentary system standing for the rights of the people and a popular demand for a purely spiritual ecclesiastical system. As a result there came about a dissolution of the old historical constitution. Cromwell and his army did away with that compromise with historical institutions which prevailed on the continent, and proceeded to the erection of a real Christian state on a revolutionary basis. Scotch and French Huguenot influences combined with the theory of the rights of the people and natural law to make up Puritanism. The most radical religious ideas, the desire for autonomy, the claim for toleration, the separation of the Church from the State, found a home in Cromwell's army. Some of these ideas are due to continental influences, to the Anabaptists, and others. A considerable mystical element was also present among the armed supporters of the Commonwealth. They were desirous of a certain amount of freedom in dogma and worship, but their moral idea was meant to be strictly and absolutely maintained. So far as Christian society went Church and State had a common aim, the erection of a Christian commonwealth where the pious minority would be in control. The new system was to be built on the basis of specific English traditions, and it held to the old English idea of the rights and duties of a Christian state. Its special marks are religious and ecclesiastical autonomy, sovereignty of the people, puritanical strict morality, a continental policy based on uniting the Protestants and opposing Roman Catholics, popularizing and Christianizing law and justice. The experiment lasted only a short time and failed because of its impracticability, since it not only destroyed the existing church organization but also conflicted with the rights and interests of individuals. The gains made by the Commonwealth could be maintained in succeeding periods only by treating the idea of church autonomy as entirely distinct from the idea of political freedom. The two spheres, the ecclesiastical and political, had to be isolated from one another. As to the moral ideal of Puritanism, it had massed together State and law, war and politics, property and trade, trying to control them and the individual in his private life through the conception of a God-serving and God-fearing people. But the leaders of Puritanism soon realized that these various elements could not be developed in such a combination. Cromwell became an opportunist and gave up his idealistic religious international policy for a realistic commercial policy. Milton allowed that true Christian morality could be practised only by the select few, not by the whole people. Among the masses the problem was solved in quite a different way. There the various religious convictions led to the foundation of numerous sects, some with extravagant political ideals like those of the Fifth Monarchy Men (q.v.), or like those of the Quakers and Ranters, who were indifferent to political forms and secular ordinances. In this confusion there came a severe crisis to a purely Christian ethics. Traditional elements had to be sacrificed, ethical problems in their practical shape were reconsidered, and, in the Restoration, the ethical consciousness was investigated objectively and scientifically, Christian and secular aims were surveyed under new relations, and the opposition, combination, or compromise between the two was treated from the scientific point of view. (Cf. on this section the literature under CROMWELL, OLIVER; and PURITANISM.)

7. The New Psychological Basis.

This scientific reconstruction of ethics depends first of all on a psychological analysis which leaves aside all metaphysical assumptions of the essence of the soul and the action of God upon it, and devotes itself to discovering the laws of its own action and nature from a study and classification of its peculiar processes. This marks a distinct separation from the old theologizing ethics. Psychological analysis of a sort entirely different from its form in the scholastic theological system assumes the chief rôle, different, too, from the old psychology, which was a compromise between the religious language of the Bible and the scientific psychology of Greek philosophy. The old system insisted on the eternal worth, the unity, and the isolation of the soul from things of sense; transcendent causes were introduced as its influences—God, angels, and demons—just as all extraordinary natural processes were referred to the immediate activity of divine or diabolic power. This naive psychological supernaturalism had been transmitted as a part of the traditional system of revelation, which worked upon the soul in a miraculous way through its association with the means of revelation in the sacraments and ecclesiastical ordinances. Ancient psychology was brought in as its support, and place was made for immanent psychological explanation, which, however, played a very subordinate rôle. The chief concern of both Roman and Protestant ethics was with the processes of salvation, and revelation and the power of grace. The opposition to this system started back as far as the thirteenth century. It had two sources, the Stoic study of the emotions and temperament and the free poetical and artistic analysis of man as found in the literature and art of the Renaissance. It ended in the principle of universal psychological analysis, based on historic induction and supported by the achievements in the study of nature. Especially original in this respect is Machiavelli, with his psychological analysis, his historical comparison, and his empirical generalization. Men like Descartes, Gassendi, Malebranche, and Bayle contributed also by their study of the emotions and passions. But the chief impulse came from Hobbes, the founder of a purely psychological analysis, intended to build up an original conception of morality. Along with Hobbes must be placed Spinoza, the creator of the mechanical method of treating the emotions and passions. These were the tendencies that were popularized by English thinkers. One of the effects of this method was a change in the view of history. The matter of history had been studied only in relation to conceptions about the character and purpose of a world derived from the revelation of the Church and the Bible. A causal determination of facts in themselves had not been attempted; but with this new view of psychology there came a causal explanation of history, with its study of historical characters on the basis of psychological analysis. Nothing consistent could be achieved here, however, unless there were a new foundation of ethical rules inductively derived from social and historical facts. This was really an extension of the principle of the consensus of mankind acknowledged to be valid by theological ethics. So there came from this psychological foundation a so-called natural system of intellectual sciences, in which the eighteenth century produced the most original work, just as the seventeenth century holds the first place in scientific analysis of the natural sciences. Even when a distinction was made between natural and supernaturally caused processes, the fixed point of departure was the results of psychological analysis founded on the assumption of regularity and normality in the phenomena under review. Morality was no longer regarded as a miracle of grace, the moral law was no longer identified with the revealed law. All of the old dogmatic scholastic problems either disappeared or became of subordinate interest, and an entirely new set of fundamental problems were treated as of primary importance.

8. Problems Presented.

First in order came psychogenetic problems. In these are discussed the sources of moral phenomena, whether they have grounds outside of their own sphere, as utilitarianism declares; or whether their source is exclusive and independent, according to the standpoint of idealistic intuitionism. This is a crucial question for Christian morality as a whole; all others, such as the connection of morality with grace and its dependence on revelation, are concerned ultimately with this. Another primary classification arises from the question of determinism; not determinism in the old sense of divine predestination, but that scheme which brings morality within a fixed causal nexus of psychological laws.

Determinism seems to destroy the value of ethics altogether, while indeterminism may be made to harmonize with the recognition of grace. There is bound to come up also the principle of autonomy, that is, whether conduct is necessarily subordinated to the principles of rational insight or to the effects of psychological motives. From this point of view, all individuals stand alike. It is really an application of the convictions of political equality and ecclesiastical toleration, as they were developed in the course of the seventeenth century. The next problem is concerned with the relation of morality and religion. Under the older system they were identical; no true morality was possible without faith. The new point of view was to treat religion as a kind of by-product, a special modification of a common natural morality. Religion itself became the subject of psychological analysis. The question arose as to the necessary relation between divine sanction or the fate of man in the next world and man's striving and willing in this. Finally, it became necessary to establish a formulation of the content of the moral law as a psychological principle in such a way that its obligations could be established as ultimate derivatives from the principles above classified and analyzed. If the Biblical standards were abandoned as necessarily authoritative, in what way could Christian ethics be brought into relation with this general analysis outlined above? The problem was finally solved by turning over the discussion of Christian ethics to theology, although at first the general formulation of moral ideas was certainly influenced by Christian types of thought. But these attempts were unsatisfactory, old scholastic conceptions were seen to lack clearness, and in proportion to the degree of removal of extraneous elements from the moral idea, the more its autonomy became plain and independent by right. These were the problems which the political and social condition of England in the seventeenth century forced into the atmosphere of thought and discussion, as they are represented in the speculations of Hobbes, the ideas of the Levellers (q.v.), and the practical program of the Erastians (see ERASTUS, THOMAS, ERASTIANISM).

III. Specific Contributions: It was Hobbes (q.v.; and see DEISM, I., § 2), writing under the influence of the French and Italian Renaissance, who opposed the practical workings of the Reformed independent ideal, the rigoristic spiritualism of their Christian social order, and tried to found morality on a purely sensualistic basis. His political ideal of the State was that of Machiavelli, and the weapons he employed against spiritualism were the sensualistic ideas of Pierre Gassendi (q.v.). But the whole structure of his thought is based on keen psychological analysis. He accomplished a complete and radical revolution in ethics, finding the source of the moral law in the secular sphere. The law of nature and divine law he interprets in an entirely novel way. The law of nature is differentiated from natural law, which by itself implies a primitive war of all against all. The law of nature is maintained because man's interests demand it. The absolute State which comes into existence through its operation has also the right to establish the true religion, for the divine law has also its sanctions from the existence of that absolute political system which man, coming out of his original confusion and discord, discovers as the sole condition of his social existence. Hobbes brings Christianity into full conformity with his absolute State. The State decides what form of Christianity shall be adopted by its subjects; even heathen states have the right of maintaining untrue religions for the sake of common welfare, and must not be resisted on this account. Hobbes' originality consists in his concentration on secular interests, his psychological analysis, and his introduction of historical illustrations into his system. Mandeville (1670–1733; see DEISM, I., § 8) is important as attempting to show that moral conceptions are artificial creations intended to hold the mass of people in subjection, and from his arguments that the specific ideas of Christian ethics can not be accommodated to political, social, commercial needs.

1. Hobbes and Mandeville.

In the Restoration there was a strong reaction against the sensualism and nominalism of Hobbes, showing itself in an attempt to establish the necessity and the apriority of moral ideas by metaphysics, and more particularly the metaphysics of Platonism. This was the work of the Cambridge school (see CAMBRIDGE PLATONISTS) which allied itself with Anglican rationalism and Arminianism and was antagonistic to Calvinistic positivism and rigorism. The law of nature is completed, according to this school, in the divine law. Stress is laid upon the necessary element of ethics and the impossibility of a purely psychological foundation. The head of the school was Cudworth (q.v.), who, like Kant and Plato, insisted upon the absolute character of morality. He asks whether the mind as the source of all necessary truth is the first factor and the experience of sense, the simple material of mind, is the second; or whether the reverse is true, so that the spiritual and the necessary must be derived from the accidental and occasional. He himself, of course, defends the necessariness of ethical ideas on the basis of the eternally necessary relations of minds to one another, which relation is based ultimately on God and is, in a fragmentary way, reflected from the conceptually necessary in God's mind to the mind of man. Henry More (q.v.) introduces the element of psychological analysis, applying it to the feelings and emotions, and combining morality with the happiness of the whole community and the individual member. It is in what he calls the "boniform faculty" that he finds the special sphere for the moral principles. The coincidence of happiness with moral conduct follows from the divine plan of the world. Richard Cumberland (1631–1718), whose special interest lay in contesting Hobbes' view of the original condition of man, shows the a priori character of the moral demands by proving that the faithful maintenance of Hobbes' contract between the individual and the State depends on a previously existing moral element. The operations and processes of sense only bring out

2. Cambridge School, Cudworth, More, and Cumberland.

some latent element, while the coincidence of happiness with morality is teleological. Good-will, love of one's neighbor, altruism, the whole field of Christian morality, work in and for the common weal.

3. Clarke, Hartley, and Price. Related to the Cambridge school is Samuel Clarke (q.v.), who accepts an absolute standard for all positive laws. Moral distinctions are therefore not accidental; the standard which is represented in the typical ideas of the good, the righteous, the truthful, and so on, the moral judgment of the plain man, come from the necessary relations between the parts of the world, themselves all arising like mathematical relations from the idea of the whole, which, in turn, is dependent on the will of God. The above relations are assumed to be normal because the welfare and maintenance of the whole depends upon them. On this law of nature is based both positive human law and positive divine law, the latter bringing the completion of happiness through the idea of immortality. David Hartley (1705–57) derives from an original self-love the moral judgment in its objective shape; obligations associated with commands apart from the individual have the immediateness of an instinct. These different products of the psychological process are parts of the accomplishment of the divine purpose in man, hence the moral law has a divine necessary character, representing a deterministic pantheism. Richard Price (1723–91) represents the defense of the intuitional character of the moral judgments of approval and disapproval. What originally is confused in instinct is clarified by thought. These judgments do not stand for considerations of interest, are quite distinct from any sensuous feeling of pleasure, and rest ultimately on the system of values established in the divine mind. This rationalizing Christian ethics aimed to establish the derivation of individual and social moral ideas from the presence of God in man's soul. It recognized no distinction between religious and secular aims, and had no intimate connection between the teaching of grace and original sin, but the coincidence in the next world of moral worth and happiness was brought out. The autonomy and divine nature of moral law was not brought into connection with the acts or facts of individual social life. These thinkers were not concerned with the erection of a Christian state nor the separation between a religious morality and the morality of man as citizen and subject of law.

4. John Locke. Against such a priori idealistic theories, John Locke (see Deism, I., § 4) worked out his a posteriori sensualistic system, opposed by his philosophy all innate ideas, making the foundation as well for ethics as for knowledge the investigation of the simplest elements of experience, viz., the feeling of pleasure and pain and the power of reflection. There was no criterion, according to him, of intuitive knowledge; this was proved by the great variety of ethical ideas in the field of ethnography and history. On the simplest elements of consciousness he based his principles of conduct. It is this common and simple basis that gives the character of necessity to morality. The law of nature is only an abstraction from the acts of men directed toward happiness. But moral law depends on a positive legislative will, adding pleasure and pain to the fulfilment of these commands and requiting them by punishment and reward. In this way the divine law of Moses and of Christ is introduced into his system as holding the supreme place, and after that the law of civil society in the State and in justice, with its ordinances resting expressly or unconsciously on a social contract. A third type of law, lying outside of both of these two, is developed from the free intercourse and judgment of society, having its sanction in public opinion and its motive in social respect. These are the chief rules of human action, because the highest attainment of happiness comes through their pursuit; they correspond with the law of nature, and harmonize with the revealed law of God; they represent the principles by which the law of the State secures social welfare; they stand for the principles by which public opinion reaches its clearest form. The State law aims at the union of the religious and political autonomy of the individual with the welfare of the whole, while the other two types of law require self-control and benevolence. In Locke's system the Christian character of morality is preserved, but it has a very loose relation to the fundamental basis of his thought. It comes into view chiefly in his discussion of tolerance, the freedom of the Church, and the political freedom of the individual. But Locke's ethics was the point of departure for two movements, one which further reduced the religious element of Deism (q.v.) contained in it, while on the other side he was appealed to by the anti-deists who established a system of utility and ethical law characterized by rational supernatural elements (William Warburton, 1698–1779, and William Paley, 1743–1805, qq.v.). But after all, in deism the chief point was its criticism of positive religion, rather than its ethical teaching; nor can any real progress be shown by the opponents of deism, in their combination of a natural and rational with a supernatural eudemonism. The greatness of Locke's work consists in his denial of innate ideas and in his establishment of moral rules adequate to the manifold examples of historical morality. He widened the sphere of ethics also by making a place for political and social morality. The practical side of his teaching made him popular in England, although in appreciating the true character of ethical study, he was less profound than the Cambridge school.

5. Shaftesbury, Butler, and Hutcheson. The separation of this sensualistic empiristic eudemonism from Christian ethics was made more complete by Lord Shaftesbury (see Deism, I., § 8), who handled the subject as a kind of arithmetic of the feelings. His work shows the esthetic standpoint of ancient times and the Renaissance, especially as he reproduces many Stoic points of view. He opposes the rationalism of the Cambridge school, and rejects the place accorded to reflection by Locke. Man approves the altruistic impulses and feelings that tend to social progress in the State and society, and disapproves whatever disturbs the harmony of so-

Zeitfracht Medien GmbH
Ferdinand-Jühlke-Straße 7
99095 Erfurt, Deutschland
produktsicherheit@kolibri360.de